Great Problems in

EUROPEAN CIVILIZATION

Great Problems in

EUROPEAN

Contributors

Crane Brinton, *Harvard University*
R. V. Burks, *Wayne University*
Peter Charanis, *Rutgers University*
Evalyn A. Clark, *Vassar College*
Stewart C. Easton, *The City College of New York*
Myron P. Gilmore, *Harvard University*
James L. Godfrey, *University of North Carolina*
E. Harris Harbison, *Princeton University*
Harry H. Kimber, *Michigan State College*
Sidney Painter, *The Johns Hopkins University*
Lowell Ragatz, *The Ohio State University*
Robert L. Reynolds, *University of Wisconsin*
Kenneth M. Setton, *Columbia University*
John Hall Stewart, *Western Reserve University*
Henry R. Winkler, *Rutgers University*
John B. Wolf, *University of Minnesota*

Englewood Cliffs, N. J.

CIVILIZATION

Editors

Kenneth M. Setton

COLUMBIA UNIVERSITY

Henry R. Winkler

RUTGERS UNIVERSITY

Prentice-Hall, Inc.

PRENTICE-HALL HISTORY SERIES

Donald C. McKay, Editor

L.C. Cat. Card No.: 54-7755

FIRST PRINTING..........APRIL, 1954
SECOND PRINTING.....SEPTEMBER, 1954
THIRD PRINTING........OCTOBER, 1954
FOURTH PRINTING........JUNE, 1955
FIFTH PRINTING..........JUNE, 1957
SIXTH PRINTING...........JULY, 1958

PRINTED IN THE UNITED STATES OF AMERICA

36460

Preface

THE CONTRIBUTORS to this volume believe that neither the general reader nor the student of history should be shielded from the facts of history, for they are the facts of life. History is not a cut-and-dried series of memorable names and dates, a mere succession of laws, institutions, and the like. It is not just a chronicle of court scandal and intrigue. It is the study of the continuous stream of human experience. The problems in this volume represent great landmarks in this long journey of mankind.

Experienced and highly trained historians have set the problems for us in this volume; they have asked the questions and supplied the material for answers pro and con. They have given us no answers, however, and have attempted no conclusions. They have tried to give us material on both sides, and on more sides still when the question cannot be resolved into alternatives. Only readers who will not think for themselves will complain that they have not been supplied with the answers. Inquiring minds will seek their own answers, and this volume has been designed to help them.

All the present readings are focused upon certain great problems, themselves a source of perennial fascination, and central to the history of European civilization. The spotlight is put upon these problems and shifted from side to side to broaden our view of them as we seek to understand them; if understanding of these problems is not everywhere easy, achievement of such understanding is enormously worth while, for these problems have supplied the pattern of much of contemporary civilization. Letters and speeches, documents and historical writings, newspapers and other sources are excerpted and organized for study or even perusal by the reader. The effort has been to assist every man to be his own historian, for every man is a historian. He cannot escape it.

The boy who finds a bundle of his grandmother's love letters in the attic becomes a historian as he reads them. His curiosity moves him to historical research: he wants to find out what a stately old lady of his acquaintance was up to, fifty years ago. There are at least two general types of questions which we put to the sources. The first are simple questions. When was Caesar or Napoleon or Stalin born? What is the date of this treaty or that, and what are its provisions? When did the war begin? Who was the king's last mistress? The answers to these questions are sometimes interesting, sometimes entertaining, but in themselves they are rarely important. The other questions are far less simple. How do you explain the phenomenal victory of Christianity over all its rivals and opponents in the early centuries of its existence? What is the validity of the historical concept of the Renaissance? What are the causes of the Protestant Movement? Was it Reformation or chiefly Revolt? How has industrialization molded the structure of modern society? How has communism achieved such strength as to place democracy and freedom of thought and enterprise in jeopardy? What caused the quick disintegration of the settlement at Versailles which helped to build the road to World War II? What has capitalism meant in the history of European peoples? Every reader will grant that these are far more important questions than the first sort posed. We have not lacked answers to important questions. If anything, we have had too many answers from historians and theologians, popular writers and publicists, and from almost everyone who has found an audience. Sometimes we come to the conclusion that the historian is a person who can ask the big questions but cannot answer them, at least not to another historian's satisfaction. The great problems of history are subjects of unending controversy. We have attempted here to present a selection of materials for the thoughtful reader to consider, in the hope that he may thus broaden his own understanding of the past as well as the present, for his future will be built upon both.

The editors wish to express their sincerest thanks to the contributors to this book, all of whom have been most helpful and cooperative; to Professor Donald C. McKay of Harvard, editor of the Prentice-Hall History Series, who has made many valuable suggestions; and to Mr. William A. Pullin, Assistant Vice President of Prentice-Hall, who first suggested this work, and who has labored long and hard to help us bring it to completion. Thanks go also to Miss Joanne Bouton of Prentice-Hall, who has seen this book through the press with great skill and understanding. Mrs. Eleanor Vuoncino gave invaluable assistance in typing manuscript corrections.

K. M. S.
H. R. W.

Acknowledgments

IN THE PREPARATION of this volume the editors and contributors have been placed under obligation, which is hereby acknowledged with thanks, to the following publishers, individuals, and others who have allowed them the use of materials from the books and other sources indicated:

George Allen and Unwin, Ltd., for Friedrich Engels, *The Condition of the Working-Class in England in 1844;* J. A. Hobson, *Imperialism;* and Arthur Ponsonby, *Now Is the Time.*

The American Historical Review, for Einar Joranson, "The Problem of the Spurious Letter of Emperor Alexius to the Count of Flanders," *ibid.,* LV (1950).

Mr. Frank Maloy Anderson for his *The Constitutions and Other Select Documents Illustrative of the History of France.*

Appleton-Century-Crofts, Inc., for F. S. Nussbaum, *A History of the Economic Institutions of Modern Europe;* and William Godwin, *An Enquiry Concerning Political Justice,* ed. R. A. Preston.

C. H. Beck'sche, for Hajo and Annemarie Holborn, eds., "Paraclesis," in *Desiderius Erasmus Roterodamus Ausgewählte Werke.*

G. Bell and Sons, Ltd., for H. Butterfield, *The Statecraft of Machiavelli;* and Giorgio Vasari, *Lives of the Most Eminent Painters, Sculptors and Architects,* trans. Margaret Foster.

Basil Blackwell, for *Napoleon Self-Revealed,* trans. and ed. J. M. Thompson; and J. H. Whitfield, *Machiavelli.*

Geoffrey Bles, Ltd., for Nicholas Berdyaev, *The Origin of Russian Communism,* trans. R. M. French.

Albert and Charles Boni, Inc., for *A King's Lessons in Statecraft: Louis XIV: Letters to His Heirs,* with introduction and notes by Jean Longnon, trans. Herbert Wilson.

The British Academy and Oxford University Press (London), for Norman H. Baynes, "Constantine and the Christian Church," *Proceedings of the British Academy,* XV (1929).

Byzantine Institute, Inc., for H. Gregoire, "The Question of the Diversion of the Fourth Crusade," *Byzantion,* XV (1941).

Mr. Somerset de Chair for his edition of *Napoleon's Memoirs.*

Mrs. Neville Chamberlain, for the Journal of Neville Chamberlain, quoted in Keith Feiling, *The Life of Neville Chamberlain* (Macmillan and Co., Ltd.).

Jacques Chambrun, Inc., for Jacques Bainville, *Napoleon,* trans. Hamish Miles.

The University of Chicago Press, for *Petrarch's Letters to Classical Authors,* trans. Mario E. Cosenza.

The Clarendon Press, for P. S. Allen, ed., *Opus Epistolarum Erasmi Roterodami;* F. B. Marsh, *The Reign of Tiberius;* R. Syme, *The Roman Revolution;* and Alfred Zimmern, *The Greek Commonwealth.*

Librairie Armand Colin, for J. E. Spenlé, *La Pensée allemande de Luther à Nietzsche.*

Columbia University Press, for Sebastian Castellio, *Concerning Heretics*, trans. R. H. Bainton; Robert of Clari, *The Conquest of Constantinople*, trans. E. A. McNeal; Grover Clark, *The Balance Sheets of Empire; The Correspondence of Gregory VII*, trans. Ephraim Emerton; Odo of Deuil, *De profectione Ludovici VII in orientem*, ed. and trans. V. G. Berry; William of Tyre, *A History of Deeds Done Beyond the Sea*, trans. E. A. Babcock and A. C. Krey; E. M. Winslow, *The Pattern of Imperialism*.

Constable and Co., Ltd., for R. W. Seton-Watson, *The Southern Slav Question and the Hapsburg Monarchy*.

Crown Publishers, for the Marquis de Sade, *Dialogue between a Priest and a Dying Man*, trans. Samuel Putnam, copyright 1927 by Pascal Covici.

The John Day Co., for James Burnham, *The Struggle for the World*.

J. M. Dent & Sons, Ltd., for *Memoirs of the Crusades by Villehardouin and Joinville*, trans. Sir Frank Marzials.

Duell, Sloan and Pearce, Inc., for S. K. Padover, ed., *The Complete Jefferson*.

E. P. Dutton and Co., for Lucien Febvre, *Martin Luther: A Destiny*, trans. Roberts Tapley; *Memoirs of the Crusades by Villehardouin and Joinville*, trans. Sir Frank Marzials; J. J. Rousseau, *The Social Contract*, trans. G. D. H. Cole; and *The Works of Liudprand of Cremona*, trans. F. A. Wright.

The Economist, for "France and Germany," *ibid.*, CLIV (1948).

W. B. Eerdmans Publishing Co., for Martin Luther, *The Bondage of the Will*, trans. Henry Cole.

Eyre and Spottiswoode, for W. E. Campbell, ed., *The Dialogue Concerning Tyndale by Sir Thomas More*.

Fathers of the Church, for Justin Martyr, *Second Apology*, trans. Thomas B. Falls.

The Folio Society, for Desmond Flower, ed., *Voltaire's England*.

Foreign Affairs, for Halvard M. Lange, "European Union: False Hopes and Reality," *ibid.*, XXVIII (1949–50); Paul Reynaud, "The Unifying Force for Europe," *ibid.*, XXVIII (1949–50); Jacques Soustelle, "France and Europe: A Gaullist View," *ibid.*, XXX (1951–52); and Dirk U. Stikker, "The Functional Approach to European Integration," *ibid.*, XXIX (1950–51).

The Free Press, for Robert Owen, *A New View of Society* (facsimile reproduction of 3rd edition).

Gyldendalske Boghandel Nordisk Forlag, for Johan Plesner, *L'Émigration de la campagne à la ville libre de Florence au XIII. siècle*.

Hafner Publishing Co., for Aristotle, *Constitution of Athens*, trans. K. von Fritz and E. Kapp; and Jeremy Bentham, *An Introduction to the Principles of Morals and Legislation*.

Harcourt, Brace and Co., for Georges Clemenceau, *Grandeur and Misery of Victory*, trans. F. M. Atkinson.

Harper and Brothers, for N.S.B. Gras, *An Introduction to Economic History*.

Harvard University Press, for material in the Loeb Classical Library.

B. Herder Book Co., for H. J. Schroeder, ed., *Canons and Decrees of the Council of Trent*.

Henry Holt and Co. for Carl Bücher, *Industrial Evolution*, trans. S. M. Wickert.

Houghton Mifflin Co., for E. L. Higgins, *The French Revolution as Told by Contemporaries*.

International Affairs (Chatham House), for Nicholas Mansergh, "Britain, the Commonwealth, and Western Union," *ibid.*, XXIV (1948).

International Publishers, for *Diderot: Selected Writings*, trans. Jean Stewart and Jonathan Kemp; and Maximilien Robespierre, *Speeches: Voices of Revolt*, I.

Journal of the History of Ideas, for material in Vol. IV (1943).

The Kenyon Review, for Erwin Panofsky, "Renaissance and Renascences," *ibid.*, VI (1944).

Alfred A. Knopf, Inc., for Harry Elmer Barnes, *Genesis of the World War;* and Frederick L. Schuman, *The Nazi Dictatorship.*

Longmans, Green and Co., Inc., for *The Epistles of Erasmus*, trans. Francis Morgan Nichols.

The Macmillan Company of Canada, Ltd., for Lord Acton, *Lectures on Modern History.*

Macmillan and Co., Ltd. (London), for Lord Acton, *Lectures on Modern History;* T. R. Malthus, *First Essay on Population;* and Tacitus, *Annals*, trans. A. J. Church and W. J. Brodribb.

The Macmillan Co. (New York), for Jacob Burckhardt, *The Civilization of the Renaissance in Italy;* Sidney B. Fay, *The Origins of the World War;* P. T. Moon, *Imperialism and World Politics;* Walter Lippmann, *The Stakes of Diplomacy;* and J. H. Stewart, *A Documentary Survey of the French Revolution.*

Manchester University Press, for James Tait, *The Medieval English Borough.*

Mediaeval Academy of America, for Carl Stephenson, *Borough and Town.*

Methuen and Co., Ltd., for Desiderius Erasmus, *Enchiridion, The Manual of the Christian Knight.*

Arnoldo Mondadori, for Luigi Salvatorelli, *Storia d'Italia*, IV.

Muhlenberg Press, for Heinrich Boehmer, *Road to Reformation*, trans. J. W. Doberstein and T. G. Tappert; and Preserved Smith, *Luther's Correspondence*, copyright 1913 by Lutheran Publishing Co.

New American Library of World Literature, for V. Gordon Childe, *What Happened in History.*

Newman Press, for Hartmann Grisar, *Martin Luther: His Life and Work*, trans. F. J. Eble, copyright 1935 by B. Herder Book Co.

Oxford University Press (New York), for Viscount Cecil, *A Great Experiment;* and Arnold Toynbee, *The World and the West.*

Oxford University Press (London), for Jonathan Swift, *Gulliver's Travels*, ed. W. A. Eddy.

Pantheon Books, Inc., for Jacob Burckhardt, *The Age of Constantine the Great*, trans. M. Hadas.

Princeton University Press, for Desiderius Erasmus, *The Praise of Folly*, trans. H. H. Hudson; August C. Krey, *The First Crusade;* Georges Lefebvre, *The Coming of the French Revolution*, trans. R. R. Palmer; LeRoy, *De la vicissitude des choses en l'univers;* and Henri Pirenne, *Medieval Cities.*

G. P. Putnam's Sons, for Paul L. Ford, ed., *The Works of Thomas Jefferson;* E. B. Hall, *Voltaire in his Letters;* Adolf Hausrath, *Treitschke: His Doctrine of German Destiny and of International Relations;* Wilhelm Roepke, *The Solution of the German Problem*, trans. E. W. Dickes; and Heinrich von Treitschke, *Germany, France, Russia and Islam.*

Random House, Inc., for Niccolò Machiavelli, *The Prince and the Discourses*, in the Modern Library.

George Routledge and Sons, Ltd. and Routledge and Kegan Paul, Ltd., for *The Works of Liudprand of Cremona,* trans. F. A. Wright.

Routledge and Kegan Paul, Ltd., for *The Alexiad of the Princess Anna Comnena,* trans. Elizabeth A. S. Dawes; and Robert E. Dickinson, *The West European City.*

St. Martin's Press, Inc., for Lord Acton, *Lectures on Modern History;* and Tacitus, *Annals,* trans. A. J. Church and W. J. Brodribb.

Claudio Sánchez-Albornoz y Menduiña, for his *Ruina y extinctión del municipio romano en España e instituciones que lo reemplazan.*

G. C. Sansoni, for Pasquale Villari, *I Primi due Secoli della Storia di Firenze.*

Charles Scribner's Sons, for F. V. A. Aulard, *The French Revolution,* trans. Bernard Miall; Pierre Gaxotte, *The French Revolution,* trans. Walter Alison Phillips; Jacques Maritain, *Three Reformers;* and Paul Van Dyke, *Ignatius Loyola.*

Sheed & Ward, for Jacques Maritain, *Three Reformers.*

The Slavonic and East European Review, for František Palacký, "Manifesto of the First Slavonic Congress," trans. William Beardmore, *ibid.,* XXVI (1948).

Peter Smith, for Gustav Schmoller, *Studies upon the Economic Policy of Frederick the Great.*

Trustees of the late Lord Tweedsmuir (John Buchan), for John Buchan, *Augustus.*

Westminster Press, for R. H. Bainton, *The Travail of Religious Liberty,* copyright 1951 by W. L. Jenkins.

University of Wisconsin Press, for A. A. Vasiliev, *History of the Byzantine Empire.*

Table of Contents

Great Problems in

EUROPEAN CIVILIZATION

1. *Freedom and Tyranny in the Ancient World*

STEWART C. EASTON

The City College of New York

I. GREECE: THE ATHENIAN LOVE OF FREEDOM—FACT OR MYTH?

WE ARE ACCUSTOMED to look back to the Athenians as the founders of democracy, and as the first people to make freedom an ideal. Yet clearly there were limitations on Athenian democracy. It excluded all who were not citizens, and the freedom of those who were citizens of foreign states was not always respected. A great deal of Athenian history is occupied with wars, not all of which were in self-defense. This first chapter will therefore be concerned with the question of how far the Athenians were really lovers of freedom, or whether the limitations were so serious that they have no right to the praise so frequently lavished upon them. Their cultural achievements will be taken for granted in this chapter; it is only their attitude towards freedom that will be considered here.

In the latter part of the sixth century B.C. the Persians established a great empire in Western Asia which spread as far as the Aegean Sea. In the process they swallowed up the flourishing coastal cities of Asia Minor which were populated by Greeks. In 499 B.C. these cities revolted against Persia and appealed to the mainland Greeks for aid. The Athenians, almost alone among the Greeks, responded. Their expeditionary force landed in Asia Minor, burned one of the Persian capitals, and won some other minor victories. But it soon returned home without having made any serious inroads into Persian power. Darius I, the powerful Persian monarch, was determined to punish the Greeks for their presumption. In 490 B.C. he sent a naval expedition against Athens, but after being defeated in the battle of Marathon, it returned to Persia, and Darius, who died soon afterwards, bequeathed his project of revenge to his son Xerxes. The latter, after collecting a huge and motley army, began a full scale invasion of Greece by land and sea. The Greeks, however, were by now better prepared. The Athenians had built a fleet, and were able to persuade the Spartans and their allies to join in the common defense of the country. The result was the rout of the Persian forces in the campaigns of 480 and 479 B.C., although during the war Athens herself was sacked and burned.

The Athenians realized that Persia was not damaged beyond repair. At any time she could renew the assault. They therefore proposed to the other Greeks that a permanent defensive alliance be formed. The Spartans, however, refused to co-operate, with the result that the Athenians went ahead without them. Under the leadership of Aristides, they succeeded in organizing the Confederation of Delos, composed of almost all the islands in the Aegean, Athens herself, and a few of the mainland cities. Some of the allies provided ships to the common pool, but the majority merely furnished money, with which the Athenians built and equipped the ships. The Confederation was entirely successful in policing the Aegean and preventing the resurgence of Persian power in that area.

The Confederation was, of course, a highly profitable enterprise for the Athenians. But its very success caused murmurs amongst the allies. Was it really necessary, they asked, to keep such a substantial navy in being? The Persian danger seemed to have receded. Could they not be relieved of some of the financial burden? The Athenians retorted by raising the assessments whenever they found it necessary, while they refused to permit secession, using the confederate fleet against those members who tried to regain their independence. Finally, under the leadership of Pericles, the Athenians began to adopt an aggressive imperial policy beyond the confines of the Aegean, still using the fleet which had been built, but for entirely different purposes. When one such expedition suffered a resounding defeat at the hands of the Persians and Phoenicians in the Mediterranean Sea off Egypt, Samos, a big island in the Confederation, at this time friendly to Athens, suggested that the treasury of the League, hitherto kept in Delos, a tiny island sacred to Apollo, should be moved to Athens for greater safety. The League meekly consented, and thereafter the Confederation was an Athenian Empire in all but name. There was no further check upon her imperial ambitions, as long as she could force her allies to pay the ever increasing tax assessments that she levied upon them.

Pericles, with the constant support of the Athenian democracy, now embarked on an expansionist policy, interfering with the internal government of the cities in the Empire, attempting by threats and promises to seduce allies of the Spartans, members of the rival Peloponnesian League, away from Sparta and into the Athenian Empire, even engaging in minor wars for the purpose. At last the exasperated Spartans, urged thereto especially by the Corinthians, trade rivals of the Athenians, undertook a preventive war, which lasted, with short intervals of truce, for 27 years. In 404 B.C. the Spartans, aided by Persian money and ships, utterly defeated the Athenians, and the Persians, thus brought back into Greek politics, became the virtual arbiters of Greece for most of the fourth century, even though they made no further attempt at military conquest. It was, therefore, possible to claim that the Athenian Empire had been the sole bulwark against Persian intervention, and with its destruction the enemy of all the Greeks had been once more permitted a foothold in the Greek world.

The facts are undisputed. But there has always been a difference of opinion, in the ancient as well as in the modern world, as to whether the Athenians were justified in their imperialism, or whether they merely exploited their Empire for their own benefit, taking advantage of their domination of the free Confederation to fasten an imperial system upon their unwilling partners, making them no longer partners but slaves—while accompanying their imperialism with protestations of their love of freedom and their devotion to democracy. There can be no doubt that the economic advantages of the Empire made possible the flowering of culture in fifth-century Athens, but was the price paid too high? Were the Athenians truly lovers of freedom, as their apologists claimed, or was this freedom an exclusive thing, of benefit only to themselves? Were they hypocrites, or genuine lovers of freedom and democracy?

All except two of the writers of the selections below were Greeks of ancient times, though only a few were contemporary with the events described. It is to be noted that the bulk of the defenders were either interested parties, or lived in a later age when the memory of the events themselves had dimmed. It may be true that imperialism always looks more attractive when viewed from the vantage point of posterity. It is possible even that some of our latter-day imperialists may be viewed with the same tolerance as Napoleon already is in the twentieth century, in spite of our unhappy experience with his successors.

A. The Nature of Athenian Imperialism

1. As a Benefit to All Greece

(a) The Ideal Beginnings: *The just tax assessments of Aristides*

Plutarch was a Greek historian, biographer, and moralist of the second century A.D., or some six hundred years after the events he describes. He had access, however, to many sources lost to us, and in general his history, when capable of being checked, has for the most part been found to be reasonably accurate. However, his bias as moralist and biographer seems sometimes to have led him to make judgments on the characters he describes which would not be sustained by modern, and probably indeed, not by some ancient historians. The following account of Aristides the incorruptible should be contrasted with the much earlier account given by Aristotle (2 [b] below), although Aristotle himself was not contemporary with the events, and is not necessarily free from bias. The critical modern reader should always be awake to the necessity of discounting personal bias in historians, especially when the historian lived close to the events he describes, and was still suffering from their political consequences.

The Hellenes used to pay a kind of contribution for the war even during the period when the Spartans held the leadership, but now they desired to be assessed city by city. So they asked the Athenians for Aristides, and commissioned him to inspect their territories and revenues, and then to fix the assessments, according to the worth and ability to pay of each member.

And yet, though he thus became controller of so much power, and though, in a sense, Hellas put all her property in his sole hands, poor though he was when he started on his mission, he came back from it poorer still. He fixed the money assessments in accordance with purity and justice, and at the same time he earned the gratitude and satisfied the needs of all concerned. Indeed, as in antiquity people used to sing the praises of the Age of Kronos—the Golden Age—so now did the Athenian allies all praise the tariff of Aristides, calling it a piece of wonderful good fortune for all Hellas, especially since, after a short time, it was doubled and even trebled.

For Aristides taxed them only to the extent of four hundred sixty talents. But Pericles must have added almost a third to this, for Thucydides says that when the war began the Athenian revenue was six hundred talents from the allies. Then, after the death of Pericles, the demagogues increased it little by little so that in the end the total amounted to thirteen hundred talents, not so much because of the excessive expenses of the long and constantly changing war, but because they incited the people to spend money on spectacular entertainments, and the erection of statues and the building of temples.

Plutarch, *Aristides,* 24, adapted from the translation by B. Perrin, *Plutarch's Lives,* Loeb Classical Library (Cambridge, Mass.: Harvard University Press, 1914), II, 287-89.

(b) The Ideal of the Empire: *The funeral speech of Pericles*

At the end of the first year of the Peloponnesian War, Pericles delivered the customary public eulogy of those who had fallen in battle. The speech which Thucydides puts in his mouth is one of the most justly famed speeches of all history. Pericles takes the occasion to praise the city of Athens for which these men had died, and the ideal of the open friendly city, the "School of Hellas," has provided posterity with a picture of Athens of this period which has too often been accepted without question as truth. Perhaps it is better to regard it as the ideal of Thucydides, and possibly of Pericles; and though no ideal has ever been better stated, the other side of the picture, as depicted also by Thucydides, should not be forgotten in the quest for the fifth century reality.

I shall begin with our ancestors; it is both just and proper that they should have the honor of the first mention on an occasion like the present. They lived in this country without a break in the succession from generation to generation, and they handed it down free to the present time by their deeds of valor. And if our more remote ancestors deserve praise, so much the more do our own fathers, who added to their inheritance the empire which we now possess, and spared no pains to be able to leave their acquisitions to us of the present generation. Finally, there are few parts of our territories that have not been increased by those of us here who are still in the prime of life, who consolidated our power throughout the greater part of the Empire and secured the city's complete independence in war and peace. I do not wish to say more about the battles fought by us and our fathers which gave us our possessions, or of the courage with which we withstood both barbarians and Greeks at home; for they are well known to you. But I would rather speak of the spirit in which we faced them, the kind of government and customs which gave rise to our greatness. . . .

Our government does not follow the laws of neighboring states; we are an example to others rather than imitators. Our constitution is a democracy, favoring the many rather than the few. Our laws secure equal justice for all in private disputes, while talent in every branch of endeavor is welcomed and honored; in such matters we pay no attention to social standing but only to merit, and this same spirit is carried over into our ordinary relations with one another. Poverty does not prevent any man from attaining office in the state if he is able to serve it. We do not watch each other jealously, nor do we resent it when others do as they please; we do not give each other black looks and angry words, nor indulge in those minor pinpricks which annoy, even if they do no actual harm. We are open and friendly in our private relations, and yet in public life we keep strictly to our laws. We pay reverence where it is due, and we are obedient to those in authority over us, paying especial attention to those laws which protect the oppressed and to the unwritten laws which we should be ashamed to break.

And yet ours is no city for work alone. Nowhere else can be found such opportunities for refreshing of the spirit. All the year round are games and sacrifices, and there is beauty in our public buildings to cheer the heart and delight the eye every day. And the city is so large and powerful that the wealth of all the world flows into it; to the Athenian the fruits of other countries are as familiar as those of his own.

Our military policy is different from that of our enemies. We fling the gates of our city open to the world. We do not deport foreigners, nor do we ever prevent them from observing what they will, even at the cost of revealing what our enemies might be able to use against us; for we do not trust so much in our material means of defense as in the spirit of our citizens. . . .

We love beauty without extravagance, we love wisdom without being effeminate. Wealth is not for us a means of ostentation, but an opportunity for further achievements; for us poverty is not

something which disgraces us to admit, though it is a real disgrace to make no effort to overcome it. Our citizens pay attention to both public and private duties. They do not become so absorbed in their private affairs that they have no time left for the city. We differ from other states in that we look upon those who take no part in public affairs as useless rather than merely quiet; we debate carefully and in person on all political matters, and then come to a decision, for we do not think that full discussion impedes a decision. On the contrary we think that without discussion our deeds are doomed to failure.

We are famous for being adventurous in action while at the same time thoughtful before action, in this respect differing from those who are only bold when they are ignorant, and lose their élan when they give themselves time to think. Surely the bravest men are those who know clearly what is before them, the glory and the danger equally, and yet do not hesitate to go forward to meet what is in store for them. In doing good, again, we differ from other people. We do not win friends by accepting favors from them, but rather by conferring them. This makes us more reliable as friends. We are creditors rather than debtors, and thus anxious to cement our friendly relations by doing kindnesses. If they do not respond with the same friendliness this can only be because they do not feel that they are giving their services spontaneously, but only because they owe it to us as a debt. Alone among mankind we benefit others not out of self-interest but because we believe firmly and fearlessly in freedom.

In short, I claim that as a city we are the school of Hellas, and that our citizens, man for man, are unequalled for their independence of spirit, versatility, and readiness to meet any emergency in complete self-reliance.

This is no idle boast. It is a fact borne out by the supremacy won for us by our customs. No other city of the present time, when tested in action, is found to be greater than her reputation; no other is so powerful that it is no shame to be defeated by her, and no indignity to be dependent upon her. The signs and evidence of her supremacy are great and visible for all to see; and posterity will be astonished, as all mankind is already today. We need no Homer or other poet to tell of our deeds and praise us; he would give a momentary pleasure only—while the truth itself is sufficient for us. Over every sea and into every land our pioneers have forced their way, and, whether they were welcomed or resisted, they have built themselves an everlasting memorial of their settlement.

This, then, is the city for which these men, resolved not to lose her, nobly fought and died; and we who survive would naturally wish to spend ourselves in service to her. And if I have spent much time in praising her I only wished to show how great is our stake in her, far greater than for those who have no such inheritance. . . . Words cannot magnify the deeds these men have done. . . .

Thucydides, *The History of the Peloponnesian War,* II, 36-42, freely adapted from the translation by R. Crawley (1876).

(c) *How Athens spent the money of the Confederation*

It is only with difficulty that modern historians have been able to piece together the details of the financial expenditure of Athens during the years of her growing empire. No ancient writer has shown any interest in this economic foundation. The next extract therefore will be taken from a modern historian, who indicates the sources he has used to come to his conclusions.

From 453 onwards, then [when the Treasury of Delos was removed to Athens], Athenians were not only practically but visibly masters of the funds of the league. The money was deposited on the Acropolis, where their other funds were kept. Athens had now, therefore, three separate treasuries, connected respectively with the City, the Goddess, and the Empire. Let us watch what came of these financial complications.

All this time Athens had been trying to collect money for the great new temple of the Goddess. The State had made generous grants out of spoils and other sources of city revenue, and individual citizens had gladly borne their share. The south wall of the Acropolis, which Cimon constructed out of booty, was built to strengthen the foundations of the projected shrine. But the work made slow progress. The temple of Zeus at Olympia, which was finished in 456, was built out of a treasure which had taken a century to accumulate; and Olympia had the contributions of all Greece to rely upon. . . .

It is from about this time that we find Athens taking definite steps to hasten the execution of her great religious and artistic projects. "Pericles," says Plutarch, "anxious to raise the spirits of the people and to encourage them to great deeds, procured a decree that all the Greeks, wheresoever they resided, whether in Europe or in Asia, whether their cities were great or small, should send representatives to Athens to confer upon the rebuilding of the Greek shrines which the barbarians had burnt, and about providing those sacrifices which had been vowed during the Persian War for the preservation of Greece; and likewise about the sea, in order that all might sail on it without fear and maintain the peace." This interesting decree, associating Pericles' policy of sea power with his building projects, cannot be dated with certainty; but it seems to belong to the decade between 460 and 450. "It took no effect," says Plutarch, "nor did the cities send their representatives; the reason of which is said to be the underhand opposition of the Lacedaemonians, for the proposal was first rejected in Peloponnesus. But I was willing to give an account of it as a specimen of the greatness of the orator's spirit and of his disposition to form magnificent designs."

But a second and less ambitious expedient, which Athens adopted about the same time, was more easily carried out. She made the allies contribute to her religious designs by paying into the treasury of the Goddess the "first fruits" of the tribute. The proportion thus deducted was one-sixtieth of each contribution, and it is to the records of these offerings that we owe our detailed knowledge of the imperial system. The lists were inscribed on stone slabs, many of which have come down to us.

The principle thus established was quickly carried further. We cannot trace its development in detail, but we know the outlines of the story. The facts speak for themselves. In 448 peace was concluded between Athens and Persia; but though their contributions should no longer have been needed, the confederates were not relieved from them. In 447 the building of the great temple, the Parthenon, was begun. In 445 peace was concluded between Athens and her enemies in Greece proper. In 444 hot discussion arose in Athens as to the use of the imperial funds. The question divided the assembly, but was decisively settled early in 443 by the banishment of the statesman who opposed the financial policy of Pericles. In the year 443–442 the Confederacy, or Empire, as it had now become, was divided into five tribute districts for the more convenient collection of funds. By 440 the reserve funds of the Goddess and of the Empire had been united in the hands of the treasurers of the Goddess. Athens had found the money for her designs.

In 440–439, however, she was startled in her building projects by the sudden revolt of two of her most important allies or subjects, Samos and Byzantium. It cost her two seasons of campaigning and one thousand two hundred seventy-six talents out of her reserve (exclusive of current imperial revenue) to repress them; and for a short time the building of the Parthenon was interrupted. But payments continued to be made for the preparation of the gold and ivory statue which was to be the great feature of the new temple. At the close of the war the other projects were resumed.

The following seven years, down to the outbreak of the Peloponnesian War, were the zenith of Athenian wealth and activity. The Parthenon building was sufficiently advanced by 438 to be inaugurated at the Panathenaic festival in the summer of that year. The gold and ivory statue of Athena was completed by Pheidias in time for the ceremony. . . . A number of other temples were begun—the Erectheum on the north side of the Acropolis, the temple of Hephaestus [etc.]. . . .

Several of these buildings still remain, and attest the boldness and patience of the perfect artists who planned and made them. Many of the payments made in connection with them remain also, to attest that they were built in very truth, as Pericles tells us, with the strictest regard to economy. It is visible in every detail, down to the careful arrangements made for selling the wood used in the scaffolding. Every item of expenditure was carefully discussed and rigidly controlled; for the work was being done, as everyone knew, not out of the native or normal resources of the city, but out of a fund which was originally intended for military purposes, and might at any moment be required for them again. . . . It would almost seem as if Pericles, knowing that a great war was imminent and that he and his artists were growing old, determined to do the work that was in them while there was yet time. By 431, when the storm broke, most, but not all, of it was done.

It is hard for us in these opulent modern days to form any conception of the temper of Athens during these few crowded years of creative activity. Those 8000 talents paid to her craftsmen and laborers represent in hard work and artistic power, above all, in self-sacrifice, far more than can be expressed in the feeble terms of present day money. From our cautious modern point of view, which puts good business before everything and lets in art as an afterthought, her finance was crazy. As a modern economist [M. Cavaignac] remarks: "The works of Pericles served no economic purpose but that of display; they could not be realized in money or exported to other lands, or utilized for the production of more wealth. The skill and treasure devoted to them were permanently sunk. . . . Pericles, in endeavoring to find profitable employment for the people, deliberately turned their energies to unproductive public works; the magnificent buildings which were reared under his direction absorbed the wealth of the city without developing any natural resources or trading facilities in return. The treasure was exhausted . . . , locked up in forms that are artistically superb, but economically worthless."

From the economic and political standpoints this criticism is sound and Pericles would have admitted it. . . . Athenians were not so blind as not to know that their temples would bring in no income except from sightseers, and that the sums out of which they were being built were only too strictly limited. They knew that they were working against time, and spending upon the work sums that wise men would have laid by for purposes of national defence and commercial and industrial development. Only on one point would they have indignantly contradicted the modern economist. He speaks as though the buildings were undertaken to "find profitable employment for the people," as though the Parthenon had been built as a relief work. The Parthenon was built by honest craftsmen, eager to do honor to their goddess, who were paid a frugal pittance for their devoted services. Artists do not work for money, even though they, like other men, need money to live by. But of the craftsmen and laborers employed on the temples, as of the city as a whole, the inscriptions justify us in saying that they were "lovers of beauty together with cheapness" [Herodotus]. . . .

It was a small handful of human beings, judged by our modern standard, which beat back the Persians, created the Empire, adorned Athens with her immortal buildings, and was ready now in 431 to take its stand, in the ranks or on shipboard, to defend and hand down its heritage. But Pericles knew how impossible it was for Athens both to fight and to do her proper work, and he did not intend that she should fight. . . . To keep the Field Service Army in the field for a season's campaigning of six months would . . . cost . . . four hundred seventy-four talents, while to keep three hundred ships at sea for a similar period would cost no less than . . . one thousand six hundred eight talents. Towards such bills as these the paltry six thousand talents on the Acropolis would not carry Athens very far in a war of indefinite continuance.[1]

---

[1] In passages omitted the author has analyzed the costs of a war, and the cash resources available to meet it.

It is quite certain that Pericles never contemplated incurring them.

In conclusion let us turn once more from the arts of war to the arts of peace, and set out in brief tabular form the results of our enquiries into the Athenian economy. . . . It can be most conveniently expressed in the form of a national balance sheet. The items are numbered in order of relative importance.

attainment, and complete self-reliance in limbs and brain." For over two thousand years we have been admiring them, in their writings and monuments, for that inimitable ease and many-sidedness and cloudless serenity of spirit. Only now that we can piece together their household bills can we admire also their steady courage which put so bold a face upon the sterner realities of life. Only now can we appreciate why

Credit	Debit
1. Tribute from allies (600 talents a year, circulated among Athenians for expenses of government, building of public works, ships, etc.)	1. Necessaries, including: (a) Two-thirds of corn supply for 350,000 people (b) Timber for shipbuilding, and other military necessities (e.g. iron for weapons, flax for sails)
2. Profits of carrying trade	
3. Exports: (a) Silver from mines (b) Olive oil (butter, soap, light) (c) Painted pottery, statuettes, etc. (d) Marble (e) Manufactures from imported raw material, e.g. shields (f) Re-exported imports (e) and (f) insignificant . . .	2. Luxuries, including: (a) Raw materials for manufactures (except clay, marble, and wool) (b) Bought labor (i.e. slaves) for crafts, household and mines (c) Finished products of all kinds
4. Payments by visitors, coming for legal business or as sightseers	

When we put together all these separate facts and figures and try to imagine for ourselves their cumulative social effect, we begin to understand in some measure the meaning of Pericles' words about his fellow citizens—how they "yield to none, man for man, for independence of spirit, many-sidedness of

Athens, who has shown us, in every line she wrote and every stone she carved, how willingly she submitted to the compelling power of art, spoke with so businesslike a caution of the homage she paid in its cause—why, not out of choice but out of necessity, she "loved beauty with cheapness".

A. Zimmern, *The Greek Commonwealth*, 5th ed. (London: The Clarendon Press, 1931), pp. 408-419.

(d) *"The world is still blessing her for it"*

In the foregoing extract Professor Zimmern explained the way in which the Athenians financed their artistic masterpieces, implying that the money, clearly not their own, was well spent in such a cause. In the following extract the same writer explains the advantages the Empire held

for the "allies," even though they may have had no interest in the beautification of Athens for which they were paying.

Thus the allies had, without knowing it, slipped into financial centralization and established the first Greek Imperial Exchequer. Moreover, it was centralization of a peculiarly insidious kind, for the predominant partners, and especially Athens, who did most of the work and bore the chief responsibility, did not contribute a penny to the costs.

Who controlled the spending of the money? Officially, of course, the allies themselves. For this purpose they elected representatives to a Parliament at Delos, which, like the Ecclesia or any other city assembly, was to discuss and decide upon matters of policy. But in practice little importance attached to its deliberations, for its executive officers, the Athenian generals, were themselves responsible to their own Sovereign People; so if the two sovereigns decided differently, a deadlock would ensue. The Imperial Parliament therefore could do little more than ratify, or, if it wished to be zealous, anticipate, the decisions of the Athenians. . . .

But side by side with the new military alliance, Athens set to work to establish a network of commercial treaties between herself and each individual member of the league. This she was able to do, not merely because of her newly won prestige, but because of the acknowledged excellence of the Solonian laws and institutions under which she lived. These formed a natural starting point for a process of unification; and as there were scores and hundreds of different forms of law and custom and procedure in use among her allies, such a process could not but be felt as a convenience. . . .

Let us look first at the sphere of civil jurisdiction. The motto of the alliance was Freedom. Athens was engaged, not only in clearing the seaboard of Persians, but in clearing the sea itself of pirates and evildoers. This was a duty which had devolved, from time immemorial, upon the chief seapower of the Aegean. . . . So Athens stood, not only for freedom from the barbarian, but for freedom of intercourse and freedom of trade; and it was to the interest of the

allies to encourage her in promoting them. To police the Aegean with her triremes was only the first step. It was an obvious corollary to add to traders' convenience by simplifying the procedure in business disputes. Athens was able, therefore, to insert in her treaties a provision that all disputes arising out of business contracts entered into at Athens must be tried by Athenian law before Athenian judges. This was accepted as early as 466 by Chios, one of the most independent of the allies. Smaller states acquiesced in still greater encroachments on their sovereign jurisdiction; and in cases of revolt or disturbance, when opportunity arose for a clean sweep, they might wake up to discover that it had almost entirely disappeared. . . .

In the criminal sphere the process of unification was slower, for here the sovereign tradition was more tenacious and intimate. Even the tiniest island liked to manage its own murderers. On the other hand, Athens was all the more anxious to interfere, for she needed authority to protect her own adherents and put down mutineers. We cannot trace the development in detail. It seems to have begun with interference in cases where loss of citizen rights was involved. Athens was called in, as Rome and so many ambitious suzerains have been called in since, as the champion of a minority when party strife had become acute. Thus Athens interfered at Erythrae in 455-50 to protect the "democrats" against a party favorable to Persia. She seized the opportunity to give the city a new constitution, enforced and defended by a garrison on the citadel. The new government had to swear not to repeal the sentence of banishment against "those who had fled to the Persians" without the consent, not only of the people of Erythrae, but of the Athenians. . . . In other words, Athens, not only by her garrison, but also by her civil jurisdiction, enforced the maintenance of the status quo. Her double hold is emphasized by the mention, side by side with the commandant of the garrison, of "Overseers", imperial civil servants appointed by the Home Government, but paid by the allies, to watch and report on the state of affairs of the cities. This shows how easy it was for Athens, with her overwhelming military predominance, to steal on from position to position. . . .

Thus Athens had gradually formed herself, whether her pupils liked it or not, to be "an education to Greece". The process was so gradual and the control so wisely exercised, that the allies could not easily put their hand on any particular cause of complaint. . . . The Athenian courts did their work well. The advantage of having a sensible code to deal with was too great to be despised. Moreover, surely it was worth the expense to have a fortnight in the capital and to see how the imperial money was being laid out on the Acropolis. So the lawcourts brought sightseers; the Parthenon and the great Vestibule proved the best of advertisements; and the waggoners and the lodging-house keepers found their own businesses more profitable than sitting still and listening hard for their day's pay in the courts. It is not surprising on the whole, though the fact remains to their credit, that the Athenians were able to boast, without fear of contradiction, before a hostile assembly, of the impartiality of their justice. . . . For Athens took her own duties, as she took everything, very seriously, and did her best, in an imperfect world, however complicated the problem, to mete out fair decisions. . . .

Athens had thus become recognized as a model state; and Greece was in the mood to adopt or imitate her ways in small things as in great. We can see this in the rapid spread of Athenian weights and measures and the Athenian coinage, or of systems arranged so as to work in with them. Athens was standardizing Greek coinage as she was unifying Greek law. She did not, of course, compel her allies to use only Attic money, or money coined on the Attic standard. But she naturally preferred that contributions should be paid in it; and there were many indirect ways by which she could encourage it. It was only decent to pay Apollo, and later Athena, in the coinage they preferred to see. . . . Attic silver began to be used not only in the Confederacy, but all over Greece and among distant barbarians. . . .

Athenian influence was thus spreading, as Pericles realized, far beyond the Aegean and the confines of the Empire. Her traders were moving East and West, finding their way into every land and every sea . . . for this also was part of the imperial mission—to mix freely with all mankind and to give of their best to men and nations. Friendships were knit and alliances made with Greek, and even with barbarian powers without a thought of the Persians or the original object of the league. . . . In the course of a generation freedom had changed its meaning; and Pericles did not feel ashamed to make a convention with the national enemy [Persia], or even to receive for the league and put away in its exchequer the contributions of Carians and Lycians. Athens had now become an Empire just like Persia or Assyria, and she did not blush to receive tribute from her inferiors. Indeed she needed it for the fulfilment of the work she had to do; and Pericles, like Darius, was determined to see that she should secure and keep it. Already in 454, when nearly the whole Athenian fleet had been destroyed in Egypt and the Aegean was for a moment exposed to pirates and Phoenicians, it was thought wiser to remove the treasury of the allies from Delos to Athens. Ostensibly this meant no more than a change of banker, Athena taking the place of Apollo. But, practically, the result was to remove it once and for all from the control of the Confederate Parliament,

Ibid., pp. 188-194.

2. ATHENS AS THE EXPLOITER OF GREECE

(a) *The league as an Athenian preserve*

The remainder of the extracts in this section will put the case against the Athenians. The first is taken from Plutarch. It will be remembered that Plutarch was a moralist writing several hundred years after the events. He points out briefly the effect of the possession of Empire on the allies, by implication blaming them for their acquiescence in Athenian imperialism.

The allies of the Athenians now began to be weary of war and military service, anxious to have some repose and look after their agriculture and commerce. For they saw their enemies driven out of the country, and no longer feared new aggression from them. They continued to pay the taxes at the rate they were assessed, but they ceased sending men and ships as they had done before.

Plutarch, *Cimon*, 11, trans. A. H. Clough, *Plutarch's Lives* (Boston, 1859), III, 213-14.

(b) *The league as means of enriching Athens*

Aristotle, writing some 120 years after the founding of the Confederacy, did not hold the same view of the disinterestedness of Aristides. He seems to have regarded the whole Confederacy as deliberately planned for the enrichment of Athens at the expense of the allies.

At this time Aristides the son of Lysimachus, and Themistocles the son of Neocles were the leaders of the people. The latter had greatest renown for

and to make everyone see and feel, what they had known in their hearts long ago, that it was the money of Athens, with which she could do what she liked. The world is still blessing her for what she did with it.

. . . Cimon . . . forced no man to go who was not willing, but he accepted money and unmanned vessels from those who wished to be excused from military service, and permitted them to yield to the temptation of staying at home and attending to their private affairs. Thus they lost their military habits, and became, through their folly and new taste for luxury, unwarlike farmers and traders; while Cimon, putting large numbers of Athenians on board his galleys, thoroughly disciplined them in his expeditions, and before long he had made them supreme over their own paymasters. The allies, whose laziness supported them while they sailed around everywhere, acquiring military and naval skills incessantly, began to fear and flatter them, finding themselves after a time no longer allies, but against their will tributaries and slaves. . . .

military skill, while the former was famous as a statesman and as the most upright man of his time. For this reason they used the one as a general, the other as a counselor. . . . It was Aristides who first assessed the contribution to be paid to the allied cities in the third year after the battle of Salamis. . . .

When the Athenian state was growing in self-confidence and in the accumulation of much wealth, he advised the Athenians to seize the leadership and to give up their residence in the countryside to come to live in the city. For they would all have their livelihood there, some by participating in military expeditions, some by doing garrison service, and in this way they would keep hold of the "leadership". They followed this advice and placed themselves in control of the empire, and from then on they got into the habit of treating their allies, with the exception of Chios, Lesbos, and Samos as if they were their masters. These three they used as guards of the Athenian empire and . . . left their constitutions untouched and allowed them to rule over whatever subjects they happened to have.

They also made it possible for the masses to live comfortably, as Aristides had proposed. For out of the income derived from the contributions made by the allies and from internal levies more than twenty thousand persons were maintained. For there were six thousand judges, sixteen hundred bowmen, twelve hundred cavalrymen, five hundred Councilmen, five hundred guards of the dockyards, plus fifty guards on the Acropolis, about seven hundred state officials at home and about seven hundred abroad. In addition when later they went to war, there were twenty-five hundred heavy armed soldiers, twenty guard ships, and other ships carrying the guardians, that is, two thousand men chosen by lot. Finally there were the Prytaneum [certain persons were honored by being entertained at public expense in the Prytaneum or City Hall, as a reward for some exceptional service to the city], the orphans, and the jailkeepers. All these persons received their livelihood from the state.

Aristotle, *Constitution of Athens,* 23-24, trans. K. von Fritz and E. Kapp (New York: Hafner Publishing Co., 1950), pp. 93-94.

(c) *Athens as exploiter of rich for benefit of poor*

The unknown writer of the following passage which is contemporary with the Empire itself is usually known as the Old Oligarch. It is not certain whether he was a disgruntled aristocrat (the usual view) or whether he was a sophist who composed his short treatise as an exercise in rhetoric. The burden of his complaint is that the richer classes both in Athens and in the Empire are exploited for the benefit of the poor, for whom the Empire was a valuable source of income and employment.

To speak next of the allies, when Athenian envoys go out and slander and vent their hatred on the upper classes, this is done because the ruler cannot help being hated by those whom he rules, but if wealth and respectability were to be dominant in the subject cities, the Athenians could hardly expect to hold their power for very long. So the upper classes are punished with infamy, robbed of their money, driven from their homes, and put to death, while the lower classes are given special honors. On the other hand, upper class Athenians protect, as far as they can, the upper class in the allied cities, because that is to the interest of their own class here. It may be urged that in the matter of might and power the real strength of Athens lies in the ability of the allies to contribute their quota of money; but to the democratic mind it is manifestly an even greater advantage for individual Athenians to lay their hands on the wealth of the allies, leaving them only enough to cultivate their estates and live upon them, but not powerful enough to entertain treasonable designs upon Athens.

Some people seem to think it a mistaken policy for the Athenians to make their allies come to Athens to have their lawsuits tried. But it is obvious what a number of advantages the Athenian people derive from this. The court fees pay them a regular salary throughout the year; they can look after the affairs of the allied states without stirring from home and without the expense of naval expeditions. And they can give their decisions in favor of their own democratic partisans, and thus ruin their opponents. While if these cases were tried at home, it would be the very friends of the Athenians who would be destroyed out of hatred for Athens. Moreover, the democracy gains the following advantages from hearing the cases involving the allies at Athens. There is the one per cent tax levied at the Peiraeus, the rooming house owner makes a nice profit, and so does the owner of animals and slaves to be let out on hire. Heralds and criers do better owing to the presence of the allies at Athens, and finally we should remember that if the allies did not have to come to Athens themselves for their lawsuits only such Athenians as visited them would be held in honor, dignitaries like generals, trierarchs and ambassadors; while, as it is, every single individual among the allies is compelled to flatter the people of Athens because he knows that it is not a casual group of judges who will try his case, but the sovereign people themselves, for this is the law and custom at Athens. He is made to behave like a suppliant in the courts of justice. When some juryman comes into court he has to shake his hand. So the allies find themselves more and more in the position of slaves to the Athenian democracy.

Anonymous [Pseudo-Xenophon], *The Constitution of the Athenians*, 14-18, trans. Stewart Easton.

(d) *Limitations of Athenian democracy*

After the panegyrics on Athenian democracy given in section 1, it is well also to be reminded that such democracy as there was did not benefit everyone in Athens. As the following extract from another economic historian suggests, the Athenian democrats were only an "exceptionally large diversified ruling class," and it was by no means a government by and for the whole people.

Fifth-century Athens thus provides the first adequately documented example of a thorough-going popular government. Its popular character must not be exaggerated. In the first place women had no place in public life. The wives of citizens were almost as completely secluded as women in Mohammedan countries today, and at law were in a worse position than their Assyrian and Babylonian sisters. Secondly, citizenship was now a hereditary privilege from which resident aliens were rigidly excluded. Yet on Gomme's estimate these included a tenth of the total population and comprised most of the craftsmen and manufacturers. Finally industry was based on slavery; even the small farmer generally owned a slave or two, and the majority of the employees in mines and factories and even the policemen were slaves. Though citizens did work on their farms, ply crafts, take on small contracts for public works, work as wage laborers for fellow citizens and even in mines, they secured leisure for politics and culture largely at the expense of their wives, of aliens who had no share in the government and of slaves who had no rights whatever.

Moreover the revenues of Athens which paid magistrates, jurors and assemblymen were swollen by two exceptional sources. The richest silver mines in the Aegean lay in Attica at Laurion; exploited mainly by slaves under local contractors, they yielded a rich harvest of royalties to the state. Secondly, Athens was an imperial city, nourished by the tribute of subjects. It is true that the Athenian Empire began as a league of free cities against Persia. The tribute was a substitute for the ships that the allies had originally equipped and manned for the common defense. But after 450 B.C. the allies felt themselves subjects and tried to rebel; the imperial people were diverting some of their contributions to the adornment of Athens and their own support.

Thus the Athenian "people" was in a sense only an exceptionally large diversified ruling class. The appearance of economic democracy had been achieved not so much by an even distribution of the wealth it produced as by using the proceeds of exploitation to relieve the poverty of its poorer sections. When external supplies were cut off by the loss of the empire, the conflict of poor and rich broke out again in violence. In the sequel Athens lost her full autonomy and returned to a moderate oligarchy with foreign support in the late fourth century.

V. G. Childe, *What Happened in History* (London: Penguin Books, Ltd., 1942), pp. 207-208.

B. The Athenian Attitude Towards the Political Freedom of Others

1. As Preservers of Greek Liberties

In the years after the Peloponnesian War, when Athens was no longer dominant in Greece, Athenians looked back to the period of their supremacy as a kind of Golden Age, and some idealized it in order to point the contrast with their present decadence. In the *Panegyric*, Isocrates, a professional orator and speech-writer, tries to persuade his readers to undertake again the leadership in Greece, this time for the purpose of getting rid of the intolerable influence of Persia in Greek affairs. In the process he praises the period of the Confederacy when Persia was kept at her proper distance. Each of the next two passages is taken from this speech.

(a) The kindness and humanity of the Athenian Empire

So public spirited were they that even in their party struggles they opposed one another, not to see which faction should destroy the other and rule over the remnant, but which should outstrip the other in doing something good for the state. . . . In the same spirit they governed their relations with other states. They treated the Hellenes with consideration and not with insolence, regarding it as their duty to command them in the field but not to tyrannize over them, desiring rather to be addressed as leaders than as masters, and rather to be greeted as saviors than reviled as destroyers; they won the Hellenic cities to themselves by doing kindness instead of subverting them by force, keeping their word more faithfully than men now keep their oaths, and thinking it right to abide by their covenants as by the decrees of necessity; they exulted less in the exercise of power than they gloried in living with self-control, thinking it their duty to feel toward the weaker as they expected the stronger to feel towards themselves; and while they regarded their home cities as their several places of abode, yet they considered Hellas to be their common fatherland.

Isocrates, *Panegyricus* (c. 380 B.C.), 79-81, trans. G. Norlin, Loeb Classical Library (Cambridge, Mass.: Harvard University Press, 1928), I, 167-169.

(b) *Imperial defense as benefit for allies*

Now up to this point I am sure that all men would acknowledge that our city has been the author of the greatest number of blessings, and that she should in fairness be entitled to the hegemony. But from this point on some take us to task, urging that after we succeeded to the sovereignty of the sea we brought many evils upon the Hellenes; and, in these speeches of theirs, they cast it in our teeth that we enslaved the Melians [see 2 c below] and destroyed the people of Scione. I, however, take the view, in the first place, that it is no sign that we ruled badly if some of those who were at war with us are shown to have been severely disciplined, but that a much clearer proof that we administered the affairs of our allies wisely is seen in the fact that among the states which remained our loyal subjects not one experienced these disasters. In the second place, if other states had dealt more leniently in the same circumstances, they might reasonably censure us; but since that is not the case, and it is impossible to control so great a multitude of states without disciplining those who offend, does it not follow that we deserve praise because we acted so harshly in the fewest possible cases, and were yet able to hold our dominion for the greatest length of time?

But I believe that all men are of the opinion that those will prove the best leaders and champions of the Hellenes under whom in the past those who yielded obedience have fared the best. Well, then, it will be found that under our supremacy the private households grew most prosperous and that the commonwealths also became greatest. For we were not jealous of the growing states, nor did we engender confusion among them by setting up conflicting polities side by side, in order that faction might be arrayed against faction and both might court our favor. On the contrary, we regarded harmony among our allies as the common boon of all, and therefore we governed all the cities under the same laws, deliberating about them in the spirit of allies, not of masters; guarding the interests of the whole confederacy but leaving each member of it free to direct its own affairs; supporting the people but making war on despotic powers, considering it an outrage that the many should be subject to the few, that those who were poorer in fortune but not inferior in other respects should be banished from the offices . . . , that furthermore in a fatherland which belongs to all in common some should hold the place of master, others of aliens, and that men who are citizens by birth should be robbed by law of their share in the government.

It was because we had these objections, and others besides, to oligarchies that we established the same polity in the other states as in Athens itself—a polity which I see no need to extol at greater length, since I can tell the truth about it in a word: They continued to live under this regime for seventy years, and during this time they experienced no tyrannies, they were free from the domination of the barbarians, they were untroubled by internal factions, and they were at peace with all the world.

On account of these services it becomes all thinking men to be deeply grateful to us, much rather than to reproach us because of our system of colonization; for we sent our colonies into the depopulated states for the protection of their territories and not for our own aggrandisement. And here is proof of this: We had in proportion to the number of our citizens a very small territory, but a very great empire; we possessed twice as many ships of war as all the rest combined, and these were strong enough to engage double their number; at the very borders of Attica lay Euboea, which was not only fitted by her situation to command the sea but which also surpassed all the islands in her general resources, and Euboea lent itself more readily to our control than did our own country; besides, while we knew that both among the Hellenes and among the barbarians those are regarded most highly who have driven their neighbors from their homes and have so secured for themselves a life of affluence and ease [an allusion to the Spartans who lived from the labor of conquered Messenians], nevertheless none of these considerations tempted us to wrong the people of the islands. On the contrary, we alone of those who have obtained great power suffered ourselves to live in more straitened circumstances than those who were reproached with being our slaves. And yet, had we been disposed to seek our own advantage, we should not, I imagine, have set our hearts on the territory of Scione (which as all the world knows, we gave over to our Plataean refugees), and passed over this great territory which would have enriched us all.

Isocrates, *Panegyricus*, 100-109, trans. G. Norlin, Loeb Classical Library (Cambridge, Mass.: Harvard University Press, 1928), I, 181-189.

2. As Enslavers of Greek Liberties

(a) *Severe exactions and refusal to permit secession*

The darker side of Athenian imperialism is drawn entirely from the pages of the contemporary Thucydides who describes without comment just what it meant for the islanders to live under Athenian rule and be unable to escape it. The first extract tells what happened to the Naxians when, having decided the Persian danger was over and that they would like to discontinue their contribution, they became the first of the allies to secede.

After this Naxos left the confederacy [466 B.C.] and a war ensued, and she had to return after a siege; this was the first instance of the engagement being broken by the subjugation of an allied city, a precedent which was followed by that of the rest in the order which circumstances prescribed. Of all the causes of defection, that connected with the arrears of tribute and vessels, and with failure of service, was the chief; for the Athenians were very severe and exacting, and made themselves offensive by applying the screw of necessity to men who were not used to and indeed not disposed to any continuous labor. In some other respects the Athenians were not the old popular rulers they had been at first; and if they had more than their fair share of service, it was correspondingly easy for them to reduce any that tried to leave the confederacy. For this the allies had themselves to blame; the wish to avoid service making most of them arrange to pay their share of the expense in money instead of in ships, and so to avoid having to leave their homes. Thus while Athens was increasing her navy with the funds which they contributed, whenever the allies revolted they found themselves without resources or experience for war. . . .

Thucydides, *The History of the Peloponnesian War*, I, 99-100, adapted from the translation by R. Crawley (1876).

(b) *An ally's view of Athenian domination*

When the Peloponnesian War broke out and the Spartans invaded Attica, the island of Lesbos revolted, led by the chief city Mitylene. The Mitylenians petitioned the Spartans to take them into their alliance. Thucydides has put into the mouths of the envoys from Mitylene the growing disillusionment of the allies with Athenian imperial policy.

Justice and honesty will be the first topics of our speech, especially as we are asking for alliance, because we know that there can never be any solid friendship between individuals, or union between communities that is worth the name, unless the parties be persuaded of each other's honesty. . . . Between ourselves and the Athenians alliance began when you withdrew from the Median [Persian] War, and they remained to finish the business. But we did not become allies of the Athenians for the subjugation of the Hellenes, but allies of the Hellenes for their liberation from the Mede, and as long as the Athenians led us fairly we followed them loyally. But when we saw them relax their hostility to the Mede, and try to compass the subjection of the allies, then our apprehensions began. As we were, however, unable to unite and defend ourselves, on account of the number of confederates who had votes, all the allies were enslaved except ourselves and the Chians, who continued to send our contingents as independent and nominally free. However we could no longer feel confidence in Athens as a leader when we looked at the examples we have mentioned; it seemed unlikely that she would refrain from reducing us to the same condition once she had enslaved our fellow confederates, as long as she had the power to do so.

Had we all remained independent we might have trusted her not to make any violent change; but since most of the allies were her subjects they would resent our independence in contrast to their own submission, and especially since they daily grew more powerful while we became poorer. Now the only safe basis for an alliance is mutual fear; a would-be aggressor is deterred by the fact that the odds are not in his favor. The only reason they left us independent was because they thought that by specious words and political manipulations

they could gain empire without having to fight for it . . . and, in addition, the system of voting made it possible for them to lead the stronger states against the weaker first, and leave the stronger states to the last when they would have lost their natural allies and be unable to defend themselves. But if they had begun with us, while all the states were still independent and commanding their own resources, and there was still a center to rally around, they would have found the task of subjugation more difficult. Moreover our navy still gave them some apprehension; it was always possible that it might unite with you or with some other power and become dangerous to Athens. For a time the flattery which we paid to the common people and their leaders also helped us to maintain our independence. But we did not expect to be able to continue this policy once war broke out, when we considered how they had treated others.

How then could we put any trust in such friendship or freedom as this? We accepted each other against our inclination; fear made them pay court to us in war, as we paid court to them in peace. Instead of sympathy, the usual basis of confidence, we were afraid, fear keeping us to the alliance more than friendship; and it was certain that as soon as one or the other of us felt that we could break faith with impunity we should do so. You should not therefore condemn us for making the break first instead of waiting for them to strike the first blow. . . . If we could resist their plots and afford to wait for them, then we should be indeed their equals and under no necessity to become their subjects. But the initiative was always theirs, not ours, so we ought clearly to be able to be free to take steps in our own defense. . . .

You should not think that this is a case of endangering yourselves for a country which is not yours. Lesbos may appear far off, but when help is wanted she will be found near enough. It is not in Attica that the war will be decided, as some imagine, but in the countries by which Attica is supported; and the Athenian revenue is drawn from the allies and will become larger still if they reduce us; since not only will no other state revolt, but our resources will be added to theirs, and we shall be treated worse than those that were enslaved before. . . .

Thucydides, *The History of the Peloponnesian War*, III, 10-14, freely adapted from the translation by R. Crawley (1876).

(c) *Wanton aggression against a neutral*

In 416 occurred the classic case of wanton Athenian aggression against the island of Melos, populated by relatively unsophisticated Dorians who had never formed part of the Confederation. This was the case for which even Isocrates felt impelled to apologize, explaining it but unable wholeheartedly to defend it (see 1 b above).

The Athenians also made an expedition against the island of Melos, with thirty ships of their own, six Chian and two Lesbian vessels, one thousand six hundred heavy infantry, three hundred archers, and twenty mounted archers from Athens, and about one thousand five hundred heavy infantry from the allies and the islanders. The Melians are a colony of Lacedaemon that would not submit to the Athenians like the other islanders, and at first remained neutral and took no part in the struggle, but afterwards upon the Athenians using violence and plundering their territory, assumed an attitude of open hostility. Cleomedes . . . and Tisias . . . the generals, encamping in their territory with the above armament before doing any harm to their land, sent envoys to negotiate. These the Melians did not bring before the people but bade them state the object of their mission to the magistrates and the few; upon which the Athenian envoys spoke as follows:

Athenians. . . . Supposing you refrain from making any set speech, but tell us whatever you do not like, and let us settle that before proceeding further. Does this proposition suit you?

Melians. There is nothing the matter with quietly instructing each other as you propose. But your military preparations are so far advanced that we can see you are here to be judges in your own cause, and that all we can reasonably expect from this negotiation is war, if we prove to have right on our side and refuse to submit, and, in the contrary case, slavery.

Athenians. If you are merely going to talk about your forebodings for the future, and have no intention of consulting about the safety of your state on the basis of realities, then we might as well stop now; otherwise we will continue.

Melians. Surely it is natural and excusable for men in our position to consider and talk about more things than one. As you say, the question in this conference is the matter of the safety of our country. We are ready to proceed in the way you propose if it is agreeable to you.

Athenians. For ourselves we shall not trouble you with specious pretenses. We shall not explain how we have a right to Empire because we overthrew the Mede, nor shall we pretend that we are now attacking you because of any wrong you have done us. We shall not bother to make a long speech which would not convince you. And we hope that you, in return, will not try to influence us by saying that you refrained from joining the Spartans even though you are their colonists, nor by telling us you have done us no wrong. Try to be practical, keeping in mind what we both really feel. You know as well as we that there is no question of right and wrong except when power is equal. That is the way the world is—the strong do what they can, while the weak suffer what they must.

Melians. Since you won't permit us to speak about right, and we must only speak of interest, we think it *expedient* that you should not destroy what is our common protection, namely the privilege of being allowed in danger to invoke what is fair and right, and even to make use of arguments which may not be strictly valid but are current usage. You are just as much interested in this as we or anyone else; for your fall would be a signal for the heaviest vengeance, and an example for the world to meditate upon.

Athenians. We are not frightened by the possible end of our Empire if it should come about. . . . In any case it is a risk we are prepared to take. We shall now proceed to show you that we have come here in the interests of our Empire, while at the same time for the preservation of your country. We wish to exercise that Empire over you, and see you preserved for the good of us both.

Melians. How could it be as good for us to serve as for you to rule?

Athenians. Because you would have the advantage of submitting before the worst has befallen you; and we should gain by not destroying you.

Melians. So you won't consent to let us be neutral, friends and not enemies, but allies of neither side?

Athenians. No, for our allies would think our friendship for you to be a sign of our weakness, while if you are our enemies, this is a sign of our power.

Melians. Do your subjects think it just to put those who have nothing to

do with you in the same category as people who are mostly your own colonists, or conquered rebels?

Athenians. As far as right goes, they think one has as much of it as the other. But they think that if anyone maintains his independence it is only because he is strong, and we only refrain from molesting them because we are afraid. So, if we reduce you to subjection our own security is increased. You are islanders, and weak, so it is more important than ever that you should not be able to baffle the masters of the sea.

Melians. Since we are debarred from talking about justice, and you have invited us to consider your interest, wouldn't our suggested policy give you a greater security? How can you avoid making enemies of all neutrals who will see what you are doing to us and conclude that some day or another you will attack them? So you make more enemies than you have already, and force others to become so who would otherwise never have thought of it. . . . If you risk so much to keep your Empire, and your subjects risk so much to get rid of your yoke, wouldn't it be cowardly and shameful for us to submit before we have tried anything?

Athenians. Not if you are well advised. The contest is unequal. The reward of honor and the penalty of shame are beside the point. It is a simple matter of preservation, and not resisting those who are far stronger than you.

Melians. But we know that it is not always numbers which decide the fortune of war. To submit is to yield to despair, while action at least gives us some chance to stand erect.

Athenians. Those who have abundant resources can afford to indulge in hope; at least they may be spared utter ruin. But hope is naturally extravagant, and people don't see it for what it is until they have staked everything upon it and been ruined. It prevents them from taking the proper precautions. Don't you be so hopeful, but remember you are weak and your whole existence depends upon a single chance. And please don't be like those crude people who abandon such security as human men can still give them, who, when visible hopes fail them, turn to the invisible, to prophecies and oracles, and other such inventions that delude men with hopes to their destruction.

Melians. You may be sure that we have no illusions about the difficulty of defending ourselves against your power and fortune, unless the terms be equal. But we trust that the gods may grant us fortune as good as yours, since we are just men fighting against unjust, and that what we lack in power will be made up by our alliance with the Spartans, who are bound, if only for very shame, to come to the aid of their kinsmen. So our confidence is not altogether irrational.

Athenians. When you speak of the favor of the gods, we may as fairly hope for that as you; neither our pretensions nor our conduct is in any way contrary to what men believe of the gods or practise among themselves. Of the gods we believe and of men we know, that by a necessary law of their nature they rule wherever they can. We were not the first to make this law or to act upon it; we found it existing before us, and it will continue to exist after us. All we do is make use of it, well aware that you would do the same if you had the power. So as far as the gods are concerned we are not afraid, nor do we fear that we shall be at a disadvantage. But when we come to your notion about the Spartans, and your belief that they will for very shame come to help you, we bless your simplicity but do not envy you your folly. When their own interests or their country's laws are at stake they are the worthiest men alive. We could say much about their conduct

towards others; but if we may put it in a nutshell, no people are more apt to consider what is agreeable to be also honorable, and what is expedient to be just. This kind of thinking does not augur well for your safety which you are counting on so unreasonably. . . . Only with numerous allies do they venture to attack a neighbor. Is it likely that they will cross the sea to protect an island while we are masters of the sea?

Melians. But they would have others to send. . . . The Cretan sea is a wide one, and it is not always so easy for the masters of the sea to intercept others. . . . And even if the Spartans miscarried in this, they would fall upon your land and upon your allies. . . . And instead of fighting for places which don't belong to you, you will have to fight for your own confederacy and your own country.

Athenians. Some day they might make such a diversion, but they will learn, as others before them, that the Athenians never once have withdrawn from a siege from fear of anyone. . . . But we are struck by the fact that . . . in all this discussion your strongest arguments depend upon hope and the future, and your actual resources are too scanty, as compared with those arrayed against you, for you to come out victorious. . . . Surely you will not let yourself be fooled by the idea of being disgraced, a fatal delusion in the face of unmistakable danger. From fear of that seductive word, too many men are enslaved by the phrase in such a way as to fall wilfully into hopeless disaster. Such error is more disgraceful than any disgrace that comes by misfortune. If you are well advised you will avoid this error, and not think it dishonorable to submit to the greatest city in Hellas, when it makes you the modest offer of becoming its tributary ally, without ceasing to enjoy the country that belongs to you; nor when you have a choice between war and security, will you be so blinded as to choose the worse. . . . Think over the matter then once again, and remember that it is for your country that you are consulting, and that you have only one. Upon this one deliberation depends its prosperity or ruin.

The Athenians now withdrew from the conference; and the Melians, left to themselves, came to the decision corresponding to the stand they had maintained during the conference, and answered, "Our resolution, Athenians, is the same as it was at first. We will not in a moment deprive of freedom a city that has been inhabited these seven hundred years; but we put our trust in the fortune by which the gods have preserved it till now, and in the help of men, that is, of the Spartans; and so we will try to save ourselves. Meanwhile we invite you to allow us to be friends to you, and foes to neither party. . . ."

The Athenian envoys now returned to the army; and the Melians showing no signs of yielding, the generals at once began hostilities . . . and besieged the place. . . .

The next winter the Spartans intended to invade the Argive territory, but arriving at the frontier found the sacrifices for crossing unfavorable and went back again. . . . About the same time the Melians again took another part of the Athenian lines which were but feebly garrisoned. Reinforcements afterwards arriving from Athens in consequence, . . . the siege was now pressed vigorously; and some treachery taking place inside, the Melians surrendered at discretion to the Athenians, who put to death all the grown men whom they took, and sold the women and children for slaves, and subsequently sent out five hundred colonists and inhabited the place themselves. . . .

Thucydides, *The History of the Peloponnesian War*, VI, 86-116, freely adapted from the translation by R. Crawley (1876.)

II. ROME: THE EARLY PRINCIPATE—AN EFFORT TO PRESERVE THE REPUBLIC, OR A DISGUISED TYRANNY?

Rome had been a self-governing republic for many centuries before Julius Caesar became permanent dictator in 46 B.C. Two years later Caesar was murdered by embittered republicans. Personal grievances may have predominated in the minds of the conspirators; but at least Brutus, and probably several of the others, were genuinely convinced that he intended to destroy the Republic and replace it by one-man rule.

Nearly forty years earlier Sulla had held a position of similarly unquestioned supremacy, but he had resigned his dictatorship after handing over the leadership in the state to a reformed Senate; the Senate, however, had long before ceased to be competent to run the empire which had been won by Roman arms, and now had lost confidence in itself. One-man rule was probably inevitable in the situation of the time, and to hindsight no possible alternative appears. But the die-hard republicans, and perhaps a majority of Roman citizens, had by no means yet accepted the inevitable. The title of king was detested by Romans who remembered their ancient domination by the Etruscans, and no better title had yet been devised. Though some Romans may have been prepared to accept the position, few indeed could have been happy about the name. So Caesar was murdered, and the murderers proclaimed the restoration of the Republic and of liberty.

Yet there was no true restoration of the Republic. After the conspirators had been defeated there was an uneasy alliance between Caesar's chief general, Mark Antony, and his designated heir, Octavian Caesar. When the issue of supremacy was ultimately decided by civil war and Octavian emerged the master of the Roman world, the problem was in no way solved. Probably more Romans had grown accustomed to the idea that the Republic had gone forever, but the institutions suitable for the new Roman one-man government had not yet been devised.

Octavian, who now accepted the title of Augustus, a title which conferred increased dignity but no power, and had for the most part previously been used of gods, was the true founder of the new imperial Roman state which has been called the Roman Empire—a misleading title for modern students, since the great bulk of the Roman possessions had been acquired under the Republic. Concerned with the problem of how to make his government legitimate and at the same time effective, he conceived the idea of assuming a few important republican powers for life. These gave him the real control of the state, though he called himself only a *princeps*, or chief citizen. He took the *proconsulare imperium* and the *tribunicia potestas*—the imperium, or military power, of a proconsul, and the civil power of a tribune, which included the right to introduce and veto legislation. Later he assumed the power of a censor, which entitled him to draw up the census of citizens and purge the ranks of the Senate, and the title of *pontifex maximus*, or chief priest, which permitted him to reform the religion. With these powers his rule was unchallenged, and he bequeathed his position intact to Tiberius, his chosen successor, by having the Senate bestow the two principal powers upon Tiberius before his own death.

There have always been varying opinions on the nature of the rule of Augustus. Was it a barely disguised tyranny, or was it, as he claimed himself, an honest attempt to restore such of the dead Republic as was possible, and give back power to the Senate and people? Was he a hypocrite, giving away the forms and shadow of power, while he retained the substance in his own hands, intentionally bamboozling the people, though concealing the fact by consummate craft? Or was he at least a genuine republican who tried to steer a middle path between the dictatorship of Julius Caesar and the anarchy of the last days of the Republic, a man who did not care for power, tried to use it as little as possible, but was forced to reform the Republic for its own good, even though the ultimate result was its abolition?

If Augustus himself was not a tyrant, and did not abuse his power, was then Tiberius the ruler who transformed the disguised monarchy into an undisguised tyranny? Many of the ancient Romans thought so; and yet even his bitterest enemies and critics admit that he was an admirer of the old Republic, and he had in earlier years at least maintained the old republican virtues of simplicity, frugality and honesty, permitted criticism of himself and his policies, and wished to avoid the task that fell to him as the successor of the divine Augustus.

The two problems that follow are closely connected. The first concerns the nature of the character and rule of Augustus, and the second asks similar questions about Tiberius. The two problems may suggest to the reader certain reflections on the nature of power, and the difficulties involved in trying to exercise it indirectly, and the inevitable pressures that beset its holders. Since none of the writers, ancient or modern, is able to adopt a totally impartial attitude, the selections may help the reader to realize the fallibility and transience of moral judgments upon public characters. John Buchan, twentieth-century imperial administrator, and Edward Gibbon, professional liberal after the manner of the eighteenth-century Enlightenment, are neither more nor less subjective in their judgments than the ancients who lived and suffered under the immediate successors of the founders of their Empire, and who were vitally interested in how they had fallen away from the old ideals of republican liberty.

A. The Achievement of Augustus

1. PUBLIC STATEMENT OF AUGUSTUS HIMSELF A YEAR BEFORE HIS DEATH

In A.D. 13 Augustus prepared a bare statement of his achievements since becoming *princeps,* and had it engraved on bronze tablets which were to be set up in front of his mausoleum. Though these tablets have disappeared, many copies were made, the most perfect of which is the *Monumentum Ancyranum,* an inscription chiseled on the walls of a temple at Ancyra (Ankara) in modern Turkey. The account contains, of course, exactly what Augustus wished to be believed about himself by posterity, and is therefore of first rate historical interest, whatever may be the opinion held about the nature of his achievements: each word is carefully chosen, and none is wasted.

In my sixth and seventh consulships, when I had extinguished the flames of civil war, after receiving by universal consent the absolute control of affairs, I transferred the republic from my own control to the will of the senate and the Roman people. For this service on my part I was given the title of Augustus by decree of the senate, and the doorposts of my house were covered with laurels by public act, and a civic crown was fixed above my door, and a golden shield was placed in the Curia Julia whose inscription testified that the senate and the Roman people gave me this in recognition of my valor, my clemency, my justice, and my piety. After that time I took precedence of all in rank, but of power I possessed no more than those who were my colleagues in any magistracy.

Res gestae divi Augusti, 34, trans. F. W. Shipley, Loeb Classical Library (Cambridge, Mass.: Harvard University Press, 1924), pp. 399-401.

2. TACITUS REPORTS OPPOSING VIEWS IN HIS TIME (ABOUT A.D. 120)

Tacitus, considered by many to be by far the greatest of Rome's historians, had been forced to endure the outright tyranny of a later Emperor, Domitian, an account of

which he gives movingly in his *Agricola.* A sentimental republican, he was yet enough of a realist to recognize that the Empire in his own time had become established, and that it was now too late to restore the republican regime. But the recognition of this fact did not prevent him from yearn-ing after the lost days of freedom, and devoting considerable attention especially to the tyrannies of Tiberius, whom he seems to have regarded as the real destroyer of Roman liberties, as will be seen from later extracts. In this first extract from Tacitus, the historian merely records the two views held in his time about Augustus, without stating his personal preference. This is a common procedure in his work, for he was evidently trained as an orator, and had a natural or acquired interest in human psychology. Frequently his pictures are unfair, but they are always vivid and thoughtful.

When, after the destruction of Brutus and Cassius, there was no longer any army of the Commonwealth, when . . . even the Julian faction had only Caesar left to lead it, then, dropping the title of triumvir, and giving out that he was a Consul, and was satisfied with a tribune's authority for the protection of the people, Augustus won over the soldiers with gifts, the populace with cheap corn, and all men with the sweets of repose, and so grew greater by degrees, while he concentrated in himself the functions of the Senate, the magistrates, and the laws. He was wholly unopposed, for the boldest spirits had fallen in battle or in the proscription, while the remaining nobles, the readier they were to become slaves, were raised the higher by wealth and promotion, so that, aggrandized by revolution, they preferred the safety of the present to the dangerous past. Nor did the provinces dislike that condition of affairs, for they distrusted the government of the Senate and the people, because of the rivalries between the leading men and the rapacity of the officials, while the protection of the laws was unavailing, as they were continually deranged by violence, intrigue, and finally by corruption. . . . At home all was tranquil, and there were magistrates with the same titles; there was a younger gener-

ation, sprung up since the victory of Actium, and even many of the older men had been born during the civil wars. How few were left who had seen the republic!

Thus the State had been revolutionized, and there was not a vestige left of the old sound morality. Stripped of equality, all looked up to the commands of a sovereign without the least apprehension for the present. . . .

On the day of the funeral . . . sensible men spoke variously of his life with praise and censure. Some said "that dutiful feeling towards a father, and the necessities of the State in which laws then had no place, drove him into civil war, which can neither be planned nor conducted on any right principles. . . . The only remedy for his distracted country was the rule of a single man. Yet the State had been organized under the name neither of a kingdom nor a dictatorship, but under that of a prince. The ocean and remote rivers were the boundaries of the empire; the legions, provinces, fleets, all things were linked together; there was law for the citizens; there was respect shown to the allies. The capital had been embellished on a grand scale; only in a few instances had he resorted to force, simply to secure general tranquillity."

It was said, on the other hand, "that filial duty and State necessity were merely assumed as a mask. It was really from a lust for sovereignty that he had excited the veterans by bribery . . . and turned against the State the arms with which he had been entrusted against Antonius. Citizens were proscribed, lands divided, without so much as the approval of those who executed these deeds. . . . No doubt there was peace after all this, but it was a peace stained with blood; there were the disasters of Lollius and Varus, the murders at Rome of the Varros, Egnatii, and Julii. . . . No honor was left for the gods when Augustus chose to be himself worshipped with temples and statues, like those of the deities, and with flamens and priests. He had not even adopted Tiberius as his successor out of affection or any regard for the State, but, having thoroughly seen his arrogant and savage temper, he had sought glory for himself by a contrast of extreme wickedness. . . ."

Tacitus, *Annals*, trans. A. J. Church and W. J. Brodribb, I, 2-4, 8-10 (New York: Modern Library, 1942), pp. 3-5, 9-11, by permission of Macmillan and Co., Ltd., London, and St. Martin's Press, Inc., New York.

3. OPINION OF THE ANCIENT WORLD

(a) *View of a faithful imperial officer*

Velleius Paterculus was an officer in the imperial army under both Augustus and Tiberius. He has no nostalgia for the lost republic, and seems to have had no doubts about the excellence of the new regime which put an end to the anarchy of the last days of the republic. He wrote a brief history of Rome which became fuller as he reached his own times. There is thus a fairly extensive account of Augustus, and the work closes with a eulogy of Tiberius in his earlier years as *princeps,* an extract from which will appear in the next section. The history is not apparently written to order, to please an imperial patron, but out of a genuine enthusiasm. Its value, therefore, is considerable in that it describes Augustus and Tiberius from the point of view of a loyal, if perhaps too uncritical, supporter of their rule.

There is nothing that man can desire from the gods, nothing that the gods can grant to a man, nothing that wish can conceive or good fortune bring to pass, which Augustus on his return to the city did not bestow upon the republic, the Roman people, and the world.

The civil wars were ended after twenty years, foreign wars suppressed, peace restored, the frenzy of arms everywhere lulled to rest; validity was restored to the laws, authority to the courts, and dignity to the senate. The power of the magistrates was reduced to its former limits, with the sole exception that two were added to the existing eight praetors. The old traditional form of the republic was restored. Agriculture returned to the fields, respect to religion, to mankind freedom from anxiety, and to each citizen his property rights were now assured. Old laws were usefully amended, and new laws passed for the general good; the revision of the senate, while not too drastic, was not lacking in severity. The chief men of the state who had won triumphs and held high office were at the invitation of Augustus induced to adorn the city. In the case of the consulship only, Caesar was not able to have his way, but was obliged to hold that office consecutively until the eleventh time in spite of his frequent efforts to prevent it; but the dictatorship which the people persistently offered him, he as stubbornly refused.

Velleius Paterculus, *History of Rome*, II, 89, trans. F. W. Shipley, Loeb Classical Library (Cambridge, Mass.: Harvard University Press, 1924), pp. 237-39.

(b) *View of an early third-century historian*

Dion Cassius was a Roman administrator and historian who wrote in the first quarter of the third century A.D. He was able to use for his history contemporary sources which are now lost to us, and, although of course he had no first-hand knowledge of the period, he makes some attempt to criticize his sources and to come to his own opinion. The following extract is taken from the eulogy of Tiberius on his predecessor as reported by Dion, together with Dion's own comments on the reign of Augustus.

After these achievements and when by kindness he had allayed all that remained of factional discord and by generosity had moderated the victorious soldiery, he might on the strength of this record and of the weapons and the money at his command have been indisputably the sole lord of all, as indeed he had become by the very course of events. Nevertheless he refused; and like a good physician who takes in hand a disease-ridden body and heals it, he first restored to health and then gave back to you the whole body politic. . . . He possessed all your armies, whose numbers you know; he was master of all your funds, so vast in amount; he had no one to fear or suspect, but might have ruled alone with the approval of all; yet he saw fit not to do this, but laid the army, the provinces, and the money at your feet.

You [i.e. the Roman people], on your part, acted well and prudently, when you withheld your assent and did not permit him to retire to private life; for you know well that a democracy could never accommodate itself to interests so vast, but that the leadership of one man would be the most likely to conserve them, and so refused to return to what was nominally independence but really factional discord; and making choice of him whom you had tested by his actual deeds and approved, you constrained him for a time at least to be your leader. And when you had thus proved him far better than before, you compelled him for a second, third, fourth and fifth time to continue in the management of affairs. And this was but fitting, for who would not choose to be safe without trouble, to be prosperous without danger, to enjoy without stint the blessings of government while escaping the life of constant anxiety for its maintenance? . . .

As regards the members of the senate, he did not take away from them the right to cast lots for the governorship of provinces, but even offered them additional prizes as a reward for excellence, nor in connection with the senate's decrees did he do away with their privilege of voting, but even added safeguards for their freedom of speech. From the people he transferred matters difficult of decision to the strict jurisdiction of the courts, but preserved to them the dignity of the elections; and at these elections he inculcated in the citizens the love of honor rather than the love of party strife, and eliminating the element of greed from their office-seeking, he put in its place the regard for reputation. . . .

[After reporting the remainder of the eulogy along the same lines, Dion Cassius then comments:]

Real grief was not in the hearts of many at the time, but later was felt by all. For Augustus had been accessible to all allies, and was accustomed to aid many persons in the matter of money. He showed great honor to his friends, and delighted exceedingly when they frankly spoke their opinions. . . . Not only for these reasons did the Romans greatly miss him, but also by combining monarchy with democracy he preserved their freedom for them, and at the same time he established order and security, so that they were free alike from the license of a democracy and from the insolence of a tyranny, living at once in a liberty of moderation and in a monarchy without terrors; they were subjects of royalty yet not slaves, and citizens of a democracy yet without discord. If any of them remembered his former deeds in the course of the civil wars, they attributed them to the pressure of cares, and they thought it fair to seek his real disposition in what he did after he was in undisputed possession of the supreme power; for this, in truth, afforded a mighty contrast.

Anybody who examines his acts in detail can establish this fact; but summing them all up briefly I may state that he put an end to all the factional discord, transformed the government in a way to give it the greatest power, and vastly strengthened it. . . . Though the people understood all this during his lifetime, they nevertheless realized it more fully after he was gone. For when they found his successor Tiberius a different sort of man, they yearned for him who was gone. . . .

Dion Cassius, *Roman History*, LVI, 39-41, 43-45, trans. E. Cary, Loeb Classical Library (Cambridge, Mass.: Harvard University Press, 1942), VII, 87-91, 99-103.

(c) *The biographer of the Caesars*

Suetonius, who wrote the *Lives of the Twelve Caesars*, is an unsatisfactory biographer for want of a critical faculty and for want of insight into the character of his subjects. Yet he has his uses as a historian since he had access to a considerable wealth of source material, especially some of the imperial archives; and his flat recitation of facts gives far less of an impression of bias than the interpretative records of Tacitus. Suetonius lacks sympathy for his subjects, but he also seems to lack equally any antipathy. Where his sources repeat gossip he faithfully does the same. Thus to him Tiberius was a tyrant, with a few redeeming features, while Augustus was the model of an enlightened monarch. These were no doubt the stereotypes prevalent in his own day (the middle of the second century A.D.). He considers the constitutional problem not at all, and he shows no interest in the question of whether human freedom had met its greatest check or had been restored. He catalogues the achievements of Augustus, without troubling to distinguish between the important and the trivial, and he attempts no summary. His value therefore for us lies in the revealing anecdotes which we can interpret for ourselves. A brief selection of these follows, the choice having been made for the light they throw upon the methods of Augustus in either preserving freedom or disguising tyranny.

He twice thought of restoring the republic; first immediately after the overthrow of Antony, remembering that his rival had often made the charge that it was his fault that it was not restored; and again in the weariness of a lingering illness, when he went so far as to summon the magistrates and the Senate to his house, and submit an account of the general condition of the empire. Reflecting, however, that as he himself would not be free from danger if he should retire, so too it would be hazardous to trust the State to the control of the populace, he continued to keep it in his hands; and it is not easy to say whether his intentions or their results were the better. His good intentions he not only expressed from time to time, but put them on record as well in an edict in the following words: "May it be my privilege to establish the State in a firm and secure position, and enjoy therefrom the rewards of which I am ambitious, that of being called the author of the best possible government, and of carrying with me when I die the hope that the foundations which I have laid for the State will remain unshaken." And he realized his hope by making every effort to prevent any dissatisfaction with the new regime. . . .

When the people did their best to force the Dictatorship upon him he knelt down, threw off his toga from his shoulders, and with bare breast begged them not to insist. He always shrank from the title of Lord [Dominus—the title used by a slave for his master] as reproachful and insulting. When the words "O just and gracious Lord!" were uttered in a farce at which he was a spectator and all the people sprang to their feet and applauded as if they were said of him, he at once checked their unseemly flattery by look and gesture, and on the following day sharply reproved them in an edict. After that he would not suffer himself to be addressed by that term even by his children or his grandchildren either in jest or earnest, and he forbade them to use such flattering terms even amongst themselves. He did not if he could help it leave or enter any city or town except in the evening or at night, to avoid disturbing anyone by the obligations of ceremony. In his consulship he commonly went through the streets on foot, and when he was not Consul, generally in a closed litter. His morning receptions were open to all, including even the Commons, and he met the requests of those who approached him with great affability. . . . He exchanged social calls with many, and did not cease to attend all their anniversaries until he was well on in years. . . .

As he was delivering a speech in the Senate someone said to him, "I did not understand," and another, "I would contradict you if I had an opportunity." Several times when he was rushing from the House in anger at the excessive bickerings of the disputants, some shouted after him, "Senators ought to have the right of speaking their mind on public affairs." . . . Yet for all that no one suffered for his freedom of speech or insolence. Even when some infamous libels against him were scattered in the Senate house he was neither disturbed nor gave himself great trouble to refute them. Without trying to discover the authors, he merely proposed that those who henceforth under a false name published notes or verses defamatory of anyone should be called to account. . . .

Whenever he took part in the election of magistrates, he went the round of the tribes with his candidates and appealed for them in the traditional manner. He also cast his own vote in his tribe, as one of the people. When he gave testimony in court, he was most patient in submitting to questions and even to contradiction. . . . He never recommended his sons for office without adding, "If they be worthy of it." . . . He wished his friends to be prominent and influential in the State, but to be bound by the same laws as the rest and equally liable to prosecution. . . . He secured the acquittal of no more than one man, and then by entreaty, making a successful appeal to the accuser in the presence of the jurors. . . .

How much he was beloved for his admirable conduct in all these respects it is easy to imagine. I say nothing of decrees of the Senate, which might seem to have been dictated by necessity or by awe. . . . The whole body of citizens with a sudden unanimous impulse proffered him the title of Father of the Country; first the commons, by a deputation sent to Antium, and then, because he declined it, again at Rome as he entered the theatre; . . . the Senate afterwards in the House, not by a decree or by acclamation, but through Valerius Messala. He speaking for the whole body said: "Good fortune and divine favor attend thee and thy house, Caesar Augustus; for thus we feel that we are praying for lasting prosperity for our country and happiness for our city. The Senate in accord with the people of Rome hails thee Father of thy Country." Then Augustus, with tears in his eyes, replied as follows (and I have given his exact words, as I did those of Messala): "Having attained my highest hopes, Fathers of the Senate, what more have I to ask of the immortal gods than that I may retain this same unanimous approval of yours to the very end of my life?"

Suetonius, *The Lives of the Caesars*, II, 28, 52-58, trans. J. C. Rolfe, Loeb Classical Library (Cambridge, Mass.: Harvard University Press, 1913), I, 165, 207-215.

4. Varying Opinion of Posterity

The modern world has by no means been as unanimous on the virtues of the rule of Augustus as were the ancients. Much appears to have depended upon the circumstances of the time of writing. In days when peace seems a rare blessing, the achievements of Augustus rank high in the opinion of mankind; in days when war seems remote, as in the days of Gibbon, the historian can permit himself the luxury of deploring the loss of freedom: in days when we are threatened by dictators any man who in the past had any share in the establishment of one-man rule is suspect and his motives impugned. On the other hand modern imperial administrators have always admired the deftness of his touch and his sure political sense as well as his administrative abilities. Historians with a liking for the dramatic and an admiration for the strong man of action have tended to depreciate Augustus by comparison with the great Julius Caesar. So we have to make allowance for personal prejudice even though Augustus died nearly two thousand years ago, and his empire collapsed a few hundred years later. No history, it seems, is ever quite dead, and there is still room for difference of opinion.

(a) The eighteenth-century rationalist

Edward Gibbon, eighteenth-century English historian, posed as a disillusioned skeptic. He greatly admired the Roman Empire especially in the second century of its existence. It was his considered view that the bulk of mankind had never been so happy as under the Good Emperors (A.D. 96–180). Yet even he was not greatly impressed by Augustus, the Empire's founder.

The tender respect of Augustus for a free constitution which he had destroyed, can only be explained by an attentive consideration of the character of that subtle tyrant. A cool head, an unfeeling heart, and a cowardly disposition prompted him, at the age of nineteen, to assume the mask of hypocrisy, which he never afterwards laid aside.

. . . His virtues, and even his vices, were artificial; and according to the various dictates of his interest, he was at first the enemy, and at last the father of the Roman world. When he framed the artful system of the imperial authority, his moderation was inspired by his fears. He wished to deceive the people by an image of civil liberty, and the armies by an image of civil government.

The death of Caesar was ever before his eyes. He had lavished wealth and honors on his adherents; but the most favored friends of his uncle were in the number of the conspirators. The fidelity of the legions might defend his authority against open rebellion; but their vigilance could not secure his person from the dagger of a determined republican; and the Romans, who revered the memory of Brutus, would applaud the memory of his virtue. Caesar had provoked his fate as much by the ostentation of his power as by his power itself. The consul or the tribune might have reigned in peace. The title of king had armed the Romans against his life. Augustus was sensible that mankind is governed by names; nor was he deceived in his expectations, that the senate and people would submit to slavery, provided they were respectfully assured that they still enjoyed their ancient freedom. A feeble senate and enervated people cheerfully acquiesced in the pleasing illusion, as long as it was supported by the virtue, or even the prudence, of the successors of Augustus. . . .

The insolence of the armies inspired Augustus with fears of a still more alarming nature. The despair of the citizens could only attempt what the power of the soldiers was, at any time, able to execute. How precarious was his own authority over men whom he had taught to violate every social duty! He had heard their seditious clamors;

he dreaded their calmer moments of reflection. One revolution had been purchased by immense rewards; but a second revolution might double those rewards. The troops professed the fondest attachment to the house of Caesar; but the attachments of the multitude are capricious and inconstant.

Augustus summoned to his aid whatever remained in those fierce minds of Roman prejudices; enforced the rigor of discipline by the sanction of law; and interposing the majesty of the senate between the emperor and the army, boldly claimed their allegiance, as the first magistrate of the republic. . . .

E. Gibbon, *History of the Decline and Fall of the Roman Empire* (1787), ed. J. B. Bury (London, 1896), I, 71-72.

5. A Twentieth-Century Professional Historian

The book from which the next extract is taken is an interesting one. Ronald Syme in his introduction states clearly that it is his view that it "is surely time for some reaction from the traditional and conventional view of the period. Much that has recently been written about Augustus is simply panegyric, whether ingenuous or edifying. Yet it is not necessary to praise political success or to idealize the men who win wealth and honors through civil war." Such a statement disarms criticism, especially when it is coupled with the admission that his design has "imposed a pessimistic and truculent tone, to the almost complete exclusion of the gentler emotions and the domestic virtues." Syme claims to be a realist, and he has had the benefit of the researches of numerous specialists who have delved into the family records of the ancient Romans. His picture and judgment must be treated with respect, even if he has not said the last word yet on the subject.

In his sixth and seventh consulates C. Julius Caesar Octavianus went through a painless and superficial transformation. The process was completed in a session of the Senate on January 13th, 27 B.C., when he solemnly announced that he resigned all powers and all provinces to the free disposal of the Senate and People of Rome. Acclamation was drowned in protest. The senators adjured him not to abandon the Commonwealth that he had preserved.

Yielding with reluctance to these manifestations of loyalty and patriotism, the master of the whole world consented to assume a special commission for a period of ten years, in the form of proconsular authority over a large *provincia,* namely Spain, Gaul, and Syria. That and nothing more. For the rest, proconsuls were to govern the provinces as before, but responsible only to the Senate; the Senate, People, and magistrates were to resume the rightful exercise of all their functions.

Three days later the Senate again met, eager and impatient to render thanks, to confer honors upon the saviour of the State. . . . A new name was devised, expressing veneration of more than mortal due. A veteran politician, the consular L. Munatius Plancus, proposed the decree that conferred on Caesar's heir the appellation of Augustus. Nothing was left to chance in preparing these exemplary manifestations. The ruler had taken counsel with his friends and allies—and perhaps with neutral politicians. They knew what they were about. In name, in semblance and in theory the sovereignty of Senate and People had been restored. . . .

The Romans as a people were possessed by an especial veneration for authority, precedent and tradition, by a rooted distaste for change unless change could be shown to be in harmony with ancestral custom, "mos majorum", which in practice meant the sentiments of the oldest living senators. . . . Yet the memory of the past reminded the Romans that change had come, though slow and combated. Rome's peculiar greatness was due not to one man's genius or to one age, but to many men and the long process of time. Augustus sought to demonstrate a doctrine— Roman history was a continuous and harmonious development. Augustus himself, so he asserted, accepted no magistracy that ran contrary to the "mos majorum". He did not need to. As it stood, the Roman constitution would serve his purpose well enough. It is therefore no paradox to discover in the Principate of Augustus both the institutions and the phraseology of Republican Rome. The historical validity of the inferences derived therefore is another question. . . .

Certain precedents of the recent past were so close as to be damaging. Pompeius Magnus governed Spain in absence through his legates. . . . But Pompeius was sinister and ambitious. That *princeps* did not cure, but only aggravated the ills of the Roman State. Very different was Augustus, a "salubris princeps" [healthy princeps] for as such he would have himself known. Not only that. The whole career of Pompeius was violent and illicit . . . it would not do to revive such memories. . . . Seeking to establish continuity with a legitimate government, Caesar's heir foreswore the memory of Caesar; in the official conception, the Dictatorship and the Triumvirate were blotted from record. This meant a certain rehabilitation of the last generation of the Republic, which in politics is the Age of Pompeius. In his youth Caesar's heir, the revolutionary adventurer, won Pompeian support by guile and coolly betrayed his allies, overthrowing the Republic and proscribing the Republicans; in his mature years the statesman stole their heroes and their vocabulary. . . . On the whole, better to say nothing of Caesar, or for that matter of Antonius,

save as criminal types. The power and domination of Augustus was in reality far too similar to that of the Dictator to stand even a casual reminder, let alone pointed and genuine comparison. The claims of the Divine Julius, the glories of Trojan descent and the obsession with Romulus, prevalent for some years in the aftermath of Actium, gradually recede and lose ground just as the victory itself, on quieter reflection an uncomfortable matter, is no longer fervently advertised.

A purified Pompeius or a ghostly and sanctified Cato were not the only victims of the Civil Wars who could be called up and enlisted in the service of the revived Republic. Cicero might be remunerative for every purpose; and the blame of his proscription was profitably laid upon Antonius, dead and disgraced. . . . In so far as Cicero had a political program, he advocated the existing order, reformed a little by return to ancient practices but not changed, namely the firm concord of the propertied classes, and the traditional distinction in function and standing between the different classes in society. Such was also the opinion of Augustus, for the Revolution had now been stabilized. Neither the Princeps nor any of his adherents desired change and disturbance. . . . Augustus labored to conserve the new order, announcing it as his dearest wish to be known as the "originator of the best state". . . . Only ghosts and words were called up to comfort the living and confound posterity. . . .

It is time to turn from words and theories. Only a robust faith can discover authentic relics of Cicero in the Republic of Augustus; very little attention was paid to him at all. . . . Augustus proudly dispensed with support of precedents—he claimed to be unique. . . . Names might change; Augustus was none the less a revolutionary leader who won supreme power through civil war. . . . To retain power, however, he must base his rule upon general consent, the support of men of property, and the active co-operation of the governing class. To that end he modified the forms of the constitution to fit his policy, his policy to harmonize with Roman sentiment. . . .

His rule was personal—and based ultimately upon a personal oath of allegiance rendered by Rome, Italy and the West in 32 B.C., subsequently by the other regions of the Empire. Caesar Augustus possessed indefinite and tremendous resources, open or secret—all that the *principes* in the last generation held, but now stolen from them and enhanced to an exorbitant degree; and he was Divi filius [son of the god] destined for consecration in his turn. The plebs of Rome was Caesar's inherited clientèle. He fed them with doles, amused them with games, and claimed to be their protector against oppression. Free elections returned—that is to say, a grateful people would unfailingly elect the candidates whom Caesar in his wisdom had chosen, with or without formal commendation. He controlled the armies of the Roman People, in fact though not in law, and provided from his own pocket the bounty for the legionaries when they returned from service. Augustus was by far the wealthiest man in the Empire, ruling Egypt as a king and owing account of it to no man; he coined in silver and gold in the provinces; and he spent his money with ostentation and for power. The military colonies in Italy and abroad were a network of his armed and devoted garrisons. Towns in Italy and the provinces knew him as their founder or their patron; kings, tetrarchs, and dynasts over the wide empire were in his portion as allies and clients. A citizen and magistrate to the senators, he was *imperator* to the legions, a king and a god to the subject populations. Above all, he stood at the head of a large and well organized political party as the source and fount of patronage and advancement.

Such was Caesar Augustus. . . . Yet it would be an elementary error to fancy that the ceremony of January 13th was merely a grim comedy devised to deceive the ingenuous or intimidate the servile. On the contrary, the purified Senate, being in a majority the partisans of Augustus, were well aware of what was afoot. To secure the domination of the Caesarian party, the consolidation of the Revolution and the maintenance of peace, it was necessary that the primacy of Caesar's heir should be strengthened and perpetuated. Not, however, under the fatal name of dictator or monarch. On all sides prevailed a conspiracy of decent reticence about the gap between fact and theory. . . .

It has been maintained in recent times that Augustus not only employed Republican language but intended that the Republican constitution should operate unhampered—and that it did, at least in the earlier years of his presidency. Augustus' purpose was just the reverse. He controlled government and patronage, especially the consulate, precisely after the manner of earlier dynasts, but with more thoroughness and without opposition. This time the domination of a faction was to be permanent and unshaken; the era of rival military leaders had closed.

The choice of means did not demand deep thought or high debate in the party councils. Augustus took what he deemed necessary for his designs, the consulate and a group of military provinces. Definition of powers and extent of *provincia* might later be modified how and when he pleased. One thing could never change, the source and origin of his domination. . . .

R. Syme, *The Roman Revolution* (Oxford: The Clarendon Press, 1939), pp. 313-325.

6. A Modern Administrator

John Buchan was a man of many sides. By way of the law, publishing, and the writing of novels and biographies he was elected to the British Parliament in 1927 and finally, with the title of Lord Tweedsmuir, became Governor-General of Canada, where his administration was a marked success. The author of three political biographies, he was in no sense a professional historian, but was greatly interested in the problems involved in the exercise of power and its relationship to human freedom (his best known biography is probably *Cromwell*). His picture of Augustus neglects those aspects of his rule emphasized in the previous extract, but on the other hand it takes very seriously Augustus' desire to preserve what was worth preserving from the republican tradition of freedom and self-government. Since politics must consider both the desirable and the practicable, the truth may be that Syme and Buchan are both in part right, and the two extracts do not contradict each other, though each emphasizes a different aspect of Augustus' work.

The twin principles of the new system were, first, that the reality of power should remain in the hands of Augustus, and, second, that such a central control should be given a constitutional façade. This meant that any scheme must be accepted and ratified by what remained of the mechanism of the Republic. He had been living on real, but for the most part, irregular, grants of authority; these must be relinquished and a new dispensation established on a basis of strict legality. His former powers had enabled him to clear the ground, but something different was needed before he could build. The new authority might be extraordinary and beyond precedent, but it must spring from the traditional sources, the Senate and the People. He was beginning to see what the ultimate form of the Roman polity must be, but he had no intention of presenting it as a clean-cut and fully articulated scheme. He would start with the rudiments, and guide the evolution on the lines he desired. He was a statesman, not a political theorist.

First for his name, since the head of the state must have a title. "Imperator", to which Julius had inclined, he unhesitatingly rejected. . . . As a term of daily use it smacked too much of dictatorship and the sword. . . . The word "princeps" as adopted by Augustus, was a popular appellation . . . and it is best translated "First Citizen",—first citizen and principal servant. . . . It combined diverse loyalties and aroused no antagonisms. Wiser than Julius, Augustus . . . recognized that names have a dangerous potency.

His next step was to decide upon the precise form which his authority should take. He must have the reality of power, but he must dress it in a cunning constitutional habit. He knew well the antiquarian propensities of his countrymen, and their passion for the minutiae of constitutionalism, and he was prepared to indulge it to the full so far as theory was concerned, provided that in practice he had the guiding of the state. His concern was less with abstract authority than with function. There was no such thing as a Roman constitution, for under the Republic the polity had always been insensibly changing, and if he set out to restore the Republic in full he would have found no general agreement as to what that Republic meant. His business, therefore, was to interweave his personal "auctoritas" with institutions which still had a strong appeal to the Roman mind, but, since these institutions were not clean cut and rigid, he could subtly adapt them in the interweaving. His task was not that of the lawyer, but of the practical statesman; the logic which guided him was not of paper but of facts.

His first step was simple. To begin with at any rate, he must hold the main office, the consulship, hold it in the old fashion by annual election. That would give him the dignity of the traditional head of the Roman state, and the handicap of colleagueship could be got over by the selection of the right kind of colleague. But the consulship alone was not enough. The kernel of his authority lay in his command of the chief— and, but for the Parthian, the only— army in the world. How was this command to be legitimated? Only by the grant of the "imperium proconsulare", so that he would be at once consul and proconsul. This was a departure from normal republican practice, but it was not without precedent, for in 52 B.C. the double office had been held by Pompey, and Pompey was still dear to conservative sentiment. . . .

But the imperium of a proconsul was not valid in the city of Rome, and in any case some authority was needed which should bring him more closely into touch with the people and conceal the truth that his ultimate power lay in the command of the army. The popular office of tribune was closed to him as a patrician, but already he had been granted many of the tribune's privileges. Now he must be invested with the others, for the key of his new policy was to acquire the power without the office. . . . The military imperium was the actual basis of his authority, but the tribunician power was at once its popular coloring and the source of its moral appeal.

There was another power which he must possess before he could deal with the hardest part of his problem, the status of the Senate. He must have some of the rights of the censor . . . for the taking of a census—neglected since 70 B.C.—and the revision of the Senate and the whole class system, he must have an *ad hoc* authority. . . .

With a Senate purged and reduced in numbers and a purified aristocracy he was now ready for his great step—the division of the burden of empire between the Senate and himself. He had no need to concern himself greatly with the popular Assemblies. In theory the supreme legislative organ . . . they had become dull inorganic things, without individuality or prestige. But the Senate was a different matter. It was the very heart and soul of the Republic, and had still in the popular eye the glamor of ancient dignity and long descent. Having revived the distinction of its membership by expelling the low-born element introduced by Julius and Antony, he could ally himself with it in the business of government. His intention was to restore all of the Republic that would work; the Republic meant nothing without the Senate. . . . The Senate should reign like a modern constitutional monarch, and it should be permitted to govern up to the full limit of its capacity. . . .

Augustus . . . had no illusions about the temporary nature of the constitution which he was about to offer to the people. It was a trial trip, a provisional arrangement strictly limited in duration, a structure which might have to be profoundly modified. The fundamental principles, which he was careful not to emphasize unduly, he did indeed believe to be essential, but the details were to be largely a matter of slow evolution and adjustment. He was summoning Rome to a partnership in a great experiment and taking her frankly into his confidence. . . . There was no figure which for a moment could compare with his in authority. More important, there was no political creed passionately held which might be an obstacle to his own. Doctrinaire republicanism had sunk almost out of sight; it had become less a dogma than a lingering sentiment, which he was ready to conciliate because he himself shared it. . . .

Did he or did he not restore the Republic? The question is really without meaning, though it has occasioned a wealth of misplaced ingenuity. What republic? That of the old simple city-state? But no antiquarian piety could have brought that to life again, for it would have meant the reduction of the Roman people to a manageable size, the abolition of the system which made rank depend on office, a return to the [earlier citizen] army, and the restoration of primitive manners and morals. No Roman of any class would have accepted such a revolution. Does the question concern the restoration of civic liberty? Then let us be careful in our definitions. The Roman "libertas" was never the Greek "eleutheria"; it was not freedom unfettered but freedom from arbitrary rule, and did not involve an atomic self-sufficiency, but could be as well, or better, attained as part of a greater whole. . . .

Augustus preserved whatever of the republican institutions still had vitality, and adapted them to a new executive purpose. . . . Of the legal sovereignty in the narrower sense there could be no doubt. It resided, as in republican days, in the Senate and the People. In theory these were supreme; all the powers of the Princeps emanated from them, and what they had granted they could withdraw. This right of resumption was emphasized by the limitation of the grant to ten years. . . . The Princeps was a magistrate in the traditional sense, with an extraordinary jurisdiction established in the republican way after sound republican precedents.

But the legal aspect was not the only, or the most vital, one. In effect Augustus had a status which the laws could not limit. . . . The logic of facts was to make this high command endure for life, since any change was unthinkable. He was resolved not to let slip those reins of power, and Rome was not less resolved, and it was therefore certain that time would increase and not diminish his influence. The old institutions, though Augustus had all the will in the world to preserve them, were bound to wither in the shadow of the new. He summoned the energies of the past to legitimize the future, but these energies were already half exhausted. If all his powers had republican precedents their combination in the hands of one man was a novelty, in one man of extraordinary administrative genius. Not all his constitutional probity and antiquarian zeal could put life into dying things. The mechanism of the small city state could not long be combined with the mechanism required by a vast empire. . . .

A great scholar has reproached him because he "willed the impossible and set up the impermanent"; but what he willed was tentative, a thing the feasibility of which was left to the test of time, and the taunt of impermanence is idle in the case of an institution which endured for centuries and is still part of the framework of the modern world.

John Buchan, *Augustus* (Boston: Houghton, Mifflin and Co., 1937), pp. 133-141, 149-152, 162.

B. Did the Principate Degenerate into a Tyranny under Tiberius?

The ancient sources, as we have seen, unanimously approved of Augustus, though Tacitus records adverse opinions held of him by some unnamed Romans. It was left for modern historians to attempt to discount the ancient tradition. In the case of Tiberius, Augustus's successor, the best historical tradition is almost equally unanimous against him, though some historians mention redeeming features of his rule. It is true that Velleius Paterculus, who had served under him, offers a much criticized eulogy of his master; but even Velleius might have changed his opinion if he had lived to see the end of the reign. Since his narrative ends before the fall of the praetorian prefect Sejanus and the subsequent treason trials (which will be referred to below), we cannot use him as a satisfactory witness for the defense.

There can, then, be no doubt of the ancient tradition that Tiberius was a suspicious tyrant. Our problem therefore is to assess the value of this tradition, and see whether it is justified. The unanimity of the sources makes the task of rehabilitation exceptionally difficult, and perhaps gratuitous, since the tradition may have represented the truth. Perhaps it would never have been attempted had not the narrative of Tacitus presented such obvious discrepancies, and had not the prejudice of Tacitus himself been apparent to anyone who reads him even for the first time. He records the reluctance of Tiberius to accept the throne, and at once explains it as windowdressing; he records dignified and humane statements of the *princeps,* and then suggests that they were but fair words concealing his true thoughts. Above all the picture of the licentious monster, aged nearly 80, disporting himself on the fair island of Capri in horrible orgies, seems utterly at variance with what we can bring ourselves to believe possible for an old, weary and embittered ruler, betrayed by those he had trusted, fearful of assassination, and hated by all. Does such a man in the evening of his life, on one of the most beautiful and peaceful islands of the world, suddenly recover vitality enough for such orgies, and would he be tempted to indulge in them? The picture simply does not fit. Nor can we easily believe that from the beginning of his reign he was always the same tyrant, but put on the mask of a lover of freedom reluctantly compelled to be a monarch, throwing off the mask only after the fall of Sejanus. Could the truth be that he was frightened as well as embittered by the conspiracy, and either by desire for vengeance or in panic, or even in the genuine belief that the state could only be preserved by such means, resorted to the treason trials? And that his voluntary seclusion on the island of Capri was simply the longed for asylum of a tired old man who knew himself to be hated in Rome?

If these things are so, then Tiberius cannot truly be called a tyrant. By using informers he set a bad precedent for later rulers to follow, but the conspiracy was no fake. The punishments he meted out were severe, but not unjustified where guilt was proved. And even if the innocent suffered sometimes with the guilty, this is not unknown in other, less dangerous, times. This is the line of argument adopted by those who would rehabilitate him.

Again the problem is insoluble. But it will reveal the difficulty of coming to a final decision in historical enquiries. The last two extracts, one of considerable length, will suggest the kind of work that can still be done in rehabilitating the reputation of one whom the author feels to have been unjustly maligned; and it will show the methods that can be used by modern historians to break up the formidable case for the prosecution presented by one of the greatest historians of antiquity.

1. OPINION OF THE ANCIENT WORLD

(a) The Official View: *Tiberius as a just and efficient ruler*

There is no reason to suppose that the work of Velleius was in any way sponsored by Tiberius, or that the following eulogy was anything other than the genuine opinion of an imperial servant who had fought under Tiberius and admired him both as general and *princeps.* As noted earlier, however, the history was written prior to the treason trials that followed the fall of Sejanus.

Who would undertake to tell in detail the accomplishments of the past sixteen years? . . . Credit has been restored in the forum, strife has been banished from the forum, canvassing for office from the Campus Martius, discord from the senate-house; justice, equity, and industry, long buried in oblivion, have been restored to the state; the magistrates have regained their authority, the senate its majesty, the courts their dignity; rioting in the theater has been suppressed; all citizens have either been impressed with the wish to do right, or have been forced to do so by necessity. Right is now honored, evil is punished; the humble man respects the great but does not fear him, the great has precedence over the lowly but does not despise him. When was the price of grain more reasonable, or when were the blessings of peace greater? The *pax augusta,* which has spread to the regions of the west and to the bounds of the north and of the south, preserves every corner of the world safe from the fear of brigandage. . . . Fair play has now precedence over influence, and merit over ambition, for the best of emperors teaches his citizens to do right by doing it, and though he is greatest among us in authority, he is still greater in the example which he sets . . .

Velleius Paterculus, *History of Rome,* II, 126, trans. F. W. Shipley, Loeb Classical Library (Cambridge, Mass.: Harvard University Press, 1924), pp. 317-19.

(b) The Sensational Biographer: *Tiberius as hypocrite*

Far different is the picture provided by Suetonius, who adopts the traditional view discussed earlier. But even Suetonius, though he devotes the bulk of his biography to the sensational details of the later part of his reign, nevertheless concedes Tiberius some merit during the earlier years. Both aspects of his narrative are included in the following selection.

Though Tiberius did not hesitate at once to assume and to exercise the imperial authority, surrounding himself with a guard of soldiers, that is, with the actual power and the outward sign of sovereignty, yet he long refused the title, at one time with barefaced hypocrisy upbraiding his friends who urged him to accept it, saying that they did not realize what a monster the empire was, at another by evasive answers and calculating hesitancy keeping the Senators in suspense when they implored him to yield, and fell at his feet. Finally, some lost patience, and one man cried out in the confusion: "Let him take it or leave it!" Another openly voiced the taunt that others were slow in doing what they promised but that he was slow to promise what he was already doing. At last, as though on compulsion, and complaining that a wretched and burdensome slavery was being forced upon him, he accepted the empire, but in such fashion as to suggest the hope that he would one day lay it down. His own words were: "Until I come to the time when it may seem right to you to grant an old man some repose". . . .

Once relieved of fear, he at first played a most unassuming part, almost humbler than that of a private citizen. Of many high honors he accepted only a few of the more modest. . . . He so loathed flattery that . . . if anyone in conversation or a set speech spoke of him in too flattering terms, he did not hesitate to interrupt him to take him to task, and to correct his language on the spot. . . . More than that, he was self-contained and patient in the face of abuse and slander, and of lampoons on himself and his family, often asserting that in a free country there should be free speech and free thought. When the Senate on one occasion demanded that cognizance be taken of such offenses and those guilty of them, he said: "We have not enough spare time to warrant involving ourselves in more affairs. If you open this loophole you will find no time for any other business. It will be an excuse for laying everybody's quarrels before you." A most unassuming remark of his in the Senate is also a matter of record: "If so and so criticizes me I shall take care to render an account of my acts and words; if he persist I shall return him in kind." All this was the more noteworthy because in addressing and in paying his respects to the Senators individually and in a body he himself almost exceeded the requirements of courtesy. . . .

He even introduced a semblance of free government by maintaining the ancient dignity and powers of the Senate and the magistrates. For there was no matter of public or private business so small or so great that he did not lay it before the Senators, consulting them about revenues and monopolies, constructing and restoring public buildings, even about levying and disbanding the soldiers. . . . He always entered the House alone. Once when he was taken there in a litter because of illness he dismissed his attendants at the door. When certain decrees were passed contrary to his expressed opinion, he did not even remonstrate. . . . Once when the Senate was divided and the act might pass by the difference of a few votes he went over to the side of the minority, but not a man followed him. . . . He himself actually rose in the presence of the Consuls, and made way for them in the street. . . . To the governors who recommended burdensome taxes for his provinces, he wrote in answer that it was the part of a good shepherd to shear his flock, not skin it. . . .

For two whole years after becoming Emperor he did not set foot outside the gates. But after being bereft of both his sons . . . he retired to Campania, and . . . after traversing Campania . . . he went to Capri, particularly attracted to that island because it was accessible by only one small beach, be-

ing everywhere else girt with sheer cliffs of great height and by deep water. . . .

Having gained the license of privacy, and being as it were out of sight of the citizens, he at last gave free rein at once to all the vices which he had for a long time ill concealed. Of these I shall give a detailed account from the beginning. [There follows an account of perversions and unnatural vices which were no doubt the common gossip of Rome, though they strain modern credulity.] His cruel and coldblooded character was not completely hidden even in his boyhood. . . . But it grew still more noticeable after he became Emperor, even at the beginning, when he was still courting popularity by a show of moderation. When a funeral was passing by and a jester called aloud to the corpse to let Augustus know that the legacies which he had left to the people were not yet being paid, Tiberius had the man haled before him, ordered that he receive what was due him, and then be put to death. . . . He did so many other cruel and savage deeds under the guise of strictness and improvement of the public morals, but in reality rather to gratify his natural instincts, that some resorted to verses to express their detestation of the present ills and a warning against those to come. . . . After the death of Sejanus he was more cruel than ever, which showed that his favorite was not wont to egg him on, but on the contrary gave him the opportunities which he himself desired. . . .

It is a long story to run through his acts of cruelty in detail. It will be enough to mention the forms that they took, as samples of his barbarity. Not a day passed without an execution, even days that were sacred and holy, for he put some to death even on New Year's Day. Many were accused and condemned with their children, and even by their children. The relatives of the victims were forbidden to mourn for them.

Special rewards were voted the accusers and sometimes even the witnesses. The word of no informer was doubted. Every crime was treated as capital, even the utterance of a few simple words. A poet was charged with having slandered Agamemnon in a tragedy, and a writer of history of having called Brutus and Cassius the last of the Romans. The writers were at once put to death and their works destroyed, although they had been read with approval in public some years before in the presence of Augustus himself. . . .

Many things go to show, not only how hated and execrable he was all this time, but also that he lived a life of extreme fear and was even exposed to insult. . . . His anxiety of mind became torture because of reproaches of all kinds from every quarter, since every single one of those condemned to death heaped all kinds of abuse upon him, either to his face or by handbills placed in the Senators' seats at the shows. By these, however, he was most diversely affected, now through a sense of shame desiring that they all be concealed and kept secret, sometimes scorning them and producing them of his own accord and giving them publicity. Why, he was even attacked by Artabanus, King of the Parthians, who charged him in a letter with the murder of his kindred and other bloody deeds, and with shameless and dissolute living, counseling him to gratify the intense and just hatred of the citizens as soon as possible by a voluntary death.

At last in utter self-disgust he all but admitted the extremity of his wretchedness in a letter which began thus: "If I know what to write to you, Fathers of the Senate, or how to write it, or what to leave unwritten at present, may all gods and goddesses visit me with more utter destruction than I feel that I am daily suffering." . . .

Suetonius, *The Lives of the Caesars*, III, 24-32, 38-42, 57-67, trans. J. C. Rolfe, Loeb Classical Library (Cambridge, Mass.: Harvard University Press, 1914), pp. 329-41, 349-51, 371-89.

(c) The Roman Senatorial Historian: *Tiberius as Rome's first tyrant*

The historical work of Tacitus is an even more severe indictment of Tiberius than the biography of Suetonius, since he is obviously a more thoughtful man. Yet his prejudice is also evident, since, although he records words and deeds which might bear a contrary interpretation, as seen in the third selection below, they do not affect his judgment of Tiberius' character, and he attributes them to hypocrisy when he troubles to make any comment upon them. Note, however, that the third selection is the earliest in time.

(i) His Disgust with His Self-Imposed Task

Much of what I have related and shall have to relate, may perhaps, I am aware, seem petty trifles to record. . . . My labors are circumscribed and inglorious; peace wholly unbroken or but slightly disturbed, dismal misery in the capital, an emperor careless about the enlargement of the empire, such is my theme. Still it will not be useless to study those at first sight trifling events out of which the movements of vast changes often take their rise.

All nations and cities are ruled by the people, the nobility, or by one man. . . . Now after a revolution, when Rome is nothing but the realm of a single despot, there must be good in carefully noting and recording this period, for it is but few who have the foresight to distinguish right from wrong, or what is sound from what is hurtful, while most men learn wisdom from the fortunes of others. Still, though this is instructive, it gives little pleasure. Descriptions of countries, the various incidents of battles, glorious deaths of great generals, enchain and refresh a reader's mind. I have to present in succession the merciless biddings of a tyrant, incessant prosecutions, faithless friendships, the ruin of innocence, the same causes issuing in the same results, and I am everywhere confronted by a wearisome monotony in my subject matter.

Tacitus, *Annals*, IV, 32-33, trans. A. J. Church and W. J. Brodribb (New York: Modern Library, 1942), pp. 162-163, by permission of Macmillan and Co., Ltd., London, and St. Martin's Press, Inc., New York.

(ii) The Reign of Terror

Former alarms then returned, as there was a charge of treason against Considius Proculus. While he was celebrating his birthday without fear, he was hurried before the Senate, condemned and instantly put to death. . . . Pompeia Macrina too was sentenced to banishment. Her husband Argolicus and her father-in-law Laco, leading men of Achaia, had been ruined by the Emperor. Her father likewise, an illustrious Roman knight, and her brother, an ex-praetor, seeing their doom was near, destroyed themselves. It was imputed to them as a crime that their great grandfather Theophanes of Mitylene had been one of the intimate friends of Pompey the Great, and that after his death Greek flattery had paid him divine honors. Sextus Marius, the richest man in Spain, was next accused of incest with his daughter, and thrown headlong from the Tarpeian rock. To remove any doubt that the vastness of the man's wealth had proved his ruin, Tiberius kept his goldmines for himself, though they were forfeited to the State. Executions were now a stimulus to his fury, and he ordered the death of all who were lying in prison under accusation of complicity with Sejanus. There lay, singly or in heaps, the unnumbered dead, of every age and sex, the illustrious with the obscure. Kinsfolk and friends were not allowed to be near them, to weep over them, or even to gaze on them too long. Spies were set around them, who noted the sorrow of each mourner and followed the rotting corpses, till they were dragged to the Tiber, where, floating or driven on the bank, no one dared to burn them or to touch them. The force of terror had utterly extinguished the sense of human fellowship, and, with the growth of cruelty, pity was thrust aside. . . .

Rome meanwhile being a scene of ceaseless bloodshed, Pomponius Labeo, . . . governor of Moesia, severed his veins and let his life ebb from him. His wife Paxaea emulated her husband. What made such deaths eagerly sought was dread of the executioner, and the fact too that the condemned, besides forfeiture of their property, were deprived of burial, while those who decided their fate themselves, had their bodies interred, and their wills remained valid. The emperor, however, argued in a letter to the Senate that it had been the practice of our ancestors, whenever they broke off an intimacy, to forbid the person their house, and so put an end to friendship. This usage he himself revived in Labeo's case, but Labeo, being pressed by charges of maladministration in his province and other crimes, had screened his guilt by bringing odium on another, and had groundlessly alarmed his wife, who, though criminal, was still free from danger. . . .

Though three years had elapsed since the destruction of Sejanus, neither time, nor intreaties, nor sated gratifications, all which have a soothing effect on others, softened Tiberius, or kept him from punishing doubtful or forgotten offenses as most flagrant and recent crimes. . . .

Tacitus, *Annals*, VI, 18-19, 29, 38, *ibid.*, pp. 204-205, 210, 218.

(iii) Contrary Instances: Justice and Humanity of Tiberius

Not satisfied with judicial proceedings in the Senate, the emperor would sit at one end of the praetor's tribunal, but so as not to displace him from the official seat. Many decisions were given in his presence, in opposition to improper influence and the solicitations of great men. This, though it promoted justice, ruined freedom. Pius Aurelius, for instance, a senator, complained that the foundations of his house had been weakened by the pressure of a public road and aqueduct, and he appealed to the Senate for assistance. He was opposed by the praetors of the treasury, but the emperor helped him, and paid him the value of his house, for he liked to spend money on a good purpose, a virtue which he long retained, when he cast off all others. To Propertius Celer, an ex-praetor, who sought because of his poverty to be excused from his rank as a senator, he gave a million sesterces, having ascertained that he had inherited his poverty. He bade others, who attempted the same, prove their case to the Senate, as from his love of strictness he was harsh, even where he acted on right grounds. Consequently everyone else preferred silence and poverty to confession and relief. . . .

Cornelius Dolabella, by way of carrying flattery yet further, sharply censured the morals of Silanus, and then moved that no one of disgraceful life and notorious infamy should be eligible for a province, and that of this the emperor should be the judge. "Laws, indeed," he said, "punish crimes committed; but how much more merciful would it be to individuals, how much better for our allies, to provide against their commission."

The emperor opposed the motion. "Although," he said, "I am not ignorant of the reports about Silanus, still we must decide nothing by hearsay. Many a man has behaved in a province quite otherwise than was hoped or feared of him. Some are roused to higher things by great responsibility; others are paralyzed by it. It is not possible for a prince's knowledge to embrace everything, and it is not expedient that he should be exposed to the ambitious schemings of others. Laws are ordained to meet facts, inasmuch as the future is uncertain. It was the rule of our ancestors that, whenever there was first an offense, some penalty should follow. Let us not revolutionize a wisely devised and ever approved system. Princes have enough burdens, and also enough power. Rights are invariably abridged, as despotism increases; nor ought we to fall back on imperial authority, when we can have recourse to the laws."

Tacitus, *Annals*, I, 75; III, 69, *ibid.*, pp. 49-50, 139-40.

2. Criticism of Ancient Opinion by a Modern Historian

(a) *"Reign of terror" an invention of Tacitus*

It seems desirable to devote some space to the consideration of the reasons why Tacitus held so firmly to the view that the last years of Tiberius were a reign of terror, and of the literary devices by which he has impressed this picture on his readers.

It is probable that he originally derived his conception of a terror from the tradition concerning Tiberius which was current in his day. . . . I have elsewhere pointed out some reasons for thinking that Tacitus, instead of making a careful study of the whole reign before beginning his work, examined and compared his various sources for the two or three years which he intended to treat in a single book, and that, as soon as this study was completed, he forthwith wrote the book, and then took up the investigations preliminary to the next. Thus, when he began, he had only a vague and general knowledge of the events of his reign, and he assumed that they would be found to harmonize with the legendary character of Tiberius. What he learned in gathering material for the first books of the *Annals* compelled him to admit that for some years Tiberius had shown himself a wise and able ruler, but this difficulty was easily overcome by the help of that hypocrisy which seems to have been attributed to Tiberius by tradition. There was, therefore, nothing in the early part of the reign which could force Tacitus to modify his preconceived ideas, and all that was necessary was to let the reader see through the mask worn by the emperor. This Tacitus accomplished by numerous comments, innuendoes, and anticipations, and, as he wrote, the picture which he was drawing became so vivid in his mind that it completely dominated his imagination. When finally he reached the sixth book and with it the dreadful climax for which he had from the first been preparing the reader and himself, he was no longer capable of weighing evidence fairly. Since a reign of terror was a logical necessity if his portrait was to stand, it only remained for him to present the facts in such a way that they would make what he thoroughly believed to be the right impression on the reader. If enough victims could not be found, he explained the deficiency by the assumption that previous historians had wearied of the monotonous catalogue of executions and suicides, and exerted himself the more to make up for the inadequacy of his material by the dexterous use of rhetoric. [The author then goes on to analyze the passage on p. 41 above, where Tiberius ordered the death of all those who were still lying in prison. He comments:]

This is a powerful and vivid description, but Tacitus himself supplies the proof that strict accuracy has been sacrificed to effect. He asserts that all who were in prison as accomplices of Sejanus were put to death, and we are, therefore, surprised to learn of the execution in prison of Sextius Paconianus in 35 A.D. (two years later). Tacitus said he had been imprisoned after the fall of Sejanus. . . . Aside from this it is very strange that such a massacre as is here described should have escaped the notice of Dio and Suetonius. The latter merely states incidentally that as many as twenty persons . . . were put to death on one day. The "untold number" of Tacitus thus shrinks very considerably. . . . The truth of the matter cannot be determined with certainty, but perhaps the best guess at what happened is that Tiberius ordered the immediate execution of some twenty persons then in prison under sentence of death. Why they had not been already executed we do not know, but it is possible that some of them had been spared in the hope that they could give important information to the government. . . .

In A.D. 34 Tacitus has no such golden opportunity, and is compelled to use considerable ingenuity. He begins with an account of the Egyptian phoenix and then continues his reign of terror with the remark that at Rome the slaughter continued and that Pomponius Labeo opened his veins, his wife following his example [p. 41 above]. If Tacitus had at once added that Labeo was accused of maladministration in Moesia and other crimes, the proper effect would hardly have been achieved, so he follows the suicide of Labeo with some general comments on the motives for suicide. . . . The proper atmosphere having now been created, the charges may now safely be stated. The statement, however, is introduced by the words, "But Tiberius declared in letters to the senate," as though the emperor, unsatisfied with the death of his victim, had maliciously sought to blacken his memory. In this way our sympathy is enlisted for Labeo without any assertion of his innocence on the part of Tacitus. Then follows a confused account of the prosecution and suicide of Scaurus, so contrived that, although Tacitus attributes the responsibility to Macro [the praetorian prefect], we are yet left with the impression that Scaurus was somehow a victim of Tiberius, whom he had angered by some lines in a tragedy he had written. Another touch is added when, having to record the banishment of three informers, Tacitus begins by saying that even *they* were punished if the opportunity offered. By these means he has succeeded in placing the events of the year in a wholly false perspective. The reasons given for suicide are adequate only if those accused were guilty or if they had no hope of a fair hearing. But immediately after the fall of Sejanus several who faced a trial before the senate were acquitted, and we have no grounds for thinking that an acquittal had become impossible since that time. If Labeo and Scaurus were guilty there was nothing horrible in their fate, and in the case of the informers it is clear that Tacitus is ready for Tiberius whatever he may do; if he punishes the delators [informers] it shows how bloodthirsty he was, and, if he spares them it shows the same thing. . . .

The narrative of Tacitus for the next year (A.D. 35) reveals the rhetorical method even more plainly. He begins by putting together the events of two eastern campaigns and apologizes for this violation of chronology by saying that he has done so to give his readers some relief from the record of domestic calamities, for, although three years had

passed since the death of Sejanus, neither time nor prayers nor satiety, which soften other men [cf. p. 41], had any effect on Tiberius, who continued to punish old and uncertain offenses as if they had been recent and serious. The suicide of Trio is then briefly told and the four other cases for the year dismissed in a few lines. This brevity of treatment robs them of most of their effectiveness, but Tacitus makes up for this by his concluding comment: "Tiberius," he says, "heard of these things, not across a strait of the sea, as formerly, or by the hands of messengers from a distance, but so close to the city that he could answer the dispatches from the Consuls on the same day, or with only a night intervening, and almost see with his own eyes the blood streaming through men's houses, or the hands of the executioner." The force of this passage is as remarkable as its irrelevance, for the proximity of Tiberius to Rome cannot increase his wickedness if he was guilty of murdering the innocent. However, Tacitus does not say that any of the victims were innocent, and it can hardly be doubted that he would have done so if he could. The rhetorical machinery is very evident at this point. The introductory remarks on the implacability of Tiberius naturally lead us to expect something horrible, we are then hurried past the facts, and by a lurid picture at the close we are left with the impression, if we do not stop to think, that the events so narrated were very horrible indeed.

It is unnecessary to give further examples of the literary devices by which Tacitus has succeeded in persuading the world that during the last years of his reign Tiberius was a ferocious tyrant, wallowing in blood. A careful reading of the sixth book of the *Annals* will show that the whole picture of the

Tiberian terror is derived from the rhetorical setting in which the facts are presented and not from the facts themselves. . . .

F. B. Marsh, *The Reign of Tiberius* (London: The Clarendon Press, 1931), pp. 284-88.

(b) *A summing up of Tiberius by the same historian*

Tacitus . . . told the truth as he saw it and was scrupulous in matters of detail. . . . Thus in the end, while, on the one hand, by his literary genius he was able to stamp his portrait of Tiberius on the minds of men for centuries, on the other, he supplied the materials for a more impartial and sober judgment. . . .

Whether such a man as Tacitus has pictured could exist at all we need not discuss. That Tiberius was not such a man the record seems to prove beyond reasonable doubt. Most of the charges against him are refuted by the facts; he did not nurse the law of treason but struggled steadily against its extension; he did not encourage delation, but punished false accusers to the last; he was not cruel or bent upon a stern severity. For years his government was singularly lenient, and even in his last years the number of his victims seems very small when we consider what had passed and the real danger of his isolated position. Tacitus will have it that his gloomy temper led him to brood over his resentments for years, and then break out in sudden vengeance, yet in every case where this charge is made, the supposed victim of these old grudges had been guilty of some fresh offense. That he forgave his enemies cannot be asserted, but there is nothing in the record to prove he was implacable or vindictive. That he was suspicious there is exceedingly little to show. Augustus in his last days warned Tiberius of several possible pretenders to the throne; one of them, Cn. Piso, was trusted in an important post; another, Manius Lepidus, was honored and respected till his death; a third, L. Arruntius, was allowed to live unmolested until the emperor himself was dying, and the Romans believed that the "suspicious tyrant" was ignorant of his fate. . . .

Nor is the charge of hypocrisy any better sustained. It seems to have been based chiefly on the emperor's bearing in the senate, which was misunderstood by a later generation, and perhaps in some degree by contemporaries as well. At the accession of Tiberius the republican forms still possessed some vitality and he was sincerely anxious to preserve the independence of the senate. With this object in view he was forced on many occasions to hide his real feelings and opinions under ambiguous phrases for fear of influencing unduly the decisions of the conscript fathers. Tacitus tells us that while his language was usually guarded even to hesitation so that his words seemed to struggle forth with difficulty, yet when he acted mercifully he spoke with readiness and fluency. The historian is somewhat puzzled by the contrast and fails to see the obvious explanation, namely, that, when Tiberius intervened in the proceedings by virtue of his imperial prerogatives, he bore himself naturally, since it was impossible to disguise his interference. By the time of Tacitus the senate had become accustomed to the open and constant assertion of the imperial authority, and it was easy for those who disliked the memory of Tiberius to construe his attempts to respect the freedom of that body as evidence of hypocrisy.

The real faults of Tiberius seem to

have been quite different. A Roman of the old school, he had little sympathy with the prevailing tendencies of the generation in which he lived, and ignored too much the smaller arts of popularity. A blunt soldier, he found the part of princeps as designed by Augustus an irksome and difficult one to play. He lacked the genial tact which had enabled his predecessor to smooth over and disguise unpleasant realities and to keep up agreeable fictions. He hated flattery and strove to maintain the independence of the senate, but disposing as he did of the patronage of the empire, he could accomplish little. In his heart he despised his contemporaries, and took too little pains to conceal his feelings. On several occasions he failed to realize, or wilfully ignored, the effect of his conduct on the public mind, as, for example, when he absented himself from the funeral of Germanicus. Whatever his reasons for leaving Rome, his long seclusion at Capri was a serious blunder, since it destroyed the illusion on which the principate was based. His blind confidence in Sejanus seems to show a real lack of discernment; perhaps it indicates that, although Tiberius was a shrewd judge of ability, he had little insight into character. . . .

Certainly the emperor cannot reasonably be blamed for punishing those who had been guilty of real crimes in connection with the long series of intrigues of which Sejanus was the instigator. The record seems to prove that Tiberius tried to secure justice and did not intentionally oppress the innocent. There is nothing to show that there was any fundamental change in either his character or his conduct; if in the last years of his reign there were more suicides and executions, the most simple and natural explanation is that many crimes had come to light, and that the isolated position of the emperor led to more frequent conspiracies. Yet the number who suffered was small, and if there was terror in Rome it was due rather to the guilty consciences of those who escaped than to the cruelty of Tiberius.

Yet it cannot be denied, that, in spite of his ability and his good intentions, Tiberius failed in his role of princeps, and that the constitution of Augustus broke down in his hands. For this failure he was not wholly or even chiefly responsible, but it is impossible not to feel that a man of greater tact and more winning manners might have reconciled the feuds in the imperial family, or at least have kept them within bounds, and that Tiberius committed a grave blunder in not dealing more promptly and firmly with the question of the succession. Sejanus was certainly the evil genius of the emperor, and but for him the reign might have had a happier ending. . . . As a result of his blind confidence in an unscrupulous minister, Tiberius, as princeps, was defeated in most of his aims. He tried to maintain the independence of the senate, but he left it more subservient than ever; he sought to restrain delation, but it steadily developed, and even if he was not himself a tyrant, it was under him that the apparatus of the later tyranny took shape; he made a sincere effort to preserve the republican monarchy of Augustus, but it was transformed into the despotism of the later Caesars, and it was this last fact, which, perhaps, contributed most to blast his memory.

Ibid., pp. 221-227.

2. *The Triumph of Christianity*

KENNETH M. SETTON

Columbia University

To THE HISTORIAN the most astonishing aspect of the early history of the Church is the rapidity with which Christianity spread. The new religion appeared at a singularly opportune time, as the first historian of the Church, Eusebius of Caesarea, emphasized in the early fourth century, in his oration *In Praise of the Emperor Constantine* (chap. xv, 4):

> At the same time one universal power, the Roman Empire, arose and flourished, while the enduring and implacable hatred of nation against nation was now removed; and as the knowledge of one God, and one way of religion and salvation, even the doctrine of Christ, was made known to all mankind; so at the same time, the entire dominion of the Roman Empire being vested in a single sovereign, profound peace reigned throughout the world. And thus, by the express appointment of the same God, two roots of blessing, the Roman Empire and the doctrine of Christian piety, sprang up together for the benefit of men.

A number of important reasons can be advanced to help explain the Christian success. First of all, Christianity was born, during the reigns of the Emperors Augustus and Tiberius, into a world at peace: travel and communication were easy. Next, the popular Greek of the day, the *koiné*, the language of the New Testament, was spoken almost universally in the cities of the Levant and the seaboard towns of the whole Mediterranean. Before this time, a belief in the gods of the Graeco-Roman pantheon had been basic to the civic life of the ancient city-state, and these gods had been served by civic colleges of priests. Religion and affairs of state had been indissolubly connected, and the ancient gods and the city-states had lost their vitality together. With the passing of the independence of the (Greek) city-states, and with the subsequent emergence of the large territorial monarchies in the Hellenistic age, men's yearnings for recognition as individuals, the human desire to feel important in society, could no longer be satisfied by participation in the now insignificant affairs of the city-states. Alexander the Great and the intellectuals around him talked of the brotherhood of man; horizons had been broadened far beyond the walls of any small group of city-states; and the universalist philosophies of Stoicism and Epicureanism gained many adherents. Then, as the city-states and the Hellenistic monarchies were drawn into the world government of the Roman Empire, the pagan cults gradually went down before the inexorable triumph of Christianity.

The way had been well prepared for Christianity. The gospel travelled rapidly along the Roman roads and the sea-lanes of the Mediterranean, from city to city, and all roads led to Rome, where our interest chiefly lies.

But if there were factors deep within the changing culture of the Graeco-Roman world which thus assisted the growth of Christianity, there were at least three forces militating against the new religion: 1) the competition which Christianity faced in the eastern "mystery cults"; 2) the Roman government's persecution of Christians for their refusal to worship the Emperor; and 3) the growth of heretical sects within Christianity, as Greek rationalist philosophy and science made their impact upon the doctrines of the new faith. Of these three obstacles to its development Christianity had the most to fear from heresy, for it challenged authority within the Church and gave rise to doctrinal strife.

It is easy to exaggerate the extent of the competition furnished to Christianity by the oriental "mystery cults." Contrary to the impression created by several modern textbooks, these salvationist cults were never really dangerous competitors of Christianity. The Romans and westerners in general were by and large prejudiced against the worship of Cybele (and her consort Attis), the "Great Mother of the Gods" from Asia Minor. The worship of Isis (and her consort Osiris), from Egypt, always kept the mark and individuality of the land of its origin; there was little connection among the Isiac congregations throughout the Roman world; and although the cult of Isis employed the Greek language, its appeal was chiefly to Egyptians. There were, it is true, many worshippers of Isis in Rome, but they were chiefly recruited from the large Egyptian colony in the city. The Syrian divinities, such as Astarte, enjoyed even less success than those of Asia Minor and Egypt, for their devotees remained socially isolated, usually kept their Semitic dialects, often practiced sacred prostitution (a fertility rite), and even made sacrifice of human beings. The oriental cults lacked content and ethical teaching; for the most part ignored the character of the initiate; and held out salvation to their devotees chiefly in half-magical rites and secret mystical experiences; they failed to possess and even to reach the whole of men's lives; and so they could easily compromise with the worship of the Roman Emperor.

These cults and others, especially Mithraism, caused the early fathers of the Church much anxiety, but never the fear of defeat. Mithraism, the Hellenized worship of the Persian god of light Mithras, was widespread among soldiers, especially those of eastern origin, and some sixty little chapels dedicated to Mithras have been identified by archaeologists in Rome. Mithraism was a form of sun-worship, especially popular in the Empire in the third century, but it is very doubtful that it was ever a serious competitor to Christianity, once the new religion had reached its stride. Modern scholarship increasingly tends to the belief, contrary to another textbook cliché that Christianity constantly borrowed the practices of the mystery cults, that in actual fact the latter probably borrowed more heavily from Christianity!

Christianity had more to fear from persecution, for its failure to subscribe to the Emperor cult, but even here the "blood of the martyrs was the seed of the Church." Each successive text in the history of persecution attests in its way the rapid growth of the early Church. In A.D. 64, when Nero sought to throw blame for the great fire in Rome upon the Christians, "a vast multitude was convicted" (Tacitus, *Annals*, XV, 44). About the year 112 the younger Pliny, then governor of the province of Bithynia, sought the advice of the Emperor Trajan concerning Christians in his province, "especially on account of the number of those endangered, for many persons of every age and of every class in society, and of both sexes, are and will be brought into danger [by charges that they are Christians]. The contagion of this superstition has spread not only through the cities but also through the towns and countryside as well. . . . But it is easy to see what a host of people could be set right if they were given a chance of repentance!" (Pliny's *Letters*, X, 96.) But Christians did not repent for the faith. Their numbers increased, and they were inclined to avoid an active participation in the affairs of the world.

Until the Roman destruction of Jerusalem in A.D. 70, the three chief centers of Christianity had been Jerusalem, Caesarea (in Palestine), and Antioch, "and it was in Antioch that the disciples were first called 'Christians' " (Acts, 11:26). After A.D. 70 the chief centers were Antioch, Ephesus, and Rome, although about the beginning of the third century Alexandria eclipsed Ephesus in importance. Antioch and Alexandria were the homes of two vigorous and opposing schools of Christian doctrine. Antioch, in Syria, close to the scenes forever associated with the birth, life, and crucifixion of Christ, clung to its view of the "Jesus of history," and tended toward the heresy of adoptionism, i.e. that Jesus, of human birth, was adopted into the Godhead, and was thus divine; the Antiochene School was of a concrete, practical, and ethical bent, inclined to a literal interpretation of the Scriptures. The Alexandrian School, less familiar with the scenes and homely facts of Jesus' life, inclined to the heresy of docetism, i.e. that Jesus was actually God, a *phantasma* of a man, and only "seemed" to be a human being (from the Greek *dokein*, "to seem"); this school was inclined to abstraction, mysticism, theology, and was moved by the "Christ of experience." Alexandrian theologians saw allegories everywhere in the Scriptures. Although many early, influential, and persistent heretical groups were unconnected with either the Antiochene or Alexandrian schools of Christian thought, some of the chief heresies in the early history of Christianity did arise in the one school or the other. Antioch and Alexandria were both Greek cities during the Roman Empire; they were the homes of Greek theologians who read and pondered not only the religious heritage of Israel, but also the philosophy of Greece. These theologians sought the synthesis of the truths of revelation and of nature, but their different interpretations only served to point up the apparent conflicts between Christianity and Greek philosophy and science. Must the latter be rejected to preserve the integrity of the Christian faith? During the first two generations after Christ, and even longer, there was a tendency among Christians to reject the world, and many Christians looked for the almost immediate second coming of Christ and the establishment of the Kingdom of God. In the middle of the second century A.D., for example, Justin Martyr wrote in his first defense of Christianity to the Emperor Antoninus Pius, "Having heard that we are looking forward to a kingdom, you Emperors have wrongly assumed that we refer to a kingdom of men, like yours, whereas we mean the kingdom of God!" (*Apol.* I, 11).

Early Christians commonly avoided participation in either local or imperial government; tending strongly to pacifism, they often resisted service in the army; they were in the world, but they sought not to be of it. Generations later this contrast between the kingdom of God and that of men was to receive its most abundant and philosophic treatment in St. Augustine's contrast between the City of God (*Civitas Dei*) and that on Earth (*Civitas terrena*). But what was the Christian educator, in actual fact, to do with the scientific and cultural inheritance of the pagan past? Should it be retained or abandoned? If retained, how should it be modified? Was Tertullian right? Did Athens have nothing in common with Jerusalem? We find the following advice in a third-century Christian source (*Didascalia Apostolorum,* iii, ed. R. H. Connolly, Oxford, 1929, p. 13):

> Avoid completely heathen books! For what have you to do with strange words or laws or false prophecies, which are a ready source of error for unsteady minds? For what do you lack in the word of God that you should betake yourself to these heathen tales? If you wish to read histories, you have the Book of Kings; if you wish to read philosophy and poetry, you have the Prophets in whom you will find a greater understanding of all poetry and philosophy, for their wisdom and words are those of the Lord, Who alone is truly wise. If you want books of songs, you have the Psalms; if you want to read about the beginning of the world's formation, you have Genesis; if you want to read of laws and precepts, you have the law of the Lord in all its glory. From all such things, therefore, which are alien to you and the work of the devil, do keep yourself entirely apart.

Was this sound advice? The question was a serious one for the Church under the Roman Empire. This is Problem 1, the conflict of the old pagan and the new Christian thought and the student will find some of the pros and cons in the texts collected below.

There was a severe persecution of Christians under the Emperors Decius and Valerian (A.D. 250–260), which closed with Gallienus' recognition of Christianity as a legal religion in the year 260–261 (Eusebius, *Eccl. Hist.,* VII, 13). From this time on there was little persecution for almost half a century, but final peace did not come to the Church until after the last great persecution, from A.D. 303 to 311, under Diocletian and Galerius, after which Christianity was never again seriously molested by the state. By the early fourth century Christians had become very numerous, and the historian Eusebius refers thus to the numbers enrolled in the ranks of Christendom on the eve of the Galerian persecution: "And how could one fully describe those assemblies thronged with countless men, and the multitudes that gathered together in every city, and the famed concourses in the places of prayer; by reason of which . . . [Christians] were no longer satisfied with the buildings of olden time, and would erect from the foundations churches of spacious dimensions throughout all the cities? And as these things went forward with the times, and day by day increasingly grew mightier, no envy could stop them, nor was any evil spirit able to cast its spell or hinder them by human devices, so long as the divine and heavenly hand was sheltering and guarding, as a worthy object, its own people" (Eusebius, *Ecclesiastical History*, VIII, 1, 5-6, trans. J. E. L. Oulton and H. J. Lawlor, Loeb Classical Library, vol. II [1932], p. 253).

During the later years of the Galerian persecution in the East there was tension, and finally civil war, in the West. After deriving no advantage from eight years of persecution, Galerius acknowledged his failure, and issued his famous edict of toleration on 30 April, 311, the interesting text of which will be found below. Eighteen months after this the Emperor Constantine crushed his rival Maxentius in the battle of the Milvian Bridge, just outside the city of Rome, on 28 October, 312, and immediately thereafter the "conversion" of Constantine became apparent to all the world. The conversion of Constantine has been one of the more highly controversial problems in the history of the Church in the critical fourth century: it began the long and difficult history of the relation of the Christian Church to the Christian state. Not without reason, therefore, have some of the chief historians of the last two generations written scores of books and articles on this subject. But when we ask of these historians why Constantine became a Christian, they give us very different answers although they all derive these answers from the same sources! Some scholars have claimed that Constantine was chiefly motivated by political opportunism (thus Niebuhr and Burckhardt, Duruy and Bouché-Leclercq, Otto Seeck, Th. Brieger, and Ed. Schwartz). But what did Constantine stand to gain? Christians were more numerous in the East, but he was Emperor in the West. Christians had never been distinguished by their numbers and service in the army, but he had been made Emperor and maintained in his position by the army.

Other scholars have held that Constantine's conversion was sincere, whether the result of a devoted search for truth or merely of fear and a gross superstition (thus Maurice and Lot, Piganiol, Alföldi, and N. H. Baynes). Pagan contemporaries recognized that Constantine claimed divine assistance in his victory, and the Roman Senate inscribed these words on the triumphal Arch of Constantine, which still stands between the Roman Forum and the Colosseum: "To the Emperor Caesar Flavius Constantinus, the greatest, pious, fortunate Augustus, because by the inspiration of Divinity and by greatness of mind, he avenged with his forces the commonwealth with just arms both on the tyrant and on all his party, the Senate and the Roman people have dedicated this triumphal Arch." Less than a year after the battle of the Milvian Bridge a pagan orator thus addressed Constantine in the summer of 313: "Certainly you have some secret understanding, O Constantine, with that divine mind, which has delegated the care of us to lesser gods, and deigns to manifest itself to you alone" (from the ninth Imperial Panegyric, chap. 3). What was the nature of Constantine's "conversion"? What was his attitude towards the Christian Church? This is Problem 2. The student may seek answers in the sources given below, especially in Constantine's own official correspondence.

Until the year 313, when Christianity finally received official recognition for all time, Christian writers had pleaded for religious freedom and toleration, and had assailed persecuting Emperors as evil tyrants and violators of the very souls of men; with the triumph of their faith, however, Christians became persecutors in their turn, and in the later fourth and early fifth centuries the pagan cults and mysteries were largely destroyed. The final victory of Christianity may be studied in the religious edicts of the Theodosian Code (book XVI, title 10, laws 10-25): pagan rites and sacrifices were prohibited; the cults suppressed, and the privileges of their priests revoked; pagans were debarred from civil and military service; scorn was cast upon veneration of "images made by the work of mortals and destined to suffer the ravages of time"; provision was sometimes made for the destruction of temples—until finally there were laws enough to suppress "any pagans who survive although we now believe that there are none" (C. Th. XVI, 10, 22). The student may now read this imperial legislation in favor of Christianity and on the destruction of paganism in the recent translation prepared under the supervision of Clyde Pharr, *The Theodosian Code*, Princeton University Press, 1952.

There were many diversities of thought and practice throughout the early Church, and a correct or orthodox understanding of the data of the faith as provided by the New Testament and the tradition of the Apostles was especially sought by the Church in Rome, where one of the earliest large Christian communities had been formed. When St. Paul wrote his Epistle to the Romans (A.D. 58 or a little later), the Church in Rome had been in existence, and he had been wanting to visit it, "for many years" (Rom. 15:24). The Church of Rome came to be of particular importance in the newly emerging Christendom, and whoever would seek to understand something of the triumph of Christianity must pay especial attention to the early history of this Church. The Bishop of Rome achieved a position of pre-eminence in western European society from the fourth century on. The fact that Rome had for generations been the capital of the Empire certainly enhanced the prestige of the Roman See, but it was not on this political accident that its Bishop was to base his claim to authority, but on the early tradition that the Church in Rome had been founded by St. Peter (and also by St. Paul): "Thou art Peter, and upon this rock [*petra*] I will build my Church . . . , and I will give thee the keys of the kingdom of heaven" [Matthew, 16:18-19].

Actually the Petrine foundation of the Church of Rome rests rather more on dogmatic than on historical fact. If St. Peter, however, wrote the First Epistle which has come down to us under his name, we appear to have at least evidence of his presence in Rome: "The Church which is at Babylon [i.e. Rome] . . . greets you. . . ." (1 Peter, 5:13). Of Paul's presence in Rome we have the testimony of Acts, 28:11-30, which informs us of his residence in the city "for two full years . . . in his own hired lodging." (The first clear assertion, however, that the Church of Rome was thus of dual apostolic foundation comes in a letter of Bishop Dionysius of Corinth, about A.D. 170, quoted in Eusebius' *Ecclesiastical History*, II, 25, 8.) What was the nature, then, of authority within the Church of Rome during the first century of its existence? We come to the problem of the episcopacy in the early Roman Church, "that most tangled of all questions" (J. T. Shotwell and L. R. Loomis, *The See of Peter*, New York, 1927, p. 59). Some attention must be given to this tangled question, however, if we are to understand the background of the growth of papal power. The more important facts and sources are noted below, in the introduction to Problem 3, which is concerned with the establishment of papal supremacy over the Western Church.

Despite persecution the Church of Rome grew enormously, always increasing in influence and in authority, during the first two centuries of its existence. At the close of the reign of the Emperor Decius (A.D. 251), a letter of Pope Cornelius tells us that, in the Church of Rome, "there are 46 presbyters, 7 deacons, 7 sub-deacons, 42 acolytes, 52 exorcists, readers and door-keepers, and more than 1,500 widows and persons in distress . . ." (quoted in Eusebius, *Eccl. Hist.*, VI, 43, 11). These figures have been interpreted as indicating that the Church of Rome must have had some 30,000 adherents by the middle of the third century. Almost one hundred years later we have striking evidence of the increased prestige of the Church of Rome when in the year 343 the western bishops, who had assembled at the Council of Sardica (the modern Sofia), agreed that if a bishop believed himself unjustly dealt with in an ecclesiastical trial conducted by his fellow bishops or superiors, he might appeal his case, for retrial, to the Bishop of Rome. This is the first general acknowledgment of the appellate jurisdiction of the Roman See.

Three quarters of a century later, in the year 417, the great Pope Innocent I wrote to a council of African bishops, who had just condemned the Pelagian heresy, commending the bishops' wisdom in appealing for support to the Roman See. The Fathers of the Church had rightly decreed, wrote the Pope, "that whatever is done, even in the most distant and remote provinces, must not be regarded as final unless it has come to the notice of this See, so that it may be confirmed as a just pronouncement by the full authority of this See, for in this way other churches may understand what to teach . . ." (*Ep.* XXIX). Finally, in 445 the Emperor Valentinian III not only acknowledged but himself helped to establish, by an imperial edict, the supremacy of the Roman papacy over the whole of western Christendom. Concerning the edict of Valentinian, B. J. Kidd has written: "The result of this enactment was . . . to rivet a papal autocracy on the Western Empire by the whole force of the Civil Law. . . . It is the crowning proof that the papacy at Rome—as distinct from the primacy of the Apostolic See in Christendom—is the creation of the State" (*A History of the Church to A.D. 461*, III [1922], 358-59). But in remonstrance against this point of view, J. W. C. Wand, now the Anglican Bishop of London, has replied: "He would be blind to the facts of history who did not realize that in one respect at least this was a great gain. It was the prestige of the Papacy more than any other single factor which tamed the barbarian and preserved for future generations the best elements of the ancient civilisation in the West" (*A History of the Early Church to A.D. 500*, London, 1937, pp. 237-38). Here is Problem 3, the establishment of papal supremacy over the western Church; here it would be easy to cull pros and cons from the works of modern historians, but we are more interested in the evidence of the sources. Was the establishment of papal authority the gradual but deliberate recognition by western Christendom of what was believed to be the will of God or was it the result of historical accident and development?

I. THE CONFLICT OF THE OLD PAGAN AND THE NEW CHRISTIAN THOUGHT

Before we study some of the conflicting opinions entertained by Christian writers concerning the value, or lack thereof, of pagan philosophy and culture, perhaps we ought first to seek at least some small knowledge of the attitude of cultivated pagans and of the imperial government towards Christianity. Our sources are very limited for the first century of Christian history. Perhaps the most illuminating text is the letter which the younger Pliny (Gaius Plinius Secundus), then governor of the Roman province of Bithynia (in Asia Minor), wrote to the Emperor Trajan in A.D. 112:

It is my solemn rule, Sire, to refer to you all matters about which I am doubtful, for who can better direct my indecision or instruct my ignorance? I have never been present at trials of Christians. Therefore I do not know either what to look for nor the extent of the punishment to be inflicted in such cases. . . . In the meantime I have followed this method in dealing with those who have been denounced to me as Christians. I have asked them whether they were Christians. In the event of confession I have repeated the question a second and even a third

time, threatening with death those who persisted; and if they still persisted [in professing Christianity], I ordered them to be executed. For I had no doubt at all that, whatever this thing might be which they were confessing, such contumacy and unbending obstinacy should certainly be punished. There were others of like madness whom I ordered to be sent to Rome, because they were Roman citizens [just as St. Paul had "appealed to Caesar" before the Roman governor Festus in Acts, 25: 6-12].

Soon, by the very fact of investigation, as usually happens, several more cases were brought to light. An anonymous accusation was placed before us; it contained many names of alleged Christians. I thought it best to discharge those who denied that they were or had ever been Christians when they repeated after me an invocation to the gods, and made supplication with incense and wine to your image, which I had ordered to be produced for this purpose, together with the statues of the gods, besides which they cursed Christ, and none of these things, it is said, can those who are really Christians be forced to do. Some persons named by the informer admitted they were Christians, and then denied it; others said they had been, but had withdrawn from the sect, some three years ago, some many years ago, and at least one twenty-five years ago! They all worshipped both your image and the statues of the gods, and they reviled Christ.

They maintained, however, that this had been the sum total of their mistake or guilt, that they had been accustomed on a set day to come together before dawn and, all together, to sing a hymn to Christ as to a god, and that they bound themselves by an oath, not for the purpose of some crime, but not to commit theft, robbery, or adultery, nor to betray a trust, nor to deny a deposit when called upon to return it to its owner. But when such rites as these were over, they said it was their custom to depart, and to come together later on to take food, but ordinary and harmless food [early Christians were sometimes accused of cannibalism!], but even this practice they had given up after my edict by which in accordance with your instructions I had forbidden secret associations. Hence I believed it the more necessary to find out the truth, and by torture, from two women slaves, who were called "deaconesses." *But I found nothing else than a depraved, immoderate superstition* [the Roman gentleman's dictum on Christianity!].

Therefore I have delayed the investigation, and I have come to you for advice. The matter has seemed to me well worth your consideration, especially on account of the number of those imperilled. . . .

To this the Emperor Trajan replied:

You have followed the method you should, my dear Secundus, in looking into the cases of those denounced to you as Christians. It is impossible to set up a rule of universal application which may result in a fixed form of action in such cases. Christians are not to be sought out; if they are informed against and found guilty, however, they must be punished; but with this provision, that a person who has denied he is a Christian, and has made the fact manifest in the proper way, i.e. by making supplication to our gods, even though he may have been suspect in the past, he is to receive pardon for repentance. Accusations made anonymously ought not to receive attention on any charge; for this sets the worst kind of precedent, and is not in keeping with the character of our reign. (Pliny, *Letters,* X, 96-97, trans. K. M. Setton.)

The search for rules of universal application was, however, the animating principle of the Roman law. Trajan's position was untenable. Less than a century after this, the early church father Tertullian (fl. A.D. 200) easily put his finger upon the flaw in the judicial procedure which Trajan had prescribed against Christians:

When Plinius Secundus was governing his province and had condemned some Christians and driven others from their steadfastness, and still the sheer numbers concerned worried him as to what he ought to do thereafter, he consulted the Emperor Trajan. He asserted that, apart from an obstinacy that refused to sacrifice, he had learnt nothing about the Christian mysteries—nothing beyond meetings before dawn to sing to Christ and to God [*sic*], and to band themselves together in discipline, forbidding murder, adultery, dishonesty, treachery, and the other crimes. Trajan replied in a rescript that men of this kind were not to be sought out, but if they were brought before Pliny they must be punished. What a decision! how inevitably entangled! He says they must not be sought out, implying they are innocent; and he orders them to be punished, implying they are guilty. He spares them and rages against them; he pretends not to see and punishes. Why cheat yourself with your judgment? If you condemn them, why not hunt them down? If you do not hunt them down, why not also acquit them? . . .

. . . You do not deal with us in accordance with your procedure in judging criminals. If the other criminals plead Not guilty, you torture them to make them confess; the Christians alone you torture to make them deny. Yet if it were something evil, we should deny our guilt, and you would use torture to force us to confess it. . . .

A man shouts, "I am a Christian." He says what he is. You, sir, wish to hear what he is *not*. Presiding to extort the truth, you take infinite pains in our case, and ours alone, to hear a lie. . . . Clearly, when others deny, you do not readily believe them; if we have denied, you at once believe us. . . . (Tertullian, *Apology,* 2, trans. T. R. Glover, Loeb Cl. Libr., pp. 11ff.)

Undoubtedly there is some special pleading here, but Tertullian's main point is well taken. Before the conversion of Constantine the relations of Church and State were rather simple: the Church was a voluntary association of intractable people to whom it was sound policy for the state to be hostile. Under persecution Christians tended to withdraw from society which was, of course, very largely pagan, but there were necessarily serious limits to this withdrawal. Education was as important to the Christian community as to pagan society at large. Ancient education was for the most part literary and philosophical; the schools of the Roman Empire were the products of centuries of pagan culture. Almost all the Fathers who oppose the Greek (and Latin) classics and philosophy do so on the grounds of their error and lack of truth, their immorality and frivolity. Those who defend them do so on the grounds of their utility as an intellectual and moral preparation for the study of Holy Scripture. The classics are not defended on the grounds of their beauty as literature.

Justin Martyr, in the middle of the second century, was a philosopher, having been a Stoic, an Aristotelian, a Pythagorean, and a Platonist in turn; converted to Christianity, he became an ardent defender of the new religion, but he remained a philosopher to the day he finally died for the faith he had adopted. On the other hand Tertullian had been a lawyer, and was very well read, but he saw no usefulness in pagan letters and in philosophy, which the Christian experience had shown, in his opinion, to be merely the seedbed of heresy. To Clement (fl. A.D. 200), head of the catechetical school of Alexandria, pagan philosophy had been necessary for the larger truths of Christianity:

Before the advent of the Lord philosophy was necessary to the Greeks for righteousness, and now it becomes conducive to piety, being a kind of preparatory training to those who attain to faith through understanding. God is the cause of all good things; but of some primarily, as of the Old and the New Testaments; and of others by consequence, as phi-

losophy. Perhaps, too, philosophy was given to the Greeks directly and primarily until the Lord should call them. Philosophy was thus a preparation, paving the way for him who is perfected in Christ. The way of truth is therefore one, but into it, as into a perennial river, streams flow from all sides. As all the branches of study contribute to philosophy, which is their mistress, so also philosophy itself co-operates in the acquisition of wisdom. Philosophy is the study of wisdom, and wisdom is the knowledge of things divine and human, and their cause also. Philosophy is characterized by investigation into truth and the nature of things—this is the truth of which the Lord Himself said, "I am the truth" [John 14, 6]. But as we say that a man can be a believer without learning, so also we assert that it is impossible for a man without learning to comprehend the things which are declared in the faith. But to adopt what is well said, and not to adopt the reverse, is caused not simply by faith, but by faith combined with knowledge. (Adapted from Clement, *Stromateis* or *Miscellanies*, I, 5, 6.)

This was the chief Christian argument in defense of pagan learning. Pagan literature was to receive its classic defense at the hands of St. Basil of Caesarea in his essay *To Young Men, On Pagan Literature*, of which a few passages are given below. Although St. Augustine, in the *City of God*, "attempts with more than ordinary diligence to tear up and eradicate depraved and ancient opinions hostile to the truth of piety, which the long-continued error of the human race has fixed deeply in unenlightened minds" (from preface to bk. VII), he nevertheless shares St. Basil's view as to the general utility of pagan thought, and expresses a high respect for Plato and his successors.

But there were other prominent fathers of the Church, such as Epiphanius of Salamis (in eastern Cyprus), and Lucifer of Cagliari (in Sardinia), who were pretty consistently hostile to the pagan classics and to pagan thought, and St. Gregory of Nazianzus and St. John Chrysostom give frequent expression to an unfriendly attitude toward pagan philosophy and letters. Sometimes Chrysostom is moved to a violent denunciation of the gross superstitions and immoralities of pagan religious legends and literature, as in his fifth *Homily on Titus* (in the *Nicene and Post-Nicene Fathers*, XIII, 535 ff). Nevertheless, Chrysostom wrote with a conscious artistry which reveals no inconsiderable study of the classical models. The fathers long debated and never solved the problem of whether, in general, to read or not to read the pagan classics and philosophy, but many of them were fascinated by the apparent pagan anticipation of some of the truths of Christian doctrine. It was as St. Paul himself had said, as he spoke to the Athenians from the hill of Areopagus: "For in Him we live and move and have our being, as indeed some of your own poets have said!" (Acts 17, 28).

A. Tertullian Asks, What Has Athens to Do with Jerusalem?

Here is a denial of the value of pagan philosophy to the Christian. On the involved and ill-understood philosophical "system of Valentinus," with its concept of the *enthymesis*, to which Tertullian alludes, the student may consult the brilliant chapter of F. C. Burkitt, "Pagan Philosophy and the Christian Church," in the *Cambridge Ancient History*, XII (1939), 469-473.

For it is philosophy which is the material of the world's wisdom, the rash interpreter of the nature and the dispensation of God. Indeed heresies are themselves instigated by philosophy. From this source came the Aeons, and I know not what infinite forms, and the trinity of man in the system of Valentinus, who was of Plato's school. From the same source came Marcion's better god, with all his tranquillity: he came of the Stoics. Then, again, the opinion that the soul dies is held by the Epicureans; while the denial of the restoration of the body is taken from the aggregate school of all the philosophers; also, when matter is made equal to God, then you have the teaching of

Zeno; and when any doctrine is alleged touching a god of fire, then Heraclitus comes in. The same subject-matter is discussed over and over again by the heretics and the philosophers. The same arguments are involved. Whence comes evil? Why is it permitted? What is the origin of man? and in what way does he come? Besides the question which Valentinus has very lately proposed—Whence comes God? Which he settles with the answer: from *enthymesis* ["conception"] and *ektroma* ["abortion"]! Unhappy Aristotle! who invented for these men dialectics, the art of building up and pulling down, an art so evasive in its propositions, so farfetched in its conjectures, so harsh in its arguments, so productive of contentions—embarrassing even to itself, retracting everything, and really treating of nothing! Whence spring those "fables and endless genealogies" [1 Tim. 1, 4], and the "unprofitable questions" [cf. Tit. 3, 9], and "words which spread like a cancer" [2 Tim. 2, 17]?

From all these, when the apostle would restrain us, he expressly names *philosophy* as that which he would have us be on our guard against. Writing to the Colossians, he says, "See that no one beguile you through philosophy and vain deceit, after the tradition of men, and contrary to the wisdom of the Holy Ghost" [Col. 2, 8]. He had been at Athens, and had in his interviews (with the philosophers) become acquainted with that human wisdom which pretends to know the truth, while it only corrupts it, and is itself divided into its own manifold heresies, by the variety of its mutually repugnant sects.

What indeed has Athens to do with Jerusalem? What concord is there between the Academy and the Church? what between heretics and Christians? Our instruction comes from the "porch of Solomon," who had himself taught that "the Lord should be sought in simplicity of heart" [Book of Wisdom, 1, 1]. Away with all attempts to produce a mottled Christianity of Stoic, Platonic, and dialectic composition! We want no curious disputation after possessing Christ Jesus, no inquisition after enjoying the gospel! With our faith, we desire no further belief. For this is our first belief, that there is nothing which we ought to believe besides.

Tertullian, *On the Prescription of Heretics,* 7, adapted from the translation of Peter Holmes, *Ante-Nicene Fathers,* III, 246.

B. St. John Chrysostom on the Superiority of the Christian Rustic over the Pagan Philosopher

In the following sermon, one of the twenty-one *Homilies on the Statues,* preached during Lent in 387, St. John Chrysostom asserts that the simple country folk who have come into the city of Antioch to attend a religious festival are of higher virtue and display a greater wisdom than the pagan philosophers.

These [country folk] are our philosophers, and theirs the best philosophy, exhibiting their virtue not by their outward appearance, but by their mind. The pagan philosophers are in character no wise better than those who are engaged on the stage, and in the sports of actors; and they have nothing to show beyond the threadbare cloak, the beard, and the long robe! But these, quite on the contrary, bidding farewell to staff and beard, and the other accoutrements, have their souls adorned with the doctrines of the true philosophy, and not only with the doctrines, but also with the real practice. And were you to question any one of these, who live a rustic life at the spade and plough, as to the dogmas respecting which the pagan philosophers have discoursed an infinite deal, and have expended a multitude of words, without being able to say anything sound, one of these would give you an accurate reply from his store of wisdom. And not only is this to be wondered at, but they confirm the credibility of these doctrines by their actions. For of the fact that we have an immortal soul, and that we shall hereafter render an account of what we have done here, and stand before a fearful Tribunal, their minds are at once thoroughly persuaded, and they have also regulated their whole course of life by such hopes as these; and have become superior to all worldly show, instructed as they have been by the sacred Scriptures, that "all is vanity, yea, vanity of vanities," and they do not greedily long for any of those things which seem to be so splendid.

These too know how to philosophize concerning God, even as God hath determined; and if, taking one of them, you were now to bring forward some pagan philosopher . . . , and then open the books of the ancient philosophers, and go through them, and institute an enquiry by way of parallel as to what these now answer, and the others in their day philosophically advanced, you would see how much wisdom belonged to the former, and how much folly to the philosophers. For while some of these would aver that the things existing were destitute of a providence, and that the creation did not have its origin from God; that virtue was not sufficient for itself, but stood in need of wealth, and nobility, and external splendor, and other things still more ridiculous; and while these [simple Christians], on the other hand, would discourse wisely respecting Providence, respecting the future Tribunals of judgment, respecting the creative power of God, bringing forth all things out of nothing, as well as respecting all other points, although at the same time they were entirely destitute of worldly schooling; who could but learn from hence the power of Christ, which hath proved these unlearned and simple persons to be as much wiser than those, who make so much boast of their wisdom, as men of discretion are seen to be in comparison to little children? For what harm can result to them from their simplicity in regard to learning, when their thoughts are full of much wisdom?

And what advantage have those philosophers from this learning, when the understanding is devoid of right thoughts? It were just as if one should have a sword that had its hilt of silver, whilst the blade was weaker than the vilest lead. For truly these philosophers have their tongue decked out with words and names, but their understanding is full of mere weakness and good for nothing. Not so with our "philosophers," but quite the reverse. Their understanding is full of spiritual wisdom and their mode of life is a transcript of their doctrines. Amongst these there are no luxurious women; there are no ornaments of dress, nor colors, nor paints; but all such corruption of manners is discountenanced. Hence the population under their charge are the more readily trained to sobriety, and the law which Paul gave, when he directed that food and covering should be had, and nothing more be sought after, they most rigidly observe. Amongst them, there are no perfumed unguents to fascinate the senses; but the earth bringing forth herbs prepares for them a varied fragrance of flowers, above all the skill of perfumers. For this reason, their bodies as well as souls enjoy a sound state of health, inasmuch as they have banished all luxury of diet, and driven off all the evil floods of drunkenness; and they eat just as much as suffices for subsistence. Let us then not despise them because of their outward appearance, but let us admire their minds. For of what advantage is the external habit, when the soul is more wretchedly clad than any beggar! The man ought to be praised and admired, not for dress, nay more, not even for his bodily form, but for his soul. Lay bare the soul of these men, and you will see its beauty, and the wealth it possesses, in their words, in their doctrines, and in the whole system of their manners!

Let the Gentiles then be ashamed, let them hide their heads, and slink away on account of their philosophers, and their wisdom, wretched as it is beyond all folly! For the philosophers that have been amongst them in their lifetime have hardly been able to teach their doctrines to a very few, who can easily be numbered; and when any trifling peril overtook them, they lost even these. But the disciples of Christ, the fishermen, the publicans, and the tent-makers, in a few years brought over the whole world to the truth; and when from that time, ten thousand perils have been constantly arising, the preaching of the Gospel was so far from being put down, that it still flourishes and increases; and they taught simple people, tillers of the ground, and occupied with cattle, to be lovers of wisdom. Such are the persons, who besides all the rest, having deeply rooted in them that love which is the source of all good things, have hastened to us, undertaking so long a journey, that they might come and embrace their fellow members.

St. John Chrysostom (d. 407), *Homily XIX on the Statues*, 3-5, adapted from the translation in the *Nicene and Post-Nicene Fathers*, IX, 465-466.

C. Justin Martyr on the Divine Inspiration of the Pagan Philosophers

While Justin Martyr deplores the error, immorality, and frivolity of some of the pagan classics, he emphasizes, in the famous doctrine of the "spermatic Logos," that all truth derived from the same divine source, and might be expressed by Socrates as well as by Plato. Christ was the Logos (or "Word"), the creative reason of God, which had sown the seed, hence "spermatic," of understanding in the pre-Christian philosophers as well as in the Christian teachers of Justin's own day. The pre-Christian philosophers were clearly worth reading:

Beyond doubt, therefore, our teachings are more noble than all human teaching, because Christ, who appeared on earth for our sakes, became the whole Logos, namely, Logos and body and soul. Everything that the philosophers and legislators discovered and expressed well, they accomplished through their discovery and contemplation of some part of the Logos. But, since they did not have a full knowledge of the Logos, which is Christ, they often contradicted themselves. And those who were born before Christ assumed human nature were dragged into law courts as irreligious and meddling persons, when they tried in human narrowness to think out and prove things by reason. Socrates, the most ardent of all in this regard, was accused of the very crimes that are imputed to us. They claimed that he introduced new deities and rejected the state-sponsored gods. But what he did was to ostracize Homer and the other poets, and to instruct men to expel the evil demons and those who perpetrated the deeds narrated by the poets; and to exhort men by meditation to learn more about God who was unknown to them, saying: "It is not an easy matter to find the Father and Creator of all things, nor, when He is found, is it safe to an-nounce Him to all men." Yet, our Christ did all this through His own power. There was no one who believed so much in Socrates as to die for his teaching, but not only philosophers and scholars believed in Christ, of whom even Socrates had a vague knowledge (for He was and is the Logos who is in every person, and who predicted things to come first through the prophets and then in person when He assumed our human nature and feelings, and taught us these doctrines), but also workmen and men wholly uneducated, who all scorned glory, and fear, and death. Indeed, this is brought about by the power of the ineffable Father, and not through the instrumentality of human reason. . . .

When I learned of the evil camouflage which the wicked demons had thrown around the divine doctrines of the Christians to deter others from following them, I had to laugh at the authors of these lies, at the camouflage itself, and at the popular reaction. I am proud to say that I strove with all my might to be known as a Christian, not because the teachings of Plato are different from those of Christ, but because they are not in every way similar; neither are those of other writers, the Stoics, the poets, and the historians. For each one of them, seeing, through his participation of the seminal Divine Word, what was related to it, spoke very well. But, they who contradict themselves in important matters evidently did not acquire the unseen [that is, heavenly] wisdom and the indisputable knowledge. The truths which men in all lands have rightly spoken belong to us Christians. For we worship and love, after God the Father, the Word who is from the Unbegotten and Ineffable God, since He even became Man for us, so that by sharing in our sufferings He also might heal us. Indeed, all writers, by means of the engrafted seed of the Word which was implanted in them, had a dim glimpse of the truth. For the seed of something and its imitation, given in proportion to one's capacity, is one thing, but the thing itself, which is shared and imitated according to His grace, is quite another.

Justin Martyr (fl. A.D. 150), *Second Apology*, 10, 13, trans. Thos. B. Falls, *Saint Justin Martyr* (in *The Fathers of the Church*), New York, 1948, pp. 129-30, 133-34.

D. St. Basil the Great's Defense of Classical Greek Literature

First, then, as to the learning to be derived from the poets, that I may begin with them, inasmuch as the subjects they deal with are of every kind, you ought not to give your attention to all they write without exception; but whenever they recount for you the deeds or words of good men, you ought to cherish and emulate these and try to be as far as possible like them; but when they treat of wicked men, you ought to avoid such imitation, stopping your ears no less than Odysseus did, according to what those same poets say, when he avoided the songs of the Sirens [cf. Homer, *Odyssey*, XII, 37 ff.]. For familiarity with evil words is, as it were, a road leading to evil deeds. On this account, then, the soul must be watched over with all vigilance, lest through the pleasure the poets' words give we may unwittingly accept something of the more evil sort, like those who take poisons along with honey. We shall not, therefore, praise the poets when they revile or mock, or when they depict men engaged in amours or drunken, or when they define happiness in terms of an over-abundant table or dissolute songs. But least of all shall we give attention to them when they narrate anything about the gods, and especially when they speak of them as being many, and these too not even in accord with one another. For in their poems brother is at feud with brother, and father with children, and the latter in turn are engaged in truceless war with their parents. But the adulteries of gods and their amours and their sexual acts in public, and especially those of Zeus, the chief and highest of all, as they themselves describe him, actions which one would blush to mention of even brute beasts—all these we shall leave to the stage-folk.

These same observations I must make concerning the writers of prose also, and especially when they fabricate tales for the entertainment of their hearers. And we shall certainly not imitate the orators in their art of lying. For neither in courts of law nor in other affairs is lying befitting to us, who have chosen the right and true way of life, and to whom refraining from litigation has been ordained in commandment. But we shall take rather those passages of theirs in which they have praised virtue or condemned vice. . . . And just as in plucking the blooms from a rose-bed we avoid the thorns, so also in garnering from such writings whatever is useful, let us guard ourselves against what is harmful. . . .

And since it is through virtue that we must enter upon this life of ours, and since much has been uttered in praise of virtue by poets, much by historians, and much more still by philosophers, we ought especially to apply ourselves to such literature. For it is no small advantage that a certain intimacy and familiarity with virtue should be engendered in the souls of the young, seeing that the lessons learned by such are likely, in the nature of the case, to be indelible, having been deeply impressed on them by reason of the tenderness of their souls. Or what else are we to suppose Hesiod had in mind when he composed these verses which are on everybody's lips, if he were not exhorting young men to virtue?—that "rough at first and hard to travel, and full of abundant sweat and toil, is the road which leads to virtue, and steep withal." Therefore it is not given to everyone to climb this road, so steep it is, nor, if one essays to climb it, easily to reach the summit. But when once one has come to the top he is able to see how smooth and beautiful, how easy and pleasant to travel it is, and more agreeable than that other road which leads to vice, which it is possible to take all at once from near at hand, as this same poet has said. For to me it seems that he has narrated these things for no other reason than to urge us on to virtue and to exhort all men to be good, and to keep us from becoming weak and cowardly in the face of the toils and desisting before reaching the end. And assuredly, if anyone else has sung the praise of virtue in terms like Hesiod's, let us welcome his words as leading to the same end as our own. Moreover, as I myself have heard a man say who is clever at understanding a poet's mind, all Homer's poetry is an encomium of virtue, and all he wrote, save what is accessory, bears to this end. . . .

It was for this reason indeed, as it seems to me, that Solon said this with respect to the rich: "But we will not exchange with them our virtue for their wealth, since the one abides always, while riches change their owners every day." And similar to these words are those of Theognis also in which he says that God, whomsoever he means indeed by this term, inclines the scale for men at one time this way, at another that way, now to be rich, but now to have nothing.

And furthermore, the sophist from Ceos, Prodicus, somewhere in his writ-

ings uttered a doctrine kindred to these others regarding virtue and vice; therefore we must apply our minds to him also, for he is not a man to be rejected. His narrative runs something like this, so far as I recall the man's thought, since I do not know the exact words, but only that he spoke in general to the following effect, not employing metre. When Heracles was quite a young man and was nearly of the age at which you yourselves are now, while he was deliberating which of the two roads he should take, the one leading through toils to virtue, or the easiest, two women approached him, and these were Virtue and Vice. Now at once, although they were silent, the difference between them was evident from their appearance. For the one had been decked out for beauty through the art of toiletry, and was overflowing with voluptuousness, and she was leading a whole swarm of pleasures in her train; now these things she displayed, and promising still more than these she tried to draw Heracles to her. But the other was withered and squalid, and had an intense look, and spoke quite differently; for she promised nothing dissolute or pleasant, but countless sweating toils and labours and dangers through every land and sea. But the prize to be won by these was to become a god, as the narrative of Prodicus expressed it; and it was this second woman that Heracles in the end followed.

And almost all the writers who have some reputation for wisdom have, to a greater or less degree, each to the best of his power, discoursed in their works in praise of virtue. To these men we must hearken and we must try to show forth their words in our lives; for he in truth who confirms by act his devotion to wisdom, which among others is confined to words, "He alone has understanding, but the others flit about as shadows. . . ."

As to the passages in literature, then, which contain admonitions of excellent things, let us accept this procedure. And since the virtuous deeds, likewise, of the men of old have been preserved for us, either through an unbroken oral tradition or through being preserved in the words of poets or writers of prose, let us not fail to derive advantage from this source also. For example, a certain fellow, a market-lounger, kept railing at Pericles, but he paid no attention; he kept it up all day long, giving Pericles a merciless dressing of abuse, but the latter took no heed of it. Then, when it was already evening and dark, though the man was scarcely desisting, Pericles escorted him home with a light, lest his own schooling in philosophy be utterly brought to naught. Again, a certain man, having become enraged against Eucleides of Megara, threatened him with death and took oath upon it; but Eucleides took a counter-oath, to the effect that verily he would appease the man and make him put aside his wrath against him. How very valuable it is that an example of this kind should be recalled to memory by a man who is on the point of being held in the grip of a fit of passion! For one must not put a simple-minded trust in the tragedy when it says "Against enemies anger arms the hand," but, on the contrary, we should not permit ourselves to be aroused to anger at all; but if this is not easy to achieve, we should at least apply reason to our anger as a sort of curb and not allow it to be carried too far beyond the bounds.

But let us bring our discussion back again to the examples of virtuous deeds. A certain man kept striking Socrates, son of Sophroniscus, full in the face, falling upon him unmercifully; yet he did not oppose, but permitted the wine-mad fellow to satiate his rage, so that his face was presently swollen and bruised from the blows. Now when the man ceased striking him, Socrates, it is said, did nothing except inscribe on his own forehead, like the name of the sculptor on a statue, "So-and-so (naming the man) made this," and only to that extent avenged himself. Since these examples tend to nearly the same end as our own precepts, I maintain that it is of great value for those of your age to imitate them. For this example of Socrates is akin to that precept of ours—that to him who strikes us on the cheek, so far from avenging ourselves upon him we should offer the other cheek also. And the example of Pericles or Eucleides is akin to the precept that we should submit to those who persecute us and gently suffer their anger; and this other one—that we should pray for blessings for our enemies instead of cursing them. For whoever has been instructed in these examples beforehand cannot after that distrust those precepts as utterly impossible to obey. I should not pass over the example of Alexander, who, when he had taken prisoner the daughters of Darius, although it had been testified to him that they possessed a marvellous beauty, did not think it fitting even to look upon them, judging it to be disgraceful for one who had captured men to be vanquished by women. Indeed, this example tends to the same purport as that well-known precept of ours—that he who looks upon a woman to enjoy her, although he does not commit adultery in act, yet in truth, because he has received the desire into his soul, is not free of guilt. . . .

But, in a single word, the body in every part should be despised by everyone who does not care to be buried in its pleasures, as it were in slime; or we ought to cleave to it only in so far as we obtain from it service for the pursuit of wisdom, as Plato advises, speaking in a manner somewhat similar to Paul's when he admonishes us to make no provision for the body unto the arousing of concupiscences [cf. Rom. 13, 14]. Or in what way do those differ, who are solicitous how the body may be as well off as possible, but overlook the soul, which is to make use of it, as utterly worthless, from those who are much concerned about their implements but neglect the art which uses them for its work? Hence we must do quite the opposite—chastise the body and hold it in check, as we do the violent chargings of a wild beast, and by smiting with reason, as with a whip, the disturbances engendered by it in the soul, calm them to sleep; instead of relaxing every curb upon pleasure and suffering the mind to be swept headlong, like a charioteer by unmanageable horses riotously running at large. . . .

But although we Christians shall doubtless learn all these things more thoroughly in our own literature, yet for the present, at least, let us trace out a kind of rough sketch, as it were, of what virtue is according to the teaching of the pagans. For by those who make it their business to gather the benefit to be derived from each source many accretions from many sides are wont to be received, as happens to mighty rivers.

St. Basil of Caesarea (d. 379), *To Young Men, On Pagan Literature*, 4-7, 9-10, trans. R. J. Deferrari and M. R. P. McGuire, *The Letters of St. Basil*, Loeb Classical Library (Cambridge, Mass.: Harvard University Press, 1934), IV, pp. 387 ff.

E. St. Augustine on the Superiority of Christian Theology over Pagan Philosophy

1. We shall require to apply our mind with far greater intensity to the present question than was requisite in the solution and unfolding of the questions handled in the preceding books; for it is not with ordinary men, but with philosophers that we must confer concerning the theology which they call natural. For it is not like the fabulous, that is, the theatrical; nor the civil, that is, the urban theology: the one of which displays the crimes of the gods, whilst the other manifests their criminal desires, which demonstrates them to be rather malign demons than gods. It is, we say, with philosophers, we have to confer with respect to this theology,—men whose very name, if rendered into Latin, signifies those who profess the love of wisdom. Now, if wisdom is God, who made all things, as is attested by the divine authority and truth, then the philosopher is a lover of God. But since the thing itself, which is called by this name, exists not in all who glory in the name,—for it does not follow, of course, that all who are called philosophers are lovers of true wisdom,—we must needs select from the number of those with whose opinions we have been able to acquaint ourselves by reading, some with whom we may not unworthily engage in the treatment of this question. For I have not in this work undertaken to refute all the vain opinions of the philosophers, but only such as pertain to theology, which Greek word we understand to mean an account or explanation of the divine nature. Nor, again, have I undertaken to refute all the vain theological opinions of all the philosophers, but only of such of them as, agreeing in the belief that there is a divine nature, and that this divine nature is concerned about human affairs, do nevertheless deny that the worship of the one unchangeable God is sufficient for the obtaining of a blessed life after death, as well as at the present time; and hold that, in order to obtain that life, many gods, created, indeed, and appointed to their several spheres by that one God, are to be worshipped.

2. As far as concerns the literature of

the Greeks, whose language holds a more illustrious place than any of the languages of the other nations, history mentions two schools of philosophers, the one called the Italic school, originating in that part of Italy which was formerly called Magna Graecia; the other called the Ionic school, having its origin in those regions which are still called by the name of Greece. The Italic school had for its founder Pythagoras of Samos, to whom also the term "philosophy" is said to owe its origin. For whereas formerly those who seemed to excel others by the laudable manner in which they regulated their lives were called sages, Pythagoras, on being asked what he professed, replied that he was a philosopher, that is, a student or lover of wisdom; for it seemed to him to be the height of arrogance to profess oneself a sage. The founder of the Ionic school, again, was Thales of Miletus, one of those seven who were styled the "seven sages," of whom six were distinguished by the kind of life they lived, and by certain maxims which they gave forth for the proper conduct of life. Thales was distinguished as an investigator into the nature of things; and, in order that he might have successors in his school, he committed his dissertations to writing. That, however, which especially rendered him eminent was his ability, by means of astronomical calculations, even to predict eclipses of the sun and moon. He thought, however, that water was the first element of things, and that of it all the elements of the world, the world itself, and all things which are generated in it, ultimately consist. Over all this work, however, which, when we consider the world, appears so admirable, he set nothing of the nature of divine mind. To him succeeded Anaximander, his pupil, who held a different opinion concerning the nature of things; for he did not hold that all things spring from one principle, as Thales did, who held that principle to be water, but thought that each thing springs from its own proper principle. These principles of things he believed to be infinite in number, and thought that they generated innumerable worlds, and all the things which arise in them. He thought, also, that these worlds are subject to a perpetual process of alternate dissolution and regeneration, each one continuing for a longer or shorter period of time, according to the nature of the case; nor did he, any more than Thales, attribute anything to a divine mind in the production of all this activity of things. Anaximander left as his successor his disciple Anaximenes, who attributed all the causes of things to an infinite air. He neither denied nor ignored the existence of gods, but, so far from believing that the air was made by them, he held, on the contrary, that they sprang from the air. Anaxagoras, however, who was his pupil, perceived that a divine mind was the productive cause of all the things which we see, and said that all the various kinds of things, according to their several modes and species, were produced out of an infinite matter consisting of homogeneous particles, but by the efficiency of a divine mind. Diogenes, also, another pupil of Anaximenes, said that a certain air was the original substance of things out of which all things were produced, but that it was possessed of a divine reason without which nothing could be produced from it. Anaxagoras was succeeded by his disciple Archelaus, who also thought that all things consisted of homogeneous particles, of which each particular thing was made, but that those particles were pervaded by a divine mind, which perpetually energized all the eternal bodies, namely, those particles, so that they are alternately united and separated. Socrates, the master of Plato, is said to have been the disciple of Archelaus; and on Plato's account it is that I have given this brief historical sketch of the whole history of these schools.

3. Socrates is said to have been the first who directed the entire effort of philosophy to the correction and regulation of manners, all who went before him having expended their greatest efforts in the investigation of physical, that is, natural phenomena. However, it seems to me that it cannot be certainly discovered whether Socrates did this because he was wearied of obscure and uncertain things, and so wished to direct his mind to the discovery of something manifest and certain, which was necessary in order thus to obtain a blessed life,—that one great object toward which the labor, vigilance, and industry of all philosophers seem to have been directed,—or whether (as some yet more favorable to him suppose) he did it because he was unwilling that minds defiled with earthly desires should essay to raise themselves upward to divine things. For he saw that the causes of things were sought for by them,—which causes he believed to be ultimately reducible to nothing else than the will of the one true and supreme God,—and on this account he thought they could only be comprehended by a purified mind; and therefore that all diligence ought to be given to the purification of the life by good morals, in order that the mind, delivered from the depressing weight of lusts, might raise itself upward by its native vigor to eternal things, and might, with purified understanding, contemplate that nature which is incorporeal and unchangeable light, where live the causes of all created natures. It is evident, however, that he hunted out and pursued, with a wonderful pleasantness of style and argument, and with a most pointed and insinuating urbanity, the foolishness of ignorant men, who thought that they knew this or that,—sometimes confessing his own

ignorance, and sometimes dissimulating his knowledge, even in those very moral questions to which he seems to have directed the whole force of his mind. And hence there arose hostility against him, which ended in his being calumniously impeached, and condemned to death. Afterwards, however, that very city of the Athenians, which had publicly condemned him, did publicly bewail him,—the popular indignation having turned with such vehemence on his accusers, that one of them perished by the violence of the multitude, whilst the other only escaped a like punishment by voluntary and perpetual exile.

Illustrious, therefore, both in his life and in his death, Socrates left very many disciples of his philosophy, who vied with one another in desire for proficiency in handling those moral questions which concern the chief good [*summum bonum*]. . . .

4. But, among the disciples of Socrates, Plato was the one who shone with a glory which far excelled that of the others, and who not unjustly eclipsed them all. By birth, an Athenian of honorable parentage, he far surpassed his fellow-disciples in natural endowments, of which he was possessed in a wonderful degree. . . . For, as Plato liked and constantly affected the well-known method of his master Socrates, namely, that of dissimulating his knowledge or his opinions, it is not easy to discover clearly what he himself thought on various matters, any more than it is to discover what were the real opinions of Socrates. We must, nevertheless, insert into our work certain of those opinions which he expresses in his writings, whether he himself uttered them, or narrates them as expressed by others, and seems himself to approve of,—opinions sometimes favorable to the true religion, which our faith takes up and defends, and sometimes contrary to it, as, for example, in the questions

concerning the existence of one God or of many, as it relates to the truly blessed life which is to be after death. For those who are praised as having most closely followed Plato, who is justly preferred to all the other philosophers of the Gentiles, and who are said to have manifested the greatest acuteness in understanding him, do perhaps entertain such an idea of God as to admit that in Him are to be found the cause of existence, the ultimate reason for the understanding, and the end in reference to which the whole life is to be regulated. Of which three things, the first is understood to pertain to the natural, the second to the rational, and the third to the moral part of philosophy. For if man has been so created as to attain, through that which is most excellent in him, to that which excels all things,—that is, to the one true and absolutely good God, without whom no nature exists, no doctrine instructs, no exercise profits,—let Him be sought in whom all things are secure to us, let Him be discovered in whom all truth becomes certain to us, let Him be loved in whom all becomes right to us.

5. If, then, Plato defined the wise man as one who imitates, knows, loves this God, and who is rendered blessed through fellowship with Him in His own blessedness, why discuss the other philosophers? It is evident that none come nearer to us than the Platonists. To them, therefore, let that fabulous theology give place which delights the minds of men with the crimes of the gods; and that civil theology also, in which impure demons, under the name of gods, have seduced the peoples of the earth given up to earthly pleasures, desiring to be honored by the errors of men, and by filling the minds of their worshippers with impure desires, exciting them to make the representation of their crimes one of the rites of their worship, whilst they themselves found

in the spectators of these exhibitions a most pleasing spectacle,—a theology in which, whatever was honorable in the temple, was defiled by its mixture with the obscenity of the theatre, and whatever was base in the theatre was vindicated by the abominations of the temples. . . . Let these two theologies, then, the fabulous and the civil, give place to the Platonic philosophers, who have recognized the true God as the author of all things, the source of the light of truth, and the bountiful bestower of all blessedness.

6. The Platonists, then, whom we see not undeservedly exalted above the rest in fame and glory, have seen that no material body is God, and therefore they have transcended all bodies in seeking for God. They have seen that whatever is changeable is not the most high God, and therefore they have transcended every soul and all changeable spirits in seeking the supreme.

7. Then, again, as far as regards the doctrine which treats of that which they call logic, that is, rational philosophy, far be it from us to compare them with those who attributed to the bodily senses the faculty of discriminating truth and thought, that all we learn is to be measured by their untrustworthy and fallacious rules. Such were the Epicureans, and all of the same school. Such also were the Stoics, who ascribed to the bodily senses that expertness in disputation which they so ardently love, called by them dialectic, asserting that from the senses the mind conceives the notions [*ennoiai*] of those things which they explicate by definition. And hence is developed the whole plan and connection of their learning and teaching. I often wonder, with respect to this, how they can say that none are beautiful but the wise; for by what bodily sense have they perceived that beauty, by what eyes of the flesh have they seen wisdom's comeliness of form? Those,

however, whom we justly rank before all others, have distinguished those things which are conceived by the mind from those which are perceived by the senses, neither taking away from the senses anything to which they are competent, nor attributing to them anything beyond their competency. And the light of our understandings, by which all things are learned by us, they have affirmed to be that self-same God by whom all things were made.

8. The remaining part of philosophy is morals, or what is called by the Greeks *ethiké*, in which is discussed the question concerning the chief good,— that which will leave us nothing further to seek in order to be blessed, if only we make all our actions refer to it, and seek it not for the sake of something else, but for its own sake. Therefore it is called the end, because we wish other things on account of it, but itself only for its own sake. This beatific good, therefore, according to some, comes to a man from the body, according to others, from the mind, and, according to others, from both together. For they saw that man himself consists of soul and body; and therefore they believed that from either of these two, or from both together, their well-being must proceed, consisting in a certain final good, which could render them blessed, and to which they might refer all their actions, not requiring anything ulterior to which to refer that good itself. This is why those who have added a third kind of good things, which they call extrinsic,—as honor, glory, wealth, and the like,—have not regarded them as part of the final good, that is, to be sought after for their own sake, but as things which are to be sought for the sake of something else, affirming that this kind of good is good to the good, and evil to the evil. Wherefore, whether they have sought the good of man from the mind or from the body, or from both together, it is still only from man they

have supposed that it must be sought. But they who have sought it from the body have sought it from the inferior part of man; they who have sought it from the mind, from the superior part; and they who have sought it from both, from the whole man. Whether, therefore, they have sought it from any part, or from the whole man, still they have only sought it from man; nor have these differences, being three, given rise only to three dissentient sects of philosophers, but to many. For diverse philosophers have held diverse opinions, both concerning the good of the body and the good of the mind, and the good of both together. Let, therefore, all these give place to those philosophers who have not affirmed that a man is blessed by the enjoyment of the body, or by the enjoyment of the mind, but by the enjoyment of God,—enjoying Him, however, not as the mind does the body or itself, or as one friend enjoys another, but as the eye enjoys light, if, indeed, we may draw any comparisons between these things. But what the nature of this comparison is, will, if God help me, be shown in another place, to the best of my ability. At present it is sufficient to mention that Plato determined the final good to be to live according to virtue, and affirmed that he only can attain to virtue who knows and imitates God,—which knowledge and imitation are the only cause of blessedness. Therefore he did not doubt that to philosophize is to love God, whose nature is incorporeal. Whence it certainly follows that the student of wisdom, that is, the philosopher, will then become blessed when he shall have begun to enjoy God. For though he is not necessarily blessed who enjoys that which he loves (for many are miserable by loving that which ought not to be loved, and still more miserable when they enjoy it), nevertheless no one is blessed who does not enjoy that which he loves. For even they who love things which ought not to be loved do not count themselves blessed by loving merely, but by enjoying them. Who, then, but the most miserable will deny that he is blessed, who enjoys that which he loves, and loves the true and highest good? But the true and highest good, according to Plato, is God, and therefore he would call him a philosopher who loves God; for philosophy is directed to the obtaining of the blessed life, and he who loves God is blessed in the enjoyment of God.

9. Whatever philosophers, therefore, thought concerning the supreme God, that He is both the maker of all created things, the light by which things are known, and the good in reference to which things are to be done; that we have in Him the first principle of nature, the truth of doctrine, and the happiness of life,—whether these philosophers may be more suitably called Platonists, or whether they may give some other name to their sect; whether, we say, that only the chief men of the Ionic school, such as Plato himself, and they who have well understood him, have thought thus; or whether we also include the Italic school, on account of Pythagoras and the Pythagoreans, and all who may have held like opinions; and, lastly, whether also we include all who have been held wise men and philosophers among all nations who are discovered to have been and taught this, be they Atlantics, Libyans, Egyptians, Indians, Persians, Chaldeans, Scythians, Gauls, Spaniards, or of other nations,—we prefer these to all other philosophers, and confess that they approach nearest to us.

10. For although a Christian man instructed only in ecclesiastical literature may perhaps be ignorant of the very name of Platonists, and may not even know that there have existed two schools of philosophers speaking the Greek tongue, to wit, the Ionic and Italic, he is nevertheless not so deaf with respect to human affairs, as not to know that philosophers profess the study, and even the possession, of wisdom. He is on his guard, however, with respect to those who philosophize according to the elements of this world, not according to God, by whom the world itself was made; for he is warned by the precept of the apostle, and faithfully hears what has been said, "Beware that no one deceive you through philosophy and vain deceit, according to the elements of the world". . . . It is from the one true and supremely good God that we have that nature in which we are made in the image of God, and that doctrine by which we know Him and ourselves, and that grace through which, by cleaving to Him, we are blessed. This, therefore, is the cause why we prefer these to all the others, because, whilst other philosophers have worn out their minds and powers in seeking the causes of things, and endeavoring to discover the right mode of learning and of living, these, by knowing God, have found where resides the cause by which the universe has been constituted, and the light by which truth is to be discovered, and the fountain at which felicity is to be drunk. All philosophers, then, who have had these thoughts concerning God, whether Platonists or others, agree with us. But we have thought it better to plead our cause with the Platonists, because their writings are better known. For the Greeks, whose tongue holds the highest place among the languages of the Gentiles, are loud in their praises of these writings; and the Latins, taken with their excellence, or their renown, have studied them more heartily than other writings, and, by translating them into our tongue, have given them greater celebrity and notoriety.

St. Augustine (d. 430), *City of God*, VIII, 1-10, adapted from the translation of Marcus Dods, *Nicene and Post-Nicene Fathers*, II, 144-151.

II WHAT PROMPTED CONSTANTINE THE GREAT TO TURN TO CHRISTIANITY?

When the Emperor Constantine turned to Christianity, the long and troubled history of the relations of the Christian Church to the Christian state began. The problem of the "conversion" of Constantine to Christianity has been much discussed and disputed. It is a problem of high significance with many implications. From a very large secondary literature two opposing points of view are presented in the following selections from two well-known studies of Constantine. In the first, the Swiss historian Jacob Burckhardt (1818–1897) depicts Constantine as a cold-blooded political opportunist, who sought to employ Christianity to serve his own purposes. (*The Age of Constantine the Great*, trans. M. Hadas, London: Routledge and Kegan Paul, Ltd., 1949, pp. 260-261, 283, 292-293):

Constantine's historical memory has suffered the greatest misfortune conceivable. That pagan writers must be hostile to him is obvious and would do him no damage in the eyes of posterity. But he has fallen into the hands of the most objectionable of all eulogists, who has utterly falsified his likeness. The man is Eusebius of Caesarea and the book his *Life of Constantine*. The man who with all his faults was always significant and always powerful is here presented in the guise of a sanctimonious devotee; in point of fact his numerous misdeeds are amply documented in a number of passages. Eusebius' equivocal praise is basically insincere. He speaks of the man but really means a cause, and that cause is the hierarchy, so strongly and richly established by Constantine. Furthermore, to say nothing of the contemptible style. there is a consciously furtive mode of expression, so that the reader finds himself treading concealed traps and bogs at the most vital passages. The reader who notices these hazards in time may be easily misled into putting the worst possible construction upon what has been withheld from him.

The introduction [to Eusebius' *Life of Constantine*] is ecstatic enough: "When I gaze in spirit upon this thrice-blessed soul, united with God, free of all mortal dross, in robes gleaming like lightning and in ever radiant diadem, speech and reason stand mute, and I would willingly leave it to a better man to devise a worthy hymn of praise." Would that had been the case! If we only possessed instead the description of a reasonable pagan like Ammianus, we should come infinitely closer to the great historical phenomenon which was the man Constantine, even though his moral character might not have emerged unsullied. Then we could perhaps see clearly what we can now only surmise, namely, that virtually throughout his life Constantine never assumed the guise of or gave himself out as a Christian but kept his free personal convictions quite unconcealed to his very last days. . . .

Eusebius is no fanatic; he understands Constantine's secular spirit and his cold and terrible lust for power well enough and doubtless knows the true causes of the war [with Licinius in 323] quite precisely. But he is the first thoroughly dishonest historian of antiquity. His tactic, which enjoyed a brilliant success in his own day and throughout the Middle Ages, consisted in making the first great protector of the Church at all costs an ideal of humanity according to his lights, and above all an ideal for future rulers. Hence we have lost the picture of a genius in stature who knew no moral scruple in politics *and regarded the religious question exclusively from the point of view of political expediency*. [Constantine] found it advisable to attach himself more closely to the Christians after this war, and . . . the elevation of Christianity to the position of state religion was thus consummated. But Constantine was a more honorable man than Eusebius; he rather allowed these events to transpire than intervened actively on their behalf, and as regards his own personal conviction, he enjoined definite beliefs upon his subjects as little as did Napoleon in his concordat. . . .

Attempts have often been made to penetrate into the religious consciousness of Constantine and to construct a hypothetical picture of changes in his religious convictions. Such efforts are futile. In a genius driven without surcease by ambition and lust for power there can be no question of Christianity and paganism, of conscious religiosity or irreligiosity; such a man is essentially unreligious, even if he pictures himself standing in the midst of a churchly community. Holiness he understands only as a reminiscence or as a superstitious vagary. Moments of inward reflection, which for a religious man are in the nature of worship, he consumes in a different sort of fire. World-embracing plans and mighty dreams lead him by an easy road to the streams of blood of slaughtered armies.... Men argue from Constantine's zealous Christian edicts, even from an address of the Emperor "to the assembly of the saints," an expression impossible on the lips of a non-Christian. But this address, it may be remarked in passing, was neither composed by Constantine nor ever delivered; and in writing the edicts Constantine often gave the priests a free hand [but how can Burckhardt be sure of this?]. And Eusebius, though all historians have followed him, has been proven guilty of so many distortions, dissimulations, and inventions that he has forfeited all claim to figure as a decisive source [is this not too strong?]. It is a melancholy but very understandable fact that none of the other spokesmen of the Church, as far as we know, revealed Constantine's true position, that they uttered no word of displeasure against the murderous egoist who possessed the great merit of having conceived of Christianity as a world power and of having acted accordingly. We can easily imagine the joy of the Christians in having finally obtained a firm guarantee against persecution, but we are not obliged to share that elation after a millennium and a half.

With Burckhardt's dogmatic certainty one may contrast the view of Norman H. Baynes, who is fully prepared to accept the possibility that Constantine's conversion was sincere ("Constantine and the Christian Church," *Proceedings of the British Academy,* vol. XV [1929], pp. 341-344):

No student of the Middle Ages can evade Constantine: he is one of the few inescapable figures in European history and one of the most intractable. To take man's past and demonstrate its inherent logic is a fascinating pursuit—to prove to one's own satisfaction that the past could not have been otherwise than it was, being a necessary development from that which had gone before, this is gratifying

to man, for he can thus look back upon human history and regard it as in a sense his own creation and can then praise its creator. In this reconstruction of the past, however, difficulties are at times caused by the interposition in the stream of history of outstanding personalities which resist rationalization and remain unexpected and embarrassing. One of these personalities is Constantine the Great. To my mind, at least, all attempts to explain away Constantine as the natural outcome of the previous history of Rome have failed completely. Constantine can only be satisfactorily interpreted in terms of the *Zeitgeist* if the *Zeitgeist* is arbitrarily fashioned in the likeness of Constantine. The more closely Constantine's life and achievement are studied, the more inevitably is one driven to see in them an erratic block which has diverted the stream of human history. It may be true that by A.D. 311 the imperial policy of persecution of the Christians had been proved a failure—Galerius, the instigator of that policy, had publicly confessed its futility—but this failure could not carry with it the implications that it was the duty of a Roman Emperor so far to disavow Rome's past as himself to adopt the faith professed by perhaps one-tenth of his subjects. Constantine presents to the student of history so interesting a problem precisely because he is an intractable individual, because he was not merely the creation of the past, but marked in himself a new beginning which was in such large measure to determine the future of the Roman world.

The representations attempted by modern scholars of the convictions and aims of Constantine have been so diverse that at times it is hard to believe that it is one and the same emperor that they are seeking to portray. As students of history we protest energetically that a man can only be rightly understood if he be regarded against the background of his world, that he can only be fairly judged in the light of the standards and the values of the society in which he lived; and then, having formulated the principle, we straightway forget it. We write our biographies in terms of the thought of our own day and impose upon another age the standards with which we are familiar. Burckhardt began his famous chapter upon Constantine and the Christian Church with the remark: "In the case of a man of genius, whose ambition and love of power refuse him a moment's peace, there can be no question of Christianity or paganism, of conscious religion or irreligion. Such a man even when he persuades himself that he has his place in an ecclesiastical community, is essentially unreligious." The issue is thus, you observe, pre-judged, and the answer to the problem cannot be for an instant in doubt. . . .

Or again, consider Otto Seeck as he discusses the authenticity of documents attributed by Eusebius to Constantine: the belief that the divine will had punished those emperors who had persecuted the Christians and preserved those who had not enforced the edicts of persecution is, he notes, common to Lactantius, Eusebius, and the documents purporting to represent the thought of Constantine; the idea was in many men's minds. "Why then should we be surprised if the good Constantine in his turn repeats the same trivialities" [says Seeck]. Trivialities? But what if a man really believes that God does actively, consistently, intervene in human affairs, that victory and defeat, prosperity and adversity are alike in His gift?—and what if that man is the ruler of the Roman world? Is that belief then insignificant? is it not rather of supreme moment? So hard it is to think ourselves back into a world which is not our own!

And there remains a yet subtler danger: we may imagine that we have discovered the key to a personality, and then we persuade ourselves that it will open every lock. And yet it is surely but rarely that every secret door of thought and motive in human life will yield to a single master-key. Life is not so simple as that. Eduard Schwartz has done as much as any scholar in our day to advance the study of the reign of Constantine; in his book, *The Emperor Constantine and the Christian Church*, he has found the Open Sesame to the understanding of the reign in Constantine's resolution to exploit in his own interest the organization which gave to the Christian Church its corporate strength: through alliance with the Church Constantine sought to attain victory and the sole mastery of the Roman world. The emperor's toleration sprang from his desire that pagan and Christian alike should be conscious that they depended upon him alone. "Never," writes Schwartz, "has an emperor so triumphed over the Church as did Constantine in and through the Council of Nicaea"; the victory lay

with the emperor's "diabolical cleverness." The one man who opposed Constantine was Athanasius, and in that contest of wills Greek met Greek; for the opposition of Athanasius was inspired not by zeal for the true faith, not by any passion for the independence of the Church, but by the pride of a hierarch in the authority of his patriarchate. The master-key in this analysis which Schwartz has given us of the personalities of Constantine and Athanasius is thus "Der Wille zur Macht" [i.e. "the will to power"]. But it may be doubted whether so extreme a simplification can do justice to the complexity of human convictions and human motives. The solution would appear rather to be imposed upon the evidence than to arise from a patient study of the documents themselves.

A. *The Evidence of Constantine's Letters*

I.

Shortly after Constantine's victory over his rival Maxentius in the battle of the Milvian Bridge (28 October 312), he wrote the following letter to Anulinus, the proconsul of Africa, ordering the restoration of property to the Church. This letter was written late in the year 312, about seven months before the so-called Edict of Milan. All the documents which follow appear to be genuine.

Greetings, Anulinus, our most honored Sir. It is the consequence of our love of goodness that whatever belongs to another by right we are not only not unwilling but we are even anxious to restore, most honored Anulinus. Therefore we wish that, when you receive this letter, you restore immediately to the churches whatever of those things which belonged to the Catholic Church of the Christians in the several cities as well as in other places have found their way into the possession of citizens or of other persons. For we have decided that whatever these same churches owned before shall be returned to them as their just due. Since therefore your

Excellency perceives that the tenor of this our command is most explicit, make haste that there be restored as soon as possible to the churches all the things which belonged to them of right, whether gardens, houses, or anything else whatsoever, so that we may learn that you have rendered the most attentive obedience to this our command. Farewell, most honored and beloved Anulinus.

Eusebius, *Eccl. Hist.*, X, 5, 15-17, trans. K. M. Setton.

2.

About the same time as the preceding letter was addressed to Anulinus, Constantine wrote also to Caecilian, the Bishop of Carthage, granting subsidies from the imperial treasury to the Christian Church in north Africa, and affording the Church the official protection of the state against heresy.

Constantine Augustus to Caecilian, Bishop of Carthage. Forasmuch as it has been our pleasure in all provinces, namely the African, the Numidian and the Mauretanian, that something be contributed for expenses to certain specified ministers of the lawful and most holy Catholic religion, I have dispatched a letter to Ursus, our esteemed finance-minister of Africa, and have notified him that he be careful to pay over to your Grace three thousand *folles* [a sum of uncertain value, but equal to many tens of thousands of dollars]. Do you, therefore, when you have secured delivery of the aforesaid sum of money, give orders that this money be distributed among all the above-mentioned persons in accordance with the schedule sent to you by Hosius [Bishop of Cordova]. But if, after all, you find that there is something lacking for the fulfilment of this my purpose in respect to them all, you should ask without any hesitation for whatever you find to be necessary from Heraclides, our fiscal procurator. For indeed when he was here I gave him orders that if your Grace should ask any money from him, he should be careful to pay it over without any scruple.

And since I have learned that certain persons of unstable mind [i.e. the Donatists in north Africa] are desirous of turning aside the laity of the most holy and Catholic Church by some vile method of seduction, know that I have given such commands to Anulinus, the proconsul, and moreover to Patricius, the Vicar of Africa, when they were here, that they should give due attention to all other matters and especially to this, and not suffer such an occurrence to be overlooked; therefore if you observe any such persons continuing in this madness, do not hesitate to go to the above-mentioned officials and bring this matter before them, so that, as I commanded them when they were here, they may turn these people from their error. May the divinity of the great God preserve you for many years.

Eusebius, *ibid.*, X, 6, 1-5, adapted from trans. J. E. L. Oulton and H. J. Lawlor, Loeb Classical Library (Cambridge, Mass.: Harvard University Press, 1932), II, 461, 463.

3.

Early in the year 313 Constantine wrote again to Anulinus in behalf of the Church in north Africa, this time granting the clergy immunity from enforced services to the state (such services being called *liturgies*): "Already in Constantine's thought the Catholic priests through their priesthood are maintaining the fortunes of Rome: this is more than mere tolerance" [N. H. Baynes].

Greetings, Anulinus, most honored Sir. Since from many facts it appears that disregard of divine worship, by which the highest reverence for the most holy and heavenly [power] is preserved, has brought great dangers upon the state, and that its lawful restoration and preservation have bestowed the greatest good fortune on the Roman name and singular prosperity on all the affairs of mankind (for it is the Divine Providence which bestows these blessings): it has seemed good that those men who, with due holiness and constant observance of this law, bestow their services on the performance of divine worship, should receive the rewards of their own labors, most honored Anulinus. Wherefore it is my wish that those persons who, within the province committed to you, in the Catholic Church over which Caecilian presides, bestow their service on this holy worship—those whom they are accustomed to call clerics—should once for all be kept absolutely free from all public burdens [*liturgies*], that they be not drawn away by any error or sacrilegious fault from the worship which they owe to the Divinity, but rather without any hindrance serve to the utmost their own law. For when they render supreme service to the Deity, it seems that they confer incalculable benefit on the affairs of state. Farewell, most honored and esteemed Anulinus.

Eusebius, *ibid.*, X, 7, 1-2, adapted from trans. Oulton and Lawlor, *op. cit.*, II, 463, 465.

4.

Constantine Augustus to Aelafius. Since it had already come to my attention, some time before this, that in our province of Africa many persons in a mad furor, with vain accusations against one another, had begun to differ in their observance of the most holy Catholic law, I decided, in order to do away with dissension of this kind, that there should appear in person [for judgment] in Rome both Caecilian, the Bishop of Carthage, against whom in particular all [the Donatists] have more than once brought action before me, and some of his opponents also, who had imagined that there were certain charges to be made against Caecilian.

[The opponents of Caecilian were eventually called Donatists, after their energetic leader Donatus "the Great." They were adjudged heretics, their heresy being the contention that a sacrament was invalid if administered by an unworthy priest. The chief charge against Caecilian was that his consecration as bishop of Carthage was invalid, because it had been performed by a bishop who had, it was alleged by the Donatists, betrayed the faith during the great persecution of Diocletian and Galerius. The imperial commission which the Emperor Constantine had intended to have investigate the case against Caecilian was transformed, at the request of Bishop Miltiades of Rome, into a church council, which declared for Caecilian against his Donatist accusers. The latter, however, refused to accept the decision of the council, and appealed therefrom to Constantine himself, who reluctantly summoned a large council to meet at Arles in the south of France on 1 August of the next year (i.e. A.D. 314), to go over the matter again. In the present letter, therefore, Constantine instructed Aelafius, the chief governor of Africa, to dispatch, by the imperial post service, Caecilian and certain of his chosen supporters, together with a representative group of his Donatist opponents, to Arles, in order that this larger body of the clergy, with imperial sanction, might make a final adjudication of the case against Caecilian. Constantine concluded his letter to Aelafius with an expression of personal anxiety, of great interest and importance to the student who seeks to depict Constantine's attitude toward Christianity and the Church:]

Since I am assured that you are also a worshipper of the supreme God, I confess to your Excellency that I consider it absolutely wrong that we should pass over in insincerity quarrels and altercations of this kind, whereby perhaps the supreme divinity may be moved not only against the human race, *but even against me myself* (!), to whose care He has, by His celestial will, entrusted rule over all earthly affairs—and yet, if angered, He may decree otherwise than up to now! For then, and only then, shall I be able truly and most fully to feel secure and always to hope for the greatest prosperity and good fortune from the ever ready kindness of the most powerful God, when I shall see all men, in the proper cult of the Catholic religion, venerate the most holy God with hearts joined like brothers in their worship.

Constantine, *Epistle to Aelafius,* trans. K. M. Setton, from Karl Ziwsa, ed., *S. Optati Milevitani libri VII,* Vienna, 1893 (*Corpus scriptorum ecclesiasticorum latinorum,* vol. XXVI), appendix, pp. 204, 206.

5.

To the bishops assembled at the Council of Arles (A.D. 314), to which reference is made in the preceding document, the Emperor Constantine sent the letter which follows, in condemnation of the Donatists. In seeking to evaluate Constantine's attitude toward Christianity, note both the general tone of the letter and such references as those to "our God" and to Christ, whose judgment he awaits.

Constantine Augustus to the Catholic Bishops, his dearest brethren, greetings. The eternal and revered and incomprehensible goodness of our God by no means permits that mankind should stray too long in the darkness, nor does it allow that the hated wishes of certain people should so far prevail as not to open up the path to salvation through its own most glorious light and cause conversion to the rule of truth. I have learned this from many examples which I can illustrate from my own experience. For in the beginning there were in me things which seemed quite removed from truth; I certainly did not think that the power in heaven could see into the secrets which I carried in my heart. What fortune, then, should these things which I have mentioned have caused to be allotted to me? Obviously one overflowing with all manner of evil! But Almighty God, who sits in the very watchtower of heaven, has made me gifts that I did not deserve. They can be neither described nor counted, these things which God in his heavenly kindness has bestowed upon me, his servant! Most holy bishops of the Savior Christ, my dearest brethren, I rejoice therefore, especially do I rejoice, that finally by the very justice of your decision you have recalled to a better hope and fortune these people [the Donatists], whom the evil purpose of the devil, with sinister power of persuasion, seemed to have turned aside from the glorious light of the Catholic law. . . .

But your just decision has been of no avail with these people [the Donatists]. . . . What force of evil persists in their hearts! . . . They ask me to judge, I who myself await the judgment of Christ, and I reply, as is the truth, that the judgment of bishops ought to be regarded as if the Lord Himself were sitting in judgment. These people have no right to any observance or to any judgment except what they have been taught by Christ's own teaching. . . . What is to be done with these detractors of the law, who renouncing the judgment of heaven have believed that they should seek judgment of me? Do they think thus so little of Christ the Savior? . . . Go now and return to your own sees, and bear me in your memories that our Savior may ever have mercy upon me. . . . I have directed my men to bring these evil deceivers of religion into my court from now on in order that they may be kept there and may see something worse than death provided for them. I have also dispatched letters addressed to the Vicar of Africa to the effect that he should send at once to my court as many as he may find who share this madness, lest they should be guilty of any further offenses under the clear light of our God which could call down upon us the grievous wrath of the Divine Providence. May Almighty God keep you safe for all time, in answer to your prayers and to my own, my dearest brethren.

Constantine, *Epistle to the Catholic Bishops,* trans. K. M. Setton, from K. Ziwsa, *op. cit.,* pp. 208-210.

B. *"In this Sign Conquer!"*

The following passage, which recounts Constantine's alleged vision of the sign of the cross in the heavens, with the exhortation to "conquer in this," is taken from Eusebius of Caesarea's *Life of Constantine.* Historians have taken the account seriously as a miracle; regarded the cross of light as a parahelion, or other strange but natural phenomenon; considered the whole affair as merely the product of an overwrought imagination; and scoffed at the text as being a later interpolation. Lactantius, *On the Deaths of Persecutors,* 44, describes Constantine as having had this manifestation of divine support merely in a dream rather than in an actual vision. However, the events related here are alleged to have occurred shortly before the Battle of the Milvian Bridge.

Constantine, being convinced, however, that he needed some more powerful aid than his military forces could afford him, on account of the wicked and magical enchantments which were so diligently practiced by the tyrant [Maxentius], sought divine assistance, deeming the possession of arms and a numerous soldiery of secondary importance, but believing the co-operating power of Deity invincible and not to be shaken. He considered, therefore, on what God he might rely for protection and assistance. While engaged in this enquiry, the thought occurred to him, that, of the many emperors who had preceded him, those who had rested their hopes in a multitude of gods, and served them with sacrifices and offerings, had in the first place been deceived by flattering predictions, and oracles which promised them all prosperity, and at last had met with an unhappy end, while not one of their gods had stood by to warn them of the impending wrath of heaven; while one alone who had pursued an entirely opposite course, who had condemned their error, and honored the one Supreme God during his whole life [namely, Constantius Chlorus, the father of Constantine], had found him to be the Savior and Protector of his empire, and the Giver of every good thing. Reflecting on this, and well weighing the fact that they who had trusted in many gods had also fallen by manifold forms of death, without leaving behind them either family or offspring, stock, name, or memorial among men: while the God of his father had given to him, on the other hand, manifestations of his power and very many tokens: and considering farther that those who had already taken arms against the tyrant, and had marched to the battle-field under the protection of a multitude of gods, had met with a dishonorable end (for one of them [Galerius] had shamefully retreated from the contest without a blow, and the other [Severus], being slain in the midst of his own troops, became, as it were, the mere sport of death); reviewing, I say, all these considerations, he judged it to be folly indeed to join in the idle worship of those who were no gods, and, after such convincing evidence, to stray from the truth; and therefore felt it incumbent on him to honor his father's God alone.

Accordingly he called on Him with earnest prayer and supplications that He would reveal to him who He was, and stretch forth His right hand to help him in his present difficulties. And while he was thus praying with fervent entreaty, a most marvelous sign appeared to him from heaven, the account of which it might have been hard to believe had it been related by any other person. But since the victorious emperor himself long afterwards declared it to the writer of this history, when he was honored with his acquaintance and society, and confirmed his statement by an oath, who could hesitate to accredit this account, especially since the testimony of aftertime has established its truth? He said that about noon, when the day was already beginning to decline, he saw with his own eyes the sign of a cross of light in the heavens, above the sun, and bearing the inscription CONQUER BY THIS. At this sight he himself was struck with amazement, and his whole army also, which followed him on this expedition, and witnessed the miracle.

He said, moreover, that he doubted within himself what the import of this apparition could be. And while he continued to ponder and reason on its meaning, night suddenly came on; then in his sleep the Christ of God appeared to him with the same sign which he had seen in the heavens, and commanded him to make a likeness of that sign which he had seen in the heavens, and to use it as a safeguard in all engagements with his enemies.

At dawn of day he arose, and communicated the marvel to his friends: and then, calling together the workers

in gold and precious stones, he sat in the midst of them, and described to them the figure of the sign he had seen, bidding them represent it in gold and precious stones. And this representation I myself have had an opportunity of seeing.

Now it was made in the following manner. A long spear, overlaid with gold, formed the figure of the cross by means of a transverse bar laid over it. On the top of the whole was fixed a wreath of gold and precious stones; and within this, the symbol of the Savior's name, two letters indicating the name of Christ by means of its initial characters, the letter P [the Greek letter Rho] being intersected by X [the Greek letter Chi] in its center: and these letters the emperor was in the habit of wearing on his helmet at a later period. From the cross-bar of the spear was suspended a cloth, a royal piece, covered with a profuse embroidery of most brilliant precious stones; and which, being also richly interlaced with gold, presented an indescribable degree of beauty to the beholder. This banner was of a square form, and the upright staff, whose lower section was of great length, bore a golden half-length portrait of the pious emperor and his children on its upper part, beneath the sign of the cross, and immediately above the embroidered banner.

The emperor constantly made use of this sign of salvation as a safeguard against every adverse and hostile power, and commanded that others similar to it should be carried at the head of all his armies.

These things were done shortly afterwards. But at the time above specified, being struck with amazement at the extraordinary vision, and resolving to worship no other God save Him who had appeared to him, he sent for those who were acquainted with the mysteries of His doctrines, and enquired who that

God was, and what was intended by the sign of the vision he had seen.

They affirmed that He was God, the only begotten Son of the one and only God: that the sign which had appeared was the symbol of immortality, and the trophy of that victory over death which He had gained in time past when sojourning on earth. They taught him also the causes of His advent, and explained to him the true account of His incarnation. Thus he was instructed in these matters, and was impressed with wonder at the divine manifestation which had been presented to his sight.

Comparing, therefore, the heavenly vision with the interpretation given, he found his judgment confirmed; and, in the persuasion that the knowledge of these things had been imparted to him by divine teaching, he determined thenceforth to devote himself to the reading of the inspired writings.

Moreover, he made the priests of God his counselors, and deemed it incumbent on him to honor the God who had appeared to him with all devotion. And after this, being fortified by well-grounded hopes in Him, he hastened to quench the threatening fire of tyranny.

Eusebius of Caesarea, *Life of Constantine*, I, chaps. 27-32, adapted from the translation in the *Nicene and Post-Nicene Fathers*, 2nd series, I, 489-491.

C. The Edict of Galerius

The Edict of Galerius, to which attention is called in the Introduction, was issued on 30 April, 311, shortly before its author's death. A translation follows of the text as preserved in the Greek version of Eusebius.

And Galerius, wrestling with terrible misfortunes, was conscience-stricken for the cruel deeds he had perpetrated against the godly. Collecting, therefore, his thoughts, he first openly confessed to the God of the universe; then he called those around him, and commanded them without delay to cause the persecution against Christians to cease, and by an imperial law and decree to urge them to build their churches and to perform their accustomed rites, offering prayers on the Emperor's behalf. Action immediately followed his word, and imperial ordinances were promulgated in each city, containing the recantation of the [persecution edicts] of our time, after this manner: "The Emperor Caesar Galerius Valerius Maximianus Invictus Augustus, Pontifex Maximus . . . to the people of the provinces, greeting:

"Among the other measures that we frame for the use and profit of the state, it had been our own wish formerly that all things should be set to rights in accordance with the ancient laws and public order of the Romans; and to make provision for this, namely, that the Christians also, such as had abandoned the persuasion of their own ancestors, should return to a sound mind; seeing that through some reasoning they had been possessed of such self-will and seized with such folly that, instead of following the institutions of the ancients, which perchance their own forefathers had formerly established, they made for themselves, and were observing, laws merely in accordance with their own disposition and as each one wished, and were assembling various multitudes in divers places: Therefore when a command of ours soon followed to the intent that they should betake themselves to the institutions of the ancients, very many indeed were subjected to peril, while very many were harassed and endured all kinds of death; and since the majority held to the same folly, and we perceived that they were neither paying the worship due to the gods of heaven nor honoring the god of the Christians; having regard to our clemency and the invariable custom by which we are wont to accord pardon to all men, we thought it right in this case also to extend most willingly our indulgence: That Christians may exist again and build the houses in which they used to assemble, always provided that they do nothing contrary to order. In another letter we shall indicate to the judges how they should proceed. Wherefore, in accordance with this our indulgence, they will be bound to beseech their own god for our welfare, and that of the state, and their own; that in every way both the well being of the state may be secured, and they may be enabled to live free from care in their own homes."

Such is the character of this edict in the Latin tongue, translated into Greek as well as may be.

Eusebius, *Eccl. Hist.*, VIII, 17, 1-11, trans. Oulton and Lawlor, Loeb Cl. Libr. II, 317, 319, 321.

D. The So-Called "Edict of Milan"

When Constantine and Licinius met at Milan in February of 313, three or four months after Constantine's victory at the Milvian Bridge, they agreed upon a policy of freedom for all religions in the Empire. Very likely a text was agreed upon for promulgation by Licinius when he returned to the East (whence he had come to render Constantine assistance, if needed, against Maxentius). Apparently no "Edict of Milan" was ever issued; it was not necessary. Constantine's religious policy in the West had already been laid down, and his attitude toward Christianity sufficiently defined, in the letters to Anulinus and Caecilian, given above. In 1891 the German scholar Otto Seeck first asserted that no Edict of Milan was ever issued, and this opinion has in general been adopted by Norman Baynes, Henri Grégoire, and Erich Caspar. However, when Licinius went back to the East, he sent the rescript which historians have improperly called the "Edict of Milan" to the governor (*praeses*) of Bithynia on 15 June, 313, as we learn from Lactantius, *On the Deaths of Persecutors*, chap. 48, where we also have a Latin version, but not the official text, of this document preserved.

But come, let us now quote also the translations made from the Latin of the imperial ordinances of Constantine and Licinius. . . .

"In our watchfulness in days gone by that freedom of worship should not be denied, but that each one according to his mind and purpose should have authority given him to care for divine things in the way that pleased him best, we had given orders that both to the Christians [and to all others liberty should be allowed] to keep to the faith of their own sect and worship. But inasmuch as many and various conditions seemed clearly to have been added in that rescript, in which such rights were conceded to the same persons, it may be that perchance some of them were shortly afterwards repelled from such observance.

"When I, Constantine Augustus, and I, Licinius Augustus, had come under happy auspices to Milan, and discussed all matters that concerned the public advantage and good, among the other things that seemed to be of benefit to the many,—or rather, first and foremost—we resolved to make such decrees as should secure respect and reverence for the Deity; namely, to grant both to the Christians and to all the free choice of following whatever form of worship they pleased, to the intent that all the divine and heavenly powers that be might be favorable to us and all those living under our authority. Therefore with sound and most upright reasoning we resolved on this counsel: that authority be refused to no one whomsoever to follow and choose the observance or form of worship that Christians use, and that authority be granted to each one to give his mind to that form of worship which he deems suitable to himself, to the intent that the Divinity may in all things afford us his wonted care and generosity. It was fitting to send a rescript that this is our pleasure, in order that when those conditions had altogether been removed, which were contained in our former letters sent to your Excellency, concerning the Christians, those things also which seemed to be wholly unfortunate and foreign to our clemency might be removed, and that now each one of those who were possessed of the same purpose—namely, to observe the Christians' form of worship—should observe this very thing, freely and simply, without any hindrance. Which things we have resolved, to signify in the fullest manner to your Excellency, to the intent that you may know that we have granted to these same Christians free and unrestricted authority to observe their own form of worship. And when you perceive that this has been granted unrestrictedly to them by us, your Excellency will understand that authority has been given to others also, who wish to follow their own observance and form of worship—a thing clearly suited to the peacefulness of our times—so that each one may have authority to choose and observe whatever form he pleases. This has been done by us, to the intent that we should not seem to have detracted in any way from any rite or form of worship.

"And this, moreover, with special regard to the Christians, we resolve: That their places, at which it was their former wont to assemble, concerning which also in the former letter dispatched to your Excellency a definite ordinance had been formerly laid down, if any should appear to have bought them either from our treasury or from any other source—that they should restore them to these same Christians without payment or any demand for compensation, setting aside all negligence and doubtfulness; and if any chance to have received them by gift, that they should restore them with all speed to these same Christians: provided that if either those who have purchased these same places or those who have received them by gift request our generosity, let them approach the prefect of the district, to the intent that through our kindness thought may be taken for them also. All which things must be handed over to the corporation of the Christians by your zealous care immediately and without delay.

"And inasmuch as these same Christians had not only those places at which it was their wont to assemble, but also are known to have had others, belonging not to individuals among them, but to the lawful property of their corporation, that is, of the Christians, all these, under the provisions of the law set forth above, you will give orders to be restored without any question whatsoever to these same Christians, that is, to their corporation and assembly; provided always, of course, as aforesaid, that those persons who restore the same without compensation, as we have mentioned above, may look for indemnification, as far as they are concerned, from our generosity.

"In all these things, you should use all the diligence in your power for the above-mentioned corporation of the Christians, that this our command may be fulfilled with all speed, so that in this also, through our kindness, thought may be taken for the common and public peace. For by this method, as we have also said before, the divine care for us, which we have already experienced in many matters, will remain steadfast. . . . And that the form which this our enactment and generosity takes may be brought to the knowledge of all, it is fitting that this which we have written be set forth by your order and published everywhere, and brought to the knowledge of all, to the intent that the enactment which embodies this our generosity may escape the notice of no one."

Eusebius, *ibid.*, X, 5, 1-14, trans. Oulton and Lawlor, II, 445 ff.

E. Constantine's Declaration to the World

Constantine and Licinius ruled the Empire together for a decade, but in A.D. 323 there broke out between them a war, which "is represented as a religious war in the history of Eusebius, and I see no reason to doubt that such was its character in the eyes of Constantine" (Baynes). Just as after the defeat of Maxentius, Constantine wrote the letters to Anulinus and Caecilian, so now after the defeat of Licinius he repeated his avowal of Christianity.

And now that through the powerful aid of God his Savior, all nations owned their subjection to the emperor's authority, he openly proclaimed to all the name of Him to whose bounty he owed all his blessings, and declared that He and not himself, was the author of his past victories. This declaration, written both in the Latin and Greek languages, he caused to be transmitted through every province of the empire. Now the excellence of his style of expression may be known from a perusal of his letters themselves, which were two in number; one addressed to the churches of God; the other to the heathen. The latter of these I think it well to insert here, as connected with my present subject, in order on the one hand that a copy of this document may be recorded as a matter of history, and thus preserved to posterity, and on the other that it may serve to confirm the truth of my present narrative. It is taken from an authentic copy of the imperial statute in my own possession; and the signature in the emperor's own handwriting attaches as it were the impress of truth to the statement I have made. . . .

"And now, with such a mass of impiety oppressing the human race, and the commonwealth in danger of being utterly destroyed, as if by the agency of some pestilential disease, and therefore needing powerful and effectual aid; what was the relief, and what the remedy which the Divinity devised for these evils? (And by Divinity is meant the one who is alone and truly God, the possessor of almighty and eternal power: and surely it cannot be deemed arrogance in one who has received benefits from God, to acknowledge them in the loftiest terms of praise.) I myself, then, was the instrument whose services He chose, and esteemed suited for the accomplishment of His will. Accordingly, beginning at the remote Britannic ocean, and the regions where, according to the law of nature, the sun sinks beneath the horizon, through the aid of divine power I banished and utterly removed every form of evil which prevailed in the hope that the human race, enlightened through my instrumentality, might be called to a due observance of the holy laws of God, and at the same time our most blessed faith might prosper under the guidance of His almighty hand.

"I said, under the guidance of His hand; for I would desire never to be forgetful of the gratitude due to His grace. Believing, therefore, that this most excellent service had been confided to me as a special gift, I proceeded as far as the regions of the East, which, being under the pressure of severe calamities, seemed to demand still more effectual remedies at my hands. At the same time I am most certainly persuaded that I myself owe my life, my every breath, in short, my very inmost and secret thoughts, entirely to the favor of the Supreme God." . . .

Eusebius, *Life of Constantine*, II, chaps. 23, 28-29, from *Nicene and Post-Nicene Fathers*, 2nd series, I, 506-507.

III. THE PROBLEM OF PAPAL SUPREMACY OVER THE WESTERN CHURCH

The problem of how the Pope in Rome became recognized as supreme pontiff over the Western Church, and laid claim to authority also over the Eastern Churches, must start with the question of the organization of the early churches in general and of that of Rome in particular. This question is complicated by the apparent disagreement of some important early sources, and also by the difficulty of deciding to what extent "church order," or government, was (and is) assumed to be of divine or apostolic institution, and to what extent it simply grew up in response to administrative necessity. How, then, was the early Church of Rome governed? At least two contemporary sources seem to indicate that this church was presided over by a board of senior members called "overseers" [*episkopoi*, bishops] and "elders" [*presbyteroi*, priests], with little or no distinction between them. Other sources would, however, lead us to believe that the Church of Rome was in fact presided over by a single person, a "monarchical bishop," being thus under "mon-episcopal rule."

Some scholars have believed that, until well into the second century A.D., rule by a board of elders or presbyters prevailed in the Churches of Rome, Corinth, and Philippi, although the rule of a single bishop, or "mon-episcopacy," was common in Asia Minor and Syria before the close of the first century. Other texts suggest, however, and other scholars affirm, a mon-episcopal organization in the Church of Rome, even in the later first century A.D., in direct descent from its apostolic foundation by Sts. Peter and Paul. Hence has come the "Petrine" theory of the papacy, to the effect that the Bishop of Rome received (and still wields) the authority of St. Peter, according to the famous text in St. Matthew, 16:18-19, which will be quoted several times in the pages which follow.

The two chief sources which seem to show that the Church of Rome was governed by a board of elders, rather than by a single bishop, are: 1) the so-called First Epistle of St. Clement, to the Corinthian Church (about A.D. 96), and 2) an early apocalypse, or work of visions, called *The Shepherd* of Hermas, written sometime between A.D. 100 and 140. These two texts are rather difficult to interpret, owing to the fact that some other early evidence appears not to be in accord with them. Another early work, *The Didaché*, or *Teaching of the Twelve Apostles*, also written between A.D. 100 and 140, appears to show the bishops and deacons at a time when they are just coming into their own as two different grades of clergy (presbyters are not mentioned in the *Didaché*), but are still regarded as of less importance in the Christian community than "the prophets and teachers," of whom St. Paul speaks (cf. 1 Cor. 12, 28): "Elect therefore for yourselves bishops and deacons who are worthy of the Lord, men gentle and without avarice, men tried and true, for they also minister to you the ministry of the prophets and teachers. Do not, then, hold them in too low esteem, for these men have been and are to be honored among you together with the prophets and teachers" (from the *Didaché*, 15).

In the Second Vision of *The Shepherd*, the Church appears to Hermas in the guise of an old woman, and directs him to "tell *those who rule the Church* [*of Rome*] that they are to direct their paths in righteousness . . . ," and makes other references to "the elders who are set over the Church" (chaps. 1-2, 4). *The Shepherd* also makes reference, in its Third Vision, chap. 5, to "the apostles and overseers [*episkopoi*, bishops] and teachers and ministers [*diakonoi*, deacons], who went their way according to the holiness of God, and did their overseeing and teaching and ministering in pure and holy fashion for the elect of God, and some of whom are dead and others are still living, and since they always agreed with one another, they both kept peace among themselves and listened to one another." These passages have been interpreted as proving that a "presbyterian" board presided over the Church of Rome.

A. The Evidence of St. Clement of Rome

The following passage from St. Clement's *Epistle to the Corinthians* is the first clear statement of the doctrine of apostolic succession, but note that the succession appears to be collegiate or "presbyterian," i.e. through the bishops and deacons as a group or governing board, rather than a mon-episcopal succession, i.e. through an individual. Observe the use of the plural "bishops and deacons." Clement seems to have written this letter, about A.D. 96, for the Church of Rome, to the Church of Corinth, protesting "that the steadfast and ancient Church of the Corinthians, because of one or two persons, has risen up against the presbyters" (chap. 47, 6), and deposed some of them; but the presbyters should be restored to their office, for their removal had been contrary to the intentions of Christ and the Apostles: the Corinthian congregation was not the source of the presbyters' authority, which came from Christ through the Apostles, and therefore the congregation could not remove divinely appointed presbyters:

The Apostles presented the Gospel to us from the Lord Jesus Christ. Jesus the Christ [i.e. the Anointed, the "Messiah"] was sent from God. The Christ then is from God, and the Apostles from the Christ. Both therefore came in due accord with the will of God. Having thus received their commands and having been fully assured by the Resurrection of our Lord Jesus Christ, and having placed their trust in the word of God, they went forth with full certainty of the Holy Spirit, announcing the glad tidings that the Kingdom of God was about to come. Throughout the country districts, then, and throughout the cities, they appointed their successors, having tested them in the Spirit, to be bishops and deacons [*episkopoi* and *diakonoi*, i.e. overseers and ministers] of those who were to receive the faith. And this was not at all new, because of old there had been written of bishops and deacons —as the Scripture says somewhere—"I will establish their bishops in righteousness and their deacons in faith" [cf. Isaiah, 60:17?].

And our Apostles knew through our Lord Jesus Christ that there would be strife for the title of bishop. For this reason, therefore, since they had received full knowledge in advance, they appointed the aforesaid, and afterwards added the provision that, if these should fall asleep [i.e. die], other approved men should succeed to their duties. Thus we believe it is not right to remove from their duties those appointed by the Apostles, or by other notable men after them with the agreement of the entire Church, for they have done their duty to the flock of Christ blamelessly, in humbleness of spirit, with peace and without seeking profit, as all have borne witness these many years.

Clement of Rome (A.D. 96), *Epistle to the Corinthians*, 42, 44, trans. K. M. Setton.

B. "The Church is Founded upon the Bishops!"

Other early sources, however, are not easily reconciled with the evidence of the First Epistle of Clement and *The Shepherd* of Hermas. Texts from Ignatius of Antioch (A.D. 112), Hegesippus (about A.D. 165), and Irenaeus of Lyon (fl. A.D. 185) show clearly the importance of the bishop from the early second century, and the texts from Hegesippus and Irenaeus seem to show a "monarchical" episcopal succession in Rome. Irenaeus, furthermore, glorifies "that tradition, derived from the Apostles, of the very great, the very ancient, and universally known Church founded and organized at Rome by the two most glorious Apostles Peter and Paul . . . , for it is a matter of necessity that every church should agree with this Church, on account of its pre-eminent authority . . ." (*Against Heresies,* III, 3). Two generations after Irenaeus, the famous St. Cyprian, Bishop of Carthage (A.D. 248–258), gave a classic statement of the establishment of the episcopal office (as he saw it) and of the central position occupied by the monarchical bishop within the Church:

Our Lord, whose precepts and admonitions we ought to observe, in establishing the office of bishop and the organization of his Church, speaks thereof in the Gospel, and says to Peter: "Thou art Peter, and upon this rock I will build my Church, and the gates of hell shall not prevail against it. And I will give unto thee the keys of the kingdom of heaven; and whatsoever thou shalt bind on earth shall be bound in heaven; and whatsoever thou shalt loose on earth shall be loosed in heaven" (Matt. 16, 18–19). Thence, with the passage of time, as bishop has succeeded bishop, the episcopal office and the organization of the Church have come down to us, so that the Church is founded upon the bishops, and every act of the Church is controlled by these same officers. Therefore, since this has been ordained by the divine law, I am amazed that certain persons have thus presumed to write me with such audacity as to send on their letters in the name of the Church itself, "while the Church," they say, "consists of the bishop and the clergy and all those who are steadfast in the faith!"

St. Cyprian, Bishop of Carthage (A.D. 248–258), *Epistle XXXIII* (also numbered XXVI and XXVII), in J.-P. Migne, *Patrologia Latina,* vol. IV, 305-306, trans. K. M. Setton.

C. St. Cyprian on the Independence of All Bishops within the Church

Although Cyprian of Carthage believed, as we have seen above, "that the Church is founded upon the bishops," he also believed that all bishops were equal in rank and authority. The Church of the middle of the third century was much exercised by the question whether baptism received at the hands of a schismatic or a heretic was valid. Cyprian believed that there was no salvation outside the Church, and that heretics and schismatics were outside the Church. Therefore, heretical baptism was an evil farce, and was no baptism at all. Those who wished to enter the true Church must thus receive true baptism, which washed away all sin, and without which the penitent's soul was forever imperilled. Rebaptism, however, was contrary to the ancient practice of the Church, and so was strongly objected to by Bishop Stephen of Rome (254–56). Stephen apparently believed, if we may state his view in rather later terms, that defect neither of doctrine nor of character rendered invalid any sacrament administered by a properly ordained priest, however far the latter may have deviated into heresy or schism.

Stephen was vigorous and tactless in his opposition to Cyprian's view, which was shared by most of the Church in Africa; he removed a number of bishops and their churches from communion with the Roman See, which aroused great animus against him, especially in Africa and in Asia Minor. The question of the rebaptism of those who had received baptism at the hands of heretics was taken up by a council of eighty-seven African bishops at Carthage under the presidency of Cyprian in the year 256, at which council Cyprian began the proceedings, after the reading of some letters, with this address, emphasizing the equality and independence of all bishops within the Church:

You have heard, my dearly beloved colleagues, what Jubaianus, our fellow bishop, has written to me ... concerning the unlawful and profane baptism of heretics, as well as what I wrote in answer to him, decreeing, to wit, what we have once and again and frequently determined, that heretics who come into the Church must be baptized and sanctified by the baptism of the Church. Moreover, another letter of Jubaianus has also been read to you, wherein, replying, in accordance with his sincere and religious devotion, to my letter, he has not only acquiesced in what I said, but, confessing that he had been instructed thereby, he has returned thanks for it.

It remains that upon this same matter each of us should bring forward what we think, judging no man, nor rejecting any one from the right of communion, if he should think differently from us. For neither does any of us set himself up as a bishop of bishops [an allusion to what Cyprian regards as an unwarranted assumption of power by the Bishop of Rome], nor by tyrannical terror does any compel his colleague to the necessity of obedience; since every bishop, according to the allowance of his liberty and power, has his own proper right of judgment, and can no more be judged by another than he himself can judge another.

But let us all wait for the judgment of our Lord Jesus Christ, who is the only one that has the power both of preferring us in the government of His Church, and of judging us in our conduct there.

Seventh Council of Carthage, trans. adapted from *Ante-Nicene Fathers*, V, 565.

D. *The Opposition of Bishop Firmilian to the See of Rome*

Cyprian's view of the equality and independence of bishops was shared not only by the African bishops present at the Council of Carthage, but also by the eastern bishops; it was at this time that one of the latter, Firmilian of Caesarea in Cappadocia, wrote Cyprian a well-known letter, of which parts are given below.[1]

Firmilian to Cyprian, his brother in the Lord, greeting. We have received by Rogatian, our beloved deacon, the letter sent by you which you wrote to us, well-beloved brother; and we gave the greatest thanks to the Lord, because it has happened that we who are separated from one another in body are thus united in spirit, as if we were not only occupying one country, but inhabiting together one and the self-same house. ...

We may in the present matter give thanks to Stephen [the Bishop of Rome] that it has now happened through his unkindness that we receive the proof of your faith and wisdom. But although we have received the favor of this benefit on account of Stephen, certainly Stephen has not done anything deserving of kindness and thanks. ... But let these things which were done by Stephen be passed by for the present, lest, while we remember his audacity and pride, we bring a more lasting sadness on ourselves from the things that he has wickedly done. ...

Since the messenger sent by you was in haste to return to you, and the winter season was pressing [A.D. 256], we have replied what we could to your letter.

[1] Although Firmilian also agreed with Cyprian's views concerning baptism, we are not concerned with this problem: suffice it to say that the wiser views of the Bishop of Rome finally prevailed (in the West, at the Council of Arles in 314).

And indeed, as respects what Stephen has said, as though the apostles forbade those who come from heresy to be baptized, and delivered this also to be observed by their successors, you have replied most abundantly that no one is so foolish as to believe that the apostles delivered this, when it is even well known that these heresies themselves, execrable and detestable as they are, arose subsequently. . . .

But they who are at Rome do not observe those things in all cases which are handed down from the beginning, and vainly pretend the authority of the apostles: this any one may know also from the fact that concerning the celebration of Easter, and concerning many other sacraments of divine matters, he may see there are some diversities among them, and that all things are not observed among them alike, which are observed at Jerusalem, just as in very many other provinces also many things are varied because of the difference of places and people. And yet on this account there is no departure at all from the peace and unity of the Catholic Church, such as Stephen has now dared to make [i.e. no one bishop and no one see could arrogate to itself the authority of the Apostles Peter and Paul], breaking the peace against you, which his predecessors have always kept with you in mutual love and honor, even herein defaming Peter and Paul, the blessed Apostles, as if the very men delivered this who in their epistles execrated heretics, and warned us to avoid them. Whence it appears that this tradition is human which maintains heretics, and asserts that the latter have baptism, which belongs to the Church alone. . . . [Firmilian distorts the argument of Stephen, seeking to reduce it to absurdity.]

And in this respect I am justly indignant at the open and manifest folly of Stephen, in that he who so boasts of the place of his episcopate and contends that he holds the succession of Peter, on whom the foundation of the Church was laid, should introduce many other rocks and establish many new churches, maintaining that there is baptism in them by his authority. For they who are baptized, without doubt, make up the number of the Church. . . . Stephen, who announces that he holds by succession the throne of Peter, is stirred with no zeal against heretics, when he concedes to them, not a moderate, but the very greatest power of grace. . . .

This indeed you Africans are able to say against Stephen, that when you knew the truth you forsook the error of custom. But we join custom to truth, and to the Romans' custom we oppose custom, but the custom of truth, holding from the beginning that which was delivered by Christ and the Apostles. Nor do we remember that this at any time began among us, since it has always been observed here, that we have known but one Church of God, and have accounted no baptism holy except that of the holy Church. . . .

Consider with what want of judgment you dare to blame those who strive for the truth against falsehood [Firmilian now writes as though addressing Stephen directly.]. . . . For how much strife and how many dissensions you have stirred up throughout the churches of the whole world! Moreover, how great sin you have heaped up for yourself, when you cut yourself off from so many flocks! For it is yourself that you have cut off! Do not deceive yourself, since he is really the schismatic who has made himself an apostate from the communion of ecclesiastical unity. For while you think that all may be excommunicated by you, you have alone excommunicated yourself from all, and not even the precepts of an Apostle have been able to mould you to the rule of truth and peace. . . .

How carefully has Stephen fulfilled these salutary commands and warnings of the Apostle, keeping in the first place lowliness of mind and meekness! For what is more lowly or meek than to have disagreed with so many bishops throughout the whole world, breaking peace with each one of them in various kinds of discord: at one time with the Easterners, as we are sure is not unknown to you; at another time with you who are in the South, from whom he received bishops as messengers so patiently and meekly as not to receive them even to the speech of common conference; and, even more, so unmindful of love and charity as to command the whole brotherhood that no one should receive them into his house, so that not only peace and communion, but also shelter and hospitality were denied to them when they came. This is to have kept the unity of the Spirit in the bond of peace, to cut himself off from the unity of love, and to make himself a stranger in all things to his brethren, and to rebel against the sacrament and the faith with the madness of contumacious discord! . . .

And yet Stephen is not ashamed to afford patronage to such [heretics] in opposition to the Church, and for the sake of maintaining heretics to divide the brotherhood, and in addition to call Cyprian "a false Christ, a false apostle, and a deceitful worker." Stephen, conscious that all these characters are in himself, has been in advance of you by falsely charging another with those things which he himself ought deservedly to hear. We all bid you, for all our sakes, with all the bishops who are in Africa, and all the clergy, and all the brotherhood [of Christendom], farewell; that, constantly of one mind, and thinking the same thing, we may find you united with us even though afar off.

Firmilian of Caesarea, *Epistle to Cyprian*, 1-3, 5-6, 17, 19, 24-26, in Cyprian, *Epistles*, no. 74, trans. adapted from *Ante-Nicene Fathers*, V. 390-397.

E. The Council of Sardica and the Right of Appeal to the Bishop of Rome

In contrast to the foregoing statements of Cyprian and Firmilian, in opposition to the ever increasing authority and influence of the Roman See within the Church, the student will find in the document which follows one of the first great markers along the road which leads to the final establishment of papal supremacy over the western Church.

In A.D. 343 a church council met at Sardica, the modern Sofia, to consider certain questions relating to the doctrine of the Council of Nicaea. The western bishops at the council affirmed the Nicene doctrine, but the eastern bishops opposed it, and withdrew to Philippopolis where they held a small council of their own. The western bishops, according to the Roman tradition of the text, passed the following canons

recognizing the appellate jurisdiction of the Roman See. There is no doubt, however, as to the authenticity of these canons.

Canon 3. Bishop Hosius [of Cordova] said: "And it is necessary to add this: that no bishop should pass from his own province into another province in which there are bishops, unless he should happen to have been invited by his brethren, so that we may not appear to be closing the gates of love. And yet we must also make this provision: that if in any province, any bishop bring suit against his brother and fellow bishop, neither one of them is to call in bishops, as arbitrators, from another province. But if any bishop appears to have had the decision in any case go against him improperly, and believes that he does not have a bad cause, but rather a good one, so that the decision should be reviewed, then, if it seems best to you all, let us honor the memory of the Apostle Peter, and agree that letters be written to Julius, the Bishop of Rome [337–352], by those who have tried the case, so that the trial may be reopened, if it should seem necessary, by the neighboring bishops, and let Bishop Julius himself appoint arbitrators. Nevertheless, if he is not able to advise that the case is of such sort that it requires a second trial, then the first settlement of the case shall not be undone, but shall thereby be confirmed.

"Are you all in agreement with this?" The synod replied: "We are!"

Canon 4. Bishop Gaudentius [of Naissus, now Nish] said: "We must add, if you please, to this decision of true sanctity, which you have just passed, that if any bishop has been deposed by the judgment of those bishops who are his neighbors, and declares that he has something to add in the matter of his defense, let no other bishop be established in his see [cathedra] before the Bishop of Rome has been apprised of the case and rendered his judgment."

Canon 5. Bishop Hosius said: "Let it be agreed, then, that if any bishop has been accused, and the assembled bishops of that region have removed him from office, and he, as it were, seeks refuge in appeal to the blessed Bishop of the Roman Church, and wishes the latter to hear him, then if the Bishop of Rome thinks it right that the investigation of the matter should be renewed, let him decide to write to those fellow bishops of the accused, who are close to his province, in order that they may conduct a careful and exact inquiry into all aspects of the case, and render a decision in the affair in accord with what they believe to be the truth. But if anyone should think it worthwhile that his case should be heard still once more, and if by his entreaty he should prevail upon the Bishop of Rome to send presbyters from his own staff, then it shall be in the power of that Bishop, if he believes and decides that it is right, to send such presbyters to render judgment together with the bishops; and those who are thus sent from Rome are to have the authority of the one from whom they have been sent. Well, we have agreed this is to be done. But if the Bishop of Rome thinks that the neighboring bishops are sufficient for hearing the case and rendering a decision concerning the bishop in question, he shall do whatever seems to be best in the great wisdom of his judgment."

The bishops answered: "We approve of what has been said!"

The Council of Sardica (A.D. 343), Canons 3–5, trans. K. M. Setton, from Heinrich Denzinger, *Enchiridion symbolorum*, 28th ed. by C. Rahner, Freiburg im B. and Barcelona, 1952, sections 57b-d, pp. 33–35.

F. St. Jerome to Pope Damasus

The following selection from a letter which St. Jerome addressed to Pope Damasus (A.D. 367–384), from the East about A.D. 376, illustrates clearly Jerome's high reverence for the See of Rome, "for this, I know, is the rock on which the Church is built."

Since the East, shattered as it is by the long standing feuds, subsisting between its peoples, is bit by bit tearing into shreds the seamless garment of the Lord, "woven from the top throughout," since the foxes are destroying the vineyard of Christ, and since among the broken cisterns that hold no water it is hard to discover "the sealed fountain" and "the garden inclosed," I think it my duty to consult the chair of Peter, and to turn to a church whose faith has been praised by Paul. I appeal for spiritual food to the church whence I have received the garb of Christ. The wide space of sea and land that lies between us cannot deter me from searching for "the pearl of great price." "Wheresoever the body is, there will the eagles be gathered together." Evil children have squandered their patrimony; you alone keep your heritage intact. The fruitful soil of Rome, when it receives the pure seed of the Lord, bears fruit an hundredfold; but here the seed corn is choked in the furrows and nothing grows but darnel or oats. In the West the Sun of righteousness is even now rising; in the East, Lucifer, who fell from heaven, has once more set his throne above the stars. "Ye are the light of the world," "ye are the salt of the earth," "ye are vessels of gold and of silver." Here are vessels of wood or of earth, which wait for the rod of iron, and eternal fire.

Yet though your greatness terrifies me, your kindness attracts me. From the priest I demand the safe-keeping of the victim, from the shepherd the protection due to the sheep. Away with all that is over-weening; let the state of Roman majesty withdraw. My words are spoken to the successor of the fisherman, to the disciple of the cross. As I follow no leader save Christ, so I communicate with none but your blessedness, that is with the chair of Peter. For this, I know, is the rock on which the church is built! This is the house where alone the paschal lamb can be rightly eaten. This is the ark of Noah, and he who is not found in it shall perish when the flood prevails. But since by reason of my sins I have betaken myself to this desert which lies between Syria and the uncivilized waste, I cannot, owing to the great distance between us, always ask of your sanctity the holy thing of the Lord.

St. Jerome, Ep. XV, to Pope Damasus, trans. W. H. Fremantle, *Nicene and Post-Nicene Fathers,* vol. VI, p. 18.

G. The Authority of the Roman See under Pope Leo the Great

In the early fifth century the western provinces of the Empire were overrun by the Vandals, Visigoths, and other barbarians. After the death of the Emperor Theodosius I (395) and his general Stilicho (408) Roman government was never again strong in the West. Roman administration faltered and finally failed; the towns declined still further; there was an increased localization of markets; and the imperial government at Ravenna lost effective touch with the provinces. As civil institutions failed, ecclesiastical institutions grew in strength; the Church took over many of the functions of the State. By the time of Pope Leo I (440–461) the Petrine theory of the papacy had reached the conclusion of the first period of its development. After gaining recognition of its authority in doctrinal matters, the papacy had gone on to achieve a position of supremacy in the entire polity of the western Church. There were still dissenting voices, but now they were fewer and less strong than they had been in earlier generations. In 445 the Emperor Valentinian III recognized the authority of the Pope over the western Church.

It is certain that the only protection both for us and for our Empire lies in the favor of God on high, and in order to earn this favor we must above all support the Christian faith and its revered religion. Since moreover the merit of St. Peter, who stands first in renown among bishops, has confirmed the primacy of the Apostolic See, as has the importance of the city of Rome, and also the authority of the holy synod, let no man's presumption make an unlawful attack upon the authority of this See. For peace will be preserved in churches everywhere only if all Christendom acknowledges its ruler. Although these principles have been observed without violation up to now, Hilary, Bishop of Arles [who had challenged the good judgment and authority of Pope Leo I], as we have learned from the faithful report of that venerable man, Pope Leo of Rome, has attempted certain unlawful undertakings with bold daring and unwarranted presumption, and in consequence of this the most wretched tumult has assailed the churches north of the Alps [Hilary having been primate of the Church in Gaul]. . . . By such audacious acts [as those of which Hilary has been guilty] confidence in our reign is diminished, and reverence for it is outraged. Not only therefore must we dispel such an attitude, which is in itself a great offense, but lest a disturbance, however slight, should arise among the churches, or religious discipline seem to be relaxed in some way, this do we decree by a law in perpetuity: that nothing is to be attempted either by the bishops of Gaul or by those of other provinces contrary to ancient custom, without the authority of the venerable Pope of the Eternal City. But whatever the authority of the Apostolic See has established or shall establish is to be taken as law for these bishops and for all others, so that whenever a bishop has been summoned to appear before the tribunal of the Roman Pope, and has failed to do so, he is to be forced to make such appearance by the governor of the province in which he resides.

Letter of Valentinian III to Aetius, dated 8 July, 445, in Migne, *Patr. Lat.*, LIV, 637-638, trans. K. M. Setton.

H. The Voice of Pope Leo the Great

I.

. . . And from Christ's overruling and eternal protection we have received the support of the Apostles' aid also, which assuredly does not cease from its operation: and the strength of the foundation on which the whole superstructure of the Church is reared is not weakened by the weight of the temple that rests upon it. For the solidity of that faith which was praised in the chief of the Apostles is perpetual: and as that remains which Peter believed in Christ, so that remains which Christ instituted in Peter. For when, as has been read in the gospel lesson [for today], the Lord had asked the disciples whom they believed Him to be amid the various opinions that were held, and the blessed Peter had replied, saying, "Thou art the Christ, the Son of the living God," the Lord said, "Blessed art thou, Simon Bar-Jona, because flesh and blood hath not revealed it to thee, but my Father, which is in heaven. And I say unto thee, that thou art Peter, and upon this rock will I build my Church, and the gates of hell shall not prevail against it. And I will give unto thee the keys of the kingdom of heaven. And whatsoever thou shalt bind on earth, shall be bound in heaven; and whatsoever thou shalt loose on earth, shall be loosed also in heaven."

The dispensation of Truth therefore abides, and the blessed Peter persevering in the strength of the Rock, which he has received, has not abandoned the helm of the Church, which he undertook. For he was ordained before the rest in such a way that from his being called the Rock, from his being pronounced the Foundation, from his being constituted the Doorkeeper of the kingdom of heaven, from his being set as the Umpire to bind and to loose, whose judgments shall retain their validity in heaven, from all these mystical titles we might know the nature of his association with Christ. And still today he more fully and effectually performs what is entrusted to him, and carries out every part of his duty and charge in Him and with Him, through Whom he has been glorified. And so if anything is rightly done and rightly decreed by us, if anything is won from the mercy of God by our daily supplications, it is of his work and merits whose power lives and whose authority prevails in his See. For this, dearly-beloved, was gained by that confession, which, inspired in the Apostle's heart by God the Father, transcended all the uncertainty of human opinions, and was endued with the firmness of a rock, which no assaults could shake. For throughout the Church Peter daily says, "Thou art the Christ, the Son of the living God," and every tongue which confesses the Lord, accepts the instruction his voice conveys.

Leo the Great, *Third Sermon*, 2-3, trans. C. L. Feltoe, in *Nicene and Post-Nicene Fathers*, 2nd Series, XII, 117.

2.

The so-called Second Ecumenical Council of Constantinople in 381 declared, in its third canon, that "the Bishop of Constantinople shall have the prerogative of honor after the Bishop of Rome, *because Constantinople is the New Rome.*" The twenty-eighth canon of the famous Council of Chalcedon in 451 was still more explicit: "For the Fathers rightly granted privileges to the throne of Old Rome, because it was the royal city, and the 150 most religious bishops, moved by the same considerations, gave equal privileges to the most holy throne of New Rome [in 381], judging with good reason that the city which is honored with the sovereignty and the Senate, and also enjoys equal privileges with old imperial Rome, should in ecclesiastical matters also be magnified as she is, and rank next after her. . . ." But the Roman See claimed its prerogative not "because it was the royal city," but because of its foundation by St. Peter, "and upon this rock [*petra*] I will build my Church." A see is apostolic if founded by an apostle; no canon of a church council can alter historical fact; the mere political pre-eminence of a city did not bestow upon the see in that city ecclesiastical superiority over other sees (for Constantinople claimed jurisdiction over much of the eastern Church). The three letters which follow are worthy of careful study; they set forth papal views of the position of the Roman See, its relation to the See of Constantinople, and hence to other sees. (Anato-lius, mentioned below, was Patriarch of Constantinople.)

To Marcianus Augustus. . . . Let the city of Constantinople have, as we desire, its high rank, and under the protection of God's right hand, long enjoy your Clemency's rule. Yet things secular stand on a different basis from things divine: and there can be no sure building save on that rock which the Lord has laid for a foundation. He that covets what is not his due, loses what is his own. Let it be enough for Anatolius that by the aid of your piety and by my favour and approval he has obtained the bishopric of so great a city. Let him not disdain a city which is royal, though he cannot make it an Apostolic See; and let him on no account hope that he can rise by doing injury to others. For the privileges of the churches determined by the canons of the holy Fathers, and fixed by the decrees of the Nicene Synod, cannot be overthrown by any unscrupulous act, nor disturbed by any innovation. And in the faithful execution of this task by the aid of Christ I am bound to display an unflinching devotion; for it is a charge entrusted to me, and it tends to my condemnation if the rules sanctioned by the Fathers and drawn up under the guidance of God's Spirit at the Synod of Nicaea for the government of the whole Church are violated with my connivance (which God forbid), and if the wishes of a single brother have more weight with me than the common good of the Lord's whole house.

Leo the Great, *Epistle 104,* 3, trans. Feltoe, *op. cit.,* p. 75.

3.

To Pulcheria Augusta. . . . Let [Anatolius, Patriarch of Constantinople] realize what a man he has succeeded, and expelling all the spirit of pride let him imitate the faith of Flavian [his predecessor], the modesty of Flavian, the humility of Flavian, which has raised him to a confessor's glory. If he will shine with his virtues, he will merit all praise, and in all quarters he will win an abundance of love not by seeking human advancement but by deserving divine favor. And by this careful course I promise he will bind my heart also to him, and the love of the Apostolic See, which we have ever bestowed on the church of Constantinople, shall never be violated by any change. Be-cause if sometimes rulers fall into errors through want of moderation, yet the churches of Christ do not lose their purity. In keeping with your own piety [he is writing to the Empress], we declare invalid the assents of the bishops [see below], since they are inconsistent with the provisions of the holy canons composed at Nicaea, and by the authority of the blessed Apostle Peter we annul them absolutely, for we obey in all ecclesiastical cases the laws which the Holy Spirit established, through the 318 bishops [at Nicaea], for the peaceful observance of all priests, so that even if a much greater number were to pass a decree different from theirs, whatever was opposed to their pronouncement would have to be disregarded.

Leo the Great, *Epistle 105,* 3, revised from translation of Feltoe, *op. cit.,* p. 77.

4.

As the student now reads the final source herewith presented to illustrate "the triumph of Christianity," he may again contemplate the question with which our general Introduction closed. Was the establishment of papal authority the gradual but deliberate recognition by western Christendom of what was believed to be the will of God, or was it the result of historical accident and development?

To Bishop Anatolius [Patriarch of Constantinople]. . . . Your purpose is in no way whatever supported by the written assent of certain bishops given, as you allege, 60 years ago [at the Council of Constantinople in 381], and never brought to the knowledge of the Apostolic See by your predecessors; and this transaction, which from its outset was doomed to fall through and has now long done so, you now wish to bolster up by means that are too late and useless, namely, by extracting from the brethren an appearance of consent which their modesty from very weariness yielded to their own injury. Remember what the Lord threatens him with, who shall have caused one of the little ones to stumble, and get wisdom to understand what a judgment of God he will have to endure who has not feared to give occasion of stumbling to so many churches and so many priests. For I confess that I am so fast bound by love of the whole brotherhood that I will not agree with any one in demands which are against his own interests, and thus you may clearly perceive that my opposition to you, beloved, proceeds from the kindly intention to restrain you from disturbing the universal

Church by sounder counsel. The rights of provincial primates may not be overthrown nor metropolitan bishops be defrauded of privileges based on antiquity. The See of Alexandria may not lose any of that dignity which it merited through St. Mark, the evangelist and disciple of the blessed Peter, nor may the splendor of so great a church be obscured by another's clouds, Dioscorus [recently deposed Patriarch of Alexandria] having fallen through his own persistence in impiety. The church of Antioch too, in which first at the preaching of the blessed Apostle Peter the Christian name arose, must continue in the position assigned to it by the Fathers, and being set in the third place [by the sixth canon of the Council of Nicaea] must never be lowered therefrom. For the See is on a footing different from that of its holders, and each individual's chief honor is his own integrity. And since that does not lose its proper worth in any place, how much more glorious must it be when placed in the magnificence of the city of Constantinople, where many priests may find both a defence of the Fathers' canons and an example of uprightness in observing you? In thus writing to you, brother, I exhort and admonish you in the Lord, laying aside all ambitious desires in order to cherish a spirit of love. . . .

Leo the Great, *Epistle 106*, 5-6, adapted from translation of Feltoe, *op. cit.*, p. 79.

3. Byzantium and the West

PETER CHARANIS

Rutgers University

THE YEAR A.D. 476 is generally taken by historians of the West as marking the end of the Roman Empire, because in that year the barbarian Odovacar put an end to the imperial office in Italy. But already the Empire had been broken up. Long before 476 the Vandals had established themselves in north Africa and the Visigoths in Spain, while the Burgundians had settled in the Rhone valley. Not long after 476 the Frank Clovis made his appearance, and conquered Gaul while the Ostrogoth Theodoric broke into Italy where, supported by his people, he set himself up as king. Meanwhile Britain had been abandoned to the Anglo-Saxons. The Roman Empire was no more.

But this was true of the West only. The eastern half of the Empire, consisting of Egypt, Syria and Palestine, Asia Minor and the major part of the Balkan peninsula, did not succumb to the barbarians. The East had by now become the center of power. Constantinople, founded by Constantine the Great (d. 337) and patterned to some extent after Rome, had been dedicated as the new capital of the Empire in 330. After Constantine the Great, and especially after the death of Theodosius I (d. 395), there was an emperor at Constantinople and another in Italy, but the former was usually in a stronger position than the latter. Constantinople outstripped Rome in population, wealth and political activity. It became also a great cultural center. The emperor who resided there represented, along with his colleague in Italy, the Roman imperial tradition. In surviving the barbarian flood which inundated the West and brought to an end the imperial office in Italy, Constantinople preserved the continuity of that tradition. The Roman Empire, reduced now to the eastern provinces and with Constantinople as sole capital, continued to exist. This is the Empire which modern historians generally call "Byzantine" and sometimes "Greek": "Byzantine" because Constantinople occupied the site of the old Greek city of Byzantium and was sometimes itself called Byzantium; "Greek" because of its Greek character, at least in language.

The Byzantine Empire is one of the great empires in history. It endured for over a thousand years. Down to about the middle of the eleventh cen-

94

tury it was the center of civilization in Christendom. It preserved the thought and literature of antiquity; it developed new forms of art; it held back the barbarians. It produced great statesmen, soldiers, and diplomats, as well as reformers and renowned scholars. Its missionaries, aided by its diplomats and sometimes by its armies, spread the gospel among the pagan tribes, especially the Slavs, who dwelt along its frontiers and beyond. As a Czech historian has put it, Byzantium "moulded the undisciplined tribes of Serbs, Bulgars, Russians, Croats even, and made nations out of them; it gave to them its religion and institutions, taught their princes how to govern, transmitted to them the very principles of civilization—writing and literature." [1] Throughout its long period of existence all, of course, was not triumph and glory. In its internal life acts of treachery and cruelty, revolts, social and religious strife, were not uncommon. There were times when it suffered serious military reverses and losses in territory. But at no time, except perhaps during the last phase of its declining years, was it an insignificant force. It finally succumbed to the Turks in 1453. Among the factors which brought about its end, the antagonism and hostility which developed between Greeks and Latins were not the least significant.

In the centuries which followed the disintegration of the Roman power in the West, Byzantium and the West went through divergent developments. There were, to begin with, some important differences between the two. There was the difference in language: Greek in Byzantium; Latin in the West. There was the difference in ethnic composition with all its cultural implications. The West was Latin and Germanic; Byzantium and the regions under its influence, especially after Egypt and Syria were lost to the Arabs, were Greek, Slavic, and Armenian. More differences developed as the two regions evolved under different historical conditions. The West came to be broken up into numerous feudatories with no, or hardly any, central organization; Byzantium remained a great Empire with a well established administrative system. The West derived its living almost entirely from agriculture; Byzantium drew its wealth from commerce and industry in addition to agriculture. The West had almost no cities; Byzantium had great urban centers as, for instance, Constantinople and Thessalonica. The West had forgotten Greek, and Byzantium was contemptuous of Latin. A Byzantine emperor in the ninth century described Latin as a "barbarous and Scythian" language. The Byzantines, proud of their superior culture, referred to the Westerners as barbarians, children of darkness, in the words of a Byzantine patriarch. The Latins, unacquainted with the fine techniques of Byzantine diplomacy, considered the Greeks treacherous and unfaithful. A Western ambassador, sent to Constantinople by the German emperor in the tenth century, scribbled on the walls of the house which had been put at his disposal: [2]

---

[1] F. Dvorník, *Les Slaves, Byzance et Rome au IXe Siècle* (Paris, 1928), p. II.

[2] F. A. Wright, trans., *The Works of Liudprand of Cremona* (New York: E. P. Dutton & Company and George Routledge and Sons, Ltd., 1930), p. 270.

"Trust not the Greeks; they live but to betray;
Nor heed their promises, whate'er they say.
If lies will serve them, any oath they swear,
And when it's time to break it feel no fear."

Two developments in particular contributed in giving rise to, and intensify-
ing, the antagonism between Byzantium and the West. One was the revival
of the Roman imperial title in the West in the year 800. The Byzantines
never quite became reconciled to this development. At times, under the force
of circumstance, they might yield to the extent of recognizing the title of
emperor, but at no time would they concede that a barbarian king of the
West could represent the Roman imperial tradition. This point is well illustrated by a passage taken from the work of Liudprand of Cremona, the ambassador of the German emperor to whom reference has already been made.[3]
An "embassy," writes Liudprand, "came from the apostolic and universal Pope
John with a letter asking Nicephorus 'the emperor of the Greeks' to conclude
an alliance and firm friendship with his beloved and spiritual son Otto, 'august
emperor of the Romans'. If you ask me why these words, and manner of
address, which to the Greeks seem sinful audacity, did not cost the bearer his
life . . . , I cannot answer. The Greeks abused the sea, cursed the waves.
. . . 'The audacity of it!' they cried, 'to call the universal emperor of the
Romans, the one and only Nicephorus, the great, the august, "emperor of the
Greeks," and to style a poor barbaric creature "emperor of the Romans!"
O sky! O earth! O sea! What shall we do with these scoundrels and criminals?' " The rivalry of the two Empires over the possession of certain territories in southern Italy intensified still more their antagonism, but the question of the imperial title always remained a fundamental issue. "Do you
want a greater scandal," said the Byzantine Emperor Nicephorus to Liudprand,
"than that he [Otto of Germany] should call himself Emperor and claim for
himself provinces belonging to our Empire? Both these things are intolerable;
and if both are insupportable, that especially is not to be borne, nay, not to
be heard of, that he calls himself Emperor."[4]

The other development was the separation of the Churches. This more than
anything else gave expression to the psychological and cultural differences
which had grown up between Byzantium and the West. The break did not
take place all at once; it was long in coming, but the Church in Byzantium
and the Church in the West never really understood each other. Except for
the last years of its existence the Byzantine Empire was not an ethnically
homogeneous unit. Within its borders there were different peoples representing different but well established cultural traditions. As a consequence differences of opinion, taking a theological form, often developed. The Byzantine
Church, in dealing with these differences, quite frequently took into account
the realities of the situation. This point of view Rome never really under-

[3] *Ibid.*, pp. 263-264.
[4] *Ibid.*, p. 249.

stood, and her intervention to bring about solutions on her own conditions led often to the disruption of relations with Byzantium. Thus, in the fifth century the question over the nature of Christ led to a schism between Rome and Byzantium which lasted for almost 40 years. In the eighth century the dispute over the problem of the worship of images led to another schism. This schism was one of the factors which prompted the papacy to seek the co-operation of the Franks, a co-operation which had as a consequence the revival of the imperial title in the West. And again in the ninth century the intervention of the papacy in a dispute which arose in the Byzantine Church over the designation of a new patriarch in Constantinople had as a consequence another schism—the famous Photian schism. Much in this schism has been shown by modern scholarship to be legendary, but its historical significance as a contributory factor in the final and permanent separation of the two Churches can hardly be overestimated.

The permanent separation of the two Churches is associated with events of the eleventh century. For reasons not quite clear a break in the relations between Rome and Constantinople occurred sometime after 1009. An attempt made some years later to re-establish relations ended in failure, and then in 1054 a new crisis was produced. The crisis was provoked by the Byzantine patriarch, Cerularius, who viewed with alarm the activities of the papacy in southern Italy, a region where the Church of Byzantium had jurisdictional interests. But the violence of the quarrel was due to the obstinacy and arrogance of Cardinal Humbert who headed the papal delegation sent to Constantinople in an effort to settle the differences which existed between the two Churches. Humbert and Cerularius excommunicated each other, and the Churches were further apart than ever before. Involved in the quarrel were the different liturgical usages of the two Churches and their difference in creed—the problem of the *filioque*—but the fundamental issue was the question of the supremacy of the papacy. The arrogance with which Cardinal Humbert insisted upon this point alienated completely the Byzantines. The papal delegates, writes the Catholic scholar Jugie, "had wished . . . to act in Constantinople as they would have acted in a city of the West. And they did not notice that in Constantinople they cut the figures of arrogant strangers with insupportable airs." [5] The quarrel of 1054 is generally regarded by scholars as the beginning of the permanent separation of the two Churches.

The divergent developments, and the consequent antagonisms which one notices in the relations between Byzantium and the West, had not yet, up to the end of the eleventh century, created an unbridgeable chasm between the two sections of Christendom. Intercourse between them was not always unfriendly. At times princes of the West co-operated militarily with the emperor of Constantinople; there were marriage alliances. Even the relations between the Churches might be best described, despite the schisms which separated them at times, as indifferent rather than hostile. The bitter quarrel of 1054

---

[5] Martin Jugie, *Le schisme byzantin* (Paris, 1941), p. 218.

itself was not regarded as ending all hope of reconciliation. One hundred years later, however, this was no longer true. A Byzantine historian wrote toward the end of the twelfth century: "Between us and the Latins a bottomless gulf of enmity has established itself; we cannot unite our souls and we entirely disagree with each other although we keep up our external relations and often live in the same house." "The Latins," wrote another Greek writer, "consider that the world is not big enough to hold both the Greeks and themselves." This state of affairs was brought about largely, if not entirely, by the Crusades.

I. THE PROBLEM OF THE ORIGIN OF THE FIRST CRUSADE

The question of the origin of the First Crusade, and with it the crusading movement, despite the voluminous literature that exists on the subject, remains still a problem. The facts themselves are clear enough. In 1071 the Seljuk Turks, already converted to Islam when they made their appearance, inflicted a disastrous defeat upon the Byzantines in a place, located deep in Asia Minor, called Mantzikert. For reasons associated primarily with the internal conditions of their Empire, the Byzantines were not able to recover from this defeat, and it was not long before the Seljuks overwhelmed virtually all Asia Minor. Three years after Mantzikert we find Pope Gregory VII urging the faithful of the West to go to the assistance of the Greeks, and some months later, writing to the German Emperor Henry IV, that he was organizing an expedition of 50,000 men in response to the appeals of the Greeks, whose Church, he said, wanted to reunite itself with Rome. He stated further that, if possible, he would command this expedition himself and would go as far as Jerusalem. The expedition contemplated by Gregory VII, of course, never took place. In the spring of 1095 at a church council held at Piacenza, in which Pope Urban II participated, Greek ambassadors representing the Byzantine Emperor Alexius are said to have been present and to have appealed for help against the Seljuks. It is further said that Pope Urban urged those present to go to the assistance of the Greeks. During the summer of 1095 Urban toured France, and in November of the same year attended the Council of Clermont, where he

made what is described as an eloquent appeal, urging the faithful to launch an expedition whose ultimate objective should be the liberation of Jerusalem. The First Crusade, and with it the beginning of the crusading movement, followed.

The question which now arises is this: What prompted Urban to make his appeal for this expedition at the time he did, and what did he hope to accomplish besides the alleged objective of liberating Jerusalem? The question has been answered variously by the different historians who have studied the problem. But let the student himself, by studying the sources at his disposal, come to his own conclusion. In studying these sources, however, he should keep in mind several things relating to conditions which existed in western Europe at the time. He should remember that the papacy was in the midst of the Investiture Struggle (see Chapter 4) whose outcome was still in doubt; that the peace and truce of God, which the Church had proclaimed in order to check the widely prevalent private warfare, had not yet succeeded; that the Church had already sanctioned the wars of the Christians against the Moslems in Spain and in Sicily; that numerous pilgrimages were taking place to the Holy Land; that western warriors were eager to seek their fortunes whenever opportunities offered themselves. He should remember also that the mercantile class which was now rising in western Europe, especially in Italy, was ready to push its interests in the Near East where trade and commerce had been thriving for centuries.

The sources themselves are scanty, a fact which explains to a large extent why the origin of the First Crusade is still a problem. We have brought together virtually all of them. Among the Latin sources we include: (1) three letters of Pope Gregory VII, urging the West to go to the assistance of Byzantium and, in one of them, broaching the possibility of liberating Jerusalem; (2) the reference to the presence of Byzantine ambassadors at the Council of Piacenza as it is reported by the Latin chronicler Bernold who, if not present himself at Piacenza, must have derived his information from his bishop who had been there; (3) the speech which Urban II delivered at Clermont as it was recorded some years later by four chroniclers, two of whom, Robert the Monk and Balderic of Bourgueil, say that they were present at Clermont, while the other two, Fulcher of Chartres and Guibert of Nogent, were probably also there; (4) the letter which Urban II wrote toward the end of December, 1095, to the assembling crusaders; and (5) the letter presumably written by the Byzantine Emperor Alexius I, to Robert, Count of Flanders, asking for the help of the West against the enemies of his Empire. This letter, in its present state, is a forgery, but whoever wrote it must have drawn his inspiration from a genuine letter, now lost, which Alexius actually wrote to Robert. This is the opinion of most scholars. We have included this document in our collection because of the problems which it presents and because it bears upon the question as to whether or not Alexius asked the West for help. Among the Greek sources, there are only two of any significance. One is the account of Anna Comnena in which she relates the coming of the crusaders to Constantinople and gives her own version of the cause of the crusade. Anna wrote the *Alexiad*—the title of her book (on her father Alexius)—some years after the First Crusade, but she was the daughter of the Byzantine Emperor Alexius and, as a consequence, must have had access to important sources of information. It must be pointed out, however, that in matters pertaining to the relations of her father with the West she is not always well informed. The other is a passage drawn from a Greek world chronicle written in the thirteenth century by a Byzan-

tine ecclesiastic, Theodore Skutariotes. The passage, of course, is not contemporary with the event to which it refers, but, as the chronicle of Skutariotes as a whole is known to derive from good sources, it deserves serious consideration.

These are virtually all the sources that bear upon the problem of the origin of the First Crusade.

A. *The Appeal of Gregory VII on Behalf of the Greeks*

1. LETTER TO COUNT WILLIAM OF BURGUNDY, FEBRUARY 2, 1074

Gregory . . . to Count William of Burgundy, greeting . . .

Your Prudence may remember how affectionately the Roman Church received your Mightiness not long since and how greatly it enjoyed your visit. Nor can you in decency forget the promise which you made to God before the tomb of Peter, chief of the Apostles, in the presence of our venerable predecessor, Pope Alexander, and of an innumerable company of bishops, abbots and people of many nations, that whenever necessary your force would not be lacking if it were called for in defense of the property of St. Peter.

Wherefore, remembering the noble repute of your honor, we beg and require of your prudence and your zeal that you bring together a military force to protect the freedom of the Roman Church and if need be that you come hither with your army in the service of St. Peter. We beg you also to send this same summons to the count of St. Giles, father-in-law of Richard, prince of Capua, and to Amadeus, son of Adelaide of Turin, and others whom you know to be loyal to St. Peter and who made the same promise with hands upraised to Heaven. If we decide to send a definite reply to Your Prudence, send back word to us by the same messenger, who will relieve us of all doubts.

And let that same messenger of yours come by the way of the countess Beatrice; who, with her daughter and her son-in-law, Duke Godfrey of Lorraine, is promoting this enterprise.

We are not, however, trying to bring together this force of fighting men for the sacrifice of Christian blood, but in order that our enemies, learning of the expedition, may fear to join battle and be the more easily won over to the right side. We are hoping also that another advantage may come from this, namely, that when the Normans are pacified we may cross over to Constantinople in aid of the Christians who, oppressed by frequent attacks of the Saracens, are urging us eagerly to reach out our hands to them in succor. The troops we have with us are sufficient against those Normans who are in rebellion against us. And be assured that you and all who shall join you in this undertaking will receive a double—nay, as we believe, a manifold—reward from Peter and Paul, chiefs of the Apostles.

The Correspondence of Pope Gregory VII, trans. Ephraim Emerton (New York: Columbia University Press, 1932), pp. 22-23.

2. THE SUMMONS TO THE FAITHFUL TO DEFEND CONSTANTINOPLE, MARCH 1, 1074

Gregory . . . to all who are willing to defend the Christian faith, greeting . . .

We desire to make known to you that the bearer of these presents upon his recent return from beyond the seas visited us at the threshold of the Apostles. From him, as also from many others, we have learned that a people of the pagans have been pressing hard upon the Christian empire, have cruelly laid waste the country almost to the walls of Constantinople and slaughtered like sheep many thousand Christians. Wherefore, if we love God and acknowledge ourselves to be Christians, we ought to be deeply grieved by the wretched fate of that great empire and the murder of so many followers of Christ. But it is not enough to grieve over this event; the example of our Redeemer and the duty of brotherly love demand of us that we should set our hearts upon the deliverance of our brethren. For as he offered his life for us, so ought we to offer our lives for our brothers. Be it known, therefore, that we, trusting in the mercy of God and in the might of his power, are preparing in every possible way to carry aid to the Christian empire as soon as may be, by God's help. We adjure you, by the faith in which you are united [to them] in the adoption of the sons of God, and by authority of St. Peter, prince of the Apostles, to be stirred with compassion by the wounds and the blood of your brethren and the peril of the empire and willingly to offer your powerful aid to your brethren in the name of Christ.

Whatever decision you may make in this matter by God's mercy, pray report it to us without delay by trustworthy messengers.

Ibid., pp. 25-26.

3. LETTER TO HENRY IV, SETTING FORTH GREGORY'S PLAN FOR AN OFFENSIVE AGAINST THE TURKS, DECEMBER 7, 1074

Gregory . . . to the glorious King Henry, greeting . . .

If God would grant by some act of his grace that my thoughts might lie open before you, I know beyond a doubt that no person could separate you from my sincere affection. But even as it is, I have entire confidence in his mercy, that it shall one day become clear that

I am truly devoted to you. For to this I am directed by the common law of all Christian men; to this the majesty of empire and the mild sway of the Apostolic See impel me; so that if I do not love you as I ought, I am trusting in vain in the mercy of God through the merits of St. Peter.

But since I desire to labor day and night in the Lord's vineyard, through many dangers even unto death, I will always strive with God's help to preserve a sacred and merited affection not only towards you whom God has placed at the summit of earthly affairs and through whom many may be led either to wander from the path of rectitude or to observe the faith of Christ, but also toward the least among Christians. For he who should try to approach the marriage feast of the king without this wedding garment will suffer a monstrous disgrace. Alas! Those who are daily plotting to sow discord between us pay no attention to these truths, that with these nets prepared at the Devil's prompting they may catch their own advantage and conceal their own vices by which they are madly calling down upon themselves the wrath of God and of St. Peter. I therefore warn and exhort you, my best beloved son, to turn your ear away from them and listen without reserve to those who seek not their own but the things that are of Jesus Christ and who do not set their own honor or profit above righteousness, so that through their counsel you may not forfeit the glory of this life, but may gain with confidence the life that is in Christ Jesus.

Further, I call to your attention that the Christians beyond the sea, a great part of whom are being destroyed by the heathen with unheard-of slaughter and are daily being slain like so many sheep, have humbly sent to beg me to succor these our brethren in whatever ways I can, that the religion of Christ may not utterly perish in our time—which God forbid! I, therefore, smitten with exceeding grief and led even to long for death—for I would rather stake my life for these than reign over the whole earth and neglect them—have succeeded in arousing certain Christian men so that they are eager to risk their lives for their brethren in defense of the law of Christ and to show forth more clearly than the day the nobility of the sons of God. This summons has been readily accepted by Italians and northerners, by divine inspiration as I believe—nay, as I can absolutely assure you—and already fifty thousand men are preparing, if they can have me for their leader and prelate, to take up arms against the enemies of God and push forward even to the sepulcher of the Lord under his supreme leadership.

I am especially moved toward this undertaking because the Church of Constantinople, differing from us on the doctrine of the Holy Spirit, is seeking the fellowship of the Apostolic See, the Armenians are almost entirely estranged from the Catholic faith and almost all the Easterners are waiting to see how the faith of the Apostle Peter will decide among their divergent views. For it is the call of our time that the word of command shall be fulfilled which our blessed Savior deigned to speak to the prince of the Apostles: "I have prayed for thee that thy faith fail not: and when thou art converted, strengthen thy brethren." And because our fathers, in whose footsteps we, though unworthy, desire to walk, often went to those regions for the strengthening of the Catholic faith, we also, aided by the prayers of all Christian men, are under compulsion to go over there for the same faith and for the defense of Christians—provided that the way shall be opened with Christ as our guide—for the way of man is not in his own hand, and the steps of a man are ordered by the Lord.

But, since a great undertaking calls for the aid and counsel of the great, if God shall grant me to begin this, I beg you for your advice and for your help according to your good pleasure. For if it shall please God that I go, I shall leave the Roman Church, under God, in your hands to guard her as a holy mother and to defend her for his honor.

Advise me at the earliest possible moment of your pleasure in this matter and what your divinely inspired judgment may determine. If I did not have better hopes of you than many suppose, these exhortations would be in vain. But since there is perchance no man whom you can completely trust in regard to the sincerity of my affection for you, I leave to the Holy Spirit, which

Ibid., pp. 56-58.

can do all things, to show you in its own way what I ask of you and how great is my devotion to you, and may it in the same way so dispose your heart toward me that the desires of the wicked may come to naught and those of the righteous may increase. These two desires are keeping incessant watch upon us two—though in different ways—and are fighting according to the wishes of those from whom they proceed.

May Almighty God, from whom cometh every good thing, cleanse you from all your sins by the merits and the authority of the blessed Apostles Peter and Paul, and make you to walk in the way of his commandments and lead you into life eternal.

B. Bernold on the Byzantine Embassy at the Council of Piacenza

There arrived at this council [Council of Piacenza, March, 1095] an embassy from the emperor of Constantinople which humbly beseeched Our Lord, the Pope, and all the faithful of Christ to procure for him some help against the pagans for the defense of our holy church which the pagans had

already destroyed in his territories. The pagans had rendered themselves masters of his territories as far as the walls of the city of Constantinople. Our Lord the Pope, therefore, urged many to furnish this aid, even engaging them to promise under oath to go there with the consent of God and bring to this same emperor, to the best of their power, their most faithful aid against the pagans.

Bernold, *Chronicon, Monumenta Germaniae historica, SS.,* V, 462, trans. Peter Charanis.

C. The Speech of Urban II at the Council of Clermont, November 27, 1095

1. THE VERSION OF FULCHER OF CHARTRES INCLUDING HIS DESCRIPTION OF CONDITIONS IN WESTERN EUROPE AT THE TIME

In the year of our Lord 1095, in the reign of the so-called Emperor Henry in Germany and of King Philip in France, throughout Europe evils of all kinds waxed strong because of vacillating

faith. Pope Urban II then ruled in the city of Rome. He was a man admirable in life and habits, who always strove wisely and energetically to raise the status of Holy Church higher and higher. . . .

But the devil, who always desires man's destruction and goes about like a raging lion seeking whom he may devour, stirred up to the confusion of the people a certain rival to Urban, Wibert by name. Incited by the stimulus of pride and supported by the shamelessness of the aforesaid Emperor of the Bavarians, Wibert attempted to usurp the papal office while Urban's predecessor, Gregory, that is Hildebrand, was the legitimate Pope; and he thus caused Gregory himself to be cast out of St. Peter's. So the better people refused to recognize him because he acted thus perversely. After the death of Hildebrand, Urban, lawfully elected, was consecrated by the cardinal bishops, and the greater and holier part of the people submitted in obedience to him. Wibert, however, urged on by the support of the aforesaid Emperor and by the instigation of the Roman citizens, for some time kept Urban a stranger to the Church of St. Peter; but Urban, although he was banished from the Church, went about through the country, reconciling to God the people who had gone somewhat astray. Wibert, however, puffed up by the primacy of the Church, showed himself indulgent to sinners, and exercising the office of pope, although unjustly, amongst his adherents, he denounced as ridiculous the acts of Urban. But in the year in which the Franks first passed through Rome on their way to Jerusalem, Urban obtained the complete papal power everywhere, with the help of a certain most noble matron, Matilda by name, who then had great influence in the Roman state. Wibert was then in Germany. So there were two Popes; and many did not know which to obey, or from which counsel should be taken, or who should remedy the ills of Christianity. Some favored the one; some the other. But it was clear to the intelligence of men that Urban was the better, for he is rightly considered better who controls his passions, just as if they were enemies. Wibert was Archbishop of the city of Ravenna. He was very rich and revelled in honor and wealth. It was a wonder that such riches did not satisfy him. Ought he to be considered by all an exemplar of right living who, himself a lover of pomp, boldly assumes to usurp the sceptre of Almighty God? Truly, this office must not be seized by force, but accepted with fear and humility.

What wonder that the whole world was a prey to disturbance and confusion? For when the Roman Church, which is the source of correction for all Christianity, is troubled by any disorder, the sorrow is communicated from the nerves of the head to the members subject to it, and these suffer sympathetically. This Church, indeed, our mother, as it were, at whose bosom we were nourished, by whose doctrine we were instructed and strengthened, by whose counsel we were admonished, was by this proud Wibert greatly afflicted. For when the head is thus struck, the members at once are sick. If the head be sick, the other members suffer. Since the head was thus sick, pain was engendered in the enfeebled members; for in all parts of Europe peace, goodness, faith, were boldly trampled under foot, within the church and without, by the high, as well as by the low. It was necessary both that an end be put to these evils, and that, in accordance with the plan suggested by Pope Urban, they turn against the pagans the strength formerly used in prosecuting battles among themselves. . . .

He saw, moreover, the faith of Christendom greatly degraded by all, by the clergy as well as by the laity, and peace totally disregarded; for the princes of the land were incessantly engaged in armed strife, now these, now those quarrelling among themselves. He saw the goods of the land stolen from the owners; and many, who were unjustly taken captive and most barbarously cast into foul prisons, he saw ransomed for excessive sums, or tormented there by the three evils, starvation, thirst, and cold, or allowed to perish by unseen death.

He also saw holy places violated, monasteries and villas destroyed by fire, and not a little human suffering, both the divine and the human being held in derision.

When he heard, too, that interior parts of Romania were held oppressed by the Turks, and that Christians were subjected to destructive and savage attacks, he was moved by compassionate pity; and, prompted by the love of God, he crossed the Alps and came into Gaul. He there called a council at Clermont in Auvergne, which council had been fittingly proclaimed by envoys in all directions. It is estimated that there were three hundred and ten bishops and abbots who bore the crozier. When they were assembled on the day appointed for the council, Urban, in an eloquent address full of sweetness, made known the object of the meeting. With the plaintive voice of the afflicted Church he bewailed in a long discourse the great disturbances which, as has been mentioned above, agitated the world where faith had been undermined. Then, as a supplicant, he exhorted all to resume the fullness of their faith, and in good earnest to try diligently to withstand the deceits of the devil, and to raise to its pristine honor the status of Holy Church, now most unmercifully crippled by the wicked.

"Dearest brethren," he said, "I, Urban, invested by the permission of God with the papal tiara, and spiritual ruler over the whole world, have come here in this great crisis to you, servants of God, as a messenger of divine admonition. I wish those whom I have believed good and faithful dispensers of the ministry of God to be found free from shameful dissimulation. For if there be in you any disposition or crookedness contrary to God's law, because you have lost the moderation of reason and justice, I shall earnestly endeavor to correct it at once, with divine

assistance. For the Lord has made you stewards over His family, that you provide it with pleasant-tasting meat in season. You will be blessed, indeed, if the Lord shall find you faithful in stewardship. You are also called shepherds; see that you do not the work of hirelings. Be true shepherds and have your crooks always in your hands. Sleep not, but defend everywhere the flock committed to your care. For if through your carelessness or neglect the wolf carries off a sheep, doubtless you will not only lose the reward prepared for you by our Lord, but, after having first been tortured by the strokes of the lictor, you will also be savagely hurled into the abode of the damned. In the words of the gospel, 'Ye are the salt of the earth'! But, it is asked, 'If ye fail, wherewith shall it be salted?' Oh, what a salting! Indeed, you must strive by the salt of your wisdom to correct this foolish people, over-eager for the pleasures of the world, lest the Lord find them insipid and rank, corrupted by crimes at the time when He wishes to speak to them. For if because of your slothful performance of duty He shall discover any worms in them, that is to say any sins, He will in contempt order them to be cast forthwith into the abyss of uncleanness; and because you will be unable to make good to Him such a loss, He will surely banish you, condemned by His judgment, from the presence of His love. But one that salteth ought to be prudent, foresighted, learned, peaceful, watchful, respectable, pious, just, fair-minded, pure. For how can the unlearned make others learned, the immodest make others modest, the unclean make others clean? How can he make peace who hates it? If anyone has soiled hands, how can he cleanse the spots from one contaminated? For it is written, 'If the blind lead the blind, both shall fall into the pit.' Accordingly, first correct yourselves, so that without reproach you can then correct those under your care. If, indeed, you wish to be the friends of God, do generously what you see is pleasing to Him.

"See to it that the affairs of Holy Church, especially, are maintained in their rights, and that simoniacal heresy in no way takes root among you. Take care lest purchasers and venders alike, struck by the lash of the Lord, be disgracefully driven through narrow ways into utter confusion. Keep the Church in all its orders entirely free from the secular power; have given to God faithfully one-tenth of the fruits of the earth, neither selling them, nor withholding them. Whoever lays violent hands on a bishop, let him be considered excommunicated. Whoever shall have seized monks, or priests, or nuns, and their servants, or pilgrims, or traders, and shall have despoiled them, let him be accursed. Let thieves and burners of houses and their accomplices be excommunicated from the church and accursed. Therefore, we must consider especially, as Gregory says, how great will be his punishment who steals from another, if he incurs the damnation of hell who does not distribute alms from his own possessions. For so it happened to the rich man in the Gospel, who was punished not for stealing anything from another, but because, having received wealth, he used it badly.

"By these evils, therefore, as I have said, dearest brethren, you have seen the world disordered for a long time, and to such a degree that in some places in your provinces, as has been reported to us (perhaps due to your weakness in administering justice), one scarcely dares to travel for fear of being kidnapped by thieves at night or highwaymen by day, by force or by craft, at home or out of doors. Wherefore, it is well to enforce anew the Truce, commonly so-called, which was long ago established by our holy fathers, and which

I most earnestly entreat each one of you to have observed in his diocese. But if any one, led on by pride or ambition, infringes this injunction voluntarily, let him be anathema in virtue of the authority of God and by the sanction of the decrees of this council."

When these and many other things were well disposed of, all those present, priests and people alike, gave thanks to God and welcomed the advice of the Lord Pope Urban, assuring him, with a promise of fidelity, that these decrees of his would be well kept. . . .

But the Pope added at once that another trouble, not less, but still more grievous than that already spoken of, and even the very worst, was besetting Christianity from another part of the world. He said: "Since, O sons of God, you have promised the Lord to maintain peace more earnestly than heretofore in your midst, and faithfully to sustain the rights of Holy Church, there still remains for you, who are newly aroused by this divine correction, a very necessary work, in which you can show the strength of your good will by a certain further duty, God's concern and your own. For you must hasten to carry aid to your brethren dwelling in the East, who need your help, which they often have asked. For the Turks, a Persian people, have attacked them, as many of you already know, and have advanced as far into the Roman territory as that part of the Mediterranean which is called the Arm of St. George; and, by seizing more and more of the lands of the Christians, they have already often conquered them in battle, have killed and captured many, have destroyed the churches, and have devastated the kingdom of God. If you allow them to continue much longer, they will subjugate God's faithful yet more widely.

"Wherefore, I exhort with earnest prayer—not I, but God—that, as heralds of Christ, you urge men by frequent exhortation, men of all ranks, knights as well as foot-soldiers, rich as well as poor, to hasten to exterminate this vile race from the lands of your brethren, and to aid the Christians in time. I speak to those present; I proclaim it to the absent; moreover, Christ commands it. And if those who set out thither should lose their lives on the way by land, or in crossing the sea, or in fighting the pagans, their sins shall be remitted. This I grant to all who go, through the power vested in me by God. Oh, what a disgrace, if a race so despised, base, and the instrument of demons, should so overcome a people endowed with faith in the all-powerful God, and resplendent with the name of Christ! Oh, what reproaches will be charged against you by the Lord Himself if you have not helped those who are counted, like yourselves, of the Christian faith! Let those who have been accustomed to make private war against the faithful carry on to a successful issue a war against infidels, which ought to have been begun ere now. Let those who for a long time have been robbers now become soldiers of Christ. Let those who once fought against brothers and relatives now fight against barbarians, as they ought. Let those who have been hirelings at low wages now labor for an eternal reward. Let those who have been wearing themselves out to the detriment of body and soul now labor for a double glory. On the one hand will be the sad and poor, on the other the joyous and wealthy; here the enemies of the Lord; there His friends. Let no obstacle stand in the way of those who are going, but, after their affairs are settled and expense money is collected, when the winter has ended and spring has come, let them zealously undertake the journey under the guidance of the Lord."

August C Krey, *The First Crusade. The Accounts of Eye-Witnesses and Participants* (Princeton: Princeton University Press, 1921), pp. 24-30. (The translation used is Krey's.)

2. As Reported by Robert the Monk

. . . "Oh, race of Franks, race from across the mountains, race chosen and beloved by God—as shines forth in very many of your works—set apart from all nations by the situation of your country, as well as by your Catholic faith and the honor of the Holy Church! To you our discourse is addressed, and for you our exhortation is intended. We wish you to know what a grievous cause has led us to your country, what peril, threatening you and all the faithful, has brought us.

"From the confines of Jerusalem and the city of Constantinople a horrible tale has gone forth and very frequently has been brought to our ears; namely, that a race from the kingdom of the Persians, an accursed race, a race utterly alienated from God, a generation, forsooth, which has neither directed its heart nor entrusted its spirit to God, has invaded the lands of those Christians and has depopulated them by the sword, pillage, and fire; it has led away a part of the captives into its own country, and a part it has destroyed by cruel tortures; it has either entirely destroyed the churches of God or appropriated them for the rites of its own religion. They destroy the altars, after having defiled them with their uncleanness. They circumcise the Christians, and the blood of the circumcision they either spread upon the altars or pour into the vases of the baptismal font. When they wish to torture people by a base death, they perforate their navels, and, dragging forth the end of the intestines, bind it to a stake; then with flogging they lead the victim around until his viscera have gushed forth, and he falls prostrate upon the ground. Others they bind to a post and pierce with arrows. Others they compel to extend their necks, and then, attacking them with naked swords, they attempt to cut through the neck with a single blow. What shall I say of the abominable rape of the women? To speak of it is worse than to be silent. The kingdom of the Greeks is now dismembered by them and deprived of territory so vast in extent that it cannot be traversed in a march of two months. On whom, therefore, is the task of avenging these wrongs and of recovering this territory incumbent, if not upon you? You, upon whom above other nations God has conferred remarkable glory in arms, great courage, bodily energy, and the strength to humble the hairy scalp of those who resist you.

"Let the deeds of your ancestors move you and incite your minds to manly achievements; likewise, the glory and greatness of King Charles the Great, and his son Louis, and of your other kings, who have destroyed the kingdoms of the pagans, and have extended in these lands the territory of the Holy Church. Let the Holy Sepulchre of the Lord, our Saviour, which is possessed by unclean nations, especially move you, and likewise the holy places, which are now treated with ignominy and irreverently polluted with filthiness. Oh, most valiant soldiers and descendants of invincible ancestors, be not degenerate, but recall the valor of your forefathers!

"However, if you are hindered by love of children, parents, and wives, remember what the Lord says in the Gospel, 'He that loveth father, or mother more than me, is not worthy of me.' 'Every one that hath forsaken houses, or brethren, or sisters, or father, or mother, or wife, or children, or lands

for my name's sake shall receive an hundred-fold and shall inherit everlasting life.' Let none of your possessions detain you, no solicitude for your family affairs, since this land which you inhabit, shut in on all sides by the sea and surrounded by mountain peaks, is too narrow for your large population; nor does it abound in wealth; and it furnishes scarcely food enough for its cultivators. Hence it is that you murder and devour one another, that you wage war, and that frequently you perish by mutual wounds. Let therefore hatred depart from among you, let your quarrels end, let wars cease, and let all dissensions and controversies slumber. Enter upon the road to the Holy Sepulchre; wrest that land from the wicked race, and subject it to yourselves. That land which, as the Scripture says, 'floweth with milk and honey' was given by God into the possession of the children of Israel.

"Jerusalem is the navel of the world; the land is fruitful above others, like another paradise of delights. This the Redeemer of the human race has made illustrious by His advent, has beautified by His presence, has consecrated by suffering, has redeemed by death, has glorified by burial. This royal city, therefore, situated at the center of the world, is now held captive by His enemies, and is in subjection to those who do not know God, to the worship of the heathen. Therefore, she seeks and desires to be liberated and does not cease to implore you to come to her aid. From you, especially, she asks succor, because, as we have already said, God has conferred upon you, above all nations, great glory in arms. Accordingly, undertake this journey for the remission of your sins, with the assurance of the imperishable glory of the kingdom of heaven."

When Pope Urban had said these and very many similiar things in his urbane discourse, he so influenced to one purpose the desires of all who were present that they cried out, "God wills it! God wills it!" When the venerable Roman pontiff heard that, with eyes uplifted to heaven he gave thanks to God and, with his hand commanding silence, said:

"Most beloved brethren, today is manifest in you what the Lord says in the Gospel, 'Where two or three are gathered together in my name there am I in the midst of them.' Unless the Lord God had been present in your minds, all of you would not have uttered the same cry. For, although the cry issued from numerous mouths, yet the origin of the cry was one. Therefore I say to you that God, who implanted this in your breasts, has drawn it forth from you. Let this then be your battle-cry in combat, because this word is given to you by God. When an armed attack is made upon the enemy, let this one cry be raised by all the soldiers of God: 'God wills it! God wills it!'

"And we do not command or advise that the old, or the feeble, or those unfit for bearing arms, undertake this jour-

Ibid., pp. 30-33.

3. As Reported by Balderic of Bourgueil

. . . "We have heard, most beloved brethren, and you have heard what we cannot recount without deep sorrow—how, with great hurt and dire sufferings our Christian brothers, members in Christ, are scourged, oppressed, and injured in Jerusalem, in Antioch, and the other cities of the East. Your own blood-brothers, your companions, your associates (for you are sons of the same Christ and the same Church), are either subjected in their inherited homes to other masters, or are driven from them, or they come as beggars among us; or,

ney; nor ought women to set out at all without their husbands, or brothers, or legal guardians. For such are more of a hindrance than aid, more of a burden than an advantage. Let the rich aid the needy; and, according to their means, let them take with them experienced soldiers. The priests and clerks of any order are not to go without the consent of their bishops; for this journey would profit them nothing if they went without such permission. Also, it is not fitting that laymen should enter upon the pilgrimage without the blessing of their priests.

"Whoever, therefore, shall determine upon this holy pilgrimage and shall make his vow to God to that effect and shall offer himself to Him as a living sacrifice, holy, acceptable unto God, shall wear the sign of the cross of the Lord on his forehead, or on his breast. When, having truly fulfilled his vow, he wishes to return, let him place the cross on his back between his shoulders. Such, indeed, by two-fold action will fulfil the precept of the Lord, as He commands in the Gospel, 'He that doth not take his cross and follow after me, is not worthy of me.'" . . .

which is far worse, they are flogged and exiled as slaves for sale in their own land. Christian blood, redeemed by the blood of Christ, has been shed, and Christian flesh, akin to the flesh of Christ, has been subjected to unspeakable degradation and servitude. Everywhere in those cities there is sorrow, everywhere misery, everywhere groaning (I say it with a sigh). The churches in which divine mysteries were celebrated in olden times are now, to our sorrow, used as stables for the animals of these people! Holy men do not possess those cities; nay, base and bastard Turks hold sway over our brothers. The blessed Peter first presided as

Bishop at Antioch; behold, in his own church the Gentiles have established their superstitions, and the Christian religion, which they ought rather to cherish, they have basely shut out from the hall dedicated to God! The estates given for the support of the saints and the patrimony of nobles set aside for the sustenance of the poor are subject to pagan tyranny, while cruel masters abuse for their own purposes the returns from these lands. The priesthood of God has been ground down into the dust. The sanctuary of God (unspeakable shame!) is everywhere profaned. Whatever Christians still remain in hiding there are sought out with unheard of tortures.

"Of holy Jerusalem, brethren, we dare not speak, for we are exceedingly afraid and ashamed to speak of it. This very city, in which, as you all know, Christ Himself suffered for us, because our sins demanded it, has been reduced to the pollution of paganism and, I say it to our disgrace, withdrawn from the service of God. Such is the heap of reproach upon us who have so much deserved it! Who now serves the church of the Blessed Mary in the valley of Josaphat, in which church she herself was buried in body? But why do we pass over the Temple of Solomon, nay of the Lord, in which the barbarous nations placed their idols contrary to law, human and divine? Of the Lord's Sepulchre we have refrained from speaking, since some of you with your own eyes have seen to what abominations it has been given over. The Turks violently took from it the offerings which you brought there for alms in such vast amounts, and, in addition, they scoffed much and often at your religion. And yet in that place (I say only what you already know) rested the Lord; there He died for us; there He was buried. How precious would be the longed-for, incomparable place of the Lord's burial, even if God failed there to perform the yearly miracle! For in the days of His Passion all the lights in the Sepulchre and round about in the church, which have been extinguished, are relighted by divine command. Whose heart is so stony, brethren, that it is not touched by so great a miracle? Believe me, that man is bestial and senseless whose heart such divinely manifest grace does not move to faith! And yet the Gentiles see this in common with the Christians and are not turned from their ways! They are, indeed, afraid, but they are not converted to the faith; nor is it to be wondered at, for a blindness of mind rules over them. With what afflictions they wronged you who have returned and are now present, you yourselves know too well, you who there sacrificed your substance and your blood for God.

"This, beloved brethren, we shall say, that we may have you as witness of our words. More suffering of our brethren and devastation of churches remains than we can speak of one by one, for we are oppressed by tears and groans, sighs and sobs. We weep and wail, brethren, alas, like the Psalmist, in our inmost heart! We are wretched and unhappy, and in us is that prophecy fulfilled; 'God, the nations are come into thine inheritance; thy holy temple have they defiled; they have laid Jerusalem in heaps; the dead bodies of thy servants have been given to be food for the birds of the heaven, the flesh of thy saints unto the beasts of the earth. Their blood have they shed like water round about Jerusalem, and there was none to bury them.' Woe unto us, brethren! We who have already become a reproach to our neighbors, a scoffing, and derision to them round about us, let us at least with tears condole and have compassion upon our brothers! We who are become the scorn of all peoples, and worse than all, let us bewail the most monstrous devastation of the Holy Land! This land we have deservedly called holy in which there is not even a foot-step that the body or spirit of the Saviour did not render glorious and blessed; which embraced the holy presence of the mother of God, and the meetings of the apostles, and drank up the blood of the martyrs shed there. How blessed are the stones which crowned you, Stephen, the first martyr! How happy, O, John the Baptist, the waters of the Jordan which served you in baptizing the Saviour! The children of Israel, who were led out of Egypt, and who prefigured you in the crossing of the Red Sea, have taken that land by their arms, with Jesus as leader; they have driven out the Jebusites and other inhabitants and have themselves inhabited earthly Jerusalem, the image of celestial Jerusaelm.

"What are we saying? Listen and learn! You, girt about with the badge of knighthood, are arrogant with great pride; you rage against your brothers and cut each other in pieces. This is not the (true) soldiery of Christ which rends asunder the sheepfold of the Redeemer. The Holy Church has reserved a soldiery for herself to help her people, but you debase her wickedly to her hurt. Let us confess the truth, whose heralds we ought to be; truly, you are not holding to the way which leads to life. You, the oppressers of children, plunderers of widows; you, guilty of homicide, of sacrilege, robbers of another's rights; you who await the pay of thieves for the shedding of Christian blood—as vultures smell fetid corpses, so do you sense battles from afar and rush to them eagerly. Verily, this is the worst way, for it is utterly removed from God! If, forsooth, you wish to be mindful of your souls, either lay down the girdle of such knighthood, or advance boldly, as knights of Christ, and rush as quickly as you can to the de-

fence of the Eastern Church. For she it is from whom the joys of your whole salvation have come forth, who poured into your mouths the milk of divine wisdom, who set before you the holy teachings of the Gospels. We say this, brethren, that you may restrain your murderous hands from the destruction of your brothers, and in behalf of your relatives in the faith oppose yourselves to the Gentiles. Under Jesus Christ, our Leader, may you struggle for your Jerusalem, in Christian battle-line, most invincible line, even more successfully than did the sons of Jacob of old— struggle, that you may assail and drive out the Turks, more execrable than the Jebusites, who are in this land, and may you deem it a beautiful thing to die for Christ in that city in which He died for us. But if it befall you to die this side of it, be sure that to have died on the way is of equal value, if Christ shall find you in His army. God pays with the same shilling, whether at the first or eleventh hour. You should shudder, brethren, you should shudder at raising a violent hand against Christians; it is less wicked to brandish your sword against Saracens. It is the only warfare that is righteous, for it is charity to risk your life for your brothers. That you may not be troubled about the concerns of tomorrow, know that those who fear God want nothing, nor those who cherish Him in truth. The possessions of the enemy, too, will be yours, since you will make spoil of their treasures and return victorious to your own; or empurpled with your own blood, you will have gained everlasting glory. For such a Commander you ought to fight, for One who lacks neither might nor wealth with which to reward you. Short is the way, little the labor, which, nevertheless, will repay you with the crown that fadeth not away. Accordingly, we speak with the authority of the prophet: 'Gird thy sword upon thy thigh, O mighty one.' Gird yourselves, everyone of you, I say, and be valiant sons; for it is better for you to die in battle than to behold the sorrows of your race and of your holy places. Let neither property nor the alluring charms of your wives entice you from going; nor let the trials that are to be borne so deter you that you remain here."

And turning to the bishops, he said, "You, brothers and fellow bishops; you, fellow priests and sharers with us in Christ, make this same announcement through the churches committed to you, and with your whole soul vigorously preach the journey to Jerusalem. When they have confessed the disgrace of their sins, do you, secure in Christ, grant them speedy pardon. Moreover, you who are to go shall have us praying for you; we shall have you fighting for God's people. It is our duty to pray, yours to fight against the Amalekites.

Ibid., pp. 33-36.

4. As Reported by Guibert of Nogent

. . . "If among the churches scattered about over the whole world some, because of persons or location, deserve reverence above others (for persons, I say, since greater privileges are accorded to apostolic sees; for places, indeed, since the same dignity which is accorded to persons is also shown to regal cities, such as Constantinople), we owe most to that church from which we received the grace of redemption and the source of all Christianity. If what the Lord says—namely, 'Salvation is from the Jews—,' accords with the truth, and it is true that the Lord has left us Sabaoth as seed, that we may not become like Sodom and Gomorrah, and our seed is Christ, in whom is the salvation and benediction of all peoples, then, indeed, the very land and city in which He dwelt and suffered is, by witness of the

With Moses, we shall extend unwearied hands in prayer to Heaven, while you go forth and brandish the sword, like dauntless warriors, against Amalek."

As those present were thus clearly informed by these and other words of this kind from the apostolic lord, the eyes of some were bathed in tears; some trembled, and yet others discussed the matter. However, in the presence of all at that same council, and as we looked on, the Bishop of Puy, a man of great renown and of highest ability, went to the Pope with joyful countenance and on bended knee sought and entreated blessing and permission to go. Over and above this, he won from the Pope the command that all should obey him, and that he should hold sway over all the army in behalf of the Pope, since all knew him to be a prelate of unusual energy and industry. . . .

Scriptures, holy. If this land is spoken of in the sacred writings of the prophets as the inheritance and the holy temple of God before ever the Lord walked about in it, or was revealed, what sanctity, what reverence has it not acquired since God in His majesty was there clothed in the flesh, nourished, grew up, and in bodily form there walked about, or was carried about; and, to compress in fitting brevity all that might be told in a long series of words, since there the blood of the Son of God, more holy than heaven and earth, was poured forth, and His body, its quivering members dead, rested in the tomb. What veneration do we think it deserves? If, when the Lord had but just been crucified and the city was still held by the Jews, it was called holy by the evangelist when he says, 'Many bodies of the saints that had fallen asleep were raised; and coming forth out of the tombs after His resurrection, they entered into the holy city and appeared unto many,' and by the prophet Isaiah when he says, 'It shall be His glorious sepulchre,' then, surely, with this sanctity placed upon it by God the Sanctifier Himself, no evil that may befall it can destroy it, and in the same way glory is indivisibly fixed to His Sepulchre. Most beloved brethren, if you reverence the source of that holiness and glory, if you cherish these shrines which are the marks of His foot-prints on earth, if you seek (the way), God leading you, God fighting in your behalf, you should strive with your utmost efforts to cleanse the Holy City and the glory of the Sepulchre, now polluted by the concourse of the Gentiles as much as is in their power.

"If in olden times the Maccabees attained to the highest praise of piety because they fought for the ceremonies and the Temple, it is also justly granted you, Christian soldiers, to defend the liberty of your country by armed endeavor. If you, likewise, consider that the abode of the holy apostles and any other saints should be striven for with such effort, why do you refuse to rescue the Cross, the Blood, the Tomb? Why do you refuse to visit them, to spend the price of your lives in rescuing them? You have thus far waged unjust wars, at one time and another; you have brandished mad weapons to your mutual destruction, for no other reason than covetousness and pride, as a result of which you have deserved eternal death and sure damnation. We now hold out to you wars which contain the glorious reward of martyrdom, which will retain that title of praise now and forever.

"Let us suppose, for the moment, that Christ was not dead and buried, and had never lived any length of time in Jerusalem. Surely, if all this were lacking, this fact alone ought still to arouse you to go to the aid of the land and city—the fact that 'Out of Zion shall go forth the law and the word of Jehovah from Jerusalem!' If all that there is of Christian preaching has flowed from the fountain of Jerusalem, its streams, whithersoever spread out over the whole world, encircle the hearts of the Catholic multitude, that they may consider wisely what they owe such a well-watered fountain. If rivers return to the place whence they have issued only to flow forth again, according to the saying of Solomon, it ought to seem glorious to you to be able to apply a new cleansing to this place, whence it is certain that you received the cleansing of baptism and the witness of your faith.

"And you ought, furthermore, to consider with the utmost deliberation, if by your labors, God working through you, it should occur that the Mother of churches should flourish anew to the worship of Christianity, whether, perchance, He may not wish other regions of the East to be restored to the faith against the approaching time of the Antichrist. For it is clear that Antichrist is to do battle not with the Jews, not with the Gentiles; but, according to the etymology of his name, he will attack Christians. And if Antichrist finds there no Christians (just as at present when scarcely any dwell there), no one will be there to oppose him, or whom he may rightly overcome. According to Daniel and Jerome, the interpreter of Daniel, he is to fix his tents on the Mount of Olives; and it is certain, for the apostle teaches it, that he will sit at Jerusalem in the Temple of the Lord, as though he were God. And according to the same prophet, he will first kill three kings of Egypt, Africa, and Ethiopia, without doubt for their Christian faith. This, indeed, could not at all be done unless Christianity was established where now is paganism. If, therefore, you are zealous in the practice of holy battles, in order that, just as you have received the seed of knowledge of God from Jerusalem, you may in the same way restore the borrowed grace, so that through you the Catholic name may be advanced to oppose the perfidy of the Antichrist and the Antichristians—then, who can not conjecture that God, who has exceeded the hope of all, will consume, in the abundance of your courage and through you as the spark, such a thicket of paganism as to include within His law Egypt, Africa, and Ethiopia, which have withdrawn from the communion of our belief? And the man of sin, the son of perdition, will find some to oppose him. Behold, the Gospel cries out, 'Jerusalem shall be trodden down by the Gentiles until the times of the Gentiles be fulfilled.' 'Times of the Gentiles' can be understood in two ways: Either that they have ruled over the Christians at their pleasure, and have gladly frequented the sloughs of all baseness for the satisfaction of their lusts, and in all this have had no obstacle (for they who have everything according to their wish are said to have their time; there is that saying: 'My time is not yet come, but your time is always ready,' whence the lustful are wont to say 'you are having your time'). Or, again, 'the times of the Gentiles' are the fulness of time for those Gentiles who shall have entered secretly before Israel shall be saved. These times, most beloved brothers, will now, forsooth, be fulfilled, provided the might of the pagans be repulsed through you, with the co-operation of God. With the end of the world already near, even though the Gentiles fail to be converted to the Lord (since according to the apostle there must be a withdrawal from the faith), it is first necessary, according to the prophecy, that the Christian sway be renewed in those regions, either through you, or others, whom it shall please God to send before the com-

ing of Antichrist, so that the head of all evil, who is to occupy there the throne of the kingdom, shall find some support of the faith to fight against him.

"Consider, therefore, that the Almighty has provided you, perhaps, for this purpose, that through you He may restore Jerusalem from such debasement. Ponder, I beg you, how full of joy and delight our hearts will be when we shall see the Holy City restored with your little help, and the prophet's, nay divine, words fulfilled in our times. Let your memory be moved by what the Lord Himself says to the Church: 'I will bring thy seed from the East and gather thee from the West.' God has already brought our seed from the East, since in a double way that region of the East has given the first beginnings of the Church to us. But from the West He will also gather it, provided He repairs the wrongs of Jerusalem through those who have begun the witness of the final faith, that is the people of the West. With God's assistance, we think this can be done through you.

"If neither the words of the Scriptures arouse you, nor our admonitions penetrate your minds, at least let the great suffering of those who desired to go to the holy places stir you up. Think of those who made the pilgrimage across the sea! Even if they were more wealthy, consider what taxes, what violence they underwent, since they were forced to make payments and tributes almost every mile, to purchase release at every gate of the city, at the entrance of the churches and temples, at every side-journey from place to place: also, if any accusation whatsoever were made against them, they were compelled to purchase their release; but if they refused to pay money, the prefects of the Gentiles, according to their custom, urged them fiercely with blows. What shall we say of those who took up the journey without anything more than trust in their barren poverty, since they seemed to have nothing except their bodies to lose? They not only demanded money of them, which is not an unendurable punishment, but also examined the calluses of their heels, cutting them open and folding the skin back, lest, perchance, they had sewed something there. Their unspeakable cruelty was carried on even to the point of giving them scammony to drink until they vomited, or even burst their bowels, because they thought the wretches had swallowed gold or silver; or, horrible to say, they cut their bowels open with a sword and, spreading out the folds of the intestines, with frightful mutilation disclosed whatever nature held therein secret. Remember, I pray, the thousands who have perished vile deaths, and strive for the holy places from which the beginnings of your faith have come. Before you engage in His battles, believe without question that Christ will be your standard-bearer and inseparable fore-runner."

Ibid., pp. 36-40.

D. Urban's Letter to the Assembling Crusaders, December, 1095

Urban, bishop, servant of the servants of God, to all the faithful, both princes and subjects, waiting in Flanders; greeting, apostolic grace, and blessing.

Your brotherhood, we believe, has long since learned from many accounts that a barbaric fury has deplorably afflicted and laid waste the churches of God in the regions of the Orient. More than this, blasphemous to say, it has even grasped in intolerable servitude its churches and the Holy City of Christ, glorified by His passion and resurrection. Grieving with pious concern at this calamity, we visited the regions of Gaul and devoted ourselves largely to urging the princes of the land and their subjects to free the churches of the East. We

The most excellent man concluded his oration and by the power of the blessed Peter absolved all who vowed to go and confirmed those acts with apostolic blessing. He instituted a sign well suited to so honorable a profession by making the figure of the Cross, the stigma of the Lord's Passion, the emblem of the soldiery, or rather, of what was to be the soldiery of God. This, made of any kind of cloth, he ordered to be sewed upon the shirts, cloaks, and *byrra* of those who were about to go. He commanded that if anyone, after receiving this emblem, or after taking openly this vow, should shrink from his good intent through base change of heart, or any affection for his parents, he should be regarded an outlaw forever, unless he repented and again undertook whatever of his pledge he had omitted. Furthermore, the Pope condemned with a fearful anathema all those who dared to molest the wives, children, and possessions of these who were going on this journey for God. . . .

solemnly enjoined upon them at the council of Auvergne (the accomplishment of) such an undertaking, as a preparation for the remission of all their sins. And we have constituted our most beloved son, Adhemar, Bishop of Puy, leader of this expedition and undertaking in our stead, so that those who, perchance, may wish to undertake this journey should comply with his commands, as if they were our own, and submit fully to his loosings or bindings, as far as shall seem to belong to such an office. If, moreover, there are any of your people whom God has inspired to this vow, let them know that he (Adhemar) will set out with the aid of God on the day of the Assumption of the Blessed Mary, and that they can then attach themselves to his following.

Ibid., pp. 42-43.

E. The Supposed Letter of Emperor Alexius I to the Count of Flanders

[Argument: This transcript of a letter was sent by the Constantinopolitan emperor, in the fourth year before the glorious Jerusalem expedition, to all Occidental churches, but especially to the Flemish count Robert. The said count, however, had by this time returned in staff and wallet from the Lord's Sepulcher, on which journey they had seen one another and had affable and friendly discourse. The said emperor, indeed, as he himself complains in this letter, had been exceedingly oppressed by an execrable pagan people whose ruler was the elder Soliman, father of the younger Soliman, whom our men afterwards, as that book mentions, defeated in martial conflict, forcing him basely to flee. Hence we marvel not a little why the oft-mentioned emperor has been always so venomous in spirit toward our men, and not feared to return evil for good. —The argument ends; the letter begins:]

To Robert, lord and glorious count of the Flemings, and to all the princes in the entire realm, lovers of the Christian faith, laymen as well as clerics, the Constantinopolitan emperor [extends] greeting and peace in our same Lord Jesus Christ and His Father and the Holy Spirit.

O most illustrious count and especial comforter of the Christian faith! I wish to make known to your prudence how the most sacred empire of the Greek Christians is being sorely distressed by the Patzinaks and the Turks, who daily ravage it and unintermittently seize [its territory]; and there is promiscuous slaughter and indescribable killing and derision of the Christians. But since the evil things they do are many and, as we have said, indescribable, we will mention but a few of the many, which nevertheless are horrible to hear and disturb even the air itself. For they circumcise the boys and youths of the Christians over the Christian baptismal fonts, and in contempt of Christ they pour the blood from the circumcision into the said baptismal fonts and contrive still further desecrations; and thereafter they violently drag them around in the church, compelling them to blaspheme the name of the Holy Trinity and the belief therein. But those who refuse to do these things they punish in diverse ways and ultimately they kill them. Noble matrons and their daughters whom they have robbed [of their possessions] they, one after another like animals, defile in adultery. Some, indeed, in their corrupting shamelessly place virgins before the faces of their mothers and compel them to sing wicked and obscene songs, until they have finished their own wicked acts. Thus, we read, it was done also against God's people in antiquity, to whom the impious Babylonians, after making sport of them in diverse ways, said: "Sing us one of the songs of Zion." Likewise, at the dishonoring of their daughters, the mothers are in turn compelled to sing wicked songs, [though] their voices sound forth not a song but rather, we believe, a plaint, as it is written concerning the death of the Innocents: "A voice was heard in Ramah, Weeping and great mourning, Rachel weeping for her children; and she would not be comforted, because they are not." However, even if the mothers of the Innocents, who are figured by Rachel, could not be comforted for the death of their children, yet they could derive comfort from the salvation of their souls; but these [mothers] are in worse plight, for they cannot be comforted at all, because they perish in both body and soul. But what further? Let us come to matters of greater depravity. Men of every age and order—i.e., boys, adolescents, youths, old men, nobles, serfs, and what is worse and more shameless, clergymen and monks, and, alas and alack, what from the beginning has never been said or heard, bishops!—they defile with the worst of sins and now they are also trumpeting abroad that one bishop has succumbed to this abominable sin. The holy places they desecrate and destroy in numberless ways, and they threaten them with worse treatment. And who does not lament over these things? Who has not compassion? Who is not horrified? Who does not pray? For almost the entire land from Jerusalem to Greece, and the whole of Greece with its upper regions, which are Cappadocia Minor, Cappadocia Major, Phrygia, Bithynia, Lesser Phrygia (*i.e.*, the Troad), Pontus, Galatia, Lydia, Pamphylia, Isauria, Lycia, and the principal islands Chios and Mytilene, and many other regions and islands which we cannot even enumerate, as far as Thrace, have already been invaded by them, and now almost nothing remains except Constantinople, which they are threatening to snatch away from us very soon, unless the aid of God and the faithful Latin Christians should reach us speedily. For even the Propontis, which is also called the Avidus and which flows out of the Pontus near Constantinople into the Great Sea, they have invaded with two hundred ships, which Greeks robbed by them had built; and they are launching them with their rowers, willy-nilly, and they are threatening, as we have said, speedily to capture Constantinople by land as well as by way of the Propontis. These few among the innumerable evil things which this most impious people is doing we have mentioned and written to you, count of the Flemings, lover of the Christian faith! The rest, indeed, let us omit, in order not to disgust the readers. Accordingly, for love of God and out of sympathy for all Christian Greeks, we beg that you lead hither to my aid and that of the Christian Greeks whatever faithful warriors of Christ you may be able to enlist in your land—those of major as well as those of minor and middle condition; and as they in the past year liberated Galicia and other kingdoms of the Westerners somewhat from the yoke of the pagans, so also may they now, for the salvation of their souls, endeavor to liberate the kingdom of the Greeks; since I, albeit I am emperor, can find no remedy or suitable counsel, but am always fleeing from the face of the Turks and the Patzinaks; and I remain in a particular city only until I perceive that their arrival is imminent. And I think it is better to be subjected to your Latins than to the abominations of the pagans. Therefore, before Constantinople is captured by them, you most certainly ought to fight with all your strength so that you may joyfully receive in heaven a glorious and ineffable reward. For it is better that you should have Constantinople than the pagans, because in that [city] are the most precious relics of the Lord, to wit: the pillar to which He was bound; the lash with which He was scourged; the scarlet robe in which He was arrayed; the crown of thorns with which He was crowned; the reed He held in his hands, in place of a scepter; the garments of which He was despoiled before the cross; the larger part of the wood of the cross on which He was crucified; the nails with which He was affixed; the linen cloths found in the sepulcher after His resurrection; the twelve baskets of remnants from the five loaves and the two fishes; the entire head of St. John the Baptist with the hair and the beard; the relics or bodies of many of the Innocents, of certain prophets and apostles, of martyrs and, especially, of the protomartyr St. Stephen, and of confessors and virgins, these latter being of such great number that we have omitted writing about each of them individually. Yet, all the aforesaid the Christians rather than the pagans ought to possess; and it will be a great muniment for all Christians if they retain possession of all these, but it will be to their detriment and doom if they should lose them. However, if they should be unwilling to fight for the sake of these relics, and if their love of gold is greater, they will find more of it there than in all the world; for the treasure-vaults of the churches of Constantinople abound in silver, gold, gems and precious stones, and silken garments, i.e., vestments, which could suffice for all the churches in the world; but the inestimable treasure of the mother church, namely St. Sophia, i.e., the Wisdom of God, surpasses the treasures of all other churches and, without doubt, equals the treasures of the temple of Solomon. Again, what shall I say of the infinite treasures of the nobles, when no one can estimate the treasure of the common merchants? What is contained in the treasures of the former emperors? I say for certain that no tongue can tell it; because not only the treasure of the Constantinopolitan emperors is there contained, but the treasure of all the ancient Roman emperors has been brought thither and hidden in the palaces. What more shall I say? Certainly, what is exposed to men's eyes is as nothing compared with that which lies hidden. Hasten, therefore, with your entire people and fight with all your strength, lest such treasure fall into the hands of the Turks and the Patzinaks; because, while they are infinite, just now sixty thousand are daily expected, and I fear that by means of this treasure they gradually will seduce our covetous soldiers, as did formerly Julius Caesar who by reason of avarice invaded the kingdom of the Franks, and as Antichrist will do at the end of the world after he has captured the whole earth. Therefore, lest you should lose the kingdom of the Christians and, what is greater, the Lord's Sepulcher, act while you still have time; and then you will have not doom, but a reward in heaven. Amen.

Einar Joranson, "The Problem of the Spurious Letter of Emperor Alexius to the Count of Flanders," *American Historical Review,* LV (1950), 812-815. (The translation is Joranson's.)

F. Anna Comnena on the First Crusade

Before he had enjoyed even a short rest, he [the Emperor Alexius] heard a report of the approach of innumerable Frankish armies. Now he dreaded their arrival for he knew their irresistible manner of attack, their unstable and mobile character and all the peculiar natural and concomitant characteristics which the Frank retains throughout; and he also knew that they were always agape for money, and seemed to disregard their truces readily for any reason that cropped up. For he had always heard this reported of them, and found it very true. However, he did not lose heart, but prepared himself in every way so that, when the occasion called, he would be ready for battle. And indeed the actual facts were far greater and more terrible than rumour made them. For the whole of the West and all the barbarian tribes which dwell between the further side of the Adriatic and the pillars of Heracles, had all migrated in a body and were marching into Asia through the intervening Europe, and were making the journey with all their household. The reason of this upheaval was more or less the following. A certain Frank, Peter by name, nicknamed Cucupeter,[1] had gone to worship

---

[1] Peter of the Cowl.

at the Holy Sepulchre and after suffering many things at the hands of the
Turks and Saracens who were ravaging
Asia, he got back to his own country
with difficulty. But he was angry at
having failed in his object, and wanted
to undertake the same journey again.
However, he saw that he ought not to
make the journey to the Holy Sepulchre
alone again, lest worse things befall him,
so he worked out a cunning plan. This
was to preach in all the Latin countries
that "the voice of God bids me announce
to all the counts in France that they
should all leave their homes and set out
to worship at the Holy Sepulchre, and
to endeavor whole-heartedly with hand
and mind to deliver Jerusalem from the
hand of the Hagarenes." And he really
succeeded. For after inspiring the souls
of all with this quasi-divine command
he contrived to assemble the Franks
from all sides, one after the other, with
arms, horses and all the other parapher-
nalia of war. And they were all so zealous and eager that every highroad was
full of them. And those Frankish soldiers were accompanied by an unarmed
host more numerous than the sand or
the stars, carrying palms and crosses on
their shoulders; women and children,
too, came away from their countries.
And the sight of them was like many
rivers streaming from all sides, and they
were advancing towards us through
Dacia generally with all their hosts. . . .

The incidents of the barbarians' approach followed in the order I have
described, and persons of intelligence
could feel that they were witnessing a
strange occurrence. The arrival of these
multitudes did not take place at the
same time nor by the same road (for
how indeed could such masses starting
from different places have crossed the
straits of Lombardy all together?).
Some first, some next, others after them
and thus successively all accomplished
the transit, and then marched through

the continent. Each army was preceded, as we said, by an unspeakable
number of locusts; and all who saw this
more than once recognized them as fore-
runners of the Frankish armies. When
the first of them began crossing the
straits of Lombardy sporadically the
Emperor summoned certain leaders of
the Roman forces, and sent them to the
ports of Dyrrachium and Valona with
instructions to offer a courteous welcome
to the Franks who had crossed, and to
collect abundant supplies from all the
countries along their route; then to follow and watch them covertly all the
time, and if they saw them making any
foraging-excursions, they were to come
out from under cover and check them
by light skirmishing. These captains
were accompanied by some men who
knew the Latin tongue, so that they
might settle any disputes that arose between them.

Let me, however, give an account of
this subject more clearly and in due
order. According to universal rumour
Godfrey, who had sold his country, was
the first to start on the appointed road;
this man was very rich and very proud
of his bravery, courage and conspicuous
lineage; for every Frank is anxious to
outdo the others. And such an upheaval of both men and women took
place then as had never occurred within
human memory, the simpler-minded
were urged on by the real desire of
worshipping at our Lord's Sepulchre,
and visiting the sacred places; but the
more astute, especially men like Bohemund and those of like mind, had another secret reason, namely, the hope
that while on their travels they might
by some means be able to seize the
capital itself, looking upon this as a
kind of corollary. And Bohemund disturbed the minds of many nobler men
by thus cherishing his old grudge against
the Emperor. Meanwhile Peter, after
he had delivered his message, crossed

the straits of Lombardy before anybody else with eighty thousand men on foot, and one hundred thousand on horseback, and reached the capital by way of Hungary. For the Frankish race, as one may conjecture, is always very hotheaded and eager, but when once it has espoused a cause, it is uncontrollable.

The Alexiad of the Princess Anna Comnena, trans. Elizabeth A. S. Dawes (London: Kegan Paul, Trench, Trubner & Co., 1928), pp. 248-250.

G. Skutariotes on the Rôle of the Emperor Alexius in the Origin of the First Crusade

Skutariotes writes that Alexius was ready to take the offensive against the Turks and continues:

Having considered, therefore, that it was impossible for him alone to undertake the battle on which everything depended, he recognized that he would have to call on the Italians as allies and he effected this with considerable cunning, adroitness and deeply laid planning. For finding a pretext in the fact that this nation considered unbearable the domination of Jerusalem and the life-giving Sepulchre of Our Saviour Jesus Christ by the Persians [the Turks are meant] and seeing therein a heaven-sent opportunity, he managed, by dispatching ambassadors to the bishop of Old Rome and to those whom they call kings and rulers of those parts [*i.e.*, the West], and by the use of appropriate arguments, to prevail over not a few of them to leave their country and succeeded in directing them in every way to the task. That is the reason why many of them, numbering thousands and tens of thousands, having crossed the Ionian Sea, reached Constantinople with all speed. And, having exchanged assurances and oaths with them, he advanced towards the east. With the aid of God and their alliance and by his own efforts he speedily expelled the Persians from Roman territories, liberated the cities and restored his sway in the East to its former glory. Such was this emperor: great in the conception of plans and the doing of deeds.

Peter Charanis, "A Greek Source on the Origin of the First Crusade," *Speculum*, XXIV (1949), 93. (Trans. Peter Charanis.)

II. THE SECULARIZATION OF THE CRUSADES AND THE ANTAGONISM BETWEEN GREEKS AND LATINS

The First Crusade was a military success. The crusading armies had met at Constantinople whence, following an understanding with the Byzantine emperor, they began their march through Asia Minor. This was in late April, 1097; in little more than two years the expedition reached its military goal. On July 15, 1099, Jerusalem fell into the hands of the crusaders.

The conquered territories in Syria and Palestine were organized into feudal principalities under the general suzerainty of the king of Jerusalem, himself one of the leaders of the crusade. These states, planted in a hostile world, loosely organized and often fighting against each other, required constant reinforcements from the West. The Moslems, who never accepted the loss of these territories, were a continuous threat, and the Byzantines were not friendly. The reason for the enmity of the Byzantines was the principality of Antioch. Up to 1085 Antioch had belonged to the Byzantine Empire and, as the leaders of the crusade while in Constantinople had promised to restore to the Empire whatever territories had belonged to it, the Byzantines had expected that Antioch would be returned to them. But Antioch was not returned; instead, it was granted to Bohemond, leader of the Norman contingent of southern Italy, who had previously campaigned against the Byzantine Empire. The Byzantines refused to accept this and sought to regain Antioch by force. Bohemond and his successors fought back and also carried on, at times with the open support of the papacy, intensive propaganda against Byzantium in the West. Thus developed the feeling in the West that, as the Greeks were treacherous, the way to prevent them from injuring the Latins, was to destroy their Empire. The Greeks in the meantime came to look upon the crusading expeditions as really aiming at their Empire. These sentiments manifested themselves in connection with the Second Crusade (1147–1149) and raised the question of the secularization of the crusading movement. Two passages, one taken from the work of Odo of Deuil, the chaplain of the French King Louis VII, whom he accompanied to the East in connection with the Second Crusade, and the other, from the Byzantine historian, John Cinnamus, also a contemporary, will introduce the reader to this problem. Both of these passages have been reproduced.

The antipathy and distrust between Greeks and Latins shown by these passages increased as the twelfth century progressed and led to violence and bloodshed, which in turn widened the chasm between the two peoples. Two incidents in particular stand out in this development: the massacre of the Latins in Constantinople in 1182 and the sack of Thessalonica by the Normans of southern Italy in 1185. The two passages which have been chosen to introduce the student to this problem are taken from the Latin historian William of Tyre, a native of the kingdom of Jerusalem, who finished about the year 1183 a general history of the crusades and the kingdom of Jerusalem, and from the Byzantine historian Nicetas Choniates, whose great history, covering the period from 1118 to 1206, was completed before 1210. The first describes the massacre of the Latins in 1182; the second gives the reaction of the Greeks to the sack of Thessalonica in 1185.

A. Odo of Deuil on the French Attitude toward Constantinople during the Second Crusade

Although the Greeks furnished us no proof that they were treacherous, I believe that they would not have exhibited such unremitting servitude if they had had good intentions. Actually, they were concealing the wrongs which were to be avenged after we crossed the Arm [*i.e.*, the Bosporus]. . . .

Distrusting their pledge, scorning their favors, and foretelling the injuries which we afterwards endured, the bishop of Langres, however, urged us to take the city. He proved that the walls, a great part of which collapsed before our eyes, were weak, that the people were inert, that by cutting the conduits the fresh water supply could be withdrawn without delay or effort. He, a man of wise intellect and saintly piety, said that if that city were taken it would not be necessary to conquer the others, since they would yield obedience voluntarily to him who possessed their capital. He added further that Constantinople is Christian only in name, not in fact, and, whereas for her part she should not prevent others from bringing aid to Christians, her emperor had ventured a few years previously to attack the prince of Antioch. He said: "First he took Tarsus and Mamistra and numerous strongholds and a broad expanse of land, and, after expelling the Catholic bishops in the cities and replacing them with heretics, he besieged Antioch. And although it was his duty to ward off the nearby infidels by uniting the Christian forces, with the aid of the infidels he strove to destroy the Christians. Nevertheless, God, who knows, judges, and avenges such things as these, willed that he should wound himself with a poisoned arrow and end his shameful life as the result of that slight wound. However, just as the present ruler, the heir of that lamentable crime, keeps for himself the ecclesiastical domains and other property which his father acquired by wickedness, just so he gazes longingly at the rest of the territory which his father wanted and already has exacted the prince's homage and, setting up one altar against another, has established his own patriarch in the city, scorning Peter's patriarch. Let it be your decision whether you ought to spare the man under whose rule the cross and sepulcher of Christ are not at all safe and after whose destruction nothing would be hostile to them."

When the bishop had finished speaking, his remarks found favor with some. Many with whom he did not find favor, however, replied with words such as the following: "Without knowledge of the law we cannot judge about their good faith. The fact that he attacked Antioch was evil, but he could have had justifiable reasons which we do not know. It is certainly true that the king recently conferred with the pope and that he was not given any advice or command concerning this point. He knows, and we know, that we are to visit the Holy Sepulcher and, by the command of the supreme pontiff, to wipe out our sins with the blood or the conversion of the infidels. At this time we can attack the richest of the Christian cities and enrich ourselves, but in so doing we must kill and be killed. And so, if slaughtering Christians wipes out our sins, let us fight. Again, if harboring ambition does not sully our death, if on this journey it is as important to die for the sake of gaining money as it is to maintain our vow and our obedience to the supreme pontiff, then wealth is welcome; let us expose ourselves to danger without fear of death."

Such was their contention, and the supporters of each side defended themselves ably. Nevertheless, I believe that the bishop would have won out if the Greeks had not gained the upper hand more by treachery than by force.

Odo of Deuil, *De profectione Ludovici VII in orientem,* ed. and trans. by Virginia Gingerick Berry (New York: Columbia University Press, 1948), pp. 67, 69-73.

B. John Cinnamus on the Second Crusade

And now began the problem of the West. For the Germans and the Franks, the nation of the Gauls and all the peoples who dwell around old Rome, the Brittii and the Brittani and generally the entire force of the West put themselves on the move. Their pretext was that they were going to cross over into Asia from Europe, fight the Turks whom they encountered, get possession of the temple in Palestine and view the Holy Places. Their real reason, however, was to occupy at the first assault the land of the Romans [*i.e.,* Byzantines] and plunder everything in sight. Their army was beyond number. When the emperor had learned that they had arrived very near the Hungarian border he sent ambassadors to them, Demetrius Macrembolites and Alexander, an Italian by descent who had come over to the emperor because, as a count of the Italian city of Gravina, he had been divested of his office . . . by the tyrant of Sicily. He ordered them to make proof of the intentions of the [Westerners] and if they had not come to do injury to the Romans, to confirm this matter by oath. When the ambassadors came to the leaders of these barbarians, they spoke as follows: "The waging of undeclared war against those who have done no wrong is neither just nor in other respects proper especially for men who claim to be of splendid lineage and to possess overwhelming power. For when they are victorious, should this happen, their victory is not won with valor, and when they are defeated, they are judged to have run risks not for virtue. Neither the one nor the other of these things is praiseworthy. As for you, you will not be permitted at all to pass over the land of the Romans before you have given pledges to the emperor that you will do no harm. And so, unless you intend to swear falsely, why do you not wage war openly? For to attack the Romans straightway will indeed be dangerous for you, but to carry the war against them with perjury will be much more so, since you will have to fight against God and the might of the Romans. But if in truth you are friendly and have no design of deceit, then confirm the matter by oath. You will then be permitted out of friend-ship to go through the land of the great emperor and will get a reception as is proper and other kindness." The ambassadors said these things and they, gathering in the tent of Conrad, the king of the Germans, for he held the place of pre-eminence among the nations of the West, said that they had not come to do any injury to the Romans and that, if it were necessary to confirm this by oath, they were disposed to do so most readily. Their expedition was directed to Palestine and against the Turks who were plundering Asia. As this was acceptable to the Romans, they put their words into deed.

John Cinnamus, *Historia* (Bonn, 1836), pp. 67-68, trans. Peter Charanis.

C. William of Tyre on the Massacre of the Latins in Constantinople in 1182

While these events were taking place in our part of the Orient, an important change occurred in the empire of Constantinople. This resulted most unfortunately for the entire Latin race and brought upon them unheard-of affronts and enormous loss. For the evils long since conceived by false and perfidious Greece travailed and "brought forth falsehood." For on the death of Manuel, that most happy emperor of illustrious memory, his son Alexius, a boy scarcely thirteen years old, succeeded to the throne, both by his father's will and by hereditary right. He was under his mother's guardianship, however, and the affairs of the empire were administered by Alexius, the *protosebastos,* son of the elder brother of the dead emperor. The principal nobles and the people of that city accordingly felt that an opportunity had come to carry into effect the evil designs which they had formed against our people.

During the reign of Manuel, beloved of God, the Latins had found great favor with him—a reward well deserved because of their loyalty and valor. The emperor, a great-souled man of incomparable energy, relied so implicitly on their fidelity and ability that he passed over the Greeks as soft and effeminate and intrusted important affairs to the Latins alone. Since he held them in such high esteem and showed toward them such lavish generosity, men of the Latin race from all over the world, nobles and men of lesser degree as well, regarded him as their great benefactor and eagerly flocked to his court. As the result of this eager deference, his affection toward the Latins increased more and more, and he was constantly improving their status.

The Greek nobles, especially the near kindred of the emperor, and the rest of the people as well, naturally conceived an insatiable hatred toward us, and this was increased by the difference between our sacraments and those of their church, which furnished an additional incentive to their jealousy. For they, having separated insolently from the church of Rome, in their boundless arrogance looked upon everyone who did not follow their foolish traditions as a heretic. It was they themselves, on the contrary, who deserved the name of heretics, because they had either created or followed new and pernicious beliefs contrary to the Roman church and the faith of the apostles Peter and Paul against which "the gates of hell shall not prevail."

For these and other reasons they had for a long time cherished this hatred in their hearts and were ever seeking an opportunity, at least after the death of the emperor, to destroy utterly the hated race of the Latins, both in the city and throughout the entire empire, that in this way they might satisfy their inexorable animosity.

. . . They summoned Andronicus the Elder, a cousin of the late emperor, from Pontus, where he was ruling, that he might assist them in their wicked plot to drive Alexius, the *protosebastos*, from the control of affairs in the realm. . . .

Thus summoned, Andronicus came to the city bringing with him large forces of barbarian troops. He encamped along the Hellespont in full sight of the city and took possession of all Bithynia. Certain powerful nobles who had been sent against him to resist his attempts traitorously deserted to his side. First and most important among these were Andronicus Angelus, commander of the troops which had been dispatched against him, and Alexius Megalducas, commander in chief of the fleet, both kinsmen of the emperor. The desertion of those who had gone over to Andronicus thus openly weakened the cause of our people greatly as did also the fact that many other notable men and a great many citizens as well showed their partisanship for Andronicus no longer secretly but in public. They longed to see him enter the city and in every possible way helped to hasten the time of his crossing.

The conspiracy continued to gain strength; the *protosebastos* was seized, blinded, and horribly mutilated. This change of affairs spread consternation among the Latins, for they feared that the citizens would make a sudden attack upon them; in fact they had already received warning of such intention from certain people who had private knowledge of the conspiracy. Those who were able to do so, therefore, fled from the wiles of the Greeks and the death which threatened them. Some embarked on forty-four galleys which chanced to be in the harbor, and others placed all their effects on some of the many other ships there.

The aged and infirm, however, with those who were unable to flee, were left in their homes, and on them fell the wicked rage which the others had escaped. For Andronicus, who had secretly caused ships to be prepared, led his entire force into the city. As soon as they entered the gates these troops, aided by the citizens, rushed to that quarter of the city occupied by the Latins and put to the sword the little remnant who had been either unwilling or unable to flee with the others. Although but few of these were able to fight, yet they resisted for a long time and made the enemy's victory a bloody one.

Regardless of treaties and the many services which our people had rendered to the empire, the Greeks seized all those who appeared capable of resistance, set fire to their houses, and speedily reduced the entire quarter to ashes. Women and children, the aged and the sick, all alike perished in the flames. To vent their rage upon secular buildings alone, however, was far from satisfying their unholy wickedness; they also set fire to churches and venerated places of every description and burned, together with the sacred edifices, those who had fled thither for refuge. No distinction was made between clergy and laymen, except that greater fury was displayed toward those who wore the honorable habits of high office or religion. Monks and priests were the especial victims of their madness and were put to death under excruciating torture.

Among these latter was a venerable man named John, a sub-deacon of the holy Roman church, whom the pope had sent to Constantinople on business relating to the church. They seized him and, cutting off his head, fastened it to the tail of a filthy dog as an insult to the church. In the midst of such frightful sacrilege, worse than parricide, not even the dead, whom impiety itself generally spares, were suffered to rest undisturbed. Corpses were torn from the tombs and dragged through the streets and squares as if the insensate bodies were capable of feeling the indignities offered them.

The vandals then repaired to the hospital of St. John, as it is called, where they put to the sword all the sick they found. Those whose pious duty it should have been to relieve the oppressed, namely the monks and priests, called in footpads and brigands to carry on the slaughter under promise of reward. Accompanied by these miscreants, they sought out the most secluded retreats and the inmost apartments of homes, that none who were hiding there might escape death. When such were discovered, they were dragged out with violence and handed over to the executioners, who, that they might not work without pay, were given the price of blood for the murder of these wretched victims.

Even those who seemed to show more consideration sold into perpetual slavery among the Turks and other infidels the fugitives who had resorted to them and to whom they had given hope of safety. It is said that more than four thousand Latins of various age, sex, and condition were delivered thus to barbarous nations for a price.

In such fashion did the perfidious Greek nation, a brood of vipers, like a serpent in the bosom or a mouse in the wardrobe evilly requite their guests—those who had not deserved such treatment and were far from anticipating anything of the kind; those to whom they had given their daughters, nieces, and sisters as wives and who, by long living together, had become their friends.

William of Tyre, *A History of Deeds Done Beyond the Sea,* trans. Emily Atwater Babcock and August C. Krey (New York: Columbia University Press, 1943), II, 461-465.

D. Nicetas Choniates on the Capture of Thessalonica by the Normans in 1185

Thus the city of Thessalonica, having held out for a short while, fell . . . into the hands of the enemy. Its fall was followed by an endless array of woes surpassing those of tragedy. Every house was abandoned. No building, no alley, no cave could offer safety from the hands of the murderers. The humblest prayers, the most subdued gestures were not able to give rise to pity. Everything was treated by the sword. And only the blows which carried away lives could check the furor of the soldiers. Churches offered no asylum and the protection of the images of the saints was of no avail. For the barbarians, confounding things divine and human, were not awed so as to respect the deity and offered no asylum to those who had fled to the churches. When they spared a life and satisfied themselves by taking the goods, they felt that they were doing a favor. But this too befell those who had fled to the churches: they were stifled to death by the congestions caused by the enormous crowds that sought refuge there. The barbarians carried their violence to the altars, massacring the conquered as if they were victims. For, as they took no heed of God and insulted the divine objects, how could they be expected to spare human beings? They plundered the sacred offerings, laid defiled hands and shameless eyes on things forbidden to be touched and seen. This was strange, indeed, but stranger still were the unholy acts which they committed against the sacred images of Christ and the saints. These they knocked down to the ground, trampled them with their feet, tore off in whatever manner they could their precious decorations and threw the rest on the crossroads to be trodden by the passers-by, or used them as fuel to cook their food. But the most profane and ill-sounding to the ear of the faithful was this, that some of them climbed upon the altars . . . and danced thereon singing obscene native barbarian songs. Then they exposed their shameful parts and sprinkled the holy places with their urine. . . . Finally the chiefs intervened and put a stop to all this.

But this was not the end of the calamities for the people of Thessalonica. For although the killing had stopped the day after the city was captured, those who escaped were oppressed with so many afflictions that they were driven to death preferring that to life. . . . Now, others, too, when victors in war, treat the vanquished with abuse and no pity and in such other ways as the arrogance of victory may inspire. But the Latins, when they have vanquished

and subjugated their adversaries, become an unbearable and indescribable evil. When their captive is a Roman who is not dressed like them and does not speak their language, they consider him an enemy of God who must drink the entire chalice of His wrath. For Latin inhumanity in its outrages against captives is like the ferocity of a viper, or a lion or a dragon when they fall upon their prey. It does not yield to either prayers or tears and is not brightened by wheedling words. . . . It is deaf to harmony and song and if charmed for the moment it soon goes back to its natural state. . . .

There is no nation which gives itself so naturally to wrath as that of the Latins. Their hatred for the Romans surpasses even that which that ancient serpent, the plotter against mankind, had conceived and spewed out long ago. The land on which we dwell and enjoy the fruit thereof these most accursed Latins compare to Paradise and the desire with which they burn to possess it ever makes them ill-disposed toward our race and architects of evil for it. They hate as the bitterest enemies even when under the necessity of the moment they pretend friendship. Their speech, even if courteous and gentle, conceals in it javelins and double-edge daggers. Between them and us a bottomless gulf of enmity has established itself; we cannot unite our souls and we entirely disagree with each other, although we keep up our external relations and often live in the same house.

Nicetas Choniates, *Historia* (Bonn, 1835), pp. 387-392, trans. Peter Charanis.

III. THE PROBLEM OF THE DIVERSION OF THE FOURTH CRUSADE

What made the chasm which had come to separate Greeks and Latins virtually unbridgeable was the Fourth Crusade (1202–1204). This expedition was to go by sea and its ultimate objective was Egypt. The crusaders, however, did not see Egypt; in-

stead they captured Constantinople and partitioned the Byzantine Empire.

Was the capture of Constantinople by the Fourth Crusade the fortuitous result of a series of events or was it deliberately planned? Historians still disagree as to the answer. To introduce the student to this problem we have chosen three important contemporary texts. One is the account of Geoffrey of Villehardouin. The other is taken from the work of Robert of Clari, and the third from the Byzantine historian Nicetas Choniates. Villehardouin was one of the chief leaders of the Fourth Crusade, and participated in the making of the important decisions. Robert was a simple knight, but he was a participant of the expedition and does not seem to be uninformed. Nicetas was a Byzantine functionary who was well acquainted with the problems which existed in the relations between Byzantium and the West, particularly Venice. The student should remember that Venice, which had obtained important commercial privileges in the Byzantine Empire, was disturbed by recent attempts of the Byzantine emperors to curtail these privileges. She resented, in particular, the granting of similar privileges to her commercial rivals, Pisa and Genoa. He should remember also that Boniface of Montferrat, the military commander of the expedition, had important connections in Byzantium and, as a consequence, he may have had personal political ambitions. We have also included two passages from modern scholars to illustrate the divergent views to which the problem of the diversion of the Fourth Crusade has given rise.

A. *Villehardouin on the Diversion of the Fourth Crusade*

Now give ear to one of the greatest marvels, and most wonderful adventures that you have ever heard tell of. At that time there was an emperor in Constantinople, whose name was Isaac, and he had a brother, Alexius by name, whom he had ransomed from captivity among the Turks. This Alexius took his brother the emperor, tore the eyes out of his head, and made himself emperor by the aforesaid treachery. He kept Isaac a long time in prison, together with a son whose name was Alexius. This son escaped from prison, and fled in a ship to a city on the sea, which is called Ancona. Thence he departed to go to King Philip of Germany,

who had his sister for wife; and he came to Verona in Lombardy, and lodged in the town, and found there a number of pilgrims and other people who were on their way to join the host.

And those who had helped him to escape, and were with him, said: "Sire, here is an army in Venice, quite near to us, the best and most valiant people and knights that are in the world, and they are going oversea. Cry to them therefore for mercy, that they have pity on thee and on thy father, who have been so wrongfully dispossessed. And if they be willing to help thee, thou shalt be guided by them. Perchance they will take pity on thy estate." And Alexius said he would do this right willingly, and that the advice was good.

Thus he appointed envoys, and sent them to the Marquis Boniface of Montferrat, who was chief of the host, and to the other barons. And when the barons saw them, they marvelled greatly, and said to the envoys: "We understand right well what you tell us. We will send an envoy with the prince to King Philip, whither he is going. If the prince will help to recover the land oversea, we will help him to recover his own land, for we know that it has been wrested from him and from his father wrongfully." So were envoys sent into Germany, both to the heir of Constantinople and to King Philip of Germany. . . .

A fortnight after came to Zara the Marquis Boniface of Montferrat, who had not yet joined, and Matthew of Montmorency, and Peter of Bracieux, and many another man of note. And after another fortnight came also the envoys from Germany, sent by King Philip and the heir of Constantinople. Then the barons, and the Doge of Venice assembled in a palace where the Doge was lodged. And the envoys addressed them and said: "Lords, King Philip sends us to you, as does also the brother of the king's wife, the son of the Emperor of Constantinople.

" 'Lords,' says the king, 'I will send you the brother of my wife; and I commit him into the hands of God—may He keep him from death!—and into your hands. And because you have fared forth for God, and for right, and for justice, therefore you are bound, in so far as you are able, to restore to their own inheritance those who have been unrighteously despoiled. And my wife's brother will make with you the best terms ever offered to any people, and give you the most puissant help for the recovery of the land oversea.

" 'And first, if God grant that you restore him to his inheritance, he will place the whole empire of Romania in obedience to Rome, from which it has long been separated. Further, he knows that you have spent of your substance, and that you are poor, and he will give you 200,000 marks of silver, and food for all those of the host, both small and great. And he, of his own person, will go with you into the land of Babylon, or, if you hold that that will be better, send thither 10,000 men, at his own charges. And this service he will perform for one year. And all the days of his life he will maintain, at his own charges, five hundred knights in the land oversea, to guard that land.'

"Lords, we have full power," said the envoys, "to conclude this agreement, if you are willing to conclude it on your parts. And be it known to you, that so favourable an agreement has never before been offered to any one; and that he that would refuse it can have but small desire of glory and conquest."

The barons and the Doge said they would talk this over; and a parliament was called for the morrow. When all were assembled, the matter was laid before them.

Then arose much debate. The abbot of Vaux, of the order of the Cistercians,

spoke, and that party that wished for the dispersal of the host; and they said they would never consent: that it was not to fall on Christians that they had left their homes, and that they would go to Syria.

And the other party replied: "Fair lords, in Syria you will be able to do nothing; and that you may right well perceive by considering how those have fared who abandoned us, and sailed from other ports. And be it known to you that it is only by way of [Egypt] or of Greece, that the land oversea can be recovered, if so be that it ever is recovered. And if we reject this covenant we shall be shamed for all time."

There was discord in the host, as you hear. Nor need you be surprised if there was discord among the laymen, for the white monks of the order of Citeaux were also at issue among themselves in the host. The abbot of Loos, who was a holy man and a man of note, and other abbots who held with him, prayed and besought the people, for pity's sake, and the sake of God, to keep the host together, and agree to the proposed convention, in that "it afforded the best means by which the land oversea might be recovered;" while the abbot of Vaux, on the other hand, and those who held with him, preached full oft, and declared that all this was naught, and that the host ought to go to the land of Syria, and there do what they could.

Then came the Marquis of Montferrat, and Baldwin Count of Flanders and Hainault, and Count Louis, and Count Hugh of St. Pol, and those who held with them, and they declared that they would enter into the proposed covenant, for that they should be shamed if they refused. So they went to the Doge's hostel, and the envoys were summoned, and the covenant, in such terms as you have already heard, was confirmed by oath, and by charters with seals appended.

And the book tells you that only twelve persons took the oaths on the side of the Franks, for more (of sufficient note) could not be found. Among the twelve were first the Marquis of Montferrat, the Count Baldwin of Flanders, the Count Louis of Blois and of Chartres, and the Count of St. Pol, and eight others who held with them. Thus was the agreement made, and the charters prepared, and a term fixed for the arrival of the heir of Constantinople; and the term so fixed was the fifteenth day after the following Easter.

Memoirs of the Crusades by Villehardouin and De Joinville, trans. Sir Frank Marzials (New York: Everyman's Library, E. P. Dutton & Company, and J. M. Dent and Sons, Ltd., 1933), pp. 17-18, 22-24.

B. Robert of Clari on the Diversion of the Fourth Crusade

In the meantime, while the crusaders and the Venetians were staying there that winter, the crusaders bethought them that they had spent a great deal. And they talked with one another and said that they could not go to [Cairo] or to Alexandria or to Syria, because they had neither provisions nor money for going there. For they had spent nearly everything, on the long delay they had made as well as on the great price they had given for the hire of the fleet. So they said they could not go, and if they went they would not be able to do anything, because they had neither money nor provisions to maintain themselves.

The Doge of Venice saw right well that the pilgrims were in sore straits, and he spoke to them and said: "Lords, in Greece there is a land that is very rich and plenteous in all good things. If we could have a reasonable excuse for going there and taking provisions and other things in the land until we were well restored, it would seem to me a good plan. Then we should be well able to go oversea." Then the marquis rose and said: "Lords, last year at Christmas I was in Germany at the court of my lord the emperor. There I saw a youth who was brother to the wife of the emperor of Germany. This youth was the son of the emperor Isaac of Constantinople, whose brother had taken the empire of Constantinople from him by treason. Whoever could get hold of this youth," said the marquis, "would be well able to go to Constantinople and get provisions and other things, for this youth is the rightful heir. . . ."

When the marquis had told the pilgrims and the Venetians that whoever had this youth, of whom we have just spoken, would have a good excuse for going to Constantinople and getting provisions, then the crusaders had two knights right well and finely equipped and sent them to Germany for this youth to come to them. And they sent him word that they would help him gain his rights. When the messengers came to the court of the emperor of Germany, there where the youth was, they told him the message they had been charged to tell. When the youth heard this, and learned the offer which the high men of the crusaders had made to him, he was very glad and made great joy over it. And he was very gracious to the messengers and he said that he would consult with the emperor his brother-in-law. When the emperor heard it, he said to the youth that this was a fine chance that had come to him and that he was greatly in favor of his going to them. And he said that he would never get anything of his heritage unless it should be by the help of God and of the crusaders.

The youth knew well that the emperor was giving him good counsel, and he arrayed himself the finest he could and went off with the messengers. Now before the youth and the messengers were come to Zara, the fleet had gone on to the island of Corfu, because Easter was already past; but when the fleet set out to go there they left two galleys behind to wait for the messengers and the youth. So the pilgrims stayed at the island of Corfu until the youth and the messengers should come. When the youth and the messengers came to Zara, they found these two galleys that had been left for them, and they put to sea and went on until they came to Corfu where the fleet was. When the high men saw the youth coming they all went to meet him, and they greeted him and did great honor to him, and when the youth saw the high men honoring him so and saw all the fleet that was there, he was glad as no man ever was before. Then the marquis came forward and took the youth and led him away to his tent.

When the youth was there, then all the high barons and the Doge of Venice assembled at the tent of the marquis, and they talked of one thing and another, until finally they asked him what he would do for them if they made him emperor and made him wear the crown in Constantinople, and he answered them that he would do whatever they wanted. So they parleyed until he said he would give the host two hundred thousand marks and would maintain the fleet a year longer at his own cost and would go oversea with them with all his

forces and would keep ten thousand men in the land oversea at his own cost all the days of his life and would give provisions for a whole year to all those who should leave Constantinople to go oversea.

Then all the barons of the host were summoned and the Venetians. And when they were all assembled, the Doge of Venice rose and spoke to them. "Lords," said the Doge, "now we have a good excuse for going to Constantinople, if you approve of it, for we have the rightful heir." Now there were some who did not at all approve of going to Constantinople. Instead they said: "Bah! what shall we be doing in Constantinople? We have our pilgrimage to make, and also our plan of going to [Cairo] or Alexandria. Moreover, our navy is to follow us for only a year, and half of the year is already past." And the others said in answer: "What shall we do in [Cairo] or Alexandria, when we have neither provisions nor money to enable us to go there? Better for us before we go there to secure provisions and money by some good excuse than to go there and die of hunger. Then we shall be able to accomplish something. Moreover, he offers to come with us and to maintain our navy and our fleet a year longer at his own cost." And the marquis of Montferrat was more at pains to urge them to go to Constantinople than anyone else who was there, because he wanted to avenge himself for an injury which the emperor of Constantinople who was then holding the empire had done to him.

Robert of Clari, *The Conquest of Constantinople,* trans. Edgar Holmes McNeal (New York: Columbia University Press, 1936), pp. 45-46, 57-59.

C. Nicetas Choniates on the Fourth Crusade

The Venetians, recalling their old alliance with the Romans, were not able to

endure that the friendship of the latter was now transferred to the Pisans. They gradually alienated themselves and looked for an opportunity for revenge. They were embittered also because the emperor Alexius [Alexius III Angelus] out of avarice had not yet paid to them the 20,000 pieces of gold which were still due to them from the fifteen pounds of gold [105,000 gold pieces] which the emperor Manuel had agreed to pay them at the time he had confiscated the property of the Venetians in the empire. But another source of evil and not the least was Enrico Dandolo, their duke, who was aged and blind, but for the Romans the most inimical and insidious man. Proud and shrewd, he called himself the most prudent among the prudent and had a madness for glory greater than any other man. When he pondered over the wrongs which his compatriots had suffered when the Angeli brothers ruled [1185–1203] and before them, during the reign of Andronicus [1183–1185] and that of Manuel [1143–1180], he felt such a desire for vengeance that he preferred to die than not to avenge these wrongs. But because he knew that any undertaking against the Romans by his people alone would rebound against his head, he sought to obtain other accomplices, people with whom he could share his secrets and whom he knew to have implacable hatred for the Romans and envy for their felicity. Time brought him these accomplices. Certain noble toparchs who had set out to go to Palestine were won over by him to join as fellow-conspirators in a common enterprise against the Romans. These toparchs were Boniface, Marquis of Montferrat; Baldwin, Count of Flanders; Henry [Hugh], Count of St. Pol; and Louis, Count of Blois. There were, besides, many others, daring warriors and in stature as tall as their spears.

Three entire years were consumed in Venice in the creation of a fleet. In the end they built one hundred and ten light ships (*dromones*) for the transport of the cavalry and sixty long ones. They gathered, besides, about seventy very big round ships of which one exceeded the others in size by so much that they called it World (*Cosmos*). On these they put one thousand cavalry clad in full armor and thirty thousand infantry including bowmen.

Now as the fleet was about to depart there supervened another evil for the Romans. This was the arrival of Alexius, son of Isaac Angelus, who came to the fleet with letters from the pope of Old Rome and the king of Germany, Philip, in which they said to the corsairs that they would do them a great favor if they received Alexius and restored him to his paternal throne. The corsairs, thinking that the presence of Alexius would give them a good pretext for their piratical expedition and quench their avarice with heaps of money, received the young man. Now Alexius, who was not so much young in years as he was in wit, caught by adroit and crafty men, made promises on oath which were beyond his power to fulfill. Not only did he promise to give them the heaps of money which they asked, but also to participate in the expedition against the Saracens with Roman troops and thirty ships. And, what is more important and most absurd, he agreed to accept the Latin deviations from the faith and the innovations concerning the privileges of the pope, and to change the old customs of the Romans.

Nicetas Choniates, *Historia* (Bonn, 1835), pp. 713-715, trans. Peter Charanis.

D. Views of Modern Historians Concerning the Diversion of the Fourth Crusade

1. A. A. VASILIEV

Many scholars have devoted much attention to the problem of the Fourth Crusade. Their chief attention has been turned to the causes of the change of direction of the crusade. One party of scholars explained the whole unusual course of the crusading enterprise by accidental circumstances and were the followers of the so-called "theory of accidents." An opposing group of scholars saw the cause of the change in the premeditated policy of Venice and Germany and became the partisans of the so-called "theory of premeditation."

Until about 1860 no dispute on that problem had existed because all historians had depended mainly on the statements of the chief western source of the Fourth Crusade and a participant in it, the French historian Geoffrey de Villehardouin. In his exposition the events of the crusade progressed simply and accidentally: not having vessels, the crusaders hired them at Venice and therefore assembled there; after having hired the vessels they could not pay the Republic of St. Mark the full amount fixed and were forced to support the Venetians in their strife with Zara; then followed the coming of the prince Alexius, who inclined the crusaders against Byzantium. Thus, there was no question of any treason of Venice nor of any complicated political intrigue.

In 1861, for the first time, a French scholar, Mas-Latrie, author of the very well-known history of the island of Cyprus, accused Venice, which had important commercial interests in Egypt, of making a secret treaty with the sultan of Egypt and thereupon skillfully forcing the crusaders to abandon the original plan of the expedition upon Egypt and to sail against Byzantium. Then the German historian, Karl Hopf, seemed definitely to prove the treason of the Venetians towards the Christian task, stating that the treaty between Venice and the sultan of Egypt was concluded on the 13th of May, 1202. Although Hopf produced no text of the treaty and did not even indicate where this text was to be found, the authority of the German scholar was so great that many scholars adopted his standpoint without any doubt. But it was shown soon after that Hopf had no new document in his hands at all and that his date was quite arbitrary. A French scholar, Hanotaux, who a little later investigated this problem, refuted the theory of Venetian treason and, consequently, "the theory of premeditation." But he thought that if the Venetians were the chief instigators of the change of direction of the Fourth Crusade, they had obvious motives: the desire to subdue Zara, which had revolted; the wish to restore their candidate to the Byzantine throne, to revenge themselves on Byzantium for the sympathy Alexius III had given the Pisans, and, possibly, the hope to obtain some profit, if the Empire fell to pieces. The theory of Hopf at the present time is considered refuted. If the Venetians can be really accused of treason, they become traitors not because of a secret treaty with the Muslims, but exclusively because they had in view their commercial interests in the Byzantine Empire.

But the followers of "the theory of premeditation" did not confine themselves to the attempt to prove the fact of the treason of Venice. In 1875 a new motive was brought forward by a French scholar, Count de Riant, who tried to prove that the chief instigator of the change of direction of the Fourth Crusade was not Dandolo, but the king of Germany, Philip of Swabia, son-in-law of the deposed Isaac Angelus. In

Germany a skillful political intrigue had been woven which was to direct the crusaders upon Constantinople. Boniface of Montferrat fulfilled Philip's plans in the East. In the change of direction of the crusade Riant sees one of the episodes of the long struggle between the papacy and the Empire. By his leading role in the crusade Philip humiliated the pope and falsified his conception of the crusade; welcoming the restored Byzantine Emperor as an ally, Philip might hope to be successful in his strife with the pope and with his rival in Germany, Otto of Brunswick. But a blow was struck to Riant's theory by an investigation of Vasilievsky, who showed that the flight of the prince Alexius to the West took place not in the year 1201, as all the historians believed, but in 1202, so that for a complicated and long-conceived political intrigue "Philip was left neither place nor time; thus the German intrigue may be proved as illusive as the Venetian." The accurate investigation of a Frenchman, Tessier, on the basis of examination of contemporary sources, refuted the theory of the German sovereign's role and returned to the acknowledgment of the great significance of the narrative of Villehardouin, that is to say, to the prevailing standpoint before 1860, "the theory of accidents." Tessier said that the Fourth Crusade was a French crusade, and the conquest of Constantinople was an achievement neither Germanic nor Venetian, but French. Of Riant's premeditation theory there remains only the fact that Philip of Swabia took part in the change of direction of the crusade and, like Henry VI, claimed the Eastern Empire; but the sources do not justify affirming the existence of a leading and subtle plan on Philip's part on which could depend the destiny of the whole Fourth Crusade.

At the end of the nineteenth century a German historian, W. Norden, definitely refuting "the theory of premeditation" and agreeing essentially with "the theory of accidents," endeavored to investigate the latter more deeply, discussed the problem of the Fourth Crusade in the light of the political, economic, and religious relations between the West and East, and tried to elucidate the inner connection between the Fourth Crusade and the history of the previous hundred and fifty years.

To sum up: in the complicated history of the Fourth Crusade there were in action various forces originating in the motives of the pope, Venice, and the German king in the West, as well as forces originating in the external and internal conditions of Byzantium in the East. The interplay of these forces created an exceedingly complex phenomenon which is not entirely clear, in some details, even at the present day. "This," said the French historian Luchaire, "will never be known, and science has something better to do than interminably to discuss an insoluble problem." Grégoire has recently even gone so far as to proclaim that "there is really no problem of the Fourth Crusade."

But among all the plans, hopes, and complications it remains clear that over all prevailed the firm will of Dandolo and his unyielding determination to develop the trade activity of Venice, to which the possession of the eastern markets promised limitless wealth and a brilliant future. Moreover, Dandolo was greatly alarmed by the growing economic power of Genoa, which at that time, in the Near East in general and in Constantinople in particular, began to gain a strong foothold. The economic competition between Venice and Genoa must also be taken into consideration when the problem of the Fourth Crusade is discussed. Finally the unpaid debt of Byzantium to Venice for the

Venetian property seized by Manuel Comnenus may also have had something to do with the diversion of the Fourth Crusade.

A. A. Vasiliev, *History of the Byzantine Empire, 324-1453* (Madison, Wisconsin: The University of Wisconsin Press, 1952), pp. 456-459. Quoted with the permission of the publishers, the University of Wisconsin Press.

2. H. GRÉGOIRE

To a Byzantinist, there can be no doubt about the fact that the course ultimately taken by the so-called Fourth Crusade, the capture of Constantinople, and the partition of the Byzantine Empire was *not* the fortuitous result of a series of unforeseen and surprising events. On the contrary, I have always been convinced, and I see that my learned colleague Professor Ostrogorsky in his excellent history of Byzantium is convinced likewise, that the "diversion" of that expedition, the détournement, as I prefer to say in allusive and ironical French, had been intended from the beginning, or rather from the moment when Boniface of Montferrat was elected to succeed Count Thibault of Champagne. Some critics call this view "la théorie byzantine." I must protest against such an expression, which seems to hint at a bias, at a tendency to look at things from the standpoint of a Byzantine. Now, the Byzantine point of view as expressed, for instance, by Nicetas Choniates, is that the capture of Constantinople fulfilled the wish of the Pope. We have no "national" bias at all. We simply try to write history, connecting as much as possible Western and Eastern affairs, Western and Eastern sources. To us, of course, the character of Boniface de Montferrat alone supplies a strong presumption in favor of the preconceived plan of conquest. But the scope of this article is limited. It is only to show that an overwhelming bulk of evidence, Latin—or French —and Greek, proves that the responsible leader of the Crusade knew, from the outset, "where he was going."

. . . The testimony of Robert de Clari . . . affords so admirable a confirmation of all the other texts that we must remind the reader of that definite, clear-cut statement, according to which Boniface declared to the crusaders, at the end of 1202 or the begining of 1203, that he had met young Alexius at Christmas of the preceding year, thus in December, 1201, at the court of Philip of Swabia, in Germany—three months after Boniface of Montferrat had been elected as the Generalissimo of the Holy War. I shall refrain today from repeating what that choice meant. Instead, I advise those who would still be in doubt to read Usseglio's splendid book on the Montferrat family, one of the most important contributions ever made to our Byzantine studies by a non-Byzantinist. Boniface was the son of a man who had enjoyed the intimate friendship of the Byzantine Emperors. He was the brother of two Caesars of Byzantium, Rainer and Conrad. Those men were looked upon in Byzantium as epic heroes. One of the most "genuine" features of Robert de Clari's vivid narration is his perfect acquaintance with those Byzantine connections of the Montferrats. There are a few confusions in his account of Conrad's "geste," but nothing really "legendary," as has often been contended in order to disparage him.

Really, there is no problem of the Fourth Crusade. As soon as Alexius the Younger, the pretender, succeeded in reaching Italy and Germany and in appearing at the Court of Philip of Swabia, his brother-in-law and brother of Henry VI, who died as he was about to carry out the Norman plan of the conquest of the Eastern Empire, Boniface of Montferrat, the leader elect of the Crusade, saw himself sitting on the Imperial throne, which his two brothers had well-nigh occupied and which he missed himself, not because of the opposition of the Pope, who hated the "Swabian" and did not trust the Montferrat, but because of the shrewd Doge of Venice.

Henri Grégoire, "The Question of the Diversion of the Fourth Crusade," *Byzantion*, XV (Boston: The Byzantine Institute, Inc., 1941), 158, 166.

4. Church and State in the Middle Ages

SIDNEY PAINTER

The Johns Hopkins University

THE CONTEST FOR supremacy between the spiritual and secular authorities has been a feature of most of the civilizations known to history. The Pharaoh Ikhnaton quarreled with the priests of Amon, Agamemnon suffered from the rage of Chryses, and Samuel humbled Saul. The popes of the eighth and early ninth centuries defended their privileges against both Byzantine and Carolingian emperors. Thus the period covered by the three following problems, roughly from the middle of the eleventh to the end of the thirteenth century is merely one phase of a long story. It is, however, an extremely significant one, especially for the history of Western European civilization.

During most of the ninth and a fair part of the tenth centuries there was in reality neither church nor state in Western Europe. The powers and functions of the state were split into fragments and divided among innumerable local lords. In France and Western Germany these lords were bound to one another and to their suzerain, the king, by the loose bonds of feudalism. In England and Eastern Germany the ties were not feudal, but they were just as loose. In general throughout Western Europe the local lord ruled the people who lived on his lands and was himself ruled by no one.

The condition of the church was little different. Each bishop was essentially independent of higher ecclesiastical authority. He ruled his diocese according to his will and its traditional laws and customs. But as the age was one of almost continuous warfare, the prelates needed the protection of an effective military leader. Hence the church became deeply involved with lay government. In the feudalized regions bishops and abbots became vassals of the feudal princes and themselves had knightly vassals. In the non-feudal parts of Germany the prelates chose neighboring lords as their advocates or lay protectors.

This fragmentation of authority resulted in something closely approaching anarchy in both church and state. The endless warfare among the members of the warrior class kept the country in perpetual disorder. There could be little discipline in the church. Most of the bishops and abbots were chosen by

135

the lay lords on whom they depended with little regard to their qualifications for ecclesiastical office. They were selected because of their loyalty to the lord and their probable usefulness to him. As the discipline of the lower clergy depended on the effectiveness of the prelates, it was exceedingly poor. Worldly-minded abbots cared little about the observance of the Benedictine rule in their houses. Bishops took little pains to enforce the laws of the church. In fact, when those laws conflicted with the interests of the lay lords, they were helpless no matter how good their intentions might be.

While most prelates had no desire to be subject to an ecclesiastic superior, they were anxious to reduce the anarchy in the state. They preferred to depend on a strong king rather than on the local lords. Hence the prelates lent their support to the kings in their efforts to develop effective royal power. They preached the sanctity of the anointed monarch and aided him with the military resources of their lands. Thus in this period of confusion there developed an alliance between church and state. But this alliance benefited the temporal interests of the bishops rather than their spiritual ones. The condition of ecclesiastical discipline was of little more interest to the kings than to the local lords.

The first strong state of medieval Western Europe was created in the middle years of the tenth century by the Saxon kings of Germany. Although the work was begun by the first monarch of the dynasty, Henry I, called the Fowler (919–936), the true founder of the state was Henry's son, Otto I, the Great (936–973). Their power had two bases. As dukes of Saxony the kings were the chosen leaders of the Saxon warriors and had extensive rights within that duchy. But outside Saxony the royal power rested almost entirely on control of the bishops and abbots and through them of the resources of the lands of the church. The kings chose the prelates and used them as their agents. The royal army consisted largely of knights supplied by the church estates.

In 961 Otto I conquered Lombardy and soon obtained firm control over the bishops of the region who became the keys to his power there. In 962 he led an army to Rome and assumed the title of emperor. His son and grandson devoted most of their attention to developing their power in Italy and quarreling with the Byzantine emperor who still ruled the southern provinces of the peninsula.

While the Saxon kings were striving to build a strong and orderly state, certain earnest and enthusiastic ecclesiastics were attempting to reform the church. This movement started with the foundation of the abbey of Cluny in 910. In the hope of avoiding lay control it was provided that Cluny should never hold land by feudal service. All its property was to be held in "free alms," that is, by prayers for the donor's soul. The monks of Cluny were to observe strictly the Benedictine rule. Under a series of able abbots Cluny gained both wealth and prestige. Daughter houses were founded and many existing monasteries joined the order. In order to establish unified rule and effective discipline there was but one abbot of Cluny and the daughter houses were ruled by priors. During the tenth and early eleventh centuries the monks of Cluny and others who were inspired by their ideals and their example improved tremendously the standards of monastic life in Western Europe.

In the eleventh century both church and empire took the paths that were to lead to conflict between them. The church reform party turned its eyes toward the secular clergy. Its long range purpose was to improve ecclesiastical discipline—especially to enforce the laws regarding clerical celibacy which were almost completely ignored in Western Europe. But they believed that reform was possible only if the church could be united under an effective head who could both discipline the clergy and defend them from the lay lords. The obvious course was to strengthen the papacy. Perhaps the chief weakness of the papacy lay in the method of selecting the pope. In theory the pope as bishop of Rome was elected by the clergy and people of his diocese. Actually he was chosen either by the emperor or by the dominant faction of the turbulent Roman nobility. In the hope of making the pope independent of lay control the reformers provided for his election by the cardinals, the more important ecclesiastics of his archdiocese. They then set to work to unify the church under the rule of the pope. To overcome one obvious difficulty, the vast extent of Latin Christendom, papal legates were appointed to exercise the papal power in various regions. Sometimes a legate was sent to solve a definite problem, but often he was given full power to reform the church in the region to which he was sent. In theory any case tried in an ecclesiastical court could be carried on appeal to the papal court in Rome, but the expense of the long journey made such appeals rare. The reformers extended the effective jurisdiction of the papal court by appointing local judges delegate to hear cases appealed to it. Moreover, efforts were made to create codes of canon or ecclesiastical law that were officially approved by the papacy and were accepted throughout the whole church. This work laid the foundation for the carrying out of the aims of the reformers—the reform of the church as a whole and its emancipation from lay control.

During the same years in which the reform party was strengthening the papacy, and through it the church as a whole, a new dynasty of German kings, the Salian house, was actively building a stronger monarchy. The Emperor Henry III (1039–1056) realized the essential weakness of a state resting almost entirely on prelates and their lands. He set to work to supply his monarchy with a firm territorial base. The Salian kings were dukes of Franconia who held extensive Swabian estates. Henry took over Thuringia and Southern Saxony and filled them with castles garrisoned with Swabian troops. He chose Goslar in Southern Saxony as his capital. Near it were great silver mines which he hoped would supply an adequate financial basis for his monarchy. Thus by the middle of the eleventh century a developing monarchy faced a developing papacy.

A clash between these two forces was practically inevitable. Even with his firm territorial base in the heart of Germany the emperor could not afford to loosen his control over the prelates and their lands. But the emancipation of the bishops from secular control was one of the prime aims of the reformers. The bishops were the key figures in the organization of the church. A bishop could perform all the sacraments, he controlled the property of the church in his diocese, and he was responsible for the discipline of his clergy. General reform could come only through the bishops. If it were to succeed, they had to be chosen for their religious zeal rather than for their political ability and loyalty to the emperor. While Henry III lived, the issue did not come to a head. He was far too powerful to defy and too pious to make outrageous appointments. But the storm broke over the head of his son and our first problem will deal with the contest between Henry IV (1056–1106) and the papacy.

The two and a quarter centuries that followed the beginning of the quarrel between Henry IV and the papacy saw almost continuous skirmishing between the pope and the lay monarchs. Occasionally a clash between a strong pope and a powerful and determined king led to a battle royal. The incidental issues of the conflict varied, but behind it lay the central theme of the struggle for supremacy. In order to vary both the contestants and the issues, problems have been chosen which show the contest between King John (1199–1216) of England and Pope Innocent III over an election to the see of Canterbury and that between King Philip IV, the Handsome, of France (1285–1314) and Pope Boniface VIII over the royal right to tax the clergy.

The period covered by these three problems was the heyday of the medieval papacy. Gregory VII was the first pope to use to the full the implements and ideas developed by the Cluniac reform party. His successors continued his work. In the twelfth century both theology and canon law were codified and prepared for universal application. Peter Lombard in his *Sentences* produced the standard statement of the church's doctrine that was to be the basis of all theological study for a long time. Gratian in his *Decretals* did the same for canon law. The popes and their servants labored to apply this theology and canon law throughout all Christendom. They also interpreted and added to the works of Peter Lombard and Gratian as changing conditions made it necessary or desirable. Innocent III was of high ability both as a theologian and canonist and he was served by men of equal quality. Of all the popes he came the closest to establishing the supremacy of the papal authority. In his reign the spiritual and temporal power of the papacy and its prestige in both these spheres reached its height. His successors plunged into a long and bitter struggle with the Emperor Frederick II (1215–1250). Although they were victorious and crushed forever the imperial power, the means required to achieve that end seriously injured the prestige of the papacy. Boniface VIII plunged recklessly into a contest with the most powerful monarch of Europe, Philip IV of France, and met defeat (1294–1303). Philip emerged from the struggle complete master of his realm and to a large degree of the papacy itself. Moving to Avignon across the Rhone from Philip's lands the popes entered upon what has been called their "Babylonian Captivity" (1305–1378).

I. POPE GREGORY VII AND THE
EMPEROR HENRY IV

Emperor Henry III died in 1156 leaving his son under age, and for some years the realm was governed by a regency headed by the young king's mother. The regency and Henry IV, when he came of age, continued the practices of Henry III in regard to the selection of prelates. They were chosen by the king who gave them the insignia of both their spiritual and temporal offices. To use the terminology of the day, he invested them with the ring and crozier, the symbols of their spiritual office, and also gave them the *regalia*, their temporal rights in their lands.

On April 21, 1073, Pope Alexander II died. His funeral was arranged and supervised by a monk named Hildebrand who had been the most influential member of Alexander's court. Hildebrand was an enthusiastic member of the reform party who had served the papacy for over 20 years. During the funeral procession the Romans loudly demanded the election of Hildebrand as Alexander's successor, and the next day the cardinals solemnly elected him pope. In strict theory the cardinals should have acted first and had the people acclaim their choice. Later the new pope's foes were to charge that he had inspired the cries of the mob and that the cardinals had no choice but to elect him. But these accusations came only in the heat of his quarrel with the Emperor and there seems no sound reason for questioning the validity of the election.

As pope, Hildebrand took the name Gregory VII. In December, 1074, he held a council at Rome. This council issued a decree forbidding any prelate to receive the insignia of his office from a layman. No archbishop was to consecrate a prelate so invested. The Emperor Henry IV simply ignored this decree and continued his customary practices. Because of its immediate cause, the quarrel between Gregory VII and Henry IV is called the "Investiture Controversy." This designation is not actually a happy one. In reality the pope was not primarily interested in who invested the bishops but rather in who chose them. It was, however, useless to insist on canonical elections if the king could invest the prelates. His power was bound to be great enough to secure a satisfactory election if he was the judge of its validity. Then as a matter of fact both Gregory and Henry soon forgot or at least

paid little attention to the original cause of their quarrel. Each was determined to establish his authority over the other.

The story of the contest can only be sketched here. When Gregory issued his decree against lay investiture, Henry was busy in Germany. He had continued vigorously his father's policies in Southern Saxony. He had built new castles in the vicinity of Goslar and brought in more Swabian troops. He had begun to exercise ancient ducal rights that had been unused since the days of the Saxon kings. The result was a great Saxon revolt. Only when this had been suppressed was Henry ready to turn to his quarrel with the papacy. In January 1076 he held a council of the prelates of Germany at the city of Worms. The prelates drew up a letter to Gregory in violent terms. The king sent an equally strong letter. Gregory replied by holding a council in Rome that declared Henry excommunicate and deposed from his royal office. During the following years the German princes who disliked Henry IV as a strong king who endangered their independence elected several anti-kings, but none was powerful enough to hold his own against Henry. Eventually Gregory died in exile in the lands of his allies, the Norman rulers of Southern Italy, after Henry's forces had occupied Rome.

The controversy between Gregory and Henry gave rise to many documents. Pope Gregory was both able and highly articulate. He expressed his views with vigor and clarity. While Henry and his advisers were more inclined to violent recriminations than to well-reasoned arguments, they too expressed their views. Then various scholars throughout Europe took a hand in the battle and aired their opinions. From this mass of material certain documents and parts of documents have been chosen to represent the views of the two parties.

The problem is to discover what the two parties believed to be the respective powers of pope and king. Here at a crucial point in the development of both the papacy and lay monarchy we have an opportunity to see the theories that lay behind the two offices

A. The Dictatus Papae

This document presents in outline Pope Gregory VII's conception of the papal authority. It has been the subject of many scholarly works; its authorship and date have been keenly debated. Today it is generally accepted as the work of Gregory himself and is believed to have been composed shortly after the council of February, 1075, which issued the decree against lay investiture. This extreme definition of papal power was accepted by few ecclesiastics and by still fewer laymen in his day. It is quite possible that the pope himself regarded it as the statement of a theoretical ideal rather than as a practical immediate goal. The problem here is to grasp Gregory's idea of papal supremacy.

That the Roman church was founded by God alone.

That only the Roman pontiff is rightly called universal.

That he alone can depose or reinstate bishops.

That his legate, even though of inferior rank, has precedence over all bishops in a council; and he can give sentence of deposition against them.

That the pope can depose those who are absent.

That in addition to avoiding intercourse with those excommunicated by him, we ought not to remain in the same house with them.

That to him alone is permitted to make new laws, to create new episcopal sees, to make a chapter of canons into a monastery, and to divide a rich bishopric or combine poor ones according to the needs of the day.

That he alone can use the imperial insignia.

That all princes shall kiss the feet of the pope and the pope only.

That only his name is to be recited in all churches.

That his name is unique in the world.

That he is allowed to depose emperors.

That he is allowed, under compelling need, to transfer bishops from one see to another.

That he can ordain as a clerk anyone he wishes from any part of the church.

That one ordained by him can rule another church but may not serve in it; and one so ordained ought not to accept a higher rank from another bishop.

That no synod ought to be called general without his command.

That no decree and no book shall be considered canonical without his authority.

That his sentence can be annulled by no one and he alone can annul the sentences of all others.

That he should be judged by no one.

That no one shall dare to condemn an appellant to the apostolic see.

That major cases concerning churches ought to be referred to the apostolic see.

That the Roman church has never erred nor, as scripture testifies, will ever err.

That the Roman pontiff, if he has been canonically ordained, is undoubtedly sanctified by the merits of St. Peter, according to the testimony of St. Ennodius, bishop of Pavia, which is supported by many holy fathers as the decrees of the blessed pope Symmachus state.

That by his command and license subjects can accuse (their rulers).

That without convening a synod he can depose and reinstate bishops.

That one shall not be considered a Catholic who does not agree with the Roman church.

That he can absolve subjects from their oaths of fidelity to iniquitous (rulers).

Gregory VII, *Dictatus papae,* trans. Sidney Painter, from Philip Jaffé, ed., *Monumenta Gregoriana* (Bibliotheca rerum Germanicarum, II), pp. 174-176.

B. Letter of Henry IV to Gregory VII

While this letter was certainly written during the course of the year 1076, its exact date has not been established. Some scholars believe it was sent immediately after the council held at Worms in January. Others place it in March after the excommunication of Henry (see our next document). I am inclined to agree with the latter view, but it makes little difference for our purpose. It is a clear and violent expression of Henry's ideas as to the proper relation between imperial and papal power. The problem here is to separate vituperation from argument in order to see Henry's conception of the royal power.

Henry king not by usurpation but by the holy ordination of God to Hildebrand at present not the apostle but a false monk. You have deserved such a greeting as this by your dishonor—you who have attained no order in the church that you have made a partaker of dishonor not of honor, of malediction not of benediction. For to speak of few and notable cases out of many not only have you not feared to lay hands on the rulers of the Holy Church, the anointed of the Lord—archbishops, bishops, and priests—but you have trodden them under your feet as slaves who know not what their lord does. In enslaving them you have stolen for yourself the favor of the vulgar mob. You have judged that all these rulers of the church know nothing while you know everything, but you have taken care to use this knowledge not for building but for destroying, so that we believe with justice that the blessed Gregory whose name you have usurped was prophesying concerning you when he said, "The spirit of the ruler is elevated in accord with the number of those subject to him and he believes that he knows more than all

because he sees that he can do more than all." And we indeed have borne all this while we have tried to preserve the honor of the apostolic see. But you have understood our humility as fear and therefore have not been afraid to revolt against the royal authority which was granted to us by God—authority which you have dared to threaten to take away from us: as if we had received the realm from you—as if both realm and empire were in your hands and not in the hand of God. Our Lord Jesus Christ called us to the kingship, but he did not call you to the priesthood. For you ascended by these steps: you have obtained money, which is abhorrent to the monastic vow, by wiles, by money you have obtained favor, by favor you have obtained a sword, and by the sword you have obtained the chair of peace and from the chair of peace you disturb the peace in that you have armed subjects against their rulers, have taught that our bishops called to their office by God are to be spurned, and have usurped for laymen authority over their priests so that these laymen depose or condemn those whom they have received as teachers from the hand of God by the imposition of episcopal hands. On me also who although I am unworthy to be among the anointed have been anointed in the kingship you have lain hands—me whom the tradition of the Holy Fathers teaches can be judged by God alone and whom this tradition asserts can be deposed for no crime unless, which God forbid, I shall have denied the faith: for the prudence of the Holy Fathers entrusted even Julian the Apostate to God rather than to themselves to be judged and deposed. He himself also, the true pope St. Peter announces "Fear God, honor the king." You, however, who fear not God, dishonor me his appointed one. Wherefore St. Paul, when he does not spare an angel from heaven if he preaches otherwise, has not excepted you preaching otherwise on earth. For he says: If anyone, either I or an angel from the sky should preach other than is preached to you, he is accursed. You, therefore, damned by this curse and by the judgment of us and all our bishops descend and leave the purchased apostolic seat: let another ascend the throne of St. Peter who does not excuse violence by religion but teaches the true doctrine of St. Peter. I, Henry, king by God's grace with all our bishops say to you: Descend, descend, damned throughout the ages.

Henry IV to Pope Gregory VII, trans. Sidney Painter, from L. Weiland, ed., *Monumenta Germaniae historica, Constitutiones et acta publica*, I (1893), pp. 110-111.

C. Excommunication of Henry IV

In February, 1076, Pope Gregory held a council in Rome. One act of this body was the formal excommunication of Henry IV. Again the problem is to separate the arguments for papal supremacy from mere self-justification.

O blessed Peter, prince of the Apostles, mercifully incline thine ear, we [sic] pray, and hear me, thy servant, whom thou hast cherished from infancy and hast delivered until now from the hand of the wicked who have hated and still hate me for my loyalty to thee. Thou art my witness, as are also my Lady, the Mother of God, and the blessed Paul, thy brother among all the saints, that thy Holy Roman Church forced me against my will to be its ruler. I had no thought of ascending thy throne as a robber, nay, rather would I have chosen to end my life as a pilgrim than to seize upon thy place for earthly glory and by devices of this world. Therefore, by thy favor, not by any works of mine, I believe that it is and has been thy will, that the Christian people especially committed to thee should render obedience to me, thy especially constituted representative. To me is given by thy grace the power of binding and loosing in Heaven and upon earth.

Wherefore, relying upon this commission, and for the honor and defense of thy Church, in the name of Almighty God, Father, Son and Holy Spirit, through thy power and authority, I deprive King Henry, son of the Emperor Henry, who has rebelled against thy Church with unheard-of audacity, of the government over the whole kingdom of Germany and Italy, and I release all Christian men from the allegiance which they have sworn or may swear to him, and I forbid anyone to serve him as king. For it is fitting that he who seeks to diminish the glory of thy Church should lose the glory which he seems to have.

And since he has refused to obey as a Christian should or to return to the God whom he has abandoned by taking part with excommunicated persons, has spurned my warnings which I gave him for his soul's welfare, as thou knowest, and has separated himself from thy Church and tried to rend it asunder, I bind him in the bonds of anathema in thy stead and I bind him thus as commissioned by thee, that the nations may know and be convinced that thou art Peter and that upon thy rock the son of the living God has built his Church and the gates of hell shall not prevail against it.

The Correspondence of Pope Gregory VII, trans. Ephraim Emerton (New York: Columbia University Press, 1932), pp. 90-91.

D. Letter of Gregory VII to Hermann, Bishop of Metz

The excommunication of Henry IV was not well received by the prelates of Germany. They had been chosen by Henry or his father. Moreover the German church was a traditional ally of the crown. Then most of them had little enthusiasm for reform, and King Henry was their most effective shield against the pope's reforming zeal. Hence Gregory felt it necessary in the summer of 1076 to argue his case and he chose to do it in the form of a letter to the bishop of Metz.

A careful study of this letter will reveal much about the points of view of both parties—the very essence of our problem.

Gregory, bishop, servant of the servants of God, to Hermann, bishop of Metz, greeting and apostolic benediction.

You have asked a great many questions of me, a very busy man, and have sent me an extremely urgent messenger. Wherefore I beg you to bear with me patiently if my reply is not sufficiently ample.

The bearer will report to you as to my health and as to the conduct of the Romans and the Normans in regard to me. As to the other matters about which you inquire—would that the blessed Peter himself, who is many times honored or wronged in me his servant, such as I am, might give the answers!

There is no need to ask me who are the excommunicated bishops, priests or laymen; since beyond a doubt they are those who are known to be in communication with the excommunicated king Henry—if, indeed, he may properly be called king. They do not hesitate to place the fear and favor of man before the commands of the eternal King nor to expose their king to the wrath of Almighty God by giving him their support.

He too feared not to incur the penalty of excommunication by dealing with followers who had been excommunicated for the heresy of simony nor to draw others into excommunication through their dealings with him. How can we think of such things but in the words of the Psalmist: "The fool hath said in his heart there is no God," or again: "They are all gone astray in their wills."

Now to those who say: "A king may not be excommunicated," although we are not bound to reply to such a fatuous notion, yet, lest we seem to pass over their foolishness impatiently we will recall them to sound doctrine by directing their attention to the words and acts of the holy fathers. Let them read what instructions St. Peter gave to the Christian community in his ordination of St. Clement in regard to one who had not the approval of the pontiff. Let them learn why the Apostle said, "Being prompt to punish every disobedience"; and of whom he said, "Do not even take food with such people." Let them consider why Pope Zachary deposed a king of the Franks and released all his subjects from their oaths of allegiance. Let them read in the records [registra] of St. Gregory how in his grants to certain churches he not merely excommunicated kings and dukes who opposed him but declared them deprived of their royal dignity. And let them not forget that St. Ambrose not only excommunicated the Emperor Theodosius but forbade him to stand in the room of the priests within the church.

But perhaps those people would imagine that when God commended his Church to Peter three times saying, "Feed my sheep," he made an exception of kings! Why do they not see, or rather confess with shame that, when God gave to Peter as leader the power of binding and loosing in heaven and on earth he excepted no one, withheld no one from his power? For if a man says that he cannot be bound by the ban of the Church, it is evident that he could not be loosed by its authority, and he who shamelessly denies this cuts himself off absolutely from Christ. If the Holy Apostolic See, through the princely power divinely bestowed upon it, has jurisdiction over spiritual things, why not also over temporal things? When kings and princes of this world set their own dignity and profit higher than God's righteousness and seek their own honor, neglecting the glory of God, you know whose members they are, to whom they give their allegiance. Just as those who place God above their own wills and obey his commands rather than those of men are members of Christ, so those of whom we spoke are members of Antichrist. If then spiritual men are to be judged, as is fitting, why should not men of the world be held to account still more strictly for their evil deeds?

Perchance they imagine that royal dignity is higher than that of bishops; but how great the difference between them is, they may learn from the difference in their origins. The former came from human lust of power; the latter was instituted by divine grace. The former constantly strives after empty glory; the latter aspires ever toward the heavenly life. Let them learn what Anastasius the pope said to Anastasius the emperor regarding these two dignities and how St. Ambrose in his pastoral letter distinguished between them. He said: "If you compare the episcopal dignity with the splendor of kings and the crowns of princes, these are far more inferior to it than lead is to glistening gold." And, knowing this, the Emperor Constantine chose, not the highest, but the lowest seat among the bishops; for he knew that God resists the haughty, but confers his grace upon the humble.

Meantime, be it known to you, my brother, that, upon receipt of letters from certain of our clerical brethren and political leaders we have given apostolic authority to those bishops to absolve such persons excommunicated by us as have dared to cut themselves loose from the king. But as to the king himself, we have absolutely forbidden anyone to dare to absolve him until we shall have been made certain by competent witnesses of his sincere repentance and reparation; so that at the same time we may determine, if divine grace shall have visited him, in what form we may grant him absolution, to God's glory and his own salvation. For it has not escaped our knowledge that there are some of you who, pretending to be authorized by us, but really led astray by fear or the favor of men, would presume to absolve him if I [sic] did not forbid them, thus widening the wound instead of healing it. And if others, bishops in very truth, should oppose them, they would say that these were actuated, not by a sense of justice, but by personal hostility.

Moreover ordination and consecration by those bishops who dare to communicate with an excommunicated king become in the sight of God an execration, according to St. Gregory. For since they in their pride refuse to obey the Apostolic See, they incur the charge of idolatry, according to Samuel. If he is said to be of God who is stirred by divine love to punish crime, certainly he is not of God who refused to rebuke the lives of carnal men so far as in him lies. And if he is accursed who withholds his sword from blood—that is to say, the word of preaching from destroying the life of the flesh—how much more is he accursed who through fear or favor drives his brother's soul into everlasting perdition! Furthermore you cannot find in the teaching of any of the holy fathers that men accursed and excommunicated can convey to others that blessing and that divine grace which they do not fear to deny by their actions.

Meantime, we order you to ask our

brother, the venerable archbishop of Trier, to forbid the bishop of Toul to interfere in the affairs of the abbess of Remiremont and, with your assistance, to annul whatever action he has taken against her.

But, concerning Matilda, daughter to us both and faithful servant of St. Peter, I will do as you wish. I am not yet quite clear as to her future status—*deo gubernante*. I wish you, however, clearly to understand that although I remember her late husband Godfrey as a frequent offender against God, I am not affected by his enmity toward me

Ibid., pp. 102-105.

E. Second Excommunication of Henry IV

The princes of Germany saw in the excommunication and deposition of Henry IV in February, 1076, a marvelous opportunity to get rid of a heavy-handed master. In October, 1076, they met and decided to invite the pope to attend a great council to be held in February, 1077, at Augsburg. There Gregory would either absolve Henry or confirm his deposition. In the latter case, they would elect a new king. King Henry realized that he had little chance of winning over Gregory in the midst of his German foes. His only hope was to seek out the pope in Italy and come to terms. The German princes also thought of this and placed guards in the Alpine passes, but Henry outflanked them by going through the kingdom of Burgundy and entering Italy from the west. Once in Lombardy he was again in control—the bishops and their knights rallied around him.

Pope Gregory had started north in December on his journey to Germany. In January, 1077, he was in the castle of Canossa, the northernmost stronghold of Matilda, countess of Tuscany, a relative of Henry but a faithful papal ally. His path to the north was blocked by Henry's Lombard levies. Through the mediation of Matilda the pope and king came to terms and Henry received absolution. He then carefully blocked the Alpine passes so that

nor by any other personal feeling, but moved by my fraternal affection for you and by Matilda's prayers I pray God for his salvation.

May Almighty God, through the mediation of Mary, Queen of Heaven, ever virgin, and the authority of the blessed Apostles Peter and Paul granted by him to them, absolve you and all our brethren who uphold the Christian faith and the dignity of the Apostolic See from all your sins, increase your faith, hope and charity and strengthen you in your defense of his law that you may be worthy to attain to everlasting life.

Gregory could not get to Germany. But the German princes refused to accept this situation. In March they met and elected as king, Rudolph, Duke of Swabia. Henry, however, proved a far more effective soldier than his rival and soon won a series of victories. By 1079 he felt strong enough to demand that the pope excommunicate Rudolph.

Gregory's answer was to hold a council at Rome in March, 1080, and once more excommunicate and depose Henry.

The reader will observe that much of this is simply justification of Gregory's policy, but these are solid arguments relative to our problem.

O blessed Peter, chief of the Apostles, and thou, Paul, teacher of the Gentiles, deign, I pray, to incline your ears to me and mercifully to hear my prayer. Ye who are disciples and lovers of the truth, aid me to tell the truth to you, freed from all falsehood so hateful to you, that my brethren may be more united with me and may know and understand that through faith in you, next to God and his mother Mary, ever virgin, I resist the wicked and give aid to those who are loyal to you. For you know that I entered holy orders not of my own pleasure, and that I accompanied the lord Pope Gregory [VI] unwillingly beyond the mountains, but still more unwillingly returned with my master Pope Leo [IX] to your special church, where I have served you as best I could; and then most unwillingly and unworthy as I was, to my great grief and with groans and lamentations I was set upon your throne.

I say this because it is not I that have chosen you, but you that have chosen me and laid upon me the heavy burden of your Church. And because you have commanded me to go up into a high mountain and denounce their crimes to the people of God and their sins to the sons of the Church, those limbs of the Devil have begun to rise up against me and have dared to lay hands upon me even unto blood.

The kings of the earth, and the princes, both secular and clerical, have risen up, courtiers and commons have taken counsel together against the Lord, and against you, his anointed, saying, "Let us burst their chains and throw off their yoke," and they have striven utterly to overwhelm me with death or banishment.

Among those especially Henry, whom they call "king," son of the Emperor Henry, has raised his heel against your Church in conspiracy with many bishops, as well ultramontanes as Italians, striving to bring it under his control by overturning me. Your authority withstood his insolence and your power defeated it. In confusion and humiliation he came to me in Lombardy begging for release from his excommunication. And when I had witnessed his humiliation and after he had given many promises to reform his way of life, I restored him to communion only, but did not reinstate him in the royal power from which I had deposed him in a Roman synod. Nor did I order that the allegiance of all who had taken oath to him or should do so in future, from which I had released them all at the same synod,

should be renewed. I held this subject in reserve in order that I might do justice as between him and the ultramontane bishops and princes, who in obedience to your Church had stood out against him, and that I might establish peace amongst them, as Henry himself had promised me to do on his oath and by the word of two bishops.

The above-mentioned ultramontane bishops and princes, hearing that he had not kept faith with me, and, as it were, in despair about him, chose Duke Rudolf for their king, without my approval as you will bear witness. Then King Rudolf immediately sent an envoy to me declaring that he had assumed the government of the kingdom under compulsion, but nevertheless was prepared to obey me in every way. And to make this the more acceptable, from that time on he repeatedly sent me the same declaration, adding that he would confirm his promise by sending as hostages his own son and the son of his liegeman Bertaldus [of Zähringen].

Meanwhile Henry was beginning to beg for my help against Rudolf. I replied that I would gladly take action after I had heard both sides in order that I might learn which was the more in accord with what was right. But he, thinking himself strong enough to overcome his opponent, paid no attention to my reply. Later, however, as he saw that he could not do as he had hoped, the two bishops of Verdun and Osnabrück came to Rome on the part of his followers and at a synod requested me in behalf of Henry to do what was right by him. The envoys of Rudolf made the same request. Finally, by divine inspiration as I believe, I decreed at the same synod that a conference should be held beyond the mountains that peace might be restored there, or else that he should be recognized as king whose cause seemed to be the more just. For I, as you, my fathers and my lords, will bear me witness, have never to the present day taken either side except as justice required. And because I reckoned that the wrong side would not be willing to have a conference in which justice was to prevail, I excommunicated and placed under the bonds of anathema all persons, whether of a king or a duke or a bishop or of any vassal, who should try by any device to prevent the holding of a conference. But the aforesaid Henry together with his supporters, not fearing the perils of disobedience—which is the crime of idolatry—incurred excommunication by preventing a conference and bound himself in the bonds of anathema and caused a great multitude of Christians to be delivered to death, churches to be scattered abroad and almost the whole kingdom of the Germans to be desolated.

Wherefore, trusting in the justice and mercy of God and of his most worshipful mother Mary, ever virgin, and relying upon your authority, I place the aforesaid Henry, whom they call "king," and all his supporters under excommunication and bind them with the chains of anathema. And again forbidding him in the name of Almighty God and of yourselves to govern in Germany and Italy, I take from him all royal power and state. I forbid all Christians to obey him as king, and I release all who have made or shall make oath to him as king from the obligation of their oath. May Henry and his supporters never, so long as they may live, be able to win victory in any encounter of arms. But that Rudolf, whom the Germans have chosen for their king in loyalty to you, may rule

Ibid., pp. 149-152.

F. A Tract about the Relation between Kings and Priests

The controversy between the Emperor Henry IV and Pope Gregory VII was not

and protect the kingdom of the Germans, I grant and allow in your name. And relying upon your assurance, I grant also to all his faithful adherents absolution of all their sins and your blessing in this life and the life to come. For as Henry is justly cast down from the royal dignity for his insolence, his disobedience and his deceit, so Rudolf, for his humility, his obedience and his truthfulness is granted the power and the dignity of kingship.

And now, most holy fathers and princes, I pray you to take such action that the whole world may know and understand that if you are able to bind and loose in Heaven, you are able also on earth to grant and to take away from everyone according to his deserts empires, kingdoms, principalities, dukedoms, marquisates, earldoms and the property of all men. You have often taken patriarchates, primacies, archbishoprics and bishoprics away from wicked and unworthy men and have granted them to pious holders. And if you can give judgment in spiritual things, what may we not believe as to your power over secular things? Or, if you can judge the angels who guide all haughty princes, what can you [not] do to their servants? Now let kings and all princes of the earth learn how great is your power, and let them fear to neglect the commands of your Church. And against the aforesaid Henry send forth your judgment so swiftly that all men may know that he falls and is overwhelmed, not by chance but by your power—and would that it were to repentance, that his soul be saved in the day of the Lord!

a local quarrel; its issues affected the relations between state and church throughout Western Europe. Scholars of many lands took part in the debate. Since the *Dictatus* of Gregory VII and his letters show the pope's point of view very fully, a tract written by the opposition has been included. The German scholar Heinrich Boehmer, who first published this document, was inclined to believe that it was written by Gerard, Archbishop of York. But as he had no real evidence as to the author he called him the Anonymous of York. George H. Williams in a recent study, *The Norman Anonymous of 1100* (1951), has come to the conclusion that the tract was written at Rouen in Normandy. As the tract is too long to be included as a whole, only the most pertinent sections are given below. The problem here is to understand the writer's conception of the royal authority.

The holy church is the bride of Christ, who is true king and priest. The church is not the bride of Christ as priest, but rather of Christ as king. Therefore, she is called queen, as it is written: "At your right hand stood the queen in golden garments surrounded by many." Blessed Augustine in a sermon declares that she is manifestly a queen. It is even foretold by the prophets that when Christ has come to His holy church, He shall have come not as a priest but as a king. Isaiah and Zachariah the prophets thus have said: "Speak daughters of Zion, behold your king comes to you. He is just and bearing salvation." And Jeremiah said: "Behold the day will come, says the Lord, and I will raise up a just branch to David and he will reign as king." Similarly in other adjoining passages you will find that it has been predicted that the king, not the priest, will come to the marriage of the holy church. These nuptials are called royal, just as it is sung in the Epiphany of the Lord: "Today the church is joined to the bridegroom of heaven in a royal wedding." For the wedding is termed royal not sacerdotal, and the bride is called a queen, not a priestess.

By divine authority and at the same time by institution of the holy fathers, kings are ordained in the church of God and are consecrated at the holy altar with sacred anointing and benediction, so that they have the power of ruling Christian people, the people of the Lord, "a chosen generation, a holy nation, a peculiar people," who are the holy church of God. What is the church of God other than a congregation of faithful Christians in one faith, hope and love, dwelling together in the house of God? For this ruling kings receive power in their consecration, that they rule and establish the church in judgment and justice, and that they order her according to the discipline of Christian law. They reign in the church which is the kingdom of God. They co-reign with Christ. In order to rule her, they watch and defend her. For to reign is to be submissive to ruling well and to serve God in fear. Even to this purpose is the bishop's rank instituted and consecrated with sacred anointing and benediction that he rule the holy church according to the form of doctrine given to him by God. On account of this, blessed Pope Gelasius says, "There are two by which the world is chiefly governed: priestly authority and royal power." Here he calls the world the holy church which is a stranger in this world. In this world priestly authority and royal power have their dominion in sacred decree. Some divide this dominion, in which, as they say, the priest has dominion over souls, and the king over bodies, as if souls can be ruled without bodies and bodies without souls. That cannot be demonstrated by reason. For it is necessary, if bodies are to be well ordered, that souls be well ordered, and vice versa, since each is ruled similarly as in the resurrection each is saved.

Nevertheless, if the king has so great dominion over governing the bodies of Christians, would he not have dominion over ruling the temple of God which is holy? For the Apostle says: "Do you not know, that your bodies are the temple of the Holy Spirit," and again, "You are the temple of the living God, which is holy," and "You are no longer strangers and foreigners . . . you are built into a habitation of God in the Holy Spirit." "Now therefore, the bodies of Christians are sanctified in baptism, consecrated with sacred anointing and after anointing are clothed with a composite garment so that they receive royal and priestly dignity," as says blessed Ambrose. Since these things are true, it is evident that the king has dominion over those who possess priestly dignity. Also the king ought not to be excluded from the governing of the holy church, that is the Christian people, because thereby the kingdom of the church would be divided and become desolate. "Every kingdom divided against itself will become desolate," says the Lord. It is not therefore good that the kingdom of the holy church be desolate, because the church lacking a kingdom quickly becomes desolate. She will lack a kingdom if kings are separated from its care and protection. The bodies of Christians would be ruled the least, if royal power were separated from the church. Hence the holy fathers and apostolic pontiffs, understanding through divine foresight, consecrated kings in protection of the holy church and defense of the Catholic faith, because unless pagans and heretics are coerced through royal power, they annihilate and bring to confusion the church, the Catholic faith, and the Christian religion. But Christian kings repulsed pagans from the church, condemned heretics and eradicated their wicked teachings deep in the fold of the church. For they were co-reigning with Christ, ever dispensing Christian laws in the kingdom of Christ. Not with priestly authority alone could these things be accomplished, and, therefore, royal power was necessary to the priestly to watch and defend so that the peace and security of the church would remain inviolate. In this manner these two persons, the priest and the king, are seen to hold the offices and image of Christ.

The king and priest have the common anointing of holy oil, spirit of sanctification, power of benediction, the common name of Christ and God, and the common authority to which this name is rightfully due. For if they have not this authority they are falsely designated by this name. But they truly possess authority and exist as participators of it, not through nature but through grace, because Christ alone, the son of God and man, has authority through grace and through nature. Nature is God and is made divine by no one. Nature is holy and is sanctified by no one. I have said "through grace" because it is in relation to man that Christ is said to be made divine and holy by the Father. King and priest, who were the image and figure of Christ —that is, of God and man—because each one was total man, were totally made divine through the grace of anointing and the consecration of benediction. If you use the etymology of the Greek word, consecration—that is, the apotheosis—it will sound as deification to you.

Priest and king are both God and Christ the Lord through grace, and whatever they do or perform according to this grace is not done by man but by God and Christ the Lord. Whatever is done in them is not done in man, but by God and Christ the Lord. Whatever the one commands or grants, either the king to the diocese or the priest to the realm, is not commanded and granted by man but by God and Christ the Lord. If we wish to be truly brothers, the king can be rightfully called priest, and the priest king, in this which is Christ the

Lord. For it is befitting the priest to rule the people in the spirit of Christ and befitting the king to sacrifice and immolate in the spirit. It is befitting of him to show "himself a living sacrifice, a holy sacrifice, a sacrifice pleasing to God," and to immolate to God the sacrifice of justice, of a united spirit, which has been completely signified through the material sacrifice which the priest keeps offering in the visible rite of the sacrament. If one wishes to discuss why the priest keeps sacrificing visibly and the king does not, it was made to demonstrate that some things are different on account of the diversity of the sacrament. For some were in part the sacrament of the king, others of the priest. The priest prefigured the human nature of Christ, the king His divine nature. The one symbolized the higher nature by which He is equal to God the Father, the other the lower which is less than the Father. The priest prefigured that Christ would pass to the limit of death and would give Himself in oblation and "sacrifice to God the Father in an odor of sweetness." The king, however, prefigured that He would reign in eternity, enthroned in a single heavenly seat "above all principality and power and might and dominion" and that He would be crowned with glory and honor and be established above all the works of God, and that all things would be subjected to Him.

Now let us turn to the New Testament because in that book priests and kings are sanctified with holy oil and chrism and are consecrated by divine benediction. I think that we are able to assert more truly and with greater certainty from these things which have been said above concerning priests and kings of the Old Testament that they have been made participators of divine grace and nature. For they themselves are one with God and his Christ; they are Gods and Christs through the spirit of adoption. In them Christ and the Holy Spirit speak. In them Christ perfects and manages His offices. In them He sacrifices and reigns and rules His people. Each is Christ and God in the spirit and in his office each is a figure or image of Christ and God: the priest of the sacerdotal and the king of the regal. The priest is of the lower office and nature—that is the human; the king is of the higher, the divine. For Christ is God and man, the true and highest king and priest. From an eternity of divinity Christ the king was not made, not created, not lower to or different from the Father but equal to and one with the Father. As priest from the putting on of His humanity, He was made according to the order of Melchizedek and created and made lower to the Father. In that He is king, He created all things, ruled all things; directing at the same time He saved both men and angels. In that He is priest He redeemed as many men as He made to reign with him. This is the full intention by which He was made priest, in that He offered Himself in sacrifice to make men participators of His kingdom and His royal power.

Everywhere in the scriptures He promises the kingdom of heaven to the faithful; nowhere the priesthood. It thus appears that for Christ the kingdom is greater and more excellent than the priestly power, so much, I am sure, as His divinity is greater and more excellent than His humanity. For what reason is it thought that similarly with men the royal power is greater and more excellent than the priestly, that the king is greater and more excellent than the priest inasmuch as he is the image of the better and more excellent nature of Christ and the emulation of His power? Why is it not, they say, against the justice of God if the priestly dignity is instituted through the royal or submissive to it, because in Christ it is enacted that he is made a priest through his royal power and through the priestly power is submissive to the father with whom he is equal through his royal power? If anyone says that the priest may be the king—for one who rules can rightly be called king—it may seem to do better that the king be invested by the king, the lesser by the greater. And they can speak contrariwise because the king is called in the writing of sacred benediction the "chief ruler." The king and the priest have the same grace and certain common gifts of privileges, but they also have certain diverse offices appropriate to each one. Although they seem to have a common grace in ruling, the priest acts in one way, the king in another, and there is a difference in the grace of each fulfilling his administration. If the priest is instituted through the king, he is not instituted through the power of man but of God. The power of the king is the power of God, belonging to God by nature and to the king by grace. Whence the king is God and Christ, albeit by grace, and whatever he does, he performs not simply as a man, but it has been done by God and it is being done by Christ through grace. Indeed, he who is by nature God and Christ works through his deputy through whom he performs his offices.

Wherefore most holy priests are submissive to kings as to Christ, and they yield compliance to them because they understand that Christ reigns and governs through all kings. Through kings the priests enter the sheepfold of the sheep—that is, through the power of government, and through the gateway—

that is, through Christ—they enter and are shepherds of the sheep. Through power the king is Christ and Christ is the gateway. Whoever, therefore, enters through the power of the king, enters through Christ. In this manner priests enter through the gateway and are the shepherds of the sheep.

The king who is blessed with so many special benedictions, who is consecrated and made divine with so many special sacraments—nothing is rightfully placed above him, because nothing is blessed with better benedictions, nothing is consecrated and made divine with greater sacraments—nay, not even with equal—and through this nothing is coequal to him. Wherefore, he should not be called a layman, because he is Christ the Lord, because through grace he is God, because he is the highest director, shepherd, master, defender, and instructor of the holy church, because he is lord of his brothers and should be adored by all, because he is the highest chief ruler. Neither should less be said by the priest because the priest consecrates him. It often happens that the lesser consecrates the greater, the lower the higher as the cardinals consecrate the pope and the suffragans the metropolitan. As it occurs they are not the authors of consecration but the ministers. God works the sacrament; they exhibit its ministry. To whom He wishes God attributes the greater sacraments, and to whom He wishes the lesser. Let not the lord pope be offended in these things which are spoken about the king since the king is the highest priest inasmuch as he is king.

York Tracts, IV: *On the Consecration of Priests and Kings*, trans. John Baldwin, from H. Boehmer, ed., in *Monumenta Germaniae historica, Libelli de lite*, III (1897), 662-679.

II. POPE INNOCENT III AND KING JOHN

The successors of Gregory VII settled the investiture controversy by making compromises with the princes of Western Europe. The earliest of these was concluded in 1107 between Pope Paschal II and King Henry I of England. This settlement grew out of a quarrel over investiture between Henry and Anselm, archbishop of Canterbury. The issue between them was an extremely important one—whether a newly elected bishop should do homage and swear fidelity to the king for the barony he held, and if so, when this ceremony should be performed. This question was one which Gregory VII had calmly ignored. He made no direct statement as to how and when a bishop should be invested with his temporal rights. It seems, however, fairly clear that he believed that this should automatically follow his consecration. In short, a bishop should be elected canonically and consecrated and invested with the spiritual insignia of his office by the archbishop. Then the prince should give him his temporal rights. It is impossible to say whether or not Gregory would have refused to allow a prelate to do homage and swear fidelity, but Anselm stoutly insisted that it was improper for him to do so. King Henry insisted that as a bishop held a barony, he should do homage and swear fidelity like any other vassal and that this should be done before consecration. Obviously this would give the king a veto power over episcopal elections—if he refused to accept a bishop, he could not be consecrated. Being a thoroughly practical man King Henry did not care very much who presented the new bishop with the ring and crozier.

The compromise was worked out on that basis. When an English prelate died, the king was to be notified. He would then summon the chief ecclesiastical personages of the diocese to meet under his presidency to elect a successor. The bishop-elect would then do homage, swear fidelity, and be invested with his barony. Only after that could he seek out the archbishop to be consecrated and invested with the ring and crozier. Actually, the English kings did not usually supervise the election in person. When he received notice of a prelate's death, he sent the chapter of the cathedral a "permission to elect." This was usually carried by a royal clerk who was himself the royal nominee for the office. In most cases the chapter elected the king's nominee without question, but if it refused and elected another, the king could refuse to accept his homage and so prevent his consecration. This system was thoroughly satisfactory to the English kings. It was, of course, a clear violation of the intention of Gregory's decree—it left the choice of bishops in lay control—but it did not violate his actual words. Investiture with the insignia of spiritual office was in the hands of the archbishop.

This system of electing bishops worked fairly smoothly through the reigns of Henry II (1154–1189) and Richard I (1189–1199). While there were occasional disputes, usually arising from a chapter's disinclination to elect a royal nominee, they were easily settled and as a rule in the king's favor. Moreover on the whole the royal nominees were highly respectable. They were usually royal clerks who earned promotion by service to the crown, but they were likely to be able administrators and men of respectable morals who served the church well. A few were scholars of some distinction and at least one became a saint. On January 8, 1198, a 37-year-old Italian nobleman named Lothar Conti was elected pope and assumed the name of Innocent III. He had a thorough training in both theology and canon law and had served in the papal court under five popes. He was determined to uphold the most lofty conceptions of the papal power and to enforce fully in all Christendom the laws of the church. On April 6, 1199, King Richard I of England died of a wound received in besieging the castle of a vassal and was succeeded by his brother John. Richard had been an able soldier completely devoted to the military life. He had paid little or no attention to the government of his realm. John was no soldier, but he was a conscientious and efficient administrator, determined to develop the power of the English crown. Of the seven episcopal elections held early in his reign only two gave him any trouble. Royal clerks were placed in the sees of Norwich, Bath, and Chichester. A faithful servant of King Richard became bishop of Worcester. Hereford went to the brother of a great baron to whom John was under obligation. But when he tried to place the brother of another baron, already bishop of St. Andrews in Scotland, in the see of Lincoln, the chapter objected and John gave way. Then when the see of Winchester fell vacant, the king nominated one of his favorite officials, Peter des Roches. Here too the chapter objected. John was determined to have his way and put the opposition in prison. Peter was elected and confirmed by the pope.

When John came to the throne, Hubert Walter, archbishop of Canterbury, enjoyed enormous prestige in England. He had started his career as a royal clerk under Henry II. King Richard made him bishop of Salisbury, archbishop of Canterbury, and justiciar of England. Papal objections finally obliged him to resign the justiciarship, but he remained a close and influential associate of his successor in that office. Hubert's interests were essentially secular, but he administered his see well and was respected by his clergy. During the early years of John's reign he was a dominant figure in the English government and had no objection to opposing the king. Naturally a monarch of John's temperament looked forward to the opportunity of obtaining a more pliable primate of all England.

Hubert Walter died on July 13, 1205. John hastened to Canterbury. There he found the chapter, the Benedictine monastery of Christ Church, engaged in an ancient debate with the bishops of the province who claimed a right to participate in the election of an archbishop. John persuaded both parties to promise to do nothing until December. But neither group kept their promise. The bishops sent a messenger to Rome to plead their cause and the monks also sent a delegation. At least a part of the monks did something more—they held a secret election and chose Reginald, their sub-prior, as archbishop and sent him at the head of their delegation. Reginald was certainly instructed to keep this election secret until he reached Rome and probably agreed not to reveal it unless the bishops tried to persuade the pope to accept a candidate of theirs. But Reginald talked as soon as he reached Flanders and John learned of the election.

He immediately rushed to Canterbury. The terrified monks denied that they had held an election and promptly elected John's nominee, John de Grey, bishop of Norwich. Chapter, bishops, and king despatched messengers to Rome to announce this election. Hence Innocent III found himself faced with two archbishops-elect. He declared both elections invalid. He ruled that the election of Reginald had been conditional and hence improper. But once an election had been made and the pope's confirmation sought, no other election could be held pending his decision. Hence John de Grey's election was invalid. The pope then ordered the chapter to send a delegation to Rome and the other parties were instructed to send delegates. When the delegation of the chapter appeared, Innocent asked them to elect an archbishop, but they split evenly between the sub-prior and John de Grey. The pope then suggested one of his cardinals, an Englishman named Stephen Langton. He was unanimously elected. Innocent then wrote to John asking him to accept Stephen as archbishop of Canterbury. John refused to do so and a bitter controversy ensued.

This struggle between John and Innocent III lasted until 1213. Eventually John gave way and made peace on the pope's terms. He did this because he was harassed by other troubles—baronial discontent and the threat of a French invasion. But as early as 1208 John offered to accept Stephen Langton. This then is the problem —why did the quarrel continue from 1208 to 1213? If John's offer to accept Stephen was not sufficient, what was the real issue in this controversy? The answer to this can be found in the following documents.

A. King John's Reply to the Letter of Pope Innocent III Announcing the Election of Stephen Langton

When King John received the letter of Innocent III informing him of the election of Stephen Langton as Archbishop of Canterbury, he was enraged. He promptly sent agents to Canterbury to eject the monks from their church and seize their property.

Except for a few who were too old and sick to move, the monks fled to France. John then wrote a violent reply to the pope's letter. We do not have this letter of King John, but we have an account of it in the chronicle of Roger of Wendover. Roger of Wendover wrote some years after these events took place. He was the official chronicler of the great abbey of St. Albans. He had access to many documents and he may well have seen a copy of John's letter. On the other hand Wendover made use of stories current in his day without worrying much about their accuracy. In short, this may be an account of what John wrote, but it may also be a summary of what popular rumor thought he wrote. Thus the problem is a double one—what was John's idea and how did it compare with that of his contemporaries?

After he had exiled the monks of Canterbury, John, king of the English, sent to the pope messengers with letters in which expressly and almost threateningly he accused him of having wickedly disavowed the election of the bishop of Norwich and of having consecrated as archbishop of Canterbury a certain Stephen de Langton who was almost unknown to him and who had long associated in the kingdom of France with his public enemies, and, what redounded more to the prejudice and subversion of the liberties belonging to his crown, the pope had presumed to promote this Stephen without having the royal assent properly requested by the monks who ought to seek it. And the king asserted that he could not be sufficiently astonished that the pope himself as well as the whole Roman court did not remember to what extent his affection for the Roman see was necessary to it as more revenues were received from the kingdom of England than from all other regions on that side of the Alps. The king added that he would, if it was necessary, stand until death for the privileges of his crown, unchangeably affirming that he could not revoke the election of the bishop of Norwich which he believed to be useful to him.

Roger of Wendover, *Flores historiarum*, trans. Sidney Painter, from Henry G. Hewlett, ed., in the Rolls Series, II, 40.

B. Letter of Pope Innocent III to King John

This letter dated May 26, 1207, at the Lateran is Pope Innocent's reply to John's refusal to accept Stephen Langton as Archbishop of Canterbury. Observe that this will enable you either to confirm or reject Wendover's account of John's letter to Innocent.

Innocent, bishop, servant of the servants of God to his most dear son in Christ John illustrious king of England greetings and apostolic benediction. When we wrote to you humbly and kindly as one asking and exhorting about the business of the church of Canterbury, you answered us contumaciously and haughtily as one threatening and disproving. . . . You pretend for certain frivolous reasons that you cannot give assent to the election by the monks of Canterbury of our dear son, Stephen, cardinal priest of St. Grisogoni; for he is an associate of your enemies and is almost unknown to you. . . . It is not a cause for blame but rather for glory that, living in Paris, he progressed so much in literary studies that he deserved to be a doctor not only in the liberal faculty but also indeed in the discipline of theology and for this reason, since his life was in accord with his teaching, he was considered worthy to obtain a Parisian prebend. Hence we are astonished if a man of so great a name coming from your realm can be unknown to you, especially since you wrote to him after he was promoted to the cardinalate by us that although you were inclined to recall him to your company nevertheless you rejoiced that he was raised to higher office. . . . Your messengers indeed expressed to us another reason why you did not give your assent—because it never was asked for by those who ought to seek it from you. . . . Although in the case of elections conducted at the Apostolic See it is not customary to seek the assent of the prince, nevertheless two monks of Canterbury were specially deputized to go

to you to ask your assent. As they were arrested at Dover, they could not carry out their instructions. We also, who have full power over the Church of Canterbury, deigned to implore the royal favor in this matter by our letters and our messenger, who presented the apostolic letters to you, bore also the letters of the prior and monks who conducted the election by the mandate of the whole chapter of Canterbury.

The Historical Works of Gervase of Canterbury, trans. Sidney Painter, from William Stubbs, in the Rolls Series, II, pp. lxxii-iv.

C. Letter of Archbishop Stephen Langton to the People of England

After his consecration by the pope, Stephen Langton went north to France prepared to cross to England if the king would allow him to. From there he wrote a number of letters arguing his case. This letter is addressed to the English people in general, but it is clearly aimed at the members of the knightly class. It has several very interesting features. One is the attempt to explain the powers of the papacy in feudal terms. Another is the reference to the right of patronage—the right of the founder of an abbey, priory, or parish church and his successors to nominate the abbot, prior, or parson. The problem is not only to understand Stephen's argument but also to comprehend the motives that Stephen believes will move those he is addressing.

Stephen, by the grace of God, Archbishop of Canterbury, primate of all England and cardinal of the Holy Roman Church to his most beloved brothers, sons, and friends in Christ and all faithful Christians in the realm of England, greeting, grace, and benediction. . . . Since the times are bad, and worse, it is believed, approach, we hasten to inform affectionately your serenity that you may hold healthily the path of truth among the present difficulties. In

the first place therefore we warn you emphatically that no one of you be executor, counselor, or minister of wickedness. For according to human laws even a serf is not bound to his lord in atrocious acts, less yet you who enjoy freedom in heart and condition. This is proved by a clear example. Whoever among you are known to rule over others, receive their homage saving the faith owed the lord king, so that if perchance they offend by the will or command of inferior lords, they are considered traitors and perjurers. So fidelity is promised or sworn to kings or other temporal lords saving the faith owed to the superior lord, that is the eternal king who is king of kings and lord of lords. Hence whatever service is performed for a temporal king, to the prejudice of the eternal king, is without question treason. Therefore dear sons, Holy Church has decreed that when any rebel persists in schism his men shall be absolved from the fidelity owed him so that as the schismatic has removed his fidelity from the eternal lord so the fidelity of his men will be taken from him. . . . Dearest sons who have been elevated to the knightly office, remember that you received its insignia from the church so that you might guard this same church with your swords and ours. If moreover it can be defended with less peril than in an armed struggle, that is by faithful counsel and devout admonition, it is just that each one of you guard it the more eagerly. We moreover on our side are prepared to conserve your rights by prompt solicitude. For neither the church of Canterbury nor of Rome intends to deprive you of the patronage of churches or the right of presentation. . . .

Stephen Langton, in Gervase of Canterbury, trans. Sidney Painter, from Stubbs, *op. cit.*, II, pp. lxxviii-lxxxiii.

D. Letter of King John to the Men of the County of Kent

On August 27, 1207, the pope addressed a letter to three English prelates, the bishops of London, Ely, and Worcester, ordering them to place England under an interdict if John continued to refuse to accept Stephen Langton. These three bishops became the pope's "executors" or agents in England in his quarrel with the king. While the bishop of Worcester had actually been consecrated after John came to the throne, these three prelates had been chosen by King Richard I. Except for a few who were too old to be effective, they were the only English bishops on whom the pope could rely fully.

Apparently the bishops had little success in their negotiations. By the beginning of 1208 they were about ready to proclaim the interdict. As we shall see later, John sent an agent to Rome to negotiate directly with the pope. This letter shows that he also negotiated with Stephen Langton through the latter's younger brother, Simon. The three bishops officially published the interdict on March 24, 1208, and promptly sailed for France. This letter from John to the men of Kent was issued at Winchester on March 13.

The king to all the men of Kent. Know that Master Simon de Langton came to us at Winchester on March 12 and in the presence of our bishops asked us to receive his brother Master Stephen de Langton as Archbishop of Canterbury. When we spoke to him of safeguarding our dignity in this matter, he said that he would do nothing for us in that respect unless we placed ourselves entirely at his mercy. We are informing you of this that you may know the harm and injury done us. . . .

Rotuli litterarum patentium, trans. Sidney Painter, from Thomas D. Hardy, ed., for the Record Commission, p. 80.

E. Letter of King John to the People of Lincolnshire

This letter is dated March 18, 1208. The king knew that the interdict was about to be proclaimed and was preparing for it. Observe John's application of feudal ideas to ecclesiastical affairs—those who do not perform the service for which they hold their lands should lose them. It seems clear that similar letters were sent to the other English sees. William de Cornhill, Archdeacon of Huntingdon, was a faithful and reliable royal clerk. Gerard de Canville was a baron who was high in John's favor.

King to all the inhabitants of the bishopric of Lincoln, both clerks and laymen. Know that beginning March 24 we have entrusted to William de Cornhill, Archdeacon of Huntingdon and Gerard de Canville all lands and property of abbots, priors, religious, and clerks of the see of Lincoln who are unwilling to celebrate divine service and we command that you obey them as our officials. . . .

Ibid., p. 80.

F. Letter of Pope Innocent III to his Agents in England

On May 27, 1208, Innocent III wrote to his agents to inform them that King John had proposed terms through the abbot of Beaulieu. The abbey of Beaulieu in Hampshire was a Cistercian house founded by King John in a fleeting fit of penitence for the sins of his youth. It was the only religious house founded by him. Its abbot was his devoted servant and his chief agent in negotiations with the pope.

Innocent, bishop, servant of the servants of God, to the bishops of London, Ely, and Worcester, greeting and apostolic benediction. Our most dear son in Christ, John, illustrious king of the English, has sent letters to us by our dear son the abbot of Beaulieu asking that we believe what the abbot shall propose to us in his name. He himself proposes that although he considers himself gravely aggrieved in the business of the church of Canterbury, nevertheless because of the devotion and reverence which he asserts he has for the Roman church and our person he is prepared to receive and treat with our venerable brother Stephen, Archbishop of Canterbury, cardinal of the Holy Roman Church, as archbishop, giving security to him and his household as may seem best and promising to make full restitution of property to clergymen and to churches. He will allow the monks of Canterbury to return to their church and remain in safety even though this seems to him very grave because he believes they treasonably intrigued against him in this business.

Innocent III, in Gervase of Canterbury, trans. Sidney Painter, from Stubbs, *ibid.*, II, pp. xc-xcii.

G. Another Letter of Innocent III to his Agents in England

This letter of Innocent III to the bishops of London, Ely, and Worcester is dated August 22, 1208. It is clear that something has gone wrong in the negotiations between the bishops and King John and someone, presumably the king, has charged Innocent with bad faith. The meaning of this letter will be made clear by the later documents. The problem here is to try to find out just what Innocent refers to.

Innocent, bishop, the servant of the servants of God, to the bishop of London, Ely and Worcester, greeting and apostolic benediction. . . . Although we are anxious to make full peace in England between realm and priesthood in so far as we can since we wish to have peace with all men; nevertheless in vain do some men scheme to suggest to others, or by their fabrications to persuade others, that we on any occasion whatsoever desire to lean to right or left to the detriment of ecclesiastical liberty, when this contentious affair undoubtedly tends to this end, that the church of God, which lay enslaved, may arise free. Therefore we direct that paying no attention to various suggestions which are put forth by bad angels you proceed faithfully according to the form and tenor of our mandate leaving aside any sinister interpretation; that the sentence of interdict be not before or otherwise relaxed than the most dear son in Christ, John, illustrious king of the English, shall receive and treat with our venerable brother Stephen, Archbishop of Canterbury, cardinal of the Holy Roman Church as archbishop of Canterbury, giving such security to him and his followers as seems best according to your judgment and shall make full restitution of property to the archbishop, the monks of Canterbury, and other churches and persons; he shall permit these monks to return to their church and remain secure. . . . This is the tenor of our mandate, prudent and simple to understand which in our letters we clearly expressed and diligently exposed to our beloved son the abbot of Beaulieu, messenger of the king, so that we consider not only unworthy but impi-ous if anyone, risking sacrilege, says or believes that we express our intentions now in one manner, now in another, since the apostolic see by the grace of God has the prudence of the serpent and the simplicity of the dove. . . .

Ibid., II, pp. xci-xcii. [This and the following texts from Gervase of Canterbury were translated by Sidney Painter.]

H. Letter of King John to the Pope's Agents

Early in January, 1209, Innocent III ordered John to carry out the offer which he had sent to Rome by the abbot of Beaulieu. If peace was not made in three months, the king would be excommunicated. The bishops of London, Ely, and Worcester were directed to publish the sentence if John did not obey. This new threat does not seem to have seriously disturbed the king, but it worried his servants who did not relish the idea of risking the penalties imposed by the church on those who served an excommunicate. On July 13, 1209, the king addressed this letter to the pope's agents asking them to come to England to negotiate. Peter, Bishop of Winchester, was a devoted servant of John and was to stand by him throughout his quarrel with Innocent. On the other hand, Jocelyn, Bishop of Bath, left England when the king was finally excommunicated. So did his brother, Hugh, who is called bishop-elect of Lincoln in this letter. Both these brothers had been chancery clerks. Geoffrey Fitz Peter as justiciar was head of the royal administration. The earl of Arundel and Aubrey de Vere, Earl of Oxford, were great barons. William Brewer was a royal servant who was rapidly building a barony. The abbot of Beaulieu, Henry, Archdeacon of Stafford, and William, Archdeacon of Huntingdon, were royal clerks. The patent and close rolls for this period have been lost—otherwise this letter would have appeared on one of them.

John by God's grace, king of England, to the venerable fathers in Christ the bishops of London, Ely, and Worcester. Know that we have talked with our venerable fathers Peter, bishop of Winchester, and Jocelyn, bishop of Bath, with our faithful men the bishop elect of Lincoln and Geoffrey Fitz Peter, our justiciar, and with our council and for the sake of God and at the lord pope's request we shall satisfy holy church; and know that we send to meet you at Dover with the above mentioned bishops of Winchester and Bath, the elect of Lincoln, and our justiciar, the earl of Arundel, Earl Aubrey, William Brewer, the abbot of Beaulieu, Henry, Archdeacon of Stafford, and William, Archdeacon of Huntingdon, to whom we have entrusted full power to satisfy holy church in all things in our name. And we ask you peremptorily to come into our land without any delay or excuses. We send you moreover our letters of conduct: and bring with you the privilege of the lord pope for conserving our rights which has been obtained and deposited at Clarum Mariscum, if it can be done, otherwise a transcript of them. Meanwhile therefore arrange that no new penalty be laid on us or our realm since we are prepared to obey the mandate of holy church and to satisfy that church. Witnessed by me at Gloucester July 13.

Ibid., II, p. c.

I. Memorandum concerning a Meeting between John's Agents and those of Innocent III in July and August, 1209

This memorandum apparently describes the meeting initiated by the last letter. In this document, Henry, archdeacon of Stafford, appears as Henry, bishop-elect of Exeter. This election was never recognized by either Archbishop Stephen or the pope. After the conclusion of peace between the king and the church, Henry was elevated to the archbishopric of Dublin. The bishop of Hereford mentioned here was Giles de Briouse, son of William de Briouse who had once been John's close friend but was now his bitter foe. John had crushed the power of the house of Briouse, and Giles had fled to France. Although his quarrel with John was hardly an ecclesiastical matter, the pope had taken up his cause. The reader should note carefully the extent to which the arrangement outlined here fulfills John's requirements as shown in previous documents.

Be it known to all who may inspect this letter that peace between the priesthood and the realm was discussed between the lord bishops of London, Ely, and Worcester, executors of the lord pope, on one part, and messengers of the lord king on the other part—to wit the lord bishops of Winchester and Bath, Hugh bishop elect of Lincoln and Henry bishop elect of Exeter, the abbot of Beaulieu, Geoffrey Fitz Peter, earl of Essex, the earl of Arundel, Earl Aubrey, and Henry, archdeacon of Huntingdon. Full restitution shall be made at once to lord Stephen, Archbishop of Canterbury of his lands and liberties with free administration of them so that he shall be in possession of them as Hubert once archbishop of Canterbury was the day he died. The monks of Canterbury also will have full possession of lands and liberties with free administration. The bishops of London, Ely, Worcester, and Hereford shall have such possession of

lands and liberties and free administration of all as they had on the day the sentence of interdict was launched. Monks, canons, and other ecclesiastical persons shall have similarly full possession. Full restitution shall be made to the lord archbishop, the bishops, and the monks of Canterbury, and all other ecclesiastical persons of all money which came into the hand of the king or was used for his purposes whether it was taken by tallage or other means except such revenue as the lord king ought to have if the church were in good peace and full liberty. And this restitution will be completed in three weeks after the feast of St. Lawrence. . . . The lord king will receive lord Stephen, Archbishop of Canterbury, cardinal of the Holy Roman Church, and will treat him as archbishop of Canterbury and will give security to him and his men and to the bishops of London, Ely, Worcester, and Hereford and their men, so that they can come and remain in safety. The lord king will announce this safe conduct through his own mouth before his magnates. Lord Stephen archbishop of Canterbury and other bishops will come in safety and remain in safety and the king shall make letters patent to this effect for each of them. The bishops, earls, and barons whom the archbishop and bishops shall name shall at the command and wish of the king be responsible for this safe conduct and will make their letters patent for each prelate. The lord archbishop on his arrival, having received his regalia [investiture with his temporal powers] shall swear fidelity to the lord king as his predecessors did to his progenitors. The monks of Canterbury shall be allowed to return to their church and remain in safety. When all this shall be completed, the interdict will be removed. The above mentioned bishops of London, Ely, and Worcester and Master Simon de Langton say that in so far as they can they will in good faith preserve the rights of the lord king to the honor of God, holy church, and the king and his realm. They will try as best they can while conserving the honor of God and the church to see that this agreement does not injure the royal prerogative in any way. The above mentioned messengers

Ibid., II, pp. ci-ciii.

of the lord king promised that they would work in good faith so that this agreement might be confirmed as drawn up. Because of this hope of peace by the counsel of the messengers the afore-mentioned executors postponed the day of announcing the excommunication of the lord king for five weeks.

J. Stephen Langton's Account of the Negotiations with King John

Despite the optimistic tone of the memorandum about the meeting in the summer of 1209, peace was not made and the sentence of excommunication against King John was published in France. But negotiations between the two parties continued. This document which was probably written in the summer of 1210 by Archbishop Langton seems to have been intended primarily to explain why he had just refused an invitation to come to England to meet with the king. It is a general account of the negotiations of 1209 and 1210. This should be carefully compared with our other statements on the same subject.

The messengers of the lord king of the English, the abbot of Stratford, and the prior of Holy Trinity of London, proposed to us in his name: first that the king himself and his magnates grieved greatly that we did not go to Dover to speak with him. For they believed that if we had come, peace with the church would certainly have come to pass. Secondly they asked us in his name that, if the power of absolving him conceded to us by the lord pope did not suffice for providing for consideration of the dignity which his predecessors had, we should take care to obtain an adequate privilege; because he would be held in greater gratitude to us, if it was done by us than if it were obtained otherwise. They added that the justiciar in the presence of the magnates said that no one of them would advise

the king to make peace unless sufficient provision was made for safeguarding his dignity; because they could fear that as a consequence the dignities of the magnates themselves would be destroyed. He added, moreover, that only the bishop of Winchester who was present failed to agree with this point of view. The above mentioned messengers asked us moreover in the king's name that we should send at once to England under our seal the privilege of the lord pope deposited at Clarum Mariscum or a transcript of it to be shown to the lord king so that if it seemed to him to be sufficient, he could satisfy the church; if it was insufficient he asks us to amend its insufficiencies by our efforts. They asked us thirdly on the part of the king that if we could not at present provide a sufficient privilege, we would relax at once the interdict on the realm, he alone remaining under sentence, so that as he alone was delinquent, he alone should be still punished until he could obtain full grace.

To these propositions we replied in this order and this manner. . . . In regard to what they said about obtaining a privilege for the lord king to conserve his dignity, we answered that this same scheme was proposed to us when we were at Dover before the king fell under sentence in the presence of our brothers of London and Ely, executors of the lord pope, the bishops of Winchester, Salisbury, Rochester and Bath, the bishop-elect of Lincoln, the chancellor, the archdeacon of Stafford, and many other clerks and many lay magnates. Then the executors answered that they could not promise that the lord pope would do anything but that indeed if the king wished to satisfy the church according to the pope's order, they would diligently beg him through messengers and letters that he deign to provide for the lord king that nothing that was done should be in detriment of his dignity. The executors added that if they begged the lord pope for a privilege before the king gave satisfaction, they would labor in vain. We on our part answered that under the conditions we could not honestly promise anything; nevertheless we stated that we were willing to work by messengers and letters to obtain a privilege after the king gave satisfaction. . . . This was the answer

Ibid., II, pp. cx-cxii.

K. *Account of a Meeting between King John and Representatives of Innocent III*

In the spring of 1211 the pope decided to send two men from his court to negotiate with King John. One of these was a cardinal named Pandulf and the other a knight of the Temple named Durand. These two emissaries met John at Northampton on August 30. This document is the account of this meeting given by a chronicler. It is certainly highly inaccurate (see Painter, *Reign of King John*, pp. 186-7). It seems likely that the chronicler had no definite information about the meeting and invented the whole thing. But he could only do this by piecing together current gossip. Hence this document shows what at least some Englishmen believed to have been the issues between king and pope and their respective attitudes and actions. Here again the problem is to separate the ideas of Innocent and John from those attributed to them by others.

The messengers of the Lord Pope Innocent III coming before John king of

before the king was excommunicated. We replied to the abbot and prior, the above mentioned messengers, that if under those circumstances we could not say honestly anything more, much less could we when the king is excommunicate, especially as it is wrong to communicate with him. Nor would the lord pope, we believe, grant him a privilege in his present state. Moreover in regard to the privilege deposited at Clarum Mariscum we replied as we replied in England that we have not this privilege. We added that the abbot of that house would act against the prohibition of the lord pope if he showed it or a copy to anyone or even allowed it to be seen without a special apostolic command. The abbot of Beaulieu who obtained the privilege knows how it was deposited at Clarum Mariscum.

England at Northampton where he had gathered all the earls and barons of England spoke to the lord king in this manner.

MESSENGERS. "Lord, we have come here from afar at your request to confirm and reform the peace of Holy Church and to hear your will in this matter."

KING. "I do not know what you seek."

MESSENGERS. "Nothing except common justice: that is that you swear that you will satisfy Holy Church and repay all that you have extorted from ecclesiastical persons and receive well and in peace Master Stephen archbishop of Canterbury, his people, and his fellow bishops who are across the seas."

KING. Hearing this the king with a haughty look replied, "I shall reveal to you my heart and the secrets of my heart. You can make me swear to return all things and whatever you wish, I shall do; but never can this Stephen such safe conduct have that I shall not, when he enters my land, have him hanged."

MESSENGERS. Hearing this the messengers replied, "We know your will; have you anything else to say?"

KING. "I have spoken."

MESSENGERS. "We wish to tell you and all your earls, barons, clerks, and laymen the cause for our coming into your land. It is true that you summoned us from Rome that we should come to hear your most just cause, as you call it, and your right; and if when your cause had been explained and heard it seemed to us that you had been delinquent in any way toward your father the lord pope, Holy Church, and the English clergy, you would be prompt to satisfy Holy Church according to our judgment and whatever penance we enjoined you would perform, and if we could find your cause just, as you claim, we would relax the interdict on England. You have given no reason why we should relax it, but rather why we should confirm it."

KING. "Listen, and rightly judge. Agreed that the lord pope is my spiritual father, that he acts as the vice-regent of St. Peter, and that I ought to obey him in all spiritual matters. This does not apply to what pertains to my crown in terrestrial affairs. The lord pope wishes to grant the archbishopric of Canterbury unjustly through an election made by traitors to me, fourteen monks of Canterbury who swore that they would never elect anyone except the bishop of Norwich. Trusting their word I gave them my letters patent to the lord pope in these words 'Whomever they should elect as archbishop of Canterbury, if he was an Englishman, I would receive' and I gave them £300 for expenses. When they reached Rome they elected Stephen Langton and rejected the bishop of Norwich without consulting me. All my

predecessors appointed archbishops, bishops, and abbots in their chambers.

"You can see by holy writings that the blessed and most glorious King St. Edward appointed St. Wulstan bishop of Worcester. When William the Bastard, the Conqueror, wished to deprive Wulstan of the bishopric because he knew no French, St. Wulstan said to William, 'You did not give me the crozier and I shall not render it to you.' He went to the tomb of St. Edward and said in his language, 'Edward, you gave me the crozier. I cannot hold it because of the king and therefore I entrust it to you: if you can defend it, do so.' He placed the crozier on the tomb of cut stone and the crozier miraculously adhered to it so that no one could move it but St. Wulstan. In our times my father Henry gave the archbishopric of Canterbury to St. Thomas. But the lord pope wishes to deprive me by his will of all the privileges my predecessors had and he does not do well."

MESSENGERS. Master Pandulf replied, "You claim that you are held to obey the lord pope in spiritual but not in temporal matters. We say that you ought to obey the lord pope in temporal as in spiritual affairs. You swore fidelity to God, and obedience to the pope and the rights of the church when you received the government of the realm. You allege that the fourteen monks are traitors because they swore never to elect anyone except the bishop of Norwich and you entrusted them with letters patent and wrote the pope that you would accept as archbishop anyone these monks elected who was an Englishman and furthermore you gave them £300 for expenses. Later they elected Master Stephen Langton. It is true you sent such letters patent to the pope. . . . The lord pope nullified the election of both the subprior and the bishop of Norwich—the subprior because his person was odious to the king and the realm and the bishop of Norwich because he was inadequate to hold so great an office and because his election was improper. Then the lord pope ordered all the monks who were there to divide in three groups and choose a suitable pastor. The first group chose the subprior; the fourteen monks chose the bishop of Norwich, and the third part Master Stephen. The lord pope ordered then that all should agree to one. The fourteen monks then prostrated themselves at the feet of the lord pope and said, 'Lord, pity us, since we swore before the lord king not to agree to elect anyone except the bishop of Norwich.' The lord pope said, 'Are you not men of the church? How do you therefore presume to make an oath to a temporal prince without the command of your prelate?' They answered, 'We did it from fear of the king and to save the dignity of our church.' The lord pope said, 'You vowed to make an oath that no one can make in this world except me alone.' And he absolved them and enjoined them to penance. Then they went and agreed to Master Stephen. The lord pope indeed presented him to you as the prince before he confirmed his election, but you repudiated him although you neither knew nor could show any cause why he should not be confirmed.

"You make claims based on St. Edward and William the Bastard, to which I reply that you are not the successor of St. Edward nor can you be compared with him. He was the protector of Holy Church; you indeed are its destroyer and foe; but we agree that you are the successor of William the Bastard since he attacked Holy Church in that he wished to deprive St. Wulstan of the see of Worcester. You succeeded him, not St. Edward. You have not degenerated in this respect—you and all your predecessors have striven to destroy Holy Church. Thus the laws of William the Bastard, although the worst, you love and use; and the laws of St. Edward, although the best, you vilely condemn.

"Then you say that your father Henry and all his predecessors were accustomed to grant archbishoprics, bishoprics, abbeys, and priories in their chambers. I reply that your father Henry by his petition secured the election of St. Thomas, and because he was elected as a result of this petition when he went in exile to Pope Alexander he resigned the archbishopric saying he had received it as a simoniac, because he was elected by the request of your father Henry. Then the lord pope gave him a dispensation. Then peace having been made between your father and St. Thomas the archbishop returned to his church and underwent martyrdom by your father's command. Then indeed when your father Henry gave satisfaction to Holy Church, he gave to the monks of Canterbury the privilege that they should elect the archbishop according to God's law without summoning the bishops but with the royal assent and the assent of the earls and barons who are present and by his charter he confirmed this privilege for himself and his heirs. . . ."

KING. "This granted Henry my father for his life but not to prejudice his successors."

.   .   .

KING. "I shall do this much for love of the lord pope: let Master Stephen resign the archbishopric and the lord pope confer the archbishopric on whom he wills and I shall receive that man as archbishop; and later let the lord pope ask me to grant Stephen a see in my land and perhaps I shall give him one in England."

PANDULF. "Holy Church is not accustomed to degrade an archbishop without cause; but it is accustomed to remove rebellious princes."

KING. "You make threats? You believe you can subject me to you as you did my nephew the Emperor Otto? I have heard from him that you have made another be elected as emperor in Germany."

PANDULF. "That is true. And the lord pope believes, in fact is certain, that he will make this new man emperor as he made Otto; and he will subject you as he did Otto."

KING. "Can you do more ill than you say?"

PANDULF. "You have revealed to us the secrets of your heart and we will reveal to you the secrets of our heart. Know that the lord pope excommunicated you, but suspended the sentence until we came into the lands subject to you. Know that you are excommunicate and the sentence against you is in effect."

KING. "What more?"

PANDULF. "We absolve all Englishmen on this day who do not communicate with you, and all who do are excommunicate."

KING. "And what more?"

PANDULF. "We absolve on this day the earls, barons, knights, clerks, free laymen, and all faithful Christians in the lands subject to you from the fidelity and homage by which they are bound to you, and the enforcement of this in England we entrust to the bishops of Winchester and Norwich as our agents. We transmit the cause of Holy Church and your right which you say you have demonstrated to the bishops of all the world so that they can absolve all who attack you as a foe of Holy Church. This will not be hard, for two years ago dukes, counts and barons asked the pope to absolve them so that they could enter this land in force and entrust the realm to whomever the lord pope may choose. The lord pope indeed proposes to send his army into England for you have few neighbors who are your friends and many who are your foes. The Holy Church wishes to declare its rights and enforce its rights through its sons. We command all that when the lord pope sends his army into England you join it and do fidelity to its leader. Otherwise you will suffer deserved and perpetual punishment."

KING. "What can you do more?"

PANDULF. "In God's word we say to you that neither you nor any heir you can have can after this day be crowned."

Annals of Burton, trans. Sidney Painter, from H. R. Luard, ed., in *Annales Monastici,* I, 209-217.

L. The Ideas of an Ecclesiastical Supporter of King John

We have seen that during the investiture controversy the clerical supporters of the royal and imperial point of view were highly articulate. King John's ecclesiastical allies seem in general to have preferred to ignore the pope's commands without advancing arguments to bolster their position. One of the chroniclers, however, gives this brief account of a clergyman who defended the royal position. His arguments resemble closely some of those advanced by the supporters of the theory of absolute monarchy in the Stuart period. Observe that the writer has no use for Alexander.

During the time of the interdict a certain pseudotheologian, Master Alexander, called the Mason, entered the king's council. He moved the king to cruelty by his wicked preaching. He said that this general scourge (the interdict) was brought on England not by the king's fault but by the wickedness of his people. He also stated that the king was the rod of God's anger and had been made a prince in order to rule his people and others subject to him with a rod of iron, to break them all like a potter's vessel, to bind those in power with shackles and the nobles with manacles of iron. By certain plausible arguments he proved that neither the temporal possessions nor the government of the subjects of kings or other potentates belonged to the pope since no power had been given by Christ to Peter, prince of the apostles, except over the church and ecclesiastical things.

Roger of Wendover, trans. Sidney Painter, from Rolls Series, II, 53.

M. Statement of Money Received by King John from the English Church during the Interdict

This document, which has been preserved among the records of the English Exchequer, was carelessly compiled. While minor discrepancies in the totals are caused by my omission of shillings and pence, the compiler clearly could not add. He used archdeaconry and archbishopric interchangeably. Then he was trying to do something that was very complicated—he was attempting to list the money received because of the quarrel with the pope. This is shown by his doubt as to whether or not to include the archbishopric of York. Geoffrey Plantagenet, archbishop of York, was in exile, but his quarrel with the king was a separate affair having nothing to do with Stephen Langton. Then, too, the compiler does not include the revenues of bishoprics vacant because of the death of their holders. The only exception to this is the 300 marks collected from the clergy of the see of Exeter. The bishopric of Norwich was not vacant and the bishop was John's good friend. I suspect its appearance here is an error. But while this record cannot be taken seriously in detail, it is valuable as a general statement. The sum of 100,000 marks was about twice John's ordinary annual revenue. The question here is whether or not the profits from the quarrel with the church were great enough to make John want to prolong it.

Receipts by King John from the bishoprics, abbeys, and clergy of England during the interdict because of Stephen, Archbishop of Canterbury.

From the archdeaconry (of Canterbury)	17,148 marks
From the priory (of Canterbury)	10,647 "
From the bishopric of London	2,989 "
From the bishopric of Salisbury	2,156 "
From the bishopric of Lincoln with the abbey of Eynsham	6,082 "
From the bishopric of Worcester	2,234 "
From the bishopric of Bath	3,186 "
From the bishopric of Ely	7,253 "
From the bishopric of Hereford	856 "
From the archbishopric of York	5,533 "
Sum without the archbishopric of York	52,585 "
Sum with this archbishopric	58,117 "
From the clergy of the archbishopric of Canterbury	1,727 marks
From the clergy of the bishopric of London	606 "
From the clergy of the bishopric of Salisbury	964 "
From the clergy of the bishopric of Lincoln	3,388 "
From the clergy of the bishopric of Worcester	711 "
From the clergy of the bishopric of Bath	418 "
From the clergy of the bishopric of Chichester	300 "
From the clergy of the bishopric of Norwich	1,500 "
Sum without archdeaconate of York	8,385 "
Sum with this archdeaconate	14,793 "
From the white monks (Cistercians)	24,027 marks
From other religious	15,044 "
Sum	39,070 "
From the clergy of the archishopric of York and the clergy of the bishopric of Durham	6,407 "
Sum total	100,005 marks

Red Book of the Exchequer, trans. Sidney Painter, from H. Hall, ed., in Rolls Series, II, 772-774.

N. *Letters Patent of a Group of Barons of Ireland in Support of King John*

From 1204 to 1211 King John was estranged from one of the most powerful of his vassals, William Marshal, Earl of Pembroke. In addition to extensive possessions in England, William was lord of Netherwent in Eastern Wales, of Pembroke in Western Wales, and of the vast lordship of Leinster in Ireland. During this period of estrangement Earl William spent most of his time in his lordship of Leinster. In 1211 King John found that he had too many enemies and decided to heal his quarrel with William. (See Sidney Painter, *William Marshal* [1933], pp. 142-174, especially pp. 172-4.) Sometime in 1212 John wrote to William sending him a copy of "letters patent issued by my barons of England." He asked William to get the barons of Ireland to issue similar letters. If the letters patent were really issued by the barons of England—a little fraud was not beneath King John—they have been lost, but we have those issued by the barons of Ireland. Presumably these letters were drawn up in John's chancery and represented his point of view, but the barons issued them and William Marshal, at least, was not one to be led by the nose. Certainly it seems safe to assume that the contents did not trouble the barons. This letter should be compared with Langton's letter to the people of England.

Declaration by William Marshall, Earl of Pembroke, Meyler Fitz Henry, Roger Pipard, Geoffrey de Mariscis, William le Petit, Nicholas de Verdun, Thomas Bloet, Adam de Hereford, Thomas Fitz Maurice, William Fitz William, Baron of Naas, Philip de Prendergast, Geoffrey de Canville, Richard de Futipo, Peter de Meset, John Fitz Leo, Thomas Fitz Anthony, Walter de Rideleff, John de Clahull, Roger Waspail, William de Katinton, David de Rupe, Maurice de London, Alexander Fitz Hugh, William de Aencurt, William Fitz Stephen, Adam le Gros, Adam le Bret, and all the magnates of Ireland.

Moved with grief and astonishment they had lately heard that the Pope proposed to absolve the subjects of the King from their fealty because the King resisted the injury done to him regarding the matter of the church of Canterbury. God had given them their Lord to defend them; therefore they ought to defend their liege Lord with all their strength. All that had been done regarding the church of Canterbury had been done against the liberty and dignity of the King and of the Crown of England. Before the coming of the Normans the Kings of England conferred at their will cathedral churches on many archbishops and bishops, now saints. But after this period the Kings granted that elections should be made, as they have hitherto been made, by assent of the King. Their Lord is faithful to them; they are his liege subjects; they and their forefathers have been nourished, enriched with wealth and honours, enfeoffed by the King and his ancestors; the King had never offended against the constitution or his subjects; and resisted in regard to the church of Canterbury that he might preserve in their integrity the liberty and dignity which the Crown of England has hitherto enjoyed. With the King they are prepared to live or die; and to the last they will faithfully and inseparably adhere to the King.

Calendar of Documents Relating to Ireland, ed. H. S. Sweetman, Rolls, Series, I, no. 448, pp. 73-74.

III. POPE BONIFACE VIII AND KING PHILIP IV OF FRANCE

Frederick I Barbarossa, who became king of Germany in 1152, and thereafter Holy Roman Emperor, had a clear and definite plan for the development of his empire. The key to this plan was the development of a strong imperial government in Italy.

The Italian provinces were rich and if properly handled could yield a large money revenue. With this money the emperor might be able to curb the independence of the German princes and develop a strong monarchy in that realm.

This policy was extremely distasteful to the towns of Lombardy which had long been practically independent and oblivious of their theoretical obligations to the emperor. It also gravely disturbed the papacy. The independence of the pope could hardly exist if any ruler had effective control of Italy. Hence the pope encouraged the Lombard towns to resist the imperial claims. After a long and bitter struggle the emperor decided that he could not subdue the great towns. He made a compromise with them and turned his attention to obtaining effective control of Tuscany and the Romagna including a great deal of land that the pope claimed as part of his patrimony. Frederick also bought off the pope's most vigorous ally, the Norman king of Sicily, by marrying his son and heir Henry to a Sicilian princess. This prince, as the Emperor Henry VI, briefly ruled Germany, most of Italy, and the Sicilian kingdom. Had he lived out his allotted span, he might well have carried out his father's plans. But Henry died in 1197 leaving as heirs a brother and an infant son.

The great Pope Innocent III devoted a large part of his pontificate to an attempt to recover the lost papal lands and to prevent a permanent union between the empire and the kingdom of Sicily. In this he failed. When he died, Henry's son Frederick II was king of Germany and Sicily and Holy Roman Emperor. Innocent's successors continued his efforts. They used all the power of their mighty office to break Frederick's power. They were particularly successful in rousing to rebellion the Lombard towns. While Frederick was able to keep his position against his foes as long as he lived, after his death his dynasty quickly disappeared. Moreover during Frederick's long struggle with the papacy, the German princes obtained almost complete independence and effectively destroyed the power of the German crown.

The last scion of Frederick's house was slain by the French prince, Charles of Anjou, count of Provence, brother of King Louis IX, who had conquered the kingdom of Sicily with the pope's blessing. Thus by 1270 the Holy Roman Empire was a hollow shell. The papacy had triumphed over its most formidable foe.

During its final struggle with the empire the papacy had relied heavily on the friendship of France. Although Louis IX had refused to give direct aid against Frederick II, he allowed his brother Charles to conquer Sicily at the pope's behest. Louis' son Philip III led a "crusade" against the king of Aragon who had seized Sicily from Charles of Anjou. The crusade was a total failure and Philip died on the campaign. The first royal task of his young heir Philip IV was to get the French army safely home. The fact that this campaign against Aragon, costly in both men and money, had been undertaken at the pope's request may well have made the new king of France less well disposed than his predecessors toward the papacy.

King Philip IV (1285–1314), called Le Bel or the Handsome, was a man of virtuous life and deep personal piety, but he was cold, calculating, ruthless and was imbued with determination to increase the royal power. He surrounded himself with men trained in Roman Law who believed in the supremacy of the secular state. Philip was not inclined to compromise in any quarrel with the papacy that affected his royal authority and his ministers were ready to encourage and support him.

In 1294 the College of Cardinals elevated to the papal throne Benedict Gaetani, an aged noble, who took the name of Boniface VIII. Boniface was arrogant and ambitious. He was determined to exalt his own position and that of his great office. Hence he had no inclination to sympathize with the demands of secular princes which conflicted with his conception of the papal power.

Ever since the Cluniac reform movement the question as to whether or not a secular monarch could force the clergy of his lands to contribute to his financial resources had been a matter of dispute.

King William II of England quarreled on this issue with Anselm, Archbishop of Canterbury in the eleventh century. In general, however, the papacy was inclined to recognize that the princes had a right to demand contributions from the secular possessions of prelates, but not from their ecclesiastical property. Then in the twelfth century pope and kings combined in efforts to raise money for crusading enterprises. These were levied on both clergy and laity on all kinds of property. This was highly profitable and similar taxes were a sore temptation to impecunious kings. Every once in a while a monarch would try to tax the clergy and there would be a controversy. But as a rule these affairs were settled by compromise. The pope would give his permission in return for some consideration.

In 1295 Philip IV and Edward I of England were preparing for war over the duchy of Gascony. Both proceeded to demand contributions from the clergy. Pope Boniface promptly issued the bull *Clericis laicos* which forbade princes to tax the clergy and the clergy to pay taxes. This started the bitter controversy from which the following documents arise. The course of the struggle cannot be traced to its end. Suffice it to say that Boniface died of shock and humiliation after having been seized by men hired by King Philip. Some years later a French pope moved the seat of the papacy to Avignon. The king of France had won and the papacy had begun its Babylonian Captivity.

The problem here again is to discover the points of view of the two sides and the arguments on which they were based. As both pope and king rather preferred vituperation to argument, the useful material is rather scanty. All general histories carry the accounts of this controversy.

A. The Bull Clericis Laicos

This bull was issued by Pope Boniface in 1296. It did not state any novel doctrine but merely expressed what had for a long time been the papal point of view. It is interesting largely as a full and careful description of the issue.

Boniface, bishop, servant of the servants of God to everlasting memory. Tradition says that in ancient times laymen injured the clergy and the experiences of the present times clearly show that they continue to do so, since not content with the limits of their power they strive for forbidden authority and indulge in illicit acts nor do they prudently pay attention to the fact that power over clerks, ecclesiastical persons, and their goods is forbidden to them. They place onerous burdens on the prelates of the Church, on churches, and on ecclesiastical persons both regular and secular. They tallage them, impose taxes on them and demand and extort a half, a tenth, a twentieth, or some other proportion or quota of their goods. They are trying in many ways to reduce the clergy to servitude and to subject them to their rule, and, we are sorry to say, some prelates of the church and ecclesiastical persons being afraid of what they should not fear, seeking temporary peace, and fearing more to offend the temporal majesty than the eternal, submit thoughtlessly rather than rashly to these abuses without obtaining either the permission or the license of the apostolic see. We therefore, being anxious to prevent such evil acts, decree by the counsel of our brothers and our apostolic authority that whatever prelate or ecclesiastical person, religious or secular, of whatever order, condition, or status shall pay, promise to pay, or consent to pay to a layman taxes or tallages, a tenth, twentieth or one hundredth or any other quantity, portion, or quota of his goods or income under the name of aid, loan, subvention, subsidy, gift or any other title or excuse without the permission of the pope shall incur the sentence of excommunication. And we decree that emperors, kings, princes, dukes, counts, barons, podestà, capitanei, officials, and governors, by whatever name they are called, of cities, castles, or any sort of place however appointed or of whatever rank, condition or status who impose, demand, or receive tallages or presume to arrest, seize, or occupy the sacred goods of churches or ecclesiastical persons or command this to be done; and all who knowingly give either publicly or secretly counsel or aid in such acts shall incur the sentence of excommunication.

P. Dupuy, *Histoire du différend d'entre le pape Boniface VIII et Philippe le Bel, Roy de France, Actes et preuves,* trans. Sidney Painter (Paris, 1655), pp. 14-15.

B. *Reply of King Philip to the Pope*

Clericis laicos enraged King Philip and he took prompt counter-measures. He forbade the export of gold and silver from his realm and banned all foreigners from trading in France without his leave. These two measures cut off all the papal revenue from France, an important item since France was the richest state of Western Christendom. The pope protested these moves in a series of letters. This letter of King Philip's is a reply to these papal protests. It was, in all probability, composed by one of the king's civil lawyers.

The problem here is to separate Philip's point of view from the rather dubious arguments with which he seeks to uphold it. Unless Philip is thinking of himself as the successor of the Roman Emperors, his first statement is manifestly untrue. The argument as to the unity of the church is one Boniface was to use later with a quite different purpose. Yet Philip states clearly and forcefully the secular princes' point of view on this question.

Before there were clerks, the king of France had the guardianship of his realm and could make laws by which he safeguarded himself and the realm from the plots and attacks of his foes and by which he deprived his enemies of all aid through which they could gravely injure him and his realm. . . .

And it seems sufficiently astonishing that the dearest son of the pope detained by violence not only the goods but even the persons of clerks but was not excommunicated for this by the lord pope. Holy Mother Church, the bride of Christ, is not only made up of clerks but also of laymen. The Scripture testifies that as there is one Lord, one faith, and one baptism so from the beginning to the end among all those faithful to Christ there is one church, the celestial bride of Christ, married to him by the ring of faith.

Not for clerks alone did Christ die and rise again. But he promised eternal salvation indifferently to all believers through good works, faith and love. And because clerks are in the church, rightly and in large numbers, they ought not nor can, except by abuse, appropriate to themselves and exclude others from the privileges of the church—privileges which Christ gave us by his grace. Many indeed are the privileges, not of the whole church, the bride of Christ, but of its ministers who were assigned or ought to be assigned to the divine cult to edify the people. These privileges were granted by the decree of the Roman pontiff with the good will or at least the permission of secular princes. And the privileges so granted or permitted cannot deprive the kings of the government and defense of their realms. Nor can they take away what is judged by the counsel of good and prudent men to be necessary for this government and defense. The Lord said to the priests in the Temple "Render unto Caesar the things that are Caesar's and to God the things that are God's." And because the part that does not belong to a whole is shameful and a member that refuses aid to the body is useless and paralyzed, anyone, clerk, layman, noble, or ignoble who refuses to aid his head, that is the lord king and the realm, is shown to be an incongruous part and a useless and paralytic member. Therefore if aid is required from

such men by reason of their position, it ought not to be called an exaction, extortion, or burden, but rather aid owed to the head by body and member. . . .

Ibid., pp. 21-23, trans. Sidney Painter.

C. Memorandum of Pierre du Bois

After Philip's reply to the pope, there was a brief lull in the controversy. The pope agreed that the clergy should contribute to the needs of the secular government when the necessity was great and that the king should decide when such an occasion arose. But soon the quarrel started again over Philip's efforts to remove a bishop who was politically objectionable. Boniface renewed the statements made in *Clericis laicos* and issued a bull forbidding Philip to nominate people for ecclesiastical office and depriving him of the custody of vacant bishoprics and abbeys. This memorandum by the legist Pierre du Bois is an answer to this last bull.

Again the point of view must be distinguished from the arguments. The arguments are not very strong, but the conception of the royal power is clear. It is noticeable that the argument is that of a lawyer and based on civil law.

It can be clearly proved by the following arguments that the pope, writing in this fashion, is and ought to be considered a heretic unless he should be willing to withdraw his letters and publicly correct his flagrant error and give satisfaction to the Most Christian King, the defender of the church, for such injurious statements which were published throughout his realm and almost all the world to the extreme scandal and infamy of Christian peoples, especially those of the realm of France. In addition the pope has presumed falsely to call certain friends of the king heretics, thus doing great injury as will appear below. . . .

The pope desires, steals, and bears away knowingly the supreme privilege

of the king which always has been and is subject to no one, and he wishes to rule all the realms without fearing the objections of men. The pope cannot deny that ever since the establishment of private property, from a time beyond the memory of man, the invasion of things in individual possession was forbidden and was mortal sin. The king has possessed his supreme jurisdiction and temporal privileges for over 1000 years. This same king and his ancestors from the time of Charlemagne from whom he descends possessed the collation of prebends and the fruits of the custody of churches. And he possessed these rights not by usage without title but by the gift by Pope Adrian who with the consent of a general council granted to Charlemagne that he and his heirs forever should nominate and elect whomever they wished as Roman pontiffs, cardinals, patriarchs, primates, archbishops, and bishops. Although Charlemagne's heir, Louis, gave up his rights in the election of prelates, he kept the collation of benefices and the fruits of the custody of churches and each king of the Franks after him used this right. And if any laws say that kings cannot confer benefices, and custom in such a matter has no weight, I answer that these laws, as it appears from the chronicles, were made 100 years or more after this time [reign of Louis the Pious?] and laws when made ought not to apply to previous but to future cases. And after these laws were made the king possessed and used his rights in good faith by both title and possession from times past.

The pope cannot claim dominion over

the realm of France except on the ground that he is the highest priest. Neither St. Peter nor his successors made any such claim. The kings of France have held possession of these rights for 1250 years. According to recent papal legislation, possession for 100 years without a title suffices for a sound defense against the claims of the papacy and the Roman church as well as against the emperor under imperial law. All this is clear from laws and canons dealing with conditions of succession. They say that empire and papacy lose the dominion over their possessions if they allow them to be detained and held. And if the Roman church and emperor ever had this dominion [over the king of France], which they never did, they lost all right by allowing the kings to possess their privileges for 100 years. . . .

Ibid., pp. 45-47, trans. Sidney Painter.

D. The Bull Unam Sanctam

This is the most important document of the controversy. Exasperated by Philip's resistance to papal claims on specific points and the king's inclination to question papal supremacy, Boniface issued this superb statement of his conception of the papal power. Most of the arguments used are conventional ones that had been produced again and again by the papal curia. But the forceful and clear expression of papal supremacy was important for its own day and for the future.

The problem is to sift out of the arguments and general statements just what Boniface's conception of the papal power was and then contrast it with the views of the king and his lawyers.

Boniface, bishop, servant of the servants of God to everlasting memory.

We are compelled by the true faith to believe and hold that there is one holy catholic and apostolic church. This we firmly believe and simply confess. And outside of this church there is neither salvation nor remission of sins as the bridegroom announces in the Song of Solomon "My dove, my undefiled is but one; she is the only one of her mother, the chosen one of her who bore her," which represents the mystic body, the head of which is Christ—and indeed Christ's head is God. In this church is one God, one faith, one baptism. For in the time of the flood there was one ark prophesying the one church. This ark was completed in one cubit and had one helmsman and master— that is Noah. And we read that all things existing on the earth outside this ark were destroyed. This church we venerate as unique because the Lord said through the prophet, "May God deliver my soul from the sword and my unique one from the power of the dog." He prayed for the soul, that is for himself as the head and for the body. And he called this body the unique church because of the unity of the bridegroom, the faith, the sacraments, and the charity of the church. This is that seamless tunic of the Lord which was not cut but given by lot. Therefore there is one body of the one, unique church and one head, not two heads, as if it were a monster. This head is Christ, Christ's vicar, Peter, and Peter's successor. For the Lord said to this Peter "Feed my sheep"—sheep in general, not any particular sheep or group of sheep. From this it is known that everything was entrusted to Peter. If therefore the Greeks or anyone else say that they were not entrusted to Peter and his successors, they necessarily admit that they are not Christ's sheep. For the Lord says in the gospel of John that there is one fold and one shepherd. We are taught by the evangelical words that there are two swords, the spiritual and the temporal, in the control of the church. For when the apostles said "Behold here two swords," which as the apostles were speaking meant two swords in the church, the Lord did not reply that it was too many but that it was enough. Certainly he who denies that the temporal sword was under the control of Peter misunderstands the word of the Lord when he said, "Put your sword into the sheath." Therefore both the spiritual and material sword are under the control of the church, but the latter is used for the church and the former by the church. One is used by the hand of the priest—the other by the hands of kings and knights at the command and with the permission of the priest. Moreover one sword ought to be subjected to the other and the temporal power ought to be subjected to the spiritual. For the apostle says, "There is no power unless from God and it must be ordained by God." Moreover the powers would not be properly ordered unless one sword was under the other sword and as it were the lower made the higher by the other. For according to St. Dionysius the divine law is that the lowest is made the highest through the medium. Nor according to the law of the universe are all things equally and directly brought into order, but the lowest is brought into place by the medium and the inferior by the superior. Moreover we ought the more clearly to admit that the spiritual power exceeds the temporal in both dignity and nobility as spiritual things surpass temporal ones. And this we are clearly taught by the giving of tithes, benediction, sanctification, the acceptance of

this power, and the governing of these things. For as the truth testifies, the spiritual power has established the temporal power and judged it if it were not good. So the prophecy of Jeremiah concerning the church and the ecclesiastical power is confirmed. "See, I have this day set thee over the nations and over the kingdoms to root out and to pull down and to destroy, and to throw down, to build, and to plant." Therefore if the temporal errs, it will be judged by the spiritual power. But if the spiritual power errs, the minor will be judged by the superior—the supreme spiritual power can be judged by God alone, not by a man. For the apostle testifies, "The spiritual man judges all things and he himself is judged by no one." Moreover this authority, even though it is given to a man and is exercised by a man, is not human but divine. For by the divine command it was given to Peter and the rock was made firm for him and his successors in Christ whom he had confessed. The Lord said to Peter, "Whatsoever thou shalt bind on earth shall be bound in heaven; and whatsoever thou shalt loose on earth shall be loosed in heaven." Therefore whoever resists this power ordained by God, resists the ordinance of God, unless as the Manichaeans pretend there are two supreme forces—a doctrine that we judge false and heretical. . . . We therefore declare, say, affirm, and announce that for every human creature to be submissive to the Roman pontiff is absolutely necessary for salvation. Given at the Lateran on the fourteenth kalends of December in the eighth year of our pontificate [Nov. 18, 1302].

Ibid., pp. 54-56, trans. Sidney Painter.

5. Town Origins

ROBERT L. REYNOLDS

University of Wisconsin

SINCE THE LATER 1700's there has been both scholarly and semi-popular interest in the problem of when and how towns developed in Western Europe. Research scholars have been attracted by the technical difficulties of the work. The sources are few, unbalanced, and ambiguous, constituting a challenge to many able historians both past and present. Interest in the subject has not stemmed alone from this narrowly professional motive. In any attempt to write a general history of Western Europe, or of any of its countries, their constitutions and laws, economy and society, the problem of when and how towns developed intrudes itself. The general writer feels himself on insecure ground unless he has digested what specialists in urban history have produced and has mentally fitted their expositions into what he wants to tell.

In this way, between two levels of scholarly work, there has been a ceaseless interaction. New findings and ideas of the students of urban history have forced modifications not only of detail but of total approach upon historians working in other fields or writing on more general topics.

The work of their colleagues has at the same time impelled the students of towns to recast their own thinking and to redirect their researches. They have had to examine new aspects of their problem or to revise conclusions which seemed adequate on the evidence of their own sources but have failed to fit with evidence developed by historical research in other fields.

In a yet wider circle, still within the scholarly world, the problem of medieval European town origins has been of great interest. Lawyers and political scientists, economists, sociologists, geographers and others too have raised questions within their own fields and have turned to the works of the students of urban origins for answers, demanding ideas and data bearing on towns of the technicians familiar with the sources. With their varying points of view and interests, these scholars have made re-examination of sources and ideas on town history necessary.

Popular interest in the problem of town origins has been continuously active. Since the late 1700's many programs for the reform of government and society, of law and economy, have been advocated by individuals or groups. Some of these programs have had little general impact; others have developed tremendous practical force. The connection between the study of town origins and a few of these movements can be demonstrated by simply noting that it was in the study of town origins that terms like these were directly or indirectly first put to modern scholarly use: bourgeoisie, capitalist, commune, and middle class.

To return to the technician-scholars who were at the center of the research on town origins. They were scholars as they have been pictured, but they were also living men who were German, Italian, French, and so on. They were also liberal democrats, conservative Prussians, and many other things as well. Consciously sometimes, but unconsciously more often, they have been influenced by what they were and what they believed in.

As one result, some scholars have studied their problems with a conscious or unconscious nationalistic or political bias. Sometimes they have then generalized recklessly in stating their conclusions, deliberately or innocently implying that what developed in the country they studied happened the same way everywhere. Research publications in any case present some difficulty, for they must cross all the language barriers in modern Europe. Workers on the same problem find it hard to read and digest the works published in all the languages now used. Indifference toward what happened far away also exists.

Most annoying has been the tendency of schools of interpretation to take sides for reasons of patriotism or of ideological allegiance. To some technically brilliant scholars the problem of how and when towns originated has become involved in the problem of propounding such things as German folk superiority over Romance peoples, or the validity of the historical dogma of Marxism. On the whole, however, propaganda for one side has been balanced by propaganda on the other. In the fervor of their work the researchers have uncovered new materials and developed useful approaches to various aspects of these problems.

It has been mentioned above that we have poor sources of information on when and how medieval European towns originated. It is also evident that much of the debate over what took place would never have been generated had it been possible to get a sufficient number of clearly understandable sources, comb them thoroughly, and then assemble a convincing analytical account. The question of sources has an immediate interest here.

Ideally, the problem of town origins should be developed now by offering, as is done in other sections of this book, quotations in English of the writings and records of the time. This is not feasible. Scraps from chronicles or law codes, passing oblique references in poems, and such are all the materials we have. As the towns arose they created problems for men of the time, but no man of the time was interested in describing, as it happened before his eyes, how even one town began. Scholars may find valuable a long list of references such as the one which tells us that "Tamworth was timbered," from the

Anglo-Saxon Chronicle entry for 913, but they would mean nothing to those outside the small circle of technical researchers.

To such researchers, when assembled with all other information that can be scraped together, this snippet of fact is important. Yet it is not even clear what "timbered" means. Therefore, in articles based on such sources the researchers have to write in painstaking detail on each small item. Their articles, written for the eyes and minds of their fellow specialists, are therefore highly technical. It is as impractical for the student to use their articles as it is to use their sources.

Consequently, what will follow here will be chiefly drawn from those passages in the scholarly publications where summaries of positions—the positions of their predecessors, the conclusions of the researchers themselves—are given.

The materials will be presented in an arrangement which roughly classifies writings on the problem of town origins according to the chronological order in which theories were presented. Since no theory was ever alone in the field, and there were and still are theories maintained in competition with one another, the chronological order has had to be mingled rather illogically with a topical order.

Many of the passages chosen spread in subject matter over into other aspects of the material than that of the section in which they appear. This cannot be helped, for all other alternatively available passages would do the same thing. It may be that the way in which these materials bear on topics outside the subjects they have been chosen to illuminate will stimulate careful readers to undertake their own work of cross-reference. In so doing they will be engaging in the very sort of scholarly enterprise in which the specialists in the field have had to engage.

The first excerpt offered, Section I, A, is intended to be taken lightly, but not too lightly. It serves to illustrate an approach to historical knowledge which had some standing until into the 1700's. The next excerpt, Section I, B, illustrates two points: (1) that serious work on the history of town origins had begun in the early 1800's, sources being used, and (2) that the first able writer, Sismondi, was inspired to go into the problem because of his enthusiasm for the cause of democratic liberties, and wrote up his findings in keeping with his enthusiasm.

In the second section the theories of the 1800's are in considerable measure covered. The origin of the medieval European town became during that period a "problem." A monumental work, by the German scholar of the history of Roman law, Savigny, offered the first thought-out explanation as to how the towns came to have the institutions which governed them by the 1200's. The essence of the Savigny thesis is given in the quotations from K. Hegel and P. Villari which appear in Section II, A, and is referred to in passing in other excerpts.

Attacks upon the Savigny thesis were constructive in that different explanations were offered by Savigny's opponents. These explanations or hypotheses concentrated, as had Savigny's, upon the origins of town law and institutions, with only incidental notice of economic and social factors. So many theories were offered that by mid-century a new problem faced the scholars themselves: the problem of appraising the merits of various of the answers to the problem of town origins. Bias frequently made controversy warmer; Hegel and Villari both mention the force of prejudices and perhaps illustrate it themselves! Section II, B, starts with a recapitulation by Stephenson of the hypotheses which had the most support until about 1890. Stephenson's résumé could also serve as an introduction to Section III, to which we turn shortly.

It is noticed that Stephenson's summary takes no notice of Italian work. It is partly to fill in this lacuna that the excerpts following deal chiefly with Italy. The last one, however, from the writings of Plesner, shows how the student of Italian towns gets drawn if not by one road then by another into formulating views that connect the medieval towns with the older Roman ones.

Section III has really been introduced by the excerpts from Stephenson previously used to open Section II, B. The importance of economic and social factors in originating and shaping medieval towns received increasing emphasis after 1890. Laws and institutions were not forgotten but were made secondary in both research and in the exposition of theories. The section opens with direct quotations from Professor Pirenne's later formulation, in a book, of the ideas he first advanced in his articles of the early 1890's.

Most of the section is given over to the presentation of excerpts from two studies of the English boroughs, by Professors Stephenson and Tait. Earlier, in Section II, B, Stephenson had asserted that as he was writing, about 1930, the scholarly world was nearer accord. His own work was immediately challenged by that of Professor Tait. The excerpts are used here for the sake of their content and because they illustrate completely the way the problem of town origins has been debated back and forth, aspect by aspect, from the days of Savigny.

Section IV offers a mere sampling of views on medieval towns taken from the writings of economists and geographers. They demonstrate how in various ways scholars other than historians have had their attention drawn to the problem of the town.

I. THE WORK ON TOWN ORIGINS BEFORE SAVIGNY

A. Accounting for Town Origins by Legends: Caesar Founds Florence

In many places, beginning even as early as the 1200's, local writers worked out histories of their beloved towns. By the middle of the 1700's the mass of these writings was considerable. Some of the work was soberly done. The best students used local records carefully but had little contact with parallel studies and documents. Consequently their histories were parochial and full of misunderstandings of their evidence. The problem of origins was especially baffling to these historians. In this matter the example of the Greeks and Romans and of the medieval romancers was generally followed. Legend was called to fill in the lack of evidence.

One legend, typical of this sort of literature, tells how the city of Florence was founded.

The legend began with Adam and then abandoned him at once to reach quickly the foundation of Fiesole, by

Atalante and his wife on the advice of Apollonius the Astrologer. Fiesole was the first city, built on the healthiest spot in Europe, whence came its name, *Fie sola*. Their sons spread over the earth, populating it. The first was called Italo and gave his name to Italy; the third was called Sicano and gave his name to Sicily, which he conquered. The second son, Dardano went off to found Troy. And here the legend runs rapidly to the Trojan War, to the flight of Aeneas, to the founding of Rome, of which Florence is the best-loved daughter. Here the story moves more slowly, to tell of Cataline. . . . After having conspired against Rome he came to Fiesole, where the Romans pursued him and attacked him, under the command of the Consuls Metellus and Florinus; the second of these died on the battlefield and the Roman army was completely defeated on the banks of the Arno. However, Julius Caesar came to revenge them, laid siege to Fiesole, destroyed it, and then founded a new city on the Arno where Florinus fell, named Florentia. . . .

Pasquale Villari, *I Primi due Secoli della Storia di Firenze*, 2nd ed. (Florence: G. C. Sansoni, 1905), pp. 52-53, trans. R. L. Reynolds.

B. Town History Written under the Influence of French Revolutionary Thought

The French Swiss, Sismondi, was the first to take up the writing of town history on a general plan. He was pro-Italian and at the time he wrote he was a supporter of the democratic ideas of the French revolutionaries. He also had the advantage that during the previous several generations, scholars had been digging out, assembling, and publishing great collections of medieval documents. The time was ripe, when he began his own studies, to work on a wide scale and with some confidence.

In the following we note reflections of his interests in republican virtues and usurped tyranny. He also stressed the importance of the military factors which had won their liberties for the townsmen and the psychological factor—patriotic love for the natal town. To perhaps too great a degree these factors have since received little notice. He has a suggestion, too, as to why we have so few sources to aid us in working in the field. His suggestion cannot be sustained by proofs but neither can any other.

By the twelfth century all the Italian cities were free. . . . We shall see them all animated by a common way of life, equally used to exercising all the republican virtues and equally worthy of the independence they had won. The revolutions in Italy which we have traced sketchily above, and the development they gave the national character, have prepared us to see how the cities became free. But this last revolution goes on somewhat hidden from our eyes. The birth of republican government, and its progress, would doubtless have been an interesting, instructive, and variegated sight, if time had not concealed its details. But we can hardly lift the veil which will always cover that first age of the history of the free cities. Northern Italy had scarcely a single historian in the tenth and eleventh centuries. In order to tell of the contests of Henry [IV] with the Papacy, we have had to turn to the German writings, for that period much more complete and detailed than those of the Italians. If events of such high importance, which also excited such lively interest at the time, found no writers to preserve the memory of them for us, it is not strange that the establishment and progress of obscure towns, which sought to keep out of sight the independence they were acquiring, were not written down in any historical account. The townsmen only got their liberty by slowly appropriating the prerogatives of the princes; they were fighting abuses by use of the same weapons with which abuses had been introduced. They were usurping liberty the way the lords had often usurped tyranny, and while they were trying to hide from the interested princes knowledge of what they were doing, they at the same time hid it from posterity. New privileges were introduced in silence, always with the help of the passage of time, and by the time they were challenged the townsmen could claim in law the backing of generations of constant usage. . . .

No revolution ever had a more marked influence upon the character of a nation, upon its constitution, and upon its future destiny than that which the union of the two crowns of Germany and Lombardy had upon the Italians. If the historical movements of the tenth and eleventh centuries were only sufficient to allow us to follow the history of the cities from that period on, it would be back in the age of the Ottos (962–1002) that we should have to start, for the cities owed their municipal constitutions to the generosity and policies of those princes, and the first germs of their republican spirit. It was the remoteness of the royal court, too, which gave the Italian towns the habit of independence. Finally, the cities owed their familiarity with arms and the legal right to fight under their own banners to the wars between royal pretenders which broke out after the extinction of the Ottonian family.

> J. C. L. Simonde de Sismondi, *Histoire des républiques italiennes du moyen-âge,* rev. ed. (Paris: Treuttel-Würtz, 1826), I, 365-367; 53-54, trans. R. L. Reynolds.

II. TOWN ORIGINS VIEWED AS A PROBLEM IN THE FIELDS OF LAW AND INSTITUTIONS

A. Savigny's "Romanist" Explanation of Town Origins

Students of laws and constitutions dominated the work on town origins during most of the 1800's. There was in fact a tendency to identify town with town institutions and to give at most only passing notice to commerce and industry or to town geography. Until the time of Napoleon it was assumed that the Roman Empire was still in some respects a living institution. Popes and Emperors and local leaders in the city of Rome harked back in various ways, both in theory and in practical matters, to this doctrine. To a marked degree Frenchmen and Italians assumed that in the essentials of their culture they were the living Romans. When some of the collectors and editors of French and Italian medieval documents wrote explanatory notes to documents which touched medieval towns they tended to attach medieval institutions to late Roman municipal governments. That Roman municipal governments had indeed survived the centuries between the 300's and the 1200's seemed to them to be so likely that they did not search for evidence to support the assumption.

The first serious examination of the sources bearing on medieval town origins was undertaken by Savigny, whose primary interest was in the history of Roman law. His Romanist theory at once generated both denial of his conclusions and intensive study of all sources which might throw light on the problem of the origin of medieval town institutions. It also generated the many alternative hypotheses treated both here and at length below in part 2, pp. 180-181.

Savigny's work appeared in successive volumes between 1815 and 1831. By mid-century it was recognized as having been the study which generated all subsequent work on the problem. A selection from Karl Hegel's fairly early work on Italian city constitutions is given here. It characterizes the Savigny thesis and gives an account of the debates as they had gone on until about 1847. Hegel was himself to take a leading part in work on the problem of medieval town origins for the rest of the century.

The repercussions of the Savigny study and then of the rival Germanist theories referred to by Hegel were particularly violent in Italy. The excerpt from Villari, writing after the heat of the debates had somewhat disappeared, covers this aspect of the problem of town origins. In other European countries the Romanist theory had a vogue; how it was accepted and was then attacked in Spain illustrates what happened in all lands which had once been Roman.

1. HEGEL REVIEWS SAVIGNY'S THESIS

. . . But what about the town constitution? It is by its nature much more unstable than are language and law, being more subject to caprice. It is often impossible to reconstruct out of its later form the sort of a constitution a town had at the beginning. Certain basic forms are found nearly everywhere, but they are too general to express a special characteristic, to indicate a specific origin. Men have looked upon the persistence of the Roman city constitution as proof of the persistence of other things. The town constitution has been made dependent upon that of Roman Law on the assumption that wherever Roman Law has been preserved in actual use the Roman court system must also have been preserved, and therefore also the municipal constitutional forms upon which they depended. The municipalities appear according to this as towering peaks, so to speak, sticking up out of the flood of the barbarian migrations from which the new deposits derived from Roman civilization spread over the rude strata.

The persistence of Roman municipal constitutions, considered from this point of view, was first put forward by Savigny in his *History of the Roman Law in the Middle Ages* and carried by analogy throughout the kingdoms of the Burgundians, the East and West Goths, the Franks, and finally the Lombards. One can estimate the scientific significance of this magnificent study from the great numbers of new investigations which have been stimulated by it in Germany as well as in Italy and France. Savigny's hypothesis must be extended to each of the individual countries in the attempt to prove it or it should be partially denied in this relationship or completely rejected. I note here only some of the most significant of these recent authors, reserving for the present work a more critical examination of the literature concerned.

Concerning Italy itself, the persistence of the Roman constitution through the municipalities of the Lombard period was first denied by Leo, and municipal freedom in the middle ages, according to Eichhorn's theory, should be derived from ecclesiastical immunities there. The most distinguished Italian learned men, particularly the scholars of Turin, Vesme, Fossati, Balbo and others, have agreed completely with this. In France the hypothesis of the survival of the Roman institutions has won a very favorable reception thanks to the dominant national prejudice which prefers to give credit for the basic elements of the admired French civilization to the Romans rather than to the Germans; this is shown fully since Raynouard, with a political rather than a scientific end in view, has heaped together a mass of utterly uncritical pieces of evidence to prove this thesis. In Germany, Gemeiner, independently of Savigny's hypothesis, had asserted the Roman origins of the freedom of his city of Regensburg—and why not also for the remaining Free Cities along the Danube and Rhine? On the other hand, Eichhorn accepting that hypothesis generally to be sure, dared extend it with certainty only to Cologne in his fine essay on the origin of municipal constitutions in Germany. Maurer then stood opposed to this view with particular reference to Regensburg and the Bavarian towns, while Hullman at the same time disputed thoroughly Eichhorn's whole general point of view concerning the development of the towns. Finally there has even been an Englishman—I refer to Cathcart, the translator of Savigny—who, going farther than his author, sought to prove the survival of the Roman constitution in England, to be sure only in such a form as would convince someone who believed in advance in that hypothesis.

Karl Hegel, Geschichte der Städteverfassung von Italien, 2 vols. (Leipzig: Weidmann, 1847), I, vi-viii, trans. R. L. Reynolds.

2. VILLARI REVIEWS CONTROVERSIES GENERATED IN ITALY BY SAVIGNY

This excerpt from Villari tells how Italian scholars dealt with the problem of the persistence of Roman municipal institutions.

Upon the condition in which Italian society found itself during the generations before the communes arose, there was once a long and lively dispute between Italian and German writers. But the methodological rigor of research work in the first half of the 19th century was continually disturbed by passions and political biases. They tried to decide whether the merit for founding modern liberty belonged to Italians or to Germans, rather than trying to discover what really were the origins. Each one tried to work out the problem so that his answers would back up what his patriotism desired, rather than working with serene scientific impartiality.

Toward the end of the eighteenth century the question was variously discussed among us Italians by deeply learned men such as Maffei, Sigonio, Pagnoncelli and many others. Muratori, without holding to any system worked out beforehand, with a true historical genius, threw beams of marvelous light on the subject, raising it to a high level by his weighty knowledge of materials. But the dispute began to grow really warm when the great Savigny took up the matter in his immortal *History of the Roman Law in the Middle Ages.* Since he was seeking to prove that

Roman jurisprudence enjoyed uninterrupted continuity through that epoch he found himself forced to maintain (so closely are all things tied together in history) that under barbarian rule the Italians had not only not lost all traces of the ancient law, as some others pretended, but neither had they lost all personal freedom, as asserted by others; and Savigny had to support the idea that the Roman municipality had never been completely destroyed. Hence the revival of our republics and of Roman jurisprudence was nothing other than a renewing of antique institutions and of antique laws which had never really disappeared. In Germany the ultimate conclusions toward which the ideas of the great historian led were quickly understood, and then Eichhorn, Leo, Bethmann-Hollweg, Karl Hegel and others rose to combat the thesis that the Italian commune had a Roman origin. These others upheld on the contrary the idea that the barbarians, and above all the Lombards in Italy, whose lordship lasted longest and was harshest of the lot, had taken all freedom from the Romans and destroyed all trace of their laws and institutions, so thoroughly that the communes and their statutes had to be a new creation whose origins were owed uniquely to the German peoples.

Opinions such as these should have had, judging only by appearances, hot opposition from Italian patriotism, and those of Savigny should have obtained universal favor. However, it didn't work out that way. Among us each school found many learned followers. Among us national feeling was flourishing, a free and united Italy was wished for, whatever the price of whatever sacrifice, and everything which seemed to be adverse to this unity was hated. In the minds of some scholars the Lombards seemed to have been right at the point of ruling all Italy and only the Popes, by calling in the Franks, had been able to halt the Lombard conquests. Had the Popes not done this, Italy could have become, like France, a united country by the ninth or tenth century. Already there had been established among us, from the days of Machiavelli, that school of thinkers which saw in the Papacy the evil cause of Italian disunity. And, naturally, these nineteenth-century Ghibellines, arguing down the thesis of Savigny, praised the Lombards, found proofs of their goodness and humaneness and belittled the Pope for having blocked general and enduring Lombard rule over all Italy. In the opposite camp there was another school of historians, led then by Gioberti, which hoped to see the Pope lead Italy to unity; and this school prevailed until about the middle of the year 1848 when disillusionment set in; members of this school, whose most illustrious representatives were Manzoni, Troya, and others, all opposed Savigny's thesis. It wasn't hard for these men to prove that, when all accounts were added up the barbarians had been really barbarous, that they had killed and destroyed and crushed every vestige of national civilization. Had such barbarians come to dominate the whole peninsula, we should have had a German Italy. Only the Pope, by calling in the Franks, whatever had been his intentions, had been able to bring some relief to the multitudes who had been too cruelly oppressed. The Franks, these scholars added, rather lifted up the Latin populations by allowing them use of the Roman law and by giving the Popes and bishops new powers which contributed certainly to the rise of the Communes. In this fashion, with opposite intentions the identical theses came to be upheld, in the first half of the nineteenth century, on both sides of the Alps. And in this dispute, without the writers being aware of it, learning was playing second fiddle to politics; historical serenity and truth suffered not a little from this fact. Balbo, Capponi, and Cappei, following a middle way, tried to hold to temperate opinions and with their learning they brought much light to bear on the subject.

Villari, *I Primi due Secoli*, pp. 15-17, trans. R. L. Reynolds.

3. Sánchez-Albornoz: The "Romanist" thesis in the Iberian Peninsula

It will soon be a century since the great Portuguese historian, Herculano, upheld the thesis that the medieval municipality of Castile and León was an inheritance of the Spanish world from the ancient world. The Roman municipal institutions had survived into Gothic Spain; the Arab-speaking Christians retained them under the rule of the Mohammedans and the inhabitants of the kingdoms of León received them from those *mozárabes*. So went the theory of Herculano. He did recognize that no text authorized the hypothesis that there was a survival of the Roman municipality among the *mozárabes*. But it was enough for him, to forge this missing link in his chain of reasoning, that two facts could be relied on. The first fact was that in later León there was a distinction between *caballeros* and *peones*, which he took as proof, without further evidence, of the survival of the old Roman distinction between *curials* and *plebeians*. The second fact was the designation of municipal magistrates by the Arabic title of *Alcalde,* in the kingdom of Léon; this, he supposed, was the word the *mozárabes* had used, during the intervening centuries, as the title for the ancient *duumvirs*. . . .

In the Asturian-Leonese kingdom no single case can be cited of a Roman-Visigothic city, of any sort, which continued more or less inhabited, which never had its living existence interrupted, between the moment right after the Mohammedan invasion and the day of its reoccupation and restoration by the Christians. All the cities, from the mountains to the Duero, had to be re-populated and colonized anew, from the second half of the 800's on. Even in the history of the most northerly cities such as Lugo there can be proved to have been a blank period of desolation. The kings of the Asturias first, and then the kings of León later, found nothing in the Duero valley but ruins—the ruins of the ancient castles, and the ruins of the ancient Roman and Gothic country estates. . . . Even had the Roman municipal organization survived, perhaps, though the evidence is against the thesis, to the end of the Visigothic period, this great disaster, or giant steamroller of the desert, would have pulverized it in the century between the reigns of Alfonso I and Ordoño I.

Claudio Sánchez-Albornoz y Menduiña, *Ruina y extinción del municipio romano en España e instituciones que lo reemplazan* (Buenos Aires: Instituto de Historia de la Cultura Española, Medioeval y Moderna, 1943) pp. 9, 122-124.

B. *Other Theories of Town Origins*

The legalistic and institutionalist emphasis of research upon medieval towns reflected interests and needs felt during the 1800's. New states such as Iceland and Canada, Czechoslovakia and Belgium were being dreamed of or were being set up. In all countries there was much modification of laws and constitutions under way. Political theorists, practical politicians, and journalists were continually in debates and in search of reasons and justifications for their positions. Savigny and then his critics were digging out and fashioning for current use many facts and ideas which could be drawn into the thinking and polemics of the day. Scholarly findings influenced policy debates; it may be that the debates stimulated some of the research, and that contemporary politics was in this respect a boon to the study of medieval history.

The excerpts which follow in this section illustrate the continuing preoccupation with the problem of the institutional origins of the medieval towns.

1. STEPHENSON ON THE NORTHERN TOWNS

Stephenson's brief follows the main lines of the arguments.

The mediaeval town has long been a controversial subject. . . . During the nineteenth century many historians, . . . offered many solutions; and in the absence of really valid evidence, each speculative effort was plausible enough to gain numerous adherents. Rival theories multiplied; polemic flourished; ultimate agreement of authorities seemed impossible. Nevertheless . . . we are sure that the second quarter of the twentieth century finds the scholarly world nearer accord. . . .

With the gradual abandonment of the Romanist theory, by which the persistence of urban institutions throughout the Dark Age was unthinkingly asserted, no less than seven substitute explanations came to be offered before 1900. . . .

(1) the immunity theory of Arnold;
(2) the *Hofrecht* [manorial court jurisdiction] theory of Nitzsch;

(3) the gild theory of Wilda and others;

(4) the *Marktrecht* [market law jurisdiction] theory of Sohm;

(5) the *Landgemeinde* [free village community] theory of Maurer and Below;

(6) the *Burgrecht* [military or garrison law] theory of Keutgen; and

(7) the mercantile settlement theory of Pirenne and Rietschel.

. . . [Of] the first four theories on the list . . . quite discredited before the opening of the present century, little need be said . . . except by way of introducing the latter three, which still have significance for the history of the English borough.

The first noteworthy clarification . . . was made by Georg von Below. . . . Arnold [1] had pictured the towns as evolving out of free communities in the Rhine and Danube valleys. These communities, he thought, had at first been subject to the great bishops who, through grants of immunity, had come to share the public authority of the king. Eventually, when the towns became independent of the bishops, they merely took over functions that had previously belonged to the latter. So municipal development was based on public law. . . . [This was] denied by Nitzsch [2]. . . . The town had begun as a servile community, administered under manorial jurisdiction (*Hofrecht*) by low-born agents of the lord (*ministeriales*). It was by no sudden revolution that the townsman had achieved freedom, but by a long slow process. Eventually, however, autonomy was secured, and the *ministeriales* became an urban aristocracy.

Below . . . proceeded first of all to demolish the *Hofrecht* theory . . . [and] also proved the utter inadequacy of Arnold's doctrine. The mediaeval town . . . had from the outset been a free community . . . [which] came to differ from the contemporary village in four respects: it had a market; it was walled; it constituted a jurisdictional unit; and it enjoyed special dispensation with regard to fiscal, military, and other political responsibilities. These four characteristics were necessitated by the new economic life of the town, and were matters of public law, coming by virtue of state endowment. But they were not fundamental elements; they were accretions which, making a village into a town, still left the village at the heart of the new agglomeration.

Thus, with some slight amendment, it was the famous doctrine of Georg von Maurer [5] that Below adopted. . . .

Meanwhile the gild theory, originally propounded by Wilda [3], had been greatly developed by other writers in Germany and outside it. . . . The town had grown from a private association or club, which, though perhaps organized for social or religious purposes, was quickly adapted to mercantile or political interests. Particularly in England, where such societies were known to have existed from an early time, and in France, where the gild was identified with the sworn commune, Wilda's doctrine won great popularity. . . . [But] Hegel, Gross, and, to a minor degree, Below, joined in demonstrating what is now universally accepted: that while town and gild were often closely associated, they were always two quite distinct entities.

At the same time a similar fate befell a much younger theory, that by which Sohm sought to identify *Stadtrecht* [town law] and *Marktrecht* [market law]. . . .

By the classic essays of 1893 and 1895 . . . Pirenne set out to explain for French readers the tangled controversy that had grown up round the beginnings of urban life in mediaeval Europe.

With precision and clarity the conflicting views mentioned above were in turn analyzed, and—in so far as each laid claim to finality—rejected. Pirenne accepted the restatement of the problem that Below had effected, but disagreed with the particular answer that he had given it. . . . He believed that the mediaeval town was pre-eminently the product of social and economic forces. . . .

In his second article Pirenne presented his own ideas on the town. Starting with the *civitas* of the late Roman Empire, he showed how, with the advent of the Dark Age, it had ceased to be either an economic or a political entity. Important still as a fortress, administrative centre, and residence for bishop or temporal prince, it had lost all but an insignificant number of its original inhabitants and all but a few vestiges of its ancient industrial activity. . . . Before it could be reborn, there had to be revival of commerce. . . . For a true urban concentration wider commerce was demanded. Towns grew up in mediaeval Europe as naturally as they have in America—on sites where the geographic location was favorable to trade and industry. . . .

The mediaeval town was essentially a trading settlement which commonly began as a stockaded quarter beside some older fortification. . . . Inevitably, as the urban community developed, antiquated systems of finance, justice, police, and administration broke down. The town came to manage its own local affairs under elected magistrates. Nor were such practices derived from rural custom, for at that time there were no autonomous villages. Self-government was as new as the bourgeoisie itself.

While Pirenne was thus sketching a more comprehensive theory of municipal origins than had as yet appeared, the work of Below was being followed up in Germany by two younger historians, Friedrich Keutgen and Siegfried Rietschel—the one in remarkable agreement with Pirenne's ideas, the other in almost diametrical opposition. To Keutgen the town was primarily a legal concept. . . . The town as a legal entity was military rather than commercial; for it was founded on the king's *Burgbann* [proclamation of fortress status], which, by offering necessary protection, eventually attracted a trading population. . . . The continuity between village and town that had been stressed by Below was broken . . . by an official revolution.

Rietschel . . . had come to conclusions which, so far as they went, coincided with those of Pirenne. Until the revival of commerce in the eleventh century, the mediaeval *civitas* lacked political autonomy, legal unity, and economic self-sufficiency. Socially its inhabitants were indistinguishable from those of the countryside. Nor did the early Germans imply that a *civitas* was a town when they called it *Burg*, for that was merely their name for any fortified enclosure. . . . He showed that the German town regularly grew from an independent source—from a mercantile settlement alongside a previously existing castle, church, village, or episcopal city.

With the close of the century it . . . became apparent that such narrow and arbitrary interpretations of the sources as had once prevailed were quite discredited. . . . And though on the constructive side there was no complete agreement, it could be seen that the really controversial matters were rapidly shrinking. . . . Little by little viewpoints were shifted and the antagonists made notable concessions to each other's opinions. . . .

In France, meanwhile, the violent controversies among German scholars had had but slight echoes. French historians, when forced by lack of evidence to abandon a Roman origin for their municipalities, could hardly be expected to substitute explanations intelligible only to German jurists. Nevertheless, Thierry, the first great writer on the subject in France, was willing to go a considerable way toward compromise with the Germanist school. According to him, the chief agents in the rise of the Third Estate were the revolutionary communes of the North; and they, in contradistinction to the consulates of the Midi, which had been founded under Italian influence, had sprung from the Teutonic gild. With some modifications, Thierry's doctrine reappeared in the well known books of Luchaire. The latter, it is true, declared that Thierry had exaggerated the importance of the communes and underestimated that of the lesser bourgeoisie, but in his own work the commune continued to hold first place and *la révolution communale* remained a favorite expression.

So far as origins were concerned, Luchaire pushed the question to one side as fundamentally insoluble. . . . The Germanists had been scarcely more accurate than the Romanists. . . . As feudalism was French, so, Luchaire would apparently have us believe, was the commune.

[Since the publication of Pirenne's articles] the mercantile settlement theory has gradually come to dominate the field. In France, therefore, the present state of opinion is much the same as in Germany.

Turning . . . to England we encounter a number of familiar views. Again the Romanist doctrine is for a time held and then abandoned. The mark-system [of free communities having aboriginally existed] is . . . by many made the basis of municipal history. The gild is prominent, and to a lesser degree the commune. The *Burg* reappears as the borough. . . .

William Stubbs . . . rejected the Romanist doctrine and in its place, though with a caution that at times verged on contradiction, put the mark theory of Georg von Maurer [5]. . . . The Anglo-Saxon *burh* was 'simply a more strictly organized form of township'. . . .

. . . It was but natural that the disciples of Stubbs should readily accept the conclusions of Below for the Continent. . . . [But] Maitland was being led to question the self-governing township, [and Keutgen] inspired him with a new theory for the origin of the borough. So far as the township was concerned, Maitland found himself unable to accept an institution for which the entire Anglo-Saxon period afforded no evidence. . . .

As to the borough, any one familiar with the Anglo-Saxon Chronicle and the royal dooms could not fail to perceive how admirably they seemed to justify Keutgen's doctrine. . . . Maitland therefore adopted Keutgen's idea that the *Burg* or borough was a military foundation . . . the maintenance and defense of which fell upon the landholders of the surrounding shires.

Furthermore, said Maitland, this military obligation toward the shire borough helps to explain a peculiar feature of Domesday: viz., that the borough, instead of being described as land of the king or land of a baron, is normally given separate treatment at the head of the county survey. . . . The thegns of the shire, in order more easily to perform their own service, came to keep houses and retainers within the walls. By the eleventh century, however, this original military constitution was virtually obsolete. Mercantile interests, as traders settled under the protection of the borough's special peace, tended to become dominant. . . .

This historical reconstruction of Maitland's—one of the most brilliant ever accomplished by that scholar—has hardly received due appreciation. . . .

Most critics . . . continued to prefer the older theory of Stubbs and Below. . . .

No doubt this failure of Maitland's thesis to bring conviction was in large measure due to his invention of the garrison theory to explain the tenurial heterogeneity of the Domesday borough. For what was actually of relative insignificance almost at once became the center of controversy. . . . Since the publication of [Maitland's] *Domesday Book and Beyond,* surprisingly little has been written on the Anglo-Saxon borough and its connection with the char-tered town of the twelfth century. Hence the occasion for the present essay. . . .

The conclusions of Pirenne and Rietschel, independently arrived at for their respective countries, immediately suggest application to England. Their theory of urban development is a flexible theory; it is not restricted to one people or to one region. . . . The extent to which the ideas of Pirenne and Rietschel have been confirmed by recent work on individual towns will be seen in the following chapter.

Carl Stephenson, *Borough and Town; A Study of Urban Origins in England* (Cambridge, Mass.: Mediaeval Academy of America, 1933), pp. 3-21, greatly condensed.

2. HEGEL ON THE COMPLEXITY OF THE PROBLEM

Hegel, already quoted above, was struck by the diversity of institutional forms he found in the Italian cities. Already in his work can be detected a reluctance to be dogmatic as to how town constitutions originated, even within a single country.

Out of the previous researches on the particular beginnings and earliest conditions of some of the most notable communes it is now sufficiently evident that just as with the founding of the city consulates so also with the representation of the particular ranks through the consulate, there had been in no wise uniformity. This partly revealed itself even in the composition of the consulates themselves. For where, as in Milan and other big communes of Lombardy and the Romagna, all three ranks of the Captains, Vassals, and Townsmen found themselves side by side as distinct associations, there the consuls were also elected by the organization of the new community from among all three ranks together. Where, from the beginning only the two ranks of Knight and Townsmen were met with, the Captains being either too insignificant a body to organize a separate rank for themselves as in Modena, or completely and entirely lacking, as in Blandrate (the counts of Blandrate were themselves only Captains of Milan), there the consulate was only two-ranked. In Mantua the consulate came up out of the single rank of the Lombard free warriors called *Arimanni,* while the feudal noble here remained completely outside the city community. In contrast in Pisa and Genoa a ruling aristocracy stood early at the top even before the commune itself emerged, which, when it did, took the form of a defense-alliance. In Florence there was no question of the equally privileged participation of various classes since a few favored noble families ruled here too until into the 13th century.

As far as I can determine, the beginning of a new commune and its consulate, speaking generally for all Italian towns, can be traced back to one of these various basic forms: the free union of the town associations and their administrators, the old free communities with a widened aldermanship, or the defense-alliance under an aristocracy of knightly and mercantile families.

Karl Hegel, *Geschichte der Städteverfassung von Italien,* II, 204-205, trans. R. L. Reynolds.

3. SALVATORELLI SUMMARIZES OPINIONS (TO ABOUT 1940).

The vicissitudes passed through by the Italian cities, as legal bodies, as administrative organizations, and as political-social forces, in the more than five hundred years between the end of the Roman municipalities and the setting up of the Communes remain obscure enough even today; probably they will always remain so for lack of sufficient documents. It is pretty certain that in Italy toward the end of the sixth century and the beginning of the seventh the Roman municipalities, already reduced to negligibility for a couple of centuries, ceased completely to exist, save at the most for the continuance in function of a minor functionary with the job of registering civil contracts (the notaries). This observation holds for the Byzantine parts of Italy and even more truly for the Lombard parts, where the Roman element in the population remained excluded, by the rule of the invaders, from public life. Still there is no reason to believe that the disappearance of the municipal governments meant also the end of all importance of the cities and of their individual existence as distinct from the open country around. Such a disappearance was barred simply by the existence of the bishops who maintained their sees inside the cities which were under an administration of city clergymen. . . .

. . . Besides this, the Lombard duchies and royal administrative shires, making up generally a single episcopal diocese, also retained for this unit a certain importance. It has also been supposed that below the ducal or shire government there was a sort of native town administration for the more humble businesses of city life, but there is no proof of it, save at the most the appearance of a *curator* in documents of the eighth century. We find to be sure, in certain judgments pronounced by Lombard governors, among the *adstantes* [responsible personages present at such official acts], Romans as well as Lombards (judging only baptismal names); even this sort of evidence is not found for generations before the eighth century.

The establishment of Frankish domination brought no substantial innovations in basic principles. The Frankish counts took the places of Lombard dukes and royal administrators. . . .

As had been the case all along, even under feudalism, the prime factor in a continuation, however reduced, of city activity and importance was constituted by the bishops. The bishops themselves became great feudal lords; and with them kings and emperors were openhanded—even more than with lay lords and especially this was true, 962–1002, under the three Ottos—in granting sovereign rights. But unlike the lay lords the bishops kept on living in the cities and the privileges granted them by the rulers came to give them in smaller or larger measure the government of the cities themselves up to the point where, in some cases, they got conceded the office and title of count. In the exercise of these functions, the bishops—who had of course also to attend to their church business—made use of a staff of special functionaries, called *vicedomini, advocati, vicecomites,* and of the subordinates next under these; in staffing this whole side of the episcopal administration lay townsmen played a major role.

At least from the middle of the ninth century on, moreover, the town populations in northern Italy showed here and there signs of either a surviving or of a revived group legal status, distinct both from the episcopal and from the comital spheres of power. This corporate legal identity existed when it came to taking care of town public property and took the more concrete form of having an administrative organization for each quarter [section or ward] in a city. In grants by kings of Italy made in the first half of the tenth century we find administrative buildings mentioned as belonging to the general body of townsmen or to sub-groups of these or also to the "gathering of the citizens". There are still other like references in documents from the period of the Ottos. We also find grants to citizen bodies of permission to fortify their cities. Nevertheless these oldest imperial concessions remained sporadic and occasional, without a true historical continuity with later developments.

Luigi Salvatorelli, *Storia d'Italia*, vol. IV: *L'Italia comunale dal Secolo XI alla metà del Secolo XIV* (Milan: Mondadori, 1940), pp. 161-165, condensed, trans. R. L. Reynolds.

4. Ottokar, Plesner, and the "Neo-Romanist" Thesis

A variety of Neo-Romanism, partly based on social and economic considerations, but brought to bear on institutional matters as well, began about the time of World War I to appear in the articles and books of the late Alfons Dopsch, whose work centered especially on the Danubian area.

Students of Italian towns also tended then to move in that direction. The picture of the "town," considered socially, economically, and institutionally, as having *always*, in Italy, covered the countryside as well as the urban, built-up, area is itself a major modification of most preceding ideas as to what town and townsmen really were and how they originated. The contrast with Pirenne's point of view, next given, is sharp.

In answer to the question upon the evolution through which in the 1200's the land in the open country had passed into the hands of the urban population, one can simply state that it came about by the process, until now unobserved, by which the majority of the proprietors of estates and the freest of the lesser holders of lands had moved into town, and then, having become *cittadini*, continued to control their old possessions. . . . Until Volpe and Ottokar began publishing [in the 1920's], historians more or less took the migration of the nobility to the city to be a secondary development; to be an effect of the conquest of the open country by the "bourgeoisie". Curiously enough, the presence in the city of a numerous noble class was seen as a manifestation of how the "bourgeoisie" had overcome and absorbed an aristocracy which was disappearing. Ottokar was the first to point out grave contradictions in the concept: It had been necessary to admit that the government of the primitive urban commune had been in the hands of feudal elements but no one had been able to reconcile that fact either with the generally agreed-on assumption that the commune had a "bourgeois" character nor with the story about the "conquest of the open country". No one could explain how those nobles came to head the "bourgeois" commune, nor how the "conquest of the open country" could be anything more than a conquest of themselves. . . . [Ottokar] explained that: "The Italian city has never stopped being the center which draws in and preoccupies the most important forces of the surrounding countryside. The feudal nobility and the big landholders do not live isolated on their fiefs and lands. They go often into town, where they have houses and fortifications, and they live in town at least part of the time. One can understand how, under these circumstances, the city—at all times in any case the fixed residence of the greatest feudatories, such as the bishops—becomes the center of a whole system of dependent feudal forces which gathered and organized themselves within the walls, bringing about increasingly ordered and firm relations between the city and the surrounding countryside. These [feudal] forces became then the core of the commune."

The limited task of this study is to demonstrate that these great landed families who headed the primitive commune were the representatives of a population of *cittadini* who were preponderantly of the same social type—landholders who had come to center their lives in the city. What characterized the earliest function of the great families in the city was that by them the whole district out to the limits of the episcopal diocese was drawn from the beginning to a certain extent about the urban center. The sphere of influence of the city and of its inhabitants is not like a circle which grows by expanding outward, but like a net which from the start goes around most of the whole area which it is later to dominate. Growth was a process by which the strands of the net were multiplied and strengthened, with more and more knots holding connections between each outlying point and the center. . . . No great landholder had a compact holding; all had scattered possessions and those of the greatest were scattered over every part of the city's countryside. . . . The network of all those holdings which thus joined in the city went on growing and strengthening, developing the importance of the city and being itself developed in step with the growing weight of the city in the system of forces operating in the countryside.

Johan Plesner, *L'Émigration de la campagne à la ville libre de Florence au XIII*e *siècle* (Copenhagen: Gyldendalske Boghandel Nordisk Forlag, 1934), pp. 106-109, trans. R. L. Reynolds.

III. THE MERCANTILE SETTLEMENT THEORY OF PIRENNE AND RIETSCHEL

The essence of the theory of Pirenne and Rietschel is found in the résumé of all leading theories given by Stephenson. It will be useful, however, to follow Pirenne's own exposition as he gave it some 30 years after publishing his first studies on the subject, and hence after a generation of scholars had gone over his evidence and reasoning—and in a large measure been convinced.

The excerpts from Stephenson already given above were drawn from his study of the origins of the English borough; he surveyed previous positions before beginning his highly technical re-examination of his own problem. Here the careful work between his opening survey and his generalized conclusions is left out. The conclusions are condensed and form the second selection given below.

The work of Stephenson was quickly studied by Professor Tait, who found himself unable to accept the most important of its conclusions. He shortly published his adverse criticisms together with his alternative theory. In the extracts from Tait, following those of Stephenson, are offered only passages in which the technical arguments are few; again, the choices center on the generalization of the opening and concluding pages of Mr. Tait's book.

The matter included in these excerpts is itself informative. But the main reason for printing them rather extensively is to provide a real sample of how debates on all aspects of town origins have been carried on since the days of Savigny. Up to this point there have been only references to controversies and résumés of conclusions. This is controversy itself.

A. The "Pirenne Theory" of Town Origins

It is therefore a safe conclusion that the period which opened with the Carolingian era knew cities neither in the social sense, nor in the economic sense, nor in the legal sense of that word. The towns and the burgs were merely forti-fied places and headquarters of admin-istration. Their inhabitants enjoyed neither special laws nor institutions of their own, and their manner of living did not distinguish them in any way from the rest of society.

Commercial and industrial activity were completely foreign to them. In no respect were they out of key with the agricultural civilization of their times. The groups they formed were, after all, of trifling importance. It is not pos-sible, in the lack of reliable information, to give an exact figure, but everything indicates that the population of the burgs never consisted of more than a few hundred men and that that of the towns probably did not pass the figure of two to three thousand souls.

The towns and the burgs played, how-ever, an essential rôle in the history of cities. They were, so to speak, the stepping-stones thereto. Round about their walls cities were to take shape after the economic renaissance, whose first symptoms appeared in the course of the tenth century, had made itself manifest. . . .

The cities of the Middle Ages show a very different picture. Commerce and industry made them what they were. They did not cease to grow under that influence. At no era in history is there so marked a contrast as that which their social and economic organization pre-sented to the social and economic or-ganization of the country. Never be-fore had there existed, it seems, a class of men so specifically and strictly urban as was the medieval bourgeoisie.

That the origin of these cities is di-rectly related, as an effect to its cause, to the commercial revival of which we have spoken in the preceding chapters, it is impossible to doubt. The proof is to be found in the striking corre-spondence which is to be noted between the expansion of trade and the rise of cities. Italy and the Netherlands, where commerce first showed itself, are pre-cisely the countries where cities made their first appearance and where they developed most rapidly and vigorously. It is easy to mark how, in step with the progress of trade, towns multiplied. They appeared along all the natural routes by which trade spread. They were born, so to speak, under its foot-steps. They are found, at first, only along sea coasts and rivers. Then, as the commercial penetrations spread, others were founded along the transverse roads which connected these first centers of activity with each other. . . .

In the need of security which the merchants felt there lies, therefore, the explanation of the fundamental charac-teristic of the towns of the Middle Ages. They were strongholds. It is impossible to imagine a town existing at that era without walls. It was an attribute by which towns were distinguished from villages. It was a right, or to use the expression of that time, it was a *privi-lege* which none of them lacked. Here again heraldry conforms very exactly to reality, in surmounting the crests of cities by a walled crown.

But the rampart was not only the sym-bol of the city; it was from it also that came the name which served and still serves to designate the population. Be-cause of the very fact that it was a forti-fied place, the town became a burg. The mercantile center, as has been shown above, was designated by the name of "new burg" to distinguish it from the original "old burg." And hence its inhabitants, at the beginning of the eleventh century at the latest, received the name of "burghers" (*bur-genses*). The first known mention of this word occurs in France in 1007. It appears again in Flanders, at St. Omer, in 1056; then it passes into the Empire by the intermediary of the region of the Moselle, where it crops up at Huy in

1066. It was therefore the inhabitants of the "new burg," that is to say of the merchant burg, who received, or more probably who created it to describe themselves, the appellation of "burghers." It is curious to see that it was never applied to those of the "old burg." These latter were known as *castellani* or *castrenses*. And this is further, and particularly significant, proof that the origins of city populations should be sought not in the older population of the early fortresses but in the immigrant population which trade brought to them and which, in the eleventh century, began to absorb them.

Henri Pirenne, *Medieval Cities, Their Origins and the Revival of Trade* (Princeton: Princeton University Press, 1925), pp. 76-77, 136-137, 156-157.

B. Controversy over the English Borough and Town

1. THE ENGLISH BOROUGH

The twelfth-century borough is very familiar. We have no trouble in recognizing it as a town—such a town as was still to be met with in any English county down to the Industrial Revolution. It was, of course, smaller and dirtier and more crowded than are most towns of to-day. It was hidden behind walls that have now largely disappeared. It was populated by men who wore strange clothes and carried stranger weapons. But fundamentally it seems to us quite comprehensible, for its life was predominantly mercantile. Its shops and warehouses, its markets and wharves, its homes of traders and artisans, spread below an occasional church tower or feudal battlement, constituted a picture that we know, and know intimately. . . .

The difficult problem for the student of mediaeval life, accordingly, has never been to describe the borough in the twelfth century, but rather to account for its sudden prominence. Thenceforth the town attained a constantly mounting importance in state and society. Why had it earlier been so obscure?

Since the majority of boroughs had long occupied well recognized positions on the map, it was at first asserted that the mediaeval towns, in all fundamental respects, were merely surviving Roman cities or newer foundations made in imitation of them. But this theory, when attacked by historians of the Germanist school, was shown to be based on little besides sheer assumption. It followed, therefore, that the borough was essentially a mediaeval product; that it somehow arose or was made in the period following the barbarian invasion of Britain. And the Germanist explanation hardly advanced beyond such a vague generalization; for every attempt to frame a simpler and more definite formula ended in confusion. To derive the twelfth-century borough from the borough-building activities of Dane and Saxon in the tenth century, despite all continuity of name, proved impossible. When one set of boroughs had been reasonably accounted for, it only became more apparent that another had not been. So Maitland's vivid picture of the old military borough left the mercantile borough an unsolved mystery. So Mary Bateson, by demonstrating the revolutionary nature of the new borough, made its connection with the original borough more obscure than ever.

Meanwhile, on the Continent, similar sources had led to similar speculation, which had ended in a similar *impasse*. But eventually the difficulty was avoided by refusing to take for granted that an older structure, whether called *civitas, urbs, burgus,* or anything else, was originally more than it was proved to be by contemporary evidence. The same procedure must be followed in dealing with the English towns. However natural it may be to regard the twelfth-century borough as a mere continuation of the earlier institution that bore the same name, such a presupposition is unwarranted and misleading. The primitive borough must be studied quite apart from all associations made familiar by later usage.

This approach to the subject inevitably leads to the acceptance of Maitland's central thesis. The older sources clearly depict a borough, the essential importance of which was military. Some boroughs were Roman fortifications adapted to the needs of combatants in the ninth and tenth centuries; others were new constructions. Many boroughs, particularly of the latter sort, were short-lived; but many, becoming identified with the freshly organized kingdom of England, continued as permanent centers of administration. And it would seem that the models for these official boroughs were those of the old Roman cities which, because of their strength, had continued to be used by the Saxon conquerors for royal residences, courts, mints, and markets. But whatever the precise origin of such administrative arrangements, it is they which appear to have dominated the tenth-century borough, not mercantile activity.

Contemporary trade was virtually restricted to the petty exchange that served to multiply local markets throughout the Dark Age; the most important transactions were in slaves and live stock. The commerce that reached an English port from overseas was as yet too slight to differentiate the mass of its inhabitants from the population of the countryside. As late as the reign of Edward the Confessor we find almost no indication of a socially distinct burgess class. On the contrary, the *burhwaru* of the older type are revealed by the records to have been predominantly agrarian. The outstanding borough-dweller was the *cniht*—a man of thegnly or semi-thegnly rank, an aristocrat who rode and fought, and who gained a living from lands tilled by poorer dependents. If he had a house within the walls, the location was dictated rather by gentlemanly preference than by business opportunity. If a peasant came to reside there, he remained a peasant. As yet there was no common borough privilege, no uniform burgage tenure, no characteristic burgess law. Judicially and fiscally *burhwaru* were still included under a territorial system devised for the country at large. Such a borough lacked all the conspicuous features of urban life. . . .

Nevertheless, while we may not know precisely how the borough came to be socially transformed, we may be reasonably sure that such a transformation took place, and we may even date it within comparatively narrow limits. The contrast between the borough pictured by the dooms and that pictured by the Norman charters is eloquent. The testimony of Domesday Book, such archaeological data as we have, and our deepening knowledge of urban development on the Continent, all support the conclusion that, in the latter half of the eleventh century, the population of the borough ceased to be predominantly military or official and became predominantly mercantile. This transition—it is here advanced—carried with it the revival of urban life in Britain and eventually established the equivalence of the terms borough and town.

Such a view avoids a dilemma of long standing. Maitland's exposition of the early borough may be taken as thoroughly sound, without implying that any one created a town by laying out a fortified camp or defining a doctrine of *Burgfriede*. At the same time Mary Bateson's portrayal of the new borough may be accepted and her principal conclusions extended even to the boroughs that were not baronial. Comprehension of all later municipal development is made simpler and clearer, for the Norman borough may be considered new in all its essential features, no matter when or by whom its walls were raised. Divorced from the origin of the borough, the origin of town life in England thus appears in its true character—a problem, not of legal interpretation, but of social history.

Carl Stephenson, *Borough and Town*, pp. 205-214, condensed.

2. Tait: Objections to Stephenson

The revival of urban life in England when the Teutonic invaders had settled down and accepted Christianity was not an isolated development. . . . The rise of towns in England cannot therefore be safely studied without some knowledge of the parallel movement on the Continent.

The strong similarities which are observable in urban organization on both sides of the Channel and North Sea may be due, at first at all events, rather to the working of like causes than to direct influence. In nomenclature, for example, the fact that towns were necessarily almost always fortified seems sufficiently to account for the general application to them of the Germanic *burh, burg, bourg,* without supposing borrowing. Certain features of their organization as it gradually developed, within or beyond the period with which we are immediately concerned, were in the nature of the case alike in all countries. Markets, fairs, a body of *probi homines* acting as administrators and, in the more advanced communities, as judges were urban requisites everywhere. In the case of these more highly organized communities there are always two main problems to be solved. When and in what circumstances did the town become a separate judicial area? At what date and by what means did it secure the right of self-government? The materials for answers to these questions, especially the first, are unfortunately imperfect in all countries and a massive literature has gathered round them, especially in Germany. The view that municipal life had survived from Roman times has long been discredited, but the hot controversy whether the town was in the beginning essentially a mere natural extension of a rural community or a fortress (or an appendage of one) or the locality of a market, has not yet been settled to everybody's satisfaction, though the last suggestion has now few, if any, continental supporters.

If the early growth of the English borough has much in common with that of the continental town, it has also some marked peculiarities, due to the insular position of the country and the course of its history. The chief of these is the limited hold which feudalism obtained here as compared with Germany and still more with France; . . . on the other hand, the crown retained its direct authority over all but a few small boroughs in the south-east down to the Norman Conquest and though some larger towns were mediatized by the new rulers of the land, the process never went to dangerous lengths. This direct relation to the king was doubtless in part accountable for the slower development of towns in England than abroad and for the complete absence during the Anglo-Saxon period of such urban charters as were being granted, sparingly enough, by feudal lords in France in the eleventh century and even occasionally in the tenth. . . .

The absence of military and political feudalism in Anglo-Saxon England explains a further marked difference between the early English borough and a large class of continental towns. In the

Low Countries the *burg* was the feudal castle or a fortified ecclesiastical settlement round which the towns (*poorte*) mostly grew up, while in France similar settlements below the feudalized walled *cités* of Roman origin came to be distinguished from them as *bourgs* when in their turn they were surrounded with walls. This distinction between old and new was unknown in pre-Conquest England where urban life began within the walls of old Roman towns and the new *burhs* founded by Alfred and his family, when not mere forts, were normally existing settlements, now for the first time surrounded by a wall or stockaded rampart.

The scientific investigation of the origins of the English borough began much later than corresponding studies abroad and was strongly influenced by them. It was not until 1896 that Maitland, much impressed by Keutgen's theory of the vital part played by the defensive *burg* in the rise of towns in Germany, gave a forecast in the *English Historical Review* of the "garrison theory" of the origin of English towns which he expounded at length in the next year in *Domesday Book and Beyond*. Briefly, his theory was that the burgesses and houses recorded in Domesday Book as paying rent to manors outside the borough in the eleventh century were relics of a duty of the shire thegns of the ninth and tenth to keep men in the boroughs for their defence, who became the nucleus of the borough community.

Though slightly guarded by his admission that "no one theory will tell the story of any and every particular town" and that "we must not exclude the hypothesis that some places were fortified and converted into burgs because they were already the focuses of such commerce as there was," Maitland's theory found practically no supporter. . . .

It was not until 1930 that the problem was attacked again, by an American scholar, Dr. Carl Stephenson, in an important article, in which the whole evidence is reviewed and a conclusion reached which has features both of agreement and disagreement with Maitland's view. Dr. Stephenson rejects the "garrison theory," but goes much further in emphasizing the military character of the early boroughs. For him the normal borough remained primarily a fortress and administrative centre until the Norman Conquest. He claims to have established from the old English laws and from Domesday that, except for a few sea-ports of the south-east, the Anglo-Saxon borough had no really urban character. Its market, like its mint, was official, its court only a unit of the general system of hundred courts. Its population was a microcosm of the countryside, containing all its social ranks from thegn down to slave. There was no land tenure peculiar to boroughs, no burgage tenure as we know it after the Conquest. *Burgenses* (*burgware*, *burhwaru*) meant no more than inhabitants of a walled centre. There was little trade and that local. For their subsistence the burgesses mainly depended on the borough fields, which the majority of them cultivated for the benefit of a wealthy land-owning minority. Free communal life did not yet exist. It was first called forth by the settlement of French traders in the old boroughs and in new ones created by Norman barons. Uniform burgage tenure was introduced and a rapid succession of other privileges was embodied in charters from the reign of Henry I. The origin of our municipal towns is thus found not in legal criteria, such as the possession of a separate court, but in the development of a mercantile community, whose chief instrument was the merchant gild. It was essentially a social, not a legal change.

This change, Dr. Stephenson goes on, falls into its place in the general growth of town life in Western Europe created by the revival of trade in the eleventh century. In England, as on the Continent, the *burgus* was a small lifeless unit until the age of mercantile settlement. This is of course the view for which, as regards the origin of continental towns, Professor Pirenne has secured wide acceptance. The great cities of the Netherlands are traced by him to the settlements of traders in *poorts* under the shelter of *burgs* fortified, like the English *burhs,* for defence against the Northmen. While reserving judgment on Dr. Stephenson's conception of the Anglo-Saxon borough until we have reconsidered the evidence, it may be well to note here that the parallel which he suggests is by no means exact. The boroughs founded by Alfred and his family—not to speak of the old Roman towns early re-occupied, were themselves called *ports* from the first in virtue of their markets. The king's reeve in the borough was *port*reeve not *borough*reeve. While the few dozen *ministeriales,* with the household serfs, of the *burg* in the Low Countries were consumers only, it was, we shall see, the definite policy of Edward and Athelstan to restrict trading as far as possible to the borough-ports. The Northmen here, but not in the Netherlands, settled down as active traders. It is only as royal and revenue-yielding creations that these early markets can be called "official," and the crown continued to retain control of the creation of markets after the Norman Conquest. Again, English boroughs were usually much larger than the *burgs* of the Netherlands. . . .

A parallel to the English *burhs* was found by Keutgen and Maitland in the purely artificial *burgs* which Henry the Fowler a little later was raising in newly conquered lands on the north-eastern frontier of Germany and peopling from without, but the likeness is somewhat superficial. England was a long-settled land. The very small *burh,* designed or adapted for military defence only and without urban possibilities may have approximated to the German type, but usually the place selected for walling had already a certain population and such elaborate arrangements as Henry was driven to make for the manning and support of the *burg* from the country round were not needed. . . .

Nearly all the chief English towns of the Middle Ages are found either among the Roman *civitates* or *burhs* re-occupied and their walls repaired, sometimes very early, or the new *burhs* of the ninth and tenth centuries. "Borough" became a technical term which covered walled and unwalled towns alike. Must we therefore conclude with Maitland that fortification was the vital moment in the origin of the borough? We may certainly agree that it gave an urgent and widespread impulse to urban aggregation, which would otherwise have been a slower process, even if peace and quiet had obtained, and that it provided shelter for the trader and artisan. In an age of constant warfare walls were everywhere a necessary condition of urban growth. But Maitland's conjectural picture of the typical tenth-century *burh* as first and foremost a fortress garrisoned by the land-owners of its district, who kept houses and warrior "boroughmen" (*burgware*) in it for its defence and wall-repair, has failed to secure general assent. It leaves out of account the early settled *civitas* like Canterbury and the general predominance of royal domain in the borough which is so evident in Domesday. It is essentially based upon a supposed foreign parallel of more than doubtful pertinence and the bold assumption that the burgesses who were paying rent to rural lords in 1066 represented armed retainers of the predecessors of these lords less than a century and a half before. It is not supported by the solitary contemporary piece of evidence on the incidence of wall-repair which has come down to us, and two important charters show that within less than twenty years after Edward's death a haw [urban holding] in a neighboring borough was regarded as a profitable appurtenance of a rural estate, not as an acquittal of a military obligation. Maitland's over-emphasis of the military aspect of the borough—we may now conveniently use the later form of *burh*—involved an underestimate of its trading importance and a one-sided theory of the origin of the borough court. . . .

Dr. Stephenson rejects the "garrison" theory, but his conception of the late Anglo-Saxon borough is equally one-sided in another direction. The normal borough, he holds, differed only from the country round in being a place of defence and therefore a natural centre of royal administration. Its trade was negligible, its social and economic system just as aristocratic and agricultural as elsewhere. Mint and market were there merely for the shelter of its walls. It is difficult, however, to reconcile this view with the legislation of Edward and Athelstan. When Edward in his first law, passed certainly before his conquests were complete and perhaps before they were begun, forbade all buying and selling outside fixed centres, he did not call them *burhs* but *ports*, a term with none but trading implications and, as we have seen, already familiar in the pre-Danish period. . . .

If the foregoing reconsideration of the evidence leaves no room for the old idea, which was still held by Miss Bateson, that a specially created urban court formed a universal legal criterion of the early borough, it does not bear out Dr. Stephenson's contention that his own criterion of mercantile settlement was generally absent, and the normal borough merely an agricultural group much of the usual manorial type. Every borough had a market and every borough was a *port*, a place of trade.

The early trade even of the more considerable of these ports must not be judged by the standard of the great cities of the Netherlands, which, with rare exceptions, they never reached. Yet by the end of the Anglo-Saxon period, many of them were evidently prosperous. Of the thirty-five for which Domesday gives statistics of population in 1066, twenty-one had more than 200 burgesses and five of these (not including unsurveyed London and Winchester) more than 900, involving total burgess populations of from about 1000 to about 9500. In a large proportion of these cases we should feel sure that the burgesses had some other means of support than agriculture, even if Domesday did not tell us that the 1320 burgesses of Norwich had only 180 acres of arable and the 538 of Ipswich (which had eight parish churches) only forty, and that among the vast majority of the burgesses of Colchester the average share of the individual was only a little more than a quarter of the villein's yardland.

In his article of 1930 Dr. Stephenson recognized no real towns outside the seaports of the south-east, but since then he has been impressed by some of the population figures and in his book *Borough and Town*, admits a considerably wider extension of urban trade. In his concluding chapter the large populations of York, Lincoln and Norwich—he might also have added Thetford with its 943 burgesses—are recognized as evidence of Scandinavian trade. The fisheries of Dunwich and the salt industry of Droitwich are noted. He is even ready to allow that the beginnings of municipal privilege may have extended beyond the south-eastern seaports, though evidence of this is wanting, and that the Norman Conquest only speeded up a process which was well under weigh. . . .

That the Norman Conquest ultimately gave a great impulse to English trade and urban development is not in dispute. The questions at issue are how far it made a new start in this development, and whether the old English borough-port from the first did not contain a germ of urban growth which might indeed come to little or perish, as it did in not a few small "free boroughs" of post-Conquest creation, but which marks it as essentially different from the *burg* of the Low Countries. On this latter point Dr. Stephenson adheres to the view he expressed in his article of 1930. On the first he has yielded a good deal of ground. He no longer maintains that there was no urban continuity between the Anglo-Saxon borough and the Anglo-Norman "town," except in a few seaports of the south-east. But he regards this urban growth before 1066 as quite recent, and he still leaves us with a large and indefinite class of "ordinary" boroughs, agricultural, save for insignificant local trade. Unfortunately, some of the evidence he adduces for this is equally applicable to larger boroughs in which he now admits trading settlement. This seems to be due to insufficient reconsideration of certain conclusions from Domesday in his original article. His study of the Anglo-Saxon borough began with the survey of 1086, and he was too much impressed by features which seemed capable of a non-urban interpretation.

It would be idle to deny that the Anglo-Saxon borough, even in the middle of the eleventh century, had features which were not in harmony with autonomous municipal organization: ecclesiastical and lay immunities, the sokes of the larger towns, burgesses dependent on rural estates, differences of rank, in some cases personal services in addition to money rents. Municipal autonomy, however, lay in a somewhat distant future. The Norman kings took over the boroughs from their predecessors, subject to rights, partly flowing from land ownership, partly from sovereignty, yielding, relatively to area, a larger revenue than their rural domains. If in some respects the borough system before long became a little more orderly, thanks partly to the influence of the new Norman foundations, in others the disorder was retained and even extended. Feudalism increased the number of sokes and preserved the Anglo-Saxon heriot in some boroughs as a feudal relief. At Norwich, Northampton, and Nottingham, English and French boroughs, with different customs, lived uneasily side by side. The gild merchant while preparing the way for the communal movement and incorporation, which ultimately swept away the relics of a disorderly past, introduced a further conflict of ideas and occasionally severe friction in practice.

If it is not possible to draw a perfectly sharp line of demarcation in the development of the borough at the Norman Conquest, it is equally difficult to draw such a line at the settlement of the Danes in the northern boroughs or indeed at any earlier date after the permanent re-occupation of the old Roman towns. It is all one story. A study of its various phases certainly discourages the old quest of a neat legal definition of the borough, applicable at all periods. Government officials in the fourteenth century found this no easier than does the student of the Burghal Hidage and Domesday Book. Yet, if, with Dr. Stephenson, it is preferred to find the common thread in the gradual development of a trading community, why should its humble beginnings be ignored?

James Tait, *The Medieval English Borough: Studies on Its Origins and Constitutional History* (Manchester, England: Manchester University Press, 1936), pp. 1-5, 21-27, 130, 136-138.

IV. DIFFERENT APPROACHES TO THE STUDY OF MEDIEVAL TOWN ORIGINS

For all the differences between them which can be noted, area by area, century by century, towns across all Europe, through all the period of origins and early development, had features—fundamental features—in common. Some of these *European* town characteristics, which they had and Chinese or Aztec towns did not, began to be analyzed by those scholars, especially sociologists, who study "urbanization" as a phenomenon of human societies. Sociologists and ethnologists sought in the medieval European towns common features which set those towns off from older European towns, such as the Roman cities of Italy, Gaul, and Britain; they sought for the aspects in which the medieval towns in turn differed from the modern European towns which bear the same names.

The subject of town origins attracted the attention of economists when the modern study of economics was still young. Soon historians, working on other aspects of the history of towns but aware of what economists were concerned with—the origins of capital and of capitalists, the organization of labor, patterns of distribution, and many other matters—began to put together in quasi-economic terms facts their research on the sources had brought to light. More and more, as has been seen, the historians themselves explained the origins of towns to be due to economic developments.

Historians of the school of Pirenne and Rietschel early began to prepare and use data drawn from historical geography. The practice became general thereafter among historians studying town origins and development.

Geographers and town-planners from the other side started to study medieval towns. They were interested in the "build" of all sorts of towns. They began to study the shapes, the street arrangements, the way man modified nature to fashion his town to meet his dream, at a given place and time, of what a town ought to be and ought to *do*. For the town as a sort of great tool for sheltering and protecting, for promoting manufacture, exchange, and supply, for entertaining and pleasing, interests such scholars.

The following excerpts are mere samples of the massive literature published on the subject of towns in general and medieval towns in particular, by scholars in non-historical disciplines or by historians presenting their materials in schematic forms derived from other disciplines.

A. Schmoller: Political Economist

As the village, so likewise does the town,—and even more conspicuously,—grow into an economic body (or organism), with a peculiar and vigorous life of its own, dominating every particular. To begin with, the choice of a locality, the laying-out of the plan, the construction of roadways, of bridges, and of walls; then the paving of the streets, the bringing of water, and the setting-up of lights; and, finally, the common arrangements which are necessary for the market, and which lead to common market-houses, public scales, etc.—these, together with the close juxtaposition of residences, and the higher forms of division of labor, of currency, and of credit, all create a mass of uniform, common institutions, and bring about an association of a far closer character than before. This necessarily makes itself felt both inside and outside the town. For centuries economic progress is bound up with the rise of the towns and the formation of civic institutions. Each town, and especially each of the larger towns, seeks to shut itself up as an economic whole, and, at the same time, in its relation to the outside world, to extend the sphere of its influence, both economic and political, as far as possible. . . .

Not only separate jurisdiction [*Immunität*], but also the right of holding a market, of collecting tolls, and of coining money, were, from early time, the privileges of the growing urban communities. This exceptional position was strengthened by the abolition of payments and services in kind, as well as by the legal advantages flowing from the principle that "town-air makes free"; and, finally, by the conquest of the right of self-government and legislation by the town council.

Gustav Schmoller, *The Mercantile System and Its Historical Significance Illustrated Chiefly from Prussian History* [published in Germany, 1884; English translation of chapter of this title from *Studies upon the Economic Policy of Frederick the Great*] (New York: Peter Smith, 1931), pp. 6-7.

B. Nussbaum Summarizes Theses of Werner Sombart

The exchanges of this developing exchange economy were largely performed by the producers themselves. It was only gradually that commerce was differentiated into a separate occupation. As in all primitive societies, piracy and occasional trading went hand in hand as a rough means of exchange, but in general, in Merovingian and Carolingian times, the merchant seems to have been a rare person, usually foreign. In the early Middle Ages he was usually a Syrian. Later came the Jews, regarded as foreigners after they had ceased to be regarded as Roman citizens. Besides the Jews, Arabs and Greeks were known as merchants in Italy, as also the North Africans in Spain. . . .

In the field of industry, the transition which we have to study is the rise of free and independent craftsmen. The dearth of materials does not permit us to say positively whether there were or were not such workmen before the beginning of town life. It is fairly clear that there were craftsmen who were freemen, but that does not dispose of the question whether or not they owed service to landlords. It is also fairly clear that the industrial worker on a manorial estate gradually acquired some independence in disposing of his products. First he could sell to the public only what his lord permitted; later the lord's claim was limited to a specified amount of his product, and the craftsman's principal occupation was dealing with the public; still later, all obliga-

tions to the lord were forgotten or commuted. The existence of such free workers throughout the Middle Ages is suggested by (1) the fact that industrial workers existed before the establishment of manorial arrangements and that not all villagers were brought into the manorial nexus, and (2) the fact of the existence of a certain number of wandering craftsmen. . . .

The climax of this transition period was the emergence of the town. In the evolution of a society from the purely agricultural conditions of the early Middle Ages to the highly urbanized conditions of the present, it is obvious that the town as such is a factor or a symptom of the highest importance. But what is a town? The definition of this familiar word has taken many different forms; a town must have walls, it must have a market, it must have a university, it must have a population of 2,000 and so on. These variations arise from variations in the point of view and have their utility for the points of view to which they correspond. Our point of view is determined by our problem, the evolution of economic institutions, and our definition of the town is consequently one which emphasizes its economic aspect. A town is a considerable settlement of human beings on a limited area without a general kinship bond, who for their sustenance look to the production of other economic units. "It is the surplus produce of the country only . . . that constitutes the subsistence of the town, which can therefore increase only with the increase of this surplus produce," says Adam Smith. It is obvious then, if our definition is to be at all serviceable, that the principal, constituent elements of the towns are those who are able by power or wealth to command the means of subsistence from elsewhere, a king who can tax, a landlord to whom dues are paid, a merchant who makes profits outside the town, a student who is supported by his parents. These are the "town-builders." After them come what we may call the "town-fillers," those who serve the needs of the town-builders: the shoemaker who makes the king's shoes, the jeweler who depends on the purchases of the merchant's wife, the landlady from whom the student rents his room. . . .

When with these concepts in mind we examine the development of the medieval towns, we note at once that they were still largely villages in the economic sense, that is, centers of residence of agricultural producers. . . .

In some of these semi-agricultural towns, however, developed groups of town-builders. They were mainly consumers of subsistence which they derived from outside agricultural areas. There were first of all the secular and ecclesiastical princes, bishops, abbots, counts, dukes, and kings. A king was inevitably a town-builder; the king of England alone in the year 1100 supported with his revenue ten to thirty times as many people as the commerce of the very important commercial town of Lübeck. Most of the churches and monasteries which became centers about which towns developed also were cen-ters to which great incomes were drawn. University students were an important element in the development of many a medieval town; their influence in town development can easily be observed in dozens of small economic communities in the United States today. The attraction to the towns of the essentially agricultural feudal lords was similarly an abstraction of consumption groups from the agricultural organization and their diversion to urban development. In the town they too were consumers of produce from outside. The medieval town grew also as a fortified center; but from the economic point of view it was rather the garrison than the walls that contributed to its evolution.

The important fact is that the consumer comes first in the evolution of the town. The merchant and the craftsman do not settle in the town until it affords them a better market than the countryside.

If the consumer comes first in the evolution of the town, it is nevertheless hard to conceive of a town in which part of the population does not support itself by industrial and commercial activity. Such classes did exist in all the medieval towns, but at first their significance and their size were alike small. The town produced some industrial articles for the peasants, but this was limited by the very small product that the peasant had to offer in exchange. Of somewhat greater significance, for some medieval towns, was international, or more correctly, interlocal commerce. . . .

Frederick L. Nussbaum, *A History of the Economic Institutions of Modern Europe: An Introduction to* Der Moderne Kapitalismus *of Werner Sombart* (New York: F. S. Crofts, 1933), pp. 34-39.

C. Bücher, Economic Theorist and Social Historian

What changes, then, were wrought in this condition of things by the mediaeval town, and in what does the economic system which we have designated as exclusive town economy consist?

The mediaeval town is above all things a *burg*, that is, a place fortified with walls and moats which serves as a refuge and shelter for the inhabitants of the unprotected places round about. Every town thus presupposes the existence of a defensive union which forms the rural settlements lying within a greater or narrower radius into a sort of military community with definite rights and duties. It devolves upon all the places belonging to this community to cooperate in maintaining intact the town fortifications by furnishing workmen and horses, and in time of war in defending them with their arms. In return they have the right, whenever occasion arises, to shelter themselves, their wives and children, their cattle and movables, within its walls. This right is called the *right of burgess,* and he who enjoys it is a burgher (*burgensis*).

Originally the permanent inhabitants of the town differ in nowise, not even in their occupations, from those living in the rural hamlets. Like the latter they follow farming and cattle-raising; they use wood, water, and pasture in common; their dwellings, as may still be seen in the structural arrangement of many old cities, are farmhouses with barns and stables and large yards between. But their communal life is not exhausted in the regulation of common pasturage and other agricultural interests. They are, so to speak, a permanent garrison stationed in the burg, and perform in rotation the daily watch-service on tower and at gate. Whoever wishes to settle permanently in the town must therefore not only be possessed of land, or a house at least; he must also be provided with weapons and armour.

The sentinel service and the extensive area of the town rendered necessary by the law of burgess demanded a great number of men; and soon the town limits no longer sufficed for their maintenance. Then it was that the one-sided development of the household establishments, already described, lent its influence, and the town became the seat of the industries and of the markets as well. In the latter the country peasant continued to dispose of his surplus supplies, obtaining from the townsman that which he himself could no longer provide and which the latter now exclusively or almost exclusively produced, namely, industrial products. . . .

We cannot here occupy ourselves further either with the development of the municipal constitution and its self-administration based upon corporative gradations, or with the political power which the towns of Germany, France, and Italy obtained in the later Middle Ages. We have to do only with the matured economic organization of which these towns formed the central points. . . .

Carl Bücher, *Industrial Evolution,* trans. from the third German edition by S. M. Wickert (New York: Henry Holt & Co., 1901), pp. 115-117, 119.

D. *N. S. B. Gras, Economic Historian*

The town developed out of the village. It was characterized by a growing economic ascendance over near-by villages. We have already seen that the urban village possessed a dominance over adjacent rural villages, that was political (or administrative), religious, and social. We are now concerned with a corresponding development in the economic field, especially in trade.

The exchange of goods has taken place in all the earlier stages of known human history. . . .

But when there came into being a class of traders who resided in a market village, and who had stores which not only supplemented the market place but became its rivals, then the economic town was born. The village (rural or urban) had become a town, and village economy had given way to town economy.

When the specialized trader came into existence, located in a market village and trading from his house, he introduced a new economic organization of vast importance, town economy. . . .

The characteristic of the town was trade. If the trade remained local, the town itself remained local and unimportant, but if favorably situated for extended trade, it grew rich and famous.

Town economy is the organization of many villages and one town, so as to constitute a single economic unit. The town was the center of local trade and the center to which were brought the products from other districts for sale to the people of the town and to the people of the villages. It was also the center to which the villages of its district sent such goods as were suitable for export to other districts, perhaps even to foreign lands.

It can hardly be too strongly emphasized that we are here dealing with purely economic considerations. . . .

Town economy occupies a stage in human history, not a period of time. A people climb the great heights of the town stage and then fall down. The process begins over again, sometimes with the same result. How long this struggle has gone on, we cannot say; but during at least the last five thousand years of recorded history, the rhythmic rise and fall of towns is the outstanding event in the history of advanced peoples. It is not a matter of wonder that this was the case because written history was a town accomplishment, and the science of history writing took its origin in the town, the home of peace, varied wealth, and unprecedented specialization. . . .

In economic history the growth of towns, their decay, and later revival constitute a cultural cycle. From about 3000 to 1500 B.C. the "Aegean" civilization of Memphis, Nippur, Mycenae, and Cnossus was at its height. Then came a period of town decay and village dominance, about 1500 to 700 B.C. the earliest middle ages of which we have any knowledge. Finally in the birth of Athens, Thebes, Corinth, Syracuse, Carthage, and Rome, the modern period, about 700 B.C., to A.D. 500, came into being, the modern period of Herodotus, Thucydides, and Caesar. To us this is, of course, the "ancient" period. And after it came our Middle Ages, about A.D. 500 to 1100, when the village, championed by the various Germanic peoples, again triumphed over the town. *Our* modern period began, as far as economic history is concerned, with the rebirth of town economy and town culture, about A.D. 1100 in southern Europe, later in the west. There will probably be no more such historic cycles, for the struggle between town and village economy has been won by a third organization, dominated not by the town but by the large commercial city.

N. S. B. Gras, *An Introduction to Economic History* (New York: Harper & Bros., 1922), pp. 104-113.

E. R. E. Dickinson, Geographer

The geographical interpretation of the urban settlement is concerned, according to Raoul Blanchard, in his essay on method in urban geography, with four main problems; first, the physical and cultural conditions involved in the origin of the nucleus of settlement; second, the reactions of this nucleus, in its functional and topographic or areal formation, to the impact of historical events; third, the life and organization of the contemporary settlement, viewed areally, both as a whole and with respect to the differentiation of its parts; fourth, the interrelations between the settlement and the surrounding territory. These four problems are concerned with the study of the individual urban settlement. There is further a comparative aspect of study. The size, function and form of settlements vary regionally with the development and present social and economic structure of the human groups which they represent and serve. It is for the geographer to investigate those features of the urban habitat that are areally repetitive and significant, just as he studies the rural habitat.

In other words, as in the field of geomorphology, the geographical study of urban, as of rural, settlements has three aspects. There is the physical *structure* of the settlement—the mode of grouping of its buildings and streets; there is the *process* which determines this structure—the social and economic character of the community; and third, there is the *stage* in the historical development of the settlement. This historical or developmental treatment may lay equal emphasis on the settlement at each phase of its development, but the final aspect of study, and that to which all else should be subordinated, is the depiction and interpretation of the settlement of to-day, both as a whole and as to the areal differentiations, by building, street, and district, within it.

Economist, historian, sociologist, and geographer study the urban settlement from different angles, and we must define the geographer's conception of such a settlement as distinct from a rural settlement, since this conditions his particular approach. Size and administrative status are not essential criteria of true urban character. Function and form are the essentials of the matter. The word urban, as opposed to rural, implies an activity divorced from the cultivation of the soil and carried out in close association with kindred activities at fixed places. These activities, in the broadest sense, are cultural (especially religious), commercial, industrial, administrative, and residential. The last include non-producers who are dependent on the urban workers and the countryside for their wants. Farming, however, is not excluded from the occupations of the urban community. A farming element is particularly characteristic of the towns of the Mediterranean lands and of east central Europe; it was important in the origin of the early medieval towns of western Europe, though it dwindled as trade and industry grew, and it is still not unimportant in many semi-urban settlements on the Continent.

The specifically urban activities are all located either in relation to a surrounding territory, or so as to carry out activities that are tied down to certain resources or where such resources can be conveniently assembled. Such activities may be carried out separately at different places. This occurs in the beginnings of permanent settlement in an area and also in thinly peopled or backward areas, where the settlement may assume a semi-permanent character. In the forested lands of north Sweden there are churches around which cluster timber buildings that are only occupied during the seasonal fairs. The tribal markets of Morocco are temporary settlements. Urban activities occur as a marked feature in the lands of Western civilization owing to the development of transport facilities. They take the form of an isolated factory, a group of workers' houses in the open country, a mining camp, or a seaside or inland resort. All these may be described as urban settlements. When, however, these activities occur in some kind of combination, in a permanent or compact settlement with some measure of community organization, the place assumes the character of a town. A city is simply a king among towns, enjoying leadership over its neighbours. A fundamental trait of both town and city, in all ages, has been that they serve as institutional centres (commercial, cultural and administrative) for a surrounding territory. It is only in recent times that industry has become a primary cause of urban growth. Upon the basis of regional service and industry there grows up a pyramidal structure of secondary occupations, catering for the needs of these specialist occupations and for the personal requirements of the inhabitants. . . .

The city cannot be interpreted adequately as a mass of materials or in terms of dead patterns. It must be interpreted as part of a social group, in terms of its four functions—dwelling, work, recreation and transport. In each of these respects every city forms part of a geographic, economic, social and cultural unit, upon which its development depends. This was the theme of our former book *City Region and Regionalism,* but the main argument may be summarized here.

Viewed from this aspect every urban centre has a two-way relation with its surroundings that extends beyond its political boundary. First, the countryside calls into being settlements which we call urban to carry out functions in its service. Second, the urban settlement, by the very fact of its existence, influences its surroundings, in varying degree, by the spread of its net-work of functional relations and the expansion of its settlement area. This regional factor varies greatly. In some cities, such as historical regional capitals, and in market and country towns, it is highly significant. In others, especially in specialized urban communities, which owe little directly to servicing the countryside, such as industrial set-

tlements and health resorts, the regional component is at a minimum. . . .

These brief town studies reveal characters that typify, in varying degree, every historic town in western Europe. Each has been, and still is to-day, primarily a seat of economic, cultural and administrative functions for its environs. Each reflects the stages in the general historical and cultural development of the country as a whole. Each emerged in the Middle Ages as a distinctive regional focus. . . .

We may now turn to consider briefly the sites and plans of these [Swiss] towns. The early medieval towns grew around pre-urban nuclei, sometimes on Roman sites, but the sites of the smaller towns were often selected primarily in the interests of defence. All of them are walled—the unwalled market settlement is a rare exception—and the majority have planned forms and characteristic architectural and architectonic features which exhibit marked regional variations.

While the route position (*Verkehrslage*) or nodality is the primary determinant of the growth of these towns, the site (*Ortslage*) has been decisive in their plan and build. Towns that have developed as route centres and as centres for a surrounding market area, have lowland sites (*Tiefenlage*) on important roads and at crossways or at the crossings of rivers or on lake shores. In valley constrictions and defiles along a lake shore, the town, as well as being a local market centre, could cut off a route and thereby acquire strategic importance (Bellinzona, St. Maurice, Rheineck). The edge of a terrace (Zofingen), an alluvial fan in the Alps (Chur), a lake delta (Steckbon) or lake embayment (Morges), are sites that determine the lay-out of the town. Some towns clustered around the nucleus of crystallization of a Roman settlement (Geneva and Basel). Others grew, as

a *Vorburg* or *Faubourg*, a parasitic settlement, around a castle on a hilltop
(Lenzburg), around a church foundation or bishop's see (Lausanne, Chur),
an abbey (St. Gallen), or a church
(Bischofszell).

Robert E. Dickinson, *The West European City: A Geographical Interpretation*, in *International Library of Sociology and Social Reconstruction*, ed. Karl Mannheim (London: Routledge and Kegan Paul, 1951), pp. 2-4, 9, 47, 56-57

6. The Meaning of the Renaissance

MYRON P. GILMORE

Harvard University

THE HISTORIAN, like other people who try to interpret human experience past or present, makes use of general concepts as well as collections of particular facts. Among these general concepts are our ideas of causation, of development or regression, of change or continuity, upon all of which we draw when we define periods and mark important turning points in any historical sequence. More than most such periodizations in the history of Europe the age of the Renaissance has depended for its meaning on the shifting content of the general hypotheses about history expressed or implied in the work of successive generations of historians. The Renaissance is in other words an abstraction, and it is an abstraction less immediately and obviously related to a series of particular events than most of the other familiar terms by which we identify particular epochs. We speak for example of the age of the French Revolution. Scholars have debated and will debate every aspect of the causes and consequences of the series of events which we call the Revolution, but no one has ever denied that the Revolution took place, unless it be that English bishop who satirized the higher critics of the Bible by writing historic doubts on the existence of Napoleon Bonaparte. Yet there are historians of repute who maintain that there is no historical reality corresponding to the conventional conception of the Renaissance, and that it would improve our understanding of the past to eliminate the term altogether from our vocabulary.

This is a more extreme position than it is possible to take about even such debated terms as the Reformation and the Industrial Revolution. After all Luther tacked up his 95 theses on 31 October, 1517, and the success of Hargreaves' spinning jenney can be measured from a definite time and place, but the student who seeks to find for the Renaissance a comparable specific event on the real or symbolic significance of which there is an equal amount of general agreement will seek in vain. If we are to avoid the unhappy results of misplaced concreteness and escape being the victims of our own metaphors, it is of the first importance to be aware of the fact that different kinds of discourse are appropriate to different levels of generalization. We cannot—or at least should not—personify the Renaissance nor treat it as an event like Magna Carta or the Declaration of Independence.   It is in reality a concept which historians use to describe a stage in the history of the European mind, and changes in intellectual history can seldom if ever be described in the same kind of language as may be used for a revolutionary act or the introduction of a new technology.   Any inward and spiritual change of great magnitude is of course accompanied and followed by outward and visible signs in every field of human activity, but the particular events that are regarded as characteristic manifestations of the Renaissance will vary with the descriptions of more elusive transformations in the attitudes, tastes, and convictions of individual men and women.

Our first problem must therefore be concerned with some of the definitions of the Renaissance proposed by its greatest historians.   In the elaboration of the concept that has become familiar in textbooks and in common parlance, the historical writing of the nineteenth century occupies the most important place, for it was in that century that there emerged a notion of the Renaissance as a period which saw a sharp break with the medieval past and the beginning of the modern world.   Earlier writers had distinguished the fifteenth and early sixteenth centuries in Italy as an age of literary and artistic achievement. Voltaire for example in his *Siècle de Louis XIV* placed Medicean Italy alongside Periclean Greece, Augustan Rome and the France of Louis XIV as the four great ages in the history of human culture, and long before Voltaire men had spoken of a "rebirth" of literature, law, painting, architecture, and scholarship, and located these phenomena in Italy in the age of humanism roughly beginning with Petrarch.   In spite of this periodization in the history of culture, it was left to the nineteenth century, the most historically minded of epochs, to define the Renaissance in a deeper and broader significance as a period which saw a decisive change in all departments of human activity and in the human spirit itself, marking the end of the Middle Ages and the beginning of the Modern World.

In this emphasis by the great nineteenth-century historians on a break in continuity there lies a paradox.   For one of the great preoccupations of nineteenth-century thought was the idea of development: the present was to be explained by the past and no criteria other than those derived from history were necessary.   The past must be understood in all its uniqueness, but at the same time a historical explanation was a complete explanation and even a justification for the present.   While Darwin explored the origin of species in the tremendously enlarged framework of geological time, those who directed their attention to the achievements of homo sapiens studied the links between modern parliamentary institutions and the customs of the Germanic tribes. The interpretation of the Renaissance as a decisive break in continuity—an epoch of transcendent significance standing as it were outside time, and marking the birth of the modern world—presents the strongest possible contrast to those evolutionary ideas which were developed and applied to so many areas of historical investigation. It was almost as if men felt themselves oppressed by the weight of historical development, imprisoned by necessity, and sought to affirm in the concept of the Renaissance the possibility of a historical miracle, *a sudden transformation* which had no satisfactory explanation in terms of antecedent causes and which violated the ordinary laws of continuity. If the greatest historians of the Renaissance in the nineteenth century did not quite depict it in this fashion without qualification, they nevertheless coined many a phrase which gave currency to the idea of the Renaissance as the period to which we were to look for the sudden beginnings of the most characteristic ideas and institutions of the modern world.

In contrast twentieth-century scholarship reacting against this view has frequently depreciated the importance of the Renaissance and emphasized the continuities between medieval and modern history. This too contains an element of the paradoxical, for one might have expected that our own age which has seen in its own life catastrophes and sudden breaks with the past would have looked at history with a heightened recognition of discontinuity.

In fact, however, each period turned towards that interpretation of the past which was at the opposite pole from its own experience. The nineteenth century which enjoyed on the whole an order and calm hardly matched since the Roman Empire constructed a Renaissance which was an apocalyptic break with the medieval past. On the other hand, the twentieth century, which has seen the predictable course of history shattered by catastrophic events, restored the continuity between medieval and modern times and in some cases even denied the Renaissance altogether.

The more comprehensive modern interpretations of the Renaissance whether "pro" or "contra" have commonly attempted to measure its significance for us by looking back over a long perspective. The very conflicts created by this attempt have produced another kind of evaluation of the Renaissance which shifts the emphasis from hindsight to contemporary opinion. If we cannot decide what the Renaissance was "in reality," we can at least ask ourselves what the "men of the Renaissance" thought about themselves and their own cultural achievement. If people believed they were living in a period of significant change of direction, this may not be evidence of actual change by any retrospective standard of measurement, but it is at least a basis on which a defensible periodization can be constructed. Our second problem is therefore concerned with the kind of generalizations that may be made about a period by those of its thinkers and writers who showed themselves most aware of the relationship between their own age and the past. The selection of excerpts included here is necessarily very limited and arbitrary, but it may serve to raise questions of interest and importance. What was the attitude of a man like Petrarch toward the classical past? How far did representative scholars think of their work as a "restoration" or "rebirth"? Did the artist look upon the great achievements in painting, sculpture and architecture with the same kind of judgments as were used by the men of letters when they evaluated the present and the past? To what extent can we discover a "common denominator" underlying quite different kinds of creative activity? How did men estimate the effects of such innovations as printing, gunpowder, and the new aids to navigation, and how did their consciousness of these things affect the idea of their age as a restoration of antiquity?

Such questions as these obviously cannot be answered by perusing a small selection of texts ranging in time from Petrarch to beyond the middle of the sixteenth century, and including not only one or two authors who are particularly representative of their time, but others who are so great as to transcend it. Nevertheless even these few texts may serve to focus the problem and to indicate the variety of possibilities inherent in any attempt to describe the significance of an age as it appeared to contemporary eyes.

General estimates of the Renaissance as an epoch in European intellectual history have always been closely related to the analysis of the importance of the work of certain of the greatest creative individuals whose achievement has come to symbolize the larger aspects of the period. This relationship, which is of course the basis for the discussion of the "spirit" of any age, is, in the case of the Renaissance, intensified precisely because so many of the characterizations of this age have turned on the meaning of "individualism." Among the eponymous heroes of the age of the Renaissance no names are more frequently mentioned than those of Machiavelli and Erasmus. The last problems in this section attempt to present some of the evidence for the conflicting interpretations of the significance of these great figures. In moving from the problems of describing and evaluating an age as a whole to that of analyzing the work of a single man, the field of observation is narrowed, but many of the fundamental questions remain. The Renaissance like the Middle Ages before it frequently appealed to the analogy between the microcosm and the macrocosm. The one has reflected the other in historical writing at least as often as in metaphysics. In the long run a revision in our judgment about a Machiavelli or an Erasmus is likely to lead to a revision in our judgment about the Renaissance as a whole.

I. WHAT DO MODERN HISTORIANS MEAN BY THE RENAISSANCE?

The following selections are intended to indicate the range of opinions on the meaning and significance of the age of the Renaissance judged as a whole. They consist of short passages, taken on the whole from much longer works, but representing the most comprehensive commitments of their respective authors.

The great French historian, Jules Michelet, devoted a large part of his life to an eloquent and passionate *History of France,* the hero of which was in fact the spirit of the French people through the ages. The seventh volume of this work entitled *The Renaissance* appeared in 1855. In its opening pages Michelet with characteristic exuberance declared that the Renaissance was nothing less than the discovery of the world and of man. With this famous phrase he became the first historian to attribute to the period a universal significance. The second of the passages from the same work shows Michelet capturing the drama of the invasion of Italy by the army of Charles VIII in 1494, and endowing this event with a crucial and almost apocalyptic quality. Henceforward 1494 became like 1492 and 1453 one of the dates most often accepted as symbolically marking the beginning of modern times.

The Swiss historian Jacob Burckhardt published in 1860 *The Civilization of the Renaissance in Italy*. This classic work gave to subsequent generations their idea of the Renaissance. Accepting Michelet's general conclusion, Burckhardt refined it and analyzed its application to Italy in the period from Giotto to Michelangelo. The selections given here, including the analysis of individualism and the significance of the revival of antiquity, illustrate the way in which Burckhardt developed his descriptive categories.

At the end of the nineteenth century Lord Acton was Regius Professor of Modern History at the University of Cambridge. The dramatic description of the break in continuity which marked the beginning of the modern period is taken from his posthumously published lectures.

Against these views of earlier students of the period must be placed the conclusions of twentieth-century scholars. Here there are included the judgments on the Renaissance of Lynn Thorndike (a historian of science), Ernst Cassirer (a historian of philosophy) and Erwin Panofsky (a historian of art).

A. *Michelet*

1. THE MEANING OF THE RENAISSANCE

The lovely word Renaissance means to those who care for beauty only the advent of a new art and the free development of the imagination. To the scholar it is the renovation of classical studies; to the lawyer the light that began to be cast on the disorder and chaos in our old customary laws.

Is this all there is to be said? Through the fogs of theological battles, the *Orlando,* the arabesques of Raphael, the nymphs of Jean Goujon continue to beguile the whims of fashion. Three very different types of mind, the artist, the priest, and the sceptic might be willing to agree on such a description of the significance of this great age. The scepticism of Montaigne was all that Pascal could see in it and Bossuet was in agreement when he wrote his *History of the Variations of the Protestant Churches.*

According to this interpretation a mighty revolutionary force, complex, extensive and profound, issued in nothing. So great an effort of the human will remained without result. What could be more discouraging for human thought?

These prejudiced views, however, forget but two little things which characterize this age more than all the preceding periods: the discovery of the world and the discovery of man.

The sixteenth century in its proper interpretation extends from Columbus to Copernicus, from Copernicus to Galileo, from the discovery of the earth to the exploration of the heavens.

In this period Man rediscovered himself. While Vesalius and Servetus revealed the bases of life, Luther and Calvin, Dumoulin and Cujas, Rabelais, Montaigne, Shakespeare, and Cervantes penetrated its moral mysteries. Mankind therefore sounded the depths of human nature and began to base itself on justice and reason. Sceptics came to the aid of faith and the boldest of all reached the point of inscribing on the portico of his Temple of the Will: "Enter to build here a profound faith."

And deep indeed were the foundations on which the new faith was supported at a time when the identity between a rediscovered antiquity and the modern age began to be recognized, when the newly discovered East extended its hands to our western civilization and when in due course began the happy reconciliation of the members of the human family.

J. Michelet, *Histoire de France*, IX, "La Renaissance" (Paris, 1879), 7-9, adapted, trans. M. P. Gilmore.

2. THE SIGNIFICANCE OF THE FRENCH INVASION OF ITALY IN 1494

On the thirty-first of December at three o'clock in the afternoon the army of Charles VIII entered Rome and the passage of its marching files was prolonged far into the night by the light of torches. The Italians viewed not without terror this sudden appearance of France and glimpsed among these barbarians the results of an art, an entirely new organization for warfare, the existence of which they had not previously suspected.

. . . Although the army had boasted sixty thousand men at the crossing of the Alps, it had detached various units all along its route and now at Rome amounted to hardly more than thirty thousand. But this was the very heart of the army, the most vigorous and the best armed; by detaching the weak and the laggards it had become still more formidable.

. . . Surrounding the king there marched with the Swiss guard three hundred archers and two hundred knights wearing gold and purple and clothed in massive armour.

There followed in rapid succession thirty-six bronze cannon, each weighing thousands of pounds, then long culverins and about a hundred falconets. Each of these pieces was drawn not by oxen in the Italian manner but by a lively team of six horses with mobile gun-carriages which in combat were detached from their fore-carriages and were immediately ready for action.

All this was to be seen in the light of the torches reflected on the walls of the Roman palaces and in the depths of the long streets with fantastic silhouettes larger than life, sinister and mournful in their effects. Everyone sensed that this was a great revolution which amounted to more than the passage of a single army and that there would emerge from this event not only the ordinary tragedies of war but a general and decisive change even in the realm of customs and ideas. The Alps were lowered forever.

Ibid., pp. 125-129.

B. *Burckhardt*

1. THE ITALIAN STATE AND THE INDIVIDUAL

In the Middle Ages both sides of human consciousness—that which was turned within as that which was turned without—lay dreaming or half awake beneath a common veil. The veil was woven of faith, illusion, and childish prepossession, through which the world and history were seen clad in strange hues. Man was conscious of himself only as member of a race, people, party, family, or corporation—only through some general category. In Italy this veil first melted into air; an *objective* treatment and consideration of the state and of all the things of this world became possible. The *subjective* side at the same time asserted itself with corresponding emphasis; man became a spiritual *individual,* and recognized himself as such. In the same way the Greek had once distinguished himself from the barbarian, and the Arabian had felt himself an individual at a time when other Asiatics knew themselves only as members of a race. It will not be difficult to show that this result was owing above all to the political circumstances of Italy.

In far earlier times we can here and there detect a development of free personality which in Northern Europe either did not occur at all, or could not display itself in the same manner. The band of audacious wrongdoers in the tenth century described to us by Liud-prand, some of the contemporaries of Gregory VII., and a few of the opponents of the first Hohenstaufen, show us characters of this kind. But at the close of the thirteenth century Italy began to swarm with individuality; the charm laid upon human personality was dissolved; and a thousand figures meet us each in its own special shape and dress. Dante's great poem would have been impossible in any other country of Europe, if only for the reason that they all still lay under the spell of race. For Italy the august poet, through the wealth of individuality which he set forth, was the most national herald of his time. . . . The Italians of the fourteenth century knew little of false modesty or of hypocrisy in any shape; not one of them was afraid of singularity, of being and seeming unlike his neighbours.

Despotism, as we have already seen, fostered in the highest degree the individuality not only of the tyrant or condottiere himself, but also of the men whom he protected or used as his tools—the secretary, minister, poet, and companion. These people were forced to know all the inward resources of their own nature, passing or permanent; and their enjoyment of life was enhanced and concentrated by the desire to obtain the greatest satisfaction from a possibly very brief period of power and influence.

But even the subjects whom they ruled over were not free from the same impulse. Leaving out of account those who wasted their lives in secret opposition and conspiracies, we speak of the majority who were content with a strictly private station, like most of the urban population of the Byzantine empire and the Mohammedan states. No doubt it was often hard for the subjects of a Visconti to maintain the dignity of their persons and families, and multi-

tudes must have lost in moral character through the servitude they lived under. But this was not the case with regard to individuality; for political impotence does not hinder the different tendencies and manifestations of private life from thriving in the fullest vigour and variety. Wealth and culture, so far as display and rivalry were not forbidden to them, a municipal freedom which did not cease to be considerable, and a Church which, unlike that of the Byzantine or of the Mohammedan world, was not identical with the State—all these conditions undoubtedly favoured the growth of individual thought, for which the necessary leisure was furnished by the cessation of party conflicts. The private man, indifferent to politics, and busied partly with serious pursuits, partly with the interests of a *dilettante,* seems to have been first fully formed in these despotisms of the fourteenth century. Documentary evidence cannot, of course, be required on such a point. The novelists, from whom we might expect information, describe to us oddities in plenty, but only from one point of view and in so far as the needs of the story demand. Their scene, too, lies chiefly in the republican cities.

In the latter, circumstances were also, but in another way, favourable to the growth of individual character. The more frequently the governing party was changed, the more the individual was led to make the utmost of the exercise and enjoyment of power. The statesmen and popular leaders, especially in Florentine history, acquired so marked a personal character, that we can scarcely find, even exceptionally, a parallel to them in contemporary history, hardly even in Jacob van Arteveldt.

. . . An acute and practised eye might be able to trace, step by step, the increase in the number of complete men during the fifteenth century. Whether they had before them as a conscious object the harmonious development of their spiritual and material existence, is hard to say; but several of them attained it, so far as is consistent with the imperfection of all that is earthly. It may be better to renounce the attempt at an estimate of the share which fortune, character, and talent had in the life of Lorenzo Magnifico. But look at a personality like that of Ariosto, especially as shown in his satires. In what harmony are there expressed the pride of the man and the poet, the irony with which he treats his own enjoyments, the most delicate satire, and the deepest goodwill!

When this impulse to the highest individual development was combined with a powerful and varied nature, which had mastered all the elements of the culture of the age, then arose the 'all-sided man'—'l'uomo universale'—who belonged to Italy alone. Men there were of encyclopaedic knowledge in many countries during the Middle Ages, for this knowledge was confined within narrow limits; and even in the twelfth century there were universal artists, but the problems of architecture were comparatively simple and uniform, and in sculpture and painting the matter was of more importance than the form. But in Italy at the time of the Renaissance, we find artists who in every branch created new and perfect works, and who also made the greatest impression as men. Others, outside the arts they

practised, were masters of a vast circle of spiritual interests.

... The fifteenth century is, above all, that of the many-sided men. There is no biography which does not, besides the chief work of its hero, speak of other pursuits all passing beyond the limits of dilettantism. The Florentine merchant and statesman was often learned in both the classical languages; the most famous humanists read the ethics and politics of Aristotle to him and his sons; even the daughters of the house were highly educated. It is in these circles that private education was first treated seriously. The humanist, on his side, was compelled to the most varied attainments, since his philological learning was not limited, as it now is, to the theoretical knowledge of classical antiquity, but had to serve the practical needs of daily life. While studying Pliny, he made collections of natural history; the geography of the ancients was his guide in treating of modern geography, their history was his pattern in writing contemporary chronicles, even when composed in Italian; he not only translated the comedies of Plautus, but acted as manager when they were put on the stage; every effective form of ancient literature down to the dialogues of Lucian he did his best to imitate; and besides all this, he acted as magistrate, secretary, and diplomatist—not always to his own advantage.

Jacob Burckhardt, *The Civilisation of the Renaissance in Italy*, trans. S. G. C. Middlemore (New York: The Macmillan Co., 1890), pp. 129-131, 134-136.

2. THE REVIVAL OF ANTIQUITY

We must insist upon it, as one of the chief propositions of this book, that it was not the revival of antiquity alone, but its union with the genius of the Italian people, which achieved the conquest of the western world. The amount of independence which the na-

tional spirit maintained in this union varied according to circumstances. In the modern Latin literature of the period, it is very small, while in plastic art, as well as in other spheres, it is remarkably great; and hence the alliance between two distant epochs in the civilisation of the same people, because concluded on equal terms, proved justifiable and fruitful. The rest of Europe was free either to repel or else partly or wholly to accept the mighty impulse which came forth from Italy. Where the latter was the case we may as well be spared the complaints over the early decay of mediæval faith and civilisation. Had these been strong enough to hold their ground, they would be alive to this day. If those elegiac natures which long to see them return could pass but one hour in the midst of them, they would gasp to be back in modern air. That in a great historical process of this kind flowers of exquisite beauty may perish, without being made immortal in poetry or tradition, is undoubtedly true; nevertheless, we cannot wish the process undone. The general result of it consists in this —that by the side of the Church which had hitherto held the countries of the West together (though it was unable to do so much longer) there arose a new spiritual influence which, spreading itself abroad from Italy, became the breath of life for all the more instructed minds in Europe. The worst that can be said of the movement is, that it was anti-popular, that through it Europe became for the first time sharply divided into the cultivated and uncultivated classes. The reproach will appear groundless when we reflect that even now the fact, though clearly recognised, cannot be altered. The separation, too, is by no means so cruel and absolute in Italy as elsewhere. The most artistic of her poets, Tasso, is in the hands of even the poorest.

The civilisation of Greece and Rome, which, ever since the fourteenth century, obtained so powerful a hold on Italian life, as the source and basis of culture, as the object and ideal of existence, partly also as an avowed reaction against preceding tendencies—this civilisation had long been exerting a partial

influence on mediæval Europe, even beyond the boundaries of Italy. The culture of which Charles the Great was a representative was, in face of the barbarism of the seventh and eighth centuries, essentially a Renaissance, and could appear under no other form. Just as in the Romanesque architecture of the North, beside the general outlines inherited from antiquity, remarkable direct imitations of the antique also occur, so too monastic scholarship had not only gradually absorbed an immense mass of materials from Roman writers, but the style of it, from the days of Eginhard onwards, shows traces of conscious imitations.

But the resuscitation of antiquity took a different form in Italy from that which it assumed in the North. The wave of barbarism had scarcely gone by before the people, in whom the former life was but half effaced, showed a consciousness of its past and a wish to reproduce it. Elsewhere in Europe men deliberately and with reflection borrowed this or the other element of classical civilisation; in Italy the sympathies both of the learned and of the people were naturally engaged on the side of antiquity as a whole, which stood to them as a symbol of past greatness. The Latin language, too, was easy to an Italian, and the numerous monuments and documents in which the country abounded facilitated a return to the past. With this tendency other elements—the popular character which time had now greatly modified, the political institutions imported by the Lombards from Germany, chivalry and other northern forms of civilisation, and the influence of religion and the Church —combined to produce the modern Italian spirit, which was destined to serve as the model and ideal for the whole western world.

Ibid., pp. 171-173.

3. THE DISCOVERY OF MAN

To the discovery of the outward world the Renaissance added a still greater achievement, by first discerning and bringing to light the full, whole nature of man.

This period, as we have seen, first gave the highest development to individuality, and then led the individual to the most zealous and thorough study of himself in all forms and under all conditions. Indeed, the development of personality is essentially involved in the recognition of it in oneself and in others. Between these two great processes our narrative has placed the influence of ancient literature, because the mode of conceiving and representing both the individual and human nature in general was defined and coloured by that influence. But the power of conception and representation lay in the age and in the people.

The facts which we shall quote in evidence of our thesis will be few in number. Here, if anywhere in the course of this discussion, the author is conscious that he is treading on the perilous ground of conjecture, and that what seems to him a clear, if delicate and gradual, transition in the intellectual movement of the fourteenth and fifteenth centuries, may not be equally plain to others. The gradual awakening of the soul of a people is a phenomenon which may produce a different impression on each spectator. Time will judge which impression is the most faithful.

Ibid., p. 308.

C. Lord Acton

1. THE BREAK IN CONTINUITY

. . . I describe as Modern History that which begins four hundred years ago, which is marked off by an evident and intelligible line from the time immediately preceding, and displays in its course specific and distinctive characteristics of its own. The modern age did not proceed from the medieval by normal succession, with outward tokens of legitimate descent. Unheralded, it founded a new order of things, under a law of innovation, sapping the ancient reign of continuity. In those days Columbus subverted the notions of the world, and reversed the conditions of production, wealth, and power; in those days Machiavelli released government from the restraint of law; Erasmus diverted the current of ancient learning from profane into Christian channels; Luther broke the chain of authority and tradition at the strongest link; and Copernicus erected an invincible power that set for ever the mark of progress upon the time that was to come. There is the same unbound originality and disregard for inherited sanctions in the rare philosophers as in the discovery of Divine Right, and the intruding Imperialism of Rome. The like effects are visible everywhere, and one generation beheld them all. It was an awakening of new life; the world revolved in a different orbit, determined by influences unknown before. After many ages persuaded of the headlong decline and impending dissolution of society, and governed by usage and the will of masters who were in their graves, the sixteenth century went forth armed for untried experience, and ready to watch with hopefulness a prospect of incalculable change.

That forward movement divides it broadly from the older world; and the unity of the new is manifest in the universal spirit of investigation and discovery which did not cease to operate, and withstood the recurring efforts of reaction, until, by the advent of the reign of general ideas which we call the Revolution, it at length prevailed. This successive deliverance and gradual passage, for good and evil, from subordination to independence is a phenomenon of primary import to us, because historical science has been one of its instruments. If the Past has been an obstacle and a burden, knowledge of the Past is the safest and surest emancipation. And the earnest search for it is one of the signs that distinguish the four centuries of which I speak from those that went before. The Middle Ages, which possessed good writers of contemporary narrative, were careless and impatient of older fact. They became content to be deceived, to live in a twilight of fiction, under clouds of false witness, inventing according to convenience, and glad to welcome the forger and the cheat. As time went on, the atmosphere of accredited mendacity thickened, until, in the Renaissance, the art of exposing falsehood dawned upon keen Italian minds. It was then that History as we understand it began to be understood, and the illustrious dynasty of scholars arose to whom we still look both for method and material. Unlike the dreaming prehistoric world, ours knows the need and the duty to make itself master of the earlier times, and to forfeit nothing of their wisdom or their warnings, and has devoted its best energy and treasure to the sovereign purpose of detecting error and vindicating entrusted truth.

Lord Acton, *Lectures on Modern History,* eds. John Neville Figgis and Reginald Vere Laurence (London: Macmillan and Co., 1906), pp. 3-5.

2. THE CLASSICAL REVIVAL

Next to the discovery of the New World, the recovery of the ancient world is the second landmark that divides us from the Middle Ages and marks the transition to modern life. The Renaissance signifies the renewed study of Greek, and the consequences that ensued from it, during the century and a half between Petrarca and Erasmus. It had survived, as a living language, among Venetian colonists and Calabrian monks, but exercised no influence on literature.

The movement was preceded by a Roman revival, which originated with Rienzi [in the middle of the fourteenth century]. Rome had been abandoned by the Papacy, which had moved from the Tiber to the Rhone, where it was governed by Frenchmen from Cahors, and had fallen, like any servile country, into feudal hands. Rienzi restored the Republic, revived the self-government of the city, the memories attached to the Capitol, the inscriptions, the monuments of the men who ruled the world. The people, no longer great through the Church, fell back on the greatness which they inherited from ancient times. The spell by which the Tribune directed their patriotism was archæology. In front of the Capitoline temple, near the Tarpeian rock and the She-Wolf's cave, he proclaimed their rights over the empire and the nations; and he invited the people of Italy to a national parliament for the restoration of Italian unity and of the ancient glory and power of Rome. Patriotism, national independence, popular liberty, all were founded on antiquarian studies and the rhetorical interpretation of the fragments of the Lex Regia.

The political scheme of Rienzi failed, but it started a movement in the world of thought deeper and more enduring than State transactions. For his ideas were adopted by the greatest writer then living, and were expounded by him in the most eloquent and gracious prose that had been heard for a thousand years. Petrarca called the appearance of the patriotic Tribune and rhetorician the dawn of a new world and a golden age. Like him, he desired to purge the soil of Italy from the barbaric taint. It became the constant theme of the humanists to protest against the foreign intruder, that is, against the feudal noble, the essential type of the medieval policy. It is the link between Rienzi, the dreamer of dreams, and the followers of Petrarca. Boccaccio had already spoken of the acceptable blood of tyrants.

But the political influence of antiquity, visible at first, made way for a purely literary influence. The desire for good Latin became injurious to Italian, and Petrarca censured Dante for his error in composing the *Divine Comedy* in the vulgar tongue. He even regretted that the *Decamerone* was not written in Latin, and refused to read what his friend had written for the level of uneducated men. The classics be-

came, in the first place, the model and the measure of style; and the root of the Renaissance was the persuasion that a man who could write like Cicero had an important advantage over a man who wrote like Bartolus or William of Ockham; and that ideas radiant with beauty must conquer ideas clouded over with dialectics. In this, there was an immediate success. Petrarca and his imitators learnt to write excellent Latin. Few of them had merit as original thinkers, and what they did for erudition was done all over again, and incomparably better, by the scholars who appeared after the tempest of the Reformation had gone down. But they were excellent letter writers. In hundreds of volumes, from Petrarca to Sadolet and Pole, we can trace every idea and mark every throb. It was the first time that the characters of men were exposed with analytic distinctness; the first time indeed that character could be examined with accuracy and certitude.

Ibid., pp. 171-173.

D. *Thorndike's Case Against the Renaissance*

Legacies from the past? Yes. Inheritances from previous periods? Yes. Survivals? Yes. Resemblances to our forebears? Yes. Reformations? Perhaps. Reactions? Unfortunately. But no rebirths and no restorations!

Books and works of art are about all that remain to us of the past. The latter are all too soon sadly altered, and their restoration, whether by some German professor or by a Thorwaldsen or Viollet-le-Duc, only makes them less like what they originally were. Books remain less changed by the lapse of time, but even their text may become corrupt, or the meaning of the very words they use alter in the interim. The humanists of the so-called Italian

Renaissance had only a bookish knowledge of antiquity; they failed almost as dismally as have Mussolini and his Fascists to make the reality of ancient Rome live again. If, even in our own day, all the resources of the art of history aided by archaeology can give us only a faint and imperfect idea of the past, how can we expect actual renaissances of it or recognize them as such, if they were to occur? At the age of sixty I am perhaps more like myself at the age of twenty than I am like anyone else. But I couldn't possibly put myself back into the frame of mind that I had then. I have a dim recollection of it; my present state of mind is an outgrowth of it; that is all. A girl of eighteen, dressed up in the clothes which her grandmother wore when a girl of eighteen, may look more like her grandmother as she was then than her grand-mother herself does now. But she will not feel or act as her grandmother felt and acted half a century or more ago. Much more tenuous is the connection between distant historical periods, and much less likely is it that historians can successfully venture upon glittering generalities about them. Who can evoke from the past more than a wraith, a phantasy, a specter, which murmurs, like the ghost in *Hamlet*, "Historian, remember me!"

. . . The concept of the Italian Renaissance or Prenaissance has in my opinion done a great deal of harm in the past and may continue to do harm in the future. It is too suggestive of a sensational, miraculous, extraordinary, magical, human and intellectual development, like unto the phoenix rising from its ashes after five hundred years. It is contrary to the fact that human nature tends to remain much the same in all times. It has led to a chorus of rhapsodists as to freedom, breadth, soaring ideas, horizons, perspectives, out of fetters and swaddling clothes, and so on. It long discouraged the study of centuries of human development that preceded it, and blinded the French *philosophes* and revolutionists to the value of medieval political and economic institutions. It has kept men in general from recognizing that our life and thought is based more nearly and actually on the middle ages than on distant Greece and Rome, from whom our heritage is more indirect, bookish and sentimental, less institutional, social, religious, even less economic and experimental.

But what is the use of questioning the Renaissance? No one has ever proved its existence; no one has really tried to. So often as one phase of it or conception of it is disproved, or is shown to be equally characteristic of the preceding period, its defenders take up a new position and are just as happy, just as complacent as ever.

> You may break, you may shatter the vase, if you will,
> But the scent of the roses will hang round it still.

Still lingers the sweet perfume of the Renaissance; still hovers about us the blithe spirit of the Prenaissance.

Lynn Thorndike, "Renaissance or Prenaissance?" *Journal of the History of Ideas*, IV (1943), 65-66, 74.

E. *Cassirer on the Originality of the Renaissance*

Our controversy as to the originality of the Renaissance and as to the dividing-line between the "Renaissance" and the "Middle Ages" seems to me in many ways rather a "logical" dispute than one about the historical facts. Ideas like "Gothic," "Renaissance," or "Baroque" are ideas of historical "style." As to the meaning of these ideas of "style" there still prevails a great lack of clarity in many respects. They can be used to *characterize* and *interpret* intellectual movements, but they express no actual historical facts that ever existed at any given time. "Renaissance" and "Middle Ages" are, strictly speaking, not names for historical periods at all, but they are concepts of "ideal types," in Max Weber's sense. We cannot therefore use them as instruments for any strict division of periods; we cannot inquire at what temporal point the Middle Ages "stopped" or the Renaissance "began." The actual historical facts cut across and extend over each other in the most complicated manner.

Nevertheless the distinction itself has a real meaning. What we can express by it, and what alone we intend to express, is that from the beginning of the fifteenth century onward the *balance* between the particular forces—society, state, religion, church, art, science—begins to shift slowly. New forces press up out of the depths and alter the previous equilibrium. And the character of every culture rests on the equilibrium between the forces that give it form. Whenever therefore we make any comparison between the Middle Ages and the Renaissance, it is never enough to single out particular ideas or concepts. What we want to know is not the particular idea as such, but the importance it possesses, and the strength with which it is acting in the whole structure. "Middle Ages" and "Renaissance" are two great and mighty streams of ideas. When we single out from them a particular idea, we are not doing what a chemist does in analyzing the water of a stream or what a geographer does in trying to trace it to its source. No one denies that these are interesting and important questions. But they are neither the only nor the most important concern of the *historian of ideas.*

The historian of ideas knows that the water which the river carries with it changes only very slowly. The same ideas are always appearing again and again, and are maintained for centuries. The force and the tenacity of tradition can hardly be over-estimated. From this point of view we must acknowledge over and over again that there is nothing new under the sun. But the historian of ideas is not asking primarily what the *substance* is of particular ideas. He is asking what their *function* is. What he is studying—or should be studying—is less the *content* of ideas than their *dynamics*. To continue the figure, we could say that he is not trying to analyze the drops of water in the river, but that he is seeking to measure its width and depth and to ascertain the force and velocity of the current. It is all *these* factors that are fundamentally altered in the Renaissance: the dynamics of ideas has changed.

Ernst Cassirer, "Some Remarks on the Question of the Originality of the Renaissance," *Journal of the History of Ideas,* IV (1943), 54-55.

F. *Panofsky*

1. THE SENSE OF HISTORY

In sum, the Italian Renaissance looked upon classical Antiquity from a historical distance; therefore, for the first time, as upon a totality removed from the present; and therefore, for the first time, as upon an ideal to be longed for instead of a reality to be both utilized and feared. The pre-Gothic Middle Ages had left Antiquity unburied, and alternately galvanized and exorcized its body. The Renaissance stood weeping at its grave and tried to resurrect its soul. And in one fatally auspicious moment it succeeded. This is why the mediaeval concept of Antiquity was so concrete and, at the same time, so incomplete and distorted; whereas the modern one is, in a sense, abstract but more comprehensive and consistent. And this is why the mediaeval revivals were real but transitory whereas the Italian, or main, Renaissance was, in a sense, academic but permanent. Resurrected souls are somewhat intangible but they have the advantage of being immortal and omnipresent. Therefore the rôle of classical Antiquity in the modern world is a little elusive but, on the other hand, pervasive—and changeable only with a change in the form of our civilization as such.

. . . One of the leading anti-Renaissancists has recently dismissed the relevance of the *"rinascimento dell' antichità"* by the following simile: "A girl of eighteen, dressed up in the clothes which her grandmother wore when a girl of eighteen, may look more like her grandmother as she was then than her grandmother herself looks now. But she will not feel or act as her grandmother did half a century ago." Taking up this simile, we may answer: If this girl decides to adopt the clothes of her grandmother for good and wears them all the time in the serious conviction that they are more appropriate and becoming than those she used to wear before, this very decision not only induces but actually presupposes a change in her whole personality and way of life —a change not sufficient to make her a duplicate of her grandmother (which no one has claimed to be true of the Renaissance period in relation to classical Antiquity), but basic enough to make her "feel and act" quite differently from the way she did as long as she believed in slacks and polo shirts.

Erwin Panofsky, "Renaissance and Renascences," *The Kenyon Review*, VI (1944), 228-229, 229-230.

2. MIDDLE AGES AND RENAISSANCE

If one wants to perceive, at one glance, the difference between the Middle Ages and the Renaissance one may compare Sebastian Brant's *Fools' Ship* of 1494 with Erasmus of Rotterdam's *Praise of Folly* of 1512. Brant, without a trace of tolerance or irony, inveighs against more than a hundred kinds of human folly, firmly convinced that he is right and that everybody else is wrong. Erasmus also ridicules human folly. But he, the most intelligent man of the century, does this by pretending to speak in the name of Folly herself. Whatever is said must therefore be interpreted as his opinion as well as hers. In one of the chapters Erasmus—or Folly—thus assails, apparently as grimly serious as Brant, the foolishness of old women still going to drinking parties, still using make-up, still hiring gigolos, still removing hair from the strangest places. But what is the conclusion? "Such capers are laughed at by everyone, and with good reason, as being the silliest in the world. Yet the old ladies are satisfied with themselves, and in the mean time they swim in pleasure and anoint themselves all over with honey; they are happy, in a word, by courtesy of me. And as for the people who find it all too ridiculous, I want them to mull over the question whether it is not better to lead this sort of honeyed life in folly than to look for a rafter, as the phrase goes, suitable for a hanging." Folly, then, first attacks foolishness and then defends it. Being Folly, her attack should really mean justification and her defense the opposite. But since she speaks in the name of Erasmus as well as in her own it also works out the other way: the attack may be serious but no less serious would then be the defense— the insight into the fact that "to be engrossed in folly, to err, to be deceived, not to know" is simply "to live as a man."

In an ironical double-twist like this there does appear a humanism—and a humanity—utterly foreign to the Middle Ages. In the Middle Ages reason could question faith and faith could question reason. But reason could not question itself and yet emerge with wisdom—even though Robert Grosseteste had a telescope.

Ibid., pp. 234-235.

II. WHAT WAS THE ATTITUDE OF THE "MEN OF THE RENAISSANCE" TOWARD THEIR OWN PLACE IN HISTORY?

The second problem turns from the modern analysis of the Renaissance to the various meanings of the concept of "rebirth" or "restoration" as that concept was used in the contemporary sources.

In the following excerpts Petrarch's Letter to Livy and Bruni's account of his own time illustrate with different emphases the intensity of the nostalgic longing among the early humanists for the recovery of the classical world. Bruni's recollections in particular bear witness to the strength of the feeling that the achievement of his generation marked an epoch in intellectual history. Modern historians recognize that there is much that is exaggerated in this account. It is not true, for example, that Greek literature had been unknown in Italy for 700 years. Yet the belief of Bruni and others like him that they were bringing a whole culture to new birth is a fact of the first importance. Vasari, the biographer of the Italian artists, writing in the sixteenth century, relies on this same metaphor of a rebirth to characterize the artistic achievement of the period.

Erasmus, Rabelais and Dolet lived in northern Europe at a time when the results of humanist scholarship had been more widely diffused. The selections taken from their writing illustrate a much more comprehensive interpretation of the idea of restoration. Not only literature and art are "reborn" but medicine, law, science, theology, and, most important of all for Erasmus, Christian piety. Furthermore the restoration of the old is now inseparably connected with the birth of the new. In Dolet's eloquent statement the revival of good literature is bound to be accompanied by a social and political improvement. With Louis LeRoy, who published his *Considerations on Universal History* in 1567 and his *Vicissitude or Variety of Things in the Universe* ten years later, we reach the point of self-conscious questioning about the balance between innovation and tradition and a willingness to recognize those achievements of his own age which were entirely unknown to the ancients.

A. Petrarch's Letter to Titus Livy

I should wish (if it were permitted from on high) either that I had been born in your age or you in ours; in the latter case our age itself, and in the former I personally should have been the better for it. I should surely have been one of those pilgrims who visited you. For the sake of seeing you I should have gone not merely to Rome, but indeed, from either Gaul or Spain I should have found my way to you as far as India. As it is, I must fain be content with seeing you as reflected in your works—not your whole self, alas, but that portion of you which has not yet perished, notwithstanding the sloth of our age. We know that you wrote one hundred and forty-two books on Roman affairs. With what fervor, with what unflagging zeal must you have labored; and of that entire number there are now extant scarcely thirty.

Oh, what a wretched custom is this of wilfully deceiving ourselves! I have said "thirty," because it is common for all to say so. I find, however, that even from these few there is one lacking. They are twenty-nine in all, constituting three decades, the first, the third, and the fourth, the last of which has not the full number of books. It is over these small remains that I toil whenever I wish to forget these regions, these times, and these customs. Often I am filled with bitter indignation against the morals of today, when men value nothing except gold and silver, and desire nothing except sensual, physical pleasures. If these are to be considered the goal of mankind, then not only the dumb beasts of the field, but even insensible and inert matter has a richer, a higher goal than that proposed to itself by thinking man. But of this elsewhere.

It is now fitter that I should give you thanks, for many reasons indeed, but for this in especial: that you so frequently caused me to forget the present evils, and transferred me to happier times. As I read, I seem to be living in the midst of the Cornelii Scipiones Africani, of Laelius, Fabius Maximus, Metellus, Brutus and Decius, of Cato, Regulus, Cursor, Torquatus, Valerius Corvinus, Salinator, of Claudius, Marcellus, Nero, Aemilius, of Fulvius, Flaminius, Attilius, Quintius, Curius, Fabricius, and Camillus. It is with these men that I live at such times and not with the thievish company of today among whom I was born under an evil star. And Oh, if it were my happy lot to possess your entire works, from what other great names would I not seek solace for my wretched existence, and forgetfulness of this wicked age! Since I cannot find all these in what I now possess of your work, I read of them here and there in other authors, and especially in that book where you are to be found in your entirety, but so briefly epitomized that,

although nothing is lacking as far as the number of books is concerned, everything is lacking as regards the value of the contents themselves.

Pray greet in my behalf your predecessors Polybius and Quintus Claudius and Valerius Antias, and all those whose glory your own greater light has dimmed; and of the later historians, give greeting to Pliny the Younger, of Verona, a neighbor of yours, and also to your former rival Crispus Sallustius. Tell them that their ceaseless nightly vigils have been of no more avail, have had no happier lot, than yours.

Farewell forever, matchless historian!

Written in the land of the living, in that part of Italy and in that city in which I am now living and where you were once born and buried, in the vestibule of the Temple of Justina Virgo, and in view of your very tombstone; on the twenty-second of February, in the thirteen hundred and fiftieth year from the birth of Him whom you would have seen, or whose birth you could have heard, had you lived a little longer.

Petrarch's Letters to Classical Authors, trans. Mario E. Cosenza (University of Chicago Press, copyright 1910 by the University of Chicago), pp. 100-103, adapted.

B. Leonardo Bruni on the History of His Own Time

I have decided to discuss in this little book in brief compass the men who excelled in Italy during my own time as well as the general condition of public affairs and of intellectual life. For I feel that I have an obligation to this age of mine to give some notice of it to posterity whatever it may turn out to have been. If only the men of earlier generations who had some skill in writing had done the same thing, we should not now find ourselves in such a profound darkness of ignorance. To me indeed the times of Cicero and Demosthenes seem much more familiar than the pe-

riod of sixty years ago. For those famous men shed such a flood of light on their own age that even after so long a time has elapsed it may be seen almost as if it were placed before our eyes. An incredible ignorance, however, depressed and concealed the centuries which came after. Moreover I note that Plato in an earlier age had the same diligence and when we read his books and letters we acquire an almost living and breathing picture of his times. For he tells us in such a way about the studies of his youth and his desire of realizing a republic and the revolutions of the times and his own journeys into Sicily and these confusing struggles of Dionysius and Dio and the final ruin of both that he seems to have wished to commend to immortality the knowledge of these things. I wish that others had been moved to do the same thing so that everyone might have left us an equally celebrated knowledge and recollection of his own age. But I think that although no one lacked the will to do this the greater number lacked the knowledge of how to write. For literature unless it is clear and elegant cannot shed light on the affairs of which it treats nor extend their memory far into the future. Therefore what I desire in others I am now about to try to present to our descendants so that if by chance they care to read some knowledge of our times may not be lacking.

. . . During the intervals of this war it was remarkable how much the cult of letters developed in Italy, for then for the first time there began to be attained a knowledge of Greek which for seven hundred years had ceased to be current among our people. Chrysoloras of Byzantium, a man of a noble house and most skilled in literature, brought back to us the knowledge of Greek. When his country was besieged by the Turks, he had first come to Venice by sea, but soon after when his reputation had spread, warmly invited and besought and influenced by the offer of a public salary, he came to Florence to present his learning to the young.

I was at that time studying the civil law although not unacquainted with other disciplines. For I was by nature inflamed by the love for learning and I had spent no small amount of time on dialectic and rhetoric. For this reason on the advent of Chrysoloras I went through a period of indecision since I concluded it would be disgraceful to desert the study of the civil law and yet thought it a kind of crime to pass over such a great opportunity for learning Greek. I frequently said to myself with youthful emotion: "Can you thus betray yourself and deprive yourself when you have the opportunity to give your attention to Homer and Plato and Demosthenes and the other poets and philosophers and orators about whom such great and wonderful qualities are reported, and it is not only an opportunity to read them but to become imbued with their marvelous teaching. Can you pass over an opportunity thus offered to you by Providence? For seven hundred years no one in Italy has known Greek literature and yet we admit that all our learning derives from it. What a useful tool for further learning, what an opportunity for fame, what an enrichment of pleasure will be yours from the knowledge of this language? There are great numbers of doctors of the civil law and you will never lack an opportunity of learning it, but this man is the one and only doctor of Greek literature and if he is removed from the scene there may afterwards be found no one from whom you could learn." Convinced by this reasoning I surrendered myself to Chrysoloras with such a great ardor for learning that what I had learned when awake during the day I turned over in my mind again when asleep at night.

Leonardo Aretino, *Rerum suo tempore gestarum commentarius,* in Muratori, *Raccolta degli storici italiani,* XIX, part iii (Città di Castello, 1914), 420, 431-432, trans. M. P. Gilmore.

C. *Vasari*

1. THE DECLINE AND RESTORATION OF THE ARTS

But as fortune, when she has raised either persons or things to the summit of her wheel, very frequently casts them to the lowest point, whether in repentance or for her sport, so it chanced that, after these things, the barbarous nations of the world arose, in divers places, in rebellion against the Romans; whence there ensued, in no long time, not only the decline of that great empire, but the utter ruin of the whole, and more especially of Rome herself, when all the best artists, sculptors, painters, and architects, were in like manner totally ruined, being submerged and buried, together with the arts themselves, beneath the miserable slaughters and ruins of that much renowned city.

. . . But infinitely more ruinous than all other enemies to the arts . . . was the fervent zeal of the new Christian religion, which, after long and sanguinary combats, had finally overcome and annihilated the ancient creeds of the pagan world, by the frequency of miracles exhibited, and by the earnest sincerity of the means adopted; and ardently devoted, with all diligence, to the extirpation of error, nay, to the removal of even the slightest temptation to heresy, it not only destroyed all the wondrous statues, paintings, sculptures, mosaics, and other ornaments of the false pagan deities, but at the same time extinguished the very memory, in casting down the honours, of numberless excellent ancients, to whom statues and other monuments had been erected, in public places, for their virtues, by the most virtuous times of antiquity. Nay, more than this, to build the churches of the Christian faith, this zeal not only destroyed the most renowned temples of the heathens, but, for the richer ornament of St. Peter's, and in addition to the many spoils previously bestowed on that building, the tomb of Hadrian, now called the castle of St. Angelo, was deprived of its marble columns, to employ them for this church, many other buildings being in like manner despoiled, and which we now see wholly devastated. And although the Christian religion did not effect this from hatred to these works of art, but solely for the purpose of abasing and bringing into contempt the gods of the Gentiles, yet the result of this too ardent zeal did not fail to bring such total ruin over the noble arts, that their very form and existence was lost. Next, and that nothing might be wanting to the completion of these misfortunes, the rage of Totila was aroused against Rome [in the sixth century], and having first destroyed her walls, he devastated her most noble and beautiful edifices, giving the whole city to fire and the sword, after having driven forth all the inhabitants, so that, during eighteen days, no living soul was to be found within the city; paintings, statues, mosaics, and all other embellishments, were so entirely wasted and destroyed by these means, that all were deprived, I do not say of their beauty and majesty only, but of their very form and being. The lower rooms of palaces and other edifices being adorned with pictures, statues, and various ornaments, all these were submerged in the fall of the buildings above them, and thence it is that, in our day, so many admirable works have been recovered: for the immediate successors of those times, believing all to be totally ruined, planted their vines on the site, when these chambers remained buried in the earth; the rooms thus buried were named "grottoes" by the moderns who discovered them, while the paintings found in them were called "grotesque."

. . . The best works in painting and sculpture, remaining buried under the ruins of Italy, were concealed during the same period, and continued wholly unknown to the rude men reared amidst the more modern usages of art, and by whom no other sculptures or pictures were produced, than such as were executed by the remnant of old Greek artists. They formed images of earth and stone, or painted monstrous figures, of which they traced the rude outline only in colour. These artists—the best as being the only ones—were conducted into Italy, whither they carried sculpture and painting, as well as mosaic, in such manner as they were themselves acquainted with them: these they taught, in their own coarse and rude style, to the Italians, who practised them, after such fashion, as I have said, and will further relate, down to a certain period. The men of those times, unaccustomed to works of greater perfection than those thus set before their eyes, admired them accordingly, and, barbarous as they were, yet imitated them as the most excellent models. It was only by slow degrees that those who came after, being aided in some places by the subtlety of the air around them, could begin to raise themselves from these depths; when, towards 1250, Heaven, moved to pity by the noble spirits which the Tuscan soil was producing every day, restored them to their primitive condition. It is true that those who lived in the times succeeding the ruin of Rome, had seen remnants of arches, colossi, statues, pillars, storied columns, and other works of art, not wholly destroyed by the fires and other devastations; yet they had not known how to avail themselves of this aid, nor had they derived any benefit from it, until the time specified above. And the minds then awakened, becoming capable of distinguishing the good from the worthless, and abandoning old methods, returned to the imitation of the antique, with all the force of their genius, and all the power of their industry.

. . . Thus much I have thought it advisable to say respecting the first commencement of sculpture and painting, and may perhaps have spoken at greater length than was here needful; but this I have done, not so much because I was carried on by my love of art, as because I desire to be useful and serviceable to the whole body of artists, for they, having here seen the manner in which art proceeded from small beginnings, until she attained the highest summit, and next how she was precipitated from that exalted position into the deepest debasement; and considering that it is the nature of art, as of human existence, to receive birth, to progress, to become old, and to die, may thus more perfectly comprehend and follow the progress of her second birth to the high perfection which she has once more attained in these our days. I have further thought, that if even it should chance at any time, which may God forbid, that by the neglect of men, the malice of time, or the will of Heaven, which but rarely suffers human things to remain long without change, the arts should once again fall into their former decay, these my labours, both what has been said and what yet remains to be said, should they be found worthy of a more happy fortune, may avail to keep those arts in life, or may at least serve as an incentive to exalted minds to provide them with more efficient aids and support, so that, by my own good intentions, and the help of such friends, the arts may abound in those facilities, of which, if it be permitted to speak the truth freely, they have ever been destitute even to this day.

Giorgio Vasari, *Lives of the Most Eminent Painters, Sculptors, and Architects*, trans. Margaret E. Foster (London: G. Bell and Sons, Ltd., 1876), I, 20-23, 30-31, 32-33.

2. THE ACHIEVEMENT OF GIOTTO

The gratitude which the masters in painting owe to Nature—who is ever the truest model of him who, possessing the power to select the brightest parts from her best and loveliest features, employs himself unweariedly in the reproduction of these beauties—this gratitude, I say, is due, in my judgment, to the Florentine painter, Giotto, seeing that he alone—although born amidst incapable artists, and at a time when all good methods in art had long been entombed beneath the ruins of war—yet, by the favour of Heaven, he, I say, alone succeeded in resuscitating art, and restoring her to a path that may be

Ibid., pp. 93-94.

D. *Erasmus*

It is no part of my nature, most learned Wolfgang, to be excessively fond of life; whether it is, that I have, to my own mind, lived nearly long enough, having entered my fifty-first year, or that I see nothing in this life so splendid or delightful, that it should be desired by one who is convinced by the Christian faith, that a happier life awaits those who in this world earnestly attach themselves to piety. But at the present moment I could almost wish to be young again, for no other reason but this, that I anticipate the near approach of a golden age; so clearly do we see the minds of princes, as if changed by inspiration, devoting all their energies to the pursuit of peace. The chief movers in this matter are Pope Leo, and Francis, King of France.

There is nothing this king does not do or does not suffer, in his desire to avert war and consolidate peace; submitting, of his own accord, to conditions which might be deemed unfair, if he preferred to have regard to his own greatness and dignity, rather than to the general advantage of the world; and exhibiting in this, as in every thing else, a magnanimous and truly royal character. Therefore, when I see that the highest sovereigns of Europe, Francis of France, Charles the Catholic King, Henry of England and the Emperor Maximilian have set all their warlike preparations aside, and established peace upon solid, and as I trust adamantine foundations,

called the true one. And it was in truth a great marvel, that from so rude and inapt an age, Giotto should have had strength to elicit so much, that the art of design, of which the men of those days had little, if any, knowledge, was, by his means, effectually recalled into life.

I am led to a confident hope, that not only morality and Christian piety, but also a genuine and purer literature may come to renewed life or greater splendour; especially as this object is pursued with equal zeal in various regions of the world,—at Rome by Pope Leo, in Spain by the Cardinal of Toledo, in England by Henry, eighth of the name, himself not unskilled in Letters, and among ourselves by our young king Charles. In France King Francis, who seems as it were born for this object, invites and entices from all countries men that excel in merit or in learning. Among the Germans the same object is pursued by many of their excellent princes and bishops, and especially by Maximilian Caesar, whose old age, weary of so many wars, has determined to seek rest in the employments of peace, a resolution more becoming to his own years, while it is fortunate for the Christian world. To the piety of these princes it is due, that we see everywhere, as if upon a given signal, men of genius are arising and conspiring together to restore the best literature.

Polite letters, which were almost extinct, are now cultivated and embraced by Scots, by Danes and by Irishmen. Medicine has a host of champions; at Rome Nicolas of Leonice; at Venice Ambrosius Leo of Nola, in France William Cop, and John Ruelle, and in England Thomas Linacre. The Imperial Law is restored at Paris by William Budé, in Germany by Udalric Zasy; and Mathematics at Basel by Henry of

Glaris. In the theological sphere there was no little to be done, because this science has been hitherto mainly professed by those who are most pertinacious in their abhorrence of the better literature, and are the more successful in defending their own ignorance as they do it under pretext of piety, the unlearned vulgar being induced to believe, that violence is offered to Religion, if any one begins an assault upon their barbarism. For in the presence of an ignorant mob they are always ready to scream and excite their followers to stone-throwing, if they see any risk of not being thought omniscient. But even here I am confident of success, if the knowledge of the three languages continues to be received in schools, as it has now begun. For the most learned and least churlish men of the profession do in some measure assist and favour the new system; and in this matter we are especially indebted to the vigorous exertions of James Lefèvre of Étaples, whom you resemble not only in name, but in a number of accomplishments.

The humblest part of the work has naturally fallen to my lot. Whether my contribution has been worth anything, I cannot say; at any rate those who object to the world regaining its senses, are as angry with me, as if my small industry had had some influence, although the work was not undertaken by me with any confidence that I could myself teach anything magnificent; but I wanted to construct a road for other persons of higher aims, so that they might be less impeded by pools and stumbling-blocks in carrying home those fair and glorious treasures.

The Epistles of Erasmus from his earliest letters to his fifty-first year Arranged in Order of Time, trans. Francis Morgan Nichols (London: Longmans, Green and Co., Inc., 1904), II, 505-508.

E. *Rabelais: Gargantua's Letter to Pantagruel*

Now it is that the minds of men are qualified with all manner of discipline, and the old sciences revived which for many ages were extinct. Now it is that the learned languages are to their pristine purity restored, viz., Greek, without which a man may be ashamed to account himself a scholar, Hebrew, Arabic, Chaldaean, and Latin. Printing likewise is now in use, so elegant and so correct that better cannot be imagined, although it was found out but in my time by divine inspiration, as by a diabolical suggestion on the other side was the invention of ordnance. All the world is full of knowing men, of most learned schoolmasters, and vast libraries; and it appears to me as a truth, that neither in Plato's time, nor Cicero's, nor Papinian's, there was ever such convenience for studying as we see at this day there is. Nor must any adventurer henceforward come in public, or present himself in company, that hath not been pretty well polished in the shop of Minerva. I see robbers, hangmen, freebooters, tapsters, ostlers, and such like, of the very rubbish of the people, more learned now than the doctors and preachers were in my time.

What shall I say? The very women and children have aspired to this praise and celestial manner of good learning. Yet so it is that, in the age I am now of, I have been constrained to learn the Greek tongue—which I contemned not like Cato, but had not the leisure in my younger years to attend the study of it—and take much delight in the reading of Plutarch's Morals, the pleasant Dialogues of Plato, the Monuments of Pausanias, and the Antiquities of Athenaeus, in waiting on the hour wherein God my Creator shall call me and command me to depart from this earth and transitory pilgrimage. Wherefore, my son, I admonish thee to employ thy youth to profit as well as thou canst, both in thy studies and in virtue. Thou art at Paris, where the laudable examples of many brave men may stir up thy mind to gallant actions, and hast likewise for thy tutor and pedagogue the learned Epistemon, who by his lively and vocal documents may instruct thee in the arts and sciences.

I intend, and will have it so, that thou learn the languages perfectly; first of all the Greek, as Quintilian will have it; secondly, the Latin; and then the Hebrew, for the Holy Scripture's sake; and then the Chaldee and Arabic likewise, and that thou frame thy style in Greek in imitation of Plato, and for the Latin after Cicero. Let there be no history which thou shalt not have ready in thy memory; unto the prosecuting of which design, books of cosmography will be very conducible and help thee much. Of the liberal arts of geometry, arithmetic, and music, I gave thee some taste when thou wert yet little, and not above five or six years old. Proceed further in them, and learn the remainder if thou canst. As for astronomy, study all the rules thereof. Let pass, nevertheless, the divining and judicial astrology, and the art of Lullius, as being nothing else but plain abuses and vanities. As for the civil law, of that I would have thee to know the texts by heart, and then to confer them with philosophy.

Now, in matter of the knowledge of the works of nature, I would have thee to study that exactly, and that so there be no sea, river, nor fountain, of which thou dost not know the fishes; all the fowls of the air; all the several kinds of shrubs and trees, whether in forests or orchards; all the sorts of herbs and flowers that grow upon the ground; all the various metals that are hid within the bowels of the earth; together with all the diversity of precious stones that are to be seen in the orient and south parts of the world. Let nothing of all these be hidden from thee. Then fail not most carefully to peruse the books of the Greek, Arabian, and Latin physicians, not despising the Talmudists and Cabalists; and by frequent anatomies get thee the perfect knowledge of the other world, called the microcosm, which is man. And at some hours of the day apply thy mind to the study of the Holy Scriptures; first in Greek, the New Testament, which is the Epistles of the Apostles; and then the Old Testament in Hebrew. In brief, let me see thee an abyss and bottomless pit of knowledge; for from henceforward, as thou growest great and becomest a man, thou must part from this tranquillity and rest of study, thou must learn chivalry, warfare, and the exercises of the field, the better thereby to defend my house and our friends, and to succour and protect them at all their needs against the invasion and assaults of evildoers.

Francis Rabelais, *Five Books of the Lives, Heroic Deeds and Sayings of Gargantua and his Son Pantagruel*, trans. Thomas Urquhart and Peter Antony Motteux (London: Lawrence and Bullen, 1892), I, 191-193.

F. *Dolet*

. . . But I wish to congratulate the state of literature in our times which is so happily and so remarkably flourishing for the study of literature today is everywhere fostered by such great efforts that nothing is lacking to attain the glory of antiquity except the ancient liberty of their men of genius and their opportunity to pursue the arts with general approbation. . . . A hundred years ago the struggle with barbarism and want of eloquence was continuous and bitter and the victory often in doubt because of the great strength and power of the barbarians, yet the ranks of virtue finally triumphed. The first to make a breach in the defences of the barbarians was Lorenzo Valla, aided by a group of his contemporaries. But this first attack was made by the light-armed troops and it was a matter of distant conflict rather than hand-to-hand fighting. Although their ranks had been opened and attacks had broken through, yet the power of the barbarians had not been sufficiently disturbed. In the end the efforts of Lorenzo Valla and his companions against barbarism which had been almost frustrated by the leaders of the barbarian horde were sustained by Angelo Poliziano, Ermolao Barbaro, Pico della Mirandola, Volaterra, Caelius Rhodiginus, Sabellicus, Critinus, Filelfo, Marsilio Ficino, and that whole generation of illustrious men who, combining their forces and recouping their losses sent against the barbarians those whom we have just listed. These men were sufficiently well-instructed and strongly motivated to defeat barbarism. Thus the shafts of good literature descended on the remaining ranks of the barbarians first from Italy, then from Germany, Britain, Spain and France. The crested helmets of the enemy were cast down, their hands were bound and they were finally led prisoners into captivity. . . . Now all the cities of Europe are freed from this horrid monster. Literature is everywhere cherished as highly as it has ever been, the study of all the arts is flourishing. By their regard for literature men are brought back to the study so long neglected of the good and the true. Now men can learn to know themselves and now those who have been heretofore in darkness and wretchedly blind to all things stand in a universal light. Now they seem truly to differ from the beasts by reason of their minds which have been so diligently cultivated by the arts and by reason of the eloquence of their speech which has been so accurately developed. Have I not reason therefore to congratulate the study of letters which has both recovered its pristine glory and blessed the life of man with so many good things (which is its true mission)? If we could only extinguish the envy which certain men educated barbarously and without discipline still bear towards literature and the educated, what then would be lacking to the happiness of this age? But at last the authority of such men begins to decline and a new generation is growing up well and properly instructed in the dignity of letters. This generation will cast out the enemies of literature from their positions of importance and it will enter upon public office and be admitted to the councils of kings; it will undertake the management of affairs and administer all things wisely. Among all those who receive the benefit of its improved status literature will warn against those things which are to be avoided and will generate a love of virtue, ordering that those who are studious and observant of virtue, justice and equity be everywhere received by kings, indeed that they be regarded and retained as kings themselves, further, that flatterers, sycophants, panderers to pleasure, with whom the halls of kings abound, be avoided like poison and banished. What more would Plato himself then ask for the felicity of his Republic?

Etienne Dolet, *Commentaria Linguae Latinae,* I (Lyons, 1536), art. "litterae," trans. M. P. Gilmore.

G. *LeRoy on the Idea of Progress*

1. THE INNOVATIONS OF THE RENAISSANCE

. . . During the last hundred years not only have things come to light which were previously covered with the darkness of ignorance but also many other things have become known which were entirely unknown to the ancients: new seas, new lands, innovations in the ways of men, habits, laws and customs, new herbs . . . trees, . . . minerals, new inventions have been found, like those of printing, artillery and the use of the compass and sextant for navigation . . . ancient languages have been restored. . . . When we consider all this we ought to endure more calmly the calamities which have come and still come upon this age. . . . Some people think that men are progressively diminishing and that human affairs are always going from bad to worse. If this had been so during the long time that the world has lasted we should all have been completely annihilated and there would no longer be anything of value among us.

LeRoy, *Considérations sur l'histoire universelle* (Paris, 1567), translated from the selection quoted in G. Atkinson, *Les Nouveaux horizons de la Renaissance française* (Paris: Droz, 1935), pp. 404-405.

2. THE BASIS OF COMPARISON

Having discussed briefly the excellence of this age we shall now compare it with the most illustrious of the preceding periods in the matters of arms, artillery, military leaders, armies, battles, sieges, empires and other states, travels by land and by sea, discoveries of unknown lands, wealth, manners and learning; to determine in what respect this age is superior or inferior or equal. . . . For five hundred years the Venetians and Genoese have been masters of the Mediterranean and they have fought bitterly one against the other to determine with whom this mastery should remain. The Venetians in the end had the best of it and are still very powerful there. In the Ocean the Portuguese and Castilians by their skill, science and sureness of navigation hold the first place in this field, having surpassed the Tyrians, Egyptians, Phoenicians, Rhodians, Romans, Carthaginians, and people of Marseilles and Brittany and all others who have ever attempted long voyages or the discovery of previously unknown lands, since they surrounded the whole earth by their navigation. And this was a thing the ancients never did nor knew how to do nor dared to undertake.

LeRoy, *De la Vicissitude ou variété des choses en l'univers,* selections with an introduction by Blanchard W. Bates (Princeton: Princeton University Press, 1944), p. 35.

III. THE PROBLEM OF UNDERSTANDING MACHIAVELLI

Few reputations in the history of literature have had as lively and controversial a history as that of Machiavelli. On the one hand there is the scheming villain of the Elizabethans, the figure who symbolizes the wickedness and corruption of Italy under the Borgias forever associated in the popular mind with a society in which men rid themselves of their enemies by such means as the poisoned ring or the stab in the back. On the other hand, there is the patriot who gave years of service to the Florentine signory and admired the institutions of republican Rome. Scholars have debated and still debate the intentions of Machiavelli in his two major works, *The Prince* and the *Discourses on the First Decade of Livy,* and they have tried also to separate Machiavelli from Machiavellianism.

The first selection included here is Machiavelli's own statement of what he is trying to do, taken from the opening of the *Discourses*. Here speaks the man who proposes to use the remote history of republican Rome as a source of generalizations which will not only enable men to increase their understanding but also to improve their present situation. Granting that Machiavelli was a retrospective sociologist, the question may be asked whether history or sociology came first, that is, whether Machiavelli evolved a political program and then turned to history to find evidence in support of it, or on the contrary went to history first to see what "lessons" it could teach. This passage contains one of his most important statements on this question.

Turning from the problems of method to those of the content of his political program, one of the most debated issues has been Machiavelli's relation to nationalism. The Italian Risorgimento made him one of its heroes and saluted him as a prophet of the unification of Italy. On the other hand it has been maintained that his program was really founded on the city-state like Florence and its expansion, that he had no real scheme for bringing the various powers of Italy into union and that his nationalistic appeals are no more than the reiteration of an already old tradition descending from Dante and Petrarch. The famous last chapter of *The Prince* which is Machiavelli's most eloquent appeal for the liberation of all Italy is given below.

What is the relationship between the *Prince* and the *Discourses*? Is there a fundamental inconsistency between the two books or can their differences be explained by the fact that the *Prince* was written in a special set of circumstances for a particular political purpose, whereas the *Discourses* reflect Machiavelli's ideal? Was he really in favor of a kind of dictator, or did he believe that the will of the community should be recognized? There is no sound method of attempting to answer these questions short of a thorough study of all of Machiavelli's writings, but some acquaintance with the nature of the real or apparent conflicts which have produced problems of interpretation may be gained from the two chapters given below. The first is from the *Discourses* and deals with the religion of the Romans; the second is from the *Prince* on whether princes should keep faith.

Finally two estimates by modern commentators who differ widely in their judgment on Machiavelli's morality are included in this section.

A. *Machiavelli's Methods and Aims*

Although the envious nature of men, so prompt to blame and so slow to praise, makes the discovery and introduction of any new principles and systems as dangerous almost as the exploration of unknown seas and continents, yet, animated by that desire which impels me to do what may prove for the common benefit of all, I have resolved to open a new route, which has not yet been followed by any one, and may prove difficult and troublesome, but may also bring me some reward in the approbation of those who will kindly appreciate my efforts.

And if my poor talents, my little experience of the present and insufficient study of the past, should make the result of my labors defective and of little utility, I shall at least have shown the way to others, who will carry out my views with greater ability, eloquence, and judgment, so that if I do not merit praise, I ought at least not to incur censure.

When we consider the general respect for antiquity, and how often—to say nothing of other examples—a great price is paid for some fragments of an antique statue, which we are anxious to possess to ornament our houses with, or to give to artists who strive to imitate them in their own works; and when we see, on the other hand, the wonderful examples which the history of ancient kingdoms and republics presents to us, the prodigies of virtue and of wisdom displayed by the kings, captains, citizens, and legislators who have sacrificed themselves for their country,—when we see these, I say, more admired than imitated, or so much neglected that not the least trace of this ancient virtue remains, we cannot but be at the same time as much surprised as afflicted. The more so as in the differences which arise between citizens, or in the maladies to which they are subjected, we see these same people have recourse to the judgments and the remedies prescribed by the ancients. The civil laws are in fact nothing but decisions given by their jurisconsults, and which, reduced to a system, direct our modern jurists in their decisions. And what is the science of medicine, but the experience of ancient physicians, which their successors have taken for their guide? And yet to found a republic, maintain states, to govern a kingdom, organize an army, conduct a war, dispense justice, and extend empires, you will find neither prince, nor republic, nor captain, nor citizen, who has recourse to the examples of antiquity! This neglect, I am persuaded, is due less to the weakness to which the vices of our education have reduced the world, than to the evils caused by the proud indolence which

prevails in most of the Christian states, and to the lack of real knowledge of history, the true sense of which' is not known, or the spirit of which they do not comprehend. Thus the majority of those who read it take pleasure only in the variety of the events which history relates, without ever thinking of imitating the noble actions, deeming that not only difficult, but impossible; as though heaven, the sun, the elements, and men had changed the order of their motions and power, and were different from what they were in ancient times.

Wishing, therefore, so far as in me lies, to draw mankind from this error, I have thought it proper to write upon those books of Titus Livius that have come to us entire despite the malice of time; touching upon all those matters which, after a comparison between the ancient and modern events, may seem to me necessary to facilitate their proper understanding. In this way those who read my remarks may derive those advantages which should be the aim of all study of history; and although the undertaking is difficult, yet, aided by those who have encouraged me in this attempt, I hope to carry it sufficiently far, so that but little may remain for others to carry it to its destined end.

Niccolò Machiavelli, *The Prince and The Discourses* (New York: The Modern Library, 1940), pp. 103-105.

B. Machiavelli and Nationalism:

[Exhortation to Liberate Italy from the Barbarians: to the Medici]

Having now considered all the things we have spoken of, and thought within myself whether at present the time was not propitious in Italy for a new prince, and if there was not a state of things which offered an opportunity to a prudent and capable man to introduce a new system that would do honour to himself and good to the mass of the people, it seems to me that so many

things concur to favour a new ruler that I do not know of any time more fitting for such an enterprise. And if, as I said, it was necessary in order that the power of Moses should be displayed that the people of Israel should be slaves in Egypt, and to give scope for the greatness and courage of Cyrus that the Persians should be oppressed by the Medes, and to illustrate the pre-eminence of Theseus that the Athenians should be dispersed, so at the present time, in order that the might of an Italian genius might be recognised, it was necessary that Italy should be reduced to her present condition, and that she should be more enslaved than the Hebrews, more oppressed than the Persians, and more scattered than the Athenians; without a head, without order, beaten, despoiled, lacerated, and overrun, and that she should have suffered ruin of every kind.

And although before now a gleam of hope has appeared which gave hope that some individual might be appointed by God for her redemption, yet at the highest summit of his career he was thrown aside by fortune, so that now, almost lifeless, she awaits one who may heal her wounds and put a stop to the pillaging of Lombardy, to the rapacity and extortion in the Kingdom of Naples and in Tuscany, and cure her of those sores which have long been festering. Behold how she prays God to send some one to redeem her from this barbarous cruelty and insolence. Behold her ready and willing to follow any standard if only there be some one to raise it. There is nothing now she can hope for but that your illustrious house may place itself at the head of this redemption, being by its power and fortune so exalted, and being favoured by God and the Church, of which it is now the ruler. Nor will this be very difficult, if you call to mind the actions and lives of the men I have named. And although those men were rare and marvellous, they were none the less men, and each of them had less opportunity than the present, for their enterprise was not juster than this, nor easier, nor was God more their friend than He is yours. Here is a just cause; *"iustum enim est bellum quibus necessarium, et pia arma ubi nulla nisi in armis spes est."* [1] Here is the greatest willingness, nor can there be great difficulty where there is great willingness,

provided that the measures are adopted of those whom I have set before you as examples. Besides this, unexampled wonders have been seen here performed by God, the sea has been opened, a cloud has shown you the road, the rock has given forth water, manna has rained, and everything has contributed to your greatness, the remainder must be done by you. God will not do everything, in order not to deprive us of freewill and the portion of the glory that falls to our lot.

It is no marvel that none of the before-mentioned Italians have done that which it is to be hoped your illustrious house may do; and if in so many revolutions in Italy and so many warlike operations, it always seems as if military capacity were extinct, this is because the ancient methods were not good, and no one has arisen who knew how to discover new ones. Nothing does so much honour to a newly-risen man than the new laws and measures which he introduces. These things, when they are well based and have greatness in them, render him revered and admired, and there is not lacking scope in Italy for the introduction of every kind of new organisation. Here there is great virtue in the members, if it were not wanting in the heads. Look how in duels and in contests of a few the Italians are superior in strength, dexterity, and intelligence. But when it comes to armies they make a poor show; which proceeds entirely from the weakness of the leaders, for those that know are not obeyed, and every one thinks that he knows, there being hitherto nobody who has raised himself so high both by valour and fortune as to make the others yield. Hence it comes about that for so long a time, in all the wars waged during the last twenty years, whenever there has been an entirely Italian army it has always been a failure, as witness first Taro,

---

[1] "War is just for those to whom it is necessary, and arms are pious where there is no hope except in arms."

then Alexandria, Capua, Genoa, Vailà, Bologna, and Mestri.

If your illustrious house, therefore, wishes to follow those great men who redeemed their countries, it is before all things necessary, as the true foundation of every undertaking, to provide yourself with your own forces, for you cannot have more faithful, or truer and better soldiers. Add although each one of them may be good, they will united become even better when they see themselves commanded by their prince, and honoured and favoured by him. It is therefore necessary to prepare such forces in order to be able with Italian prowess to defend the country from foreigners. And although both the Swiss and Spanish infantry are deemed terrible, none the less they each have their defects, so that a third method of array might not only oppose them, but be confident of overcoming them. For the Spaniards cannot sustain the attack of cavalry, and the Swiss have to fear infantry which meets them with resolution equal to their own. From which it has resulted, as will be seen by experience, that the Spaniards cannot sustain the attack of French cavalry, and the Swiss are overthrown by Spanish infantry. And although a complete example of the latter has not been seen, yet an instance was furnished in the battle of Ravenna, where the Spanish infantry attacked the German battalions, which are organised in the same way as the Swiss. The Spaniards, through their bodily agility and aided by their bucklers, had entered between and under their pikes and were in a position to at-

Ibid., pp. 94-98.

C. The "Strong Man" and the Community

1. OF THE RELIGION OF THE ROMANS

Although the founder of Rome was Romulus, to whom like a daughter, she

tack them safely without the Germans being able to defend themselves; and if the cavalry had not charged them they would have utterly destroyed them. Knowing therefore the defects of both these kinds of infantry, a third kind can be created which can resist cavalry and need not fear infantry, and this will be done by the choice of arms and a new organisation. And these are the things which, when newly introduced, give reputation and grandeur to a new prince.

This opportunity must not, therefore, be allowed to pass, so that Italy may at length find her liberator. I cannot express the love with which he would be received in all those provinces which have suffered under these foreign invasions, with what thirst for vengeance, with what steadfast faith, with what love, with what grateful tears. What doors would be closed against him? What people would refuse him obedience? What envy could oppose him? What Italian would withhold allegiance? This barbarous domination stinks in the nostrils of every one. May your illustrious house therefore assume this task with that courage and those hopes which are inspired by a just cause, so that under its banner our fatherland may be raised up, and under its auspices be verified that saying of Petrarch:

Valour against fell wrath
Will take up arms; and be the combat
  quickly sped!
For, sure, the ancient worth,
That in Italians stirs the heart, is not
  yet dead.

owed her birth and her education, yet the gods did not judge the laws of this prince sufficient for so great an empire, and therefore inspired the Roman Senate to elect Numa Pompilius as his successor, so that he might regulate all those things that had been omitted by Romulus. Numa, finding a very savage people, and wishing to reduce them to civil obedience by the arts of peace, had recourse to religion as the most necessary and assured support of any civil society; and he established it upon such foundations that for many centuries there was nowhere more fear of the gods than in that republic, which greatly facilitated all the enterprises which the Senate or its great men attempted. Whoever will examine the actions of the people of Rome as a body, or of many individual Romans, will see that these citizens feared much more to break an oath than the laws; like men who esteem the power of the gods more than that of men. This was particularly manifested in the conduct of Scipio and Manlius Torquatus; for after the defeat which Hannibal had inflicted upon the Romans at Cannae many citizens had assembled together, and, frightened and trembling, agreed to leave Italy and fly to Sicily. When Scipio heard of this, he went to meet them, and with his drawn sword in hand he forced them to swear not to abandon their country. Lucius Manlius, father of Titus Manlius, who was afterwards called Torquatus, had been accused by Marcus Pomponius, one of the Tribunes of the people. Before the day of judgment Titus went to Marcus and threatened to kill him if he did not promise to withdraw the charges against his father; he compelled him to take an oath, and Marcus, although having sworn under the pressure of fear, withdrew the accusation against Lucius. And thus these citizens, whom neither the love of country nor the laws could have kept in Italy, were retained there by an oath that had been forced upon them by compulsion; and the Tribune Pomponius disregarded the hatred which he bore to the father, as well as the insult offered him by the son, for the sake of complying with his oath and preserv-

ing his honour; which can be ascribed to nothing else than the religious principles which Numa had instilled into the Romans. And whoever reads Roman history attentively will see in how great a degree religion served in the command of the armies, in uniting the people and keeping them well conducted, and in covering the wicked with shame. So that if the question were discussed whether Rome was more indebted to Romulus or to Numa, I believe that the highest merit would be conceded to Numa; for where religion exists it is easy to introduce armies and discipline, but where there are armies and no religion it is difficult to introduce the latter. And although we have seen that Romulus could organize the Senate and establish other civil and military institutions without the aid of divine authority, yet it was very necessary for Numa, who feigned that he held converse with a nymph, who dictated to him all that he wished to persuade the people to; and the reason for all this was that Numa mistrusted his own authority, lest it should prove insufficient to enable him to introduce new and unaccustomed ordinances in Rome. In truth, there never was any remarkable lawgiver amongst any people who did not resort to divine authority, as otherwise his laws would not have been accepted by the people; for there are many good laws, the importance of which is known to the sagacious lawgiver, but the reasons for which are not sufficiently evident to enable him to persuade others to submit to them; and therefore do wise men, for the purpose of removing this difficulty, resort to divine authority. Thus did Lycurgus and Solon, and many others who aimed at the same thing.

The Roman people, then, admiring the wisdom and goodness of Numa, yielded in all things to his advice. It is true that those were very religious times, and the people with whom Numa had to deal were very untutored and superstitious, which made it easy for him to carry out his designs, being able to impress upon them any new form. And doubtless, if any one wanted to establish a republic at the present time, he would find it much easier with the simple mountaineers, who are almost without any civilization, than with such as are accustomed to live in cities, where civilization is already corrupt; as a sculptor finds it easier to make a fine statue out of a crude block of marble than out of a statue badly begun by another. Considering then all these things, I conclude that the religion introduced by Numa into Rome was one of the chief causes of the prosperity of that city; for this religion gave rise to good laws, and good laws bring good fortune, and from good fortune results happy success in all enterprises. And as the observance of divine institutions is the cause of the greatness of republics, so the disregard of them produces their ruin; for where the fear of God is wanting, there the country will come to ruin, unless it be sustained by the fear of the prince, which may temporarily supply the want of religion. But as the lives of princes are short, the kingdom will of necessity perish as the prince fails in virtue. Whence it comes that kingdoms which depend entirely upon the virtue of one man endure but for a brief time, for his virtue passes away with his life, and it rarely happens that

it is renewed in his successor, as Dante so wisely says:—

" 'T is seldom human wisdom descends
    from sire to son;
Such is the will of Him who gave it,
That at his hands alone we may implore
    the boon."

The welfare, then, of a republic or a kingdom does not consist in having a prince who governs it wisely during his lifetime, but in having one who will give it such laws that it will maintain itself even after his death. And although untutored and ignorant men are more easily persuaded to adopt new laws or new opinions, yet that does not make it impossible to persuade civilized men who claim to be enlightened. The people of Florence are far from considering themselves ignorant and benighted, and yet Brother Girolamo Savonarola succeeded in persuading them that he held converse with God. I will not pretend to judge whether it was true or not, for we must speak with all respect of so great a man; but I may well say that an immense number believed it, without having seen any extraordinary manifestations that should have made them believe it; but it was the purity of his life, the doctrines he preached, and the subjects he selected for his discourses, that sufficed to make the people have faith in him. Let no one, then, fear not to be able to accomplish what others have done, for all men (as we have said in our Preface) are born and live and die in the same way, and therefore resemble each other.

Ibid., pp. 145-149.

2. In What Way Princes Must Keep Faith

How laudable it is for a prince to keep good faith and live with integrity, and not with astuteness, every one knows. Still the experience of our times shows those princes to have done great

things who have had little regard for good faith, and have been able by astuteness to confuse men's brains, and who have ultimately overcome those who have made loyalty their foundation.

You must know, then, that there are two methods of fighting, the one by law, the other by force: the first method is that of men, the second of beasts; but as the first method is often insufficient, one must have recourse to the second. It is therefore necessary for a prince to know well how to use both the beast and the man. This was covertly taught to rulers by ancient writers, who relate how Achilles and many others of those ancient princes were given to Chiron the centaur to be brought up and educated under his discipline. The parable of this semi-animal, semi-human teacher is meant to indicate that a prince must know how to use both natures, and that the one without the other is not durable.

A prince being thus obliged to know well how to act as a beast must imitate the fox and the lion, for the lion cannot protect himself from traps, and the fox cannot defend himself from wolves. One must therefore be a fox to recognise traps, and a lion to frighten wolves. Those that wish to be only lions do not understand this. Therefore, a prudent ruler ought not to keep faith when by so doing it would be against his interest, and when the reasons which made him bind himself no longer exist. If men were all good, this precept would not be a good one; but as they are bad, and would not observe their faith with you, so you are not bound to keep faith with them. Nor have legitimate grounds ever failed a prince who wished to show colourable excuse for the nonfulfillment of his promise. Of this one could furnish an infinite number of modern examples, and show how many times peace has been broken, and how many promises rendered worthless, by the faithlessness of princes, and those that have been best able to imitate the fox have succeeded best. But it is necessary to be able to disguise this character well, and to be a great feigner and dissembler; and men are so simple and so ready to obey present necessities, that one who deceives will always find those who allow themselves to be deceived.

I will only mention one modern instance. Alexander VI did nothing else but deceive men, he thought of nothing else, and found the occasion for it; no man was ever more able to give assurances, or affirmed things with stronger oaths, and no man observed them less; however, he always succeeded in his deceptions, as he well knew this aspect of things.

It is not, therefore, necessary for a prince to have all the above-named qualities, but it is very necessary to seem to have them. I would even be bold to say that to possess them and always to observe them is dangerous, but to appear to possess them is useful. Thus it is well to seem merciful, faithful, humane, sincere, religious, and also to be so; but you must have the mind so disposed that when it is needful to be otherwise you may be able to change to the opposite qualities. And it must be understood that a prince, and especially a new prince, cannot observe all those things which are considered good in men, being often obliged, in order to maintain the state, to act against faith, against charity, against humanity, and against religion. And, therefore, he must have a mind disposed to adapt itself according to the wind, and as the variations of fortune dictate, and, as I said before, not deviate from what is good, if possible, but be able to do evil if constrained.

A prince must take great care that nothing goes out of his mouth which is not full of the above-named five qualities, and, to see and hear him, he should seem to be all mercy, faith, integrity, humanity, and religion. And nothing is more necessary than to seem to have this last quality, for men in general judge more by the eyes than by the hands, for every one can see, but very few have to feel. Everybody sees what you appear to be, few feel what you are, and those few will not dare to oppose themselves to the many, who have the majesty of the state to defend them; and in the actions of men, and especially of princes, from which there is no appeal, the end justifies the means. Let a prince therefore aim at conquering and maintaining the state, and the means will always be judged honourable and praised by every one, for the vulgar is always taken by appearances and the issue of the event; and the world consists only of the vulgar, and the few who are not vulgar are isolated when the many have a rallying point in the prince. A certain prince of the present time, whom it is well not to name, never does anything but preach peace and good faith, but he is really a great enemy to both, and either of them, had he observed them, would have lost him state or reputation on many occasions.

Ibid., pp. 63-66.

D. *Two Modern Views of Machiavelli*

1. Defense of Machiavelli's Intentions

There is, in one of the startling chapters of the *Prince,* an opening sentence which has seemed to many the confirmation of Machiavelli's cynicism. It is on the subject of faith in princes. The first half pays lip-service to the virtue of keeping one's word, and then his terrible *nevertheless* steps in to point to the reality: "Still the experience of our times shows those princes to have done great things who have had little regard for good faith, and have been able by astuteness to confuse men's brains and who have ultimately overcome those who have made loyalty their foundation." This is, indeed, one of those texts on which it is customary to base the attack not only on Machiavelli, but on the Italian Renascence as well: so pagan, and ergo, so wicked, how could it reckon in terms of keeping faith? . . . And those whose business it is to blacken the Renascence have been quick to follow up the issue. So neat, so symmetrical a position: the Italians were corrupt (it was Machiavelli's own word for them) because they had abandoned the Age of Faith, so that their punishment came at the hands of the incorrupt; at the hands of those who, presumably, still lived in the Age of Faith, and of faith. Does not Alexander VI come later in the chapter as a concrete example of faithlessness? All that is most convenient for those who like the ready-made in pictures, or who have the cause of medievalism at heart. But it is precisely because of this that the background of the *Legations* is essential to any comprehension of the ideas current in Machiavelli's mind at the time he wrote the *Prince.* When we know that background is it not clear that it is Florence who built on loyalty, and that it is Florence who has gone down before the faithlessness of Charles VIII, Louis XII, Ferdinand of Aragon, and Maximilian, to keep the list short? This chapter which has given so much offense to the moralists north of the Alps has an opposite function to the one always lent to it. It is not Machiavelli codifying Italian corruption for the use of would-be despots. Once more, there would be little use his codifying formulas that had led to defeat as a recipe for securing success. . . . The praise that he gives to the virtue of keeping faith is quite sincere; but the bitterness arises from the fact that the policy of keeping faith has proved inadequate.

J. H. Whitfield, *Machiavelli* (Oxford: Basil Blackwell, 1947), pp. 60-61.

2. MACHIAVELLI'S IMMORALITY

Above all, there is Machiavelli's most curious statement on the subject of morality, a thesis which appears in Chapter XV of *The Prince;* and this contains an assertion which, because it is vague, will cover everything. It is more important in that the author points out that in his case in particular his opinion differs from that of his contemporaries. It is the thesis that in the world a man must behave as other people behave; and that if he allows his conduct to be guided by the thought of what men *ought* to do, this will conduce rather to his ruin than to his advantage or preservation. In itself the statement might be meaningless, and on one construction indeed, might be regarded as innocuous. A man can scarcely be accused of any great immorality if he accepts the standards of his time and consents to live as the world lives. The thesis might prove, however, more pointed and more dangerous if it implied that men should take as their standard of conduct the morality of their day conceived at its worst; and it is important to note in this respect that Machiavelli had a remarkably low view of human nature. He does not recommend us to break a treaty merely when we think that the other party is going to break it; he says that since men are wicked the other party may always be presumed to be about to break it. And his whole attitude is more significant if we note that this is a thesis concerning general conduct; it is not conditioned by any reference to the safety or even the welfare of the state. It would have been expressed in different terms if it had meant that everything is allowable which is intended for the public good. Finally it is based on the simple fact that the wicked have prospered and the loyal have been defeated. We may account for the attitude by historical circumstances, we may befog the question with mystical interpretations, but in Machiavelli the doctrine "live as the world lives" is the ordinary vulgar doctrine that morality does not pay; its only purport is the reduction of the conduct of good men to the standards of that of the worst, and it is difficult to see how an invitation to immorality could have been expressed in other terms or placed on a more comprehensive basis. Just as the tendency of Machiavelli's system was to make men more consistent and scientific in their political cunning, so the effect—the very intention—of his remarks on morality was to clear the path for the more general acceptance of the kind of statecraft that he had to teach.

H. Butterfield, *The Statecraft of Machiavelli* (London: G. Bell and Sons, Ltd., 1940), pp. 110-113.

IV. ERASMUS AND THE CHRISTIAN INHERITANCE

The figure of Erasmus of Rotterdam dominated the intellectual world of his time and has ever since been regarded as symbolizing the mighty achievements of Renaissance scholarship. His work is intimately related to both the Reformation and the Counter-Reformation, and many men who began by being his disciples found themselves on opposing sides when the lines of the great sixteenth-century battle were drawn. Yet, if we ask ourselves to what extent Erasmus was a Christian and what kind of Christian, the answers are not altogether simple. No man did more to exalt the noblest of the pagan philosophers (Saint Socrates, pray for us), and no man did more to hold up to ridicule and scorn the abuses and even some of the uses of the Christian Church as he found it. On the other hand, he provided the first Greek Testament, devoted a lifetime to restoring a direct knowledge of the early texts of Christianity, and left eloquent and moving exhortations to the pious life. He has been accused of being in effect a pagan, of being a Lutheran before Luther, and of being a renegade to the Reform which he had helped to make possible. He died in communion with the Roman Church, but although he had been offered a cardinal's hat by Paul III, many of his works were put on the Index by Paul IV. In him we see changes of emphasis and new tensions in the relation between the classic and Christian traditions, and many of the arguments about the religious or "pagan" character of the Renaissance are focused in the attempt to evaluate his convictions.

The first selections included here illustrate the kind of attack Erasmus directed at contemporary religious practices. The first passage is taken from one of the so-called *Colloquies,* dialogues which Erasmus had written originally for an instructional manual in Latin but which he had continued because they served as dramatic vehicles for the expression of his own views. The interlocutors in the *Shipwreck* discuss the behavior of a ship's company and crew under the threat of imminent death, and the contrast between simple trust in God and the elaborate invocation of the saints. The second selection is from the most famous of Erasmus' works, *The Praise of Folly,* and contains Folly's indictment of the theologians. This is followed by an excerpt from the dialogue called *Julius Exclusus* which Erasmus never acknowledged but which he very probably wrote. Here Pope Julius II is represented as excluded from heaven because of the scandalous contrast between his behavior and his pretensions.

The second section presents some characteristic statements of Erasmian piety. The first is from the *Enchiridion,* a manual of Christian practice for the layman written by Erasmus in 1501. The second is the eloquent statement of what Erasmus called the philosophy of Christ contained in one of the prefaces to the edition of the New Testament which he published in 1516.

A. The Erasmian Critique of Church and Theology

1. THE INVOCATION OF SAINTS: ADOLPH AND ANTHONY

ADOL. The Mariners striving in Vain with the Storm, at length the Pilot, all pale as Death comes to us.

ANT. That Paleness presages some great Evil.

ADOL. My Friends, says he, I am no longer Master of my Ship, the Wind has got the better of me; all that we have now to do is to place our Hope in God, and every one to prepare himself for Death.

ANT. This was cold Comfort.

ADOL. But in the first Place, says he, we must lighten the Ship; Necessity requires it, tho' 'tis a hard Portion. It is better to endeavour to save our Lives with the Loss of our Goods, than to perish with them. The Truth persuaded, and a great many Casks of rich Merchandize were thrown over-Board.

ANT. This was casting away, according to the Letter.

ADOL. There was in the Company, a certain *Italian,* that had been upon an Embassy to the King of *Scotland.* He had a whole Cabinet full of Plate, Rings, Cloth, and rich wearing Apparel.

ANT. And he, I warrant ye, was unwilling to come to a Composition with the Sea.

ADOL. No, he would not; he had a Mind either to sink or swim with his beloved Riches.

ANT. What said the Pilot to this?

ADOL. If you and your Trinkets were to drown by yourselves, says he, here's no Body would hinder you; but it is not fit that we should run the Risque of our Lives, for the Sake of your Cabinet: If you won't consent, we'll throw you and your Cabinet into the Sea together.

ANT. Spoken like a Tarpawlin.

ADOL. So the *Italian* submitted, and threw his Goods over-Board, with many a bitter Curse to the Gods both above and below, that he had committed his Life to so barbarous an Element.

ANT. I know the *Italian* Humour.

ADOL. The Winds were nothing the less boisterous for our Presents, but by and by burst our Cordage, and threw down our Sails.

ANT. Lamentable!

ADOL. Then the Pilot comes to us again.

ANT. What, with another Preachment?

ADOL. He gives us a Salute; my Friends, says he, the Time exhorts us that every one of us should recommend himself to God, and prepare for Death. Being ask'd by some that were not ignorant in Sea Affairs, how long he thought the Ship might be kept above Water, he said, he could promise nothing, but that it could not be done above three Hours.

ANT. This was yet a harder Chapter than the former.

ADOL. When he had said this, he orders to cut the Shrouds and the Mast down by the Board, and to throw them, Sails and all, into the Sea.

ANT. Why was this done?

ADOL. Because, the Sail either being gone or torn, it would only be a Burden, but not of Use; all our Hope was in the Helm.

ANT. What did the Passengers do in the mean Time?

ADOL. There you might have seen a wretched Face of Things; the Mariners, they were singing their *Salve Regina*, imploring the Virgin Mother, calling her the Star of the Sea, the Queen of Heaven, the Lady of the World, the Haven of Health, and many other flattering Titles, which the sacred Scriptures never attributed to her.

ANT. What has she to do with the Sea, who, as I believe, never went a Voyage in her Life?

ADOL. In ancient Times, *Venus* took Care of Mariners, because she was believ'd to be born of the Sea, and because she left off to take Care of them, the Virgin Mother was put in her Place, that was a Mother, but not a Virgin.

ANT. You joke.

ADOL. Some were lying along upon the Boards, worshipping the Sea, pouring all they had into it, and flattering it, as if it had been some incensed Prince.

ANT. What did they say?

ADOL. O most merciful Sea! O most generous Sea! O most rich Sea! O most Beautiful Sea, be pacified, save us; and a Deal of such Stuff they sung to the deaf Ocean.

ANT. Ridiculous Superstition! What did the rest do?

ADOL. Some did nothing but spew, and some made Vows. There was an *Englishman* there, that promis'd golden Mountains to our Lady of *Walsingham*, so he did but get ashore alive. Others promis'd a great many Things to the Wood of the Cross, which was in such a Place; others again, to that which was in such a Place; and the same was done by the Virgin *Mary*, which reigns in a great many Places, and they think the Vow is of no Effect, unless the Place be mentioned.

ANT. Ridiculous! As if the Saints did not dwell in Heaven.

ADOL. Some made Promises to become *Carthusians*. There was one who promised he would go a *Pilgrimage* to St. *James* at *Compostella*, bare Foot and bare Head, cloth'd in a Coat of Mail, and begging his Bread all the Way.

ANT. Did no Body make any Mention of St. *Christopher?*

ADOL. Yes, I heard one, and I could not forbear laughing, who bawling out aloud, lest St. *Christopher* should not hear him, promised him, who is at the Top of a Church at *Paris,* rather a Mountain than a Statue, a wax Taper as big as he was himself: When he had bawl'd out this over and over as loud as he could, an Acquaintance of his jogg'd him on the Elbow, and caution'd him: Have a Care what you promise, for if you should sell all you have in the World, you will not be able to pay for it. He answer'd him softly, lest St. *Christopher* should hear him, you Fool, says he, do you think I mean as I speak, if I once got safe to Shore, I would not give him so much as a tallow Candle.

ANT. O Blockhead! I fancy he was a *Hollander.*

ADOL. No, he was a Zealander.

ANT. I wonder no Body thought of St. *Paul,* who has been at Sea, and having suffered Shipwreck, leapt on Shore. For he being not unacquainted with the Distress, knows how to pity those that are in it.

ADOL. He was not so much as named.

ANT. Were they at their Prayers all the While?

ADOL. Ay, as if it had been for a Wager. One sung his *Hail Queen;* another, *I believe in God.* There were some who had certain particular Prayers not unlike magical Charms against Dangers.

ANT. How Affliction makes Men religious! In Prosperity we neither think of God nor Saint. But what did you do all this While? Did you not make Vows to some Saints?

ADOL. No, none at all.

ANT. Why so?

ADOL. I make no Bargains with Saints. For what is this but a Bargain in Form? I'll give you, if you do so and so; or I will do so and so, if you do so and so: I'll give you a wax Taper, if I swim out alive; I'll go to *Rome,* if you save me.

ANT. But did you call upon none of the Saints for Help?

ADOL. No, not so much as that neither.

ANT. Why so?

ADOL. Because Heaven is a large Place, and if I should recommend my Safety to any Saint, as suppose, to St. *Peter,* who perhaps would hear soonest, because he stands at the Door; before he can come to God Almighty, or before he could tell him my Condition, I may be lost.

ANT. What did you do then?

ADOL. I e'en went the next Way to God the Father, saying, *Our Father which art in Heaven.* There's none of the Saints hears sooner than he does, or more readily gives what is ask'd for.

The Colloquies of Erasmus, trans. N. Bailey (London, 1878), I, 276-280.

2. THE THEOLOGIANS

Perhaps it were better to pass over the theologians in silence, and not to move such a Lake Camarina, or to handle such an herb, *Anagyris foetida,* as that marvelously supercilious and irascible race. For they may attack me with six hundred arguments, in squadrons, and drive me to make a recantation; which if I refuse, they will straightway proclaim me an heretic. By this thunderbolt they are wont to terrify any toward whom they are ill-disposed. No other people are so loth to acknowledge my favors to them; yet the divines are bound to me by no ordinary obligations. They are happy in their self-love, and as if they already inhabited the third heaven they look down from a height on all other mortal creatures as on creatures that crawl on the ground, and they come near to pitying them. They are protected by a wall of scholastic definitions, arguments, corollaries, implicit and explicit propositions; they have so many hideaways that they could not be caught even by the net of Vulcan; for they slip out on their distinctions, by which also they cut through all knots as easily as with a double-bitted axe from Tenedos; and they abound with newly invented terms and prodigious vocables. Furthermore, they explain as pleases them the most arcane matters, such as by what method the world was founded and set in order, through what conduits original sin has been passed down along the generations, by what means, in what measure, and how long the perfect Christ was in the Virgin's womb, and how accidents subsist in the Eucharist without their subject.

But those are hackneyed. Here are questions worthy of the great and (as some call them) illuminated theologians, questions to make them prick up their ears—if ever they chance upon them. Whether divine generation took place at a particular time? Whether there are several sonships in Christ? Whether this is a possible proposition: God the Father hates the Son? Whether God could have taken upon Himself the likeness of a woman? Or of a devil? Or of an ass? Of a gourd? Of a piece of flint? Then how would that gourd have preached, performed miracles, or been crucified? Also, what would Peter have consecrated if he had administered the sacrament while Christ's body hung upon the Cross? Also whether at that moment Christ could be said to be a man? And whether after the resurrection it will be forbidden to eat and drink? (Now, while there is time they are providing against hunger and thirst!) These finespun trifles are numberless, with others even more subtle, having to do with instants of time, notions, relations, accidents, quiddities, entities, which no one can perceive with his eyes unless, like Lynceus, he can see in blackest darkness things that are not there. We must put in also those hard say-

ings, contradictions indeed, compared to which the Stoic maxims which were called paradoxes seem the merest simplicity. For instance: it is less of a crime to cut the throats of a thousand men than to set a stitch on a poor man's shoe on the Lord's day; it is better to choose that the universe should perish, body, boots, and breeches (as the saying is), than that one should tell a single lie, however inconsequential. The methods our scholastics pursue only render more subtle these subtlest of subtleties; for you will escape from a labyrinth more quickly than from the tangles of Realists, Nominalists, Thomists, Albertists, Occamists, Scotists,—I have not named all, but the chief ones only. But in all these sects there is so much learning and so much difficulty that I should think the apostles themselves must needs have the help of some other spirit if they were to try disputing on these topics with our new generation of theologues.

Paul could exhibit faith; but when he said, "Faith is the substance of things hoped for, the evidence of things not seen," he did not define it doctorally. The same apostle, though he exemplified charity supremely well, divided and defined it with very little logical skill in his first epistle to the Corinthians, Chapter 13. And no doubt the apostles consecrated the Eucharist devoutly enough; but suppose you had questioned them about the *terminus a quo* and the *terminus ad quem,* or about transubstantiation—how the body is in many places at once, the difference between the body of Christ when in heaven, when on the Cross, when in the sacrament of the Eucharist, about the point when transubstantiation occurs (seeing that the prayer effecting it is a discrete quantity having extension in time)—they would not have answered with the same acuteness, I suggest, with which the sons of Scotus distinguish and define these matters. The apostles knew the mother of Jesus, but who among them has demonstrated philosophically just how she was kept clear from the sin of Adam, as our theologians have done? Peter received the keys, received them from One who did not commit them to an unworthy person, and yet I doubt that he ever understood—for Peter never did attain to subtlety—that a person who did not have knowledge could have the key to knowledge. They went about baptizing everywhere, and yet they never taught what is the formal, the material, the efficient, and the final cause of baptism, nor is mention made by them that it has both a delible character and an indelible one. They wor-shipped, to be sure, but in spirit, follow-ing no other teaching than that of the Gospel, "God is a spirit and they that worship Him must worship Him in spirit and in truth." It seems never to have been revealed to them that a picture drawn with charcoal on a wall ought to be worshipped with the same worship as Christ himself—at least if it is drawn with two fingers outstretched and the hair unshorn, and has three sets of rays in the nimbus fastened to the back of the head. For who would comprehend these things if he had not consumed all of thirty-six years upon the physics and metaphysics of Aristotle and the Sco-tists?

Desiderius Erasmus, *The Praise of Folly*, trans. from the Latin, with an essay and commentary, by H. H. Hudson (Princeton: Princeton University Press, 1941), pp. 77-81.

3. Julius II Excluded from Heaven: Julius, his Tutelary Spirit, and Saint Peter

JULIUS. What's the trouble here? Won't the doors open? The lock must have been changed or at least tampered with.

SPIRIT. Perhaps you haven't brought the right key, for this door will never be opened by the same key as you use for your money-box. So why haven't you brought both keys here, for this one that you have is the key of power not of knowledge?

JULIUS. This is the only one I ever had and I see no need of another as long as I have this.

SPIRIT. Nor indeed do I except that in the meantime we are shut out.

JULIUS. I am getting very angry. I will beat down these gates. Hey, some-one in there, open this door at once! What is the matter? Will no one come? Why does the porter dally like this? No doubt he's snoring and probably drunk.

SPIRIT. (As always he judges every-one else by himself!)

SAINT PETER. It's a good thing we have adamantine doors here; otherwise this man would have broken in. He must be some giant or satrap, a con-queror of cities. But, O immortal God, what a stench! I will not open the door at once, but by looking out of this little barred window find out what kind of a monster this may be. Who are you and what do you want?

JULIUS. Open as quickly as you can. If you had done your duty, you ought to have come out to meet me with all the pomp due an emperor.

SAINT PETER. Spoken imperiously enough. But first explain to me who you are.

JULIUS. As if you could not see for yourself!

SAINT PETER. See? Indeed I see a strange and hitherto unknown, not to say monstrous, spectacle.

JULIUS. Unless you are wholly blind, you must recognize this key even if you don't know the golden oak. And you see the triple crown and the pallium gleaming with gems and with gold.

SAINT PETER. Indeed I see a key silvered all over although it is only one and very different from those keys which Christ as the true pastor of the Church once gave over to me. And how should I recognize this proud crown? No barbarian tyrant ever wore such a one still less anyone who demanded to be admitted here. Nor does this pallium in the least move me who have always scorned and despised gold and gems as rubbish. But what is this? I see everywhere on key and crown and pallium the signs of that most wicked rogue and impostor Simon [Magus] who shares my name but not my way of life, and whom I long ago turned out of the temple of Christ.

JULIUS. If you are wise you will put aside this joking, for, in case you don't know, I am Julius the Ligurian and you will surely recognize the two letters P.M. if you learned to read at all.

SAINT PETER. I believe they stand for "Pestis Maxima" [Supreme Plague].

SPIRIT. Ha ha ha! How this soothsayer has hit the nail on the head!

JULIUS. No, "Pontifex Maximus" [Supreme Pontiff].

SAINT PETER. If you were three times "Maximus" and more even than Mercury Trismegistus, you would not come in here unless you were also "optimus," that is holy [sanctus].

JULIUS. If in fact it matters at all to be called "sanctus," you who are delaying opening the doors for me have passed the bounds of impudence since you during so many centuries have been called only "sanctus," while no one has ever called me anything but "sanctissimus." And there are six thousand bulls . . . in which I am not only named "most sacred lord" but am described by the very name of holiness itself, not sanctus, so that I did whatever I pleased.

SPIRIT. Even indulging in drunkenness.

JULIUS. They said that that made the sanctity of the most sacred lord Julius.

SAINT PETER. Then ask admission of those flatterers who made you most sacred and let them give you happiness who gave you sanctity. Although you think this is a question of no concern, will you be called "sanctus" whether you are or not?

JULIUS. I am exasperated. If I were only permitted to live, I should envy you neither that sanctity nor that felicity.

SAINT PETER. O what a revelation of a "most sacred mind"! Although I have now for some time been inspecting you from all sides, I notice in you many signs of impiety and none of holiness. And what does this strange crowd so very unpontifical want for itself? You bring some twenty thousand with you nor do I see anyone in such a great mob who has the countenance of a Christian. I see the loathsome dregs of men, smelling of nothing but brothels, drink-shops and gunpowder. It seems to me that hired robbers or rather infernal skeletons have rushed hither from hell to make war on heaven. Also the more I contemplate you yourself, the less do I see any vestige of an apostle. In the first place what kind of monster are you who, although you wear outside the garments of a priest, underneath bristle and clink with a covering of bloody armor? In addition to this how savage are your eyes, how stubborn your mouth, how threatening your brow and how haughty and arrogant your glance! It is shameful to have to say and at the same time disgusting to see that no part of your body is not defiled by the signs of your unrestrained and abominable lust. Not to speak of the fact that you always belch and smell of inebriation and drunkenness and indeed seem to me to have just vomited. This is so truly the condition of your whole body that you seem withered, wasted, and broken not so much by age and disease as by drunkenness.

SPIRIT. How graphically he has depicted him in all his colors.

SAINT PETER. Although I see that you have long been threatening me with your look, yet I cannot keep back what I feel. I suspect that you are that most pestilential heathen Julius returned from hell to make sport of me.

Erasmi Opuscula, ed. W. K. Ferguson (The Hague, 1933), pp. 65-68, trans. M. P. Gilmore.

B. The Erasmian Affirmation

1. AGAINST THE EVIL OF IGNORANCE

But inasmuch as faith is the only gate unto Christ, the first rule must be that thou judge very well both of him and also of scripture given by his spirit, and that thou believe not with mouth only, not faintly, not negligently, not doubtfully, as the common rascal of Christian men do: but let it be set fast and immovable throughout all thy breast, not one jot to be contained in them that appertaineth not greatly unto thy health. Let it move thee nothing at all that thou seest a great part of men so live, as though heaven and hell were but some manner of tales of old wives, to fear or flatter young children withal: but believe thou surely and make no haste, though the whole world should be mad at once, though the elements should be changed, though the angels should rebel: yet verity cannot lie, it cannot but come which God told before should come. If thou believe he is God, thou must needs believe that he is true also, and on this wise think without wavering, nothing to be so true, nothing to be so sure, and without doubt of the things which thou hearest with thine ears, which thou presently beholdest with thine eyes, which thou handlest with thy hands, as those things be true which thou readest in the scriptures, that God of heaven, that is to say verity, gave by inspiration, which the holy prophets brought forth, and the blood of so many martyrs hath approved: unto which now so many hun-

dred years the consent of all good men hath agreed and set their seals: which Christ here being in flesh, both taught in his doctrine and expressly represented or counterfeited in his manners and living. Unto which also miracles bear witness, the devils confess and so much believe, that they quake and tremble for fear. Last of all which be so agreeable unto the equity of nature, which so agree between themselves, and be everywhere like themselves, which so ravisheth the minds of them that attend, so moveth and changeth them. If these so great tokens agree unto them alone, what devil's madness is it to doubt in the faith? Yea of those things past thou mayst easily conjecture what shall follow: how many and great things also, how incredible to be spoken did the prophets tell before of Christ: which of these things came not to pass? Shall he in other things deceive which in them deceived not? In conclusion, the prophets lied not, and shall Christ the Lord of prophets lie? If with this and such other like cogitations thou often stir up the flame of faith, and then fervently desire of God to increase thy faith, I shall marvel if thou canst be any long time an evil man. For who is all together so unhappy and full of mischief that would not depart from vices, if so be he utterly believed, that with these momentary pleasures, beside the unhappy vexation of conscience and mind, are purchased also eternal punishments: on the other side, if he surely believed for this temporal and little worldly vexation to be rewarded or recompensed to good men an hundred fold joy of pure conscience presently: and at the last life immortal.

Erasmus, *Enchiridion Militis Christiani* [*The Manual of the Christian Knight*], English translation (London: Methuen and Co., 1905), Chapter IX, pp. 115-117.

2. THE PHILOSOPHY OF CHRIST

. . . In this epoch of ours when men turn their attention with such eagerness to studies, each according to his choice, the philosophy of Christ is the only one to be scorned by some although they are Christians, to be neglected by the mass of men and discussed but without warmth not to say hypocritically by very few. Yet in all the other sciences which human industry has produced there is nothing so hidden and abstruse that the keeness of the intellect has not discovered it, nothing so difficult that an immense effort has not conquered it. What brings it about that we do not embrace this philosophy alone with the eagerness which it deserves although we profess to call ourselves Christians? Platonists, Pythagoreans, Academics, Stoics, Cynics, Peripatetics, and Epicureans have a profound knowledge of the dogmas of their own sects or at least have memorized them; on behalf of these they engage in combat and would prefer to give their lives rather than to desert the inheritance of their founders. But why should we not show a similar devotion to Christ, the author of our being and our leader? Who would not think it a betrayal on the part of a man who professed himself an Aristotelian not to know what that philosopher thought about the causes of thunder, origins of matter or infinity? Yet these are not things the knowledge or ignorance of which renders us happy or unhappy. Shall not we who have been brought in so many ways to the knowledge of Christ and drawn to him by so many sacraments regard it as a base betrayal to deny his dogmas which offer to all men an assured felicity? And how can anyone charge here that we exaggerate when the impious madness of some has reached the point of wanting to compare Christ with Zeno or Aristotle and his doctrine with what I can only call as politely as possible their little precepts. Let them attribute as much as they can or as much as they like to the leaders of their sects; in reality Christ is the only doctor to come to us from heaven, he is the only one to teach the certain truth, since he is himself eternal wisdom; as the unique author of human salvation he alone has taught the things necessary for salvation and he alone perfectly realized in practice what he taught and was able to show forth in reality what he had promised.

. . . I strongly dissent from those who are unwilling to have the Scriptures translated into the vernacular and read by the ignorant, as if Christ taught so complicated a doctrine that it can hardly be understood even by a handful of theologians or as if the arcanum of the Christian religion consisted in its not being known. It is perhaps reasonable to conceal the mysteries of kings but Christ seeks to divulge his mysteries as much as possible. I should like to have even the most humble women read the Evangel and the Epistles of St. Paul. And these ought also to be translated into all languages so that they might be read and known not only by Scots and Irishmen but also by Turks and Saracens. The first step is certainly to know the Scriptures in whatever manner. Although many will mock at them some will be captivated. Would that the ploughboy recited something from them at his ploughshare, that the weaver sang from them at his shuttle and that the traveller whiled away the tedium of his journey with their tales, indeed would that the converse of Christian men were drawn from them, for we are on the whole what our daily discourse reveals us to be. Let each attain what he can and express what he can. Let him who is behind not envy him who is ahead and let the leader encourage the follower without making him despair. Why should we restrict to a few a profession which is common to all? For since baptism in which the first profession of the philosophy of Christ is made is equally common to all Christians, since they share alike the other sacraments and finally the supreme reward of immortality, it is not fitting that the possession of dogma be relegated to those few whom we call theologians or monks. Although these latter constitute only a minute proportion of the Christian people nevertheless I could wish that they conform more closely to what they hear. For I fear lest there be found among the theologians those who are far from deserving this title, who discourse of earthly not of divine things and among the monks who profess poverty and contempt for the world you may find instead even more of the world. To me

he is truly a theologian who teaches not with syllogisms and contorted arguments but with compassion in his eyes and his whole countenance, who teaches indeed by the example of his own life that riches are to be despised, that the Christian man must not put his faith in the defenses of this world but depend entirely on heaven, that he is not to return an injury for an injury, that he is to pray well for those who pray badly and do his best for those who deserve ill, that all good men ought to love and cherish each other as members of the same body and evil men tolerated if they cannot be corrected. Those who lose their goods, who are despoiled of their possessions, who mourn,—these are not to be pitied for they are the blessed and death is even to be desired by the pious for it is the passage to immortality. If anyone inspired by the spirit of Christ preaches things of this kind, if he inculcates, urges, invites, encourages, then he is a true theologian even if he should be a ditch digger or a weaver.

. . . For that which is especially according to nature easily comes into the minds of all. And what else is the philosophy of Christ which he himself calls a re-birth (*renascentia*) but a restoration of a nature which was originally created good?

From the text of "Paraclesis," in *D. Erasmus Roterodamus Ausgewählte Werke,* eds. Hajo and Annemarie Holborn (Munich: C. H. Beck'sche, 1933), pp. 140-141, 142, 145, trans. M. P. Gilmore.

7. Protestant and Catholic

E. HARRIS HARBISON

Princeton University

THE PROTESTANT REFORMATION and the Catholic response to it in the sixteenth century were vast and complex historical movements with origins which lay deep in the economic, political, and intellectual conditions of the preceding centuries. The historical consequences of the two movements were as various and wide-ranging as their causes. But it is well to remember that each began in the inner religious consciousness of individual human beings, and that each was primarily a religious movement.

The chapter which follows considers the Protestant and Catholic reform movements from within, so to speak, through the thoughts of the leaders on both sides: their appeals, their confessions, their reasoned arguments, and their impassioned propaganda. The words come from an age in which the relation of man to God and salvation of the soul from eternal damnation were profoundly important concerns of most intellectuals as well as of ordinary people. To understand the problems suggested by the selections, therefore, requires a strenuous effort of the historical imagination. The reader must attempt to get inside men of four centuries ago who were convinced that the questions how a man is "saved," whether man has "free will" or not, and where a Christian must look for religious "authority," are crucially important questions.

To a modern Christian, of course, such language is not hard to understand. But even those today who have lost touch with all religion are aware that individuals still undergo "conversion" (to or away from one ideology or another of the age), that "free will vs. determinism" is still a disturbing question to scientists, philosophers, and statesmen, and that our world is just as distraught as was the sixteenth century over the clash of apparently irreconcilable "authorities" (ideologies of nation, race, or class). The thought-world of Luther and Loyola is remote from us, but their problems remind us of ours since many of them were and are perennial human concerns.

Three main questions are outlined below.

(1) What actually happened to Martin Luther in his room in the tower of the Augustinian Friary at Wittenberg some time in 1512 or 1513? And what happened to Ignatius of Loyola at Manresa some ten years later in 1522? An

obvious difficulty presents itself here: neither man wrote down an account of his experience at the time (as Pascal did a century later), and perhaps religious "conversion" is indescribable in any case. But the peculiarities of Luther's experience to a large extent determined the later beliefs and practices of Protestants, and the peculiarities of Loyola's experience were responsible for many of the tenets of the Order he founded, and even for some of the general tendencies of the Catholic Reformation, or "Counter-Reformation" as Ranke called it. It is important, therefore, to puzzle out as accurately as possible what the similarities and differences were in the two religious "conversions" to which the religious upheaval of the sixteenth century can be traced. To this end, the most important documents relating to Luther's experience are given, followed by several sharply contrasting modern interpretations. Loyola's account of his conversion concludes the section.

(2) Careful study of these two conversion experiences will suggest the second main question: Why did most Protestants believe so strongly in predestination and Catholics in free will? What was the religious and psychological stake in the controversy, and why did men literally slit each other's throats over it? It is one of the strangest paradoxes of historical experience that *both* the belief in predestination and the belief in free will can stimulate vigorous and dynamic movements—as the history of the Puritans (who believed in predestination) and of the Jesuits (who believed in free will) appears to prove. In the long run, which is the greater spur to action on the stage of history: belief that the individual is the helpless instrument of irresistible supernatural power, or belief that this power is helpless without the free and willing cooperation of the self-determined individual? How is the historian to explain the heat of the controversy, and what is its long-range significance?

(3) The argument over free will leads naturally into the more crucial argument over religious authority. Granted (as everyone did grant in the sixteenth century) that all power is of God, how does God actually make known His will to men? Through the visible, historical institution known as the Church, centered at Rome and headed by the Pope? Or rather through the Old and New Testaments considered as the direct revelation of the divine will? Or is it through man's reason, the divine gift which distinguishes human beings from beasts? Or through direct, intimate experience of God, through the "inner light," through mystical experience, intuition, or "conscience"? These were the four main answers: Church, Bible, reason, and individual intuition or conscience. Generally the Protestants held to the Bible and conscience, the Catholics to the Church and reason, but like all generalizations this is far too simple, as careful reading of the documents given below will suggest. Were there only two main positions on religious authority, or was there a wide spectrum of opinions? How did different individuals combine two or more of the four main answers suggested, and why? Why were "reasonable" positions on the question apparently so difficult to maintain?

In answering this last question, one very important broad fact must be constantly borne in mind: it occurred to almost no one on either side of the bitter religious controversy of the sixteenth century that there could be some truth on both sides. Truth was one and indivisible. Like the totalitarians of a later day, Lutherans, Calvinists, and Catholics could hardly ever entertain the idea that their opponents might be possessed of a fraction of the truth; the fight would have to be fought out to a finish. The few who did envisage the possibility of irreconcilable believers agreeing to disagree and yet living peaceably with each other were lonely voices crying in the wilderness.

I. THE CONVERSION EXPERIENCES OF LUTHER AND LOYOLA

The facts concerning the background of Luther's "conversion" upon which historians are generally agreed are the following: Martin Luther (1483–1546) entered the Order of Augustinian Friars in 1505 at the age of 21. He was a conscientious monk—zealous, if not overzealous, in the performance of his duties. At the same time he became increasingly troubled by a sense of guilt, which no amount of confession or ascetic practices could alleviate. The popular theology of his day tended to emphasize the importance in salvation of "good works," i.e., the sacramental and monastic practices, such as penance or pilgrimage, universally recognized throughout the Church as practices pleasing to God. The particular scholastic theology which he had been taught—Nominalism—emphasized the power, majesty, and inscrutability of God's will. Luther was terror-stricken by the recurring thought that nothing which he as a human being and sinner might do could possibly please God and win His forgiveness.

Then something happened. While working up lectures on the Bible for his students at Wittenberg, probably in the winter of 1512-13 (the date is disputed), the true meaning of what St. Paul had insisted upon—that God considers not men's "works" but their "faith"—flooded in upon him. Undoubtedly, the way to this illumination had been prepared by his reading, thinking, and personal contacts for months or years before, but as he looked back upon it, it came suddenly. Notice carefully the dates of the selections that follow: only a few of them are really contemporary with the event. What weight is to be given to later reminiscences in such a case? What really happened to Luther? What did he mean when he insisted over and over throughout the rest of his life that a man is "justified" by "faith alone," and not by "works"? Why did this become a slogan subversive of the whole medieval ecclesiastical system?

A. A Tract of 1533

Certain it is, I was a pious monk and followed the rule of my order so strictly that I could say, if ever a monk got to heaven by his monkery, I should certainly have got there. All my fellow-monks who knew me will bear me out. If I had kept on any longer, I should have killed myself with vigils, prayers, reading, and other work.

Martin Luthers Werke: Kritische Gesamtausgabe. (Weimar, 1883 ff), XXXVIII, 143. Hereafter cited as *WA.* Translation of this and the next five selections by E. Harris Harbison.

B. A Sermon of 1539

In the monastery we had enough to eat and drink, but the heart and conscience suffered pain and martyrdom, and the greatest suffering is that of the soul. I was often frightened by the name of Jesus, and when I looked upon him hanging on the cross, he seemed to me like a flash of lightning. When I heard his name mentioned, I would rather have heard the Devil named, for I thought that I would have to do good works until Christ became friendly and gracious to me because of them. In the monastery I thought not about women nor money nor wealth, but my heart troubled and writhed, worrying how I might make God gracious to me. For I had fallen from the faith, and it left me no way but to think that I had offended God and that I would have to appease Him with my good works. But thank God we once more have His Word, which pictures and points out Christ as our righteousness.

WA, XLVII, 589-590.

C. A Conversation of 1533

I often confessed to Staupitz [Vicar-General of the Augustinian Friars, Luther's monastic order], not about women, but about my really knotty problems. He used to say, "I don't understand." That was fine comfort! If I went to someone else, I got the same answer. In fact, no confessor wanted to know about my problems. So I thought, "No one has this temptation but you!" So I became like a dead body. At last Staupitz, seeing how sad and downcast I was, leaned over to me at table [one day] and asked, "Why are you so sad?" I replied, "Ah, what will become of me?" He said, "You don't realize how necessary all this is to you. Without it nothing good will come of you." He didn't understand. He thought I was learned, and was becoming proud.

WA, Tischreden, I, 240.

D. Preface to Luther's Collected Works, 1545

[While working on the Psalms] I was absorbed by a passionate desire to understand Paul in his Epistle to the Romans. Nothing stood in my way but that one expression, "The justice of God is revealed in the Gospel" (Romans 1:17). For I hated those words, "the justice of God," because I had been taught to understand them in the scholastic sense as the formal or active justice whereby God, who is righteous, punishes unrighteous sinners. I was in the frame of mind of feeling that although I was living a blameless life as monk, I was still a sinner with a troubled conscience before God, and I had no confidence that I could appease Him by my efforts. I did not love—nay, I hated the righteous God who punishes sinners, and I murmured with unbridled resentment, if not with unspoken blasphemy, against Him, saying, "As if it were not enough for miserable sinners who are eternally lost through original sin to be afflicted with every kind of calamity through the law of the Ten Commandments, without God's adding woe to woe through the Gospel and even threatening us with His justice and wrath in the Gospel." Thus I raged, my conscience wild and disturbed. Still I kept hammering away at those words of Paul, wishing passionately to know what he meant.

After I had pondered the problem for days and nights, God took pity on me and I saw the inner connection between the two phrases, "The justice of God is revealed in the Gospel" and "The just shall live by faith." Then I began to understand that this "justice of God" is the righteousness by which the just man lives through the free gift of God, that is to say "by faith"; and that the justice "revealed in the Gospel" is the passive justice of God by which He takes pity on us and justifies us by our faith, as it is written, "The just shall live by faith." Thereupon I felt as if I had been born again and had entered Paradise through wide-open gates. Immediately the whole of Scripture took on a new meaning for me. I raced through the Scriptures, so far as my memory went, and found analogies in other expressions: "the work of God," i.e., what God works in us; "the strength of God," by which He gives us strength; "the wisdom of God," by which He makes us wise; "the power of God," "the blessing of God," "the glory of God."

Whereas the expression "justice of God" had filled me with hate before, I now exalted it as the sweetest of phrases with all the more love. And so this verse of Paul's became in truth the gate to Paradise for me.

WA, LIV, 185-186.

E. *A Conversation of 1532*

These words, "the just" and "the justice of God," were a flash of lightning in my consciousness. The moment I heard them I was terribly frightened: if God is just, then He will punish. But thank God, once when I was turning these words over in my mind in the heated room in this tower [another version adds, "in which was the monks' latrine"]—"the just shall live by faith,"

WA, Tischreden, III, no. 3232c.

"the justice of God"—it soon occurred to me that if we must be "justified by faith" and if the "justice of God" must save all those who have faith, then it will not be as a reward to us but by the free mercy of God. This raised up my spirit. For the justice of God is what justifies and saves us through Christ. And so these words became more pleasing to me. The Holy Spirit revealed the meaning of this passage to me in this tower.

F. *Lecture-notes on the Psalms, 1513–1515*

What our scholastic theologians call the act of penance—that is, to be displeased with oneself, to detest, condemn, and accuse oneself, to wish to avenge, punish, and chastise oneself, and in effect to hate evil and be wroth with oneself—this in one word the Scripture calls justification. Therefore so long as we fail to condemn ourselves before God, we cannot rise and be justified. ... The justification of God will never rise in us unless our own justification first falls and perishes utterly. . . . Otherwise God's justice would be

WA, III, 31.

G. *Letter to Staupitz, May 30, 1518*

I remember, reverend Father, among those happy and wholesome stories of yours, by which the Lord used wonderfully to console me, that you often

mocked and Christ would have died in vain. This is the argument of that very profound theologian, the Apostle Paul—an argument unknown in the highest degree to our theologians today, in practice if not in theory. For Paul wants to be found in Christ, with no justification of his own. He calls himself the first of sinners—a great and happy point of pride. For the more sin abounds [he says], the more God's grace and justice abounds in us. That is, the less justification we have of our own, the more we judge and curse and detest ourselves, the more abundantly God's grace flows into us.

mentioned the word *poenitentia*, whereupon, distressed by our consciences and by those torturers who with endless and intolerable precept taught nothing but what they called a method of confession, we received you as a messenger from Heaven, for penitence is not genuine save when it begins from the love of justice and of God, and this which they consider the end and consummation of repentance is rather its commencement.

Your words on this subject pierced me like the sharp arrows of the mighty, so that I began to see what the Scriptures had to say about penitence, and behold the happy result: the texts all supported and favored your doctrine, in so much that, while there had formerly been no word in almost all the Bible more bitter to me than *poenitentia* (although I zealously simulated it before God and tried to express an assumed and forced love), now no word sounds sweeter or more pleasant to me than that. For thus do the commands of God become sweet when we understand that they are not to be read in books only, but in the wounds of the sweetest Saviour.

After this it happened by the favor of the learned men who taught me Hebrew and Greek that I learned [from Erasmus' edition of the New Testament in Greek, note on Matthew 3:2] that the Greek word is *metanoia* from *meta* and *noun,* i.e., from "afterwards" and "mind," so that penitence or *metanoia* is "coming to one's right mind, afterwards," that is, comprehension of your own evil, after you had accepted loss and found out your error. This is impossible without a change in your affections. All this agrees so well with Paul's

theology, that, in my opinion, at least, nothing is more characteristically Pauline.

Then I progressed and saw that *metanoia* meant not only "afterwards" and "mind," but also "change" and "mind," so that *metanoia* means change of mind and affection. . . .

Sticking fast to this conclusion, I dared to think that they were wrong who attributed so much to works of repentance that they have left us nothing of it but formal penances and elaborate confession. They were seduced by the Latin, for *poenitentiam agere* means rather a work than a change of affection and in no wise agrees with the Greek.

When I was glowing with this thought, behold indulgences and remissions of sins began to be trumpeted abroad with tremendous clangor, but these trumpets animated no one to real struggle. In short, the doctrine of true repentance was neglected, and only the cheapest part of it, that called penance, was magnified. . . . As I was not able to oppose the fury of these preachers, I determined modestly to take issue with them and to call their theories in doubt, relying as I did on the opinion of all the doctors and of the whole Church, who all say that it is better to perform the penance than to buy it, that is an indulgence. . . . This is the reason why I, reverend Father, who always love retirement, have unhappily been forced into the public view. . . .

Preserved Smith, *Luther's Correspondence* (Philadelphia: Lutheran Publishing Co., 1913), I, 91-93.

H. A Tract of 1520

Lo! my God, without merit on my part, of His pure and free mercy, has given to me, an unworthy, condemned, and contemptible creature, all the riches of justification and salvation in Christ,

so that I no longer am in want of anything, except of faith to believe that this is so. For such a Father, then, who has overwhelmed me with inestimable riches of His, why should I not freely, cheerfully, and with my whole heart, and from voluntary zeal, do all that I know will be pleasing to Him and acceptable in His sight? I will therefore give myself, as a sort of Christ, to my neighbour, as Christ has given himself to me; and will do nothing in this life except what I see will be needful, advantageous, and wholesome for my neighbour, since by faith I abound in all good things in Christ.

Luther, *On Christian Liberty* (1520), in Henry Wace and C. A. Buchheim, eds., *Luther's Primary Works* (London: Hodder and Stoughton, 1896), pp. 281-282.

[MARTIN LUTHER]

Naturally modern historians still differ sharply in interpreting the preceding documents, although there is much on which all are agreed. To Catholic historians, Luther was unbalanced and "abnormal," a "heretic" in the literal sense of one who seizes upon a single aspect of truth and blows it up out of all proportion to its significance. The trouble, they insist, was with Luther, not with the Catholic tradition on salvation, although there admittedly were abuses in practice. To Protestant historians, Luther was essentially "normal," in a badly mechanized ecclesiastical system which was offering salvation in exchange for "good works"—and cash. The trouble was with the Church, not with Luther. Moderate historians of both persuasions and some of neither are able to see the tragic conflict of personal and institutional standards involved, and to point out the truth on both sides. But it is not easy to reconcile the following twentieth-century interpretations of Luther's experience. Can it be done at all?

I. *Febvre: A "Humanistic" Interpretation*

In the monastery Luther had striven anxiously to compass his soul's salvation by meritorious works. What had been the result? An immense discouragement, fearful moods of despair, and, little by little, the partial but growing conviction that all struggle is vain, that there is no end to depravity and that sin is a permanent fact. Sin itself, not mere fallibility for which some external remedy can be found, but the infernal illimitable force which forever separates man from his Creator.

How to find relief then from doubt and despair and terror? In a lightning flash, which revealed suddenly the whole extent of his past reflections and reveries, Luther saw the answer. He never forgot it. . . .

Theretofore he had brought all his energies to bear in a desperate effort to succeed by main force and unaided. He would purify his soul; he would stamp out the evil in it; he would transform himself from the sinner into a righteous man. It sounded easy enough but was harder in practice. Experience—and a cruelly gained experience—proved to Luther that all his efforts to win salvation resulted in sanguinary defeat.

Suddenly he perceived a quite different solution. Might not the Christian who, instead of constantly bracing and overtaxing his own feeble will, should subject himself, with a mingling of joy and terror, to the operation of an omnipotent, infinitely holy and truly regenerating supernatural will—might not such a one, despairing utterly of himself and his personal efforts, if he ceased to exhaust himself in repelling the promptings of evil and accepted Hell itself as no more than his just deserts and, instead of struggling vainly, sought shelter in God as chickens seek shelter under the hen, and trusted God's infinity to supply what he lacked—might not such a one in the end find consolation and peace?

A singularly bold and complete metamorphosis. A moment before, the vain and furious strain of the gladiator tensing every muscle only to fail the more pitiably. Now, instead, the utter and blessed passivity and the resignation of one who, confessing himself to be beaten even before the encounter, somehow builds his hope on the very magnitude of his defeat.

Lucien Febvre, *Martin Luther: A Destiny*, trans. Roberts Tapley (New York: E. P. Dutton and Co., 1929), pp. 51-53.

J. Grisar: A Moderate Roman Catholic Account

In none of his other Epistles does St. Paul penetrate so deeply into the questions of grace, justification, and election, as in his magnificent Epistle addressed to the Christians of Rome. Luther believed that this profound Epistle furnished the thread that would lead him out of his labyrinth. Disregarding the tradition of the Church concerning the meaning of the Epistle, he buried himself in its contents and brooded over its many mysterious expressions. For him the sacred document was to become the subject-matter of academic lectures with entirely new ideas. How often may he not have wandered up and down the venerable corridors of the monastery meditating on the significance of the words of the Apostle. His emaciated form may have become animated, his deep-set eyes may have flashed, as he imagined to discover in the Epistle to the Romans the desired solution of his problems. With ever-increasing confidence he imputed to the Apostle the ideas to which he was urged for the sake of the supposed quieting of his scruples. Simultaneously, an arsenal of new weapons against the self-righteous Pharisees within the Church seemed to open itself to him. . . .

The ancient Church, above all things, upheld the freedom of the human will to do good. She steadfastly maintained that God wills the salvation of all men without exception and to this end offers them the necessary grace, with which men should freely cooperate. Baptism makes a man a child of God by virtue of sanctifying grace; but the inclination to evil remains through no fault of his own, provided he does not consent to sin. Concupiscence is diminished by the means of grace offered by the Church. If any one has been seduced into committing mortal sin, he may confidently hope to regain the state of grace through the merits of the death of Christ, provided he submits to penance and resolves to amend his life. Mere faith in the application of the merits of Christ is not sufficient. Actual grace assists man to be converted and to persevere in doing good. . . .

Luther, with the Epistle to the Romans in his hand, proclaimed that man was not free to do good; that all his efforts were sinful, because evil concupiscence dwelled in his soul; that God did everything in him, governing him as the rider governs his steed. He did not differentiate between natural and supernatural good. Christ, he said, has fulfilled the law for me and atoned for every weakness and sin. Through His righteousness the believing and trustful sinner is covered, apart from his own works and his own righteousness. He remains a sinner as before, but is justified by the imputation of the justice of Christ and necessarily brings forth good works through the infinite causality of God, just as trust in God is imparted to the hesitating only through the divine omnipotence.

Hartmann Grisar, *Martin Luther: His Life and Work*, trans. F. J. Eble (St. Louis and London: B. Herder Book Co., 1935), pp. 71, 73.

K. *Maritain: A Militant Roman Catholic Analysis*

From his own witness and the studies of Denifle and Grisar I note here two things in the inner life of Brother Martin [Luther].

First, he seems to have sought in the spiritual life chiefly what authors call sensible consolations, and to have been desperately attached to that experimental savouring of piety, that assurance in feeling, which God sends to souls to draw them to Himself, but takes from them when He wills, and which are only means. For Luther, on the other hand, the whole point was to *feel* oneself in a state of grace—as if grace itself were an object of sensation! . . .

Second, and as a result of the same vicious disposition, he relied on his own strength to arrive at Christian virtue and perfection, trusting his own efforts, in his penances, in the works of his will, far more than in grace. Thus he practiced the very Pelagianism [emphasis on man's will] with which he was to charge Catholics, from which he himself was never really to be free. In his spiritual life he was, in practice, a Pharisee relying on his works, as his scrupulous fidgetiness shows. . . .

Is it then that in the decisive moment of his crisis he falls into some grave outward sin? We do not think so. But inwardly he fell; he despaired of grace. When a man begins to know the wounds and wretchedness of the sons of Adam, the serpent whispers in his ear: "Be content to be what you are, spoiled angel, misbegotten creature; your business is to do ill, since your every being is bad." A spiritual temptation preeminently. Luther makes that act of perverse resignation; he gives up the fight; he declares that the fight is impossible. Submerged by sin on all sides, or by what he thinks to be sin, he lets himself go with the tide. And he comes to the practical conclusion: *Concupiscence cannot be conquered.* . . .

Concupiscence Luther identified with original sin. Original sin is always in us, ineffaceable; it has made us radically bad and corrupted us in the very essence of our nature. God commanded the impossible when He gave us His law. But now Christ has paid for us and His justice redeems us. *He* is just instead of us. Justification is wholly exterior to us and we are still sin to our very bones: it infuses no new life into us, it simply covers us as with a cloak. There is nothing for us to do to be saved. On the contrary, to want to co-operate with the divine action is a lack of faith, a denial of the Blood of Christ, and damnation.

From henceforth "Heaven opens." Good-bye to torments and remorse! Absolute uselessness of works; salvation by faith alone, that is through confidence in Christ. "Sin courageously, believe more firmly than ever" [says Luther] and you will be saved. . . . One might say that that immense disaster for humanity, the Protestant Reformation, was only the effect of an interior trial which turned out badly in a monk who lacked humility.

Reprinted from Jacques Maritain, *Three Reformers* (New York: Charles Scribner's Sons, 1929), pp. 6-13 *passim*.

L. *Boehmer: A Protestant Interpretation*

If we ask what that decisive hour produced, Luther himself gives us the answer: a new insight and a new sense of life. The new insight is reflected in the argument to Psalm 31, probably written on the same day: "Concerning the means of true repentance, that sins are remitted, not by any works, but alone by the mercy of God without any merit." But this sentence still does not clearly express what is, in the last analysis, treated of here; namely, not merely the conditions of the forgiveness of sin, but rather the nature of God and His gracious will toward us. However, he was always of the opinion that in this he had uttered nothing new, but had "only restored the Holy Gospel again." In reality, in this, the head and heart of his message, he is not an innovator but a renovator. Therefore of all the names that his or later generations have invented to characterize his unique position in the history of the Christian religion and religion in general, none fits him so well as the name *Reformer,* which was coined especially for him.

In the first place, this term clearly expresses that he was not the founder of a new religion, nor even that he was one of those many well-meaning, alleged renovators of "true" Christianity who think that they can restore original Christianity by an external, mechanical imitation of primitive Christian ordinances for congregational life, or by a literal, verbal application of primitive Christian doctrines. He was rather the rediscoverer and reviver of what was essential and specifically Christian in primitive Christianity. This is evangelical faith in God, or, to put it in another way, the Gospel of the grace of God in Christ.

In the second place, this name is also very fortunate in that it fixes and symbolizes in the simplest manner the significant distinction which exists between Luther's religious self-consciousness and the self-consciousness of most other great personalities in the history of religion, Christian and non-Christian. If there is anything that is characteristic of the latter, it is the consciousness of being a bearer and instrument of a spe-cial revelation which is believed to have been received in visions, dreams, and other ecstatic experiences and confirmed by miracles and signs. Luther never had such ecstatic experiences. Nevertheless, he never doubted that the "insight" which had made him a reformer had been "given to him by the Holy Ghost," or "revealed" to him. The suddenness with which this "insight" emerged, after days of agonizing thought and search, and the profound emotion and the feeling of being liberated which accompanied it certainly contributed toward strengthening him in this conviction. But it is unquestionable that his conviction was confirmed by the impression that God had been especially near to him in that moment; and that it was corroborated by the certainty that "his teaching was not his but rather the true, pure Word of God," and that he had received it not in visions and dreams, but in a completely normal state of mind. For in his opinion visions and dreams are always very dubious and delusive, dependent upon the temperament and disposition of the individual who has them, often caused by evil spirits, never equal in value to the Gospel even when they are genuine, and, for that matter, no longer necessary to Christianity now that it possesses the Gospel. . . .

As is shown in a classical manner by the ecstatic experiences of Loyola, visions, auditions, and inspirations . . . almost never have a single meaning, and like all visionary complexes are not easily retained in their original form. "Insights," however, always have a single meaning and are not easily altered. . . . Naturally, this frequently results in the "insights" being handed down as a mere formula, appropriated merely by rote and not inwardly assimilated. On the other hand, it also means that they reach much wider circles, that they may be readily translated into action, indeed that they can actually change the face of the whole world without their originator having moved a finger.

Heinrich Boehmer, *Road to Reformation: Martin Luther to the Year 1521*, trans. J. W. Doberstein and T. G. Tappert (Philadelphia: Muhlenberg Press, 1946), pp. 111-112, 115-116.

[IGNATIUS LOYOLA]

Boehmer's interpretation of the significance of Luther's experience suggests comparison with the experience of Ignatius of Loyola (1491-1556), founder of the Society of Jesus or Jesuit Order (1540). Loyola was a Spaniard of the lesser nobility, with romantic sensibilities and courtly ambitions, apparently headed for a humdrum career in camp and court. This never came about, for a French cannon ball shattered his leg at Pampluna in May, 1521 (a month after Luther defied the assembled Diet at Worms). During a long and painful convalescence, he found none of his favorite chivalric romances to read and so devoured a life of Christ and legends of the saints. What if he should become a saint instead of a knight? The romantic idea was translated into action shortly after he was able to walk again. He determined to become a soldier of Christ and dedicated himself to the Virgin as a knight to his Lady. But like Luther, he soon went through the valley of doubt, as the following account makes clear. It is his "Confessions," dictated during the closing years of his life to a friend, Father Gonzalez de Camara. Some 30 years separate the account itself from the events described, which took place at Manresa in Spain in 1522. As in the case of Luther, what confidence is to be placed in such reminiscences? How did Loyola's experience differ from Luther's, and what might this difference mean for any future movements founded by the two men?

M. *Ignatius of Loyola's Account of his Conversion*

The 24th of March, 1522, the eve of Our Lady, as secretly as possible he [Loyola] gave to a poor man all his clothes and put on the clothes he longed for and went to kneel before the altar of Our Lady, and now there and now on foot, staff in hand, passed the whole night, and left for Barcelona at daybreak. In order not to be recognized he went, not by the direct road where he would find many people who would know him and show him honour, but by a roundabout way to a town called Manresa; where he determined to stay in a hospital some days and note down some things which he took with him very carefully and in which he found much consolation. . . .

But he began to be much troubled by scruples. Because, even though the general confession which he had made in Montserrat had been made very carefully and all in writing, nevertheless it seemed to him sometimes that he had not confessed some things, and that idea afflicted him very much because, though he confessed this idea itself, he found no inward satisfaction. And so he began to seek out spiritual men who might aid these scruples of conscience but nothing helped him, and at last a doctor of theology, who was preaching in the church of Manresa, a very spiritual man, told him one day in confession to write everything he could recollect. He did it and after confession his scruples of conscience came back, so that he was in great tribulation and although he knew that these things caused him great loss and that it would be well for him to free himself from them, he could not. He thought sometimes that there might be a cure in having his confessor order him in the name of Jesus Christ not to confess again any things in his past life and he wanted to have his confessor so order him, but he had not the boldness to say it to his confessor. But the confessor, without being told, ordered him not to confess anything in his past life unless it was a very clear, distinct sin in his memory. He did not profit at all by that order and remained troubled. At that time he lived in a room which the Dominican monks had given him in their convent and kept up his daily seven hours of prayer on his knees, rising always at midnight, and all other exercises of the spirit, but in all these he found no cure for the scruples of his conscience and many months passed in torment. And once, when he was in great tribulation because of them, he took to prayer and in his fervour called aloud on God, saying, "Help me, O Lord, for I find no help in man nor in any other creature; though if I thought I could find help no work would seem too great for me. Show me, Lord, where to find help, because, even though it should be necessary to follow a little dog in order that he might lead me to the remedy, I would do it."

Possessed by these thoughts there came to him many times with great force, the temptation to throw himself into a large opening there was in his room to the place where he prayed. But realizing that it was a sin to kill himself, he began to say aloud, "Lord, I will not do anything which is an offense to Thee," repeating those words many times. And there came to his memory the story of a saint who, to obtain from God something he much desired, went many days without food until he obtained it. And thinking of that a good while, at last he made up his mind to do it, saying to himself, that he would neither eat nor drink until God provided for him or he saw himself near to death: because if he saw himself so far *in extremis* that if he did not eat he must die, he determined that then he would beg bread and eat it. (This was a foolish plan, for in truth how could he in the very article of death either beg or eat bread?) That happened on a Sunday after he had communed and the whole week he persevered without putting anything in his mouth and without giving up his accustomed exercises, even going to divine services and praying on his knees at midnight, etc. But when the next Sunday arrived when it was necessary to go to make his confession, as he was wont to tell his confessor very much in detail what he had done, he told him also how in that week he had eaten nothing. The confessor told him to break his fast: and although he found himself still with force, nevertheless he obeyed his confessor and found himself that day free from his scruples of conscience. But the third day, which was a Tuesday, while he was praying he commenced to remember his sins and as if he were threading beads, he kept on passing in thought from sin to sin of his past life and it seemed to him that he was obliged to confess them again. But at the end of these thoughts there came to him disgust with the life he led and impulses to leave it. And with that, it pleased God that he awoke as if out of sleep. And as he already had some experience in the diversity of spirits by the lessons which God had given him, he began to regard the way in which that spirit had come and so determined very clearly not to confess any more anything of his past life, and so from that day on he remained free from those torments of conscience; holding it for certain that our Lord had freed him by His mercy.

Aside from his seven hours of prayer he occupied himself in aiding the souls of some who came to him seeking help in spiritual things and all the rest of the day not occupied in these two things, he gave to meditation on the things of God and what he had read and heard. But when he came to go to bed, often great spiritual consolation came to him and intimations of divine things which made him lose a large share of the time destined for sleep—which was not much. And considering this, he thought that he had a certain time set aside for communion with God and in addition the rest of the day. And by this road he came to doubt if those intimations came from the good spirit, and he came to the conclusion that it was better to neglect them and sleep the hours allotted to sleep. And he did so. He still persevered in his determination to eat no meat and was so firm in it that he had no thought of changing it in any way. One day when he got up in the morning there appeared to him meat ready to be eaten; as if he saw it with his bodily eyes without any wish to eat meat preceding the appearance of it. And there came to him, at the same moment, a strong assent of his will to eat meat for the future. And though he recalled his former determination, he could not doubt that he ought to eat meat. Afterwards his confessor said he wondered if it was not a temptation, but he (Ignatius) examining the whole matter carefully, could not doubt that it was a sign.

In those days God was treating him like a boy in school, teaching him; and this because of his rudeness and gross mind, either because there was no one to teach him or because of the firm will which had been given him by God Himself for His service. At all events he clearly judged and has always judged that God was so teaching him. First if he doubted it he would think he was sinning against the divine majesty and then it can be seen by the five following points.

He was very much devoted to the Holy Trinity and offered prayer every day to the three persons separately. And offering prayer to the most Holy Trinity the thought came to him "How would it be to offer four prayers to the Trinity?" But the thought gave him little or no trouble as a thing of small importance. And standing one day praying the hours of Our Lady on the steps of the monastery, his understanding began to be raised as if he saw the most Holy Trinity as the three keys of an organ and that with so many tears and sobs that he could not restrain them. And, taking part that morning in a procession, he could not until dinner time keep back the tears, nor, after dinner, cease to talk about the Trinity: and that with much joy and consolation, so that all his life the impression remained with him to feel great devotion in offering prayer to the most Holy Trinity.

Once he saw in his understanding with great spiritual joy the way in which God had created the world, because he seemed to see a white thing from which issued rays and from that God made light. But he would not know how to explain these things, nor does he remember entirely well everything about that information which at that time God was impressing on his soul.

Also at Manresa, where he stayed almost a year after he began to be consoled by God and saw the fruit of his efforts to help souls, he gave up those extremes which he had before practiced and cut his nails and hair [which had been uncut]. One day when he was in the church of the monastery hearing mass and the body of Our Lord was raised, he saw, with the inner eyes, so to speak, rays of light which came from above. And although he cannot after so long a lapse of time explain it well, nevertheless what he saw clearly with the understanding was how Our Lord Jesus Christ was in that most Holy Sacrament.

On many occasions and for a long time when in prayer he saw with the interior eyes the humanity of Christ and the figure which appeared to him was like a white body, neither very big nor very small, but he could not see any distinction of members. He saw that in Manresa many times. If he should say twenty or forty he would not dare to judge that it was a falsehood. Another time he saw it when he was in Jerusalem and again when he was journeying near Padua. He also saw Our Lady in a similar form without distinguishing the parts of her body. Those things which he has seen gave so much confirmation to his faith that he has often thought within himself that if he had not read the scriptures which teach us those things of the faith, he would determine to die for them solely because of what he has seen.

Once he went to a church which stood a little more than a mile from Manresa which was called, I think, St. Paul, and the road runs next to the river. And walking and saying his prayers, he sat down for a little with his face toward the river. And thus sitting the eyes of his understanding began to open and, without seeing any vision, he understood and knew many things—as well spiritual things as things of the faith and things in the realm of letters and that with a brightness of illustration so great that they seemed to him entirely new things. And the details of what he then understood cannot be explained though they

were many. All that can be said is that he received a clarity in his understanding of such a sort that in all the reasoning of his life up to the age of more than sixty-two years, collecting all the help he had received from God and all he has known and joining them into one, it does not seem to him that he has gained as much from all these advantages as from that single illumination when he sat by the river.

And that left him with an understanding so enlightened that it seemed to him he was another man and that he had an intellect different from the one he had before. And after this had lasted for some time, he went on his knees before a roadside cross which stood nearby to give thanks to God and there appeared to him the vision [of a serpent] which had appeared to him many times but which he had never understood; the thing of which it has been said before that it appeared very beautiful with many eyes. But he saw plainly, being before the cross, that the thing had not as beautiful a colour as usual. And he recognized very clearly, with a powerful assent of the will, that it was the devil and since, although for a long time the devil continued to appear to him often, he, as a sign of contempt, drove him away with a pilgrim staff he always carried in his hand.

Reprinted from Paul Van Dyke, *Ignatius Loyola* (New York: Charles Scribner's Sons, 1926), 36, 39-44. Original in *Scripta de Sancto Ignatio de Loyola* (Madrid, 1904), vol. I, pp. 47-55.

II. FREE WILL VS. PREDESTINATION

Reflection on the preceding selections will suggest that Luther and Loyola thought quite differently about the relative part which *his own will*, as distinguished from God's, had played in the process of his conversion. What was there in Luther's experience to induce him to emphasize God's power and his own helplessness?

Did this logically imply a theology of "predestination" and the elimination of "free will"? Why might Loyola be more inclined to defend "free will"?

Enough has been said to suggest that the Protestant and Catholic positions on the question grew to a large extent out of personal religious experience. But the question of free will was already expounded before Luther began to wrestle with his soul in the monastery. Humanists had been re-reading Greek and Roman arguments about the problem. On the whole these humanists thought highly of man, his reason, his goodness, and his will. They were in conscious revolt against the more sombre view of man held by medieval thinkers; they tended to emphasize man's freedom. To one who had gone through such a shattering conversion experience as Luther, such an optimistic view of human nature was almost blasphemous: unaided by God, man was utterly helpless except to sin.

It is for this reason that the great humanist Erasmus (1469?–1536) deliberately chose the issue of free will when he finally decided that he must break with Luther (1524). The Reformer's gloomy view of human nature went against the grain of the humanist's belief in the dignity, rationality, and freedom of man, qualified though such a belief was by trust in God's grace. Luther saw the importance of the issue and struck back at Erasmus (1525) in a large book which turned out to be the closest thing to a systematic exposition of his theology which he ever wrote. Sir Thomas More (1478–1535), humanist and close friend of Erasmus, saw the problem more specifically from the point of view of the Church, as did Loyola and the fathers of the Church assembled at the Council of Trent (1545–7, 1551–2, 1562–3). John Calvin (1509–1564) summed up the case for predestination with the hard legal logic which convinced so many thousands of his readers of God's majesty and man's misery.

What, if anything, is at stake in this controversy in terms of human happiness and understanding?

A. Erasmus Attacks Luther (1524)

What shall I say of the prodigal son? How could he have wasted his share of the inheritance had it not been his to do with as he pleased? But what he had, he held of his father; and we, too, remember that all our natural qualities are so many gifts of God. Besides, he enjoyed his share even when it was in his father's possession, and then it was in safer hands. What does it mean, then—his departure from his father after suddenly having demanded his share? Quite simply, to give oneself credit for one's natural qualities, and to use them, not in obeying the commandments of God, but in satisfying carnal lusts. And what means the hunger of the prodigal son? It is the sickness by which God directs the mind of the sinner towards self-knowledge, self-hatred, and regret for having left his Father. What is the meaning of the son's inner questioning, when he envisions confession and return? It is the human will adapting itself to the motivating grace that is also called, as we have said, "prevenient" grace. What about this Father who goes before his son on the way? It is the grace of God, which allows our will to do the good when we have determined to do it.

Besides, I ask, what merit could a man claim for himself who is indebted to Him from whom he received natural intelligence and free will for all he can do with these faculties? And yet God considers it meritorious in us not to turn our soul from His grace, and to enlist our talents in His service. That is enough to show that we make no mistake in attributing something to man, although we refer all his works to God as to their author: it is from Him, in fact, that man derives the power of making his strivings one with the operations of divine grace. . . . [The divine wisdom assists man] as guide and advisor, just as an architect directs his workman, draws his plans for him, explains the reason for them, corrects his faulty beginnings, and bolsters him if he loses courage: the work is attributed to the architect, without whose aid nothing would have been created, but no one pretends that the worker and pupil were worthless. What the architect is to his pupil, grace is to our will. That is why Paul writes to the Romans (Chapter 8: 26): "Even so His Spirit cometh to aid our weakness." Now no one calls a person who does nothing weak; that term, rather, is applied to him who lacks strength sufficient to accomplish what he undertakes; in the same sense, you do not say that some one helps you when he does everything. Now Scripture continually speaks of aid, support, succour, shelter. In order for there to be aid, the person aided has to do something. You would not say that the potter helps the clay to become a pot, or that the carpenter aids the axe in making a stool.

That is why, when our opponents declare that man can do nothing without the grace of God, therefore there are no good works by men, we confront them with this proof, which I believe more probable, that men can do everything with the aid of grace, therefore all human works can be good. As many passages as there are in Holy Scripture which mention succour, there are an equal number to establish free will, and they are countless; and I shall carry the day without any possible disagreement if the matter is judged by the number of proofs. . . .

In my opinion, similarly, free will could be preserved while completely avoiding this flagrant confidence in our own merits and the other dangers seen by Luther, without even considering those which we have cited above, and while retaining the main advantages of the Lutheran teaching. This is what

the doctrine means to me which attributes to grace all the first inspiration which enflames the soul, but which leaves to the human will, when it is not devoid of divine grace, a certain place in the unfolding of the drama. Now since this drama has three parts, the beginning, the development, and the fulfilment, we give the two extremities to grace and let free will enter only into the development. Thus two causes collaborate in the same given action, divine grace and the human will; but grace is the principal cause, the will a secondary one which could do nothing without the first, while grace is sufficient in itself—thus fire burns by its natural virtue, although God is the essential cause which sustains its action, without which the fire would lose all its power, if God happened to withdraw his support. . . .

But why, we are asked, leave a place for free will? In order to have something with which justly to accuse the impious who by their own decision stand outside divine grace; to acquit God of the false charges of cruelty or injustice; to drive despair or arrogance far from us; to inspire us to effort. These are the reasons which have led almost all writers to admit free will; but it would remain ineffective without the perpetual aid of the grace of God, which justly prevents us from pride. But still it will be said: what good, then, is free will, if it can do nothing by itself? I shall only reply, And what would be the use of man himself and all his faculties, if God acted on him as the potter on the clay, or even as He might act on a pebble?

Erasmus, *De Libero Arbitrio* (1524), in J. Clericus, ed., *Desiderii Erasmi Roterodami Opera Omnia* (Lugduni Batavorum, 1703–1706), IX, 1240, 1244, 1248, trans. Brice M. Clagett.

B. *Luther Replies to Erasmus* (*1525*)

You [Erasmus] alone in pre-eminent distinction from all others, have entered upon the thing itself; that is, the grand

turning point of the cause; and have not wearied me with those irrelevant points about popery, purgatory, indulgences, and other like baubles, rather than causes, with which all have hitherto tried to hunt me down,—though in vain.

You, and you alone, saw what was the grand hinge upon which the whole turned, and therefore you attacked the vital part at once; for which, from my heart, I thank you. . . .

The human will is, as it were, a beast between [God and Satan]. If God sit thereon, it wills and goes where God will: as the Psalm saith, "I am become as it were a beast before thee, and I am continually with thee." (Ps. 73:22-23.) If Satan sit thereon, it wills and goes as Satan will. Nor is it in the power of its own will to choose, to which rider it will run, nor which it will seek; but the riders themselves contend, which shall have and hold it. . . .

God is that Being, for whose will no cause or reason is to be assigned, as a rule or standard by which it acts; seeing that, nothing is superior or equal to it, but it is itself the rule of all things. For if it acted by any rule or standard, or from any cause or reason, it would be no longer the will of God. Wherefore, what God wills is not therefore right, because He ought or ever was bound so to will; but on the contrary, what takes place is therefore right, because He so wills. A cause and reason are assigned for the will of the creature, but not for the will of the Creator; unless you set up, over Him, another Creator. . . .

As to myself, I openly confess, that I should not wish "free-will" to be granted me, even if it could be so, nor anything else to be left in my own hands, whereby I might endeavour something towards my own salvation. And that, not merely because in so many opposing dangers, and so many assaulting devils, I could not stand and hold it fast (in which state no man could be saved, seeing that one devil is stronger than all men); but because, even though there were no dangers, no conflicts, no devils, I should be compelled to labour under a continual uncertainty, and to beat the air only. Nor would my conscience, even if I should live and work to all eternity, ever come to a settled certainty, how much it ought to do in order to satisfy God. For whatever work should be done, there would still remain a scrupling, whether or not it pleased God, or whether He required any thing more; as is proved in the experience of all those who believe in works, and as I myself learned to my bitter cost, through so many years of my own experience.

But now, since God has put my salvation out of the way of *my* will, and has taken it under *His own,* and has promised to save me, not according to my working or manner of life, but according to His own grace and mercy, I rest fully assured and persuaded that He is faithful, and will not lie, and moreover great and powerful, so that no devils, no adversities can destroy Him, or pluck me out of His hand. "No one (saith He) shall pluck them out of My hand, because My Father which gave them Me is greater than all" (John, 10:27-28). Hence it is certain, that in this way, if all are not saved, yet some, yea, many shall be saved; whereas by the power of "free-will," no one whatever could be saved, but all must perish together. And moreover, we are certain and persuaded, that in this way, we please God, not from the merit of our own works, but from the favour of His mercy promised unto us; and that, if we work less, or work badly, He does not impute it unto us, but, as a Father, pardons us and makes us better.

Luther, *The Bondage of the Will* (1525), trans. Henry Cole (Grand Rapids: W. B. Eerdmans Publishing Co., 1931), pp. 391, 74, 231, 384-5. Original in *WA,* XVIII, 551 ff.

C. Sir Thomas More Criticizes Luther (1528)

Every man that any faith hath, and any manner knowledge of Christian belief, may well and surely perceive that Luther and all his offspring, with all those that favour and set forth his sect, be very limbs of the devil, and open enemies to the faith of Christ. And not only to the faith and manhood of our Saviour Christ, but also against the Holy Ghost and the Father Himself, and utterly against all goodness of the Godhead, as those that wretchedly lay all the weight and blame of our sin to the necessity and constraint of God's ordinance, affirming that we do no sin of ourself by any power of our own will but by the compulsion and handiwork of God. And that we do not the sin ourself, but that God doth the sin in us Himself. And thus these wretched heretics, with this blasphemous heresy alone, lay more villainous rebuke to the great majesty of God, than ever any one ribald laid unto another.

For who was there ever that laid unto another all the particular evil deeds of any one other man, where these ribalds lay to the charge and blame of God all the malice and mischiefs, from the first fault to the last, that ever was wrought or thought by man, woman or devil? And by this give they [to] wretches great boldness to follow their foul affections as things after their opinion more verily wrought in them by God than the best minds be in good men, and that it were therefore in vain for them to resist their sinful appetites. And if they shall be damned, yet they say it shall be long ere they feel it. For Luther saith that all souls shall sleep and feel neither good nor bad after this life till doomsday. And then they that shall be damned, shall be damned, he saith, for no deserving of their own deeds but for such evil deeds as God only forced and constrained them unto and wrought in them Himself, using them in all those evil deeds but as a dead instrument, as a man heweth with an hatchet; and that God shall damn all that shall be damned for His own deeds only which Himself shall have done in them; and, finally, for his own pleasure because it liked him not to choose them as he did his chosen people. Whom they say that he chose in such wise before the beginning of the world, that they can never sin.

W. E. Campbell, ed., *The Dialogue Concerning Tyndale by Sir Thomas More* (1528), (London: Eyre and Spottiswoode, 1927), pp. 279-280.

D. Loyola Warns Those Who Attack Free Will

Although it is very true that no one can be saved unless he is predestined and has faith and grace, there is great need for caution in the way we speak and write about all this. We ought not to speak much about predestination as a matter of course; but if mention is made of it at some time in some way, we should speak so that ordinary people may not fall into any error and say, as sometimes they do, "If I am going to be saved or lost, the question is already settled, and whether I do good or evil, there can be no other outcome"; and therefore becoming paralyzed, they neglect the good works which lead to their salvation and to the spiritual profit of their souls. . . . So we may speak of faith and grace so far as we can with the help of God, for the greater praise of His divine majesty, but not in such a way nor in such terms, especially in these perilous times of ours, that good works and free will shall receive any detriment or come to be considered of no account.

> Ignatius of Loyola, "Rules for the true understanding which we should have of the Church Militant," nos. 14, 15, 17, *Monumenta Ignatiana* (2nd series), *Exercitia Spiritualia* (Madrid, 1919), 556-560. Trans. E. Harris Harbison.

E. The Council of Trent Reaffirms Free Will (1547)

Since there is being disseminated at this time, not without the loss of many souls and grievous detriment to the unity of the Church, a certain erroneous doctrine concerning justification, the holy, ecumenical and general Council of Trent . . . intends, for the praise and glory of Almighty God, for the tranquillity of the Church and the salvation of souls, to expound to all the faithful of Christ the true and salutary doctrine of justification, which the Sun of justice, Jesus Christ, the author and finisher of our faith taught, which the Apostles transmitted and which the Catholic Church under the inspiration of the Holy Ghost has always retained; strictly forbidding that anyone henceforth presume to believe, preach or teach otherwise than is defined and declared in the present decree. (Sixth Session, Introduction to Decree concerning Justification.)

If anyone says that man can be justified before God by his own works, whether done by his own natural powers or through the teaching of the law, without divine grace through Jesus Christ, let him be anathema [cursed].

If anyone says that man's free will moved and aroused by God, by assenting to God's call and action, in no way cooperates toward disposing and preparing itself to obtain the grace of justification, that it cannot refuse its assent if it wishes, but that, as something inanimate, it does nothing whatever and is merely passive, let him be anathema.

If anyone says that after the sin of Adam man's free will was lost and destroyed, or that it is a thing only in name, indeed a name without a reality, a fiction introduced into the Church by Satan, let him be anathema.

If anyone says that the sinner is justified by faith alone, meaning that nothing else is required to cooperate in order to obtain the grace of justification, and that it is not in any way necessary that he be prepared and disposed by the action of his own will, let him be anathema.

If anyone says that the justice received is not preserved and also not increased before God through good works, but that those works are merely the fruits and signs of justification obtained, but not the cause of its increase, let him be anathema.

If anyone says that the Catholic doctrine of justification as set forth by the holy council in the present decree, derogates in some respect from the glory of God or the merits of our Lord Jesus Christ, and does not rather illustrate the truth of our faith and no less the glory of God and of Christ Jesus, let him be anathema. (Sixth Session, Canons 1, 4, 5, 9, 24, 33, concerning Justification.)

> H. J. Schroeder, ed., *Canons and Decrees of the Council of Trent* (St. Louis and London: B. Herder Book Co., 1941), pp. 29, 42-46.

F. *Calvin Reasserts Predestination* (*1559*)

Indeed, God asserts his possession of omnipotence, and claims our acknowledgment of this attribute; not such as is imagined by sophists, vain, idle, and almost asleep, but vigilant, efficacious, operative, and engaged in continual action; not a mere general principle of confused motion, as if he should command a river to flow through the channels once made for it, but a power constantly exerted on every distinct and particular movement. For he is accounted omnipotent, not because he is able to act, yet sits down in idleness, or continues by a general instinct the order of nature originally appointed by him; but because he governs heaven and earth by his providence, and regulates all things in such a manner that nothing happens but according to his counsel. For when it is said in the Psalms, that he does whatsoever he pleases, it denotes his certain and deliberate will. For it would be quite insipid to expound the words of the Prophet in the philosophical manner, that God is the prime agent, because he is the principle and cause of all motion; whereas the faithful should rather encourage themselves in adversity with this consolation, that they suffer no affliction, but by the ordination and command of God, because they are under his hand. But if the government of God be thus extended to all his works, it is a puerile cavil to limit it to the influence and course of nature. And they not only defraud God of his glory, but themselves of a very useful doctrine, who confine the Divine providence within such narrow bounds, as though he permitted all things to proceed in an uncontrolled course, according to a perpetual law of nature; for nothing would exceed the misery of man, if he were exposed to all the motions of the heaven, air, earth, and waters. . . .

Predestination, by which God adopts some to the hope of life, and adjudges others to eternal death, no one, desirous of the credit of piety, dares absolutely to deny. But it is involved in many cavils, especially by those who make foreknowledge the cause of it. We maintain, that both belong to God; but it is preposterous to represent one as dependent on the other. When we attribute foreknowledge to God, we mean that all things have ever been, and perpetually remain, before his eyes, so that to his knowledge nothing is future or past, but all things are present; and present in such a manner, that he does not merely conceive of them from ideas formed in his mind, as things remembered by us appear present to our minds, but really beholds and sees them as if actually placed before him. And this foreknowledge extends to the whole world, and to all the creatures. Predestination we call the eternal decree of God, by which he has determined in himself, what he would have to become of every individual of mankind. . . .

In conformity, therefore, to the clear doctrine of the Scripture, we assert, that by an eternal and immutable counsel, God has once for all determined, both whom he would admit to salvation, and whom he would condemn to destruction. We affirm that this counsel, as far as concerns the elect, is founded on his gratuitous mercy, totally irrespective of human merit; but that to those whom he devotes to condemnation, the gate of life is closed by a just and irreprehensible, but incomprehensible, judgment. . . .

These things will amply suffice for persons of piety and modesty, who remember that they are men. But as these virulent adversaries are not content with one species of opposition, we will reply to them all as occasion shall require. Foolish mortals enter into many contentions with God, as though they could arraign Him to plead to their accusations. In the first place they inquire, by what right the Lord is angry with his creatures who had not provoked him by any previous offence; for that to devote to destruction whom he pleases, is more like the caprice of a tyrant than the lawful sentence of a judge; that men have reason, therefore, to expostulate with God, if they are predestinated to eternal death without any demerit of their own, merely by his sovereign will. If such thoughts even enter the minds of pious men, they will be sufficiently enabled to break their violence by this one consideration, how exceedingly presumptuous it is only to inquire into the causes of the Divine will; which is in fact, and is justly entitled to be, the cause of every thing that exists. For if it has any cause, then there must be something antecedent, on which it depends; which it is impious to suppose. For the will of God is the highest rule of justice; so that what He wills must be considered just, for this very reason, because He wills it. When it is inquired, therefore, why the Lord did so, the answer must be, Because He would. But if you go further, and ask why He so determined, you are in search of something greater and higher than the will of God, which can never be found. Let human temerity, therefore, desist from seeking that which is not, lest it should fail of finding that which is. This will be a sufficient restraint to any one disposed to reason with reverence concerning the secrets of his God. Against the audaciousness of the impious, who are not afraid openly to rail against God, the Lord will sufficiently defend himself by his own justice, without any vindication by us, when, depriving their consciences of every subterfuge, he shall convict them and bind them with a sense of their guilt. Yet we espouse not the notion of the Romish theologians concerning the absolute and arbitrary power of God, which, on account of its profaneness, deserves our detestation. We represent not God as lawless, who is a law to himself; because, as Plato says, laws are necessary to men, who are the subjects of evil desires; but the will of God is not only pure from every fault, but the highest standard of perfection, even the law of all laws. . . .

Wherefore some people falsely and wickedly charge God with a violation of equal justice, because, in his predestination, he observes not the same uniform course of proceeding towards all. If he finds all guilty, they say, let him punish all alike; if innocent, let him withhold the rigour of justice from all. But they deal with him just as if either mercy were forbidden to him, or, when he chooses to show mercy, he were constrained wholly to renounce justice. What is it that they require: if all are guilty, that they shall suffer the same punishment. We confess the guilt to be common, but we say, that some are relieved by Divine mercy. They say, Let it relieve all. But we reply, Justice requires that he should likewise show himself to be a just judge in the infliction of punishment. When they object to this, what is it but attempting to deprive God of the opportunity to manifest his mercy, or to grant it to him, at least, on the condition that he wholly abandon his justice? . . .

Another argument often urged to overthrow predestination is that its establishment would destroy all solicitude and exertion for rectitude of conduct. For who can hear, they say, that either life or death is appointed for him by God's eternal and immutable decree, without immediately concluding that it is of no importance how he conducts himself; since no action of his can in any respect either impede or promote the predestination of God? Thus all will abandon themselves to despair, and run into every excess to which their licentious propensities may lead them. And truly this objection is not altogether destitute of truth; for there are many impure persons who bespatter the doctrine of predestination with these vile blasphemies, and with this pretext elude all admonitions and reproofs: God knows what he has determined to do with us; if he has decreed our salvation, he will bring it to us in his own time; if he has destined us to death, it will be in vain for us to strive against it. But the Scripture, while it inculcates superior awe and reverence of mind in the consideration of so great a mystery, instructs the godly in a very different conclusion, and fully refutes the wicked and unreasonable inferences of these persons. For the design of what it contains respecting predestination is, not that, being excited to presumption, we may attempt, with nefarious temerity, to scrutinize the inaccessible secrets of God, but rather that, being humbled and dejected, we may learn to tremble at his justice and admire his mercy. At this object believers will aim. But the impure cavils of the wicked are justly restrained by Paul. They profess to go on securely in their vices; because if they are of the number of the elect, such conduct will not prevent their being finally brought into life. But Paul declares the end of our election to be that we may lead a holy and blameless life. If the object of election be holiness of life, it should rather awaken and stimulate us to a cheerful practice of it, than be used as a pretext for slothfulness. But how inconsistent is it to cease from the practice of virtue because election is sufficient to salvation, while the end proposed in election is our diligent performance of virtuous actions! Away, then, with such corrupt and sacrilegious perversions of the whole order of election. They carry their blasphemies much further, by asserting that any one who is reprobated by God will labour to no purpose if he endeavour to approve himself to him by innocence and integrity of life; but here they are convicted of a most impudent falsehood. For whence could such exertion originate but from election?

John Calvin, *Institutes of the Christian Religion,* trans. John Allen, 6th American ed. (Philadelphia: Presbyterian Board of Christian Education, 1930), I, 185; II, 144-145, 149, 165, 173-175.

III. THE PROBLEM OF AUTHORITY

The medieval theory of the authority of the Pope in the Church and of the Church in human society is clearly summarized in *Unam Sanctam* (p. 171). Luther did not challenge this authority until six or seven years after his conversion experience. In 1517 he attacked corruptions in the doctrine of indulgences in 95 Theses. Unexpectedly and immediately, he was applauded by thousands of his fellow Germans. The Papacy saw the danger, but handled it clumsily. In three years of disputing and negotiating Luther was driven step by step to see the full implications of his belief that man is saved by faith, not by works. As his position became more and more revolutionary, he was officially condemned by ecclesiastical authority; and as he was condemned, he appealed first to a future Pope who might be better informed, then to a General Council, finally in effect to the Bible and his own conscience. He had raised the problem of religious authority in a way more pregnant with danger to the Church than any heretic had done for over a thousand years.

In 1520 Luther openly broke with the Papacy in a pamphlet from which selections are given below. A year later he defied the demand of the highest authorities in Church and State at the Imperial Diet of Worms that he recant his views—in words which rang throughout Europe. Humanists like Erasmus, who had greeted Luther's attack on indulgences with enthusiasm, were shocked. Erasmus's subtle mind saw the difficulties and dangers in Luther's appeal to the Bible and to individual judgment. As a professional scholar, Erasmus valued reason, and he had a high regard for the authority of the early Church Fathers. His friend, Sir Thomas More, saw the problem more from the point of view of the Church, the divine institution founded by Christ to continue His authority. The Council of Trent finally settled the issue of the interpretation of Scripture for Roman Catholics. No one stated the belief in the virtues of obedience to ecclesiastical authority with more warmth and conviction than Loyola, writing in the closing years of his life to the members of his Order in Portugal. It remained for Calvin to state the argument for the sole authority of Scripture more sharply than it had ever been stated before, and for his erstwhile pupil and later incisive critic, Sebastian Castellio (1515–1563), to attack Calvin's argument from a point of view still Christian and Protestant, but suggestive of the scepticism and tolerance of a later age.

In reading what follows, it is important to notice the key words which betray an author's cast of mind or point of view. What are these words? What is at stake in the argument? What modern parallels suggest themselves?

A. Luther Challenges the Authority of the Roman Church (1520–21)

The Romanists have, with great adroitness, drawn three walls round themselves, with which they have hitherto protected themselves, so that no one could reform them, whereby all Christendom has fallen terribly.

Firstly, if pressed by the temporal power, they have affirmed and maintained that the temporal power has no jurisdiction over them, but, on the contrary, that the spiritual power is above the temporal.

Secondly, if it were proposed to admonish them with the Scriptures, they objected that no one may interpret the Scriptures but the Pope. ?

Thirdly, if they are threatened with a council, they pretend that no one may call a council but the Pope.

Thus they have secretly stolen our three rods, so that they may be unpunished, and intrenched themselves behind these three walls, to act with all the wickedness and malice, which we now witness. . . .

Let us, in the first place, attack the first wall: [that the temporal power has no jurisdiction over the spiritual].

It has been devised that the Pope, bishops, priests, and monks are called the *spiritual estate;* princes, lords, artificers, and peasants are the *temporal estate.* This is an artful lie and hypocritical device, but let no one be made afraid by it, and that for this reason: that all Christians are truly of the spiritual estate, and there is no difference among them, save of office alone. As St. Paul says (1 Cor. 12), we are all one body, though each member does its own work, to serve the others. This is because we have one baptism, one Gospel, one faith, and are all Christians alike; for baptism, Gospel, and faith, these alone make spiritual and Christian people.

As for the unction by a Pope or a bishop, tonsure, ordination, consecration, and clothes differing from those of laymen—all this may make a hypocrite or an anointed puppet, but never a Christian or a spiritual man. Thus we are all consecrated as priests by baptism. . . .

Therefore a priest should be nothing in Christendom but a functionary; as long as he holds his office, he has precedence of others; if he is deprived of it, he is a peasant or a citizen like the rest. Therefore a priest is verily no longer a priest after deposition. But now they have invented *characteres indelibiles,* and pretend that a priest after deprivation still differs from a simple layman. They even imagine that a priest can never be anything but a priest—that is, that he can never become a layman. All this is nothing but mere talk and ordinance of human invention.

It follows, then, that between laymen and priests, princes and bishops, or, as they call it, between spiritual and temporal persons, the only real difference is one of office and function, and not of estate. . . .

Now see what a Christian doctrine is this: that the temporal authority is not above the clergy, and may not punish it. This is as if one were to say the hand may not help, though the eye is in grievous suffering. Is it not unnatural, not to say unchristian, that one member may not help another, or guard it against harm? Nay, the nobler the member, the more the rest are bound to help it. Therefore I say, Forasmuch as the temporal power has been ordained by God for the punishment of the bad and the protection of the good, therefore we must let it do its duty throughout the whole Christian body, without respect of persons, whether it strike Popes, bishops, priests, monks, nuns, or whoever it may be. . . .

The second wall is even more tottering and weak: that they alone pretend to be considered masters of the Scriptures; although they learn nothing of them all their life. They assume authority, and juggle before us with impudent words, saying that the Pope cannot err in matters of faith, whether he be evil or good, albeit they cannot prove it by a single letter. That is why the canon law contains so many heretical and unchristian, nay unnatural laws; but of these we need not speak now. For whereas they imagine the Holy Ghost never leaves them, however unlearned and wicked they may be, they grow bold enough to decree whatever

they like. But were this true, where were the need and use of the Holy Scriptures? Let us burn them, and content ourselves with the unlearned gentlemen at Rome, in whom the Holy Ghost dwells, who, however, can dwell in pious souls only. If I had not read it, I could never have believed that the devil should have put forth such follies at Rome and find a following. . . .

Therefore it is a wickedly devised fable—and they cannot quote a single letter to confirm it—that it is for the Pope alone to interpret the Scriptures or to confirm the interpretation of them. They have assumed the authority of their own selves. And though they say that this authority was given to St. Peter when the keys were given to him, it is plain enough that the keys were not given to St. Peter alone, but to the whole community. Besides, the keys were not ordained for doctrine or authority, but for sin, to bind or loose; and what they claim besides this from the keys is mere invention. . . .

Only consider the matter. They must needs acknowledge that there are pious Christians among us that have the true faith, spirit, understanding, word, and mind of Christ; why then should we reject their word and understanding, and follow a pope who has neither understanding nor spirit? Surely this were to deny our whole faith and the Christian Church. Moreover, if the article of our faith is right, "I believe in the holy Christian Church," the Pope cannot alone be right; else we must say, "I believe in the Pope of Rome," and reduce the Christian Church to one man, which is a devilish and damnable heresy. Besides that, we are all priests, as I have said, and have all one faith, one Gospel, one Sacrament; how then should we not have the power of discerning and judging what is right or wrong in matters of faith? . . . Balaam's ass was wiser than the prophet. If God spoke by an ass against a prophet, why should He not speak by a pious man against the Pope?

The third wall falls of itself, as soon as the first two have fallen. . . .

When need requires, and the pope is a cause of offence to Christendom, in these cases whoever can best do so, as a faithful member of the whole body, must do what he can to procure a true free council. This no one can do so well as the temporal authorities, especially since they are fellow-Christians, fellow-priests, sharing one spirit and one power in all things, and since they should exercise the office that they have received from God without hindrance, whenever it is necessary and useful that it should be exercised. . . .

As for their boasts of their authority, that no one must oppose it, this is idle talk. No one in Christendom has any authority to do harm, or to forbid others to prevent harm being done. There is no authority in the Church but for reformation. Therefore if the Pope wished to use his power to prevent the calling of a free council, so as to prevent the reformation of the Church, we must not respect him or his power; and if he should begin to excommunicate and fulminate, we must despise this as the doings of a madman, and, trusting in God, excommunicate and repel him as best we may. . . .

And now I hope the false, lying spectre will be laid with which the Romanists have long terrified and stupefied our consciences. And it will be seen that, like all the rest of us, they are subject to the temporal sword; that they have no authority to interpret the Scriptures by force without skill; and that they have no power to prevent a council, or to pledge it in accordance with their pleasure, or to bind it beforehand, and deprive it of its freedom; and that if they do this, they are verily of the fellowship of antichrist and the devil, and have nothing of Christ but the name.

Luther, *To the Christian Nobility of the German Nation* (1520), in Henry Wace and C. A. Buchheim, eds., *Luther's Primary Works* (London: Hodder and Stoughton, 1896), pp. 162-175, *passim*.

[Closing words at the Diet of Worms, April 18, 1521]: . . . Since your Majesty and your lordships ask for a simple reply, I shall give you one without horns and without teeth: unless I am convinced by the evidence of the Scriptures or by plain reason—for I do not accept the authority of the Pope or the councils alone, since it is established that they have often erred and contradicted themselves—I am bound by the Scriptures I have cited and my conscience is captive to the Word of God. I cannot and will not recant anything, for it is neither safe nor right to go against conscience. I can do no other. Here I stand. God help me. Amen. [The words "I can do no other. Here I stand" are not in the earliest accounts of what Luther said.]

WA, VII, 838, trans. E. Harris Harbison.

B. Erasmus on the Difficulties of Biblical Authority

Not that I do not know that the whole source and vein of Christian philosophy is hidden in the Gospel and the Epistles. But the strange and often confused terms, the metaphors and oblique figures of speech, hold so much difficulty that we must often perspire with effort before we understand the meaning. In my opinion it would be best if some men of both piety and learning were assigned the task of distilling from the purest sources of the Evangelists and the Apostles and from the most approved interpreters the essence of the whole philosophy of Christ —as simply as is compatible with scholarship, as briefly as is compatible with clarity. Let those things which have to do with faith be summed up in as few articles as possible. Let those which have to do with conduct be set down also in few words and in such a way that men may know that the yoke of Christ is pleasant and easy, not painful; that their forebears are fathers, not tyrants—pastors, not pirates; and that they themselves are called to salvation, not to slavery. They are human beings, after all; their hearts are not iron or adamant. They can melt, they can be won by kindnesses, as even the beasts. And the most effective agent is Christian truth. . . .

Erasmus to Paul Volz, 14 August 1518, P. S. Allen, ed., *Opus Epistolarum Desiderii Erasmi Roterodami* (Oxford: The Clarendon Press, 1913), III, 365-366, trans. E. Harris Harbison.

I take so little pleasure in dogmatizing that I should rather rank myself with the sceptics, whenever I am justified in so doing by the inviolable authority of Holy Scripture and by the decisions of the Church, to which I always submit my judgment quite willingly, whether or not I understand the reasons for what she decrees. And this temper of mind appears to me preferable to that of certain others, who, narrowly attached to their own views, never let any one deviate from them in anything, and who violently twist all the texts of Scripture in support of the position they have embraced once and for all. . . .

Here it will be objected: "Why the need of interpretation, when Scripture itself is perfectly clear?" But if it is as clear as all that, why, over the centuries, have such eminent men been blind on so important a point, as our opponents contend? If Scripture is without obscurity, why was there need for prophecies in apostolic times? That, I shall be told, was a gift of the Holy Spirit. But I should like to know whether, just as the gift of healing and the gift of tongues have ceased, this divine gift has not ceased also. And if it has not ceased, we must seek to learn to whom it could have passed. If it has passed to merely anyone at all, then every interpretation will be uncertain; if it has been received by no one, since today so many obscurities still torment the learned, no interpretation will be more certain. If I maintain that it resides in the successors of the apostles, it will be objected that over the centuries many men have succeeded the apostles who nevertheless had none of the apostolic spirit. And yet, everything else being equal, it will be sought in them, for it is more probable that God has infused His Spirit in those to whom He has given holy orders; just as we believe that grace is more clearly given to the baptized than to the unbaptized.

But, as we must, we shall admit no less than the possibility that the Spirit may actually reveal to some humble and illiterate person truths withheld from a host of learned men, as when Christ thanked His Father for the things He made known to the simple, to those whom the world thought mad—things he had hidden from the wise and the judicious, from the knowledge of scribes, Pharisees, and philosophers. And perhaps Dominic, perhaps Francis [the thirteenth-century saints], were the kind of madmen who are allowed to follow their inspirations. But if Paul, in the day when this gift of the Spirit was in its full vigor, already warns men to check on whether these inspirations really come from God, what must we do in our worldly age? By what standard shall we judge opinions? By learning? But there are none but master scholars in both parties. By conduct? On both sides, likewise, there are only sinners. But we find the chorus of saints all on the same side, defending free will. I am told, it is true, "They were nothing but men." But I only meant to compare men with one another, never with God. I am asked, what does the majority prove, with regard to spiritual insight? I answer, what does the minority prove? I am asked, how can a bishop's mitre be of use in understanding Holy Scripture? I answer, what good is a mantle or cowl? Again, how can philosophical studies make it easier to understand Holy Writ? And I reply, what use is ignorance? And again, how is the comprehension of texts connected with the meeting of a council, where it might be that no member had received the Spirit of God? I answer, what then is the value of private pseudo-councils of a few individuals, where there is only too clearly no possessor of the Spirit?

Do we remember this plea of Paul's, "Don't ask for proof that Christ lives in me"? Then the apostles were only believed to the extent to which their miracles confirmed their teaching. These days, on the contrary, anyone at all demands credence just because he declares he is filled with the spirit of the Gospel. Because the apostles drove out serpents, cured the sick, brought the dead to life, and gave the gift of tongues by the laying on of hands, men decided to believe, and not without difficulty, the paradoxes they taught. And today, when we see new teachers declaring things that common sense cannot even class as paradoxes, we have not yet seen one of them capable of curing a lame horse. And would to Heaven that,

if they cannot work miracles, some of them would at least show the purity and simplicity of apostolic life, which to us, poor late-comers, would be miraculous enough!

I am not speaking specifically of Luther, whom I have never met and whose works give me a confused impression, but of certain others whom I have known more closely. It is they who in biblical controversies reject the interpretation of the Fathers which we suggest to them, they who cry unrestrainedly, "The Fathers were only men!" If they are asked what criterion can be used to establish the true interpretation of Scripture, since there are only men on both sides, they rely on the revelations of the Spirit. But if they are asked why the Spirit should favor them rather than those whose miracles have shone forth throughout the world, they answer as if the Gospel had disappeared from the earth thirteen centuries ago. If you insist that their life be worthy of the Spirit, they retort that they are justified by faith, not by works. If you require miracles, they tell you that the time for them has long passed, and that there is no longer any need for them, now that the Scriptures are fully clarified. And then if you doubt that Scripture is clear precisely on the point where so many great minds have erred, you fall back into the same vicious circle.

Besides, if we admit that he who possesses the Spirit is sure of understanding the Scriptures, how shall I be certain of what he has seen only partially? What shall I do when several learned men bring me different interpretations, each one swearing all the time that he has the Spirit? Especially, if we add that the Spirit does not reveal all truth to them fully, even he who has the Spirit can go wrong, and err on some point.

These are my objections to those who so easily reject the traditional interpretation of the Holy Books, and who

propose their own as if it had plum-
meted from Heaven. Finally, assuming
that the Spirit of Christ could have left
His people in error on some secondary
point without immediate repercussions
on human salvation, how can we admit
that for thirteen hundred years He
abandoned His Church to error, and
that in all the host of holy people not
one could reveal to the Church that
truth which, our recent arrivals pretend,
constitutes the heart of all the Gospel
teaching?

But to finish this matter: whatever
others may arrogate to themselves is
their own affair; as for me, I claim for
myself neither wisdom nor sanctity, and
I take no pride in my intellect, but I
shall simply and carefully set forth the
views which capture my allegiance. If
any one wishes to teach me, I shall not
meet the truth with a closed mind.

Erasmus, *De Libero Arbitrio* (1524), in J. Clericus, ed., *Desiderii Erasmi Roterodami Opera Omnia* (Lugduni Batavorum, 1703–6), IX, 1215, 1219-1220,
trans. Brice M. Clagett.

C. *Sir Thomas More Defends and Defines the Church (1528)*

And therefore is holy scripture, as I
said, the highest and the best learning
that any man can have, if one take the
right way in the learning.

It is, as a good holy saint saith, so
marvellously tempered, that a mouse
may wade therein, and an elephant be
drowned therein. For there is no man
so low but if he will seek his way with
the staff of his faith in his hand, and
hold that fast and search the way therewith, and have the old holy fathers
also for his guides, going on with a
good purpose and a lowly heart, using
reason and refusing no good learning
with calling of God for wisdom, grace
and help, that he may well keep his
way and follow his good guides, then
shall he never fall in peril, but well and
surely wade through and come to such
end of his journey as himself would well
wish. But surely if he be as long as
Longyus, and have an high heart and
trust upon his own wit as he doth, look
he never so lowly, that setteth all the
old holy fathers at nought, that fellow
shall not fail to sink over the ears and
drown. And of all wretches worst shall
he walk that, forcing little of the faith
of Christ's church, cometh to the scripture of God to look and try therein
whether the church believe aright or
not. For either doubteth he whether
Christ teach his church true, or else
whether Christ teacheth it at all or not.
And then he doubteth whether Christ
in his words did say true when he said
he would be with his church till the
end of the world. And surely the thing
that made Arius, Pelagius, Faustus,
Manichaeus, Donatus, Eluidius and all
the rabble of the old heretics to drown
themselves in those damnable heresies,
was nothing but high pride of their
learning in scripture, wherein they followed their own wits and left the common faith of the catholic church, preferring their own gay glosses before the
right catholic faith of all Christ's
church, which can never err in any substantial point that God would have us
bounden to believe. And therefore, to
end where we began, whoso will not
unto the study of scripture take the
points of the catholic faith as a rule of
interpretation, but, of diffidence and
mistrust, study to seek in scripture
whether the faith of the church be true
or not, he cannot fail to fall in worse
errors and far more jeopardous than any
man can do by philosophy, whereof the
reasons and arguments in matters of our
faith have nothing in like authority. . . .

And finally—to put out of question
which is Christ's very [i.e. true] church,

since it is agreed between us and granted through christendom and a conclusion very true that by the church we know the scripture—which church is that by which ye know the scripture?

Is it not this company and congregation of all these nations that, without factions taken and precision from the remnant, profess the name and faith of Christ? By this church know we the scripture; and this is the very church; and this hath begun at Christ and hath had him for their head, and saint Peter his vicar, after him, the head under him, and alway since, the successors of him continually—and have had his holy faith, and his blessed sacraments, and his holy scriptures delivered, kept, and conserved therein by God and his holy spirit. And albeit some nations fall away, yet likewise as how many boughs soever fall from the tree—though they fall more than be left thereon—yet they make no doubt which is the very tree, although each of them were planted again in another place and grew to a greater than the stock he came first of; right so, while we see and well know that all the companies and sects of heretics and schismatics—how great soever they grow—came out of this church that I spake of, we know evermore that the heretics be they that be severed, and the church the stock that all they came out of. And since that only the church of Christ is the vine that Christ spake of in the gospel, which he taketh for his body mystical; and that every branch severed from that tree loseth his lively nourishing, we must needs well know that all these branches of heretics fallen from the church— the vine of Christ's mystical body— seem they never so fresh and green, be yet indeed but witherlings that wither and shall dry up, able to serve for nothing but for the fire.

W. E. Campbell, ed., *The Dialogue Concerning Tyndale by Sir Thomas More* (1528) (London: Eyre and Spottiswoode, 1927), pp. 102-103, 143-144.

D. The Council of Trent Defines the Relation of Church and Scripture (1546)

. . . Following the examples of the orthodox Fathers, [the Council] receives and venerates with a feeling of piety and reverence all the books both of the Old and New Testaments, since one God is the author of both; also the traditions, whether they relate to faith or to morals, as having been dictated either orally by Christ or by the Holy Ghost, and preserved in the Catholic Church in unbroken succession. . . .

[The Council], considering that not a little advantage will accrue to the Church of God if it be made known which of all the Latin editions of the sacred books now in circulation is to be regarded as authentic, ordains and declares that the old Latin Vulgate Edition, which, in use for so many hundred years, has been approved by the Church, be in public lectures, disputations, sermons and expositions held as authentic, and that no one dare or presume under any pretext whatsoever to reject it.

Furthermore, to check unbridled spirits, it decrees that no one relying on his own judgment shall, in matters of faith and morals pertaining to the edification of Christian doctrine, distorting the Holy Scriptures in accordance with his own conceptions, presume to interpret them contrary to that sense which holy mother Church, to whom it belongs to judge of their true sense and interpretation, has held and holds, or even contrary to the unanimous teaching of the

Fathers, even though such interpretations should never at any time be published. Those who act contrary to this shall be made known by the [bishops] and punished in accordance with the penalties prescribed by the law. (Fourth Session, Decrees concerning the Scriptures.)

H. J. Schroeder, ed., *Canons and Decrees of the Council of Trent* (St. Louis and London: B. Herder Book Co., 1941), pp. 17-19.

E. Ignatius of Loyola Praises Obedience to Ecclesiastical Authority (1553)

Although the understanding has not the freedom of choice possessed by the will and naturally gives its assent to that which appears to it true, nevertheless, in many things wherein the evidence of known truth does not force it, the understanding may be inclined to one side or the other and, in such things, every obedient brother should incline himself to think what his superior thinks. Certainly, since obedience is a sacrifice in which the man, without any division of himself, offers his entire being in the fire of love to his Creator by the hand of His ministers . . . it cannot be said that obedience comprises only doing what is commanded or contentment of the will in doing it. Obedience also includes the judgment; thinking what the superior orders so far (as has been said) as the mind can be inclined by the effort of the will. . . . Just as among the heavenly bodies there can be no movement without subordination of one body to another, so in the movement of a rational being by another (which is obedience) subordination is necessary for transferring the influence and virtue from the mover to the moved and this cannot occur without conformity of will and understanding.

The understanding may be misled as well as the will. The scriptures say "Lean not upon thine own understanding" and also, in other human affairs, wise men know it is true wisdom not to trust one's own wisdom. This counsel is even more necessary in regard to spiritual things and persons. . . .

He who has not this obedience of judgment cannot have a perfect obedience which is to obey with love and joy. He loses perseverance, promptness and skill. He loses the much praised simplicity of blind obedience, questioning in himself if the command is wise or unwise, perhaps blaming his superior because he commands that which is not to his mind. He loses humility and fortitude in difficult affairs.

Unless the understanding is subjected in obedience there arise discontent, pain, delay, slackness, murmuring, excuses, which rob obedience of its value and merit.

Lack of surrender of the judgment disturbs the peace and tranquillity of the one who obeys and differences of judgment disturb the peace and union of the congregation; hence St. Paul urges let all think and speak the same thing.

Finally to subject the judgment in obedience, is to offer to God the noblest of oblations: not keeping back anything of oneself and conquering by love for Him the natural inclination all men have to follow their own judgment.

Three rules will help towards this perfect obedience. First: Do not look on the superior as on a man subject to errors and miseries, but look at what you obey in the man, which is Christ the highest wisdom, the highest goodness, infinite love; . . .

Second: Always be ready to look for reasons to defend what a superior orders, and not for disapproving it; third, assume that the order is in accord with God's will and begin with enthusiasm to obey it.

Loyola to the Portuguese Jesuits, 26 March 1553. Reprinted from Paul Van Dyke, *Ignatius Loyola* (New York: Charles Scribner's Sons, 1926), pp. 226-228. Original in *Monumenta Ignatiana* (Madrid, 1906), First Series, IV, 669-681.

F. Calvin Insists Upon the Sole Authority of Scripture (1559)

There has very generally prevailed a most pernicious error, that the Scriptures have only so much weight as is conceded to them by the suffrages of the Church; as though the eternal and inviolable truth of God depended on the arbitrary will of men. For thus, with great contempt of the Holy Spirit, they inquire, Who can assure us that God is the author of the Scriptures? Who can with certainty affirm, that they have been preserved safe and uncorrupted to the present age? Who can persuade us that this book ought to be received with reverence, and that expunged from the sacred number, unless all these things were regulated by the decisions of the Church? It depends, therefore (say they), on the determination of the Church, to decide both what reverence is due to the Scripture, and what books are to be comprised in its canon. Thus sacrilegious men, while they wish to introduce an unlimited tyranny under the name of the Church, are totally unconcerned with what absurdities they embarrass themselves and others, provided they can extort from the ignorant this one admission, that the Church can do every thing. But, if this be true, what will be the condition of those wretched consciences, which are seeking a solid assurance of eternal life, if all the promises extant concerning it rest only on the judgment of men? Will the reception of such an answer cause their fluctuations to subside, and their terrors to vanish? Again, how will the impious ridicule our faith, and all men call it in question, if it be understood to possess only a precarious authority depending on the favor of men!

But such cavillers are completely refuted even by one word of the Apostle. He testifies that the Church is "built upon the foundation of the apostles and prophets." If the doctrine of the prophets and apostles be the foundation of the Church, it must have been certain, antecedently to the existence of the Church. Nor is there any foundation for this cavil, that though the Church derive its origin from the Scriptures, yet it remains doubtful what writings are to be ascribed to the prophets and apostles, unless it be determined by the Church. For if the Christian Church has been from the beginning founded on the writings of the prophets and the preaching of the apostles, wherever that doctrine is found, the approbation of it has certainly preceded the formation of the Church; since without it the Church itself had never existed. It is a very false notion, therefore, that the power of judging of the Scripture belongs to the Church, so as to make the certainty of it dependent on the Church's will. Wherefore, when the Church receives it, and seals it with her suffrage, she does not authenticate a thing otherwise dubious or controvertible, but, knowing it to be the truth of her God, performs a duty of piety, by treating it with immediate veneration. But with regard to the question, How shall we be persuaded of its divine original, unless we have recourse to the decree of the Church? this is just as if any one should inquire, How shall we learn to distinguish light from darkness, white from black, sweet from bitter? For the Scripture exhibits as clear evidence of its truth, as white and black things do of their color, or sweet and bitter things of their taste. . . .

The testimony of the Spirit is superior to all reason. For, as God alone is a sufficient witness of himself in his own word, so also the word will never gain credit in the hearts of men, till it be confirmed by the internal testimony of the Spirit. It is necessary, therefore, that the same Spirit, who spake by the mouths of the prophets, should penetrate into our hearts, to convince us that they faithfully delivered the oracles which were divinely intrusted to them. . . .

Without this certainty, better and stronger than any human judgment, in vain will the authority of the Scripture be either defended by arguments, or established by the consent of the Church, or confirmed by any other supports; since, unless the foundation be laid, it remains in perpetual suspense. Whilst, on the contrary, when, regarding it in a different point of view from common things, we have once religiously received it in a manner worthy of its excellence, we shall then derive great assistance from things which before were not sufficient to establish the certainty of it in our minds. For it is admirable to observe how much it conduces to our confirmation, attentively to study the order and disposition of the Divine Wisdom dispensed in it, the heavenly nature of its doctrine, which never savours of any thing terrestrial, the beautiful agreement of all the parts with each other, and other similar characters adapted to conciliate respect to any writings.

John Calvin, *Institutes of the Christian Religion,* trans. John Allen, 6th Amer. ed. (Philadelphia: Presbyterian Board of Christian Education, 1930), I, 75-77, 79, 81.

G. Sebastian Castellio Upholds Sense and Reason (c.1563)

All sects hold their religion according to the Word of God and say that it is certain. . . . Calvin says that his is certain, and they, theirs. He says they are wrong and wishes to be judge, and so do they. Who shall be judge? Who made Calvin the arbiter of all the sects, that he alone should kill? He has the Word of God and so have they. If the matter is certain, to whom is it certain? To Calvin? But why does he then write so many books about manifest truth? There is nothing unknown to Calvin. He talks as if he might be in paradise and writes huge tomes to explain what he says is absolutely clear.

In view of all this uncertainty we must define the heretic simply as one with whom we disagree. And if, then, we are going to kill heretics, the logical outcome will be a war of extermination, since each is sure of himself. Calvin would have to invade France and other nations, wipe out cities, put all the inhabitants to the sword, sparing neither sex nor age, not even the babes and the beasts. All would have to be burned save Calvinists, Jews, and Turks, whom he excepts.

Sebastian Castellio, *Contra libellum Calvini* . . . [composed c.1562, pub. in Holland, 1612], H, p. 125, trans. R. H. Bainton, *The Travail of Religious Liberty* (Philadelphia: The Westminster Press, 1951), pp. 114-115. Copyright 1951 by W. L. Jenkins.

All the Christian sects are agreed as to the authority [of Scripture]. The question is not whether Scripture is true, but how it is to be understood.

All agree that it is true, but contend as to the meaning. Learned men have not been so blind as to debate for centuries about matters which are perfectly plain. . . .

Now since Scripture is obscure on controverted points . . . we must consider where lies the plain incontrovertible and unshakable truth. Then when this is discovered we can see which side of the controversy accords with Scripture and with the plain incontrovertible truth as above determined, for this must decide. Nor is there doubt that a double support is preferable to a single. I am thinking of the support of sense and intellect. These are the instruments of judging. . . .

When men have been persuaded to shut their eyes and reject the evidence of the senses of the body and of the mind, to believe words, though all the senses refute the words, then nothing is so absurd, impossible, or false as not to be accepted. Why not believe that the white which you see is not white? . . . That what you perceive with the mind is not what you perceive? And then do we wonder that such monstrous errors survive until now among those who are persuaded of the like, or that today such stubborn controversies flourish among theologians? When each adheres tenaciously to words and words disagree, how can you decide if the judgment of the senses is rejected? . . . One says that you must eat Christ's flesh to be saved, and he has the plain words of Christ, "Except ye eat the flesh of the Son of Man," etc. Another denies that Christ's flesh profits a man for salvation and he, too, cites the plain words of Christ, "The flesh profiteth nothing." What will you do? . . .

I will fight with all my might against this monster [of literalism]. If I cannot kill it I hope at least to wound it severely.

We must make it clear, however, that in denying what is contrary to the senses we do not deny that which is above the senses. There is a vast distinction. In human and divine things we say that those matters are above the senses, which cannot be perceived by the senses, for example the questions what God is and whether He created the world; in how many days He made it; whether the souls of men sleep with their bodies, to rise with them. . . .

I never find that Christ did anything contrary to the senses and intellect, and rightly, for the senses and intellect are the works of the Father, and Christ came to destroy not the works of the Father, but of the devil. No wonder then that he did not deprive men of sense and intellect. . . .

Reason is, so to speak, the daughter of God. She was before letters and ceremonies, before the world was made; and she is after letters and ceremonies, and after the world is changed and renewed she will endure and can no more be abolished than God Himself. Reason, I say, is a sort of eternal word of God, much older and surer than letters and ceremonies, according to which God taught His people before there were letters and ceremonies, and after these have passed away He will still so teach that men may be truly taught of God. According to reason Abel, Enoch, Noah, and Abraham and many others lived before the letters of Moses, and after these many have lived and will continue to live. According to reason Jesus Christ himself, the Son of the living God, lived and taught. They are the same, for reason is a sort of interior and eternal word of truth always speaking. By reason Jesus refuted the Jews who placed greater trust in letters and ceremonies. Reason worked upon the Sabbath day and taught the Jews that they might remove a sheep from the ditch on the Sabbath without offense. . . .

Let us hold to this very general rule: if any statement either in profane or sacred authors is of such a kind that, unless taken figuratively, it clearly runs counter to reason or the senses, then it must be taken figuratively and so interpreted as to be reconcilable with reason and the senses. This rule will be incredibly useful in solving many problems.

Sebastian Castellio, *De Arte Dubitandi et Confidendi, Ignorandi et Sciendi* [composed 1563], Elisabeth Feist, ed., in *Per la storia degli eretici italiani del secolo xvi in Europa* (Rome, 1937), Book I, chaps. 22-25 [trans. R. H. Bainton, *Concerning Heretics* (New York: Columbia University Press, 1935), pp. 293-297], and Book II, chap. 41, trans. E. Harris Harbison.

8. The Problem of Government in Seventeenth Century Europe

JOHN B. WOLF

University of Minnesota

THE CENTURY BETWEEN the deaths of Henry IV (1610) and Louis XIV (1715) saw the emergence of the bureaucratic state as the central agency of government. For over a thousand years European political society had been loosely organized, with the realities of power largely in the hands of men who ruled the towns and villages rather than in the central authority of the king. The economic, technical, and military development, as well as the legal and administrative machinery, had been inadequate to support any really strong central authority. Thus, even though his predecessors for several hundred years had been working to strengthen the monarchy, Henry IV was often quite unable to enforce obedience to his commands, and at the same time was very careful not to encroach upon the authority of local governments. Since the royal authority in France was more fully developed than that of most of the rest of Europe, this meant, in effect, that the traditional authorities on the land and in the towns of Europe still could and did act like quasi-independent powers.

A century later Louis XIV, the grandson of Henry IV, with an army of 400,000 men and a complex administrative and police machine that reached into the villages and towns alike, ruled the kingdom of France. The local traditional authorities in the towns and on the land were either broken or tamed; they had to recognize the power of the central government. The revolution that is implied in this contrast within France occurred elsewhere in Europe more or less in the same way. The Hapsburg lands in central Europe in 1610 were decentralized to a point that implied practically complete abdication of power by the central authority. When Leopold I died in 1705, the government in Vienna was already the central authority for the Danubian Monarchy, ruling a multinational state by a complex bureaucratic organization. On a smaller scale the same alteration in the locus of power occurred in Sweden, Denmark, Brandenburg-Prussia, and, after 1700, in Spain and in some of the Italian states. This was the dramatic political revolution of the seventeenth century.

It is, of course, impossible adequately to discuss a problem of this magnitude in a short essay. We should note, however, that the characteristic institutions that forced the rise of the bureaucratic administrative machine were the standing army and the standing navy. Up to the seventeenth century princes relied upon feudal levies, the "free companies" of condottieri, and their palace guards for military power. Even a great king like the ruler of France did not possess military powers greater than many of his subjects. Louis XIII (1610–43), for example, made war on relatively even terms against coalitions of his barons, the city of La Rochelle, the Huguenot towns of the south, and the Protestants in Navarre. He had difficulty assembling an army stronger than the ones available to either Huguenots or noblemen. By the end of the seventeenth century, however, all over Europe there were armies of professional soldiers wearing the king's coat, supplied and fed from the king's storehouse, paid by the king's treasury, and ruled by the king's war minister. The time was past when a great baron or a city could defy the royal authority with military power.

In a way this appearance of standing armies was a return of the Roman legions to the Continent, and it is undoubtedly related to the same economic forces that had allowed the government of Rome to guard the frontier and to keep the peace with the professional soldiers. When the monetary economy gave way to one of sustenance and barter, the Roman soldiers and the Roman bureaucracy disappeared, for the absolute *sine qua non* for a standing army is money that can be collected by taxation. By the seventeenth century the extension of trade and manufacturing, lubricated by gold and silver from the new world, had re-established a monetary economy in most of Europe. It is probably not surprising that soldiers reappeared at the same time, for soldiers and sailors can protect commerce and society and therefore trade will carry the burden of their support.

At the same time the political rivalries between the communities of Europe that had been building up for a century or more emerged as full-blown problems unrelated to the religious issues that had beclouded them in the preceding century. The rise of bureaucratic governments interested in extending the empire of taxation, and concerned with problems of strategic defenses, colonial rivalries, and commercial competition, as well as with the dynastic interests of the monarch, led to the conception of policy based upon reason of state. The treaties of Westphalia (1648), Nijmwegen (1678), and Ryswick (1697) successively mark the rise of the idea that the state has a reason of its own, and therefore its central government has need of power to implement it.

Actually, of course, in the second half of the seventeenth century, the preponderant power of France forced the rest of Europe to reorganize both politically and militarily to avoid falling under French domination. Louis XIV probably made his most important contribution to the historical process of his age not in France, but in the neighboring states that had to reorganize to meet his power.

One must be careful not to simplify so complex a problem as the emergence of the bureaucratic state. It was not only the great increase of commerce and a monetary economy, and the emergence of the idea of reason of state. Indeed, one should consider changes in the art of warfare, the development and expansion of legal conceptions, the religious rebellion that had placed princes at the head of state churches, and perhaps a host of other, lesser, forces that contributed to the process. For several hundred years princes had been striving consciously or unconsciously to enlarge the power of their central administration. The chief instruments of this process had always been the bourgeois figures trained in law, finance, or administration who entered the royal government. These "men of the pen" in contrast to the "men of the sword" had every interest in seeing the king's government strong. The seventeenth century saw an acceleration of the process. All over Europe learned graduates of the law schools or men trained in the counting houses entered governmental service, and in the second half of the century these men came to predominate in the royal councils. When the "men of the pen" crowded the noblemen and princes of the blood from the benches around the king's council table, the bureaucratic centralized monarchy had arrived.

Naturally such a development of centralized bureaucracy did not occur without protest. In England, in France, in Hungary, and in many other states this protest took the form of armed rebellion. In France rebellious noblemen and Huguenots challenged Louis XIII's government time and again. The tenacity of the King and the genius of his great minister, Richelieu, brought victory to the royal arms, but when both the King and the Cardinal were dead, the forces of opposition again tried to rebel. These revolts, called the Fronde (1649–52), failed as much because of disunion in the camp of the opposition as because of the skill of the Cardinal Mazarin, the first minister of the regency government. The English civil war that led to the execution of Charles I and the creation of a new government made the middle years of the century even more turbulent in England than they were in France. In Brandenburg-Prussia, in Sweden, in Russia and elsewhere, the revolts came in the second half of the century. The results were nearly everywhere the same. In most of the continental states the king's government was triumphant; both nobles and townsmen were brought to heel. In England the central authority emerged as the real power in the kingdom, but its direction came to be controlled by Parliament rather than by an absolute king. Nonetheless, the rise of the English treasury and of the admiralty bespeaks the victory of the centralizing forces in society. Poland is the striking example of the state in which this centralizing process failed to achieve a victory. The Polish kingdom was left so weak and disorganized that the partitions of the eighteenth century were the inevitable results. Obviously the form of the political process demanded conformity of development in the various states of Europe; failure to create a centralized bureaucratic government invited disaster.

A revolution such as this one naturally required rationalization to make it acceptable to men. The political theorist explains what is happening in politics and in a measure helps to establish the pattern of the process. He also presents a measure of the civilization that he represents, for the political theorist picks up arguments in his environment and, by his assumptions, indicates what his society believed to be true beyond all need of questioning. Thus the theorist provides an excellent mirror in which we can see the political process as well as the intellectual climate of an era. The following selections have been chosen to bring out the rationale that men developed to explain the political developments of their age.

The great moral question that rulers and theorists alike had to face involved the relationship between the power or "might" to establish a government and rule a people, and the authority or "right" to conduct that rule. Political theorists of the Graeco-Roman era as well as of the Christian Middle Ages had almost universally condemned the exercise of naked power as tyranny and despotism. Thus men nourished in the classical tradition (as European men of culture were) had to find "right" or authority for the exercise of power. The first three selections illustrate three different approaches to this question.

The first selection, by Thomas Hobbes, brutally bases power and authority upon a necessity that he finds in the nature of man and society. Hobbes is a product of the scientific thought of his century. He pushes aside legal and theological argument and stands firmly upon a theory of psychology and society that made him both one of the most read and one of the most unpopular theorists of his age. To many of his contemporaries his frank materialism and cynical realism about men's motives, as well as his scarcely concealed rejection of Christianity, seemed monstrous and insupportable. No political philosopher after Hobbes, however, could afford to ignore the problem that *The Leviathan* posits. Like most medieval and Renaissance theorists, and, for that matter, political thinkers of the next hundred years, Hobbes assumes the medieval legal formula of the contract as the basic legal principle of society. This was the natural form for a political theory in the seventeenth century just as the idea of evolution and emergence provides a frame for theorists of our day. His analysis of the contract, however, is made dependent upon his conception of man and society rather than upon any medieval legalism. The student should be sure to understand how Hobbes has combined both power and authority in the hands of the Leviathan and given sanctity to the situation.

The second selection is from the works of the great Bishop of Meaux, Jacques Bénigne Bossuet. It was written for the instruction and edification of the Dauphin, the son of Louis XIV. The Bishop's solution is much less complex than that of the English materialist. He saw the world through the eyes of the Bible, St. Augustine, and St. Thomas, and he himself was convinced that order and authority were essential for society. Louis' government, therefore, was good, and both Louis' power and his authority were the gift and the institution of God. The Divine Right theory never found a more eloquent protagonist than Bossuet, but by the time that he propounded it, the process of history was already making kings into the first servants of states, and Divine Right was on the verge of becoming an ornamental anachronism to which men gave only lip service. Nonetheless, in Bossuet's pages we find seventeenth century Europe's testimony to its religious faith just as Hobbes manifests its growing materialism.

The third selection is a justification for the English Revolution of 1688. John Locke ably states the Whig case that a king must obey the law or forfeit the throne. Both power and authority, according to Locke, are derived from the people who delegate power to kings, but who can never give up their authority or right to anyone. Thus, as long as princes obey the law, that is, satisfy the people, they are allowed to rule, but the people do not thereby surrender their right to change rulers if princes abuse their power. Locke has been hailed as the theorist of modern constitutionalism. Indeed, the men who made the revolutions in Europe and America at the end of the eighteenth century were certainly inspired by his thinking. It must be noted, however, that neither Locke nor the men who made the English Revolution of 1688 had any intention of disrupting royal authority; they merely wanted to be sure that the king did not act arbitrarily and beyond the law. In reality the Revolution of 1688 is well within the form of the political process of the seventeenth century, for Parliament willingly strengthened the central authority to achieve its ends in war, and thereby gave England the most effective government in Europe. The "democratic" tendencies inherent in Locke's argument did not manifest themselves until almost a century after his death.

The next four items do not wander far from the first three. Less theoretical, they deal with the problem of the king's "right" as a question of conscience and policy rather than as a philosophical or theological proposition. Omer Talon, one of the foremost jurists of the Parlement of Paris, presented his argument in full Parlement before the Regent, Anne of Austria, and the boy King, Louis XIV. It was a bold statement for its day: only a few years before, Richelieu and Louis XIII would never have tolerated such "advice" from a jurist. Talon does not question the right of the king to rule, but he tries to insist that law, custom, and tradition place limits upon the exercise of royal power. He belongs to that company of men who feared the Leviathan and tried to forge a ring to put in its nose so that the creature could be managed more easily.

The next selection was written by Louis XIV as instructions for his infant son. Both Louis and his father before him had ascended the throne while still children, and he felt that he, too, must count upon the possibility of his death before his son came of age. Actually he outlived both his son and his grandson. Louis' discussion is interesting as much for the window that it provides into the mind of the King as for the subject of his discussion. He cheerfully takes full credit for the work of his predecessor, Mazarin, and assumes that the improvements in the entourage that surrounded him in 1661 were the result of his wisdom. He also, however, shows us clearly his attitude toward the problem of government and the rôle of the king in society. This piece should be compared with the advice that Louis prepared for his grandson, Philip, when the latter accepted the throne of Spain (the last item in the present section). It is interesting to see the differences between the advice of Louis as a young ruler and as a mature monarch.

Fénelon's *Examination of Conscience* was one of the most searching criticisms of the régime of Louis XIV ever written. For many years, indeed until an autographed copy was found, it was not believed that this document could have been circulated in the French court during Louis' lifetime. Fénelon, the Archbishop of Cambrai, was tutor to Louis' talented grandson, the Duke of Burgundy. He was a theologian, a moralist, an historian, and a philosopher. He does not question the King's *right* to rule, but, like Talon before him, he insists that custom and law both human and divine must curb the willfulness of a prince. This document, written for the edification of the Duke of Burgundy, was only one of Fénelon's treatises on politics in which he insisted upon the moral obligations that government imposes upon a ruler.

In considering the selections in this section one should keep in mind the central problems of "right" and "power" as the basis for government. The men who wrote these documents were confronted with grave political problems that threatened to undo society: rebellion and tyranny are equally destructive. The paramount fact of their world was the imperative necessity for the exercise of power; the greatest problem confronting them was the moral right with which that power was to be used.

I. BY WHAT RIGHT DOES GOVERNMENT EXIST?

A. *Thomas Hobbes'* Leviathan

Educated at Oxford and a frequent visitor to the Continent, Thomas Hobbes (1588–1679) was one of the most important political theorists of all time. He was acquainted with Bacon, Gassendi, Campanella, Descartes, Galileo, and many others who were giving the western mind a new orientation through science. He himself was never more than an amateur in the natural sciences, but his attempt to place political philosophy on a scientific basis made him one of the first modern political theorists. Obviously Hobbes was attacking the violence and the anarchy that accompanied the English civil wars, but even more, he was attempting to establish a secure intellectual basis for the government of his king. His materialistic premises and his rigorous logic made him one of the most controversial figures of the age.

[13.] *Of the natural condition of mankind as concerning their felicity and misery*

. . . in the nature of man, we find three principal causes of quarrel. First, competition; secondly, diffidence; thirdly, glory.

The first, maketh men invade for gain; the second, for safety; and the third, for reputation. The first use violence, to make themselves masters of other men's persons, wives, children, and cattle; the second, to defend them; the third, for trifles, as a word, a smile, a different opinion, and any other sign of undervalue, either direct in their persons, or by reflection in their kindred, their friends, their nation, their profession, or their name.

Hereby it is manifest, that during the time men live without a common power to keep them all in awe, they are in that condition which is called war;

and such a war, as is of every man, against every man. For war consisteth not in battle only, or the act of fighting; but in a tract of time, wherein the will to contend by battle is sufficiently known: and therefore the notion of *time* is to be considered in the nature of war; as it is in the nature of weather. For as the nature of foul weather lieth not in a shower or two of rain; but in an inclination thereto of many days together: so the nature of war, consisteth not in actual fighting; but in the known disposition thereto, during all the time there is no assurance to the contrary. All other time is peace.

Whatsoever therefore is consequent to a time of war, where every man is enemy to every man; the same is consequent to the time, wherein men live without other security, than what their own strength, and their own invention shall furnish them withal. In such condition, there is no place for industry, because the fruit thereof is uncertain: and consequently no culture of the earth; no navigation, nor use of the commodities that may be imported by sea; no commodious building; no instruments of moving, and removing, such things as require much force; no knowledge of the face of the earth; no account of time; no arts; no letters; no society; and which is worst of all, continual fear, and danger of violent death; and the life of man, solitary, poor, nasty, brutish, and short.

It may seem strange to some man, that has not well weighed these things; that nature should thus dissociate, and render men apt to invade, and destroy one another: and he may therefore, not trusting to this inference, made from the passions, desire perhaps to have the same confirmed by experience. Let him therefore consider with himself, when taking a journey, he arms himself, and seeks to go well accompanied; when going to sleep, he locks his doors; when even in his house he locks his chests; and this when he knows there be laws, and public officers, armed, to revenge all injuries shall be done him; what opinion he has of his fellow-subjects, when he rides armed; of his fellow citizens, when he locks his doors; and of his children, and servants, when he locks his chests. Does he not there as much accuse mankind by his actions, as I do by my words? But neither of us accuse man's nature in it. The desires, and other passions of man, are in themselves no sin. No more are the actions, that proceed from those passions, till they know a law that forbids them: which till laws be made they cannot know: nor can any law be made, till they have agreed upon the person that shall make it.

The passions that incline men to peace, are fear of death; desire of such things as are necessary to commodious living; and a hope by their industry to obtain them. And reason suggesteth convenient articles of peace, upon which men may be drawn to agreement. These articles, are they, which otherwise are called the Laws of Nature: whereof I shall speak more particularly in the two following chapters.

[14.] *Of the first and second natural laws, and of contracts*

The Right of Nature, which writers commonly call *jus naturale*, is the liberty each man hath, to use his own power, as he will himself, for the preservation of his own nature; that is to say, of his own life; and consequently, of doing anything, which in his own judgment, and reason, he shall conceive to be the aptest means thereunto.

By Liberty, is understood, according to the proper signification of the word, the absence of external impediments: which impediments, may oft take away part of a man's power to do what he would; but cannot hinder him from using the power left him, according to his judgment, and reason shall dictate to him.

A Law of Nature, *lex naturalis*, is a precept or general rule, found out by reason, by which a man is forbidden to do that, which is destructive of his life, or taketh away the means of preserving the same; and to omit that, by which he thinketh it may be best preserved. For though they that speak of this subject, use to confound *jus*, and *lex*, *right* and *law*: yet they ought to be distinguished; because Right consisteth in liberty to do, or to forbear; whereas Law, determineth, and bindeth to one of them: so that law, and right, differ as much, as obligation, and liberty; which in one and the same matter are inconsistent.

And because the condition of man, as hath been declared in the precedent chapter, is a condition of war of every one against every one; in which case every one is governed by his own reason; and there is nothing he can make use of, that may not be a help unto him, in preserving his life against his enemies; it followeth, that in such a condition, every man has a right to every thing; even to one another's body. And therefore, as long as this natural right of every man to every thing endureth, there can be no security to any man, how strong or wise soever he be, of living out the time, which nature ordinarily alloweth men to live. And consequently it is a precept, or general rule of reason, *that every man ought to endeavour peace, as far as he has hope of obtaining it; and when he cannot obtain it, that he may seek, and use, all helps, and advantages of war.* The first breach of which rule, containeth the first, and fundamental law of nature; which is, *to seek peace, and follow it.* The second, the sum of the right of nature; which is, *by all means we can, to defend ourselves.*

From this fundamental law of nature, by which men are commanded to endeavour peace, is derived this second law; *that a man be willing, when others are so too, as far forth, as for peace, and defence of himself he shall think it necessary, to lay down this right to all things; and be contented with so much liberty against other men, as he would allow other men against himself.* For as long as every man holdeth this right, of doing any thing he liketh; so long are all men in the condition of war. But if other men will not lay down their right, as well as he; then there is no reason for any one, to divest himself of his: for that were to expose himself to prey, which no man is bound to, rather than to dispose himself to peace. This is that law of the Gospel; *whatsoever you require that others should do to you, that do ye to them.* And that law of all men *quod tibi fieri non vis, alteri ne feceris.*

To *lay down* a man's *right* to any thing, is to *divest* himself of the *liberty*, of hindering another of the benefit of his own right to the same. For he that renounceth, or passeth away his right, giveth not to any other man a right which he had not before; because there is nothing to which every man had not right by nature: but only standeth out of his way, that he may enjoy his own original right, without hindrance from him; not without hindrance from another. So that the effect which redoundeth to one man, by another man's defect of right, is but so much diminution of impediments to the use of his own right original.

Right is laid aside, either by simply renouncing it; or by transferring it to another. By *simply* Renouncing; when he cares not to whom the benefit thereof redoundeth. By Transferring; when he intendeth the benefit thereof to some certain person, or persons. And when a man hath in either manner abandoned, or granted away his right; then is he said to be Obliged, or Bound, not to hinder those, to whom such right is granted, or abandoned, from the benefit of it . . . : and that such hindrance is Injustice, and Injury, as being *sine jure;* the right being before renounced, or transferred. So that *injury,* or *injustice,* in the controversies of the world, is somewhat like to that, which in the disputations of scholars is called *absurdity.* For as it is there called an absurdity, to contradict what one maintained in the beginning: so in the world, it is called injustice, and injury, voluntarily to undo that, which from the beginning he had voluntarily done. The way by which a man either simply renounceth, or transferreth his right, is a declaration, or signification, by some voluntary and sufficient sign, or signs, that he doth so renounce, or transfer; or hath so renounced, or transferred the same, to him that accepteth it. And these signs are either words only, or actions only; or, as it happeneth most often, both words, and actions. And the same are the Bonds, by which men are bound, and obliged: bonds, that have their strength, not from their own nature, for nothing is more easily broken than a man's word, but from fear of some evil consequence upon the rupture. . . .

The mutual transferring of right, is that which men call Contract. . . . One of the contractors may deliver the thing contracted for on his part, and leave the other to perform his part at some determinate time after, and in the mean time be trusted; and then the contract on his part is called Pact, or Covenant: or both parts may contract now, to perform hereafter: in which cases, he that is to perform in time to come, being trusted, his performance is called *keeping of promise,* or faith; and the failing of performance, if it be voluntary, *violation of faith.*

When the transferring of right, is not mutual: but one of the parties transferreth, in hope to gain thereby friendship, or service from another, or from his friends; or in hope to gain the reputation of charity, or magnanimity; or to deliver his mind from the pain of compassion; or in hope of reward in heaven; this is not contract, but Gift, Free-Gift, Grace: which words signify one and the same thing. . . .

If a covenant be made, wherein neither of the parties perform presently, but trust one another; in the condition of mere nature, which is a condition of war every man against every man, upon any reasonable suspicion, it is void: but if there be a common power set over them both, with right and force sufficient to compel performance, it is not void. For he that performeth first, has no assurance the other will perform after; because the bonds of words are too weak to bridle men's ambition, avarice, anger, and other passions, without the fear of some coercive power; which in the condition of mere nature, where all men are equal, and judges of the justness of their own fears, cannot possibly be supposed. And therefore he which performeth first, does but betray himself to his enemy; contrary to the right, he can never abandon, of defending his life, and means of living.

But in a civil estate, where there is a power set up to constrain those that would otherwise violate their faith, that fear is no more reasonable; and for that cause, he which by the covenant is to perform first, is obliged so to do.

The cause of fear, which maketh such a covenant invalid, must be always something arising after the covenant made; as some new fact, or other sign of the will not to perform; else it cannot make the covenant void. For that which could not hinder a man from promising, ought not to be admitted as a hindrance of performing.

He that transferreth any right, transferreth the means of enjoying it, as far as lieth in his power. As he that selleth land, is understood to transfer the herbage, and whatsoever grows upon it: nor can he that sells a mill turn away the stream that drives it. And they that give to a man the right of government in sovereignty, are understood to give him the right of levying money to maintain soldiers; and of appointing magistrates for the administration of justice.

The force of words being, as I have formerly noted, too weak to hold men to the performance of their covenants; there are in man's nature, but two imaginable helps to strengthen it. And those are either a fear of the consequence of breaking their word; or a glory, or pride in appearing not to need to break it. This latter is a generosity too rarely found to be presumed on, especially in the pursuers of wealth, command, or sensual pleasure; which are the greatest part of mankind. The passion to be reckoned upon is fear; whereof there be two very general objects: one, the power of spirits invisible; the other, the power of those men they shall therein offend. Of these two, though the former be the greater power, yet the fear of the latter is commonly the greater fear. The fear of the former is in every man, his own religion: which hath place in the nature of man before civil society. The latter hath not so; at least not place enough, to keep men to their promises; because in the condition of mere nature, the inequality of power is not discerned, but by the event of battle. So that before the time of civil society, or in the interruption thereof by war, there is nothing can strengthen a covenant of peace agreed

on, against the temptations of avarice, ambition, lust, or other strong desire, but the fear of that invisible power, which they every one worship as God; and fear as a revenger of their perfidy. All therefore that can be done between two men not subject to civil power, is to put one another to swear by the God he feareth. . . .

[15.] *Of other laws of nature*

From that law of nature, by which we are obliged to transfer to another, such rights, as being retained, hinder the peace of mankind, there followeth a third; which is this, *that men perform their covenants made:* without which, covenants are in vain, and but empty words; and the right of all men to all things remaining, we are still in the condition of war.

And in this law of nature, consisteth the fountain and original of Justice. For where no covenant hath preceded, there hath no right been transferred, and every man has right to every thing; and consequently, no action can be unjust. But when a covenant is made, then to break it is *unjust:* and the definition of Injustice is no other than *the not performance of covenant.* And whatsoever is not unjust, is *just.*

But because covenants of mutual trust, where there is a fear of not performance on either part, as hath been said in the former chapter, are invalid; though the original of justice be the making of covenants; yet injustice actually there can be none, till the cause of such fear be taken away; which while men are in the natural condition of war, cannot be done. Therefore before the names of just, and unjust can have place, there must be some coercive power, to compel men equally to the performance of their covenants, by the terror of some punishment, greater than the benefit they expect by the breach of their covenant; and to make good that propriety, which by mutual contract men acquire, in recompense of the universal right they abandon: and such power there is none before the erection of a commonwealth. And this is also to be gathered out of the ordinary definition of justice in the Schools: for they say, that *justice is the constant will of giving to every man his own.* And therefore where there is no *own,* that is no propriety, there is no injustice; and where is no coercive power erected, that is, where there is no commonwealth, there is no propriety; all men having right to all things: therefore where there is no commonwealth, there nothing is unjust. So that the nature of justice, consisteth in keeping of valid covenants: but the validity of covenants begins not but with the constitution of a civil power, sufficient to compel men to keep them: and then it is also that propriety begins.

[18.] *Of the rights of sovereigns by institution*

A *commonwealth* is said to be *instituted,* when a *multitude* of men do agree, and *covenant, every one,* with every one, that to whatsoever *man,* or *assembly of men,* shall be given by the major part, the *right* to *present* the person of them all, that is to say, to be their *representative;* every one, as well he that *voted for it,* as he that *voted against it,* shall *authorize* all the actions and judgments, of that man, or assembly of men, in the same manner, as if they were his own, to the end, to live peaceably amongst themselves, and be protected against other men.

From this institution of a commonwealth are derived all the *rights,* and *faculties* of him, or them, on whom sovereign power is conferred by the consent of the people assembled.

First, because they covenant, it is to be understood, they are not obliged by former covenant to anything repugnant hereunto. And consequently they that have already instituted a commonwealth, being thereby bound by covenant, to own the actions, and judgments of one, cannot lawfully make a new covenant, amongst themselves, to be obedient to any other, in any thing whatsoever, without his permission. And therefore, they that are subject to a monarch, cannot without his leave cast off monarchy, and return to the confusion of a disunited multitude; nor transfer their person from him that beareth it, to another man, or other assembly of men: for they are bound, every man to every man, to own, and be reputed author of all, that he that already is their sovereign, shall do, and judge fit to be done: so that any one man dissenting, all the rest should break their covenant made to that man, which is injustice: and they have also every man given the sovereignty to him that beareth their person; and therefore if they depose him, they take from him that which is his own, and so again it is injustice. Besides, if he that attempteth to depose his sovereign, be killed, or punished by him for such attempt, he is author of his own punishment, as being by the institution, author of all his sovereign shall do: and because it is injustice for a man to do anything, for which he may be punished by his own authority, he is also upon that title, unjust. And whereas some men have pretended for their disobedience to their sovereign, a new covenant, made not with men, but with God; this also is unjust: for there is no covenant with God, but by mediation of somebody that representeth God's person; which none doth but God's lieutenant, who hath the sovereignty under God. But this pretence of covenant with God is so evident a lie, even in the pretenders' own consciences, that it is not only an act of an unjust, but also of a vile and unmanly disposition.

Secondly, because the right of bearing the person of them all, is given to him they make sovereign, by covenant only of one to another, and not of him to any of them; there can happen no breach of covenant on the part of the sovereign; and consequently none of his subjects, by any pretence of forfeiture, can be freed from his subjection. That he which is made sovereign maketh no covenant with his subjects beforehand, is manifest; because either he must make it with the whole multitude, as one party to the covenant; or he must make a several covenant with every man. With the whole, as one party, it is impossible; because as yet they are not one person: and if he make so many several covenants as there be men, those covenants after he hath the sovereignty are void; because what act soever can be pretended by any one of them for breach thereof, is the act both of himself, and of all the rest, because done in the person, and by the right of every one of them in particular. Besides, if any one, or more of them, pretend a breach of the covenant made by the sovereign at his institution; and others, or one other of his subjects, or himself alone, pretend there was no such breach, there is in this case, no judge to decide the controversy; it returns therefore to the sword again; and every man recovereth the right of protecting himself by his own strength, contrary to the design they had in the institution. It is therefore in vain to grant sovereignty by way of precedent covenant. The opinion that any monarch receiveth his power by covenant, that is to say, on condition, proceedeth from want of understanding this easy truth, that covenants being but words and breath, have no force to oblige, contain, constrain, or protect any man, but what it has from the public sword; that is,

from the untied hands of that man, or assembly of men that hath the sovereignty, and whose actions are avouched by them all, and performed by the strength of them all, in him united. But when an assembly of men is made sovereign; then no man imagineth any such covenant to have passed in the institution; for no man is so dull as to say, for example, the people of Rome made a covenant with the Romans, to hold the sovereignty on such or such conditions; which not performed, the Romans might lawfully depose the Roman people. That men see not the reason to be alike in a monarchy, and in a popular government, proceedeth from the ambition of some, that are kinder to the government of an assembly, whereof they may hope to participate, than of monarchy, which they despair to enjoy.

Thirdly, because the major part hath by consenting voices declared a sovereign; he that dissented must now consent with the rest; that is, be contented to avow all the actions he shall do, or else justly be destroyed by the rest. For if he voluntarily entered into the congregation of them that were assembled, he sufficiently declared thereby his will, and therefore tacitly covenanted, to stand to what the major part should ordain: and therefore if he refuse to stand thereto, or make protestation against any of their decrees, he does contrary to his covenant, and therefore unjustly. And whether he be of the congregation, or not; and whether his consent be asked, or not, he must either submit to their decrees, or be left in the condition of war he was in before; wherein he might without injustice be destroyed by any man whatsoever.

Fourthly, because every subject is by this institution author of all the actions, and judgments of the sovereign instituted; it follows, that whatsoever he doth, it can be no injury to any of his subjects; nor ought he to be by any of them accused of injustice. For he that doth anything by authority from another, doth therein no injury to him by whose authority he acteth: but by this institution of a commonwealth, every particular man is author of all the sovereign doth: and consequently he that complaineth of injury from his sovereign, complaineth of that whereof he himself is author; and therefore ought not to accuse any man but himself; no nor himself of injury; because to do injury to one's self, is impossible. It is true that they that have sovereign power may commit iniquity, but not injustice, or injury in the proper signification.

Fifthly, and consequently to that which was said last, no man that hath sovereign power can justly be put to death, or otherwise in any manner by his subjects punished. For seeing every subject is author of the actions of his sovereign; he punisheth another for the actions committed by himself.

And because the end of this institution is the peace and defense of them all; and whosoever has right to the end, has right to the means; it belongeth of right, to whatsoever man, or assembly that hath the sovereignty, to be judge both of the means of peace and defense, and also of the hindrances, and disturbances of the same; and to do whatsoever he shall think necessary to be done, both beforehand, for the preserving of peace and security, by prevention of discord at home, and hostility from abroad; and, when peace and security are lost, for the recovery of the same. And therefore,

Sixthly, it is annexed to the sovereignty, to be judge of what opinions and doctrines are averse, and what conducing to peace; and consequently, on what occasions, how far, and what men are to be trusted withal, in speaking to multitudes of people; and who shall examine the doctrines of all books before they be published. For the actions of men proceed from their opinions; and in the well-governing of opinions, consisteth the well-governing of men's actions, in order to their peace, and concord. And though in matter of doctrine, nothing ought to be regarded but the truth; yet this is not repugnant to regulating the same by peace. For doctrine repugnant to peace can no more be true, than peace and concord can be against the law of nature. It is true, that in a commonwealth, where by the negligence, or unskilfulness of governors, and teachers, false doctrines are by time generally received; the contrary truths may be generally offensive. Yet the most sudden, and rough bursting in of a new truth, that can be, does never break the peace, but only sometimes awake the war. For those men that are so remissly governed, that they dare take up arms to defend, or introduce an opinion, are still in war; and their condition not peace, but only a cessation of arms for fear of one another; and they live, as it were, in the precincts of battle continually. It belongeth therefore to him that hath the sovereign power, to be judge, or constitute all judges of opinions and doctrines, as a thing necessary to peace; thereby to prevent discord and civil war.

Seventhly, is annexed to the sovereignty, the whole power of prescribing the rules, whereby every man may know, what goods he may enjoy, and what actions he may do, without being molested by any of his fellow-subjects; and this is it men call *propriety*. For before constitution of sovereign power, as hath already been shown, all men had right to all things; which necessarily causeth war: and therefore this propriety, being necessary to peace, and depending on sovereign power, is the act of that power, in order to the public peace. These rules of propriety, or *meum* and *tuum,* and of *good, evil, lawful,* and *unlawful* in the actions of subjects, are the civil laws; that is to say, the laws of each commonwealth in particular; though the name of civil law be now restrained to the ancient civil laws of the city of Rome; which being the head of a great part of the world, her laws at that time were in these parts the civil law.

Eighthly, is annexed to the sovereignty, the right of judicature; that is to say, of hearing and deciding all controversies, which may arise concerning law, either civil, or natural; or concerning fact. For without the decision of controversies, there is no protection of one subject, against the injuries of another; the laws concerning *meum* and *tuum* are in vain; and to every man remaineth, from the natural and necessary appetite of his own conservation, the right of protecting himself by his private strength, which is the condition of war, and contrary to the end for which every commonwealth is instituted.

Ninthly, is annexed to the sovereignty, the right of making war and peace with other nations, and commonwealths; that is to say, of judging when it is for the public good, and how great forces are to be assembled, armed, and paid for that end; and to levy money upon the subjects, to defray the expenses thereof. For the power by which the people are to be defended, consisteth in their armies; and the strength of an army, in the union of their strength under one command; which command the sovereign instituted, therefore hath; because the command of the *militia,* without other institution, maketh him that hath it sovereign. And therefore whosoever is made general of an army, he that hath the sovereign power is always generalissimo.

Tenthly, is annexed to the sovereignty, the choosing of all counsellors, ministers, magistrates, and officers, both in peace and war. For seeing the sovereign is charged with the end, which is the common peace and defense, he is understood to have power to use such means, as he shall think most fit for his discharge.

Eleventhly, to the sovereign is committed the power of rewarding with riches, or honour, and of punishing with corporal or pecuniary punishment, or with ignominy, every subject according to the law he hath formerly made; or if there be no law made, according as he shall judge most to conduce to the encouraging of men to serve the commonwealth, or deterring of them from doing disservice to the same.

Lastly, considering what value men are naturally apt to set upon themselves; what respect they look for from others; and how little they value other men; from whence continually arise amongst them, emulation, quarrels, factions, and at last war, to the destroying of one another, and diminution of their strength against a common enemy; it is necessary that there be laws of honour, and a public rate of the worth of such men as have deserved, or are able to deserve well of the commonwealth; and that there be force in the hands of some or other, to put those laws in execution. But it hath already been shown, that not only the whole *militia,* or forces of the commonwealth; but also the judicature of all controversies, is annexed to the sovereignty. To the sovereign therefore it belongeth also to give titles of honour; and to appoint what order of place, and dignity, each man shall hold; and what signs of respect, in public or private meetings, they shall give to one another.

These are the rights, which make the essence of sovereignty; and which are the marks, whereby a man may discern in what man, or assembly of men, the sovereign power is placed, and resideth. For these are incommunicable, and inseparable. The power to coin money; to dispose of the estate and persons of infant heirs; to have præemption in markets; and all other statute prerogatives, may be transferred by the sovereign; and yet the power to protect his subjects be retained. But if he transfer the *militia*, he retains the judicature in vain, for want of execution of the laws: or if he grant away the power of raising money; the *militia* is in vain; or if he give away the government of doctrines, men will be frighted into rebellion with the fear of spirits. And so if we consider any one of the said rights, we shall presently see that the holding of all the rest will produce no effect, in the conservation of peace and justice, the end for which all commonwealths are instituted. And this division is it, whereof it is said, *a kingdom divided in itself cannot stand:* for unless this division precede, division into opposite armies can never happen.

[21.] *Of the liberty of subjects*

Liberty, or freedom, signifieth, properly, the absence of opposition; by opposition, I mean external impediments of motion; and may be applied no less to irrational, and inanimate creatures, than to rational. For whatsoever is so tied, or environed, as it cannot move but within a certain space, which space is determined by the opposition of some external body, we say it hath not liberty to go further. And so of all living creatures, whilst they are imprisoned, or restrained, with walls, or chains; and of the water whilst it is kept in by banks, or vessels, that otherwise would spread itself into a larger space, we use to say, they are not at liberty, to move in such manner, as without those external impediments they would. But when the impediment of motion, is in the constitution of the thing itself, we use not to say; it wants the liberty; but the power to move; as when a stone lieth still, or

a man is fastened to his bed by sickness.

And according to this proper, and generally received meaning of the word, a Freeman, *is he, that in those things, which by his strength and wit he is able to do, is not hindered to do what he has a will to.* But when the words *free,* and *liberty,* are applied to any thing but bodies, they are abused; for that which is not subject to motion is not subject to impediment: and therefore, when it is said, for example, the way is free, no liberty of the way is signified, but of those that walk in it without stop. And when we say a gift is free, there is not meant any liberty of the gift, but of the giver, that was not bound by any law or covenant to give it. So when we *speak freely,* it is not the liberty of voice, or pronunciation, but of the man, whom no law hath obliged to speak otherwise than he did. Lastly, from the use of the word *free-will,* no liberty can be inferred of the will, desire, or inclination, but the liberty of the man; which consisteth in this, that he finds no stop, in doing what he has the will, desire, or inclination to do.

But as men, for the attaining of peace, and conservation of themselves thereby, have made an artificial man, which we call a commonwealth; so also have they made artificial chains, called *civil laws,* which they themselves, by mutual covenants, have fastened at one end, to the lips of that man, or assembly, to whom they have given the sovereign power; and at the other end to their own ears. These bonds, in their own nature but weak, may nevertheless be made to hold, by the danger, though not by the difficulty of breaking them.

In relation to these bonds only it is, that I am to speak now, of the *liberty* of *subjects.* For seeing there is no commonwealth in the world, wherein there be rules enough set down, for the regulating of all the actions, and words of men; as being a thing impossible: it followeth necessarily, that in all kinds of actions by the laws praetermitted, men have the liberty, of doing what their own reasons shall suggest, for the most profitable to themselves. For if we take liberty in the proper sense, for corporal liberty; that is to say, freedom from chains and prison; it were very absurd for men to clamour as they do, for the liberty they so manifestly enjoy. Again, if we take liberty, for an exemption from laws, it is no less absurd, for men to demand as they do, that liberty, by which all other men may be masters of their lives. And yet, as absurd as it is, this is it they demand; not knowing that the laws are of no power to protect them, without a sword in the hands of a man, or men, to cause those laws to be put in execution. The liberty of a subject, lieth therefore only in those things, which in regulating their actions, the sovereign hath praetermitted: such as is the liberty to buy, and sell, and otherwise contract with one another; to choose their own abode, their own diet, their own trade of life, and institute their children as they themselves think fit; and the like.

Nevertheless we are not to understand, that by such liberty, the sovereign power of life and death, is either abolished, or limited. For it has been already shown, that nothing the sovereign representative can do to a subject, on what pretence soever, can properly be called injustice, or injury; because every subject is author of every act the sovereign doth; so that he never wanteth right to any thing, otherwise, than as he himself is the subject of God, and bound thereby to observe the laws of nature. And therefore it may, and doth often happen in commonwealths, that a subject may be put to death, by the command of the sovereign power; and yet neither do the other wrong; as when

Jeptha caused his daughter to be sacrificed: in which, and the like cases, he that so dieth, had liberty to do the action, for which he is nevertheless, without injury put to death. And the same holdeth also in a sovereign prince, that putteth to death an innocent subject. For though the action be against the law of nature, as being contrary to equity, as was the killing of Uriah, by David; yet it was not an injury to Uriah, but to God. Not to Uriah, because the right to do what he pleased was given him by Uriah himself: and yet to God, because David was God's subject, and prohibited all iniquity by the law of nature. . . .

The liberty, whereof there is so frequent and honourable mention, in the histories, and philosophy of the ancient Greeks, and Romans, and in the writings, and discourse of those that from them have received all their learning in the politics, is not the liberty of particular men; but the liberty of the commonwealth: which is the same with that which every man then should have, if there were no civil laws, nor commonwealth at all. And the effects of it also be the same. For as amongst masterless men, there is perpetual war, of every man against his neighbour; no inheritance, to transmit to the son, nor to expect from the father; no propriety of goods, or lands; no security; but a full and absolute liberty in every particular man: so in states, and commonwealths not dependent on one another, every commonwealth, not every man, has an absolute liberty, to do what it shall judge, that is to say, what that man, or assembly that representeth it, shall judge most conducing to their benefit. But withal, they live in the condition of a perpetual war, and upon the confines of battle, with their frontiers armed, and cannons planted against their neighbours round about. The Athenians, and Romans were free; that is, free commonwealths: not that any particular men had the liberty to resist their own representative. . . . There is written on the turrets of the city of Lucca in great characters at this day, the word LIBERTAS; yet no man can thence infer, that a particular man has more liberty, or immunity from the service of the commonwealth there, than in Constantinople. Whether a commonwealth be monarchical, or popular, the freedom is still the same.

To come now to the particulars of the true liberty of a subject; that is to say, what are the things, which though commanded by the sovereign, he may nevertheless, without injustice, refuse to do; we are to consider, what rights we pass away, when we make a commonwealth; or, which is all one, what liberty we deny ourselves, by owning all the actions, without exception, of the man, or assembly, we make our sovereign. For in the act of our *submission*, consisteth both our *obligation*, and our *liberty*; which must therefore be inferred by arguments taken from thence; there being no obligation on any man, which ariseth not from some act of his own; for all men equally are by nature free. And because such arguments, must either be drawn from the express words, *I authorize all his actions*, or from the intention of him that submitteth himself to his power, which intention is to be understood by the end for which he so submitteth; the obligation, and liberty of the subject, is to be derived, either from those words, or others equivalent; or else from the end of the institution of sovereignty, namely, the peace of the subjects within themselves, and their defense against a common enemy.

First therefore, seeing sovereignty by institution, is by covenant of every one to every one; and sovereignty by acquisition, by covenants of the van-

quished to the victor, or child to the parent; it is manifest, that every subject has liberty in all those things, the right whereof cannot by covenant be transferred. I have shown before in the 14th chapter, that covenants, not to defend a man's own body, are void. Therefore,

If the sovereign command a man, though justly condemned, to kill, wound, or maim himself; or not to resist those that assault him; or to abstain from the use of food, air, medicine, or any other thing, without which he cannot live; yet hath that man the liberty to disobey.

If a man be interrogated by the sovereign, or his authority, concerning a crime done by himself, he is not bound, without assurance of pardon, to confess it; because no man . . . can be obliged by covenant to accuse himself.

Again, the consent of a subject to sovereign power, is contained in these words, *I authorize, or take upon me, all his actions;* in which there is no restriction at all, of his own former natural liberty: for by allowing him to *kill* me, I am not bound to kill myself when he commands me. It is one thing to say, *kill me, or my fellow, if you please;* another thing to say, *I will kill myself, or my fellow.* It followeth therefore, that

No man is bound by the words themselves, either to kill himself, or any other man; and consequently, that the obligation a man may sometimes have, upon the command of the sovereign to execute any dangerous, or dishonourable office, dependeth not on the words of our submission; but on the intention, which is to be understood by the end thereof. When therefore our refusal to obey, frustrates the end for which the sovereignty was ordained; then there is no liberty to refuse: otherwise there is.

Upon this ground, a man that is commanded as a soldier to fight against the enemy, though his sovereign have right enough to punish his refusal with death may nevertheless in many cases refuse, without injustice; as when he substituteth a sufficient soldier in his place: for in this case he deserteth not the service of the commonwealth. And there is allowance to be made for natural timorousness; not only to women, of whom no such dangerous duty is expected, but also to men of feminine courage. . . .

To resist the sword of the commonwealth, in defense of another man, guilty, or innocent, no man hath liberty; because such liberty, takes away from the sovereign, the means of protecting us; and is therefore destructive of the very essence of government. . . .

As for other liberties, they depend on the silence of the law. In cases where the sovereign has prescribed no rule, there the subject hath the liberty to do, or forbear, according to his own discretion. And therefore such liberty is in some places more, and in some less; and in some times more, in other times less, according as they that have the sovereignty shall think most convenient. . . .

If a monarch, or sovereign assembly, grant a liberty to all, or any of his subjects, which grant standing, he is disabled to provide for their safety, the grant is void; unless he directly renounce, or transfer the sovereignty to another. For in that he might openly, if it had been his will, and in plain terms, have renounced, or transferred it, and did not; it is to be understood it was not his will, but that the grant proceeded from ignorance of the repugnancy between such a liberty and the sovereign power; and therefore the sovereignty is still retained; and consequently all those powers, which are necessary to the exercising thereof; such as are the power of war, and peace, of judicature, of appointing officers, and councillors, of levying money, and the rest named in the 18th chapter.

The obligation of subjects to the sovereign, is understood to last as long, and no longer, than the power lasteth, by which he is able to protect them. For the right men have by nature to protect themselves, when none else can protect them, can by no covenant be relinquished. The sovereignty is the soul of the commonwealth; which once departed from the body, the members do no more receive their motion from it. The end of obedience is protection; which, wheresoever a man seeth it, either in his own, or in another's sword, nature applieth his obedience to it, and his endeavour to maintain it. And though sovereignty, in the intention of them that make it, be immortal; yet is it in its own nature, not only subject to violent death, by foreign war; but also through the ignorance, and passions of men, it hath in it, from the very institution, many seeds of a natural mortality, by intestine discord. . . .

Thomas Hobbes, *Leviathan* (1651), *passim.*

B. Bossuet's Politics Drawn from the Holy Scriptures

One of the greatest orators of seventeenth century France, Jacques Bénigne Bossuet (1627–1704), Bishop of Meaux and tutor to Louis XIV's son, the Dauphin, was perhaps the most important Catholic thinker of Louis' court. His numerous sermons, theological treatises, and historical studies entitle him to the position of leader of the conservative party in the France of his day.

[BOOK I]

I. *Man is made to live in society*

1st Proposition: Men have only one real goal and one real object, which is God. "Hear O Israel: The Lord our

God is one Lord. Thou shalt love the Lord thy God with thy whole heart, and with thy whole soul, and with thy whole strength" (Deut. 6:4, 5).

2nd Proposition: The love of God obliges men to love one another. ". . . we ought to love each other because we ought all to love the same God who is our common father."

3rd Proposition: All men are brothers. First of all they are all children of the same God. "All you are brethren and call none your father upon earth; for one is your father in heaven" (Matt. 23:8, 9). Those we call fathers and from whom we are descended according to the flesh do not know who we are. God alone knows us from all eternity.

5th Proposition: Each man has need of other men. If we are all brothers, all made in the image of God and equally his children, we need to take care of each other, and it is not without reason that it is written, "And He gave to every one of them commandment concerning his neighbor" (Ecc. 17:12).

II. *From the general society of mankind is born civil society*

III. *To form nations and unite peoples it was necessary to establish government*

2nd Proposition: Only the authority of government can put restraints on passions and on the violence that became natural to men.

6th Proposition: Government perpetuates itself and makes states immortal. When God told Moses that he was going to die, Moses said to him: "May the Lord . . . provide a man that may be over this multitude" (Num. 27:16). Then by order of God, Moses established Joshua to succeed him. . . . After the death of Moses all the people recognized Joshua.

[BOOK II]

I. *Who has held authority since the beginning of the world?*

1st Proposition: God is the true king. A great king recognized this, since he spoke thus in the presence of all his people: ". . . Blessed are Thou, O Lord, the God of Israel, our father from eternity to eternity. . . . Thine are riches and Thine is glory; Thou hast dominion over all" (1 Par. 29:10, 12). "The Empire of God is eternal, from that comes that he is called the King of the Centuries" (Apoc. 15:3).

7th Proposition: Monarchy is the most common, the oldest, and the most natural form of government. The people of Israel subjected themselves to monarchy as being the universally accepted government. "Make us a king, to judge us, as all nations have" (1 Sam. 8:5). If God was irritated it was because up till then He had governed this people himself, and that He was their true king. That is why He said to Samuel: ". . . for they have not rejected thee, but Me, that I should not reign over them" (1 Sam. 8:7).

Indeed this form of government is so natural that one finds it first of all with all peoples. . . . Rome began that way, and it finally returned to it as its natural state. . . .

8th Proposition: Monarchical government is the best.

If it is the most natural, it is consequently the most durable, and from that also the strongest. It is thus most opposed to division which is the essential evil of states and the most certain cause of their ruin. . . . "Every kingdom divided against itself shall be made desolate and every city or house divided against itself shall not stand." (Matt. 12:25.) We have seen that Our Savior has followed in this sentence the natural progress of government. . . .

[BOOK III]

II. *Royal authority is sacred*

1st Proposition: God establishes kings as His ministers, and reigns by them over His people. We have already seen that all power comes from God. St. Paul says: "For he [the prince] is God's minister to thee for good. But if thou do that which is evil, fear: for he beareth not the sword in vain: For he is God's minister, an avenger to execute wrath upon him that doeth evil" (Romans 13:4). Princes act then as ministers of God and His lieutenants on the earth. It is by them that He exercises His empire. "And now you say that you are able to withstand the kingdom of the Lord which He possesseth by the sons of David" (2 Par. 13:8). It is by that that we have seen that the royal throne is not the throne of a man, but the throne of God Himself. "He hath chosen Solomon my son, to sit upon the throne of the kingdom of the Lord over Israel" (1 Par. 28:5). And again: "Solomon sat on the throne of the Lord." (*Ibid.* 29:23)

2nd Proposition: The person of kings is sacred. It follows from all that the person of kings is sacred and that to attempt to murder a king is a sacrilege. God has anointed them by His prophets with a sacred unction, just as he has anointed the pontiffs and His altars. But even without the exterior application of unction, they are sacred by their profession; as representatives of the divine majesty, deputized by Providence to exercise His designs. It is thus that God called Cyrus His anointed one: "Thus saith the Lord to My anointed Cyrus whose right hand I have taken hold of, to subdue nations" (Is. 45:1).

3rd Proposition: One owes obedience to the prince by the principles of religion and of conscience. St. Paul, after having said that the prince is the minister of God, concludes thus: "Where-fore ye must needs be subject: not only for wrath but also for conscience sake" (Romans 13:5). That is why "Servants be obedient to them that are your lords, not serving to the eye, as it were pleasing to men, but as servants of Christ, doing the will of God from the heart" (Ephes. 6:5-6). And again: "Servants obey in all things your masters according to the flesh, not serving to the eye, as pleasing to men, but in simplicity of heart fearing God. What-soever you do, do it with good heart: as to the Lord and not to men: knowing that you shall receive of the Lord the reward of inheritance, serve ye the Lord Christ" (Coloss. 3:22-24).

If the apostle spoke thus of servitude, an estate contrary to nature, what ought we to think of the legitimate subjugation to princes, and to the magistrates, protectors of public liberty?

4th Proposition: Kings ought to respect their own power and employ it only for public good. Their power coming from on high, as it has been said, they ought not to believe that they receive it to be used at their own discretion, but rather that they ought to make use of it with fear and restraint as a thing that comes to them from God, and of which God will demand of them an accounting.

[BOOK IV]

The royal authority is absolute

1st Proposition: The prince owes no account to any person for that which he orders. "I observe the mouth of the king and the commandments of the oath of God. Be not hasty to depart from his face and do not continue in an evil work. For he will do all that pleaseth him; and his word is full of power. Neither can any man say to him: Why dost thou so? He that keepeth the commandments shall find no evil" (Eccles. 8:2-5). Without this absolute authority, he could neither effect the good nor suppress the evil: it is necessary that his power be such that no one could hope to escape him. . . .

This doctrine is confirmed by St. Paul: "Wilt thou then not be afraid of power? Do that which is good" (Rom. 13:3).

2nd Proposition: When the prince has judged, there is no other judgment.

Sovereign judgments are attributed to God. And Josaphat established judges to judge the people. "You do not exercise the judgment of man but of the Lord" (2 Par. 19:6). Ecclesiasticus says: "Judge not against a judge" (Eccl. 8:17). It is necessary to obey princes as justice itself, otherwise there is neither order nor goal in affairs. They are gods, and participate in some fashion in the divine independence. "I have said: You are gods and all of you the sons of the most high" (Psl. 81:6).

Bishop de Bossuet, *Politics Drawn from the Holy Scriptures,* trans. John B. Wolf, from *Oeuvres complètes de Bossuet,* vol. XVI (Paris, 1838).

C. *John Locke's Study of Civil Government*

Principal theorist for the Whig party, John Locke (1632–1704) undoubtedly deserves a primary place in the annals of revolutionary thought. He was attached as a tutor to the fortunes of one of the great Whig families—Shaftesbury—sharing both its exile and its triumph in the Revolution of 1688. The *Two Treatises on Government,* of which the selection below is a part, was his defense of that Revolution. It proved to be so telling an argument that Locke has inspired the thought and action of revolutionary figures in Europe and the Americas from his day until our own, when Marxian justifications have supplanted his ideas in some parts of the world.

[CHAPTER I]

. . . Political power, then, I take to be a right of making laws, with penalties of death, and consequently all less penalties for the regulating and preserving of property, and of employing the force of the community in the execution of such laws, and in the defence of the commonwealth from foreign injury, and all this only for the public good.

[CHAPTER II: OF THE STATE OF NATURE]

To understand political power aright, and derive it from its original, we must consider what state all men are naturally in, and that is, a state of perfect freedom to order their actions, and dispose of their possessions and persons as they think fit, within the bounds of the law of Nature, without asking leave or depending upon the will of any other man.

A state also of equality, wherein all the power and jurisdiction is reciprocal, no one having more than another, there being nothing more evident than that creatures of the same species and rank, promiscuously born to all the same advantages of Nature, and the use of the same faculties, should also be equal one amongst another, without subordination or subjection, unless the lord and master of them all should, by any manifest declaration of his will, set one above another, and confer on him, by an evident and clear appointment, an undoubted right to dominion and sovereignty.

. . . The state of Nature has a law of Nature to govern it, which obliges every one, and reason, which is that law, teaches all mankind who will but consult it, that being all equal and independent, no one ought to harm another in his life, health, liberty or possessions; for men being all the workmanship of one omnipotent and infinitely wise Maker; all the servants of one sovereign Master, sent into the world by His order and about His business; they are His property, whose workmanship they are, made to last during His, not one another's pleasure. And, being furnished with like faculties, sharing all in one community of Nature, there cannot be supposed any such subordination among us that may authorize us to destroy one another, as if we were made for one another's uses, as the inferior ranks of creatures are for ours. Every one as he is bound to preserve himself, and not to quit his station wilfully, so by the like reason, when his own preservation comes not in competition, ought he as much as he can to preserve the rest of mankind, and not unless it be to do justice on an offender, take away or impair the life, or what tends to the preservation of the life, the liberty, health, limb, or goods of another.

And that all men may be restrained from invading others' rights, and from doing hurt to one another, and the law of Nature be observed, which willeth the peace and preservation of all mankind, the execution of the law of Nature is in that state put into every man's hands, whereby every one has a right to punish the transgressors of that law to such a degree as may hinder its violation. For the law of Nature would, as all other laws that concern men in this world, be in vain if there were nobody that in the state of Nature had a power to execute that law, and thereby preserve the innocent and restrain offenders; and if any one in the state of Nature may punish another for any evil he has done, every one may do so. For in that state of perfect equality, where naturally there is no superiority of jurisdiction of one over another, what any may do in prosecution of that law, every one must needs have a right to do. . . .

Besides the crime which consists in violating the law, and varying from the right rule of reason, whereby a man so far becomes degenerate, and declares himself to quit the principles of human nature and to be a noxious creature, there is commonly injury done, and some person or other, some other man, receives damage by his transgression; in which case, he who hath received any damage has (besides the right of punishment common to him, with other men) a particular right to seek reparation from him that has done it. And any other person who finds it just may also join with him that is injured, and assist him in recovering from the offender so much as may make satisfaction for the harm he hath suffered.

From these two distinct rights (the one of punishing the crime, for restraint and preventing the like offence, which right of punishing is in everybody, the other of taking reparation, which belongs only to the injured party) comes it to pass that the magistrate, who by being magistrate hath the common right of punishing put into his hands, can often, where the public good demands not the execution of the law, remit the punishment of criminal offences by his own authority, but yet cannot remit the satisfaction due to any private man for the damage he has received. That he who hath suffered the damage has a right to demand in his own name, and he alone can remit. The damnified person has this power of appropriating to himself the goods or service of the offender by right of self-preservation, as every man has a power to punish the crime to prevent its being committed again, by the right he has of preserving all mankind, and doing all reasonable things he can in order to that end. And thus it is that every man in the state of Nature has a power to kill a murderer, both to deter others from doing the like injury (which no reparation can compensate) by the example of the punishment that attends it from everybody, and also to secure men from the attempts of a criminal who, having renounced reason, the common rule and measure God hath given to mankind, hath, by the unjust violence and slaughter he hath committed upon one, declared war against all mankind, and therefore may be destroyed as a lion or a tiger, one of those wild savage beasts with whom men can have no society nor security. And upon this is grounded that great law of Nature, "Whoso sheddeth man's blood, by man shall his blood be shed."

To this strange doctrine—viz., That in the state of Nature every one has the executive power of the law of Nature—I doubt not but it will be objected that it is unreasonable for men to be judges in their own cases, that self-love will make men partial to themselves and their friends; and, on the other side, ill-nature, passion, and revenge will carry them too far in punishing others, and hence nothing but confusion and disorder will follow, and that therefore God hath certainly appointed government to restrain the partiality and violence of men. I easily grant that civil government is the proper remedy for the inconveniences of the state of Nature, which must certainly be great where men may be judges in their own case, since it is easy to be imagined that he who was so unjust as to do his brother an injury will scarce be so just as to condemn himself for it. But I shall desire those who make this objection to remember that absolute monarchs are but men; and if government is to be the remedy of those evils which necessarily follow from men's being judges in their own cases, and the state of Nature is therefore not to be endured, I desire to know what kind of government that is, and how much better it is than the state of Nature, where one man commanding a multitude has the liberty to be judge in his own case, and may do to all his subjects whatever he pleases without the least question or control of those who execute his pleasure?

[CHAPTER III: OF THE STATE OF WAR]

The state of war is a state of enmity and destruction; and therefore declaring by word or action, not a passionate and hasty, but sedate, settled design upon another man's life puts him in a state of war with him against whom he has declared such an intention, and so has exposed his life to the other's power to be taken away by him, or any one that joins with him in his defence, and espouses his quarrel; it being reasonable and just I should have a right to destroy that which threatens me with destruction; for by the fundamental law of Nature, man being to be preserved as much as possible, when all cannot be preserved, the safety of the innocent is to be preferred, and one may destroy a man who makes war upon him, or has discovered an enmity to his being, for the same reason that he may kill a wolf or a lion, because they are not under the ties of the common law of reason, have no other rule but that of force and violence, and so may be treated as a beast of prey, those dangerous and noxious creatures that will be sure to destroy him whenever he falls into their power.

And hence it is that he who attempts to get another man into his absolute power does thereby put himself into a state of war with him; it being to be understood as a declaration of a design upon his life. For I have reason to conclude that he who would get me into his power without my consent would use me as he pleased when he had got me there, and destroy me too when he had a fancy to it; for nobody can desire to have me in his absolute power unless it be to compel me by force to that which is against the right of my freedom—*i.e.*, make me a slave. To be free from such force is the only security of my preservation, and reason bids me look on him as an enemy to my preservation who would take away that freedom which is the fence to it; so that he who makes an attempt to enslave me thereby puts himself into a state of war with me. He that in the state of Nature would take away the freedom that belongs to any one in that state must necessarily be supposed to have a design to take away everything else, that freedom being the foundation of all the rest; as he that in the state of society would take away the freedom belonging to those of that society or commonwealth must be supposed to design to take away from them everything else, and so be looked on as in a state of war.

[CHAPTER IV: OF SLAVERY]

The natural liberty of man is to be free from any superior power on earth, and not to be under the will or legislative authority of man, but to have only the law of Nature for this rule. The liberty of man in society is to be under no other legislative power but that established by consent in the commonwealth, nor under the dominion of any will, or restraint of any law, but what that legislative shall enact according to the trust put in it. Freedom, then, is not what Sir Robert Filmer tells us: "A liberty for every one to do what he lists, to live as he pleases, and not to be tied by any laws"; but freedom of men under government is to have a standing rule to live by, common to every one of that society, and made by the legislative power erected in it. A liberty to follow my own will in all things where that rule prescribes not, not to be subject to the inconstant, uncertain, unknown, arbitrary will of another man, as freedom of nature is to

be under no other restraint but the law of Nature.

This freedom from absolute, arbitrary power is so necessary to, and closely joined with, a man's preservation, that he cannot part with it but by what forfeits his preservation and life together. For a man, not having the power of his own life, cannot by compact or his own consent enslave himself to any one, nor put himself under the absolute, arbitrary power of another to take away his life when he pleases. Nobody can give more power than he has himself, and he that cannot take away his own life cannot give another power over it. Indeed, having by his fault forfeited his own life by some act that deserves death, he to whom he has forfeited it may, when he has him in his power, delay to take it, and make use of him to his own service; and he does him no injury by it. For, whenever he finds the hardship of his slavery outweigh the value of his life, it is in his power, by resisting the will of his master, to draw on himself the death he desires. . . .

[CHAPTER VII: OF POLITICAL OR CIVIL SOCIETY]

Man being born, as has been proved, with a title to perfect freedom and an uncontrolled enjoyment of all the rights and privileges of the law of Nature, equally with any other man, or number of men in the world, hath by nature a power not only to preserve his property —that is, his life, liberty, and estate, against the injuries and attempts of other men, but to judge of and punish the breaches of that law in others, as he is persuaded the offence deserves, even with death itself, in crimes where the heinousness of the fact, in his opinion, requires it. But because no political society can be, nor subsist, without having in itself the power to preserve the property, and in order thereunto punish the offences of all those of that society, there, and there only, is political society where every one of the members hath quitted this natural power, resigned it up into the hands of the community in all cases that exclude him not from appealing for protection to the law established by it. And thus all private judgment of every particular member being excluded, the community comes to be umpire, and by understanding indifferent rules and men authorised by the community for their execution, decides all the differences that may happen between any members of that society concerning any matter of right, and punishes those offences which any member hath committed against the society with such penalties as the law has established; whereby it is easy to discern who are, and are not, in political society together. Those who are united into one body, and have a common established law and judicature to appeal to, with authority to decide controversies between them and punish offenders, are in civil society one with another; but those who have no such common appeal, I mean on earth, are still in the state of Nature, each being where there is no other, judge for himself and executioner; which is, as I have before showed it, the perfect state of Nature.

And thus the commonwealth comes by a power to set down what punishment shall belong to the several transgressions they think worthy of it, committed amongst the members of that society (which is the power of making laws), as well as it has the power to punish any injury done unto any of its members by any one that is not of it (which is the power of war and peace); and all this for the preservation of the property of all the members of that society, as far as is possible. But though every man entered into society has quitted his power to punish offences against the law of Nature in prosecution of his own private judgment, yet with the judgment of offences which he has given up to the legislative, in all cases where he can appeal to the magistrate, he has given up a right to the commonwealth to employ his force for the execution of the judgments of the commonwealth whenever he shall be called to it, which, indeed, are his own judgments, they being made by himself or his representative. And herein we have the original of the legislative and executive power of civil society, which is to judge by standing laws how far offences are to be punished when committed within the commonwealth; and also by occasional judgments founded on the present circumstances of the fact, how far injuries from without are to be vindicated, and in both these to employ all the force of all the members when there shall be need.

Wherever, therefore, any number of men so unite into one society as to quit every one his executive power of the law of Nature, and to resign it to the public, there and there only is a political or civil society. And this is done wherever any number of men, in the state of Nature, enter into society to make one people one body politic under one supreme government: or else when any one joins himself to, and incorporates with any government already made. For hereby he authorises the society, or which is all one, the legislative thereof, to make laws for him as the public good of the society shall require, to the execution whereof his own assistance (as to his own decrees) is due. And this puts men out of a state of Nature into that of a commonwealth, by setting up a judge on earth with authority to determine all the controversies and redress the injuries that may happen to any member of the commonwealth, which judge is the legislative or magistrates appointed by it. And wherever there are any number of men, however associated, that have no such decisive power to appeal to, there they are still in the state of Nature.

And hence it is evident that absolute monarchy, which by some men is counted for the only government in the world, is indeed inconsistent with civil society, and so can be no form of civil government at all. For the end of civil society being to avoid and remedy those inconveniences of the state of Nature which necessarily follow from every man's being judge in his own case, by setting up a known authority to which every one of that society may appeal upon any injury received, or controversy that may arise, and which every one of the society ought to obey. Wherever any persons are who have not such an authority to appeal to, and decide any difference between them there, those persons are still in the state of Nature. And so is every absolute prince in respect of those who are under his dominion. . . .

For he that thinks absolute power purifies men's blood, and corrects the baseness of human nature, need read but the history of this, or any other age, to be convinced to the contrary. . . .

[CHAPTER VIII: OF THE BEGINNING OF POLITICAL SOCIETIES]

Men being, as has been said, by nature all free, equal and independent, no one can be put out of this estate and subjected to the political power of another without his own consent, which being done by agreeing with other men, to join and unite into a community for their comfortable, safe, and peaceable living, one amongst another, in a secure enjoyment of their properties, and a greater security against any that are not of it. This any number of men may do, because it injures not the freedom of the rest; they are left, as they were, in the liberty of the state of Nature. When any number of men have so consented to make one community or government, they are thereby presently incorporated, and make one body politic, wherein the majority have a right to act and conclude the rest.

For, when any number of men have, by the consent of every individual, made a community, they have thereby made that community one body, with a power to act as one body, which is only by the will and determination of the majority. For that which acts any community, being only the consent of the individuals of it, and it being one body, must move one way, it is necessary the body should move that way whither the greater force carries it, which is the consent of the majority, or else it is impossible it should act or continue one body, one community, which the consent of every individual that united into it agreed that it should; and so every one is bound by that consent to be concluded by the majority. And therefore we see that in assemblies empowered to act by positive laws where no number is set by that positive law which empowers them, the act of the majority passes for the act of the whole, and of course determines as having, by the Law of Nature and reason, the power of the whole.

And thus every man, by consenting with others to make one body politic under one government, puts himself under an obligation to every one of that society to submit to the determination of the majority, and to be concluded by it; or else this original compact, whereby he with others incorporates into one society, would signify nothing, and be no compact if he be left free and under no other ties than he was in before in the state of Nature. For what appearance would there be of any compact? What new engagement if he were no farther tied by any decrees of the society than he himself thought fit and did actually consent to? This would be still as great a liberty as he himself had before his compact, or any one else in the state of Nature, who may submit himself and consent to any acts of it if he thinks fit.

For if the consent of the majority shall not in reason be received as the act of the whole, and conclude every individual, nothing but the consent of every individual can make anything to be the act of the whole, which, considering the infirmities of health and avocations of business, which in a number though much less than that of a commonwealth, will necessarily keep many away from the public assembly; and the variety of opinions and contrariety of interests which unavoidably happen in all collections of men, it is next impossible ever to be had. And, therefore, if coming into society be upon such terms, it will be only like Cato's coming into the theatre, *tantum ut exiret*. Such a constitution as this would make the mighty leviathan of a shorter duration than the feeblest creatures. . . .

[CHAPTER XIII: OF THE SUBORDINATION OF THE POWERS OF THE COMMON-WEALTH]

Though in a constituted commonwealth standing upon its own basis and acting according to its own nature—that is, acting for the preservation of the community, there can be but one supreme power, which is the legislative, to which all the rest are and must be subordinate, yet the legislative being only a fiduciary power to act for certain ends, there remains still in the people a supreme power to remove or alter the legislative, when they find the legislative act contrary to the trust reposed in them. For all power given with trust for the attaining an end being limited by that end, whenever that end is manifestly neglected or opposed, the trust must necessarily be forfeited, and the power devolve into the hands of those that gave it, who may place it anew where they shall think best for their safety and security. And thus the community perpetually retains a supreme power of saving themselves from the attempts and designs of anybody, even of their legislators, whenever they shall be so foolish or so wicked as to lay and carry on designs against the liberties and properties of the subject. For no man or society of men having a power to deliver up their preservation, or consequently the means of it, to the absolute will and arbitrary dominion of another, whenever any one shall go about to bring them into such a slavish condition, they will always have a right to preserve what they have not a power to part with, and to rid themselves of those who invade this fundamental, sacred, and unalterable law of self-preservation for which they entered into society. And thus the community may be said in this respect to be always the supreme power, but not as considered under any form of government, because this power of the people can never take place till the government be dissolved.

It may be demanded here, what if the executive power, being possessed of the force of the commonwealth, shall make use of that force to hinder the meeting and acting of the legislative, when the original constitution or the public exigencies require it? I say, using force upon the people, without authority, and contrary to the trust put in him that does so, is a state of war with the people, who have a right to reinstate their legislative in the exercise of their power. For having erected a legislative with an intent they should exercise the power of making laws, either at certain set times, or when there is need of it, when they are hindered by any force from what is so necessary to the society, and wherein the safety and preservation of the people consists, the people have a right to remove it by force. In all states and conditions the true remedy of force without authority is to oppose force to it. The use of force without authority always puts him that uses it into a state of war as the aggressor, and renders him liable to be treated accordingly. . . .

[CHAPTER XVIII: OF TYRANNY]

As usurpation is the exercise of power which another hath a right to, so tyranny is the exercise of power beyond right, which nobody can have a right to; and this is making use of the power any one has in his hands, not for the good of those who are under it, but for his own private, separate advantage. When the governor, however entitled, makes not the law, but his will, the rule, his commands and actions are not directed to the preservation of the properties of his people, but the satisfaction of his own ambition, revenge, covetousness, or any other irregular passion.

If one can doubt this to be truth or reason because it comes from the obscure hand of a subject, I hope the authority of a king will make it pass with him. King James, in his speech to the Parliament, 1603, tells them thus: "I will ever prefer the weal of the public and of the whole commonwealth, in making of good laws and constitutions, to any particular and private ends of mine, thinking ever the wealth and weal of the commonwealth to be my greatest weal and worldly felicity—a point wherein a lawful king doth directly differ from a tyrant; for I do acknowledge that the special and greatest point of difference that is between a rightful king and an usurping tyrant is this— that whereas the proud and ambitious tyrant doth think his kingdom and people are only ordained for satisfaction of his desires and unreasonable appetites, the righteous and just king doth,

by the contrary, acknowledge himself to be ordained for the procuring of the wealth and property of his people."

May the commands, then, of a prince be opposed? May he be resisted, as often as any one shall find himself aggrieved, and but imagine he has not right done him? This will unhinge and overturn all polities, and instead of government and order, leave nothing but anarchy and confusion.

To this I answer: That force is to be opposed to nothing but to unjust and unlawful force. Whoever makes any opposition in any other case draws on himself a just condemnation, both from God and man. . . .

[CHAPTER XIX: OF THE DISSOLUTION OF GOVERNMENT]

He that will, with any clearness, speak of the dissolution of government, ought in the first place to distinguish between the dissolution of the society and the dissolution of the government. That which makes the community, and brings men out of the loose state of Nature into one politic society, is the agreement which every one has with the rest to incorporate and act as one body, and so be one distinct commonwealth. The usual, and almost only way whereby this union is dissolved, is the inroad of foreign force making a conquest upon them. For in that case (not being able to maintain and support themselves as one entire and independent body) the union belonging to that body, which consisted therein, must necessarily cease, and so every one return to the state he was in before, with a liberty to shift for himself and provide for his own safety, as he thinks fit, in some other society.

This being usually brought about by such in the commonwealth, who misuse the power they have, it is hard to consider it aright, and know at whose door to lay it, without knowing the form of government in which it happens. Let us suppose, then, the legislative placed in the concurrence of three distinct persons:—First, a single hereditary person having the constant, supreme, executive power, and with it the power of convoking and dissolving the other two within certain periods of time. Secondly, an assembly of hereditary nobility. Thirdly, an assembly of representatives chosen, *pro tempore,* by the people. Such a form of government supposed, it is evident:

First, that when such a single person or prince sets up his own arbitrary will in place of the laws which are the will of the society declared by the legislative, then the legislative is changed. For that being, in effect, the legislative whose rules and laws are put in execution, and required to be obeyed, when other laws are set up, and other rules pretended and enforced than what the legislative, constituted by the society, have enacted, it is plain that the legislative is changed. Whoever introduces new laws, not being thereunto authorised, by the fundamental appointment of the society, or subverts the old, disowns and overturns the power by which they were made, and so sets up a new legislative.

Secondly, when the prince hinders the legislative from assembling in its due time, or from acting freely, pursuant to those ends for which it was constituted, the legislative is altered. . . .

Thirdly, when, by the arbitrary power of the prince, the electors or ways of election are altered without the consent and contrary to the common interest of the people, there also the legislative is altered. For if others than those whom the society hath authorised thereunto do choose, or in another way than what the society hath prescribed, those chosen are not the legislative appointed by the people.

Fourthly, the delivery also of the people into the subjection of a foreign power, either by the prince or by the legislative, is certainly a change of the legislative, and so a dissolution of the government. For the end why people entered into society being to be preserved one entire, free, independent society, to be governed by its own laws, this is lost whenever they are given up into the power of another.

Why, in such a constitution as this, the dissolution of the government in these cases is to be imputed to the prince is evident, because he, having the force, treasure, and offices of the State to employ, and often persuading himself or being flattered by others, that, as supreme magistrate, he is incapable of control; he alone is in a condition to make great advances towards such changes under pretence of lawful authority, and has it in his hands to terrify or suppress opposers as factious, seditious, and enemies to the government; whereas no other part of the legislative, or people, is capable by themselves to attempt any alteration of the legislative without open and visible rebellion, apt enough to be taken notice of, which, when it prevails, produces effects very little different from foreign conquest. Besides, the prince, in such a form of government, having the power of dissolving the other parts of the legislative, and thereby rendering them private persons, they can never, in opposition to him, or without his concurrence, alter the legislative by a law, his consent being necessary to give any of their decrees that sanction. But yet so far as the other parts of the legislative any way contribute to any attempt upon the government, and do either promote, or not, what lies in them, hinder such designs, they are guilty, and partake in this, which is certainly the greatest crime men can be guilty of one towards another.

There is one way more whereby such a government may be dissolved, and that is: When he who has the supreme executive power neglects and abandons that charge, so that the laws already made can no longer be put in execution; this is demonstratively to reduce all to anarchy, and so effectively to dissolve the government. For laws not being made for themselves, but to be, by their execution, the bonds of the society to keep every part of the body politic in its due place and function; when that totally ceases, the government visibly ceases, and the people become a confused multitude without order or connection. Where there is no longer the administration of justice for the securing of men's rights, nor any remaining power within the community to direct the force, or provide for the necessities of the public, there certainly is no government left. Where the laws cannot be executed it is all one as if there were no laws, and a government without laws is, I suppose, a mystery in politics inconceivable to human capacity, and inconsistent with human society.

In these, and the like cases, when the government is dissolved, the people are at liberty to provide for themselves by erecting a new legislative differing from the other by the change of persons, or form, or both, as they shall find it most for their safety and good. For the society can never, by the fault of another, lose the native and original right it has to preserve itself, which can only be done by a settled legislative and a fair and impartial execution of the laws made by it. But the state of mankind is not so miserable that they are not capable of using this remedy till it be too late to look for any. To tell people they may provide for themselves by erecting a new legislative, when, by oppression, artifice, or being delivered over to a foreign power, their old one is gone, is only to tell them they may ex-

pect relief when it is too late, and the evil is past cure. This is, in effect, no more than to bid them first be slaves, and then to take care of their liberty, and, when their chains are on, tell them they may act like free men. This, if barely so, is rather mockery than relief, and men can never be secure from tyranny if there be no means to escape it till they are perfectly under it; and, therefore, it is that they have not only a right to get out of it, but to prevent it.

There is, therefore, secondly, another way whereby governments are dissolved, and that is, when the legislative, or the prince, either of them act contrary to their trust.

For the legislative acts against the trust reposed in them when they endeavour to invade the property of the subject, and to make themselves, or any part of the community, masters or arbitrary disposers of the lives, liberties, or fortunes of the people.

The reason why men enter into society is the preservation of their property; and the end why they choose and authorise a legislative is that there may be laws made, and rules set, as guards and fences to the properties of all the society, to limit the power and moderate the dominion of every part and member of the society. For since it can never be supposed to be the will of the society that the legislative should have a power to destroy that which every one designs to secure by entering into society, and for which the people submitted themselves to legislators of their own making: whenever the legislators endeavour to take away and destroy the property of the people, or to reduce them to slavery under arbitrary power, they put themselves into a state of war with the people, who are thereupon absolved from any farther obedience, and are left to the common refuge which God hath provided for all men against force and violence. . . . What

I have said here concerning the legislative in general holds true also concerning the supreme executor, who having a double trust put in him, both to have a part in the legislative and the supreme execution of the law, acts against both, when he goes about to set up his own arbitrary will as the law of the society. He acts also contrary to his trust when he employs the force, treasure, and offices of the society to corrupt the representatives and gain them to his purposes, when he openly pre-engages the electors, and prescribes, to their choice, such whom he has, by solicitations, threats, promises, or otherwise, won to his designs, and employs them to bring in such who have promised beforehand what to vote and what to enact. Thus to regulate candidates and electors, and new model the ways of election, what is it but to cut up the government by the roots, and poison the very fountain of public security? For the people having reserved to themselves the choice of their representatives as the fence to their properties, could do it for no other end but that they might always be freely chosen, and so chosen, freely act and advise as the necessity of the commonwealth and the public good should, upon examination and mature debate, be judged to require. This, those who give their votes before they hear the debate, and have weighed the reasons on all sides, are not capable of doing. To prepare such an assembly as this, and endeavour to set up the declared abettors of his own will, for the true representatives of the people, and the law-makers of the society, is certainly as great a breach of trust, and as perfect a declaration of a design to subvert the government, as is possible to be met with. To which, if one shall add rewards and punishments visibly employed to the same end, and all the arts of perverted law made use of to take off and destroy all that stand in

the way of such a design, and will not comply and consent to betray the liberties of their country, it will be past doubt what is doing. What power they ought to have in the society who thus employ it contrary to the trust [which] went along with it in its first institution, is easy to determine; and one cannot but see that he who has once attempted any such thing as this cannot any longer be trusted.

To this, perhaps, it will be said that the people being ignorant and always discontented, to lay the foundation of government in the unsteady opinion and uncertain humour of the people, is to expose it to certain ruin; and no government will be able long to subsist if the people may set up a new legislative whenever they take offence at the old one. To this I answer, quite the contrary. People are not so easily got out of their old forms as some are apt to suggest. They are hardly to be prevailed with to amend the acknowledged faults in the frame they have been accustomed to. And if there be any original defects, or adventitious ones introduced by time or corruption, it is not an easy thing to get them changed, even when all the world sees there is an opportunity for it. This slowness and aversion in the people to quit their old constitutions has in the many revolutions which have been seen in this kingdom, in this and former ages, still kept us to, or after some interval of fruitless attempts, still brought us back again to our old legislative of king, lords and commons; and whatever provocations have made the crown be taken from some of our princes' heads, they never carried the people so far as to place it in another line.

But it will be said this hypothesis lays a ferment for frequent rebellion. To which I answer:

First, no more than any other hypothesis. For when the people are made miserable, and find themselves exposed to the ill usage of arbitrary power, cry up their governors as much as you will for sons of Jupiter, let them be sacred and divine, descended or authorised from Heaven; give them out for whom or what you please, the same will happen. The people generally ill treated, and contrary to right, will be ready upon any occasion to ease themselves of a burden that sits heavy upon them. They will wish and seek for the opportunity, which in the change, weakness, and accidents of human affairs, seldom delays long to offer itself. He must have lived but a little while in the world, who has not seen examples of this in his time. . . .

Secondly, I answer, such revolutions happen not upon every little mismanagement in public affairs. Great mistakes in the ruling part, many wrong and inconvenient laws, and all the slips of human frailty will be borne by the people without mutiny or murmur. But if a long train of abuses, prevarications, and artifices, all tending the same way, make the design visible to the people, and they cannot but feel what they lie under, and see whither they are going, it is not to be wondered that they should then rouse themselves, and endeavour to put the rule into such hands which may secure to them the ends for which government was at first erected, and without which, ancient names and specious forms are so far from being better, that they are much worse than the state of Nature or pure anarchy; the inconveniences being all as great and as near, but the remedy farther off and more difficult.

Thirdly, I answer, that this power in the people of providing for their safety anew by a new legislative when their legislators have acted contrary to their trust by invading their property, is the best fence against rebellion, and the probablest means to hinder it. For rebellion being an opposition, not to persons, but authority, which is founded only in the constitutions and laws of the government: those, whoever they be, who, by force, break through, and, by force, justify their violation of them, are truly and properly rebels. For when men, by entering into society and civil government, have excluded force, and introduced laws for the preservation of property, peace, and unity amongst themselves, those who set up force again in opposition to the laws, do *rebellare*— that is, bring back again the state of war, and are properly rebels, which they who are in power, by the pretence they have to authority, the temptation of force they have in their hands, and the flattery of those about them being likeliest to do, the properest way to prevent the evil is to show them the danger and injustice of it who are under the greatest temptation to run into it.

In both the forementioned cases, when either the legislative is changed, or the legislators act contrary to the end for which they were constituted, those who are guilty are guilty of rebellion. For if any one by force takes away the established legislative of any society, and the laws by them made, pursuant to their trust, he thereby takes away the umpirage which every one had consented to for a peaceable decision of all their controversies, and a bar to the state of war amongst them. They who remove or change the legislative take away this decisive power, which nobody can have but by the appointment and consent of the people, and so destroying the authority which the people did, and nobody else can set up, and introducing a power which the people hath not authorised, actually introduce a state of war, which is that of force without authority; and thus by removing the legislative established by the society, in whose decisions the people acquiesced and united as to that of their own will, they untie the knot, and expose the people anew to the state of war. . . .

But if they who say it lays a foundation for rebellion mean that it may occasion civil wars or intestine broils to tell the people they are absolved from obedience when illegal attempts are made upon their liberties or properties, and may oppose the unlawful violence of those who were their magistrates when they invade their properties, contrary to the trust put in them, and that, therefore, this doctrine is not to be allowed, being so destructive to the peace of the world; they may as well say, upon the same ground, that honest men may not oppose robbers or pirates, because this may occasion disorder or bloodshed. If any mischief come in such cases, it is not to be charged upon him who defends his own right, but on him that invades his neighbour's. If the innocent honest man must quietly quit all he has for peace sake to him who will lay violent hands upon it, I desire it may be considered what a kind of peace there will be in the world which consists only in violence and rapine, and which is to be maintained only for the benefit of robbers and oppressors. Who would not think it an admirable peace betwixt the mighty and the mean, when the lamb, without resistance, yielded his throat to be torn by the imperious wolf? . . .

The end of government is the good of mankind; and which is best for mankind, that the people should be always exposed to the boundless will of tyranny, or that the rulers should be sometimes liable to be opposed when they grow exorbitant in the use of their power, and employ it for the destruction, and not the preservation, of the properties of their people?

Nor let any one say that mischief can arise from hence as often as it shall please a busy head or turbulent spirit to desire the alteration of the government. It is true such men may stir whenever they please, but it will be only to their own just ruin and perdition. For till the mischief be grown general, and the ill designs of the rulers become visible, or their attempts sensible to the greater part, the people, who are more disposed to suffer than right themselves by resistance, are not apt to stir. The examples of particular injustice or oppression of here and there an unfortunate man moves them not. But if they universally have a persuasion grounded upon manifest evidence that designs are carrying on against their liberties, and the general course and tendency of things cannot but give them strong suspicions of the evil intention of their governors, who is to be blamed for it? Who can help it if they, who might avoid it, bring themselves into this suspicion? Are the people to be blamed if they have the sense of rational creatures, and can think of things no otherwise than as they find and feel them? And is it not rather their fault who put things in such a posture that they would not have them thought as they are? I grant that the pride, ambition, and turbulency of private men have sometimes caused great disorders in commonwealths, and factions have been fatal to states and kingdoms. But whether the mischief hath oftener begun in the people's wantonness, and a desire to cast off the lawful authority of their rulers, or in the rulers' insolence and endeavours to get and exercise an arbitrary power over their people, whether oppression or disobedience gave the first rise to the disorder, I leave it to impartial history to determine. . . .

That subjects or foreigners attempting by force on the properties of any people may be resisted with force is agreed on all hands; but that magistrates doing the same thing may be resisted, hath of late been denied: as if those who had the greatest privileges and advantages by the law had thereby a power to break those laws by which alone they were set in a better place than their brethren; whereas their offence is thereby the greater, both as being ungrateful for the greater share they have by the law, and breaking also that trust which is put into their hands by their brethren.

Whosoever uses force without right—as every one does in society who does it without law—puts himself into a state of war with those against whom he so uses it, and in that state all former ties are cancelled, all other rights cease, and every one has a right to defend himself, and to resist the aggressor. This is so evident that Barclay himself—that great assertor of the power and sacredness of kings—is forced to confess that it is lawful for the people, in some cases, to resist their king, and that, too, in a chapter wherein he pretends to show that the Divine law shuts up the people from all manner of rebellion. Whereby it is evident, even by his own doctrine, that since they may, in some cases, resist, all resisting of princes is not rebellion. . . .

To conclude. The power that every individual gave the society when he entered into it can never revert to the individuals again, as long as the society lasts, but will always remain in the community; because without this there can be no community—no commonwealth, which is contrary to the original agreement; so also when the society hath placed the legislative in any assembly of men, to continue in them and their successors, with direction and authority for providing such successors, the legislative can never revert to the people whilst that government lasts; because, having provided a legislative with power to continue for ever, they have given up their political power to the legislative, and cannot resume it. But if they have set limits to the duration of their legislative, and made this supreme power in any person or assembly only temporary; or else when, by the miscarriages of those in authority, it is forfeited; upon the forfeiture of their rulers, or at the determination of the time set, it reverts to the society, and the people have a right to act as supreme, and continue the legislative in themselves or place it in a new form, or new hands, as they think good.

John Locke, *Of Civil Government* (1689), *passim.*

II. HOW SHALL A KING CONDUCT HIMSELF?

A. *Omer Talon's Speech Before the Parlement of Paris*

Magistrate of the Parlement of Paris and one of the most influential jurists of his era, Omer Talon (1595–1652) played an important rôle in the Parlementary Fronde (1649–51). He was famous for his fearless defense of the rights of the Parlement and his insistence upon the rule of law rather than the arbitrary rule of the prince. After listening to his protest, the Regent, Anne of Austria, became so furious that she was reduced to tears. She is said to have whispered, "My son will punish them! He will do it!"

You are, Sire, our sovereign lord, the power of your Majesty comes from on high, your Majesty owes no account for your acts except to God and your conscience, but it is important for your glory that we be free men and not slaves; the grandeur of your crown is measured by the quality of those who obey it.

Most sovereigns exercise limited powers. Some rule in republics to which they render full account of their administration. Others have obligatory councils, fixed and ordered assemblies of estates, circles and diets to which they are obliged to defer, which take account of their affairs and censor their acts.

Those who are believed to possess an absolute power, having despotic authority in their states, command in ruined provinces, in desert lands baked by the ardor of the sun, or in Lapp lands or south sea islands, where there is nothing of man but the face of man.

France, the gift of heaven, the abundance of the earth, favorite of nature, is the heritage of the greatest of all princes, of the eldest son of the church, which gives to your Majesty the title Augustus, the quality of the King of the French, that is to say, commandant of men of heart and spirit, and not of forced slaves who obey by fear or who fear the hand of power, or who curse every day the authority that they respect. Such is the thought of a great queen, speaking to Cyrus her son, that there is a great difference between the kingdom of the Medes and the Persians; the first establishing their government in an exact power which does not suffer contradiction, the other contents itself with a legitimate authority which reconciles the benevolence of the people, a benevolence which is diminished and easily lost as soon as men are persuaded that the order of government fixes on them miseries that they resent and weighs upon them evils that persecute them. For these are the maxims of State and of Justice which prepare the thrones of kings, which are the foundations and the key stones of legitimate monarchies. They give to ministers the obligations, and to magistrates an honest liberty to execute their office and to acquit faithfully the commission of which honor obliges them to carry out.

Omer Talon's Speech before the Parlement of Paris (15 January, 1648), trans. John B. Wolf, from *Mémoires de feu M. Omer Talon*, IV (The Hague, 1732), 186-189.

B. Louis XIV's Instructions to the Dauphin

The most famous of the Bourbon kings of France, Louis XIV (1638–1715) was also the most literate of his house. Neither his father nor his grandfather before him nor his descendants in the eighteenth and nineteenth centuries wrote as much or as cogently as the Sun King. In his own day Louis was the perfect embodiment of the idea that the central authority must be supreme. His experience as a boy with the revolts of the Fronde as well as all the teaching of his gifted preceptor, Cardinal Mazarin, convinced him that no other solution for political life was either possible or desirable. In his career even more than in his writings, Louis created the ideal of kingship connected with the Bourbon name.

Many reasons, all very important, my son, have decided me, at some labour to myself, but one which I regard as forming one of my greatest concerns, to leave you these Memoirs of my reign. . . . I have never considered that kings . . . are dispensed from the obligation common to fathers of instructing their children by example and by precept. On the contrary, it has seemed to me that in the high rank in which we are placed, you and I, a public duty is added to private, and that in the midst of all the respect which is given us, all the abundance and brilliancy with which we are surrounded . . . this solicitude would not be very lofty if it did not extend beyond ourselves by making us communicate all our enlightenment to the one who is to reign after us.

I have even hoped that in this purpose I might be able to be more helpful to you, and consequently to my subjects, than any one else in the world; for there cannot be men who have reigned of more talents and greater experience than I, nor who have reigned in France; and I do not fear to tell you that the higher the position the greater are the number of things which cannot be viewed or understood save by one who is occupying that position.

I have considered, too, what I have so often experienced myself—the throng who will press round you, each for his own ends, the trouble you will have in finding disinterested advice, and the entire confidence you will be able to feel in that of a father who has no other interest but your own, no ardent wish but for your greatness.

I know not whether I should account as a fault of my own not to have assumed at the beginning the conduct of my realm. If it be a fault, I have striven earnestly to repair it afterwards, and I make bold to assure you that this was never the result either of negligence or of slackness.

From my early infancy the very name of *rois fainéants* or *maires du palais* displeased me when mentioned in my presence. But I must point out the state of affairs: grievous disturbances throughout the kingdom before and after my majority; a foreign war in which these troubles at home had lost to France thousands and thousands of advantages; a Prince of my blood and of great name at the head of my enemies; many Cabals in the State; the Parliaments still in the possession and enjoyment of a usurped authority; at my Court very little disinterested fidelity and, on this account, my subjects, though outwardly most submissive, as much a responsibility and cause of misgiving to me as the most rebellious; a minister reestablished in power despite so many factions, very skilful and very adroit, but whose views and methods were naturally very different from mine, whom, nevertheless, I could not gainsay, nor abate the least portion of his credit,

without running the risk of again raising against him by some misleading appearance of disgrace those very storms which had been allayed with so much difficulty. I myself was still very young, though I had reached the majority of kings, which the State laws anticipate in order to avoid still greater evils, but not the age at which mere private persons begin to regulate freely their own affairs. I only knew to its full extent the greatness of my burden, without having yet learned my own capabilities. . . .

I did not, however, neglect to prove myself in secret and without a confidant, reasoning alone and in my heart over all events as they occurred, full of hope and joy when I discovered sometimes that my first views became those which men of skill and experience arrived at in the end; and I held firmly from the bottom of my heart that I should never have been placed and preserved on the throne animated by so great a passion to acquit myself well without being able to find the means to do so. Some years therefore having thus rolled by, the state of general peace, my marriage, my authority more firmly established, and the death of Cardinal Mazarin constrained me to defer no longer the putting into execution of the hopes and fears which I had entertained for so long.

I made a beginning by casting my eyes over all the different parties in the State, not indifferently, but with the glance of experience, sensibly touched at seeing nothing which did not invite and urge me to take it in hand, but carefully watching what the occasion and the state of affairs would permit. Everywhere was disorder. . . .

Two things without doubt were absolutely necessary: very hard work on my part, and a wise choice of persons capable of seconding it.

As for work, it may be, my son, that you will begin to read these Memoirs at an age when one is far more in the habit of dreading than loving it, only too happy to have escaped subjection to tutors and to have your hours regulated no longer, nor lengthy and prescribed study laid down for you.

On this heading I will not warn you solely that it is none the less toil *by which* one reigns, and *for which* one reigns, and that the conditions of royalty, which may seem to you sometimes hard and vexatious in so lofty a position, would appear pleasant and easy if there was any doubt of your reaching it.

There is something more, my son, and I hope that your own experience will never teach it to you: nothing could be more laborious to you than a great amount of idleness if you were to have the misfortune to fall into it through beginning by being disgusted with public affairs, then with pleasure, then with idleness itself, seeking everywhere fruitlessly for what can never be found, that is to say, the sweetness of repose and leisure without having the preceding fatigue and occupation.

I laid a rule on myself to work regularly twice every day, and for two or three hours each time with different persons, without counting the hours which I passed privately and alone, nor the time which I was able to give on particular occasions to any special affairs that might arise. There was no moment when I did not permit people to talk to me about them, provided that they were urgent; with the exception of foreign ministers who sometimes find too favourable moments in the familiarity allowed to them, either to obtain or to discover something, and whom one should not hear without being previously prepared.

I cannot tell you what fruit I gathered immediately I had taken this reso-lution. I felt myself, as it were, uplifted in thought and courage; I found myself quite another man, and with joy reproached myself for having been too long unaware of it. This first timidity, which a little self-judgment always produces and which at the beginning gave me pain, especially on occasions when I had to speak in public, disappeared in less than no time. The only thing I felt then was that I was King, and born to be one. I experienced next a delicious feeling, hard to express, and which you will not know yourself except by tasting it as I have done. For you must not imagine, my son, that the affairs of State are like some obscure and thorny path of learning which may possibly have already wearied you, wherein the mind strives to raise itself with effort above its purview, more often to arrive at no conclusion, and whose utility or apparent utility is repugnant to us as much as its difficulty. The function of Kings consists principally in allowing good sense to act, which always acts naturally and without effort. What we apply ourselves to is sometimes less difficult than what we do only for our amusement. Its usefulness always follows. A King, however skilful and enlightened be his ministers, cannot put his own hand to the work without its effect being seen. Success, which is agreeable in everything, even in the smallest matters, gratifies us in these as well as in the greatest, and there is no satisfaction to equal that of noting every day some progress in glorious and lofty enterprises, and in the happiness of the people which has been planned and thought out by oneself. All that is most necessary to this work is at the same time agreeable; for, in a word, my son, it is to have one's eyes open to the whole earth; to learn each hour the news concerning every province and every nation, the secrets of every court, the mood and the weaknesses of each Prince and of every foreign minister; to be well informed on an infinite number of matters about which we are supposed to know nothing; to elicit from our subjects what they hide from us with the greatest care; to discover the most remote opinions of our own courtiers and the most hidden interests of those who come to us with quite contrary professions. I do not know of any other pleasure we would not renounce for that, even if curiosity alone gave us the opportunity.

I have dwelt on this important subject longer than I had intended, and far more for your sake than for my own; for while I am disclosing to you these methods and these alleviations attending the greatest cares of royalty I am not unaware that I am likewise depreciating almost the sole merit which I can hope for in the eyes of the world. But in this matter, my son, your honour is dearer to me than my own; and if it should happen that God call you to govern before you have yet taken to this spirit of application and to public affairs of which I am speaking, the least deference you can pay to the advice of a father, to whom I make bold to say you owe much in every kind of way, is to begin to do and to continue to do for some time, even under constraint and dislike, for love of me who beg it of you, what you will do all your life from love of yourself, if once you have made a beginning. . . .

Regarding the persons whose duty it was to second my labours, I resolved at all costs to have no prime minister; and if you will believe me, my son, and all your successors after you, the name shall be banished for ever from France, for there is nothing more undignified than to see all the administration on one side, and on the other, the mere title of King.

To effect this, it was necessary to divide my confidence and the execution of my orders without giving it entirely to one single person, applying these different people to different spheres according to their diverse talents, which is perhaps the first and greatest gift that Princes can possess.

I also made a resolution on a further matter. With a view the better to unite in myself alone all the authority of a master, although there must be in all affairs a certain amount of detail to which our occupations and also our dignity do not permit us to descend as a rule, I conceived the plan, after I should have made choice of my ministers, of entering sometimes into matters with each one of them, and when they least expected it, in order that they might understand that I could do the same upon other subjects and at any moment. Besides, a knowledge of some small detail acquired only occasionally, and for amusement rather than as a regular rule, is instructive little by little and without fatigue, on a thousand things which are not without their use in general resolutions, and which we ought to know and do ourselves were it possible that a single man could know and do everything.

It is not so easy for me to tell you, my son, what ought to be done in the choice of different ministers. In this matter fortune plays always, in spite of us, as large or a greater part than sagacity; and in the part that sagacity is able to play, intuition can do far more than taking thought. . . .

To lay bare to you all that was in my mind, it was not to my interest to choose subjects of a more eminent quality. Before all else it was needful to establish my own reputation, and to let the public know from the very rank from which I chose them, that it was my intention not to share my authority with them. It was important that they should not conceive hopes of higher things than what it pleased me to give them—a matter which is difficult in the case of people of high birth. And these precautions were so necessary that even on that question the world was a fairly long time in getting to know me thoroughly.

Several were able to persuade themselves that within a short time some one of those who approached me would take possession of my mind and my affairs. The greater number regarded the assiduity of my labours as a fervour which would soon relax, and those willing to judge it more favourably were waiting to form their opinion by results.

Time has shown what to believe, and I have now been pursuing for ten years fairly consistently, as it seems to me, the same course, without relaxing my application; kept well informed of everything; listening to the least of my subjects; at any hour knowing the number and quality of my troops, and the state of my fortified towns; unremitting in issuing my orders for all their requirements; dealing at once with foreign ministers; receiving and reading dispatches; doing myself a portion of the replies and giving to my secretaries the substance of the others; regulating the State receipts and expenditure; requiring those whom I placed in important posts to account directly to me; keeping my affairs to myself as much as any one before me had ever done; distributing my favours as I myself chose, and retaining, if I mistake not, those who served me in a modest position which was far removed from the elevation and power of prime ministers, although loading them with benefits for themselves and their belongings. . . .

A King's Lessons in Statecraft: Louis XIV: Letters to His Heirs, with Introduction and Notes, by Jean Longnon, trans. Herbert Wilson (New York: Albert and Charles Boni, 1925), *passim.*

C. Archbishop Fénelon on the Duties of Royalty

Archbishop of Cambrai and tutor of Louis XIV's grandson, the Duke of Burgundy, François de Salignac de la Mothe-Fénelon (1651–1715) was one of the real literary and philosophical lights at the French court during the later years of the reign of Louis XIV. His political and philosophical works had so strong an influence upon the generation of literary men who followed him in the eighteenth century that he deserves to be classed with the philosophers who made the era of the Enlightenment. The piece below was written in the hope of influencing the heir to Louis' throne. It was a daring act to criticize the old King so obviously under the guise of educating his successor. The Duke of Burgundy died before Louis; therefore, the effect of Fénelon's teaching could not be tested.

ARTICLE I: INSTRUCTION NECESSARY FOR A PRINCE

1. Do you know all the truths of Christianity? You will be judged by the Gospels, just as the least of your subjects. Have you studied your duties in this divine law? . . . Do you hope that God will allow you to be ignorant of His law, according to which He wishes you to live and to govern His people?

2. Have you believed that the Gospel ought not to be the rule for kings as it is for their subjects, and that politics dispenses kings from being humble, just, sincere, moderate, compassionate, ready to pardon injuries? . . .

3. Have you not sought councillors of all sorts disposed to flatter you in your ambitions, vanity? . . . Have you not failed to listen to men firm and disinterested, who . . . would tell you the

truth with respect, and would not fail to prevent you from making errors?

5. Have you not neglected to pray to God for knowledge of His wishes . . . not having prayed well, you have merited the darkness in which God has left you. . . .

6. Have you chosen for your council of conscience pious men . . . as you search the best generals for your army . . . and doctors for your illness? Have you nominated several persons to that council so that one may save you from the error of the other? . . . Have you fear of the consequences of surrendering yourself to one man? Finally, have you given the council complete liberty to expose to you without softening the full extent of your obligations to your conscience?

7. Have you worked to instruct yourself in the laws, customs, and usages of your kingdom? The King is the first judge of his state; it is he who makes the laws, it is he who interprets them . . . it is he who judges . . . according to the laws that he establishes or finds already established in his kingdom. It is he who ought to put to right all other judges; in a word, his function is to be the head of all justice in peace, as he is the head of the armies in war. . . . To judge well; that is, to judge according to the laws, it is necessary to know the laws. Do you know them, and are you ready to redress the judgment of men who are ignorant of them? . . . The voice of a single well-informed man ought often to be preferred to that of ten timid and feeble, or infatuated and corrupted judges. This is the case where one ought to weigh rather than count the opinions.

8. Have you studied the true form of the government of your kingdom? It is not enough to know the laws that regulate property and other goods of particular [persons]; this is undoubtedly the least part of justice. It is really important that you protect the relations between you and your nation, between you and your neighbors. Have you seriously studied the law of peoples, a law which it is less permissible for a king to be ignorant of since it is the law which regulates his conduct in its most important functions, and since this law may be reduced to the most evident principles of natural law for the entire human race. . . . Do you believe that God will allow you to reign if you reign without being instructed in that which must regulate your power? You cannot, then, regard the study of history, of customs, and of all the details of ancient governmental forms as an indifferent curiosity, but rather as an essential duty of royalty.

9. It is not enough to know the past; it is necessary to know the present. Do you know how many people are in your kingdom, how many men, how many women, how many laborers, (etc.). . . . [A king] ought to know the natural condition of the inhabitants of his provinces, their customs, their privileges, their commerce, the laws regulating their contacts within and without the kingdom. He ought to know the tribunals established in each province . . . etc. Otherwise he would not know the importance of most of the things that pass before his eyes, his ministers will impose upon him constantly, he will believe to see all, and see only a half. A king ignorant of all these things is only half a king. . . .

ARTICLE II: THE EXAMPLE THAT A KING OWES TO HIS SUBJECTS

10. It is customarily said of kings that they have less to fear of the vices of ordinary men than of the faults to which they abandon themselves in their royal functions. For myself I say stubbornly the contrary. I maintain that all their faults in their most private lives have an infinite consequence for

them. . . . Subjects are servile imitators of their prince, above all in things that flatter their passions. Have you given them the bad example of a dishonest and criminal love? If you have done it, your authority has been used to elevate infamy; you have broken the barrier of decency and honesty; you have made vice and impudence triumph; you have taught your subjects not to blush at that which is shameful, a bad lesson that they will never forget. "It would be better," said Jesus Christ, "to be thrown with a millstone around the neck, into the depths of the sea, than to have scandalized the least of the little ones." What, then, is the scandal of a king who shows vice seated with him on the throne, not only to all his subjects, but also to all the courts and all the nations of the known world, . . . Perhaps you believe that your disorders have been secret. No, evil is never secret for princes. Good can be secret, for one has some difficulty to believe the good of them; but for evil, one divines it, one believes it on the least suspicions. . . .

11. Have you not authorized immodest liberty in women? Have you admitted them to your court only for good reasons? . . . Have you excluded young women whose beauty would be a temptation for you and your courtiers? It would be better that such people remain in a retired life, in the heart of their own families, far from the court. . . .

12. Have you taken care to restrain luxury and check the numerous consequences of fashion? It is this which corrupts the most of the women. They incur expenses at the court that they cannot sustain without crime. Luxury augments in them passions. . . .

13. Have you not given bad example either by words too free or by piquant raillery or by indecent manners in speaking of religion? Courtiers are servile imitators who glory in having all the faults of princes.

ARTICLE III: OF JUSTICE THAT OUGHT TO TAKE PRECEDENCE IN ALL ACTS OF GOVERNMENT

14. Have you taken anything from your subjects by pure authority and contrary to law? Have you made amends as a private person would have when you have taken a man's house or enclosed his field in your park or suppressed his charge [office that he had bought] or extinguished his interest payments? Have you examined the true needs of the state to compare them with the weight of taxation before loading the tax on your people? Have you consulted . . . the most informed, the most zealous for the public good, and the most competent men to tell you the truth without flattery? . . . Have you not called necessary for the state that which only flatters your vanity? . . .

15. Have you not tolerated injustices even if you have refrained from doing them? . . . Have you informed yourself of the acts of your administration? Have you let it be understood that you are ready to listen to complaints . . . and to give justice? Have you done it when you discovered the faults [of your ministers]?

16. Have you not given your ministers, or at least allowed them to take, excessive profits that their services have not merited? The compensations that a prince gives to those who serve his state ought always to have certain limits. . . . It is still less permitted to give such fortunes to favorites who ordinarily have served the state even less.

18. Have you searched for means to care for your people, and to take from them only that which the true needs of state require? The goods of the people ought only to be used for their own needs. You have your *domaine* [private lands of the king] . . . it is intended for the sustenance of your house.

You ought to moderate these domestic expenses, above all when your *domaine* revenues are mortgaged. . . . The tax payments of the people ought to be used for the true business of state. You ought to study to retrench in times of public poverty all costs which are not absolutely necessary. . . .

19. Have you not multiplied expenses and offices in order to draw from their creation new sums of money [sale of offices]? Such creations are only disguised taxes. They result in the oppression of the people. . . .

20. Have you never tolerated and wished to ignore that your ministers had taken private property for your use without paying just value? . . .

21. In contracts that you make with private persons, are you just, as though you were the equal of the one with whom you contract? . . .

23. Have you not tolerated enlistments [in the army] that were not truly free? It is true that the people ought to defend the state, but that is only for just and absolutely necessary wars. It would be necessary to choose from each village the free young men whose absence will not hurt anything. . . . But to take men without choice and in spite of themselves, to leave an entire family to languish and often perish without its head, to take a laborer from the plow, to take him for ten, fifteen years in the service, where he perishes often of misery in hospitals unsupplied with necessary services. . . . This cannot be excused either before God or man.

24. Have you been careful to free each galley slave as soon as the term imposed by the courts for his punishment is finished? The condition of these men is terrible; nothing is more inhuman than to prolong their term. . . .

25. Have you always paid your troops so that they can live without pillage? If you have not you place your soldiers in a condition necessitating pillage and violence. . . . Do you punish them for doing that which you know well they could not avoid doing? . . .

26. Have you not done injustice to a foreign nation? One hangs a poor wretch for having stolen a coin . . . and one treats as a hero a man who makes a conquest; that is to say, subjugates unjustly a neighboring state. . . . War which you have commenced with bad intention and which you have sustained with success, far from giving you a good conscience, rather engages you not only to restore the usurped lands but also to pay all the damages caused by reason of your violence. . . .

27. When war is in question have you first of all examined your rights and submitted them to the most intelligent and least disposed to flatter of your councillors? Have you mistrusted the councils of certain ministers who had an interest in involving you in a war or at least sought to flatter your vanity? . . . Have you considered all the reasons which can be made against you? . . . Have you not looked to your personal glory as a reason for undertaking an adventure, for fear of passing your life without distinguishing yourself from other princes? . . .

28. Have you well studied whether the war in question was necessary for your people? Perhaps it only concerned some contention about succession that involved you personally; your people have no real interest in it. Does it matter to them that you have another province? . . .

29. Have you faithfully kept your word with your enemies, given in capitulations, etc? There are laws of war that must be respected no less religiously than those of peace. . . .

30. It is not enough to respect the capitulations made with enemies; it is also necessary to respect them religiously with regard to the conquered peoples. . . . They owe you obedience only ac-

cording to the contract, and if you violate it, you do not deserve to have them observe it.

31. During a war have you not done unnecessary evil to your enemies? These enemies are still men, still your brothers, if you are truly a man yourself. . . . You must render account to God, and to repair, according to all in your power, all the evils that you have authorized and that have been done unnecessarily.

32. Have you punctually fulfilled peace treaties? Have you never violated them under vain pretexts? With respect to articles of ancient treaties which are ambiguous, in place of finding in them reasons for war, it is necessary to interpret them by the practices that followed their signing [customary law].

Bishop Fénelon, *An Examination of Conscience on the Duties of Royalty Composed for the Instruction of Louis of France, Duke of Burgundy* (1692), trans. John B. Wolf, from *Oeuvres de Fénelon,* III (1838), 335 ff.

D. Louis XIV's Instructions to the Duke of Anjou

1. Never omit any of your duties, especially towards God.

2. Preserve yourself in the purity of your bringing up.

3. Cause God to be honoured in all places where you have power; procure His glory; give the example. It is one of the greatest forms of good that Kings can do.

4. On every occasion declare yourself on the side of virtue and against vice.

5. Have no attachment ever to any one.

6. Love your wife, lead a good life with her, and ask God to give you one suitable to you. . . .

7. Love the Spaniards and all your subjects attached to your Crowns and to your person; do not give preference to those who flatter you most; esteem those who for a good cause venture to displease you; these are your real friends.

8. Make your subjects happy; and, with a view to this, only engage in war when you are obliged, and after you have well considered and weighed the reasons with your Council.

9. Endeavour to keep your finances in good order; watch over the Indies and your fleets; keep your commerce in mind; live in close union with France, since there is nothing so advantageous to our two Powers as this union which nothing can withstand.

10. If you are compelled to go to war, place yourself at the head of your armies.

12. Never leave your affairs for your pleasure; but make for yourself a rule of some kind which will give you occasions of liberty and distraction.

13. Of these there is hardly a more innocent one than the chase and the pleasure of some country house, provided that you do not incur too much expense thereon.

14. Pay great attention to your affairs; when people discuss them with you listen to them at length at the beginning, without deciding anything.

15. When you have attained to more knowledge, remember that it is for you to decide; but whatever be your experience, always hearken to all the advice and all the arguments of your Council before coming to this decision.

16. Do all in your power to get to know well the most important people, in order that you may make suitable use of them.

17. See that your Viceroys and Governors shall always be Spaniards.

18. Treat every one well; never say anything vexing to any one, but do honour to people of quality and merit.

25. Treat your domestic servants well,

but do not allow them too much familiarity, and trust them still less; use them so long as they are well-behaved; dismiss them on the least fault they commit and never uphold them against the Spaniards.

29. Throw some money to the people when you are in Spain, and especially when entering Madrid.

30. Do not appear astonished at the extraordinary figures you will meet; never make fun of them; each country has its peculiar manners and you will soon become accustomed to what at first will seem most surprising to you.

31. Avoid as far as you can granting favours to those who give money to obtain them; dispense suitably and liberally, and be chary of accepting presents except they be trifling; if sometimes you cannot help accepting them, give a more valuable one to the donor after allowing a few days to pass.

32. Keep a privy purse in which to put your own money, of which you alone have the key.

33. I will end with one of the most important pieces of advice that I can give you: never allow yourself to be ruled; be the master; have no favourites or prime minister; listen to, and consult your Council, but do you decide yourself. God, who made you King, will give you the lights which are necessary to you, so long as you have a right intention.

Louis XIV, *Instructions to the Duke of Anjou* (1700), trans. Herbert Wilson, *op. cit.*, pp. 173-176.

9. The Enlightenment: The Nature of Man and the State

CRANE BRINTON

Harvard University

IN THE LATTER HALF of the eighteenth century, revolutions in the British North American colonies and in France, together with the earlier revolutions in England in the seventeenth century, gave Western civilization the basic institutions of modern democracy. From the American and the French revolutions there emerged documents—the American Declaration of Independence, the state Bills of Right, the Bill of Rights incorporated in the first ten amendments to our Constitution, the French Declaration of the Rights of Man and the Citizen, the "principles of 1776 and 1789"—which are among the most important charters of modern democracy. These documents in turn emerge from, and reflect, a century-long debate over the nature of man and the state known even to its participants—and to historians ever since —as the "Enlightenment." The debate was no narrowly political one. It was conducted through all the media of public opinion, through essays, novels, drama, and poetry, through pamphlets, magazines, and the nascent newspaper, through pulpits, schools, clubs, and fraternal societies as well as (where there were such institutions, as in England, the thirteen colonies, Switzerland, certain French provinces) political assemblies. Since out of this great debate there took shape many of the ideas most Americans have been brought up on, and tend to take for granted, it is particularly important, now that the "principles of 1776 and 1789" are facing the challenge of totalitarian principles, for us to re-examine them in their historical origins. Such a re-examination should strengthen rather than weaken our belief in their fundamental validity. It should enable us to revise them where they are wrong, or incomplete.

A concrete series of historical events sets the framework for the later critical attack on the ideas of the Enlightenment. The great French Revolution was begun in 1789 in an atmosphere of world-wide hope that these events would usher in an era of universal peace and happiness, when men would live according to the great watchwords of the Enlightenment, Reason and Nature.

But by 1793 France was in the midst of a bloody Reign of Terror, and by 1799 the democratic experiment had turned into the dictatorship of a successful general, Napoleon Bonaparte. The long and exhausting Napoleonic wars added to the disillusion the Reign of Terror had begun. Nineteenth-century thinkers began, quite naturally indeed, to blame their eighteenth-century predecessors of the Enlightenment for what had gone wrong.

The Enlightenment, they maintained, had made a false estimate of the nature and capacity of human beings. It had disastrously oversimplified moral and political problems. It had supposed men to be by natural endowment rational creatures, essentially much alike. It had found the sole source of the obviously existing evils of the eighteenth century—grave inequalities of wealth and prestige, war, crime, vice, all the long tale of human suffering—in environment, in society, in something "artificial," not "natural." It had believed it possible, by a process ultimately one of education, to free men everywhere from this bad environment, from kings and nobles and priests, from privilege, convention, ignorance, and superstition, and substitute a good environment under which men's natural goodness and reasonableness would shortly bring universal happiness. It had succeeded, at least for a brief time in France, in persuading men to attempt to eliminate much of the old network of tradition and institutions, the old, bad "environment" we call society. But instead of creating a new society based on Reason and Nature, the French seemed to have lapsed into barbarism. Surely the Enlightenment had been wrong about the fundamental nature of man and the state?

The matter was put in a neat figure of speech by the French historian Taine in his *Origins of Contemporary France,* written in the 1870's and 1880's: You see a man in sound health drink from a cup; he falls suddenly to the ground in a fit; you conclude that the drink contained a poison. The drinker, says Taine, was the French revolutionary, the Jacobin, and the drink was the evil brew prepared for him by the thinkers of the Enlightenment, by Locke, by Voltaire, by Rousseau, by Jefferson, and their fellow thinkers.

It will be our purpose in the following problems to judge the broad lines of the thought of the Enlightenment by excerpts from the actual writings of the thinkers of the Enlightenment. Now it is supremely difficult to judge the thought of an age, especially in a culture like that of the modern Western world, where the range of individual taste and opinion is so wide. The reader will see the difficulty at once if he tries to summarize in broad generalities the beliefs and attitudes even of a small group he knows well, say his own college, even his own fraternity. He will always find exceptions, individuals who don't fit the pattern he is trying to make. But the effort must be made, for we cannot do without such patterns.

It is always easy to pick out the concrete instances which support the general propositions one is working with, and push aside those which conflict with it. Such a process, it seems to the present writer, went on in the mind of the Taine we have just cited on the Jacobin. Taine, who accused the thinkers of the Enlightenment of oversimplification, himself was guilty of oversimplification. It is hard not to "rig" the interpretation of so broad a problem as the one we are here concerned with. These excerpts from the thought of the Enlightenment are so few in comparison with the millions of printed words of the period still preserved in our libraries! The student cannot be too strongly urged to take these excerpts as a mere springboard from which he can leap off into the abundant and varied thought of the Enlightenment. It is a rich and rewarding period to study, and its thought is basic to our own.

We shall in the following problems concentrate on the central problem of definition. What did these thinkers mean by "reason," "nature," "God," "good," "evil," "society," and the like? Did they simplify human beings into mere thinking machines? Did they fail to allow for the part emotions, passion, prejudice, and habit play in human life? Did they think of the past as a mere tissue of errors which enlightenment could quickly dispel? Were they devoted to the kind of thinking the geometrician uses, deductive reasoners from a few simple postulates, neglectful of "facts," of observation and experiment? Were they devoid of a sense of history, of the complicated processes of growth in men and in society which has made us what we are? Did they think of reform of human institutions as essentially a simple engineering task, themselves as makers of neat blueprints anybody could follow to build the perfect society? Were they, in short, "terrible simplifiers," a phrase in which the nineteenth-century Swiss historian Burckhardt anticipated the totalitarians of our own day?

To those who want definite answers, the kind of answer you get to a problem in arithmetic, any sensible conclusion from the following investigation of the meaning the thinkers of the Enlightenment gave to "reason" and "nature," their attitudes toward the nature of man and state, will be a conclusion that concludes nothing. One can indeed conclude that the Enlightenment was a movement of protest against things-as-they-are, that its thinkers sought to change, often quite radically, things-as-they-are. But one cannot conclude that they were in anything like complete agreement. They were, like ourselves, divided in the answers they gave in the great debate over the philosophical, ethical, and political questions of man's place in the universe. But they enjoyed the debate, they threw themselves into it with gusto, and they believed the debate was good. Perhaps some of them believed that the debate would quite soon be settled, that all men once enlightened would agree on the answers, and would live according to the answers. But the important thing for us is that these eighteenth-century thinkers believed in the debate itself, and in men's freedom—indeed, their *need*—to take part in it. There is a famous saying attributed to Voltaire, which cannot indeed be found in his writings, but which surely is in character. He is said to have written Helvetius: "I disagree with everything you say, but I would fight to the death for your right to say it." Perhaps this is a better answer to our problem here than it may seem at first to be.

I. REASON: DEDUCTION OR OBSERVATION AND EXPERIMENT?

One of the great reproaches made against the thinkers of the Enlightenment is that they thought in long chains of deduction, as do mathematicians. It is claimed that, though they gave lip-service to the careful experiments and observations of natural science, they did not really recognize the dangers of thinking without frequent refreshing returns to the earth of facts, of sense data. We begin with an excerpt from the seventeenth-century French philosopher, René Descartes, in which this "rationalistic" mathematical method of reasoning is clearly stated. Descartes is one of the important intellectual sources of the Enlightenment. His influence, especially on the continent, was perhaps greater than that of the scientist Newton. In Descartes men found clearly stated, not only the logic of mathematical reasoning, but the basic theme of the Enlightenment: think it out for yourself, regardless of what your parents, your teachers, your priests have told you, regardless of Authority and Tradition. Our other selections suggest how different indeed were men's interpretation of "reason"; we have Jonathan Swift, the brilliant Anglo-Irish satirist, and two Frenchmen, Voltaire, symbol for the whole Enlightenment, and Denis Diderot, one of the subtlest and most imaginative of the French *philosophes*, a writer whose reputation has risen greatly in our own century. Do these thinkers advocate an oversimple, mathematical approach to the problems of human relations? Is man for them a mere thinking machine?

A. Descartés. Right Reason, 1637

Good sense is better distributed than anything in the world; for each thinks himself so well provided therewith, that as a rule even those who are the most difficult to satisfy with regard to everything else, do not desire more of it than they already have. This does not show that every one deceives himself; it testifies rather to the fact that the power of judging well and of distinguishing the true from the false, which is properly that which we call good sense, or reason, is naturally equal in all men. And thus the diversity of our opinions is not because some are more reasonable than others, but only because we conduct our thought by different ways, and do not all consider the same things. For it is not sufficient that the understanding be good—the thing is to apply it well. The greatest minds are capable of the greatest vices as well as of the greatest virtues, and those who proceed but slowly can advance much further, if they follow the right road, than those who hasten in the wrong direction.

For my own part, I have never presumed that my understanding was in any way more perfect than that of most people: indeed, I have often wished that my thought were as quick, or my imagination as exact and vivid, or my memory as comprehensive or as ready, as those of others. And I know no qualities but these which make for the perfection of the mind, for inasmuch as reason or sense is the only thing which renders us human and distinguishes us from animals, I would believe that it is quite complete in every individual, and follow herein the common opinion of the philosophers, who say that there are variations only as regards accidentals, and not between the forms and natures of individuals. . . .

Above all, I took pleasure in mathematics, because of the certainty and evidence of their reasons, but I did not yet remark their true use; and thinking that they served the mechanical arts alone, I was surprised that since their foundations were so firm and solid, nothing more lofty had been built upon them. So, on the other hand, I compared the writings of ancient pagans who treated of morals to very superb and magnificent palaces built only on sand and mud, for they highly exalted the virtues and made them appear estimable above all existing things, but they did not sufficiently teach how to know them, and often that which they call by so fine a name is only insensibility, or pride, or despair, or parricide. . . .

I could in nowise approve those blundering and restless persons who, being called neither by birth nor fortune to the management of public affairs, are always devising some new reformation. And if I thought that this writing contained the least thing which could make me suspected of this folly, I should be very sorry to permit its publication. My design never extends further than the endeavour to reform my own thoughts, and to build on ground which is wholly mine. If, since my work has pleased me, I here show you its plan, it is not because I wish to counsel any one to imitate it. Those to whom God has allotted more of His grace would perhaps have loftier designs, but I much fear that this one is already but too hard for many. Even the resolve to free oneself from all opinions formerly accepted and believed is not an example which every man ought to follow, and the world is almost solely made up of two classes of minds for whom it is by no means expedient,—to wit, of those who, thinking themselves cleverer than they are, cannot refrain from precipitating their judgments, and have not patience enough to conduct all their thoughts methodically, so that if they once took the liberty of doubting the principles they have received, and of escaping from the beaten track, they would never be able to keep to the path they ought to follow in order to proceed more directly, and would remain astray all their life; and those who, having sufficient reason or modesty to judge that they are less capable of distinguishing the true from the false than others by whom they might be instructed, ought much rather to content themselves with following the opinions of those others than seek better for themselves. . . .

I do not know whether I ought to discuss with you the earlier of my meditations, for they are so metaphysical and so out of the common that perhaps they would not be to every one's taste; and yet, in order that it may be judged whether the bases I have taken are sufficiently firm, I am in some measure constrained to speak of them. I had remarked for long that, in conduct, it is sometimes necessary to follow opinions known to be very uncertain, just as if they were indubitable, as has been said above: but then, because I desired to devote myself only to the research of truth, I thought it necessary to do exactly the contrary, and reject as absolutely false all in which I could conceive the least doubt, in order to see if afterwards there did not remain in my belief something which was entirely indubitable. Thus, because our senses sometimes deceive us, I wanted to suppose that nothing is such as they make us imagine it; and because some men err in reasoning, even touching the simplest matters of geometry, and make paralogisms, and judging that I was as liable to fail as any other, I rejected as false all the reasons which I had formerly accepted as demonstrations; and finally, considering that all the thoughts which we have when awake, can come to us also when we sleep, without any of them then being true, I resolved to feign that everything which had ever entered into my mind was no more true than the illusions of my dreams. But immediately afterwards I observed, that while I thus desired everything to be false, I, who thought, must of necessity be something; and remarking that this truth, *I think, therefore I am*, was so firm and so assured that all the most extravagant suppositions of the sceptics were unable to shake it, I judged that I could unhesitatingly accept it as the first principle of the philosophy I was seeking.

Then, examining attentively what I was, and seeing that I could feign that I had no body, and that there was no world or any place where I was, but that nevertheless I could not feign that I did not exist, and that, on the contrary, from the fact that I thought to doubt of the truth of other things, it followed very evidently that I was; while if I had only ceased to think, although all else which I had previously imagined had been true, I had no reason to believe that I might have been, therefore I knew that I was a substance whose essence or nature is only to think, and which, in order to be, has no need of any place, and depends on no material thing; so that this I, that is to say, the soul by which I am what I am, is entirely distinct from the body, and even easier to know than the body, and although the body were not, the soul would not cease to be all that it is.

After that I considered generally what is requisite to make a proposition true and certain; for since I had just found one which I knew to be so, I thought that I ought also to know in what this certainty consisted. And having remarked that there is nothing at all in this, *I think, therefore I am,* which assures me that I speak the truth, except that I see very clearly that in order to think it is necessary to exist, I judged that I might take it as a general rule, that the things which we conceive very clearly and very distinctly are all true, and that there is difficulty only in seeing plainly which things are that we conceive distinctly.

René Descartes, *Discourse on Method and Metaphysical Meditations* (London: Walter Scott Publishing Co., n. d.), pp. 2-3, 9, 17-19, 37-39.

B. Swift. *The Anti-Intellectual Attack on Scientific Reason, 1726*

This Academy is not an entire single building, but a continuation of several houses on both sides of a street, which growing waste was purchased and applied to that use.

I was received very kindly by the Warden, and went for many days to the Academy. Every room hath in it one or more projectors, and I believe I could not be in fewer than five hundred rooms.

The first man I saw was of a meagre aspect, with sooty hands and face, his hair and beard long, ragged and singed in several places. His clothes, shirt, and skin were all of the same colour. He had been eight years upon a project for extracting sun-beams out of cucumbers, which were to be put into vials hermetically sealed, and let out to warm the air in raw inclement summers. He told me he did not doubt in eight years more he should be able to supply the Governor's gardens with sunshine at a reasonable rate; but he complained that his stock was low, and entreated me to give him something as an encouragement to ingenuity, especially since this had been a very dear season for cucumbers. I made him a small present, for my lord had furnished me with money on purpose, because he knew their practice of begging from all who go to see them.

I went into another chamber, but was ready to hasten back, being almost overcome with a horrible stink. My conductor pressed me forward, conjuring me in a whisper to give no offence, which would be highly resented, and therefore I durst not so much as stop my nose. The projector of this cell was the most ancient student of the Academy; his face and beard were of a pale yellow; his hands and clothes daubed over with filth. When I was presented to him, he gave me a close embrace (a compliment I could well have excused). His employment from his first coming into the Academy, was an operation to reduce human excrement to its original food, by separating the several parts, removing the tincture which it receives from the gall, making the odour exhale, and scumming off the saliva. He had a weekly allowance from the society, of a vessel filled with human ordure, about the bigness of a Bristol barrel. . . .

We crossed a walk to the other part of the Academy, where, as I have already said, the projectors in speculative learning resided.

The first professor I saw in a very large room with forty pupils about him. After salutation, observing me to look earnestly upon a frame, which took up the greatest part of both the length and breadth of the room, he said perhaps I might wonder to see him employed in a project for improving speculative knowledge by practical and mechanical operations. But the world would soon be sensible of its usefulness, and he flattered himself that a more noble exalted thought never sprang in any other man's head. Every one knew how laborious the usual method is of attaining to arts and sciences; whereas by his contrivance the most ignorant person at a reasonable charge, and with a little bodily labour, may write books in philosophy, poetry, politics, law, mathematics, and theology, without the least assistance from genius or study. He then led me to the frame, about the sides whereof all his pupils stood in ranks. It was twenty foot square, placed in the middle of the room. The superficies was composed of several bits of wood, about the bigness of a die, but some larger than others. They were all linked together by slender wires. These bits of wood were covered on every square with paper pasted on them,

and on these papers were written all the words of their language, in their several moods, tenses, and declensions, but without any order. The professor then desired me to observe, for he was going to set his engine at work. The pupils at his command took each of them hold of an iron handle, whereof there were forty fixed round the edges of the frame, and giving them a sudden turn, the whole disposition of the words was entirely changed. He then commanded six and thirty of the lads to read the several lines softly as they appeared upon the frame; and where they found three or four words together that might make part of a sentence, they dictated to the four remaining boys who were scribes. This work was repeated three or four times, and at every turn the engine was so contrived that the words shifted into new places, as the square bits of wood moved upside down.

Six hours a day the young students were employed in this labour, and the professor showed me several volumes in large folio already collected, of broken sentences, which he intended to piece together, and out of those rich materials to give the world a complete body of all arts and sciences; which however might be still improved, and much expedited, if the public would raise a fund for making and employing five hundred such frames in Lagado, and oblige the managers to contribute in common their several collections.

He assured me, that this invention had employed all his thoughts from his youth, that he had emptied the whole vocabulary into his frame, and made the strictest computation of the general proportion there is in books between the numbers of particles, nouns, and verbs, and other parts of speech.

I made my humblest acknowledgement to this illustrious person for his great communicativeness, and promised if ever I had the good fortune to return to my native country, that I would do him justice, as the sole inventor of this wonderful machine; the form and contrivance of which I desired leave to delineate upon paper, as in the figure here annexed. I told him, although it were the custom of our learned in Europe to steal inventions from each other, who had thereby at least this advantage, that it became a controversy which was the right owner, yet I would take such caution, that he should have the honour entire without a rival.

We next went to the school of languages, where three professors sat in consultation upon improving that of their own country.

The first project was to shorten discourse by cutting polysyllables into one, and leaving out verbs and participles, because in reality all things imaginable are but nouns.

The other project was a scheme for entirely abolishing all words whatsoever; and this was urged as a great advantage in point of health as well as brevity. For it is plain that every word we speak is in some degree a diminution of our lungs by corrosion, and consequently contributes to the shortening of our lives. An expedient was therefore offered, that since words are only names for *things*, it would be more convenient for all men to carry about them such things as were necessary to express the particular business they are to discourse on. And this invention would certainly have taken place, to the great ease as well as health of the subject, if the women, in conjunction with the vulgar and illiterate, had not threatened to raise a rebellion, unless they might be allowed the liberty to speak with their tongues, after the manner of their ancestors; such constant irreconcilable enemies to science are the common people.

Jonathan Swift, *Gulliver's Travels,* ed. W. A. Eddy (London: Oxford Standard Authors, 1933), Part III, chap. V, pp. 212-221.

C. Voltaire. On Locke, *1733*

Perhaps there never was a more sage, a more methodical genius, never a more accurate logician, than Locke; yet he was by no means a great mathematician. He could never submit to the fatigue of calculations, nor endure the dry and barren nature of mathematical truths, which do not at first present the mind with any sensible image; and no man was ever a more decisive evidence, that it is possible to have a geometrical mind, without the assistance of geometry. Before his time, great philosophers had decided positively in what the soul of man consisted. But as they knew nothing at all about the matter, they were, just as might be expected, all of different opinions.

In Greece, the cradle both of arts and errors, and in which the strength and weakness of the human mind have been so strikingly displayed, men reasoned, as we ourselves do now, upon the subject of the soul. The divine Anaxagoras —to whom an altar was raised, for having taught mankind that the sun was larger than the Peloponnesus, that snow was black, and that the heavens were composed of stone—asserted that the soul was an aerial spirit, but nevertheless immortal. Diogenes, a different man from him who became a cynic, after having been a dealer in base coin, asserted, that the soul was a portion of the very substance of God himself; an idea which was, at least, brilliant and dazzling. Epicurus composed it of parts, like the body. Aristotle, who has been explained in innumerable ways, because he was utterly unintelligible, believed, if we refer for his belief to some of his disciples, that the understanding of all men was one and the same substance. The divine Plato, master of the divine Aristotle—and the divine Socrates, master of the divine Plato, pronounced the soul corporeal and eternal. The demon of Socrates had undoubtedly informed him what it was. There are, indeed, people who pretend that a man who boasted of having a familiar genius, must inevitably have been a little foolish, or a little knavish; but such people are extremely difficult to please.

With respect to our fathers of the church, many in the early ages thought the human soul, and angels, and God himself, corporeal. The world improves and refines every day. St. Bernard, according to the confession of Father Mabillon, taught, on the subject of the soul, that after death it did not see God, in heaven, but communed solely with the humanity of Jesus Christ. For this once, he was not believed upon his word; and, indeed, the adventure of the crusade had rather discredited his oracles. Numberless schoolmen appeared afterwards upon the stage in pompous succession, such as the irrefragable doctor, the subtle doctor, the angelic doctor, the seraphic doctor, and the cherubic doctor, all of whom were perfectly confident they understood the nature of the human soul, but at the same time always spoke about it as if they wished no one else should understand it. Our own countryman, Descartes—born to detect the errors of antiquity, but unfortunately also to substitute his own in their room, and urged on by that spirit of system which blinds the strongest understandings—conceived he had demonstrated that the soul was the same thing as thought; as matter, according to him, is the same thing as extension. He affirms strongly, that a man always thinks, and that the soul arrives in the body provided with a whole stock of metaphysical notions, acquainted with God, with space and infinity, in possession of all sorts of abstract ideas, full, in short, of beautiful and sublime knowledge, which, most unluckily, it totally forgets immediately on its departure from the mother's womb. Father Malebranche, of the Oratory, in his sublime illusions, does not admit the doctrine of innate ideas; but he had no doubt but that we saw in God everything, and that God, if we may so express it, was in fact our soul.

After so many random reasoners had been thus forming what might have been called the Romance of the Soul, a sage appears who has modestly presented us with the history of it. Mr. Locke has developed human reason to man, just as a skilful anatomist explains the springs and structure of the human body. He avails himself of all the light that can be derived from natural philosophy; he sometimes ventures to speak affirmatively; but he also ventures to express doubt. Instead of displaying definitions of what we are little or not at all acquainted with, he examines, step by step, what we wish to be acquainted with. He begins with an infant at its birth; he follows slowly and cautiously the progress of its understanding; and he sees what it has in common with brutes, and what it has above them. He consults particularly his own testimony—the evidence of consciousness. 'I leave those', says he, 'who are better informed on the subject than myself, to discuss whether the soul exists before, or not until after the organization of the body; but I acknowledge it has fallen to my lot to have one of those heavy and inert souls which do not always think; and I am even unfortunate enough to conceive, that it may very possibly be no more necessary that the soul should be always thinking, than that the body should be always in motion'.

With regard to myself, I pride myself

in being on this subject as simple as Mr. Locke. No one can ever induce me to believe that I am always thinking, and I feel no more disposed than he was, to imagine that a few weeks after my conception I was a very knowing soul, acquainted with a thousand things which I forgot on being born; and that I have to no purpose whatever possessed, while in the womb, invaluable stores of information, which abandoned me the instant I really wanted them, and which I have never since been able to recover.

Locke, after having destroyed innate ideas; after having wisely renounced the vanity of believing that man always thinks; having well established the principle, that all our ideas are derived to us through the senses; having examined our simple and analysed our compound ideas; having followed the human mind through all its operations; having pointed out the imperfections of the various languages employed by mankind, and the abuse we make of words almost every moment of our lives— Locke, I say, at last considers the extent, or rather the nothingness, of human knowledge. It is in this chapter that he ventures modestly to observe:— 'We shall, perhaps, never be capable of knowing, whether a being purely material thinks or not'. This judicious and guarded observation was considered by more than one divine, as neither more nor less than a scandalous and impious declaration, that the soul is material and mortal. Some English devotees, after

their usual manner, sounded the alarm. The superstitious are in society what poltroons are in an army—they both feel and excite causeless terror. The cry was that Mr. Locke wished to overturn religion: the subject, however, had nothing to do with religion at all; it was purely a philosophical question, and perfectly independent of faith and revelation. It was only necessary to examine, without acrimony or heat, whether there is any contradiction in say—'Matter may think, and God may communicate thought to matter'. But theologians too often begin with passionately charging the man who does not join in their opinion with blaspheming or insulting God. . . .

Every philosopher is destined to endure reviling and calumny. For one man capable of replying with reason, there are a hundred who have nothing to advance but abuse, and every one pays with the money which he possesses. My ears are every day dinned and wearied with the exclamations—'Locke denies the immortality of the soul; Locke destroys morality'; and what is surprising, if anything could surprise, is that out of all those who in this manner bring accusations against the morality of Locke, there are very few indeed that have ever read him, fewer still that have understood him, and none whom it is not our duty to wish possessed of such virtues as were possessed by that great man, who so truly merited the epithets of wise and good.

Desmond Flower, ed., *Voltaire's England* (London: The Folio Society, 1950), pp. 175-183.

D. Diderot. *The Interpretation of Nature, 1754*

VII. So long as things are only in our understanding, they are our opinions; these are notions which can be true or false, granted or denied. They take on consistency only by being related to externally existing things. This connection is made either by an uninterrupted chain of reasoning, which is connected at one end with observation and at the other with experiment; or by a series of experiments dispersed at intervals along the chain of reasoning, like weights along a thread suspended by its two ends. Without these weights the thread would be the sport of the slightest motion of the air.

VIII. One may compare ideas which have no foundation in nature, to those forests of the North whose trees have no roots. It needs only a breath of wind, only a small fact, to overturn a whole forest of trees and of ideas.

IX. Men are disturbed to feel how severe are the laws of the investigation of truth, and how limited is the number of our means. Everything is reduced to a return from the senses to reflection, and from reflection to the senses: to turn into oneself and to turn outwards again, ceaselessly; it is the labour of the bee. Much country has been covered in vain, if a load of wax is not brought back to the hive. A useless accumulation of wax has been made if it is not known how to make a comb of it.

X. But, unfortunately, it is easier and quicker to consult oneself than to consult nature. Also, reason is inclined to dwell within itself, and instinct to spread outward. Ceaselessly instinct goes, observing, tasting, touching, listening and there would be perhaps more experimental physics to be learnt by studying animals than by following a course of lectures by a professor. There is no deception in their behaviour. They proceed to their ends without caring about what surrounds them; if they surprise us, it is not in the least their intention. Astonishment is the first effect of some great phenomenon: it is the task of philosophy to dissipate this. In a course of experimental philosophy, it is a question of sending the student away more enlightened and not more puzzled. To pride oneself about the phenomena of nature, as if one were the author of them oneself, is to imitate the stupidity of that editor of the *Essais*,

who could not hear the name of Montaigne without blushing. A great lesson which there is often occasion to give, is the confession of one's insufficiency. Is it not better to gain the confidence of others by the sincerity of a "I know nothing about it," than to babble words and excite pity for oneself, by trying to explain everything? He who freely admits that he does not know the things of which he is ignorant, disposes me to believe that what he undertakes to make me admit is correct.

XI. Astonishment often comes from supposing several marvels where there is only one; from imagining in nature as many particular acts as there are phenomena, while perhaps it has ever produced but a single act. It seems, even, that if it had been under the necessity of producing several acts, the different results of these acts would have been isolated; that there would have been collections of phenomena independent of one another, and that the general connection of things, of which philosophy supposes the continuity, would be broken at several places. The absolute independence of a single fact is incompatible with the idea of the whole; and without the idea of the whole, no more philosophy. . . .

XIV. I represent to myself the vast body of science as a large area strewn with dark places and with illuminated places. Our labours should have as their aim, either to extend the limits of the lighted places, or to multiply the number of centres of illumination. The latter is for the creative genius; the other for the wisdom which improves, develops, amplifies.

XV. We have three principal means: the observation of nature, thought and experiment. Observation collects the facts, thought combines them, and experiment verifies the result of the combination. The observation of nature must be assiduous, the thinking must be profound and the experiment must be exact. One rarely sees these methods combined. And creative geniuses are not common. . . .

XXIII. We have distinguished two kinds of philosophy, the experimental and that based on reasoning. The former has its eyes bandaged, walks always feeling its way, grasps whatever falls into its hands and finds precious things in the end. The other gathers these precious things, and tries to make a torch of them; but this pretended torch has up to the present served it less well than the gropings of its rival, and this must be so. Experiment mul-

tiplies its actions infinitely, it is ceaselessly in action, it is busy seeking phenomena all the time that reasoning uses in seeking analogies. Experimental philosophy knows neither what will come nor will not come out of its labours; but it works on without relaxing. The philosophy based on reasoning, on the contrary, weighs possibilities, makes a pronouncement and stops short. It boldly said: "light cannot be decomposed": experimental philosophy heard, and held its tongue in its presence for whole centuries; then suddenly it produced the prism, and said, "light can be decomposed."

Jonathan Kemp, ed., *Diderot: Interpreter of Nature,* in *Selected Writings,* trans. Jean Stewart and Jonathan Kemp (New York: International Publishers, 1943), pp. 43-47.

II. RELIGION IN THE ENLIGHTENMENT: GOD AND NATURE

Organized Christianity was one of the great targets for the critical thought of the Enlightenment. To many of the thinkers of the eighteenth century, Christianity was an "unnatural" superstition, its miracles unconfirmed by their "modern" science, its dogmas unreasonable, its whole structure dedicated to maintaining existing—and evil —society. "Revelation" they denied as a valid criterion of truth. They sought for what they called a "natural" in contrast with a "revealed" religion. But their actual range of religious opinion was great. Some sought to retain Christianity purified of its "superstitions," but with its ethics and much of its theology intact. These men are *theists*. Others sought to create a new religion, based on the orderly universe Newton had made familiar to their generation, a universe in which Nature was deified as a kind of Supreme Being. These men are *deists,* who believe in what a critic has called the "clockmaker God"—a God who has made the universe, including man, and has set it in motion, but who never interferes with its running according to the laws he made for it. Voltaire was a deist, at least for practical purposes. Jean Jacques Rousseau was a deist of more seri-

ous turn. Finally, there are the *atheists*, men who maintain that all we can know is the material universe, and that if there is a God who began everything, we cannot possibly know anything at all about him, and had better give up talking about him. Atheism was actually a most unpopular doctrine in the eighteenth century, and its open profession illegal almost everywhere. One of its earliest and most outright advocates was the French physician La Mettrie's *L'Homme Machine (Man a Machine),* published in 1748. Though legally banned almost everywhere, the book circulated, as did most banned books, quite freely among the educated public throughout the Europe of the Enlightenment. *Man a Machine* is, however, packed with allusions to writers ancient and modern, and any excerpt would require too many explanatory footnotes for our use. We take instead to represent the atheist's position a short dialogue by the Marquis de Sade, who was quite as outspoken as La Mettrie. Finally, it must not be forgotten that the position of Christian theism was by no means without defenders in the eighteenth century. We take as an example a brief pamphlet of John Wesley, the English divine who founded the most numerous Protestant sect to emerge from this century, the Methodists. These excerpts give a kind of incomplete spectrum of eighteenth-century attitudes toward religion. Are any of these men really *skeptics?*

A. Voltaire. "On the Soul and God," *1770*

Monseigneur, the royal family of Prussia has excellent reasons for not wishing the annihilation of the soul. It has more right than anyone to immortality.

It is very true that we do not know any too well what the soul is: no one has ever seen it. All that we do know is that the eternal Lord of nature has given us the power of thinking, and of distinguishing virtue. It is not proved that this faculty survives our death: but the contrary is not proved either. It is possible, doubtless, that God has given thought to a particle to which, after we are no more, He will still give the power of thought: there is no inconsistency in this idea.

In the midst of all the doubts which we have discussed for four thousand years in four thousand ways, the safest course is to do nothing against one's conscience. With this secret, we can enjoy life and have nothing to fear from death.

There are some charlatans who admit no doubts. We know nothing of first principles. It is surely very presumptuous to define God, the angels, spirits, and to pretend to know precisely why God made the world, when we do not know why we can move our arms at our pleasure.

Doubt is not a pleasant condition, but certainty is an absurd one.

What is most repellent in the *System of Nature* [of Holbach]—after the recipe to make eels from flour—is the audacity with which it decides that there is no God, without even having tried to prove the impossibility. There is some eloquence in the book: but much more rant, and no sort of proof. It is a pernicious work, alike for princes and people:

"Si Dieu n'existait pas, il faudrait l'inventer." [If God did not exist, it would be necessary to invent him.]

But all nature cries aloud that He does exist: that there *is* a supreme intelligence, an immense power, an admirable order, and everything teaches us our own dependence on it.

From the depth of our profound ignorance, let us do our best: this is what I think, and what I have always thought, amid all the misery and follies inseparable from seventy-seven years of life.

Your Royal Highness has a noble career before you. I wish you, and dare prophesy for you, a happiness worthy of yourself and of your heart. I knew you when you were a child, monseigneur: I visited you in your sick room when you had smallpox: I feared for your life. Your father honoured me with much goodness: you condescend to shower on me the same favours which are the honour of my old age, and the consolation of those sufferings which must shortly end it. I am, with deep respect, etc.

Letter to Frederick William, Prince of Prussia, in E. B. Hall [S. G. Tallentyre, *pseud.*], *Voltaire in His Letters* (New York: G. P. Putnam's Sons, 1919), pp. 232-233.

B. Rousseau. The Deist Position, *1762*

The first causes of motion do not exist in matter; bodies receive from and communicate motion to each other, but they cannot originally produce it. The more I observe the action and reaction of the powers of nature acting on each other, the more I am convinced that they are merely effects; and we must ever recur to some volition as the first cause: for to suppose there is a progression of causes to infinity, is to suppose there is no first cause at all. In a word, every motion that is not produced by some other, must be the effect of a spontaneous, voluntary act. Inanimate bodies have no action but motion; and there can be no real action without volition. Such is my first principle. I believe, therefore, that a *Will* gives motion to the universe, and animates all nature. This is my first article of faith.

In what manner volition is productive of physical and corporeal action I know not, but I experience within myself that it is productive of it. I *will* to act, and the action immediately follows; I *will* to move my body, and my body instantly moves; but, that an inanimate body lying at rest, should move itself, or produce motion, is incomprehensible and unprecedented. The *Will* also is known by its effects and not by its essence. I know it as the cause of motion; but to conceive matter producing motion, would be evidently to conceive an effect without a cause, or rather not to conceive any thing at all.

It is no more possible for me to conceive how the will moves the body, than how the sensations affect the soul. I even know not why one of these mysteries ever appeared more explicable than the other. For my own part, whether at the time I am active or passive, the means of union between the two substances appear to me absolutely incomprehensible. Is it not strange that the philosophers have thrown off this incomprehensibility, merely to confound the two substances together, as if operations so different could be better explained as the effects of one subject than of two.

The principle which I have here laid down, is undoubtedly something obscure; it is however intelligible, and contains nothing repugnant to reason or observation. Can we say as much of the doctrines of materialism? It is very certain that, if motion be essential to matter, it would be inseparable from it; it would be always the same in every portion of it, incommunicable, and incapable of increase or diminution; it would be impossible for us even to conceive matter at rest. Again, when I am told that motion is not indeed essential to matter, but necessary to its existence, I see through the attempt to impose on me by a form of words, which it would be more easy to refute, if more intelligible. For, whether the motion of matter arises from itself, and is therefore essential to it, or whether it is derived from some external cause, it is not further necessary to it than as the moving cause acting thereon: so that we still remain under the first difficulty.

General and abstract ideas form the source of our greatest errors. The jargon of metaphysics never discovered one truth; but it has filled philosophy with absurdities, of which we are ashamed as soon as they are stripped of their pompous expressions. . . .

I believe therefore, that the world is governed by a wise and powerful *Will*. I see it, or rather I feel it; and this is of importance for me to know. But is the world eternal, or is it created? Are things derived from one self-existent principle, or are there two or more, and what is their essence? Of all this I know nothing, nor do I see that it is necessary I should. In proportion as such knowledge may become interesting I will endeavor to acquire it: but further than this I give up all such idle disquisitions, which serve only to make me discontented with myself, which are useless in practice, and are above my understanding.

You will remember, however, that I am not dictating my sentiments to you, but only explaining what they are.

Whether matter be eternal or only created, whether it have a passive principle or not, certain it is that the whole universe is one design, and sufficiently displays one intelligent agent: for I see no part of this system that is not under regulation, or that does not concur to one and the same end; viz. that of preserving the present and established order of things. That Being, whose will is his deed, whose principle of action is in himself,—that Being, in a word, whatever it be, that gives motion to all parts of the universe, and governs all things, I call GOD.

J. J. Rousseau, *Profession of Faith of a Savoyard Vicar,* trans. Olive Schreiner (New York: Peter Eckler, 1889), pp. 15-16, 17-18, 28-30, 35.

C. De Sade. The Atheist Position, 1782

THE PRIEST. Now that you have come to that fatal moment when the veil of illusion is rent only to permit straying man a sight of the cruel picture of his errors and his vices, do you not repent, my child, the many misdemeanors you have been led to commit through weakness and human fragility?

THE DYING MAN. Yes, my friend, I repent.

THE PRIEST. Ah, then, profit from that happy remorse by obtaining from Heaven, during the brief interval that remains to you, a general absolution of your sins, and remember that it is only through meditation on the most blessed Sacrament of penitence that it will be possible for you to obtain the gift of eternal life.

THE DYING MAN. I do not understand you, any more than you have understood me.

THE PRIEST. What!

THE DYING MAN. I told you that I repented.

THE PRIEST. I heard you.

THE DYING MAN. Yes, but without understanding.

THE PRIEST. What do you mean ... ?

THE DYING MAN. Just this. . . . Since I have been created by nature with very lively tastes, with very strong passions, and have been placed in this world for the sole purpose of giving myself over to, and satisfying, those tastes and passions, and since these consequences of my having been created are, merely, necessities in keeping with the first designs of nature, or, if you prefer, essential corollaries to her plans for me, the whole being in accordance with her own laws, I repent not having sufficiently recognized her omnipotence, and the only remorse I feel has to do with the mediocre employment I have made of those faculties (criminal according to you, wholly natural according to me) which she gave me for her own service: I have, at times, resisted her, and for this I am penitent. Blinded by the absurdities of your doctrines, I have combatted, for the sake of those doctrines, the violence of those desires which I received by an inspiration a good deal more divine, and this I repent: I have reaped only flowers, when I might have gathered an ample harvest of fruits . . . there you have the just cause of my regret; please do me the honor not to suppose there is any other cause.

THE PRIEST. Oh, where are those errors, those sophistries of yours, leading you? You impute to the thing created all the power of the Creator, and this unfortunate tendency, which leads you astray is, though you will not see it, simply the result of that corrupt Nature which you endow with omnipotence.

THE DYING MAN. My friend, it appears to me your dialectic is as false as your mind itself. I wish you would either reason more justly or leave me to die in peace. What do you mean by "creator," and what do you understand by "corrupt nature"?

THE PRIEST. The Creator is the master of the universe; it is He who has made everything, created everything, and who preserves everything, as the simple consequence of His omnipotence.

THE DYING MAN. He's quite a chap, upon my word! Ah, well, tell me, then, why it is that this fellow, who is so powerful, still has created, according to you, a Nature that is corrupt.

THE PRIEST. What merit would men have had, if God had not left them a free choice, and if they had not encountered, upon the earth, the possibility either of doing good or of avoiding evil?

THE DYING MAN. And so, that god of yours must do everything crosswise, solely for the purpose of tempting, or of proving, his creature? He did not know his own creature, then? He doubted the result?

THE PRIEST. He undoubtedly knew what the result would be, but He wished to leave man the merit of choice.

THE DYING MAN. Of what use was that, since he knew what the choice would be? Why, if he is all-powerful, as you say—why did he not keep man in the right path and force him to choose the good?

THE PRIEST. Who can fathom the immense and infinite wisdom of God towards man, and who can understand all that we behold?

THE DYING MAN. The one who simplifies things, my friend, the one, above all, who does not multiply causes in order to confuse effects the more. What need have you of a second difficulty, when you cannot explain the first; and since it is possible that Nature alone has done all that you attribute to your god, why must you go seeking a master for her? The cause of what you do not understand is, it may be, the simplest thing in the world. Perfect your physics, and you will understand Nature better; purify your reason, banish your prejudices, and you will have no need of that god of yours.

THE PRIEST. Poor fellow! . . . I have arms to fight you, but I see clearly that you are an atheist, and since your heart refuses the infinite and authentic proofs we every day receive of the existence of the Creator, I have nothing more to say to you. One does not give light to a blind man.

THE DYING MAN. My friend, you must grant me one point: the blinder of us is, surely the one who puts a bandage over his eyes, not the one who snatches the bandage away. You build up, you invent, you multiply; as for me, I destroy, I simplify. You pile error upon error, while I combat all errors. Which is the blinder of the two?

THE PRIEST. You have no belief whatever, then, in God?

THE DYING MAN. None. And for a very simple reason, namely, that it is utterly impossible for me to believe what I do not understand. Between comprehension and faith, there should be a direct relation; comprehension is the first food of faith: where there is no comprehension, faith is dead, and those who, in such a case, pretend to have faith, are self-imposters. I defy you, yourself, to believe in the god you preach to me—because you cannot demonstrate him to me, because the power is not in you to define him for me, because, in short, you do not understand him. And since you do not understand him, you are unable to furnish me with any reasonable argument. In a word, whatever is beyond the limits of the human mind is a chimera or a futility, and your god can be only one or the other of these things. In the former case, I should be a fool to believe in him; in the latter, an imbecile. My friend, prove to me the inertia of matter, and I will grant you your creator; prove to me that Nature is not sufficient to herself, and I will permit you to assume that she must have a master. Until that time, look for nothing from me: I only yield to evidence, and I receive evidence only through my senses: where they stop, my faith is powerless. I believe in the sun because I see it; I conceive it to be the unifying center of all the inflammable material in Nature; its periodical revolution pleases, without astonishing, me. It is an operation of physics, as simple, possibly, as that of electricity, but one which is not permitted us to understand. What need have I to go further? When you shall have built me a scaffolding for your god above all that, shall I be any the further along, and will it not require quite as much effort to understand the workman as to define the work? As a consequence, you do me no service by setting up your edifying chimera; you have troubled my mind, but you have not enlightened it, and I owe you nothing but hatred as compensation. Your god is a machine which you have manufactured to serve your own passions; it moves at their direction, but when it interferes with my own passions, grant me the right to overthrow it. And so, at the moment when my weakened soul has need of philosophic calm, please do not come to terrify it with your sophistries, which frighten without convincing, which irritate without improving. This soul, my friend, is what Nature has willed it should be, that is to say, the result of those organs and their needs which she has been pleased to create for me. And since she has equal need of virtues and of vices, when it has pleased her to impell [sic] me to the former, she has done so; when she would impel me to the latter, she does

it by inspiring in me certain desires; and I, likewise, have surrendered to these. Do not seek beyond her laws for the sole cause of all human inconsistency; and in her laws, look for no other principles than her own volition and her own needs.

THE PRIEST. Then everything in the world is inevitable.

THE DYING MAN. Assuredly.

THE PRIEST. But if everything is inevitable, then everything must be regulated.

THE DYING MAN. Has any one denied that?

THE PRIEST. And what could regulate everything that is, except an all-powerful and all-wise hand?

THE DYING MAN. Is it necessary for powder to blaze when one touches fire to it?

THE PRIEST. Yes.

THE DYING MAN. And what wisdom do you find in that?

THE PRIEST. None.

THE DYING MAN. It is, then, possible that there are certain things which are necessary, without any wisdom being involved; and it follows that it is also possible for all things to derive from a first cause, without there being either reason or wisdom in that first cause.

THE PRIEST. What point are you trying to make?

THE DYING MAN. I am proving to you that everything may be as it is, and as you see it to be, without any wise and reasonable cause, and that natural results must have natural causes, without need of supposing unnatural ones, such as your god would be who, as you already have admitted, stands in need of explanation, without himself being able to furnish any: I would prove to you, as a consequence, that your god is good for nothing and absolutely useless; and since there is every evidence that what is useless is non-existent, I have need, in order to convince myself of the fact that your god is a chimera, of no other reasons than those furnished me by the certainty I possess of his futility.

THE PRIEST. If you are off on that foot, it seems to me there is little use in speaking to you of religion.

THE DYING MAN. Why not? Nothing amuses me like evidence of the excessive fanaticism and imbecility of which men can be guilty on this score; there are, for me, some mistakes so prodigious that the contemplation of them, however horrible the picture, is always interesting. Answer my questions frankly, and above all, banish egotism. If I were so weak as to permit myself to be taken in by those ridiculous beliefs of yours concerning the fabled existence of a being who makes religion necessary, under what form should you advise me to render him my tribute of worship? Would you have me adopt the dreams of Confucius rather than the absurdities of Brahma? Should I adore the great serpent of the Africans, the star of the Peruvians or Moses' god of armies? What sect of Mahomet would you have me join, or which of the Christian heresies would, in your eyes, be preferable? Look well to your answer.

THE PRIEST. Can there be any doubt about my answer?

THE DYING MAN. There you have the perfect egotist.

THE PRIEST. No. It is merely because I love you as much as I do myself that I advise you in accordance with what I believe.

THE DYING MAN. We must love ourselves very little if we listen to such errors.

THE PRIEST. Ah, who could be so blind as not to be convinced by the miracles of our divine Redeemer?

THE DYING MAN. One who sees in him only the most ordinary of all knaves and the shallowest of impostors.

THE PRIEST. *Ye Gods! Who hear him, yet do not strike him dead!*

THE DYING MAN. No, my friend, all is at peace, because that god of yours, whether divine impotence or divine reason, or all that you would have him be—though I do not for a moment admit his existence, except out of condescension toward you or, if you prefer, to lend myself the better to your narrow views—because, I say, that god, if he did exist, as you are foolish enough to believe, would never, to convince us of his existence, have adopted means so ridiculous as those your Jesus supposes.

Marquis de Sade, *Dialogue between a Priest and a Dying Man,* ed. Maurice Heine, trans. Samuel Putnam (Chicago: Pascal Covici, 1927), pp. 33-50, by permission of Crown Publishers.

D. Wesley. A Defense of Methodism, 1749

1. There has lately appeared (as you cannot be ignorant) a set of men preaching up and down in several parts of this kingdom, who for ten or twelve years have been known in England by the title of Methodists. The vulgar in Ireland term them Swaddlers;—a name first given them in Dublin, from one of them preaching on those words:

"Ye shall find the young child wrapped in swaddling clothes, lying in a manger."

2. Extremely various have been the reports concerning them. Some persons have spoken favourably: but the generality of men treat them in a different manner,—with utter contempt, if not detestation; and relate abundance of things in order to prove that they are not fit to live upon the earth.

3. A question, then, which you may naturally ask, is this: "In what manner

ought a man of religion, a man of reason, a lover of mankind, and a lover of his country, to act on this occasion?"

4. Before we can properly answer this, it should be inquired, concerning the persons in question, what they are; what they teach; and what are the effects which are generally observed to attend their teaching.

5. It should first be inquired, what they are. In order to reach a speedy determination of this, we may set aside whatever will admit of any dispute, as, whether they are good men or bad, rich or poor, fools, madmen, and enthusiasts, or sober, rational men. Now, waiving all this, one point is indisputable: it is allowed on all hands, they are men who spend all their time and strength in teaching those doctrines, the nature and consequences whereof are described in the following pages.

6. The doctrines they constantly teach are these: that religion does not consist in negatives only,—in not taking the name of God in vain, in not robbing or murdering our neighbour, in bare abstaining from evil of any or every kind; but is a real, positive thing: that it does not consist in externals only,—in attending the church and sacrament, (although all these things they approve and recommend,) in using all the means of grace, or in works of charity, (commonly so called,) superadded to works of piety; but that it is, properly and strictly, a principle within, seated in the inmost soul, and thence manifesting itself by these outward fruits, on all suitable occasions.

7. They insist, that nothing deserves the name of religion, but a virtuous heart, producing a virtuous life: a complication of justice, mercy, and truth, of every right and amiable temper, beaming forth from the deepest recesses of the mind, in a series of wise and generous actions. . . . .

8. These are their constant doctrines.

It is true, they occasionally touch on abundance of other things. Thus they frequently maintain, that there is an inseparable connexion between virtue and happiness; that none but a virtuous (or, as they usually express it, a religious) man can be happy; and that every man is happy in the same proportion as he is truly religious; seeing a contented mind, (according to them,) a cheerful, thankful, joyous acquiescence in every disposal of that Sovereign Wisdom who governs both heaven and earth, if it be not an essential branch of religion, is, at least, a necessary consequence of it. On all proper occasions they strongly recommend, on the one hand, the most intense love of our country; on the other, the firmest loyalty to our Prince, abstracted from all views of private interest. They likewise take every opportunity of enforcing the absolute necessity of sobriety and temperance; of unwearied industry in the works of our calling; of moral honesty in all its branches; and, particularly, in the discharge of all relative duties, without which, they say, religion is vain. But all these they recommend on that one single ground,—the love of God and of all mankind; declaring them to be of no avail, if they do not spring from this love, as well as terminate and centre therein.

9. Whoever is at the pains of hearing these Preachers, or of reading what they have wrote, with any degree of attention and impartiality, must perceive that these are their doctrines. And it is equally easy to discern what the effects of their preaching have been. These doctrines they spread wherever they come. They convince many in every place, that religion does not consist (as they imagined once) either in negatives or externals, in barely doing no harm, or even doing good; but in the tempers of the heart, in right dispositions of mind towards God and man,

producing all right words and actions.

10. And these dispositions of mind are, more or less, the continual consequence of their preaching: (that is, if we may know the tree by its fruit, which is doubtless the most rational way of judging:) the lives of many who constantly attend it show, that God has wrought a real change in their heart; and that the grand principle of love to God and man already begins to take root therein.

11. Hence those who were before of quite the opposite temper, are now generous, disinterested lovers of their country; and faithful, loyal subjects to their Prince, His sacred Majesty King George: they are now sober and temperate in all things, and punctually honest in all their dealings: they are strict in every relative duty, and laborious and diligent in their callings, notwithstanding the continual discouragement they receive from many who still cry out, "Ye are idle, ye are idle; therefore ye say, Let us go and serve the Lord." They are content in every state, whether of plenty or want, and thankful to God and man. These are plain, glaring, undeniable facts, whereof, if any Magistrate will be at the trouble to take them, numerous affidavits may be made, in Dublin, Cork, Limerick, and many other places.

But if these things are so, it is easy to conceive in what manner every man of religion, every man of reason, every lover of mankind, every lover of his country, ought to act on this occasion.

12. For, first, ought not every man of religion, with all the earnestness of his soul, to praise God, who, after so long a night of ignorance and error had overspread our country, has poured light on so many of those that sat in darkness and the shadow of death? has shown such numbers even of the lowest and most brutish of men, wherein true religion lies; has taught them both to lay the right foundation, and to build the whole fabric thereon; has convinced them, "Other foundation can no man lay than that which is laid, even Jesus Christ;" and, "The end of the commandment is love," of the whole commandment or law of Christ; love, the life, the soul, the spirit of religion, the river that makes glad the city of God, the living water continually springing up into everlasting life?

13. Admit that they do not exactly judge right as to some of the appendages of religion; that you have a clearer and juster conception than they of several things pertaining to the beauty of holiness; yet ought you not to bless God for giving these outcasts of men to see at least the essence of it? nay, to be living witnesses of the substance of religion, though they may still mistake as to some of the circumstances of it.

14. Ought not every man of reason (whether he assents, or no, to that system of opinions commonly called Christianity) sincerely and heartily to rejoice in the advancement of solid, rational virtue? in the propagation, not of this or that set of opinions, but of genuine pure morality? of disinterested benevolence, of tender affections, to the whole of the human race? Ought you not to be glad, that there are any instruments found, till others appear who are more equal to the task, whose one employment it is (from whatever motive) to diffuse generous honesty throughout the land? . . .

17. If you are a lover of mankind, must you not sympathize with those who suffer evil in various kinds, for this very thing, because they do good to mankind, looking for no reward on this side of heaven? As to the idle tale of their laying up treasures on earth, it neither agrees with fact nor reason. Not with fact; for it is notorious, that those who before piqued themselves on owing no man anything, are now in-

debted in larger sums, than, humanly speaking, they can ever pay. Not with reason; for if riches had been their aim, they would have sought out the rich, not the poor; not the tinners in Cornwall, the colliers of Kingswood, the keelmen in Newcastle-upon-Tyne. At the same time, they showed they were not afraid or ashamed to appear before the greatest or wisest of men: witness their appearing in the most public manner, both at Dublin, Bristol, Oxford, and London.

18. Ought not every lover of his country, not only not to oppose, but to assist with all the power and interest he has, those who continually, and not without success, recommend the love of our country, and what is so closely connected therewith, duty and loyalty to the best of Princes? Ought you not to forward, so far as ever your influence will go, sobriety and temperance among your countrymen? What can be more for the interest of this poor nation, and for the good of all, whether rich or poor? You do well to promote that excellent design of spreading the linen manufacture among us. None can doubt but this is admirably well calculated for the good of the whole kingdom: but are not temperance and honesty still more conducive to the good of this and of every kingdom? Nay, and how directly conducive are these virtues to that very end, the flourishing of our manufactures!

19. And what can conduce more to the general good of all the inhabitants of this land, than industry joined to content? to peace with God, peace with yourselves, peace with one another? O how needful in this, above all lands! For, what a stranger has it been in our coasts! Ye men of Ireland, help! Come all, as one man, all men of religion and reason, all lovers of God and of mankind, all lovers of your country. O suffer not yourselves to be thus grossly abused, thus miserably imposed upon, any longer! Open your eyes; look around and judge for yourselves; see plain and undeniable facts; be convinced by the force of truth and love, that the work is indeed of God. Rejoice in the good of your country, in peace and good-will continually advanced among men. Beware you do not oppose, or speak or think evil of, what God hath done in the earth. Rather, each in the station wherein he is placed, join hearts and hands in the work, till holiness and happiness cover our land as the waters cover the sea.

JOHN WESLEY.

Dublin, July 6, 1749.

John Wesley, "A Short Address to the Inhabitants of Ireland," *Works* (London: John Mason, 1856), IX, 165-170.

III. MAN IN NATURE AND IN SOCIETY

The men of the Enlightenment found their own society seriously deficient, and in need of reform. But did they, as so many of their later critics have maintained, believe that man had once, in a primitive savage state, before art, law, and the sciences had corrupted him, been happy and good? Did they believe in the natural goodness of man even in their own day, if he could only go back to the simple life, if he could only rely on his heart instead of his head? Rousseau in his first work, *A Discourse on the Arts and Sciences* (1750), certainly concluded that the progress of the arts and sciences had been accompanied by a moral decadence; and in his second, *A Discourse on the Origin of Inequality* (1755), he maintained that the physical (i.e. "natural") inequalities among men were relatively unimportant in comparison with the social and economic (i.e. "unnatural") inequalities the growth of civilization had produced. Primitivism— the belief that men were better and happier in days of old, or in parts of the world as yet untouched by European civilization—

was a doctrine in the air of the Enlightenment. But do the following excerpts suggest that this primitivism was unchallenged among the men of the Enlightenment? As to man's own nature, did these thinkers again oversimplify, making man by nature free, equal, and virtuous, corrupted only by society, by "environment," by arrangements made by unenlightened men and presumably therefore alterable by enlightened men? Rousseau, Voltaire, and Diderot are joined by Claude Helvetius, author of the materialistic study, *De l'Esprit,* Jeremy Bentham, the founder of the Utilitarian system of thought in England, and Thomas Jefferson to help us cope with these questions.

A. Rousseau. Good Man and Bad Civilization, 1755

If the reader thus discovers and retraces the lost and forgotten road, by which man must have passed from the state of nature to the state of society; if he carefully restores, along with the intermediate situations which I have just described, those which want of time has compelled me to suppress, or my imagination has failed to suggest, he cannot fail to be struck by the vast distance which separates the two states. It is in tracing this slow succession that he will find the solution of a number of problems of politics and morals, which philosophers cannot settle. He will feel that, men being different in different ages, the reason why Diogenes could not find a man was that he sought among his contemporaries a man of an earlier period. He will see that Cato died with Rome and liberty, because he did not fit the age in which he lived; the greatest of men served only to astonish a world which he would certainly have ruled, had he lived five hundred years sooner. In a word, he will explain how the soul and the passions of men insensibly change their very nature; why our wants and pleasures in the end

seek new objects; and why, the original man having vanished by degrees, society offers to us only an assembly of artificial men and factitious passions, which are the work of all these new relations, and without any real foundation in nature. We are taught nothing on this subject, by reflection, that is not entirely confirmed by observation. The savage and the civilised man differ so much in the bottom of their hearts and in their inclinations, that what constitutes the supreme happiness of one would reduce the other to despair. The former breathes only peace and liberty; he desires only to live and be free from labour; even the *ataraxia* [imperturbability] of the Stoic falls far short of his profound indifference to every other object. Civilised man, on the other hand, is always moving, sweating, toiling and racking his brains to find still more laborious occupations: he goes on in drudgery to his last moment, and even seeks death to put himself in a position to live, or renounces life to acquire immortality. He pays his court to men in power, whom he hates, and to the wealthy, whom he despises; he stops at nothing to have the honour of serving them; he is not ashamed to value himself on his own meanness and their protection; and, proud of his slavery, he speaks with disdain of those, who have not the honour of sharing it. What a sight would the perplexing and envied labours of a European minister of State present to the eyes of a Caribbean! [sic] How many cruel deaths would not this indolent savage prefer to the horrors of such a life, which is seldom even sweetened by the pleasure of doing good! But, for him to see into the motives of all this solicitude, the words *power* and *reputation,* would have to bear some meaning in his mind; he would have to know that there are men who set a value on the opinion of the rest of the world; who can be made happy and satisfied with themselves rather on the testimony of other people than on their own. In reality, the source of all these differences is, that the savage lives within himself, while social man lives constantly outside himself, and only knows how to live in the opinion of others, so that he seems to receive the consciousness of his own existence merely from the judgment of others concerning him. It is not to my present purpose to insist on the indifference to good and evil which arises from this disposition, in spite of our many fine works on morality, or to show how, everything being reduced to appearances, there is but art and mummery in even honour, friendship, virtue, and often vice itself, of which we at length learn the secret of boasting; to show, in short, how, always asking others what we are, and never daring to ask ourselves, in the midst of so much philosophy, humanity and civilisation, and of such sublime codes of morality, we have nothing to show for ourselves but a frivolous and deceitful appearance, honour without virtue, reason without wisdom, and pleasure without happiness. It is sufficient that I have proved that this is not by any means the original state of man, but that it is merely the spirit of society, and the inequality which society produces, that thus transform and alter all our natural inclinations.

I have endeavoured to trace the origin and progress of inequality, and the institution and abuse of political societies, as far as these are capable of being deduced from the nature of man merely by the light of reason, and independently of those sacred dogmas which give the sanction of divine right to sovereign authority. It follows from this survey that, as there is hardly any inequality in the state of nature, all the inequality which now prevails owes its strength and growth to the development of our faculties and the advance of the human mind, and becomes at last permanent and legitimate by the establishment of property and laws. Secondly, it follows that moral inequality, authorised by positive right alone, clashes with natural right, whenever it is not proportionate to physical inequality; a distinction which sufficiently determines what we ought to think of that species of inequality which prevails in all civilised countries; since it is plainly contrary to the law of nature, however defined, that children should command old men, fools wise men, and that the privileged few should gorge themselves with superfluities, while the starving multitude are in want of the bare necessities of life.

J. J. Rousseau, "A Discourse on the Origin of Inequality," in *The Social Contract*, trans. G. D. H. Cole, Everyman's ed. (New York: E. P. Dutton and Co., n. d.), pp. 236-238.

B. *Voltaire. Letter to Rousseau on the Latter's "Discourse on the Origin of Inequality," 1755*

I have received, sir, your new book against the human species, and I thank you for it. You will please people by your manner of telling them the truth about themselves, but you will not alter them. The horrors of that human society—from which in our feebleness and ignorance we expect so many consolations—have never been painted in more striking colours: no one has ever been so witty as you are in trying to turn us into brutes: to read your book makes one long to go on all fours. Since, however, it is now some sixty years since I gave up the practice, I feel that it is unfortunately impossible for me to resume it: I leave this natural habit to those more fit for it than are you and I. Nor can I set sail to discover the aborigines of Canada, in the first place because my ill-health ties me to the side of the greatest doctor in Europe, and I should not find the same professional assistance among the Missouris: and secondly because war is going on in that country, and the example of the civilised nations has made the barbarians almost as wicked as we are ourselves. I must confine myself to being a peaceful savage in the retreat I have chosen—close to your country, where you yourself should be.

I agree with you that science and literature have sometimes done a great deal of harm. Tasso's enemies made his life a long series of misfortunes: Galileo's enemies kept him languishing in prison, at seventy years of age, for the crime of understanding the revolution of the earth: and, what is still more shameful, obliged him to forswear his discovery. Since your friends began the Encyclopædia, their rivals attack them as deists, atheists—even Jansenists.

If I might venture to include myself among those whose works have brought them persecution as their sole recompense, I could tell you of men set on ruining me from the day I produced my tragedy *Œdipe:* of a perfect library of absurd calumnies which have been written against me: of an ex-Jesuit priest whom I saved from utter disgrace rewarding me by defamatory libels: of a man yet more contemptible printing my *Century of Louis XIV* with *Notes* in which crass ignorance gave birth to the most abominable falsehoods: of yet another, who sold to a publisher some chapters of a *Universal History* supposed to be by me: of the publisher avaricious enough to print this shapeless mass of blunders, wrong dates, mutilated facts and names: and, finally, of men sufficiently base and craven to assign the production of this farago to me. I could show you all society poisoned

by this class of person—a class unknown to the ancients—who, not being able to find any honest occupation—be it manual labour or service—and unluckily knowing how to read and write, become the brokers of literature, live on our works, steal our manuscripts, falsify them, and sell them. I could tell of some loose sheets of a gay trifle which I wrote thirty years ago (on the same subject that Chapelain was stupid enough to treat seriously) which are in circulation now through the breach of faith and the cupidity of those who added their own grossness to my *badinage* and filled in the gaps with a dullness only equalled by their malice; and who, finally, after twenty years, are selling everywhere a manuscript which, in very truth, is theirs and worthy of them only. . . .

Confess, sir, that all these things are, after all, but little personal pin-pricks, which society scarcely notices. What matter to humankind that a few drones steal the honey of a few bees? Literary men make a great fuss of their petty quarrels: the rest of the world ignores them, or laughs at them.

They are, perhaps, the least serious of all the ills attendant on human life. The thorns inseparable from literature and a modest degree of fame are flowers in comparison with the other evils which from all time have flooded the world. Neither Cicero, Varro, Lucretius, Virgil, or Horace had any part in the proscriptions of Marius, Sulla, that profligate Antony, or that fool Lepidus; while as for that cowardly tyrant, Octavius Cæsar—servilely entitled Augustus—he only became an assassin when he was deprived of the society of men of letters.

Confess that Italy owed none of her troubles to Petrarch or to Boccaccio: that Marot's jests were not responsible for the massacre of St. Bartholomew: or the tragedy of the *Cid* for the wars of the Fronde. Great crimes are always committed by great ignoramuses. What makes, and will always make, this world a vale of tears is the insatiable greediness and the indomitable pride of men, from Thomas Koulikan, who did not know how to read, to a customhouse officer who can just count. Letters support, refine, and comfort the soul: they are serving you, sir, at the very moment you decry them: you are like Achilles declaiming against fame, and Father Malebranche using his brilliant imagination to belittle imagination.

If anyone has a right to complain of letters, I am that person, for in all times and in all places they have led to my being persecuted: still, we must needs love them in spite of the way they are abused—as we cling to society, though the wicked spoil its pleasantness: as we must love our country, though it treats us unjustly: and as we must love and serve the Supreme Being, despite the superstition and fanaticism which too often dishonour His service.

M. Chappus tells me your health is very unsatisfactory: you must come and recover here in your native place, enjoy its freedom, drink (with me) the milk of its cows, and browse on its grass.

I am yours most philosophically and with sincere esteem.

E. B. Hall [S. G. Tallentyre, *pseud.*], *Voltaire in His Letters* (New York: G. P. Putnam's Sons, 1919). pp. 149-154.

C. Helvetius. Men Are Alike, 1773

RECAPITULATION

After having in the Introduction to this work said a few words on its importance, and on the ignorance of mankind relative to the true principles of education, and lastly, of the dryness of the subject, and the difficulty of treating it, I have examined,

SECTION I

"Whether education, necessarily different in different men, be not the cause of that inequality of understandings hitherto attributed to the unequal perfection of their organs."

To this purpose I have inquired at what age the education of man begins, and who are his instructors.

I see that man is the pupil of every object which surrounds him, of all the positions in which chance has placed him, in short, of every incident that happens to him.

That these objects, positions, and incidents are not exactly the same for any two persons, and consequently no two receive the same instructions.

That if it were possible for two men to have the same objects before their eyes, these objects not striking them at the precise moment when their minds are in the same situation, will not, in consequence, excite in them the same ideas: therefore the pretended uniformity of instruction received, either in the schools or in the paternal house, is one of those suppositions whose impossibility is proved by facts, and by the influence that chance, independent of instructors, has, and always will have, on the education of childhood and youth.

These matters settled, I consider the extreme extent of the power of chance, and I examine,

Whether illustrious men do not frequently owe to it their taste for a particular sort of study, and consequently their talents and their success in that study.

If the science of education can be perfected without restraining the bounds of the empire of chance.

If the contradictions at present perceived among all the precepts of education, do not extend the empire of chance.

If these contradictions, of which I

have given some examples, ought not to be regarded as effects of the opposition that is found between the religious system and that of the public prosperity.

If religions might not be rendered less destructive of the national felicity, and founded on principles more conformable to the general interest.

What those principles are.

If they might not be established by an intelligent prince.

If among the false religions there are not some whose worship has not been less opposite to the welfare of society, and consequently to the improvement of the science of education.

If after these several examens, and on the supposition that all men have an equal aptitude to understanding, the mere difference in their education ought not to produce a difference in their ideas and their talents. From whence it follows, that the inequality in understanding cannot be regarded, in men commonly well organized, as a demonstrative proof of their unequal aptitude to acquire it.

I have examined,

SECTION II

"If all men, commonly well organized, have not an equal aptitude to understanding?"

I agree in the first place, that as all our ideas come to us by the senses, we ought to regard the mind or understanding either as the mere effect of the greater or less degree of perfection in the five senses; or of an occult and indeterminable cause, to which has been vaguely given the name of organization.

To prove the falsity of this opinion, we must have recourse to experience, form a clear idea of the word Mind or Understanding and distinguish it from the soul. This distinction made, we must observe,

On what objects the mind acts.

How it acts.

If all its operations are not reducible to the observing of the resemblances and differences, the agreements and disagreements that different objects have among themselves and with us; and if, in consequence, all judgments formed on corporeal objects are not mere sensations.

If it be not the same with judgments formed on ideas to which are given the names of abstract, collective, &c.

If in every case to judge and compare can be any thing else than *alternate inspection*, that is to say, *sensation.*

If we can feel the impression of objects without comparing them with each other.

If such comparison does not suppose an interest to compare them.

If that interest be not the sole and unknown cause of all our ideas, our actions, our pains, our pleasures, and, in short, our sociability.

From whence I observe, that as this interest, in its last analysis, takes its source in corporeal sensibility; that this sensibility is consequently the sole principle of human ideas and actions.

That there is no rational motive for rejecting this opinion.

That this opinion, once demonstrated and acknowledged for true, we must necessarily regard the inequality of understandings as the effect,

Either of the unequal extent of the memory;

Or of the greater or less perfection of the five senses.

That in fact, it is neither the extent of the memory, nor the extreme fineness of the senses, that produces, and ought to produce the extent of the understanding.

That with regard to the fineness of the senses, men commonly well organized differ only in the degrees of their sensations.

That this small difference does not change the relation of their sensations to each other, and consequently has no influence over the understanding, which is not, and cannot be any thing else than a knowledge of the true relations objects have to each other.

The cause of the different opinions of men.

That this difference is the effect of the uncertain signification of words; such as

Good,

Interest, and

Virtue.

That if words were precisely defined, and their definitions ranged in a dictionary, all the propositions of morality, politics, and metaphysics would become as susceptible of demonstration as the truths of geometry.

That from the moment the same ideas are annexed to the same words, all minds adopting the same principles, would draw from them the same conclusions.

That it is impossible, as all objects appear to all men to have the same relations, that by comparing objects with each other, men (either in the material world, as is proved by geometry, or in the intellectual world, which is proved by metaphysics), should not form the same conclusions.

That the truth of this proposition is proved by the resemblance of the tales of the fairies, philosophic tales, and religious tales of all countries, and by the uniformity of impositions, employed everywhere by the ministers of false religions, to preserve and increase their authority over the people.

From all these facts it results, that as the greater or less fineness of the senses does not at all change the proportion in which objects strike us, all men, commonly well organised, have an equal aptitude to understanding.

To augment proofs of this important truth, I have added a demonstration of it in the same section, by another series of propositions. I have shewn that the most sublime ideas, once simplified, are, by the consent of all philosophers, reducible to this clear proposition, *that white is white, and black is black.*

That every truth of this kind is comprehensible by all understandings; and that therefore there is not any one, how great and general soever it may be, which clearly represented, and disengaged from the obscurity of words, cannot be equally conceived by all men commonly well organised. Now to be equally able to comprehend the highest truths, is to have an equal aptitude to understanding. Such is the conclusion of the second section.

SECTION III

The object of this section is an inquiry concerning the causes to which the inequality of understandings is to be attributed.

These causes are reducible to two.

The one is the unequal desire that men have to knowledge.

The other, the diversity of positions in which chance places them; a diversity from which results that of their instruction, and their ideas. To shew that it is to these two causes only we ought to refer the difference and inequality of understandings, I have proved that most of our discoveries are the gifts of chance.

That these same gifts are not granted to all.

This distribution however is not so unequal as imagined.

That in this respect chance is less neglectful of us, than we are, if I may use the expression, neglectful of chance.

That in fact all men commonly well organised have an equal power of understanding, but that power is dead in them, when not put in action by some passion, such as the love of esteem, glory, &c.

That men owe to such passions only the attention proper to fecundate the ideas offered to them by chance.

That without passions their minds might be, so to say, regarded as perfect machines, whose movement is suspended till the passions put them in action.

From whence I conclude, that the inequality of understandings in men is the produce of chance, and of the unequal vivacity of their passions; but whether those passions are the effects of the strength of temperament, is what I examine in the following section.

SECTION IV

I there demonstrate,

That men commonly well organised are susceptible of the same degree of passion.

That their unequal force is always the effect of the difference of situations in which chance has placed them.

That the original character of each man, (as Pascal observes), is nothing more than the produce of his first habits: that man is born without ideas, without passions, and without other wants than those of hunger and thirst, and consequently without character:

that he often changes it without any change in his organisation: that those changes, independent of the greater or less fineness of his senses, operate according to the changes that happen in his situation and ideas.

That the diversity of characters depends solely on the different manners in which the sentiment of self-love is modified in men.

That this sentiment, the necessary effect of corporeal sensibility, is common to all, and produces in all the love of power.

That this desire produces envy, the love of wealth, of glory, importance, justice, virtue, intolerance, in short, all the factitious passions, whose several names mean nothing more than the different applications of the love of power.

This truth established, I shew, by a short genealogy of the passions, that if the love of power be nothing more than the mere effect of corporeal sensibility, and if all men commonly well organised are sensible, all are consequently susceptible of the sort of passion proper to put in action the equal aptitude they have to understanding. . . .

Claude Helvetius, *A Treatise on Man,* trans. W. Hooper (London: B. Law, 1777), II, 443-452.

D. Diderot. *Men Are Not Alike, about 1774*

[Text of Helvetius]   Page 154.—*Are men of different opinion on the same question? This difference is always due to the fact that either they do not understand one another, or they do not have the same objects before them, or they do not give to the question itself the necessary interest.*

[Comment of Diderot]   This is not all, and men's arguments have a breeding place perhaps more fertile than any of those noted above.

However well organized two heads

might be, it is impossible for the same ideas to be equally evident in one as in the other.   I do not think that this principle can be refuted.

Therefore it is impossible for the same reasoning to appear equally conclusive to both.

One line of reasoning, tying in with the chain of ideas of one of the disputants, will appear evident to him. The other disputant, if only because he would have to admit several errors if this reasoning, which does not tie in with or even thwarts his chain of ideas, were true, naturally will be inclined to think it false.

[Text of Helvetius] Page 155.—*All men are born with equality of understanding.*

[Comment of Diderot] All men are born without understanding; they have it neither false nor just: it is the experience of the things of life that disposes them toward justness or falseness.

He who has always made bad use of his senses will have false understanding.

He who, mediocrely educated, thinks he knows all, will have false understanding.

He who, carried away by self-sufficiency and hastiness, is hurried in his judgments, will have false understanding.

He who attaches too much or too little importance to certain things will have false understanding.

He who dares pronounce himself on a question which exceeds the capacity of his natural talent will have false understanding.

There is nothing so rare as logic: an infinity of men lack it, almost all women have none at all.

He who is subject to prejudices will have false understanding.

He who is obstinate out of conceit, out of a desire to be different, or out of inclination for paradoxes, will have false understanding.

And he who trusts his reason too much and he who trusts it too little will have false understanding.

All interests, all prejudices, all passions, all vices, all virtues are capable of perverting the understanding.

Thence I conclude that equality of understanding is in every respect a figment of the imagination. . . .

CHAPTER II

Page 13.—*Is man good or evil at birth?*

If one can give the name of good only to him who has done good, and the name of evil only to him who has done evil, then assuredly man, at birth, is neither good nor evil. I will say as much of understanding and of stupidity.

But does man bring with him at birth organic and natural tendencies to say and do foolish things, to harm himself and his fellow-men, to listen to or disregard the advices of his parents, to diligence or laziness, to justice or anger, to respect or despise laws? Only he who in his life has never seen two children nor has ever heard them cry in their cradles can doubt this. Man is born nothing, but every man is born with a special aptitude for something.

"M. Helvetius, you are a hunter, I think?"

"Yes, I am one."

"Do you see that little dog?"

"The one with the twisted legs, the low and long body, the pointed muzzle and the paws and hide spotted with fire?"

"Yes. What is he?"

"He is a basset hound; this species has good scent, high spirits, courage: he will thrust himself in the burrow of a fox, at the risk of emerging with torn ears and sides."

"And this other one?"

"He is a brach hound. He is an indefatigable animal: his hard and bristling fur permits him to plunge into thorny and thick bushes; he stops the partridge, he bays the hare, he takes the place of three or four dogs."

"And this other one?"

"He is one of the most beautiful greyhounds."

"And this third one?"

"A setter. I cannot tell you anything about him: will he be docile, will he not? will he have good scent, will he not? It is a matter of race."

"And this fourth one?"

"He promises to be a very beautiful hound."

"They are all dogs?"

"Yes."

"And, tell me. I have an excellent gamekeeper, he will do everything I wish; could I not order him to make a brach out of the basset, a greyhound out of the brach, a field dog out of the greyhound, a hound out of the field dog, and a barbet out of the hound?"

"Do nothing of the kind."

"And why? . . . They have just been born, they are nothing; fit for everything, rearing will dispose of them at my will."

"You are making fun of me."

"M. Helvetius, you are right. But what if there should be in the human species the same variety of individuals as there is in the canine race, what if each had his own gait and game?"

"Réfutation de Helvétius," Diderot, *Oeuvres Complètes,* ed. J. Assézat (Paris: Garnier Frères, 1875), II, 243-244, 406-407. Translated.

E. Bentham. *The Principle of Utility, 1789*

I. Nature has placed mankind under the governance of two sovereign masters, *pain* and *pleasure.* It is for them alone to point out what we ought to do, as well as to determine what we shall do. On the one hand the standard of right and wrong, on the other the chain of causes and effects, are fastened to their throne. They govern us in all we do, in all we say, in all we think: every effort we can make to throw off our subjection, will serve but to demonstrate and confirm it. In words a man may pretend to abjure their empire: but in reality he will remain subject to it all the while. The *principle of utility* recognises this subjection, and assumes it for the foundation of that system, the object of which is to rear the fabric of felicity by the hands of reason and of law. Systems which attempt to question it, deal in sounds instead of sense, in caprice instead of reason, in darkness instead of light.

But enough of metaphor and declamation: it is not by such means that moral science is to be improved.

II. The principle of utility is the foundation of the present work: it will be proper therefore at the outset to give an explicit and determinate account of what is meant by it. By the principle of utility is meant that principle which approves or disapproves of every action whatsoever, according to the tendency which it appears to have to augment or diminish the happiness of the party whose interest is in question: or, what is the same thing in other words, to promote or to oppose that happiness. I say of every action whatsoever; and therefore not only of every action of a private individual, but of every measure of government.

III. By utility is meant that property in any object, whereby it tends to produce benefit, advantage, pleasure, good, or happiness, (all this in the present case comes to the same thing) or (what comes again to the same thing) to prevent the happening of mischief, pain, evil, or unhappiness to the party whose interest is considered: if that party be the community in general, then the happiness of the community: if a particular individual, then the happiness of that individual.

IV. The interest of the community is one of the most general expressions that can occur in the phraseology of morals: no wonder that the meaning of it is often lost. When it has a meaning it is this. The community is a fictitious *body,* composed of the individual persons who are considered as constituting as it were its *members.* The interest of the community then is, what?—the sum of the interests of the several members who compose it.

V. It is in vain to talk of the interest

of the community, without understanding what is the interest of the individual. A thing is said to promote the interest, or to be *for* the interest, of an individual, when it tends to add to the sum total of his pleasures: or, what comes to the same thing, to diminish the sum total of his pains.

VI. An action then may be said to be conformable to the principle of utility, or, for shortness sake, to utility, (meaning with respect to the community at large) when the tendency it has to augment the happiness of the community is greater than any it has to diminish it.

VII. A measure of government (which is but a particular kind of action, performed by a particular person or persons) may be said to be conformable to or dictated by the principle of utility, when in like manner the tendency which it has to augment the happiness of the community is greater than any which it has to diminish it.

VIII. When an action, or in particular a measure of government, is supposed by a man to be conformable to the principle of utility, it may be convenient, for the purposes of discourse, to imagine a kind of law or dictate, called a law or dictate of utility: and to speak of the action in question, as being conformable to such law or dictate.

IX. A man may be said to be a partizan of the principle of utility, when the approbation or disapprobation he annexes to any action, or to any measure, is determined by and proportioned to the tendency which he conceives it to have to augment or to diminish the happiness of the community: or in other words, to its conformity or unconformity to the laws or dictates of utility.

X. Of an action that is conformable to the principle of utility one may always say either that it is one that ought to be done, or at least that it is not one that ought not to be done. One may say also, that it is right it should be done; at least that it is not wrong it should be done: that it is a right action; at least that it is not a wrong action. When thus interpreted, the words *ought,* and *right* and *wrong,* and others of that stamp, have a meaning: when otherwise, they have none.

XI. Has the rectitude of this principle been ever formally contested? It should seem that it had, by those who have not known what they have been meaning. Is it susceptible of any direct proof? it should seem not: for that which is used to prove every thing else, cannot itself be proved: a chain of proofs must have their commencement somewhere. To give such proof is as impossible as it is needless.

XII. Not that there is or ever has been that human creature breathing, however stupid or perverse, who has not on many, perhaps on most occasions of his life, deferred to it. By the natural constitution of the human frame, on most occasions of their lives men in general embrace this principle, without thinking of it: if not for the ordering of their own actions, yet for the trying of their own actions, as well as of those of other men. There have been, at the same time, not many, perhaps, even of the most intelligent, who have been disposed to embrace it purely and without reserve. There are even few who have not taken some occasion or other to quarrel with it, either on account of their not understanding always how to apply it, or on account of some prejudice or other which they were afraid to examine into, or could not bear to part with. For such is the stuff that man is made of: in principle and in practice, in a right track and in a wrong one, the rarest of all human qualities is consistency.

XIII. When a man attempts to combat the principle of utility, it is with reasons drawn, without his being aware of it, from that very principle itself. His arguments, if they prove any thing, prove not that the principle is *wrong,* but that, according to the applications he supposes to be made of it, it is *misapplied.* Is it possible for a man to move the earth? Yes; but he must first find out another earth to stand upon.

Jeremy Bentham, *An Introduction to the Principles of Morals and Legislation* (New York, 1948), pp. 1-7. Printed with permission of Hafner Publishing Co., publishers of the Hafner Library of Classics.

F. Jefferson. Natural Goodness More Evident among Farmers than Merchants, 1786

How happens it that Rhode Island is opposed to every useful proposition? Her geography accounts for it, with the aid of one or two observations. The cultivators of the earth are the most virtuous citizens, and possess most of the amor patriæ. Merchants are the least virtuous, and possess the least of the amor patriæ. The latter reside principally in the seaport towns, the former in the interior country. Now, it happened that of the territory constituting Rhode Island and Connecticut, the part containing the seaports was erected into a State by itself, called Rhode Island, and that containing the interior country was erected into another State called Connecticut. For though it has a little seacoast, there are no good ports in it. Hence it happens that there is scarcely one merchant in the whole State of Connecticut, while there is not a single man in Rhode Island who is not a merchant of some sort. Their whole territory is but a thousand square miles, and what of that is in use is laid out in grass farms almost entirely. Hence they have scarcely any body employed in agriculture. All exercise some species of commerce. This circumstance has decided the characters of these two States. The remedies to this evil are hazardous. One would be to consolidate the two States into one. Another would be to banish Rhode Island from the Union. A third, to compel her submission to the will of the other twelve. A fourth, for the other twelve to govern themselves according to the new propositions, and to let Rhode Island go on by herself according to the ancient articles. But the dangers and difficulties attending all these remedies are obvious.

Thomas Jefferson, "Answers to Questions Propounded by M. de Meusnier," in S. K. Padover, ed., *The Complete Jefferson* (New York: Duell, Sloan & Pearce, Inc., 1943), pp. 43-44.

IV. INDIVIDUAL LIBERTY OR COLLECTIVE AUTHORITY: POLITICAL ULTIMATES

The last phase of our general problem of what the thinkers of the Enlightenment really meant in their great debate over the nature of man and the state is more specifically political. These thinkers made frequent use of terms like "social contract" —by which they meant at bottom that government is, or should be, founded on the consent of the governed; and "natural law" —by which they meant at bottom that there are principles of justice, of right and wrong, which men can learn to know and agree on, to which actual existing laws (which they commonly called "civil law") ought to conform. Under this natural law, men had "natural rights." But these terms are highly technical, and rewarding though their study is, call for special training in formal political theory and in jurisprudence. We shall try here to go behind these terms to a central problem most important to us: were these thinkers seeking to promote the freedom of the individual citizen, his "right" to do as he likes subject to a minimum of restraint from government; or were they rather seeking to impose on men—for their own greater good, indeed, as these thinkers saw it—a more enlightened, more efficient, and perhaps even more rigid system of government than the existing ones? Were these thinkers on the side of liberty or of authority? Did they want a society edging toward anarchism, or did they want a kind of authoritarianism, even totalitarianism, an "enlightened despotism?" Did they trust the common man or did they distrust him? The problem is especially acute in what is perhaps the most famous political writing of the age, Rousseau's *Social Contract* (1762). Some have seen in this work a defense of individual freedom; others have seen in it a defense of collective authority. The problem, which is a very knotty one indeed, can perhaps be put with undue simplicity: are liberty and equality, coupled as ideals in the great democratic documents of the time, at bottom incompatible? If so, toward which side did the thinkers of the Enlightenment lean, or what compromises did they advocate? To an excerpt from Rousseau we have added selections which illustrate the range of thought on this problem in our period. William Godwin was the English philosophical anarchist whose ideas considerably influenced the youthful writings of Wordsworth, Coleridge, and Shelley. The passage quoted is from his best-known work, *Political Justice*. Maximilien Robespierre, the "Incorruptible," was the principal leader of revolutionary France during the days of the Terror in 1793 and 1794. His position on the question of liberty and equality appears in a speech delivered in 1793. Thomas Jefferson, finally, is the author of the letter which contains our concluding selection.

A. French Declaration of the Rights of Man and the Citizen

The representatives of the French people, organized in National Assembly, considering that ignorance, forgetfulness, or contempt of the rights of man are the sole causes of public misfortunes and of the corruption of governments, have resolved to set forth in a solemn declaration the natural, inalienable, and sacred rights of man, in order that such declaration, continually before all members of the social body, may be a perpetual reminder of their rights and duties; in order that the acts of the legislative power and those of the executive power may constantly be compared with the aim of every political institution and may accordingly be more respected; in order that the demands of the citizens, founded henceforth upon simple and incontestable principles, may always be directed towards the maintenance of the Constitution and the welfare of all.

Accordingly, the National Assembly recognizes and proclaims, in the presence and under the auspices of the Supreme Being, the following rights of man and citizen.

1. Men are born and remain free and equal in rights; social distinctions may be based only upon general usefulness.

2. The aim of every political association is the preservation of the natural and inalienable rights of man; these rights are liberty, property, security, and resistance to oppression.

3. The source of all sovereignty resides essentially in the nation; no group, no individual may exercise authority not emanating expressly therefrom.

4. Liberty consists of the power to do whatever is not injurious to others; thus the enjoyment of the natural rights of every man has for its limits only those that assure other members of society the enjoyment of those same rights; such limits may be determined only by law.

5. The law has the right to forbid only actions which are injurious to society. Whatever is not forbidden by law may not be prevented, and no one may be constrained to do what it does not prescribe.

6. Law is the expression of the general will; all citizens have the right to concur personally, or through their representatives, in its formation; it must be the same for all, whether it protects or punishes. All citizens, being equal before it, are equally admissible to all public offices, positions, and employments, according to their capacity, and without other distinction than that of virtues and talents.

7. No man may be accused, arrested, or detained except in the cases determined by law, and according to the forms prescribed thereby. Whoever solicit, expedite, or execute arbitrary orders, or have them executed, must be punished; but every citizen summoned or apprehended in pursuance of the law must obey immediately; he renders himself culpable by resistance.

8. The law is to establish only penalties that are absolutely and obviously necessary; and no one may be punished except by virtue of a law established and promulgated prior to the offence and legally applied.

9. Since every man is presumed innocent until declared guilty, if arrest be deemed indispensable, all unnecessary severity for securing the person of the accused must be severely repressed by law.

10. No one is to be disquieted because of his opinions, even religious, provided their manifestation does not disturb the public order established by law.

11. Free communication of ideas and opinions is one of the most precious of the rights of man. Consequently, every citizen may speak, write, and print freely, subject to responsibility for the abuse of such liberty in the cases determined by law.

12. The guarantee of the rights of man and citizen necessitates a public force; such a force, therefore, is instituted for the advantage of all and not for the particular benefit of those to whom it is entrusted.

13. For the maintenance of the public force and for the expenses of administration a common tax is indispensable; it must be assessed equally on all citizens in proportion to their means.

14. Citizens have the right to ascertain, by themselves or through their representatives, the necessity of the public tax, to consent to it freely, to supervise its use, and to determine its quota, assessment, payment, and duration.

15. Society has the right to require of every public agent an accounting of his administration.

16. Every society in which the guarantee of rights is not assured or the separation of powers not determined has no constitution at all.

17. Since property is a sacred and inviolable right, no one may be deprived thereof unless a legally established public necessity obviously requires it, and upon condition of a just and previous indemnity.

J. H. Stewart, *A Documentary Survey of the French Revolution* (New York: The Macmillan Company, 1951), pp. 113-115, by permission of The Macmillan Company.

B. Rousseau. Forcing a Man To Be Free, 1762

CHAPTER VI

The Social Compact

I suppose men to have reached the point at which the obstacles in the way of their preservation in the state of nature show their power of resistance to be greater than the resources at the disposal of each individual for his maintenance in that state. That primitive condition can then subsist no longer; and the human race would perish unless it changed its manner of existence.

But, as men cannot engender new forces, but only unite and direct existing ones, they have no other means of preserving themselves than the formation, by aggregation, of a sum of forces great enough to overcome the resistance. These they have to bring into play by means of a single motive power, and cause to act in concert.

This sum of forces can arise only where several persons come together: but, as the force and liberty of each man are the chief instruments of his self-preservation, how can he pledge them without harming his own interests, and neglecting the care he owes to himself? This difficulty, in its bearing on my present subject, may be stated in the following terms—

"The problem is to find a form of association which will defend and protect with the whole common force the person and goods of each associate, and in which each, while uniting himself with all, may still obey himself alone, and remain as free as before." This is the fundamental problem of which the *Social Contract* provides the solution.

The clauses of this contract are so determined by the nature of the act that the slightest modification would make them vain and ineffective; so that, although they have perhaps never been formally set forth, they are everywhere the same and everywhere tacitly admitted and recognised, until, on the violation of the social compact, each regains his original rights and resumes his natural liberty, while losing the conventional liberty in favour of which he renounced it.

These clauses, properly understood, may be reduced to one—the total alienation of each associate, together with all his rights, to the whole community; for, in the first place, as each gives himself absolutely, the conditions are the same for all; and, this being so, no one has

any interest in making them burdensome to others.

Moreover, the alienation being without reserve, the union is as perfect as it can be, and no associate has anything more to demand: for, if the individuals retained certain rights, as there would be no common superior to decide between them and the public, each, being on one point his own judge, would ask to be so on all; the state of nature would thus continue, and the association would necessarily become inoperative or tyrannical.

Finally, each man, in giving himself to all, gives himself to nobody; and as there is no associate over whom he does not acquire the same right as he yields others over himself, he gains an equivalent for everything he loses, and an increase of force for the preservation of what he has.

If then we discard from the social compact what is not of its essence, we shall find that it reduces itself to the following terms—

"Each of us puts his person and all his power in common under the supreme direction of the general will, and, in our corporate capacity, we receive each member as an indivisible part of the whole."

At once, in place of the individual personality of each contracting party, this act of association creates a moral and collective body, composed of as many members as the assembly contains votes, and receiving from this act its unity, its common identity, its life and its will. This public person, so formed by the union of all other persons, formerly took the name of *city*, and now takes that of *Republic* or *body politic;* it is called by its members *State* when passive, *Sovereign* when active, and *Power* when compared with others like itself. Those who are associated in it take collectively the name of *people,* and severally are called *citizens,* as sharing in the sovereign power, and *subjects,* as being under the laws of the State. But these terms are often confused and taken one for another: it is enough to know how to distinguish them when they are being used with precision.

CHAPTER VII

The Sovereign

This formula shows us that the act of association comprises a mutual undertaking between the public and the individuals, and that each individual, in making a contract, as we may say, with himself, is bound in a double capacity; as a member of the Sovereign he is bound to the individuals, and as a member of the State to the Sovereign. But the maxim of civil right, that no one is bound by undertakings made to himself, does not apply in this case; for there is a great difference between incurring an obligation to yourself and incurring one to a whole of which you form a part. . . .

In fact, each individual, as a man, may have a particular will contrary or dissimilar to the general will which he has as a citizen. His particular interest may speak to him quite differently from the common interest: his absolute and naturally independent existence may make him look upon what he owes to the common cause as a gratuitous contribution, the loss of which will do less harm to others than the payment of it is burdensome to himself; and, regarding the moral person which constitutes the State as a *persona ficta,* because not a man, he may wish to enjoy the rights of citizenship without being ready to fulfil the duties of a subject. The continuance of such an injustice could not but prove the undoing of the body politic.

In order then that the social compact may not be an empty formula, it tacitly includes the undertaking, which alone can give force to the rest, that whoever refuses to obey the general will shall be compelled to do so by the whole body. *This means nothing less than that he will be forced to be free;* * for this is the condition which, by giving each citizen to his country, secures him against all personal dependence. In this lies the key to the working of the political machine; this alone legitimises civil undertakings, which, without it, would be absurd, tyrannical, and liable to the most frightful abuses. . . .

BOOK IV

CHAPTER II

Voting

. . . There is but one law which, from its nature, needs unanimous consent. This is the social compact; for civil association is the most voluntary of all acts. Every man being born free and his own master, no one, under any pretext whatsoever, can make any man subject without his consent. To decide that the son of a slave is born a slave is to decide that he is not born a man.

If then there are opponents when the social compact is made, their opposition does not invalidate the contract, but merely prevents them from being included in it. They are foreigners among citizens. When the State is instituted, residence constitutes consent; to dwell within its territory is to submit to the Sovereign.

Apart from this primitive contract, the vote of the majority always binds all the rest. This follows from the contract itself. But it is asked how a man can be both free and forced to conform to wills that are not his own. How are the opponents at once free and subject to laws they have not agreed to?

* *Note: italics not in original.*

I retort that the question is wrongly put. The citizen gives his consent to all the laws, including those which are passed in spite of his opposition, and even those which punish him when he dares to break any of them. The constant will of all the members of the State is the general will; by virtue of it they are citizens and free. When in the popular assembly a law is proposed, what the people is asked is not exactly whether it approves or rejects the proposal, but whether it is in conformity with the general will, which is their will. Each man, in giving his vote, states his opinion on that point; and the general will is found by counting votes. When therefore the opinion that is contrary to my own prevails, this proves neither more nor less than that I was mistaken, and that what I thought to be the general will was not so. If my particular opinion had carried the day I should have achieved the opposite of what was my will; and it is in that case that I should not have been free.

This presupposes, indeed, that all the qualities of the general will still reside in the majority: when they cease to do so, whatever side a man may take, liberty is no longer possible.

J. J. Rousseau, *The Social Contract*, trans. by G. D. H. Cole, Everyman's ed. (New York: E. P. Dutton & Co., n. d.), pp. 14-18, 93-94.

C. Godwin. Toward Individual Freedom? 1793

. . . It is . . . necessary before we enter upon the subject carefully to distinguish between society and government. Men associated at first for the sake of mutual assistance. They did not foresee that any restraint would be necessary to regulate the conduct of individual members of the society towards each other or towards the whole. The necessity of restraint grew out of the errors and perverseness of a few. An acute writer has expressed this idea with peculiar felicity. "Society and government," says he, "are different in themselves and have different origins. Society is produced by our wants, and government by our wickedness. Society is in every state a blessing; government even in its best state but a necessary evil." [1]

. . . If there be any truth more unquestionable than the rest, it is that every man is bound to the exertion of his faculties in the discovery of right and to the carrying into effect all the right with which he is acquainted. It

may be granted that an infallible standard, if it could be discovered, would be considerably beneficial. But this infallible standard itself would be of little use in human affairs unless it had the property of reasoning as well as deciding, of enlightening the mind as well as constraining the body. If a man be in some cases obliged to prefer his own judgment, he is in all cases obliged to consult that judgment before he can determine whether the matter in question be of the sort provided for or no. So that from this reasoning it ultimately appears that no man is obliged to conform to any rule of conduct farther than the rule is consistent with justice.

Such are the genuine principles of human society. Such would be the unconstrained concord of its members in a state where every individual within the society and every neighbour without was capable of listening with sobriety to the dictates of reason. We shall not fail to be impressed with considerable regret if, when we descend to the present mixed characters of mankind, we find ourselves obliged in any degree to depart from so simple and grand a principle. The universal exer-

---

[1] [Thomas Paine] *Common Sense,* p. 1.

cise of private judgment is a doctrine so unspeakably beautiful that the true politician will certainly resolve to interfere with it as sparingly and in as few instances as possible. Let us consider what are the emergencies that may be thought to demand an exception. They can only be briefly stated in this place, each of them requiring to be minutely examined in the subsequent stages of the enquiry.

In the first place then it seems necessary for some powerful arbitrator to interfere where the proceedings of the individual threaten the most injurious consequences to his neighbours, and where the instant nature of the case will not accord with the uncertain progress of argument and conviction addressed to the mind of the offender. . . . [But all punishment, even when necessary is evil.]

Notwithstanding all these objections, it would be difficult to find a country respecting which we could say that the inhabitants might with safety be dismissed from the operation of punishment. So mixed is human character, so wild are its excursions, so calamitous and detestable are the errors into which it occasionally falls, that something more than argument seems necessary for their suppression. Human beings are such tyros in the art of reasoning that the wisest of us often prove impotent in our attempts where an instant effect was most powerfully wanted. While I stand still to reason with the thief, the assassin or the oppressor, they hasten to new scenes of devastation, and with unsparing violence confound all the principles of human society. I should obtain little success by the abolition of punishment unless I could at the same time abolish those causes that generate temptation and make punishment necessary. Meanwhile the arguments already adduced may be sufficient to show that punishment is always an

evil, and to persuade us never to recur to it but from the most evident necessity.

The remaining cases in which it may seem requisite to have recourse to the general will of the society and to supersede the private judgment of individuals are when we are called upon to counteract the hostilities of an internal enemy or to repel the attacks of a foreign invader. Here, as in the former instance, the evils that arise from an usurpation upon private judgment are many and various. It is wrong that I should contribute in any mode to a proceeding, a war for example, that I believe to be unjust. Ought I to draw my sword when the adversary appears to me to be employed in repelling a wanton aggression? The case seems not to be at all different if I contribute my property, the produce it may be of my personal labour, though custom has reconciled us to the one rather than the other.

The consequences are a degradation of character and a relaxation of principle in the person who is thus made the instrument of a transaction which his judgment disapproves. In this case, as has been already stated generally, the human mind is compressed and unnerved till it affords us scarcely the semblance of what it might otherwise have been. And in addition to the general considerations in similar cases, it may be observed that the frequent and obstinate wars which at present desolate the human race would be nearly extirpated if they were supported only by the voluntary contributions of those by whom their principle was approved.

The objection which has hitherto been permitted practically to supersede these reasonings is the difficulty of conducting an affair in the success of which millions may be interested upon so precarious a support as that of private judgment. The men with whom we are usually concerned in human society are of so mixed a character, and a self-love of the narrowest kind is so deeply rooted in many of them, that it seems nearly unavoidable upon the scheme of voluntary contribution that the most generous would pay a very ample proportion, while the mean and avaricious, though they contributed nothing, would come in for their full share of the benefit. He that would reconcile a perfect freedom in this respect with the interest of the whole, ought to propose at the same time the means of extirpating selfishness and vice. How far such a proposal is feasible will come hereafter to be considered.

BOOK III

CHAPTER II

Of the Social Contract

Upon the first statement of the system of a social contract various difficulties present themselves. Who are the parties to this contract? For whom did they consent, for themselves only or for others? For how long a time is this contract to be considered as binding? If the consent of every individual be necessary, in what manner is that consent to be given? Is it to be tacit or declared in express terms?

Little will be gained for the cause of equality and justice if our ancestors, at the first institution of government, had a right indeed of choosing the system of regulations under which they thought proper to live, but at the same time could barter away the understandings and independence of all that came after them to the latest posterity. But if the contract must be renewed in each successive generation, what periods must be fixed on for that purpose? And if I be obliged to submit to the established government till my turn comes to assent to it, upon what principle is that obligation founded? Surely not upon the contract into which my father entered before I was born?

Secondly, what is the nature of the consent in consequence of which I am to be reckoned the subject of any particular government? It is usually said that acquiescence is sufficient, and that this acquiescence is to be inferred from my living quietly under the protection of the laws. But if this be true, an end is as effectually put to all political science, all discrimination of better and worse, as by any system invented by the most slavish sycophant that ever existed. Upon this hypothesis every government that is quietly submitted to is a lawful government, whether it be the usurpation of Cromwell or the tyranny of Caligula. Acquiescence is frequently nothing more than a choice on the part of the individual of what he deems the least evil. In many cases it is not so much as this, since the peasant and the artisan, who form the bulk of a nation, however dissatisfied with the government of their country, seldom have it in their power to transport themselves to another. It is also to be observed upon the system of acquiescence that it is in little agreement with the established opinions and practices of mankind. Thus what has been called the law of nations lays least stress upon the allegiance of a foreigner settling among us, though his acquiescence is certainly most complete; while natives removing into an uninhabited region are claimed by the mother country, and removing into a neighbouring territory are punished by municipal law if they take arms against the country in which they were born. Now surely acquiescence can scarcely be construed into consent while the individuals concerned are wholly unapprised of the authority intended to be rested upon it.

Mr. Locke, the great champion of the doctrine of an original contract, has been aware of this difficulty, and therefore observes that "a tacit consent indeed obliges a man to obey the laws of any government as long as he has any possessions or enjoyment of any part of the dominions of that government; but nothing can make a man a member of the commonwealth but his actually entering into it by positive engagement, and express promise and compact." A singular distinction; implying upon the face of it that an acquiescence such as has just been described is sufficient to render a man amenable to the penal regulations of society, but that his own consent is necessary to entitle him to its privileges.

A third objection to the social contract will suggest itself as soon as we attempt to ascertain the extent of the obligation, even supposing it to have been entered into in the most solemn manner by every member of the community. Allowing that I am called upon, at the period of my coming of age for example, to declare my assent or dissent to any system of opinions or any code of practical institutes; for how long a period does this declaration bind me? Am I precluded from better information for the whole course of my life? And if not for my whole life, why for a year, a week or even an hour? If my deliberate judgment or my real sentiment be of no avail in the case, in what sense can it be affirmed that all lawful government is founded in my consent?

But the question of time is not the only difficulty. If you demand my assent to any proposition, it is necessary that the proposition should be stated simply and clearly. So numerous are the varieties of human understanding in all cases where its independence and integrity are sufficiently preserved that there is little chance of any two men coming to a precise agreement about ten successive propositions that are in

their own nature open to debate. What then can be more absurd than to present to me the laws of England in fifty volumes folio and call upon me to give an honest and uninfluenced vote upon their whole contents at once?

But the social contract, considered as the foundation of civil government, requires more of me than this. I am not only obliged to consent to all the laws that are actually upon record, but to all the laws that shall hereafter be made. It was under this view of the subject that Rousseau, in tracing the consequences of the social contract, was led to assert that "the great body of the people, in whom the sovereign authority resides, can neither delegate nor resign it. The essence of that authority," he adds, "is the general will; and will cannot be represented. It must either be the same or another; there is no alternative. The deputies of the people cannot be its representatives; they are merely its attorneys. The laws that the community does not ratify in person are no laws, are nullities."

. . . Lastly, if government be founded in the consent of the people, it can have no power over any individual by whom that consent is refused. If a tacit consent be not sufficient, still less can I be deemed to have consented to a measure upon which I put an express negative. This immediately follows from the observations of Rousseau. If the people, or the individuals of whom the people is constituted, cannot delegate their authority to a representative, neither can any individual delegate his authority to a majority in an assembly of which he is himself a member. The rules by which my actions shall be directed are matters of a consideration entirely personal, and no man can transfer to another the keeping of his conscience and the judging of his duties. But this brings us back to the point from which we set out. No consent of ours can divest us of our moral capacity. This is a species of property which we can neither barter nor resign, and of consequence it is impossible for any government to derive its authority from an original contract.

William Godwin, *An Enquiry Concerning Political Justice and Its Influence on General Virtue and Happiness,* ed. R. A. Preston (New York, Copyright 1926: Used by permission of Appleton-Century-Crofts), I, 39, 78-86, 92-96.

D. Robespierre. *Toward Authoritarian Collectivism? 1793*

What is the purpose, what is the goal for which we strive? We wish a peaceful enjoyment of freedom and equality, the rule of that eternal justice whose laws are graven not in marble or in stone, but in the hearts of all men. We wish a social order that shall hold in check all base and cruel passions, which shall awaken to life all benevolent and noble impulses, that shall make the noblest ambition that of being useful to our country, that shall draw its honorable distinctions only from equality, in which the generality shall safeguard the welfare of the individual, and in which all hearts may be moved by any evidence of republican spirit. . . . We want morality in the place of egotism, principles in the place of mere habit, the rule of reason in the place of the slavery of tradition, contempt for vice in the place of contempt for misfortune, the love of glory in the place of avarice. Honest men instead of "good society," truth instead of empty show, manly greatness instead of the depravity of the great, a sublime, powerful, victorious and happy people!

The splendor of the goal pursued by our Revolution is simultaneously the source of our strength and our weakness. It is the source of our weakness, because it unites all the perfidious and vicious individuals, all the advocates of tyranny who think of plunder, who think to find in the Revolution a trade and in the Republic a booty. Thus we may explain the disaffection of many persons who began the struggle together with us, but who have left us when our path was but half accomplished, because they did not pursue the objects we were pursuing. . . .

You are surrounded beyond the boundaries; at home, all the friends of the tyrants conspire, and will continue to conspire, so long as treason still has a hope. We must stifle the domestic and foreign enemies of the Republic, or we must be destroyed with the Republic. And therefore, under the present circumstances, the principle of our Republic is this: to influence the people by the use of reason, to influence our enemies by the use of terror.

In times of peace, virtue is the source from which the government of the people takes its power. During the Revolution, the sources of this power are virtue and terror: virtue, without which terror will be a disaster; and terror, without which virtue is powerless. But terror is nothing more nor less than swift, severe and indomitable justice. . . .

It has been said that terror is the means by which a despotic government rules. Has your rule anything in common with such a government? Yes, indeed, but only in the sense that the sword in hands of the protagonists of liberty resembles the sword in the hands of the champion of tyranny. When despots rule because their subjects are terrified, the despots are justified—as despots. You put down all the enemies of freedom by means of terror, and you are justified—as founders of the Republic. *The government of the Revolution is the despotism of liberty against tyranny*.* Must might be used only in order to protect crime? . . .

If tyranny prevails for but a single day, all the patriots will have been wiped out by the next morning. And yet some persons dare declare that despotism is justice and that the justice of the people is despotism and rebellion. . . .

Either we or our enemies must succumb. "Show consideration for the Royalists!" shout some persons; "have compassion with the criminal!" "No, I tell you; you have compassion with innocence, compassion with the weak, and compassion with humanity! . . ."

The whole task of protecting the Republic is for the advantage of the loyal citizen. In the Republic, only republicans may be citizens. The Royalists and conspirators are foreigners to us,

---

* *Note: italics not in original.*

enemies. Is not the terrible war in which we now are involved a single indissoluble struggle? Are the enemies within not the allies of those who attack us from without? The murderers who rend the flesh of their country at home; the intriguers who seek to purchase the conscience of the representatives of the people; the traitors who sell themselves; the pamphleteers who besmirch us and are preparing for a political counter-revolution by means of a moral counter-revolution;—are all these individuals any less dangerous than the tyrants whom they serve? All those who would intervene between these criminals and the sword of justice are like unto those who would throw themselves between the bayonets of our soldiers and the troops of the enemy, and the enthusiasm of their false feelings amounts in my eyes only to sighs directed toward England and Austria!

Maximilien Robespierre, *Speeches: Voices of Revolt,* I (New York: International Publishers, 1927), pp. 72-75.

E. Jefferson. On the Need for Revolution, 1816

Some men look at constitutions with sanctimonious reverence, and deem them like the ark of the covenant, too sacred to be touched. They ascribe to the men of the preceding age a wisdom more than human, and suppose what they did to be beyond amendment. I knew that age well; I belonged to it, and labored with it. It deserved well of its country. It was very like the present, but without the experience of the present; and forty years of experience in government is worth a century of book-reading; and this they would say themselves, were they to rise from the dead. I am certainly not an advocate for frequent and untried changes in laws and constitutions. I think moderate imperfections had better be borne with; because, when once known,

we accommodate ourselves to them, and find practical means of correcting their ill effects. But I know also, that laws and institutions must go hand in hand with the progress of the human mind. As that becomes more developed, more enlightened, as new discoveries are made, new truths disclosed, and manners and opinions change with the change of circumstances, institutions must advance also, and keep pace with the times. We might as well require a man to wear still the coat which fitted him when a boy, as civilized society to remain ever under the regimen of their barbarous ancestors. It is this preposterous idea which has lately deluged Europe in blood. Their monarchs, instead of wisely yielding to the gradual change of circumstances, of favoring progressive accommodation to progressive improvement, have clung to old abuses, entrenched themselves behind steady habits, and obliged their subjects to seek through blood and violence rash and ruinous innovations, which, had they been referred to the peaceful deliberations and collected wisdom of the nation, would have been put into acceptable and salutary forms. Let us follow no such examples, nor weakly believe that one generation is not as capable as another of taking care of itself, and of ordering its own affairs. Let us, as our sister States have done, avail ourselves of our reason and experience, to correct the crude essays of our first and unexperienced, although wise, virtuous, and well-meaning councils. And lastly, let us provide in our constitution for its revision at stated periods. What these periods should be, nature herself indicates. By the European tables of mortality, of the adults living at any one moment of time, a majority will be dead in about nineteen years. At the end of that period then, a new majority is come into place; or, in other words, a new generation. Each generation is as independent of the one preceding, as that was of all which had gone before. It has then, like them, a right to choose for itself the form of government it believes most promotive of its own happiness; consequently, to accommodate to the circumstances in which it finds itself, that received from its predecessors; and it is for the peace and good of mankind, that a solemn opportunity of doing this every nineteen or twenty years, should be provided by the constitution; so that it may be handed on, with periodical repairs, from generation to generation, to the end of time, if anything human can so long endure. It is now forty years since the constitution of Virginia was formed. The same tables inform us, that, within that period, two-thirds of the adults then living are now dead. Have then the remaining third, even if they had the wish, the right to hold in obedience to their will, and to laws heretofore made by them, the other two-thirds, who, with themselves, compose the present mass of adults? If they have not, who has? The dead? But the dead have no rights. They are nothing; and nothing cannot own something. Where there is no substance, there can be no accident. This corporeal globe, and everything upon it, belong to its present corporeal inhabitants, during their generation. They alone have a right to direct what is the concern of themselves alone, and to declare the law of that direction; and this declaration can only be made by their majority. That majority, then, has a right to depute representatives to a convention, and to make the constitution what they think will be the best for themselves. But how collect their voice? This is the real difficulty. If invited by private authority, or county or district meetings, these divisions are so large that few will attend; and their voice will be imperfectly, or falsely pronounced. Here, then, would be one of the advantages of the ward divisions I have proposed. The mayor of every ward, on a question like the present, would call his ward together, take the simple yea or nay of its members, convey these to the county court, who would hand on those of all its wards to the proper general authority, and the voice of the whole people would be thus fairly, full, and peaceably expressed, discussed, and decided by the common reason of the society. If this avenue be shut to the call of sufferance, it will make itself heard through that of force, and we shall go on, as other nations are doing, in the endless circle of oppression, rebellion, reformation; and oppression, rebellion, reformation, again; and so on forever.

Thomas Jefferson, "Government by the People" (letter to Samuel Kercheval, July 12, 1816), in S. K. Padover, ed., *The Complete Jefferson* (New York: Duell, Sloan & Pearce, Inc., 1943), pp. 291-293.

10. *The French Revolution and Napoleon*

JOHN HALL STEWART

Western Reserve University

In 1789 THERE burst upon France a tremendous cataclysm which, as we shall see in the first part of this problem, had been developing for three-quarters of a century. Change was long overdue in many parts of the French institutional structure. In other parts, whether absolutely necessary or not, it was desired by numerous sections of the populace. Need and desire for change became coupled with the growth of an ideology, the essence of which was the theory of the natural rights of man. This idea gave momentum to the demand for change, especially on the part of the middle class, which wished political power and social status concomitant with the economic influence that it already possessed.

Had France been dominated by a "benevolent despot" such as the late Frederick the Great of Prussia, it is possible that the unfortunate circumstances might not have evolved—or if they *had,* their solution doubtless would have been provided with speed and efficiency. But France was not to experience enlightened despotism. Instead of intelligent and competent leadership, it had only the indifferent government of Louis XV. When he died in 1774, after a relatively inglorious reign of nearly 60 years, he was succeeded by his grandson, Louis XVI, who, although decidedly more virtuous, was no more effective a sovereign than his predecessor.

Louis XVI is more to be pitied than censured. He had the misfortune to inherit a position and responsibilities for which he was not fitted by either training or temperament. It was during the later years of his reign that matters reached a crisis, which resulted in the metamorphosis of French institutional life known as the French Revolution.

Stemming immediately from financial distress, which neither Louis nor his ministers could (or were permitted to) solve, the first step towards the Revolution took the form of the summoning of the Estates General. This outmoded agency had not met for 175 years, and it was now revived essentially as a financial expedient, when all others had failed. Constituted, as previously, of representatives of the two privileged orders (the clergy and the nobles) and the "unprivileged" third estate, the Estates General of 1789, however, differed from its predecessors in one vital respect: the commoners had as many delegates as the nobles and clergy combined. Granted as a sort of compromise, this circumstance resulted, in a few short weeks, in a momentous accomplishment. Owing to the inertia and vacillation of the king, the commoners were able to enlist the support of the more progressive aristocrats and clerics, to defy the royal authority, to gain control of the Estates General, and to transform it into a National Assembly, the avowed purpose of which was to provide France with a constitution and a program of reforms.

During the ensuing six years, this assembly and two succeeding ones—the Legislative Assembly (1791–1792) and the National Convention (1792–1795) —managed to achieve many of the objectives contemplated by the leaders of 1789. Politically, France received not only one constitution, but, after the virtually inevitable fall of the monarchy in 1792, two others. Both of these latter ones provided for a republican form of government. The first, in 1793, was more democratic in form, but because of critical conditions it was never put into effect; the second, in 1795, was less democratic in character, but endured until 1799, by which time (as we shall see) the Revolution was "ended," and the destinies of France passed into other hands. Likewise in the sphere of politics the French people received (at least on paper) certain guarantees of personal liberties, and they were permitted some experience in practical politics. The legal system underwent a thorough and progressive reorganization. Religious liberty was established, and the Roman Church, the church of the majority of Frenchmen, became, at least for a time, substantially a department of the state. The entire economy was recast in a new mold of "free enterprise." The social structure was re-established on bases of equality and "careers open to talents." Even the cultural aspects of life were revitalized by plans for universal education, encouragement of the arts, and such accomplishments as the creation of the metric system.

The foregoing items represent but a suggestion of the fundamental change which France underwent, the *real* revolution. As might be expected, this revolution was not achieved without a struggle. First came the conflict between revolutionaries and *anti*-revolutionaries. In time this was augmented by quarrels among the revolutionaries themselves, the moderates and the radicals. As seems to be the case in most revolutions, the radicals triumphed, and for a brief period in 1793 and 1794 dominated the situation through means that we know as "The Reign of Terror." The circumstances were complicated by the outbreak of foreign war with the states of Europe which viewed the Revolution as a danger to European stability and wished to suppress it. Part Two of this section suggests something of the manner in which the English-speaking world viewed the Revolution.

Paradoxically, despite all that the revolutionary leaders were able to achieve in the face of seemingly insurmountable obstacles, they never did solve the problem of finances, the problem which had precipitated the entire movement in 1789. In the end it was met, as is too often the case in revolutions, by a forced currency, which rapidly depreciated in value, and repudiation of the bulk of national obligations. The fact remains, however, that, for good or ill, within an astonishingly short period of time, a tremendous amount had been achieved, and France had been transformed into a modern state.

The years from 1795 to 1799 in the history of France (the period of the "Directory") represent, at one and the same time, three different things. First, it was during this time that the second republican constitution was given an opportunity to function and many of the essential features of the Revolution were brought to completion. Second, it was the time during which there rose to power the man who was to take charge of events in 1799, namely, Napoleon Bonaparte. (Accordingly, these years may be considered as the last phase of the French Revolution and the first phase of the Napoleonic Era.) Third, and this is most significant, it represents the phase of transition between the two epochs.

By 1799 France was weary—of terror, of internal conflict, of foreign war, of financial and economic unsettlement. The time was ripe for a "strong man" to assume control of events. And, as seems never to fail, such a man was on hand, ready and eager to meet the emergency. The years that follow, from 1799 to 1815, present not only the history of the "fate" of the Revolution in the hands of a dictator; they also portray the life of one of the most striking figures in the entire story of the human race.

An obscure Corsican, Napoleon Bonaparte experienced much hardship and frustration during his early years—a most fitting background for a potential dictator. Entering the army, he took advantage of every opportunity to advance himself. In 1795, when the heirs of the "Terror" were faced with the necessity of employing force to perpetuate themselves in power, Napoleon had the good fortune to be selected as the man to direct the action—which he did with great dispatch. Possibly fearing that he might endeavor to capitalize upon his newly acquired prominence, the executive "Directors" of the new government gave him a dubious reward in the form of the command of the French Army of Italy. So, a general at the age of 26, Napoleon embarked upon his career. Transforming what had long been a graveyard of military reputations into a scene of brilliant victories and diplomatic triumphs, Napoleon returned to France in 1797 in a cloud of glory, and with the government even more deeply in his debt. Two years later, despite an ill-fated Egyptian expedition which, had the full truth of it been known, might have ruined his chances, once again he was in the right place at the right time. The faltering government of the Directory, dispossessed by a clever *coup d'état,* yielded to the rule of Bonaparte.

From 1799 to 1814, and again briefly in 1815, Napoleon Bonaparte ruled France. This period is the famed "Napoleonic Era." At first maintaining a pretense of governing through a republican constitution as "First Consul" (nominally for ten years), he soon acquired the title and status of "Consul for Life." By 1804 he had established himself as "Emperor of the French," with the inheritance vested in his family. These achievements alone are suggestive of the character and tactics of the man.

The acquisition of power, however, is only one of the significant features of Napoleon's régime. With regard to France itself, he consolidated and modified the principal gains of the Revolution in such a way that it is difficult to determine to which period France today is more deeply indebted. Suffice it to say that the legal system, local government, educational institutions, and many other features of modern France bear the unmistakable marks of Napoleon's endeavors.

As with most dictators, Napoleon's path soon led to war (after a brief interlude of "pacification"), war with a series of European coalitions over ten long and bloody years. Successful at the outset, Napoleon gained control of more European territory than had been in the hands of a single state or individual since the days of Charlemagne. Throughout his vast empire he disseminated the ideas and institutions of revolutionary France in a manner which was to have profound effects upon the future of Europe.

Age, illness, war-weariness, and an exaggerated sense of his own destiny proved, however, in the long run, to be Napoleon's undoing. Between 1812, when he staged a disastrous invasion of Russia, and 1814, when a desperate and overwhelming European coalition brought him to his knees, his doom was sealed. He was shipped off to the little island of Elba to reign over a "comic kingdom." Meanwhile, representatives of the great powers convened at Vienna to attempt to restore Europe to its pre-Revolutionary, pre-Napoleonic status, and to devise ways and means of maintaining such a restoration.

Napoleon's escape from Elba, and his recapturing of France by the force of his personality, were only portions of an anticlimax which was settled in a few months on the decisive field of Waterloo. This time he was destined to be sentenced to isolation on St. Helena, a rocky island in mid-Atlantic, a "prison" from which escape was to be provided only by death, in 1821—in his fifty-second year! Part Four of this section is designed to suggest something of the character of the man.

Thus in 1815 apparently ended the Age of the French Revolution and Napoleon, an age during which the oldest and most civilized of European states had been turned inside out, and Western Europe as a whole had been turned upside down. It would seem, in view of the brief summary of the epoch, that it well merits the special attention which historians have given it. On the other hand, as is suggested in Part Three of this section, historians are by no means agreed concerning the significance of the French Revolution.

Time and space preclude the possibility of dealing with more than a few aspects of the French Revolution and Napoleon in this book. Accordingly, we shall approach them through four problems, each of which represents a basic feature of their study. The result may suggest to the reader something of the complexity of one of the most significant periods in the history of modern Europe.

Attempts at solving these problems will doubtless produce more or less definite conclusions concerning at least four aspects of the French Revolution and Napoleon. Obviously, however, these are not enough—they must be supplemented by further conclusions, not only about other phases of these historical phenomena, but also about each of them as a whole. Unless additional problems are sought and solved, any comprehension of this period of European history will remain sketchy to say the least. Nor would one have any idea of what ultimately came of it.

What additional types of problem will serve as a means of suggesting the breadth of these topics—perhaps also as an introduction to subsequent problems in this book? To what extent did the French Revolution *actually* effect fundamental change in French institutions; in other words, how was the France of 1799 different from and still similar to that of 1789? By what processes were these changes brought about—by legislation or by fiat, by accident or by necessity, by peaceful or by violent action? Why did the "Terror" develop; and was it, in its various forms, unavoidable? To what extent did the changes represent the wishes of the people of France as a whole? Did the aims and objectives of the revolutionaries change during the decade from 1789 to 1799; and if so, how and why? Who were the leaders of the Revolution during its several phases, what type of men were they, and what were their contributions? Why was Napoleon able to take control of the situation in 1799? To what extent did he retain the gains of the Revolution intact; to what extent did he alter them; and how and why? How and why was Napoleon able to dominate the European scene as he did, for so many years? Why at last did he and his empire fall; or did they really *fall*? And why have both the French Revolution and Napoleon continued to fascinate both the casual and the serious student of history these many generations?

Above all, did the French Revolution and the Napoleonic Era come to a full stop in 1815? Or did they both continue to affect the course of European and world history in the years that followed?

I. WHAT CAUSED THE FRENCH REVOLUTION?

One of the most important factors in the study of history is causation—the reasons why things happen. It is especially significant in the study of revolutions in general and the French Revolution in particular. A revolution, strictly speaking, is any movement which results in *fundamental* change. What causes such movements? Obviously, dissatisfaction with things as they are must have something to do with it. If everyone were satisfied, there would be neither need nor demand for change. Dissatisfaction, however, is apparently never enough in itself to effect change. In order to produce results, it must be made active, through the leadership of individuals who hope for better things. Peculiarly, these persons usually belong to a group which is enjoying enough benefits to make it desirous of more. They seldom represent the downtrodden elements in the population.

In time the leaders develop or adopt an ideology, which serves as a justification for their demands and provides patterns for their plans. This is where ideas enter the scene. But, no matter how much dissatisfaction, leadership, or ideology, the change is seldom achieved until the existing regime breaks down and provides the "revolutionaries" with an opportunity to assume control of the situation. Then the revolution begins.

Here the problem consists of examining evidence, both primary and secondary, with a view to determining why a revolution came to France, why it came there rather than elsewhere, why it came when it did and in the form which it assumed.

The Evidence of Contemporaries

In dealing with contemporary evidence, certain factors must always be taken into consideration: the authenticity of the evidence; the qualifications of the writer; the extent to which he was an observer or a participant; the degree to which he was motivated by self-interest or prejudice. Here we have accounts by an observer (Young), a participant (Siéyès), and a man who, in a sense, belongs in both categories (Weber). To what extent do these excerpts indicate what contemporaries thought the causes of the French Revolution were?

A. Arthur Young

Unsuccessful as a practical farmer, nevertheless the Englishman Arthur Young (1741–1820) was among the foremost agricultural enthusiasts, authorities, and writers of the eighteenth century. Observant, understanding, and a fine reporter, he set down in *Travels in France* one of the best descriptions of conditions in France prior to the Revolution.

Peasantry in Guienne (10 June, 1787)

Pass Payrac, and meet many poor beggars, which we had not done before. All the country, girls and women, are without shoes or stockings; and the ploughmen at their work have neither sabots nor feet to their stockings. This is a poverty that strikes at the root of national prosperity; a large consumption among the poor being of more consequence than among the rich: the wealth of a nation lies in its circulation and consumption; and the case of poor people abstaining from the use of manufactures of leather and wool ought to be considered as an evil of the first magnitude. It reminded me of the misery of Ireland. . . .

Peasantry in Béarn (12 August, 1787)

A succession of many well built, tight, and COMFORTABLE farming cottages, built of stone, and covered with tiles, . . . and young trees nursed up with such care, that nothing but the fostering attention of the owner could effect anything like it. To every house belongs a farm, perfectly well inclosed, with grass borders mown and neatly kept around the corn fields, with gates to pass from one inclosure to another. . . . There are some parts of England . . . that resemble this country of Bearne; but we have very little that is equal to what I have seen in this ride of twelve miles from Pau to Moneng. It is all in the hands of little proprietors, without the farms being so small as to occasion a vicious and miserable population. It is visible in their new built houses and stables; . . . even in the coops for their poultry, and the sties for their hogs. A peasant does not think of rendering his pig comfortable, if his own happiness hangs by the thread of a nine year lease. . . .

(Paris, 17 October, 1787)

. . . One opinion pervaded the whole company, that they are on the eve of some great revolution in the government: that everything points to it: the confusion in the finances great; with a *deficit* impossible to provide for without the states-general of the kingdom, yet no ideas formed of what would be the consequence of their meeting: no minister existing, or to be looked to in or out of power, with such decisive talents as to promise any other remedy than palliative ones: a prince on the throne, with excellent dispositions, but without the resources of a mind that could govern in such a moment without ministers: a court buried in pleasure and dissipation; and adding to the distress instead of endeavouring to be placed in a more independent situation: a great ferment amongst all ranks of men, who are eager for some change, without knowing what to look to or to hope for: and a strong leaven of liberty, increasing every hour since the American revolution; altogether form a combination of circumstances that promise e'er long to ferment into motion if some master hand of very superior talents and inflexible courage, is not found at the helm to guide events, instead of being driven by them. It is very remarkable that such conversation never occurs but a bankruptcy is a topic: the curious question on which is, *would a bankruptcy occasion a civil war, and a total overthrow of the government?* The answers that

I have received to this question appear to be just: such a measure conducted by a man of abilities, vigour, and firmness would certainly not occasion either one or the other. But the same measure, attempted by a man of a different character, might possibly do both. All agree that the states of the kingdom cannot assemble without more liberty being the consequence; but I meet with so few men that have any just ideas of freedom that I question much the species of this new liberty that is to arise. They know not how to value the privileges of THE PEOPLE: as to the nobility and the clergy, if a revolution added anything to their scale I think it would do more mischief than good. . . .

Arthur Young, *Travels during the Years 1787, 1788, and 1789. Undertaken More Particularly with a View of Ascertaining the Cultivation, Wealth, Resources, and National Prosperity of the Kingdom of France* (London, 1792), pp. 18, 41-42, 66.

B. Abbé Siéyès

The career of Abbé Emmanuel Joseph Siéyès (1748–1836) spanned the Old Régime, the Revolution, the Napoleonic Era, and the Restoration. In public life almost continuously from 1789 to 1815, he first gained recognition through the publication of his provocative pamphlet, "What is the Third Estate?" 1789.

The plan of this pamphlet is very simple. We have three questions to ask:

1st. What is the third estate? Everything.
2nd. What has it been heretofore in the political order? Nothing.
3rd. What does it demand? To become something therein. . . .

CHAPTER I. THE THIRD ESTATE IS A COMPLETE NATION

What are the essentials of national existence and prosperity? *Private* enterprise and *public* functions.

Private enterprise may be divided into four categories: 1st. Since earth and water furnish the raw material for

man's needs, the first category will comprise all families engaged in agricultural pursuits. 2nd. Between the original sale of materials and their consumption or use, further workmanship . . . adds to these materials a second value . . . Human industry thus succeeds in improving the benefits of nature and in increasing the gross produce. . . . Such is the work of the second class. 3rd. Between production and consumption, as well as among the different degrees of production, a group of intermediate agents . . . comes into being; these are the dealers and merchants. . . . 4th. In addition to these three classes of industrious and useful citizens . . . a society needs many private undertakings and endeavors which are *directly* useful or agreeable to the *individual*. This fourth class includes from the most distinguished scientific and liberal professions to the least esteemed domestic services. Such are the labors which sustain society. Who performs them? The third estate.

Public functions likewise . . . may be

classified under four well-known headings: the Sword, the Robe, the Church, and the Administration. It is unnecessary to discuss them in detail in order to demonstrate that the third estate everywhere constitutes nineteen-twentieths of them, except that it is burdened with all that is really arduous, with all the tasks that the privileged order refuses to perform. Only the lucrative and honorary positions are held by members of the privileged order. . . .

It suffices here to have revealed that the alleged utility of a privileged order to public service is only a chimera: that without it, the higher positions would be infinitely better filled; that they naturally ought to be the lot of and reward for talents and recognized services; and that if the privileged classes have succeeded in usurping all the lucrative and honorary positions, it is both an odious injustice to the majority of citizens and an act of treason against the state.

Who, then, would dare to say that the third estate has not within itself all that is necessary to constitute a complete nation? . . . If the privileged order were abolished, the nation would not be something less but something more. Thus, what is the third estate? Everything; but an everything shackled and oppressed. What would it be without the privileged order? Everything; but an everything free and flourishing. Nothing can progress without it; everything would proceed infinitely better without the others. . . .

What is a nation? a body of associates living under a *common* law and represented by the same *legislature*.

Is it not exceedingly clear that the noble order has privileges, exemptions, even rights separate from the rights of the majority of citizens? Thus it deviates from the common order, from the common law. Thus its civil rights already render it a people apart in a great nation. . . .

Also, it enjoys its political rights separately. It has its own representatives, who are by no means charged with representing the people. Its deputation sits apart; . . . it is foreign to the nation in principle, since its mandate does not emanate from the people, and in aim, since its purpose is to defend not the general but a special interest.

The third estate, then, comprises everything that appertains to the nation; and whatever is not the third estate may not be regarded as being of the nation. What is the third estate? Everything!

John Hall Stewart, *A Documentary Survey of the French Revolution* (New York: The Macmillan Company, 1951), pp. 42-44.

C. Joseph Weber

Joseph Weber was the foster brother of Marie Antoinette. He was born in 1755, but the place and date of his death remain unknown. He lived at the French Court, and hence witnessed many of the leading events of the Revolution. In the light of modern scholarship, his analysis of revolutions is unusual.

. . . thirty different writers might assign thirty different causes for this shock which the world has experienced, and each render his explanation plausible.

The truth is that there are numerous causes of which one may say, "Without that the Revolution would not have happened"; but there is not one which could be put forward as the sole cause of the Revolution.

. . . I . . . recognize three primary and immediate causes of the French Revolution: the disorder in the finances, the state of mind, and the war in America.

If order had reigned in the treasury; if the equilibrium between expenditure and receipts had been perfect; then the ideas of independence, which filled all minds, would have been vented in private circles, in academic sessions, or in a few parliamentary remonstrances; . . .

If the general disposition of mind had been, under Louis XVI, what it had been under Louis XIV, or even under half the reign of Louis XV, the disorder of the finances would not have led to any political catastrophe. . . .

. . . if . . . there had been no war in America; and there had been sixteen millions less in the national debt; then the disposition of mind would not have suddenly carried theories of peaceful independence to the convulsions and excesses of an actual revolt.

To have prevented the French Revolution, then, one of these three things was necessary: to arrange the finances, to control the trend of thought, or to abandon the American insurgents. By avoiding one of these three causes of disturbance, the other two would have been rendered powerless. Instead, all three were united when they were most potent. A Leopold, a Frederick, a Gustavus might still have found a way to triumph over these; but Louis XVI was born to be the father of a submissive people, and not to be the master of rebellious subjects; the Providence which had destined him to be a great example, had given him the constancy of martyrs rather than the courage of heroes, . . .

. . . The character of the unfortunate Louis XVI, and the variance between his particular virtues and the requirements of events, have obviously contributed so much to the success of the Revolution, that I ought perhaps to present them here as a fourth primary cause. . . . But beyond that, . . . lack-

ing one personage, another would have come forward. Whenever, in a great state, the sources of the public treasury have dried up; when the old restraints of rank and subordination are broken down, and there is no firm hand to impose new ones immediately, then it must be expected that vices, passions, and even virtues will enter into a fermentation whose effects will be incalculable. . . . There will be enthusiasts, dangerous by the very purity of their intentions, and corrupt beings who will willingly cause public misfortune to further their personal interests. There will be youth, avid for novelties, drunk with presumption, and disdaining the experience of centuries; old men, bowed down by the yoke of routine, and understanding nothing except that which exists no longer; . . . One will see those ambitious for power and for riches seize, some without discernment and others without scruple, all means of satiating the passion which torments them. Into this tumult, already so terrible, the discontented, the vindictive, the envious, the ingrate will throw themselves. At first, they will all belong to the classes superior in rank, in fortune, or in education. Soon each will devote all his efforts to move what one calls the brute mass of society, in order to detach some portion of it, and use it against his rivals. Once put into movement, this mass will overwhelm everything, men and projects, opposition and counsel, enemies and leaders.

That is a general description of the French Revolution; it is that of every revolution which breaks out under like circumstances and with like principles.

E. L. Higgins, *The French Revolution as Told by Contemporaries* (Boston: Houghton Mifflin Company, 1938), pp. 1-2. The excerpt comes from Joseph Weber, *Mémoires de Weber concernant Marie Antoinette*, 2 vols. (Paris, 1822), I, 75-79 (originally published 1804), being vols. 55 and 56 of *Collection des mémoires relatifs à la Révolution française* . . . , ed. Saint-Albin Berville and Jean Francois Barrière. 56 vols. (Paris. 1820–1828).

The Verdict of Historians

Evaluation of verdicts of historians necessitates consideration of their competence and prejudices. It also requires a knowledge of their nationality, their remoteness from the events, the sources available and the extent to which they utilized them, and the possibility that the circumstances of their own time may have motivated their work. Here analyses by historians, a century apart and considerably removed from the events, are presented. How do they compare with each other and with the contemporary evidence? What answer or answers do they provide to the question, "What caused the French Revolution?"

A. Alexis de Tocqueville

In 1855 Alexis de Tocqueville (1805–1859) published perhaps the first serious scholarly analysis of the causes of the Revolution. Influenced by his study of democracy in America, and probably likewise by the fate of the Second Republic, Tocqueville's work also indicated a belief in history as a process of continual evolution.

Let it be borne in mind that France was the only country in which the feudal system had preserved its injurious and irritating characteristics, while it had lost all those which were beneficial or useful; and it will seem less surprising that the Revolution which was to abolish the old constitution of Europe should have broken out there rather than elsewhere.

Let it also be borne in mind that France was the only feudal country in which the nobility had lost its old political rights, . . . but had nevertheless retained and even largely increased its pecuniary indemnities and the individual privileges of its members; . . . and it will at once be understood why its privileges seemed so inexplicable and detestable to the French. . . .

Let it be borne in mind, finally, that the nobility was separated from the middle classes, which it had eschewed, and from the people, whose affections it had lost; that it stood alone in the midst of the nation, seemingly the staff of an army, really a group of soldierless officers; and it will be easy to conceive how, after an existence of a thousand years, it was overthrown in a single night.

. . . the royal government abolished the provincial liberties, usurped the place of the local authorities in three fourths of the kingdom, and monopolized public business, great and small; . . . Paris consequently became of necessity the master of the country instead of the capital. . . These two facts, which were peculiar to France, would alone suffice to show how a revolt could achieve the overthrow of a monarchy which had endured so violent shocks during so many centuries. . .

Political life had been so long and so thoroughly extinguished in France—individuals had so entirely lost the habit of mixing in public affairs, of judging for themselves, of studying popular movements, and even understanding the people at all, that the French quite naturally drifted into a terrible revolution without seeing it—the very parties who had most to fear from it taking the lead, and undertaking to smooth and widen the way for its approach.

In the absence of free institutions, and, consequently, of political classes, active political bodies, or organized parties, the duty of leading public opinion, when it revived, naturally fell to the lot of philosophers. Hence it might be expected that the Revolution would be conducted less in view of specific facts than in conformity with abstract principles and general theories. It might be conjectured that, instead of assailing specific laws, it would attack all laws together, and would assume to substitute for the old Constitution of

France a new system of government which these writers had conceived.

The Church was mixed with all the old institutions that were to be destroyed. Hence it was plain that the Revolution would shake the religious while it overthrew the civil power; and this done, and men's minds set free from all the restraints which religion, custom, and law impose on reformers, it was impossible to say to what unheard-of lengths of boldness it might not go. . . .

. . . The old government had deprived the French of the power and the desire to help each other. When the Revolution broke out, there were not ten men in the greater part of France who were in the habit of acting in concert, in a regular manner, and providing for their own defense; every thing was left to the central power. And so, when that power made way for an irresponsible sovereign assembly, and exchanged its former mildness for ferocity, there was nothing to check or delay it for an instant. The same cause which had overthrown the monarchy had rendered every thing possible after its fall. . . .

To comprehend the contrast between the benign theories and the violent acts of the Revolution, one must remember that it was prepared by the most civilized classes of the nation, and executed by the roughest and unpolished. The former having no bond of mutual union, no common understanding among themselves, no hold on the people, the latter assumed the whole direction of affairs when the old authorities were abolished. Even where they did not govern they inspired the government; and a glance at the way they had lived under the old regime left no room for doubt as to what they would prove. . . .

The careful student of France during the eighteenth century must have noticed . . . the birth and development of two leading passions, which were not coeval, and not always similar in their tendencies.

One—the deepest and most solidly rooted—was a violent, unquenchable hatred of inequality. . . .

The other—of more recent date, and less solidly rooted—prompted men to seek to be free as well as equal.

Toward the close of the old regime these two passions were equally sincere, and apparently equally active; they met at the opening of the Revolution, and, blending together into one, they took fire from contact, and inflamed the whole heart of France. . . .

Alexis C. M. H. C. de Tocqueville, *The Old Regime and the Revolution,* trans. John Bonner (New York: Harper and Brothers, 1856), pp. 246-251.

B. Georges Lefebvre

Although retired from the Professorship of the French Revolution at Paris, Georges Lefebvre (born 1874) remains the leading scholar in the field. Of his numerous writings, many consider *Quatre-Vingt-Neuf* (1939) one of his most significant contributions, and the best analysis of the causes of the Revolution since Tocqueville. The excerpt is from the English translation of this work.

The ultimate cause of the French Revolution of 1789 goes deep into the history of France and of the western world. At the end of the eighteenth century the social structure of France was aristocratic. It showed the traces of having originated at a time when land was almost the only form of wealth, and when the possessors of land were the masters of those who needed it to work and to live. It is true that in the course of age-old struggles . . . the king had been able gradually to deprive the lords of their political power and subject nobles and clergy to his authority. But he had left them the first place in the social hierarchy. . . .

Meanwhile the growth of commerce and industry had created, step by step, a new form of wealth, mobile or commercial wealth, and a new class, called in France the bourgeoisie, which since the fourteenth century had taken its place as the Third Estate in the General Estates of the kingdom. This class had grown much stronger with the maritime discoveries of the fifteenth and sixteenth centuries and the ensuing exploitation of new worlds, and also because it proved highly useful to the monarchical state in supplying it with money and competent officials. In the eighteenth century commerce, industry and finance occupied an increasingly important place in the national economy. It was the bourgeoisie that rescued the royal treasury in moments of crisis. From its ranks were recruited most members of the liberal professions and most public employees. It had developed a new ideology which the "philosophers" and "economists" of the time had simply put into definite form. The role of the nobility had correspondingly declined; and the clergy, as the ideal which it proclaimed lost prestige, found its authority growing weaker. These groups preserved the highest rank in the legal structure of the country, but in reality economic power, personal abilities and confidence in the future had passed largely to the bourgeoisie. . . . The Revolution of 1789 restored the harmony between fact and law. . . .

But this deeper cause of the French Revolution does not explain all its distinctive features. In England, though there have been political revolutions, social evolution has gone on in relative calm. The French Revolution was realized by violence. . . . In France the Third Estate liberated itself. Hence the older aristocracy long preserved more wealth and influence in other countries than in France. These special features of the Revolution in France arose from its immediate causes, and especially from the collapse of the central power which in other countries was able to keep events under control.

There would have been no French Revolution—such as actually took place —if the king, "handing in his resignation," had not convoked the Estates General. The immediate cause lay in a government emergency for which Louis XVI could find no other solution. But the Third Estate was by no means the first to profit from the emergency, contrary to the general opinion, taken over from the Revolutionists themselves, who declared *ad nauseam* that "the people rose up and overthrew despotism and aristocracy." No doubt it did end that way. But the people were not the original motive force. The bourgeoisie, having no legal means of expression, was in no position to force the king to appeal to the nation. Still less were the peasants and the working classes. The privileged groups did have the necessary means: the clergy in its Assembly, the nobility in the Parliaments and the Provincial Estates. It is these bodies that forced the king's hand. . . . The first act of the Revolution, in 1788, consisted in a triumph of the aristocracy, which, taking advantage of the government crisis, hoped to reassert itself and win back the political authority of which the Capetian dynasty had despoiled it. But, after having paralyzed the royal power which upheld its own social preeminence, the aristocracy opened the way to the bourgeois revolution, then to the popular revolution in the cities and finally to the revolution of the peasants —and found itself buried under the ruins of the Old Regime. . . .

Georges Lefebvre, *The Coming of the French Revolution,* trans. R. R. Palmer (Princeton: Princeton University Press, 1947), pp. 1-3

II. HOW DID THE ENGLISH-SPEAKING WORLD RESPOND TO THE REVOLUTION?

The French Revolution was not a purely local movement. Rapidly it assumed an international aspect, bringing to the peoples of other states the hope that they, too, might come to enjoy the benefits of liberty, equality, and emancipation from despotism. As may be seen in the history of Europe from 1815 to 1870, the results, though delayed, were none the less pronounced.

In the case of the English-speaking world, the impact of the Revolution assumed special significance. The response of England was undoubtedly affected by several factors. France had been a mortal enemy for years—hence, to some Englishmen any disaster was much too good for her. England still smarted with the memory of the loss of her American colonies in a revolution (in which France had participated), and the idea of revolution was distasteful to many. On the other hand, 1789 brought the hundredth anniversary of England's own "Glorious Revolution," which had eliminated absolutism. Accordingly, to some Englishmen it appeared that France was at last to enjoy the same happy experience.

To the people of the American colonies, at that time struggling with the inauguration of their new constitutional, republican regime, the French Revolution was naturally a source of great interest and considerable enthusiasm.

The problem in this connection is chiefly one of public opinion. What were the opinions in the English-speaking world concerning the French Revolution? How did they vary, and why? What did they represent? To what extent were they effective in determining the attitude of the governments towards France?

The Response of Contemporaries in England

Public opinion is always difficult to gauge. Especially is this true in endeavoring to determine the extent to which either Burke's *Reflections* or Paine's rejoinder represented English opinion on the French Revolution. It is possible, however, to decide just what each of these writers thought of the movement, as well as what they thought of each other's ideas about it. At least they suggest that there was more than one point of view in England. Paine, although an American by adoption, is included here because he was in England when he wrote *Rights of Man*.

A. Edmund Burke

A Protestant Irishman, Edmund Burke (1729–1797) was a leading statesman, orator, and political theorist in Great Britain. Perhaps his greatest work was *Reflections* (1790), attacking the French Revolution, provoking replies from Mackintosh and Paine, and considered by many the most influential political pamphlet ever written.

. . . Abstractedly speaking, government, as well as liberty, is good; yet could I, in common sense, ten years ago, have felicitated France on her enjoyment of a government . . . without inquiry what the nature of that government was, or how it was administered? Can I now congratulate the same nation upon its freedom? . . .

. . . I must be tolerably sure, before I venture publicly to congratulate men upon a blessing, that they have really received one. . . . I should therefore suspend my congratulations on the new liberty of France, until I was informed how it had been combined with government; with publick force; with the discipline and obedience of armies; with the collection of an effective and well-distributed revenue; with morality and religion; with solidity and property; with peace and order; with civil and social manners. All these (in their way) are good things too; and, without them, liberty is not a benefit whilst it lasts, and is not likely to continue long. The effect of liberty to individuals is, that they may do what they please; we ought to see what it will please them to do, before we risk congratulations, which may be soon turned into complaints. . . . liberty, when men act in bodies, is *power*. Considerate people, before they declare themselves, will observe the use which is made of *power;* and particularly of so trying a thing as *new* power in *new* persons, of whose principles, tempers, and dispositions they have little or no experience, and in situations, where those who appear the most stirring in the scene may possibly not be the real movers. . . .

. . . from Magna Charta to the Declaration of Right, it has been the uniform policy of our constitution to claim and assert our liberties, as an *entailed inheritance* derived to us from our forefathers, and to be transmitted to our posterity; as an estate specially belonging to the people of this kingdom, without any reference whatever to any other more general or prior right. By this means our constitution preserves a unity in so great a diversity of its parts. . . .

. . . A spirit of innovation is generally the result of a selfish temper, and confined views. People will not look forward to posterity, who never look backward to their ancestors. . . . the idea of inheritance furnishes a sure principle of conservation, and a sure principle of transmission; without at all excluding a principle of improvement. . . . by preserving the method of nature in the conduct of the state, in what we improve, we are never wholly new; and in what we retain, we are never wholly obsolete. By adhering in this manner and on those principles to our forefathers, we are guided not by the superstition of antiquarians, but by the spirit of philosophick analogy. . . .

Compute your gains: . . . France has bought undisguised calamities at a higher price than any nation has purchased the most unequivocal blessings! France has bought poverty by crime!

. . . France, when she let loose the reins of regal authority, doubled the licence of a ferocious dissoluteness in manners, and of an insolent irreligion in opinions and practices; and has extended through all ranks of life . . . all the unhappy corruptions that usually were the disease of wealth and power. This is one of the new principles of equality in France.

. . . Laws overturned; tribunals subverted; industry without vigour; commerce expiring; the revenue unpaid, yet the people impoverished; a church pillaged, and a state not relieved; civil and military anarchy made the constitution of the kingdom; everything human and divine sacrificed to the idol of publick credit, and national bankruptcy the consequence; and, to crown all, the paper securities of new, precarious, tottering power, the discredited paper securities of impoverished fraud and beggared rapine, held out as a currency for the support of an empire. . .

Were all these dreadful things necessary? Were they the inevitable results of the desperate struggle of determined patriots, compelled to wade through blood and tumult, to the quiet shore or a tranquil and prosperous liberty? No! nothing like it. The fresh ruins of France, which shock our feelings wherever we can turn our eyes, are not the devastation of civil war; they are the sad but instructive monuments of rash and ignorant counsel in time of profound peace. . . .

. . . those who attempt to level, never equalise. In all societies, consisting of various descriptions of citizens, some descriptions must be uppermost. The levellers, therefore only change and pervert the natural order of things; . . .

It is said that twenty-four millions ought to prevail over two hundred thousand. True; if the constitution of a kingdom be a problem of arithmetick.

. . . to men who *may* reason calmly, it is ridiculous. . . .

. . . In denying their false claims of right, I do not mean to injure those which are real, and are such as their pretended rights would totally destroy. . . . Men . . . have a right to do justice, as between their fellows. . . They have a right to the fruits of their industry; and to the means of making their industry fruitful. They have a right to the acquisitions of their parents; to the nourishment and improvement of their offspring; to instruction in life, and to consolation in death. Whatever each man can separately do, without trespassing upon others, he has a right to do for himself; and he has a right to a fair portion of all which society, with all its combinations of skill and force, can do in his favour. In this partnership all men have equal rights; but not to equal things. He that has but five shillings in the partnership, has as good a right to it, as he that has five hundred pounds has to his larger proportion. But he has not a right to an equal dividend in the product of the joint stock; and as to the share of power, authority, and direction which each individual ought to have in the management of the state, that I must deny to be amongst the direct original rights of man in civil society; . . .

Government is not made in virtue of natural rights, which may and do exist in total independence of it; and exist in much greater clearness, and in a much greater degree of abstract perfection: but their abstract perfection is their practical defect. By having a right to everything they want everything. Government is a contrivance of human wisdom to provide for human *wants*. Men have a right that these wants should be provided for by this wisdom. Among these wants is to be reckoned the want, out of civil society,

of a sufficient restraint upon their passions. . . . In this sense the restraints on men, as well as their liberties, are to be reckoned among their rights. But as the liberties and the restrictions vary with times and circumstances, and admit of infinite modifications, they cannot be settled upon any abstract rule; and nothing is so foolish as to discuss them upon that principle. . . .

The science of constructing a commonwealth, or renovating it, or reforming it, is, like every other experimental science, not to be taught *à priori*. Nor is it a short experience that can instruct us in that practical science; . . . The science of government being therefore so practical in itself, and intended for such practical purposes, a matter which requires experience, . . . it is with infinite caution that any man ought to venture upon pulling down an edifice which has answered in any tolerable degree for ages the common purposes of society, or on building it up again, without having models and patterns of approved utility before his eyes. . . .

I do not know under what description to class the present ruling authority in France. It affects to be a pure democracy, though I think it in a direct train of becoming shortly a mischievous and ignoble oligarchy. But for the present I admit it to be a contrivance of the nature and effect of what it pretends to. I reprobate no form of government merely upon abstract principles. There may be situations in which the purely democratick form will become necessary. There may be some . . . where it would be clearly desirable. This I do not take to be the case of France, or of any other great country. Until now, we have seen no examples of considerable democracies. The ancients were better acquainted with them. . . . If I recollect rightly, Aristotle observes, that a democracy has many striking points of resemblance with a tyranny. Of this

I am certain, that in a democracy, the majority of the citizens is capable of exercising the most cruel oppression upon the minority, whenever strong divisions prevail in that kind of polity, as they often must; and that oppression of the minority will extend to far greater numbers, and will be carried on with much greater fury, than can almost ever be apprehended from the dominion of a single sceptre. . . .

Edmund Burke, *Reflections on the Revolution in France, and on the Proceedings in Certain Societies in London relative to that Event. In a Letter Intended to Have Been Sent to a Gentleman in Paris* (1790), in *The Works of the Right Honourable Edmund Burke*, 8 vols. (Boston: Wells and Lilly, 1826–27), III, 24, 25, 50, 51, 55, 67, 70, 77, 78-80, 145-147.

B. Thomas Paine

Migrating from England to America in 1774, Thomas Paine (1737–1809) became a leading republican propagandist. In 1787 he returned to his native land, and in 1791–1792 published *Rights of Man* as a reply to Burke. Forced to flee to France, he became a member of the Convention. He died in America.

1. (*Preface to the French edition*)

The astonishment which the French Revolution has caused throughout Europe should be considered from two different points of view: first as it affects foreign peoples, secondly as it affects their governments.

The cause of the French people is that of all Europe, or rather of the whole world; but the governments of all those countries are by no means favorable to it. It is important that we should never lose sight of this distinction. We must not confuse the peoples with their governments; especially not the English people with its government.

The government of England is no friend to the revolution of France. . . .

The English nation, on the contrary, is very favorably disposed towards the French Revolution, and to the progress of liberty in the whole world; . . .

2. (*Rights of Man*)

There never did, there never will, and there never can, exist a Parliament, or any description of men, or any generation of men, in any country, possessed of the right or the power of binding and controlling posterity to the *"end of time"*, or of commanding for ever how the world shall be governed, or who shall govern it; . . . Every age and generation must be as free to act for itself, *in all cases,* as the ages and generations which preceded it. The vanity and presumption of governing beyond the grave is the most ridiculous and insolent of all tyrannies. . . . It is the living, and not the dead, that are to be accommodated. . . .

I am not contending for nor against any form of government, nor for nor against any party, here or elsewhere. That which a whole nation chooses to do, it has a right to do. Mr. Burke says, No. Where, then, does the right exist? I am contending for the rights of the *living,* and against their being willed away, and controlled and contracted for, by the manuscript assumed authority of the dead; and Mr. Burke is contending for the authority of the dead over the rights and freedom of the living. . . .

It was not against Louis XVIth but against the despotic principles of the Government, that the nation revolted. These principles had not their origin in him, but in the original establishment, many centuries back: and they were become too deeply rooted to be removed, and the Augean stables of parasites and plunderers too abominably filthy to be cleansed by anything short of a complete and universal Revolution. . . .

Mr. Burke does not attend to the distinction between men and principles, and, therefore, he does not see that a revolt may take place against the despotism of the latter, while there lies no charge of despotism against the former. . . .

. . . There were . . . a thousand despotisms to be reformed in France, which had grown up under the hereditary despotism of the monarchy, and became so rooted as to be in a great measure independent of it. . . . But Mr. Burke, by considering the king as the only possible object of a revolt, speaks as if France was a village, in which everything that passed must be known to its commanding officer, and no oppression could be acted but what he could immediately control. . . .

. . . Man did not enter into society to become *worse* than he was before, nor to have fewer rights than he had before, but to have those rights better secured. His natural rights are the foundation of all his civil rights. . . .

. . . Natural rights are those which appertain to man in right of his existence. Of this kind are all the intellectual rights, or rights of the mind, and also those rights of acting as an individual for his own comfort and happiness, which are not injurious to the natural rights of others. Civil rights are those which appertain to man in right of his being a member of society. Every civil right has for its foundation some natural right pre-existing in the individual, but to the enjoyment of which his individual power is not, in all cases, sufficiently competent. Of this kind are all those which relate to security and protection. . . .

It was the error of . . . all those who were unacquainted with the affairs of France to confound the French nation with the French Government. The French nation, in effect, endeavoured to render the late Government insolvent for the purpose of taking government into its own hands: and it reserved its means for the support of the new Government. . . .

There is a general enigma running through the whole of Mr. Burke's book. He writes in a rage against the National Assembly; but what is he enraged about? If his assertions were as true as they are groundless, and that France by her Revolution, had annihilated her power, and become what he calls a *chasm*, it might excite the grief of a Frenchman . . . and provoke his rage against the National Assembly; but why should it excite the rage of Mr. Burke? Alas! it is not the nation of France that Mr. Burke means, but the Court; and every Court in Europe, dreading the same fate, is in mourning. He writes neither in the character of a Frenchman nor an Englishman, but in the fawning character of that creature known in all countries, and a friend to none—a courtier. . . . Nothing can be more terrible to a Court or Courtier than the Revolution of France. . . .

From the Revolutions of America and France, and the symptoms that have appeared in other countries, it is evident that the opinion of the world is changing with respect to systems of Government, and that revolutions are not within the compass of political calculations. The progress of time and circumstances, which men assign to the accomplishment of great changes, is too mechanical to measure the force of the mind, and the rapidity of reflection, by which revolutions are generated: All the old governments have received a shock from those that already appear; and which were once more improbable, and are a greater subject of wonder, than a general revolution in Europe would be now.

When we survey the wretched condition of man, under the monarchical and hereditary systems of Government, . . . it becomes evident that those systems are bad, and that a general revolution in the principle and construction of Governments is necessary.

What is government more than the management of the affairs of a Nation? It is not, and from its nature cannot be, the property of any particular man or family, but of the whole community, at whose expense it is supported; and though by force and contrivance it has been usurped into an inheritance, the usurpation cannot alter the right of things. Sovereignty, as a matter of right, appertains to the Nation only, and not to any individual; and a Nation has at all times an inherent indefeasible right to abolish any form of Government it finds inconvenient, and to establish such as accords with its interest, disposition and happiness. . . .

When men think of what Government is, they must necessarily suppose it to possess a knowledge of all the objects and matters upon which its authority is to be exercised. In this view of Government, the republican system, as established by America and France, operates to embrace the whole of a Nation; and the knowledge necessary to the interest of all the parts, is to be found in the center, which the parts by representation form: But the old Governments are on a construction that excludes knowledge as well as happiness; . . .

What were formerly called Revolutions, were little more than a change of persons, or an alteration of local circumstances. . . . But what we now see in the world, from the Revolutions of America and France, are a renovation of the natural order of things, a system of principles as universal as truth and the existence of man, and combining moral with political happiness and national prosperity. . . .

As it is not difficult to perceive, from the enlightened state of mankind, that hereditary Governments are verging to their decline, and that Revolutions on the broad basis of national sovereignty and Government by representation, are making their way in Europe, it would be an act of wisdom to anticipate their approach, and produce Revolutions by reason and accommodation, rather than commit them to the issue of convulsions.

From what we now see, nothing of reform in the political world ought to be held improbable. It is an age of Revolutions, in which everything may be looked for. . . .

Thomas Paine, *Rights of Man; Being an Answer to Mr. Burke's Attack on the French Revolution,* ed. with an intro. and notes by Moncure Daniel Conway (New York: G. P. Putnam's Sons, 1895), pp. 272, 273, 277, 278, 283-285, 306, 379, 381, 385, 386, 389.

The Response of Contemporaries in the United States

Americans were by no means unanimous in their attitude towards the French Revolution. Here we have the opinions of two eminent American revolutionary statesmen, each experienced in French affairs, one writing from America, the other from France. Were their comments similar or dissimilar? To what extent were they indicative of American opinions? How may their attitudes be explained? What had they in common with and apart from their English contemporaries? And, taken together with these, how do they explain the response of the English-speaking world to the Revolution?

A. Thomas Jefferson

Thomas Jefferson (1743–1826), American revolutionary leader, principal drafter of the Declaration of Independence, Minister to France (1784–1789), and President of the United States (1801–1809), was well qualified to evaluate the French Revolution which he had observed at close range during its early days.

1. (*Letter to Edmund Pendleton, from Philadelphia, 24 July, 1791*)

. . . The success of [the French Revolution] will ensure the progress of liberty in Europe, and its preservation here. The failure of that would have been a powerful argument with those who wish to introduce a king, lords, and commons here, a sect which is all head and no body. . . .

2. (*Letter to Edward Rutledge, from Philadelphia, 29 August, 1791*)

. . . I still hope the French Revolution will issue happily. I feel that the permanence of our own leans in some degree on that, and that a failure there would be a powerful argument to prove that there must be a failure here. . . .

3. (*Letter to Marquis de Condorcet, from Philadelphia, 30 August, 1791*)

. . . I am looking ardently to the completion of the glorious work in which your country is engaged. I view the general condition of Europe as hanging on the success or failure of France. Having set such an example of philosophical arrangement within, I hope it will be extended without your limits also, to your dependents and to your friends in every part of the earth. . . .

4. (*Letter to T. M. Randolph, from Philadelphia, 7 January, 1793*)

. . . the event of the revolution . . . is now little doubted of, even by its enemies. The sensation it has produced here, and the indications of them in the public papers, have shown that the form our own government was to take depended much more on the events of France than anybody had before imagined. The tide which, after our

former relaxed government, took a violent course towards the opposite extreme, and seemed ready to hang everything round with the tassels & baubles of monarchy, is now getting back as we hope to a just mean, a government of laws addressed to the reason of the people, and not to their weaknesses. . . .

5. (*Letter to J. P. Brissot de Warville, from Philadelphia, 8 May, 1793*)

. . . I continue eternally attached to the principles of your revolution. I hope it will end in the establishment of some firm government, friendly to liberty, & capable of maintaining it. If it does, the world will become inevitably free. If it does not, I feel that the zealous apostles of English despotism here, will increase the number of its disciples. However, we shall still remain free. Tho' they may harass our spirits, they cannot make impression on our center. . . .

6. (*Letter to Elbridge Gerry, from Philadelphia, 26 January, 1799*)

. . . I was a sincere well-wisher to the success of the French Revolution, and still wish it may end in the establishment of a free and well-ordered republic; . . .

7. (*Letter to M. de Barbé-Marbois, from Monticello, 24 June, 1817*)

. . . When I left France at the close of '89, your revolution was, as I thought, under the direction of able and honest men. But the madness of some of their successors, the vices of others, the malicious intrigues of an envious and corrupting neighbor, the tracasserie of the Directory, the usurpations, the havoc, and devastations of your Attila, and the equal usurpations, depredations and oppressions of your hypocritical deliverers, will form a mournful period in the history of man, a period of which the last chapter will not be seen in your day or in mine, and one which I still fear is to be written in characters of blood. . . .

8. (*Autobiography, 1821*)

. . . I considered a successful reformation of government in France, as insuring a general reformation thro' Europe, and the resurrection, to a new life, of their people, now ground to dust by the abuses of the governing powers. I was much acquainted with the leading patriots of the assembly. Being from a country which had successfully passed thro' a similar reformation, they were disposed to my acquaintance, and had some confidence in me. I urged, most strenuously, an immediate compromise; to secure what the government was now ready to yield, and trust to future occasions for what might still be wanting. It was well understood that the King would grant at this time 1. Freedom of the person by Habeas corpus: 2. Freedom of conscience: 3. Freedom of the press: 4. Trial by jury: 5. A representative legislature: 6. Annual meetings: 7. The origination of laws: 8. The exclusive right of taxation and appropriation. And 9. The responsibility of ministers; and with the exercise of these powers they would obtain in future whatever might be further necessary to improve and preserve their constitution. They thought otherwise, however, and events have proved their lamentable error. For after 30. years of war, foreign and domestic, the loss of millions of lives, the prostration of private happiness, and the foreign subjugation of their own country for a time, they have obtained no more, nor even that securely. They were unconscious of (for who could foresee?) the melancholy sequel of their well-meant perseverance; that their physical force would be usurped by a first tyrant to trample on the independence, and even the existence, of other nations: that this would afford fatal example for the atrocious conspiracy of Kings against their people; and would generate their unholy and homicide alliance to make common cause among themselves, and to crush, by the power of the whole, the efforts of any part to moderate their abuses and oppressions.

The letter to Barbé-Marbois is from Andrew A. Lipscomb and Albert Ellery Bergh, eds., *The Writings of Thomas Jefferson . . . Definitive Edition*, 20 vols. (Washington: Thomas Jefferson Memorial Association, 1905–1907), XV, 129–130. All the other excerpts are from Paul L. Ford, ed., *The Works of Thomas Jefferson*, 12 vols. (New York and London: G. P. Putnam's Sons, 1904–1905), I, 138–139; V, 309; VI, 287, 311–312; VII, 206–207, 322; IX, 19.

B. Gouverneur Morris

Eminent statesman and diplomat, Gouverneur Morris (1752–1816) was American Minister to France, 1792–1794. His reports on the French Revolution are of significance not only because he was an eyewitness, but because he had played an important part in the American Revolution.

1. (*Letter of July, 1789, to Mr. Carmichael*)

. . . There are great intrigues against the administration here, but hitherto without any effect. I have steadily combated the violence and excess of those persons who, either inspired with an enthusiastic love of freedom, or prompted with sinister designs, are disposed to drive everything to extremity. Our American example has done them good, but, like all novelties, Liberty runs away with their discretion, if they have any. They want an American constitution, with the exception of a king instead of a president, without reflecting that they have not American citizens to support that constitution. Mankind sees distant things in a false point of light, and judge either more or less favorably than they ought . . . ; . . . we try everything by the standard of preconceived notions, so that there is an impossibility almost of knowing by description a distant people or country. Whoever, therefore, desires to apply in the practical science of government those rules and forms which prevail and succeed in a foreign country, must fall into the same pedantry which our young scholars just fresh from an university, who would fain bring everything to a Roman standard. Different constitutions of government are necessary to the different societies on the face of this planet. . . .

2. (*Diary, 19 November, 1790*)

How will it all end? This unhappy country, bewildered in the pursuit of metaphysical whimsies, presents to one's moral view a mighty ruin. Like the remnants of ancient magnificence, we admire the architecture of the temple, while we detest the false god to whom it was dedicated. Daws and ravens, and the birds of the night now build their nests in its niches; the sovereign, humbled to the level of a beggar's pity, without resources, without authority, without a friend; the Assembly, at once a master and a slave—now in power, wild in theory, raw in practice, it engrosses all functions, though incapable of exercising any, and has taken from this fierce, ferocious people every restraint of religion and of respect. Here conjecture may wander through unbounded space. What sum of misery may be requisite to change popular will, calculation cannot determine. What circumstances may arise in the order of Divine will to give direction to that will, our sharpest vision cannot discover. What talents may be found to seize those circumstances to influence that

will, and, above all, to moderate the power which it must confer, we are equally ignorant. One thing only seems to be tolerably ascertained, that the glorious opportunity is lost, and (for this time at least) the Revolution has failed. . . .

3. (*Letter to Washington, 1791*)

. . . In the midst, however, of all these confusions, what with confiscating the church property, selling the domains, curtailing pensions and destroying offices, but especially by that great liquidator of public debt, a paper currency, this nation is working its way to a new state of active energy which will, I think, be displayed as soon as a vigorous government shall establish itself. The intervening confusion will probably call forth men of talent to form such government and exert its powers.

4. (*Letter to Washington, 4 February, 1792*)

This ministry . . . is convinced that the Constitution is good for nothing; and unfortunately there are many of them so indiscreet as to disclose that opinion, when at the same time they declare their determination to support and execute it, which is, in fact, the only rational mode (which now remains) of pointing out its defects. It is unnecessary to tell you that some members of the National Assembly are in the pay of England. . . . The situation of their finances is such that every considerate person sees the impossibility of going on in the present way, and as a change of system after so many pompous declarations is not a little dangerous among people so wild and ungoverned, it has appeared to them that a war would furnish some plausible pretext for measures of a very decisive nature, in which state necessity will be urged in the teeth of policy, humanity, and justice. Others consider a war as the means of obtaining for the government the eventual command of a disciplined military force, which may be used to restore order; in other words, to bring back despotism, and then they expect that the King will give the nation a constitution which they have neither the wisdom to form nor the virtue to adopt for themselves.

Others, again, suppose that in case of a war there will be such a leaning from the King towards his brother, from the Queen towards the Emperor, from the nobility (the very few) who remain towards the mass of their brethren who have left the kingdom, that the bad success naturally to arise from the opposition of undisciplined mobs to regular armies may be easily imputed to treasonable counsels, and the people be prevailed on to banish them altogether and set up a Federal Republic. . . .

5. (*Letter to Jefferson, 17 June, 1792*)

On the whole . . . we stand on a vast volcano. We feel it tremble, we hear it roar, but how and when and where it will burst, and who may be destroyed by its eruptions, it is beyond the pen of mortal foresight to discover. . . . while a great part of the nation is desirous of overturning the present government in order to restore the ancient form, and while another part, still more dangerous from position and numbers, are desirous of introducing the form of a federal republic, the moderate men, attacked on all sides, have to contend alone against an immense force. I cannot go on with this picture, for my heart bleeds when I reflect that the finest opportunity which ever presented itself for establishing the rights of mankind throughout the civilized world is perhaps lost, and forever.

Gouverneur Morris, *The Diary and Letters of Gouverneur Morris . . .* , ed. Anne Carey Morris, 2 vols. (New York: Charles Scribner's Sons, 1888), I, 113-114, 359-360, 383, 508-509, 545.

III. WHAT HAVE FRENCH HISTORIANS THOUGHT OF THE REVOLUTION?

Inevitably a writer's treatment of his native land is different from his analysis of some other country. In the case of French historical writers, "La Belle France" has come in for even more than her share of adulation. Yet on several topics these historians are bitterly divided—particularly on the French Revolution and (as indicated in Part IV) Napoleon.

One of the reasons for this partisanship is because to them the Revolution is still a living force—as evidenced in its extension through French history since 1815. To the conservatives, it was a great mistake. To the liberals, it has been only partly achieved. To radicals its fulfillment is far distant. It is difficult, therefore, to speak of a French *history* of the Revolution, when the truth would seem to be that there are only French *histories*.

If French historians of the Revolution (apart, of course, from those who were its contemporaries) may be classified, the most convenient groupings would seem to be the "Classic" (up to the latter part of the nineteenth century) and the "Modern" (since that time). But even in such classifications the distinctions may be more apparent than real.

The essential problem, then, would appear to be threefold: to determine why each historian wrote as he did; to ascertain what conclusions he reached and why; and to decide how, if at all, the work of such writers may be used in understanding the French Revolution.

The "Classic" Historians

The "classic" historian is more than one whose works are seldom read. He is one whose writings are of value more for the opinions they present and the manner in which they reflect trends in historical writing than for the historical data they contain. Frequently written to justify or to denounce something, they were often based on inadequate research—if only because sources were not available. "Classic" historians of the French Revolution are legion. The two here presented are suggestive of the diverse points of view concerning that event. What were their attitudes? Why did they hold them?

A. François Mignet

Scholar, journalist, liberal, François Mignet (1796–1884) left his native Provence for Paris in 1821. Three years later he published his history of the Revolution, one of the first formal studies of the movement, as a critique of the reactionary Bourbon monarchy of Charles X. The work long enjoyed popularity.

. . . This revolution not only modified the political power, but it entirely changed the internal existence of the nation. . . . France was in an utter confusion of arbitrary administration, of class legislation and special privileges to special bodies. For these abuses the revolution substituted a system more conformable with justice, and better suited to our times. It substituted law in the place of arbitrary will, equality in that of privilege; delivered men from the distinctions of classes, the land from the barriers of provinces, trade from the shackles of corporations and fellowships, agriculture from feudal subjection and the oppression of tithes, property from the impediment of entails, and brought everything to the condition of one state, one system of law, one people.

In order to effect such mighty reformation as this, the revolution had many obstacles to overcome, involving transient excesses with durable benefits. The privileged sought to prevent it, Europe to subject it; and thus forced into a struggle, it could not set bounds to its efforts, or moderate its victory. Resistance from within brought about the sovereignty of the multitude, and aggression from without, military domination. Yet the end was attained, in

spite of anarchy and in spite of despotism: the old society was destroyed during the revolution, and the new one became established under the empire. . . .

The constitution of 1791 . . . was, however, less democratic than that of the United States, which had been practicable, despite the extent of the territory, proving that it is not the form of institutions, but the assent which they obtain, or the dissent which they excite, which permits or hinders their establishment. In a new country, after a revolution of independence, as in America, any constitution is possible; there is but one hostile party, that of the metropolis, and when that is overcome, the struggle ceases, because defeat leads to its expulsion. It is not so with social revolutions among nations who have long been in existence. Changes attack interests, interests form parties, parties enter into contest, and the more victory spreads the greater grows opposition. This is what happened in France. The work of the constituent assembly perished less from its defects than from the attacks of faction. Placed between the aristocracy and the multitude, it was attacked by the one and invaded by the other. The latter would not have become sovereign, had not civil war and the foreign coalition called for its intervention and aid. To defend the country, it became necessary that it should govern it; then it effected its revolution, as the middle class had effected its own. . . .

The French Revolution . . . had two wholly distinct objects; that of a free constitution, and that of a more perfect state of civilization. . . . The privileged classes wished to establish their régime against the court and the bourgeoisie, by preserving orders and the states-general; the bourgeoisie sought to establish its régime against the privileged classes and the multitude, by the constitution of 1791; and the multitude wished to establish its régime against all the others by the constitution of 1793. Not one of these governments could become consolidated, because they were all exclusive. But during their attempts each class, in power for a time, destroyed of the higher classes all that was intolerant or calculated to oppose the progress of modern civilization.

When the directory succeeded the convention the struggle between the classes was greatly weakened. The higher ranks of each formed a party which still contended for the possession and for the form of government; but the mass of the nation, which had been so profoundly agitated from 1789 to 1795, longed to become settled again, and to arrange itself according to the new order of things. This period witnessed the end of the movement for liberty, and the beginning of the movement towards civilization. The revolution now took its second character, its character of order, foundation, repose, after the agitation, the immense toil, and system of complete demolition of its early years.

This second period was remarkable, inasmuch as it seemed a kind of abandonment of liberty. . . . it was liberal under the directory and at the commencement of the Consulate, and military at the close of the Consulate and under the empire. . . . after having made a nation of sectaries it made a nation of working men, and then it made a nation of soldiers.

Many illusions were already destroyed; men had passed through so many different states, had lived so much in so few years, that all ideas were confounded and all creeds shaken. The reign of the middle class and that of the multitude had passed away. . . . They were far from that France of the 14th of July, with its deep conviction, its high morality, its assembly exercising the all-powerful sway of liberty and of reason. . . . They were far from the more sombre and more tempestuous France of the 10th of August, when a single class held the government and society, and had introduced therein its language, manners, and costume, the agitation of its fears, the fanaticism of its ideas, the distrust of its position. Then private life entirely gave place to public life; the republic presented, in turn, the aspect of an assembly and of a camp; the rich were subject to the poor; the creed of democracy combined with the gloomy and ragged administration of the people. At each of these periods men had been strongly attached to some idea; first to liberty and constitutional monarchy, afterwards, to equality, fraternity, and the republic. But at the beginning of the directory there was belief in nothing; . . .

François A. M. A. Mignet, *History of the French Revolution from 1789 to 1814,* trans. from the French (London: G. Bell and Sons, 1885) [Bohn's Standard Library], pp. 1-3, 313-315.

B. Hippolyte A. Taine

Following a treatise on the Old Régime (1875), Hippolyte A. Taine (1828–1892), scholar extraordinary, produced three volumes on the Revolution (1878–1884). "Scientific" in approach, analytical rather than narrative, his work reflects an attempt to explain the misfortunes of France at the close of the Second Empire.

. . . In several of its laws . . . it [the Constituent Assembly] planted good seed. But in all that relates to political institutions and social organization its proceedings are those of an academy of Utopians, and not those of practical legislators. . . . it carried out its principle to the end, the principle of Rousseau. It deliberately refused to consider man as he really was under its own eyes, and persisted in seeing nothing in him but the abstract being created in books. . . . the Assembly destroyed on the one hand the time-honoured, spontaneous, and lasting societies formed by geographical position, history, common occupations and interests, and on the other, those natural chiefs whose name, repute, education, independence, and earnestness designated them as the best qualified to occupy high positions. In one direction it despoils and permits the ruin and proscription of the superior class. . . . In another it dispossesses and breaks up all historic or natural corporations. . . . Nothing remains but individual particles, twenty-six millions of equal and disconnected atoms. Never was so much disintegrated matter, less capable of resistance, offered to hands undertaking to mould it. . . . As awkward in destruction as it is in construction, it invents for the restoration of order in a society which is turned upside down a machine which would, of itself, create disorder in a tranquil society. . . . The masterpiece of ideal abstractions and of practical absurdities is perfected; spontaneous anarchy, by means of the Constitution, becomes legalized anarchy. . . .

. . . whatever the grand terms of liberty, equality, and fraternity may be, with which the Revolution graces itself, it is, in its essence, a *transfer of property;* in this alone consists its chief support, its enduring energy, its primary impulse and its historical significance. . . .

The worst feature of anarchy is not so much the absence of the overthrown government as the rise of new governments of an inferior grade. Every fallen State produces bands which conquer and which are sovereign; . . . born enemies of work, of subordination, and of the law—form leagues for breaking down the worm-eaten barriers which still surround the sheep-like masses; and as they are unscrupulous, they slaughter on all occasions. On this foundation their authority rests; . . . their government, in keeping with its brutal masters, consists in robbery and murder; nothing else can be looked for from barbarians and brigands.

But never are they so dangerous as when, in a great State recently fallen, a sudden revolution places the central power in their hands; for they then regard themselves as the legitimate inheritors of the shattered government, and, under this title, they undertake to manage the commonwealth. . . . The important and dominant personage, the one whose ideas prevail, . . . is here the subordinate Jacobin, the pillar of the club, the maker of motions, the street rioter, . . . the faubourg cannoneer, the drinking market-porter who elaborates his political conceptions in the interval between his hiccoughs.—For information he has the rumours circulating in the streets which assign a traitor to each domicile, and for other acquisitions the club bombast, through which he becomes the leader of the great machine. This machine so vast, so complex, . . . transcends his limited comprehension; . . . In his narrow brain, perverted and turned topsy-turvy by the disproportionate notions put into it, only one idea suited to his gross instincts and aptitudes finds a place there, and that is the desire to kill his enemies; and these are also the State's enemies, however open or concealed, present or future, probable or even possible. He carries this savagery and bewilderment into politics, and hence the evil arising from his usurpation. . . .

. . . the rulers of the country have brought with them into power the prejudices and sensibilities of the epoch; under the empire of the prevailing dogma they have deferred to the will of the multitude and, with too much faith in the rights of man, they have had too little in the rights of the magistrate; moreover, through humanity, they have abhorred bloodshed and, unwilling to repress, they have allowed themselves to be repressed. . . . while their constitutions, so many unhealthy products of theory and fear, have done no more than transform spontaneous anarchy into legal anarchy. . . . On the strength of this a faction arises which ends in becoming an organized band: under its clamorings . . . the majorities are all silenced, while the minorities vote, decree, and govern; . . . Of all the garrisons of the central citadel . . . not one has been able to defend itself, to refashion the executive instrument, to draw the sword and use it in the streets: on the first attack, often at the first summons, all have surrendered, and now the citadel, with every other public fortress, is in the hands of the Jacobins.

This time, its occupants are of a different stamp. Aside from the great mass of well-disposed people fond of a quiet life, the Revolution has sifted out and separated from the rest all who are fanatical, brutal or perverse enough to have lost respect for others; these form the new garrison. . . . None of this class are scrupulous concerning human life or property; for . . . they have shaped the theory to suit themselves, and reduced popular sovereignty to their sovereignty. The commonwealth, according to the Jacobin, is his; . . . everything belongs to him; the fact of being a Jacobin makes him legitimately czar and pope. . . . his mandate does not emanate from a vote; it descends to him from aloft, conferred on him by Truth, by Reason, by Virtue. As he alone is enlightened, and the only patriot, he alone is worthy to take command, while resistance, according to his imperious pride, is criminal. If the majority protests it is because the majority is imbecile or corrupt; in either case, it merits a check, and a check it shall have. Accordingly, the Jacobin does nothing else from the outset; . . . there is no outrage not committed by him. . . . if he hesitates he knows he is lost; to save himself from the scaffold he has no refuge but in a dictatorship. . . .

Hippolyte A. Taine, *The French Revolution*, trans. John Durand, 3 vols. (New York: Henry Holt and Co., 1878–1885), I, 214-216; II, 196-198; III, 2-3.

The Modern Historians

As indicated in Problem I, many factors must be considered in evaluating the verdicts of historians. As suggested in the Introduction to this problem, this is particularly true of Frenchmen. Here we have the work of two modern French historians, both learned, both provided with a variety of sources. Why do they differ? What points of view do they represent? In what respects are they like or unlike the earlier writers? What kind of account of the Revolution might be written on the basis of a combination of their work and that of their "classic" counterparts?

A. Alphonse Aulard

Alphonse Aulard (1849–1928) was the first holder of the Professorship of the French Revolution at the University of Paris. A prodigious worker and exceptionally erudite, he completed his general history of the Revolution in 1901. This represented a new, authoritative statement of the "political" aspects of the movement.

(Preface)

. . . I propose to show how the principles of the Declaration of Rights were, between 1789 and 1804, put into operation by the institutions of the time; or interpreted by speeches, by the press, by the policies of the various political parties, and by the manifestations of public opinion. Two of these principles, the principle of the equality of rights, and the principle of national sovereignty, were those most often invoked in the elaboration of the new state politic. They are, historically, the essential principles of the Revolution; . . . The chief object of this book is the narration of the vicissitudes which these two principles underwent.

In other words, I wish to write the political history of the Revolution from the point of view of the origin and the development of Democracy and Republicanism.

Democracy is the logical consequence of the principle of equality. Republicanism is the logical consequence of the principle of national sovereignty. . . .

(Conclusion)

Had I a historical thesis to sustain, or a train of reasoning to develop, in order to demonstrate the truth of a proposition, a logical conclusion would have been necessary. But I have merely attempted to narrate, objectively, and without any preconceived idea, the political history of the Revolution, from the point of view of the origin and development of democracy and the Republic. . . .

I wish . . . not to write a conclusion . . . , but to suggest a few ideas which are too general in their nature to have found a fitting place at any particular point of the narrative, but which disengage themselves only from the whole mass of facts.

1. It is a mistake to say that the French Revolution was effected by a few distinguished individuals, by a few super-men. . . . no individual emerges from the history of the ten years between 1789 and 1799 as the master of events: . . . Can we say that the French nation was the hero, the true super-man of the French Revolution? Yes; if we see the French nation not as a multitude, but in a condition of organized groups. . . .

2. The Revolution was realised only partly and for a time. It was even suspended, and appeared to be abolished, during the rule of Napoleon I; . . . Why?—because the French people was not sufficiently educated to wield its own sovereignty. . . .

3. It has been said that the generation which performed such great and terrible deeds was a generation of giants; or, to be more literal, that it was a more competent and remarkable generation than that which preceded it or that which followed. This is a retrospective illusion. The citizens who formed the various groups . . . by which the Revolution was effected, do not seem to have been superior either in talent or in enlightenment to the Frenchmen of the time of Louis XV or that of Louis-Philippe. . . . The generation of 1789 and 1793 was neither superior nor inferior; it was an average generation. Perhaps we may safely say that when first the guillotine and then proscription had deprived it of its most distinguished individuals it fell somewhat below the average; and that this was one of the circumstances which allowed Bonaparte to dominate it and cast it into slavery. . . .

4. . . . People used to denote, by the same phrase, both the principles which constitute the French Revolution and the actions consistent with those principles, and the period during which the Revolution was effected, with all the actions, consistent with or in contradiction to those principles, performed during that period. This confusion was as harmful to the truth as it was useful to the supporters of the retrograde policy, as it allowed one to attribute to the Revolution, considered as a sort of his-

torical personage, the most grievous or even the most anti-revolutionary laws or actions. . . . This abusive manner of speaking—"The Revolution did or didn't do so-and-so"—has had the result that many people see in the Revolution a kind of incoherent power; capricious, violent and sanguinary. It has been attempted thus to discredit the very principles of the Revolution; especially by the pains and to the profit of those who regard these principles as *satanic*, and who would govern society by the reverse of these principles. For the rest, all the political parties of the nineteenth century have pleaded their cause by means of arguments drawn from anything or everything that happened between 1789 and 1799; and these facts, taken at random or ingeniously selected, they have called *the French Revolution*. Now, I fancy, matters are clearer: the Revolution consists in the Declaration of Rights drafted in 1789 and completed in 1793, and the attempts made to realise that declaration; the counter-Revolution consists in the attempts made to prevent the French from acting in conformity with the principles of the Declaration of Rights; that is to say, according to reason, elucidated by history.

The French Revolution is, so to speak, a political, social, and rational ideal, which Frenchmen have attempted partially to realise, and which historians have attempted to confound either with its application, often incoherent, as far as it was effected, or with the events provoked by the very enemies of that ideal, with a view to abolishing or obscuring it. This book will, I hope, have contributed to dissipate this dangerous ambiguity.

5. The Imperial despotism arrested the Revolution, and marked a retrogression towards the principles of the *ancien régime;* provisionally abolishing liberty and partially abolishing equality. But they were rather the political results of the Revolution than the social which were thus suppressed. . . . and this it is that explains why, after its fall, when these results were contested by the returned royalists, that very Napoleon Bonaparte who disorganized the political work of the Revolution as completely as he possibly could, appeared to be, and was able to call himself, "the man of the Revolution."

François Victor Alphonse Aulard, *The French Revolution, A Political History, 1789–1804,* trans. Bernard Miall, 4 vols. (London and New York: Charles Scribner's Sons, 1910), I, 9; IV, 277-282.

B. *Pierre Gaxotte*

Pierre Gaxotte (born 1895) published his interpretation of the Revolution in 1928. Providing an interesting comparison with Taine, it must be viewed in the light of Gaxotte's attitude towards the Third Republic as the heir of the Revolution, and his concern with communism as part of the inheritance.

The France of the old regime was a very great and ancient structure in building which fifty generations had been engaged for more than fifteen centuries. . . . taking it all in all, the total effect was rich, the façade was imposing, and those who lived in it were better off and more numerous than elsewhere. . . .

Distress may cause riots, but cannot produce revolutions. These latter are due to more deep-lying causes, and in 1789 the French were not in distress. On the contrary, . . . the country had considerably increased in wealth since the middle of the century and . . . , with the exception of the country gentry, the material condition of all classes of society had sensibly improved. . . .

Before the Revolution France was not unhappy. She had reason to complain, but not to revolt. Of the two great problems which demanded her attention —the abolition of the relics of feudalism and financial reform—neither would have been insoluble if the soul of France had not been stirred to its depths by an intellectual and moral crisis. This complicated the slightest conflicts and rendered a situation which was merely difficult, first disquieting and then desperate.

The tragedy of the eighteenth century lies, indeed, not in its wars nor in the "days" (*journées*) of the Revolution, but in the dissolution and reversal of the ideas which had illumined and dominated the seventeenth. Riots and massacres were but the bloody and signal expression of this fact; for, long before these happened, the real harm had already been done. . . .

. . . the writers, reacting on the societies, and the societies on the writers, it came about that the unconscious band of brothers found themselves carried away by an increasingly rapid movement "towards the advent of a certain intellectual and moral type which no one had foreseen, of which everyone would disapprove, yet for which all were preparing the way": the socialistic Jacobin of 1793.

This evolution was hastened by the revolt of the American colonies against Great Britain. . . .

The trial of the King is one of the most moving tragedies in all history. . . . But for those who are interested in the sequence of events it is above all necessary to throw light on the political reasons for his prosecution and punishment. The reasoning of the Montagnards was terrible in its simplicity: it was necessary to guillotine the King in order to make regicide the emblem and proof of republican sincerity. The question of whether or no the King was to die would divide the deputies and show the numbers on either side. Those who rejected the death penalty were to

be accused of royalism, treason, and commerce with the *émigrés* and Austrians. Those who voted for it would remain indissolubly united by fear of a reaction. . . . The trial of the King was to mark the end of the *bourgeois* Republic, just as the declaration of war had meant the end of the Constitutional Monarchy. . . .

. . . The more firmly the Revolutionary Government was established, the more sanguinary it became, and the more actively the guillotine was kept at work. . . . The Terror was of the very essence of the Revolution, because the Revolution was not merely a change in the system of government, but a social revolution, an attempt at expropriation and extermination.

While the armies, under pressure from the enemy, recovered the normal conditions of effective action . . . , France was subjected at home to a communistic experiment which was to leave her bled white, ruined, and ready to surrender to the first saviour who would present himself. . . .

Communism was inconceivable without an unexampled display of coercion and force, and it was this which was the real significance of the Terror, and explained its development and duration. The terrorist dictatorship was connected with the social laws, and not with military events. . . . the Terror was organized at the very time when the danger from abroad was diminishing. It was reduced to a code when the frontiers had been cleared of the enemy, and it reached its high-water mark when the French arms were victorious. . . .

The despotism of Liberty, the dogmatism of Reason—such were the names given by the revolutionists to the system of government which they had set up. . . . Let us say, more simply, that it was the reign of the Social Contract—"the handing over of the individual, with all his rights, to the community," in strict accordance with the rule laid down by Rousseau. . . .

For forty years the clubs and societies had been elaborating their ideas and purging themselves of the dissident elements, and their work was now accomplished. In accordance with strict logic their doctrines had developed, through successive stages, from anarchic Liberalism to Communist dictatorship. . . .

Communism, being a regime contrary to nature, could engender nothing but distress and ruin. The whole system of regulation, bureaucracy, inquisition, coercion, tribunals and the guillotine was bankrupt, completely and absolutely bankrupt. Never had so many and such terrible expedients been adopted to attain so piteous and humiliating an end —a France reduced to famine and living only by fraud or on succour from abroad. . . .

. . . In the course of ten years the Revolution had falsified all calculations and disappointed all hopes. The benefits which had been expected of it were an ordered and stable government, sound finance, wise laws, peace abroad, and tranquillity at home. Instead of which there had been anarchy, war, communism, the Terror, insolvency, famine, and two or three bankruptcies. The Napoleonic dictatorship reconciled the need for authority with democratic ideology. It was an expedient of theorists at their wits' end. The doctrinaires of 1789 had aimed at regenerating humanity and reconstructing the world. In order to escape the Bourbons, the doctrinaires of 1799 were reduced to trusting to the sword.

Pierre Gaxotte, *The French Revolution,* trans. Walter Alison Phillips (London and New York: Charles Scribner's Sons, 1932), pp. 2, 21, 38, 40, 53, 54, 235, 288, 289, 303, 306, 307, 314, 410.

IV. WHAT MANNER OF MAN WAS NAPOLEON BONAPARTE?

Whereas historians may understandably disagree over the interpretation of an historical era or movement, such as the French Revolution, differences of opinion invariably become more pronounced (and more acrimonious) when the biographical element enters into the discussion—especially if the individual happens to be a dynamic and enigmatic person, such as Napoleon Bonaparte.

A critic once said of H. G. Wells' *Outline of History* that the writer's relative *objectivity* in discussing the Java Ape-Man and his decided *subjectivity* in referring to Napoleon as a cockerel strutting on the dunghill of his opportunity were quite comprehensible—it is easier to be dispassionate about a man who had left only a jaw-bone as evidence than about one who has left 30 volumes of letters. He might have added, "and who kept all Europe in a turmoil for 15 years or more!"

Few persons have had as much written about them as has Napoleon I; and few have been praised or denounced in as many ways or in as many languages. When we try to arrive at a balanced opinion of the man (and our estimate of the era is of little value unless we *do* have a comprehension of him—especially as the heir of the French Revolution), we can try at least three types of sources: those written by Napoleon himself; those written by his immediate associates; and those written by "posterity." These should give some idea of what type of man he was.

According to Napoleon Himself

Opinions of a person, written by the individual himself, are always open to question. Either the person does not fully understand himself, or he is giving opinions gratuitously, with a view to explaining (or explaining away) some characteristic or deed. Yet a man's own words frequently suggest his qualities and character more effectively than the words of others. This is particularly true of Napoleon. What features are apparent in the sources presented? What kind of verbal sketch might be drawn from this type of evidence? Would it stand by itself?

A. In Correspondence

Napoleon's correspondence was extensive. Because most of it was dictated, it is probable that little of the contents reflects premeditation. In many respects the letters give a better indication of his character than do his other writings.

1. (*To Nicolo Paravicini, his uncle, concerning his brother Joseph, Brienne, 25 June, 1784*)

. . . As for his future profession, he has put the Church first, as you know; and hitherto he has persisted in his resolution. Now he wants to enter the King's service. I think he is making a big mistake, for several reasons.

(1) First, as my dear father points out, he is not strong enough to face the dangers of war. His weak health doesn't allow him to bear the strain of foreign service, and so he contemplates military life merely in the form of garrison duty. Certainly my brother would make an excellent garrison officer: he is cheerful and good looking, the kind of boy who will come in for plenty of foolish flattery: . . . But what if it comes to fighting? . . .

(2) He has been educated for a clerical career. It is very late to change his mind. The Bishop of Autun would have presented him to a rich living, and he was certain of a bishopric. How that would have helped the family! . . . If he has a real taste for the army— which, after all, is the best profession in the world—and if the Great Mover of human affairs gave him at birth (as he gave me) a definite turn for the military life, then I approve of his choice.

(3) He wants to go into the army. Very well, but into what branch of the service? The Marines? But he knows no mathematics; and it would take him two years to learn it. Besides, he hasn't the health for a life at sea. If it is to be the Engineers, he will need four or five years to learn what is necessary, and at the end of that time he will still be only an Engineer cadet: besides, I don't believe it is compatible with his frivolous character to spend the whole day at work. The same reason excludes the Artillery, except that he would only have to work 18 months to become a cadet, and another 18 to get his commission. No! that's not the sort of thing for him either. No doubt, then, he would like to enter the Infantry. Very good: I understand. He wants to do nothing all day but parade the town. Besides, what is a smart young infantry officer up to, three quarters of his time, except misconducting himself? And that is something that neither my dear father, nor you, nor my mother, nor my dear uncle the Archdeacon, can ever allow, especially as he has already shown some signs of extravagance and frivolity. We shall therefore make a last effort to get him to stick to the clerical career; and failing that, my dear father will take him back to Corsica with him, and keep an eye on him, and try to turn him into a lawyer. . . .

P.S. Tear up this letter. . . .

2. (*To Citizen Ripault, concerning the regulation of public opinion, Paris, 23 July, 1801*)

Citizen Ripault is to see that he is supplied every day with all the papers that come out, except the political papers. He will read them carefully, make an abstract of everything they contain likely to affect the public point of view, especially with regard to religion, philosophy, and political opinion. He will send me this abstract between 5 and 6 o'clock every day.

Once every ten days he will send me an analysis of all the books or pamphlets which have appeared during that period, calling attention to any passages that might bear on moral questions, or interest me in a political or moral connexion.

He will take pains to procure copies of all the plays which are produced, and to analyse them for me, with observations of the same character as those above mentioned. This analysis must be made, at latest, within 48 hours of the production of the plays.

He is to send me every 1st and 6th day, between 5 and 6 o'clock, a list of all the bills, posters, advertisements, etc. which deserve attention, as well as anything that has come to his knowledge, and anything that has been done or said in the various Institutes, literary meetings, sermons, new educational establishments, or fashionable trials, that might be of interest from a political and moral point of view. . . .

3. (*To Barbier, the emperor's librarian, concerning the establishment of a portable library, Bayonne, 17 July, 1808*)

The Emperor wishes to provide himself with a portable library of 1,000 volumes, in small 12° size, and good type. His Majesty's intention is to have works specially printed for his own use, and without margins, so as not to waste space. The volumes should contain 5 or 600 pages each, and should be bound with loose backs, so that they open flat, and in the thinnest possible boards. This library would be composed of about 40 volumes on religion, 40 of epics, 40 of plays, 60 of poetry, 100 of novels, and 60 of history. The balance, up to 1,000, would be made up of historical memoirs of all ages.

The religious works would be the *Old* and *New Testaments* in the best translations: a selection of the Epistles and other most important works of the Church Fathers; the *Koran;* some mythology: select treatises on the sects which have had most historical influence, such as the Arians, Calvinists, Reformed bodies, etc.; and a history of the Church, if there is room for it within the thousand volumes.

The Epics should be Homer, Lucan, Tasso, *Télémaque*, the *Henriade*, etc.

The Tragedies: of Corneille, only the plays that have stood the test of time; Racine; but leave out the *Frères ennemis, Alexandre*, and the *Plaideurs;* of Crébillon, only *Rhadamiste*, and *Atrée et Thyeste;* and what has survived of Voltaire.

History: put in some good books on chronology, and the chief ancient authorities—sufficient for a detailed history of France. You can include under the head of history Machiavelli's *Discours sur Tite-Live*, the *Esprit des Lois*, the *Grandeur des Romains*, and whatever is worth keeping of Voltaire's historical writings.

Novels: Rousseau's *Confessions*, and *Nouvelle Héloise*. There is no need to mention the masterpieces of Fielding, Richardson, Lesage, etc., which are of course included. The *Contes* of Voltaire.

Note.—Don't put in Rousseau's *Émile*, or the whole crowd of letters, memoirs, speeches, and useless treatises that he wrote. The same remark applies to Voltaire. . . .

Napoleon Self-Revealed in Three Hundred Selected Letters, trans. and ed. J. M. Thompson (Boston and New York: Houghton Mifflin Company, 1934), pp. 1-3, 81, 223-224, by permission of Basil Blackwell, Ltd., Oxford, England.

B. In Memoirs and Other Writings

Usually written long after the facts, and often, as in the case of Napoleon's, designed to perpetuate the kind of memory the writer wishes mankind to hold of him, memoirs must be used with caution. Public documents, such as the Imperial Catechism, frequently provide more accurate impressions.

1. (*Concerning Napoleon's return to Paris from Italy, 1797*)

During the two years of my command in Italy, I had filled the whole world with the renown of my victories; and the coalition had been broken up by them. . . . At no period of history had the French soldier been more thoroughly impressed with the sense of his superiority over all other soldiers in Europe. It was owing to the influence of the victories in Italy. . . .

Extraordinary contributions to the amount of upwards of 120 millions had been levied in Italy; 60 millions had sufficed to pay, feed, and provide for the army of Italy . . . ; and 60 millions, which had been sent to the Treasury at Paris, had enabled it to supply the wants of the interior, and the army of the Rhine: . . . Independently of this important supply of sixty millions, the treasury owed to my victories an annual saving of seventy millions, the amount of the expense of the armies of the Alps and Italy in 1796. The naval department at Toulon had received considerable supplies in hemp and timber, and the shipping taken at Genoa, Leghorn, and Venice. The national museum had been enriched with the *chefs-d'oeuvre* of the arts which had embellished Parma, Florence, and Rome, and which were valued at upwards of 200 millions.

The commerce of Lyons, Provence, and Dauphiny began to revive the moment the grand debouché of the Alps was opened to it. The Toulon squadron ruled the Mediterranean, the Adriatic, and the Levant. Happy times for France seemed to be at hand, and she acknowledged with pleasure that she owed them to the conquerors of Italy.

On my arrival, the leaders of all parties immediately called upon me; but I refused to listen to them. The public was extremely eager to see me; the streets and squares through which I was expected to pass were constantly crowded with people, but I never showed myself. The Institute having appointed me a member of the class of mechanics, I adopted its costume. I received no constant visits, except from a few men of science . . . , several generals . . . , and a very few deputies.

I was received in public audience by the Directory who had had scaffoldings erected in the Place du Luxembourg for this ceremony, the pretext for which was the delivery of the treaty of Campo-Formio. . . .

2. (*Conditions in France on his return from Egypt, 1799*)

When lamentable weakness and endless versatility are manifested in the councils of a government; when an administration, yielding by turns to the influence of every opposing party, and going on from day to day without any fixed plan or determined system, has shown its utter insufficiency; and when the most modern citizens in the state are obliged to confess that it is without a government; when rulers, insignificant at home, have shamefully brought on their country the contempt of foreigners—the greatest of injuries in the eyes of a proud people; a vague uneasiness spreads throughout society: agitated by the instinct of self-preservation, it looks into its own resources, and seeks for someone able to save it from destruction.

A populous nation always possesses this tutelary genius in its own bosom, though he may sometimes be tardy in appearing. It is not indeed sufficient for him to exist, he must be known to others, and he must know himself. Until then all endeavours are vain, all schemes ineffectual. The inertness of the multitude is the protection of the nominal government, and in spite of its inexperience and weakness, the efforts of its enemies cannot prevail against it. But let this deliverer, so impatiently expected, suddenly give a proof of his existence, and the nation instinctively acknowledges and calls on him; all obstacles vanish at his approach, and a great people thronging round his steps, seems exultingly to proclaim 'This is the man'. . . .

Napoleon's Memoirs, ed. [and trans.] Somerset de Chair (London: Faber and Faber, Ltd., 1948), pp. 267-269, 361-362, by permission of Mr. Somerset de Chair.

3. (*From the "Fourth Commandment" of Napoleon's Imperial Catechism, 4 April, 1807*)

Question: What are the duties of Christians with respect to the princes who govern them, and what in particular are our duties towards Napoleon I, our Emperor?

Answer: Christians owe to the princes who govern them, and we owe in particular to Napoleon I, our Emperor, *love, respect, obedience, fidelity, military service,* and the tributes laid for the preservation and defence of the Empire and of his throne; we also owe to him fervent prayers for his safety and the spiritual and temporal prosperity of the State.

Question: Why are we bound to all these duties towards our Emperor?

Answer: First of all, because God, who creates empires and distributes them according to His will, in loading our Emperor with gifts, both in peace and in war, has established him as our sovereign and has made him the minister of His power and His image upon the earth. *To honour and to serve our Emperor is then to honour and to serve God himself.* Secondly, because our Lord Jesus Christ by His doctrine as well as by His example, has Himself taught us what we owe to our sovereign; He was born the subject of Caesar Augustus; He paid the prescribed impost, and just as He ordered to render to God that which belongs to God, so he ordered to render to Caesar that which belongs to Caesar.

Question: Are there not particular reasons which ought to attach us more strongly to Napoleon I, our Emperor?

Answer: Yes; for it is he whom God has raised up under difficult circumstances to re-establish the public worship of the holy religion of our fathers and to be the protector of it. He has restored and preserved public order by his profound and active wisdom; he defends the State by his powerful arm; he has become the anointed of the Lord through the consecration which he received from the sovereign pontiff, Head of the universal church.

Question: What ought to be thought of those who may be lacking in their duty towards our Emperor?

Answer: According to the Apostle Saint Paul, they would be resisting the order established by God himself and would render themselves *worthy of eternal damnation.*

Frank Maloy Anderson, *The Constitutions and Other Select Documents Illustrative of the History of France, 1789-1901* (Minneapolis: The H. W. Wilson Co., 1904), pp. 313, 314, by permission of the author.

According to His Contemporaries

Contemporaries, especially those of familiar association, frequently provide the best descriptions of and opinions on individuals.

It must be remembered, however, that the closer the association, the greater is the possibility of the impressions being colored by the relationship. Contrariwise, if the writer is *not* close to his subject, the ac-

count may suffer in the opposite direction.
Both Bourrienne and Madame de Rémusat
were well qualified to speak about Napoleon. What were their impressions? How
and why did they differ? To what extent
must they be discounted? What manner
of man emerges when their accounts are
blended?

A. Louis Bourrienne

In many respects the most important
and most useful memoirs about Napoleon
are those of Louis Antoine Fauvelet de
Bourrienne (1769–1834). Schoolmate,
friend, secretary, and diplomatic representative, Bourrienne ultimately lost favor because of peculation. He was in an unusually favorable position to observe and
record the habits of Napoleon.

My long and intimate connection with
Bonaparte from boyhood, my close relations with him when General, Consul,
and Emperor, enabled me to see and
appreciate all that was projected and
all that was done during that considerable and momentous period of time. I
not only had the opportunity of being
present at the conception and the execution of the extraordinary deeds of one
of the ablest men nature ever formed,
but . . . I found means to employ the
few moments of leisure which Bonaparte
left at my disposal in making notes,
collecting documents, and in recording
for history facts respecting which the
truth could otherwise with difficulty be
ascertained . . .

Bonaparte had two ruling passions,
glory and war. He was never more
gay than in the camp, and never more
morose than in the inactivity of peace.
Plans for the construction of public
monuments also pleased his imagination,
and filled up the void caused by the
want of active occupation. He was
aware that monuments form part of the
history of nations. . .

. . . In all his actions he lost sight
of the present moment, and thought
only of futurity; . . .

Before he fought a battle, Bonaparte
thought little about what he should do
in case of a success, but a great deal
about what he should do in case of a
reverse of fortune. . . .

He did not esteem mankind, whom,
indeed, he despised more and more in
proportion as he became acquainted
with them. . . .

One of Bonaparte's greatest misfortunes was, that he neither believed in
friendship nor felt the necessity of loving. . . .

In his social relations Bonaparte's
temper was bad; but his fits of ill-
humour passed away like a cloud, and
spent themselves in words. His violent
language and bitter imprecations were
frequently premeditated. . . .

. . . He possessed every requisite for
being what is called in society an agreeable man, except the will to be so. His
manner was imposing rather than pleasing, and those who did not know him
well experienced in his presence an involuntary feeling of awe. . . .

He often talked a great deal, and
sometimes a little too much; but no one
could tell a story in a more agreeable
and interesting way. His conversation
rarely turned on gay or humourous subjects, and never on trivial matters. He
was so fond of argument that in the
warmth of discussion it was easy to
draw from him secrets which he was
most anxious to conceal. . . .

Bonaparte had no faith in medicine.
He spoke of it as an art entirely conjectural, and his opinion on this subject
was fixed and incontrovertible. His
vigorous mind rejected all but demonstrative proofs.

He had little memory for proper
names, words, or dates, but he had a
wonderful recollection of facts and
places. . . .

Bonaparte was insensible to the
charms of poetic harmony. He had not
even sufficient ear to feel the rhythm of

poetry, and he never could recite a verse without violating the metre; yet the grand ideas of poetry charmed him. . . .

Gallantry to women was by no means a trait in Bonaparte's character. He seldom said anything agreeable to females, and he frequently addressed to them the rudest and most extraordinary remarks. . . .

On the subject of religion Bonaparte's ideas were very vague. . . . He was very fond of talking of religion. . . . He readily yielded up all that was proved against religion as the work of men and time: but he would not hear of materialism. . . . He was perfectly tolerant towards every variety of religious faith. . . .

. . . Bonaparte was neither malignant nor vindictive. . . . None but those who are blinded by fury will call him a Nero or a Caligula. . . . He was very fond of children, a trait which seldom distinguishes a bad man. In the relations of private life, to call him amiable would not be using too strong a word, and he was very indulgent to the weakness of human nature. . . . To judge impartially, we must take into account the influence which time and circumstances exercise on men; and distinguish between the different characters of the Collegian, the General, the Consul, and the Emperor. . . .

. . . He had no idea of power except in direct force. All benevolent men who speculate on the amelioration of human society were regarded by Bonaparte as dangerous, because their maxims and principles were diametrically opposed to the harsh and arbitrary system he had adopted. . . . he always said that men were only to be governed by fear and interest. . . . Bonaparte held the liberty of the press in the greatest horror; . . . Great man as he was, he was sorely afraid of little paragraphs. . . .

The historian of these times ought to put no faith in the bulletins, despatches, notes, and proclamations which have emanated from Bonaparte, or passed through his hands. . . .

The bulletins always announced what Bonaparte wished to be believed true; but to form a proper judgment on any fact, counter-bulletins must be sought for and consulted. It is well-known, too, that Bonaparte attached great importance to the place whence he dated his bulletins; . . .

The official documents were almost always incorrect. There was falsity in the exaggerated descriptions of his victories, and falsity again in the suppression or palliation of his reverses and losses. A writer, if he took his materials from the bulletins and the official correspondence of the time, would compose a romance rather than a true history. . . .

. . . the slight estimation in which he held literary men. . . . he called them mere manufacturers of phrases. He could not pardon them for excelling him in a pursuit in which he had no claim to distinction. . . .

Louis Antoine Fauvelet de Bourrienne, *Memoirs of Napoleon Bonaparte*, ed. and trans. Ramsay W. Phipps, new ed. rev., 4 vols. (New York: Charles Scribner's Sons, 1889); I, xxvi, xxvii, 313, 315, 316, 317, 319, 320, 322, 323, 324, 327, 328, 367; II, 112, 113, 233 (originally published 1829).

B. *Madame de Rémusat*

Claire Élisabeth Jeanne Gravier de Vergennes, Comtesse de Rémusat (1780–1821) was the wife of one of Napoleon's officials. An aristocratic, cultured woman of independent judgment, she indicates in her memoirs a changing attitude towards the Emperor over the years.

. . . I am far from saying that he always appeared to me in the light in which I see him now; my opinions have progressed, even as he did; but I am so far from being influenced by personal feelings that I do not think it is possible for me to deviate from the exact truth. . . .

. . . there was a sort of fascination in the smile of Bonaparte; but, during all the time I was in the habit of seeing him, he rarely put forth that charm. Gravity was the foundation of his character; not the gravity of a dignified and noble manner, but that which arises from profound thought. In his youth he was a dreamer; later in life he became a moody, and later still an habitually ill-tempered man. . . .

. . . The geometrical turn of his mind disposed him to analyze even his emotions. No man has ever meditated more deeply than Bonaparte on the "wherefore" that rules human actions. . . . he could never understand that natural nonchalance which leads some persons to act without a project and without an aim. He always judged others by himself, and was often mistaken. . .

Bonaparte was deficient in education and in manners; it seemed as if he must have been destined either to live in a tent where all men are equal, or upon a throne where everything is permitted. . . .

In trying to depict Bonaparte, it would be necessary, following the analytical forms of which he was so fond, to separate into three very distinct parts his soul, his heart, and his mind; for no one of these ever blended completely with the others. Although very remarkable for certain intellectual qualities, no man, it must be allowed, was ever less lofty of soul. There was no generosity, no true greatness in him. . . .

All Bonaparte's methods of government were selected from among those which have a tendency to debase men. . . . He can not be said to have truly loved glory, for he never hesitated to prefer success to it. . . . Of generous courage he was not capable; . . .

According to the order I have laid down, I ought now to speak of Bonaparte's heart; but if it were possible to believe that a being, in every other way similar to ourselves, could exist without that portion of our organization which makes us desire to love and to be loved, I should say that in his creation the heart was left out. Perhaps, however, the truth was that he succeeded in suppressing it completely. He was always too much engrossed by himself to be influenced by any sentiment of affection. . .

. . . The Emperor despised women, and contempt can not exist together with love. He regarded their weakness as an unanswerable proof of their inferiority, and the power they have acquired in society as an intolerable usurpation. . .

I am disposed to believe that Bonaparte . . . was never awakened to love except by vanity. . . .

The intellect of Bonaparte was most remarkable. It would be difficult, I think, to find among men a more powerful or comprehensive mind. It owed nothing to education; for, in reality, he was ignorant, reading but little, and that hurriedly. But he quickly seized upon the little he learned, and his imagination developed it so extensively that he might easily have passed for a well-educated man.

. . . With him one idea gave birth to a thousand, and a word would lift his conversation into elevated regions of fancy, in which exact logic did not indeed keep him company, but in which his intellectual power never failed to shine. . . .

I have said that Bonaparte was incapable of generosity; and yet his gifts were immense, and the rewards he bestowed gigantic. But, when he paid for a service, he made it plain that he expected to buy another, and a vague uneasiness as to the conditions of the bargain always remained.

. . . He believed that Frenchmen would not murmur were but their slavery brilliant, and that we would willingly barter all the liberty that the Revolution had so hardly won for us, for his dazzling military success.

. . . he saw in war a means of stifling the reflections which his mode of government was sure sooner or later to evoke, and he reserved it to dazzle us, or at least to reduce us to silence. As he felt himself perfectly master of the science of war, he had no fear of its results; . . . The first, the real ambition of Napoleon was for power, and he would have preferred peace if it could have increased his authority. . . . He looked with disdain on the progress of the age, regarding the French Revolution, which was so solemn a warning to sovereigns, only as an event whose results he might use to his own advantage; and he came to despise the cry for liberty which for twenty years had been uttered at intervals by the people. He was persuaded that he could . . . trick them by accomplishing the destruction of what had existed, and replacing

it by sudden creations, which would appear to satisfy the longing for equality which he believed with reason to be the ruling passion of the time.

He tried to turn the French Revolution into a mere freak of fortune, a useless disturbance which had merely upset individuals. . . .

There would seem to have been in him two different men. The one, rather gigantic than great, but nevertheless prompt to conceive and also prompt to execute, laid from time to time some of the foundations of the plan he had formed. This man, actuated by one single idea, untouched by any secondary impression likely to interfere with his projects, had he but taken for his aim the good of mankind, would, with such abilities as he displayed, have become the one greatest man of the earth; even now he remains, through his perspicacity and his strength of will, the most extraordinary.

The other Bonaparte, forming a kind of uneasy conscience to the first, was devoured by anxiety, agitated by continual suspicion, a slave to passions which gave him no rest, distrustful, fearing every rival greatness, even that which he had himself created. . . .

Memoirs of Madame de Rémusat, 1802–1808 . . ., trans. Mrs. Cashel Hoey and John Lillie, complete in one vol. (New York: D. Appleton and Co., 1880), pp. 1-5, 8, 10, 14, 15, 334, 335, 337.

According to Posterity

As in the case of French historians of the Revolution and writers of memoirs about Napoleon (and for the same reasons), historians of the Napoleonic Era are by no means in agreement concerning the character and achievements of the Emperor. Whether Lanfrey in 1867 or Bainville in 1931, opinions vary. What factors (both general and special) caused this? How do the accounts of these writers compare with those of Bourrienne, Madame de Rémusat, and Napoleon himself? Can one determine satisfactorily, on the basis of all this evi-

dence, what manner of man Napoleon Bonaparte actually was?

A. Pierre Lanfrey

Pierre Lanfrey (1828–1877) was a French journalist, historian, and critic of the Second Empire. His writings included studies of the Church in the eighteenth century, the French Revolution, and Napoleon. The last named (5 vols., 1867–1875) is still important because of its highly controversial approach to the subject.

In all times the true and distinctive mark of political genius has been aptitude for founding a solid and durable work, adapting it to the deep needs of a people and an epoch. The incomparable elements that Bonaparte possessed to realize such a work he only employs to astonish and to dazzle men. He tries to strike their imagination, not to satisfy their reason or their interests. The fate of his country is only a secondary object in comparison with the apotheosis which he dreams of for himself. Beyond this purely personal ideal of glorification, we fail to discover in him any persistent or definite spring of action. It is almost impossible for him to stop at a determined end: he has no sooner advanced a step than he goes further still, again still further, without ever waiting till the ground is firm under his feet. For him, a conquest is a stepping-stone for a fresh conquest. Hence the hasty, feverish, impromptu character of his political creations, at home as well as abroad. All that he does in this respect, with the impatience and rapidity of an ambition greedy enough to devour a world, is in his mind only a transition, a beginning capable of an indefinite extension. Consequently everything remains unfinished, in a state of outline and experiment. He never acts with the idea of the definite, he wishes to retain to the last the power of changing everything according to opportunity, and above all things according to the humour of his insatiable cravings. He never aims at stability, but at size, at splendour; grandeur does not satisfy him, he must have the immeasurable, the gigantic; and beyond this perilous domain, something else attracts him still more; it is the unknown and the marvellous. Under the sting of this irresistible disquietude, he forgets the road to follow and the end to attain in the movement itself. He cares less about the final result than about the means that he will display, and the prodigious effect that he will produce. It matters little to him whether the work is ephemeral, provided he finds in it more activity, more noise, more glory. The task to accomplish and the means necessary to insure success are trifles beside the grand adventures for which they furnish him the opportunity or the pretext. This infatuation was so much the more terrible that it had taken possession of a cold and positive mind, whose most chimerical dreams clothed forms of mathematical rigour, and had at their service a military genius without equal. With enthusiastic temperaments exaltation is only temporary; but the studied frenzy of a calculating mind is without remedy, because it does not depend on a sentiment but on the very form of the intellect itself. . . .

. . . If there is, in fact, a striking and characteristic trait in the innumerable conversations which have been preserved by men who approached him most familiarly, it is the absence of all effusion or unreserved confidence. He was always engrossed with the endeavour either to penetrate the views of his interlocutor or so to work upon his mind as to bring him round to a calculated object; we look in vain for anything like sympathy, enthusiasm, or a moment of frank confidence about himself or about others. Even when he gave way to that coquettishness of feline grace of which his contemporaries have so often described the seduction, he never lost sight of the effect he wished to produce; he calculated everything, even his imprudence in language. He was as reserved with his own relations as with strangers. In short, we cannot find in his whole life a single instance of that philosophical irony which charms us so in a Caesar or a Frederick, because it shows that the man is superior to his part, that he knows his own value, that he is not the dupe of his own fortune. . . . Napoleon, on the contrary, is always on the stage, constantly thinking of himself; . . . he had not that supreme greatness of the man who has a just appreciation of his worth; he remained, by his incurable infatuation, on a level with narrow minds; . . .

The *régime* inaugurated under the name of Empire was no other than pure Caesarism. . .

. . . In order to create this power . . . it was necessary to do violence to the spirit of the people no less than to the spirit of the times; in order to preserve it, it was necessary to hinder this people from recovering a consciousness of its own existence. . .

. . . This transformation of the Consulate into an Empire . . . was inspired by a puerile vanity, for which real power was no longer enough if it was not accompanied by that external homage invented and brought to perfection by so many centuries of monarchical superstition. In this Bonaparte was very inferior to Cromwell, of whom he spoke with so much disdain; in the English statesman there was more seriousness, more sense, more manliness. . . . Bonaparte's genius is prodigious, but within narrow limits. He was endowed with an extraordinary penetration, and yet he had no foresight; he was calculating, and yet he was incapable of governing himself. . . . He made great political interests subservient to a miserable satisfaction of self-love. Never did the innate littleness of his soul betray itself more visibly than in the feverish haste with which he adopted all the forms of ancient etiquette. What did he care for the perils which this petty ambition was going to create for us, provided that he, the son of the obscure lawyer of Ajaccio, could call kings 'our dearly-beloved brother'—provided that he could sign his letters to the Pope, 'Your devoted son'—provided that he could say, 'My good town of Paris, my subjects, my people, my ministers, my palace, my forest of Fontainebleau'?

Pierre Lanfrey, *The History of Napoleon the First,* trans. from the French, 2nd ed., 4 vols. (London and New York: The Macmillan Co., 1886), II, 150-153, 431, 433, 434.

B. Jacques Bainville

First published in 1931, Jacques Bainville's study of Napoleon is one of the most widely read biographies of the man. The author (1879–1936) was a royalist; hence his views on Napoleon, the vigorous opponent of the Bourbons, are of great significance.

. . . If Bonaparte was distinguished by anything, it was by the clarity of his ideas, the precision of his exposition, the sense of sequence with which he asserted the essentials of success. . . .

. . . Bonaparte never knew whither he was moving, because he could not know; and that was why he always went further on. . . .

. . . Time took him by the shoulder and pushed him. His days were counted out for him. They would flow past with dreamlike speed, so prodigiously crowded, broken by so few truces and breathing spaces, in a sort of impatient frenzy to reach the catastrophe quickly, laden in the end with such a burden of grandiose happenings that his reign, really so brief, seemed to have lasted a century.

On the throne, Napoleon was more at ease than if he had been born to it, because the very traditions which he revived were considered and intentional. . . .

. . . If the mind of a sovereign came to birth in him, it was not only by that capability of man to shape himself to the part he must play. He thought of the condition and duties of a monarch, and of the flaws which a monarchy must not develop. . . . There must be no backsliding, only upward advance. . . .

Nor was the coronation the idea of a romantic megalomaniac. In reviving Charlemagne, Bonaparte doubtless sought to impress the imagination of the nations. But his real aim was the dropping of one more anchor in deep water. Perhaps he cherished the illusion that anointing would guarantee his power by giving it a sacred and legitimate character. Perhaps, too, he deliberately used that tool as he used all others. . . .

Ideas came to Napoleon one after another; he adapted and abandoned them with disconcerting rapidity. At one moment he was regarded as a knave, the next as a man drunk with power, as he struggled in an inextricable entanglement of which he was not the author. On the contrary, his task was to extricate France from it, by means of the unbounded credit allowed to him, and that endless, even absurd, supply of credit left him powerless to extricate even himself. . . .

Napoleon excelled always in the art of striking the imagination. . . .

With catastrophe the true stature of Napoleon appeared. He was the man who understood his own history, who dominated it and took it all in at one glance. . . . One secret of his incredible rise had been that he always saw things largely. . . .

If the extraordinary man finished the "romance of his life" and gave it an epic turn, it was because he was superior to the rest of mortals, and especially superior in the infallible sense of his destiny. In this crashing of worlds, what other man would not have weakened? It was not enough to have will and force of character. The Emperor had an historical view of his own situation. . . .

Except from the point of view of glory, or of "art", it would probably be better

that Napoleon should never have existed. All in all, his reign, which was meant to continue the Revolution, ended in dire failure. His genius prolonged a contest which he was foredoomed to lose. All these victories, all these conquests (which he had not begun himself)—to what end? To go back to just beyond the point from which the militant Revolution had started. . . It was not worth the cost of so much upheaval, unless to bequeath to history the legacy of some noble pictures. Bonaparte restored an order in Europe; but was it worth the disorder that he spread, the forces that he quickened only to bring them back upon the heads of Frenchmen? As for the Napoleonic State, which endured through four regimes and seemed to be built upon a base of bronze, it is in decadence. Gradually its laws are falling apart. Before long France will be farther away from the Napoleonic Code than Napoleon was from Justinian and the Institutes, and the day is approaching when the impulse of new ideas will leave the work of the legislator as a thing outmoded.

A man of imagination, a potent maker of images, a poet, he had a strong sense of this flight of the centuries. . . . He knew that in the imagination of the peoples he had eclipsed Frederick the Great, that his picture would hang upon their walls and his name upon sign-boards, until some other hero should arise to take his place. That other hero has not come. The fabulous adventure, the Emperor with the Roman mask, the god of battles, the man who taught humanity that possibilities have no bounds, the demiurge of politics and war, remains unique in his kind. It may be that, in the course of time, Ampère will count for more than Napoleon. The Napoleonic era may prove to be no more than a brief episode in what will be styled the Age of Electricity. In the end, perhaps, Napoleon will be but one of the figures of the solar myth, appearing in an island of the rising run and fading out in an island of the sunset. He was hardly dead when men turned to such hypotheses and fancies. All men, all things, come to dust. Napoleon Bonaparte has no armor against oblivion. Nevertheless, after a hundred years, the glamour of his name remains intact, and his aptitude for survival is as extraordinary as his aptitude for ruling. When he left Malmaison for Rochefort, before delivering himself into the hands of his enemies, he lingered mournfully as he turned away from his memories and off the world's stage. From the memory of mankind he will pass no less slowly; and across the years, through revolutions and through strange rumor, the ears of men still catch the footsteps of the Emperor as he passes beyond the world's edge to reach new horizons.

Jacques Bainville, *Napoleon,* trans. Hamish Miles (Boston: Little, Brown and Co., 1933), pp. 37, 103, 165, 166, 172, 285, 339-341, 403-405, by permission of Jacques Chambrun, Inc.

11. The New Industrial and Social Order

HARRY H. KIMBER

Michigan State College

IN THE MIDDLE YEARS of the nineteenth century a series of changes in the methods by which man satisfied his basic economic needs of food, clothing, and shelter came to a climax in Great Britain. As these changes developed from one place to another in Great Britain, and as the whole and ever-growing complex of changes spread among the nations on the continent and across the sea to America, the life and civilization of Western man was affected perhaps more radically than by any other series of events in history. Historians have given the name of Industrial Revolution—an analogy with the consequences of political changes which overturn states—to this much more profound and complicated movement affecting the whole of society. In order to indicate better the broad scope of changes involved, the expression Economic Revolution is sometimes preferred. Whatever term may be thought proper, five basic revolutionary changes occurred.

In the first place, machinery came to replace hand work throughout whole industries. This was increasingly accompanied, in the second place, by the application on a large scale of water power and steam power to machinery. In the third place, new ways and means of transportation were brought into existence by the invention of the steam engine and the development of canal systems, and new kinds of roads. The social changes which were a consequence and a condition of the foregoing aspects of the Industrial Revolution would not have been possible on an extensive scale unless there had occurred, in the fourth place, correspondingly revolutionary changes in methods of agriculture. The great social change brought about by industrialization was the concentration of the manufacturing and trading population in great urban centers of enormous size and complexity: the modern city. Agriculture on an unprecedented scale was necessary to support these urban populations, and, accordingly, the revolution in transportation already mentioned was likewise indispensable to the mass-delivery of food-stuffs.

In the fifth place, another kind of revolutionary change that was an integral part of the Industrial Revolution affected the methods and character of business organization. This was the means by which the capital required to carry on manufacture and trade under the new system was amassed from many sources, and the methods by which the great enterprises characteristic of the new order were owned, controlled, and directed.

Taken together the changes described above represent a new economic order. Likewise the social changes which came about in consequence of the economic changes effected by the Industrial Revolution were themselves revolutionary in scope and in result. Such changes spread into virtually every area of society, modifying old and creating new social groupings, bringing into being new classes in society, disarranging the political balance in the state, and calling forth new forms of government, however much the newness was concealed by accustomed form and usage. A new civilization was born.

The new civilization of the nineteenth century posed for its contemporaries many problems. Rising out of the foundations of Western Europe, it was inextricably bound up with the culture pattern of the past at the same time that it was essentially a new thing upon the earth. Greek, Roman, and Christian ideals dominated the minds of men, but they were now of necessity applied to a contemporary social and intellectual world that in points of difference was further from Queen Anne's England than the people of that age were from the Romans of Caesar's time.

The new order posed questions in at least three major areas: the economic, the social, and the political. The readings which follow are not intended to summarize in any degree of completeness the many and various facets which these questions presented in the course of the century, but they are rather to be regarded as introductions to the nature of the questions faced by the people of the nineteenth century, stated in the terms in which they appeared and reappeared in the economic, social, and political conflicts of the day. Since most of these problems were posed first in Great Britain, most of our materials are taken from the writings and speeches of Englishmen of the period.

In the part on "The New Society" the problem of the new economic order is discussed by John Stuart Mill, Friedrich Engels, and Leo XIII in terms of the right of private property and its corollary, competition. Under the heading of "The Myth of Progress" Thomas Malthus and Robert Owen debate the basic question posed by the secularist view of society: can man by the exercise of reason alone progress toward the perfection of a social order? In the third part of this problem two members of Parliament and a political philosopher deal with the problem of the new political balance created by the rise of the working man in the age of capitalism to an increasingly dominant position in the body politic.

I. THE NEW SOCIETY

The nineteenth century in England was marked by a new and vigorous concern for social ethics. This concern for the social question—the Condition of England Question, as it was then called—was evidenced not only in the writings of intellec-

tuals and men of letters, but also in the popular movements of protest and reform which arose from among the working classes. Under the Industrial Revolution the standard of living of the working classes had so far improved as to make them more sensitive to injustice and more capable of imagining a better ordering of society than had been the case with their semi-feudal predecessors of the previous century. There was violence and lawlessness in the eighteenth century, but it was the violence of fanatical or ignorant men, and the lawlessness of gin and hysteria; the trades union movement, the agitation for parliamentary reform preceding the passage of the Bill of 1832, Chartism in its various phases, the rise of Socialism, all strike a different note. The great popular movements of the nineteenth century reflect "the resentment of men convinced that there is something false and degrading in the arrangement and justice of their world." [J. L. and Barbara Hammond, *The Bleak Age* (London, New York, and Toronto: Longmans, Green & Co., 1934), p. 3.]

This is in short the social question. A new social order was gradually arising upon the ruins of the old—the old order based on the land economy of the Middle Ages, the new order the result of the industrialization of the modern world. In the readings that follow there are presented aspects of three of the basic ideas involved in the nineteenth-century debate on social issues: the idea of private property and free competition, a criticism of the competitive system of capitalism, and a statement of economic and social rights and responsibilities from a Christian point of view. The last, although it represents one of the positions taken in England, comes from a non-English source, largely because the document from which it has been taken is one of the most important pronouncements on the social question which appeared during the nineteenth century.

A. *John Stuart Mill Defends Economic Liberalism*

John Stuart Mill (1806–1873) is one of the great exponents of nineteenth century liberalism, perhaps best known for his defense of individual freedom in the classic *Essay on Liberty* (1859). Mill belonged to the school of thought known as the Philosophical Radicals, which professed to accept no socio-political institution on the basis of authority or custom but subjected all things to the scrutiny of reason in the light of the criterion of utility as set forth in the writings of Jeremy Bentham.

In writing the *Principles of Political Economy,* Mill was aware of the problems posed by the new order, the condition of the workers, the rise of the capitalist class, and the remedies proposed by early Socialists and Communists. In the following passages he goes to the heart of the matter, the place of the individual in society. He defends private property and the principle of competition on utilitarian grounds. From the right of private property and the workings of competition in economic life there arises the highest value of civilized social order, the freedom of the individual.

Private property, in every defence made of it, is supposed to mean, the guarantee to individuals of the fruits of their own labour and abstinence. The guarantee to them of the fruits of the labour and abstinence of others, transmitted to them without any merit or exertion of their own, is not of the essence of the institution, but a mere incidental consequence, which when it reaches a certain height, does not promote, but conflicts with the ends which render private property legitimate. To judge of the final destination of the institution of property, we must suppose everything rectified, which causes the institution to work in a manner opposed to that equitable principle, of proportion between remuneration and exertion, on which in every vindication of it that will bear the light, it is assumed to be grounded. We must also suppose two conditions realized, without which neither Communism nor any other laws or institutions could make the condition of the mass of mankind other than degraded and miserable. One of these conditions is, universal education; the other, a due limitation of the numbers of the community. With these, there could be no poverty even under the present social institutions: and these being supposed, the question of Socialism is not, as generally stated by Socialists, a question of flying to the sole refuge against the evils which now bear down humanity; but a mere question of comparative advantages, which futurity must determine. We are too ignorant either of what individual agency in its best form, or Socialism in its best form, can accomplish, to be qualified to decide which of the two will be the ultimate form of human society.

If a conjecture may be hazarded, the decision will probably depend mainly on one consideration, viz. which of the two systems is consistent with the greatest amount of human liberty and spontaneity. After the means of subsistence are assured, the next in strength of the personal wants of human beings is liberty; and (unlike the physical wants, which as civilization advances become more moderate and more amenable to control) it increases instead of diminishing in intensity, as the intelligence and the moral faculties are more developed. . . . The restraints of Communism would be freedom in comparison with the present condition of the majority of the human race. The generality of labourers in this and most other countries, have as little choice of occupation or freedom of locomotion, are practically as dependent on fixed rules and on the will of others, as they could be on any system short of actual slavery; to say nothing of the entire domestic subjection of one half the species, to which it is the signal honour of Owenism and most other forms of Socialism that they assign equal rights, in all respects, with those of the hitherto dominant sex. But it is not by comparison with the present bad state of society that the claims of Communism can be estimated; nor is it sufficient that it should promise greater personal and mental freedom than is now enjoyed by those who have not enough of either to deserve the name. The question is,

whether there would be any asylum left for individuality of character; whether public opinion would not be a tyrannical yoke; whether the absolute dependence of each on all, and surveillance of each by all, would not grind all down into a tame uniformity of thoughts, feelings, and actions. This is already one of the glaring evils of the existing state of society, notwithstanding a much greater diversity of education and pursuits, and a much less absolute dependence of the individual on the mass, than would exist in the Communistic régime. No society in which eccentricity is a matter of reproach, can be in a wholesome state. It is yet to be ascertained whether the Communistic scheme would be consistent with that multiform development of human nature, those manifold unlikenesses, that diversity of tastes and talents, and variety of intellectual points of view, which not only form a great part of the interest of human life, but by bringing intellects into stimulating collision, and by presenting to each innumerable notions that he would not have conceived of himself, are the mainspring of mental and moral progression. . . .

The institution of property, when limited to its essential elements, consists in the recognition, in each person, of a right to the exclusive disposal of what he or she have produced by their own exertions, or received either by gift or by fair agreement, without force or fraud, from those who produced it. The foundation of the whole is, the right of producers to what they themselves have produced. It may be objected, therefore, to the institution as it now exists, that it recognises rights of property in individuals over things which they have not produced. For example (it may be said) the operatives in a manufactory create, by their labour and skill, the whole produce; yet, instead of its belonging to them, the law gives them only their stipulated hire, and transfers the produce to some one who has merely supplied the funds, without perhaps contributing anything to the work itself, even in the form of superintendence. The answer to this is, that the labour of manufacture is only one of the conditions which must combine for the production of the commodity. The labour cannot be carried on without materials and machinery, nor without a stock of necessaries provided in advance, to maintain the labourers during the production. All these things are the fruits of previous labour. If the labourers were possessed of them, they would not need to divide the produce with any one; but while they have them not, an equivalent must be given to those who have, both for the antecedent labour, and for the abstinence by which the produce of that labour, instead of being expended on indulgences, has been reserved for this use. The capital may not have been, and in most cases was not, created by the labour and abstinence of the present possessor; but it was created by the labour and abstinence of some former person, who may indeed have been wrongfully dispossessed of it, but who, in the present age of the world, much more probably transferred his claims to the present capitalist by gift or voluntary contract: and the abstinence at least must have been continued by each successive owner, down to the present. If it be said, as it may with truth, that those who have inherited the savings of others have an advantage which they may have in no way deserved, over the industrious whose predecessors have not left them anything; I not only admit, but strenuously contend, that this unearned advantage should be curtailed, as much as is consistent with justice to those who thought fit to dispose of their savings by giving them to their descendants. But while it is true that the la-

bourers are at a disadvantage compared with those whose predecessors have saved, it is also true that the labourers are far better off than if those predecessors had not saved. They share in the advantage, though not to an equal extent with the inheritors. The terms of co-operation between present labour and the fruits of past labour and saving, are a subject for adjustment between the two parties. Each is necessary to the other. The capitalist can do nothing without labourers, nor the labourers without capital. If the labourers compete for employment, the capitalists on their part compete for labour, to the full extent of the circulating capital of the country. Competition is often spoken of as if it were necessarily a cause of misery and degradation to the labouring class; as if high wages were not precisely as much a product of competition as low wages. The remuneration of labour is as much the result of the law of competition in the United States, as it is in Ireland, and much more completely so than in England. . . .

Instead of looking upon competition as the baneful and antisocial principle which it is held to be by the generality of Socialists, I conceive that, even in the present state of society and industry, every restriction of it is an evil, and every extension of it, even if for the time injuriously affecting some class of labourers, is always an ultimate good. To be protected against competition is to be protected in idleness, in mental dulness; to be saved the necessity of being as active and as intelligent as other people; and if it is also to be protected against being underbid for employment by a less highly paid class of labourers, this is only where old custom or local and partial monopoly has placed some particular class of artizans in a privileged position as compared with the rest; and the time has come when the interest of universal improvement is no longer promoted by prolonging the privileges of a few. If the slop-sellers and others of their class have lowered the wages of tailors, and some other artizans, by making them an affair of competition instead of custom, so much the better in the end. What is now required is not to bolster up old customs, whereby limited classes of labouring people obtain partial gains which interest them in keeping up the present organization of society, but to introduce new general practices beneficial to all; and there is reason to rejoice at whatever makes the privileged classes of skilled artizans feel, that they have the same interests, and depend for their remuneration on the same general causes, and must resort for the improvement of their condition to the same remedies, as the less fortunately circumstanced and comparatively helpless multitude. . . .

John Stuart Mill, *Principles of Political Economy,* from the 5th London ed. (New York: D. Appleton & Co., 1865), I, 268-271, 278-280.

B. *Friedrich Engels Attacks Competition*

Friedrich Engels (1820–1895) was, with Karl Marx, a co-founder of modern or "scientific" Socialism. Engels' association with Marx began shortly after the writing of the book from which the following passages are taken. This description of the condition of the English working class was first published in Germany in 1845, and appeared in an American edition 40 years later. The book was to some extent the result of Engels' own observations while in England on business, but in the main its material is drawn from evidence presented before government commissions of inquiry. Not only does the book present something less than a balanced picture of the good and evil which flowed from the Industrial Revolution and the rise of capitalism, but in a later edition the author himself makes the point that the things described are largely matters of the past. Improvement in the standards of life and labor of the mass of the people should not, however, he warns his readers, lead us into justifying an economic system based on private wealth and competition. Concessions to justice and philanthropy are made only to speed capital concentration in the hands of the few by crushing the smaller competitors who could not afford to grant such amenities to their employees. The major grievance is the capitalistic system itself.

The capitalistic system gradually destroyed the old society of landowners, agricultural laborers, and petty bourgeoisie, and erected in its place a social structure dominated by two classes, the capitalist and the proletariat. The old medieval culture of status, weakened by Renaissance emphasis upon individualism, was now dissolved by the facts of urban life in the age of the Industrial Revolution. Engels describes the workings of individualism in the following words:

"The brutal indifference, the unfeeling isolation of each in his private interest becomes the more repellant and offensive, the more these individuals are crowded together, within a limited space. And, however much one may be aware that this isolation of the individual, this narrow self-seeking is the fundamental principle of our society everywhere, it is nowhere so shamelessly barefaced, so self-conscious as just here in the crowding of the great city. The dissolution of mankind into monads, of which each one has a separate principle, the world of atoms, is here carried out to its utmost extreme. Hence it comes, too, that the social war, the war of each against all, is here openly declared. . . . People regard each other only as useful objects; each exploits the other, and the end of it all is, that the stronger treads the weaker under foot, and that the powerful few, the capitalists, seize everything for themselves, while to the weak many, the poor, scarcely a bare existence remains." [Friedrich Engels, *The Condition of the Working-Class in England in 1844* (London: George Allen & Unwin, Ltd., 1950), p. 24.]

Competition is the completest expression of the battle of all against all which rules in modern civil society. This battle, a battle for life, for existence, for everything, in case of need a battle of life and death, is fought not between the different classes of society only, but also between the individual members of these classes. Each is in the way of the other, and each seeks to crowd out all who are in his way, and to put himself in their place. The workers are in constant competition among themselves as the members of the bourgeoisie among themselves. The power-loom weaver is in competition with the hand-loom weaver, the unemployed or ill-paid hand-loom weaver with him who has work or is better paid, each trying to supplant the other. But this competition of the workers among themselves is the worst side of the present state of things in its effect upon the worker, the sharpest weapon against the proletariat in the hands of the bourgeoisie. Hence the effort of the workers to nullify this competition by associations, hence the hatred of the bourgeoisie towards these associations, and its triumph in every defeat which befalls them. . . .

Fine freedom, where the proletarian has no other choice than that of either accepting the conditions which the bourgeoisie offers him, or of starving, of freezing to death, of sleeping naked among the beasts of the forests! A fine "equivalent" valued at pleasure by the bourgeoisie! And if one proletarian is such a fool as to starve rather than agree to the equitable propositions of the bourgeoisie, his "natural superiors," another is easily found in his place; there are proletarians enough in the world, and not all so insane as to prefer dying to living.

Here we have the competition of the workers among themselves. If *all* the proletarians announced their determination to starve rather than work for the bourgeoisie, the latter would have to surrender its monopoly. But this is not the case—is, indeed, a rather impossible case—so that the bourgeoisie still thrives. To this competition of the worker there is but one limit; no worker will work for less than he needs to subsist. If he must starve, he will prefer to starve in idleness rather than in toil. . . .

From this it is evident what the minimum of wages is. The maximum is determined by the competition of the bourgeoisie among themselves; for we have seen how they, too, must compete with each other. The bourgeois can increase his capital only in commerce and manufacture, and in both cases he needs workers. Even if he invests his capital at interest, he needs them indirectly; for without commerce and manufacture, no one would pay him interest upon his capital, no one could use it. So the bourgeois certainly needs workers, not indeed for his immediate living, for at need he could consume his capital, but as we need an article of trade or a beast of burden, —as a means of profit. The proletarian produces the goods which the bourgeois sells with advantage. When, therefore, the demand for these goods increases so that all the competing working-men are employed, and a few more might perhaps be useful, the competition among the workers falls away, and the bourgeoisie begin to compete among themselves. The capitalist in search of workmen knows very well that his profits increase as prices rise in consequence of the increased demand for his goods, and pays a trifle higher wages rather than let the whole profit escape him. He sends the butter to fetch the cheese, and getting the latter, leaves the butter ungrudgingly to the workers. So one capitalist after another goes in chase of workers, and wages rise; but only as high as the increasing demand permits. If the capitalist, who willingly sacrificed a part of his extraordinary profit, runs into danger of sacrificing any part of his ordinary average profit, he takes very good care not to pay more than average wages.

From this we can determine the average rate of wages. Under average circumstances, when neither workers nor capitalists have reason to compete, especially among themselves, when there are just as many workers at hand as can be employed in producing precisely the goods that are demanded, wages stand a little above the minimum. How far they rise above the minimum will depend upon the average needs and the grade of civilisation of the workers. If the workers are accustomed to eat meat several times in the week, the capitalists must reconcile themselves to paying wages enough to make this food attainable, not less, because the workers are not competing among themselves and have no occasion to content themselves with less; not more, because the capitalists, in the absence of competition among themselves, have no occasion to attract working-men by extraordinary favours.

This standard of the average needs and the average civilisation of the workers has become very complicated by reason of the complications of English industry, and is different for different sorts of workers, as has been pointed out. Most industrial occupations demand a certain skill and regularity, and for these qualities which involve a certain grade of civilisation, the rate of wages must be such as to induce the worker to acquire such skill and subject himself to such regularity. Hence it is that the average wages of industrial workers are higher than those of mere porters, day labourers, etc., higher especially than those of agricultural labourers, a fact to which the additional cost of the necessities of life in cities contributes somewhat. In other words, the worker is, in law and in fact, the slave of the property-holding class, so effectually a slave that he is sold like a piece of goods, rises and falls in value like a commodity. If the demand for workers increases, the price of workers rises; if it falls, their price falls. If it falls so greatly that a number of them become unsaleable, if they are left in stock, they are simply left idle; and as they cannot live upon that, they die of starvation. For, to speak in the words of the economists, the expense incurred in maintaining them would not be reproduced, would be money thrown away, and to this end no man advances capital; and, so far, Malthus was perfectly right in his theory of population. The only difference as compared with the old, outspoken slavery is this, that the worker of to-day seems to be free because he is not sold once for all, but piecemeal by the day, the week, the year, and because no one owner sells him to another, but he is forced to sell himself in this way instead, being the slave of no particular person, but of the whole property-holding class. For him the matter is unchanged at bottom, and if this semblance of liberty necessarily gives him some real freedom on the one hand, it entails on the other the disadvantage that no one guarantees him a subsistence; he is in danger of being repudiated at any moment by his master, the bourgeoisie, and left to die of starvation, if the bourgeoisie ceases to have an interest in his employment, his existence. The bourgeoisie, on the other hand, is far better off under the present arrangement than under the old slave system; it can dismiss its employees at discretion without sacrificing invested capital, and gets its work done much more cheaply than is possible with slave labour, as Adam Smith comfortingly pointed out.

Hence it follows, too, that Adam Smith was perfectly right in making the assertion: "That the demand for men, like that for any other commodity, necessarily regulates the production of men, quickens it when it goes on too slowly, and stops it when it advances too fast." *Just as in the case of any other commodity!* If there are too few labourers at hand, prices, i.e. wages, rise, the workers are more prosperous, marriages multiply, more children are born and more live to grow up, until a sufficient number of labourers has been secured. If there are too many on hand, prices fall, want of work, poverty, and starvation, and consequent diseases arise, and the "surplus population" is put out of the way. And Malthus, who carried the foregoing proposition of Smith farther, was also right, in his way, in asserting that there are always more people on hand than can be maintained from the available means of subsistence. Surplus population is engendered rather by the competition of the workers among themselves, which forces each separate worker to labour as much each day as his strength can possibly admit. If a manufacturer can employ ten hands nine hours daily, he can employ nine if each works ten hours, and the tenth goes hungry. And if a manufacturer can force the nine hands to work an extra hour daily for the same wages by threatening to discharge them at a time when the demand for hands is not very great, he discharges the tenth and saves so much wages. This is the process on a small scale, which goes on in a nation on a large one. The productiveness of each hand raised to the highest pitch by the competition of the workers among themselves, the division of labour, the introduction of machinery, the subjugation of the forces of nature, deprive a multitude of workers of bread. These starving workers are then removed from the market, . . . and so it

goes on, always the same old round, or rather, so it would go if other circumstances did not intervene. The introduction of the industrial forces already referred to for increasing production leads, in the course of time, to a reduction of prices of the articles produced and to consequent increased consumption, so that a large part of the displaced workers finally, after long suffering, find work again. If, in addition to this, the conquest of foreign markets constantly and rapidly increases the demand for manufactured goods, as has been the case in England during the past sixty years, the demand for hands increases, and, in proportion to it, the population. Thus, instead of diminishing, the population of the British Empire has increased with extraordinary rapidity, and is still increasing. Yet, in spite of the extension of industry, in spite of the demand for working-men which, in general, has increased, there is, according to the confession of all the official political parties (Tory, Whig, and Radical), permanent surplus, superfluous population; the competition among the workers is constantly greater than the competition to secure workers.

Whence comes this incongruity? It lies in the nature of industrial competition and the commercial crises which arise from them. In the present unregulated production and distribution of the means of subsistence, which is carried on not directly for the sake of supplying needs, but for profit, in the system under which every one works for himself to enrich himself, disturbances inevitably arise at every moment. For example, England supplies a number of countries with most diverse goods. Now, although the manufacturer may know how much of each article is consumed in each country annually, he cannot know how much is on hand at every given moment, much less can he know how much his competitors export thither. He can only draw most uncertain inferences from the perpetual fluctuations in prices, as to the quantities on hand and the needs of the moment. He must trust to luck in exporting his goods. Everything is done blindly, as guess-work, more or less at the mercy of accident. Upon the slightest favourable report, each one exports what he can, and before long such a market is glutted, sales stop, capital remains inactive, prices fall, and English manufacture has no further employment for its hands. In the beginning of the development of manufacture, these checks were limited to single branches and single markets; but the centralising tendency of competition which drives the hands thrown out of one branch into such other branches as are most easily accessible, and transfers the goods which cannot be disposed of in one market to other markets, has gradually brought the single minor crises nearer together and united them into one periodically recurring crisis. Such a crisis usually recurs once in five years after a brief period of activity and general prosperity; the home market, like all foreign ones, is glutted with English goods, which it can only slowly absorb, the industrial movement comes to a standstill in almost every branch, the small manufacturers and merchants who cannot survive a prolonged inactivity of their invested capital fail, the larger ones suspend business during the worst season, close their mills or work short time, perhaps half the day; wages fall by reason of the competition of the unemployed, the diminution of working-time and the lack of profitable sales; want becomes universal among the workers, the small savings, which individuals may have made, are rapidly consumed, the philanthropic institutions are overburdened, the poor-rates are doubled, trebled, and still insufficient, the number of the starving increases,

and the whole multitude of "surplus" population presses in terrific numbers into the foreground. This continues for a time; the "surplus" exist as best they may, or perish; philanthropy and the Poor Law help many of them to a painful prolongation of their existence. Others find scant means of subsistence here and there in such kinds of work as have been least open to competition, are most remote from manufacture. And with how little can a human being keep body and soul together for a time! Gradually the state of things improve; the accumulations of goods are consumed, the general depression among the men of commerce and manufacture prevents a too hasty replenishing of the markets, and at last rising prices and favourable reports from all directions restore activity. Most of the markets are distant ones; demand increases and prices rise constantly while the first exports are arriving; people struggle for the first goods, the first sales enliven trade still more, the prospective ones promise still higher prices; expecting a further rise, merchants begin to buy upon speculation, and so to withdraw from consumption the articles intended for it, just when they are most needed. Speculation forces prices still higher, by inspiring others to purchase, and appropriating new importations at once. All this is reported to England, manufacturers begin to produce with a will, new mills are built, every means is employed to make the most of the favourable moment. Speculation arises here, too, exerting the same influence as upon foreign markets, raising prices, withdrawing goods from consumption, spurring manufacture in both ways to the highest pitch of effort. Then come the daring speculators working with fictitious capital, living upon credit, ruined if they cannot speedily sell; they hurl themselves into this universal, disorderly race for profits, multiply the disorder and haste by their unbridled passion, which drives prices and production to madness. It is a frantic struggle, which carries away even the most experienced and phlegmatic; goods are spun, woven, hammered, as if all mankind were to be newly equipped, as though two thousand million new consumers had been discovered in the moon. All at once the shaky speculators abroad, who must have money, begin to sell, below market price, of course, for their need is urgent; one sale is followed by others, prices fluctuate, speculators throw their goods upon the market in terror, the market is disordered, credit shaken, one house after another stops payments, bankruptcy follows bankruptcy, and the discovery is made that three times more goods are on hand or under way than can be consumed. The news reaches England, where production has been going on at full speed meanwhile, panic seizes all hands, failures abroad cause others in England, the panic crushes a number of firms, all reserves are thrown upon the market here, too, in the moment of anxiety, and the alarm is still further exaggerated. This is the beginning of the crisis, which then takes precisely the same course as its predecessor, and gives place in turn to a season of prosperity. So it goes on perpetually,— prosperity, crisis, prosperity, crisis, and this perennial round in which English industry moves is, as has been before observed, usually completed once in five or six years.

Friedrich Engels, *The Condition of the Working-Class in England in 1844,* (London: George Allen & Unwin, Ltd., 1950), pp. 75-84.

C. Pope Leo XIII Asserts the Right of Private Property

The pontificate of Pope Leo XIII extended from 1878 to 1903. The whole Christian world was by the Industrial Revolution confronted with a situation in which that scheme of social ethics which had been developed in the predominantly agrarian and static social order of the Middle Ages was often unrealistic and sometimes reactionary. Unchanging in its view of the nature of man and of society and uncompromising in its assertion of right principles of Christian conduct, in the face of industrialism, nationalism, and democracy, the Church required a restatement of its position in modern terms. In *Rerum Novarum* (1891) and in other encyclicals Pope Leo XIII applied Christian principles to the social problems that were arising out of the new economic order. He taught that all power must be exercised with regard to the demands of justice, that the dignity of labor, derived as a means of the accomplishment of the supernatural destiny of man, must not be violated; and, in contrast to the Marxian theory of inevitable class struggle, he preached the peaceful ordering of society through the mutual recognition of the moral rights and the spiritual responsibilities of both Capital and Labor.

The encyclicals of Leo helped to effect a reconciliation between the ancient Church and the modern age, and assumed for the Christian Religion a place of leadership in the solution of the social question and the reconstruction of society. The Roman Catholic Church was not alone, of course, in addressing itself to the problem of Christian implications of the new social issues. In one way or another, the questions raised in *Rerum Novarum* have been faced by almost all of the Christian Churches time and again in the nineteenth and twentieth centuries.

1. It is not surprising that the spirit of revolutionary change, which has so long been predominant in the nations of the world, should have passed beyond politics and made its influence felt in the cognate field of practical economy. The elements of a conflict are unmistakable: the growth of industry, and the surprising discoveries of science;

the changed relations of masters and workmen; the enormous fortunes of individuals, and the poverty of the masses; the increased self-reliance and the closer mutual combination of the working population; and, finally, a general moral deterioration. The momentous seriousness of the present state of things just now fills every mind with painful apprehension; wise men discuss it; practical men propose schemes; popular meetings, legislatures, and sovereign princes, all are occupied with it —and there is nothing which has a deeper hold on public attention.

2. Therefore, Venerable Brethren, as on former occasions, when it seemed opportune to refute false teaching, We have addressed you in the interest of the Church and of the common weal, and have issued Letters on Political Power, on Human Liberty, on the Christian Constitution of the State, and on similar subjects, so now We have thought it useful to speak on the CONDITION OF LABOR. It is a matter on which We have touched once or twice already. But in this Letter the responsibility of the Apostolic office urges Us to treat the question expressly and at length, in order that there may be no mistake as to the principles which truth and justice dictate for its settlement. The discussion is not easy, nor is it free from danger. It is not easy to define the relative rights and the mutual duties of the wealthy and of the poor, of capital and of labor. And the danger lies in this, that crafty agitators constantly make use of these disputes to pervert men's judgments and to stir up the people to sedition.

3. But all agree, and there can be no question whatever, that some remedy must be found, and quickly found, for the misery and wretchedness which press so heavily at this moment on the large majority of the very poor. The ancient workmen's Guilds were destroyed in the last century, and no other organization took their place. Public institutions and the laws have repudiated the ancient religion. Hence by degrees it has come to pass that Working-Men have been given over, isolated and defenseless, to the callousness of employers, and the greed of unrestrained competition. The evil has been increased by rapacious Usury, which, although more than once condemned by the Church, is nevertheless, under a different form but with the same guilt, still practiced by avaricious and grasping men. And to this must be added the custom of working by contract, and the concentration of so many branches of trade in the hands of a few individuals, so that a small number of very rich men have been able to lay upon the masses of the poor a yoke little better than slavery itself.

4. To remedy these evils the *Socialists*, working on the poor man's envy of the rich, endeavor to destroy private property, and maintain that individual possessions should become the common property of all, to be administered by the State or by municipal bodies. They hold that, by thus transferring property from private persons to the community, the present evil state of things will be set to rights, because each citizen will then have his equal share of whatever there is to enjoy. But their proposals are so clearly futile for all practical purposes, that if they were carried out the workingman himself would be among the first to suffer. Moreover they are emphatically unjust, because they would rob the lawful possessor, bring the State into a sphere that is not its own, and cause complete confusion in the community.

5. It is surely undeniable that, when a man engages in remunerative labor, the very reason and motive of his work is to obtain property, and to hold it as his own private possession. If one man hires out to another his strength or his

industry, he does this for the purpose of receiving in return what is necessary for food and living; he thereby expressly proposes to acquire a full and real right, not only to the remuneration, but also to the disposal of that remuneration as he pleases. Thus, if he lives sparingly, saves money, and invests his savings, for greater security, in land, the land in such a case is only his wages in another form; and consequently, a working-man's little estate thus purchased should be as completely at his own disposal as the wages he receives for his labor. But it is precisely in this power of disposal that ownership consists, whether the property be land or movable goods. The *Socialists,* therefore, in endeavoring to transfer the possessions of individuals to the community, strike at the interests of every wage-earner, for they deprive him of the liberty of disposing of his wages, and thus of all hope and possibility of increasing his stock and of bettering his condition in life.

6. What is of still greater importance, however, is that the remedy they propose is manifestly against justice. For every man has by nature the right to possess property as his own. This is one of the chief points of distinction between man and the animal creation. For the brute has no power of self-direction, but is governed by two chief instincts, which keep his powers alert, move him to use his strength, and determine him to action without the power of choice. These instincts are self-preservation and the propagation of the species. Both can attain their purpose by means of things which are close at hand; beyond their surroundings the brute creation cannot go, for they are moved to action by sensibility alone, and by the things which sense perceives. But with man it is different indeed. He possesses, on the one hand, the full perfection of animal nature, and therefore

he enjoys, at least as much as the rest of the animal race, the fruition of the things of the body. But animality, however perfect, is far from being the whole of humanity, and is indeed humanity's humble handmaid, made to serve and obey. It is the mind, or the reason, which is the chief thing in us who are human beings; it is this which makes a human being human, and distinguishes him essentially and completely from the brute. And on this account—viz., that man alone among animals possesses reason—it must be within his right to have things not merely for temporary and momentary use, as other living beings have them, but in stable and permanent possession; he must have not only things which perish in the using, but also those which, though used, remain for use in the future.

7. This becomes still more clearly evident if we consider man's nature a little more deeply. For man, comprehending by the power of his reason things innumerable, and joining the future with the present—being, moreover, the master of his own acts—governs himself by the foresight of his counsel, under the eternal law and the power of God, Whose Providence governs all things; wherefore it is in his power to exercise his choice not only on things which regard his present welfare, but also on those which will be for his advantage in time to come. Hence man not only can possess the fruits of the earth, but also the earth itself; for of the products of the earth he can make provision for the future. Man's needs do not die out, but recur; satisfied today, they demand new supplies to-morrow. Nature, therefore, owes to man a storehouse that shall never fail, the daily supply of his daily wants. And this he finds only in the inexhaustible fertility of the earth.

8. Nor must we, at this stage, have

recourse to the State. Man is older than the State; and he holds the right of providing for the life of his body prior to the formation of any State. And to say that God has given the earth to the use and enjoyment of the universal human race is not to deny that there can be private property. For God has granted the earth to mankind in general; not in the sense that all without distinction can deal with it as they please, but rather that no part of it has been assigned to any one in particular, and that the limits of private possession have been left to be fixed by man's own industry and the laws of individual peoples. Moreover the earth, though divided among private owners, ceases not thereby to minister to the needs of all; for there is no one who does not live on what the land brings forth. Those who do not possess the soil, contribute their labor; so that it may be truly said that all human subsistence is derived either from labor on one's own land, or from some laborious industry which is paid for either in the produce of the land itself or in that which is exchanged for what the land brings forth.

9. Here, again, we have another proof that private ownership is according to nature's law. For that which is required for the preservation of life, and for life's well-being, is produced in great abundance by the earth, but not until man has brought it into cultivation and lavished upon it his care and skill. Now, when man thus spends the industry of his mind and the strength of his body in procuring the fruits of nature, by that act he makes his own that portion of nature's field which he cultivates —that portion on which he leaves, as it were, the impress of his own personality; and it cannot but be just that he should possess that portion as his own, and should have a right to keep it without molestation.

10. These arguments are so strong and convincing that it seems surprising that certain obsolete opinions should now be revived in opposition to what is here laid down. We are told that it is right for private persons to have the use of the soil and the fruits of their land, but that it is unjust for any one to possess as owner either the land on which he has built or the estate which he has cultivated. But those who assert this do not perceive that they are robbing man of what his own labor has produced. For the soil which is tilled and cultivated with toil and skill utterly changes its condition; it was wild before, it is now fruitful; it was barren, and now it brings forth in abundance. That which has thus altered and improved it becomes so truly part of itself as to be in great measure indistinguishable and inseparable from it. Is it just that the fruit of a man's sweat and labor should be enjoyed by another? As effects follow their cause, so it is just and right that the results of labor should belong to him who has labored.

11. With reason, therefore, the common opinion of mankind, little affected by the few dissentients who have maintained the opposite view, has found in the study of nature, and in the law of Nature herself, the foundation of the division of property, and has consecrated by the practice of all ages the principle of private ownership, as being pre-eminently in conformity with human nature, and as conducing in the most unmistakable manner to the peace and tranquility of human life. The same principle is confirmed and enforced by the civil laws—laws which, as long as they are just, derive their binding force from the law of nature. The authority of the Divine Law adds its sanction, forbidding us in the gravest terms even to covet that which is another's:—*Thou shalt not covet thy neighbor's wife; nor his house, nor his field, nor his man-servant, nor his maid-*

*servant, nor his ox, nor his ass, nor any-
thing which is his.*

12. The rights here spoken of, belonging to each individual man, are seen
in a much stronger light if they are
considered in relation to man's social
and domestic obligations.

13. In choosing a state of life, it is
indisputable that all are at full liberty
either to follow the counsel of Jesus
Christ as to virginity, or to enter into
the bonds of marriage. No human
law can abolish the natural and primitive right of marriage, or in any way
limit the chief and principal purpose
of marriage, ordained by God's authority from the beginning: *Increase and
multiply.* Thus we have the Family;
the "society" of a man's own household; a society limited indeed in numbers, but a true "society," anterior to
every kind of State or nation, with
rights and duties of its own, totally independent of the commonwealth.

14. That right of property, therefore,
which has been proved to belong naturally to individual persons, must also
belong to a man in his capacity of head
of a family; nay, such a person must
possess this right so much the more
clearly in proportion as his position mul-
tiplies his duties. For it is a most
sacred law of nature that a father must
provide food and all necessaries for those
whom he has begotten; and, similarly,
nature dictates that a man's children,
who carry on, as it were, and continue
his own personality, should be provided
by him with all that is needful to enable them honorably to keep themselves
from want and misery in the uncertain-
ties of this mortal life. Now, in no
other way can a father effect this except by the ownership of profitable
property, which he can transmit to his
children by inheritance. A family, no
less than a State, is, as We have said,
a true society, governed by a power

within itself, that is to say by the
father. Wherefore, provided the limits
be not transgressed which are prescribed
by the very purposes for which it exists, the Family has at least equal rights
with the State in the choice and pursuit of those things which are needful to
its preservation and its just liberty. . . .

20. Let it be laid down, in the first
place, that humanity must remain as it
is. It is impossible to reduce human
society to a level. The *Socialists* may
do their utmost, but all striving against
nature is vain. There naturally exist
among mankind innumerable differences
of the most important kind; people differ in capability, in diligence, in health,
and in strength; and unequal fortune is
a necessary result of inequality in condition. Such inequality is far from being disadvantageous either to individuals
or to the community; social and public life can only go on by the help of
various kinds of capacity and the playing of many parts; and each man, as a
rule, chooses the part which peculiarly
suits his case. As regards bodily labor,
even had man never fallen from *the
state of innocence,* he would not have
been wholly unoccupied; but that which
would then have been his free choice
and his delight, became afterwards compulsory, and the painful expiation of
his sin. *Cursed be the earth in thy
work; in thy labor thou shalt eat of it
all the days of thy life.* In like manner, the other pains and hardships of
life will have no end or cessation on
this earth; for the consequences of sin
are bitter and hard to bear, and they
must be with man as long as life lasts.
To suffer and to endure, therefore, is
the lot of humanity; let men try as they
may, no strength and no artifice will
ever succeed in banishing from human
life the ills and troubles which beset it.
If any there are who pretend differently
—who hold out to a hard-pressed peo-

ple freedom from pain and trouble, undisturbed repose, and constant enjoyment—they cheat the people and impose upon them, and their lying promises will only make the evil worse than before. There is nothing more useful than to look at the world as it really is—and at the same time to look elsewhere for a remedy to its troubles.

21. The great mistake that is made in the matter now under consideration is to possess one's self of the idea that class is naturally hostile to class; that rich and poor are intended by nature to live at war with one another. So irrational and so false is this view, that the exact contrary is the truth. Just as the symmetry of the human body is the result of the disposition of the members of the body, so in a state it is ordained by nature that these two classes should exist in harmony and agreement, and should, as it were, fit into one another, so as to maintain the equilibrium of the body politic. Each requires the other; capital cannot do without labor, nor labor without capital. Mutual agreement results in pleasantness and good order; perpetual conflict necessarily produces confusion and outrage. Now, in preventing such strife as this, and in making it impossible, the efficacy of Christianity is marvelous and manifold. First of all, there is nothing more powerful than Religion (of which the Church is the interpreter and guardian) in drawing rich and poor together, by reminding each class of its duties to the other, and especially of the duties of justice. Thus Religion teaches the laboring man and the workman to carry out honestly and well all equitable agreements freely made; never to injure capital, or to outrage the person of an employer; never to employ violence in representing his own cause, or to engage in riot or disorder; and to have nothing to do with men of evil

principles, who work upon the people with artful promises, and raise foolish hopes which usually end in disaster and in repentance when too late. Religion teaches the rich man and the employer that their work people are not their slaves; that they must respect in every man his dignity as a man and as a Christian; that labor is nothing to be ashamed of, if we listen to right reason and to Christian philosophy, but is an honorable employment, enabling a man to sustain his life in an upright and creditable way; and that it is shameful and inhuman to treat men like chattels to make money by, or to look upon them merely as so much muscle or physical power. Thus, again, Religion teaches that, as among the workman's concerns are Religion herself and things spiritual and mental, the employer is bound to see that he has time for the duties of piety; that he be not exposed to corrupting influences and dangerous occasions; and that he be not led away to neglect his home and family or to squander his wages. Then, again, the employer must never tax his work people beyond their strength, nor employ them in work unsuited to their sex or age. His great and principal obligation is to give to every one that which is just. Doubtless before we can decide whether wages are adequate, many things have to be considered; but rich men and masters should remember this —that to exercise pressure for the sake of gain upon the indigent and the destitute, and to make one's profit out of the need of another is condemned by all laws, human and divine. To defraud any one of wages that are his due is a crime which cries to the avenging anger of Heaven. *Behold, the hire of the laborers . . . which by fraud hath been kept back by you, crieth; and the cry of them hath entered into the ears of the Lord of Sabaoth.* Finally, the rich must religiously refrain from cutting down the workman's earnings, either by force, by fraud, or by usurious dealing; and with the more reason because the poor man is weak and unprotected, and

because his slender means should be sacred in proportion to their scantiness.

22. Were these prospects carefully obeyed and followed, would not strife die out and cease?

From the encyclical letter "Rerum Novarum" addressed to the Roman Catholic world in 1891 by Pope Leo XIII, in Henry George, *The Condition of Labor, an Open Letter to Pope Leo XIII* (New York: United States Book Co., 1891), pp. 121-132.

II. THE MYTH OF PROGRESS

The changing society of the nineteenth century was the product not alone of the economic changes effected by the Industrial Revolution; it was also in large part the adolescent child of the Enlightenment, and, as such, was apt to manifest a brash rejection of ancient wisdom. Calvinistic doctrine, influential in English thinking long after the restoration of King and Church, although tending to encourage political democracy, was apt to dull the edge of religion as an instrument of social reform. Earthly prosperity was regarded as the evidence of grace and the reward of virtue; earthly poverty became the consequence of imprudence or the penalty for vice. Now came Rousseau's doctrine of the essential goodness of man and from this root grew many branches, among them the Socialism of Saint-Simon and the Positivism of Comte. The mists of old beliefs were swept away, and unaided by Divine Providence, man sought to find in the laws governing the social world the key to his own way to perfection. The "Myth" of Redemption was replaced by the Myth of Progress. The ultimate end of the cycle in the twentieth century was not the good society but crashing catastrophe, and so the question remains with us: Can man by his own unaided efforts create a perfect world?

The following selections represent two points of view taken in the debate. Malthus, the pessimist, asserts on scientific grounds the proposition that mankind is doomed, by the operation of natural laws irresistible except by moral means, to limits to self-improvement. Owen, the optimist, expresses the view that by education in right principles the perfect society can be established among men.

A. Thomas Malthus Describes the Principle of Population

Thomas Robert Malthus (1766–1834) was a parish priest of the Church of England who later relinquished parochial duties in favor of a teaching post. Few men have had a more continuous and pervasive influence upon the discussion of a public question than has had Malthus upon the problem of social improvement. Against the optimism of those who held that if reason adduces right principles and education inculcates character in accordance with knowledge, society can be improved, Malthus interposed the view that population increases disproportionately to the supply of food, and that misery and want are natural devices to keep it in check.

The great and unlooked for discoveries that have taken place of late years in natural philosophy; the increasing diffusion of general knowledge from the extension of the art of printing; the ardent and unshackled spirit of inquiry that prevails throughout the lettered, and even unlettered world; the new and extraordinary lights that have been thrown on political subjects, which dazzle, and astonish the understanding; and particularly that tremendous phenomenon in the political horizon, the French revolution, which, like a blazing comet, seems destined either to inspire with fresh life and vigour, or to scorch up and destroy the shrinking inhabitants of the earth, have all concurred to lead many able men into the opinion, that we were touching on a period big with the most important changes,

changes that would in some measure be decisive of the future fate of mankind.

It has been said, that the great question is now at issue, whether man shall henceforth start forwards with accelerated velocity towards illimitable, and hitherto unconceived improvement; or be condemned to a perpetual oscillation between happiness and misery, and after every effort remain still at an immeasurable distance from the wished-for goal.

Yet, anxiously as every friend of mankind must look forwards to the termination of this painful suspense; and, eagerly as the inquiring mind would hail every ray of light that might assist its view into futurity, it is much to be lamented, that the writers on each side of this momentous question still keep far aloof from each other. Their mutual arguments do not meet with a candid examination. The question is not brought to rest on fewer points; and even in theory scarcely seems to be approaching to a decision.

The advocate for the present order of things, is apt to treat the sect of speculative philosophers, either as a set of artful and designing knaves, who preach up ardent benevolence, and draw captivating pictures of a happier state of society, only the better to enable them to destroy the present establishments, and to forward their own deep-laid schemes of ambition: or, as wild and mad-headed enthusiasts, whose silly speculations, and absurd paradoxes, are not worthy the attention of any reasonable man.

The advocate for the perfectibility of man, and of society, retorts on the defender of establishments a more than equal contempt. He brands him as the slave of the most miserable, and narrow prejudices; or, as the defender of the abuses of civil society, only because he profits by them. He paints him either as a character who prostitutes his un-

derstanding to his interest; or as one whose powers of mind are not of a size to grasp any thing great and noble; who cannot see above five yards before him; and who must therefore be utterly unable to take in the views of the enlightened benefactor of mankind.

In this unamicable contest, the cause of truth cannot but suffer. The really good arguments on each side of the question are not allowed to have their proper weight. Each pursues his own theory, little solicitous to correct, or improve it, by an attention to what is advanced by his opponents.

The friend of the present order of things condemns all political speculations in the gross. He will not even condescend to examine the grounds from which the perfectibility of society is inferred. Much less will he give himself the trouble in a fair and candid manner to attempt an exposition of their fallacy.

The speculative philosopher equally offends against the cause of truth. With eyes fixed on a happier state of society, the blessings of which he paints in the most captivating colours, he allows himself to indulge in the most bitter invectives against every present establishment, without applying his talents to consider the best and safest means of removing abuses, and without seeming to be aware of the tremendous obstacles that threaten, even in theory, to oppose the progress of man towards perfection.

It is an acknowledged truth in philosophy, that a just theory will always be confirmed by experiment. Yet so much friction, and so many minute circumstances occur in practice, which it is next to impossible for the most enlarged and penetrating mind to foresee, that on few subjects can any theory be pronounced just, that has not stood the test of experience. But an untried theory cannot fairly be advanced as probable, much less as just, till all the arguments against it, have been maturely weighed, and clearly and consistently refuted.

I have read some of the speculations on the perfectibility of man and of society, with great pleasure. I have been warmed and delighted with the enchanting picture which they hold forth. I ardently wish for such happy improvements. But I see great, and, to my understanding, unconquerable difficulties in the way to them. These difficulties it is my present purpose to state; declaring, at the same time, that so far from exulting in them, as a cause of triumph over the friends of innovation, nothing would give me greater pleasure than to see them completely removed.

The most important argument that I shall adduce is certainly not new. The principles on which it depends have been explained in part by Hume, and more at large by Dr. Adam Smith. It has been advanced and applied to the present subject, though not with its proper weight, or in the most forcible point of view, by Mr. Wallace: and it may probably have been stated by many writers that I have never met with. I should certainly therefore not think of advancing it again, though I mean to place it in a point of view in some degree different from any that I have hitherto seen, if it had ever been fairly and satisfactorily answered.

The cause of this neglect on the part of the advocates for the perfectibility of mankind, is not easily accounted for. I cannot doubt the talents of such men as Godwin and Condorcet. I am unwilling to doubt their candour. To my understanding, and probably to that of most others, the difficulty appears insurmountable. Yet these men of acknowledged ability and penetration, scarcely deign to notice it, and hold on their course in such speculations, with unabated ardour, and undiminished confidence. I have certainly no right to say that they purposely shut their eyes to such arguments. I ought rather to doubt the validity of them, when neglected by such men, however forcibly their truth may strike my own mind. Yet in this respect it must be acknowledged that we are all of us too prone to err. If I saw a glass of wine repeatedly presented to a man, and he took no notice of it, I should be apt to think that he was blind or uncivil. A juster philosophy might teach me rather to think that my eyes deceived me, and that the offer was not really what I conceived it to be.

In entering upon the argument I must premise that I put out of the question, at present, all mere conjectures; that is, all suppositions, the probable realization of which cannot be inferred upon any just philosophical grounds. A writer may tell me that he thinks man will ultimately become an ostrich. I cannot properly contradict him. But before he can expect to bring any reasonable person over to his opinion, he ought to shew, that the necks of mankind have been gradually elongating; that the lips have grown harder, and more prominent; that the legs and feet are daily altering their shape; and that the hair is beginning to change into stubs of feathers. And till the probability of so wonderful a conversion can be shewn, it is surely lost time and lost eloquence to expatiate on the happiness of man in such a state; to describe his powers, both of running and flying; to paint him in a condition where all narrow luxuries would be contemned; where he would be employed only in collecting the necessaries of life; and where, consequently, each man's share of labour would be light, and his portion of leisure ample.

I think I may fairly make two postulata.

First, That food is necessary to the existence of man.

Secondly, That the passion between the sexes is necessary, and will remain nearly in its present state.

These two laws ever since we have had any knowledge of mankind, appear to have been fixed laws of our nature; and, as we have not hitherto seen any alteration in them, we have no right to conclude that they will ever cease to be what they now are, without an immediate act of power in that Being who first arranged the system of the universe; and for the advantage of his creatures, still executes, according to fixed laws, all its various operations.

I do not know that any writer has supposed that on this earth man will ultimately be able to live without food. But Mr. Godwin has conjectured that the passion between the sexes may in time be extinguished. As, however, he calls this part of his work, a deviation into the land of conjecture, I will not dwell longer upon it at present, than to say, that the best arguments for the perfectibility of man, are drawn from a contemplation of the great progress that he has already made from the savage state, and the difficulty of saying where he is to stop. But towards the extinction of the passion between the sexes, no progress whatever has hitherto been made. It appears to exist in as much force at present as it did two thousand, or four thousand years ago. There are individual exceptions now as there always have been. But, as these exceptions do not appear to increase in number, it would surely be a very unphilosophical mode of arguing, to infer merely from the existence of an exception, that the exception would, in time, become the rule, and the rule the exception.

Assuming then, my postulata as granted, I say, that the power of population is indefinitely greater than the power in the earth to produce subsistence for man.

Population, when unchecked, increases in a geometrical ratio. Subsistence increases only in an arithmetical ratio. A slight acquaintance with numbers will shew the immensity of the first power in comparison of the second.

By that law of our nature which makes food necessary to the life of man, the effects of these two unequal powers must be kept equal.

This implies a strong and constantly operating check on population from the difficulty of subsistence. This difficulty must fall some where; and must necessarily be severely felt by a large portion of mankind.

Through the animal and vegetable kingdoms, nature has scattered the seeds of life abroad with the most profuse and liberal hand. She has been comparatively sparing in the room, and the nourishment necessary to rear them. The germs of existence contained in this spot of earth, with ample food, and ample room to expand in, would fill millions of worlds in the course of a few thousand years. Necessity, that imperious all pervading law of nature, restrains them within the prescribed bounds. The race of plants, and the race of animals shrink under this great restrictive law. And the race of man cannot, by any efforts of reason, escape from it. Among plants and animals its effects are waste of seed, sickness, and premature death. Among mankind, misery and vice. The former, misery, is an absolutely necessary consequence of it. Vice is a highly probable consequence, and we therefore see it abundantly prevail; but it ought not, perhaps, to be called an absolutely necessary consequence. The ordeal of virtue is to resist all temptation to evil.

This natural inequality of the two powers of population, and of production in the earth, and that great law of our nature which must constantly keep their effects equal, form the great difficulty that to me appears insurmountable in the way to the perfectibility of society. All other arguments are of slight and subordinate consideration in comparison of this. I see no way by which man can escape from the weight of this law which pervades all animated nature. No fancied equality, no agrarian regulations in their utmost extent, could remove the pressure of it even for a single century. And it appears, therefore, to be decisive against the possible existence of a society, all the members of which, should live in ease, happiness, and comparative leisure; and feel no anxiety about providing the means of subsistence for themselves and families.

Consequently, if the premises are just, the argument is conclusive against the perfectibility of the mass of mankind.

Thomas Robert Malthus, *First Essay on Population,* 1798, reprinted for the Royal Economic Society from the 1798 ed. (London: Macmillan & Co., Ltd., 1926), pp. 1-17.

B. *Robert Owen Prescribes Education for the New World*

Robert Owen (1771–1858), a significant figure in the development of the new social order in England, is typical of what is sometimes called the Utopian school of Socialism because he believed in the essential goodness of man, regarded religion as a universal force, rather than as a delusion foisted by the exploiters on the exploited, and looked to education and improvement of the social environment as means to reform. Owen was a philanthropist. He rejected, on the one hand, competition as a principle of social order, and, on the other hand, the theory of history as the product of materialistic forces, while struggle or war between classes as the inevitable outcome of the march of progress had no place in his theories and methods of reform.

As proprietor of the mills at New Lanark, Scotland, Owen created a model factory community, introduced labor reforms, and established a school for the cultivation of a spirit of universal benevolence. He believed that environment determined character, that social ills were due to social wrongs, and that education provided the means by which a controlled environment would pour the characters of men in a mold suitable for "the New Society."

In order to create a community based on good will he bought a 30,000 acre estate in the New World, and at New Harmony, Indiana, established his pioneer co-operative community. New Harmony was soon rent with dissension and three years after its establishment, Owen withdrew with a loss of nearly his entire fortune. Upon his return to England, Owen was instrumental in establishing Co-operative Societies, set up an exchange system whereby workmen sold to one another the products of their own labors, and became actively associated with the organization of workmen into labor unions.

Whatever the failures and futilities of his life, Robert Owen has had a potent influence on English and American social attitudes and thought. Here, in contrast to Malthus, is his prescription for the improvement of the lot of man.

Those who have duly reflected on the nature and extent of the mental movements of the world for the last half century, must be conscious that great changes are in progress; that man is about to advance another important step towards that degree of intelligence which his natural powers seem capable of attaining. Observe the transactions of the passing hours; see the whole mass of mind in full motion; behold it momentarily increasing in vigour, and preparing ere long to burst its confinement. But what is to be the nature of this change? A due attention to the facts around us, and to those transmitted by the invention of printing from former ages, will afford a satisfactory reply.

From the earliest ages it has been the practice of the world, to act on the supposition that each individual man forms his own character, and that therefore he is accountable for all his sentiments and habits, and consequently merits reward for some, and punishment for others. Every system which has been established among men has been founded on these erroneous principles. When, however, they shall be brought to the test of fair examination, they will be found not only unsupported, but in direct opposition to all experience, and to the evidence of our senses. This is not a slight mistake which involves only trivial consequences; it is a fundamental error of the highest possible magnitude; it enters into all our proceedings regarding man from his infancy, and will be found to be the true and sole origin of evil. It generates and perpetuates ignorance, hatred, and revenge, where, without such error, only intelligence, confidence, and kindness would exist. It has hitherto been the Evil Genius of the world. It severs man from man throughout the various regions of the earth; and makes enemies of those who, but for this gross error, would have enjoyed each other's kind offices and sincere friendship. It is, in short, an error which carries misery in all its consequences.

This error cannot much longer exist; for every day will make it more and more evident THAT THE CHARACTER OF MAN IS, WITHOUT A SINGLE EXCEPTION, ALWAYS FORMED FOR HIM; THAT IT MAY BE, AND IS CHIEFLY, CREATED BY HIS PREDECESSORS; THAT THEY GIVE HIM, OR MAY GIVE HIM, HIS IDEAS AND HABITS, WHICH ARE THE POWERS THAT GOVERN AND DIRECT HIS CONDUCT. MAN, THEREFORE, NEVER DID, NOR IS IT POSSIBLE HE EVER CAN, FORM HIS OWN CHARACTER. . . .

Had not mankind been misinstructed from infancy on this subject, making it necessary that they should unlearn what they have been taught, the simple statement of this truth would render it instantaneously obvious to every rational mind. Men would know that their predecessors might have given them the habits of ferocious cannibalism, or of the highest known benevolence and intelligence: and by the acquirement of this knowledge they would soon learn that, as parents, preceptors, and legislators united, they possess the means of training the rising generations to either of those extremes; that they may with the greatest certainty make them the conscientious worshippers of Juggernaut, or of the most pure spirit possessing the essence of every excellence which the human imagination can conceive; that they may train the young to become effeminate, deceitful, ignorantly selfish, intemperate, revengeful, murderous,—of course ignorant, irrational, and miserable; or to be manly, just, generous, temperate, active, kind, and benevolent, —that is, intelligent, rational, and happy. The knowledge of these principles having been derived from facts which perpetually exist, they defy ingenuity itself to confute them; nay, the most severe scrutiny will make it evident that they are utterly unassailable.

Is it then wisdom to think and to act in opposition to the facts which hourly exhibit themselves around us, and in direct contradiction to the evidence of our senses? Inquire of the most learned and wise of the present day, ask them to speak with sincerity, and they will tell you that they have long known the principles on which society has been founded to be false. Hitherto, however, the tide of public opinion in all countries has been directed by a combination of prejudice, bigotry, and fanaticism, derived from the wildest imaginations of ignorance; and the most enlightened men have not dared to expose those errors which to them were offensive, prominent, and glaring.

Happily for man, this reign of ignorance rapidly approaches to dissolution; its terrors are already on the wing, and soon they will be compelled to take their flight, never more to return. For now the knowledge of the existing errors is not only possessed by the learned and reflecting, but it is spreading far and wide throughout society; and ere long it will be fully comprehended even by the most ignorant.

Attempts may indeed be made by individuals, who through ignorance mistake their real interests, to retard the progress of this knowledge; but as it will prove itself to be in unison with the evidence of our senses, and therefore true beyond the possibility of disproof, it cannot be impeded, and in its course will overwhelm all opposition.

These principles, however, are not more true in theory than beneficial in practice whenever they are properly applied. Why, then, should all their substantial advantages be longer withheld from the mass of mankind? Can it, by possibility, be a crime to pursue the only practical means which a rational being can adopt to diminish the misery of man, and increase his happiness?

These questions, of the deepest interest to society, are now brought to the fair test of public experiment. It remains to be proved, whether the character of man shall continue to be formed under the guidance of the most inconsistent notions, the errors of which for centuries past have been manifest to every reflecting rational mind; or whether it shall be moulded under the direction of uniformly consistent principles, derived from the unvarying facts of the creation; principles, the truth of which no sane man will now attempt to deny.

Robert Owen, *A New View of Society,* a facsimile reproduction of the 3rd ed. printed in London in 1817 (Glencoe, Ill.: The Free Press, n.d.), pp. 90-95.

III. THE NEW STATE

The Industrial Revolution, creating as it did new forms of wealth and correspondingly new social classes, shifted the political balance in the state. The earlier phase of this shift in power was reflected in the English Constitution by the Parliamentary Reform Act of 1832, whereby the virtual monopoly of power in the legislature—which controlled the executive—hitherto enjoyed by landed wealth, was gradually destroyed, and the new middle classes, together with the better-off artisans, were permitted to share in the control of the state. Bitterly disappointed at this limited extension of the franchise, the working classes, whose agitation had helped to accomplish the passage of the Act of 1832, continued to press for more radical reform. The Chartist movement went through its several phases. A combination of repression, years of prosperity, and the distraction of other movements, drained off enthusiasm and support for further extension of the franchise.

But the urbanization of culture which accompanied the growth of the factory system had gradually raised the material standards of living of the working classes; increased both the need and the opportunity for education; and made the "lower orders" of society more conscious of their standard of living, more articulate in the definition of their rights, and more sophisticated in the choice of means to achieve them than ever before in history. The working-class leaders looked to legislation for relief and to political reform for legislation. By the mid-sixties the demand for further extension of the representative base of Parliament revived and, as events proved, could no longer be ignored.

With the exception of a few Philosophical Radicals, such as J. S. Mill, responsible men in both the Conservative and Liberal parties repudiated any intention of creating a "democratic" England. It became increasingly obvious, however, that once the aristocratic principle was repudiated no logical stopping place for the extension of political power could be found; in the end the parties vied with each other for the partisan advantage of being the first to accomplish the inevitable. The Liberal Reform Bill of 1866 proposed a moderate extension of the franchise, but it was defeated by a combination of the anti-democratic Liberals with the Conservative opposition. The Conservatives, thereby brought into office, passed in 1867 a bill far more radical in its effects than the Liberal bill would have been. By the Reform Act of 1867, which enfranchised the "rate-paying householder," the urban working classes were given the right to vote for members of the House of Commons. The balance of political power was shifted to the working man and the democratic era was ushered in.

The question of political democracy, the prospects of a state based on a popular franchise rather than a restricted one, was one of the great questions of the nineteenth century. Was the course that was chosen the wisest one? How far and to what extent have the predictions, the hopes and the fears, of both the proponents and opponents of the democratic state been realized in fact? For the greatest good of the state, should votes be weighed as well as counted?

A. Robert Lowe Warns Against Democracy

Robert Lowe (1811–1892), born the son of an Anglican clergyman, was educated at Winchester School and Oxford University, became a lawyer, emigrated to Australia, and while there served in the Legislative Council of New South Wales. Returning to England, he became an editorial writer for *The Times* and then, entering English political life, was elected to the House of Commons in 1852. He held ministerial rank under Palmerston and played a considerable role in educational reform. He

was not included in the Russell Ministry of 1865, and led the fight against the Liberal Reform Bill of 1866. He was likewise a prominent opponent of the Conservative Reform Bill of 1867. It is from his speech delivered in the course of the debate on this bill that the passages which follow are taken. Later Lowe held the important post of Chancellor of the Exchequer in the Gladstone Cabinet of 1868, going to the Home Office in 1873. In 1880 he retired to the House of Lords as Viscount Sherbrooke.

Lowe is best remembered today for his frank and vitriolic opposition to the progress of democracy. He was a man of great integrity. The views which he expresses on the extension of the franchise were widely shared among the leading political and literary figures of his day. They must not be supposed to represent mere reactionism or blind obstruction to progress. "I have been a Liberal all my life," said Lowe in a debate on a similar issue in 1865, "I was a Liberal at a time and in places where it was not so easy to make professions of Liberalism as in the present day; I suffered for my Liberal principles but I did so gladly because I had confidence in them. . . . But . . . because I am a Liberal, and know that by pure and clear intelligence alone can the cause of true progress be promoted, I regard as one of the greatest dangers with which the country can be threatened a proposal to subvert the existing order of things, and to transfer power from the hands of property and intelligence, and to place it in the hands of men whose whole life is necessarily occupied in daily struggles for existence." [Parliamentary Debates, Commons, third series, Vol. 178, cols. 1439-1440.]

. . . I should have thought that, before we handed our Constitution over, as I have said, to persons who are more numerous probably than the present constituency, and before we effected a complete and absolute transfer of power, we ought to have had some little inquiry. The hon. and learned Member for Edinburgh (Mr. Moncreiff) has told us that the notion, which every statesman in England has held up to the present time, that property and intelligence ought to be represented in this House as well as numbers, is one of those platitudes that has long since been buried. I only wish that all other platitudes were buried with it. As it is, things are daily said which make me hardly able to believe my ears. Scotland, it is said, is a highly-favoured country; and England is an ill-used country; because, in Scotland, according to the declaration made the other night, a greater amount of poverty and ignorance will be admitted into the constituencies than in England. The hon. and learned Member for Sheffield (Mr. Roebuck) is congratulated beyond measure. He is happy above all the children of men, because he is to have 28,000 electors let loose upon him in addition to and below his present constituency. On the other hand, the hon. Member for Birmingham (Mr. Bright) has been treated with the most cruel ingratitude by the House, because it has withheld from his embraces 36,000 men of Birmingham who are burning to record their votes for somebody. People are happy according to the proportion of poverty and ignorance they are allowed to represent, and are miserable in proportion to the prevalence in their constituencies of those elements which used to be sovereign in this country— property and intelligence. I should like to bury that platitude with the rest. In like manner words have faded from our recollection. Nobody could get up last year without making use of the strong vernacular expression—"swamping." Who talks of "swamping" now? The only idea now is to see how many persons we can enfranchise, to take care that they shall be as poor and ignorant as possible, to adopt, indeed, a principle like household suffrage—occupation of a house being, no doubt, in the abstract, some proof of respectability—but then

to strain that principle until you do away with the respectability by bringing in the dregs of the house-occupying class to control the respectable householders. That seems to be the idea on which we are acting. Lamenting this as I do, I must beg the House to consider for a few moments what will follow. . . .

You are going to transfer power mainly to the non-electors, who are more numerous than the present constituencies. Now, what do you know of the non-electors of this country? What are their politics? What are their views? What will be their influence for good or for evil upon our institutions? Last year my right hon. Friend, the Member for South Lancashire, wished to enfranchise skilled labour, the *élite* of the working class. That has dropped out of our discussions. Nobody talks of skilled labour. The object of this Bill, so far as I understand it, or except as it may be modified in some degree by the lodger franchise, is to enfranchise unskilled labour. We know what the politics of skilled labour are. I confess they are not much to my taste. Trade unions, mechanics' institutes, and the gregarious life which working men lead, have helped to form a school of opinion which I will not examine, because we have got past it. The question now is not what is the opinion of the *élite* of the working classes, but what is the opinion of the unskilled labour class. For instance, in the borough I represent you will, I rather think, give us some Wiltshire labourers with 8s. a week wages. Will any Gentleman favour me with a *précis* of the politics of these men? (*Laughter.*) But it is really no joke. You are handing over to new and untried persons the institutions of this country, and everything which is dear to us as Englishmen, and it is well that we should know something about them. The fact is, that the great mass of those you are going to enfranchise are people who have no politics at all. Their politics are yet to be learnt. It has not been worth anybody's while to teach them or to agitate them because they have had no vote, and they are unacquainted with even the rudiments of political instruction. You are about to take away the management of affairs from the upper and middle classes, who have managed affairs since the Reform Bill, as I think with some little success, and you are about to place it in the hands of people of whose politics you know nothing, for the best of all possible reasons—because they do not know what their politics are themselves. But they will not be always without politics; and what will they be? What must be the politics of people who are struggling hard to keep themselves off the parish —whose every day is taken up with hard, unskilled labour, and who are always on the verge of pauperism? With every disposition to speak favourably of them, their politics must take one form —socialism. What other aspect can politics bear in their eyes? What can be their view of a state of society in which all the good things are given to others, and all the evil things are given to them? They know nothing of the laws that regulate the distribution of wealth. They attribute to society the inequalities of society. Unless they are absolute angels, they will suppose that they are being treated with great harshness and great cruelty. What man will speak acceptably to them except the man who promises somehow or other to re-distribute the good things of this world more equally, so that the poor will get more, and the rich and powerful will get less? Is it possible to suppose that any other language will be acceptable to them? It would be idle to deceive ourselves. Once give them power, and the use they will make of it will be to try to remedy evils which no doubt

grind them very sorely, and which, I suppose, we should all like to remedy if we could, but which most of us believe to be beyond the reach of legislation. Do you suppose that the working classes will not take any steps in this direction? We are going to make a revolution, and on the Continent when a revolution is made (a thing of which we have no experience from 1688 till to-day) the first step is always to take the duties off spirituous liquors. That is the first flight which young freedom has always taken. "Why," it will be said, "why should your beer, your sugar, your tea, and spirits be taxed when there are so many rich people who can pay these taxes perfectly well." And will not all this come with the force of absolute conviction to the minds of these people? "Why," it will be said, "should the comforts and luxuries of the poor man be taxed? Let the duties be taken off these things and put upon the rich. Where is the difficulty of imposing a graduated income tax? Is it not monstrous that while you are paying £20,000,000 a year upon sugar, tea, spirits, tobacco, and so forth, here is a great nobleman with a house full of the most valuable pictures, plate, jewels, statuary—all sorts of what the French call 'dead values'—upon which he pays no tax at all? Put a tax upon these things and relieve yourselves from the heavy taxes which you bear." Do not you see that the first step after the enfranchisement of the unskilled labour class must necessarily be to turn indirect taxation into direct taxation, so assessed as to fall mainly upon the upper classes? Are you so "soft" as to suppose that, when you have stripped yourselves of political power and transferred it to these people—and they have twenty times the motive to use it that you have, for their necessity is sorer and the stake to them greater—they will consider political questions fairly, and will not consider first of all how they can benefit themselves? Of course they will. . . .

There is a feeling among hon. Gentlemen opposite that something will be gained for party by their measure. They think that the middle classes have been uniformly hostile to them, and that something may be gained if they get to a lower class—that one will counteract the other. I have faith in no such speculation. We have inaugurated a new era in English politics this Session, and depend upon it the new fashion will henceforth be the rule and not the exception. This Session we have not had what we before possessed—a party of attack and a party of resistance. We have instead two parties of competition, who, like Cleon and the Sausage-seller of Aristophanes, are both bidding for the support of Demos. Do not suppose this is the mere product of the Reform Bill, and that when you get a new Parliament this unwelcome symptom will disappear. This will be a permanent condition of things. It is the condition of things in America. There the old condition of things has vanished. You have now no Conservative party there—the very tradition of such a thing is forgotten. You have two parties candidates for popular

favour, seeking to outbid each other. Each of them is willing to do anything in the world to secure popular favour—the only difficulty is to find out what the people want; and the difference between them is that one calculates well and the other makes mistakes and does not succeed in doing what the people desire. As to not immediately setting themselves to do what the people desire, because what they desire is wrong or foolish, that never enters their heads. As to the working man, for instance—no sooner does he show a disposition to go very near socialism, than a party and press immediately start up to advocate and develop his views. This is what we are coming to. . . .

Have you so totally unlearnt the simplest lessons of experience as to believe that it is by diving into the depths of ignorance and poverty you can find wisdom to manage the delicate and weighty affairs of this great Empire? . . . I took upon myself two years ago—only two years—to make a prophecy. I said that if we embarked on the course of democracy we should either ruin our party or our country. Sir, I was wrong, as prophets very often are. It is not a question of alternatives; we are going to ruin both.

Parliamentary Debates, Commons, third series, Vol. 187, cols. 786–799.

B. A Minister Defends Extension of the Franchise

Sir Austen Henry Layard (1817–1894) was Under-Secretary of State for Foreign Affairs in the Russell Cabinet at the time that the Reform Bill of 1866 was under consideration. Layard's interests and accomplishments ranged from law to archaeology and from domestic politics to diplomacy. Educated on the Continent, he later worked in a London law office, traveled in Turkey and Persia, and became a political agent of the British ambassador to Turkey, by whom he was commissioned to undertake excavations in Assyria. His

archaeological activities were later sponsored by the British Museum. In 1852 he entered Parliament as member for Aylesbury, in 1860 shifting his constituency to Southwark. Later on in his career he was knighted and became British ambassador to the Sublime Porte (Turkey).

In the speech which follows, Layard takes up point by point the major arguments which had been advanced against the extension of the franchise to the working classes. In considering this issue as an historical question, it always must be borne in mind that it is the climate of opinion of the nineteenth century which is relevant to the issue—not twentieth century ideas of democracy.

I will now endeavour to meet the principal arguments and objections which, as I understand, have been urged against the Bill of the Government. . . .

Now, as regards the first objection, that the working classes are already sufficiently represented, and that by admitting a larger number of them to the franchise we should be running the risk of swamping and overpowering other classes, which have an equal right to representation. . . .

Until we have men in this House who are of the working classes themselves, who are in constant association with them, who have that intimate knowledge of their habits of thought, their necessities, their real or imagined grievances, and their views, and who can consequently state them to the House of Commons in a manner which will be satisfactory to the artizans themselves, I contend that the working classes are not properly represented in Parliament. . . .

The rest of my noble Friend the Member for Haddingtonshire seems to be disturbed by nightmares of Mr. Odger, and he is haunted by visions of Mr. Potter and the Trades Unions. But I confess that I should feel no alarm at seeing those Gentlemen amongst us. On the contrary I think their presence here would be of great advantage to us and to those whom they represent. If the grievances of which they complain on behalf of the working classes are just grievances, they would be listened to; and if redress were possible, I cannot doubt but that the justice of the House of Commons would seek to give that redress. If those grievances were ill founded, or were attributable to causes over which legislation had no control, the truth would appear after impartial and open discus-

sion, and I have sufficient confidence in the good sense and fairness of the working classes to feel convinced that they would yield to argument and admit themselves wrong. We have nothing to fear from fair public debate of these delicate and important social questions, which affect and agitate the working classes; but we have everything to fear from the effect which a sense of injustice produces upon those classes when they think that they have not a fair hearing, and when they believe that the House of Commons refuses to listen to and to remedy what they consider, whether erroneously or not is beside the question, their just grievances.

But allowing that the reduction of the franchise as proposed by the Government would admit a far larger number than 25 per cent of the working classes to the register, there is no chance whatever that such men as I have mentioned would be elected to Parliament in any sufficient numbers to affect the balance of classes in this House in the slightest imaginable degree. I will go further and say, that if we were to adopt the most extreme democratic views, and have universal suffrage, there are no statistics to show that the working classes, as opposed to the agricultural and other classes, would obtain such a majority in the constituencies of the country as seriously to affect the character and composition of the House of Commons, and through it the institutions of the country. The alarm felt lest the workingmen should obtain such an ascendancy in the constituencies as to be able to return a House composed of a majority of their own body, is surely a mere delusion. It is founded upon an assumption which is quite baseless, viz. that but one set of opinions upon political and social questions exists amongst the working classes, and that they are at all times prepared to act and vote together. Now my experience of the working classes proves to me the contrary. I believe that the political opinions of those who compose them differ as much as the political opinions of any other classes in this country. . . .

But then we are told that the working classes might take advantage of the disunion amongst other classes or amongst political parties, and give their support to one side or the other, first exacting promises and conditions favourable to their designs, and that by thus commanding the majority they could secure the objects they had in view. It appears to me that this argument also has been fully answered by the Member for Westminster (Mr. Mill) when he pointed out that in the face of great public interests a minority never could be a majority, and that it was the most improbable of all things that if the working classes, in an absolute minority, were to put forward views and claims which were dangerous to the real interests of the other classes, they would be able to carry them in Parliament. The truth of this has been proved over and over again. . . .

Let me now turn to the second objection—that the working classes are from various causes not fitted for the exercise of the franchise. I have no desire to recur again to the words of the right hon. Member for Calne (Mr. Lowe), which have been the subject of such frequent comment in this House and elsewhere, and have made so deep an impression on the working classes throughout the country. The right hon. Gentleman has endeavoured to explain away the meaning of those words; I leave it to the country to decide with what success. But I wish to show that, supposing those words bore the interpretation placed upon them by the Chancellor of the Exchequer and by the working classes, they would only express an opinion upon the condition of

those classes, and upon their unfitness to be admitted to political rights, which has more than once been expressed by the right hon. Gentleman. . . .

There is an argument which has been advanced more than once in this debate against the working classes, grounded upon the charge against them of "impulsiveness," which ought not, I think, to be left unnoticed or unanswered. I mean the argument, or rather the assertion, that if they had any preponderating influence in this House, and in the government of the country, they would soon plunge this country into war. . . . Let us test the validity of this argument by the facts. Let us look at the annals of the last Parliament, and see whether motions in this House and opinions outside of this House in favour of war have been supported by the working classes or by hon. Gentlemen opposite and those whom they represent. . . .

Whilst the civil war was raging in America, what classes in this country called upon the Government to take steps which would have inevitably involved us in war with the United States? Was it the working classes? . . . It is a fact not to be forgotten —and it is one, I think, which furnishes a complete answer to the charge made against the working classes of their readiness to drive the Government into war—that during all the suffering entailed upon a great body of the working men of this country by the suspension of their labour in consequence of the cotton famine, not a single petition was presented to this House by them asking for any interference in the affairs of the United States; and that, with the sole exception of Liverpool, every constituency in this kingdom in which the working classes have any influence, most warmly and cordially supported the Government in their determination to maintain strict neutrality during the civil war in America.

Having now disposed, so far as I am able, of objections to the lowering of the franchise founded upon the impulsiveness of the working classes, let me say a few words on the charge of venality brought against them. This accusation has been urged by several Members of the House during the debate, but by none with greater force and eloquence than my right hon. Friend the Member for Hertfordshire (Sir E. Bulwer-Lytton) in his great speech of the other evening. He described, in his telling manner, the contest for the vote of the working man between Smith with the £5 note and Brown with the rights of man, in which Smith, of course, prevailed. . . .

Sir, I say that until this House is prepared, until society itself is prepared, to condemn and punish him who corrupts, it has no right to condemn and punish him who is corrupted. Nor have we any right to exclude from the franchise a large portion of our fellow-countrymen, whose honesty as a class I will venture to declare will bear comparison with that of any other class, because we can show that some of them have been corrupted.

I now come to the next objection, viz. that the working classes do not pay direct taxes, and have not sufficient stake in the country to entitle them to a larger share in its government. The best answer has already been given to that objection by the Chancellor of the Exchequer, when he showed that the aggregate incomes of the working classes amount to almost as much as the aggregate incomes of all other classes of the community; that is to say, that it is nearly half the actual income of the country. . . .

I may further point out this remarkable fact—one most deserving of attention, and in my opinion reflecting the highest credit upon the working men—that theirs is the only class which, as a class, provides for the poor, the needy, the sick, and the suffering, by an organised and regular saving from individual incomes—by the daily putting by of something which leads to an actual privation and sacrifice. . . . We impose no such self-denial upon ourselves. I say, Sir, that with all that other classes may give in charity—and no one will deny the charity of our middle and upper classes—none make so great a daily uninterrupted sacrifice. . . .

Have the working classes then no stake in the country, as it has been asserted? Would their property, large as I have shown it to be, be less affected, less liable to loss, than that enjoyed by any other portion of the community, in the event of foreign war or domestic commotion? They know as well as we do how sensitive credit is, how the funds rise and fall, how misgovernment, how any interruption to the public peace can lower the value of all property. I will go further, and maintain that they have even a greater stake in the country than other classes have, and would feel more acutely than any other class any derangement in the public credit or any event which might check the prosperity of the nation. To us a decrease in the value of our property or of our incomes means a luxury the less; with them it means a necessity the less: with us reduced rent means food and clothing less luxurious, less costly; with them reduced wages or no wages at all means too often no food and no clothing at all. And will any one say in the face of these facts, that the working classes have no interest in the well-being, prosperity, and peace of the country?

I will now come to another argument against the Bill to which I have alluded, viz. that by lowering the franchise and increasing the size of and lowering constituencies, you render it impossible for any but rich men and demagogues to enter the House of Commons. . . .

For my part, Sir, I believe the time will come when all the legitimate expenses of elections will be met by a county and borough rate, and when all expenses not absolutely necessary and legitimate will be prohibited by laws which we shall be prepared to enforce, and when those who incur illegal expenses will be duly punished. Until the corruption of voters is not only a punishable offence, but is considered to be disgraceful by this House and by society, and until this House and society unmistakably mark their sense of the conduct of those who have engaged in such practices, corruption and bribery will never be put an end to. You have no right to throw it in the teeth of the working men that they are unfit to exercise the franchise because they are corrupt, whilst you are their corruptors. . . .

But now let me turn to the second part of the objection, that besides wealthy men only demagogues, who would pander to the passions and prejudices of the mob, would be returned to this House. This again is an assertion which can be tested by facts, and I venture to say that facts are entirely opposed to it. In the first place no constituency in which the working classes at this time have a decided influence at elections return a "demagogue," or any Member who can be considered as bearing any resemblance to that character; nor, as far as I am aware, has any "demagogue" offered himself for election to any such constituency. That was not so thirty or forty years ago, when men who would certainly be now thought demagogues of the most violent character were returned to this House. In truth, as you trust the working classes, as you extend to them their just rights, men of this kind have less influence over them, and are less likely to

become sufficiently important to command the support of any number of working men. . . .

And all this dread of democracy— all these predictions of terrible results to the Constitution—are founded upon the supposition that a certain number of the working classes must be admitted by the Government Bill to the franchise. Have you, then, so much fear of the working classes—do you think that their admission to a share in the Government of the country would be productive of such vast evils?

You now declare that you do not doubt their individual fitness, if character and conduct are to be the tests of fitness, to exercise the franchise. You now repudiate the description of their habits and their vices which you cheered not long ago. You go further; you now praise them, and declare that you have unbounded faith in them. I do not doubt the generous sympathy felt by the right hon. Baronet the Member for Hertfordshire (Sir E. Bulwer-Lytton) for the working man; and few who heard his speech will forget the noble words in which he described the aspirations of the working man as "the eternal link between the aims of educated labour and the dreams of philosophy and genius." But it is of little use to talk of sympathy for the working classes, and to admit their fitness for the enjoyment of the franchise, whilst at the same time you refuse to put any trust in them, and to give the franchise to them. Your opinion of our duty to the working man somewhat resembles the view which the Scotch pedagogue took of our duty towards our neighbour, which his pupil had described to be, "to fear him, to love him, and to trust him." "You may fear him and love him as much as you like," said he, "but you must not trust him." As long as the working man is just what you wish him to be, you will say a good word in his favour; but he must be the model working man after your own notion. He must have all the virtues of his own class and of all other classes put together. If he pays his rent punctually for twenty years, brings up respectably a large family of children, has never been seen at the beerhouse, and is unknown to the relieving officer, he shall receive a prize of 10s., presented to him by a great peer, or by an illustrious man of letters. He will be allowed to read newspapers, to study history, and to attend lectures at the institute. All this he may do, and a great deal more; but if he attempts to apply the principles that he has learned —if he attempts to put into practice the lessons of political economy which he has been taught—if he begins to think that he is entitled to make the most of the sweat of his brow and the labour of his hand—if it dawns upon him that he has as much right to combine with

his fellow-men to obtain a fair price for his work as the owners of capital have a right to combine against him for the regulation of his wages—then, indeed, the benevolent admirers of the working classes, and the dispensers of so many good things to him, lift up their hands in amazement, stand aghast at his audacity and his ingratitude, and behold the flood of democracy about to sweep over the land, and to wash away, even to the very last vestiges, the glorious institutions of this country. . . .

I appeal to the justice, not to the liberality, of the House of Commons. If you will only do justice to the working classes, if you will only place confidence in them, depend upon it that they will not show themselves unworthy of that confidence, but that they will give you even greater proofs than they have hitherto given of the love they bear to the Throne, the institutions, and the greatness of their country.

Parliamentary Debates, Commons, third series, Vol. 182, cols. 1434-1459.

C. Sir Henry Maine Evaluates the New Order

Sir Henry James Sumner Maine (1822–1888) is one of the great nineteenth-century writers on the history and philosophy of political institutions. Regius Professor of Civil Law at Cambridge University, he later held posts of increasing honor and responsibility in both the political and the academic world. His most notable and still influential book on *Ancient Law* was published in 1861. Among his other books are *Village Communities in East and West,* 1871; *Early History of Institutions,* 1875; *Early Law and Custom,* 1883; and the book from which the following passage is taken, *Popular Government,* 1885. Limitations of space have required the deletion of extensive passages in which Maine supports and illustrates his argument by numerous examples and copious allusions drawn from his rich store of historical data. Produced in the intellectual climate of the 'eighties, the argument of *Popular*

Government has distinct "Darwinian" overtones, just as earlier writers on social science were apt to sound a Malthusian note.

The real fear of democracy that lay at the root of the opposition of such men as Maine to universal suffrage was, however, a fear of the tyranny of the majority. Such an extension of political power to the mass of the people would lead, so they believed, to a repression of individual rights and become a barrier to true progress. It was in the constitutional safeguards against precipitate popular action that Maine found strength in the American Constitution. "On the whole," he wrote, "there is only one country in which the question of the safest and most workable form of democratic government has been adequately discussed, and the results of discussion tested by experiment. This is the United States of America. American experience has, I think, shown that, by wise Constitutional provisions thoroughly thought out beforehand, Democracy may be made tolerable. The public powers are carefully defined; the mode in which they are to be exercised is fixed; and the amplest securities are taken that none of the more important Constitutional arrangements shall be altered without every guarantee of caution and every opportunity for deliberation."

Political liberty, said Hobbes, is political power. When a man burns to be free, he is not longing for the "desolate freedom of the wild ass"; what he wants is a share of political government. But, in wide democracies, political power is minced into morsels, and each man's portion of it is almost infinitesimally small. One of the first results of this political comminution . . . is that two of the historical watchwords of Democracy exclude one another, and that, where there is political liberty, there can be no Equality.

"The man who can sweep the greatest number of fragments of political power into one heap will govern the rest. The strongest man in one form or another will always rule. If the government is a military one, the qualities which make a man a great soldier will make him a ruler. If the government is a monarchy, the qualities which kings value in counsellors, in administrators, in generals, will give power. In a pure democracy, the ruling men will be the Wire-pullers and their friends; but they will be no more on an equality with the people than soldiers or Ministers of State are on an equality with the subjects of a Monarchy. . . . In some ages, a powerful character, in others cunning, in others power of transacting business, in others eloquence, in others a good hold upon commonplaces and a facility in applying them to practical purposes, will enable a man to climb on his neighbours' shoulders and direct them this way or that; but under all circumstances the rank and file are directed by leaders of one kind or another who get the command of their collective force."

There is no doubt that, in popular governments resting on a wide suffrage, either without an army or having little reason to fear it, the leader, whether or not he be cunning, or eloquent, or well provided with commonplaces, will be the Wire-puller. The process of cutting up political power into petty fragments has in him its most remarkable product. The morsels of power are so small that men, if left to themselves, would not care to employ them. . . .

The Wire-puller is not intelligible unless we take into account one of the strongest forces acting on human nature —Party feeling. Party feeling is probably far more a survival of the primitive combativeness of mankind than a consequence of conscious intellectual differences between man and man. It is essentially the same sentiment which in certain states of society leads to civil, intertribal, or international war; and it is as universal as humanity. . . .

It is through this great natural tendency to take sides that the Wire-puller works. Without it he would be powerless. His business is to fan its flame; to keep it constantly acting upon the man who has once declared himself a partisan; to make escape from it difficult and distasteful. His art is that of the Nonconformist preacher, who gave importance to a body of commonplace religionists by persuading them to wear a uniform and take a military title, or of the man who made the success of a Temperance Society by prevailing on its members to wear always and openly a blue ribbon. In the long-run, these contrivances cannot be confined to any one party, and their effects on all parties and their leaders, and on the whole ruling democracy, must be in the highest degree serious and lasting. The first of these effects will be, I think, to make all parties very like one another, and indeed in the end almost indistinguishable, however leaders may quarrel and partisan hate partisan. In the next place, each party will probably become more and more homogeneous; and the opinions it professes, and the policy which is the outcome of those opinions, will less and less reflect the individual mind of any leader, but only the ideas which seem to that mind to be most likely to win favour with the greatest number of supporters. Lastly, the wire-pulling system, when fully developed, will infallibly lead to the constant enlargement of the area of suffrage. What is called universal suffrage has greatly declined in the estimation, not only of philosophers who follow Bentham, but of the *a priori* theorists who assumed that it was the inseparable accompaniment of a Republic, but who found that in practice it was the natural basis of a tyranny. But extensions of the suffrage, though no longer believed to be good in themselves, have now a permanent place in the armoury of parties, and are sure to be a favourite weapon of the Wire-puller. The Athenian statesmen who, worsted in a quarrel of aristocratic cliques, "took the people into partnership," have a close parallel in the modern politicians who introduce household suffrage into towns to "dish" one side, and into counties to "dish" the other.

Let us now suppose the competition of Parties, stimulated to the utmost by the modern contrivances of the Wire-puller, to have produced an electoral system under which every adult male has a vote, and perhaps every adult female. Let us assume that the new machinery has extracted a vote from every one of these electors. How is the result to be expressed? It is, that the average opinion of a great multitude has been obtained, and that this average opinion becomes the basis and standard of all government and law. There is hardly any experience of the way in which such a system would work, except in the eyes of those who believe that history began since their own birth. The universal suffrage of white males in the United States is about fifty years old; that of white and black is less than twenty. The French threw away universal suffrage after the Reign of Terror; it was twice revived in France, that the Napoleonic tyranny might be founded on it; and it was introduced into Germany, that the personal power of Prince Bismarck might be confirmed. But one of the strangest of vulgar ideas is that a very wide suffrage could or would promote progress, new ideas, new discoveries and inventions, new arts of life. Such a suffrage is commonly associated with Radicalism; and no doubt amid its most certain effects would be the extensive destruction of existing institutions; but the chances are that, in the long-run, it would produce a mischievous form of Conservatism. . . .

A moment's reflection will satisfy any competently instructed person that this is not too broad a proposition. Let him turn over in his mind the great epochs of scientific invention and social change during the last two centuries, and consider what would have occurred if universal suffrage had been established at any one of them. Universal suffrage, which to-day excludes Free Trade from the United States, would certainly have prohibited the spinning-jenny and the power-loom. It would certainly have forbidden the threshing-machine. It would have prevented the adoption of the Gregorian Calendar; and it would have restored the Stuarts. It would have proscribed the Roman Catholics with the mob which burned Lord Mansfield's house and library in 1780, and it would have proscribed the Dissenters with the mob which burned Dr. Priestley's house and library in 1791.

There are possibly many persons who,

without denying these conclusions in the past, tacitly assume that no such mistakes will be committed in the future, because the community is already too enlightened for them, and will become more enlightened through popular education. But without questioning the advantages of popular education under certain aspects, its manifest tendency is to diffuse popular commonplaces, to fasten them on the mind at the time when it is most easily impressed, and thus to stereotype average opinion. It is of course possible that universal suffrage would not now force on governments the same legislation which it would infallibly have dictated a hundred years ago; but then we are necessarily ignorant what germs of social and material improvement there may be in the womb of time, and how far they may conflict with the popular prejudice which hereafter will be omnipotent. . . .

It is perfectly possible, I think, as Mr. Herbert Spencer has shown in a recent admirable volume, to revive even in our day the fiscal tyranny which once left even European populations in doubt whether it was worth while preserving life by thrift and toil. You have only to tempt a portion of the population into temporary idleness by promising them a share in a fictitious hoard lying (as Mill puts it) in an imaginary strongbox which is supposed to contain all human wealth. You have only to take the heart out of those who would willingly labour and save, by taxing them *ad misericordiam* for the most laudable philanthropic objects. For it makes not the smallest difference to the motives of the thrifty and industrious part of mankind whether their fiscal oppressor be an Eastern despot, or a feudal baron, or a democratic legislature, and whether they are taxed for the benefit of a corporation called Society, or for the advantage of an individual styled King or Lord. Here then is the great question about

democratic legislation, when carried to more than a moderate length. How will it affect human motives? What motives will it substitute for those now acting on men? The motives, which at present impel mankind to the labour and pain which produce the resuscitation of wealth in ever-increasing quantities, are such as infallibly to entail inequality in the distribution of wealth. They are the springs of action called into activity by the strenuous and never-ending struggle for existence, the beneficent private war which makes one man strive to climb on the shoulders of another and remain there through the law of the survival of the fittest.

These truths are best exemplified in the part of the world to which the superficial thinker would perhaps look for the triumph of the opposite principle. The United States have justly been called the home of the disinherited of the earth; but, if those vanquished under one sky in the struggle for existence had not continued under another the same battle in which they had been once worsted, there would have been no such exploit performed as the cultivation of the vast American territory from end to end and from side to side. There could be no grosser delusion than to suppose this result to have been attained by democratic legislation. It has really been obtained through the sifting out of the strongest by natural selection. The Government of the United States, which I examine in another part of this volume, now rests on universal suffrage, but then it is only a political government. It is a government under which coercive restraint, except in politics, is reduced to a minimum. There has hardly ever before been a community in which the weak have been pushed so pitilessly to the wall, in which those who have succeeded have so uniformly been the strong, and in which in so short a time there has arisen so great an inequality of private fortune and do-mestic luxury. And at the same time, there has never been a country in which, on the whole, the persons distanced in the race have suffered so little from their ill-success. All this beneficent prosperity is the fruit of recognising the principle of population, and the one remedy for its excess in perpetual emi-gration. It all reposes on the sacred-ness of contract and the stability of private property, the first the imple-ment, and the last the reward, of suc-cess in the universal competition. These, however, are all principles and institu-tions which the British friends of the 'artisan' and 'agricultural labourer' seem not a little inclined to treat as their ancestors did agricultural and industrial machinery. The Americans are still of the opinion that more is to be got for hu-man happiness by private energy than by public legislation. The Irish, how-ever, even in the United States, are of another opinion, and the Irish opinion is manifestly rising into favour here. But on the question, whether future democratic legislation will follow the new opinion, the prospects of popular government to a great extent depend. There are two sets of motives, and two only, by which the great bulk of the ma-terials of human subsistence and com-fort have hitherto been produced and reproduced. One has led to the cultiva-tion of the territory of the Northern States of the American Union, from the Atlantic to the Pacific. The other had a considerable share in bringing about the industrial and agricultural progress of the Southern States, and in old days it produced the wonderful prosperity of Peru under the Incas. One system is economical competition; the other con-sists in the daily task, perhaps fairly and kindly allotted, but enforced by the prison or the scourge. So far as we have any experience to teach us, we are driven to the conclusion, that every society of men must adopt one system or the other, or it will pass through penury to starvation.

I have thus shown that popular gov-ernments of the modern type have not hitherto proved stable as compared with other forms of political rule, and that they include certain sources of weakness which do not promise security for them in the near or remote future. My chief conclusion can only be stated nega-tively. There is not at present sufficient evidence to warrant the common belief, that these governments are likely to be of indefinitely long duration. There is, however, one positive conclusion from which no one can escape who bases a forecast of the prospects of popular gov-ernment, not on moral preference or *a priori* assumption, but on actual ex-perience as witnessed to by history. If there be any reason for thinking that constitutional freedom will last, it is a reason furnished by a particular set of facts, with which Englishmen ought to be familiar, but of which many of them, under the empire of prevailing ideas, are exceedingly apt to miss the significance. The British Constitution has existed for a considerable length of time, and there-fore free institutions generally may con-tinue to exist. I am quite aware that this will seem to some a commonplace conclusion, perhaps as commonplace as the conclusion of M. Taine, who, after describing the conquest of all France by the Jacobin Club, declares that his in-ference is so simple, that he hardly ven-tures to state it. "Jusqu'à présent, je n'ai guère trouvé qu'un (Principe) si simple qu'il semblera puéril et que j'ose à peine l'énoncer. Il consiste tout entier dans cette remarque, qu'une so-ciété humaine, surtout une société mod-erne, est une chose vaste et com-pliquée." This observation, that "a human society, and particularly a mod-ern society is a vast and complicated thing," is in fact the very proposition which Burke enforced with all the splendour of his eloquence and all the power of his argument; but as M. Taine says, it may now seem to some too simple and commonplace to be worth putting into words. In the same way, many persons in whom familiarity has bred contempt, may think it a trivial observation that the British Constitution, if not (as some call it) a holy thing, is a thing unique and remarkable. A series of undesigned changes brought it to such a condition, that satisfaction and impatience, the two great sources of political conduct, were both reasonably gratified under it. In this condition it became, not metaphorically but literally, the envy of the world, and the world took on all sides to copying it. The imitations have not been generally happy. One nation alone, consisting of Englishmen, has practised a modification of it successfully, amidst abounding material plenty. It is not too much to say, that the only evidence worth mentioning for the duration of popular government is to be found in the success of the British Constitution during two centuries under special conditions, and in the success of the American Constitution during one century under conditions still more peculiar and more unlikely to recur. Yet, so far as our own Constitution is concerned, that nice balance of attractions, which caused it to move evenly on its stately path, is perhaps destined to be disturbed. One of the forces governing it may gain dangerously at the expense of the other; and the British political system, with the national greatness and material prosperity attendant on it, may yet be launched into space and find its last affinities in silence and cold.

Sir Henry Sumner Maine, *Popular Government* (New York: Henry Holt & Co., 1886), pp. 29-55.

12. Liberalism and Nationalism in the Mid-Nineteenth Century

EVALYN A. CLARK

Vassar College

LIBERALS IN THE PERIOD of contemporary history since the First World War have tended to attack nationalism as reactionary and unenlightened. In the period from 1815 to 1880 liberals, especially liberal intellectuals, ordinarily took it for granted that nationalism was progressive, even radical, humanitarian, the foe of reaction and autocracy. Liberalism and nationalism were to them the obverse and reverse sides of the same coin. National independence of the oppressed minorities from the aged, reactionary empires of Hapsburg, Czar, and Sultan was the essential first step toward achieving liberal reforms within a national state. This was Giuseppe Mazzini's and John Stuart Mill's position, the prevalent belief of nineteenth-century liberals and one which still strongly influenced Woodrow Wilson's idealistic conviction that national self-determination would lessen injustice, tyranny, and war. Mill defined nationality in liberal, even democratic, terms as the feeling of common sympathies, the desire to form a nationality, to live under a government of one's own choosing, not primarily in the romantic or traditionalist terms of race, descent, geography, or language. A famous passage in his *Considerations on Representative Government* sets forth this liberal concept of nationalism: "It is in general a necessary condition of free institutions that the boundaries of governments should coincide in the main with those of nationalities." Mill himself was liberal enough to subordinate this quest for national independence to the struggle for human liberty. Many of the continental liberals were not, especially in lands that lacked both.

The Revolutions of 1848 were certainly warning enough to anyone that nations or groups that have gained their liberty may not grant liberty to others, that the Germans and the Hungarians in the course of their struggle for freedom might come to despise and oppress the Czechs, Poles, Serbs, and Croatians, and that the doubly oppressed minorities might in desperation prefer to return to their ancient oppressor.

Some warning voices were raised by liberals such as Lord Acton, Alexis de Tocqueville, John Stuart Mill, and Richard Cobden that crusades for liberty, wars for an ideal—what we would now call ideological wars—intervention in other countries' affairs, or forcing peoples to be free, could destroy the desired aims of liberty and peace. They warned that the idea of a national mission expressed by Michelet, Palmerston, Mickiewicz, Mazzini, and Kossuth was merely the old "divine right" transferred to the "people" and could be as absolute and hostile to individual liberty as its hated ancestor.

The dilemma of which was more important, the freedom of man or the freedom of states, if one had to choose between them, was posed particularly by the Revolutions of 1848 and even more by Bismarck's rise to power in Germany. In both cases the struggle for liberty came to be opposed to the quest for national independence and unity. In both cases liberalism was defeated by its supposed ally, nationalism. In 1848 both contestants were finally defeated, in the 1860's and 1870, nationalism defeated liberalism.

Another dilemma, freedom or peace, appeared constantly in the course of the century, especially in the Revolutions of 1848. Liberals of the earlier half of the century had rejected, whether for romantic or for rational and "Manchesterian" reasons, the bloodshed and tyranny of war and revolution. Liberalism meant pacifism, anti-militarism, free trade in international affairs, peaceful reform in internal affairs by moderate extensions of suffrage, Parliamentary responsibility, and orderly legislation to assure freedom of speech, assembly, education, and religion.

The liberals, however, disliking as they did the despotism and feudalism of the central and eastern European empires, sympathized with the struggles of oppressed nationalities to preserve their own cultures and to free themselves. In turn, as the cultural nationalism of the first half century became increasingly political, the inherently revolutionary character of the ideal of national self-determination showed itself more clearly. Mill's and Mazzini's ideal of national states could only be achieved by overturning every government in Europe east of the Rhine, and this in fact was just what the Revolutions of 1848 proceeded to do. The pacifist liberal had to face the moral question whether or not he should support and intervene in wars and insurrections—Greek, Polish, German, Czech, Hungarian, Serbian, Croatian, Italian—especially those of 1830 and 1848 and increasingly often thereafter. To some liberals the problems of intervention and foreign policy, especially in the test case of the nineteenth-century liberal conscience—Poland—pointed out the incompatibility of liberalism with nationalism. Some turned to nationalism and preferred national freedom—their own or others—to peace or even to individual freedom. One of the striking developments of the period was the chauvinism and interventionism of the more radical of the liberal advocates —of Louis Auguste Blanqui and Louis Blanc in 1848 and 1871 and of Gustav Struve and the German republicans in 1848, who staged insurrections against their own moderate governments on the issue of "Aid to Poland," "No peace with the Danes," "No peace with the Germans."

Until 1848 liberalism, socialism, radical republicanism, and nationalism were often blended and their future conflicts concealed by common aims and common enemies, especially on the continent. In general the English liberals distrusted socialism, radical democracy, and statism as inimical to individual freedom, and felt they were confirmed in this distrust by the bloody events of 1848 and 1849, particularly in France. These revolutions, the kaleidoscopic combination of all the forces issuing from the French Revolution and the Industrial Revolution, revealed the latent antagonisms of forces often in uneasy alliance until then—not only nationalism and liberalism, but liberalism and democracy or even democracy and socialism. Moreover the Utopian socialism of Louis Blanc, the conspiratorial idealism of Blanqui and Mazzini were as opposed to one another as they came to be to political democracy and liberalism, and each school of thought was as full of hidden antitheses as Rousseau's political philosophy and the French Revolutionary tradition. Many liberals came to find, as Ernest Renan did in 1849, after his initial sympathy with the social revolution, that "the revolutionary philosophy, great and liberating as it was, contained the hidden poison of belief in violence, and an idea of justice based on a materialistic conception of property and a neglect of individual rights—all these carry the seeds of destruction." (*Essais de morale et de critique,* Paris, 1859, p. x.) This dilemma of the liberals over the "social question" may perhaps be paralleled by the twentieth-century debate over the relation of democracy to socialism and to communism.

The disappointment of all participants in the Revolutions of 1848 contributed largely to the reaction against the earlier romanticism, liberalism, and cultural nationalism and to the success of the cult of realism. The post-revolutionary nationalism differs markedly from the optimistic idealism of the pre-revolutionary years. Since the thinkers and talkers failed, it was felt that men of action and power, practical politicians and generals—Bismarcks and Cavours—must be necessary.

Racism, imperialism, militarism, neo-mercantilism, and aggressive and intolerant treatment of minorities in the name of national unity became increasingly the concomitants of nationalism. With the new methods of mass communication and propaganda provided by cheap journalism, the telegraph, the typewriter, with increasing resort to universal military service, with popular education, universal suffrage, urbanization, and decline of religion, the nationalist movements tended to become mass movements and increasingly intolerant and illiberal. Liberals distrusted equally the chauvinism of the Left, as seen in the Paris Commune, and of the Right as seen in Napoleon III, Bismarck, or the Russian Pan-Slavs.

By the beginning of the last quarter of the century Germany and Italy had finally achieved their unity and independence by war and forceful unification. France and England, the oldest nations in terms of unity, had achieved many liberal reforms. Even some of the oppressed Slav peoples had achieved independence or autonomy, though the Poles, Czechs, and South Slavs were still bitterly resentful of their oppression.

But liberalism tended more and more to think of nationalism as foe, not friend, while the Right came more and more to claim a monopoly of patriotism and the Left to turn against it in disillusioned diatribes. The Paris Commune, the Marxist Second International, the rise of anarchism, and the Dreyfus case produced a reversal of partners like the Diplomatic Revolution of the 18th century. The radical and socialist Left became anti-patriotic, anti-militarist, and international—"the worker has no fatherland." The Right became the self-appointed defenders of the shrines of Revanche, Pan-Germanism, Pan-Slavism, anti-Semitism, and imperialism.

Liberalism remained a friend of nationalism chiefly in lands where both were long established, as in England and France, or in lands not yet free.

I. YEARS OF CRISIS: 1848 AND 1849

The year 1848 has been called by G. M. Trevelyan "the turning point at which modern history failed to turn" from despotism to freedom. Or perhaps we may borrow Winston Churchill's expressive phrase, "the hinge of fate," for these crucial years in the movements toward liberalism and nationalism. Many of the problems of our own day were then given a decisive turn—the "problem of Germany," the perpetual instability of French governments, the hostility of Czechs to Germans and of Hungarians and Germans to Slavs, the relations of Russia and the West, the hostility of conservatism and of revolutionary socialism to reforming liberalism, the growing estrangement of liberalism and nationalism.

In 1848, when revolutionary uprisings blazed their way across most of Europe, the three great problems of the day were the "social question," the "national question," and the "political question." The "political question" could comprise republicanism, constitutionalism, and universal suffrage, singly or in combination, but these were often grouped together by the conservatives under the opprobrious label of "republicanism." Actually, with Cavour the question was constitutionalism and he was opposed to republicanism and universal suffrage; Mazzini saw the problem in terms of the last two; Kossuth's republicanism emerged only by force of circumstance. All three of these problems were intertwined in the Revolutions of 1848, but the political and social questions remained uppermost in France, while in the Austrian Empire the national question soon came to overshadow everything else.

In France with its revolutionary and republican traditions the revolutionists at least agreed on a republic in the beginning. They disagreed on whether it was to be a "liberal" republic or a "democratic and social" republic. The Provisional Government, established after the overthrow of Louis Philippe, showed itself as an uneasy compromise from the first night of February 24 when the ministers chosen by the Chamber of French deputies had to accept two socialists as the price of their confirmation by the people of Paris at the Hotel de Ville. The resultant fusion of rival groups had little authority and less unity. The majority of the Provisional Government were moderate republicans who were really in the tradition of 1789, favoring private property and as much laissez faire as possible, but willing to accept universal suffrage and the republic. Alexandre Auguste Ledru-Rollin, in the key post of Minister of the Interior, was a Jacobin or Montagnard republican who thought himself a second Robespierre and aroused the fears of the provinces and the bourgeoisie by his leanings toward socialism and his demands for continuing the tradition of 1793. He defended the Terror of the past, but shrank from it in the present. Louis Blanc, the socialist leader forced into the Provisional Government by the workers, was usually allied with the Jacobins to form the Left minority in the government. He was the idol of the people of Paris— an uncompromising enemy of laissez faire, a preacher of gradual transition to socialism through producers' co-operatives financed by the state. His ideal was a democratic republic, based on the principle of association of all workers and achieved by political measures, not by armed force or the dictatorship of a minority. In this ideal republic all would work as a moral duty and there would be no social distinctions and privileges of inherited wealth: "From each according to his ability, to each according to his need." Though Louis Blanc steadfastly denied any responsibility for the May 15 insurrection or the June Days, which put an end to the uneasy truce of February, the workers' delegates to his Luxembourg Commission of Inquiry on Labor grew more insurrectionary and listened more to his bitter attacks on capitalism and privilege than to his pleas for moderation and political maturity.

Moreover the Paris workers were not in a mood to make fine distinctions between the theoretically peaceful preachings of Louis Blanc or the Utopian Socialists and those of class war and unrelenting hostility to the bourgeois state preached by Pierre Joseph Proudhon and Auguste Blanqui who were outside the Provisional Government. Blanqui, one of the greatest revolutionaries of the nineteenth century and the dread of all governments, democratic as well as reactionary, spent most of his life in prison but managed to take part in the French revolutions of 1830, 1848, and the Commune of 1871. His proclaimed aims were the dictatorship of the workers over Paris and of Paris over the provinces, achieved by a coup d'etat and then the confiscation of property and the destruction of existing social and political institutions. Through his control over the largest of the revolutionary clubs, the Central Republican Society, usually called the Blanqui Club, he was able to stir up constant insurrections or threats of insurrections against the government. He was as hostile to the Jacobin and socialist minority of the Provisional Government or National Assembly as he was to the moderate republican majority. He has often been compared to Lenin in his intransigent temperament and his techniques of revolution.

A rival and sometimes unwilling ally of Blanqui was the Creole, Armand Barbès, leader of the second largest revolutionary group, the Club of the Revolution, who came to control also the Society of the Rights of Man. This had been the largest of the radical political associations driven underground by the Orleans monarchy.

Avowedly Robespierrist, it became more socialist as its membership came to include more workers. Like Barbès, it grew increasingly hostile to the parliamentary republic after the resounding defeat of the radicals in the April elections to the National Assembly.

Blanqui and Barbès precipitated the May 15 insurrection which invaded the Assembly, and for a few hours overturned the government and replaced it by a provisional government of leaders of the revolutionary clubs. This insurrection alarmed not only the Rightist Party of Order and the moderates in the National Assembly but even the Montagnards like Ledru-Rollin. It fatally compromised the mediating influence of Louis Blanc, since both workers and deputies suspected him of betraying them, probably unjustly. Henceforth the Assembly and the workers of Paris moved to an open split, Blanqui and Barbès were imprisoned, and Louis Blanc narrowly escaped. The aroused Assembly forced the government to close the National Workshops, set up as a concession to Louis Blanc, and the Luxembourg Commission. The Paris workers rose in desperate armed revolt and the bloody June Days of civil war brought terrible defeat to the leaderless socialists but also fatal discredit and disunion to the republicans.

Alphonse de Lamartine, the poet statesman and historian of the Girondists, catapulted into power and popularity by the February Revolution, thought of himself as the savior of France. His way was to try to reconcile the republican factions within the creaking Provisional Government in the name of national unity. Like Michelet, the romantic nationalist historian, he had a glorified ideal of the First Republic. His only message was essentially that of Michelet in *The People:* "One people, one Fatherland, one France! Let us never become two nations, I beseech you! Without unity we perish!" But Lamartine in his attempt at reconciling all, at least all the republicans, succeeded in winning the distrust of all. His "Manifesto to Europe" of March, 1848, which he issued as Minister for Foreign Affairs, tried to pacify the apprehensions of European chancelleries that the revolutionary Republic might continue the military and propagandist interventionism of the First Republic by declaring a crusading war on Prussia, Austria, and Russia to free the Poles and the Italians or tear up the frontiers of 1815. Yet it breathed forth the resurgent glory of France and warned against any aggression against France or other nations who wanted to be free. Palmerston shrewdly noted that this Manifesto was designed for internal consumption as well and was Lamartine's attempt to satisfy both the bellicose and pacifist groups of the French republicans. The emotional appeal of revolutionary intervention was shown in the great May 15 insurrection of workmen and students against the National Assembly led by Blanqui and Barbès, under the marching cry of "Long live Poland!" In their brief moment of power they decreed war on the Russian and German monarchs unless Poland were immediately freed. In 1848, when patriotism was still claimed as a monopoly of the Left, the Extreme Left, especially in France and Germany, proved to be the most chauvinistic and interventionist.

Lamartine opposed this extreme antirepublican Left of Barbès and Blanqui; he also opposed the attempts of the socialists to take over the revolution and to make the red flag the flag of the new republic, yet he tried to keep both Ledru-Rollin and Louis Blanc inside the government by supporting Blanc's demands for the "right to work," and for the Luxembourg Commission to investigate and propose reforms in labor conditions. But Lamartine meant by "the people" all Frenchmen, whereas Louis Blanc meant all workers and Blanqui meant a minority of professional revolutionists. In June, when the clash of concepts became clear, Lamartine had to choose to fight for the Republic against the Paris populace. By then he had also earned the distrust of the moderate republicans such as Tocqueville as well as of the resurgent Right by his denunciations of the bourgeoisie and his wooing of the Left.

After the June Days, the moderate republicans, disunited even in their own ranks, succumbed before Louis Napoleon's drive for power and the bitter hostility of the workers against the Republic. The Center lost most of its supporters who moved either to the extreme of Left or Right. Louis Napoleon became the rallying point of all those discontented with the domestic and foreign policy of the Republic, from Extreme Left to Extreme Right. The embittered workmen cheered him as the heir of the great Revolution as they fought on the barricades against the bourgeois republic. The Right hailed him as the foe of the Revolution and the restorer of order and past glory. Louis Napoleon could be all things to all men more successfully than Lamartine.

Did the Left, in France and Germany especially, defeat liberalism by frightening the peasants and middle class by their premature radicalism and chauvinism? Or were the liberals themselves too timid and too fearful of democracy and social reforms? Were they too inexperienced in practical politics or too stagestruck in reenacting the romantic and heroic drama of the Great Revolution? Or perhaps the democratic faith in the panacea of universal suffrage and republicanism was too optimistic. Certainly Tocqueville's unheeded warning to the constitutional committee of the National Assembly that direct election of the President by universal suffrage of the people could lead to dictatorship was only too soon and too thoroughly vindicated.

All over Europe, both during the Revolutions and afterward, the forces of liberalism were so divided over the "political question" and the "social question" that they furnished no strong center coalition to resist the crossfire of the Extreme Right of autocratic rulers—Napoleon III, the Czar, the Hapsburg Emperor, the Prussian King—or the Extreme Left of the revolutionary radicals.

In the rest of Europe, it was the "national question" that came to dominate the revolutions. The ideal of liberal nationalism expressed by Mazzini, that the nations must achieve their own freedom, but must also work fraternally for a common ideal transcending all nations, an internationalism of republicanism, liberalism, and peace, was badly betrayed by the events of 1848–49. In Central Europe, particularly in the Hapsburg Empire, after a brief March honeymoon of liberal declarations of fraternity among the oppressed nationalities, came the increasing bitterness and strife of nationality against nationality within the polyglot Empire and the consequent defeat of both national and liberal aims by national animosities, Russian arms, and Hapsburg politics. The mutual suspicion, rivalry, and accusations of Slav, Magyar, and German that culminated in the First World War first crystallized in the years 1848–49.

When the news of the Paris Revolution of late February reached Vienna, a chain reaction of uprisings and revolutionary events followed, all over the Austrian Empire and indeed all over Europe. Appropriately enough, the dramatic events centered around the Ides of March: Louis Kossuth's speech in the Hungarian Diet demanding freedom and a constitution for all the Empire, the meetings of Czechs and Germans in Prague demanding autonomy for Bohemia, uprisings in Berlin, north Italy, the Viennese revolution of March 13 when the students and workmen toppled Metternich overnight and forced the Emperor to promise a constitution to his dominions, the winning of Hungarian autonomy and the People's Charter, the Bohemian and Croatian demands for autonomy.

The Hungarian parliament and ministry began the great reform period of the "March and April laws," which showed the strength and weakness of Hungarian liberalism and of Kossuth, who soon came to dominate the course of Hungarian events. They drew up a new constitution and ended the old regime of feudalism and aristocratic privilege in Hungary, freed the peasants, set up an elected parliament based on a greatly extended suffrage, and a ministry responsible to parliament. They equalized taxation, granted freedom of the press, and set up a National Guard, all typically liberal reforms.

But Kossuth and his Radicals were less constructive in their relations with the Austrian monarchy and with the dependent nations within Hungary. They moved more and more toward a break with the Empire and alienated their own moderates as they set up a separate Hungarian army and ministries of foreign affairs and finance.

Kossuth like all the Hungarian nationalists assumed the unquestioned domination of the Magyars over all the peoples of the Hungarian crown. He enforced the new language laws which made the Magyar language the exclusive official language of the whole kingdom, a deep affront to the linguistic nationalism of all the Slavs. A delegation of Serbs living within Hungary, who came to ask the Hungarian Diet in April for the right to use their own language, was told by Kossuth that the question of equality of the Slav language with Magyar could only be settled by the sword. The Diet of Transylvania was forced to decree its own end and the complete union of the province with Hungary. This aroused the Saxons and Rumanians of Transylvania against the Magyars. Less than a month later the Croatian Diet at Agram demanded the constitutional rights of Croatia and were treated as traitors and rebels. The nine million Slav, Rumanian, and Saxon subjects of Hungary ringed around the Magyars in armed rebellion to vindicate their rights to equality and freedom and to resist forcible Magyarization.

Kossuth alarmed all the Slavs of the Empire by his advocacy of the completion of German unity and his alliance with the Germans of Frankfurt and the Pan-German radicals of Vienna to achieve the disintegration of the Hapsburg monarchy and the Magyar ascendancy in Hungary. The German radicals in Vienna and Bohemia hoped for the merging of German Austria, including Bohemia, in a united Germany, and Kossuth supported this on condition that the Magyars should keep Croatia and Slavonia. The Slavs, however, hoped for a transformation of the Austrian monarchy into a group of national states under the personal monarchy of the House of Austria in order to achieve at least Slav equality with the Germans and Magyars, perhaps eventually Slav predominance, since they formed the great majority of the inhabitants of the Empire. This policy of Austroslavism, as it was called later, seemed to most of them their only hope, since they knew they were too weak as individual Slav states to resist the growing threat of German unity and of Russian despotism. The unity of all Germany dreamed of by the Frankfurt Congress "would not only destroy the unity of Austria but would annihilate also the union of the Slavic races, whose national independence would be threatened." So declared the May First call for a Slav Congress to be held at Prague in June, 1848, to counterbalance the German Congress.

This warning had first been sounded by Frantisek Palacky, Czech historian and an advocate of Austrian federalism, in April. He wrote to the Committee of Fifty at Frankfurt declining to take part in the planning of the German National Assembly on the ground that Bohemia was a Slav kingdom, not a province of Greater Germany, and uttered the famous phrase, "Assuredly, if the Austrian state had not existed for ages, it would have been necessary, in the interests of Europe and of humanity, for us to invent it."

The Czech moderates were neither separatists nor Russophiles. Palacky indeed justified the existence of Austria as a necessary bulwark against the "ever accelerated expansion of the Russian monarchy," which threatened western civilization and the cause of freedom by a "universal monarchy, that is to say, an infinite and inexpressible evil." His ideal was a Danubian federation of equal nationalities around a liberal and reformed Austria to unite the whole area between the Russian Empire and the German Confederation and thus to preserve peace and liberty for the Slavs and for Europe.

The Slav Congress, then, was called by the Czech moderates to counteract Magyarizing and Germanizing centralization and to declare the rights and the brotherhood of the Slav peoples long submerged beneath German and Magyar. It was in no sense a revolt against the Hapsburgs. Though the Czechs demanded and obtained an autonomous government in April, the moderates declared their loyalty to Austria at the Slav Congress in June. But the insurrection of a tiny Czech radical minority of students and workers discredited the Slav Congress. It brought swift reprisal in Prague from the imperial government and shattered Czech dreams of freedom. Yet the Czechs still felt they needed protection against the Germans, as their brother Slavs needed it against the Magyars, so they perforce supported the imperial government.

The Croats were more careful to make clear their loyalty to the Hapsburgs, when the Croatian Diet in July revolted against the increasingly oppressive Magyar rule and asked to be united as an autonomous kingdom directly to the Austrian crown. Kossuth was by then virtually a dictator over the Hungarian parliament, which the conservative and moderate members had left in protest. He treated the Croatian declaration of independence as treason and in his impassioned speech of July 11 demanded money and men as a national necessity to make war against the Croatians.

The imperial government recognized the value of the help of the rebellious Slavs against the rebellious Hungarians, who were not merely demanding their own independence but threatening the existence of Austria by scheming with the pan-Germans in Austria and in Frankfurt.

With the triumph of Austrian arms over Lombardy in August the Austrian government felt freer to proceed against Hungary. It sanctioned the Croatian invasion of Hungary and then declared war on Hungary in October 1848. The second Viennese insurrection of October broke out when the Pan-German radicals revolted to prevent the war against Hungary. In spite of the help of the Slavs of the Empire, the imperial government was not able to crush the fierce national resistance of Kossuth's minority until the young Francis Joseph called upon the Russian Emperor in March for help. The Czar was glad enough to put down the republican insurrectionary flames that were already threatening his own restive minorities, especially in Poland, and indeed all monarchical and conservative institutions. In vain Kossuth proclaimed a Hungarian republic, the deposition of the Hapsburgs, a holy war against Russia, and finally, as the Russian and Austrian armies were closing in for the kill, his willingness to remedy the grievances of the non-Magyar nationalities. In August, 1849, the Hungarian army surrendered to the Czar and Kossuth fled to Turkey, then England and America.

In spite of Kossuth's eloquent defense of

himself as champion of freedom, it can be maintained that he did more disservice to the liberal cause than any nineteenth-century leader. His evolution from liberal nationalism to Magyar chauvinism formed the storm center of the whirlwind of national hatreds aroused in Europe in the Revolutions of 1848.

Ironically, it was the liberal emancipation of the peasants in the Hapsburg Empire that led to the emergence of the Slavs as a political force and set the Germans and Magyars, who were landowners and bourgeois, against the Slavs, who were overwhelmingly peasants. Extension of the suffrage and the constitutional equality of the Slav majority with the Magyar and German minorities originated as liberal political and social reforms but led to nationalistic struggles for predominance. In the end everyone lost, but the chief victim was liberalism.

The two parts of our first problem, then, will illustrate the conflict over the "social" and the "political" questions in France and over the "national" question in Central Europe. The argument, appearing in the words of the leading protagonists of the conflicting viewpoints, will illustrate the complex interplay of liberalism and of nationalism in these critical years of the mid-nineteenth century.

The French Republic Liberal or Social?

A. Alphonse de Lamartine: Liberal Republican Leader

France is a Republic. The French Republic does not need to be recognized in order to exist; it *is* by natural right and by national might. It is the will of a great nation authorized by itself alone. However, since the French Republic wishes to enter into the family of established nations as a regular power and not as a force disruptive of European order, it is fitting that you should promptly make known to the governments to which you are accredited the principles and policies which hereafter will govern the foreign policies of the French government.

The proclamation of the French Republic is not an act of aggression against any form of government anywhere in the world. The diversity of forms of government is just as legitimate as is the diversity of character, geographical situation and intellectual, moral and material development among peoples. Nations, like individuals, are not all the same age; the principles which govern them pass through successive phases. Monarchic, aristocratic, constitutional and republican forms of government express the varying degrees of maturity of the mind of the people. They demand more liberty in proportion to their readiness for it; they demand more equality and democracy as they become more animated by justice and love towards fellow man. It is a question of time. A people is as much lost by setting ahead the clock of this maturity as it would be dishonored by failing to profit by it. Monarchies and the republics do not, in the eyes of true statesmen, represent absolute principles locked in a death struggle; rather they are contrasting facts which can co-exist providing they have mutual respect and understanding.

War, then, is not now one of the principles of the French Republic as it was its fatal and glorious necessity in 1792. Between 1792 and 1848 lies half a century. To go back, after this half century, to the principles of 1792, to the period of Empire and conquest, would not be advancing but regressing. Yesterday's revolution [February, 1848] was a step forward, not backward. We and the world alike wish to go forward in brotherhood and peace. . . .

In 1792, the nation was not united, two peoples existed on the same soil. . . . Today there are no longer any distinct and unequal classes, all are enfranchised by liberty, all are leveled by equality before the law. . . . There is not a single French citizen, whatever his political belief, who does not put his fatherland first and who, by this very unity, makes her impregnable in the face of attempted invasion. . . .

In 1792 neither France nor Europe was ready to understand and accept a harmonious inter-relation of nations with its resultant of benefits to mankind. . . . Fifty years freedom of thought, freedom of speech, freedom of the press have had their effect; books, newspapers and speeches have propagated European enlightenment. Reason, shining over all, passing over national boundaries, has given men's minds a fatherland of the spirit which will be the crowning achievement of the French Revolution and the establishment of international brotherhood throughout the world.

In 1792, liberty was a novelty, equality a scandal, the Republic a problem. . . . [Thrones and peoples] will realize that there is such a thing as conservative liberty; that there may exist in a Republic not only a better system but also that there is more true order in government by all for all than in government by and for a few.

Make no mistake, however. These ideas which the Government charges you to present to the European powers as a pledge of European security are not to be taken as suing for forgiveness by the Republic for daring to be born, still less as a humble petition for the right to exist as a great state. . . .

The French people will declare war on no one; needless to say, she would accept the challenge were she to be attacked. The thoughts of those now governing France run as follows: France would be fortunate, in case war should be imposed upon her, thus forcing her to grow in strength and glory despite her moderation. France would be guilty were she to declare war without being forced to do so. . . .

Although the French Republic proclaims that the treaties of 1815 no longer exist except as facts to be modified by mutual consent, and that it is her right and her duty to bring about this modification, legally and peacefully, nevertheless, the good sense, moderation, conscientiousness and prudence of the Republic exist and these are, for Europe, a better and more honorable guarantee than the letter of those treaties which have been frequently violated or modified.

Endeavor, Sir, to achieve comprehension and acceptance of the Republic's emancipation from the treaties of 1815 and, at the same time, show that this freedom is not irreconcilable with the peace of Europe. Thus, we proclaim it aloud, were Providence to decree that the hour of reconstruction of certain oppressed European nations had struck— were Switzerland, our faithful ally since the days of Francis I, either hindered or threatened in her political progress . . ., were Italy's independent states to be invaded, their internal transformation to be limited or thwarted, or were these states to be forcibly prevented from joining in the formation of an Italian nation, then the French Republic would believe she had the right to take arms herself in order to protect these legitimate movements of state growth and nationality.

The Republic, you see, in one bound has passed by the age of proscription and dictatorships. She is equally resolved never to let liberty be veiled at home nor her democratic principles be obscured abroad. Let no man place his hand between the peaceful radiance of her liberty and the eyes of mankind. She declares herself to be allied by heart and mind to all rights, progress and legitimate development of the institutions of all nations who wish to live by the same principles as her own. Never will she carry on hidden and inflammatory propaganda among her neighbors. Well she knows that the only liberties which endure are those which spring from their native soil. Nonetheless, she will strive, by the example of order and peace she sets to the world to indulge in the only real and honest propagandizing, that of winning admiration and sympathy. This is no war, it is nature; this is no agitation of Europe, it is life; this is no torch to set the world aflame, it is a beacon light to summon and guide the peoples of the world! . . .

These three words [Liberty, Equality and Fraternity] in their application to our foreign affairs mean this: setting France free from the chains which outrage her principles and her dignity; restoration of the position she should hold among the great European powers; finally, the proclamation of her alliance and amity with all peoples. If France is aware of her role in the liberal, civilizing mission of this century, no one of these words means war. If Europe is wise and just, there is not one which does not say peace.

Manifesto to Europe or *Circular of the Minister of Foreign Affairs to the Diplomatic Agents of the French Republic,* in *Le Moniteur universel,* 4 March, 1848, pp. 544-45, in part, trans. E. A. Clark.

B. *Alexis de Tocqueville: A Liberal Republican Critic*

I had spent the best days of my youth amid a society which seemed to increase in greatness and prosperity as it increased in liberty; I had conceived the idea of a balanced, regulated liberty, held in check by religion, custom and law; the attractions of this liberty had touched me; it had become the passion of my life; I felt that I could never be consoled for its loss, and that I must renounce all hope of its recovery.

I had gained too much experience of mankind to be able to content myself with empty words; I knew that, if one great revolution is able to establish liberty in a country, a number of succeeding revolutions make all regular liberty impossible for very many years. . . .

I began to pass in review the history of our last sixty years, and I smiled bitterly when I thought of the illusions formed at the conclusion of each period in this long revolution.

The Constitutional Monarchy had succeeded the Ancien Régime; the Republic, the Monarchy; the Empire, the Republic; the Restoration, the Empire; and then came the Monarchy of July. After each of these successive changes it was said that the French Revolution, having accomplished what was presumptuously called its work, was finished; this had been said and it had been believed. Alas! I myself had hoped it under the Restoration, and again after the fall of the Government of the Restoration; and here is the French Revolution beginning over again, for it is still the same one. As we go on, its end seems farther off and shrouded in greater darkness. Shall we ever—as we are assured by other prophets, perhaps as delusive as their predecessors—shall we ever attain a more complete and more far-reaching social transformation than our fathers foresaw and desired, and than we ourselves are able to foresee; or are we not destined simply to end in a condition of intermittent anarchy, the well-known chronic and incurable complaint of old races? . . .

All the deputies who came to Paris [for the National Assembly in early May] with the desire to put down the excesses of the Revolution and to combat the demagogic party regarded him [Lamartine] beforehand as their only possible leader, and looked to him un-hesitatingly to place himself at their head to attack and overthrow the So-cialists and demagogues. They soon discovered that they were deceived, and that Lamartine did not see the part he was called upon to play in so simple a light. It must be confessed that his was a very complex and difficult position. It was forgotten at the time, but he could not himself forget, that he had contributed more than any other to the success of the Revolution of Feb-ruary. . . .

He was then following the tortuous road that was so soon to lead him to his ruin, struggling to dominate the Moun-tain without overthrowing it, and to slacken the revolutionary fire without extinguishing it, so as to give the coun-try a feeling of security strong enough for it to bless him, not strong enough to cause it to forget him. . . .

The nation saw in Ledru-Rollin the bloody image of the Terror; it beheld in him the genius of evil as in Lamartine the genius of good, and it was mistaken in both cases. . . .

Lamartine, who had seen nothing but Paris during the last two months, and who had there, so to speak, lived in the very heart of the revolutionary party, exaggerated the power of the Capital and the inactivity of the rest of France. He over-estimated both. But I am not sure that I, on my side, did not strain a point on the other side. . . . In any case, I am led to believe that it was Lamartine's tergiversations and his semi-connivance with the enemy that saved us, while it ruined him. Their effect was to amuse the leaders of the Moun-tain and to divide them. The Montag-nards of the old school, who were re-tained in the Government, separated themselves from the Socialists, who were excluded from it. . . .

Lamartine saw these dangers more closely and clearly than I, and I believe today that the fear of arousing a mortal conflict influenced his conduct as much as did his ambition. . . .

It was then [at the May 15 uprising against the National Assembly on the pretext of demonstrations of sympathy for the Prussian repression of Polish riots] that I saw appear, in his turn, in the tribune a man whom I have never seen since, but the recollection of whom has always filled me with horror and disgust. He had wan, emaciated cheeks, white lips, a sickly, wicked and repul-sive expression, a dirty pallor, the ap-pearance of a mouldy corpse; he wore no visible linen; an old black frock-coat tightly covered his lean, withered limbs; he seemed to have passed his life in a sewer and to have just left it. I was told it was Blanqui.

Blanqui said one word about Poland; then, turning sharply to domestic af-fairs, he asked for revenge for what he called the massacres of Rouen, recalled with threats the wretchedness in which the people had been left, and complained of the wrongs done to the latter by the Assembly. After thus exciting his hear-ers, he returned to the subject of Po-land and, like Raspail, demanded an immediate vote. . . .

A long interval passed; at last Barbès darted up and climbed, or rather leapt, into the tribune. He was one of those men in whom the demagogue, the mad-man and the knight-errant are so closely intermingled that it is not possible to say where one ends or the other com-mences, and who can only make their way in a society as sick and troubled as ours. . . .

"I demand," said he, in panting, jerking tones, "that, immediately and before rising, the Assembly shall vote the departure of an army for Poland, a tax of a milliard upon the rich, the re-moval of the troops from Paris, and shall forbid the beating to arms; if not,

the representatives to be declared traitors to the country." ...

The whole time elapsing between the
[insurrections of May] and the days of
June was filled with the anxiety caused
by the approach of these latter days. ...
The National Assembly was so constantly possessed by this thought that
one might have said that it read the
words "Civil War" written on the four
walls of the House. ...

The danger was perceived afar off as
well as near at hand. The provinces
grew indignant and irritated with Paris;
for the first time for sixty years they
ventured to entertain the idea of resisting it. ... The ruin of commerce, universal war, the dread of Socialism made
the Republic more and more hateful in
the eyes of the provinces. This hatred
manifested itself especially beneath the
secrecy of the ballot. The electors were
called upon to re-elect in twenty-one departments; and in general they elected
the men who in their eyes represented
the Monarchy in some form or other. ...

It was then that suddenly, for the
first time, the name of Louis Napoleon
came into notice. The Prince was
elected at the same time in Paris and in
several departments. Republicans, Le-
gitimists and demagogues gave him
their votes; for the nation at that time
was like a frightened flock of sheep,
which runs in all directions without following any road. ...

I come at last to the insurrection of
June, the most extensive and the most
singular that has occurred in our history, and perhaps in any other. ...

What distinguished it also, among all
the events of this kind which have succeeded one another in France for sixty
years, is that it did not aim at changing
the form of government, but at altering
the order of society. It was not, strictly
speaking, a political struggle, in the
sense which until then we had given to
the word, but a combat of class against

class, a sort of Servile War. It represented the facts of the Revolution of
February in the same manner as the
theories of Socialism represented its
ideas; or rather it issued naturally from
these ideas, as a son does from his
mother. We behold in it nothing more
than a blind and rude, but powerful,
effort on the part of the workmen to
escape from the necessities of their condition, which had been depicted to them
as one of unlawful oppression, and to
open up by main force a road towards
that imaginary comfort with which they
had been deluded. It was this mixture
of greed and false theory which first
gave birth to the insurrection and then
made it so formidable. These poor people had been told that the wealth of the
rich was in some way the produce of a
theft practised upon themselves. They
had been assured that the inequality of
fortunes was as opposed to morality and
the welfare of society as it was to nature. Prompted by their needs and
their passions, many had believed this
obscure and erroneous notion of right,
which, mingled with brute force, imparted to the latter an energy, a tenacity and a power which it would never
have possessed unaided.

It must also be observed that this
formidable insurrection was not the enterprise of a certain number of conspirators, but the revolt of one whole
section of the population against another. ...

Such were the days of June, necessary
and disastrous days. They did not extinguish revolutionary ardour in France,
but they put a stop, at least for a time,
to what may be called the work apper-
taining to the Revolution of February.
They delivered the nation from the tyranny of the Paris workmen and restored it to possession of itself.

Socialist theories continued to penetrate into the minds of the people in
the shape of envious and greedy desires,

and to sow the seed of future revolutions; but the socialist party itself was beaten and powerless. The Montagnards, who did not belong to it, felt that they were irrevocably affected by the blow that had struck it. The moderate Republicans themselves did not fail to be alarmed lest this victory had led them to a slope which might precipitate them from the Republic, and they made an immediate effort to stop their descent, but in vain. Personally I detested the Mountain, and was indifferent to the Republic; but I adored Liberty, and I conceived great apprehensions for it immediately after these days. I at once looked upon the June fighting as a necessary crisis, after which, however, the temper of the nation would undergo a certain change. The love of independence was to be followed by a dread of, and perhaps a distaste for, free institutions; after such an abuse of liberty a return of this sort was inevitable. This retrograde movement began, in fact, on the 27th of June. At first very slow and invisible, as it were, to the naked eye, it grew swifter, impetuous, irresistible. Where will it stop? I do not know.

Alexis de Tocqueville, *Recollections,* trans. Alexander Teixeira de Mattos (New York: The Macmillan Co., 1896), pp. 85-87, 145-46, 149-54, 163-65, 180-83, 187-88, 230-31.

C. Louis Blanc: For a Social and Democratic Republic

The cry of our days is: "LAISSEZ FAIRE, LAISSEZ PASSER! To the strongest the reward of their strength." That means: Woe to the weaker, woe to the loser. For in a society where the conditions are unequal, individualism is not liberty—it is war!

We are entering now upon fateful days. Will society be destroyed or transformed? And note well that I do not speak solely as representative of one faction or even one class. No—progress exists, for me, only on condition that everyone profits from it—everyone without exception. Progress, to me, means solidarity recognized and realized by all interests. Do you know why I have declared, in my heart, war to the death against the principle of antagonism? Not only because it is the misfortune of the worker; it is also frequently the misfortune of the employer; because it merely shifts tyranny, when it does not make it permanent. Now, whatever the source, tyranny is odious to me. Therefore, I believe in the happiness of all by the association of all, in accord with the noble motto inscribed on our flag, that motto created by our ancestors, the most glorious advance of the human spirit: Liberty, Equality, Fraternity.

Beware, gentlemen, of that dangerous doctrine: "We wish laissez faire, laissez passer because we wish liberty." Liberty cannot, in fact, exist for all, when their forces are completely unequal. I have written before and I repeat here confidently: Look now, in all honesty, is the worker free not to die from hunger who in the universal disorder created by unlimited competition cannot find the work which alone can give him bread? Is the vagabond who has no refuge free not to sleep on the street pavement, I ask you? Or is he even free to sleep on the street since he is punished for the crime of vagrancy? . . .

I address myself to your heart, to your patriotism. . . .

We have a glorious mission to perform. To France, now a republic, falls the eternal honor of inaugurating in the world the principle of association. Let us hasten to establish it in order to cut short all cause and pretext of hatred in our midst; in order to produce for a known market, in order that nothing in our destiny be given over to chance, to the unforeseen, to blind and brutal force; in order that we may turn away in wholesome fear from these paths which lead to civil war; in order that we may prepare for our fatherland by common effort, the place we desire.

The solution we are looking for is this, and I say it from the bottom of my heart: to make an end of revolutions—Progress; to end wars—Justice!

Address of the President of the Government Commission on Labor at the Luxembourg Palace, meeting of March 17, *Le Moniteur universel*, (no. 79) 19 March, 1848, p. 639, trans. E. A. Clark.

M. Louis Blanc: "Until now, my friends, power has always been on one side and the nation on the other. These two forces, instead of interpenetrating and comprehending one another, always consider themselves enemies. That is why until now society has always lived between power by oppression and liberty by revolt. Now all this is going to change! 'Till now power has been resistance, we have been movement. 'Till now, power has distrusted the people, because it had the insolence to believe itself above them. Now we lend all our strength, all our hopes, in the confidence that the people gives us and that we have in the people, because we are sure that our heart beats in unison with theirs. Yes, fraternal accord between those who compose society and those who are called to the honor of leadership—fraternal accord, permanent, indestructible, for henceforth power can only be the union of good men, elected by their equals, to guide and regulate the march of mankind toward liberty." (Prolonged acclamations: Long live Louis Blanc, long live the Republic!)

The delegates begin to leave the room when Louis Blanc returns suddenly, his face shining with joy, and stops them on the stairs with these words: "My friends, return! I have great news for you!" Everyone immediately rushes into the hall. M. Louis Blanc: "Two words only!" Profound silence.

"The Republic we have proclaimed is going to triumph over all of Europe. I have just learned from my honorable colleague M. de Lamartine, Minister of Foreign Affairs, who has just received the news, that Austria has revolted. (Explosion of applause. Cries of joy.)

"Austria has revolted and Metternich has fled!" (Immense enthusiasm. From all sides: "Long live the Republic! Long live the universal Republic!")

[Stenographic report of the meeting of March 19, when members of the Provisional Government were acclaimed by the Commission.] *Ibid.*, March 20, p. 645, trans. E. A. Clark.

Certainly no one admires more than I the genius of M. Lamartine, his integrity, the chivalrous character of his attempts and the splendor of his imagination so well supported by the brilliance of his style. But these very qualities had a fatal side, seeming to veil both to himself and others the nature of his faults. Gifted with a prodigious power of illusion, he imagined that he had suddenly given France the Republic he had so long rejected as impossible; dragged at the end of the movement, he thought he was its head and imagined it would be easy to master it. . . . He dreamed of his role, with the passion of the man of letters— it can be summed up in two words—to be applauded. . . . He coveted the support of all, he was sympathetic to all opinions, he sought to place himself at the point of intersection of all parties. With equal ardor he pursued the approbation of the salon and the revolutionary clubs. . . .

His natural generosity leads me to suppose that M. Lamartine was aiming to achieve general reconciliation. But he yielded also to an inner reason which he probably did not admit to himself— the human heart is so ready to deceive itself. . . . It was one of the faults and misfortunes of M. Lamartine that for the sake of his own vanity and glory he would flatter and connive with intelligent and strong characters like M. Barbès, but also with sharp wits, like M. Blanqui, who made use of him while he thought he was using them.

In any case, this calculated and superficial good will of M. Lamartine never extended to the Luxembourg when this palace of the aristocracy became the palace of the people. Why? Because M. de Lamartine knew nothing of real public opinion, because he could not forgive the Luxembourg for being the heart and soul of that February Revolution—all else was shadow and noise—because, finally, he was afraid of socialism, that great reality, as children are afraid of phantoms.

If it were only a question of loving the People with a poetic love, he could have done that certainly, and no one more willingly than he would have lavished on human sufferings the treasures of a sentimentality gushing forth in metaphors. But to espouse boldly the cause of the poor and oppressed against the strong, to brave with the valor of an indomitable soul, injustice armed with a sword, or even injustice crowned with flowers; to expose oneself, for the sake of eternal truth, to being misunderstood, wronged, vilified, ridiculed, stung to the quick by myriad vipers; to endure the hatred of the dishonest in order to keep one's inner peace, to be willing to make adversaries of the whole world if necessary—that is what he lacks. M. Lamartine defied death nobly with the courage of a soldier; he trembled at detractors, with the weakness of a poet. He did not know how to make mortal enemies. This explains why he had on his side all parties for a day. He went to bed thinking he had France on his bedside table. He fell asleep in self-intoxication. He dreamed of dictatorship. He woke up and he was alone.

Louis Blanc, *Histoire de la Révolution de 1848,* 2 vols. (Paris: Flammarion, 1880), II, 63-65, trans. E. A. Clark.

D. *The Revolutionary Radicals: The Clubs and Committees*

This Society has for its object—first, to defend the rights of the people, the exercise of which has been restored to them by the Revolution of February; secondly, to draw from this Revolution all its social consequences. As its point of departure, the Society takes the Declaration of the Rights of Man as laid down in 1793 by Robespierre. It ensues that, in a political point of view, the Repub'ic, one and indivisible, comprehends the inalienable laws of the people. In a social point of view, the old constitution is abolished; and that which is called to replace it must rest on equality and fraternity, the fundamental principles of the new social compact. Consequently, the social revolution, now at its commencement, places itself between the Pariahs and the Privileged of the ancient state of society. To the first it says—Be united, but calm; for in this lies your strength. Your number is such that it must suffice to manifest your will, and make you obtain all you desire. It is also such that you cannot desire anything but what is just.

Your voice and your will are the voice and the will of God. To the others it says—The old social form has disappeared. The reign of privilege and exploitation is past. In the point of view of the ancient social form, if the privileges with which you were invested were acquired in a legal manner, do not avail yourselves of them: these laws were your own work; the immense majority of your brethren were strangers to them, and, therefore, are not bound to respect them. Rally, then, together, for you have need of the pardon of those whom you have so long sacrificed. If, in spite of this promise of pardon, you persist in remaining isolated in order to defend the old social form, you will find in the vanguard, on the day of conflict, our sections organized: and your brethren will no longer hold towards you the language of pardon, but that of justice. [The Members of the Central Committee: Villain, Lebon, Huber, Chipron, Barbès]

Placard of the Society of the Rights of Man and of the Citizen (April 29), *The Annual Register, or a View of the History and Politics of the Year 1848* (London, 1849), pp. 262-63.

The Revolutions of 1848 in Central Europe: Nationalist Antagonisms

A. *The Slavic Viewpoint: The Czechs*

. . . The Slavs, among whom liberty was ever cherished the more fervently as they showed little aspiration for conquest and dominion, and among whom the desire for independence always prevented the formation of a higher central power of any kind, fell in the course of the ages, people after people, under alien dominion. A policy which has long been condemned, as it should be condemned, in the eyes of the world, has most recently of all deprived the heroic Polish nation, our noble kinsmen, of their independence as a State. The whole great Slavonic world, it seemed, found itself in bondage for all time when the ready servants of that system of bondage did not hesitate to deny to the Slavs the very capacity to be free. . . . Now the long under-yoked Slav is again raising his head, he is scaring violence away from his presence, and with lusty emphasis is claiming his ancient heritage, his liberty. Strong in feeling, stronger still in will-power and his newly acquired fraternal unanimity, he remains none the less true to his natural character and the principles of his forefathers. He demands neither conquest nor dominion, but he asks for liberty for himself and for all others: he demands that liberty shall be unconditionally recognized as the most sacred right that man possesses. Therefore we Slavs reject and hold in abhorrence all dominion based on main force and evasion of the law; we reject all privileges and prerogatives as well as all political differentiation of classes; we demand unconditional equality before the law, an equal measure of rights and duties for all. Where a single slave is born among millions, true liberty does not exist in that place. Yes, liberty, equality, fraternity for all who live in the State is our watchword today, as it was a thousand years ago.

Nor is it only for the individuals in the State that we lift up our voices and put forward our demands. Not less sacred to us than man in the enjoyment of his natural rights is the nation, with its sum total of spiritual needs and interests. Even if history has attributed a more complete human development to certain nations than to others, it has none the less always been seen that the capacity of those other nations for development is in no way limited. Nature in and for herself draws no distinction between nations as though some were noble and others ignoble; she has not called any one nation to dominate over others, nor set aside any nation to serve another as an instrument for that other's ends. . . . Yet the German threatens many a Slavonic people with violence if it will not agree to assist in the upbuilding of the political greatness of Germany, and thus the Magyar is not ashamed to arrogate to himself exclusive national rights in Hungary. We Slavs utterly decry all such pretensions; and we reject them the more emphatically the more they are wrongfully disguised in the garb of freedom. Faithful, however, to our natural character, and declining to seek revenge for wrongs done us in the past, we extend a brotherly hand to all neighboring nations who are prepared to recognise and effectively champion with us the full equality of all nations, irrespective of their political power or size.

Similarly we reprehend and hold in abhorrence that policy which claims to deal with lands and nations as mere material, subject to a ruling power, to take, to change, to partition at pleasure or fancy irrespective of the race, the language, the customs and the inclinations of the nations, and regardless of their natural connection or of the independence which is their right. . . .

Taking our stand on the conviction that the mighty current of thought of today demands new political formations and that the State must be reconstructed, if not within new bounds at least upon new foundations, we have proposed to the Austrian Emperor, under whose constitutional rule the majority of us live, that the imperial State be converted into a federation of nations all enjoying equal rights, whereby regard would be paid not less to the different needs of these nations than to those of the united Monarchy. We see in such a federal union not only our own salvation but also liberty, enlightenment and humanity generally; and we are confident that civilised Europe would readily contribute to the realisation of that union. In any case we are determined to ensure for our nationality in Austria, by all the means available to us, a full recognition of the same rights in the State as the German and Magyar nations already enjoy, and in this we rely upon the powerful demand for all genuine rights which wells up warmly in every truly free breast.

The enemies of our nationality have succeeded in terrifying Europe with the bogy of political Panslavism which, they have declared, threatens to destroy all that has been won anywhere for freedom, enlightenment and humanity. We, however, are acquainted with the one magic word which of itself suffices to lay that bogy; and for the sake of freedom, enlightenment and humanity we do not desire to keep it secret from the nations disquieted by the pricks of their own conscience. That word is justice, justice towards the Slavonic nations generally and justice towards its oppressed branches in particular. . . . We raise our voices emphatically on behalf of our unhappy brethren the Poles, whom malicious violence has robbed of independence; we ask the governments concerned finally to remedy this old sin, this curse which has descended as a burdensome heritage upon their Cabinet policy, and in this matter we rely upon the sympathies of all Europe. . . . We look to the Governments of Prussia and Saxony to abandon at long last the systematic denationalisation of the Slavs in . . . East and West Prussia, which they have carried on up till now; we demand of the Hungarian Ministry that without delay they cease to employ inhuman and violent methods against the Slavonic peoples in Hungary, in particular the Serbs, the Croats, the Slovaks and Ruthenians, and that the national rights which are their due shall be fully assured them as speedily as possible.

We, the youngest but by no means the weakest, in entering once more the political arena of Europe, propose that a general European Congress of Nations be summoned for the discussion of all international questions; being thoroughly convinced that free nations will more easily come to agreement than paid diplomats. May this proposal meet with due consideration before the reactionary policy of the individual Courts causes the nations, incited by hatred and malice, mutually to destroy one another!

In the name of liberty, equality and fraternity of all nations. Frantísek Palacký, President of the Slavonic Congress.

"Manifesto of the First Slavonic Congress to the Nations of Europe, June 12, 1848," *The Slavonic and East European Review*, XXVI (April 1948), 309-313, trans. Dr. William Beardmore.

B. The Slavic Viewpoint: The Croatians

YOUR MAJESTY—

It is a well-known fact, that the three united kingdoms of Dalmatia, Croatia and Slavonia, though united with Hungary during seven and a half centuries in good and bad fortune, have yet always preserved their former rights and national liberty, and up to the present day have never recognized the usurped hegemony of Hungary.

We have always been accustomed to see the best guarantee for the national independence of these Kingdoms in our noble Kings whose innate sense of justice, as well as their solemn coronation oath imposed on them the duty of maintaining not only the Kingdom of Hungary but also these united Kingdoms in their rights and liberties. And so it happened that this unimpaired Royal power, which seemed threatening to the Magyars' desire for separation, was for us a sacred refuge, to which we could always appeal for help against our oppressors.

But Your Majesty! the days of last March have robbed us loyal Croats, Slavonians and Dalmatians even of this our sole though powerful support. Our former oppressors have also become oppressors of your Majesty's Royal power. The old Hungary is falling to dust before the breath of the new age, and with it goes the old bond between Austria and Hungary.

Your Majesty! The Croat clings stubbornly to that freedom which has been transmitted to him by his ancestors for so many centuries, and he understands too well the requirements of modern times, not to be heartily grateful to his sovereign for the ever memorable concessions made during the March days to the peoples of the unitary state [Gesamtstaat]. But we confess that a cold shudder ran through our veins, and a dull foreboding came over us, when towards the end of last March we unexpectedly learnt that Hungary's new position towards Austria, instead of being complete amalgamation in the unitary state (as we could not but expect in view of the prevailing constitutional regime in Austria) is that of a state which is entirely independent and separate from Austria.

We loyal Croatians, Slavonians and Dalmatians neither can nor will recognize for these countries any Ministry which seeks to loosen the bonds which have hitherto connected us with the State as a whole [Gesamtstaat]. Let Hungary separate from the Monarchy, and consequently from these Kingdoms, if it has the inclination and the strength; but Croatia, Slavonia and Dalmatia are independent countries, and as such they not merely do not wish to loosen the existing bond with Austria, but far rather declare openly and unreservedly that they wish to enter into a still closer connexion with the now constitutional Empire of Austria, on the basis of complete equality of all nationalities. For if we and our fathers were only deterred from a similar step by the fact that the old Austria was governed absolutely, we for our part no longer see any obstacle to such a rapprochement, in view of [Austria's] metamorphosis today. We therefore submit in all humility for Your Majesty's sanction the following resolutions of our Diet, composed of elected representatives and meeting on June 5, 1848:—

1. Since for the above reasons we do not recognize the present Hungarian Government for these countries, we regard all decrees, issued by the Hungarian Ministry in violation of our rights and with insult to the dignity of the Ban, as unlawful and illegal, and at the same time would beg Your Majesty to declare invalid all such actions of the Hungarian Ministry as are injurious to us, and to shield and protect us in future from its fatal influences. Consequently the present provisional Government . . . should continue its present activity for which we confidently await your Majesty's approval, and for the future requests, that a Government may be formed for these Kingdoms, under the presidency of the Ban. . . . But in order to better ensure the unity of the Monarchy as a whole, we are ready to subordinate even this our own provincial Government in matters affecting the whole State, to the responsible Central Government of the Monarchy as a whole. . . .

4. The official language in the entire public life without any exception shall be the national Slav language [spoken] in these countries; and in such a way that even the decrees of the Central Government relative to these countries shall be published exclusively in this language.

5. All matters relating to internal administration will fall within the sphere of the Diet of these Kingdoms. But in respect of those affairs which proceed from the mutual relation of these Kingdoms to the State as a whole, these Kingdoms submit to the decisions of the Central Parliament, to which also the Central Ministry will be responsible for its actions.

But in order to prove that they definitely adhere to the Unitary State, these Kingdoms have already elected their deputies for the Central Parliament of the whole Monarchy, which is to be held on June 26; and these [deputies] are to convey, in the name of the whole nation, to the representatives of the other allied peoples of Austria, our just and earnest wishes of support and greeting.

6. Since it is natural that kindred nationalities should exercise a mutual attraction on each other, and since the Kingdom of Dalmatia, both in view of ancient chartered rights and the coronation oath and solemn promises of Your Majesty, forms an integral part of these Kingdoms, the said Kingdom of Dalmatia shall, both in respect of legislation and administration, be completely reunited to these Kingdoms, while the remaining Southern Slav portions of the Monarchy . . . shall be brought into closer connexion with these Kingdoms. . . .

We respectfully remain Your Majesty's loyal subjects.

THE BAN AND DEPUTIES OF THE KINGDOMS OF DALMATIA, CROATIA AND SLAVONIA. Agram, 5th and following days of June, 1848.

Address of the Croatian Diet to His Majesty, June, 1848, trans. in R. W. Seton-Watson, *The Southern Slav Question and the Hapsburg Monarchy* (London: Constable and Co. Ltd., 1911), pp. 350-56.

C. The Magyar View: Louis Kossuth's Speech of the 11th July, 1848

Gentlemen, the country is in danger. Perhaps it would suffice to say thus much; for, with the dawn of liberty, the dark veil has dropped from the nation. You know what the condition of our country is; you know that besides the troops of the line, a militia of about twelve thousand men has been organized; you know that the authorities have been empowered to place corps of the National Guard on a war footing, in order to establish an effective force to defend the country, and to punish sedition, which is rife on our frontiers. This command found an echo in the nation.

Under such circumstances we took the reins of government, menaced by treachery, rebellion, reactionary movements, and by all those passions which the policy of Metternich leagued to us as a cursed inheritance. Scarcely had we assumed the government—nay, not all of us had even assembled—when we already received the most authentic information that the Panslavonic agitation had no other object than to excite the whole of the upper provinces to open rebellion, and that even the day had been fixed when the outbreak should take place. . . .

Croatia is in open rebellion! Many years have elapsed, gentlemen, when not only one or the other, but numbers, called the attention of the government to the fact, that in encouraging—I say not forgiving, but encouraging—the Illyric agitation, it would nourish a serpent in its bosom which would compass the ruin of the dynasty. And since the revolutionary state in which we find Europe shaking on her foundations, the gentlemen in those parts fancied they might with impunity break out in open rebellion. Had Hungary given any

cause whatever for this rebellion, she would, without considering the fact that there is a revolution, ask you to be just to Croatia, and to subdue the revolt, not with the force of arms, but with the sacred name of justice.

Where is a reason to be found that, even if we take up arms to quell the disturbance, we should feel in our own hearts the conviction of having ourselves provoked the disturbance? I say, no! The rights we have acquired for ourselves, we have likewise acquired for Croatia; the liberty that was granted to the people, was likewise granted to the Croats; we extended the indemnity allowed by us to our nobility, at our own expense, to Croatia—for that country is too small and powerless to raise herself the indemnity.

With regard to nationality, Croatia entertained apprehensions—though produced by various conceptions and by erroneous ideas—for the Parliament has expressly decreed that in public life the Croats should have the fullest right to make use of their own language in accordance with their own statutes; and thus their nationality has been sanctioned, by this public recognition. Their municipal rights the Parliament has not only not impaired, but extended and augmented. . . .

In one word, we have not neglected any thing whatever which, within the limits of integrity, of liberty, and of the rights of the people, we could do to pacify their minds. We, gentlemen, can not, therefore, admit that on the part of the cabinet the slightest cause has been given to provoke the Croatian rebellion.

If a people think the liberty they possess too limited, and take up arms to conquer more, they certainly play a doubtful game—for a sword has two edges. Still I can understand it. But if a people say, Your liberty is too much for us, we will not have it if you give it us, but we will go and bow under the old yoke of Absolutism—that is a thing which I endeavor in vain to understand.

The case, however, stands nearly thus: in the so-called petition which was sent to his majesty by the Conventicle of Agram, they pray that they may be allowed to separate from Hungary—not to be a self-consistent, independent nation, but to submit to the Austrian ministry.... I do not, indeed, ascribe to the sentiment of freedom so great an influence on the masses, as not to be persuaded that even this sham loyalty, in its awkward affectation, is but an empty pretext under which other purposes are concealed. On the part of the leaders it covers the reactionary tendency; but on the other hand, this idea is connected with the plan of erecting an Austro-Slavonian monarchy. They say: "Let us send deputies to Vienna; let us procure the majority for the Slavonian element, and Austria will cease to be a German empire; and what with the Bohemians, and our people down here, a new Slavonian empire will rise." This is a rather hazardous game, and Europe will probably soon decide on the question; for if we should not master these affairs, they will become a European question. This much is certain, that this combination (if of any consequence at all) will doubtless involve the ruin of the Austrian dynasty. There can be no doubt about it.

The Viennese ministers have thought proper, in the name of the Austrian emperor, to declare to the cabinet of the King of Hungary, that unless we make peace with the Croats at any price, they will act in opposition to us. This is as much as to say, that the Austrian emperor declares war to the King of Hungary, or to his own self. Whatever opinion you, gentlemen, may have formed of the cabinet, I believe you may so far rely on our patriotic feelings and on our honor, as to render it superfluous on my part to tell you that we have replied to this menace in a manner becoming the dignity of the nation.

The Austrian relations, the affairs of the countries on the Lower Danube, the Servian disturbances, the Croation rebellion, Panslavonian agitators, and the reactionary movements—all these circumstances, taken together, cause me to say the nation is in danger, or rather, that it will be in danger unless our resolution be firm!

The danger, therefore is great, or rather, a danger threatening to become great gathers on the horizon of our country, and we ought, above all, to find in ourselves the strength for its removal. That nation alone will live which in itself has sufficient vital power; that which knows not to save itself by its own strength, but only by the aid of others, has no future. I therefore demand of you, gentlemen, a great resolution. Proclaim that, in just appreciation of the extraordinary circumstances on account of which the Parliament has assembled, the nation is determined to bring the greatest sacrifices for the defense of its crown, of its liberty, and of its independence, and that, in this respect, it will at no price enter with any one into a transaction which even in the least might injure the national independence and liberty, but that it will be always ready to grant all reasonable wishes of every one. But in order to realize this important resolution, either by mediating, if possible, an honorable peace, or by fighting a victorious battle, the government is to be authorized by the nation to raise the effective strength of the army to two hundred thousand men, and for this purpose to equip immediately forty thousand men, and the rest as the protection of the country and the honor of the nation may demand. . . .

Gentlemen, what I meant to say is, that this request on the part of the government ought not be considered as a vote of confidence. No; we ask for your vote for the preservation of the country! And I would ask you, gentlemen, if anywhere in our country a breast sighs for liberation, or a wish waits for its fulfillment, let that breast suffer yet a while, let that wish have a little patience, until we have saved the country. (Cheers.) This is my request! You all have risen to a man, and I bow before the nation's greatness! If your energy equals your patriotism, I will make bold to say, that even the gates of hell shall not prevail against Hungary!

> W. H. Stiles, *Austria in 1848–49* (New York: Harper and Brothers, 1852), II, 384-94.

II. A FOREIGN POLICY FOR LIBERAL NATIONALISM

The dilemma of the liberal in international affairs is illustrated in the early Victorian period by the post-revolutionary debate in the British House of Commons occasioned by Palmerston's highhanded conduct of the Don Pacifico affair. This four-day Great Debate widened to a comprehensive discussion of the fundamental lines of British foreign policy, past, present, and future, and revealed deep-seated conflicts within the liberal camp then emerging from a realignment of the old Whigs and Tories—Manchester, Palmerstonian, Peelite, Gladstonian—all liberals of a sort, and all in an uneasy alliance with nationalism and idealism.

Viscount Palmerston, the Secretary of State for Foreign Affairs, had entered Parliament at the age of 23 and had a lifetime of experience in cabinets and the House of Commons. Starting as a Conservative and follower of William Pitt, he came to accept moderate parliamentary reform and entered the Foreign Office under Earl Grey, the Whig leader. He was a disciple of Canning in maintaining that a strong foreign policy would lead to peace. This meant upholding the power and prestige of England, and defending British interests by intervention at times or by secret diplomacy at other times. He sympathized with oppressed nationalities and constitutionalism, but not to the extent of quixotic adventures that would sacrifice British interests, as the Hungarians, Poles, and Italians found to their cost in 1849.

When the Tories were split in 1846 by Sir Robert Peel's defection to the Free Traders, Lord John Russell and the Whigs came into power and Palmerston again returned to the Foreign Office to preside through the stormy years of revolution on the continent. The debate on the Don Pacifico affair reveals the crosscurrents and realignments of English opinion and policy during the revolutions, when practically every vital question of British relations with the continent came to the fore, not only with the major powers of France, Prussia, Austria, and Russia, but with all the smaller powers and submerged nations as well.

William Ewart Gladstone, like Palmerston, had begun as a Conservative, but was on the path that led to his emergence as a Liberal and the formation of the Liberal Party. The following was his first major speech on foreign policy in the House of Commons. John Bright and Richard Cobden were the leaders of the Manchester liberals who believed that free trade, disarmament, and non-intervention would lead to peace, internationalism, and the true prestige of England.

Alexander Cockburn, who had just entered the House of Commons a year before as a rising lawyer, gained an opportunity for distinction by the legal and forensic ability manifested in this decisive speech and in consequence became Palmerston's Attorney-General. Henry Drummond was a Tory of the old school, who also was elected to the House for the first time in 1847. He did not enter politics until he was in his 60's and remained an independent and sarcastic observer, portrayed by

Carlyle as "a singular mixture of all things."

In England nationalism was seldom a conscious and articulate doctrine even among the intellectuals, but nationalist feeling had penetrated so deeply all the levels of the population that Palmerston could appeal to uninformed public opinion and the popular newspapers to support his flamboyant statement of British national interest and thus win out against *The Times,* the leaders of most of the Parliamentary groups, the Queen and the Prince Consort, and even his own divided cabinet. It is doubtful, however, if even he could have succeeded if he had not tempered what some opponents have labelled chauvinism and bullying by his appeal to justice, generosity, and individual rights.

The occasion for this great debate was a motion of confidence by Mr. Roebuck, one of Palmerston's supporters in the House of Commons, in answer to the condemnation of Palmerston's foreign policy by the House of Lords. He moved: "That the principles which have hitherto regulated the foreign policy of Her Majesty's Government are such as were required to preserve untarnished the honor and dignity of this country, and in times of unexampled difficulty the best qualified to maintain peace between England and the various countries of the world." The debate ranged widely over Palmerston's quarrels with the French constitutional monarchy and republic, his stormy interventions and retreats on the continent during the Revolutions of 1848–49, especially in Italy and Hungary, and by no means limited itself to his arbitrary ordering of the British fleet to Greece to force settlement of the undoubtedly exaggerated claims of Don Pacifico, a Portuguese Jew from Gibraltar and therefore a British subject, against the Greek government for the damage to his home inflicted by a Greek mob in 1847, and Palmerston's willingness to risk war with France and Russia, the co-guarantors of Greek independence. Should England follow the reformist pledge of 1830 by the Whig Earl Grey, "Peace, non-intervention and retrenchment," or should it actively intervene by political or military means to advance the cause of liberalism and national independence? Was Palmerston at heart a crusader or an opportunist pursuing the balance of power for England's benefit? In any case, Palmerston won a resounding victory in Britain, but whether this 19th century "John Bull" with all his faults, virtues, and contradictions furthered the cause of liberalism, national freedom, or friendship for Britain has been debated ever since.

The Great Debate Over British Intervention: The Don Pacifico Affair

A. Palmerston Defends His Foreign Policy

When I say that this is an important question, I say it in the fullest expression of the term. It is a matter which concerns not merely the tenure of office by one individual, or even by a Government; it is a question that involves principles of national policy, and the deepest interests as well as the honour and dignity of England.

With regard to our policy with respect to Italy, I utterly deny the charges that have been brought against us, of having been the advocates, supporters, and encouragers of revolution. It has always been the fate of advocates of temperate reform and of constitutional improvement to be run at as the fomentors of revolution. It is the easiest mode of putting them down; it is the received *formula.* It is the established practice of those who are the advocates of arbitrary government to say, "Never mind real revolutionists; we know how to deal with them; your dangerous man is the moderate reformer; he is such a plausible man; the only way of getting rid of him, is to set the world at him, by calling him a revolutionist."

Now, there are revolutionists of two kinds in this world. In the first place, there are those violent, hotheaded, and unthinking men who fly to arms, who overthrow established Governments; and who recklessly, without regard to consequences, and without measuring difficulties and comparing strength, deluge their country with blood, and draw down the greatest calamities on their fellow-countrymen. These are the revolutionists of one class. But there are revolutionists of another kind; blind-minded men, who, animated by antiquated prejudices, and daunted by ignorant apprehensions, dam up the current of human improvement; until the irresistible pressure of accumulated discontent breaks down the opposing barriers, and overthrows and levels to the earth, those very institutions which a timely application of renovating means would have rendered strong and lasting. Such revolutionists as these are the men who call us revolutionists. It was not to make revolutions that the Earl of Minto went to Italy, or that we, at the request of the Governments of Austria and Naples, offered our mediation between contending parties. . . .

I believe that the principles on which we have acted are those which are held by the great mass of the people of this country. I am convinced these principles are calculated, so far as the influence of England may properly be exercised with respect to the destinies of other countries, to conduce to the maintenance of peace, to the advancement of civilisation, to the welfare and happiness of mankind. . . .

It is a noble thing to be allowed to guide the policy and to influence the destinies of such a country; and, if ever it was an object of honourable ambition, more than ever must it be so at the moment at which I am speaking. For while we have seen . . . the political earthquake rocking Europe from side to side—while we have seen thrones shaken, shattered, levelled; institutions overthrown and destroyed—while in almost every country of Europe the conflict of civil war has deluged the land with blood, from the Atlantic to the Black Sea, from the Baltic to the Mediterranean; this country has presented a spectacle honourable to the people of England, and worthy of the admiration of *mankind*.

We have shown that liberty is compatible with order; that individual freedom is reconcilable with obedience to the law. We have shown the example of a nation, in which every class of society accepts with cheerfulness the lot which Providence has assigned to it; while at the same time every individual of each class is constantly striving to raise himself in the social scale—not by injustice and wrong, not by violence and illegality—but by persevering good conduct, and by the steady and energetic exertion of the moral and intellectual faculties with which his Creator has endowed him. To govern such a people as this, is indeed an object worthy of the ambition of the noblest man who lives in the land; and therefore I find no fault with those who may think any opportunity a fair one, for endeavouring to place themselves in so distinguished and honourable a position. But I contend that we have not in our foreign policy done anything to forfeit the confidence of the country. . . . I maintain that the principles which can be traced through all our foreign transactions, as the guiding rule and directing spirit of our proceedings, are such as deserve approbation. I therefore fearlessly challenge the verdict which this House, as representing a political, a commercial, a constitutional country, is to give on the question now brought before it; whether the principles on which the foreign policy of Her Majesty's Government has been conducted, and the sense of duty which has led us to think ourselves bound to afford protection to our fellow subjects abroad, are proper and fitting guides for those who are charged with the Government of England; and whether, as the Roman, in days of old, held himself free from indignity, when he could say *Civis* *Romanus sum* [I am a Roman citizen]; so also a British subject, in whatever land he may be, shall feel confident that the watchful eye and the strong arm of England, will protect him against injustice and wrong.

Parliamentary Debates, Commons, third series, Vol. 112, June 25, 1850, cols. 380, 432-33, 443-44.

B. Gladstone's Criticism

Sir, I am well prepared, following the example of other and more distinguished men, to bear my share in the abuse which, I doubt not, may attend the part which we shall take on this occasion. I am prepared to hear it said that we are espousing the cause, as against England, of countries other than our own; that we cabal against the noble Lord because he is the protector of Englishmen domiciled abroad. Sir, I deny that he has truly protected Englishmen by the course he has pursued. I hold that no Minister in his place can really give to Englishmen resident in foreign lands either an effectual or a permanent protection, except by a careful observance of the principles that have been consecrated by the universal assent of mankind for governing the conduct of nation to nation. In vain do you talk to us of a knot of foreign conspirators against the noble Lord, . . . [it] is the combined opinion of civilised Europe. . . .

Sir, great as is the influence and power of Britain, she cannot afford to follow, for any length of time, a self-isolating policy. It would be a contravention of the law of nature and of God, if it were possible for any single nation of Christendom to emancipate itself from the obligations which bind all other nations, and to arrogate, in the face of mankind, a position of peculiar privilege. And now I will grapple with the noble Lord on the ground which he selected for himself, in the most triumphant portion of his speech, by his reference to those emphatic words, *Civis* *Romanus sum* [I am a Roman citizen]. He vaunted, amidst the cheers of his supporters, that under his administration an Englishman should be, throughout the world, what the citizen of Rome had been. What then, Sir, was a Roman citizen? He was the member of a privileged caste; he belonged to a conquering race, to a nation that held all others bound down by the strong arm of power. For him there was to be an exceptional system of law; for him principles were to be asserted, and by him rights were to be enjoyed that were denied to the rest of the world. Is such, then, the view of the noble Lord, as to the relation that is to subsist between England and other countries? Does he make the claim for us, that we are to be uplifted upon a platform high above the standing-ground of all other nations? It is, indeed, too clear, not only from the expressions, but from the whole spirit of the speech of the noble Viscount, that too much of this notion is lurking in his mind; that he adopts in part that vain conception, that we, forsooth, have a mission to be the censors of vice and folly, of abuse and imperfection, among the other countries of the world; that we are to be the universal schoolmasters; and that all those who hesitate to recognise our office, can be governed only by prejudice or personal animosity, and should have the blind war of diplomacy forthwith declared against them. . . . What, Sir, ought a Foreign Secretary to be? Is he to be like some gallant knight at a tournament of old, pricking forth into the lists, armed at all points, confiding in all his sinews and his skill, challenging all comers for the sake of honour, and having no other duty than to lay as many as possible of his adversaries sprawling in the dust? If such is the idea of a good Foreign Secretary, I, for one, would vote to the noble Lord his present appointment for his life. But, Sir, I do not understand the duty of a Secretary for Foreign Affairs to be of such a character. I understand it to be his duty to conciliate peace with dignity. I think it to be the very first of all his duties studiously to observe, and to exalt in honour among mankind, that great code of principles which is termed the law of nations which . . . I find . . . a great and noble monument of human wisdom, founded on the combined dictates of reason and experience. . . .

Sir, the English people, whom we are here to represent, are indeed a great and noble people; but it adds nothing to their greatness or their nobleness, that when we assemble in this place we should trumpet forth our virtues in elaborate panegyrics, and designate those who may not be wholly of our mind as a knot of foreign conspirators. When, indeed, I heard the hon. and learned Gentleman the Member for Sheffield [Mr. Roebuck, supporter of Palmerston] glorifying us, together with the rest of the people of this country, and announcing that we soared in unapproachable greatness, and the like, I confess I felt that eulogies such as those savoured somewhat of bombast; and thought it much to the honour of this House that the praises thus vented seemed to fall so flat; that the cookery of the hon. and learned Gentleman was evidently seasoned beyond the capacity and relish of our palates. It is this insular temper, and this self-glorifying tendency, which the policy of the noble Lord, and the doctrines of his support-

ers, tend so much to foment, and which has given to that policy the quarrelsome character that marks some of their speeches; for, indeed, it seems as if there lay upon the noble Lord an absolute necessity for quarrelling. No doubt it makes a difference, what may be the institutions of one country or another. If he can, he will quarrel with an absolute monarchy. If he cannot find an absolute monarchy for the purpose, he will quarrel with one which is limited. If he cannot find even that, yet, sooner than not quarrel at all, he will quarrel with a republic. He has lately shown us this in the case of France; he showed it once before in the case of America. . . .

Sir, I say the policy of the noble Lord tends to encourage and confirm in us that which is our besetting fault and weakness, both as a nation and as individuals. Let an Englishman travel where he will as a private person, he is found in general to be upright, highminded, brave, liberal, and true; but with all this, foreigners are too often sensible of something that galls them in his presence, and I apprehend it is because he has too great a tendency to self-esteem —too little disposition to regard the feelings, the habits, and the ideas of others. Sir, I find this characteristic too plainly legible in the policy of the noble Lord. I doubt not that use will be made of our present debate to work upon this peculiar weakness of the English mind. The people will be told that those who oppose the Motion are governed by personal motives, have no regard for public principle, no enlarged ideas of national policy . . . but, Sir, let the House of Commons be warned —let it warn itself—against all illusions. There is in this case also a course of appeal. There is an appeal, such as the hon. and learned Member for Sheffield has made, from the one House of Parliament to the other. There is a further appeal from this House of Parliament to the people of England; but, lastly, there is also an appeal from the people of England to the general sentiment of the civilised world; and I, for my part, am of opinion that England will stand shorn of a chief part of her glory and her pride if she shall be found to have separated herself, through the policy she pursues abroad, from the moral supports which the general and fixed convictions of mankind afford—if the day shall come in which she may continue to excite the wonder and the fear of other nations, but in which she shall have no part in their affection and their regard.

No, Sir, let it not be so: let us recognise, and recognise with frankness, the equality of the weak with the strong; the principles of brotherhood among nations, and of their sacred independence. When we are asking for the maintenance of the rights which belong to our fellow-subjects resident in Greece, let us do as we would be done by, and let us pay all the respect to a feeble State and to the infancy of free institutions, which we should desire and should exact from others towards their maturity and their strength. Let us refrain from all gratui-

Ibid., cols. 586-90.

tous and arbitrary meddling in the internal concerns of other States, even as we should resent the same interference if it were attempted to be practised towards ourselves. If the noble Lord has indeed acted on these principles, let the Government to which he belongs have your verdict in its favour; but if he has departed from them, as I contend, and as I humbly think and urge upon you that it has been too amply proved, then the House of Commons must not shrink from the performance of its duty, under whatever expectations of momentary obloquy or reproach, because we shall have done what is right; we shall enjoy the peace of our own consciences, and receive, whether a little sooner or a little later, the approval of the voice of the public, for having entered our solemn protest against a system of policy which we believe . . . must of necessity in its final results be unfavourable even to the security of British subjects resident abroad . . . unfavourable to the dignity of the country . . . and equally unfavourable to that other great and sacred object . . . the maintenance of peace with the nations of the world.

C. A Manchester Liberal's Criticism: Richard Cobden

. . . But what would Earl Grey have said to the doctrine of the hon. and learned Gentleman, that we have no prospect of peace with the countries of Europe till they have adopted constitutional Governments? What sort of constitutional Governments? Is it our own? Why, even if they came so far as this, and suppose they adopt our form of government, might not hon. Members in the Assembly at Washington get up and say, "We will have no peace till we make the world republican." The hon. and learned Gentleman

seems to have set out with the doctrine that we ought to interfere with the forms of government of the nations of Europe; and, judging from the noble Lord's speech, I must say he appears to be no unwilling pupil in that school of policy. If the House of Commons votes its approbation of such sentiments, and the noble Lord acts on them, I think the Foreign Office will have undertaken the reform and constitutionalising of every country on the face of the earth. But do you think the people of this country, when they get cool, will see the wisdom of carrying out such a course? . . .

If you claim the right of intervention in your Government, you must tolerate it in other nations also. With what face could you get up and denounce the Emperor of Russia for invading Hungary after the doctrine advocated by the hon. and learned Member to-night, had been adopted by this country? I say, if you want to benefit nations struggling for their freedom, establish as one of the maxims of international law the principle of non-intervention. If you want to give a guarantee for peace, and, as I believe, the surest guarantee for progress and freedom, lay down this principle and act on it—that no foreign State has a right by force to interfere with the domestic concerns of another State, even to confer what you conceive to be a benefit upon it, against its own consent. . . .

But I come back to the principle. Do you want to benefit the Hungarians? I will tell you the sentiments of the leading Hungarians. I have seen them all, and I must say that, much as I admired them during their noble struggle, what I have seen of them in adversity has entitled them to still greater respect, for I never saw men endure adversity with more manly fortitude and dignified self-respect. They have avoided all expressions of sympathy from public meetings, and (loathing the idea of being dependent on the charity of others) have sought, by emigration to America and elsewhere, an opportunity of subsisting by the labour of their own hands. These men say, "We don't ask you to help us, or to come to our assistance. Establish such a principle as shall provide we shall not be interfered with by others." And what do the Italians say? They don't want the English to interfere with them or to help them. "Leave us to ourselves," say they. "Establish the principle that we shall not be interfered with by foreigners." [Mr. Roebuck: Hear, hear!] I will answer the hon. and learned Gentleman's cheer. He seems to ask, how

will you keep out Austria from Italy, and Russia from Hungary? Why, by setting a good example ourselves, and then, if necessary, by protesting against the violation of the principle by others. I will give him an illustration of what I mean. Does he remember when Kossuth took refuge in Turkey, and Austria and the Emperor of Russia demanded him back? I beg him to understand that that illustrious refugee was not saved by any intervention of the Foreign Secretary. Has it not been admitted that the Emperor of Russia gave up his claim before the courier arrived from England? What was it then that liberated him? It was the universal outburst of public opinion and public indignation in Western Europe. And why had public opinion this power? Because this demand for the extradition of political offenders was a violation of the law of nations, which declares that persons who have committed political offences in one State shall find a sanctuary in another, and ought not to be delivered up. . . . Let us begin and set the example to other nations of non-intervention. I have no doubt that our example and protest would influence the Governments of Austria and Russia; but what possible moral influence can this country have with those States when the Government goes abroad to interfere with the domestic affairs of other countries? It is said, however, that the noble Lord the Foreign Secretary goes abroad as the champion of liberalism and constitutionalism. But I cannot fall into this delusion. I cannot trace this battle that we are taught to believe is going on under the noble Viscount's auspices between liberalism and despotism abroad. I do not think that the noble Lord is more democratic than his colleagues. . . . I do not find that the noble Lord has taken up any great question of constitutional freedom abroad. Did he ever protest against the invasion of Hungary by Russia? He made a speech against Austria, I remember, on one occasion, but he did not breathe a syllable against Russia. The only allusion he made to Russia was in the nature of an apology, uttered in a sense that seemed to justify the part taken by Russia rather than otherwise. . . .

I believe the progress of freedom depends more upon the maintenance of peace, the spread of commerce, and the diffusion of education, than upon the labours of cabinets and foreign offices.

Ibid., cols. 670, 671-74.

D. A Radical Supporter of Palmerston Defends Intervention: Mr. Cockburn

I admit that to those hon. Gentlemen who consider that peace is the great end and aim of existence, and that to peace all else is to be sacrificed— who hold that man was created by Heaven for the sole purpose of producing, and manufacturing, and consuming cotton—who recognise no nobler aspirations, no impulses of humanity—I admit to them, that peace is of the greatest importance to this country—not merely peace between this country and foreign Governments, but peace between foreign Governments and the people who are subjected to those Governments. I admit to them that peace is essential to the development of our industry, and to the progress of our manufactures. But I tell those men that every revolution and struggle in Europe is fatal to our interests, and I tell them that as matters now are, such things will frequently occur. Mark my words, unless the relations between the governors and the governed be placed on a more satisfactory basis, you may secure peace for the day, as men have before now bought peace at the price of their independence; but that is an

And if you prevent those perturbations which have recently taken place abroad in consequence of your foreign policy, and if you will leave other nations in greater tranquillity, those ideas of freedom will continue to progress, and you need not trouble yourself about them. . . . In private life we no longer find it necessary to carry arms for our protection, as did our forefathers. There has been the discontinuance of the practice of duelling; and something should be done to carry the same spirit into the intercourse of nations.

unsafe and an uncertain condition of things. You had far better obtain peace, based and founded on principles which are likely to endure; otherwise you only put off the evil day. You may execute the leaders, and imprison their followers. You may decimate by military executions—it matters not. The time will come when the struggle will be renewed and renewed, over and over again, till freedom is at last secured. It would be far better to settle it at once, and to settle it as it can only be settled, by inducing arbitrary monarchs to act righteously by their subjects—by inducing the people to accept the counsels of mediation and peace. . . .

. . . When the right hon. Gentleman the Member for the University of Oxford [Gladstone] says we are a byword and a scorn among nations, and that "Englishman" is a hated name, he says what is utterly incorrect. He identifies a nation with its arbitrary rulers. I tell him that the nations, that is, the people of Europe, do not dislike the English, but, on the contrary, our policy for the last few years has endeared us to them. They know the difficulties of our position, they make all allowance for the Government, they know it cannot interfere by force of arms, but they know that constitutional liberty in every quarter of the world has the sympathy of the minds and hearts of the British people, and they know that the Government exhibits the faithful echo of these sympathies. We have now arrived at a most momentous epoch in the history of this country—aye, and of the world. We are called upon to take our choice between two great antagonistic principles. Is the foreign policy of this country to be the foreign policy which the noble Lord and the Government have pursued—that middle policy between absolutism and republicanism, encouraging constitutional governments, but not interfering to establish them by military force; using only our moral in-fluence, and taking the proud position as the head of the constitutional nations of the world? The arbitrary rulers of foreign nations may endeavour to destroy Her Majesty's Government; but rest assured of this—when the nations of the Continent have at length succeeded in establishing constitutional governments, and in securing free institutions for themselves, and when their voices can speak out, they will look back gratefully to the sympathy we have shown them in their time of suffering and distress; and the influence which we shall maintain amongst them will be commensurate with that sympathy.

Ibid., cols. 638, 642-43.

E. A Tory Criticism of All Liberalism: Mr. Drummond

The present Ministry was founded on agitation originally, and is supported by agitation now; and it is impossible that a Government which is the creature of agitation at home, can be the promoters of peace abroad. Amongst the chief supporters of the Government are the Manchester School, the heads of which have openly declared the ultimate object that they have in view. The hon. Member for Manchester [John Bright] declared lately at a public meeting—

"We live in an age of agitation. I am one of those who greatly approve of this state of things, and rejoice at it. There is a party in this country rapidly moving onward towards a peaceable, wide, and enduring democracy. The glorious constitution of Crown, Lords, and Commons, is in fact an imposture, which it is part of my duty to expose."

Another speaker of the same class said—

"If the working classes will but join the middle classes in right good earnest, the upper classes, the corinthian capital of the column, would soon begin to crumble; and fall they must, for they are rotten at the core."

I am at a loss to discover any difference between these principles and those enunciated by the noble Lord the other night at the conclusion of his speech. I was lately looking at a bed of red roses; many were of different shades, some deep red, and called the Black Prince, and some quite light, and rejoicing in the name of the Maiden's Blush. I am willing to conclude that Her Majesty's Ministers are of the delicate tint of the maiden's blush; but still they are all red: some darker and some lighter, but all alike red; and I am totally unable to discover any difference between them and the red republicans, save as one red rose differs from another. . . .

It is absurd to suppose that we can adopt agitation as a political principle at home, and make tranquillity the principle of our transactions abroad. The principle of the Government from first to last has been to keep up a system of political agitation; and the Ministers are only the stormy petrels, the harbingers of universal European convulsion. I have no doubt that they will so continue, and that nothing will stop them. But I deprecate any attempt to overturn the Government so long as the country is unconvinced of the delusiveness of the path which we are pursuing —a path which I am convinced can lead

Ibid., cols. 593-96.

III. THE FRANCO-PRUSSIAN WAR AND THE ANNEXATION OF ALSACE-LORRAINE

The decades following the Revolutions of 1848 witnessed a disillusionment with idealism and liberalism. The Czechs, the Poles, the South Slavs fell into a sullen resentment under renewed oppression by the old absolute monarchies; the Hungarians, the Germans, and the Italians achieved political power under "realistic" political leaders who were willing to sacrifice freedom to power and unity.

The War of 1870 between France and Germany is often taken as the beginning of "contemporary history" because it proved a turning point not only in the national affairs of the two chief rivals but in its international repercussions, in both thought and action. The new age of power politics was an age marked by the trend to forceful, illiberal, aggressive nationalism in much of Europe.

Heinrich von Treitschke's career epitomizes the development of a liberal nationalist to an apologist for Prussia's and Bismarck's policy of unification by "blood and iron." His opposition to Bismarck's unconstitutional defiance of the Reichstag was changed to passionate support with Bismarck's success in the Danish War of 1864 and the Austro-Prussian War of 1866. By 1870 Trietschke at the age of 36 was one of the most influential political writers and speakers in Germany, through his forceful journalism and his widely attended university lectures at Heidelberg on politics and history. In 1871 he began his career in the Reichstag and shortly after he was appointed to the University of Berlin.

The article here quoted in part was written August 30, 1870, before the decisive

but to one result, which is the involving of all the countries in Europe in one scene of universal bloodshed. . . .

. . . I will not consent to overthrow one set of men merely to uphold another equally culpable with themselves.

Prussian victory at Sedan, and popularized in a widely read pamphlet Bismarck's demand for the annexation of Alsace-Lorraine as punishment for France's alleged war guilt. The arguments are a kind of recapitulation of all the stages of the evolution of Treitschke's—and Germany's—nationalism. Side by side, often in contradiction, like successive geological layers confused by rough excavation, appear arguments of successive stages, romantic, liberal, and Bismarckian.

Ernest Renan was one of the leading Germanophile intellectuals, venerating the idealism of Kant, Fichte, Herder, and Goethe, as did Michelet and Victor Hugo. He recognized the German theologian and philosopher David Strauss, author of the agnostic and controversial *Life of Jesus*, as his "master" and was carrying on a warm correspondence with him as the war began. Renan had cherished as the great ideal of his life "the intellectual, moral and political alliance of Germany and France, including England, which should constitute a force capable of governing the world and directing it in the ways of a liberal civilization, equally distant from the uninformed blind order of democracy and from the childish yearnings to return to a dead past." (*La réforme intellectuelle et morale*, Paris 1884, 4th ed. [first published 1871], preface, p. v.) He expected Strauss to maintain the same Olympian internationalism and dislike of militarism, whether of the Prussian or the French variety. His two open letters, published a year apart, in response to two open letters published by Strauss challenging him to speak for France, reveal his tragic but not bitter disillusionment at the passionate Prussianism of the German intellectuals he had admired and had defended at the cost of considerable unpopularity during the war. He came to believe there were "two opposite poles of the German character," the gentle and liberal one he had idealized and the "man of iron."

The problems of war guilt, peace terms, national character, self-determination, national security, and unity were focussed in the impassioned arguments for and against the annexation of Alsace-Lorraine.

A. Heinrich von Treitschke

Wherever Germans live, as far as the remote colonies beyond the seas, the flags are flying from every window, and the clanging of bells and the thunder of cannon are proclaiming victory after victory. All of us know that after three more frightful struggles—at Metz, at Strassburg, at Paris—the war will be gloriously closed. To him who remembers at this moment the bitter shame which we have hidden in our hearts for so many years since the day of Olmütz, it must often appear as if all this were a dream. . . .

The thought, however, which, after first knocking timidly at our doors as a shamefaced wish, has, in four swift weeks, grown to be the mighty war-cry of the nation, is no other than this: "Restore what you stole from us long ago: give back Alsace and Lorraine."

Were I to marshal the reasons which make it our duty to demand this, I should feel as if the task had been set me to prove that the world is round. What can be said on the subject was said after the battle of Leipzig, in Ernst Moritz Arndt's glorious tract, "The Rhine the German River, not the German Boundary"; said exhaustively, and beyond contradiction, at the time of the Second Peace of Paris, by all the considerable statesmen of non-Austrian-Germany—by Stein and Humboldt, by Munster and Gagern. . . . If a reckless, robber-war like this is to cost that people nothing more than a war indemnity, the cynical jesters, who wor-

ship chance and fortune as the only governing powers among the nations, and laugh at the rights of States as a dream of kind-hearted ideologues, would be proved to be in the right. The sense of justice to Germany demands the lessening of France. . . .

What is demanded by justice is, at the same time, absolutely necessary for our security. . . .

Every State must seek the guarantees of its security in itself alone. The silly fancy, that gratitude and magnanimity could secure the German countries against a defeated France, has, twice over, been its own fearful punishment. What German can read without rage the account of those peace proceedings at Paris in which victor and vanquished exchanged parts, and a respectful attention was paid to all the prejudices of France, while nobody thought of the feelings of Germany? . . . If the France of 1815, which still possessed a great treasure of moral forces, fell back so soon on greedy dreams of conquest, what have we to expect from the society of the Second Empire, which has lost all its faith in the ideal treasures of life . . . ? The nation is our enemy, not this Bonaparte, who rather obeyed than led it. . . .

The distracted world already foresees a whole brood of wars springing out of the bloody seed of this. We owe it some guarantee of permanent peace among the nations. . . . The statesmen of the present day, whenever they have realised the altered equilibrium of the Powers, will feel that the strengthening of the boundaries of Germany contributes to the security of the peace of the world. We are a peaceful nation. The traditions of the Hohenzollerns, the constitution of our Army, the long and difficult work before us in the upbuilding of our united German State, forbid the abuse of our warlike power. . . .

In view of our obligation to secure

the peace of the world, who will venture to object that the people of Alsace and Lorraine do not want to belong to us? The doctrine of the right of all the branches of the German race to decide on their own destinies, the plausible solution of demagogues without a fatherland, shiver to pieces in presence of the sacred necessity of these great days. These territories are ours by the right of the sword, and we shall dispose of them in virtue of a higher right—the right of the German nation, which will not permit its lost children to remain strangers to the German Empire. We Germans, who know Germany and France, know better than these unfortunates themselves what is good for the people of Alsace. . . . Against their will we shall restore them to their true selves. We have seen with joyful wonder the undying power of the moral forces of history, manifested far too frequently in the immense changes of these days, to place much confidence in the value of a mere popular disinclination. The spirit of a nation lays hold, not only of the generations which live beside it, but of those which are before and behind it. We appeal from the mistaken wishes of the men who are there to-day to the wishes of those who were there before them. We appeal to all those strong German men who once stamped the seal of our German nature on the language and manners, the art and the social life, of the Upper Rhine. Before the nineteenth century closes the world will recognise that . . . we were only obeying the dictates of national honour when we made little account of the preferences of the people who live in Alsace to-day.

When Alsace fell under the dominion of the French our Empire lay powerless on the ground. The fire of the German spirit, which had once flamed through the whole world, seemed extinguished. Germany bowed herself before the con-

quering policy and the victorious culture of France. . . . We have broken with the rules of their Art, and we can confidently challenge comparison between the free movement of our scientific and religious life and the spiritual culture of France. We have succeeded in giving our richer and stronger language such a freedom and delicacy that it need no longer fear the rivalry of French. Even the advantage of their elder culture, the fine tone and polish of social intercourse, is passing away. . . .

At all times the subjection of a German race to France has been an unhealthy thing; to-day it is an offence against the reason of History—a vassalship of free men to half-educated barbarians. . . .

When our united strength has won that outwork of the German State, which is now in such mortal peril, the nation will have pledged its soul to the idea of unity. The resistance of the new province will strengthen the impulse of our policy towards unity, and constrain all sensible men to range themselves in disciplined loyalty behind the Prussian throne. The advantage is all the greater as it is still possible that some new Republican attempt in Paris might tempt the moonstruck glance of the German radicals once more to turn gradually towards the West. . . .

A politico-economical consideration may be added. . . . Nature has dealt with our country much more like a stepmother than a mother. The singularly barren outline of our shore coast-line on the North Sea, and the course of most of our German rivers and hill-chains, are just as unfavourable to political unity as they are to commerce. Only a few strips of our German soil can compare in natural fertility with wealthy Normandy, the luxurious plains of England, and the teeming cornfields of the interior of Russia. But here, in Alsace, there is a real German district, the soil of which, under favouring skies, is rich with blessings. . . .

. . . We are not now so exhausted in money and in men as not to be able to defy the opposition of the whole of Europe. The neutral Powers might have stopped this French attempt at robbery by one strong and timely word. They failed to utter it, and they cannot complain to-day because we alone decide what we shall take as the prize of the victory which we alone have won. We owe it to the clear-sighted audacity of Count Bismarck that this war was begun at the right time—that the Court of the Tuileries was not allowed the welcome respite which would have permitted it to complete the web of its treacherous devices. And as the war began as a work of clear and statesmanlike calculation, so it will end. . . .

We desire to renew the power and glory of the Hohenstaufens and the Ottos, but not their World-Empire. Our new State owes its strength to the national idea. . . . For this reason it finds its western frontier indicated to it by the language and manners and life of the rural population. Every State is kept fresh and young from below. New forces never cease to arise out of the healthy depths of the peasant class. . . .

. . . It is not the business of a wise national policy to go very far beyond this extent of territory; but, at the same time, such a policy ought not to cling with *doctrinaire* obstinacy to the boundary of language as a limit which must in no case be crossed. There is no perfect identity between the political and the national frontier in any European country. Not one of the Great Powers, and Germany no more than the rest of them, can ever subscribe to the principle that "language alone decides the formation of States." It would be impossible to carry that principle into effect. From a military point of view the German territory in France is secured by two strongholds [Metz and Belfort], which lie a few miles beyond the line of language. . . .

The German territory which we demand is ours by nature and by history . . . [of the time of the Nibelungs, the Hohenstaufens, the Hanseatic League, the Meistersingers, the Reformation, the Holy Roman Empire]. In the tempests of the great Revolution the people of Alsace, like all the citizens of France, learned to forget their past. . . .

Most assuredly, the task of reuniting there the broken links between the ages is one of the heaviest that has ever been imposed upon the political forces of our nation. . . .

Perverse obstinacy, and a thousand French intrigues creeping in the dark, will make every step on the newly conquered soil difficult for us: but our ultimate success is certain, for on our side fights what is stronger than the lying artifices of the stranger—nature herself and the voice of common blood.

Heinrich von Treitschke, "Was Fordern Wir von Frankreich," ["What We Demand from France,"] *Preussische Jahrbuecher*, (26) 1870, 367 ff., reprinted in *Zehn Jahre deutscher Kaempfe*, 3e Auflage (Berlin, 1897), translated into English in *Germany, France, Russia and Islam* (New York: G. P. Putnam's Sons, 1915), pp. 96-99, 101-121, 134-39, 154, 158.

B. Ernest Renan

Your fiery Germanists allege that Alsace is a German territory unjustly detached from the German Empire. Take note that all nationalities are imperfect arrangements; if you start applying such logic to the ethnography of each district, you will be paving the way for wars without end. Many a fair province, linguistically French, does not form a part of France and this is an advantage even for France itself.

There are Slavic lands which belong to Prussia. . . . Is it worthy of Germany to take over by force a province which, already rebellious and irritable, has become irreconcilable since the destruction of Strasbourg? The mind sometimes stands aghast before the audacity of your statesmen. The King of Prussia seems to be on the point of taking on the heavy task of settling the French problem, of giving—and consequently guaranteeing—a government to France. Could any one lightheartedly assume such a burden? How can you fail to see the result of this policy would be the necessity of occupying France forever with some three or four hundred thousand men? . . .

I am amazed that your best minds do not see this and especially that they are opposed to European intervention on these questions. Peace cannot, it seems to me, be concluded directly between France and Germany; it can only be the work of Europe, which condemned the war and must wish that no member of the European family of nations be seriously weakened. You speak with good right of guarantees against the return of dreams of aggression; but what guarantee would be worth that of Europe consecrating anew the present frontiers and forbidding everyone without exception to dream of upsetting the boundaries fixed by ancient treaties? All other solutions will leave the door open to vengeance without end. Let Europe do this and she will have sown the seed for the future of the most fruitful institution—a central authority, a sort of congress of the United States of Europe, judging the nations, exercising control over them and correcting the principle of nationality by the principle of federation.

Ernest Renan, "Lettre à M. Strauss," 13 September, 1870, *Journal des Débats*, 16 September, 1870, reprinted in *La Réforme intellectuelle et morale*, 4th ed. (Paris: Calmann Levy, 1884), pp. 180-182, trans. E. A. Clark.

We were evidently wrong in our belief that the 19th century had ushered in an era of civilization, peace and popular sovereignty. "How can you declare that the shifting of human beings is a crime and a shame when previously such transfers were acceptable to races as noble as your own and were even profitable to you" you may ask. Let us look at the dates. Today's concept of justice is not that of yesterday. The sentiment of nationalism is not a hundred years old. . . . In those days [before the Revolution] the transfer of a province simply meant the assignment of real estate from one prince to another; the people themselves usually remained indifferent. This consciousness of nationality has been given the world by our own Revolution; it is we who have given it to those whom we have fought (and often fought unjustly); it is our own doctrine. That is why we French liberals were in favor of the Venetians, for the Milanese against Austria; for Bohemia, for Hungary against Viennese centralization; for Poland against Russia; for the Greeks and the Slavs in Turkey against the Turks. We were also in favor of the Romans against the Pope or rather against the foreign coercion which kept these vassals of the Pope in spite of themselves; we were unwilling to concede that a population could, against its will, be subjugated to a religious idea which asserted its need of territory in order to exist. . . .

Wars would continue without end unless there is some limit set for revenge for past violence. Lorraine certainly did once form part of the German empire but so also did Holland. Switzerland, even Italy (down to Benevento) and—if you go beyond the treaty of Verdun—all of France with Catalonia thrown in! Nowadays Alsace is a Germanic land both by language and by race, but before it was overrun by the Germanic peoples, Alsace was a Celtic land as was also part of South Germany. Now we do not conclude from this that South Germany ought to be French; but let no one come tell us that by ancient right Metz and Luxembourg ought to be German! There is no end to such archaeology! In almost every case where the fiery patriots of Germany set up German claims we could just as easily set up a Celtic claim to antedate them; before the Celtic period —so they say—were non-Aryan Finns and Lapps; before the Lapps there were cavemen and before cavemen there were orangoutangs! If one carries out this historical philosophy the only legitimate rights would be those of the orangoutangs unjustly dispossessed by the perfidy of civilized men!

Let us be less arbitrary; alongside of the rights of the dead, let us pay some attention to the rights of the living. The treaty of 843 [Verdun], a pact of division of territory between three barbarian chieftains who certainly were only concerned with their personal convenience, cannot everlastingly be a cornerstone of national rights. . . .

The European nations, as history has made them, are like peers in one great senate where each member is inviolable. Europe is a confederation of States held together by their common concept of civilization. The individuality of each nation is, doubtless, formed by race, language, history and religion but also by something much more tangible: the determination of different provinces of a State to live united. . . . Alsace is German linguistically and racially but she has no desire to be a part of the German state; that settles the question. We hear talk of the rights of France, the rights of Germany; these abstractions are far less important to us than is the right of the Alsatians, living creatures of flesh and blood, to obey that power to which they have consented.

Do not blame our French liberals for considering that the right of peoples not to be transferred without their own consent amounts almost to divine right. For those who, like us, no longer admit the dynastic principle, which bases the unity of the state on the personal rights of the sovereign, there is no other right of nations . . . [than the principle of nationality].

Our policy is based on the rights of nations, yours is based on the theory of racism. Overemphasis on humanity's division into races, aside from the fact that it is based on scientific error, since very few countries possess a race which is really pure, can only result in wars of extermination, "zoological" wars if I may say so, similar to those waged by the different species of carnivorous animals in their struggle for survival. It would be the end of that fruitful mingling of numerous and essential elements which we call humanity. You have raised aloft in the world the banner of archaeological and ethnographical politics in place of that of liberal politics; this system will be fatal for you. Comparative philology which you have created and which you have mistakenly transported into the realm of politics is going to do you a bad turn. The Slavs have taken it up with passion; every Slav schoolmaster is your enemy, a termite which will bring down your house. How can you believe that the Slavs will not do to you what you have done to others, they who follow your lead in every respect, follow step by step? Each assertion of Pan-Germanism is at the same time an assertion of Pan-Slavism, each of your moves towards concentration is at the same time a catalytic agent "precipitating" the Slav, setting him apart as a separate entity. A glance at the affairs of Austria emphasizes this fact. In fifty years, the Slav will recognize that it is you who have made his name synonymous with *slave;* he will see the long historical exploitation of his race by yours; the number of Slavs is twice yours, the Slav, like the dragon of the Apocalypse whose tail swept away a third of the stars, will one day bring the hordes of central Asia in his wake, those former followers of Genghis Khan and Tamerlane. How much better it would have been had you kept for that day appeals to reason, to morality, to love of principle. Think what a weight will be thrown into the balance of the world on that day when Bohemia, Moravia, Croatia, Serbia, all the Slav peoples of the Turkish empire —peoples surely destined for liberation, races heroic and warlike still, needing only a leader, gather around that Moscow-centered conglomeration; which already unites so many different elements into a Slav matrix and which may well be the appointed kernel for future Slav unity just as Macedonia, only partially Greek, Piedmont partially Italian, Prussia partially German, were the focal points for Greek, Italian and German unity. And you are too wise to count on any gratitude from Russia. One of the hidden causes of Prussian ill will towards us is that part of their culture is due to us. One of Russia's grievances, one day, will be that she was civilized by the Germans. They may deny it but at the same time they will prove it by their very denial and this memory will irritate them. The Academy of St. Petersburg will, one day, feel resentful towards the Academy of Berlin for its own Germanness just as the Academy of Berlin holds it against us that it used to be half French. Our century is the century of the triumph of the serf over the master: in certain respects the Slav is still your serf.

Now, on the day of the Slav victory we are going to be worth more than you are, just as Athens, under the Roman Empire, still played a leading part whereas Sparta no longer played any role.

Watch out for ethnography or rather do not apply it too much to politics. Under the pretense of German etymology you take over for Prussia such and such a village of Lorraine. The name of Vienna (Vindobona), Worms (Borbitomagus), Mainz (Mogontiacum) are Gallic; we are never going to claim these towns; but if, one fine day, the Slavs put in a claim for Prussia, Pomerania, Silesia, Berlin on the ground that their names are Slav; if they did along the Elbe and the Oder what you have done along the Moselle, if they started pointing out on the map villages formerly settled by Slavic tribes, what would you have to say? A nation and a race are not synonymous. Little Switzerland, so solidly built, has three languages, three or four races, two religions. A nation is an association, centuries old but not eternal, between provinces partly of common origin serving as a kernel and others which group themselves around it; the whole bound together by common interests or by ancient actions which have been accepted and transformed into interests. England which is the most perfect of nations is the most mixed, judged ethnographically and historically: pure Bretons, Romanized Bretons, Irish, Scotch, Anglo-Saxons, Danes, pure Normans, French Normans, all blend together.

But I stop; these days it would be naive to speak of moderation, justice, fraternity, of the gratitude and consideration which peoples owe each other. The way you will have to behave in those provinces annexed against their wish will finally demoralize you. You will have to give the lie to all your principles, to treat as criminals men whom you should respect (men who will have done nothing but what you did so nobly after Jena); all moral ideas will be perverted. Our whole system of European equilibrium and concert will be banished to cloud-cuckoo land; our liberal tenets will be an out-of-date jargon. Because of the action of Prussian statesmen, France for many a day will have only one objective: winning back the lost provinces. Stirring up the ever-growing hate of the Slavs for the Germans, favoring Pan-Slavism, truckling to every Russian ambition, dazzling the eyes of the Catholic party everywhere with the re-establishment of the Pope in Rome; in domestic affairs, yielding to the legitimist clerical party of the West since it alone is intensely fanatical; these are the policies necessitated by such a situation. It is just the opposite of what we dreamed of! . . . but,

what can we do? We would, on the other hand, be culpable were we to attempt, by advocating, even now, generous and disinterested pursuits, to prevent the country from listening to the voice of two million Frenchmen crying out for the assistance of their former Fatherland.

France is on the point of saying, like your Herwegh, "Enough of love, now let us try hate." I have no intention of following her in this new experiment —whose success one may, moreover, question since the resolve France finds it the most difficult to follow is that of hate. In any case life is too short to waste time and strength in such a sorry pursuit. In my modest way, I have worked for friendship between France and Germany; if the time has come "to leave off kissing," I shall withdraw. I shall not advocate hate after having preached love; I shall be silent.

"Nouvelle Lettre à M. Strauss," 15 September, 1871, *ibid.*, pp. 193-202, 207-9.

C. Declaration of the Alsace-Lorraine Deputies at the National Assembly

Bordeaux, February 17, 1871
We, the undersigned French citizens, chosen and delegated by the departments of "Bas Rhin," "Haut Rhin," "Moselle" and "Meurthe" to bring to the National Assembly of France the expression of the unanimous will of the populations of Alsace and of Lorraine, after having met together and debated the question, have resolved to set forth, in a solemn declaration, their sacred and inalienable rights in order that the National Assembly, France and Europe, having before their eyes the wishes and resolves of our constituents, may not accomplish nor allow to be accomplished any act which, by its nature, would wrong the rights, the care and defense of which have been entrusted to us through a firm mandate.

DECLARATION

I. *Alsace and Lorraine do not want to be ceded.*

Associated with France for more than two centuries through good and bad fortune, these two provinces, everlastingly exposed to the blows of the enemy, have constantly sacrificed themselves for national greatness. They have sealed with their blood the indissoluble pact that binds them to French unity. Today, brought into question by foreign claims, they proclaim in spite of every obstacle, every danger, under the very yoke of the invader, their unshakable loyalty.

All are unanimous. The citizens who remained at home, as well as the soldiers who flocked to our colors, the former by voting, the others by fighting, declare to Germany and to the world the unchangeable will of Alsace and

Lorraine to remain French. (Bravo! Bravo! on the Left and in other parts of the Chamber.)

II. *France cannot consent to nor sign the transfer of Lorraine and Alsace.*

(Very true!) France cannot, without endangering the continuity of her national existence, herself deal a mortal blow to her own unity by abandoning those who have won, by two hundred years of patriotic devotion, the right to be defended by the whole country against all attempts of victorious might.

Even an Assembly born from universal suffrage cannot invoke its sovereignty to shield or ratify demands tending to the disruption of national integrity. (Applause on the Left.) It would take upon itself a right that does not even belong to the whole people gathered in its national assembly. (Applause on Left.) Such an abuse of power, which would result in the mutilation of our common mother, would turn over to the just severities of history those who have made themselves guilty of it.

France may suffer from the blows of might, she cannot sanction its decrees.

III. *Europe cannot either allow or ratify the abandonment of Alsace and Lorraine.*

Guardians of the rules of justice and of the rights of nations, the civilized peoples cannot any longer remain unmoved by the fate of their neighbors without in turn running the risk of being the victims of the outrages that they would tolerate. Modern Europe cannot allow a people to be seized as a wretched herd; Europe cannot remain deaf to the repeated protests of menaced populations; Europe owes it to her own preservation to forbid any such abuses of might. It knows, moreover, that French unity is, today, as well as in the past, a guarantee of the general order of the world, a barrier against the spirit of conquest and invasion.

Peace brought about at the price of a transfer of territory would be but a ruinous truce and not a final peace. For all, it would be a source of internal agitation, a legitimate and permanent incentive to war. And as for us, Alsatians and Lorrainers, we would be ready to renew the war today, tomorrow, at any time, at any moment. (Very good! on various benches.)

To sum up, Alsace and Lorraine loudly protest against any transfer, France cannot consent to it, Europe cannot sanction it.

In faith of which we call our fellow citizens of France, and the peoples of the world to witness that we hold as null and void any act, treaty, vote or plebiscite that would consent, in favor of a foreign power, to the abandonment of the whole or of any part of our provinces of Alsace and Lorraine. (Bravos on the Left.)

We proclaim that the right of the Alsatians and Lorrainers to remain French is forever inviolable, and we swear for ourselves as well as for our constituents, our children and their descendants, that we will, by every available means against any and all usurpers, eternally claim that right. (Bravo! Bravo! Great applause on the Left.)

[Drawn up by Gambetta and signed by 38 deputies from Alsace and Lorraine.]

Journal officiel de la République française, III Année, (58), 22 février 1871, p. 109, Séance du 17 février. Trans. E. A. Clark.

13. Imperialistic Rivalries and the Road to the First World War

LOWELL RAGATZ

The Ohio State University

Up to the close of the Napoleonic era modern European wars were largely dynastic in nature. They arose through conflict between rulers, each of whom sought narrow private benefits from the struggles. The concept of the nation in arms did not emerge until the period of international upheaval attending the spread of the French Revolution. After 1815, wars increasingly came to be waged between national states rather than between monarchs. The stakes became higher, although they were much the same in character—control of outlying lands, commonly overseas, coveted by two or more Powers in the national interest. In this dynamic age, as the individual began closely to associate himself with the nation at large, "national interests" were more and more identified as his own interests. As a result, the power politics of the old dynastic struggles now emerged as a peculiarly personal matter for the individual in state after state.

Rivalry for control of remote African, Asiatic, and Pacific areas, and the economic opportunity they afforded, became an increasingly disturbing factor in international relations. Clashing extra-European ambitions led to rising strife, particularly among the various Powers of Europe. The importance of the imperialist rivalries of the period is attested by the fact that virtually every one of the major international conferences of 1815–1914 dealt with problems raised by such conflict. Most of the leading treaties of the time sought to adjust these imperialist problems in one way or another.

To illustrate these developments, we can turn to some of the highlights in the international affairs of the century after 1815. Opposing Levantine interests occasioned bitter controversy between France and Great Britain in the late 1830's and early 1840's, bringing them dangerously close to war. When, however, Russia began active encroachments in the Holy Land in the 1850's, the old enemies, who regarded the Near East as their particular preserve, joined forces against her in the Crimean War (1853–1856) and rejuvenated the Turk, "the sick man of Europe," to hold the Romanovs in check.

Similarly, when the Austro-Prussian War of 1866 terminated Austria's leader-ship in Germanic affairs, Hapsburg interest turned to southeastern Europe where the Austrians soon were at swords' points with the Russians. Russia, for her part, capitalized on Ottoman atrocities against restless Christian minorities in Bulgaria by unleashing a war against the Turks. She apparently emerged with hegemony over the Balkans by the Treaty of San Stefano in 1878, but this result of her military triumph was denied her. Thoroughly aroused, Britain and Austria-Hungary summoned the Powers to the Congress of Berlin, where they collectively deprived the Tsarist regime of the spoils of victory. The Russians, therefore, sought compensation in eastern and southwestern Asia where they promptly collided with rising Japan and India-conscious Britain.

These developments only begin to tell the story of the impact of imperialism on the international relations of the modern world. From 1878 to 1914, as in the earlier period, the struggle for colonies, or for strategic bases, or for com-mercial rights in various parts of the world were at the very forefront of the intercourse of the major powers. Thus, although they had helped to block Russian expansion in the Near East at Ottoman expense, the Austrians in 1878 themselves began an administration of Turkey's northwest Balkan prov-inces, Bosnia and Herzegovina, which ended in ultimate annexation. The British, also in 1878, established a protectorate over Turkey's insular pos-session, Cyprus. Four years later, the British began a military occupation of Turkey's Nile dependency, Egypt, in order presumably to safeguard the inter-ests of various European nationals. Originally intended as a temporary meas-ure, the occupation was still in force when World War I broke out.

The Franco-Prussian War of 1870–1871, which upset the European diplo-matic balance by wresting continental leadership from France and according it to the newly-united German Empire, was a strictly European affair, but it soon had important overseas repercussions. Republican leaders in defeated France sought to regain prestige by creating a new empire in Africa and Asia. Through a series of shrewdly-conceived moves in 1884 and 1885, Ger-man patriots, arguing that colonial possessions symbolized greatness, forced Count Otto von Bismarck, the Chancellor who had united Germany, reluc-tantly to accept control over extensive lands in Africa and over a portion of New Guinea. Germany's sudden emergence as a colonial power, coupled with rapid expansion of German trade in traditional British areas of exploita-tion, in turn brought Germany into rivalry with Great Britain. When the imperious new German Emperor, William II (r. 1888–1918), later encouraged a naval building program which challenged British supremacy on the seas, the traditional Anglo-German friendship came to an abrupt close.

Meanwhile, on the continent, Bismarck, ever fearful of French vengeance, sought to divert France by supporting her adventures in Africa and Asia. At the same time, he worked to safeguard the German Empire by creating the Three Emperors' League of 1872, designed to insure peace between Germany, Austria-Hungary, and Russia should any of them become involved in war.

Unhappily for Germany, Balkan rivalries drew the Romanovs and Hapsburgs steadily apart, another evidence of the role of imperialism in the international politics of the period. The unstable Three Emperors' League was relegated to the background in 1879 by a more logical German and Austrian alliance, aimed primarily at Russia.

Bismarck, none the less, with amazing adroitness, maneuvered a renewal of the League in 1881. When this renewal finally lapsed six years later, he devised the German-Russian Reinsurance Treaty of 1887 which, unknown to Austria, recognized Russia's dominant position in the eastern Balkan lands. But William II refused to renew the Reinsurance Treaty in 1890, holding that it was incompatible with the Dual Alliance of Germany and Austria-Hungary.

This Teutonic alignment was expanded into a Triple Alliance in 1882. Again, the major impelling factor was an imperialistic one. Italy, embittered over France's recent seizure of Tunisia, which she herself coveted, sought admission to the fold. Soon a second armed camp appeared. In 1894, after some years of gestation, a Franco-Russian Alliance aimed at Germany, the common foe sandwiched between the two partners, was born. This agreement with Germany's western rival was Russia's answer to the Kaiser's failure to continue the Reinsurance Treaty.

Britain, standing alone among the European Great Powers, now found herself in dangerous isolation. She sought first to improve her position by a close understanding with the United States. In the Hay-Pauncefote Treaty of 1901 she yielded her joint right under the Clayton-Bulwer Treaty of 1850 to construct a trans-Isthmian canal. When her ardent wooing of the United States proved unavailing because of ingrained American opposition to entangling alliances, she reversed her centuries-old anti-French policy. The Entente Cordiale of 1904 halted bitter Anglo-French colonial rivalries in Africa, Asia, America, and the Pacific by a more rational policy of compromise. This agreement soon made it possible for Britain to act in concert with France against Germany, from whom both powers felt a threat as the twentieth century progressed. Finally, the Anglo-Russian Entente of 1907 resolved colonial rivalries in three Asiatic spheres—Persia, Afghanistan, and Tibet—and the Triple Entente now confronted the Triple Alliance. Colonial questions had been a major determinant of the structure of both groups.

Meanwhile, Japan, treading the path of empire in the wake of the Western Powers, was checked in her ambitious project of annexing China's outlying province, Manchuria. At the close of the first Sino-Japanese War (1894–1895), Japan had seized the Liaotung Peninsula in lower Manchuria from China. In 1895, Russia, Germany, and France forced Japan to return this territory to China and accept an additional cash indemnity instead. Three years later, these powers, joined by Britain, forced a disintegrating China to grant them long-term leases to strategic areas. To complete the irony, Russia herself then acquired the Liaotung Peninsula. Such duplicity led Japan to accept an alliance with Britain clearly aimed at Russia, then the common foe. Shortly thereafter, Japan defeated Russia in the war of 1904–1905 and at length acquired the Liaotung Peninsula. Afterwards, in the decade before World War I, Japan steadily increased her pressure designed to achieve control of large parts of a China which was deep in the throes of civil war and revolution.

As the various diplomatic alliances among the major powers began to take shape in the twentieth century, the imperialist struggles provided a further testing ground of their strength. The Algeciras Conference of 1906, the Bosnian crisis of 1908, the Agadir crisis of 1911, the Turko-Italian War of 1911–1912, and finally the Balkan Wars of 1912–1913 not only evidenced the imperialistic strife of the period, but influenced profoundly the diplomacy of all the powers. Certainly this ceaseless conflict became a dominant factor conditioning the European mind to accept a great war. It is less evident that it formed the basic cause of the war, and its influence in that connection has been keenly debated by scholars and laymen. Our problem here, in any event, is to assess the nature of imperialism, to study the various points of view with regard to its reason for being, and to examine at least one facet of its relation to the coming of World War I. The selections which follow will enable the reader to understand some of the issues involved and give him a start toward grasping the complicated interrelations between pre-1914 imperialism and the eruption of the first great twentieth-century world war.

I. THE NATURE OF IMPERIALISM

"Imperialism" is a word of many meanings. The term is highly elastic and, as one writer phrases it, "so elusive of definition and covers practices and procedures of such variant and even contradictory character, that it has become a downright nuisance." (Jacob Viner, in the review section of the *Journal of Political Economy,* December, 1929, pp. 745ff.) Adjectives such as agricultural, ancient, commercial, cultural, economic, industrial, military, modern, open door, and religious are frequently employed to make it less nebulous and are commonly encountered in contemporary writing.

"Imperialism" is, however, most commonly used in the sense of extending economic and political control over outlying lands and people—in modern times, empire building carried out by national states. While operating freely before 1815, imperialism has been a dominant force in European life only during the nineteenth and twentieth centuries. With Nationalism, Democracy, and Industrialization, it has given Old World history its distinctive pattern and has underlain many of the most important developments of the period.

Imperialism arose through the need for industrial raw materials, for markets for surplus manufactures, and for outlets for oversupplies of capital. At times, too, expansion was viewed as a means of relieving overpopulation. It appeared at different times in different countries, roughly paralleling their economic development, always raised both ardent champions and bitter foes, and regularly became a hotly contested domestic issue in each country coming under its sway.

Its importance in shaping foreign relations cannot be overemphasized. Since 1815, it extended European rule over most of Africa and over vast portions of Asia and Oceanica, led to European financial penetration of all quarters of the earth, and made Europe the world's workshop. If Europe gained paramount economic, political, and social position in global affairs between 1815 and 1914, if the world was, literally, Europe's oyster in the Age of Middle Class Democracy, this was due largely to the play of imperialism.

There can be no real understanding of Old World events and extra-European happenings since 1815 without according overseas expansion careful consideration. Imperialism provides a key to world affairs following the collapse of the Napoleonic regime and today forms one of the most important branches of historical studies.

A. Imperialism, Militarism and Nationalism

With mounting realization of imperialism's great role in recent and contemporary world affairs, great interest has developed in its origins, its development and its many ramifications. Outstanding among books on the subject has been *The Pattern of Imperialism,* by Earle M. Winslow (1896–), from which the following selection has been excerpted.

The story of Imperialism and Militarism constitutes the history of power as it has been exercised by one group over another. . . . "Imperialism" and "Militarism" . . . are coeval terms, representing the same general pattern of thought and behavior in the ordering of human relationships. It makes little difference whether we speak of "Militarism and war" or "Imperialism and war." A nation that is militaristic is likely to want to give its militarism an aggressive outlet, which can only mean an attitude of belligerency and an act of hostility towards some other nation. Imperialism is only a more concrete term for the same behavior; it suggests not only ability and willingness to use military power, but also the territory on and against which such power must be employed. It is not a synonym for Colonialism—many colonies have been established by people innocent of imperialistic aggression, in places empty of other people against whom aggression needed to be used in order to make the settlement a success. Even where the intruders fought the natives, as so often . . . happened in the colonization of the Americas, the conflict was rarely waged primarily as an expedition of military or naval power. . . .

We have come to regard . . . this colonial activity and conflict as Colonialism rather than as Imperialism. The latter term quite properly suggests something more organized, more military, more self-consciously aggressive, bent on objectives above and beyond the mere occupation of virgin territory in which conflict was incidental . . . and subordinate to the desire of Europeans to find a new place to live. We readily associate Imperialism with what the Romans did in Gaul and elsewhere and what Napoleon, Hitler and Mussolini were up to; with British policies in India, French and Dutch policies in Africa, Asia and the Pacific and Japanese policies in China. And we must not be too modest—we Americans are accused, and we accuse ourselves, of following imperialistic policies in Latin America, in the Caribbean, in the Philippines and in other parts of the world too numerous to mention. Soviet Russia, despite the protests of Marxists that Communism is incapable of following an imperialistic policy, appears to the more imaginative to be no less imperialistic than the so-called capitalist powers, which the critics of Capitalism have long regarded as the only groups capable of committing the sin of Imperialism. . . .

The theory of Imperialism in some form or other has long been almost a monopoly of the radicals—Socialists, Communists, Marxists or other critics of Capitalism who ascribe modern Imperialism to the workings of the private enterprise economy. . . . But there are other theories, hypotheses, explanations and interpretations of Imperialism, which have not had their origin in radical or Marxian thought, which . . . range from almost-Socialistic theories to a complete denial of the view that Capitalism or any economic system can be a cause of Imperialism, accompanied by the affirmation . . . that the causes must be looked for in behavior patterns which are far older than Capitalism.

One of the common assumptions of those who undertake to interpret History is that Nationalism . . . reflects on the political side what Capitalism reflects in the economic sphere, and that Nationalism and Capitalism combine to produce "economic imperialism". . . . It is only comparatively recently that History has been told in terms of Nationalism and Internationalism; in terms, that is, of conflict as well as peaceful intercourse between nations, with emphasis sometimes on international trade, international co-operation and international peace, and again on economic Nationalism, international rivalries and international war.

But it is important to make clear at the beginning that . . . Imperialism . . . is not an extension or expansion of Nationalism. . . . Nationalism . . . did not emerge until the eighteenth century, when the French Revolution brought its first real manifestation. It developed simultaneously with Democracy and Industrialism and the phenomenon which marked all three movements was the overthrow of absolute monarchic forms of government by the ideas and realities of popular sovereignty. . . .

To all this, Imperialism is entirely foreign. . . . Consciousness of belonging to an empire . . . is completely subordinate to the consciousness of belonging to a nationality. . . . The modern nation contains no foreigners, except as a transient phenomenon. But empires always contain "foreigners"—people alien to the mother or ruling country. And these foreigners are universally regarded . . . either as objects of charity and solicitude (the White Man's Burden, the recipients of a civilizing mission, etc.) or as slaves, never quite as equals. This is clearly a much more ancient attitude than that expressed in Nationalism or nationality.

No—Nationalism does not necessarily lead to Imperialism; it may be the road to Internationalism. On the other hand, Imperialism never leads to Interimperialism. Nationalism has within it the same feeling as has Democracy, that of mutuality, but Imperialism is an exclusive concept. Wherever the spirit of exclusiveness creeps into a nation, as it well may, it is a sign that that nation is losing the attributes of Nationalism, Internationalism and Democracy and is setting forth on the ancient business of telling "foreigners" what to do and what not to do, which is the path of empire. . . .

Many people have [regarded] . . . Nationalism . . . and Imperialism as almost synonymous, or at least merely as different stages in the same process, with Nationalism paving the way to Imperialism. But nation-building and empire-building by no means involve the same set of attitudes; in fact, they involve attitudes which are essentially opposed to each other, and which find their opposite expressions in popular rather than scholarly reactions. . . . The greater part of the popular reaction to . . . Imperialism and Militarism has been emotional, favorable or unfavorable according to whether the person concerned was on the giving or the receiving end of the process or in the favored or exploited class. . . . No explanation has been more widespread than that based on the view that human selfishness and cupidity . . . constitute the source of Imperialism and war. This is a modern development of thought, but its beginnings can be detected wherever men have spoken of their desires which express themselves in terms of property and gain.

Earle M. Winslow, *The Pattern of Imperialism* (New York: The Columbia University Press, 1948), pp. 3-8.

B. Expansion the Major Cause of World Unrest

One school of writers regards overseas rivalry between acquisitive nations as the basic factor behind mounting global tensions since 1815 and Imperialism as the force giving birth to World Politics. Among the more able exponents of these views has been Parker T. Moon (1892–1936), sometime Professor of International Relations at Columbia, who wrote the most widely-used treatise in the field.

The American public is barely beginning to realize the significance of . . . present-day Imperialism. . . . Of ancient Imperialism . . . we have heard much and of Napoleon's spectacular exploits every schoolboy has read. But the realms conquered by military emperors of past ages were baubles . . . compared with the far-flung dominions which have been won . . . in our own supposedly prosaic generation. . . .

Little as the general public may realize the fact, Imperialism is the most impressive achievement and the most momentous world-problem of our age. . . . More than half of the world's land surface and more than a billion human beings are included in the colonies and "backward countries" dominated by a few imperialist nations. Every man, woman and child in Great Britain has ten colonial subjects, black, brown and yellow. For every acre in France there are twenty in the French colonies and protectorates. Italy is one-sixth as large as her [ex-] colonies; Portugal, one twenty-third; Belgium, one-eightieth. The nations of western Europe are dwarfs beside their colonial possessions.

How prevalent Imperialism was in Europe before the [First World] War, and still remains, it is difficult for Americans to appreciate, since the "average" American has been accustomed . . . to think that seizure of territory was somewhat akin to theft, that Militarism and aggressive war were out of date among democratic nations, that conquest was contrary to the normal principles of international morality. . . .

This, however, . . . has not been the attitude of the imperialist nations of Europe or of Europeanized Japan. French statesmen have vehemently declared the conquest of colonies to be . . . imperative for France and the Third Republic has won almost five million square miles. Italian patriots . . . proclaimed it a sacred duty and Italy . . . [at one time held] almost a million square miles. Englishmen have regarded it, in Kipling's words, as "the White Man's Burden" which civilized peoples dare not shirk; and in the last half-century four million square miles have been added to the British Empire, besides many a veiled protectorate and sphere of influence not formally annexed. Germany at first, under Bismarck's cautious guidance, abstained from . . . empire-building, but at length plunged into World Politics . . . to appropriate a million square miles in Africa and the East Indies, to dominate the rich Asiatic empire of the Ottoman sultans; and finally to stake all and lose all in the titanic conflict of 1914. Austria-Hungary, as lesser partner in the Central European coalition, strove to master the Balkans. Russian tsars . . . stretched acquisitive hands into Central Asia, Persia, Manchuria and Mongolia and looked hungrily on Turkey, Tibet and Afghanistan. Japan . . . took Formosa, Korea, part of Manchuria, Shantung, German islands in the Pacific and . . . attempted . . . to make . . . China . . . a Japanese protectorate. All the Great Powers save the United States boldly and frankly set themselves to the epic task, in the nineteenth century, of carving out stupendous colonial empires; and even the United States, feeling the same urge to action, reached into the Pacific and into the Caribbean for modest parcels of colonial territory.

Nor were the Great Powers more imperialist than several of the smaller nations. Belgium, with her vast property in Central Africa; Portugal, with colonies larger than the German Kaiser's; Spain, clinging tenaciously to a strip of Morocco together with pitiable fragments of her former colonial grandeur; and Holland glorying in a magnificent East-Indian island empire, have vied with stronger states in seeking the rewards which all hoped to win in the stirring game of World Politics.

"World Politics"—it is a phrase to conjure with! Imperialism has given birth to world-wide empires, to world-wide diplomacy. Great Britain is not, in truth, a European nation, but the nucleus of a universal power. The tricolor of France flies in the Congo jungle, on Sahara's sands, above Indo-Chinese rice-fields. European diplomatists act the drama of international relations on a stage as broad as earth. . . . Such is the meaning of World Politics. And Imperialism is the root and *raison d'être* of World Politics.

If, from this commanding standpoint, one reviews the recent history of international relations, the alliances, ententes, crises and wars reveal a new meaning. Almost without exception, they were but surface manifestations of the swift, deep current of Imperialism. When France and England trembled on the verge of war in 1898, during the Fashoda Crisis, imperialist rivalry for a million or so square miles of the African Sudan was the cause. The German Emperor's celebrated telegram to President Kruger, congratulating him on having repulsed a British invasion, was . . . a revelation of tense imperialist competition in South Africa and as such it both angered and alarmed British statesmen. The Moroccan "crises" of 1905 and 1911, which so nearly embroiled all Europe in war, were not unique results of some peculiarly German—or peculiarly French—aggressiveness; rather, they were two of the innumerable explosions which have been caused when the aims of imperialist nations happened to cross.

The South African War of 1899 . . . would never have been fought had English Imperialism not been active in South Africa; nor would the Spanish-American War have occurred if there had been no American interests in Cuba. The greatest war the twentieth century had witnessed before 1914 was the purely imperialist Russo-Japanese struggle for Korea and Manchuria. . . . [In the First World War, the] alignment of European powers was dictated by Imperialism, not by race or democracy or kinship of culture. Germany, Austria-Hungary and Turkey were allied by Teutonic domination in the Near East. Republican France and monarchist England were bound together by the far-reaching imperialist bargain of 1904; liberal England and tsarist Russia by an agreement of 1907 regarding imperialist interests in Persia, Afghanistan and Tibet. . . .

The climax has not yet been reached; the dénouement is still uncertain. Never was imperialist rivalry so keen as after the . . . [First World] War. We are now entering a period of intensified international economic competition in which the problem of Imperialism is becoming all the more acute because most of the backward areas available for colonies have already been appropriated. Competition is stimulated by scarcity. . . . Moreover, tariff barriers are being erected in hitherto open colonies; governments are . . . officially participating in the international scramble for oil, railway and mining concessions; the tide of immigrant "surplus population" from Europe and Asia is being turned back . . . by American restrictions . . . [and is seeking] new outlets; backward peoples are fast becoming educated to the point of providing a really important and rapidly increasing market for manufactures; raw materials are becoming more and more the stakes of diplomacy. [Imperialism has thus become the greatest force making for unrest in the post World War I era.]

Parker T. Moon, *Imperialism and World Politics* (New York: The Macmillan Company, 1926), pp. 1-5.

C. Aggressive Overseas Enterprise Increases National Prestige

The sudden outbreak of war in 1914 left the American public bewildered. Engrossed in the development of their incredibly rich continent, United States nationals had taken little interest in foreign affairs and were entirely unprepared for the catastrophe which was destined soon to engulf them. The citizenry at large displayed a pathetic eagerness to be thoroughly informed and "accelerated International Relations courses," to use a phrase familiar in student circles, became the order of the day. Such adult education was carried out by innumerable lecturers, journalists, and pulpit orators with excellent results. A leader among these mass educators was Walter Lippmann (1889–   ), then on the threshold of a brilliant career as a publicist. The following passage is taken from his *The Stakes of Diplomacy* which became a best seller.

How does it happen . . . that the people not concerned in a special interest are so ready to defend it against the world? Plain men who have no financial interest in copper will feel aggrieved if American copper interests in a foreign land are attacked. The German people felt "humiliated" because German trade was thwarted in Morocco.

The most obvious reason for this is that the private citizens are in the main abysmally ignorant of what the real stakes of diplomacy are. They do not think in terms of railroad concessions, mines, banking and trade. When they envisage Morocco they do not think of the Mannesmann Brothers [promoters of German mining rights in the sultanate], but of "German prestige" and "French influence." When the Triple Entente compelled Germany to recede in the Moroccan affair of 1911, the rage of the German people was not due to a counting of their economic losses. They were furious, not that they had lost Morocco, but that they had lost the dispute.

There is small doubt that the masses of people in no country would risk war to secure mining concessions in Africa. But the choice is never presented to them that way. Each contest for economic privileges appears to the public as a kind of sporting event with loaded weapons. The people wish their team, that is, their country, to win. Just as strong men will weep because the second baseman fumbles at the crucial moment, so they will go into tantrums of rage because corporations of their own nationality are thwarted in a commercial ambition.

They may have nothing tangible to gain or lose by the transaction; certainly they do not know whether they have. But they feel that "our" trade is their own and, though they share few of its profits, they watch its career with tender solicitude. Above all, they feel that if "our" German traders are beaten in Morocco, the whole value of being a German has been somewhat lessened. This is where business and national prestige flow together. Business is the chief form which competition between nations can assume. To be worsted in that competition means more than to lose money; it means a loss of social importance as well.

Trademarks like "Made in Germany" were a constant humiliation to Englishmen, even though they were glad to buy the goods because they were cheaper and better. But when, from all over the world, Englishmen came home beaten by a greater vitality and more modern organization, their damaged pocketbooks were only the smallest part of their loss. The real wound was the wound of self-respect, the lurking fear that there has been a depreciation in Englishmen. The fear is emphasized by the public opinion of the world which judges by trade efficiency and asks heartrending questions like: Is England decadent? Friendly critics rub salt into the wound by commenting on the obsolete machinery of British manufacture, the archaic habits of British merchants. Is it any wonder that what starts as a loss of dollars and cents is soon transfigured into a loss of the Englishman's importance in the world? But when you attack that, you attack the sources of his patriotism, and when he starts to reassert his importance, the proceeding has ceased to appear as a commercial enterprise. It has become a defense of British civilization.

This is the mood for a strong foreign policy, which means a policy that uses political power to increase national prestige. The way to increase national prestige is to win economic victories by diplomatic methods. British diplomacy has been winning them for . . . [many] years—in Egypt, Persia, Africa. While Germany was capturing trade, Great Britain was scoring the diplomatic victories—the greatest of them being that in Morocco. From an economic point of view, England had more to lose than to gain by a French dominion in Morocco. The real economic interest probably lay in that internationalization of Moroccan opportunity for which Germany contended. But England's interest was not primarily economic. Her interest was the defeat of German aggrandizement. She fought German prestige, and by threatening war in Mr.

Lloyd George's Mansion House Speech [1] she won. She sent German diplomats home to receive the jeers of the German people.

The actual trade of Morocco was insignificant in the mêlée. Morocco became the bone on which Germany and England tested the sharpness of their teeth. The two populations cared very little for any particular iron mine, but they cared enormously about the standing of Englishmen and Germans in settling world problems. The consequences of the Moroccan affair have been terrible beyond words. National feeling was unloosened which overflowed the original dispute. Morocco meant not money but bad will, suspicion, fear, resentment. To the British it was evidence of German aggression; to the German it represented the tightening of the iron ring, the policy of encirclement. The strongest passions of defense in both countries were called into the European arena, and when both sides claim to be defensive I see no reason for questioning their sincerity. It is perfectly possible for two nations both to feel attacked at the same time.

In some such way as this, patriotism becomes involved in business. Specific disputes over specific trade opportunities become the testing points of national pride. Just as a man will fight a lawsuit at tremendous cost for a trivial sum, so nations will risk war to score a diplomatic victory. They feel that a defeat on one point will exhibit weakness and carry in its train defeat on other points. So they throw into the scales of decision their armaments. Navies and armies are prepared for peace as well as war. They are pre-

---

[1] Delivered on 21 July 1911, shortly after the German gunboat *Panther* had anchored in Morocco's Agadir harbor. The then Chancellor of the Exchequer feared that Germany planned to establish a naval base there and threatened war should this transpire.

pared to underline and emphasize diplomatic negotiation. They are a kind of initiation fee to the diplomatic corps. The weak threat of a strong Power counts for more than the strong threat of a weak one. When two diplomats meet, the decisive thing is not their good manners nor the justice of their pleas, it is the potential power of the nation for which they speak. Costa Rica may have envoys at European capitals, but they are not listened to eagerly. Imagine Costa Rica with a great navy, and her minister's view would be consulted with real interest.

There are in the world today not more than eight Powers which really count—Great Britain, France, Russia, Italy, Germany, Austria-Hungary, Japan and the United States. When I say "count," I mean that the effective force of the world is in their hands and that the decision of world affairs is for them. The other nations lie in the orbit of the Great Powers. They follow but do not lead. Central America can have no foreign policy without consulting the United States. The immediate cause of the war was over the question of whether Serbia should become a satellite of the Germanic-Magyar combination or of the Russian Empire. Turkey in the last few years has followed a German lead. England's prime interest in Belgium was that it should not fall within the German sphere.

There is an incessant competition between governments to attach these smaller states to themselves. At no point can one say that specific trade opportunities are the prize. The real prize for the diplomats is an increase of power, a greater emphasis to their word. Their nations rally behind them—the interested business men see it as dollar diplomacy, the mass of the people, hardly aware of the concrete issues, see it as a gigantic competition involving their own sense of importance. The diplomatic struggle is played in Morocco, at Constantinople, in Pekin, wherever there are stakes for which to play. At home there is joy in victory, anger at defeat. Armament is added as an "insurance" for diplomacy, and of course military preparation always calls forth military preparation. Every international incident is seen then, not on its "merits," but in its relation to the whole vast complicated game, forever teetering on the edge of war.

Walter Lippmann, *The Stakes of Diplomacy* (New York: Henry Holt and Company, 1915), pp. 76–83. Reprinted by permission of The Macmillan Company.

D. Empire Builders Missionaries of Civilization

The seamy side of imperialism was most conspicuous and was most commonly discussed. There was, however, another aspect to the problem, and occasional writers lauded expansion as an instrument of human betterment in backward regions. Such appraisers viewed a given country's effort in perspective, regarding it as part of a common undertaking for the benefit of mankind, and developed a strong sense of group achievement in which there was no place for national rivalry. Prominent among such writings was an article by the editors of *The Edinburgh Review* (1802–1929) appearing in 1907.

Let us . . . say boldly that the modern European movement of expansion is not . . . primarily a colonizing movement. It is not a movement merely in favor of annexing territory, of opening up new countries, of settling on the soil and bringing backwoods and prairies under cultivation. It is much more a movement towards organizing, directing and controlling where organization, direction and control are needed and are lacking. What pushes us on in Egypt, and France on in Morocco, is not so much the lust of dominion and desire for acquiring fresh possessions, as the sense that we . . . can restore order where there is chaos, and fertility where there is sterility. Our Cromers [British Agent and Consul-General in Egypt, 1883–1907, and "the maker of modern Egypt"] and Willcockses [builder of the Aswan Dam in the 1890's, irrigating vast areas in the Nile valley] and Garstins [the engineer who cleared the upper Nile of vegetable growth and opened it to navigation] act not from narrowly selfish motives of personal or even national aggrandizement. They act because they are charged with certain ideas and capacities which, in the sphere where they are called upon to work, are precisely the ideas and capacities of which there is most urgent need. . . .

But . . . these ideas of government and these applications of science . . . are not the special property of the English nation. . . . The idea of a Government and administration honestly devoted to the welfare of society, which has proved such a blessing to the Egyptian people, the idea of a scientific knowledge and skill applied to the practical affairs of life, which has so marvellously extended the productivity of the Nile Valley, are in truth European ideas. They are ideas which the Western races have spent centuries in testing, analyzing and perfecting, and they in fact constitute the main elements in what we call in the lump European civilization.

Europe had absorbed these political and scientific ideas until she was full to bursting with them when the greatly increased facilities in locomotion resulting from her own practical science brought her into contact with regions where these ideas had never been heard of, and where life in consequence was lived under conditions of anarchy, with none of its possibilities realized and resources developed. The result of this contact has been a lively recognition on the part of Europe of the field for effective action thus opened to her and an overmastering desire to bring her political and scientific ideas to bear on these new scenes of social anarchy and wasted opportunity. Nothing is easier than, in the way this desire has been carried out, to see only shallow and selfish motives at work; but there could be no more infallible proof of intellectual inferiority and second-rateness than is implied in the resting satisfied with such explanations. Under the selfish rivalries and jealousies which are apt to distort and color a national application of European ideas there has always been the deeper motive at work, the consciousness of possessing the powers and the knowledge most needed and which could be most favorably exercised.

This deeper European motive has been stronger than the selfish national motive. We have profited by the work we have done in India, and shall profit perhaps by the work we are doing in Egypt. France has on the whole profited by the work she has done in Algeria and Tunisia, and will probably profit some day by the work that awaits her in Morocco. But the work was not done for the profit. . . . It was done . . . because those who did it . . . were acting, not on behalf of England or on behalf of France, but on behalf of European ideas and European science. . . . Even the South African [Boer] War was . . . not the selfish and sordid business that many people represent it to have been. It was not the selfish and sordid motive that aroused popular enthusiasm and excitement here in England, but the belief that Kruger's government was inefficient, corrupt and oppressive beyond all bearing. . . . With the general public, the European motive was throughout the strongest.

Most of us, probably, are ready enough to admit our own disinterestedness. We are no greedy landgrabbers, but the apostles of an idea, the missionaries of Western civilization. We make that claim for ourselves, and we make it also for those with whom we are in friendship and sympathy. We make it for France. France, introducing order into chaos, transforming a pirates' den into a beautiful and prosperous city, and reviving by her wells and springs the date palms of a thousand perishing oases, is also a missionary of Western civilization. Her action, like ours, is to be accounted for, not by selfish and sordid motives, but by an appreciation of the great opportunities that have been set before her for bringing European ideas and European science to bear upon regions which most need their influence. . . .

Germany's share in European civilization is equal to England's share or France's. Germany, as much as England or France, believes in and lives by the great political and scientific ideals which have inspired that civilization; and, this being so, is it not evident that . . . when she builds her new railway [direct to Baghdad] she too will be actuated by the desire . . . to apply Western ideas to the conditions of life where they are most needed? Whether the new railway will ever profit her much it is impossible to say, but whether it does or not, it will not have been undertaken mainly for mere profit. It will have been undertaken mainly because the anarchy and ignorance of Asia Minor and Mesopotamia are a perpetual challenge to the ideas and capacities of which Germany is full. . . .

We have no wish here to enforce Germany's claims to be the chosen instrument for the carrying out of this task. There is, however, one characteristic of her Turkish policy which the Baghdad railway so forcibly illustrates that it is impossible not to refer to it. We English have been so accustomed to calculate quite openly upon the speedy decline and disintegration of the Turkish Empire, and even to hurry the process by plucking off such fragments as were most accessible or as seemed ripe for the operation, that we have a difficulty in understanding the directly contrary hypothesis that Turkish affairs may be mended . . . by infusing into the Turkish Government and administration certain qualities which have hitherto been lacking to them and so building them up and strengthening them from within. . . .

The Baghdad railway is a kind of hypodermic syringe for the infusion of these ideas into the Turkish system. But it is not the only means Germany is employing. She is working to the same end in many other ways. German engineers for several years have been mapping out the Turkish railway systems of Syria and Arabia; and . . . [are about] . . . to survey the section to Medina. This southern railway system, extending to the Holy Cities, may . . . prove as strengthening an influence . . . as the Baghdad railway itself to the Turkish Empire. In conception and execution it has been throughout a German work. Similarly, in matters of revenue and finance, German counsel is attended to. . . . In all other departments of the Turkish government, especially in the instruction, organization and equipment of the Turkish army, we find the same prevalence of German activity, the same aid and advice constantly proffered and accepted; the same instilling, everywhere, through German channels, of European ideas of order and efficiency.

Already this stiffening of Turkish counsels has produced a marked effect. . . . Although the good resolutions of an Abdul Hamid, with only his own shifty Oriental impulses to depend upon, may be of negligible importance, . . . the good resolutions of an Abdul Hamid, steadied by German tenacity and common sense, . . . [are] of a different value and worthy of a quite different consideration.

"The Benefits of the Baghdad Railway," *The Edinburgh Review,* October, 1907, pp. 371 ff.

II. THE GREAT DEBATE: PROS AND CONS OF EMPIRE

There had been a lull in empire building following the break-up of the old overseas domains between 1775 and 1825. Renewed interest appeared about 1850 and led to the rapid creation of second empires commonly larger and more widely-scattered than the first.

Distinct interests in almost every western country sought to further expansion as a national enterprise. Such groups had widely-divergent objectives and not all were primarily activated by self-interest. Conspicuously procolonial were the great industrialists (especially the textile, ceramic, liquor, and armaments manufacturers), import-export houses, investors, bankers, promoters, shipbuilders, army officers, big navy groups, church leaders, exponents of "the White Man's Burden," militant patriots, and rabble-rousing politicians. Collectively, they exercised tremendous influence in shaping public thinking and at times succeeded in forcing a reluctant government's hands.

Conversely, intellectuals, agrarian interests, "Little Germans" and their counterparts in other lands, Socialists, and Communists offered vigorous opposition. Vociferous Colonial Nationalism, so widespread in our own day, had not yet emerged to lend force to their arguments. The debate progressed from country to country and went on intermittently to 1914 with little variation in argument and with the imperialists normally emerging triumphant.

A. Overseas Possessions Insure National Greatness and Strength

An early vehement demand for German colonies appears in Friedrich List's *National System of Political Economy,* a renowned exposition of protectionist doctrines published in 1841. The author (1789–1846), a distinguished figure in the free-trade controversy of the day, regarded the acquisition and exploitation of overseas possessions as the certain and best means for any country to attain a commanding economic position.

The highest means of development of the manufacturing power, of the internal and external commerce proceeding from it, of any considerable coast and sea navigation, of extensive sea fisheries and consequently of a respectable naval power, are *colonies.*

The mother nation supplies the colonies with manufactured goods and obtains in return their surplus produce of agricultural products and raw materials; this interchange gives activity to its manufactures, augments thereby its population and the demand for its internal agricultural products and enlarges its mercantile marine and naval power. The superior power of the mother country in population, capital and enterprising spirit obtains through colonization an advantageous outlet, which is again made good with interest by the fact that a considerable portion of those who have enriched themselves in the colony bring back the capital which they have acquired there and pour it into the lap of the mother nation, or expend their income in it.

Agricultural nations, which . . . need . . . colonies, . . . do not possess the power of utilizing and maintaining them. What the colonies require cannot be offered by them, and what they can offer, the colony itself possesses.

The exchange of manufactured goods for natural products is the fundamental condition on which the position of the present colonies continues. On that account, the United States of North America seceded from England as soon as they felt the necessity and the power of manufacturing for themselves [and] of carrying on for themselves navigation and commerce with the countries of the torrid zone. On that account, Canada will also secede after she has reached the same point. On that account, independent agricultural-manufacturing-commercial states will also arise in the countries of temperate climate in Australia in the course of time.

But this exchange between the countries of the temperate zone and the countries of the torrid zone is based upon natural causes, and will be so for all time. Hence India has given up her manufacturing power with her independence to England; hence all Asiatic countries of the torrid zone will pass gradually under the dominion of the manufacturing-commercial nations of the temperate zone; hence all the islands of the torrid zone which are at present dependent colonies can hardly ever liberate themselves from that condition; and the states of South America will always remain dependent to a certain degree on the manufacturing-commercial nations.

England owes her immense colonial possessions solely to her surpassing manufacturing power. If the other European nations wish also to partake of the profitable business of cultivating waste territories and civilizing barbarous nations, or nations once civilized but which are again sunk in barbarism, they must commence with the development of their own internal manufacturing powers, of their mercantile marine and of their naval power. And should they be hindered in these endeavors by England's manufacturing, commercial and naval supremacy, in the union of their powers lies the only means of reducing such unreasonable pretensions to reasonable ones.

Friedrich List, *National System of Political Economy,* trans. Sampson Lloyd (London: Longmans, Green and Company, 1904), pp. 216-217.

B. Colonies a Bread and Butter Proposition

W. T. Stead (1849–1912) was a world-famous journalist and social reformer. Imperialism was one of his many enthusiasms and he found a great hero in Cecil Rhodes (1853–1902), leading British exponent of an "all red" African domain from Cairo to the Cape. In the late 1890's, Stead wrote *A History of the Mystery,* a fictionized account of the Jameson Raid into Transvaal—an attempt at conquest (1895) and a provocative prelude to the Boer War (1899–1902). This became a best-seller. Rhodes here appears thinly disguised as "Mr. Cecil," a highly vocal imperialist voicing a telling contemporary British argument for expansion.

"So you really saw a genuine meeting of the unemployed in London's East End last night?" [queried Stirling.]

"Yes," said Cecil, very soberly. "Mark my words, Stirling, you will be eating each other before very long on these islands. . . . It weighs on me like a nightmare, and the meeting last night, the wild speeches, which were nothing but semi-articulate wails for bread, and the hungry look on the faces of those present, gave me a bad turn. . . . And your Little Englanders . . . are such fools they do not see it. It makes me mad to think of it sometimes, and you who know what traitors these people are, . . . speak to them . . . [and] meet them at dinner instead of treating them as they deserve—as traitors to their country."

Stirling said nothing, while Cecil paced backwards and forwards.

"Oh, you are all alike," he said savagely. . . . "You are all so full of the politics of the parish pump, you have never a thought for the great problem which over-shadows everything. They call it an Imperial question; a bread-and-butter question it is, or rather a bread-without-butter question for the people, as you will find out before very long. . . .

"Never was I so convinced as last night, when I walked home from that meeting, . . . that the very existence of your people depends upon us beyond the seas. How many are there of you here? Forty millions in these little islands, and in another twenty or thirty years, how many will there be? Twenty or thirty millions more. What are you to feed them on? Your trade, your foreign trade. You could not feed your people . . . for six months but for that, and yet who thinks about it?

"I suppose what these people would like would be for me to take my money . . . and break it up into sixpences and give it away to your forty millions as . . . [one gives] sixpences to the children in the workhouse at Christmas. Sixpence a head all round for your forty millions would just wipe out a million; and what better would you be . . . a week after the sixpences had been distributed? The million would be gone and all its potentialities of usefulness, but your forty millions of people would remain without any prospect of getting anything more to eat because they had sixpence a head last week. . . .

"A great fortune that is frittered away in doles is like a shower of rain falling in the desert; but a great fortune that is devoted to hewing out a channel for enterprise and industry is like the creation of a river on whose banks generations yet unborn shall find sustenance and prosperity. . . . In order to keep your forty millions here from eating each other for lack of other victuals, we beyond the seas must keep open as much of the surface of this planet as we can for the overflow of your population to inhabit and . . . create markets where you can dispose of the produce of your factories and of your mines. The Empire, I am always telling you, is a bread-and-butter question. If you have not to be cannibals, you have got to be Imperialists."

W. T. Stead, *A History of the Mystery*. The Masterpiece Library, Penny Popular Novels No. 58. Abridged (London: The Review of Reviews Office, 1897), pp. 3-4.

C. The German People Must Have "Lebensraum!!"

The spectacle of German youth flocking from their homes and being lost to the Fatherland was abhorrent to Heinrich von Treitschke (1834–1896), the "patriotic" historian glorifying the House of Hohenzollern and Prussia. A major force in molding the minds of the rising generation, he became a strong advocate of overseas expansion and made Young Germany world-empire conscious. As a leading German Imperialist, he was bitterly hostile to Great Britain which he regarded as a nation of insolent shopkeepers. His essay, "First Attempts at German Colonization," appearing on the eve of the Berlin Conference of 1884–1885 on African affairs, is a classic in the literature of imperialism.

Without any pressure from authority, there has risen from the people . . . a spontaneous demand for German colonies. . . . By the persistent endeavors of our brave travellers, missionaries and merchants, the first attempt at German colonization,[2] has . . . been rendered possible. Germany's modest gains on the [West] African Coast . . . aroused attention in the world at large, because everyone knew that they were not due, as in the case of the colonizing experiments of the Electorate of Brandenburg,[3] to the bold idea of a great mind, but because a whole nation greeted them with a joyful cry, "At last! At last!"

For a nation that suffers from continual over-production, and sends yearly 200,000 of her children abroad, the question of colonization is vital. During the first years which followed the restoration of the German Empire [in 1871], well-meaning people began to hope that the constant draining away of German forces into foreign countries would gradually cease, together with the political persecutions, the discontent and the petty domestic coercive laws of the good old times. This hope was disappointed, and was doomed to be so, for those political grievances were not the only, nor even the most important causes of German emigration.

In the short time since the establishment of the Empire, the population has increased by a full eighth, and this rapid growth, in spite of all the misery which it involves, is nevertheless the characteristic of a healthy national life. . . . Our population . . . must, in no distant future, rise to a hundred millions and more, . . . [and] their fatherland

[2] In German Southwest Africa, Togo, and Kamerun, where protectorates were proclaimed in 1884.

[3] In the late 17th century, the Elector of Brandenburg, which later developed into Prussia, tried to break into the lucrative slave trade by opening a trading post at Cape Three Points and a distribution center in the Caribbean. Brandenburg was in no economic position to press the venture, and it collapsed early in the 1700's. The experiment is of historical significance only because it represented the first attempt at overseas activity by a German state.

. . . [will then] be too narrow for the Germans. . . . According to all appearance, German emigration will still, for a long while, remain an unavoidable necessity, and it becomes a new duty for the motherland to take care that her wandering children remain true to their nationality and open new channels for her commerce. This is . . . more important than our political control of the lands we colonize. A state whose frontiers march with those of three Great Powers, and whose seaboard lies open towards a fourth, will generally only be able to carry on great national wars and must keep its chief military forces carefully collected in Europe. The protection of a remote, easily-threatened colonial empire would involve it in embarrassments and not strengthen it. . . .

The German emigrants in North America are completely lost to our State and our nationality. Set in the midst of a certainly less intellectual but commercially more energetic people, the nationality of the German minority must inevitably be suppressed by that of the majority. . . . The German emigration to North America is an absolute loss for our nation—a present given to a foreign country without any equivalent compensation. . . . Therefore it is quite justifiable on the ground of national self-preservation . . . [to] seek for ways and means to divert the stream of German emigrants into lands where they run no danger of losing their nationality. Such a territory has been already found in the south of Brazil. There, unassisted and sometimes not even suspected by the motherland, German nationality remains quite intact . . . and our rapidly increasing export trade with [this area] . . . shows that the commerce of the old home profits greatly by the loyalty of her emigrant children. Other such territories will also be discovered if our nation enters with prudence and boldness on the new era now opening to the colonizing energy of Europeans.

With the crossing of Africa begins the last epoch of great discoveries. When once the center of the Dark Continent lies open, . . . it will be our turn to show what we can do; in those remote regions, the power of the state can only follow the free action of the nation and not precede it. In this new world it must be seen whether the trivial pedantry of an unfortunate past . . . has at last been overcome forever, and whether the German trader has enough self-confidence to venture on rivalry with the predominant financial strength of England.

The future will show whether the founding of German agricultural colonies is possible in the interior of Africa; there will certainly be an opportunity for founding mercantile colonies which will yield a rich return. After destiny has treated us badly for so many centuries, we may well count for once on the favor of fortune. In South Africa also circumstances are decidedly favorable for us. English colonial policy, which has been successful everywhere else, has not been fortunate at the Cape. The civilization which flourishes there is Teutonic and Dutch. The attitude of England, wavering between weakness and violence, has evoked among the brave Dutch Boers a deadly ineradicable hatred. . . . [We may well], in some form or other, undertake the protectorate of the Teutonic population of South Africa and succeed as heirs of the English in a neglected colony which, since the opening of the Suez Canal, has little more value for England.

If our nation dares decidedly to follow the new path of an independent colonial policy, it will inevitably become involved in a conflict of interests with England. It lies in the nature of things that the new Great Power of central Europe must come to an understanding with all the other Great Powers. We have already made our reckoning with Austria, with France and with Russia; our last reckoning, that with England, will probably be the most tedious and the most difficult; for here we are confronted by a line of policy which for centuries, almost unhindered by the other Powers, aims directly at maritime supremacy. . . .

England's state policy since the days of William III has never been anything else than a remarkably shrewd and remarkably conscienceless commercial policy. The extraordinary successes of this state-policy have been purchased at a high price, consisting in the first place of a number of sins and enormities. The history of the English East India Company is the most defiled page in the annals of the modern European nations, for the shocking vampirism of this merchant-rule sprang solely from greed. . . .

A still more serious factor in the situation is that, owing to her transatlantic successes, England has lost her position as a European Great Power; in negotiations on the continent her voice counts no longer. . . . The worst consequence, however, of British commercial policy is the immense and well-justified hatred which all nations have gradually been conceiving towards England. From the point of view of international law England is today the place where barbarism reigns. . . . [Her] national policy, like every policy which aims at the unreasonable goal of world supremacy, always reckoned, as its foundation principle, on the misfortunes of all other nations.

England's commercial supremacy had its origin in the discords on the continent and, owing to her brilliant successes, which were often gained without a struggle, there has grown up in the English people a spirit of arrogance, for which "chauvinism" is too mild an expression. Sir Charles Dilke, the well-known Radical member of Mr. Gladstone's Cabinet, in his book, *Greater Britain,* . . . claims as necessary acquisitions for "Greater Britain," China, Japan, Chili, Peru, the La Plata States, the tablelands of Africa—in short, the whole world.

In spite of the outrageous ill-usage of Ireland, and the bestial coarseness of the London mob, he calls Great Britain the land which from the earliest time exhibits the greatest amount of culture and insight, together with the least intermixture of ignorance and crime. He looks confidently forward to the time when Russia and France will only be pigmies by the side of England. In only three passages does he deign to make a cursory mention of the Germans. One of them is when he indignantly asks whether we really wish to be so selfish as to decline to support with German money the Euphrates Railway [planned as a precursor to the later German-constructed Baghdad line] which is indispensable to Greater Britain. Thus, then, the manifold glories of the world's history, which commenced with the empire of the monosyllabic Chinese, are to conclude their melancholy cycle with the empire of the monosyllabic British! . . .

German policy is national and cosmopolitan at the same time; it counts, otherwise than British policy does, on the peaceful prosperity of her neighbors. We can rejoice without reserve at each advance of the Russians in Central Asia and each French success in Tonkin. Our ambition only reaches thus far, that in the still uncolonized quarters of the earth, wind and sun should be fairly divided between the civilized nations. . . .

The great German seaport towns . . . have the prospect of a new period of revival; it is from the Hansa [Baltic] towns that the bold pioneers of our nation in Africa come. What Schiller at the commencement of the nineteenth century wrote about the greedy polyp-like arms of England is not out of date today; but we hope that when the twentieth century dawns the transatlantic world will have already learned that the Germans today no longer, as in Schiller's day, escape from the stress of life into the still and holy places of the heart.

From Adolf Hausrath, *Treitschke: His Doctrine of German Destiny and of International Relations* (New York: G. P. Putnam's Sons, 1914), pp. 205-216.

D. Counterviews

Great Britain was the dominant colonial power in the world after the close of the Napoleonic Wars. There a large-scale controversy centering about the retention of overseas possessions was in full swing by mid-century following the triumph of free trade doctrines. Now that colonies no longer existed for the exclusive advantage of the Motherland, had they not become a liability rather than an asset? Precisely the same arguments were used in other countries in turn almost to the outbreak of World War I. A penetrating article by the editors, in *The Edinburgh Review* for April 1851, admirably summarizes the views of both imperialists and anti-colonists.

In former times, and under the old mercantile system, we valued our colonies as outlets for our manufactures, and as sources of supply for needful products which we could not obtain, or could not obtain so cheaply or so well, elsewhere. We valued them as the principal and the surest channels for that commerce which we felt to be the life-blood of the nation. They were secure, increasing and favored markets for those articles of British produce which other nations excluded as far as they could by severe and prohibitory tariffs; and they produced for us exclusively those valuable raw materials and articles of luxury which we wished to debar other nations from procuring.

In conformity with these ideas, we bound them to the mother country in the bands of a strict and mutually favoring system of customs' duties: we compelled them to trade with us exclusively; to take from us exclusively all the articles with which we could supply them; and to send to us exclusively all the produce of their soil. In return, we admitted their produce to our markets at lower rates than that of other countries or excluded the produce of other countries altogether. This was a consistent, intelligible and mutually fair system. Under it our colonies were *customers who could not escape us* and vendors who could sell to us alone.

But a new system has risen up, not only differing from the old one, but based upon radically opposite notions of commercial policy. We have discovered that under this system our colonies have cost us, in addition to the annual estimate for their civil government and their defence, a sum amounting to many millions a year in the extra price which we have paid for their produce beyond that at which other countries could have supplied it to us. In obedience to our new and wiser commercial policy, we have abolished all discriminating and protective duties; we have announced to our colonies that we shall no longer favor their productions and, as a necessary and just corollary, that we shall no longer compel them to favor ours— that we shall supply ourselves with our sugar, coffee, cotton and indigo wherever we can buy them cheapest and that they are at liberty to follow the same principle in the purchase of their calicoes, silks and woollens. They are therefore to us now, in a commercial point of view, friendly trading communities and nothing more. The very object for which we founded, governed, defended and cherished them, has been abandoned: why, then, should we any longer incur the cost of their maintenance?

Being, then, on the footing of independent states as far as their tariffs are concerned, they yield us nothing and benefit us in nothing as colonies that they would not yield us and serve us were they altogether independent. Nay, they are even less serviceable to us; for the experience of the United States has shown us how immeasurably faster colonies advance in population, in enterprise, in agriculture and in commerce— in everything which makes them valuable as customers—when separated from the mother country than when still attached to it by the bonds of allegiance and the clumsy fetters of remote and injudicious control. . . .

In the next place, our colonies used to be regarded as inexhaustible storehouses of waste and fertile land and as outlets for our dense and often-suffering population; and it is in this view, perhaps, that most persons are still disposed especially to value them. But what is the fact? Have we not the plainest indications that even in this respect they would be more valuable if they were independent and that even now the United States, because independent, are preferred by our emigrants? According to Sir William Molesworth's statement in 1848, of 1,673,600 persons who had emigrated during the preceding twenty years, 825,564 went direct to the United States, and how many more went indirectly through Canada we can only guess. . . .

Again—we used to make some of our colonies serviceable as prisons for our convicts—distant and safe receptacles for the disposal of our metropolitan villany and filth—places for "burying our dead out of our sight." *Now* we can use them as such no longer. Our colonies have one and all remonstrated; have refused to receive the sweepings of our gaols any longer; have threatened to rebel if we persist in sending them; and we have ourselves, on more than one occasion, admitted the system to be an indefensible one and have announced our determination to abandon it.

We have been taught to believe that our colonial empire, "on which the sun never sets," is about the most important element in our national greatness and that these vast dominions in every part of the world add incalculably, though in some mysterious way, to our imperial dignity and strength. . . . [Now we are told] that this "prestige of empire" is a hollow show . . . ; that outlying dependencies which require to be garrisoned in time of peace and protected in time of war draft off from this country the forces which are needed for our defence at home; dissipate our army and navy . . . ; and waste the funds which should be devoted to the protection of the mother country.

It is idle, [we learn,] to pretend that a system which gives us such a vast additional territory to defend without giving us any additional means of defending it can be other than a source of dangerous weakness; that if we had no dependencies, we should be impregnable and invulnerable at home; and that half our navy and a fourth of our army would suffice for the protection of our hearths and homes. If, indeed, the colonies paid tribute into our treasury, if they furnished contingents to our military force and supplied a fixed quota of ships and stores toward the augmentation of our navy, the case might be different. But they do nothing of all this. . . . Our colonial empire costs us at least £4,000,000 a year—a sum nearly equal to the income-tax, . . . the malt tax . . . [or] the sugar tax; any one of which might be repealed, to the infinite relief of our people, in case our colonies were abandoned.

Lastly, we govern them ill. . . . They are perpetual sources of difficulty and dispute; they are always quarrelling with us and complaining of us, and not unfrequently breaking out into open rebellion; they yearn for independence and would gladly purchase immunity from our vexatious interference and ignorant control by encountering all the risks and difficulties to which a severance of the imperial connection might expose them. Since, then, the colonies are commercially as free as America or Spain; since they are no longer favored or enforced customers for our productions; since they would be at least as available to our emigrants if independent as if still subject to our rule; since they refuse to help us by relieving us of our convict population; since they are sources of weakness and not of strength to us in times of peril or of war; since they pay no part of the expenses of the mother country and only a small portion of their own; since we mismanage their affairs and impede their progress; and since they themselves wish to be set free from a fettering and galling yoke; what argument, which will bear the test of close investigation, can be adduced to warrant our retaining them in tutelage?

Such is . . . the reasoning we have to meet. . . . The position is undoubtedly a strong one: nevertheless, we hold that there are sufficient grounds for maintaining inviolate the connection actually existing between the colonies and the mother country. . . . Since . . . there is no foundation for the idea that we need to abandon our colonies from sheer inability to retain them, we may proceed to point out a few of the reasons which may be urged for preserving the connection inviolate. . . .

In the first place, not a single one of our colonies is inhabited by a homogeneous population. In none is the British race the sole one; in scarcely any is it the most numerous. Some of the dependencies have been taken from savage tribes; others have been conquered from other European nations. . . . With what show of decency or justice could England abandon to their own guidance and protection countries peopled by such various, heterogeneous and often hostile races, even if any considerable number of their inhabitants were unwise enough to wish it? What inevitable injustice such a step must entail upon one or other section of the colonists, what certain peril to the interests of them all and of humanity at large! . . .

Colonies with mixed and aboriginal populations . . . we simply could *not* abandon; colonies with a population exclusively or overwhelmingly British come under a different category. But even with these we think it is not difficult to see that the interests of civilization will be far more effectually served by their retention than by their abandonment, by still maintaining them as integral portions of the British Empire than by casting them adrift to run the chances of a hazardous voyage unassisted and alone. They would "go ahead" far faster, we are told, if independent than if still subject to the hampering rule of the mother country; and the example of the United States is triumphantly appealed to in confirmation of the assertion. We reply that we can well believe that they would go ahead far faster if free than if fettered, but not than they will now, when colonial legislatures have been created and endowed with the powers of managing all strictly colonial concerns. There is scarcely an advantage, conferrable by freedom, possessed by the United States since their separation from Britain, that will not now be enjoyed in an equal degree by our North American and our Australian dependencies. . . .

If, indeed, it were true, as is often ignorantly alleged, that the colonies hated Great Britain and were anxious to cast off their allegiance to her, much might be urged against the policy of retaining unwilling and therefore troublesome and dangerous dependencies. But we believe the statement to be the reverse of true. They may hate the Colonial Office: they do not hate England. They are often indignant, and sometimes we think they have been so with justice, at the vexatious interference, the injudicious control, the irritating vacillations, the sad mistakes of the authorities at home; they often bluster and sometimes rebel; they nurture in their bosom, as does every community, a noisy knot of turbulent and disaffected men; they talk largely at times of their desire of independence, and occasionally even forget themselves so far as to hint at "annexation." But this is the mere effervescence of political excitement. . . .

If, in an evil hour, the counsels of the counterfeit economists were to prevail, and England were to resign her children to the vanity and feebleness of independence, we feel certain that the very first peril they encountered from without, the very first time they were menaced either with insult or with conquest by a foreign Power, they would instinctively and undoubtingly appeal to England for assistance and protection; and England would respond to their confidence with the most prompt and generous aid. . . . We should have to bear the expense of defending them from attack without having any control over their conduct in incurring it.

Finally: there is one other consequence which would ensue from the abandonment of our colonial Empire which demands to be most deliberately weighed. . . . If we emancipate our colonies and cast them on their own unaided resources both for self-government and self-defence, they will of course immediately look about them for the means of securing these primary objects. However economically they may manage, . . . they can neither govern themselves, nor defend themselves, without a considerable revenue. . . . How [can this] revenue be raised?

There are three sources from the combination of which it might be derived: the sale of waste lands, direct taxation or customs duties on imported articles. The first of these sources could never produce much. . . . Direct taxation is always burdensome, irritating and unwelcome. . . . In colonies where the population is scanty and scattered, there would arise peculiar and insuperable obstacles in the way of levying a capitation-tax, a land-tax or an income-tax. . . . The source of indirect taxation alone remains; and from this accordingly we should find that the revenue of the emancipated colonies would inevitably be raised. A further option has to be made in the choice between import and export duties; . . . the former, among a commercially educated people, will obviously be the most popular and will certainly be adopted. . . .

In a densely populated and luxurious country like England, moderate duties suffice to procure a large revenue . . . but this could not be the case in a thinly peopled colony; a low scale of duties could never raise an ample or adequate revenue; the money must be obtained, and objectionable and burdensome as such a way of obtaining it would be, . . . it would be adopted as a matter of course. The first effect, then, of our proclaiming the independence of our colonies, must inevitably be the enactment by them of a high tariff on all imported commodities; and as the commodities required by new countries are, by the nature of the case, articles of manufactured rather than of agricultural produce, and as England is the chief manufacturing country in the world, it would be chiefly on our productions that this high tariff would

press. . . . [This would effectively close to us] the markets we ourselves have planted in the wilderness. . . .

We hope we have succeeded in making it clear that our colonies are far too valuable portions of our Empire to be lightly laid down or put away. . . . Many of them, in simple justice to the native population or to those British subjects who have settled there on the faith of the imperial connection, we could not possibly abandon. Others the interests of civilization and humanity compel us to retain. All of them ought to be, and will be if we govern them aright, sources of strength and pride to us. The very interests of that free and enlightened commercial policy for which we have fought so long and sacrificed so much forbid us to entertain the thought of severing the time-hallowed connection between Great Britain and the communities which have gone forth from her bosom. . . .

The cost of our colonies . . . we could easily sustain were it twice as great; the affection of the colonists it is easy to preserve or to recover where, through misjudgment or misunderstanding, it has been shaken or impaired. By ruling them with forbearance, steadiness and justice; by leading them forward in the path of freedom with an encouraging but cautious hand; by bestowing on them the fullest powers of self-government wherever the infusion of British blood is large enough to warrant such a course . . . we may secure the existence and rivet the cohesion of a vast dominion blest with the wisest, soberest, most beneficial form of liberty which the world has yet enjoyed, and spread to distant lands and future ages the highest, most prolific, most expansive development of civilization which Providence has ever granted to humanity. . . .

To cast our colonial Empire to the winds . . . [to save some millions] a year is a line of policy which, we sincerely think, is worthy only of a narrow and a niggard school which will be counselled only by men who are merchants rather than statesmen and whose mercantile wisdom even is confined, short-sighted and unenlightened; one which, we feel assured, can never be adopted by England till the national spirit which has made her what she is shall have begun to wane and fade away.

"Shall We Retain Our Colonies?" *The Edinburgh Review,* April, 1851, pp. 475 ff.

III. DOES IMPERIALISM PAY?

Empire building is costly business, involving heavy expenditures in men and money. Returns on investments are generally not immediate and normally continue low for long periods. Taxpayers view attendant drains upon the public treasury with apprehension and soon begin to query "What is there in it for *us*?" and then, "What am *I* getting out of this?"

Expansionists seek to curb such critical tendencies by fostering pride in empire and a feeling of partnership in a national enterprise predestined to pay off handsomely. Conversely, anti-imperialists seek to demonstrate either that there is no gain whatsoever in colonial undertakings or that, while every citizen shares in the staggering cost, the huge profits fill the pockets of only a few who chance to be strategically placed. The debate arises in every country venturing upon the path of empire and periodically breaks out anew without any final decision ever being reached.

A. An Affirmative American Opinion

The Spanish-American War (1898) unexpectedly brought a new colonial empire into being and the United States was suddenly confronted with the many problems attendant upon overseas expansion. The public at large was entirely unprepared for this startling development and the pros and cons of imperialism were avidly argued East, West, North, and South. The question most commonly put by the practical down-to-earth citizen was "Is there money in it?" O. P. Austin (1848–1933), Chief of the United States Bureau of Statistics and a popular writer, sought to show that it was indeed a profitable venture and (hoping to allay the doubts of timorous souls opposing the extension of alien rule upon moral grounds) that it at the same time bestowed incalculable benefits upon the inhabitants of the area involved. His article today stands as the foremost popular exposition of these views.

Does colonization pay? This is a question which Americans are now asking. . . . The best answer is provided by the experience of those other nations that long ago reached the point where such a step was found necessary. . . .

The three modern colonizing powers from whose experience we are able to draw lessons are Great Britain, France and Spain. Germany has so recently begun to colonize that her experiments have not yet sufficiently advanced to justify us in including her colonies in this study. Great Britain is the largest and by far the most successful of the colonizing powers; France comes next in order; Spain's colonial experiments are generally conceded to have been unsuccessful.

A study of these three groups of colonies shows that all those of Great Britain (except Canada and Australia), like those of France and Spain, were established with a view to their commercial usefulness rather than as permanent homes for any considerable percentage of the population of the governing country. Great Britain's principal colonies, named in the order of their imports from the governing country, are: India, Australasia, British Africa, Canada, British Asia and the British West Indies. Canada absorbs less than 7 per cent of the goods which England sends to her colonies but sells to England vastly more than she buys from her. Australasia absorbs 26 per cent of Great Britain's exports to her colonies and supplies 31 per cent of Great Britain's imports from the colonies. Canada has become practically self-supporting in the way of meeting her own requirements and those which she cannot meet she can secure more conveniently from the United States. Therefore, as a market, she is of comparatively little value to the United Kingdom. For many years Australasia will continue to be an important market for British manufactures: she also supplies raw materials to Great Britain. Of the total commerce of Great Britain with her colonies, a large proportion is with those established and maintained because of advantage to her commerce.

The points to be considered in determining the somewhat mercenary question, "Does colonization pay?", as viewed with regard to the interests of the colonizing country, are (1) the market that the colonies afford for the goods which the colonizing country has to sell and whether control gives to the mother country a larger share of the market than she would have without that control; (2) the supplies the colonies are able to furnish for use in the mother country and whether the purchase of these supplies from the colonies proves more advantageous to the mother country than if they should be purchased from other parts of the world; (3) the advantages, if any, which accrue to the native population of the country controlled.

The commercial ambitions of countries which have reached a stage of development to warrant them in entering the field of modern colonization are . . . (1) to enlarge the markets for their manufactures; (2) to obtain reliable supplies of the materials which their

people must consume for food or use in manufacturing and (3), in obtaining them, to give some share of the profit of production or transportation to the people of the home country. With these cold business considerations in view, let us study . . . the commerce of the countries whose modern colonial experiences seem likely to prove instructive along these lines.

In 1897, Great Britain's exports of domestic produce and manufactures amounted to $1,135,970,000, of which $391,274,000, or 34.4 per cent, was sent to her colonies. . . . Here is a market found by Great Britain in her colonies, during 1897, for nearly $400,000,000 worth of goods, all of which are the product of labor; and all are of a kind for which the producers and manufacturers of the United States are now seeking a market. . . . Great Britain's sales of manufactures to her colonies alone in 1897 [were] 40 per cent greater than our total sales of manufactures to the entire world in that year.

"But," the objector will say, "would not Great Britain have made these same sales if the countries had not held colonial relations with her, especially since the tariff laws of her colonies at that time made no discrimination in favor of products from the mother country?" Let us see.

In 1897, the total imports of the world, exclusive of the United Kingdom, were $8,172,000,000, of which $962,-000,000 was taken by the British colonies; leaving the total imports of the non-British world during that year $7,210,000,000. In that year, Great Britain's exports . . . to the non-British world amounted to $1,005,000,000 or . . . 14 per cent of the total. . . . [Of the] total importations of the British colonies in that year, . . . the United Kingdom supplied $391,000,000 or 41 per cent. . . .

Even to the United States, an English-speaking country from which her purchases are enormous, she supplied in that year less than 22 per cent of the total imports.

It will thus be seen that . . . the colonizing country . . . sells to her colonies a much larger percentage of what they buy than she is able to sell to countries with which she does not have this relation—even under the most favorable conditions. . . . A study of the exports of France to the whole world and to her colonies shows even more strikingly the advantage in her colonial trade over that with other parts of the world. The imports of the non-French world, in 1897, amounted to $9,249,000,000, of which 9.33 per cent was supplied by France; the total imports of the French colonies were $111,157,000, and of this $68,685,000 or 62 per cent was supplied by France. In 1897, Spain's exports to the whole world amounted to $208,382,-000, of which $71,962,000 or 35 per cent went to her colonies.

A further study of the commerce of 1897 shows that the total exports of the non-British world were in round terms $8,245,000,000, of which the United Kingdom took . . . about 21 per cent, [and that] the total exports from the British colonies . . . [were] $800,250,-000, of which the United Kingdom took . . . 57 per cent. . . . How much her own people were benefited by her giving so large a proportion of her trade to her own colonies cannot be statistically determined; though the estimate made by distinguished British writers that the investment of British capital in the colonies today is more than $2,-000,000,000 shows that a considerable percentage of this benefit must have accrued to her citizens, directly or indirectly. To the profits must be added those of the carrying trade between the United Kingdom and her colonies, which is almost exclusively in the hands of her vessel owners.

In attempting, then, to answer the question, "Does colonization pay the colonizing country?" we find that [in the case of] Great Britain, the colonial relationship brought her from the colonies a market for merchandise valued at fully $250,000,000 in excess of that which she would have sold had they belonged to the non-British . . . world. Most of this accrues to the benefit of home labor. . . . On the other hand, she expended among them . . . about $460,000,000, by which she must have materially benefited not only her people residing in those colonies, but those of her home citizens having [investments] in the colonies. . . .

The development of modern commerce and of the carrying trade makes the interchange of commodities and natural products between the great sections of the globe much greater today than ever before; and every year's developments add to the facilities for quick and inexpensive interchange. The older and well-developed countries, especially those in a temperate climate, require three classes of articles from other parts of the world: (1) foodstuffs of a class which they cannot produce at home; (2) materials for use in manufacturing and (3) certain lines of manufactured articles not convenient to be produced at home. On the other hand, the newer countries, especially those in the tropical zone, where manufacturing has not developed, require chiefly two classes of imports: (1) foodstuffs of the class which they cannot produce at home and (2) manufactures which they cannot produce.

The well-developed countries of the temperate zone require sugar, coffee, tea, silks, tropical fruits, spices [and] fibres for use in manufacturing—all of which are produced in the tropical countries freely and with less expenditure of labor than they could be produced if grown in the temperate zones.

On the other hand, the articles which the tropical countries require—breadstuffs, meats, clothing, manufactures of iron and steel, machinery and the various classes of household and business conveniences which modern ingenuity offers them—are all produced abundantly and cheaply in the temperate zone and by the very people who want and require the products of the tropical countries.

Thus the great colonizing countries, all lying in the temperate zones, are dependent upon territory lying near the equator for certain lines of products which they must have; while the tropical countries are dependent upon those of the temperate zone for other and equally important lines of products. It is . . . due to this fact . . . that the drift has been so rapid during this century toward the control of tropical territory by governments located in the temperate zone.

To put it in homely form, and with no intention to put it offensively, it may be said that the disposition of modern progressive nations lying in the temperate zone is to control "garden spots" in the tropics, where there may be produced, under their direction and through the operation of their accumulated wealth, the articles of tropical growth which their citizens require and, in return, to furnish to the people occupying those garden spots the foodstuffs and manufactures which they require; to de-velop for them their territory by the construction of roads, canals, railways and telegraphs and by the establishment of schools [and] newspapers; and to give them the benefit of other blessings of civilization which they have not the facilities for creating.

Now let us apply the foregoing facts to the United States and to the islands which the events of the past year have brought into closer relationship with us. The United States has become a great manufacturing as well as producing and consuming nation. Her manufacturers supply the home market and send abroad more than a million dollars' worth per day of their product. In doing this, however, they require constantly increasing quantities of tropical materials; and the people who are co-operating with them in developing the higher stages of her progress, whether in the factory, on the farm, in the mines or forests, require also a constantly increasing quantity of tropical productions. . . . These articles these islands can produce, while on the other hand they now import, under normal conditions, $100,000,000 worth of foodstuffs and manufactures of the class which we produce and desire to sell. They will double or treble that demand when internal transportation and invested capital will develop within them new areas of production and consumption and stimulate those already existing.

O. P. Austin, "Does Colonization Pay?" *The Forum,* January, 1900, pp. 621 ff.

B. Three Tragic Fallacies Attending Empire Building

Expansionists have always laid special emphasis upon the value of colonies as (1) yielders of huge commercial profits; (2) outlets for surplus population and (3) sources of supply for essential raw products. These doctrines have been resoundingly challenged by Professor Grover Clark (1891–1938), Far Eastern journalist and sometime Professor of Economics at the University of Denver, in his famed *A Place in the Sun,* and his elaborate parallel statistical study, *The Balance Sheets of Empire.* The latter contains an admirable summary of his dispassionate findings.

Western expansion in the past four centuries, culminating in the swiftly moving drive during the three decades which just preceded the [First] World War, undoubtedly has brought certain substantial advantages to the Western peoples. But, especially in the decades just before and since the [First] World War, this expansion also brought heavy costs in money, in lives and in . . . antagonisms. These costs are the debit entries which must be made in the ledger of Imperialism.

For the three centuries up to 1800 the record, if it were available (as it is not, except in very general terms), probably would show a cash profit to the Western governments and taxpayers, provided no money value were put on the lives lost in the taking as well as in the taken countries.

For the eight decades preceding the new drive for colonies which started in the 1880's, the governments as such spent considerably more on expansion than they received directly from it. These losses ultimately fell on the taxpayers. But private interests were making good profits on trade with the overseas territories and the governmental expenditures were much less than they came to be later. Perhaps the private profits roughly equalled the governments' losses. In any case, between 1800 and 1880, the balance for the people as a whole in the colony-holding countries was not large on either the debit or the credit side of the ledger.

Since 1880, however, the cash costs to the countries which have used force to get or keep control of colonies unquestionably have been very substantially more than any possible cash profits derived from the trade with the territories controlled. Germany and Italy have spent more directly on their colonies than the total value of the trade with them; Italy's margin of expense over trade value was very large even before the . . . drive into Ethiopia started. Japan has not spent as much directly on getting and keeping her col-

onies as the total value of her trade with them, but considerably more than the possible profits on that trade. The direct colonial expenses for France and Britain probably have been some, but not much, more than the profits on the trade with the overseas territories, especially if the trade with the Dominions be counted in the British total.

For all these countries, however, the direct expenditures on the colonies are only a part of the real colonial costs. A part of the general naval and military defence expenses must be charged against the colonies since not one of these nations would feel required to maintain such expensive armed forces if it did not have the overseas territories. If a conservatively estimated share of the general expenditures for defence be allocated to the colonies as their proper share of the overhead expenses of keeping up the nation's armed forces, the ledgers of the colonies show a large red ink balance for every one of the principal colony-holding countries. And this debit balance for the cash accounts includes no portion of the expenses of the [First] World War, even though the jealousies aroused by the drive for colonies were so important a factor in bringing that war about.

The record shows, too, that the gains in other than direct money terms which frequently are claimed to result from the possession of colonies have not been anything like enough to compensate for the heavy cash losses which the ledger records.

In spite of all that was said about the value of colonies as outlets for population, and as places to which people could go without being lost to the fatherland, the number of those who left all Europe permanently to live in the overseas territories controlled by European governments (which does not include the British Dominions) in the past half century has been extremely small compared either with the increase in population at home or with the migration to regions which were completely independent or, like the Dominions, practically so. Europe's population in this period has increased about 173 millions. The net emigration from Europe has been about 19.3 millions. The net emigration to the territories controlled from Europe has been about 500,000, which is less than 0.3 per cent of the population increase in Europe and only 2.6 per cent of all the permanent emigrants.

In spite, too, of the insistently repeated assertion that the possession of colonies and the consequent control of raw materials in them materially increases a nation's security in time of war and gives it substantial advantages in time of peace, the records show that this claim, like the claims that colonies provide important outlets for population and yield large and profitable trade to the holding country, is fundamentally fallacious.

The wartime situation is obvious enough. Access to the sources of raw materials depends on the ability to keep communications open with those sources, not on the presence or absence of political control over the territories where the sources are.

In times of peace, substantial advantages can be derived from ownership of the source of any particular raw material, in insuring either supplies or large profits for the owning country's nationals, only to the extent that something approaching monopoly control can be maintained of all the sources of supply. But, through the development of new sources or of substitute products for all the important raw materials, whether agricultural or mineral, it has become practically impossible for any country today to keep anything like monopoly control of any raw material. The tendency . . . is strongly toward

rather than away from increased competition in the world's raw materials markets.

Furthermore, the fallacy of the claim that a country really can make itself materially less dependent on foreign sources of supply and on foreign markets by adding to the territory under its control is strikingly demonstrated by the actual trade record of the colony-holding countries.

Not one of them does as much as a fourth of its trade with its colonies. Japan has the best record in this respect, but even she, . . . in 1929–1934, when her trade with her colonies was at its highest in proportion of her total trade, did only 22 per cent of her external business with the lands under her control. Even if all the British trade with the Dominions be included, the United Kingdom, even since the Ottawa Agreements of 1932 [which accorded nearly all Dominion produce free entry into Great Britain and gave increased preferential rates to British manufactures entering the Dominions], has done with all the British countries just over a third of her external trade, and the share with the British territories under London's control has been only 15 per cent of the total.

Nor does one of the colony-holding countries get from the overseas territories which it controls as much as a fifth of the raw materials and the foodstuffs which it requires, or sell to these regions as much as a third of the products of its factories. Even including the trade with the independent Dominions, the United Kingdom gets only a little more than a third of its food and raw materials imports from within the British Commonwealth, and sells less than half its exported manufactured goods to the British countries.

In brief, every country depends far more on foreign sources of supply and foreign markets than it does on overseas territories and sources under its own control, in spite of all the claims that have been made to justify the taking of colonies and in spite of all the money and lives that have been spent to get and keep colonies.

Moreover, no country gets *all* of its trade with its colonies, or with any colony, *because* it has political control. Control gives some advantages in getting trade, but the very fact that all the colonies trade with other countries than the one in control demonstrates that the controlling country could and probably would get a fair amount of trade with the regions which make up its colonies even if it did not have control.

Obviously it is impossible to determine precisely what proportion of the trade, in any particular case, goes to the holding country because it has control. But it is interesting to observe the British record in this connection. In the past half century, the share which the territories controlled from London have had in the trade of the United Kingdom has decreased, while that of the self-governing Dominion areas has increased.

The record of the overseas countries tells the same story: the share of the United Kingdom in the trade of the regions which it controls has fallen off, while that in the trade of the Dominions has increased. On its face, this record suggests that the trade importance of the British overseas countries has been in inverse, not direct, ratio to the amount of political control. But to draw that conclusion would be to give far more weight to the influence of political control in determining the movement of trade than the facts warrant.

Stated briefly, these are the conclusions which are inescapable from a careful analysis of the record for the past half century of what their colonies actually have meant to the principal colony-holding countries. The three main arguments for possessing colonies turn out to be three great fallacies, and they are seen to be dangerous as well as costly fallacies when account is taken of the results of the struggle for colonies not only or even primarily in cash but in lives lost, in wars caused and in the pyramided hatreds which so gravely threaten new wars.

Grover Clark, *The Balance Sheets of Empire* (New York: The Columbia University Press, 1936), pp. 3-5.

C. A Few Gain But the Nation Loses

Imperialism, by J. A. Hobson (1858-1940), distinguished British economist and journalist, appeared in 1902, at the close of the Boer War. It created a tremendous sensation and gave birth to anti-expansionist movements in many lands. Democrats in the United States and Socialists and Communists in Europe, in particular, drew ammunition from its devastating pages and used Hobson's arguments with telling effect.

Most spectacular of his charges was that, while empire building was carried on at public expense, huge profits accrued to members of narrowly-restricted groups and that the nation as a whole gained little if anything. This scholarly study continues the classic indictment of imperialism in our own day.

. . . Imperialism . . . is clearly condemned as a business policy in that, at enormous expense, it has procured a small, bad, unsafe increase of markets and has jeopardized the entire wealth of the nation in rousing the strong resentment of other nations. . . . [This being the case], we may ask, "How is the British nation induced to embark upon such unsound business?" The only possible answer is that the business interests of the nation as a whole are subordinated to those of certain sectional interests that usurp control of the national resources and use them for their private gain. . . .

Although . . . Imperialism has been bad business for the nation, it has been good business for certain classes and certain trades within the nation. The vast expenditure on armaments, the costly wars, the grave risks and embarrassments of foreign policy, the checks upon political and social reforms within Great Britain, though fraught with great injury to the nation, have served well the present business interests of certain industries and professions. . . .

What is the direct economic outcome of Imperialism? A great expenditure of public money upon ships, guns, military and naval equipment and stores, growing and productive of enormous profits when a war, or an alarm of war, occurs; new public loans and important fluctuations in the home and foreign bourses; more posts for soldiers and sailors and in the diplomatic and consular services; improvement of foreign investments by the substitution of the British flag for a foreign flag; acquisition of markets for certain classes of exports and some protection and assistance for British trades in these manufactures; employment for engineers, missionaries, speculative miners, ranchers and other emigrants.

Certain definite business and professional interests feeding upon imperialistic expenditure, or upon the results of that expenditure, are thus set up in opposition to the common good and, instinctively feeling their way to one another, are found united in strong sympathy to support every new imperialist exploit. . . . Some . . . , especially the shipbuilding, boilermaking and gun and ammunition making trades, are conducted by large firms with immense capital whose heads are well aware of the uses of political influence for trade purposes.

These men are Imperialists by conviction; a pushful policy is good for them.

With them stand the great manufacturers for export trade who gain a living by supplying the real or artificial wants of the new countries we annex or open up. Manchester, Sheffield, Birmingham, to name three representative cases, are full of firms which compete in pushing textiles and hardware, engines, tools, machinery, spirits, guns, upon new markets. The public debts which ripen in our colonies, and in foreign countries that come under our protectorate or influence, are largely loaned in the shape of rails, engines, guns and other materials of civilization made and sent out by British firms. The making of railways, canals and other public works, establishment of factories, the development of mines, the improvement of agriculture in new countries, stimulate a definite interest in important manufacturing industries which feeds a very firm imperialist faith in their owners.

The proportion which such trade bears to the total industry of Great Britain is not great, but some of it is extremely influential and able to make a definite impression upon politics through chambers of commerce, parliamentary representatives and semi-political, semi-commercial bodies like the Imperial South African Association or the China Society.

The shipping trade has a very definite interest which makes for Imperialism. This is well illustrated by the policy of state subsidies now claimed by shipping firms as a retainer and in order to encourage British shipping for purposes of imperial safety and defence.

The services are, of course, imperialist by conviction and by professional interest and every increase of the army, navy and air force enhances the political power they exert. . . . To the military services we may add the Indian Civil Service and the numerous official and semi-official posts in our colonies and protectorates. Every expansion of the Empire is also regarded by these same classes as affording new openings for their sons as ranchers, planters, engineers or missionaries. . . . From this standpoint our colonies [are] a vast system of outdoor relief for the upper classes.

In all the professions, military and civil, the army, diplomacy, the church, the bar, teaching and engineering, Greater Britain serves for an overflow, relieving the congestion of the home market and offering chances to more reckless or adventurous members, while it furnishes a convenient limbo for damaged characters and careers. . . .

By far the most important economic factor in Imperialism is the influence relating to investments. . . . In dealing with . . . foreign investments we are facing the most important factor in the economics of Imperialism. Whatever figures we take, two facts are evident. First, that the income derived as interest upon foreign investments enormously exceeded that derived as profits upon ordinary export and import trade. Secondly, that while our foreign and colonial trade, and presumably the income from it, were growing but slowly, the share of our import values representing income from foreign investments was growing very rapidly. . . .

. . . the modern foreign policy of Great Britain has been primarily a struggle for profitable markets of investment. To a larger extent every year Great Britain has been becoming a nation living upon tribute from abroad, and the classes who enjoy this tribute have had an ever-increasing incentive to employ the public policy, the public purse and the public force to extend the field of their private investments and to safeguard and improve their existing investments. This is, perhaps, the most important fact in modern politics and the

obscurity in which it is wrapped has constituted the gravest danger to our State.

What was true of Great Britain was true likewise of France, Germany, the United States and of all countries in which modern Capitalism has placed large surplus savings in the hands of a plutocracy or of a thrifty middle class. . . .

Aggressive Imperialism, which costs the taxpayer so dear, which is of so little value to the manufacturer and trader, which is fraught with such grave incalculable peril to the citizen, is a source of great gain to the investor who cannot find at home the profitable use he seeks for his capital and insists that his Government should help him to profitable and secure investments abroad.

If, contemplating the enormous expenditure on armaments, the ruinous wars, the diplomatic audacity or knavery by which modern governments seek to extend their territorial power, we put the plain, practical question, *Cui bono?*, the first and most obvious answer is the investor. . . . The big money-lender and speculator . . . [are] determinants of imperial policy. They have the largest definite stake in the business of Imperialism and the amplest means of forcing their will upon the policy of nations. . . .

Such is the array of distinctively economic forces making for Imperialism— a large loose group of trades and professions seeking profitable business and lucrative employment from the expansion of military and civil services and from the expenditure on military operations, the opening up of new tracts of territory and trade with the same and the provision of new capital which these operations require, all these finding their central guiding and directing force in the power of the general financier.

The play of these forces does not openly appear. They are essentially parasites upon patriotism and they adapt themselves to its protecting colors. In the mouths of their representatives are noble phrases, expressive of their desire to extend the area of civilization, to establish good government, promote Christianity, extirpate slavery and elevate the lower races. Some of the business men who hold such language may entertain a genuine, though usually a vague, desire to accomplish these ends, but they are primarily engaged in business and they are not unaware of the utility of the more unselfish forces in furthering their ends. Their true attitude of mind was expressed by Mr. Rhodes in his famous description of Her Majesty's Flag as "the greatest commercial asset in the world."

J. A. Hobson, *Imperialism* (London, 1938), pp. 46-61. Used by permission of George Allen and Unwin, Ltd., publishers.

IV. IMPERIALISM AND WORLD WAR I

The European colonial empires were at their height in 1914, with Great Britain, France, Russia, Germany, the Netherlands, Italy, Belgium, and Portugal controlling large portions of the world. Imperialistic rivalry, which had stood at its peak at the turn of the century, had been materially lessened through the Anglo-French Entente Cordiale (1904), the Anglo-Russian Convention (1907), and the proposed Anglo-German partitionment of Portugal's colonies (1913–1914). The fears of millions that such rivalries would ultimately lead to large-scale international strife had all but been calmed when the oft-foreseen but oft-averted World War suddenly burst out in the summer of 1914 following the assassination of the Archduke Franz Ferdinand, heir apparent to the Hapsburg throne, at the hands of Serb terrorists. This was the *immediate* cause for war, but did not clashing imperialistic ambitions constitute the real, underlying cause? Keen debate on that score opened immediately and still continues.

A. A German Chauvinist's Charges

Many Germans have held, since the tragic summer of 1914, that World War I was rooted in British jealousy over Imperial Germany's colonial and commercial expansion which challenged Britain's dominant position. Among those viewing the titanic struggle as one precipitated by imperialistic rivalry was Count Ernst zu Reventlow (1869–1943), whose vitriolic denunciations of Britain created a sensation both at home and in neutral nations and are today remembered as leading examples of vituperative authorship in the realm of international relations.

The prosperity of German industry, of German trade, of German shipping and the development of German capital began, about the middle of the nineties, to attract the attention of an ever-growing number of persons in Great Britain. Such attention on the part of the English is, as we know, invariably tainted by animosity. From all oversea countries arrived reports from British consuls and commercial agents, telling of German competition in the foreign markets. Everywhere was the German merchant to be found, who was unusually active, who spoke all languages and who endeavored most skillfully to find out the wants and wishes of the native population, to which wants the manufactured goods were subsequently adapted.

The immense growth of German industry had been rendered possible by the protectionist policy inaugurated by Bismarck in 1879. The protection of those national forces which demanded to be developed, against foreign competition [and] especially against British industry, was an imperative necessity. Bismarck had not let himself be caught in the English net so carefully spread for continental birds, i.e., by the doctrine of the blessing of free trade for German industry. As soon as it was protected, German industry revealed a strength hitherto unsuspected; it could now thrive and the more it . . . [throve] the more could it expand; and thus was it ever more and more in a position to satisfy all requirements as to quality.

After a very short time, the English jeers about German industrial products, which were scoffed at as being "cheap and nasty," produced no effect. Then came England's great and irremediable mistake. In order to protect English buyers against worthless German products, the British Government decided that all manufactured goods imported into Great Britain, Ireland and the colonies should be marked "Made in Germany." Thus did England, the champion of the magnificent ideal of Free Trade, decide. As is well known, the plan failed, and the German products, thanks to their good quality and their cheapness, obtained instead an unlooked-for success; for the English buyer got into the habit of asking for German instead of English goods. This failure, with the involuntary comedy and the still more involuntary English irony attached to it, produced its repercussion in the whole world and became a universal and well-deserved advertisement for German industry. . . .

It is by no means the superior capacity or the originality of the English people which . . . permitted them to obtain possession of the markets of the world. An exceptionally favorable geographical position; the ability to inflict in the most cunning and unscrupulous manner damage on other nations which were either exploited, if possible, by their best forces being drawn by England into her own service or which, if this was impossible, were paralyzed in

such a way that they destroyed themselves: such have been the factors of the development of British wealth and power. The incurable madness of the Continental Powers, which perpetually tore each other to pieces and exhausted their resources for the greater glory of the British grocer, did the rest. But never did the superior productivity, the superior intelligence and the honest work of the English have a share in the building up of England's monopoly. . . .

The Entente Cordiale [1904] . . . between France and England was an event of the highest importance in the history of the world for it marked the first great step taken on the road leading up to the war of 1914 which England so carefully organized and prepared and set in motion. The convention of 1904 put an end, once and for all, to all the colonial quarrels between England and France. . . . Bismarck had understood, by a skillful handling of African colonial problems, how to prevent a rapprochement between the two Western Powers; especially had he understood the art of keeping the Egyptian question, that chief bone of contention, alive. Fourteen years after Bismarck's departure, the last seeds of dissension sowed by this policy of his were dug up and destroyed. With the exception of a few unimportant reservations, France renounced all her claims to intervene in Egyptian matters. England promised, partly in public and partly in secret agreements, to assist her French friends in obtaining Morocco. . . . The most important point was the fact of the union of the two Western Powers. . . .

British statesmanship had not succeeded in reducing the German Empire to the position of England's humble servant. Consequently Germany was henceforth England's enemy. . . .

Ernst zu Reventlow, *The Vampire of the Continent* (New York: The Jackson Press, 1916), pp. 132-157.

B. *An American Publicist's Views*

Harry Elmer Barnes, Professor of Historical Sociology at Smith College, was a prolific textbook writer and for some years a Scripps-Howard columnist. His trenchant books and articles materially shaped American thought on international relations in the era after 1918. He first won fame as a pioneer revisionist historian, repudiating the then current thesis that Germany was guilty of methodically plotting the 1914 War, and his *Genesis of the World War* seeks to study its causes.

The general underlying causes of the European military menace may be summarized under four main headings: economic and commercial rivalry, nationalism and patriotism, military and naval preparations and the two great systems of counter-alliances.

In regard to the first of these, the chief guilt, if it may be thus designated, falls unquestionably upon Great Britain and Germany. From the close of the War of 1812 onward, Great Britain had been far and away the most powerful industrial and commercial country in the world. During the late 70's and 80's, Germany experienced the Industrial Revolution which brought to her the mechanical technique and the factory system. A stupendous industrial and commercial transformation ensued which, in rapidity and extent, has only been rivalled by the development of American industry since the Civil War and the parallel transformation of Japanese industry. Particularly in the textile industry, the iron and steel industry and the new chemical industry did Germany rapidly forge ahead, to become a notable contender with Great Britain for the industrial primacy of Europe. Likewise Germany developed rapidly a great merchant marine which struggled with England for the carrying trade of the oceans, and she sought territory overseas for colonial empire and areas of investment to afford markets for her surplus products and outlets for her capital accumulations. And, in the same way that Great Britain had developed a great navy to protect her colonies and merchant marine, so toward the close of the nineteenth century Germany began to lay plans for a navy.

Many . . . have referred to the German naval plans as "foolish" or worse. Doubtless this is true in an absolute sense, as all forms of military and naval preparedness must be viewed as fundamentally idiotic. Yet the German naval plans were only a natural and normal outgrowth of the general spirit of the times and of the particular circumstances of German development following 1890. No modern state has yet developed a colonial empire, extensive world trade and a great merchant marine without feeling that it is desirable to secure protection through the provision of an adequate navy. The German naval expansion was unquestionably a psychological, diplomatic and pecuniary liability, but the same may be said of all navies. Further, . . . the German navy was never any real challenge to the naval supremacy of Great Britain alone, to say nothing of the combined navies of Great Britain, France, Russia and Japan. Finally, the German naval policy cannot be regarded as a direct cause of the war as Germany and England had reached a satisfactory, if informal, understanding before 1914 on the 16:10 basis. . . .

These developments in commerce and naval plans greatly alarmed Great Britain and led her to look upon Germany rather than France as the chief menace to her interests and safety in the west. Up to this time she had regarded France as the main danger in this area, but shortly after the beginning of the present century France was supplanted by Germany as the chief object of British concern in the traditional British policy to maintain England free from danger from any power on the coasts of the North Sea.

Added to this British jealousy of German industrial and commercial progress and her fear of the German menace to her safety on the North Sea due to the development of German naval plans, was the growing influence of Germany in the Near East, which was involved in the German plans for the railroad from Berlin to Baghdad, with the resulting desire to exploit the great resources of Asia Minor. During the nineteenth century Great Britain had looked upon Russia as the great menace to her interest in the Near East but, with the launching of the German plans for the railroad from Hamburg to the Persian Gulf, England became more and more fearful about the possible results of German advances in Turkey and Mesopotamia. Dr. John S. Ewart, a most distinguished Canadian jurist, whose recent book, *The Roots and Causes of the Wars, 1914–1918*, is the most thorough book in English on the subject, presents the following admirable summary of these causes of Anglo-German rivalry:

"1. Germany's rivalry in manufactures, in commerce, in finance, in mercantile shipping and in war-navy, added to her predominance in military power, aroused British apprehension and created British antagonism. That was one root of the war between the United Kingdom and Germany.

"2. British policy in western Europe had for many years pivoted upon the determination to maintain freedom from menace on the North Sea coasts. While France was the danger in this regard, France was the potential enemy. As Germany waxed, and France relatively waned, British apprehension became fixed on the power to the east of Belgium and Holland instead of, as formerly, the power to the west. That was another root of the war between the United Kingdom and Germany.

"3. British traditional policy in eastern Europe and the Near East had been the protection of Constantinople and India against the advances of Russia. The advent of Germany as a competitor for domination at Constantinople, and for political as well as economic expansion in Asia Minor, Persia and Mesopotamia, diverted British apprehension from Russia to Germany. That was another root of the war between the United Kingdom and Germany. . . ."

Harry Elmer Barnes, *Genesis of the World War*, rev. ed. Copyright 1926, 1927 by Alfred A. Knopf, Inc., New York. Reprinted by permission of the publisher.

C. The Orthodox Communist Version

The Marxists, like the Socialists, were bitterly opposed to imperialism. Still in exile in Switzerland, Vladimir [Nikolai] Lenin (1870–1924) in 1916 wrote his *Imperialism, the Highest Stage of Capitalism*, which denounced the struggle then at its height as a war for the division of the world. Today this is regarded as one of his major works. Originally in Russian, an English edition appears as Volume V of Lenin's *Selected Works* and, in voluminous explanatory notes, J. Fineberg, the editor, deftly sets forth the following official Marxist interpretation of the causes of the struggle.

The main causes that gave rise to the war of 1914–1918 were the struggle for world domination, the struggle for the re-division of the world and for *colonies*, principally between Great Britain, at the head of the Triple Entente (Great Britain, France and Russia) and Germany, at the head of the Triple Alliance (Germany, Austria-Hungary and Turkey).

Until the end of the last century, Great Britain was regarded as the possessor of the most powerful colonial empire. She possessed the largest mercantile fleet in the world. British goods and capital ruled in every part of the globe. Germany had hardly any colonies at all. But, during the quarter of a century preceding the War, German capitalist economy had been developing at a very rapid rate, far exceeding the rate of development of British capitalist economy. On the continent of Europe, including Russia, German goods began successfully to compete with British goods and gradually to squeeze them out of the market. The export of German goods to England itself began to grow. Great Britain's market in Europe began to shrink, while for rapidly growing German Imperialism the European market became inadequate. The struggle between British and German Imperialism for world domination and for colonies became inevitable.

Having a magnificent army, Germany, during the ten or twelve years before the World War, built a powerful navy, but was not able to bring it to the level of the British navy. She realized that it would be difficult for her to fight Great Britain on the sea. She therefore chose the other way, of threatening the British colonies, India and Egypt. In 1908, Germany finally came to an agreement with Turkey concerning the building of the Berlin-Baghdad railway. Great Britain fully appreciated this danger. The rivalry between the British and the German Imperialists for world domination increased and inevitably had to lead to an open conflict.

In addition to these main antagonisms between the British and German bourgeoisie, there were economic and political antagonisms between the ruling classes of France and Germany, Russia and Austria, and Russia and Turkey.

The French bourgeoisie had long been striving to secure the return of Alsace-Lorraine, important industrial areas which had been annexed by Germany after the Franco-Prussia War of 1870–1871. Moreover, for the further development of her metallurgical industries, France needed the coal and iron ore of the German provinces of the Saar and Ruhr. The interests of France and Germany also came into conflict over the question of colonies. A struggle had long been going on between them over Morocco, for example.

The ground for the open struggle was prepared by the growth of all those antagonisms. In order to surround Germany, her powerful neighbor, France in 1892 concluded an alliance with Russia; huge subsidies were paid to the Russian Government. In 1913, on the eve of the War, the French Government guaranteed the issue of loans on the Paris Stock Exchange to the amount of 400,-000,000 to 500,000,000 francs every year. On her part, Russia undertook to build strategical railways to the German frontiers and to increase the peace strength of her standing armies. The visit of the French Premier, Poincaré, to Russia in July 1914 had for its object the coordination of the attack of these two allies against Germany.

As far back as 1907, this alliance was joined by Great Britain. Thus, on the basis of a struggle against Germany, a triple alliance was formed between England, France and Russia, which came to be known as the Triple Entente. The three countries put all their age-long quarrels among themselves into the background for a time in order to establish a united front against Germany. Russia was brought into the alliance in order, of course, to increase the military forces against Germany, and also because Tsarist Russia was a semi-colonial country which was a market for foreign goods and a field for the investment of foreign capital. Tsarist Russia represented a huge reserve of western Imperialism and the junction point of all the contradictions of Imperialism.

But the ruling classes of Russia were no less interested, economically and politically, in a war against Germany, Austria and Turkey than the French and British bourgeoisie. The peculiar situation in Russia consisted in that the interests of the landlord class became interwoven with those of the young imperialist bourgeoisie. Germany had long served as a market for the produce of Russian agriculture but, as a consequence of the tariff policy pursued by Germany, the German market for Russian agricultural produce had begun to shrink towards the end of the last century. For thirty years before the War, an uninterrupted struggle went on between Russia and Germany for the reduction of German import duties on Russian grain. The shrinking of the German markets affected the pockets, not only of the Russian landlords, but also of the Russian finance capitalists, for the export of grain was carried on through the medium of the banks which were closely connected with both Russian industry and Russian agriculture. Moreover, the Russian industrial and finance capitalists had their own independent interests in the struggle against Germany. The increasing import of German manufactures was seriously affecting the interests of the Russian bourgeoisie as well as the interests of the British, French and Belgian bourgeoisie who had invested large amounts of capital in Russian industry.

Another cause of the impending conflict was the Near Eastern interests of growing Russian Imperialism. The latter was in need of markets. After the defeat of Russia in the Far East in 1905, in her war against Japan, practically the only foreign markets left for Russian manufactures were Persia and Turkey in the Near East. Here Russian industry could successfully compete with foreign industry. Moreover, the Russian landlords and capitalists strove to secure an independent outlet from the Black Sea to the Mediterranean Sea, which was commanded by Turkey by her possession of the Dardanelles Straits; in 1913 about fifty per cent of Russian exports passed through these Straits. Russia strove for the possession of Constantinople but Turkey was an ally of Germany and Austria which, in their turn, were interested in exercising their economic influence and domination over her, and so Russia's predatory striving in relation to Turkey brought her into conflict with the Triple Alliance.

Thus the World War inevitably arose out of the growing antagonisms between two groups of countries headed by Great Britain and Germany respectively.

V. I. Lenin, *Selected Works,* ed. J. Fineberg, A. Fineberg and I. Levin, 12 vols. (Moscow: Co-operative Publishing Society of Foreign Workers in the U.S.S.R., 1934–1939), V, 328-330.

D. An Historical Appraisal

By the late 1920's, the greater portion of the documents in the European archives covering the period 1870–1914 had been published and historians were able dispassionately to appraise them. Their professional verdicts were eagerly awaited and attracted wide attention. Best known among such findings in the United States was *The Origins of the World War* by Sidney B. Fay, Professor of History at Smith College who was shortly thereafter awarded a professorship at Harvard. One of his most incisive sections, that which assesses economic imperialism as an underlying cause of the conflict, is here presented.

Economic Imperialism embraces a series of international rivalries which resulted in large part from the Industrial Revolution in England and its subsequent introduction into the other great countries of the world. It led to quantity production of goods which in turn involved the struggle for new markets and new sources of raw materials. It resulted in a great increase of population, part of which sought to emigrate to the still unoccupied regions of the world, thereby sharpening the colonial rivalry of the Great Powers. It brought about the accumulation of capital which sought investment abroad, thus leading to economic exploitation and political competition. In consequence of these and other factors, the Great Powers began to partition Africa among themselves, to secure territory or exclusive spheres of influence in China and to build railroads in Turkey and elsewhere.

This struggle for markets, raw materials and colonies became more acute during the last quarter of the nineteenth and the beginning of the twentieth century, owing to the fact that Germany and Italy entered the competition. Hitherto politically weak and divided, they had now secured national unity and wished to come forward to share with the other Powers in the partitioning of the world.

It can hardly be said that any one of the Great Powers was more responsible than another for the international jealousies and friction which arose out of this economic Imperialism. By 1914, all the Great European Powers had secured slices of Africa. In China, Italy only had failed to gain something for herself. In the matter of railway construction, which was one of the most important forms of economic Imperialism because it involved political as well as economic interests, one sees the English building the Cape-to-Cairo railway, the Russians the Trans-Siberian and the

Germans the . . . Baghdad Railway. The first of these came into conflict with German, Belgian and French ambitions; the second was partly responsible for the Russo-Japanese War; the third caused endless suspicions and friction between Germany and the Triple Entente.

Protective tariffs which usually accompanied the modern industrial system, except in England, were another form of economic Imperialism. Tariff wars and retaliatory measures caused irritation between countries, especially in the mind of the man in the street and in newspaper discussion. There was always the danger that great merchants and industrialists would use official government support to secure economic advantages for themselves. This tended to bring governments into conflict with one another.

Generally speaking, however, this economic Imperialism is usually exaggerated as one of the underlying causes of the War. It is often said, for instance, that the industrial development of Germany and the jealousy with which it was regarded by England made a war between these two countries inevitable sooner or later. This, however, is an unsound view. It arises from the fact that economic rivalry tends to become exaggerated in the mind of the public, because it is a subject which touches the pockets of wide classes, and is more generally discussed and perhaps understood than other questions like secret treaties, militarism or nationalism.

It often happens that great merchants or industrialists own or control newspapers which are selfishly interested in contributing to the exaggeration of these economic questions. But if one reads the diplomatic correspondence of the years before the War, one is struck by the relatively slight importance which is given to these economic rivalries which haunt so largely the mind of the average business man and newspaper editor. It is not so much questions of economic rivalry as those of prestige, boundaries, armies and navies, the Balance of Power and possible shiftings in the system of alliances, which provoke reams of diplomatic correspondence and raise the temperature in Foreign Offices to the danger point.

Sidney B. Fay, *The Origins of the World War,* rev. ed., 2 vols. in 1 (New York: The Macmillan Company, 1930), I, 44-46.

14. The Emergence of Fascism and Communism

R. V. BURKS

Wayne University

As MASS MOVEMENTS, Fascism and Communism were both by-products of World War I. Their intellectual pedigrees go back for about a century before 1914, but their adherents were regarded as curious if not crackpot sectarians until the close of the War. In 1917 Communists seized control of the government of tsarist Russia; in 1922 Fascists usurped the authority of the Italian state. The power and prestige which accrued to both movements as a consequence of their conquest, albeit by force and terror, of two major states, marked the beginning of a struggle the end of which is not yet in sight.

In the interwar period both Fascists and Communists made significant progress, particularly after the onset of the Great Depression in 1929. The Communists in China developed a guerrilla army capable of holding its own against government forces, while, at the other end of the Eurasian land mass, in Western Europe, the Communist following achieved a size sufficient to threaten the stability of existing governments. There were, moreover, Communist factions in every quarter of the globe, all of them supplied with funds and directives by a Communist International which was located in Moscow. The Fascists accomplished even more. They seized Portugal in 1929; but their great victory came four years later when they captured the populous and industrial German state and, by the eve of World War II, they had enlarged their domain to include Austria, Czechoslovakia, Spain, and, by some standards, Greece. They had, in addition, a significant body of sympathizers in the Argentine, and a military alliance with the Japanese. While Fascism and Communism had originated in Europe, they had both acquired, by 1939, a global character.

During World War II the Fascists reached a pinnacle of success. Virtually all Europe was theirs, and most of North Africa, not to speak of the Japanese conquests in Asia. From these heights the Fascists plunged into a chaos of defeat. Even Germany, the center of their power, was crushed and entirely occupied by enemy troops. Newspapermen, and the public with them, were then inclined to write *finis* to the Fascist story. But the historian cannot overlook the fact that the Fascists still held the Iberian peninsula; nor can he ignore the emergence in Germany and Italy of neo-Fascist parties, whose strength imperiled the stability of the established governments; nor the rise in France, South Africa, and the Argentine of powerful proto-Fascist movements.

Communist Russia, on the other hand, emerged from World War II as a victor-state. To a remarkable extent what had been lost by the Fascists fell prey to the Communists: the whole of eastern Europe, except Greece, plus the eastern third of Germany, together with mastery over the Chinese fourth of the human race, so that the Communist empires stretched from the Elbe river in the west to the Pacific ocean in the east, and from the Arctic seas in the north to the Himalayan peaks on the borders of India. In Korea, Indo-China, and Malaya, Communist troops continued to advance. In Western Europe, Communist strength increased so sharply that substantial foreign aid, both as food and as armament, had to be rushed to the beleaguered governments there in the hope of saving them.

The nature of the Fascist and Communist movements will become clearer if we bring into the drama of their advance a third protagonist, Democratic Liberalism. Based rather on islands than on the Eurasian land mass, Democratic Liberalism had its strongholds in such countries as Great Britain, the United States, and Australia; it was a maritime and commercial phenomenon primarily. To be sure, Democracy had its adherents on the Eurasian land mass, and in a country like France these adherents were more numerous than either the Fascists or the Communists. Even so Democrats had grave difficulty in holding the French government against the fanatic and violent assaults of the totalitarian opposition. This was especially so because the Democrats were, by nature, neither fanatics nor, except in the last resort, believers in violence. On the whole, though there are obvious exceptions to the generalization, the bastions of Democracy were found where the English language was spoken, where the populations were preponderantly Protestant, and where the standard of living was highest.

Its more pacific nature to the contrary notwithstanding, Democratic Liberalism had been involved in struggle with Fascism and Communism from the very beginning. With the collapse of their tsarist Russian ally, the Democratic states had converted World War I into a crusade to make the world safe for Democracy. At the conclusion of this crusade they had created in the League of Nations what they hoped would become the nucleus of a world government, an extension to international politics of that rule of law and that respect for the rights of the individual which characterized their domestic establishments. In the interwar period, in the face of the Fascist offensive, the machinery of the League broke down badly, and the Democracies were forced to accept Communist control of Russia as an accomplished fact. Broadly speaking, the world by 1939 had been partitioned between the forces of Democratic Liberalism, of Communism, and of Fascism. And the two latter were on the march.

When the Fascists undertook to overrun the whole of Europe, the Democracies abruptly found themselves in an unnatural but desperately necessary alliance with the Russian Communists. Only by means of this alliance was it possible to rescue the British Isles from Fascism. Only by means of this alliance was the military isolation of America in a Fascist-dominated world prevented. But in all this there was, from the viewpoint of the Democracies, a cruel paradox: the crushing defeat of the Fascists and their Japanese allies created on the Eurasian land mass a power vacuum into which the Democracies had not the strength to keep Communism from flooding. The Democracies could only hold on to the peripheries of the Eurasian land mass, and then only at the back-breaking cost of rearmament, the development of nuclear weapons, and localized wars. The danger that this "cold war" with the Russian Communists might flare into World War III seemed omnipresent.

The emergence of Fascism and Communism was thus joined with a breathtaking and murderous ideological struggle which seemed bound to dominate the whole of the twentieth century. Awed observers noted that the essential core of these new movements was a body of doctrine concerned with the fate of the human race. The nature of this doctrine obviously had something to do with the world-wide appeal, and the mounting military strength, of the Fascist and Communist movements. To a brief analysis of this doctrine we must now turn.

Doctrinally speaking, both Fascists and Communists were concerned above all with the future. They held the present state of man to be unworthy of his nature, and they openly aimed at the creation of an infinitely better, if not a perfect, society. For Communists this society would be classless. There would be no exploitation of man by man and, in consequence, neither war, nor poverty, nor government. The German Fascists, to deal with them alone, looked forward to a Thousand-Year Empire in which the blond Aryan race would exercise that sway over inferior peoples which was its biologic due.

For both Fascists and Communists the achievement of this utopian goal could only be the outcome of a bitter struggle between the forces of good, represented by themselves, and the minions of evil, represented by their enemies. The German Fascists believed that this struggle between good and evil had indeed begun long ago, when the "pure" blood of the Teutonic tribes had been sullied by intermarriage with inferior "races," particularly the Jewish. All history was for these Fascists a battle between superior races, which were the creators of human culture, and inferior breeds which, out of envy, constantly conspired to wreck civilization. Communists, on the other hand, thought the struggle between good and evil had begun with the invention of a social institution, that of private property. Its development had ended the halcyon days of primitive tribal communism and had divided men into social classes, into owners who exploited and workers who suffered exploitation, and so paved the way for an epic final struggle between vast masses of industrial proletarians (led by the Communists) and a handful of monopoly capitalists.

Thus the adherents of both movements regarded existing society as a purely provisional arrangement. History was reducible to a struggle for social salvation, and historical change had to be forced in the direction of utopia. Only through the shedding of blood could utopia be won. For the German Nazis, the control and annihilation of inferior races entailed their military conquest and, in consequence, the subordination of all things German—knowledge, trade unions, the family—to the art and to the act of war. Communists, for their part, girded for the fray with the encircling capitalist powers, both Fascist and Democratic, with whom "peaceful coexistence" was in the long run impossible. But Russia herself, the stronghold of Communism, was a backward country, and would have to be industrialized quickly if she would match the more highly developed economies of the capitalist states. Thus the Five-Year Plans. Since Russia was short on capital but long on manpower, rapid industrialization could be accomplished only through the substitution of manpower for machines. Hence her forced labor camps.

But to return to the Democracies, whose very existence had been threatened by the emergence of Fascism and Communism. The discerning student will recognize at once that Democratic Liberalism also possessed an essential core of doctrine which prescribed the nature of history and the destiny of man. Democrats also had a hope for the future; they hoped for a truly democratic and forever prosperous society in which war had been eliminated by world government or international cooperation, poverty by the machine, and disease by the miracle of modern medicine. For Democratic Liberals history tended to be a duel between ignorance and enlightenment, between superstition and science, a race, as it were, between education and catastrophe. Democrats also tried to channel change in the direction of utopia, though for them this meant, not war or revolution, but support of the United Nations as the nucleus of world government; or more money for education and cancer research; or Point Four programs for raising the living standards of backward peoples.

Since the observable core of Democratic Liberalism, as well as of Fascism and Communism, was a body of doctrine which was concerned with the ultimate fate of human kind, we may say that the twentieth century had become an epoch of warfare waged in the name of sacred causes—sacred because men were willing to die for them. What was more, these sacred causes tended to become identified with the fortunes of great and powerful peoples. America became in two world wars the arsenal of Democracy. Germany became the bulwark of Fascist power, Russia the fatherland of the international proletariat. The prestige and influence of the sacred causes rose and fell with the triumphs and defeats of the bastion states. As an age of ideological warfare— for these sacred causes are referred to as ideologies—the twentieth century might well prove to be a watershed in the history of civilization.

Affirmation of the semi-religious character of Fascism and Communism is only the beginning, if we are to explain their emergence as mass movements.

The doctrine which is their core must be related to the social, political, and economic environment in which it arose. Communism is officially the ideology of the industrial proletariat, but the historian knows that its greatest successes have been achieved among backward agrarian peoples, where for statistical purposes a proletariat did not exist. The Nazis brutally slaughtered some six million Jews, an act of barbarism unprecedented at least in modern history. Yet the Germans had been among the greatest creators of human culture. In science, in music, in philosophy, in literature, in all the humane arts, their achievements as a people could be matched by very few. What we are saying is, quite simply, that historians cannot take ideological doctrine as the explanation of ideological movements. Ideological tenets may bring masses of men to war or to revolution, but they do not explain why these masses accept those tenets. The fact that the acts of a Communist may be explained by his faith in a classless society does not explain why a Communist believes in such a society. Ideologies are not primarily a product of reasoning, as is shown by the fact that their doctrine constantly changes even when such change is proclaimed to be unnecessary and impossible.

The real problem, then, is the non-doctrinal origin of Fascism and Communism. Since World War I this problem has been the subject of tenacious controversy. Most of the writers involved in this controversy have, of course, been adherents of the Democratic faith, which places ultimate trust in human reason, the scientific method, and open discussion; these men have been troubled by the miraculous spread of competing faiths. Communists, to be sure, have a simple account of the non-doctrinal origin of Democratic Liberalism. They say that Democratic doctrine is a rationalization of the class interests of the ruling capitalist oligarchy. The Fascist explanation of the non-doctrinal origins of Democratic Liberalism is also simple: it is an extension of Jewish commercial practice, a device for smothering potential elites by implying that inferior peoples possess the same rights as their racial betters.

The dispute over the non-doctrinal origin of Fascism and Communism is by no means purely academic. Each school, the national as well as the international, has its partisans in the political arena, in the diplomatic and military professions, and in business circles, as well as among the intellectuals. The student who ponders the passages which follow will see that each of these authors is in effect and by indirection advocating a policy, a policy which he thinks will solve the threat created for Democracy by the emergence of Fascism and Communism.

By way of illustrating the practical nature of the dispute over the non-doctrinal origin of these movements we may contrast the policy implications of two such conflicting points of view as those of Toynbee and Burnham, given below. If Toynbee is on the right track, then the foreign policy of the Democracies should emphasize relief and technical assistance programs in the hope of proving that the living standards of backward areas can be raised without resort to the methods of Communist dictatorship and without the subjection of these areas to Western imperialist exploitation. In domestic matters Toynbee's thesis implies that the Democracies must work to rid their social structures of those inequalities and injustices the existence of which troubles Western consciences and leads Westerners to embrace Communism. If, on the other hand, Burnham's position is correct, the Democracies must first of all root out the Communist conspiracy in their midst (perhaps even at some cost to the traditional liberties of the citizen) and then, secondly, concentrate sufficient military force to destroy the Communist power in Russia, before the Communists accumulate enough strength to destroy the Democracies. Toynbee leads to Point Four programs, Burnham to preventive war; Toynbee to further social reform, Burnham to a counter-espionage offensive.

Similarly, the adherents of Spenlé will urge the Democracies to pursue one kind of German policy, while those who sympathize with Roepke will propose a German policy of an entirely different nature. Spenlé would keep Germany weak and divided. Roepke would unite and rearm her.

The question still remains whether Fascism and Communism are primarily products of national history and expressions of national interest, or whether they are not tending to replace, on a world-wide scale, the principle of nationality. It is obvious that no ideology can play a role on the world stage unless and until it finds a locus of power. Otherwise the group will remain a sect, like the followers of Trotsky or the anarchosyndicalists in Spain and Portugal. Ideology must claim universal validity and world-wide allegiance and yet, at the same time, it must function within the framework of national states, that is to say, within the realm of particular communities and their immediate interest. In another form the question posed by the emergence of Fascism and Communism, and their struggle with Democracy, is whether the national state can survive an age of ideological warfare, or whether indeed we are not witnessing the emergence of supranational ideological empires and commonwealths.

I. FASCISM AND COMMUNISM AS ESSENTIALLY NATIONAL MOVEMENTS

Generally speaking, the controversy concerning the non-doctrinal origins of Communism and Fascism has revolved around two poles. At the one extreme there is the view that these movements possess a decidedly national character. Nazism, the particular German form of Fascism, is regarded as having peculiarly German roots that go deep into the German past. Nazism is a twentieth-century synthesis of ethical attitudes derived from German Lutheranism, of political practices inherited from the Prussian barracks-state, of a treatment of the conquered which harks back to centuries of German military advance against the stubborn Slav. Similarly, Communism can be considered a stream-lined version of tsarist imperialism, a compound of Russian Orthodox messianism —as expressed in the doctrine of the Third Rome—and of the hasty modernization of a backward society by the autocratic methods of Peter the Great.

A. Spenlé: Fascism as an Outgrowth of German History

Our first writer, J. E. Spenlé, is a Frenchman who has specialized in the history of German thought. In the excerpt which follows he argues that there is an intimate connection between the Lutheran Reformation and the Nazi movement. The effect of Luther's teaching, Spenlé asserts, was to subordinate the church to the state, so that heretical ideas acquired a treasonable character; to separate public from private morality, so that the state was freed of any moral restrictions; to represent God as an arbitrary and fickle despot, so that there was no approach to Him, or to any other problem, by way of human reason; and, finally, to foster a religious imperialism which, in secular dress, has become the essence of German patriotism. Spenlé does not insist that the Lutheran Reformation was the only development in German history predisposing the Germans to Nazism, but his analysis of this particular factor suggests the type of argument used by those who regard Fascism and Communism as pre-eminently national movements.

The attempt to find in Luther's doctrine an anticipation of the idea of freedom of conscience is badly mistaken. Traditional Lutheran theology has been all too often confused with a certain watered-down Protestantism, of more or less liberal tendencies, completely reshaped by the philosophy of the eighteenth century. The freedom which Luther claims for the believer is solely the freedom to come in touch with God directly, without any human being as intermediary, by means of reading and pondering Holy Scripture. In the place of the authority of tradition and of the hierarchy of the Catholic Church, Luther puts the infallible authority of the written Word, of a Bible conceived of as literally inspired; but the principle of authority remains. It is merely transferred. Traditional "theocracy" gives way to Lutheran "Bibliocracy," which ends up as an "orthodoxy" much more dogmatic than the orthodoxy of the living and adaptable tradition of the [Catholic] Church.

Even more erroneous is the opinion of those who have found in Luther's Reformation a doctrine which is favorable to modern Liberalism or Democracy. Exactly the opposite is the case. The reformer was indeed faced with a difficult problem. After having proclaimed

the "priesthood of all believers" and after having abolished the hierarchy of the Roman Church, he should logically have arrived at an entirely free and, if we may say so, democratic organization of the religious community. The individual congregation should at least have had the right to choose its pastor and the duty of covering the expenses of worship, of religious education, and of poor relief. The idea of Democracy could thus have been derived from the theological premises of the Reformation, as in fact happened in those countries where the Calvinist type of Protestantism was victorious. But this was not the case in Lutheran Germany. Rather Luther entrusted the task of judging souls, of defending the faith, and of organizing the new rites to the worldly power of the German princes, to the *Weltliche Obrigkeit* [secular authority] (whom the Apostle Paul called the magistrate). . . .

[Luther] lives in a period when the [Holy Roman] Empire is declining, when there are wild outbursts of passion and all kinds of revolts. Worse yet: mutinous peasants and anarchist sectarians all take his preachments, the doctrines of "evangelical freedom" and the "priesthood of all believers," which he has proclaimed, as points of departure. Had he not said that he recognized no authority other than that of the Bible? But it is on the authority of Biblical texts and Biblical prophecy that the rebellious peasantry claim to base the famous "Twelve Articles" containing their revolutionary demands, and on this same authority that Thomas Muenzer's Anabaptists base themselves in order to establish, arms in hand, the Kingdom of God on earth in the form of a theocratic communism. Luther flies into a rage when he sees his work of reformation so badly botched by the Bolsheviks of his age. He throws the helm sharply to the right. He thunders against all these partisans of anarchy and appeals to the only force for order existing in the Empire, a force which he has already partly won for his work of reform: the German princes.

As a consequence of this fact, the relationship between church and state, between the religious and the political communities, or, in the words of the middle ages, between the spiritual and the secular powers, will be profoundly modified. In the middle ages the Church is independent of the state; she has her own organization, her own hierarchy, her canon law, her own taxation system. And furthermore she is a *universal* institution. She stands above the diverse nationalities and the changing, temporal sovereignties. The Lutheran Church, on the other hand, will acquire a "territorial" and a "confessional" character. She finds herself under the tutelage of the state, which organizes worship, exercises the right of censorship, appoints and pays the church personnel, and protects the faith. The right to reform—*jus reformandi*—and the episcopal authority—*jus episcopale*—are delegated to the sovereign princes, who exercise them within their territorial frontiers. These princes are subject to no judge except their own consciences and are responsible to God alone. There is, above them, no higher spiritual authority. They are not even obliged to be practicing Lutherans or to have a spiritual confessor; of the thunderbolt of excommunication they need have no fear. If it is a question of defining a dogma or of finding some formula which will establish religious peace and harmony, then it is they, the lay princes, who deliberate, as in the diet at Augsburg. They seek advice in matters of faith from the theologians, that is to say, from the professors of theology, whom they call to this religious tribunal. Thus the University, or at least the faculty of Protestant theology, thanks to Lutheranism, will play a preponderant role in German religious life. Doubtless there continues to exist, theoretically, the fiction of a universal church, of an "invisible" community of believers. But in fact there can be seen only a diversity of religious confessions entrenched behind their particular territorial frontiers. Thus the Lutheran Reformation replaces the principle of Catholic universalism with the principle of confessionalism and territorialism. The superiority of the spiritual over the secular is replaced with the principle of princely absolutism.

For this absolutism has, in Luther's eyes, a mystical character. Absolutism is of divine origin. *Alle Obrigkeit kommt von oben* ("All authority comes from God"). Not indeed because recognized and sanctified by the Church, but rather because ordained directly, and outside the Church, by God himself for the realization of His creative plan for the world. The Lutheran Reformation emphasizes the divine authority of the sovereign, a *direct* creation of the will of God. Politics has its own requirements, its own principles, its own rules, yes even its own ethics, and in these matters religion is not to intervene. What determines the divine character of the sovereign is not that he represents law, justice, or love, but rather that he is the possessor of power. In place of the word "power" Luther prefers to use the word *"sword"*—the sword which God has placed in the hands of the princes in order to fight the devil, that is, to chastise dissension, rebellion, anarchy. Now a sword is never something merciful. It is by definition something hard and trenchant. The Christian church, it is true, preaches love, forgiveness of sins, and peace. But the state for its part must impose peace and it can do so only by compulsion, with the sword, by means of war. If the state is belligerent, if it appears to be hard and despotic, that is not its fault, but the fault of the corrupt condition in which the world finds itself. As a believer, the Christian lives, then, in an invisible kingdom of grace; he follows the ethics of love and forgiveness. But as member of the state, or rather as the subject of authority, his attitude ought to be that of absolute submission, of unconditional obedience to the source of authority established by God. As a subject he knows no other morality than the strict fulfillment of his duty, of his function, of his *"Beruf"* [calling], be he prince, magistrate, soldier, or hangman. There is no place here for "conscientious objection." Well known is the famous epistle of Luther's, in which he fulminates against the "murderous and pillaging bands of rebellious peasants" and advises the German princes what to do. Let them try yet once more to bring the erring rebels to their senses. But if this effort fails, let them resort to the most severe reprisals. The Evangel enjoins it. "Lay about with the sword, slaughter, strangle as many as you can. If you thereby lose your life, so much the better for you—never could a more beautiful death befall you, for you will die as a consequence of your faith in the word of God and in the service of the love of your fellow man." . . .

And in consequence his theology is basically anti-rational and anti-humanistic. Between the world of reason and the world of faith there looms up an eternal abyss. It is not rational intellect, it is not search for divine truth which makes the Christian, but *faith alone* (*sola fides*). But faith is by no means the rational acceptance of a truth; it is a living force, which is derived from a need for salvation, and from a deep-going moral pessimism. The "theoretical" optimism of reason is for God an annoyance. If reason were sufficient, the divine work of salvation would then be superfluous. As a consequence, Luther saw in Aristotle his great enemy, he who had usurped *cathedra Christi* [the throne of Christ]. "I believe," so he wrote in 1518, "that it is impossible to reform the church if one does not begin by pulling up by the roots all the *canones* and *decretales,* the whole body of scholastic theology, together with philosophy and logic, such as today are held in great esteem, in order to replace them with something else." The certainty and security which reason provides are misleading. God is not concerned with being known. He is all-powerful and absolutely despotic. He is unfathomable—more obscure than the deepest abyss. Man must become aware of his absolute misery, of his utter worthlessness, in order that he may hear God's call, which is an entirely *personal* call and in no way an impersonal verity. What so sharply distinguishes the Lutheran faith is that it makes itself master of God. God exists *for* mankind. Christ died *for* mankind. "If God were seated like a bump on a log alone in heaven," Luther said, "He would not be God." For if man is nothing in comparison with God, so God on the other hand would not be God without man—just as the master is no master without servants and the father no father without children.

"The German," writes Thomas Mann, "comes to God only after having abandoned dogma and after having overcome the misery of his own nothingness; he finds his balance in social life only when he has traversed the abyss of loneliness; he achieves health only after he has explored the extremes of sickness and death." We have here a dialectic entirely characteristic of the German manner of thinking and which proceeds by opposites, as a consequence of some internal crisis, fetching affirmation from negation, transforming want into abundance, misery into triumph, sinfulness into innocence, painful anxiety into unshakable confidence. This is precisely the miracle of the Lutheran faith; it is also the secret of that "transmutation of values" of which Nietszche will later speak. And if we take a closer look, this Lutheran faith is even beyond morality. *"Peccate fortiter"* ["sin bravely"], wrote Luther to the wise and timorous Melanchthon. It is not so much a matter of wisely avoiding evil (for evil is perhaps as indispensable to salvation and to God's plan for the world as the good) but rather of freeing ourselves once and for all of this oppressive and unbearable antithesis between good and evil, between the divine law and sin, which denotes that we are not yet perfect in the faith, that we are not yet completely one with the will of God and with His grace, and do not share in His grace and His creative power.

This is what distinguishes the theology of faith from the theology of love. The two are not mutually exclusive, but the first is superior to the second. Luther himself gave both of these aspects of Christianity formulation in the two basic propositions which he inscribed at the beginning of his essay *"On Christian freedom"*:

"The Christian," we read, "is lord and master of all things and subject to none." This is the definition of faith.

"The Christian," we read further, "is the obedient servant of all and subject to everyone." And that is the principle of love.

But the reformer obviously prefers the first to the second proposition. For faith alone raises us to the heavenly and the divine, while love holds us down to the earthly and the human and binds us to the thousand attachments and the thousand dependencies of daily life. "I do not stop repeating," Luther says, "that faith makes masters (*Herren*) of us, while love makes slaves (*Knechte*) of us. I would go so far as to say: through faith we become gods." It is precisely the kingdom, the dominion, the empire which is the final goal. Faith makes us victorious over all our enemies and, at the same time, frees us from all earthly bonds. And is it not this religious imperialism which breaks out in Luther's famous hymn? Let us recall the last verse of the last stanza:

"Take they then our life, goods, fame, child, and wife. When their worst is done, they yet have nothing won: *the Empire ours remaineth.*

"Das Reich muss uns doch bleiben!"

What messianic power [is contained] in this Lutheran mysticism, whose song of triumph peals out like a provocation thrown into the face of the whole world! Luther set going the great religious war which shattered the world-wide universality of the [Catholic] Church and of the [Holy Roman] Empire. But the German faith endures. And it will not in the future prove compatible with the ideas of reason, law or humanity which were developed by the Renaissance. . . . The spirit of the Lutheran Reformation has from the beginning been amalgamated with German national feeling. German nationalism is secularized Lutheranism transferred to the political sphere.

Jean Edouard Spenlé, *La Pensée allemande de Luther à Nietzsche,* 3rd. ed. (Paris: Librairie Armand Colin, 1942), pp. 15-19, 22-25, trans. R. V. Burks.

B. Berdyaev: Communism as Russian Imperialism

We have next a Russian theologian whose approach to Communism is much like the approach of the Frenchman Spenlé to German Fascism. Nicholas Berdyaev was probably the greatest Orthodox theologian of the first half of the twentieth century; he was also a leading figure in the existentialist school of philosophy, a role he acquired after taking up residence in the West in 1922. In his *Origin of Russian Communism,* an excerpt from which is given below, Berdyaev expounds the thesis that Communism, although it came to Russia from the West, was completely transformed by conditions in Russia. In the beginning, Communism made little sense in Russia, for an industrial proletariat hardly existed there. But when Lenin, the founder of the Bolshevik party, replaced the traditional but outworn Russian myth of the Third Rome with the new messianic myth of the international proletariat, and when he replaced a discredited tsarist autocracy with the dictatorship of the proletariat, he was able to re-establish a tottering and demoralized tsardom on a new, and firm, religious base. Thus for Berdyaev the ideological doctrine and the governmental practices of Soviet Russia are only secondarily Marxist or Communist. They derive mainly from the tsarist past.

And in actual fact Russian Marxism, since it had arisen in a country still not industrialized and with no developed proletariat, was bound to be torn by a moral self-contradiction which weighed upon the conscience of many Russian socialists. How is it possible to desire the growth of capitalism, to welcome this growth, and at the same time to regard capitalism as an evil and a moral wrong against which every socialist is called to fight? This complicated question gives rise to moral conflict. The growth of capitalist industry in Russia presupposed the turning of the peasantry into a proletariat, depriving them of their means of production, i.e. reducing a considerable part of the nation to a condition of beggary.

This double-mindedness in assigning the values of capitalism and the bourgeoisie is to be seen in Marxism in its most classical form. Marx, in so far as he took his stand upon the evolutionary point of view and recognized the existence of various stages in history, to which different values are to be as-

signed, set a high value upon the mission of the bourgeoisie in the past and the role of capitalism in the development of the material strength of mankind. The whole conception of Marxism is very much dependent on the growth of capitalism and adjusts the messianic idea of the proletariat—which has nothing in common with science— to capitalist industry. Marxism believes that the factory, and the factory alone, will create the new man. . . . But the first Russian Marxists were faced with a moral problem and a problem of cognition, and it set up a moral and logical conflict. We shall see that this moral conflict was decided only by Lenin and the Bolsheviks. It is precisely the Marxist Lenin who will assert the possibility of establishing socialism in Russia independently of the development of capitalism and before a working class of any great size was organized.

Plekhanov [the leader of the Mensheviks] declared himself against confusing the revolution which was to overthrow the absolute monarchy with the social revolution. He was opposed to a revolutionary socialist seizure of power, i.e. to the Communist revolution in the course it actually took. The social revolution must be waited for. The liberation of the workers should be the work of the workers themselves, not of a revolutionary clique. This needs an increase in the number of workers, the development of their consciousness; it presupposes a greater development of industry. Plekhanov was fundamentally the enemy of Bakuninism, which he regarded as a mixture of Fourier and Stenka Razin. He was opposed to sedition and conspiracy, to Jacobinism and belief in committees. A dictatorship can achieve nothing unless the working class has been prepared for revolution. He stresses the reactionary character of the peasant commune as a hindrance to economic development. One must rely upon the objective social process. Plekhanov did not accept the Bolshevik revolution, because he was always opposed to the seizure of power for which neither strength nor consciousness had been prepared. What is needed above all is the revolutionizing of thought, not an elemental upheaval, and a revolutionizing of the thought of the working class itself, not of a partisan organized minority.

But with such an application of Marxist principles to Russia, there would be long to wait for the social revolution. The very possibility of direct socialist activity in Russia would be made a matter of doubt. The revolutionary will might be finally crushed by intellectual theory. Thus, the more revolutionary-minded Russian Marxists were obliged to interpret Marxism in some other way and to set up other theories of the Russian revolution, to work out other tactics. In this wing of Russian Marxism, the revolutionary will overcame the intellectual theories and the armchair interpretation of Marxism. There occurred unnoticed a combination of the traditions of revolutionary Marxism with those of the old revolutionary outlook which had no desire to tolerate a capitalist stage in the development of Russia, with Chernishevsky, Bakunin, Nechaev, Tkachev. This time it was not Fourier but Marx who was united with Stenka Razin. The Marxists who were Bolsheviks stood much more clearly in the line of Russian tradition than those who were Mensheviks. On the basis of the evolutionary determinist interpretation of Marxism it is impossible to justify a proletarian socialist revolution in a peasant country, industrially backward and with a feebly developed working class. With such an understanding of Marxism one must rely first of all on a bourgeois revolution, on the development of capitalism and then, when the time comes, bring about the socialist revolution. This was not very favorable to the stimulation of the revolutionary will. . . .

This 'orthodox' [Leninist] Marxism, which was in actual fact Marxism which had been changed by being given a Russian form, adopted primarily not the determinist, evolutionary scientific side of Marxism, but its messianic myth-creating religious side, which gave scope to the stimulation of the revolutionary will, and assigned a foremost place to the proletariat's revolutionary struggle as controlled by an organized minority, which was inspired by the conscious proletariat idea. This orthodox totalitarian Marxism always insisted on the preaching of materialist belief, but it contained strong idealist elements also. It showed how great was the authority of an idea over human life, if it is an integrated idea, and answers to the instincts of the masses. In Bolshevist Marxism the proletariat ceased to be an empirical reality, for as an empirical reality the proletariat was a mere nothing; it was above all the idea of a proletariat that mattered, and those who became vehicles for the expression of this idea might be an insignificant minority. If this insignificant minority is entirely possessed by the gigantic idea of the proletariat, if its revolutionary will is stimulated, if it is well organized and disciplined, then it can work miracles; it can overpower the determinism which normally controls social life. And Lenin proved in practice that this is possible. He brought about the revolution in Marx's name, but not in Marx's way. The Communist revolution was brought about in Russia in the name of totalitarian Marxism—Marxism as the religion of the proletariat, but it was a contradiction of everything that Marx had said about the development of human society. It was not revolutionary *narodnichestvo* [a utopian peasant socialism], but orthodox totalitarian Marxism which succeeded in achieving the revolution, in which Russia skipped that stage of capitalist development which to the first Russian Marxists had appeared so unavoidable. And it was clear that this agreed with Russian tradition and the instincts of the people.

At that time the illusions of the revolutionary *narodnichestvo* had already been outlived; the myth about the peasantry had collapsed. The people had not accepted a revolutionary intelligentsia. A new revolutionary myth was needed. And the myth about the people was changed into the myth about the proletariat. Marxism broke up the conception of the people as an integral organism; it analysed it into classes with opposed interests. But in the myth of the proletariat, the myth of the Russian people arose in a new form. There took place, as it were, an identification of the Russian people with the proletariat, and of Russian messianism with proletarian messianism. The Soviet Russia of workers and peasants came into being. In it the notion of the people as a peasantry was combined with the idea of it as a proletariat, and that in spite of everything that had been said by Marx, who regarded the peasantry as a petty-bourgeois, reactionary class. Orthodox totalitarian Marxism forbade any reference to the opposition between the interests of the proletariat and those of the peasantry. That was the rock on which Trotsky struck, desiring as he did to be true to classical Marxism. The peasantry was declared to be a revolutionary class, although the Soviet Government had constantly to fight it, sometimes very bitterly. Lenin turned anew to the old tradition of Russian revolutionary thought. He pronounced that the industrial backwardness of Russia, the rudimentary character of its capitalism, is a great asset for the social revolution.

There will be no need to deal with a strong, organized bourgeoisie. There Lenin was obliged to repeat what Tkachev had said, and by no means what Engels had said. Bolshevism is much more traditional than is commonly supposed. It agreed with the distinctive character of the Russian historical process. There had taken place a Russification and orientalizing of Marxism. . . .

Lenin's purpose, which he followed up with unusual logical consistency, was the formation of a strong party representing a well organized and iron disciplined minority and relying upon the strength of its integrated revolutionary Marxist outlook. The party had to have a doctrine in which nothing whatever is to be changed and it had to prepare for dictatorship over life as a complete whole. The very organization of the party, which was centralized in the extreme, was a dictatorship on a small scale. Every member of the party was subjected to this dictatorship of the center. The Bolshevik party which Lenin built up in the course of many years was to provide the pattern of the future organization of the whole of Russia, and in actual fact Russia was organized on the pattern of the Bolshevik party organization. The whole of Russia, the whole Russian people, was subjected not only to the dictatorship of the Communist party but also to the dictatorship of the Communist dictator, in thought and in conscience. Lenin denied freedom within the party and this denial of freedom was transferred to the whole of Russia.

This is indeed the dictatorship of a general outlook for which Lenin had prepared. He was able to do this only because he combined in himself two traditions: the tradition of the Russian revolutionary intelligentsia in its most maximalist tendency, and the tradition of Russian Government in its most despotic aspect. The Social Democrat

Mensheviks and the Socialist Revolutionaries remained in the stream of the first tradition only, and that in a mitigated form. But combining in himself traditions which in the nineteenth century had been in mortal conflict, Lenin was able to fashion a scheme for the organization of a Communist state and to realize it. However paradoxical it may sound, still Bolshevism is the third appearance of Russian autocratic imperialism; its first appearance being the Muscovite Tsardom and its second the Petrine Empire. Bolshevism stands for a strong centralized state. A union was achieved of the will to social justice and the will to political power, and the second will was the stronger. Bolshevism entered into Russian life as a power which was militarized in the highest degree, but the old Russian state also had always been militarized.

The problem of power was fundamental with Lenin and all his followers; it distinguished the Bolsheviks from all other revolutionaries. They too created a police state, in its methods of government very like the old Russian state. But to organize government, to subject to it the laboring and peasant masses, could not be a matter of the use of armed force alone, or of sheer coercion. An integrated doctrine was needed, a consistent general outlook, and symbols which held the state together were required. In the Muscovite Tsardom and in the empire the people were held together by a unity of religious faith; so also a new single faith had to be expressed for the masses in elementary symbols. Marxism in its Russian form was wholly suitable for this. . . .

Lenin did not believe in man. He recognized in him no sort of inward principle; he did not believe in spirit and the freedom of the spirit, but he had a boundless faith in the social regimentation of man. He believed that a compulsory social organization could create any sort of new man you like, for instance, a completely social man who would no longer need the use of force. Marx believed the same thing, that the new man could be manufactured in factories. This was Lenin's utopianism, but it was a utopianism which could be and was realized. One thing he did not foresee; he did not foresee that class oppression might take an entirely different form, quite unlike its capitalist form. The dictatorship of the proletariat, having increased the power of the state, is developing a colossal bureaucracy which spreads like a network over the whole country and brings everything into subjection to itself. This new Soviet bureaucracy is more powerful than that of the tsarist regime. It is a new privileged class which can exploit the masses pitilessly. This is happening. An ordinary workman very often receives 75 roubles a month, but a Soviet civil servant, a specialist, gets 1,600 roubles a month, and this portentous inequality exists in a Communist state. Soviet Russia is a country of state capitalism which is capable of exploitation no less than private capitalism. The transitional period may be drawn out indefinitely. Those who are in power in it acquire a taste for power and desire no changes, which are unavoidable for the final realization of Communism. The will-to-power becomes satisfying in itself and men will fight for it as an end and not as a means.

All this was beyond Lenin's view. In this he was particularly utopian and very naive. The Soviet state has become like any other despotic state. It uses the same methods of falsehood and violence. It is first and foremost a state of the military police kind. Its international politics are as like the diplomacy of bourgeois states as two peas. The Communist revolution was distinctively Russian, but the miraculous birth of the new life did not take place. The old Adam has remained and continues to act, if in another form. . . .

Bolshevism made use of everything for its own triumph. It made use of the weakness of the Liberal Democratic government [of 1917], of the unsuitability of its watchwords to weld the insurgent masses together. It made use of the objective impossibility of carrying on the war any longer when the spirit of it was hopelessly lost by the unwillingness of the soldiers to go on fighting, and it proclaimed peace. It made use of the disorganization and discontent of the peasantry and divided all the land among the peasants, destroying what was left of feudalism and the dominance of the nobility. It made use of the Russian traditions of government by imposition, and instead of an unfamiliar Democracy of which they had had no experience it proclaimed a dictatorship which was more like the old rule of the tsar. It made use of the characteristics of the Russian spirit in all its incompatibility with a secularized bourgeois society. It made use of its religious instinct, its dogmatism and maximalism, its search after social justice and the kingdom of God upon earth, its capacity for sacrifice and the patient bearing of suffering, and also of its manifestations of coarseness and cruelty. It made use of Russian messianism, which still remained, though in an unconscious form, and of the Russian faith in Russia's own path of development. It made use of the historic cleavage between the masses and the cultured classes, of the popular mistrust of the intelligentsia, and it easily destroyed such of the intelligentsia as did not submit to it.

It absorbed also the sectarian spirit of the Russian intelligentsia and Russian *narodnichestvo* while transforming them in accordance with the requirements of a new epoch. It fitted in with the absence among the Russian people of the Roman view of property and the bourgeois virtues; it fitted in with Russian collectivism which had its roots in religion; it made use of the breakdown of patriarchal life among the people and the dissolution of the old religious beliefs. It also set about spreading the new revolution by methods of violence from above, as Peter had done in his time; it denied human freedom, which had been unknown to the masses before, and had been the privilege of the upper cultured classes of society, and for which the masses had certainly not been roused to fight. It proclaimed the necessity of the integral totalitarian outlook of a dominant creed, which corresponded with the habits, experience and requirements of the Russian people in faith and in the dominating principles of life. The Russian spirit is not prone to scepticism, and a sceptical liberalism suits it less than anything. The spirit of the people could very readily pass from one integrated faith to another integrated faith, from one orthodoxy to another orthodoxy which embraced the whole of life. Russia passed from the old Middle Ages to the new Middle Ages, avoiding the ways of the new history with its secularization, its differentiation of various fields of culture, with its liberalism, its individualism, its triumph of the bourgeoisie and of capitalism.

The old consecrated Russian empire fell and a new one was formed, also a consecrated empire, an inverted theocracy. Marxism, itself so un-Russian in origin and character, assumed a Russian style, an oriental style approaching Slavophilism. Even the old Slavophil's dream of transferring the capital from St. Petersburg to Moscow, to the Kremlin, was realized by the Red Communists, and Russian Communism proclaimed anew the old idea of the Slavophils and Dostoyevsky—*ex Oriente lux*. Light proceeds from Moscow, from the Kremlin, a light to lighten the bourgeois darkness of the West. At the same time Communism creates a despotic and bureaucratic state, called into being to dominate the whole life of the people, not only in body but also in soul, in accord with the traditions of Ivan the Terrible and the rule of the tsars. Marxism in its Russian form proclaims the dominance of politics over economics, the power of the government to change the life of the country in any way it likes. In its grandiose schemes which were always on a world-wide scale, Communism makes use of the Russian disposition for making plans and castle-building which had hitherto had no scope for realization or practical application. Lenin desired to overcome Russian sloth, the product of the life of the gentry and of serfdom, to conquer Oblomov and Rudin, the 'superfluous people', and in this positive task it seems he was successful.

A metamorphosis has taken place, i.e. an Americanization of the Russian people, the production of a new type of practical man with whom daydreaming and castle-building passed into action and constructiveness, of a technician, a bureaucrat of a new type. But here also the special characteristics of the Russian spirit had their say. The faith of the people was given a new direction, the Russian peasants now reverence the machine as a totem. Technical undertakings are not the ordinary matter-of-fact customary affair that they are to Western people; they have been given a mystic character and linked on with plans for an almost cosmic revolution. . . .

The Russian people [had] not realized their messianic idea of Moscow the Third Rome. The ecclesiastical schism of the seventeenth century revealed that the Muscovite tsardom is not the Third Rome: still less, of course, was the Petersburg empire a realization of the idea of the Third Rome. In it a final cleavage took place. The messianic idea of the Russian people assumed either an apocalyptic form or a revolutionary; and then there occurred an amazing event in the destiny of the Russian people. Instead of the Third Rome in Russia, the Third International was achieved, and many of the features of the Third Rome pass over to the Third International. The Third International is also a consecrated realm, and it also is founded on an orthodox faith. The fact that the Third International is not international but a Russian national idea is very poorly understood in the West. Here we have the transformation of Russian messianism. Western Communists, when they join the Third International, play a humiliating part; they do not understand that in joining the Third International they are joining the Russian people and realizing its messianic vocation.

I have heard that at a French Communist meeting a French Communist asserted, 'Marx said that the workmen have no fatherland. This used to be true, but now it is no longer true; they have a fatherland, that is, Russia, Moscow, and the workers should defend their fatherland.' This is absolutely true and ought to be understood by everybody. Something has happened which Marx and the Western Marxists could not have foreseen, and that is a sort of identification of the two messianisms, the messianism of the Russian people and the messianism of the proletariat. The Russian working class and peasantry are a proletariat; and the proletariat of the whole world from France to China is becoming the Russian people—a unique people in the world; and the messianic consciousness of the working class and proletariat is bringing about an almost Slavophil attitude towards the West. The West is always identified with the bourgeoisie and capitalism. The nationalization of Russian Communism, to which all bear witness, has its course in the fact that Communism has come into existence in only one country, in Russia, and the Communist realm is surrounded by bourgeois capitalist states. A Communist revolution in a single country inevitably leads to nationalism and a nationalist standpoint in political relations with other countries. . . . In Soviet Russia now they talk about the socialist fatherland and they want to defend it; they are ready to sacrifice their lives for it. But the socialist fatherland is still the same Russia, and in Russia perhaps popular patriotism is coming into being for the first time. . . .

Nicholas Berdyaev, *The Origin of Russian Communism,* trans. R. M. French, new ed. (London: Geoffrey Bles, Ltd., 1948), pp. 102-04, 106-07, 119-21, 127-28, 140-42, 144-45.

C. Toynbee: Communism as a Weapon Against the West

The presentations of Spenlé and Berdyaev, arguing that ideological movements are primarily national in character, should be supplemented with a third interpretation of the same sort. This third interpretation is the work of the most famous of contemporary British historians, Arnold Toynbee. Essentially Toynbee views Communism as a function of an age-old conflict between Russia and the West, a conflict in which Muscovite technological inferiority has constantly placed the Russians at a great disadvantage. To preserve their independence in the face of constant Western aggression, the Russians have had, willy-nilly, to put up with a tyrannical government which has constantly tried to catch up with the West by forced marches of modernization. Yet somehow the Russians have never quite managed to catch up; the West has continued to put itself through more and more complex industrial revolutions. The West has replaced the musket with the machine gun, and the machine gun in turn with the atom bomb. By adopting a peculiarly Western ideological heresy, however, the Russians under Lenin at last found a spiritual means of offsetting the technological superiority of the West, for that heresy not only makes Russian fifth columns of those Communists who dwell within the West itself, but it likewise, by appealing to backward peoples whose independence is threatened or destroyed by Western imperialism, puts Russia in competition with the West for the allegiance of the non-Western world.

Let us begin with Russia's experience, for Russia is part of the world's great non-Western majority. Though the Russians have been Christians and are, many of them, Christians still, they have never been Western Christians. Russia was converted not from Rome, as England was, but from Constantinople; and, in spite of their common Christian origins, Eastern and Western Christendom have always been foreign to one another, and have often been mutually antipathetic and hostile, as Russia and the West unhappily still are today, when each of them is in what one might call a 'post-Christian' phase of its history.

This on the whole unhappy story of Russia's relations with the West did, though, have a happier first chapter; for, in spite of the difference between the Russian and the Western way of life, Russia and the West got on fairly well with one another in the early Middle Ages. The peoples traded, and the royal families intermarried. An English King Harold's daughter, for instance, married a Russian prince. The estrangement began in the thirteenth century, after the subjugation of Russia by the Tatars. The Tatars' domination over Russia was temporary, because the

Tatars were nomads from the steppes who could not ever make themselves at home in Russia's fields and forests. Russia's lasting losses as a result of this temporary Tatar conquest were, not to her Tatar conquerors, but to her Western neighbors; for these took advantage of Russia's prostration in order to lop off, and annex to Western Christendom, the western fringes of the Russian world in White Russia and in the western half of the Ukraine. It was not till 1945 that Russia recaptured the last piece of these huge Russian territories that were taken from her by Western powers in the thirteenth and fourteenth centuries.

These Western conquests at Russia's expense in the late Middle Ages had an effect on Russia's life at home, as well as on her relations with her Western assailants. The pressure on Russia from the West did not merely estrange Russia from the West; it was one of the hard facts of Russian life that moved the Russians to submit to the yoke of a new native Russian power at Moscow which, at the price of autocracy, imposed on Russia the political unity that she now had to have if she was to survive. It was no accident that this newfangled autocratic centralizing government of Russia should have arisen at Moscow; for Moscow stood in the fairway of the easiest line for the invasion of what was left of Russia by a Western aggressor. The Poles in 1610, the French in 1812, the Germans in 1941, all marched this way. Since an early date in the fourteenth century, autocracy and centralization have been the dominant notes of all successive Russian regimes. This Moscovite Russian political tradition has perhaps always been as disagreeable for the Russians themselves as it has certainly been distasteful and alarming to their neighbors; but unfortunately the Russians have learned to put up with it, partly perhaps out of sheer habit, but also, no doubt, because they have felt it to be a lesser evil than the alternative fate of being conquered by aggressive neighbors.

This Russian attitude of resignation towards an autocratic regime that has become traditional in Russia is, of course, one of the main difficulties, as we Westerners see it, in the relations between Russia and the West today. The great majority of people in the West feel that tyranny is an intolerable social evil. At a fearful cost we have put down tyranny when it has raised its head among our Western selves in the forms of Fascism and National Socialism. We feel the same detestation and distrust of it in its Russian form, whether this calls itself tsarism or calls itself Communism. We do not want to see this Russian brand of tyranny spread; and we are particularly concerned about this danger to Western ideals of liberty now that we Franks find ourselves thrown upon the defensive for the first time in our history since the second Turkish siege of Vienna in 1682–3. Our present anxiety about what seems to us to be a post-war threat to the West from Russia is a well-justified anxiety in our belief. At the same time, we must take care not to allow the reversal in the relation between Russia and the West since 1945 to mislead us into forgetting the past in our natural preoccupation with the present. When we look at the encounter between Russia and the West in the historian's instead of the journalist's perspective, we shall see that, over a period of several centuries ending in 1945, the Russians have had the same reason for looking askance at the West that we Westerners feel that we have for looking askance at Russia today.

During the last few centuries, this threat to Russia from the West, which has been a constant threat from the thirteenth century till 1945, has been made more serious for Russia by the outbreak, in the West, of a technological revolution which has become chronic and which does not yet show any signs of abating.

When the West adopted fire-arms, Russia followed suit, and in the sixteenth century she used these new weapons from the West to conquer the Tatars in the Volga valley and more primitive peoples in the Urals and in Siberia. But in 1610 the superiority of the Western armaments of the day enabled the Poles to occupy Moscow and to hold it for two years, while at about the same time the Swedes were also able to deprive Russia of her outlet on the Baltic sea at the head of the Gulf of Finland. The Russian retort to these seventeenth-century Western acts of aggression was to adopt the technology of the West wholesale, together with as much of the Western way of life as was inseparable from Western technology.

It was characteristic of the autocratic centralizing Muscovite regime that this technological and accompanying social revolution in Russia at the turn of the seventeenth and eighteenth centuries should have been imposed upon Russia from above downwards, by the fiat of one man of genius, Peter the Great. Peter is a key figure for an understanding of the world's relations with the West not only in Russia but everywhere; for Peter is the archetype of the autocratic Westernizing reformer who, during the last two and a half centuries, has saved the world from falling entirely under Western domination by forcing the world to train itself to resist Western aggression with Western weapons. Sultans Selim III and Mahmud II and President Mustafa Kemal Ataturk in Turkey, Mehmed 'Ali Pasha in Egypt, and 'the Elder Statesmen', who made the Westernizing revolution

in Japan in the eighteen-sixties, were, all of them, following in Peter the Great's footsteps consciously or unconsciously.

Peter launched Russia on a technological race with the West which Russia is still running. Russia has never yet been able to afford to rest, because the West has continually been making fresh spurts. For example, Peter and his eighteenth-century successors brought Russia close enough abreast of the Western world of the day to make Russia just able to defeat her Swedish Western invaders in 1709 and her French Western invaders in 1812; but, in the nineteenth-century Western industrial revolution, the West once more left Russia behind, so that in the First World War Russia was defeated by her German Western invaders as she had been defeated, two hundred years earlier, by the Poles and the Swedes. The present Communist autocratic government was able to supplant the tsardom in Russia in consequence of Russia's defeat by an industrial Western technology in 1914–17; and the Communist regime then set out, from 1928 to 1941, to do for Russia, all over again, what the Tsar Peter had done for her about 230 years earlier.

For the second time in the modern chapter of her history Russia was now put, by an autocratic ruler, through a forced march to catch up with a Western technology that had once more shot ahead of hers; and Stalin's tyrannical course of technological Westernization was eventually justified, like Peter's, through an ordeal by battle. The Communist technological revolution in Russia defeated the German invaders in the Second World War, as Peter's technological revolution had defeated the Swedish invaders in 1709 and the French invaders in 1812. And then, a few months after the completion of the liberation of Russian soil from German Western occupation in 1945, Russia's American Western allies dropped in Japan an atom bomb that announced the outbreak of a third Western technological revolution. So today, for the third time, Russia is having to make a forced march in an effort to catch up with a Western technology that, for the third time, has left her behind by shooting ahead. The result of this third event in the perpetual competition between Russia and the West still lies hidden in the future; but it is already clear that this renewal of the technological race is another of the very serious difficulties now besetting the relations between these two ex-Christian societies.

Technology is, of course, only a long Greek name for a bag of tools; and we have to ask ourselves: What are the tools that count in this competition in the use of tools as means to power? A power-loom or a locomotive is obviously a tool for this purpose, as well as a gun, an aeroplane, or a bomb. But all tools are not of the material kind; there are spiritual tools as well, and these are the most potent that man has made. A creed, for instance, can be a tool; and, in the new round in the competition between Russia and the West that began in 1917, the Russians this time threw into their scale of the balances a creed that weighed as heavily against their Western competitors' material tools as, in the Roman story of the ransoming of Rome from the Gauls, the sword thrown in by Brennus weighed against the Roman gold.

Communism, then, is a weapon; and, like bombs, aeroplanes, and guns, this is a weapon of Western origin. If it had not been invented by a couple of nineteenth-century Westerners, Karl Marx and Friedrich Engels, who were brought up in the Rhineland and spent the best part of their working lives in London and in Manchester respectively,

Communism could never have become Russia's official ideology. There was nothing in the Russian tradition that could have led the Russians to invent Communism for themselves; and it is certain that they would never have dreamed of it if it had not been lying, ready-made, there in the West, for a revolutionary Russian regime to apply in Russia in 1917.

In borrowing from the West a Western ideology, besides a Western industrial revolution, to serve as an anti-Western weapon, the Bolsheviki in 1917 were making a great new departure in Russian history; for this was the first time that Russia had ever borrowed a creed from the West. We have already noticed that Christianity had come to Russia, not from the West, but from Byzantium, where Christianity had a distinctive, non-Western form and spirit; and a fifteenth-century Western attempt to impose Western Christianity on Russia had been a failure. In A.D. 1439, at an ecclesiastical council held at Florence, representatives of the Eastern Orthodox Church in what then still remained of the Byzantine empire had unwillingly recognized the ecclesiastical supremacy of the Roman see in the hope that, in return, the Western world would save Constantinople from conquest by the Turks. The metropolitan archbishop of Moscow, who was a suffragan of the Greek patriarch of Constantinople, had been attending the Council, and he had voted the same way as his brethren who were representing the Greek Orthodox church; but when he came home to Moscow, his recognition of the pope's supremacy was repudiated there and he himself was deposed.

Two hundred and fifty years later, when Peter the Great went to the West to learn the 'know-how' of Western technology, there was no longer any question of Russia's being required to adopt a Western form of Christianity as the price of being initiated into the secrets of Western technological efficiency. Before the end of the seventeenth century there had been a revulsion in the West, not merely against religious fanaticism, but against religion itself, in consequence of the West's weariness of its own domestic wars of religion. The Western world, whose apprentice Russia became in Peter's day, was thus an irreligious world, and the sophisticated minority of Russians who became the agents of the Westernization of Russia followed the example of their sophisticated Western contemporaries by turning lukewarm towards the Russian form of Christianity without adopting any Western form of Christianity instead. So, in adopting Communism in 1917, Russia was making a breach with her traditions by taking up a Western creed for the first time in her history.

The reader will also have noticed that this Western creed, which Russia did take up in 1917, was one that was particularly well suited to serve Russia as a Western weapon for waging an anti-Western spiritual warfare. In the West, where Communism had arisen, this new creed was a heresy. It was a Western criticism of the West's failure to live up to her own Christian principles in the economic and social life of this professedly Christian society; and a creed of Western origin which was at the same time an indictment of Western practice was, of course, just the spiritual weapon that an adversary of the West would like to pick up and turn against its makers. With this Western spiritual weapon in her hands, Russia could carry her war with the West into the enemy's country on the spiritual plane. Since Communism had originated as a product of uneasy Western consciences, it could appeal to other uneasy Western consciences when it was radiated back into

the Western world by a Russian propaganda. And so now, for the first time in the modern Western world's history since the close of the seventeenth century, when the flow of Western converts to Islam almost ceased, the West has again found itself threatened with spiritual disintegration from inside, as well as with an assault from outside. In thus threatening to undermine the Western civilization's foundation on the West's own home ground, Communism has already proved itself a more effective anti-Western weapon in Russian hands than any material weapon could ever be.

Communism has also served Russia as a weapon for bringing into the Russian camp the Chinese quarter of the human race, as well as other sections of that majority of mankind that is neither Russian nor Western. We know that the outcome of the struggle to win the allegiance of these neutrals may be decisive for the outcome of the Russo-Western conflict as a whole, because this non-Western and non-Russian majority of mankind may prove to hold the casting vote in a competition between Russia and the West for world power. Now Communism can make a twofold appeal to a depressed Asian, African, and Latin American peasantry when it is the voice of Russia that is commending Communism to them. The Russian spokesman can say to the Asian peasantry first: 'If you follow the Russian example, Communism will give you the strength to stand up against the West, as a Communist Russia can already stand up against the West today.' The second appeal of Communism to the Asia peasantry is Communism's claim that it can, and that private enterprise neither can nor would if it could, get rid of the extreme inequality between a rich minority and a poverty-stricken majority in Asian countries. Discontented Asians, however, are not the only public for whom Communism has an appeal. Communism also has an appeal for all men, since it can claim to offer mankind the unity which is our only alternative to self-destruction in an atomic age.

It looks as if, in the encounter between Russia and the West, the spiritual initiative, though not the technological lead, has now passed, at any rate for the moment, from the Western to the Russian side. We Westerners cannot afford to resign ourselves to this, because this Western heresy—Communism—which the Russians have taken up, seems to the great majority of people in the West to be a perverse, misguided, and disastrous doctrine and way of life. A theologian might put it that our great modern Western heresiarch Karl Marx has made what is a heretic's characteristic intellectual mistake and moral aberration. In putting his finger on one point in orthodox practice in which there has been a crying need for reform, he had lost sight of all other considerations and therefore has produced a remedy that is worse than the disease.

The Russians' success in capturing the initiative from us Westerners by taking up this Western heresy called Communism and radiating it out into the world in a cloud of anti-Western poison-gas does not, of course, mean that Communism is destined to prevail. Marx's vision seems, in non-Marxian eyes, far too narrow and too badly warped to be likely to prove permanently satisfying to human hearts and minds. All the same, Communism's success, so far as it has gone, looks like a portent of things to come. What it does tell us is that the present encounter between the world and the West is now moving off the technological plane on to the spiritual plane. . . .

Arnold Toynbee, *The World and the West* (New York: Oxford University Press, 1953), pp. 4-16.

II. FASCISM AND COMMUNISM AS PRIMARILY INTERNATIONAL MOVEMENTS

Thus we see how Fascism and Communism may be interpreted as essentially national movements, as products of the particular historical experience of a given nation or as useful devices for spreading the influence, and raising the prestige, of a given nation among its neighbors. But there is, as mentioned earlier, another approach to these ideologies. At the opposite pole from the national interpretation we have those who tend to regard the identification of Communism with Russia and of Fascism with Germany as largely accidental. The Russians are merely the first victims of Communist world conspiracy, and the Germans have simply had to endure the most from Fascist tyranny. It is simply not true that "it can't happen here," in America, or in Britain, or Australia. The Communists, or the Fascists, can seize power in any country, if the local popula-tion is not eternally vigilant. For the motivations which make Fascists and Communists are everywhere present; it is only a question of degree and of circumstance. Fascist and Communist intellectuals, usually disguised as liberals or socialists or patriots, are everywhere spreading their doctrines, and many times in the places least expected.

A. Schuman: Fascism as a Phase of Monopoly Capitalism

Frederick L. Schuman is an American political scientist who has specialized in the study of international politics. He views Fascism as the disease of a sick society, bred of petty-bourgeois neuroses, and fostered by the propertied classes in order to protect and enlarge their monopolistic industrial concerns. Fascism appears first in marginal states, where a slight dislocation will stagger the whole economy, but it can appear anywhere that capitalism exists, because it is intimately associated with the latest, or monoply, stage of capitalism, a stage in which warfare, and warfare alone, remains an economically profitable activity. Another Great Depression may well bring America, or Britain, to the same pass. The student should bear in mind that Schuman wrote the following passage in 1936.

Fascism is the social philosophy and the state-form of the bourgeoisie in the monopolistic epoch of late capitalism. It emerges first, not in the lands where monopolistic enterprise has reached its highest point of development, but rather where the deprivations produced by the dilemma of an economy strangling for lack of markets first manifest themselves most acutely. The dictatorship of the proletariat arrived first, not in Great Britain or the United States, where capitalism was oldest (and therefore in Marxist theory most ripe for the revolutionary transition to socialism), but in backward Russia. Here the moneyed elite was feeblest. Here the proletariat was most bitterly exploited and oppressed and at the same time most revolutionary, most disciplined, most unified. Here above all, impact of the First Imperialist War [1914–18] produced the most disastrous social and economic consequences, shattering the power of the state and of the ruling classes and opening the way for the seizure of power by the Bolshevists.

Similarly the dictatorship of Fascism arrived first, not where monopolistic industry had evolved most elaborately, but in backward Italy. The Italian elite in 1920–23 felt itself most acutely menaced by proletarian and peasant social revolution—whether justifiably or not is irrelevant. The Italian petty bourgeoisie was numerous, poor, embittered. In Italy the impact of the Great War led to a degradation of national symbols and to painful frustrations of patriotic expectations. Italy had "won the war, but lost the peace." Mass

paranoia and megalomania, combined with the fear and desperation of the ruling classes, enabled the black-shirts of Mussolini to seize power.

A decade later Germany succumbed to the same disease of a sick society. Here trusts, monopolies, and cartels had long been features of industrial organization. Even before 1914 acute observers—for example, Brentano and Rathenau—were noting that industrial combinations were becoming more powerful than the state and were assuming state functions. During the blood-bath which followed Sarajevo, the state, the general staff, heavy industry, and the landed nobility were so closely integrated as to become one. After 1919 the industrial and landed elite was obliged to rule through a tepid, imported democracy for which it had scant respect. The royalty of the masses to Weimar was destroyed by the inflation and by the diplomatic and military impotence of the republic. The *Kleinbuergertum* [petty bourgeoisie] had long since begun to exhibit neurotic symptoms of a class suffering chronically from material and psychic insecurities. These insecurities were enormously multiplied by the economic consequences of military defeat. Here, as in Italy, poverty in natural resources made the margin between prosperity and depression a narrow one and caused economic and social maladjustments to reflect themselves more immediately in psychological and political disorders than where comfortable reserves of wealth can be drawn upon in a crisis—for example, the United States. Germany, like Italy, was economically a "marginal" state. Here Fascism blossomed into full flower as a demagogic movement bred of petty-bourgeois neuroses and as an instrument of power used by the ruling classes to serve their purposes. Here the Fascist state is most clearly the coercive and co-ordinating agency of the plutocracy in the age of monopolistic capitalism.

It is worthy of note, moreover, that Fascism appears first not only in "marginal" nations, but in "marginal" classes and "marginal" industries. It is nurtured by the social groups which are affected first and most severely by the maladjustments of a diseased economy. The petty bourgeoisie is everywhere in the West the least sharply defined and the most insecure segment of the social hierarchy. Its social status is most ambiguous. Its defences against pressure from above and below are weakest. Its identification with the symbols of nationalism is most intimate and its psychic frustrations are most acute when these symbols are debased. On the other hand, investment banking and heavy industry—that is, iron, steel, shipbuilding, armaments, and construction—are the economic activities which are first affected by down swings of the business cycle and the last to recover in up swings. These are the most sensitive centers of financial and industrial power in highly developed capitalistic societies. Bankers and heavy industrialists are most prosperous when capitalistic economy is expanding and least prosperous when it is contracting. It is here that competition first becomes destructive with the shrinking of the market. Here governmental aid, foreign markets, protective tariffs are demanded first and most insistently. Here trusts, cartels, holding companies, interlocking directorates, and all the other devices of monopoly first become general. Both Mussolini and Hitler were heavily subsidized by the powers of iron and steel, banking and investment. Thyssen and Krupp, Schroeder and Schacht constituted the liaison between those powerful but "marginal" business groups and the NSDAP [Nazi Party]. Without this alliance the Fascist state would never have come into being.

The seeds of Fascism are obviously falling upon fertile soil in other nations similarly afflicted with the dilemma of late capitalism. In Japan "economic planning," state control of business, militant nationalism, and belligerent imperialism marched hand in hand with industrial capitalism from the beginning. Japan effected the transition from an indigenous feudalism to an indigenous Fascism without the intervening phase of Democratic Liberalism. In the Brittain, the France, the America of the Great Depression heavy industry and investment banking are likewise prostrate. Here, too, the lower middle classes are reduced to desperation, while workers and farmers suffer unemployment and impoverishment and sink to a level of misery which paralyzes all will to action. In all of the Western states Democratic governments continue to wrestle with the problems of depression by the application of half-hearted, tentative, and "temporary" policies which have been carried to their logical conclusion by Fascism: business codes, price-fixing, production quotas, import and export quotas, restriction of competition, subsidies to agriculture, work-creation schemes, and the like.

In all of the Western states the failure of such steps to effect a restoration of prosperity has bred incipient Fascist movements which need for their rapid development only financial support from business and a further disintegration of Democratic ideology among the masses. The spread of Fascism in these states has not been thwarted save in France by any greater powers of resistance on the part of the proletariat, but only by the greater antiquity and stability of the Democratic tradition. The temporary success of the new experiments, such as the NRA [New Deal law for the control of industry under government leadership], or another "automatic" up swing of the business cycle in spite of the new experiments, may delay the advent of Fascism in the Western Democracies for a considerable period. But if the analysis of the genesis and import of Fascism here essayed has any validity, these developments will not prevent the adoption by the ruling classes of such political and economic techniques as are necessary for the preservation of capitalistic economy in the epoch of business contraction and monopoly. Neither will they prevent the emergence of political ideologies and state-forms comparable in fact, if not in name, to those of Italy and Germany.

Even in this event, however, the slow descent of the Fascist societies toward the new mediaevalism can by no means be forecast with any degree of certainty. The continuity of economic and cultural retrogression is far more likely to be interrupted by the advent of the Second Imperialist War. In the Third Reich the aristocracy is driven toward conquest by hunger for land and glory. The plutocracy is driven toward conquest by the shrinking of its markets, by the diminution of its profits through the impoverishment of domestic consumers, by the bright prospects of gain to be got by forging the weapons of war and by using them to conquer new markets in the East. The neurotic middle-class masses are driven toward conquest by nationalist megalomania, by morbid longings for murder and suicide bred of the insecurities and tensions of a diseased society. The Nazi leaders are driven toward conquest by all these pressures and by the exigencies of internal politics in a dictatorship which must become increasingly unstable and insecure with the further disintegration of the economic and social order of monopolistic capitalism. Salvation is to be had only through eco-nomic expansion in new markets. New markets are to be had only by the military subjugation of the Danube basin and of such portions of the Soviet Union as can be conquered from Communism.

Fascism is driven toward war by its own ideology and by the tightening ropes of economic strangulation in which its ruling classes are entangled. Fascism was born of the trauma of the First Imperialist War. It may perish in the trauma of the Second Imperialist War. War again on a world-wide scale would doubtless bring irremediable catastrophe in its wake. Neither Britain nor the United States could long remain aloof if Russia were attacked or if two continental coalitions fell upon one another's throats. Japan would seek to seize Siberia and to oust America from the western Pacific. The U.S.S.R., if compelled to fight, would fight with all possible weapons, including colonial revolt and proletarian revolution organized by the Comintern. Finally might come a long and bloody descent into chaos for Western civilization—or world-wide social revolution—or both. . . .

The prospect may give pause to the preachers of war. But for the ruling classes of the West war is still profitable. Conquest may still be lucrative after all other economic activity has ceased to pay dividends. When the armed pilgrims on Fascism's road reach this goal, when pathological hatreds, lusts, and longings for extinction create the means of their own satisfaction, the great guns will again thunder their doom, the terror of the skies will sow fire over the earth, and the shells will shriek their dirge over a world in agony. Fascism itself will be consumed by its war-made sons. . . .

Frederick L. Schuman, *The Nazi Dictatorship. A Study in Social Pathology and the Politics of Fascism,* 2nd. ed., rev. Copyright 1935, 1936 by Alfred A. Knopf, Inc., New York. Reprinted by permission of the publisher.

B. Roepke: Fascism as Modernized Tyranny

The second representative of the international school is Wilhelm Roepke, a renowned German economist who was deprived of his professorial chair by Hitler in 1933 and shortly thereafter fled into exile. For Roepke, Communism and Fascism are cut from the same cloth. They are both collectivist or totalitarian movements which constitute a twentieth-century, mechanized revival of a very ancient phenomenon, that of political tyranny. The intellectual progenitors of totalitarianism are to be found in all Western countries and the partisans of the movement are those dregs of society, criminals, crackpots, and perverts, who band together and, by a cunning mixture of deceit and violence, manage to seize control of the state. They then vent their insane fury, first on their own, afterwards on neighboring peoples. Only the use of force will stop them, and the Western Democracies must bear a heavy share of the responsibility for the destruction wrought by the Fascists because they did not intervene when it became clear that the German anti-Fascists were unable to halt the march of the Brown Shirts. Instead the Western Democracies approved and applauded the new tyranny until the day when Fascism, having got a firm grip on the German people, launched a vicious assault on the Democracies themselves.

It did indeed call for no exceptional clarity of vision to recognize Nazism as a frightful barbarian invasion of the laboriously hedged garden of civilization. But why was there general blindness to this in Germany, as later in the rest of the world, and why, in both cases, were men's eyes opened only when it was too late, when Germany had suffered the catastrophe of tyranny, and the world the catastrophe of war? The main reason lay in the *weakening of the moral reflexes.* That was what prevented so many people, faced with a barbarism that in the preceding generation would have made its perpetrators utterly impossible in the civilized world, from taking up the only proper attitude of flaming and uncompromising indignation, and nipping the evil in the bud. People were blind because they were determined to be blind. But that determination in face of unprecedented barbarism proved the serious weakening of the moral sense, of which the world had already given a first sign in the case of Fascist Italy when men praised the punctuality of the trains and the improvement of tourist travel, but forgot what that regime meant for the Italians.

Thus the failure to recognize the true features of Nazism was in the last resort a moral failure, which men sought to cover up with all sorts of theories by way of excuse, euphemism, or even justification, and with stale witticisms. *But this is a responsibility the world must share in full with the Germans.* There was certainly a good deal in this National Socialism that was anything but edifying, and certainly its victims deserved sympathy and assistance. But, on the other hand, had not Germany been given order and discipline? Were not the *Autobahnen,* the motor roads, perfect? Was not the economic and social policy of the Third Reich a thoroughly interesting experiment, perhaps worth emulating? Was it really so monstrous for the Third Reich to repudiate the limitations on its armaments (they could not be maintained forever), to claim full sovereignty over the Rhineland, to work for reunion with the Germans of Austria and perhaps even of Sudeten, and to treat Danzig more and more openly as a German city under its rule? . . .

One of these questions of ours had reference to the fact that one ground for coming to terms with Nazism was the idea that it was an efficient bulwark against Bolshevism, or at least was, in comparison with Bolshevism, the lesser evil. In this belief there was all too ready acceptance of the Nazi propaganda claim that the *coup d'etat* of 1933 saved Germany from a Communist revolution. That theory was indeed one of the trump cards played by National Socialism against unfavorable world opinion—we know with what success. At the outset and for a long time very few realized that this was no more than casting out devils through Beelzebub, and that the differences between the Red collectivism and the Brown totalitarianism could not remove from the world the essential similarity of their principles of structure. . . .

It remains a serious fault that the world should have allowed itself to be so led astray in its judgment and its moral susceptibilities by this playing off of Communism against National Socialism. How grave is this fault and how ready our times show themselves to submit to this mental and emotional confusion is shown by the fact that today we see the same unsureness and denseness in regard to Communism. Nobody who actively defends Communism or even finds excuses for it has any right to be indignant with the people for its seduction by the Brown collectivism, and a world that today shows the same attitude to Communism that it showed in the past to National Socialism, an attitude of palliation and of appeasement, if not of actual encouragement, proves to us that it is in a moral and mental condition that might have made it an accomplice in Nazism.

This play between Fascism (National Socialism) and Communism was facilitated by a certain interpretation of National Socialism. We refer to the idea that National Socialism, like Fascism, was fundamentally simply a spurious and insincere collectivism, with the aid of which "capitalism" was trying to maintain its position in a last desperate struggle against genuine collectivism, without troubling too much about the methods of government or the ideologies to be worked off on the masses who were to be fooled. Such a theory was well adapted to make the fundamental opponents of collectivism more ready to come to terms with National Socialism, if it did not actually throw them into its arms, while winning the allegiance of the others for "true" collectivism. One side was persuaded in this way to see in National Socialism an ally in the struggle against collectivism, and the other to see in collectivism an ally against Nazism. One side thus became partisans or promoters of Nazism and the other of Communism.

We may feel the latter to be less unattractive than the former, but this does not prevent the two sides from both being wrong, because the interpretation of Nazism from which both proceed is untenable. It is an altogether primitive sociological principle, although, unfortunately, propagated by Marxism, that a government is simply the executive organ of the "ruling class." "The class that in truth rules politically is the class of the rulers, with their religious, philosophic, or moral ideas, whatever these may be," but not a group that stands for any sort of common economic interests. It is cheap romanticism to suppose that the leaders of a state are marionettes, dancing at the ends of wires pulled by the "capitalists." The idea is completely untenable, even though there are actually "capitalists" who themselves entertained it. In Germany itself it was mainly "capitalists" who were so stupid as cynically to promote Hitler's rise to power, and later one of them, when the National Socialism he had supported had driven him into emigration, was actually simple enough to publish a book describing the wretched part he had played, instead of keeping a shamed silence. All these "capitalists" were driven long ago to the painful conclusion that Nazism was an entirely genuine collectivism, and was determined to rule by its own uncontrolled power. Thus those socialists who still adhered to the theory that National Socialism was a last desperate struggle of "monopoly capitalism" and was a pseudo-collectivism made the same mistake in their theories that the "capitalists" of the type of Fritz Thyssen had made earlier in practice. . . .

Thus intellectual confusion and moral obtuseness united to clear away the obstacles in the path of the Nazis—obstacles that otherwise would soon have made an end of their dominance. We who knew what Nazism meant had assumed in those critical years after the *coup d'etat* of 1933 that the conclusions we had drawn must force themselves upon the whole world. We took it for granted that at the very outset the Third Reich must come to grief through the resistance of the outer world, after the internal resistance had proved inadequate. We imagined the world's reactions and power of decision to be still more or less normal, so that we could not believe that the Nazi regime would last long. We thought the object lesson the Nazis had given in Germany would be sufficient to open the eyes of the rest of the world; the failure in Germany would increase the resolution abroad; since the battle had been lost in Germany, in the international field the determination not to lose it could not, we thought, but increase accordingly.

It had been impossible for us to make any mistake in our estimate of National Socialism; but unfortunately we were entirely mistaken in our estimate of the world outside Germany. We had not expected such inertia, indecision, and lack of unity. Indeed, time after time, from 1933 to this day the points were set wrongly with such incredibly mistaken instinct that disaster rushed upon us all like an express train. Thus we had the depressing spectacle of the representatives of foreign countries willingly shaking hands with murderers, liars, Reichstag-burners, torturers, blackmailers, sexual perverts, and such fry, hurrying to attend Nazi festivals, and taking pains to make it seem that these figures from the dregs of society were entitled to consideration. . . .

During the first years of the regime it would have been child's play to make an end of the monstrous thing, and in all probability even in 1936 the simple mobilization of France would have sufficed to turn the treaty-breaking reoccupation of the Rhineland from a triumph into an annihilating political defeat of Hitler. When in 1938 Austria was violated, nobody stirred, and when in the autumn of that same year the same game of extortion and menace was played against ·Czechoslovakia, in the Munich capitulation world policy in regard to the Third Reich descended to the uttermost extreme of weakness. During the whole period countless Germans had set their last desperate hopes on a firm attitude on the part of the great powers, but again and again they had to witness the triumph of their hated tyrants over a spineless world. Finally, Russia too made concessions to Hitler in the Molotov-Ribbentrop agreement, enabling Hitler at last to let loose war and, with the support of Russian deliveries, to carry it on successfully for a considerable time. The dismal picture is completed by the sudden chorus of praise from the Communists of all countries of the coalition of Nazism and Communism against the "imperialist and capitalist world."

If we consider all this soberly and with scientific objectivity, we can no longer doubt that *the world-wide catastrophe of today is the gigantic price the world has to pay for its deafness to all the warning signals that prophesied with ever increasing shrillness from 1930 to 1939 the hell the satanic forces of National Socialism were to let loose, first against Germany herself and then against the rest of the world. The horrors of the war correspond exactly with those that the world permitted Germany to suffer, while it actually maintained normal relations with the Nazis and organized with them international festivals and congresses. . . .*

Today it seems almost incredible that the world should have been able for so long to harbor the illusion that the Nazis might treat foreign countries better than they treated their own people; its doing so is inexcusable. Today, however, it should be clear to everybody that Nazism began its march of conquest in Germany itself, that the Germans were the first victims of that barbarian invasion which poured over them from below, that they were the first to be overwhelmed by terrorism and by mass hypnosis, and that all that the occupied countries had later to endure was suffered first by the Germans themselves, including the worst fate of all, that of being impressed or seduced into becoming tools of further conquests and oppression. . . .

It would be a misjudgment of the German problem if we were pharisaically to ignore the share of guilt that has to be borne by the world outside Germany; and this guilt is at the same time an offense against that section of the German people which stood out against Nazism. . . . But it would also be an error to see in Nazism nothing more than the sudden madness of a single nation in the midst of an entirely healthy world, and to forget that it was the special German form of a tendency that was of an international character. The Third Reich was the German form of the social and administrative system that we know as totalitarianism; and

just as that system is not the mark of a nation but of a period, it came into existence in Germany owing to conditions that can be shown to have existed throughout the civilized world. For reasons peculiar to Germany, she succumbed to germs of disease from which other countries were not free, but against which they were able to set greater powers of resistance. The disease obtained an exceptional hold over Germany because in that country national characteristics, international infection, and the exceptional circumstances of the time made up a particularly dangerous combination. The world could not have had so appalling a degree of complicity in German totalitarianism and its career if it had not already been itself infected.

Some years ago the great French historian and sociologist Elie Halévy coined the phrase "era of tyrannies," which has since become famous. But long before this it had become clear that those state systems of which the first had made its appearance in Russia in 1917, and which then appeared in several other countries in a great variety of forms, have essential traits common to all of them, later comprehended under the name "totalitarianism." Whether in Bolshevism, Fascism, or Nazism, we meet continually with the forcible and ruthless usurpation of the power of the state by a minority drawn from the masses, resting on their support, flattering them and threatening them at the same time; a minority led by a "charismatic [divinely endowed] leader" (Max Weber) and brazenly identifying itself with the state. It is a tyranny that does away with all the guarantees of the constitutional state, constituting as the only part the minority that has created it, furnishing that party with far-reaching judicial and administrative functions, and permitting within the whole of the nation no groups, no activities, no opinions, no associations or religions, no publications, no educational institutions, no business transactions that are not dependent on the will of the government. . . .

If National Socialism is essentially a particular form of totalitarianism, the story of its intellectual birth must to that extent be also that of totalitarianism. It is a specially complicated story, and this is not the place for its detailed narration. But the very circumstance that German totalitarianism was preceded by the Russian and Italian forms shows to how great an extent Nazism took over and worked out with German thoroughness ideas that were by no means of German origin. It would be wearisome to compile the names that mark the various stages passed through by the ideology of the totalitarian state. But if we merely mention the chief writers, such as the Frenchman Georges Sorel (who by their own acknowledgment strongly influenced both Lenin and Mussolini) and the Italian Pareto, and if we add how deeply the theorists and practicians alike both of Russian Bolshevism and of Italian Fascism influenced the German National Socialists, we have made it easy to see that the outer world worked just as ardently on the building of the intellectual foundations of the Third Reich as did Germany herself.

Even the racial mania that seems to be an exclusive domain of German totalitarianism was presented to the Germans by foreigners—particularly by the French writer Gobineau, who himself simply elaborated the idea that dates back to the eighteenth century. The racial delusion may be described as a cross between those foreign germs and the specifically German ethical romanticism that will occupy us later. While these and other precursors of the Nazi racial doctrine have nothing in common with the appalling delusionary charac-

ter of that doctrine, the fact remains that that is the abyss into which we are inevitably plunged in the end if we once pursue the mistaken path of the biologism of which Darwin and his school laid the foundations. The Nazi racial doctrine is the final putrid product of the decay of an intellectual process by which in the course of the nineteenth century man was degraded, with the zeal of a misunderstood science, to a subject of zoology and stud farming; but in this process all the principal countries of the West took part. The death chambers of Auschwitz and Maidanek are the final gruesome result of certain scientific ideas having ultimately found their way in the course of a century to the morally and mentally lowest levels of humanity, to a group that then, through a social catastrophe of inconceivable dimensions, became the rulers of a great people. . . .

The all-important thing we must always keep in mind is the incontrovertible fact that *the National Socialists did not come into power by the clear will of a majority of the German nation, but by the disreputable backstairs method of the coup d'état.* At the beginning of the Third Reich the majority of the German nation was opposed to Nazism, and the importance of this fundamental fact is in no way diminished because, by the iron logic of totalitarianism, the nation that had become its victim suffered on top of all else immeasurable injury to its soul and was brought down to the acceptance of its own servitude. And was the development different in Italy or in the Communistic countries? Have the Poles, the Rumanians, the Latvians, or the Yugoslavs, all, or even a majority of them, become Communists, simply because the ruthless machinery of totalitarianism has descended upon them? And is even the case of Russia so unambiguous that we may identify the Russians with Communism, or more precisely with Stalinism? Is not the answer obvious? . . .

There are people who say that the Germans ought to have made a more courageous stand against Nazism and its atrocities, and we fully share this opinion. But ought we not, in order to be quite just, also bear in mind that diabolical hostage system of the Nazis, which threatened the family of every rebel with a cruel death? How far was a man entitled to show courage at the expense of his wife and children?

Who, again, can judge the way the soul of man reacts to an unceasing flow of subtle monopolist propaganda, shutting out all other information? It may be admitted that the German, for reasons we shall consider later, is particularly easily influenced and particularly lacking in judgment in all political questions; but we do not know how the experiment would have worked out with any other nation that was unable, like the occupied countries of Europe, to draw strength from resistance, from the patriotic revolt against the impudent pretensions of an alien conqueror speaking another language. The whipping up of the German's patriotism, on the contrary, bound him all the more strongly to his own tyrannical government. . . .

But how can we get over the appalling fact that the Germans, wherever they carried their conquests, committed the most horrible crimes and hair-raising cruelties, that the German name is associated with the cold-blooded extermination of millions, with the infliction of indescribable tortures, with unfeeling destruction of irreplaceable values, and with causing infinite mental torment? All those of us who learned with boundless indignation and the deepest horror of these crimes know how near we were to wishing for that execrable country the fate of Sodom and Gomorrah. And yet the National Socialists would have attained one of the aims they were probably pursuing with their atrocities if we allowed ourselves to be carried away by our anger into identifying Germany with Nazism. This is the very point at which our sense of justice is subjected to its hardest test and must not fail us. The test is very hard even if we recall that unfortunately this is not the first time in history that terror, mass murder, and the most appalling cruelties have made their appearance in the midst of a nation; that in England Henry VIII delivered seventy thousand to the hangman, that in Soviet Russia millions of peasants have been "liquidated" in cold blood, and that a few decades ago millions of Armenians were cruelly murdered in Turkey. . . .

If we probe to the bottom of the question, we shall probably come up against the following general truth: Every society, however civilized and Phaeacian it may seem to us, conceals in its depth a sewer of subhuman types, which must be kept firmly closed like the fisherman's bottle in the *Arabian Nights*. In other words, the powers of evil lurk everywhere, awaiting their chance from some earthquake or conflagration, revolution or war. Bore into these depths and it will be seen how masses of the dregs of humanity are hurled into the air. Ask the French with their bloodthirsty militia of the Laval regime, the Norwegians with their *hirden,* the Dutch, the Croats, the Hungarians, or the Austrians, and let not the Englishman or American be too sure that "it can't happen here." Instead, let them be glad that they have been spared that experience so far. And we will not be so tactless as to ask how things are in Russia.

The upheaval of society by totalitarianism must of necessity bring the worst elements to the top. That is a general law, which has only been confirmed by Nazism and is of universal application all over the world. Whenever anything resembling the Nazi upheaval has happened (as in Russia, in Italy, or elsewhere), the biggest blackguards have regularly set the tone, dragging the honor of their country through the mire. Thus what happened in Germany was simply that such men as the execrable von Papen and his backers, who can never do adequate penance for their stupidity and perversity, opened up the sewers of the German community, a process that some of them, by unpardonable stupidity, even mistook for the fresh-water supply. . . .

Wilhelm Roepke, *The Solution of the German Problem*, trans. E. W. Dickes (New York: G. P. Putnam's Sons, 1947), pp. 6-11, 13-14, 17-18, 25-26, 32-34, 42-43, 45-46.

C. Burnham: Communism as World Conspiracy

Our last writer, James Burnham, is an American and a professor of philosophy. His view is that Communism is a dangerous and world-wide conspiracy directed against the Democracies. He rejects utterly the nationalist interpretation of a Berdyaev or a Toynbee. So far from espousing Communism, Burnham argues, the vast majority of the Russians are desperately opposed to this doctrine, as the forced labor camps and the secret police of the Soviet regime make abundantly clear. So far from succumbing to and amalgamating with Russian national sentiment, Communism is absorbing within itself the nationalism of all countries by granting each nationality everything except the one thing that really counts, political power. Communism is not identifiable with Russian imperialism. The Communists say they mean to conquer the world, and they mean what they say; possession of the Russian base, with its immense reservoir of raw materials and manpower, give them a better than even chance of achieving their objective. In short, if the Democracies do not destroy Communism, at home as well as abroad, and set up a world government, Communism will destroy the Democracies and establish a world Communist empire. This is why Burnham entitles his book *The Struggle for the World*.

During recent years there has been much dispute about the question: has Communism taken over Russia, or Russia taken over Communism? Are we to understand Communism as primarily an international movement, acknowledging no fatherland, that happens to have had its chief local success to date in Russia; or are we to believe, as many analysts contend, that Communism is, or has become, no more than a new outward form for the older nationalism and imperialism of Russia?

These two views seem incompatible; and there seems at hand much evidence, especially from the last decade, for the second. It is a fact that the Russian Communists control the world Communist movement. It is a fact that during the past ten years there has been within the Soviet Union a revival of Russian nationalist tradition. The cult of the traditional heroes of Russian history, tsars and soldiers and even legendary figures, has reappeared with official approval. Literature and the arts express pride in Russian themes. Tsarist military decorations, uniforms and even modes of address have been reinstated. The Orthodox Church has been permitted to resume a less hampered activity. During the war, internal propaganda stressed the patriotic defense of the holy motherland. In addition, many of the aims of Soviet foreign policy, both those achieved and those still in process, are seen to be continuations of the foreign policies of imperial Russia. . . .

The Communist world movement first came to complete power in the great and populous Russian empire. There is nothing surprising in the subsequent result that the Russian Communists became dominant in the world movement. This would have been true of the German Communists, if Germany had been the first nation conquered; or of the British Communists if it had been England. And the succeeding stage of Communist development would then have had a German or an English bias. Since 1917 the Russian Communists have had at their immediate disposal the greater percentage of the material substance of power—human beings, funds, lands, factories, armies. Naturally, so backed, their voices have been louder in international Communist councils than those of any others. Naturally, also, when it came to choices on international policy—in connection with Germany or China or Austria or Argentina—they would tend to support a decision which would be favorable to their own special interests, even if that decision meant difficulty for Communists in Germany or China or Argentina. The Russian Communists discovered, moreover, that to control the masses of the Russian people, to get them to endure uninterrupted sufferings and to die in wars, the symbols of Russian nationalism and even Russian religion were useful instruments.

But to conclude from this that international Communism is only "the Russian state party," an extension throughout the world of the Russian foreign office, and that Communism is "nothing but Russian imperialism," would be a disorienting mistake.

From the point of view of Communists themselves, Communist Russia is not a "national fatherland" in the ordinary sense, but a "fortress of the world revolution," just as a conquered trade union in a non-Communist country might be considered a pillbox, or a Communist cell in the State Department, a sentry post. The dispute between Trotsky and Stalin, so far as it was more than a struggle for personal power, was not over "world revolution" versus nationalism. Both Trotsky and Stalin, like all Communists, believed in both world revolution and the defense of a Communist Russia. The principal issue between them was a purely tactical problem. What percentage of Communist resources and energies should be assigned directly to the Russian fortress, and what to operations in the still unconquered sections of the earth? Trotsky argued for a faster pace, and for a bigger allotment to the non-Communist hinterland. Stalin wanted more time, and a relatively greater share given to increasing the armaments and strengthening the walls of the fortress already won.

> The internal consolidation of the proletarian dictatorship in the U.S.S.R., the success achieved in the work of socialist construction, the growth of the influence and authority of the U.S.S.R. among the masses of the proletariat and the oppressed peoples of the colonies signify the continuation, intensification and expansion of the *international social revolution.* . . . The U.S.S.R. inevitably becomes the base of the world movement of all oppressed classes, the center of international revolution, the greatest factor in world history. In the U.S.S.R., the world proletariat for the first time acquires a country that is really its own. . . . The U.S.S.R. is the only fatherland of the international proletariat, the principal bulwark of its achievements and the most important factor for its international emancipation. . . .

These words are not from Trotsky, but from the 1928 Program of the Communist International, written under the direct supervision of Stalin.

Soviet patriotism, with its Russian component, is therefore not merely consistent with Communist internationalism, but obligatory upon genuine Communists. When the Communists conquered power in one nation, the strategy of the world Communist struggle for a monopoly of world power was thereby necessarily altered. Before that, Communists were against the governments of all nations, and for their overthrow. Thereafter the Communists had an existing state of their own; and every extension of the power or boundaries of that state became automatically an extension of world Communism. . . .

Soviet "neo-Russian" imperialism is thus identical with "revolutionary emancipation." Nor is it surprising that there is a continuity between Soviet imperialism and tsarist imperialism, since the general lines of both are in considerable part dictated by evident geopolitical considerations. Soviet state policy is identical with world Communist policy. That is why we can get light on Soviet policy by reading the New York *Daily Worker* and observing the activities of American Communists, just as we get light on American Communists by noting what the Soviet government is doing. . . .

Within the Soviet domain, there are, it is true, especially among the youth, some millions of total believers, whose minds and souls are shaped absolutely by the Communist myth. But there is every reason to think that this is not true of the majority of the people. The outside world may be led to believe that workers rule in Russia; but the Russian workers know by life that they are serfs and slaves. Comfortable American journalists can believe that Stalin liquidated counter-revolutionary kulaks as a class; but Russian peasants know that he tortured and killed and robbed their families and starved [their] neighbors. English and American preachers and diplomats can accept the confessions at the Moscow trials and complacently explain them as expresssions of the peculiarities of the Russian soul; but Russians who knew and worked with the defendants understand that the confessions are fables of the N.K.V.D. [Soviet

secret police]. French poets can rejoice at the unanimity of will shown by a Soviet election; but Russians know how that unanimity is obtained. . . .

Let us ask: why are the secret police, the purges, and the prohibition of foreign travel considered necessary by the regime, and not merely admitted publicly in the controlled press, but constantly and spectacularly emphasized, especially in internal propaganda? The only possible explanation is that the regime recognizes the existence of profound mass discontent, however inarticulate and unorganized. If everyone, or nearly everyone, liked the regime, why would it be necessary to have the enormous secret police apparatus operating in every social, cultural, economic and political institution? Why would it be necessary to institute the periodic purges which, by the official accounts, involve hundreds of thousands, even millions, of persons, and often sweep away the entire staffs of magazines, theaters, movie trusts, factories, farms, party committees, commissariats, and so on, which in many cases, have been praised a few months before as the best defenders of the revolution? If the masses of the people believe Stalin to be the messiah that is described by our own fellow-travellers (exercising their decadent right of free speech from their vantage point of another continent), why, we may wonder, does Stalin need to make the attempt to get away from him a criminal offense?

The regime confronts here an insoluble dilemma. In order to propagate the Communist myth in the non-Communist world, it must swamp the ether, the newsstands and the bookstalls of all countries with the story of the happy, contented land of socialism. In order to terrorize its own unhappy subjects into submission, it must fill the colums of *Pravda, Izvestia,* and *Red Star* with denunciations of wrecking, sabotage, graft, "diversions," plots and deviations, on a scale so huge that it would seem to indicate a belief by the regime that nine-tenths of the population must be criminals and traitors. Both versions are lies, but the second, in its own indirect way, informs us very plainly about the true relation between the regime and the people. . . .

The internationalism of earlier Communism—of Communism while it was still comparatively weak, still a relatively isolated sect—was doctrinaire, abstract. It was based upon a presumed identity of international "class forces," independent of all national divisions. The Communists proclaimed that the masses had no true fatherland, that nationalism was just a trick whereby the class enemy forged heavier chains, that the main enemy was always one's own government, that sentiments of patriotism were shameful treachery to the revolution. These ideas were at variance both with reality and more especially with the deep traditional feelings of the masses. Consequently, this earlier internationalism, or rather antinationalism, often found itself crashing head on against the powerful sweep of national sentiment, which, far from subsiding, has reached a new intensity in our times. Potential recruits or followers of the Communists were offended and repelled by [this] anti-nationalism; it was a difficult barrier between Communism and "the mind of the masses."

Social Democracy, in accordance with Marx's own precepts, was also originally internationalist in this same doctrinaire sense, and met the same troubles. In 1914, at the outbreak of the First World War, Social Democracy ended the dilemma by succumbing to nationalism. Within each of the warring nations, the Socialists abandoned their previous abstract formulas about the unity of the workers of the world, the duty of opposing "their own" governments and fighting against "imperialist wars," and so on. They decided to be patriotic citizens and soldiers, fighting for their respective governments against the national enemies. The end result of this solution has been the disintegration of Social Democracy as an independent historical force. Social Democracy (called simply "socialism" in the United States), in any crisis such as war or revolution, henceforth became subordinated to one or another national state. Thus the Socialist parties in many of the Allied powers in the Second World War became the governmental leaders in the fight for national survival. After the war the British (Socialist) Labor party or the French Socialist party is first of all English or French, and only secondarily Socialist.

Communism has taken a different path, of far greater historical weight. It is not succumbing to nationalism, but absorbing nationalism, and thereby integrating into one movement two of the greatest—perhaps the two greatest—historical forces of the present age. There is here a typical "triumph of Stalinist realism." The Stalinist method has always been to try, as far as possible, to swim with the tide, never directly counter to it, but always to keep on top of the water, not to be dragged under. Since nationalist sentiments do exist, let us not weaken and isolate ourselves by bucking them, but rather let us exploit them, let us make them an avenue of approach to the masses instead of a wall of separation.

A decade ago the national flag, in each country, began to appear on party platforms along with the Red banner; comrades sang "The Star-Spangled Banner" or "God Save the King" as well as "The Internationale"; the portraits of the traditional patriotic heroes were hung beside those of Marx, Lenin and Stalin; the Communist school in New York was re-named "The Jefferson

School," and the N.K.V.D. recruited a contingent for the Spanish civil war as "The Abraham Lincoln Brigade." The Red army, during the war, organized Czech divisions and Polish divisions and Hungarian and Spanish, and for that matter German divisions. Communism becomes a kind of world political chameleon, more American than Washington or Lincoln ("Communism is [twentieth-century] Americanism"), more French than Joan of Arc, more Chinese than Sun-Yat-sen, more German than Frederick—and, needless to say, more Russian than Peter the Great. . . .

Stalin has written several tens of thousands of words about the national question; and on these there have been many million words of commentary. His "solution" of the national question, however, boils down to a very simple formula: grant nationalities everything expedient except power. Let them keep native costumes, songs, language, food, dances (it is all these that make big conferences in Moscow so colorful); anything so long as they do not have power. Power, under the Communist system, is a monopoly; that is the constant. The method was gradually worked out for the nationalities within the borders of the twelve original Soviet republics; it was extended to the four new republics formed during the war; and it is being used, with suitable adaptations and at various stages, for the nationalities that are brought under the expanding Communist influence. Many puzzling and seemingly irreconcilable features of present-day Communist policy make ready sense when they are understood in terms of multinationalism. It would, moreover, be a grave mistake to underestimate the power of this remarkable hybrid. Its career is not ended, but only beginning. . . .

Part III of the Program of the International has as its title: "The ultimate aim of the Communist international—

world Communism." The official *History of the Communist Party*, required reading for all Communists everywhere, declares: "Study of the history of the Communist party strengthens the certainty of the final victory of the great task of the Lenin-Stalin party: the victory of Communism in the whole world."

The fact that this is the Communists' belief, that world conquest is, in their own minds, their goal, is not, by itself, particularly important. There have been, and still are, other groups and even individuals who have believed in this same goal of world conquest. Several such individuals can be found in almost any insane asylum. There the belief is not taken seriously in objective terms. It is regarded as a delusion which, far from being coherently related to the total behavior of the maniac, is symptomatic of the breach between his diseased mind and its social environment.

The situation is analogous when this goal is professed, as it has often been, by small and weak sects. Then, too, it can be treated as a more or less troublesome delusion. It is not materially possible for the sect to do anything about the goal, and the rest of the world does not have to be concerned. Often the actions of the sect, in spite of the professed goal, do not have any positive relation to it; the grandiose goal is no more than an inverted answer to some obscure psychotic need. Implicit in at least one interpretation of the doctrines of Mohammedanism, Judaism, and even Calvinism is a goal of world conquest, but none of these groups is acting in practice to realize the goal; and none of them is in a material position to have a chance in this historical period to achieve it, even if they should attempt to do so. Therefore, in these cases also, the goal may be disregarded.

When, however, we find that a belief in the goal of world conquest is combined with both sufficient means to give a chance of achieving it, and actions which in fact work toward it, then the purpose must be taken quite literally, at face value. This was the case with Nazism; and it seems also to have been true of at least one section of the Shintoist-militarist Japanese leadership. It is much more obviously true of Communism. In Communist doctrine, there is not the slightest ambiguity about the goal of world conquest. In action, Communists work always and everywhere toward that goal. And at the present time the means at their disposal, in numbers, material resources, and psychological influence, are enough to give them a very substantial probability of reaching it.

However often this plain truth is repeated, very few of the leaders and citizens of the Democratic nations really believe it. They do not believe it, I suppose, because they do not want to believe it. It is, we may grant, an uncomfortable belief, putting a pistol to the will, and demanding just Yes or No as an answer. Nevertheless, and in spite of however many exorcisms by Henry Wallace or the Dean of Canterbury, it is true, and will continue to be true, until the issue is decided. . . .

Even if world empire were not the positive goal of Communism, it would, from the Communist standpoint, be a necessary aim as a defensive measure. The Communists believe, and have always believed, that there are only two alternatives for modern society: Communism or capitalism. In spite of what people may "subjectively" think, they are all "objectively" lined up on one side or the other: there is no in-between. When, therefore, Communism became a serious world force by conquering a large section of the earth and its inhabitants, an inescapable historical dilemma was presented. Either capitalism would destroy the new Communist world, or Communism would conquer the remainder of capitalism. (Somewhat paradoxically, the Communists hold the latter result to be in the long run "inevitable.") The showdown might be drawn out or for a while postponed, but it cannot be avoided. . . .

The Communist objectives in relation to the United States may be summed up as follows:

First, to try to prevent interference by the United States with the Communist plans for the consolidation of Fortress Eurasia, and even to gain United States assistance in fulfilling those plans.

Second, to weaken, undermine and demoralize the United States to the maximum extent possible prior to the open war struggle.

Third, to become imbedded within the social fabric of United States life in order to be ready for direct action—espionage, sabotage, stimulation of riots and revolts, etc.—when open war begins.

These objectives are furthered, of course, by Communist activities and propaganda throughout the world. Within the United States and its dependencies they are promoted by a powerful and complex network. Many Americans, understanding nothing of totalitarian politics, dismiss the Communists as "a negligible force in American life," because the Communist party gets few votes in elections. For Communists, elections—particularly the vote one gets in elections—are among the most minor of political exertions. It might be recalled that in 1917, at the beginning of the Russian revolution, the Russian Bolshevik faction, which became the Communist party, numbered only about 25,000 members. In general it is a law of politics that a small minority, tightly organized and disciplined, knowing in advance what it wants and planning consciously how to get it, has far greater weight than loose, amorphous majorities. . . .

It is of course true that many of these rifts, or potential rifts, exist, independently of Communism, within the fabric of our society. There would be a Negro problem, a labor problem, a religious problem, a Jewish problem, if there were no Communist movement. It is further true that many good citizens, non-Communists and anti-Communists, concern themselves with these problems. Their concern, however, is to try to solve them. What they do not grasp is that the concern of the Communists —with whom they so often join their activities, frequently without themselves knowing of the united front into which they enter—is not to solve them but to make them insoluble. They do not understand that the Communists do not want to mend the nation, but to smash it beyond repair. The good citizen is glad to find Communist allies when he seeks, say, a fair trial for a Negro; he does not know that the Communist will use him for the precise purpose, not of helping the Negro, but of embittering and poisoning race relationships. The good citizen joins a committee to support, perhaps, the families of strikers; he does not know that the Communists in the committee have as their objective not the well-being of labor but the hopeless exaggeration of class conflicts, and the undermining of the American economy. Or the good citizen, as a humanitarian, joins some committee "for Soviet-American friendship," equally unaware that the function of the committee is to protect and defend not the peoples of Russia and the United States, but the Communist dictatorship today crushing the Russian people and tomorrow aiming for the people of America.

So, if all goes according to plan, the full war will open with the United States so isolated, and so internally weakened, divided, demoralized, that it will be unable even to make a good showing in the struggle. Meanwhile, in the war itself, with public Communist activities limited or abolished, the infiltrated divisions will be in a position to take direct action to break down the industrial and military machine, and the morale of the nation.

The downfall of the United States will remove the last great obstacle. The Communist world empire will begin.

James Burnham, *The Struggle for the World* (New York: The John Day Co., 1947), pp. 75-78, 120, 112-13, 86-88, 90-91, 93-94, 105, 110.

15. The Disintegration of the Versailles Settlement and the Road to World War II

HENRY R. WINKLER

Rutgers University

As in the case of other major conflicts, the outcome of World War I bore little relationship to the issues which had precipitated the conflict. The long years of bitter struggle had unleashed forces whose impact brought into being an almost entirely new international order. On the European continent, the three great eastern empires had collapsed. In Germany, a fledgling republic, established partly as a result of Allied demands, reluctantly faced the consequences of the defeat of the Hohenzollern armies. In Central Europe, independent succession states, with indeterminate boundaries, mutually exclusive claims, and little prospect of stable economic foundations, sprang into existence as the Hapsburg monarchy broke up like a ship on the rocks. Russia, in control of the Bolsheviks but deep in the throes of civil war and intervention, was almost completely isolated from the international affairs of the rest of Europe. In large parts of Europe starvation threatened, and the spectre of further revolution was more than the fearful nightmare of timid men.

These were some of the circumstances which faced the representatives of the victorious Allies who gathered in Paris to plan for the reconstruction of the war-torn world. If the result did not usher in the bright new future of wartime aspiration, these difficulties must be considered in assessing the settlement finally achieved. The postwar treaties were attempts to accomplish a number of ends: to "punish" those responsible for the war, to guarantee insofar as possible the right of national self-determination, to establish machinery for the pacific conduct of international relations. Almost from the beginning, these treaties became the focus of an impassioned debate, which reflected conflicting judgments of the conditions under which a peaceful future might be assured. The first part of our problem, therefore, calls for an assessment of the major element in the postwar settlement, the treaty of Versailles designed to cope with the "German question."

Once the Paris Conference had completed its tasks, Europe settled down to a decade of comparative quiet. But it was a calm that concealed fundamental weaknesses in the international situation. Nothing had been done to deal with the problem of Bolshevist Russia. The Soviet State remained isolated and hostile on the flank of a shattered continent. Perhaps equally serious was the withdrawal of the United States from participation in the "affairs of Europe." Woodrow Wilson's dream of a League of Nations had come to fruition, but the League that was established was little more than a rump in the absence of half of the major Powers. Not only the U.S.S.R. and the United States but Germany also (until 1926) was absent from the councils of the League. As a result, from the beginning Great Britain and France were its key members. It is one of the tragedies of the interwar years that they should have differed so sharply in their approach to the problems of this critical decade.

The major concern of France, understandably enough, was with the danger of a German revival. French statesmen for the most part acknowledged the importance of Germany to the economic life of Europe, but their fears of German aggression tended to compel them to make economic considerations secondary to strategic questions in the determination of policy. They supported the League with varying degrees of enthusiasm, but in virtually every case they regarded it as merely one of the instruments to ensure French security against aggression from the east. Meanwhile, parallel with the untested guarantees of the League, they proceeded to organize a system of alliances with the states of Central and Eastern Europe. At the same time, they insisted on a rigid adherence to the military and economic terms of Versailles in order to redress the balance, based on a larger population and a greater industrial potential, favoring Germany in her relations with France.

As for Great Britain, her policy reflected cleavages deeply rooted in British political life. The Conservative governments, which were in office for the greater part of this period, were reluctant to commit themselves to a policy which might involve automatic military support of the European *status quo*. In particular, they refused to accept the French thesis that an attempt by Germany to upset the settlement in Eastern Europe was as great a threat to the interests of the western powers as an attack across the Rhine. As a consequence, they were willing to guarantee the Franco-German border, but rejected any direct responsibility for the maintenance of the territorial arrangements in the east. In contrast, a substantial core of the Labour and Liberal opposition insisted that a peaceful and prosperous European order could only be established within the framework of a strengthened League of Nations. Some recognized that their position implied adequate military guarantees to make the League effective and to temper French fears of aggression. Others, strongly influenced by pacifist revulsion from the horrors of war, thought of the League as a substitute for military sanctions, placing their hopes in the gradual development of a general spirit of international collaboration.

Whatever the merits of these respective positions, the decade of the 'twenties seemed to offer the possibility that Europe would settle down to a peaceful future. The signature of the Locarno treaties in 1925, guaranteeing the critical frontiers of Western Europe and providing for arbitration agreements between Germany and Poland and Czechoslovakia, was followed by Germany's entrance into the League of Nations. Europe experienced a certain measure of economic prosperity which augured well for future stability and the "spirit of Locarno" appeared to be a backdrop for further triumphs in the establishment of a real international peace. But the hopes of the 'twenties were transmuted by the great depression into the fears and tensions of the 'thirties. Nationalism in Germany, always a problem, reached new heights and eventually brought Adolf Hitler into power. Democracy, which seemed to be taking root in Central and Eastern Europe, collapsed under the pressure of economic crisis. And in Britain and France the economic catastrophe created circumstances which made it difficult for those countries to take a firm lead at a period when the times demanded a complete rethinking of the bases of previous policies. The second part of this problem, then, has to do with some of the programs for the establishment of European security which gained support in the decade or so after the Paris Conference. Selections will be mainly from British and French materials, since the basic decisions were made in these two countries. But in order to achieve a measure of perspective, several excerpts from Russian and German sources will be included.

Italy, Japan, and Germany, to say nothing of Soviet Russia, were all dissatisfied with the international situation. In the 1930's, the first three of these Powers were determined to rewrite the terms of Paris and redraw the frontiers of 1919—by arms if necessary. The weaknesses and vacillations of the western States played directly into their hands. The Japanese invasion of Manchuria in 1931 was the first major attempt to change the *status quo* by force. When the League of Nations failed to halt the Japanese in their seizure of Chinese territory, the signal was given for an outburst of aggression that led finally to the renewed horror of war in 1939.

In Europe, the festering nationalism of Germany, once the National Socialist party had triumphed in 1933, became the chief touchstone of international relations. Faced with a Nazi threat to its own territory, the Soviet Union shifted from its dogmatic isolationism and emerged as the advocate of "collective security" against aggression. Conversely, during the next three years, Fascist Italy moved from an uneasy opposition to German ambitions in Central Europe to an equally uneasy partnership with the Nazis in the so-called Rome-Berlin Axis. As for the western Powers, they stood by while Adolf Hitler built up German power and undermined the resistance of his future victims. Hitler's abandonment of the League and his open program of large-scale rearmament should perhaps have been their cue for effective action. But France was so ideologically divided—and so defensively minded—

that her leaders failed to take any real initiative in crushing the ambitions of Germany. With the United States still aloof from European affairs, leadership inevitably fell to Great Britain. Here too there were factors which blocked a firm stand against the Nazi menace. The fear of war, a strong current of pacifism, mistrust of Russian collaboration, the belief that Germany would be satisfied when her "legitimate grievances" were removed—these were some of the elements in the picture. From 1933 to 1939, Britain witnessed an impassioned debate over the respective merits of "appeasing" the dictators or of uniting with other nations to resist their attacks upon the European order.

For the most part, the advocates of appeasement were the formulators of western policy. Whether their policy was correct or whether "collective security" would have been more successful in curbing aggression and perhaps even avoiding war is the implied question in our third part. From 1935, the dictators moved from triumph to triumph. The Italian seizure of Abyssinia was followed by German reoccupation of the demilitarized Rhineland. In Spain, the Nazis and Fascists shared with General Franco victory in a war that seemed to foreshadow the ideological alignments of a future European struggle. After Germany, Italy, and Japan had drawn together in an Anti-Comintern Pact, Hitler began to tighten the screws against Germany's neighbors. When he annexed Austria in March, 1938, the democratic Powers stood helplessly by. A few months later, it was the turn of Czechoslovakia. Hitler's ever growing claims for the German minority in Czechoslovakia brought demands for a strong stand from the advocates of collective security, in the West and in Russia. But, as we have seen, their opponents determined the policy that was followed. At Munich in September, 1938, Hitler was given all that he demanded—under the threat of precipitating war if his requirements were not met. The conflicting interpretations of the Munich policy and its consequences appear in the third part of this problem.

After Munich, events in Europe rushed to a rapid climax. In March, 1939, Hitler seized the rump Czecho-Slovak State that had survived the surgery of Munich. Almost immediately, the Nazi leader began to demand that Poland come to heel, but this time the western Powers reacted differently. Britain gave a military guarantee—which could hardly be implemented—to Poland, the first basic change in her East European policy since 1919. But it was clear that without Russian participation any alliance against Nazi Germany would have difficulty defending Poland or preventing Nazi hegemony in Central and Eastern Europe. Through the summer of 1939 negotiations were carried on by Britain and France for an agreement with the Russians. Mutual suspicion, and the fears of Poland, the Baltic countries, and Romania, all contributed to the slow pace of these conversations. Suddenly, on August 23, came the announcement that Russia and Germany had signed a Non-Aggression Pact. The outbreak of war was now inevitable, since Germany, freed of the threat of Russian intervention, was prepared to invade Poland. In the last part of this problem, we turn to the Anglo-French-Russian negotiations to examine the conflicting western and Russian positions and then study the implications of the Nazi-Soviet Pact as it is analyzed in various quarters. There, on the eve of a second world conflict, we leave the problem of international diplomacy between the wars.

The attempt to achieve peace and security between 1919 and 1939 is a chronicle of failure. Why it failed is as vital a question today as it was in 1939. There are no easy answers. But it may be hoped that the conflicting views presented in the course of this chapter will at least illustrate the complexity of a problem upon whose solution in our time depends perhaps the future of all mankind.

I. THE CARTHAGINIAN PEACE?

Throughout our period, the Treaty of Versailles was a symbol in many quarters of all that was wrong with the postwar world. As early as 1919, the influential pen of John Maynard Keynes produced an indictment of the Treaty, and his charges affected the attitudes of a large segment of western opinion. *The Economic Consequences of the Peace* presented an interpretation which held that the Allied Powers intended deliberately to reduce the German people to servitude. German nationalism was not slow in elaborating the charges. Perhaps the chief weapon in Adolf Hitler's arsenal was his constant fulmination against the iniquities of Versailles. As time went on, observers began to wonder. In 1944, for example, a young Frenchman, Etienne Mantoux, wrote an answer to Keynes which argued, first, that the major problems of the postwar era were the outcome of the war itself and not of the Treaty, and secondly, that the terms of Versailles were proper and could have been implemented if there had been the will to do so in the west and the desire, in Germany, to live peacefully with her neighbors. Whatever the merits of the argument, it is clear that the stereotype of Versailles—what men thought it was—had a profound effect on the international policies pursued during the two decades under discussion in this chapter.

A. *Versailles For and Against*

The following selections illustrate the two conflicting theses which were developed during the debate on the Versailles Treaty.

Both statements, made on the morrow of the signature of the Treaty, reflect arguments which continued to be used in the years that followed. The first excerpt is from the official defence of the Treaty made before the British House of Commons by David Lloyd George. Prime Minister of Great Britain, he had shared with Georges Clemenceau of France and Woodrow Wilson of the United States the major responsibility for deciding upon the terms of the settlement. He had certain reservations about the document, but in this statement to Parliament he emphasizes the two main justifications for a stern peace—Germany's responsibility for unleashing the war and the need for guarantees that it "would not happen again." In contrast with this view was the attitude of the British Labour party. From the beginning it was a major opponent of the Treaty. It branded the settlement as punitive, vindictive, grasping, and above all, certain to fail completely. All of this appears in our second selection, which is taken from a pamphlet published by the Labour party in 1919. Its author, Arthur Henderson, was secretary of the Labour party and at this time was serving as its leader as well. He had represented Labour in the coalition cabinet set up by Lloyd George during the war and was to be an influential figure on the international scene in the years that followed Versailles.

1. LLOYD GEORGE

The last time I had the opportunity of addressing the House upon this Treaty, its main outlines had been settled. I ventured then to call it a "stern, but a just Treaty." I adhere to that description. The terms are in many respects terrible terms to impose upon a country. Terrible were the deeds which it requites. Terrible were the consequences that were inflicted upon the world. Still more terrible would have been the consequences had they succeeded. What do these terms mean to Germany? Let us look at the matter quite frankly. . . . I am not minimising the terms. If hon. Members want to exercise their imagination to realise what the terms mean, they have only to apply the terms to Great Britain, and they will begin to realise what they mean. There is no doubt that they are stern. Are they just? Let us examine separately those which have been challenged.

Take the Territorial terms. In so far as territories have been taken away from Germany, it is a restoration. Alsace-Lorraine—forcibly taken away from the land to which its population were deeply attached. Is it an injustice to restore them to their country? Schleswig-Holstein—the meanest of the Hohenzollern frauds; robbing a poor, small, helpless country, with a pretense that you are not doing it, and then retaining that land against the wishes of the population for fifty or sixty years. I am glad the opportunity has come for restoring Schleswig-Holstein. Poland—torn to bits, to feed the carnivorous greed of Russian, Austrian, and Prussian autocracy. This Treaty has reknit the torn flag of Poland, which is now waving over a free and a united people; and it will have to be defended, not merely with gallantry, but with wisdom. For Poland is indeed in a perilous position, between a Germany shorn of her prey and an unknown Russia which has not yet emerged. All these territorial adjustments of which we have heard are restoration. Take Danzig—a free city, forcibly incorporated in the

Kingdom of Prussia. They are all territories that ought now to belong to Germany, and they are now restored to the independence of which they have been deprived by Prussian aggression. . . .

I come now to the question of reparation. Are the terms we have imposed unjust to Germany? If the whole cost of the War, all the costs incurred by every country that has been forced into war by the action of Germany, had been thrown upon Germany, it would have been in accord with every principle of civilised jurisprudence in the world. There was but one limit to the justice and the wisdom of the reparation we claimed, and that was the limit of Germany's capacity to pay. The experts of all the great Allied countries examined with very close attention that question, and they arrived with fair unanimity at the approximate limits of the reparation which could be recovered from Germany, and under the Treaty we have never exceeded nor fallen short of their verdict. We have set out certain categories of damage which Germany has to repair; damage to property on land and sea; damage for loss of life amongst civilians—that includes the damage sustained by the relatives of those gallant sailors who lost their lives in the merchant shipping of this country; damage for the loss of shipping and of cargoes; and also the damage which is represented by the pensions and the separation allowances paid by each country in respect of casualties in the War. Is there anything unjust in imposing upon Germany those payments? I do not believe anyone could claim it to be unjust. Certainly no one could claim that it was unjust unless he believed that the justice of the War was on the side of Germany.

I come to another condition—disarmament. Having regard to the use which Germany made of her great army, is there anything unjust in scattering that army, disarming it, making it incapable of repeating the injury which it has inflicted upon the world? . . .

Then I am told, "Oh, yes, take them individually and they may be quite fair, but the cumulative effect is so crushing that you ought to have taken that into account." [Hon. Members: "Hear, hear!"] I will deal with that. That is a criticism, and I am prepared to meet it. They say it may be just, but is it wise? I agree that justice ought to be guided by wisdom. If these conditions do not meet that test, I agree they fail, although we could defend each individual decision upon its merits. Let us examine them. There were three alternative methods of dealing with Germany, bearing in mind her crime. What was that crime? Germany not merely provoked, but planned the most devastating war the earth has ever seen. She planned it and prepared for it for years. She deliberately embarked upon it, not to defend herself against assailants, but to aggrandise herself at the expense of her neighbours. I cannot think of a worse crime, certainly in the conditions of Europe as they were. They knew there were millions of armed men in other lands, and they deliberately hurled 4,000,000 of their own youth against millions in France, millions in Russia, and possibly millions in the United Kingdom. They knew not how far it would extend. They lit a fire: They knew not what it would devour, what it would scorch, what it would burn, what sufferings would be caused, or what would be the desolation. They recked it not. . . .

There are three ways of dealing with that crime. One was to say, "You tried, you failed; go, and sin no more." [An Hon. Member: "Hear, hear."] Hon. Members may think that that is a good way of doing it, but let us see what it means. I am not afraid of examining that. Do not let us imagine, because it

looks ridiculous, that there are not people who believe in it—I mean outside this House. [An Hon. Member: "And inside it too."] You have got to answer it. Had that happened, you must remember that Germany suffered less than her victims. Louvain is not in Prussia. France is not in Pomerania, the devastated territories are not in Brandenburg. Look at that land of desolation and wilderness. I have traversed it pretty well from one end to the other. I felt it my duty to do so, in order to know with what I was dealing. That is not across the Rhine. Go across the Rhine. There are no devastated cities and no scorched plains there. The country is whole; the factories are there, the machinery is there—their own and other peoples—and if you had done that Germany would have been better off than the people she had victimised. The cost of the War would have been less, because she would have had a perfect military machine. She would have said, "Look at the triumph of militarism! We have kept all this devastation from you. France is paying more now than we are!" Why, to have done that would have been to put a premium on militarism. The point I do not think is worth arguing.

Let us take the second. The second is to go to the other extreme—to treat Germany as Rome treated Carthage, or, may I say, Prussia treated Poland—destroy her national existence, tear her to pieces, fling one piece to one conqueror, another to another, and a third to another. Fling the bits to the winds of heaven, and have done with them. That is how Prussia treated Poland. It was not merely a crime, it was a blunder, and after a century and a half Poland reappears a formidable and bitter foe. She had 20,000,000 population; Germany had 60,000,000. It is not merely that it would have been wrong and an injustice, but it would have been a folly, and I am glad that we have not soiled our hands with Prussian methods in dealing with Prussia.

What is the third method? To compel Germany, in so far as it is in her power to restore, to repair, to redress. Yes, and to take every possible precaution of every kind that is in our power against the recurrence of another such crime—to make such an example as will discourage ambitious rulers—yea, and ambitious peoples—from ever attempting to repeat this infamy. That is not vengeance. It is discouragement. This crime must be marked. The world cannot take these risks again. I said that Germany failed. I shudder to think how near she got to success. When you are thinking of the terms of peace you must think of making it impossible for any country to repeat an experiment of this kind without running the most terrible risks to her destiny. Every delegate entering the Council felt in his heart the supreme need for imposing terms that would make not merely rulers, but nations, shrink from attempting a crime of this kind again. That was the principle upon which we proceeded.

But it is said, "Are you not punishing Germany for the crime of her rulers?"

Well, I am sorry to have to answer this, but I must. If Germany had been committed to this War against the will of her people, I say at once we ought to have taken that into account in the terms of peace. But was that so? [Hon. Members: "No, no!"] The nation approved, the nation applauded; the nation had been taught to approve and to applaud. From the Baltic to the Boden Sea the nation was united and enthusiastic behind the enterprise. It was not like the unity and enthusiasm of France to repel an invader on French soil. It was an enthusiasm which was at its highest when German troops were marching through Belgium. . . . I should have been glad had it been possible to say that this was a war which had been entered into against the will of the German people. But it was not, and therefore it is essential that nations must know, if they enter into unprovoked wars of aggression against their neighbours, what may lie in store for them when defeat falls upon their arms. I therefore have no hesitation in challenging anyone, either inside or outside this House, to point to a single Clause in this Treaty that is not in accordance with the stern and highest demands of justice and fair play. . . .

Parliamentary Debates, Commons, fifth series, Vol. 117, July 3, 1919, cols. 1213-16, 1218-22.

2. HENDERSON

The Treaty is obviously based on a principle which President Wilson has repeatedly repudiated, namely, that peace will best be secured by the mere destruction of German military power and the punishment of the German people. It responds in this to the theory naturally popular in war time—and in which we are apt to acquiesce as a perhaps necessary part of war moral—that the main obstacle to permanent peace and a better organisation of the world was German military power and the special wickedness of the German race.

But the actual situation of the world which confronts us now, after the utter and complete destruction of German military power, assuredly proves the inadequacy of such a theory. Although German power has disappeared with a completeness that is one of the most astounding dramas of history, we have neither peace nor disarmament nor the prospect of these things. New wars in which Russians, Italians, Jugo-Slavs, Hungarians, Japanese, and Chinese are likely to be involved; a new naval rivalry which may create a gulf between ourselves and the Americans; vast new campaigns stretching from Archangel to the Caspian Sea; conscription for the purpose of military occupation of millions of square miles of territory; costly military interventions to prevent the trying by other peoples of political experiments of which we do not approve —it is these things which have followed that destruction of German militarism which was to give us permanent peace and a more rational world order.

The fact of itself condemns the whole principle and spirit upon which the Treaty is based. For although the theory of establishing peace by preponderant military power has been so tragically exploded by the results which have followed the German collapse, the democracies are asked to believe that, if only the new German Republic is treated with sufficient severity, if its territory, or much of it, is occupied militarily by half a dozen different countries; if this section of the German race is handed over to the Poles, that to the French, the other to the Czecho-Slovaks, some more to the Italians; if the sources of Germany's wealth are taken from her; if the population, especially the younger part of it, and more particularly the children, are exposed to conditions so severe as to amount to the employment of what Mr. Churchill calls "the weapon of starvation," the world will have peace. Beyond this merely negative and repressive method the Treaty does not in fact go. European history has no meaning if there were the slightest chance of such methods succeeding.

The settlement is supported on the ground that it is and should be punitive; that militarism needs an "example." Such a plea is prompted by the application of a false analogy of persons to states and nations, and is irreconcilable with justice, humanity, or expediency. It is morally bad for two main reasons:—

1. The chief punitive measures—the blockade or economic restrictions—creating want and suffering, will fall mainly upon those who have no possible responsibility whatever for the war: those who are now children or who were unborn when the offences were committed; and upon the politically uninstructed mass of workers who, owing to the control of the press by the Government, were honestly convinced that they were going into a defensive war, and were doing nothing less than their duty. These groups will suffer much more punishment than the official and wealthy classes who have the largest share of the guilt. Starvation or restriction will not touch the latter; it will the former. Such a result, far from creating a sense of guilt and predisposing to repentance and reform, will create a profound sense of injustice fatal to any "conversion" of the German people, which alone could justify punishment.

2. Even if we accept the idea of 70 millions of men, women, children, invalids, decrepit, all being equally guilty, we know from our experience in dealing with the individual criminal that if no provision is made for enabling him to earn an honest living—his offence once purged—he cannot be won from crime, but must remain an outlaw to the common danger. If the law does not protect even the criminal in his just rights it compels the criminal to protect himself; to take the law, that is, into his own hands. This Treaty makes no constructive provision whatever. As it stands, it justifies the plea of the Ger-

man militarist that a Germany which is not preponderantly powerful will be crushed by her enemies, and that her only security is in her own strength.

The Treaty is based upon utterly inconsistent principles. The principles of justice and the League of Nations and the 14 points are, it is true, included in the document, but only in the form of generalisations, aspirations, and vague formulae. Most of the actualities created by the terms, down to the minutest details, are governed by the idea of punishment, of strategy, or the snatching of some economic or territorial advantage for one or the other of the Allies. The result of such a settlement can be predicted with certainty.

Many of its provisions are patently unenforceable, e.g., the indemnity. The history of the Treaty of Berlin shows that the existence of impossible obligations guaranteed by the Great Powers is a perpetual source of unrest and of danger to the peace of the world. In so far as the conditions are enforceable, they can only be enforced by the permanent military subjection of Germany or a permanent threat of starvation. No nation of 60 millions can be expected to acquiesce in the violations of nationality and the economic servitude imposed by this Treaty. The Allied Governments and the new League of Nations will therefore have to devote all their energies to the task of "keeping Germany down," and the peoples of the world will live under the shadow of a renewal of the war at the first favorable opportunity. Even if Germany and Russia are not driven into an alliance, every international dispute among the Allied Powers—the question of Fiume proves this—will attain a dangerous and exaggerated importance as opening an opportunity to upset the unjust terms of this peace, in the shadow of the settlement. Then the conditions now exposed

must have important effects upon the internal situation in Germany. Political and economic chaos is threatening to engulf the whole of Europe east of the Rhine. The recovery of stability and order depends largely upon what happens in Germany during the next six or twelve months. A peace, such as this, which offers the German people no possibility of economic recovery, no guarantee of justice or equality, plays straight into the hands of the reactionaries on the one side and the extremists on the other. The complete economic ruin of Germany will inevitably bring the downfall of the moderates, and a struggle for power between the militarist reactionaries and the extremists. The only certainty with regard to the issue of such a struggle is that it would be fatal to the peace and recovery of Europe.

Even if we view the Treaty only from the limited standpoint of our own nation, without reference to its wide implications for the world as a whole, there is sufficient cause to fear its effects upon the British people. It is difficult, if not impossible, to see how it could be carried out except by the permanent militarisation of the Allied peoples, the continuance of conscription in this country, the lasting organisation of Europe as an armed camp, with all the economic and social results which the predominance of the military over the civil power involves for this country. If there is a hope that these effects will not follow their causes contained in the Treaty, it is because its provisions are unworkable as well as unjust, and because its speedy revision after it has been signed is not merely desirable, but also inevitable as soon as its implications are fully ascertained. The Brest-Litovsk peace was indefensible and merited the unstinted condemnation it received from world democracy.

From the beginning it was obvious it could not stand, and the same must be said of the Peace of Paris, for it also in many respects does violence to the fundamental principles of an enduring and just peace.

Arthur Henderson, *The Peace Terms* (London: Labour party, [1919]), pp. 6-9.

II. THE SEARCH FOR EUROPEAN SECURITY

With the signature of the postwar treaties, Europe faced the task of organizing the peace. From the start, conflicting views were evident as to how best this might be accomplished. There is no clear cut pattern to be traced, for within most countries champions of virtually every proposed road to peace were to be found. With sweeping oversimplification, nevertheless, we may say that the major split was between those who saw disarmament and conciliation as the avenues to European security, and those who thought in terms of maintaining superior military power against any threat to the postwar settlement. The first view found its most active advocates in Great Britain; the second in France. On the whole, the British proponents of national disarmament were also the outstanding supporters of the League of Nations as a substitute for "power politics." Frenchmen, for the most part, considered the League as the armed guarantor of the European *status quo,* particularly after the failure of the American and British governments to ratify a tripower guarantee treaty, originally projected by Woodrow Wilson. Within these broad positions, however, there was substantial variation. Some of the "League of Nations group" in Britain agreed with the French insistence on armed superiority, but for the League rather than for any nation or group of nations. Others rejected force completely. The argument for disarmament, which became in the eyes of many almost a symbol of goodwill, had its critics. That it was rejected by the conventional supporters of Allied preponderance goes without saying. But it was also questioned by those who argued that any system based on international law would be a sham without some provision for its enforcement. Here we can indicate only a few of the opposing currents of argument, but the selections below may give some indication of the complexity of the problem of organizing the postwar security of Europe.

A. Roads to Peace

Certain of the approaches to maintaining European peace are mirrored in the following excerpts. The first selection is from a memorandum handed to the representatives of the major Powers at Paris during the peace negotiations. Its author was Marshal Ferdinand Foch, who had led the Allied nations to victory after being named Generalissimo of all their troops on the western front. Despite the establishment of a German Republic after the defeat of the Kaiser's armies, Foch had little faith in a German change of heart. He believed that a populous and militaristic Germany would threaten the peace and security of France unless it were deliberately kept weak. He was especially concerned about German strength in the west and here argues the case for preponderant French military superiority on the German frontier. While Foch and other Frenchmen saw military superiority over Germany as the most effective safeguard of the peace, many other European statesmen during the decade of the 'twenties placed their hopes in the League of Nations. Most prominent among these League advocates was Lord Robert Cecil (later Viscount Cecil of Chelwood), the son of a former British Prime Minister, Lord Salisbury, and in his own right a distinguishd member of the Conservative party. He had been one of the leading figures in the establishment of the international organization and became one of its most influential supporters in the years that followed the war. His experience in this period convinced him that the League, if it were to be effective, must have force behind it as a means of guaranteeing the peace. His point of view is illustrated in a selection from a volume published in 1941, summarizing his reflections on the League experiment. A strikingly different approach was that of another Englishman, Arthur Ponsonby (later Lord Ponsonby). A former Liberal who had joined the Labour party because of its position on international affairs, he was Under-Secretary of State for Foreign Affairs in the first Labour government of 1924. Ponsonby, like Cecil, supported the League of Nations, but he rejected the use of force even by an international body. A pacifist, he looked to the gradual spread of anti-war sentiment as the only sure way to permanent peace. His reasons, outlined in a book which was designed to promote the cause of pacifism, appear in our third selection. Finally, Maxim Litvinov, the well-known Soviet diplomat who was later, in the 'thirties, to be a leading supporter of the League as an instrument of collective resistance to aggression, here, in a press conference held in 1924, gives us some insight into how the Communist regime of Russia regarded the League of Nations in the 1920's.

1. Foch

. . . Now that the Hohenzollerns have gone, in circumstances peculiarly damning to that dynasty and, indeed, to any military monarchy, the danger of a return to the imperial system must at least be remote. But a republic built up on the same principles of militarism and the centralisation of power, and taking the whole of Germany in hand, will be no less dangerous and will remain no less a menace to peace. Experience shows that it would not be difficult to give that character to a republic in a country soaked with the Prussian system, Prussian methods and militarist doctrines—a country in which discipline and the centralisation of power, thanks both to the national temperament and to tradition, are still the basis of society.

In short, pending the completion of her political and psychological metamorphosis, Germany will remain for a long time yet a redoubtable menace to civilisation. In these circumstances, the most elementary prudence renders it essential for the allied nations, nucleus of a League of Nations, to prepare a scheme of purely defensive measures and of primary precautions. These, if they are sufficiently precise, will at the same time give proof of the determination to reach the desired goal, which is peace, and to make it impossible for Germany to embark on a fresh war of conquest, to resume her designs of domination by force of arms. . . .

To sum up, the Allied Powers—France, in spite of the justice of her claims and her imprescriptible rights; Belgium, under the restraint of her neutrality; Great Britain, secure in her insular position—had never contemplated war on Germany. But, in 1914, they were brutally attacked by her. For some time to come the possibility of history repeating itself cannot be excluded. If in 1914, 1915, 1916 and 1917 the Allies were able to hold Germany in check; if they were able to give Great Britain time to build up her armies by means of conscription and other measures; if they were able to wait for the United States to throw their decisive forces into the scale, it was only because Russia was fighting on their side and because, for this reason, they continued for some time to have the advantage of superiority in numbers on the western front. Russia can no longer be counted on for an indefinite time to come. It is therefore necessary that the western barrier against a German invasion should be made stronger than it was in the past, and that the Allied Powers who, on account of their geographical position, are in the front rank of the protagonists of civilisation, should lose no time in making such military preparations as will enable the other powers inspired with the same ideals to come to their support while there is yet time.

A concerted scheme of defence by the Allied Powers is therefore imperative.

The prime necessity is a natural frontier, a first barrier against a German invasion. There exists but one, the Rhine. It must be held by the Allied forces until a new order of things is established. . . .

The object of this arrangement, which is purely defensive and must be brought into existence at once, is to guard against, and to meet, the requirements that would be created by a German aggression. It is indispensable, inasmuch as war, when it comes, lives on realities only, on material forces turned to advantage within a given time: natural lines of defence or defensive plans, troops, armaments; all of these have been shown above to be necessary. The arrangement would be carried out, as we have seen, under the auspices of the nations, founders of the League of Nations—France, Great Britain, Belgium, the United States.

Under the shelter of these measures of security, which it will reinforce with its moral support, the League of Nations, once firmly established, will be enlarged by the accession of the other nations who have joined in the defence of the principles of right and justice. It will create an order of things henceforward indestructible.

The League, once founded on that basis, with its statutes and its means of coercion, might progressively develop into the League of Nations by the successive accession of other nations, the neutral nations first, the enemy nations later. Its aim, once realised, would enable the military burden of the member nations to be gradually alleviated.

This is the ideal which we must pursue for a period which at present cannot be determined.

It can only be attained under shelter of the measures of security described above; in the absence of those measures, civilisation will be in constant danger of a renewed German aggression, which, this time, might not be repelled in time.

The fortune of war has placed the line of the Rhine in our hands, thanks to a combination of circumstances and to a rallying of forces under the Allied command which could only be witnessed again in the remote future. To throw away the opportunity of utilising this strong natural frontier, without any guarantees save those of a moral character and of distant and uncertain effect is, in the military sphere, to court the gravest of risks.

Nor have the armies forgotten the blood which it has cost them.

"Note handed by Marshal Foch, Commander-in-Chief of the Allied Armies, to the Plenipotentiaries of the Powers," Command 2619, France No. 1 (1924). *Papers respecting Negotiations for an Anglo-French Pact* (London: His Majesty's Stationery Office, 1924), pp. 20-21, 23.

2. CECIL

It had become clear that preparedness in some form or another was essential for national safety. Continental nations with no sea to protect them had long realized this. They had sought safety in arms and alliances. But those expedients were unsatisfactory. To make a nation secure, armament must make it stronger than any probable enemy. That means that its probable enemy will become relatively weaker and in consequence be in danger. Hence the inevitable armaments race with all its attendant evils. Alliances are only another way of increasing armament. To meet them, the only resource is to form counter-alliances, with the result that two or more groups of countries are created, anxiously watching one another and each justifying the growth of its armaments expenditure by dwelling on the enmity of its neighbours.

We saw the process in full operation before 1914. . . .

It was to meet this situation, after it had produced the catastrophe of 1914–1918, that the League of Nations was proposed. It was no new idea. Something of the kind had been repeatedly suggested. But the colossal scale of modern war made it urgent to find some means of national security. Here, then, was a plan by which might be obtained all and more than all the security given by alliances without the very grave disadvantages that ordinary alliances lead to. Let the peace-loving nations combine, not against this or that Power, but against all aggressors. Let them form, as it were, an international mutual assurance society.

It was an essential part of this conception that, in the last resort, adequate force should be on the side of those who were attacked. In such a defensive force we must play an important part. That meant that we might have to join in resisting aggression in any part of the civilized world. Here was the difficulty for us as for other nations. Immediately came the cry that it was unreasonable or even immoral to ask that British blood and treasure should be expended to defend distant countries like Manchuria or Abyssinia or Czechoslovakia. What, it was asked, does it matter to us what happens to people who dwell in such places? Let us, then,

avoid 'commitments' to act in defence of others and confine ourselves to the protection of our own so-called interests. Evidently such a view struck at the very foundation of the League of Nations or indeed of any international organization of peace. Unless it is agreed that peace is essential to us as it is to all civilized peoples, and that any serious breach of it wherever it occurs is a threat to the peace of the whole world, no world cooperation for peace is possible. Conversely, if these propositions are admitted, then resistance to aggression is vital to our interests wherever in the civilized world that aggression may take place. At the Peace Conference in 1919, this proposition had been easily accepted. We had all just been through four years of agonizing warfare, embracing almost the whole world, which had originated in a political murder in the extreme corner of the south-east of Europe. Evidently what had happened once might happen again. Peace was indivisible and the new structure for peace should if possible extend all over the civilized world. Perhaps the representatives of the nations in 1919 overestimated the value of experience. Perhaps they ought to have limited the obligations to take the first active steps for peace to those nations who were nearest to the outbreak of war. Certain it is that only by vigorous and courageous leadership could the Governments of the world have been kept up to their duties under the Covenant. As we have seen, that leadership failed. . . .

Viscount Cecil, *A Great Experiment* (New York: Oxford University Press, 1941), pp. 342–344.

3. PONSONBY

If, as experience shows, you do not prevent war by preparing for war, the deduction seems pretty certain that you can help to prevent war by not preparing for it. Disarmament, therefore, should become the first aim and object

of the pacifist. Not as some say security first, then disarmament. This means you will get neither. But disarmament first, and security must follow, and indeed can only follow on disarmament.

Disarmament is a drastic and extreme

policy. Nations in their present mood and temper are far from showing any disposition to adopt so sudden a change. Can we for a moment imagine Authority in our own country fathering, fostering, and encouraging such an idea as disarmament? The notion till recently was relegated to the propaganda of unpractical pacifist cranks. But the word has been officially pronounced—very tentatively, it is true, but loudly enough to give hope that in time a chorus will take it up which cannot be ignored. The people have been told hitherto that they would be safe if they were armed, they have found time after time that this is not true. . . . The extent and nature of the deception practised on them is beginning to be understood, and, therefore, the task of persuading them that safety lies in disarming may not prove to be so difficult as it seemed at first. A League of Nations is undoubtedly the channel through which disarmament might be hastened and eventually realised. The League as at present constituted, however, recognises force as the basis of international authority. While supporting the Covenant as the first consolidation of an international conception, and while favouring the Protocol [the proposed "Geneva Protocol" for the Pacific Settlement of International Disputes] as a small advance towards disarmament, I am under no illusion as to what the consequence would be if ever the League decided to bring the sanction of force into operation. A League of Nations war will not be just a tidy little police affair, but will be the signal for a world war in which Governments would join ostensibly for international justice, but really to test the efficiency of their armaments and pay off old scores, and the League would perish. Disarmament would remove this weak spot from the constitution of the League, as well as the power of individual states to wage war.

The danger about disarmament does not lie in its consummation but in the methods advocated for approaching it. Half-way houses in this case are extremely precarious. It is much more difficult to insist on and supervise limitation in armaments than to decide on disarmament. A haze of controversy always surrounds discussions on standards, ratios and degrees of expenditure. So long as armaments continue to exist, no nation will take the risk of being inferior to its neighbours, and in every nation there will be a sufficiently influential body, if not Authority itself, which will see to it that what is called "adequate" armaments are kept up. Whether it be men, ships, guns, bombs, submarines or gases matters very little. . . .

If causes of war were genuine—and I have most emphatically pointed out that they never are—they might occur at any time, sometimes in rapid succession. The fact that we find the greater European wars spaced out at decent intervals is very significant: it means *that the Governments have to wait till they feel sure the people are ready, and, however great the provocation may be in between whiles, they will adjust their diplomacy so as to compromise over a settlement.* . . . As long as there is reason to believe that there is any widespread reluctance on the part of the people, no *casus belli* will appear on the horizon. . . .

This clear demonstration of the unreality of causes of war shows us that it rests with the people as to how long the interval lasts between the last war and the next war. It rests with us to prolong that interval indefinitely. That is to say, if a sufficient number of people declare themselves, now early in the intermediate period, as determined not to fight another war, and if the youth of the country are taught some of the disagreeable truths about war, and in their turn declare their intention not to be taken in, each successive Government will have to reckon with this growing opinion, and they will manipulate their diplomatic moves accordingly. . . .

The people are the masters. They have complete power. But so accustomed have they been to subservience and acquiescence, that they do not know they have the power. It is our business to teach them, so that Governments may become their servants. *If the people want enduring peace, they can have it. It rests with them.* . . .

Yes, I am against the next war *now*, because I *know* it will be a sham fight, with the wrong forces drawn up in conflict against one another, because I *know* severe punishment will come, not to the culprits, but to the innocent, because I *know* nothing will be settled by it, and because I believe warfare is a resort to barbaric violence and a spiritual and economic outrage on mankind.

Yes, indeed, I am against all war between nations, because I am convinced there can be no cause of international dispute which can justify the loss of millions of lives and the wholesale destruction of cities and of irreplaceable national treasures.

If, then, we fail to persuade the people to abandon the credulity of the primitive man with regard to the war superstition, and to resist the false appeal of the militarist, and if Government will not move fast enough, then the next war is only a matter of time. After the pause, after the suitable interval, after the lapse of the period necessary to imbue youth with the old ideas, the enemy will be chosen, the motive found, and the signal will be given. War weariness is already diminishing. Young men are growing up who have not known war, and are being taught to look forward to the next war as a great adventure. The years are passing quickly; there is not a moment to be lost. Now is the time for action. If mentally, rationally and spiritually, there is no great change soon in the people's mood, the hour will strike. Our vision and imagination recoil from the prospect, which will be beyond any description. I will not attempt to picture it because I could not. But I would ask in all seriousness whether it is not worth a supreme effort to avoid, for all time, such a monstrous iniquity.

> Arthur Ponsonby, *Now Is the Time. An Appeal for Peace,* 5th imp. (London: Leonard Parsons, 1926), pp. 137-140, 178-179, 188, 190-191, by permission of George Allen and Unwin, Ltd.

4. Litvinov

We regard the League of Nations, as before, not as a friendly association of peoples working for the general good, but as a masked league of the so-called great Powers, who have appropriated to themselves the right of disposing of the fate of weaker nations. The fact that Germany, a defeated country that is in the military sense weak, is now entering the League, does not imply a change in the character of the League; it only means that certain Powers are counting on using Germany to assist in carrying

out their plans in general, and their hostile designs against the USSR in particular.

More than any other Government, the Soviet Government is interested in strengthening peace, on the basis of independence and self-determination for all nations. That is why it would welcome the creation of an international organization in which and through which every nation could realize its national sovereign rights and all nations could settle the differences arising between them by peaceful and friendly means. But less than any other Government does the Soviet Government see in the existing League of Nations an approximation to such an organization. Up to now the League of Nations has not in the slightest degree justified the hopes and expectations placed in it by its protagonists. It has not only failed even once to protect the rights and security of a small or weak nationality against coercion and the military verdict of stronger Powers, but on the chief question which is of vital interest to all mankind, and in particular to us, on the question of disarmament, it has not yet taken one single serious step.

The League is a cover for the preparation of military action for the further suppression of small and weak nationalities. To a considerable degree it is only a diplomatic *bourse,* where the strong Powers arrange their business and conduct their mutual accounts behind the back and at the expense of the small and weak nations. The USSR, as a State of the working masses, cannot take responsibility for the League of Nations, which sanctifies the enslavement and exploitation of foreign nations. Inspired solely by the desire to avoid any complications which might break the general peace, and in particular the progress of its great work of internal construction, and pursuing its policy of non-intervention in the internal affairs of other nations, the USSR does not feel the slightest desire to enter an organization in which it would have to play the part either of hammer or of anvil. In particular, the Soviet Government knows that it would then be confronted, in the form of partners or even of judges, with States, many of which have not even recognized it, and consequently do not even conceal their enmity towards it, and with others, even among those which have recognized it, which even now behave towards it with ill-concealed hostility.

Jane Degras, ed., *Soviet Documents on Foreign Policy, Volume II. 1925-1932.* Issued under the auspices of the Royal Institute of International Affairs. (London: Oxford University Press, 1952), p. 65.

B. *The Disarmament Dilemma*

Total disarmament, of the kind advocated by Arthur Ponsonby, was never a real possibility in the interwar years. "Disarmament" in the official vocabulary of the period meant a reduction and limitation of the instruments of war by international agreement. Most efforts in this direction centered about the World Disarmament Conference, which convened in February, 1932, and finally collapsed in 1935. During the years of preparation before 1932 and at the Conference itself, the differences which separated the nations of the world were graphically illustrated. Arthur Henderson was one of the most passionate supporters of an agreement to cut down on armaments. His speech to the League of Nations Assembly in 1930, at a time when he was Foreign Secretary of the British government, conveys the feeling of moral fervor behind the drive for disarmament. His enthusiasm, however, was doomed to disappointment, in part because of the irreconcilable hostility between France and Germany. The remaining two excerpts in this part of our problem reveal something of this hostility. Georges Clemenceau, wartime Premier of France, anticipated the resurgence of German military power and fought bitterly against any weakening of the French hegemony in Europe. Rudolph Nadolny, as German representative to the Disarmament Conference in 1932, argued that any program of arms reduction must treat Germany in exactly the same terms as it did the other major Powers of Europe. In these statements, by Clemenceau in 1930 and by Nadolny in 1932, may be seen one of the basic obstacles to success—the French fear of German power and the German demand for "equality" with her neighbors, whether in disarmament or rearmament.

1. HENDERSON

The Assembly will forgive me if I say quite frankly what is in my mind on this issue. We can never fulfil the purpose for which the League has been created unless we are prepared to carry through a scheme of general disarmament by international agreement. The authors of the Covenant never believed that international cooperation could succeed if national armaments should remain unrestricted, and if armament competition should revive. It was for that reason that they inserted in Article 8 the obligation to accept a general reduction and limitation of national forces by international treaties. That obligation has not been honoured, though it was incurred eleven years ago. The years are slipping by and yet that obligation forms part of the treaties of peace, and it is no less sacred than any other obligation which those treaties contain. By that obligation every Government Member of this League is bound. It is a pledge which has often been renewed; it was interpreted and reinterpreted in correspondence which passed between the Powers that signed the Peace Treaties of 1919. It was renewed in the solemn pledge of the Final Act of the Conference at Locarno in 1925. Time and again the Assembly has renewed that undertaking.

It was only two years ago that a solemn resolution was adopted by the Assembly which declared that the present conditions of security set up by the Covenant, by the treaties of peace, by the reduction in the armament of certain countries under those treaties, and also by the Locarno agreement, would allow of the conclusion at the present time of a first general Convention for the reduction and limitation of armaments. Yet, need I remind this great Assembly, two years have gone by and we have not made that general Convention. The pace is slow and the peoples of the world are growing impatient and doubtful, in many cases, of our good faith. . . .

Reductions by individual Powers, by small groups of Powers, or in respect of certain forces only, do not fulfil the pledges that have been made. Unless naval disarmament can be made general, unless it can be completed by the reduction and limitation of land and air forces, the peace treaties will not have been executed, the Covenant will remain unfulfilled, and the peace of Europe and of the world will not be safe. . . .

Finally, I have ventured to direct the attention of the Assembly to this the most vital and most urgent of all the political questions which confront the world today. We who are gathered here are the custodians of the peace of the world and of the lives and happiness not only of the present generation but of our children and of generations still unborn. While the memories of the great war are still with us, we have a golden opportunity to make impossible the next war, which, if it should come, will be even more terrible, and more destructive than the last.

I appeal to all those delegates of the nations represented here to join this Assembly in a strong and united effort to achieve the great purpose for which this League of Nations stands.

League of Nations, *Official Journal,* Records of the Eleventh Ordinary Session of the Assembly (Geneva, 1930), p. 42.

2. CLEMENCEAU

What are we doing, then, if not proceeding, article by article, to restore Germany's power, which, by a truly miraculous exercise of will, after its complete collapse during the War, is about to be built up again in the retrograde peace, which is surrendering, stage by stage, everything that human justice has gained by our victory. After the restoration of Germany's moral prestige by a lie we have the upsetting of the financial reparations by the progressive series of mutilations of the Treaty down to the payment of the so-called debts to America!

Finally, when this account is settled, or simply opened for the first cut of the final, fatal wound, it will be represented to us that the fabric of European justice according to the Treaty of Versailles has on all sides caused nothing but social disturbance and recriminations leading to outbreaks of violence. That will be the day toward which Germany has been ceaselessly striving since the Treaty of Versailles.

What forces are at the disposal of the new nations of Central Europe? What help will they afford us, and what support are we in a position to offer them? All the problems raised by the German aggression of 1914 will have to be dealt with at one and the same time. Germany, having regained her strength, will have inevitably bargained for arrangements from which her concern to isolate France will not be excluded. . . .

If Germany, still obsessed by her traditional militarism, persists in her *Deutschland über alles,* well—let the die be cast. We shall take up the atrocious War again at the point where we left it off. We must have the courage to prepare for it, instead of frittering away our strength in lies that no one believes, from conference to conference.

If Germany desires to prepare herself to live in peace let her say it, LET HER PROVE IT, and we shall not need the Geneva Chinese to reconcile us. I simply entreat Providence to preserve us from the talkers, and find us, if we still have any, vigilant men. Citizens of the new *régime* of European

justice, your day has come. Fashion your destiny yourselves. . . .

The notion of an extravagant act of generosity toward the defeated nation with a view to founding a lasting peace was well calculated to arouse our hopes. But could we really be asked to embark on such a venture without having first assured ourselves of the attitude of a partner who had displayed sentiments with regard to us very far removed from those it was our sincere purpose to awake in him? His acts of folly spring from the innate weakness of the German, which hands him over to the violences of what I shall call the primitive manifestations of human animality.

When I am told that a policy of concessions, more or less happily graduated, is going to regain for us the goodwill of our former enemies I can only be glad to hear it, for I desire nothing so much as a state of stable equilibrium in Europe. But I must be able to perceive some sign of a favourable response to the goodwill that I am asked to manifest. Judge then of my surprise when I discover that *Germany goes on arming and France disarming.* The position is that the most scientific preparations for war are being carried out on the other side of the frontier. With us frontiers lie open, armaments are insufficient, effectives are well below the numbers recognized as necessary, while on the other side a feverish life of reconstruction is developing and reorganizing, by the adaptation of fresh material, every department of their war equipment as well as their means of transport. Never was work more generally agreed upon. No complaining. No resistance. Goodwill. Universal enthusiasm the moment the word "war" is thrown to the passions of the mob, and no sign of a Franco-German reconciliation.

"Germany is arming and France disarming": that is the decisive feature

of this moment of history when the two states of mind confront one another in such stark brutality that I defy any sane man to cast doubt on the evidence. . . .

Georges Clemenceau, *Grandeur and Misery of Victory*, trans. F. M. Atkinson (New York: Harcourt Brace and Co., 1930), pp. 384-385, 389-392.

3. NADOLNY

It might, perhaps, have been natural for Germany to content herself with combining in a draft convention the various disarmament clauses in the Treaty of Versailles and submitting such a draft to this high assembly as the German counter-draft. For that system of disarmament has been in effect for some years in several States. Furthermore, it was the intention of those who enjoined this disarmament, and who at the same time drew up Article 8 of the Covenant, that this method should inaugurate general disarmament.

We have chosen another road because we intend to do our best to assist the Conference in reaching a tangible result. . . .

Allow me to add a few explanations of the German point of view. We are here to reach an agreement on general disarmament. Our Convention must apply to the whole world, and therefore to Germany also. Germany is a Member of the League and belongs to it on the same footing and with the same rights as all the other Members. Consequently, Article 8 of the Covenant must apply to Germany in the same way as to all the other Members. . . .

Germany is prepared, on condition that the Convention to be concluded applies to her in exactly the same way as to all other States, to cooperate to the best of her powers in the task before the Conference. I need hardly say that she is prepared to make all possible allowance for the national security of other States—that is to say, in so far as is compatible with Article 8 of the Covenant, or, in other terms, with effec-

tive general disarmament and with her own security.

The requirements of security cannot and must not prevent disarmament. We share the opinion which has been expressed by many speakers and is implied in the wording of Article 8 of the Covenant—namely, that security is primarily guaranteed by the most effective possible measure of general disarmament on a large scale. When one has only small guns, one cannot use big guns, and if there were no revolvers in the world there would plainly be fewer accidents. That is obvious.

We are well aware that, in the present atmosphere of general mistrust, there is a certain tendency to look for stronger guarantees against the risks of war in the form of general measures of security; but, as you will remember, it is apparent from the Locarno Final Protocol that it was then thought that the time had come to carry out disarmament by means of a general understanding, and you will also remember that the League of Nations expressly stated in 1928 that the position of general security was such as to allow of a reduction of armaments. . . .

In drafting these proposals, the German delegation started from the fact that Germany and three other countries have already carried through disarmament for some years past, under a regulation which was set up by the same Powers that drafted Article 8 of the Covenant and declared at the same time that the disarmament of the above-mentioned four countries was to be the first step towards general disarmament as provided for in the Covenant. Germany therefore considers her own disarmament as indicative of the course which the disarmament of all Members of the League will have to follow, having regard to the fundamental equality of rights of all Members of the League which excludes all discrimination in regard to any of them. The principles governing the general reduction and limitation of armaments, which the Conference is called upon to lay down, must be equally applicable to all Members of the League and to all countries associating themselves with the League's action for disarmament. . . .

The following proposals . . . are based upon the principle that there can be only one system of disarmament in future which must be equally applicable to all countries; such a system would produce an equitable and effective solution of the problem of disarmament if armament figures to be incorporated in it for all countries were fixed at the lowest possible level. These proposals are furthermore taking into account the necessity to safeguard the national safety of nations as provided for in Article 8 of the Covenant.

In submitting these proposals to the Conference, the German delegation wishes to make it clear that the German Government cannot accept a Convention unless its provisions are equally applicable to Germany and to other signatory countries.

Records of the Conference for the Reduction and Limitation of Armaments. Series A, Verbatim Records of the Plenary Meetings, I, 143-147.

III. APPEASEMENT AND THE MUNICH SETTLEMENT

In the wake of the great depression came a tragic deterioration in European relations. The depression was by no means the sole force behind the increase in international tension, but it served as a precipitant of aggression on the part of the "revisionist" Powers, in Asia as well as Europe. A major turning point in the history of the western world was September, 1931. The Japanese seizure of Manchuria ushered in an almost unbroken series of successes for the enemies of the existing international order. Japan, Italy, and above all Germany moved step by step to achieve their purposes, not by negotiation, discussion, and compromise, but by force and the threat of force. The spectre of war settled heavily over a western society that had dreamed briefly of an international future based on law instead of force. The vision was dissipated by the strident and menacing demands of the Fascist Powers and their supporters. Into the hands of the governments of the Western European democracies, above all into those of Great Britain, fell the task of dealing with these new challenges to the stability of Europe and of the world. They retreated almost continually. By 1937, when Neville Chamberlain became the British Prime Minister, they had erected their retreat into a system. "Appeasement" did not begin in 1937 —it had been urged in the 'twenties by the very groups which castigated it in the 'thirties. But its positive virtues, in the face of naked aggression, were proclaimed most systematically after Chamberlain took over the reins of government. It reached its culmination at Munich in the autumn of 1938, where Chamberlain and Edouard Daladier, the French Premier, agreed finally to the Nazi seizure of a part of Czechoslovakia in order to avert the possibility of war. Was the policy of retreat before the aggressors wise? Was it inevitable in the light of the European situation? What were the alternatives? In the debate centering about the German-Czech crisis can be found the basic approaches to the whole problem of aggression in the disastrous era of the 1930's, the era of appeasement.

A. The Grand Alliance

The threatening growth of German power under the Nazis brought Winston Churchill into the lists as the outstanding champion of British rearmament and European collective opposition to the pressures of Hitler's Reich. The following excerpt illustrates the nature of Churchill's position as the Nazis swallowed Austria and turned their attention to Czechoslovakia. Neville Chamberlain's views of the Churchill proposal can be seen in a selection from a letter to his sister, published in 1946 by his biographer.

1. CHURCHILL

Our affairs have come to such a pass that there is no escape without running risks.

On every ground of prudence as well as of duty I urge His Majesty's Government to proclaim a renewed, revivified, unflinching adherence to the Covenant of the League of Nations. What is there ridiculous about collective security? The only thing that is ridiculous about it is that we have not got it. Let us see whether we cannot do something to procure a strong element of collective security for ourselves and for others. We have been urged to make common cause in self-defense with the French Republic. What is that but the beginning of collective security? I agree with that. Not so lightly will the two great liberal democracies of the West be challenged, and not so easily, if challenged, will they be subjugated. That is the beginning of collective security. But why stop there? Why be edged and pushed farther down the slope in a disorderly expostulating crowd of embarrassed States? Why not make a stand while there is still a good company of united, very powerful countries that share our dangers and aspirations? Why should we delay until we are confronted with a general landslide of those small countries passing over, because

they have no other choice, to the overwhelming power of the Nazi regime?

If a number of States were assembled around Great Britain and France in a solemn treaty for mutual defense against aggression; if they had their forces marshaled in what you may call a Grand Alliance; if they had their Staff arrangements concerted; if all this rested, as it can honourably rest, upon the Covenant of the League of Nations, in pursuance of all the purposes and ideals of the League of Nations; if that were sustained, as it would be, by the moral sense of the world; and if that were done in the year 1938—and, believe me, it may be the last chance there will be of doing it—then I say that you might even now arrest this approaching war. Then perhaps the curse which overhangs Europe would pass away. Then perhaps the ferocious passions which now grip a great people would turn inwards—and not outwards in an internal rather than an external explosion, and mankind would be spared the deadly ordeal towards which we have been sagging and sliding month by month. I have ventured to indicate a positive conception, a practical and realistic conception, and one which I am convinced will unite all the forces of this country without whose help your armies cannot be filled or your munitions made. Before we cast away this hope, this cause and this plan, which I do not at all disguise has an element of risk, let those who wish to reject it ponder well and earnestly upon what will happen to us if, when all else has been thrown to the wolves, we are left to face our fate alone.

Parliamentary Debates, Commons, fifth series, Vol. 333, March 4, 1938, cols. 99-100.

2. CHAMBERLAIN

. . . with Franco winning in Spain by the aid of German guns and Italian

planes, with a French government in which one cannot have the slightest confidence and which I suspect to be in closish touch with our Opposition, with the Russians stealthily and cunningly pulling all the strings behind the scenes to get us involved in war with Germany (our Secret Service doesn't spend all its time looking out of the window), and finally with a Germany flushed with triumph, and all too conscious of her power, the prospect looked black indeed. In face of such problems, to be badgered and pressed to come out and give a clear, bold, and unmistakable lead, show "ordinary courage", and all the rest of the twaddle, is calculated to vex the man who has to take the responsibility for the consequences. As a matter of fact, the plan of the "Grand Alliance", as Winston calls it, had occurred to me long before he mentioned it. . . . I talked about it to Halifax, and we submitted it to the chiefs of the staff and the F. O. experts. It is a very attractive idea; indeed, there is almost everything to be said for it until you come to examine its practicability. From that moment its attraction vanishes. You have only to look at the map to see that nothing that France or we could do could possibly save Czechoslovakia from being overrun by the Germans, if they wanted to do it. The Austrian frontier is practically open; the great Skoda munition works are within easy bombing distance of the German aerodromes, the railways all pass through German territory, Russia is 100 miles away. Therefore we could not help Czechoslovakia —she would simply be a pretext for going to war with Germany. That we could not think of unless we had a reasonable prospect of being able to beat her to her knees in a reasonable time, and of that I see no sign. I have therefore abandoned any idea of giving guarantees to Czechoslovakia, or the French in connection with her obligations to that country.

Keith Feiling, *The Life of Neville Chamberlain* (London: Macmillan and Co., Ltd., 1946), pp. 347-348, by permission of Macmillan and Co., Ltd. and Mrs. Neville Chamberlain.

B. Munich and After

In Britain, as elsewhere in the world, the Munich settlement was greeted with relief: war had been averted. Among many, however, relief was accompanied by fear for the kind of a future it portended for the peoples of Europe, to say nothing of the Czechs themselves. Neville Chamberlain's defense of Munich, made in the British Parliament immediately after the Pact was signed, appears in the first selection below. From the many criticisms leveled at it during the debate in the House of Commons, portions of the biting indictment by Clement Attlee, leader of the Labour party, are selected to indicate the position of those who felt that it did not mean "peace in our time."

1. CHAMBERLAIN

Before I come to describe the Agreement which was signed at Munich in the small hours of Friday morning last, I would like to remind the House of two things which I think it very essential not to forget when those terms are being considered. The first is this: We did not go there to decide whether the predominantly German areas in the Sudetenland should be passed over to the German Reich. That had been decided already. Czechoslovakia had accepted the Anglo-French proposals. What we had to consider was the method, the conditions and the time of the transfer of the territory. The second point to remember is that time was one of the essential factors. All the elements were present on the spot for the outbreak of a conflict which might have precipitated the catastrophe. We had populations inflamed to a high degree; we had extremists on both sides ready to work up and provoke incidents; we had considerable quantities of arms which were by no means confined to regularly organised forces. Therefore, it was essential that we should quickly reach a conclusion, so that this painful and difficult operation of transfer might be carried out at the earliest possible moment and concluded as soon as was consistent, with orderly procedure, in order that we might avoid the possibility of something that might have rendered all our attempts at peaceful solution useless. . . .

Before giving a verdict upon this arrangement, we should do well to avoid describing it as a personal or a national triumph for anyone. The real triumph is that it has shown that representatives of four great Powers can find it possible to agree on a way of carrying out a difficult and delicate operation by discussion instead of by force of arms, and thereby they have averted a catastrophe which would have ended civilisation as we have known it. The relief that our escape from this great peril of war has, I think, everywhere been mingled in this country with a profound feeling of sympathy—[Hon. Members: "Shame."] I have nothing to be ashamed of. Let those who have, hang their heads. We must feel profound sympathy for a small and gallant nation in the hour of their national grief and loss.

Mr. Bellenger: It is an insult to say it.

The Prime Minister: I say in the name of this House and of the people of this country that Czechoslovakia has earned our admiration and respect for her restraint, for her dignity, for her magnificent discipline in face of such a trial as few nations have ever been called upon to meet. . . .

I pass from that subject, and I would like to say a few words in respect of the various other participants, besides ourselves, in the Munich Agreement. After everything that has been said about the German Chancellor today and in the past, I do feel that the House ought to recognise the difficulty for a man in that position to take back such emphatic declarations as he had already made amidst the enthusiastic cheers of his supporters, and to recognise that in consenting, even though it were only at the last moment, to discuss with the representatives of other Powers those things which he had declared he had already decided once for all, was a real and a substantial contribution on his part. . . .

In my view the strongest force of all, one which grew and took fresh shapes and forms every day was the force not of any one individual, but was that unmistakable sense of unanimity among the peoples of the world that war must somehow be averted. The peoples of the British Empire were at one with those of Germany, of France and of Italy, and their anxiety, their intense desire for peace, pervaded the whole atmosphere of the conference, and I believe that that, and not threats, made possible the concessions that were made. I know the House will want to hear what I am sure it does not doubt, that throughout these discussions the Dominions, the Governments of the Dominions, have been kept in the closest touch with the march of events by telegraph and by personal contact, and I would like to say how greatly I was encouraged on each of the journeys I made to Germany by the knowledge that I went with the good wishes of the Governments of the Dominions. They shared all our anxieties and all our hopes. They rejoiced with us that peace was preserved, and with us they look forward to further efforts to consolidate what has been done.

Ever since I assumed my present office my main purpose has been to work for the pacification of Europe, for the removal of those suspicions and those animosities which have so long poisoned the air. The path which leads to appeasement is long and bristles with obstacles. The question of Czechoslovakia is the latest and perhaps the most dangerous. Now that we have got past it, I feel that it may be possible to make further progress along the road to sanity.

My right hon. Friend has alluded in somewhat bitter terms to my conversation last Friday morning with Herr Hitler. I do not know why that conversation should give rise to suspicion, still less to criticism. I entered into no pact. I made no new commitments. There is no secret understanding. Our conversation was hostile to no other nations. The objects of that conversation, for which I asked, was to try to extend a little further the personal contact which I had established with Herr Hitler and which I believe to be essential in modern diplomacy. We had a friendly and entirely non-commital conversation, carried on, on my part, largely with a view to seeing whether there could be points in common between the head of a democratic Government and the ruler of a totalitarian State. We see the result in the declaration which has been published, in which my right hon. Friend (Mr. Duff Cooper) finds so much ground for suspicion. . . .

I believe that there are many who will feel with me that such a declaration, signed by the German Chancellor and myself, is something more than a pious expression of opinion. In our relations with other countries everything depends on there being sincerity and good will on both sides. I believe that there is sincerity and good will on both sides in this declaration. That is why to me its significance goes far beyond its actual words. If there is one lesson which we should learn from the events of these last weeks it is this, that

lasting peace is not to be obtained by sitting still and waiting for it to come. It requires active, positive efforts to achieve it. No doubt I shall have plenty of critics who will say that I am guilty of facile optimism, and that I should disbelieve every word that is uttered by rulers of other great States in Europe. I am too much of a realist to believe that we are going to achieve our paradise in a day. We have only laid the foundations of peace. The superstructure is not even begun.

For a long period now we have been engaged in this country in a great programme of rearmament, which is daily increasing in pace and volume. Let no one think that because we have signed this agreement between these four Powers at Munich we can afford to relax our efforts in regard to that programme at this moment. Disarmament on the part of this country can never be unilateral again. We have tried that once, and we very nearly brought ourselves to disaster. If disarmament is to come it must come by steps, and it must come by the agreement and the active co-operation of other countries. Until we know that we have obtained that co-operation and until we have agreed upon the actual steps to be taken, we here must remain on guard. . . .

While we must renew our determination to fill up the deficiencies that yet remain in our armaments and in our defensive precautions, so that we may be ready to defend ourselves and make our diplomacy effective—(Interruption) —yes I am a realist—nevertheless I say with an equal sense of reality that I do see fresh opportunities of approaching this subject of disarmament opening up before us, and I believe that they are at least as hopeful today as they have been at any previous time. It is to such tasks—the winning back of confidence, the gradual removal of hostility between nations until they feel that they can safely discard their weapons, one by one, that I would wish to devote what energy and time may be left to me before I hand over my office to younger men.

Parliamentary Debates, Commons, fifth series, Vol. 339, October 3, 1938, cols. 41-42, 45, 47-50.

2. ATTLEE

We all feel relief that war has not come this time. Every one of us has been passing through days of anxiety; we cannot, however, feel that peace has been established, but that we have nothing but an armistice in a state of war. We have been unable to go in for carefree rejoicing. We have felt that we are in the midst of a tragedy. We have felt humiliation. This has not been a victory for reason and humanity. It has been a victory for brute force. At every stage of the proceedings there have been time limits laid down by the owner and ruler of armed force. The terms have not been terms negotiated; they have been terms laid down as ultimata. We have seen today, a gallant, civilised and democratic people betrayed and handed over to a ruthless despotism. We have seen something more. We have seen the cause of democracy, which is, in our view, the cause of civilisation and humanity, receive a terrible defeat. . . .

I fear that the House is faced with this, that the real outstanding problem in this business, the real big issue, the central fact of the situation, is that the map of Europe has been forcibly altered by the threat of war. Herr Hitler has successfully asserted the law of the jungle. He has claimed to do what he will by force and in doing so has struck at the roots of the life of civilised peoples. In doing this to one nation he threatens all, and if he does this, and he has with impunity, there is no longer any peace in the world even although there may be a pause in actual warfare. The whole of Europe is now under the constant menace of armed force. That

is why many people cannot feel very happy about the present situation. They feel that there has been an immense victory for force and wrong. Ever since the last War people have realised that if peace is to be preserved there must be something above the will of the individual ruler of an armed State. That is the whole basis of the League of Nations and many people are surprised today to be under this menace —people who have grown to political consciousness in the years from 1918 to 1932, because between those years there was peace. Now we have gone back.

I say we are witnessing a degeneration of the world due to two things. The first thing is the failure to deal with the political and economic questions arising out of the follies of the Peace Treaties, and arising out of the widespread injustice and maladjustments of the economic system. The other thing is the failure to deal with force, the failure to restrain aggression. . . .

When the National Government overthrew the whole policy of collective security and abandoned it and the League, we told this House over and over again that we were entering on a very dangerous course. We realised that we were back in 1914 with all its dangers, and we knew that sooner or later a challenge would come to this country; and that is what has happened. The real pity of it is that, having decided to leave the League system which we practised and in which we believed, and to embark on a policy of alliances and power politics, instead of strengthening the people whose natural interests were with ours, we have had nothing but constant flirtations with this and that dictator. The Prime Minister has been the dupe of the dictators, and I say that today we are in a dangerous position.

... We are left isolated. The Union of Soviet Socialist Republic [sic] may well hold aloof in future when it considers what little trust can be placed on our Western democracies, and we shall be left alone with France; all our potential allies have gone; and France, which in my view has the greatest responsibility for this debacle of policy, finds herself in the position of a second-class State.

And what have we got in place of the alliances and covenants and collective security and all the rest of it which buttressed this country in the past? We are left with two promises, one from Signor Mussolini and one from Herr Hitler. That is really all that we have got. We have to walk by faith—the faith of the Prime Minister in Signor Mussolini and his faith in Herr Hitler. The Prime Minister has said how difficult it was for Herr Hitler to recede from a statement which he had once made. I have five pages of statements made by Herr Hitler, from every one of which he has receded. I need not go through them; you know them—pages of them; but the Prime Minister says against all experience that he has faith in Herr Hitler's promise, grounded on two or three interviews—a pretty flimsy support for this country.

I ask, what is to happen next? What reason have we to think that Herr Hitler will stop now? Suppose he does not. What will happen? ...

... The real question that faces us in this Debate is not just a review of the past, not just our apprehensions of the present; it is, What can we do for the future of the human race?

Parliamentary Debates, Commons, fifth series, Vol. 339, October 3, 1938, cols. 51, 55-56, 62-64, 66.

IV. THE COMING OF THE WAR

After Munich, the Nazis moved quickly toward their next objectives. In March, 1939, they brutally put an end to the fiction of Czech independence. Immediately, the familiar campaign of hysterical vituperation—this time against Poland—began. Now, however, the western reaction had changed. The British Government gave an outright guarantee of support to Poland. More realistically, perhaps, it joined with its French ally in opening negotiations looking toward an Anglo-French-Soviet pact against Nazi aggression. The negotiations dragged on through the summer. The western democracies were unwilling to meet Soviet demands with regard to the defence of the Baltic states. The Russian leaders, apparently mistrusting western intentions, refused proposals which in their view would have committed them to "pulling British and French chestnuts out of the fire." The western statesmen did not fully grasp the urgency of their problem, for meanwhile the Soviet leaders, with spectacular disregard of ideological questions, were in touch with the Nazi hierarchy. On August 23, the Russians cast their lot—temporarily at least—with the Nazis. In a treaty, whose secret clauses gave them a free hand to seize parts of Poland and Romania, they pledged in essence to remain neutral in the event of a war over Poland. Soviet motives in these tangled negotiations leading up to the bombshell of August 23 are of prime importance in considering how World War II was precipitated. This last part, therefore, contains material which aid the student to understand the nature of the situation on the eve of conflict.

A. Anglo-French-Soviet Negotiations

Two views of the Anglo-French-Soviet conversations follow. The problem as seen by the West is explained to the British House of Commons by Neville Chamberlain on May 19, 1939. At this juncture, the negotiations seemed to have stalled completely. The western Powers were unwilling to accede to the Soviet demand that the three signatories guarantee the defence of the Baltic states against aggression, whether those states wanted to be defended or not. The governments of these countries feared the Soviet Union as much as they did Nazi Germany. The British and French governments, for their part, had little confidence in the motives of the Soviet Union. But even if they wanted a pact against Nazi aggression, they had to decide whether the Soviet conditions were immutable or whether they were merely counters to be used in bargaining. The information available seems to indicate that neither Britain nor France ever really decided how to assess the Soviet position until it was too late to conclude an agreement. Something of the feeling of western indecision and ambiguity, of the failure of the British and French governments to realize how urgent their problem actually was, can be sensed in Chamberlain's speech. As for the Soviet leaders, their suspicion of the West was no less marked than the western distrust of the Soviet Union. By June, 1939, when Andrey A. Zhdanov, an important member of the Soviet Politburo, published a strong denunciation of the western position, the Soviet leaders had already begun secret conversations with the Nazi regime. Whether the Zhdanov article was an attempt to bring Britain and France to terms or a preparatory justification for the future pact with Germany, its appearance in the official newspaper, *Pravda*, gave it the stamp of an important policy statement by the Soviet leadership.

1. CHAMBERLAIN

. . . I turn to the discussions with the Government of the Soviet Union. . . . We are not concerned at all with Russian internal doctrine. We are concerned with the best method of building up what my right hon. Friend for Warwick and Leamington (Mr. Eden) has called a peace front. If we can evolve a method by which we can enlist the co-operation and assistance of the Soviet Union in building up that peace front, we welcome it; we want it; we attach value to it. The suggestion that we despise the assistance of the Soviet Union is without foundation. Without accepting any view of an unauthorised character as to the precise value of the Russian military forces, or the way in which they would best be employed, no one would be so foolish as to suppose that that huge country, with its vast population and enormous resources, would be a negligible factor in such a situation as that with which we are confronted. . . .

The House may remember a recent statement by M. Stalin, that it was the policy of the Soviet Union 'to support States which might be victims of aggression, provided that they were prepared to defend their independence.' That is our own point of view, and it appeared to indicate that the Soviet Union might be prepared to collaborate in carrying this aim into effect. But we were also aware . . . that the direct participation of the Soviet Union in this matter might not be altogether in accordance with the wishes of some of the countries for whose benefit, or on whose behalf, these arrangements were being made. We would desire to have the collaboration of all these countries, and we do not want to have any division among them. Accordingly, we suggested to the Soviet Government that they should make a declaration with regard to Poland and Rumania similar to the one which had been made by ourselves and France, namely, that if Great Britain and France should be involved in conflict in consequence of undertakings which we had given to those countries, or either of them, the Soviet Union express its readiness to lend its assistance to Poland or Rumania, as the case might be, always provided, of course, that their assistance was desired. . . . The British Government have never desired to ask the Soviet Government to do anything which they were not prepared to do themselves. They have always wanted the arrangement to be reciprocal. . . . If it be argued that it did not provide for the case of a direct attack on the Soviet Union, agreed; but it did not provide for the case of a direct attack on this country. . . . It may be argued that it did not cover the case of certain States, other than Poland and Rumania, which are neighbours of Russia, and through which perhaps she might be attacked. Again, I say, it is quite true that it did not cover that, but, on the other hand, it equally did not apply to certain western States which, if attacked, might cause us ultimately to be involved in war. . . . Our suggestion did not contemplate that the Soviet Government should intervene irrespective of whether Great Britain and France did so—although, as a matter of fact, our own commitments which follow upon the assurances we have given are irrespective of whether the Soviet Union come in. Therefore, if there be an inequality between the two States in the proposals which have been made, the inequality was in favour of the Soviet Union and not of this country. . . .

Nevertheless, since the proposal was not acceptable to the Soviet Union, we tried again. What we, above all, were anxious for was, that we should be able to come to an agreement quickly, and it is always easy to come to an agreement quickly if you accept everything that the other side puts up. [An Hon. Member: 'That is what you did at Munich'.] No doubt that is what some would have done. I do ask the House to remember that in this matter we are trying to build up, not an alliance between ourselves and other countries, but a peace front against aggression, and we should not be succeeding in that policy if, by ensuring the co-operation of one country, we rendered another country uneasy and unwilling to collaborate with us. Therefore, I suggest . . .

that in this matter, which is one of great difficulty and delicacy, a certain amount of caution is necessary, caution arising not out of ideological differences, not out of pure obstinacy, not even because we think that one course serves narrow British interests better than another, but because the object of our policy is to build up this peace front. We would rather delay for a few days longer than hastily take a step which might result in the work that we have already done crumbling before our very eyes.

We thought that perhaps the Soviet Government might have been willing to declare its agreement with us on those matters on which we could agree, and that it would be prepared to let us discuss further, and at greater leisure, the subjects on which difficulties still existed. That, in our view, would have been a wise course to take to show agreement and I cannot help thinking that, if we agreed even on a part of the policy to be pursued, it would have made it easier to come to a complete agreement on the rest. I cannot help saying how much I regret the decision of the Soviet Government not to let M. Potemkin go to Geneva. My Noble Friend [the Foreign Secretary] will, therefore, be deprived of the opportunity of discussing personally with him these matters, which I think, might have been valuable for both of us. . . . This is one of the cases in which I cannot help feeling that there is a sort of veil, a sort of wall between the two Governments which it is extremely difficult to penetrate, and that if only that opportunity had been afforded us we might have, perhaps, managed to shake hands across the gap. . . .

I have nothing more to say except this. Throughout this matter we have been in close touch with the Government of France, with whom we are happy to have collaboration and counsel. There is no difference between us. ... I do trust that ... it may be found possible to overcome these obstacles which have hitherto prevented us from reaching an agreement with the Government of the Soviet Union, and that we shall be able in due course to report to the House that we have at last made a final agreement with them.

Parliamentary Debates, Commons, fifth series, Vol. 347, May 17, 1939, cols. 1836-1840.

2. Zhdanov

The Anglo-Franco-Soviet negotiations on the conclusion of an effective pact of mutual assistance against aggression have reached a deadlock. Despite the utmost clarity of the position of the Soviet Government, despite all efforts of the Soviet Government aimed at the earliest conclusion of a pact of mutual assistance, no substantial progress is discernible in the course of the negotiations. In the present international situation this fact cannot but be of serious importance. It encourages the hopes of the aggressors and all enemies to peace in the possibility of the disruption of agreement among the democratic states against aggression and it impels aggressors to the further unleashing of aggression.

A question arises in this connection: What is the reason for the delay in the negotiations whose favourable termination is impatiently and hopefully awaited by all pacific nations and all friends of peace?

I permit myself to express my personal opinion in this matter, although my friends do not share it. They still think that when beginning the negotiations on a pact for mutual assistance with the U.S.S.R. the English and French Governments had serious intentions to create a powerful barrier against aggression in Europe. I believe, and shall try to prove it by facts, that the English and French Governments had no wish for an equal treaty with the U.S.S.R., that is, for the only kind of treaty to which a self-respecting state can agree, and that is precisely what has caused the state of stagnation into which the negotiations have entered.

What are these facts?

Anglo-Soviet negotiations in the direct sense of this word, that is, since we were presented on 15 April with the first British proposals, have been going on for seventy-five days. Of these, the Soviet Government took sixteen days in preparing answers to the various English projects and proposals while the remaining of fifty-nine have been consumed by delays and procrastination on the part of the English and French. The question is: Who, in such a case, if not the English and French, bears responsibility for such slow progress in the negotiations?

Further, it is well known, from the practice of concluding international agreements similar to the Anglo-Franco-Soviet one, that this same England concluded pacts of mutual assistance with Turkey and Poland within a very short space of time. Hence it follows that when England *desired* to conclude treaties with Turkey and Poland she was able to secure the necessary speed for the negotiations. The impermissible delays and endless procrastination in negotiations with the U.S.S.R. permit doubts in the sincerity of the real intentions of England and France and compel us to put the question as to what exactly forms the basis of such policy: Is it a serious endeavour to ensure a peace front or a desire to utilize the negotiations as well as the delay in the negotiations for some different purposes having nothing in common with the creation of a front of pacific powers?

This question suggests itself all the more in that in the course of the negotiations the English and French Governments pile up artificial difficulties, make it appear that serious differences exist between England and France on the one hand and the U.S.S.R. on the other, questions which, given goodwill and sincere intention by England and France, could be solved without delay or hindrance. It is known, for instance, that the question of a tripartite guarantee of immediate assistance to Latvia, Estonia and Finland, in the event of violation of their neutrality by aggressors, forms just such an artificially invented 'stumbling block' in the negotiations. Statements to the effect that the said Baltic states do not desire those guarantees and that precisely this circumstance allegedly hinders England and France from accepting the Soviet proposal, are obviously unsubstantial and could only be inspired by one intention; to hamper the negotiations in order to disrupt them. In any case facts are known to us which show that when, for instance, England believes it to be in her interest to guarantee some country or other, she finds proper ways for it without waiting for these countries themselves to demand guarantees.

The English newspaper, the *Sunday Times*, in its issue of 4 June this year, states that 'Poland . . . agreed that if Great Britain was drawn into war on account of the invasion of Holland she would come to Britain's assistance' and that 'Great Britain agreed that if Poland was drawn into war on account of the invasion of Danzig or Lithuania she would come to Poland's assistance'. Thus Poland and Great Britain give a guarantee simultaneously both to Lithuania and Holland. I do not know whether Lithuania and Holland were asked about this bilateral guarantee. In any case, the press reported nothing to this effect. Moreover, as far as I know, both Holland and

Lithuania deny the existence of such guarantees. Still, the *Sunday Times* reports a pact of bilateral guarantee for these countries has already, in the main, been concluded, and it is no secret for anyone that the *Sunday Times* report has not been denied anywhere.

Not long ago, in an interview with a certain French journalist, the Polish Minister for Foreign Affairs, Beck, declared quite unequivocally that Poland neither demanded nor requested from the U.S.S.R. anything in the sense of granting her any guarantees whatever and that she was fully satisfied with the fact that Poland and the U.S.S.R. recently concluded a trade agreement. Wherein then differs the position of Poland from the position of the ruling circles of the three Baltic states? In nothing whatsoever. However, this does not prevent England and France from demanding from the U.S.S.R. guarantees not only for Poland and four other states of whose desire to receive a guarantee from the U.S.S.R. we know nothing, but also for Holland and Switzerland, with whom the U.S.S.R. does not even maintain ordinary diplomatic relations.

All this shows that the English and French do not desire a treaty with the U.S.S.R. that is based on principles of equality and reciprocity, although they vow every day, that they too are for 'equality'. They desire a treaty in which the U.S.S.R. would play the labourer shouldering the entire burden of obligations. But no self-respecting country will agree to such a treaty if it does not wish to become a plaything in the hands of people who like others to pull their chestnuts out of the fire for them. Still less can the U.S.S.R. agree to such a treaty, whose strength, power and dignity are known to the whole world.

It seems to me that the English and French desire not a real treaty acceptable to the U.S.S.R., but only talks about a treaty in order to speculate before public opinion in their countries on the alleged unyielding attitude of the U.S.S.R. and thus make easier for them-selves the road to a deal with the aggressors.

The next few days must show whether this is so or not.

> *Pravda*, June 29, 1939, in *Documents on International Affairs 1939–1946, Volume 1, March–September 1939.* Issued under the auspices of the Royal Institute of International Affairs (London: Oxford University Press, 1951), pp. 418-420.

B. The Nazi-Soviet Pact

The meaning of the Russo-German agreement on August 23 was debated bitterly at the time, and has continued to be argued since. Was it a defensive maneuver by the Soviets, designed to gain time to prepare for a German attack considered inevitable? Or was it a move to embroil all of Europe in an exhausting conflict, the major beneficiary of which would be a Communist regime nursing its strength in neutral isolation? Or did it represent a typical imperialist bargain directed toward the cold-blooded division of Eastern Europe between German and Russian masters? Here is a series of conflicting views. Vyacheslav Molotov was the Soviet Commissar for Foreign Affairs. His speech to the Supreme Soviet of the U.S.S.R. is the official Russian explanation of the Pact. Waclaw Gryzbowski, the Polish Ambassador to Moscow at the time, sees in the agreement a cynical green light to Germany, the signal for the unleashing of a world conflict. His acid comments, it should be noted, were made before the secret articles of the Pact, providing among other things for the partition of Poland, became known to the world. Two other excerpts have been added to throw some light on the reaction to the Pact in the West. While official comment was guarded, individual figures were outspoken. To illustrate how sharply divided was their response, we quote from two speeches in the British House of Commons, both by members of the more extreme "left." John McGovern, a member of the tiny Independent Labour party, had at one time been a strong sympathizer of the Communist "experiment" in Russia. He had become disillusioned with the Soviet regime and a recent trip around the Continent had convinced him of its single-minded intention to promote the expansion of Russian power. His analysis of the Pact reflects this view of Soviet policy. Ellen Wilkinson, who was once described as the "most vigorous man in the Labour party," was usually well to the left of the more moderate leadership of that party. Vehemently opposed to the policy of Neville Chamberlain's National Government, she tended to lay the blame for what had happened at its feet rather than at those of the Soviet leaders. Her speech in the House of Commons, made like McGovern's the day after the announcement of the Pact, reflects some of the bitterness with which she responded to the collapse of the common East-West front against Nazi aggression.

1. MOLOTOV

. . . What is the root of these contradictions in the position of Great Britain and France? In a few words, it can be put as follows:—

On the one hand the British and French Governments fear aggression, and for that reason would like to have a pact of mutual assistance with the Soviet Union, in so far as it would strengthen them—Great Britain and France. But on the other hand the British and French Governments are afraid that the conclusion of a real pact of mutual assistance with the U.S.S.R. may strengthen our country—the Soviet Union—which it appears does not answer their purpose. One cannot but see that these fears outweighed other considerations. Only in this way can we understand the position of Poland, which has been acting on the instructions of Great Britain and France.

I shall now go on to the Soviet-German Non-Aggression Pact.

The decision to conclude a non-aggression pact between the U.S.S.R. and Germany was adopted after military negotiations with France and Great Britain had reached an impasse owing to the insuperable difficulties I have mentioned. As the negotiations had shown that the conclusion of a pact of mutual assistance could not be expected, we could not but explore other possibilities of ensuring peace and eliminating the danger of war between Germany and the U.S.S.R. If the British and French Governments refused to reckon with this, that is their affair. *It is our duty to think of the interests of the Soviet people, the interests of the Union of Soviet Socialist Republics*—all the more because we are firmly convinced that the interests of the U.S.S.R. coincide with the fundamental interests of the peoples of other countries.

But that is only one side of the matter. Another circumstance was required before the Soviet-German Non-Aggression Pact could come into existence. It was necessary that in her foreign policy Germany should make a turn towards good neighbourly relations with the Soviet Union. Only when this second condition was fulfilled, only when it became clear to us that the German Government desired to change its foreign policy so as to secure an improvement of relations with the U.S.S.R., was a basis found for the conclusion of the Soviet-German Non-Aggression Pact. Everybody knows that during the last six years, ever since the National-Socialists came into power, political relations between Germany and the U.S.S.R. have been strained. Everybody also knows that, despite the differences of outlook and political systems, the Soviet Government had endeavoured to maintain normal business and political relations with Germany. . . .

Since 1926 the political basis of our relations with Germany has been the Treaty of Neutrality which was prolonged by the present German Government in 1933. This Treaty of Neutrality remains in force to this day. The Soviet Government considered it desirable even before this to take a further step towards improving political relations with Germany, but circumstances have been such that this has become possible only now.

It is true that, in the present case, we are dealing *not with a pact of mutual assistance,* as in the case of the Anglo-French-Soviet negotiations, but *only with a non-aggression pact.* Nevertheless, conditions being what they are it is difficult to over-estimate the international importance of the Soviet-German pact. That is why we favoured the visit of the German Minister for Foreign Affairs, Herr von Ribbentrop, to Moscow.

August 23, 1939, the day the Soviet-German Non-Aggression Pact was signed, is to be regarded as a date of great historical importance. The non-aggression pact between the U.S.S.R. and Germany marks a turning point in the history of Europe, and not of Europe alone. Only yesterday German Fascists were pursuing a foreign policy hostile to us. Yes, only yesterday we were enemies in the sphere of foreign relations. Today, however, the situation has changed and we are enemies no longer.

The art of politics in the sphere of foreign relations does not consist in increasing the number of enemies for one's country. On the contrary, the art of politics in this sphere is to reduce the number of such enemies and make the enemies of yesterday good neighbours, maintaining peaceable relations one with the other. History has shown that enmity and wars between our country and Germany have been to the detriment of our countries, not to their benefit.

The countries which suffered most of all in the war of 1914–18 were Russia and Germany. Therefore, the interests of the peoples of the Soviet Union and Germany do not lie in mutual enmity. On the contrary, the peoples of the Soviet Union and Germany stand in need of peaceable relations. The Soviet-German Non-Aggression Pact puts an end to the enmity between Germany and the U.S.S.R. and this is in the interests of both countries. The fact that our outlooks and political systems differ must not and cannot be an obstacle to the establishment of good political relations between both States, just as like differences are no impediment to the good political relations which the U.S.S.R. maintains with other non-Soviet capitalist countries.

Only the enemies of Germany and the U.S.S.R. can strive to create and foment enmity between the peoples of these countries. We have always stood for amity between the peoples of the U.S.S.R. and Germany, and for the growth and development of friendship between the peoples of the Soviet Union and the German people.

The chief importance of the Soviet-German Non-Aggression Pact lies in the fact that the two largest States of Europe have agreed to put an end to enmity between them, to eliminate the menace of war and to live at peace one with the other, making narrower thereby the zone of possible military conflicts in Europe. . . .

V. Molotov, *Soviet Foreign Policy, Four Speeches* (London: Lawrence and Wishart, 1941), pp. 9-20, in *Documents on International Affairs 1939-1946*, I, 439-442, by permission of Oxford University Press.

2. GRYZBOWSKI

. . . (c) At the beginning of May M. Litvinov himself vanished from the political scene. Today we realize that the Soviets' imperialistic plans must have been already sufficiently formulated for them to retain a final and decisive understanding with Chancellor Hitler as a trump card in their policy of instigation of war. It is obvious that such an understanding could not be negotiated by M. Litvinov. . . .

M. Molotov took over the Commissariat for Foreign Affairs on May 5th. . . .

Some days later . . . I gave M. Molotov a résumé of our attitude.

We could not accept a one-sided guarantee. Nor could we accept a mutual guarantee, because in the event of a conflict with Germany our forces would be completely engaged, and so we would not be in any position to give help to the Soviets. Also we could not accept collective negotiations, and made our adoption of a definite attitude conditional on the results of the Anglo-French negotiations. We rejected all discussion of matters affecting us other than by the bilateral method. Our alliance with Rumania, being purely defensive, could not in any way be regarded as directed against the U.S.S.R.

In addition I indicated our favourable attitude to the Anglo-Franco-Soviet negotiations, and once more emphasized our entire loyalty in relation to the Soviets. In the event of conflict we by no means rejected specified forms of Soviet aid, but considered it premature to determine them definitely. We considered it premature to open bilateral negotiations with the Soviets before the Anglo-Franco-Soviet negotiations had achieved a result. M. Molotov made no objection whatever. . . .

It has to be borne in mind that so long as the Anglo-French negotiations lasted it was almost impossible for us to go beyond a waiting attitude. We felt no optimism whatever in regard to the result of those negotiations. It was difficult to expect that the Soviets would do anything in the direction of preventing a conflict or even rendering its outbreak difficult. We observed rather that their tactics aimed at the exact opposite.

The German-Soviet Pact of Non-Aggression justly made a deep impression.

The fact that two mutually contradictory sets of negotiations had been carried on simultaneously was a true measure of the cynicism of Soviet policy. The conclusion of the pact was beyond all doubt an encouragement to Germany to make war. The scope of the obligations undertaken, the extent of the understanding between the Soviets and Germany remained vague.

The Soviets endeavored to give it the appearance of a pact assuring them peace, but not effecting any fundamen-

tal change in their policy. In this regard M. Molotov even appealed to Poland's example.

The undefined character of the obligations resulting from the pact was emphasized by M. Voroshilov's interview given a few days later. Evidently influenced by news emanating from Berlin and London of the conversations between the British Ambassador and Chancellor Hitler, Marshal Voroshilov gave the Soviet Press an interview, in which he stated that the Anglo-Franco-Soviet negotiations were only suspended, and that their renewal would not be in contradiction with the Soviet-German pact.

Moreover, Marshal Voroshilov simultaneously stated that the supply of raw material and war material to Poland in the event of a conflict was a 'commercial matter', equally not in contradiction with the pact.

The warning was understood in Berlin. . . .

Polish White Book, no. 184, in *Documents on International Affairs 1939–1946*, I, 435-437, by permission of Oxford University Press.

3. McGovern

. . . I am not disappointed with the Russian Pact. I am one who believes in knowing who are your friends and who are your enemies, and while I could not assist any campaign which would involve the world in strife for purposes which I do not approve, at the same time I have no use for treachery or double-dealing of any kind. I am sure that at this moment it must give great pleasure to Torgler and Thaelmann in the concentration camps and to Dimitroff who was accused of the Reichstag fire, as well as to Goering who made such a great outburst of physical violence against him, to see von Ribbentrop flying in Hitler's aeroplane over what is regarded as the sacred soil of Russia. It must be gratifying to them

to see the Nazis who have brutally maltreated and murdered thousands of communists in Germany, exchanging handshakes of friendship with the Russians. It must be gratifying to them to see the Russian entertaining those brutal people who have done to death so many men in the concentration camps and back streets of Germany. . . .

I think the leaders of this nation are entitled to realise where they stand, and this pact between Germany and Russia does at least remove any doubt from the minds of the people of this country as regards counting on assistance which cannot be obtained. I took the view last year rightly or wrongly—and there was reason and evidence behind it—that the one country in the world which desired war was Russia. I took that view strongly. At that time I cycled from

Prague to Vienna and from Vienna to Berlin spending a week in each city and developing contacts with well-informed quarters. I took the view that Russia wanted the major Powers to be involved in conflict. The Russians did not want a short war. They wanted a prolonged struggle in which the conditions would be suitable for world revolt, or, if they did not secure world revolt, they wanted at least to weaken those nations who were dominant and were feared by them. I say, honestly and sincerely, that I believe the leaders at the Kremlin were prepared to sacrifice 20,000,000 or 30,-000,000 lives in that gamble for themselves.

. . . In relation to Russia's aim I disagreed—not because I wanted to—with members of both the Labour party and the Liberty party about the aid that Russia would give in a war. I know there are people who have both misinterpreted and misunderstood my point of view, but I had it clearly in mind. Even if you did conclude a pact with Russia it would, in my estimation, give no real aid. Russia is like the man who goes to sea and proclaims that he is going in to bathe, but only paddles his feet in the water. That is all Russia would have done. She fans the flames. She would bring about that extended period of war, to which I have referred.

Today we have the position that the Swastika and the Hammer and Sickle fly side by side and that the free democratic nations are left to see the realisation of this policy on the part of Russia. I leave that to the apologists of the Commmunist party. No doubt they can apologize for that as they can for almost anything under the sun. . . .

Parliamentary Debates, Commons, fifth series, Vol. 351, August 24, 1939, cols. 37-41.

4. WILKINSON

. . . There is one feature of our Debate which is rather curious, and that is that everybody has spoken as though this Russo-German pact was such a tremendous triumph for Hitler. But is it? After all, he has had to swallow almost everything he has said, and in fact has got what might be described as "The German Munich." He has had to send Ribbentrop, of all people, to Moscow, on a penance to Canossa, though he went in a Nazi-decorated aeroplane instead of a white sheet. Really, is that a sign of such internal strength as could cause that bogy-bogy speech which has just been made by the right hon. Member for Sparkbrook? The big mistake that has been made is that this country has steadily under-estimated the Russian strength. Whatever else can be said of Herr Hitler he has tended to put a much higher valuation upon it than we have. . . .

One of the tragedies of the policy of this country has been continually to underestimate what really was happening in that enormous country of Russia, covering one-sixth of the surface of the globe and the only country—certainly in Europe and, I believe, taking the United States into consideration—that can be self-sufficient in war production. We have treated that country with studied insult for as long as Members on the other side have been in power in this country. There was no insult too foul for them to repeat in the old days. I accept unhesitatingly the Prime Minister's word that in the last few weeks or days—since the beginning of August —he has done everything in his power to get conclusions through the Military Mission sent to Russia, but you cannot alter the effect of years and years of insult when, because you are obviously in a tight corner, you are prepared to go a long way to meet the point of view of the other people. Really, that had got to be said.

An attitude of high moral propriety has been taken in this House. There has been the suggestion that in some way or another it was Russia's moral right to save the British Empire. Why? Was it a moral obligation and a right and a duty which she owed to the human race to save the British Empire? To do Russia justice—if we can in this House—she has never proclaimed her affection for either the British Empire or for the present Government. What Russia has done on certain occasions is to make concrete offers of help to this country. There was, first, the concrete offer of general disarmament, and when that was laughed out of court there were concrete proposals of assistance provided that the alliance, or pact, or whatever you like, was to be a concrete reality. That has been done again and again. I would refer hon. Members to the columns of their daily Bible, the "Times," for proof of that. Each one of those offers has been either coldly ignored or laughed at. If we behave like that to a country when we are in a tight corner we cannot really complain if she does not hasten to our assistance. . . .

The right hon. Gentleman over and over again has said at that Box that he did not wish to see Europe divided into two ideological blocs. He has got his way. Europe is no longer divided into ideological blocs, because Russia and Germany are now on the same side. There was a time when he could have had that division, which would have meant that the whole of the armed forces of the democracies, not only Russia but the Oslo group and America— I for one find it difficult to recognise it as a democracy. . . .

Viscountess Astor: Is Russia a democracy?

Miss Wilkinson: It is very much so. The point I want to get out is that Russia was supremely concerned, as an anti-Fascist democracy at that time, to try everything she could to get an anti-Fascist group. The Prime Minister said: "We will not have this ideological grouping." Very well, he has seen what Herr Hitler calls potentially the greatest force in the world swing over probably to the other side—we do not as yet know for certain. I suggest that it is about time that we got to an ideological grouping. Men will not fight for the Bank of England, Montagu Norman and the City of London, but they will fight for something they consider is supremely worth fighting for. . . .

Parliamentary Debates, Commons, fifth series, Vol. 351, August 24, 1939, cols. 46-48, 51.

16. *The Aftermath of World War II*

JAMES L. GODFREY

University of North Carolina

WAR SOLVES SOME PROBLEMS; others it exacerbates. During the fighting governments and people have the task of achieving victory and problems are resolved within the comparatively simple frame of that imperative necessity. With the cessation of open hostilities, nations confront the problems of peace. These are more difficult to solve for there is no clearly defined and generally accepted goal as clearly mandatory upon all as that of victory in war. Unity of will gives way to diffusion of purpose; haste to procrastination; and suspicion thrives where co-operation once grew.

The basic and continuing problem to emerge from World War II was the antagonism and incompatibility of communism with the culture of western Europe. This could not be expressed in the simple slogan communism *vs.* capitalism because the economic, political, and social system of much of western Europe had been too modified by historical forces to meet any longer the connotations of the term "capitalism." The problem before Europe was in accepting or rejecting the "sovietization" of itself. This struggle centered in western and central Europe, but it was important for the entire world. Though the influence of what happens in Europe has somewhat diminished, it is still true that an extension of communism throughout that continent would have profound repercussions in all other areas. The United States was especially concerned and intervened directly and effectively in the contest.

This basic problem may, for our purpose, be divided into four related problems: the economic rehabilitation of Europe, the creation of an international organization capable of taking vigorous action for the prevention of aggression and the preservation of peace, the establishment of institutions for regional co-operation in western Europe, and the restoration of the independence and prosperity of Germany with an orientation acceptable to her neighbors. While all of these problems have an importance that goes beyond the struggle between "East" and "West" they are at the same time the essential elements in that struggle.

Perhaps the most immediate problem was that of the economic rehabilitation of much of Europe. The war had been severely damaging to the economic

structures of several countries and the restoration of normal economic relationships both within and between countries would take great effort and much
time.   Meanwhile a depressed standard of living and economic dislocation
brought political ferment and the possible growth of communism.   Humani-
tarianism and political considerations made it almost certain that the United
States would have to use its resources to aid its former allies—even former
enemies—in their efforts to restore economic and political stability.   How
much aid, in what form, and under what conditions became an important consideration for the western world.   Great Britain was the first nation to be
helped, but soon wider sections of the continent followed.

Out of the political and economic situation of western Europe there arose
a second problem.   To what extent should the nations co-operate in an effort
to help each other, and what institutions should be created to further this
co-operation?   Some, as we shall see, favored the development of economic
and military arrangements for mutual advantage, while others advocated the
political integration of western Europe into a form of federal union.   While
the political arrangements actually made in the Council of Europe fell far
short of any effective union, they seemed to be more fundamental to Europe's
necessities and appeared to be more promising for her future; they are thus
given preference over more limited solutions of the problem of co-operation.

Europe has played a role of the utmost importance in establishing and maintaining international institutions for the service of mankind and the preservation of peace.   Though the League of Nations gradually expired during the
1930's, man did not lose his conviction that some international organization
was indispensable in the modern world.   The United Nations, whose charter
was formed at San Francisco in 1945, was generally accepted as a necessary
world organization.   During its first years, however, it became a battleground
in which the rising incompatibilities displayed themselves and reflected the
increasing tensions of the struggle between the Soviet Union and the West.
In the Security Council the use of the veto became a highly controversial
matter.   Some views on this issue are given below.

Perhaps the most difficult problem was that of Germany.   In a sense the
solution of the German problem was a key to all the others.   If the German
problem could be solved in a manner satisfactory to all interested countries, the
temperature of Europe would be lowered and the prospects for the future peace
and welfare of that continent much improved.   The treatment of this problem
should reveal why this was so.

These four problems were by no means all that plagued postwar Europe and
the world.   In each instance they are problems that are still in the process of
solution, and the student will have a chance to consider vexatious questions
without having a solution presented.   In this respect our own age is very like
earlier ages were to those who lived during them, for there never was a time
when there were no difficulties to be faced and no failures to be repaired.

I. THE ECONOMIC REHABILITATION OF EUROPE

A. The American Loan to Britain

During the war, as a necessary effort to supplement and keep effective the economies of certain countries at war with Germany, the United States created a vast system of economic aid known as "lend-lease." On August 24, 1945, a few days after the conclusion of the war against Japan, President Harry S. Truman terminated the operation of lend-lease. To soften the distress that such a move would inevitably give and to bolster the economy of Great Britain now faced with the gigantic task of converting from a war to a peace footing, Truman held forth the prospect of a loan. This would mean that it would be repayable, would bear interest, and, in this instance, be accompanied by certain requirements concerning both international trade and currencies. In the House of Commons, Hugh Dalton, one of the leading members of the new Labour government, became the official, though diffident, champion of the acceptance of the loan, while Mr. Robert Boothby, a Conservative with independent leanings, pointed out the "impossible" character of the transaction. The argument *pro* and *con* developed basic considerations surrounding the extension of financial aid by the United States to her former allies in the war against Germany and Japan.

1. THE CHANCELLOR APPROVES THE LOAN

Hugh Dalton served as Chancellor of the Exchequer from July 1945 to November 1947. The following statements are part of his official defense of the loan negotiated in Washington by an English commission under the leadership of Lord Keynes.

I will begin with the loan agreement; and it may be convenient and logical if we first ask ourselves why we need a dollar loan at all. The answer is, because, during the war, our national economy has been distorted and violently twisted out of shape for the sake of the common war effort. And this distortion was deliberately worsened by Lend-Lease itself. We deliberately forced down our exports to the bare minimum. Why? To make munitions; to make supplies of all kinds connected with the war, for ourselves and for our Allies; and to man the Navy, the Army and the Air Force.

With the conclusion of the war against Japan, and with the sudden ending of Lend-Lease, we found ourselves in a most abnormal situation. We were faced with not only one problem but two serious problems. . . . The first problem was the simple question—how were we to pay, from VJ-Day [Victory-over-Japan Day] onwards, for all food and raw materials and other necessities which we must import in order to live and employ our people? Lend-Lease and Mutual Aid had ceased; but our urgent need of supplies from the dollar countries continued and will continue. Some of these supplies cannot be got except from the dollar countries; and ultimately, of course, we can pay for them only from the proceeds of our exports, visible and invisible. I do not need to stress to this House that it will take time—though I do stress that we must make sure that it takes the least possible time—not merely to regain the pre-war level of our exports, but to reach that higher level which is required if we are effectively and securely to balance our external trade in the postwar days.

During the interval, while we are re-establishing this balance, we shall need to import supplies from all parts of the world, and to pay, somehow or other, for what we import. Inevitably, therefore, we shall be running, for some time, an overdraft on our current trading account. The thing is inescapable. If any hon. Member has doubts as to the magnitude of that overdraft, I would ask him to study the facts and figures given in the White Paper on the Statistical Material presented by our repre-

sentatives during the Washington Negotiations. That is one of our problems
—what I have called the question mark
for the future, the problem of how soon
we can re-establish our export trade in
sufficient volume to pay for our imports,
and how, meanwhile, we are to meet the
critical situation which confronts us.

But there is also the second problem
of the legacy from the war years. This
legacy, a wholly disagreeable one, consists essentially of the debt which we
find ourselves owing to our Allies and
associates in the war, not to speak of
certain neutrals. These debts we have
accumulated during the war, entirely for
war purposes. This great load of debt,
which we are bringing out of the war,
is, indeed, a strange reward for all we,
in this land, did and suffered for the
common cause, to which all parties and
sections of this community were totally
devoted. . . . A large part of this debt,
though not all of it, is owed to the
sterling area.

I would like, here, to say a word
about the sterling area. This is a term
which is, I think, sometimes misunderstood. The sterling area is no new
thing. It is no creation of the war. It
is not even a creation of the immediate
prewar years. The sterling area has existed for over a century as a banking
and currency arrangement. Right up
to 1939, when the war broke out, holders of sterling were free to spend it anywhere for any purpose. But when war
came, we and the rest of the sterling
area enforced, for the first time, a complete system of exchange control. It
was necessary for the efficient conduct
of the war; but it was a new thing, born
of war conditions. All members of the
sterling area were free to spend sterling
anywhere within the area or outside it,
for any purpose approved by their own
control; but—and this is important to
an understanding of the present position
—we asked the other members of the

sterling area to cut to a minimum their
demands on our reserves of gold and
dollars, since we were the central reserve for the whole area. That was
the origin of what is now called "the
sterling area dollar pool." As hon.
Members will see from the Financial
Agreement, it is proposed that this arrangement, in the form in which it has
existed during the war, shall shortly
come to an end, and that we shall revert
to the prewar convertibility of sterling
for current transactions. Later, I shall
indicate how shortly it is to come to an
end; but here I wish to emphasise that
what we are doing is reverting, in this
respect, to the prewar situation. We
are not doing something which is fresh
and new.

May I say a word about our own reserves in this country? We began the
war with a little over £600,000,000 of
gold and dollars, as against external lia-
bilities of £496,000,000. But in April,
1941, immediately before Lend-Lease
began, our reserves had almost disappeared, as a result of the need to use
them up, in pre-Lend-Lease conditions,
for the purchase, on whatever terms we
could, of essential supplies from the
United States and elsewhere. In April,
1941, our reserves had practically vanished. They had fallen to the dangerously low figure of only £3,000,000 net.
From that point, however, following
upon the introduction of Lend-Lease,
our reserves began, fortunately and not
unnaturally, to recover. This recovery
was due partly to proceeds of sterling
area exports, and partly to the fact that
American troops in the sterling area
were paid in sterling and other local
currencies, which the American Government bought with dollars; and these
dollars came back into our reserves.
By 31st October of this year, our net
gold and dollar reserves had risen to
about £450,000,000 net—not an excessive figure in all the conditions that

confront us! For meanwhile, our external debts had risen, as a result of the circumstances I have been describing, to £3,500,000,000.

This, then, is the essence of the situation which I am seeking to lay before the House. On the one hand, we have a vast wartime debt, which we have no hope of paying off from our own unaided resources in the near future. On the other hand, we have a prospective overdraft on our current trading account for the first few years of the future, until our exports enable us once more to pay our way. That was the two-fold problem, which our negotiators took with them to Washington. That was the reason why we needed the American loan.

. . . I now turn with a flicker less of enthusiasm to the main provisions of the Loan Agreement. . . . I ask the House to approve this Agreement, as giving us, on balance, substantial and indispensable advantages. In addition to the 650,000,000 dollars . . . for the final settlement of Lend-Lease, we obtain a further credit for 3,750,000,000 dollars, making a total of 4,400,000,000 dollars in all. This credit is open to be drawn upon, up to this amount, until the end of 1951. It bears interest at 2 per cent. No payment is due, either of interest or principal, until 31st December, 1951, six years hence. Thereafter the loan is due to be repaid in equal annual instalments of 140,000,000 dollars—about £35,000,000—over 50 years.

I would draw the attention of the House to the fact that the Agreement contains a novel and important provision, not previously included in an arrangement of this sort, for a waiver of interest. The annual interest is to be completely cancelled in any year in which our exports, visible and invisible, are insufficient to pay for our pre-war level of imports, adjustments being made for price changes—on the understanding, naturally, that our reserves also are insufficient to make good the payment. On this last point we are the sole judges. . . .

So much for the waiver clause. I will now say a word about those sections in the Agreement dealing with the sterling area arrangements, which I should like to touch upon in the light of what I have said about the sterling area as a whole and its character. It is, at first sight, surprising that, according to Section 6(1) of the Agreement, no part of this credit is to be used to reduce our debt to the sterling area. At an earlier stage of the negotiations, we thought it was particularly desirable that part of the loan should be set aside for this purpose; but as the discussion proceeded, the American representatives took the view that Congress would not look kindly upon proposals to apply any any part of this dollar credit to reducing our debt to the sterling area. Hence Section 6(1). But the Agreement does help us to take the first step towards the much desired restoration of the convertibility of sterling. And there is considerable desire for this within the sterling area—let not the House be mistaken on this point. The restrictions on convertibility are not popular with our friends in the sterling area. They desire to see them loosened up. Their relaxation is not something demanded by the Americans only, it is also much desired by our friends in the sterling area. It is important, therefore, that we are enabled, under this Agreement, to take the first steps in that direction, through being helped to balance our current trading account at an earlier stage than would otherwise be possible.

Parliamentary Debates, Commons, fifth series, Vol. 417, December 12, 1945, cols. 423-429.

2. Boothby's Indictment

Sir Robert Boothby, a Conservative, represented East Aberdeenshire in the House of Commons for more than two decades where he established a reputation as a vigorous debater on foreign affairs and economic subjects. He here fears two things: Britain's inability to repay the loan and American interference in British economic affairs.

I feel rather strongly about this question, and I would like to say to my hon. Friends that, as no Amendments are being called in this Debate, I do propose myself to seek to divide the House on the main question tomorrow and to ask as many of my hon. Friends as I can get to do so, to vote with me against the proposals of His Majesty's Government. The main ground on which I do that, among many others, is because I conscientiously believe that this country is not, and will not be, in a position to discharge the obligation she is being invited to undertake by the Government; and if one believes that, I do not think that one has any alternative but to carry one's beliefs into the Division Lobby. . . .

Let us now look at the financial burden we are being invited to assume. From 1951 to 2000 A.D. we have to pay £33,000,000 a year. There is in addition to this, a little item to which the Chancellor referred, the sterling debts, the sterling balances. These after an agreed scaling down, have to be paid now, not in sterling, but in dollars. Annual payments for interest and amortisation, on the basis of two per cent. of the principal, will amount to about £70,000,000 a year.

Therefore, I estimate that the cost of the amortisation of the sterling balances in dollars plus the cost of the American Loan, will come to just over £100,000,-000 a year; and that is a burden which, I say, this country will not, in any foreseeable future, be able to sustain. It is an obligation we shall not be able to meet. It represents about 10 per cent. of our present target for exports and over 20 per cent. of our pre-war exports; and it is about half as heavy, as an eminent economist pointed out in one of the newspapers yesterday, as the burden of reparations imposed on Germany after the last war, by the Dawes Plan. I do not really see that our war performance during the past six years has called for the imposition of such a burden.

I submit that the conditions put forward for our approval are far too onerous. It is not untrue to say that comparable terms have never hitherto been imposed on a nation that has not been defeated in war. To get through, and pay our debt, on the admission of the Government, we shall have to increase our exports by 75 per cent.; not 50 per cent. any more, but 75 per cent., over pre-war. If there ever was any chance of our achieving this aim, it has been removed by the conditions attached to the Loan which is now being given us. Lord Baldwin has been much criticised for the 1923 debt settlement; but the terms he obtained then were princely in comparison with these terms. And our position was incomparably better then. But we were compelled to repudiate, as we shall be compelled to repudiate this time. Look at the inevitable effect of our convertibility undertaking—to convert dollars freely, sterling into dollars —on our trade. No doubt hon. Members on both sides of the House have read the extremely able letter of Sir Hubert Henderson in "The Times" this morning. He wrote:

". . . all incentive to these countries to buy from us because we buy from them will be removed in about a year from now. Moreover, any part of the huge accumulated sterling balances which countries in the sterling area are allowed to spend at all must be made equally available for dollar as for sterling purchases."

I was told only yesterday that some of our engineering firms have orders from countries in the sterling area up to 1950 and 1951 for capital goods and machinery, for delivery two, three, four, even five, years hence. As soon as this program begins, a very considerable number of these contracts will be transferred immediately to the United States. Can you imagine, for example, that India, or Egypt, as soon as they get convertible currency in exchange for their sterling balances, will not go straight to the United States of America; not because they dislike this country particularly, but because they can get the goods more quickly delivered. For the United States are well on the way to complete reconversion; in fact, they have already practically converted their industries to a peace basis, and we have a long way still to go in this direction. . . .

I would ask the President of the Board of Trade to answer this question. Is there anything in the Agreement which obliges the United States, in any circumstances, to make cuts in her tariffs of a magnitude that would assure a substantial importation of goods into the United States of America? Anyway, what is the value of the United States of America as a market to this country? Compare it with the value of the Empire market, which we are throwing away. There is only one certain export to the United States, and that is whisky. It stood by us during the war, and before; but the Government and particularly the Board of Trade, have been doing their best during the last five months to ruin the whisky industry by cutting down the supply of raw materials. It is madness, if dollars are what we are after. And

the Government seems to be very keen on dollars. In the Bretton Woods Agreement, and in every one of these White Papers, the onus is put upon the debtor nation to re-establish equilibrium in the balance of trade; and there is no onus at all upon the creditor nations.

I am going to speak bluntly, and say that there are two main objectives underlying the agreement which we are being asked to approve. The first is to get back as quickly as possible to the economic system of the 19th century— the system of *laissez faire* capitalism. The second is to break up, and prise open, the markets of the world for the benefit of the United States of America, who have an intense desire to get rid of their surplus products, which will be enormous, at any cost. . . .

What is the purpose of trade? Surely it is to raise the standard of living by the mutually advantageous exchange of goods. That is a principle that the United States will not realise. They think that trade is the building up of an export surplus, in exchange for debt or gold. That is their idea of trade, and that is the policy they are now about to resume on a colossal scale. There can be only one result of it, and it will be the same as it was the last time. Between the two wars, international trade became a ruthless pursuit for gold. But the struggle for export markets did nothing to increase the real wealth of the world. It meant simply that some countries exported their unemployment to others, which got into unpayable debt as a result. . . . And this, in turn, led to stagnation, and to dislocation of the entire world economy, and ultimately to world war.

I want now to put two propositions to the Chancellor of the Exchequer. The first is that multilateral trade and free convertibility, to which this Agreement admittedly commits us, are impractical in the modern world. Mr. Amery, . . . wrote, a little while ago:

"The unregulated and unbalanced flow of international trade on *laissez faire* principles may, like the unregulated flow of water, prove disastrous to all concerned. Deluge and drought, boom and slump, over-production side by side with under-consumption, are in each case the natural concomitants of leaving water, or trade and investment, to find their own level."

I believe that that is profoundly true. . . .

My second proposition is that we cannot have a planned national economy with international economic anarchy. It has been left to a Socialist Government to lead us back to international economic anarchy and to the economic system of the 19th century, the system of *laissez faire* capitalism, which crashed to destruction in 1929. The next time that an American slump comes—will anybody deny, by the way, the possibility of another American slump? Or do we all think that America's economic stability is now so great that they will

never have another? . . . It is great optimism on their part if they place such reliance in the operation of free, knock-about Capitalism. I have no such confidence in the economic system of the United States of America. . . .

These terms are hard. They are very hard. As the "Economist" truly says:

"Our present needs are the direct consequences of the fact that we fought earliest, that we fought longest, and that we fought hardest".

The Americans have had full value from Lend-Lease. In addition, they have made a substantial capital profit on the securities we were forced to sell in order to save them in 1941. We made nothing out of that transaction, because we shot off what we got in defense of the United States of America. As the "Economist" rightly says:

"It is for them to say what pleasure they derive from a bargaining victory won over their best friend"—

I would add at such a moment and at such a price.

Parliamentary Debates, Commons, fifth series, Vol. 417, December 12, 1945, cols. 455-469.

B. *The Marshall Plan*

While the end of the war in 1945 brought to the fore certain economic problems of an immediate nature, it was not until 1947 that the full extent of Europe's economic plight was revealed. At the same time it became emphatically clear that economic stability and political stability in Europe went hand in hand. By mid-summer of 1947 the containment of the Soviet Union and the economic rehabilitation of Europe were seen as one problem by the United States and the European countries that were beyond the orbit of Russian control.

The winter months of 1947 were bitterly cold and brought with them much suffering combined with a temporary retardation of economic activity. The first real shock of

the year came with the announcement that Great Britain would from March 31 suspend responsibility for the solvency and security of Greece. This posed the possibility of an important expansion of Soviet power into the Eastern Mediterranean and forced the American government to the annunciation, on March 12, of the "Truman Doctrine," which extended American military and financial aid to both Greece and Turkey. The primary purpose of the new responsibilities was to "contain" the Soviet Union, which at the time had created considerable frustration and alarm through the exercise of her veto powers in the Security Council and the use of her political power in the Balkans.

The spring months were further plagued by trouble in Palestine, the rise of the de

Gaullist movement in France, and further anxiety on the subject of communist intransigeance. It was in this tense atmosphere that General Marshall, who had become Secretary of State on January 7, made the speech at the Harvard University commencement exercises in which he held out to Europe the prospect of American financial aid extending over the next three or four years. This offer contained the condition that the European countries must agree upon their requirements and help themselves and each other before relying upon the United States. While the offer was extended to all Europe, it was widely believed that the Soviet Union would find it impossible to accept, and that some embarrassment might be created for the communists by the reactions of the states under Russian domination to the offer. Marshall's speech was thus a move in the struggle for Europe that was now going on between the Soviet Union and the United States, and was made at a time of pronounced tension. Quite beyond the struggle, however, it had economic implications of vast importance for the future of Europe.

Great Britain took the lead in welcoming the offer. Various views of its meaning and implication for Britain and the "West" are set forth along with the rejection of the offer for the "East." The latter view is expressed by Molotov, who represented the Soviet Union at the Paris meeting summoned to formulate Europe's answer to Marshall's proposition.

1. *The Times* VIEWS WITH APPROVAL

The Times is one of the world's most famous newspapers. At this period in its existence it was independent in its political outlook. Its editorials, or leaders, are frequently inspired by official sources and are always mature and serious comments upon the affairs of the day. Here, as elsewhere, it champions the case for Anglo-American co-operation.

. . . The United States Government is itself clearly aware that further American aid, beyond that already contemplated, will be needed for European reconstruction. It is no less clear that the difficulty of giving such aid in a form that will be acceptable to the American public is fully recognized, and that Mr. Marshall's plan must represent a careful choice of method.

The urgency of this matter scarcely needs elaboration. The United Kingdom's dollar credits, which represent a major part of the dollars available for the whole of the non-American world, are being rapidly exhausted. The pace of withdrawal has grown alarmingly, and drawings appear to have risen to a rate of well over £50,000,000 a month. Of the original amount of £937,500,000, only £450,000,000 is left, and proportionately an even larger part of the Canadian credit has been consumed. Such dollars as are still left to other European countries are almost certainly being spent just as rapidly, for the United States is running a current trade surplus of not much less than £100,000,000 a month with the world at large, and most of the European countries are heavily in deficit on their current international trading accounts. From this position there is little prospect of any early relief. This country's adverse balance is as high as ever, and many other European countries are in a similar condition. Production in most of the war-ravaged countries is gaining ground gradually, it is true, and it is reasonable to look for an eventual fall in the price of foodstuffs. This would greatly assist the United Kingdom and indeed all the European countries which import food heavily and are principally dependent on manufactured goods for their export trade. But relief from these sources can only be gradual.

In the circumstances it cannot be hoped that the balance between the two hemispheres can be significantly redressed at any early date by a large increase in American imports. The appeal to the United States to import more heavily, so cogent in the long run, is of only limited relevance in the short. The United States has indeed a better long-term record as an importer than is often suggested. During the eight years before the war, she covered no less than nineteen-twentieths of her current oversea receipts by imports of goods and services other than gold. It is doubtful whether her current imports of goods and services now represent more than half her exports. But, as the National City Bank of New York points out in its current review, the reason is to be found largely in sheer inability to buy because other countries cannot produce and deliver. For the moment both the huge American export surplus and the huge import surpluses of the impoverished countries of Europe and elsewhere are the result not of trade policy but simply of their respective wealth and poverty. In the circumstances, for a year or two at least, a gap will remain which can only be filled satisfactorily by American loans and investments for the benefit of the impoverished countries of Europe and the East. There has been no sign that arrangements made so far will be likely to fill the gap adequately. Government-sponsored lending agencies might delay the dollar crisis for six months or even twelve, but they could not avert it.

. . . Mr. Marshall and his advisers have evidently concluded that a plan aimed openly at financing European reconstruction in accordance with an inclusive plan sponsored by the European Governments themselves would stand more chance of popular support in the United States than any attempt to finance individual countries directly in the more orthodox manner. This idea of a general European agreement as the basis for American assistance has evidently been gaining ground in America; it was elaborated in detail recently by Mr. Walter Lippmann. It is to be hoped that the United States is not intending to insist on a fully coordinated economic plan as a condition of assistance. Americans will no doubt be conscious of the differences between the policies and interests of the separate countries, of the absence of elaborate economic plans in the individual countries themselves, and the difficulty of framing them, let alone that of coordinating them into an agreed plan covering most of a continent. But general agreement within Europe on the principal directions in which help is required should not be impossible to secure.

Europe cannot afford a merely passive response. It is for European Governments to ascertain what the United States Government really requires, to undertake such negotiation and organisation among themselves as may be needed, and, if necessary, to explain where and why any of the requirements cannot be met. The element of time is crucial. The American public is clearly still far from the stage where large-scale American financial assistance would find general support. Europe herself may be far from the stage where she could produce any common policy which the United States would find convincing. Mr. Marshall has produced an idea which is politically courageous as well as economically constructive. It can hardly be a simple task to win American public support for so far-reaching and substantial an interest in European affairs as this plan implies. It is for the European Governments to show the same sort of courage and imagination in organising a cooperative response.

The Times (London), June 7, 1947, p. 5.

2. *The Guardian* VIEWS WITH CONCERN

The Manchester Guardian enjoys the same sort of prestige that surrounds *The Times*. It is a Liberal paper and its editorials frequently reflect a great concern with basic Liberal principles. Well to the fore in its argument is its concern with the basic conditions for international trade.

That the United States Government has moved a long way toward a positive policy of aid for European reconstruction was shown by the Secretary of State's speech on Thursday. Mr. Marshall recognised that to restore Europe's economic structure would take a longer time and a greater effort than had been foreseen. Outside help would be needed for "the next three or four years." It is plain enough that whether Europe can slowly recover or must suffer a further collapse depends on getting this help, and that only the United States can give it. But many people in Britain and on the Continent, as well as in North America, have been trying to hide their heads in the sand. Mr. Marshall's speech promises a great advance on the piecemeal aid that seemed to be all that Europe might get in the future. The United States, he said, should do whatever it could to "assist in the return of normal economic health to the world." It is reasonable that the United States, in order to make sure that the aid is well used, should want European countries to draw up a definite programme of reconstruction which American goods would then help them to carry out. The Secretary of State seems now to have accepted Mr. Lippmann's view that the United States should provide "working capital for a reorganised European economy" and not merely hand out doles to bankrupt governments. That is fair enough. And it is plain that reconstruction will be easier if the European countries can make a concerted programme. But it would be a pity to put too much stress on this "unification." In the present state of American opinion the aid would then seem to be mainly a subsidy to an anti-Russian group. That would make it politically impossible, the American must realise, for some of the Governments of Western and Central Europe to take part. In any case such a grouping would, if it became at all exclusive, be more dependent on American loans than either its members or the United States could wish. Western Europe has little hope of eventually paying its way in the world unless its trade with Eastern Europe can be revived. An attempt should therefore at least be made to carry out the reconstruction programme through the United Nations' European Economic Commission, of which Russia is a member.

If this is done Europe will respond to Mr. Marshall's suggestion with enthusiasm, yet not with confidence. There is too much reason for fearing that the present dollar crisis will be relieved only to be succeeded by another. Nothing could do more to allay this fear than the success of the attempts of the trade conference at Geneva to reduce tariffs. Its work in the last two months, however, has been less promising than seemed possible. Its achievements cannot in any case become clear until almost the last moment, when the various concessions which each country might make can be fitted together into a whole pattern of tariff cuts. What is discouraging, therefore, is not that there has been no definite progress but that the main difficulty has come from an internal conflict about American policy. The Australians asked for a cut of 50 per cent in the American tariff on wool, and the American delegates replied by offering to bind it at its present level. That was a reasonable beginning for bargaining. But in the meantime the House of Representatives passed a Bill that would add a new duty of 50 per cent to wool imports. The Senate has rejected this and it is unlikely that in fact any increase in the tariff will be made while Mr. Truman is in office. But it is also unlikely that any cut can be made, and that may greatly reduce the size and number of the other tariff cuts that might have been agreed at Geneva.

The proposed international trade organisation would still serve a useful purpose even if few tariff cuts were agreed to at Geneva. It would provide a means of international consultation about commercial policies that might gradually reduce the severity of restrictions on trade. Moreover, it would be a way of positive co-operation to increase and stabilise the volume of world demand for goods. It is on that, even more than on a reduction in tariffs and quotas, that

the expansion of world trade depends. That means, above all, American demand. The American Government knows well enough that world prosperity depends on a large and fairly stable supply of dollars, but so far it has not been able to convince Congress or, probably, most Americans. Other countries cannot feel confident that either of the two ways in which they may get dollars is at all assured. Their exports to the United States may always be small because of high tariffs, and an American slump may cut their whole trade sharply. In the same slump, if not before, the United States may stop lending abroad. These risks have to be taken in any case. Europe cannot afford not to try to expand trade. But it is for the Americans to see that the attempt does not break down.

The Manchester Guardian, June 7, 1947, p. 6.

3. *The Statist* VIEWS WITH ALARM

The Statist is not for the general reader; it is published in the City of London and finds its clientele among the financial and commercial interests that surround it. It is intensely conservative in tone and frequently expresses partisan views in a rather strident manner. Its attack upon the Marshall Plan has, perhaps, more of politics than economics in it.

To say "What's the motive?" to Mr. Marshall would be as ungracious as looking a gift horse in the mouth. . . . Nonetheless, the mental question is not only a fair one, but is inevitable. To say that the prime need of every nation is world rehabilitation is to include the United States in that shared want. Indeed, the test of Mr. Marshall's sincerity is the tacit avowal that dollars to Europe, on a new lend-lease basis, are to be offered as much from a motive of national self-preservation as from that of philanthropy. Mr. Michael Foot, amongst others, has put the position succinctly—Europe lacks dollars

and America has too many. Rephrased, that means that America is faced with a plethora of production and Europe offers a continuance of want. . . . If [dollars are] not forthcoming by one means or another, Europe may plunge rapidly, under the impetus of Russia, into a welter of Bolshevised Communism, and the United States may topple headlong again into the very kind of slump which cenotaphed Mr. Hoover's tenure of the White House.

The choice for Europe, as many here view it (unfairly, in our opinion, to America), is an awkward one. It is a choice between physical helotry to the Soviets or economic serfdom to the loan-providers of Washington and Wall Street. . . . More bluntly, again as many see it, whichever of the choices is Europe's destiny, the political and social shape of things to come must be alien to the traditions of the communities affected.

. . . By linking, in the closest possible economic way, the rehabilitated Europe to America, it would make the Pacific coast the dominant factor in European international relations. Britain need not be much concerned about such an effect. ... It might, however, strongly change the value of the Danubian and Mediterranean factors, by shifting the focal point of our concern in world affairs from (so to speak) Vienna to a Washington-Ottawa axis. ... Mr. Marshall himself is wise enough to realise that the attitude of many Britons to his proposal cannot be other than that of the burnt child which dreads the fire. Our present expiring dollar loan was borrowed at one rate and is being spent at another. ... Similarly, the Anglo-American bargain on the allocation of costs in the joint Anglo-American zone in Germany pressed heavily on this country, which could have been relieved of a strong drain on the dollar, but was not, as Washington insisted upon equal contributions.

Great Britain has a further cause, if not for fear, for caution. The existing, but rapidly shrinking, dollar loan was bought at a heavy cost. For it we sacrificed our age-old sovereignty over our own currency and our right to make what trading arrangements within the Imperial connections we and our racial kinsmen might please. To gratify America, and, of course, to give ourselves immediate relief, we sold in 1945 a portion of our Imperial birthright for a mess of dollars that have proved less valuable in the spending than in the negotiating. We do not want, in 1947 or 1948, to purchase a rehabilitated Europe at the cost of a completely disintegrated British Commonwealth and the final loss of the sovereignty of the United Kingdom over its own external relations. ... In the last resort, America must lend, that is, America must find a series of recipients for her power-produced products, whereas Europe need not borrow, that is, need not, if the political fabric can stand the strain. ...

... When the Marshall project is restated in more specific terms, with the knowledge that not only the Secretary of State and the President are behind it, but Congress also, the attitude of our own Executive should be one of caution mingled with courtesy rather than one of mere sentimental gratitude coloured by political fear of an unstemmed Communism from beyond the Urals.

The Statist, CVL (June 14, 1947), 627-628.

4. Molotov Rejects

V. M. Molotov, Soviet Minister for Foreign Affairs, went to Paris to consider the arrangements to be made to carry out the Marshall Plan. At the end of the meetings he was interviewed by *Le Monde*. His rejection of the Plan is an indictment of the intentions of the United States, Great Brittain, and France for their supposed attempt to dominate the arrangements for the distribution of the aid.

It is a matter, he [Molotov] said, of creating a new organization which would be placed over the European countries and which would intervene in their internal affairs even to the point of giving directives concerning the development of their principal industries. At the same time, Great Britain and France and the countries closely associated with them have the pretension to create for themselves a predominant position at the center of this organization. Some verbal assurances have been given that this organization would not intervene in the internal affairs of the member states nor in any way threaten their sovereignty. But it is clearly apparent that the European countries would become, nevertheless, controlled countries and would lose their former economic and political independence to satisfy the designs of certain great powers. In all instances it is intended to control the grant of American credits to countries by their obedient conduct toward the organization and its directing committee.

. . . the Soviet government considers

Le Monde, July 4, 1947, p. 1.

II. UNITED NATIONS: THE PROBLEM OF THE VETO

The League of Nations failed in the sense that it did not prevent the occurrence of World War II. Despite this failure, there was widespread determination to create a new set of international institutions at the end of the war. In fact, the lives of the various nations had become so intertwined that it would be almost impossible to think of a world without some integrating principle and without machinery for the furtherance of international co-operation.

The creation of the United Nations was not in itself a problem, since there was never a serious question of having or not having an international organization. The problems, rather, were the form that it should take and the procedures it should use. Among its procedures the one that has given the most trouble has been the method of voting. The basic question was whether any one of the five great powers, by casting a negative vote, should be permitted to block action by the Security Council to prevent war or punish an aggressor. To many the effectiveness of the United Nations would depend upon the power of the Security Council to act in dealing with circumstances threatening peace. If a great power could veto action, would not this deprive the United Nations of its greatest usefulness to the world?

This problem could not be settled at the Dumbarton Oaks Conference (1944) at which so much concerning the future United Nations was formulated. The question of voting was referred to the Yalta Conference (February, 1945) for consideration by Roosevelt, Churchill, and Stalin. It was here that the decision was made to give the veto power to each of the five

it contrary to the interests of the European countries that the decisive role in the economic reconstruction should be played by the United States and not by the countries themselves. This is incompatible with the maintenance of national sovereignties.

great powers. Apparently the decision was much desired by both the Soviet Union and the United States as a protection against being committed to a future line of action on behalf of the United Nations without the approval of the government concerned. At the San Francisco Conference the Yalta decision stood despite vigorous attack and objections by many of the 45 lesser powers, and the Charter contained the provision that no enforcement action could be undertaken by the Council except upon the approval of seven of the eleven members. The five great powers must be included in the seven, though it has since been determined that an abstention does not count as a veto.

There were some hopes at the time that the veto power would remain in reserve and would not be used except upon the most important occasions. These were quickly dispelled. By 1946 the Assembly was requesting the Council not to employ the veto in an immoderate manner, and as we see by the following excerpts the veto had become a serious problem. It is symptomatic, however, of the more basic problem of the antipathy between the East and West.

A. Attlee's Misgivings

Clement Attlee was Prime Minister at the time when he criticized the use of the veto power. It was possible for him, speaking in the House of Commons, to be more forthright in his criticisms than it would have been for the British delegate speaking before the Assembly, or a commission, of the United Nations. At the same time, he could be certain that his remarks would be noticed.

I would call attention this afternoon to another matter which is down for discussion and which is of vital importance to the very existence of the United Nations organisation. That is the question of the veto in the Security Council. It raises the whole question of the value of the Security Council. I have in my mind very vivid recollections of the San Francisco Conference. I attended there with my right hon. Friend the Member for Warwick and Leamington (Mr. Eden), my right hon. Friend the Minister of Works, and other Members of the Coalition Government. We worked as a team, and much hard work was done. There was a spirit in that meeting of hopefulness and good will. I cannot help expressing a feeling of disappointment at the recent performances in the Security Council. It has undoubtedly given an impression of disunity and ineffectiveness—such as to raise doubts about its value as an instrument for preserving international peace and security. This, I think, is not due to any fault in the machinery which was devised, but in the use to which it has been put.

After all, the underlying hypothesis that unless the five leading Powers were in general agreement on the policy to be pursued by the Security Council there was little hope for the preservation of peace, was, I think, correct. I think it took account of the realities of the situation. But it all depends on what is meant by "in agreement," what is meant by "unanimity." If the Security Council is only going to be able to decide on a line of action in the case where the five great Powers have all made up their minds in advance, and find themselves in agreement before discussion in the Security Council, the occasions on which the Council can reach positive decision will, I am afraid, be very few.

At San Francisco we agreed to the creation of the veto, but I am quite certain that we all regarded this as something to be used only in the last resort in extreme cases where the five great Powers might be involved in conflict. We never conceived it as a device to be used constantly whenever a particular Power was not in full agreement with the others. Yet that is just what has happened recently. The veto was used for every trifling thing and that is reducing to a nullity the usefulness of the Security Council. What is more, it is leading to disrespect, whereas the Security Council was created in order to create confidence, to command confidence as a quasi-judicial body in matters of differences between States which involved the danger of war.

The use of the Security Council as a propaganda instrument is to be regretted. It is the desire of His Majesty's Government that this body should return to and fulfil its original intention so that the world may feel that there exists an instrument which, when matters cannot be settled by negotiation between countries, stands ready to intervene and bring impartial minds to bear upon the issues involved. Nothing will be so disastrous to the peace of the world as to allow the respect, dignity and power of the Security Council to be brought to nought.

While His Majesty's Government are not at the present time prepared to move that there should be any change in the Charter, we certainly are of the opinion that there should be a review of the use of the veto with a view to restraining it to its original intent. After all, what was our conception of the Security Council? Our conception was that the meetings of the great Powers and their discussions in Council were for the purpose of exchanging points of view and making concessions where necessary, and of realising that it was more important that the Security Council should reach a corporate decision than that the viewpoint of individuals should be maintained through thick and thin. In fact, if the Security Council is to be worked, it must be worked with a belief in the democratic method of arriving at results. There must be good will. There must be acceptance of the democratic principle of the rights and obligations of the majority and minority. We in this

House over many years have worked on that principle. Broadly speaking the will of the majority prevails, but the majority give full opportunity for the minority to put their views and both sides understand the point beyond which it is unwise to insist.

Parliamentary Debates, Commons, fifth series, Vol. 427, October 23, 1946, cols. 1673-1675.

B. A French Analysis

Le Monde, probably the most responsible of the Paris papers, devoted an editorial to the analysis of the veto problem. It went on to a suggested solution that might have much said for it in terms of logic, but little in terms of practical international politics.

The debate on the veto holds an important place in the considerations of the political commission of the United Nations. The Australian and Cuban delegates sustained before this commission their proposals to modify or revise the use of the veto power. The Australians demanded only that the use of the veto be restrained and that the members of the Security Council give their agreement to this. The Cuban delegation goes farther by asking that the General Assembly reconsider the article of the Charter dealing with the veto, and that a sub-committee before February 1 prepare, for submission to the General Assembly, a report covering the question of an amendment to the Charter.

In the discussions since the opening of the session, the opposition of the small powers to the veto has become increasingly obvious. If this opposition began at San Francisco, it has only been strengthened by the experience of the total paralysis worked by the veto upon the Security Council. Russia, on the other hand, will not consider the slightest restriction on the veto. The attitude of the other great powers is inconsistent if not contradictory. Sir Hartley Shaw-

cross, the British delegate, declares that in principle he is against the veto but does not wish it changed. It is the same with Mr. Connally, the American delegate, who wishes that the number of troublesome problems involving a possible use of the veto be kept to a minimum by employing the full possibilities of conciliation before the problems reach the stage of Council consideration. M. Parodi [French delegate] suggests that certain problems not compatible with the use of the veto—such as the control of atomic energy—be excluded from its operation.

These positions of the great powers are explained by their desire to save the United Nations which might not survive a conflict over the veto. That is why the delegates of the United States and Great Britain have spoken contrary to the views of their governments and the desires of public opinion in their own countries. It has been a necessary reiteration of the slogan of San Francisco: "No peace is possible without an agreement of the five great powers; there can be no agreement without the veto."

A formula which pretends to impose agreement by saying that it ought to exist is illusory. In reality the great powers are not in accord despite the veto. Their debates, without conclusions, merely postpone the disagreements until a future time when some conflict, graver than the others, will place peace—or, at least, the continuing existence of the United Nations—in peril.

. . . If the United Nations had an armed force at its disposal the arguments of the champions of the veto would become useless. Four great powers would be able to impose their will upon a fifth who would be able to resist only to the extent that it had been permitted to arm. With [national] armaments restricted and the existing level of armaments known to all, the erring nation would be obliged to submit to the United Nations. The veto, which is today considered detrimental would become a matter of indifference. . . .

Le Monde, December 3, 1946, p. 1.

C. The Russian Defense

In a speech before the General Assembly, Molotov pointed out the part played by the question of the veto in the establishment of the United Nations and warned that the United Nations would not survive any tampering with the operation of the veto power.

The principle of the unanimity of the great Powers was adopted not by chance, but after a thorough and lengthy discussion. The recognition of this principle reflected the desire of the United Nations to ensure co-ordination and unity of action on the part of the great Powers in counteracting any possible aggression. Before the second world war the great Powers were not animated by this desire for unity of action in defence of peace and security, and therein lay the greatest misfortune for the whole of mankind. The United States stood aloof from the high road, so to speak. In regard to the Soviet Union, the principal members of the League of Nations pursued a short-sighted and out-and-out reactionary policy.

The hard trials of the war led the Governments of the great western Powers to the conviction that it was necessary to act in harmony against the common enemy during the war, and to the recognition of the necessity of forming such an international organization to deal with post-war problems as would maintain the profoundly progressive principle forged in the war, the principle of the unity of the great Powers which rallied around them all the democratic States. It follows from this that the principle of the unanimity of the great Powers in matters relating to the defence of peace and security is deeprooted, and that this principle was recognized by the United Nations, which were activated by the desire for a more reliable defence of the interests of all the peace-loving States, both great and small.

Of late, a wide-scale campaign has been launched against the recognition of this principle. No chance was lost of engaging in long-winded discussions of this principle, while the problem of the necessary unity of the great Powers is glossed over in every way and is constantly being replaced by the specific question of the manner in which the so-called "veto" is to be applied in deciding questions in the Security Council.

What is the meaning of this campaign against the veto, that is to say, against the right of any of the great Powers not to permit a decision to be adopted in the Security Council which it considers undesirable in the interests of the maintenance of peace and international security? What will be the outcome of renunciation of the principle of unanimity of the great Powers in deciding questions of this nature?

It is easy to foresee the results of such a renunciation. No one will now suggest that we should go back to the bankrupt League of Nations with its unanimity of all members in adopting decisions. Consequently there is a desire to utilize the renunciation of this principle in order to impose a procedure whereby decisions would be adopted by a majority vote. Proposals to this effect have already been made here in the General Assembly. There are even people who represent such a procedure for the adoption of decisions within an international organization as the most democratic one, as if the best democracy worthy of universal recognition would be to consider, in an international organization, that the vote of Honduras is equal to that of the United States of America, or the vote of Haiti to that of the Union of Soviet Socialist Republics, which represents a federation of sixteen Republics. It seems obvious that it is not worth while wasting words on arguments regarding this sort of "democracy."

However, this does not mean that the campaign conducted under the guise of the struggle against the veto can be ignored. It would be extremely shortsighted to regard this campaign as a fortuitous and insignificant matter. It would also be naive to overlook the fact that the campaign has assumed a character which is definitely hostile to the Soviet Union. None of us are blind from birth; nobody here could fail to see that the downright reactionaries are already making capital out of this campaign. . . .

Imagine what would happen if the campaign to abolish the so-called veto were crowned with success! What would be the political consequences?

It is quite obvious that the repudiation of the principle of unanimity of the great Powers, and this is what is actually behind the proposal for the abolition of the veto, would mean, in fact, the liquidation of the United Nations, because this principle is the cornerstone of that Organization. Perhaps not all the participators in this noisy campaign sufficiently realize whence it is leading. But inasmuch as the United Nations is based on the principle of unanimity of the great Powers, the abolition of this principle will result in the collapse of the very edifice of the United Nations.

But this is not the only question at issue. The success of this campaign would mean victory for a policy which would enable one group of States, led by the strongest of the Powers, to dominate the other Powers, which would then find themselves in the minority. Instead of a policy of international cooperation in the spirit of the democratic principles of the United Nations, the triumphant policy would be that of the new claimants to world domination as represented by a corresponding *bloc* or, if you wish, by a group of Powers to which the retention of the principle of unanimity of the great Powers already seems to be irksome.

The disputes and struggles that are going on around the so-called veto indicates the intensification of the antagonisms between the two fundamental political tendencies, one of which consists in the defence of the principle, which we all recognize, of international cooperation among the big and small States, while the other one consists in the desire of certain influential groups to have a free hand in order to wage a frantic struggle for world domination. An attitude of neutrality in such a question is ambiguous and inappropriate.

United Nations. *Plenary Meetings of the General Assembly,* 23 October–16 December, 1946, pp. 836-838, 840-841.

III. UNITED EUROPE (COUNCIL OF EUROPE)

The United Nations was formed in response to the demand for international institutions to promote peace and cooperation. Within the United Nations it was possible to have organizations of a regional character to deal with problems common to a group of nations. The idea that a political organization common to all should be created for western Europe was not new; it arose from the realization that economically and culturally western Europe is largely one. Many believed, however, that nationalism and the antagonisms of the past were too strong for any effective political union; others favored the formation of a union but differed as to its functions and strength. The range of attitudes toward the problems of a more united Europe is illustrated by four European political figures, and an English historian.

Students should bear in mind, however, that the particular aspect of the problem selected for comment deals specifically with the political union of western Europe. This part of the problem has been selected because it would seem to offer the greatest range of development for the future. The central organ for the political organization of western Europe is the Council of Europe which meets in Strasbourg. In addition, one should bear in mind the existence of other arrangements—chiefly economic—for securing some degree of European cooperation.

One of these grew out of the practical demands of the Marshall plan. It will be recalled that this plan called for a set of estimates of economic needs by various nations and a program of economic cooperation. The European nations participating in the plan created for themselves a common economic arrangement called the Organization for European Economic Cooperation (O.E.E.C.). This Organization was entrusted with the task of drawing up an economic program for individual countries providing for the creation of sound foundations that would preclude in the future the necessity for extraordinary outside aid. The O.E.E.C. in addition made arrangements for the allocation of American aid under the Marshall plan and established arrangements to make it easier for European countries to trade with, and thus aid, each other. Through O.E.E.C. a very commendable degree of European economic cooperation has been secured.

Another economic arrangement of a later date (1951) is known as the Schuman plan. Taking its name after one of the more remarkable of the post-war French political leaders, the plan calls for the integration of the coal and iron and steel industries of France, Germany, Italy, Belgium, Holland and Luxembourg. These countries have placed these industries under a common management and have opened their markets in such a fashion that coal and iron may move freely from one to the other. The Schuman plan is, perhaps, the most encouraging evidence of voluntary cooperation since the war.

In addition, evidences of military cooperation may be found in the European Defense Community and the North Atlantic Treaty Organization. Long run hopes for great achievements, however, would seem to rest upon the political integration of western Europe and for this reason the Council of Europe has been selected as the central problem in securing a united Europe.

A. Reynaud Supports a Federation

Paul Reynaud was once premier of France. His argument for a Council of Europe, possessing great power and resting upon a direct vote of the European people, is in the French tradition of giving support to international organizations in such a way that they become endowed with some of the machinery and many of the powers of a national state. Reynaud is arguing for the creation of a supranational state.

It is clear that, because of the decrease in America's national income during 1949 and the budgetary deficit due to military expenditures, Congress will make substantial reductions in Marshall Plan appropriations unless Western Europe, in return for the sacrifices demanded of American taxpayers, takes a decisive step toward unification. Many Europeans, particularly on the Continent itself, have understood the need to build a united Europe. Following my return from captivity, in 1945, I, for one, went to see Sir Alfred Duff Cooper, then British Ambassador to France, and told him this was one of the conclusions I had reached during the years of meditation that I owed to Adolf Hitler. The 1948 Congress of Europe at The Hague, of which Winston Churchill was the moving spirit and in which nationals of all the Western European countries participated except Germany, Spain and Portugal, gave powerful expression to the desire of Europeans of every party except the Communist to build a single Europe. The Governments were obliged as a result to create a Committee of Five, in which France, Great Britain and the Benelux nations were represented, to study the question. This Committee, of which I was a member, met in Paris in December 1948 and January 1949 under the chairmanship of Mr. Herriot. The British Government instructed its representatives in such a fashion that it was impossible to reach agreement, and the Committee had to submit to the respective Governments the resolution of the British delegation on the one hand and that of all the other delegations on the other. The British resolution stipulated that the Consultative Assembly should consist of only 40 members and that each delegation should have as its chief a minister empowered to cast the vote of the entire delegation. . . .

The Governments did reach agreement on May 5, 1949, upon a statute similar to that originally opposed by the British. With the addition of the Scandinavian countries, Ireland, Italy, Greece and Turkey, the Consultative Assembly now has 101 members belonging to 12 nations, and each member has the right to vote as he pleases. The members are appointed either by the parliaments, as is the case in France and Italy, or by the Governments, as is the case in Great Britain and Belgium. The only right enjoyed by this assembly is that of discussion. Here too it is limited. For the present it may debate only such subjects as have been accepted for the agenda by the Committee of Foreign Ministers. It may not encroach upon the functions of existing agencies such as the O. E. E. C. nor concern itself with problems related to national defense. It can merely submit recommendations to the Committee of Foreign Ministers which, in turn, submits them to the respective Governments. The latter are free to accept or reject them.

As we have seen, Great Britain agreed to the creation of the Council of Europe with extreme distrust. Under these circumstances and with these very limited powers the Assembly met at Strasbourg for a month, from August 10 to September 9, 1949. At that time, Leon Blum expressed surprise that no Mirabeau rose up in the Assembly to demand extension of its powers. . . . Leon Blum forgot that this was because Mirabeau had been elected by the people. If Mr. Churchill had spoken in such terms, his opponent, Mr. Morrison, would have answered: "Why no, Mr. Churchill, you are here by the will of Mr. Attlee." The weakness of this Assembly lies in the method by which its members are chosen.

At the Congress at The Hague I pointed out how difficult it would be to make the interest of Europe prevail over the selfish interests of each nation, and declared that the only chance of success was to shock public opinion in all countries. I said that we must therefore appeal to the peoples through the democratic mechanism of elections. I proposed that the Assembly should be elected by universal suffrage, with one deputy for each million inhabitants voting not as Englishmen, Frenchmen or Italians but as Europeans. This proposal was rejected by an overwhelming majority. A Conservative British M.P. objected with the old French proverb: "Make haste slowly." To which I retorted that this was strange advice to give to a drowning man trying to grasp a branch. A French Socialist, former Premier Paul Ramadier, accused me of being "ahead of the times." I accepted his criticism in good part, remembering what price my country and the world had paid for the mistakes of those who, before the war, were behind the times.

Today a current of opinion is forming in favor of repairing this initial error; but it seems unlikely that the British Government will allow itself to be convinced.

. . . As I listened [to critics] I could not help thinking of Bismarck's phrase that Germany's unity would be forged only by blood and iron, and also of the formula of our own French historian, Jacques Bainville: "In order to build a federation there must be a federating state." There is such a state in Eastern Europe. Are we in Western Europe incapable, I asked, of achieving by an act of our own will what, in another part of the world, is imposed by a dictator?

Paul Reynaud, "The Unifying Force for Europe," *Foreign Affairs*, XXVIII (1949–1950), 260-262.

B. Stikker Argues for a Functional Approach

Smaller countries are often conservative in their approach to international problems. Dirk Strikker, a former foreign minister in the government of the Netherlands, contends that the political organization of Western Europe must proceed slowly by giving the Council of Europe things of a practical and limited nature to do.

There is no single center of European gravity around which the nations can group to speed up this process [of federation]. That is the reason why the functional approach offers the most direct path to the goal. "Functional integration" is based on the existence of very real national interests, and at the same time recognizes the necessity of subordinating separate interests more and more to the common welfare. It is based on a mixture of realism and idealism. It seeks to restrict national sovereignty, but does not attempt the feat of abolishing it at one stroke; to await the ideal situation in which complete federation became possible would

mean never starting at all. It proposes that the countries of Western Europe at once proceed to cooperate wherever they can. Whenever a nation enters a new field of cooperation national sovereignty is transferred to a certain extent by that very fact. These new organizations create what might be called a limited federation—limited not geographically but functionally. In short, this approach does not claim to provide the final answer to Europe's problems but simply a series of practical steps forward. It is not a theoretical answer but an outcome of the concrete developments of the last few years.

. . . The proponents of federation have met with opposition from the British and Scandinavian Governments. The suggestion for a geographically limited federation—a "little Europe" which would omit Britain and Scandinavia—has also failed to win strong backing. The functional approach to European integration has, however, met with general approval. There is a general understanding of Britain's views that her relations with the rest of the

Commonwealth are too important to be risked in experiments in Europe, and that she must search for a form of organization which does justice both to her position in Europe and that within the Commonwealth. And there is hope that organs set up to meet limited concrete needs will help solve this problem for her and for the Scandinavian countries. No one wants a "rump Europe."

Dirk U. Stikker, "The Functional Approach to European Integration," *Foreign Affairs*, XXIX (1950–1951), 440-441.

C. Lange Cautions Delay and a Wider Framework

Norway frequently has had an English outlook. Here a teacher and former foreign minister, Halvard Lange, argues for a slow approach to the problems of Union. Much harm, he warns, can come from not realizing the formidable obstacles in the way.

In the Strasbourg Assembly there emerged in the course of last summer's debates two distinct schools of thought. The Latins (irrespective of party), most of the Benelux representatives and the British Conservatives favored what might be termed the constitutional, or the federal, approach to the problem. They wanted to start with a draft constitution for the United States of Europe. The Scandinavians, with hardly an exception and again irrespective of party, and most of the British Labor representatives, favored what might be called the functional approach. They wanted to take up concrete projects for practical cooperation in various fields and to evolve such inter-European machinery as would be necessary to carry out the projects.

At its session in Paris in November 1949, the Committee of Ministers of the Council of Europe inclined toward the functional rather than the constitutional approach. It favored a policy of caution, of making haste slowly. Norwegians were very glad that such was the case. In the Norwegian view, there would be considerable danger of provoking a popular revulsion against the idea of European union, if precipitate action were taken. It takes time to put before the public measures for a pooling of national sovereignties, to explain fully their implications, and to make clear why the measures are needed.

In this connection I think it is important to point out that the so-called European Movement may be dangerous in so far as it creates the illusion in the United States that there exists in Europe much more of a mass movement for European union than is actually the case. No doubt, opinion in favor of union is considerably stronger on the Continent than it is in Scandinavia. I seriously doubt, however, that the European Movement has as wide popular support as it claims. Some of the resolutions adopted by the Strasbourg Consultative Assembly may give a similar impression to that created by rallies of the European Movement. The Assembly, consisting as it does of individuals without defined constitutional responsibilities in their own countries, moves on a much less responsible level than does the Committee of Ministers. I am convinced that the Committee of Ministers is more truly representative of what popular opinion as a whole in Western Europe considers possible of achievement than is the European Movement or the Consultative Assembly.

. . . The problem of European union is our common problem. It is one problem among many which face us within our North Atlantic community, and I am convinced it can find its solution only in the wider context of Atlantic cooperation. Western Europe does not on its own possess enough natural resources to constitute a self-sufficient economic unit. Nor would it be desirable to make any attempt in the direction of European autarchy. Europe certainly must break down internal barriers which are out of harmony with technological and economic realities. But there would be scant advantage and might be real danger if integration within Europe should, in any way, result in any kind of European isolationism. There must be ever closer cooperation across the ocean. . . . To many Americans, the inevitable slowness of the process may seem depressing. Viewed in a historic perspective and from the Norwegian side of the Atlantic, developments of the last two and a half years are momentous. The establishment of O.E.E.C., the creation of the Western Union, the conclusion of the Atlantic Treaty and the setting up of the Council of Europe are no mean achievements in such a short span. Let us hope that the march of world events will give us the time we need to solve the problem of European unity by truly democratic methods.

Halvard M. Lange, "European Union: False Hopes and Reality," *Foreign Affairs*, XXVIII (1949–1950), 448-450.

D. Spaak Calls United Europe an Indispensable Need

Paul-Henri Spaak, a former prime minister of Belgium, is an outspoken champion of the project for Western Europe and a former president of the Council of Europe. The statement from him was not delivered in person as illness prevented his appearance before the meeting of the National Industrial Conference Board.

In this world there is no possible balance between the United States on the one hand, Great Britain, France, Italy and Western Germany isolated and divided, on the other. But there is a conceivable and desirable balance between the United States on the one hand, and a European community on the other. I attach the greatest importance to this point of view and see there an essential condition to the successful result of our efforts in the future.

Personally, I never felt that a Europe organized on the new basis should be considered like a Third Force, trying to take and keep a neutral position between the U.S.S.R. and the United States. Such an idea seems to me both utterly impracticable and utterly false. But I think that a new Europe must constitute a force which deliberately chooses its side and this must be that of the United States, since it is there that are found freedom, democracy, the respect of men and peace. But, it goes without saying that if on that side everyone must be able to act in a climate of friendship, they must also be able to act on a perfectly equal footing.

Thus a United Europe is not only necessary for the prosperity of the various European countries, it is indispensable to their political independence as well as to the balance of the world.

Speech by Paul-Henri Spaak, New York, September 27, 1951. The text may be found in *Vital Speeches of the Day*, XVIII (Oct. 15, 1951), 28.

E. Mansergh Points Out the Peculiar Position of Great Britain and the Empire

Nicholas Mansergh, an English historian, discusses the dilemma confronting Great Britain with her obligations to her worldwide Dominions and Empire and her responsibilities toward the political unification of Western Europe. May not these two obligations be in conflict? Need they be?

The most important conclusion to be drawn from . . . the reactions of the Dominions to Western Union is that the initiative lies with the United Kingdom. It is her responsibility to formulate policy in relation to Western Union, and the responsibility and the opportunity are the greater because of the very wide measure of support which the concept has elicited from the Dominions. In the formulation of policy her predominant concern must be to reconcile her interests in Europe and her interests overseas. On the strategic side this presents few difficulties; on the political and economic sides competing claims must be balanced. That can hardly be done if the approach is rigid or theoretic. It demands on the contrary a readiness to weigh practical issues as they arise and a prudent aversion to finalities. All this is in full accord with the traditional pragmatism . . . [so] characteristic of British statesmanship.

If not of equal, it is at least of considerable importance that the gaze of British statesmen should not rest exclusively on European problems, even if today Western Europe constitutes at once the danger zone and the most effective bastion of security for the Commonwealth as a whole. Mr. Mackenzie King has spoken of "leagues of free peoples" for which Western Union should be the pattern and of which it would remain the most important, but not the only one. This is a conception that seems to merit closer consideration. It is possible to conceive of a security system, in which the Commonwealth countries would in co-operation with the United States play a full part, composed of "leagues of free peoples" co-operating for their own defence in the Mediterranean, in the Indian Ocean, and in the Pacific areas. The interests and responsibilities of these "leagues of free peoples" could be dove-tailed, and as a whole, buttress the wider concept of the United Nations. For the Commonwealth, however important Western Europe must be, it is not and cannot be the only region in which leadership and organization is required. In this context the language of the Brussels Treaty is perhaps not wholly satisfactory. It speaks of an obligation on the part of the signatory powers to *"resist aggression in Europe."* It is argued that because, in the first place, Western Europe is the most likely target of attack and, in the second, that because outside Europe no major act of aggression could be countered effectively except through the active intervention of the United States, this restrictive phrase is at least innocuous. But in the event of aggression in the Middle East, in the Far East, or even in Southern Asia, in all of which areas the Commonwealth countries would almost certainly be involved, the possible neutrality of the other Western European Powers might be a positive disadvantage. It is not so much a question of what forces they might be able to send overseas, but of what forces they might be able to tie down by active participation in Europe. Whatever the merits of this particular provision, it does seem essential in general that the extra-European field should be consistently kept in the forefront in any future negotiations.

Behind all this lies a more far-reaching problem. The nations of the Commonwealth have cordially welcomed the consolidation of Western Europe on the assumption that it does not involve the United Kingdom in commitments which will either compel her to abandon, or leave her unable to fulfil, the extra-European role she has played in the past. Alliances involving a merging of authority with the Western Union States may prove acceptable and welcome, but any union involving the loss of the United Kingdom's freedom of action must raise for them the most formidable misgivings. The long-term question, therefore, that deserves the consideration of Empire statesmen is the extent to which Britain can, if she so wishes, co-operate in a Western Union whilst retaining a sufficient margin of resources and freedom of action to maintain effective leadership in the Commonwealth overseas.

Nicholas Mansergh, "Britain, the Commonwealth, and Western Union," *International Affairs*, XXIV (1948), 503-504.

IV. THE PROBLEM OF GERMANY

The unconditional surrender of the German forces in 1945 left Germany in the throes of defeat, occupation, economic ruin, and political disorganization. The succeeding years worked a remarkable transformation in Germany's condition without giving any considerable satisfaction in the solution of the major problem confronting Germany and the world: How was Germany to be brought back into the full enjoyment of her political independence and economic recovery without threatening the security of her neighbors or the peace of the world?

By 1947, with the failure of the London Conference, it seemed clear that the revival of Germany would not be accomplished by co-operative efforts. The difficulty of collaboration between the Soviet Union and the Western World in restoring Germany to a reasonable place in European society was now obvious, and the more important question emerged of whether the rehabilitation of Germany could take place at all without bringing East and West to war. Since that time the Western Allies fostered the establishment of a federal government at Bonn and transferred to that government a large measure of political power despite the fact that Germany remained under modified military occupation. This government had no authority over the Soviet Zone in the eastern part of Germany and had simultaneously to make its way toward a more complete power of its own and the unification of all Germany. Since 1949 this effort was made through a policy of co-operation with the Western powers and of opposition to the Soviet Union. The Bonn government was admitted to the economic arrangements of the West, entered the Schuman plan with France as a principal partner, and was concerned with the integration of her military forces, as they were revived, with the forces of the European Defense Community and the North Atlantic Treaty Organization.

These evidences of growing German strength and continuing tension between West and East did not leave all consciences at ease. Europe—especially France—had memories of German military strength that led to grave concern. Could Germany be made strong without being made dangerous? Would the concept of a European or North Atlantic defense force prove workable by mixing in Germany's military divisions with those of other nations? Would it deprive Germany of the possibility of aggressive action against her neighbors? Could Germany continue to live divided into a western part under the Bonn government with a westward affiliation, and an eastern part under the control of the Soviet Union? Would not the German desire to secure the unity of the country endanger the peace and threaten the new war which the strengthening of western Germany was designed to avoid? No limited selection of comments could possibly deal with all phases and aspects of the "German problem"; those that follow must be taken as suggestive only.

A. The Basic Necessity for a Franco-German Agreement

Jacques Soustelle, a former minister in various French governments and Secretary-General of the party supporting General Charles de Gaulle, argues here for a bilateral agreement between France and Germany at a time when the prevailing opinion favors a general Western European agreement.

Any consideration of the German question must begin with the elementary geographical fact that Germany is located in the heart of Europe, between the Slav world and the West. After 1945 there was but one possible policy to be followed toward Germany—the one advocated by the Provisional French Government under the leadership of General de Gaulle. It favored the rebirth of the German states—Baden, Wurttemberg, the Palatinate, etc.—and sought to make it possible for each of them to develop its own political and economic existence so that they would be incorporated in a federated Europe as distinct states, not as "Germany." This policy was neither understood nor supported by our British and American allies. On the contrary, they urged the fusion of the three Western zones and the creation of the Republic of Bonn. Inevitably, this raised the question of the unity of all Germany. Even after the birth of the Western republic a safer policy was still available, however. If a European confederation had been set up without delay, Western Germany would have found her place in it and accustomed herself to it before nationalism was reborn. Instead, unfortunately, the West resorted to such fictions as the Council of Europe, and dangerous efforts were made to "pool" coal, steel and armed forces. Now Russia has decided to exploit her chosen weapon—the appeal of German unity. In the field of politics it is comparable to the atomic bomb.

It is useless to shut one's eyes to reality. Unity—the reconstitution of the Reich with its own armed force—is the primordial objective for the immense majority of Germans, even if it is proposed by the Soviets and even if it is encumbered with a Russian mortgage. . . .

We French people know from the experience of three wars the meaning for us, and for the peace of the world, of the recurrent appearance of the German nebula which gathers itself together and then explodes. That was the phenomenon of the Bismarckian Germany of 1870, of Wilhelm's Empire of 1914 and of Hitler's Third Reich. Now the outlines of the Fourth Reich appear on the horizon, the product of Western errors and cynical Soviet calculation.

There is still time to deal with this problem; but only a little. The sole possible solution is a Franco-German agreement. In March of this year General de Gaulle said: "For centuries there has been a deplorable conflict between France and Germany. Europe cannot be built if these nations remain in opposition to one another." And he pointed out the path by which this "enormous and permanent historic fact" can be surmounted: "A *direct* agreement between France and Germany, on the subjects which have always divided them as well as on those which tend to bring them together." In General de Gaulle's view the "Atlantic policy" does not really tend in that direction. "This policy," he said, "pretends to arbitrate between a Germany and a France which are not in agreement, notably in the military field, rather than let them come to an understanding and themselves make that understanding the basis of a European confederation having in its charge matters of economy, defense, culture."

. . . Perhaps because they have been adversaries so long, it is possible for Frenchmen and Germans to reach a mutual understanding when they speak together directly. They know each other so well that the very dissimilarity of their qualities enables them to estimate each other more accurately than others can ever do. Only a Franco-German accord can provide the basis for a confederated Europe which would be a reality and not a fiction of the chancelleries. But the perpetual intervention of the other Powers, especially in view of the hope now entertained by the Germans of being able to secure a specially profitable alliance with America, makes such an accord impossible.

And it is no less hindered by the French fear that the American will, in effect, recreate with their own hands the very idol which they brought down yesterday.

Jacques Soustelle, "France and Europe: A Gaullist View," *Foreign Affairs,* XXX (1951–1952), 546-548.

B. *The Soviet View of Western Policy*

A. Y. Vishinsky was, next to Molotov, the most important of the Russian diplomatic figures. The speech in which he sets forth the Russian fears of a military alliance between Germany and the Western powers was given before the General Assembly of the United Nations where he was an aggressive representative of his country.

As was well known, the United States Government, together with the Governments of the United Kingdom and France, had organized a military-political bloc of five states, the aim of which was not to prevent German aggression and render mutual assistance against such aggression. The bloc could not pursue such an aim because it was not directed against the danger of the recurrence of German aggression and it even intended that Western Germany, which since time immemorial had served as a stronghold of German militarism and only recently had served as a bulwark for Hitler's aggression, should be included in it. It was quite clear that the forming of such alliance was in direct contradiction with the objectives of strengthening world peace and security.

However, other alliances of peace-loving European states were being concluded to prevent the possibility of recurring German aggression. Similar treaties had been concluded by the USSR with the countries of Eastern Europe as well as with Finland; and it was on the same basis that the Anglo-Soviet treaty and the Twenty-Year Franco-Soviet Treaty of mutual assistance had been concluded. Such treaties and the alliances based upon them aimed at preventing the possibility of further German aggression; they were in full conformity with the interests of all peace-loving peoples and would not lead to the oppression of peace-loving countries. They were not designed to set States against each other or to split Europe.

However, treaties such as the treaty of military alliance of the Western States, which included the United Kingdom, France, Belgium, the Netherlands and Luxembourg, did not only have in mind Germany, but could be directed against States which had been allies during the Second World War. All the British, French and American Press openly stated that the military alliance of the five Western Powers was directed against the USSR, and against the new European democracies. Such a treaty could in no way be regarded as one concluded for the purpose of defence alone. Those who concluded such agreements and those who established such alliances were pursuing a policy which was utterly incompatible with the strengthening of peace. Those who were concluding such treaties were assisting the instigators and organizers of a new war.

United Nations. *Plenary Meetings of the General Assembly,* 21 September– 12 December, 1948, pp. 129-130.

C. Freedom Before Unity

Marion Dönhoff was the political editor of *Die Zeit* of Hamburg. As a private individual she allows herself the luxury of forthright statement which is frequently denied to those who hold high public office.

Citizens of the Western German state are confronted today by vital questions which every one of them has to answer. First and foremost is this: "Is the unity of Germany of more importance to me than the consolidation of the Western state?"

Reunification will always be the goal of all Germans. But they seek it not out of longing for the old German Reich, which represents a degree of nationalism that almost no one is interested in any more, but primarily because the thought that 18,000,000 compatriots are at the mercy of the Soviet terror is unbearable. Once again in Eastern Germany there is growing up a generation which, from the time it enters school and proceeds via youth organizations up to forced recruitment for military service, is subjected to totalitarian indoctrination. Now the "youth organization" is Communist instead of Nazi, and the military service is for "Eastern police." But the fear of denunciation to the authorities, of forced labor and imprisonment is the condition of existence, just as before—and this time under Russian masters. Added to the neutral wish to rescue one's fellow countrymen from this bitter predicament is the question (which will be dealt with in detail later) whether Western Germany can live by herself. In the circumstances, then, the desire of Western Germans to join together the two parts of the whole is of course strong.

But the majority of people in Western Germany realize by now that they cannot have both unity and freedom. For the time being we must choose either the one or the other. Faced with this alternative it seems more opportune to be content with freedom now, and to work for unity later, rather than to begin by striving for a unity which can be gained only under Russian domination, and to renounce freedom forever.

Marion Dönhoff, "Germany Puts Freedom Before Unity," *Foreign Affairs,* XXVIII (1949–1950), 399–400.

D. The German Chancellor Speaks

Konrad Adenauer, leader of the Christian Democratic Party in the Federal Republic of Germany, speaks in support of the western orientation of his country.

Since the breakdown of Germany, i.e. since 1945, Soviet Russia has been the only state which has continued to arm. Contrary to what happened in Russia, the Western Allies reduced their armaments after the breakdown of Germany. It was only last year, when the case of Korea revealed Soviet Russia's intentions to the world, that the Western Allies and the nations of the North Atlantic Treaty Organization started rearming. It is only since the outbreak of this war in Korea that the world has clearly realized Soviet Russia's true aims.

There is something else I must point out here: Since 1945, Soviet Russia, by the methods of the cold war has linked the following countries to herself: Albania, Bulgaria, Roumania, Poland, Hungary, Czechoslovakia, and the eastern half of Germany. In this eastern part of Germany, Soviet Russia has been maintaining over 25 highly armed divisions only for the purpose of striking fear into our hearts, and of making us subservient. She maintains Fifth Columns in the Federal Republic and in other European countries. As I have just pointed out, the eastern half of

Germany has already fallen a victim to Soviet Russian policies. The Soviet Zone is a satellite State of Russia, its government is one of Russia's publicity agents. At the same time, the Federal Republic of Germany is a no-man's-land from both a political and military point of view. It is completely disarmed. It is not a sovereign power. It is suspended between the Eastern Block and the Western Allies without in any way being able to protect and defend itself. In the long run, this is an impossible situation. A conclusion of treaties with the Western Allies as envisaged in the above-mentioned communiques of 14th September, would put an end to this situation which, I insist again, is impossible and unbearable in the long run. Once these treaties are concluded, the Federal Republic would be a treaty-partner of the Western Allies for mutual defense against any attack upon Germany or Europe. At the same time, the Federal Republic would recover its full sovereignty. In this case, Soviet Russia would suffer as decisive a defeat regarding her Western Policy as she did in San Francisco regarding her Eastern Policy through the Japanese Peace Treaty. The aim of Soviet Russian world policies is perfectly clear. She wants to perpetuate the present uncertain situation of German political and military affairs because this will prevent an integration of Western Europe. The Soviet Union calculates that the United States would no longer be interested in a Western Europe that is falling to pieces, and without unification and integration, Western Europe is crumbling away and the Western European States are more or less powerless. The Soviet Union assumes that the United States would no longer be interested in a weak Europe and would withdraw from Europe. The Soviet Union would then, without a war, draw not only the Federal Republic, but also the other Western European countries, into the sphere of its influence, and would finally dominate the whole of Europe. We know very well what would be in store for us in that case. We only need remember Czechoslovakia, Hungary, Poland, and the other satellite States. Germany would then certainly be doomed. All Europe would then be politically an appendix to that part of Asia which is ruled by the Soviet Union. Communism in its Asiatic form would descend upon us with all its horrors. All those things that are sacred and dear to us would be destroyed. There would be no freedom for anyone. Christian civilization of the occident, and Christianity itself, would be destroyed. If Germany remains a no-man's-land, and if at last, after all, hostilities commenced in Europe, Germany would become the battle-field for the clashing powers. The fate of unhappy Korea would then be our fate.

Speech by Dr. Konrad Adenauer delivered over the German radio from Bonn, September 18, 1951. The text may be found in *Vital Speeches of the Day*, XVII (December 1, 1951), 109.

E. *The American Program*

Dean Acheson was Secretary of State during the final years of the Truman administration. Much of the policy of containing Communism came under his direction.

The European Defense Community will be closely interlocked with NATO. Each will be important to the other. They will meet together, as needed. Security guarantees between the two organizations now agreed upon will be presented to legislative bodies. And in this way, West Germany will be closely associated with the whole defense arrangements for Western Europe.

This, in turn, was closely related to the fourth main point dealt with in these meetings; that is, the restoration of Germany to a responsible and equal place among nations. What we would like to see is the peaceful unification of all Germany under conditions of freedom. This remains our aim, but the history of Soviet obstruction and Communist policy in post-war Europe does not encourage us to hope that this goal can be achieved in the immediate future. Therefore, what the three occupying powers—Britain, France and ourselves—are now seeking to do is to put an end to the occupation of Germany through a series of contractual agreements between these three governments and the Federal Republic. These agreements would establish German sovereignty to the fullest extent possible in the present world situation. Coupled with the European Defense Community arrangements, they would provide the necessary safeguards against aggressive militarism.

We succeeded, at London and Lisbon, in reaching decisions which open the way to the conclusion of these agreements. This involved some extremely difficult and tangled problems, such as the amount of the German contribution to the common defense. In all these problems, our European colleagues demonstrated statesmanship of a high order. It was inspiring to see people face resolutely and courageously the problems of the future, not dwelling in the fears and resentments of the past.

It was a thrilling thing to feel the hope and excitement with which Europe responded to the progress made against these ancient national rivalries which have caused so much mischief for so long. The job is not completed, but two years of patient work have brought us close to the point where these measures for creating a European Defense Community and ending the occupation of West Germany can be reduced to words and laid before national legislatures for their action. They have brought us to the dawn of a new day in Europe.

Radio speech by Dean Acheson. Text may be found in *The New York Times*, March 1, 1952, p. 3.

F. The Russian "Offer" and Its Rejection

The New York Times frequently carries the text of documents of significant importance in international relations. In this case the Russian note and the Western reply were printed together, and constitute a striking illustration of the deadlock of Soviet and Western policies.

THE BASIS FOR THE PROPOSED TREATY

Almost seven years have passed since the end of the war with Germany, but Germany still does not have a peace treaty, finds itself divided, continues to remain in an unequal situation as regards other governments. It is necessary to end such an abnormal situation. This responds to the aspirations of all peace-loving peoples. It is impossible to assure a just status to the legal national interests of the German people without the earliest conclusion of a peace treaty with Germany.

Conclusion of a peace treaty with Germany has an important significance for the strengthening of peace in Europe. A peace treaty with Germany will permit final decision of questions which have arisen as a consequence of the second World War. The European states which have suffered from German aggression, particularly the neighbors of Germany, have a vital interest in the solution of these questions. . . .

The necessity of hastening the conclusion of a peace treaty with Germany is required by the fact that the danger of reestablishment of German militarism which has twice unleashed world wars has not been eliminated in as much as appropriate provisions of the Potsdam conference still remain unfilled. A peace treaty with Germany must guarantee elimination of the possibility of a rebirth of German militarism and German aggression.

Conclusion of a peace treaty with Germany will establish for the German people permanent conditions of peace, will aid the development of Germany as a unified democratic and peace-loving government in accordance with the Potsdam provisions and will assure to the German people the possibility of peaceful cooperation with other peoples. . . . The Governments of the Union of Soviet Socialist Republics, United States of America, Great Britain and France consider that preparations of the peace treaty should be accomplished with the participation of Germany in the form of an all-German Government and that a peace treaty with Germany should be formed on the following basis:

Participants

Great Britain, the Soviet Union, the United States of America, France, Poland, Czechoslovakia, Belgium, Holland and the other governments which participated with their armed forces in the war against Germany.

Political Provisions

1. Germany is re-established as a unified state, thereby an end is put to the division of Germany and a unified Germany has a possibility of development as an independent democratic peace-loving state.

2. All armed forces of the occupying powers must be withdrawn from Germany not later than one year from the date of entry into force of the peace treaty. Simultaneously all foreign military bases on the territory of Germany must be liquidated.

3. Democratic rights must be guaranteed to the German people to the end that all persons under German jurisdiction without regard to race, sex, language or religion enjoy the rights of man and the basic freedoms including freedom of speech, press, religious persuasion, political conviction and assembly.

4. Free activity of democratic parties and organizations must be guaranteed in Germany with the right of freedom to decide their own internal affairs, to conduct meetings and assembly, to enjoy freedom of press and publications.

5. The existence of organizations inimical to democracy and to the maintenance of peace must not be permitted on the territory of Germany.

6. Civil and political rights equal to all other German citizens for participation in the building of peace-loving democratic Germany must be made available to all former members of the German army, including officers and generals, all former Nazis, excluding those who are serving court sentences for commission of crimes.

7. Germany obligates itself not to enter into any kind of coalition or military alliance directed against any power which took part with its armed forces in the war against Germany.

Territory

The territory of Germany is defined by the borders established by the provisions of the Potsdam conference of the great powers.

Economic Provisions

No kind of limitations are imposed on Germany as to the development of its peaceful economy, which must contribute to the growth of the welfare of the German people.

Likewise, Germany will have no kind of limitations as regards trade with other countries, navigation and access to world markets.

Military Provisions

1. Germany will be permitted to have its own national armed forces (land, air and sea) which are necessary for the defense of the country.

2. Germany is permitted to produce war materials and equipment, the quan- tity and style of which must not exceed the limitations required for the armed forces established for Germany by the peace treaty.

Germany and the United Nations Organization

The Governments concluding a peace treaty with Germany will support the application of Germany for acceptance as a member of the United Nations organization.

The New York Times, March 26, 1952, p. 4.

THE REPLY

. . . The Soviet Government's proposals do not indicate what the international position of the all-German Government would be before the conclusion of a peace treaty. The United States Government considers that the all-German Government should be free both before and after the conclusion of a peace treaty to enter into association compatible with the principles and purposes of the United Nations.

In putting forward its proposals for a German peace treaty, the Soviet Government expressed its readiness also to discuss other proposals. The United States Government has taken due note of this statement. In its view, it will not be possible to engage in detailed discussion of a peace treaty until conditions have been created for free elections and until a free all-German Government which could participate in such discussions has been formed. There are several fundamental questions which would also have to be resolved.

For example, the United States Government notes that the Soviet Government makes the statement that the territory of Germany is determined by frontiers laid down by the decisions of the Potsdam conference. The United States Government would recall that in fact no definitive German frontiers were laid down by the Potsdam decisions, which clearly provided that the final determination of territorial questions must await the peace settlement.

The United States Government also observes that the Soviet Government now considers that the peace treaty should provide for the formation of German national land, air and sea forces, while at the same time imposing limitations on Germany's freedom to enter into association with other countries. The United States Government considers that such provisions would be a step backwards and might jeopardize the emergence in Europe of a new era in which international relations would be based on cooperation and not on rivalry and distrust.

Being convinced of the need of a policy of European unity, the United States Government is giving its full support to plans designed to secure the participation of Germany in a purely defensive European community which will preserve freedom, prevent aggression and preclude the revival of militarism. The United States Government believes that the proposal of the Soviet Government for the formation of German national forces is inconsistent with the achievement of this objective. The United States Government remains convinced that this policy of European unity cannot threaten the interests of any country and represents the true path of peace.

The New York Times, March 26, 1952, p. 4.

Index